James Dickey

"Show me a hero and I will write you a tragedy"

From the *Notebooks* of F. Scott Fitzgerald

Why, I can . . . frame my face to all occasions.
I'll drown more sailors than the mermaid shall;
I'll slay more gazers than the basilisk;
I'll play the orator as well as Nestor,
Deceive more slily than Ulysses could
And, like a Sinon, take another Troy.
I can add colors to the chameleon,
Change shapes with Proteus for advantages,
And set the murderous Machiavel to school.
Can I do this, and not get a crown?
Tut, were it farther off, I'll pluck it down . . .

The future King Richard III
in Shakespeare's *3 King Henry VI*

TITLES BY HENRY HART

CRITICISM

The Poetry of Geoffrey Hill

Seamus Heaney: Poet of Contrary Progressions

Robert Lowell and the Sublime

POETRY

The Ghost Ship

The Rooster Mask

The James Dickey Reader (Editor)

James Dickey

THE WORLD AS A LIE

Henry Hart

June 4, 2011

For Clay —

Here's a life
you shouldn't emulate!

Best wishes —
Henry Hart

Picador USA | New York

For Jay Parini and Terry Meyers

For a full list of permissions, see p. 809.

Picador® is a U.S. registered trademark and is used by St. Martin's Press under license from Pan Books limited.

Production Editor: David Stanford Burr

Library of Congress Cataloging-in-Publication Data

Hart, Henry, 1954–.
    James Dickey: the world as a lie / Henry Hart.—1st ed.
      p. cm.
    Includes bibliographical references and index.
    ISBN 0-312-20320-9
    1. Dickey, James. 2. Authors, American—20th century—Biography. I. Title: World as a lie. II. Title.

    PS3554.I32Z695 2000
    811'.54—dc21
    [B]   99-054788

First Edition: April 2000

10 9 8 7 6 5 4 3 2 1

CONTENTS

ACKNOWLEDGMENTS

Among the many people who contributed to this book, I'm especially indebted to Steve Ennis for procuring and making available James Dickey's papers at the Emory University Library, Special Collections. He has been unstinting in his assistance. Anne Posega aided my research when I visited the Dickey archive at the Washington University Library in Saint Louis. Matthew Bruccoli generously gave me access to the papers at the University of South Carolina Library. I also owe a debt to the special collection librarians and archivists at Vanderbilt, Yale, the Library of Congress, the University of Texas at Austin, the University of Minnesota, the University of New Hampshire, Harvard, the College of William and Mary, the University of South Carolina, Darlington School, Clemson, the Jimmy Carter Library, the National Archives, and NASA. Theron Raines, Dickey's literary agent, also assisted me by letting me rummage through his collection of documents. Franklin Garrett and Anne Salter at the Atlanta History Center diligently answered my questions and provided me with useful photocopies.

I'm particularly grateful for the information provided by Dickey's two sons, Chris and Kevin, and also by Dickey's sister, Maibelle, and his sister-in-law, Patsy. Their intimate knowledge of James Dickey was invaluable. Al Braselton knew Dickey better than most, and to him I extend special thanks for many conversations and documents. Early in my research, Lewis King, George Garrett, Jim Mann, Bill Barnwell, and Richard Lamb agreed to extensive taped interviews and provided encouragement. Jacques de Spoelberch kindly discussed his editorial role in the prolonged genesis of *Deliverance*, and then agreed to serve as my agent. Having been unable for several years to interest agents and editors in a biography of Dickey, I was pleased that Jacques quickly found an editor, George Witte, who devoted many long hours to the shaping of this book. I also owe a good deal to Inman Mays and Sheldon Kelly for their broad knowledge of Dickey's life, and to Hubert and Phyllis Shuptrine for giving me detailed accounts of working with Dickey on *Jericho*. I'm equally grateful for the information provided by Dickey's close University of South Carolina friends: Ward Briggs, Matthew Bruccoli, Don Greiner, and Ben Franklin. Several of Dickey's former USC students—Paula Goff, Jim Mann, and David Havird—provided numerous insights and facts as well. All of these people agreed to reminisce into my tape recorder. I must also express hearty thanks to Earl Bradley, Stanley Logan, George Kamajian, and Herbert Vaughn for writing me so much about Dickey's World War II experiences. Bill Pratt was exceptionally helpful with Dickey's student years at Vanderbilt, Donald Hall with Dickey's publishing years at Wesleyan University Press. I would also like to give warm thanks to Anne Wright for letting me quote from her husband's substantial correspondence with Dickey, and Robert Bly, Donald Hall, and the Andrew Lytle estate for the same privilege. I thank all of the others, whose names are mentioned in this book, who granted permission to quote from their letters to Dickey or to me.

The interviews I recorded and then transcribed provided one of the most important resources for this biography, so I must thank all those who agreed to commit their memories and thoughts to tape: Elizabeth Adams, Shaye Areheart, Bill Baer, Richard Bausch, William F. Buckley, Pat Conroy, George Core, Bill Emerson, Nancy Galbraith, Ben Greer, Carolee Guilds, Lester Hardwick, Robert Herzberger, Richard Hodges, Stefan Kanfer, Robert Lescher, R. W. B. Lewis, Laurence Lieberman, Marie Tyler McGraw, Terry Miller, Joyce Pair, Wyatt Prunty, Mary MacLamore, Theron Raines, John Simon, Dave Smith, William Styron, Ernest Suarez, Elizabeth Sutton, Eleanor Taylor, Henry Taylor, Claude Terry, David Tillinghast, Mona Van Duyn, Jarvis Thurston, Gordon Van Ness, and Calhoun Winton.

I benefited from dozens of phone interviews and letters. For them I must thank Elizabeth Adams, Gary Adelman, Michael Allin, Franklin Ashley, James Applewhite, Doc Ayers, Peter Balakian, Dugan Barr, William Bake, George Bailey, Judy Baughman, Don Berry, David Bottoms, Gordon Bigelow, Bookie Binkley, Hugh Blackburn, Virginia Kirkland Blackwood, Richard Blakeslee, Joseph Blotner, Joseph Bloxsom, Robert Bly, Mark Bollman, John Boorman, Bob Bradley, Ron Brentano, Van K. Brock, John Broderick, Joseph Broesamle, Paul Brooks, Arlen Brown, Ashley Brown, Jody Brown, Mark Brunhele, Amy Burk, Stanley Burnshaw, Jack Burton, Keen Butterworth, Bedford Calhoun, Richard Calhoun, Katherine Camp, Lynn Cansler, Mary Cantwell, Pat Carr, Virginia Spencer Carr, David Casseres, Vernon Cassill, Turner Cassity, Fred Chapell, Bill Childers, John Clendenning, Wayne Cody, Jean Cohen, Jim Coleman, Mary Ann Coleman, James Colvert, Pat Conroy, Tony Corcoran, Bill Cromartie, Allen Curnow, Irvin Dahmen, Rosemary Daniell, Lloyd Davis, Peter Davison, Yvonne Dell, Lawrence Dembo, David Dickey, Fred Dickey, Richard Dillard, Violetta Brown Dodge, Carl Dolmetsch, Richard and Mary Domingos, Scott Donaldson, Mason Dorsey, Wilfred Dowden, Bernie Dunlap, John Edwardson, R. Bryan Ellis, Bill Emerson, Carol Fairman, Betsy Fancher, Johnny Feiber, Harry Finestone, Enfield "Flickey" Ford, Marshall Frady, Charles Fries, Catherine Fry, Bill Fuqua, Nancy Galbraith, John Gallogly, Tony Ganz, Tim Gautreaux, Frank Gillespie, Dana Gioia, Robert Giroux, Vernon Glenn, Jonis Gold, Herman Gollob, Jim Gonia, Wallace Graves, Randal Greene, Roberta Greifer, William Griswold, Charles Guerry, John Hall, Barry Hannah, Michael Hanson, Andrew Harbelis, Kelsie Harder, Michael Harper, Roger Harris, Pegram Harrison, Thomas Hart, Senator Hartke, Glenn Helgeland, Jerome Hellman, Brian Henry, Kevin Herbert, Dr. Wallace Hill, John Hodgins, Daniel Hoffman, Barbara Holcombe, Martha Holden, Thad Horton, Richard Howard, Dr. William Hunter, Howard Hyle, Bill Hyman, Dr. Iannone, Marc Jaffe, Elizabeth Janeway, Maria Cooper Janice, Jan Jarecki, John Jarrell, Comer Jennings, Madison Jones, Hugh Keenan, Ken Keener, David Keller, Edward

Kern, Robert Kimbrough, John Kimmey, Ken Kipnis, Smith Kirkpatrick, Robert Kirschten, Carolyn Kizer, Marvin Klotz, Bruce Konkle, Philip Kunhardt, Sydney Lea, Jack Leigh, Robert Lescher, Arnold Levine, Edward Lewis, Tom Lewis, Laurence Lieberman, Gordon Lish, Kasper Locher, Willard Lockwood, John Logan, John Logue, William Logan, Susan Ludvigson, Al Lukas, Nan Lyon, John Lyons, Andrew Lytle, Marshall MacFarlane, Peter Mackuk, Ed Madden, Mike McDonald, Peter McKeever, Tim McLaurin, Norman Mailer, Joseph Maiolo, Robert Manning, Martin Mansfield, Paul Mariani, Peter Bird Martin, William Matthews, George Meredith, Susan Mitchell, George Montgomery, Kevin Mooney, Lewis Morgan, Willie Morris, Monica Moseley, Robert Moss, Albert Murray, Patricia Muske, Robert Newman, John North, J. Bruce Nunley, Charles Orme, Joseph Parris, Charlotte Patton, Edmund Peckham, Janet Peery, Margaret Jane Pepperdine, Mark Pendergrast, Robert Peters, Jim Peterson, Richard Pincus, Robert Pinsky, George Plimpton, Roger Porter, Dr. Craig Powell, Reynolds Price, Jim Rawley, Ennis Rees, James Reiss, Bruce Renner, Carl Richter, John Rickman, Walter Rideout, George Rodman, Frank Rogers, Tom Roper, Ned Rorem, Jack Rosenbalm, Philip Roth, Richard Roth, Larry Rubin, Louis Rubin, Mike Russo, Vern Rutsula, Stephen Sandy, Joseph Santora, Walter Schirra, Richard Schramm, Charles Scott, Ward Scott, James Seay, Tom Shapcott, Ralph Shaw, Pam Shelden, Joy Shelton, Heyward Siddons, Robert Siegel, Louis Simpson, Rembert Sims, Arthur Smith, Daniel Smith, Doug Smith, William Jay Smith, Joseph Sokolowicz, Monroe Spears, James Stevens, Malcolm Stuart, William Styron, Walter Sullivan, Marshall Swanson, Wes Taft, Anne Locke Taylor, James Taylor, Marsh Terry, Richard Tillinghast, Irene Thompson, Lucy and Clinton Trowbridge, Frederick Turner, Robert Tyndall, John Ullman, John Updike, Krishna Vaid, Henry Van Slotten, Gloria Vando, Glen Verrill, Ellen Bryant Voight, Richard Vowles, David Wagoner, Andy Wallace, Gwen Leege Walti, Carl Warren, Paul Warshow, Eric Weissberg, Jon Westling, Bill White, Harold Whittern, Patricia Wilcox, Richard Wilbur, Nancy Wilds, Fritz Van Winkle, Ken Witt, Anne Wright, Don Yearwood, Thomas Daniel Young, Carl and Mrs. Zibart, Richard Ziebart.

Several of my William and Mary students, chief among them Dave Gunton, helped me proofread and correct the manuscript. Michael Mott, David Morrill, and Emily Mieras also contributed information and editorial advice. Bonnie Chandler kindly helped with the typing. The College of William and Mary and the Virginia Center for the Humanities provided grants so that I could finish my manuscript in a timely fashion. My wife, Susannah, gave practical assistance and moral support during the six years of my labors. To all my fellow collaborators I offer heartfelt thanks.

INTRODUCTION

When James Dickey died on January 19, 1997, most of the obituaries—from the six-column one in the *New York Times* to the shorter ones in *Time* and *Newsweek*—paid tribute to the big, life-loving, hard-drinking bard who had written the best-selling novel *Deliverance*. The eulogists pointed out that he had been a star college football player, a combat pilot with one hundred missions during World War II and the Korean War, an advertising executive for The Coca-Cola Company, a tournament archer and expert bow hunter, a National Book Award–winning poet, a poetry consultant at the Library of Congress, a popular professor, and an author of poetry books, coffee-table books, literary criticism, novels, and children's books. In Dickey's hometown newspaper, the *Atlanta Journal-Constitution*, David Kirby announced that "a boozy, bold 'Dylan Thomas of the South'" had died, and that Dickey had "staked out the position of premier tough-guy writer that Ernest Hemingway had held in the previous generation."[1] Kirby also contended that Dickey was an aesthete and impersonator in the tradition of Oscar Wilde.

During a memorial service at the University of South Carolina, the novelist Pat Conroy remarked on Dickey's personae and impersonations as well: "He tried to live a hundred lives and succeeded in living about ninety-five of them. No American life has been so restless in its pursuit of expertise in so many fields." Because Dickey aspired to be a Jeffersonian Renaissance man as well as a Rabelaisian hell-raiser, Conroy expressed sympathy for the recorder of his life: "Pity the biographer of James Dickey. If this biographer . . . gets all of the far-flung outrageous stories on paper, then the life of James Dickey will make Ernest Hemingway look like a florist from the Midwest. This is a promise, not a premise, a certainty, not a guess."[2] If Dickey had modeled his life on Hemingway's, he had also sought to outperform the great performer.

By the time of Dickey's death, at least half-a-dozen writers had proposed gathering "the far-flung outrageous stories" into a biography, but Dickey had stipulated as early as 1980 that he would authorize no biography. In interviews he allied himself with T. S. Eliot and Matthew Arnold in opposing such a book, and in private he did what he could to keep the biographical hounds off his trail. "No one will ever be able to reconstruct my life. It is more complicated and more unknowable than that of Lawrence of Arabia,"[3] he wrote in a journal published in 1971. If Dickey confounded researchers, he also courted them by saving almost every scrap of paper he wrote on and every scrap that was ever written to him. To make them accessible to the public, he began selling his papers to Washington

University in 1964. In 1993, he sold so many letters, manuscripts, notebooks, military documents, teaching materials, appointment books, financial statements, and other records to Emory University that it took 233 boxes and about one hundred feet of shelf space to contain all the material. About five years later, Emory bought many more papers that had been stored in Dickey's house when he died. Hundreds of his letters had already made their way to other archives around the country. In these various havens, I have found lines of poetry Dickey scribbled on Applebee's napkins, a little book about toothpaste and toothbrushing he assembled when he was five years old, love letters he received from Atlanta girls when he was a teenager, his international Playboy key, and even a sixteen-ounce can of Budweiser beer.

For all his halfhearted objections to potential biographers, Dickey loved to read biographies, and in his essays, most notably those he wrote on Lawrance Thompson's *Robert Frost: The Early Years* and Allen Seager's *The Glass House: The Life of Theodore Roethke,* he laid out a blueprint for the kind he most admired. In his review of Thompson's book, focusing on Frost-the-man versus Frost-the-myth, Dickey could have been addressing his own hagiographers when he cautioned Frost's: "'Beloved' is a term that must always be mistrusted when applied to artists, and particularly to poets. Poets are likely to be beloved for only a few of the right reasons, and for almost all the wrong ones: for saying things we want to hear, for furnishing us with an image of ourselves that we enjoy believing in, even for living for a long time in the public eye." He praised Thompson for scrutinizing Frost with both approbation and disapproval:

> As partial as it is [toward Frost], Dr. Thompson's account is yet the fully documented record of what Frost was like when he was not beloved: when he was, in fact, a fanatically selfish, egocentric, and at times dangerous man; was from the evidence, one of the least lovable figures in American literature. What we get from Dr. Thompson is the . . . construction of a complex mask, a *persona,* an invented personality that the world, following the man, was pleased, was overjoyed, finally, to take as an authentic identity, and whose main interest, biographically and humanly, comes from the fact that the mask is almost the diametrical opposite of the personality that lived in and motivated the man all his life.

Dickey concluded: "Looking back on Frost through the lens of Dr. Thompson's book, one finds it obvious that the mode, the manner in which a man lies, and what he lies about—these things and the *form* of his lies—are the main things to investigate in a poet's life and work."[4]

In his review of Seager's biography, Dickey restated his position. Although he entitled his review "Roethke: The Greatest American Poet," he was anything but fawning. He drew attention to Roethke's egotism, drinking, violence, and insanity, but his worst offense, according to Dickey, was his pathetically unbelievable lying, which Dickey witnessed on a trip to Seattle in 1963:

> [Roethke] would enter into a long involved story about himself. "I used to spar with Steve Hamas," he would say. I remember trying to remember

who Steve Hamas was, and by the time I had faintly conjured up an American heavyweight who was knocked out by Max Schmeling, Roethke was glaring at me anxiously. "What the hell's wrong?" he said. "You think I'm a damned liar?"

I did indeed, but until he asked me, I thought he was just rambling on in the way of a man who did not intend for others to take him seriously. He *seemed* serious enough, for he developed the stories at great length, as though he had told them, to others or to himself, a good many times before.

Dickey fell into a bitter silence as he listened to Roethke's long-winded, self-centered tales. Although Roethke wanted him to corroborate the lies in order "to help protect him from his sense of inadequacy, his dissatisfaction with what he was as a man," Dickey refused. "My own disappointment," he remembered, "was not at all in the *fact* that Roethke lied, but in the obviousness and uncreativeness of the manner in which he did it. Lying of an inspired, habitual, inventive kind, given a personality, a form, and a rhythm, is mainly what poetry *is*, I have always believed. All art, as Picasso is reported to have said, is a lie that makes us see the truth."[5]

For Dickey, Roethke embodied his masterful lies in his poems, and while he commended Seager for explaining the biographical context—the "glass house"—in which the poetic lies grew, he attacked those responsible for imposing limits on Seager's book. "Something is wrong here," Dickey commented. "One senses too much of an effort to mitigate certain traits of Roethke's, particularly in regard to his relations with women. It may be argued that a number of people's feelings and privacy are being spared." Because of Seager's reticence, Dickey believed that "a whole—and very important—dimension of the subject has thereby been left out of account." For those who preferred a whitewashed, mythic Roethke, Dickey had harsh words: "It is no good to assert, as some have done, that Roethke was a big lovable clumsy affectionate bear who just incidentally wrote wonderful poems. It is no good to insist that Seager show 'the good times as well as the bad' in anything like equal proportions; these are not the proportions of the man's life. The driving force of him was agony, and to know him we must know all the forms it took."[6] Dickey blamed Seager's reluctance to tell the whole truth on Roethke's wife, Beatrice, and attacked her for placing obstacles in Seager's way.

Writing a biography is a complex business, especially when your subject or your subject's family and friends are still alive. It was Oscar Wilde who noted that the biographer added one more fear to the prospect of death. Wilde also said that the great writer has many apostles, and usually it's Judas who writes the biography. In her book about the numerous problems facing Sylvia Plath's biographers, Janet Malcolm called the biographer a professional burglar. I would add to the list of epithets the name of Adam. Many biographers begin their perilous adventures in relative innocence—in a kind of adorational Eden. Out of a fascination with their subject's writings, they want to pluck the apple that contains the secrets, or seeds, of their subject's life and art. Biographers quickly realize that there are those who would rather they left the apple alone. Much biographical information, after all, is private knowledge, forbidden knowledge, harmful knowledge.

Out of my own enchantment with Dickey's early work and curiosity about his life, I informed Dickey around 1992 that I planned to write his biography. He never responded, but mutual friends told me of his dismay. Over the next four years, partly because he realized I was persevering with my research, he warmed to the project. About a year before he died, a Dickey scholar, Gordon Van Ness, told me that Dickey wanted to speak to me. Since I had been working on the book for several years, and since I feared he might try to restrict or block it, I made my first phone call to his house with great trepidation. When I told him my name and where I was calling from, there was a pause, and then he nearly shrieked: "Henry Hart! That's not your name!" He made up a menacing name that sounded like a character's in *The Godfather:* "You're not Henry Hart. You're Henrico Corleone! You're a hit man for the Mafia!"[7] (In two months, after telling me that he had read Edgar Rice Burroughs's Tarzan books as a boy, he signed some of his letters to me "Bolgani, the Gorilla," presumably because Tarzan had killed the gorilla.) To my great relief, despite his discombobulating jokes that portrayed me as his executioner, Dickey expressed little animosity toward my project. But he obviously had worries, the main one being the way I would address the romanticized versions of his life that he had aired so free-spiritedly in conversations and publications.

Although Dickey liked to ridicule T. S. Eliot's self-conscious aesthete J. Alfred Prufrock, he shared Prufrock's need to "prepare a face to meet the faces that you meet." In an anecdote about his first poetry reading, which he said he had approached with diffidence and fear, he admitted in 1989: "The public image, whatever that may be, notwithstanding, I'm really a rather shy person. It made me very nervous to get up in front of even as few as ten or fifteen people. My wife noticed how nervous it was making me. We were on a relatively modest salary at the time at a small West Coast experimental school [Reed College, where he taught in 1963], and even though I got a couple of hundred dollars that we very much needed for a week's work, I just didn't know if it was worth what I was going through to get it."[8] Dickey finally told his wife that he would decline the offer to read at Oregon State. When she advised him to relax and just be himself on stage, he responded: "But what self, which one?" To mask his insecurities, he confessed that he "had to invent a self" and chose for his model the "big, strong, hard-drinking, hard-fighting" Ernest Hemingway. He added: "Nothing could be less characteristic of the true James Dickey, who is a timid, cowardly person."[9]

Right after telling this story to the interviewer, Ernest Suarez (and it *was* a story; he had given numerous poetry readings before teaching at Reed), he named Hemingway and T. E. Lawrence as the twentieth century's "two great invented selves, people who wished to become other than they really were and who wrote and acted out of the assumed personality."[10] He could also have included William Butler Yeats, who once argued: "All happiness depends on the energy to assume the mask of some other life, on a rebirth as something not one's self, something created in a moment and perpetually renewed. . . . The poet finds and makes his mask in disappointment, the hero in defeat."[11] Like his self-conscious and self-inventing forebears, Dickey regularly chose to overcome disappointment and defeat by creating and then flaunting heroic masks. When he wrote that no biographer could do justice to his life because he was more complicated than Lawrence of Arabia, what he meant was that he wore more masks and played more roles than Lawrence. To close friends like Paula Goff he agreed that he was "the sum of all the roles he played"[12]—a sum that, presumably, no one would ever be able to tally.

On July 15, 1996, during my second phone conversation with Dickey, he again brought up the matter of lying. He wanted to know what I planned to call my biography. I said I might call it *James Dickey: A Rage to Live* after a couplet from Alexander Pope's "Epistle II: To a Lady" that he greatly admired: "You purchase Pain with all that Joy can give,/And die of nothing but a Rage to live." He thought for a moment, and then said, "No. Henry, we've got to shake them up out there. We've got to call it: *James Dickey: The World as a Lie.*"[13] The title reminded me of a line from Schopenhauer quoted by one of Dickey's favorite writers, Joseph Campbell, in *The Mythic Image.* (I learned later that he had borrowed the phrase from the title of a poem by Paula Goff.) The world of time and space, Schopenhauer proposed, was "a vast dream, dreamed by a single being, in such a way that all the dream characters dream too."[14] What Dickey meant was what Schopenhauer meant: the world could be viewed as a dream or lie or invention—something created mysteriously and majestically out of the void by a First Maker—in which all the characters dreamed or lied, too. The Greek word behind *poetry* is *poesis*, "a making," and Dickey implied that we all are poets or artist-gods making or "making-up" or at least remaking the world. With a childlike sense of wonder, as well as with the many sextants he bought as an adult, he obsessively contemplated stars and cosmic origins. With his head in the heavens, he laughed like a mystic comedian at the mundane facts at his feet.

Nearly everything Dickey said about his life was an embroidery of fiction and fact. Trying to comprehend his penchant for tall tales and cavalier behavior, friends and foes alike attributed it to his Southernness. "Most Southern literature comes right off the front porch," Dickey once said. "[It arises from] people sitting and talking, long-windedly, but always willing to listen to each others' stories because they've all got good ones to tell."[15] Dickey's conviction that he was free to invent his past and future also had foreign sources—the existentialist writings of Albert Camus and Jean-Paul Sartre. In a televised conversation with Bill Moyers, Dickey once recalled listening with rapt attention to a Sorbonne lecture by Camus "about the Existentialist proposition that we no longer have any supernatural sanctions . . . , that man is essentially what he has made of himself. The famous Sartrian formula—Man is free to act, but he must act to be free—was pretty much the subject of that evening's lecture."[16] Skeptical of this libertarian position, Moyers asked Dickey if all acts were therefore permissable. Dickey fudged. It depended, he said, on the quality and quantity of the actions. On other occasions he boldly proclaimed that in a universe without traditional sanctions he, as a poet, could say, do, and make of himself whatever he pleased.

In his controversial endorsement of lying, Dickey found a sympathetic ally in Oscar Wilde, who bemoaned, with his usual wit, what he called the "decay of lying" in modern letters:

> One of the chief causes that can be assigned for the curiously commonplace character of most of the literature of our age is undoubtedly the decay of Lying as an art, a science, a social pleasure. . . . Lying and poetry are arts—arts, as Plato saw, not unconnected with each other—and they require the most careful study, the most disinterested devotion. . . . The fashion of lying has almost fallen into disrepute. Many a young man starts in life with a natural gift for exaggeration which, if nurtured in congenial and sympathetic surroundings, or by the imitation of the best models might grow into something really great and wonderful. But as a rule he comes to nothing. He either falls into careless habits of accuracy . . . or takes to frequenting the society of the aged and the well-informed. Both things are equally fatal to his imagination.[17]

Unleashing the imagination without concern for conventional truths or morals was a goal of fin-de-siècle aesthetes. It was also a goal of James Dickey.

Dickey considered his long novel *Alnilam* his most significant work, partly because it was to be his most extensive exploration of the imagination's ability to transform facts into captivating lies. The two main characters, Frank and Joel Cahill, reinvent the world in ways Dickey espoused. In a lengthy abstract for the novel and its projected sequel, *Crux Australis*, Dickey wrote of his alter ego, Joel:

> He evidently has some notion of a society which he calls "circulatory," or "cyclic." The society would depend very heavily on *role-playing* and *lying*. Joel believes that lying exercises the creative and imaginative faculties, and, when indulged in on either an individual or a group basis, raises the consciousness of the party or parties concerned. The process is what Joel calls "continuous invention," and he believes, apparently, that such systematic practice of fabrication will create a new human world and the transfigured world of the human ability to fabricate. There is a kind of sketchy notion to the effect that there will be "truth areas," where empirical fact is rigorously adhered to and communicated truthfully. This is the area that will enable the state to function. All the citizens are indoctrinated both to truth and invention, so that they can be circulated in and out of both areas, as the state desires. It might even be a kind of law that one must spend equal time in both, or perhaps more time in the "invention area" than in the "truth area," but surely, some time in both. The real basis for the *mind* or imagination of the state will be in the invention area, where people are constantly exercising their creative abilities by making up stories about themselves, about their neighbors, about anything and everything there is. People would soon learn to live with this, Joel says, exploit it, and rejoice in it. It is a kind of freedom human beings have never before had on a large-scale, systematic basis. There might be a kind of hierarchy of lying here where one class of "inventors" would be compelled to

enter the truth area or indicate by some sign or other, in case vital or necessary information was required, that this was indeed truth. The rest could be lies, but the highest group of all, the group that corresponds to the philosopher-kings or sages are those that need make no sign as to whether what they say is true or whether it is fantasy. These are the master inventors, and the state reveres them.[18]

Joel's conception of utopia turns Plato's *Republic*, with its truth-telling philosopher-kings, on its head. "What shocks the virtuous philosop[h]er," Dickey would say with John Keats, "delights the camelion Poet."[19]

For Dickey, the world was a theater in which he bestowed upon his multitudinous selves the costumes and actions of high or low drama. In his poems he often wrote about kings, and in his life he played mad or bad or good kings with equal gusto. Asked what Dickey was really like, a friend from his advertising years, Al Braselton, answered: "Which Dickey?" He professed to know four Dickeys—Jamey, Jim, James, and Jimbo: "Jamey, the nickname he was given by his family in early childhood, is the Proust-like preternaturally-aware poetic sensibility who misses nothing and remembers everything." Jim is "the friend and good companion," who is embarrassed by Jamey's sensitivity and determined to avoid all literary affectation. James is "the writer . . . who keeps himself in a most secretive manner." Jimbo is "the celebrity," the larger-than-life figure out to prove to a culture biased against poets that he is no "sissy."[20] As if to outdo his friend's assessment, Dickey usually boasted that he had a whole troupe of personae. "Everyone is several Walter Mittys,"[21] he told an interviewer in 1967. To another interviewer he confided: "Everybody has in himself a saint, a murderer, a pervert, a monster, a good husband, a scoutmaster, a provider, a businessman, a shrewd horse trader, a hopeless aesthete. . . . There are all kinds of contradictory selves. Essentially, the most exciting thing for a writer, especially a young writer, is to get as many of these energized as he can, to let the monster speak as well as let the prospective husband speak."[22] Assessing Dickey's contradictions, his sister-in-law, Patsy, once wrote: "Jim created James, the mad nobleman living in an impenetrable fortress of legend. Then with Viking ruthlessness, with outrageous pleasure, James slew Jim, the man who could create life in stone. Then there was only James Dickey."[23]

Everyone who followed literature after World War II heard stories about Dickey's awful and even unlawful behavior. To a certain extent, he emulated his peers, who suffered from what he called "the occupational hazards" of poetry—alcoholism, mania, suicide, and depression. Referring to Hart Crane, Dylan Thomas, John Berryman, Randall Jarrell, and Sylvia Plath (as he often referred to Theodore Roethke, Robert Lowell, Anne Sexton, Delmore Schwartz, and Weldon Kees), he told a *Playboy* interviewer in 1973:

> I think there is a terrible danger in the over-cultivation of one's sensibilities, and that's what poets are forced to do in order to be poets. You will find that poets, almost without exception, are cast into the most abject despair over things that wouldn't bother an ordinary person at all. Living with such an exacerbating mind and sensibility gets to be something that

one cannot bear any longer. In order to create poetry, you make a monster out of your own mind. You can't get rid of him. He stays right with you every minute. Every minute of every day and every night. He produces terrible things—nightmare after nightmare. I'm subject to having them no less than any of the rest of them. But I don't fool myself. I know what's doing it. Writers start out taking something to aid the monster, to give them the poetry. Poets use alcohol, or any other kind of stimulant, to aid and abet this process, then eventually take refuge in the alcohol to help get rid of it. But by that time the monster is so highly developed he cannot be got rid of.[24]

While Dickey seemed bent on out-monstering his fellow monsters, he also subscribed to the notion that poetry was an act of redemption and atonement. He transgressed, knowing that his sins would inspire poems, that he could purge his sins and gain forgiveness through writing. If he pledged his soul to the devil, he believed that in return he would acquire Faustian power. He justified the hazards of poetry writing by saying that "the moments of intensity which do lead to delight and joy and fulfillment are so much better than those that other people have."[25]

One of the insidious effects of alcoholism on writers is the way it dissipates creative and critical faculties while bolstering delusions of greatness. Dickey's literary career reached its zenith in the 1960s and early 1970s, before alcohol and other forces in his chaotic life eroded his judgment. The poet and editor Peter Davison summed up the critical consensus in a 1967 *Atlantic Monthly* essay when he argued that, of all the contemporary poets, only Robert Lowell and James Dickey deserved the title "major." During this period, Dickey became a literary celebrity. *Life* and *Time* published profiles of him. He appeared on the Johnny Carson, Merv Griffin, and Dick Cavett shows. He could count as friends such writers and politicians as William Styron, Norman Mailer, John Updike, Robert Lowell, John Berryman, Robert Penn Warren, William F. Buckley, Jimmy Carter, and Eugene McCarthy. He commanded the highest fees of any poet on the reading circuit, and, like Dylan Thomas before him, he titillated, scandalized, and mesmerized his audiences. For the poet who aspired to be a notorious *poète maudit* or Roaring Boy, alcohol was an enabling tonic. About Dickey's drinking, the poet Richard Wilbur observed:

Especially among Southern writers, after a little Daniels or Dickel, one hears Jim Dickey stories having to do with outrageous and alcoholic behavior at this place or that. I have seen a bit of such behavior, and have heard tell of it from people who do not fabricate or embellish. It seems to me that I understand . . . what goes on in Jim at such times: an impatience with the correct and civilized self, a wish to be unbounded. Norman Mailer, and Norman Mailer's fictional heroes, often feel challenged to do precisely the wrong thing, and I suspect that Jim has sometimes said to himself, "What is the worst thing I could say or do at this moment?" There is a relation, I think, between the breaking-out character of some of his actions and the breaking-out character of some of the poems we published [at Wesleyan University Press] during Jim's days with Wesleyan: certain poems seem to violate the poet's own sense of the normal and possible, offering preternatural events not as truths but as exciting fabrications.[26]

If alcohol fueled Dickey's engines during the 1960s, helping him become one of the most sensational performers on the poetry circuit, during the 1970s, many critics felt those engines were spinning out of control.

With every advancing year, Dickey liked to say that he was the oldest adolescent alive, and those who witnessed his bad behavior at poetry readings agreed. On these occasions the Dionysian boy usurped the throne from the Apollonian adult. Although he was famous, fame did little to appease his vanity and ambition. He lied and cavorted out of a desperate need for love, even while recognizing that his monstrous conduct repelled as often as it entranced, and that his flaws had turned his life into a tragedy of classic proportions. Adulation from those who enjoyed his flouting of taboos was a balm to his conscience. Gradually, however, his Dionysian and Faustian excesses estranged family and friends, especially after the death of his first wife, Maxine. Dickey's son, Chris, has told the story of family suffering in his memoir *Summer of Deliverance.* Dickey gave me his version of his first and second marriages during five days of taped interviews in August 1996. Although I wrote Dickey's second wife, Deborah, asking for interviews, she declined and did not contribute to the contents of the book. Deborah's full story of frustrated ambition, feminist anger, violent recrimination, and prolonged self-abasement still needs to be told for a clearer understanding of James Dickey's last two decades. Her profound love for Dickey and her arduous recuperation from drug addiction after Dickey's death are only hinted at here.

Dickey's bibulous exploits were not his whole life, even though, as Dickey said of Roethke's agonies, they came to dominate it. While Dickey could be cruel and egocentric to the point of solipsism, he could also be a sensitive, understanding, and hilarious companion. Of the many eminent poets from his generation who taught in universities, he was one of the most charismatic and encouraging, as almost all his students attest. His unaffected manner could make the shyest admirer feel at ease, just as his curiosity and empathy could make the same person feel that whatever he or she had to say was eminently important. He could be generous to beginning writers. Barnstorming around the country to read to the humblest community college or high school audience, he was a successful ambassador for poetry, and by insisting on high reading fees he helped other poets as well as himself. His vast knowledge of literature, which his memory kept at the tip of his tongue, had few rivals among writers of any age.

I.

ORIGINS

1. Cityfolk and Countryfolk

James Dickey entered the world on February 2, 1923, the day the groundhog was supposed to crawl from his burrow and predict the advent of spring. Although the groundhog never became one of his totem animals—fiercer animals like the wolverine, the shark, and the lynx claimed that distinction—he liked to regale audiences in the 1960s with tales of growing up among the animals of the North Georgia hills. In aphoristic moods he would say: "The fox knows many things, but the groundhog knows one big thing."[1] For some Dickey played the groundhog, the contemplative burrower, the loner in touch with a great secret. For others he played the fox, the Renaissance man, the wily predator with irrepressible curiosities and appetites. Dickey shared his Groundhog Day birthday, as he liked to point out, with Farrah Fawcett and James Joyce. Browsing in the Doubleday bookstore in New York, he once met Fawcett, the actress who appeared as a glamorous detective in the television series *Charley's Angels*. When he proudly announced to her that they shared a birthday, she reputedly said, "I beg your pardon?" In his seductive Southern voice, Dickey replied, "Yes, we do." She was taken aback by this unexpected revelation: "My goodness. And who are you?" Dickey said he was "just a fan,"[2] and watched her exit the store flanked by her bodyguards. His other birth mate was no Hollywood star, but a penurious, highbrow writer devoted to avant-garde principles. Because Fawcett and Joyce represented two sides of his personality that merged and clashed throughout his life, Dickey was forever joking about the date they shared with the groundhog.

His claims to an impoverished childhood in Georgia's Appalachian Mountains notwithstanding, Dickey was born in Atlanta's Davis-Fisher Sanitorium (it became the Crawford Long Hospital in 1931). Along with his father, Eugene, and mother, Maibelle, Dickey spent his first three years in his maternal grandmother's palatial, white-columned house at 1459 Peachtree Street. His grandmother, Mrs. Huntley, enjoyed all the benefits of a life made leisurely by wealth and servants. Like many Atlanta families, the Huntleys and Dickeys did their best to resurrect the comforts undermined by the Civil War. Near their fashionable neighborhood, Pershing Point, where Peachtree and West Peachtree Streets converged, Margaret Mitchell's parents had built a house in 1912. Jim Dickey had reason to feel a sense of kinship with his fellow Atlantan beyond the coincidence of family names (Mitchell's early nickname was Jimmy, her lawyer father was Eugene, and her mother was May Belle). As Dickey grew up, like Mitchell, he was torn between the romantic myths of the old South and the more enlightened ways of the new.

Margaret Mitchell's house at 1149 Peachtree, grand as it was with its Palladian entrance and Doric columns, was less prominent than the house at 1459, at least during the period before *Gone with the Wind* was published.

Dickey's first house earned a place on an Atlanta postcard and became a showpiece for tourists. His maternal grandmother, Lena Huntley (nee Burckhardt), came from a German family—her mother was German-born, which in the 1930s and 1940s must have complicated his childhood. Like Theodore Roethke, his favorite American poet, Dickey as an adult both romanticized and reviled his German roots. In 1996, several months before he died, he told an interviewer: "I didn't speak English until I was five or six years old. I was raised in a German-speaking household."[3] In fact, Dickey learned only a few German words, which he often confused, from the woman he and his siblings called *grossmutter*. She taught him *richtig tun*, which means "do it right," and a phrase from a German poet: "*Es muss sein, es muss sein*" ("it must be, it must be"), a dictum that haunted Dickey all his life. Equally haunting was the book *Struwwelpeter*, a group of sadistic stories about punishments meted out to children. "That was a horrible book," he would say. "Scariest damn thing you've ever seen."[4] Dickey exaggerated the Germanic nature of his upbringing because he believed that his own penchant for iron-willed discipline, cruelty, and fatalism was rooted there.

Grandmother Huntley imparted an affection for German culture that remained with Dickey until he died. She read him Schiller and Goethe (her favorite line from Schiller was "Against ignorance even the gods have struggled in vain") and taught him that a writer should have noble ideas and write about them in noble ways.[5] She cultivated his ear for German music, especially Mozart. Dickey's voluminous novel *Alnilam*, which he worked on nearly his entire creative life, was his most sustained examination of the Apollonian and Dionysian contraries he'd inherited from his German forebears. Charismatic power and the chaos that resulted from it were his two principal themes. From his boyhood on, Dickey was obsessed with what Nietzsche called the "ubermensch," the "higher man" or superman, and his tragic falls. Publicly, Dickey sometimes pooh-poohed German culture by joking about its dullness, but privately its extremes enthralled him. He once told a reporter for the *Washington Post*: "I love to read dull books. . . . I think it's because my heritage on my mother's side is German, and they run to that sort of thing. That's why they've produced so many philosophers, like Kant and Hegel. Especially them, but also Schopenhauer and Fichte and many another. To say nothing of the impenetrable Heidegger, who doesn't really have anything much to say."[6] Many of these philosophers expressed sentiments sympathetic to authoritarianism, and Heidegger was a Nazi apologist at one point. During *Alnilam*'s gestation, Dickey expressed a keen interest in the Nazis and all other cults that led multitudes to ruin by first turning them into zealots; his other novels and poetry are shot through with supermen, whose impact on the world is at once heroic and profoundly destructive.

For the young Dickey, Mrs. Huntley, who had married a dentist after Mr. Burckhardt's death, could be a gentle eccentric as well as a martinet. Her second husband was equally eccentric—he liked to get drunk and walk around the house playing a zither in the nude. Normally kind and understanding, Mrs. Huntley was sickly, as was her daughter, Maibelle, Dickey's mother. Huntley suffered from diabetes, which made her blind. When she contracted gangrene, she had to have a leg amputated. The possibility and reality of amputation horrified the young Dickey. He later filled his novels and poems with an array of severed appendages, as well as characters who suffered from diabetes. In middle age, Dickey himself would claim—falsely—that he was diabetic.

Family antagonisms simmered beneath the orderliness of 1459 Peachtree. The aristocratic Huntley had opposed her daughter's marriage to Eugene Dickey, a rather lackadaisical man and an undistinguished lawyer whose main ambition in life was to become an esteemed cockfighter. Among other detractions, he had little standing in Atlanta society and little desire to gain any. Maibelle's family felt their daughter had married a "damn Yankee" and "Negro sympathizer," or, as Dickey bluntly put it in later life, "a Negro."[7] (Dickey's father, in fact, had old-fashioned ideas about race, which led him to support such notorious segregationists as Lester Maddox in the 1960s.)

Maibelle as a young woman was shy, solitary, and homely. She never dated Eugene; he simply showed interest, proposed, and on December 29, 1910, married her. The Peachtree house was spacious, but the inevitable tensions in the family gave the Dickeys a reason to find a house of their own. In 1925, they moved from Peachtree to a stately red-brick house at 166 West Wesley Road in the Atlanta suburb known as Buckhead. Opulent mansions lined both sides of the street, and the Dickey house held its own among them. Its two stories, symmetrical wing rooms, and mansard roof typified houses built in Atlanta's affluent suburbs during the early twentieth century. The front doorway, which was surrounded by small glass windows, exhibited aspects of Palladian architecture, while the entablature was Greek Revival and the chimney and overall proportions of the house were modernist. Ivy-covered pine and oak trees shaded the house from the sun and gave the Dickey children an ideal place to play.

Even as a child Dickey was aware of Atlanta's relatively short, turbulent history. On his trips to the Chattahoochee River, where his father owned land, he could envision the Civil War battles that had erupted around earthworks still jutting from the river valley, and the Indian battles that preceded them. The Chattahoochee River had once formed the ancient boundary between Creeks and Cherokees and had been the site of Sherman's triumphs during his march toward Atlanta in July 1864. Here, decades later, the young Dickey played, camped, entertained fantasies of heroic combat, and developed a keen sense of ruins and resurrections. If he looked one way, he could see signs of the war that reduced Atlanta to broken walls and blackened chimney stems. If he looked another, he could see the phoenix-like city that had soared from the ashes.

Part of Atlanta's recrudescence began in 1886 when a druggist, John Pemberton, began selling a tonic called Coca-Cola to the public. By 1920, three years before Dickey's birth, Atlanta had recovered sufficiently from the Civil War to become a fair-sized city with over 200,000 people. During Dickey's boyhood, Atlanta burgeoned on many fronts. In 1922, radio stations went on the air for the first time. In 1923, a new baseball park was built after fire destroyed the Atlanta Crackers' old park on Ponce de Leon Avenue. Hotels, office buildings, and homes sprouted everywhere. The city built the airport known as Candler Field (named for the creator of The Coca-Cola Company) in the mid-1920s. Delta Air Lines, for whom Dickey would write advertising copy in the 1950s after working on the Coca-Cola account, set up its headquarters in Atlanta in 1929.

At the beginning of the twentieth century, Atlanta was an odd mix of progressive and reactionary factions. Partly due to the efforts of Margaret Mitchell's mother, an ardent feminist, Atlanta women obtained the right to vote a year before the 1920 constitutional amendment that granted suffrage to women. Despite their political advances, many women were content with their traditional roles. Among the activities prized by fashionable women were the dances at the Piedmont Driving Club, where Dickey's sister Maibelle (named after her mother) socialized, and the Capital City Club, where Dickey's father was a member. At the first Piedmont dinner dance after the Great War, Dickey's mother was among the guests. Because of her war service making bandages and other supplies, she greeted the guest of honor, the commander of the American Expeditionary Forces, Gen. John Pershing.

While some Atlantans dined and danced at posh clubs, an organized crime family known as the "bunco ring" flourished in the city. After Prohibition took effect on January 16, 1920, illegal stills and bootleggers proliferated. Corrupt, racist politicians extended their tentacles throughout Atlanta. During Dickey's childhood, the Democratic-Populist demagogue Thomas Watson continued to influence Atlanta politics with his anti-Catholic, anti-Semitic, and antiblack tirades. The Ku Klux Klan had a powerful hand in city government into the 1920s. The young Dickey absorbed these contradictory social attitudes and never completely resolved them. As an adult, old South and new South continued to battle in his psyche.

With the stock market crash of 1929 and the ensuing Depression, Atlanta plunged with the rest of America into financial chaos. The Dickeys were a notable exception. Having inherited money from the SSS Tonic Company, Dickey's mother provided for the family as if the Roaring Twenties had never ended. Embarrassed by his family's affluence and how they came by it, Dickey usually repudiated any suggestion that he had been raised by wealthy parents. To his closest friends he mocked his grandfather's tonic company, saying that its slogan should be "Go where the ignorance is,"[8] since it targeted poor, uneducated blacks. In his unpublished novel *The Entrance to the Honeycomb*, written in the early 1950s, and a draft of it he called *The Casting*, he expressed his repugnance for inherited wealth through his alter ego, Julian Glass. Asked about the amenities of 166 West Wesley, Dickey usually feigned ignorance. In fact, his parents hired numerous servants. A chauffeur, Andrew James Burney, drove the Dickeys around Atlanta, gardened, and did odd jobs around the house. A Hungarian cook, Julia, lived in the house and prepared the meals. Temperamental and superstitious (she was known to throw skillets when angry and hang chicken heads on the clothesline to keep away evil spirits), she was also a superb chef. Old George was another "character" who worked at West Wesley. Allowed into the house only on holidays, he drank one beer, played the harmonica, and always told a gothic tale about a black snake. The rest of the time he tended the yard. A succession of maids (one named Coreer was Dickey's favorite) were in charge of domestic chores. Two nursemaids—one for Jim and one for his younger brother, Tom—also worked for the Dickeys.

According to Tom, the family had a budget of about fifteen hundred dollars per month for maintaining their household during the Depression (today this would amount to about two hundred thousand dollars per year). Low taxes in the 1930s made the Dickeys even more comfortable. Dickey once admitted, "I don't remember really that there was any special pinch on us financially. Maybe because my mother's income was from patent medicine and depression years are very good for patent medicine because people can't afford to pay doctors. We never really suffered, but we were not rich."[9] The Dickeys were not fabulously wealthy like Ernest Woodruff, who presided over The Coca-Cola Company at the time, but they earned a princely sum from their tonic company nevertheless—and without having to work for it. Despite sudden memory lapses when the subject of servants arose, Dickey remembered them well. His bond with his private nurse, Mamie Doster, was particularly close and affectionate, partly because she read to him. His claims of a philistine childhood were as apocryphal as his claims of early poverty. "He was born with a book in his hand,"[10] declared his older sister, Maibelle. Indeed, he constantly implored his nurse to bring him books just as he commanded secretaries to ransack his shelves near the end of his life when illness made walking difficult. His boyhood tastes were eclectic. He wanted to hear children's stories about anthropomorphic animals as much as encyclopedia articles about astronomy. Mrs. Dickey also read to her precocious son. She introduced him to *Hamlet,* as if to prepare him for his later mother-son and father-son conflicts. Fearing accusations of being a pampered and effeminate child, Dickey sometimes said he had been an untutored, rough-and-tumble pauper, whose parents couldn't afford to buy him a new pair of shoes (throughout his life he blamed his foot problems on this early hardship). He wanted to be regarded as a Horatio Alger hero rather than Little Lord Fauntleroy.

Dickey's need to envision his past in terms of heroic sacrifices influenced the way he viewed his birth. Throughout his life he claimed that his birth had depended on the death of his older brother, Eugene: "I *did* gather by implication and hints of family relatives that my mother, an invalid with angina pectoris, would not have dared to have another child if Gene had lived. I was the child who was born as a result of this situation. And I always felt a sense of guilt that my birth depended on my brother's death."[11] Dickey's mother kept a picture of Eugene dressed in a sailor suit on her bedroom wall, but like her husband she said little about the pain of losing him. Her silence may have created the appropriate void for her son's imaginings. The idea that he had been conceived because of his brother's death made his birth seem miraculous and Christ-like as well as freighted with original sin, and that's how he treated it in his poetry and prose.

Eugene was born on September 14, 1914, and died of infantile paralysis on April 4, 1921, at the age of six. Dickey's mother suffered from a mild ailment, a valve malfunction in her heart brought on by rheumatic fever. She did not have the more serious angina pectoris. She "dared" to have several more children—Jim and Tom—after Eugene's death (Maibelle was born in 1912). Indeed, she outlived her husband and even outlived Dickey's first wife, Maxine. She died of cancer in 1977 at the age of eighty-nine. According to her grandson, Kevin, who later became a doctor, she did in fact complain of angina and of being constantly fatigued, but exaggerated her illness—a propensity she passed on to her son. Kevin's older brother, Chris, who often stayed with his grandmother, suspected that she retired to her room for long naps in order to get sympathy and keep her distance from her husband. Often during her "naps," she read and listened to the newly established radio stations. Like her husband and like Jim, she was reclusive by nature. Jim's boyhood friends noticed that she stayed inside most of the time and usually wore nothing more than a nightgown. When she and her daughter went out shopping, they "dressed as though they were to meet the queen,"[12] as one of Jim's friends remarked, but still she kept her distance by wearing a veil. In the manner of Poe, a writer both mother and son cherished, Maibelle no doubt understood the power a beautiful, aloof, and possibly dying woman could exert.

Despite her manipulative hypochondria, Maibelle Dickey was a caring and generous mother. Her children, especially her daughter, remembered her with great affection. Maibelle once said,

> If you tried a million years, you could never relate how really wonderful she was. She treated each of her children as an only child, gave each a home of his own, and supplemented all of Jim's grants. She was a marvelous letter writer. Jim probably gets his talent from her, although Papa could write an excellent letter too. . . . [She] was a very bright and happy-hearted person, especially around her children, in spite of the fact that she had a leaking valve in her heart, which caused her a great deal of concern. She had a great sense of humor also, especially in her letters. My cousin reports that during the war (WWII) his fellow soldiers would often say, "please read more from your aunt's letter!" Then they would all be greatly entertained and have a good time laughing.[13]

Her son remembered her similarly: "She was a deeply feeling, quiet sort of retiring person who stayed alone in her thoughts most of the time, but humorous and sweet as she could be, and helpful. She was almost the ideal mother because she stayed out of the way. You asked her something; she would tell you what she thought, but she sure wouldn't impose it on you."[14] To a journalist writing a profile of her, Dickey portrayed her as a paragon of virtue "who lived for her children and would do anything for them, give them anything . . . , suffer for them, die for them. She was very proud of all of us, and worried continually about us. . . . Her imaginative and very caring and also very practical kindness—remains with me as the best example that I possess of unqualified and continuous human goodness."[15] Dickey's childhood friends confirmed these sentiments.

Having attended Washington Seminary in Atlanta and then Brenau College in Gainesville, Georgia, Dickey's mother was typical of her generation in that she gave up her career ambitions (singing, painting, and writing were among her talents) in order to raise a family. She channeled her literary abilities into letters rather than poems, stories, or novels. Dickey claimed that he expressed his literary talent at the start of his career in the same way—by writing letters during the war. If his mother was his early tutor, she was also his first literary model and muse. The fact that Dickey, in his later life and writings, often tried to sever his bonds with those women—whether wives or lovers—who attracted him betrays a closeness to his biological mother rather than any original antagonism. As a young man, Dickey found it hard to love any woman other than Maibelle. As an adult, he played prodigal son and unfaithful husband, but never disentangled himself from the principal woman in his life.

Maibelle Swift was born in 1889, two decades after the Civil War, in a mansion on Capitol Avenue that later became the first Piedmont Hospital. The original family house was built by her father, Charles Thomas Swift, who died a year after her birth. The remaining Swifts—she had three sisters and a brother—subsequently moved into a house resembling Mount Vernon on the mansion-lined West Paces Ferry Road. Maibelle Dickey owed her fortune to her father, who had cofounded and codirected the company that made "Swift's Southern Specific," known throughout the South as "Three-S Tonic." A Civil War captain in the Georgia Light Artillery, Charles Swift originally bought the formula for his tonic from Irwin Dennard, a plantation owner from Perry, Georgia. According to legend, in 1821 Dennard gave some Creek Indians a suit of clothes for the recipe of herbs and roots (swamp sumac from Alabama, Queen's Delight from South Georgia, and sumac from North Georgia). His slaves found the medicine he bottled highly palatable, perhaps because of its high alcohol content, and regularly used it to cure indigestion.

Charles Swift and his business partner, Col. H. J. Lamar of Macon, Georgia, brought their SSS business to Atlanta around 1873 because of the city's numerous railroads. Like the original Coca-Cola tonic, the Atlanta-based Botanic Blood Balm (BBB), and the many other tonics that circulated after the Civil War, the SSS tonic was supposed to cure all sorts of ailments, from dyspepsia to cancer and syphilis. Sales grew steadily during the late nineteenth century, boomed in the prosperous 1920s, and survived the Depression. Dickey, who jokingly renamed his family's patent medicine "Swift's Syphilitic Specific," once told a friend that sales plummeted when the Pure Food and Drug Act forced the company to eliminate the part of the label referring to cancer.[16] The brick building erected in 1879 to house the company still stands on the northeast corner of Butler and Hunter Streets. The recipe of roots and herbs has changed little, although now it is fortified with iron and vitamins to enrich the blood. Having expanded its product list to include such amenities as toothache gel, skin lotion, and vitamin supplements, in 1997 the company earned nine million dollars in annual sales and still paid dividends to the family.

At the beginning of *Deliverance*, the novel that made him famous, Dickey intimated that his family's tonic company, with its origins in the quackery of the Old South and commercialism of the new, was one of the sources of privilege he wanted to flee. His persona, Ed, sees a sign for 666, a tonic similar to SSS, and muses: "We hummed along, borne with the inverted canoe on a long tide of patent medicines and religious billboards. From such a trip you would think that the South did nothing but dose itself and sing gospel songs; you would think that the bowels of the southerner were forever clamped shut; that he could not open and let natural process flow through him, but needed one purgative after another in order to make it to church."[17]

Dickey took a certain ambivalent pride in knowing that his grandfather was a successful businessman who'd fought in the Civil War. He inherited from his grandfather a compulsion to prove himself in martial and entrepreneurial arenas, but he never knew Charles Swift, and neither did his mother. Because Swift married relatively late and because Dickey's mother was his youngest child, Dickey explained: "She didn't remember him. The only time she ever saw her father was when she was lifted up as a little girl to kiss his face in the coffin."[18] His grandfather was his most ostensible link to the Old South and to its mixture of idealism, charlatanry, and prejudice. Dickey would spend much of his life wrestling with the inheritance bequeathed by his family's most eminent ghost.

Dickey shared an interest in genealogy with his sister and knew the histories of both sides of his family. Charles Swift traced his lineage to England, Ireland, Germany, and Scotland. His family name derived from a species of bird (like the chimney swift) and the ability to run swiftly. Dickey and his brother, Tom, lived up to their ancestral name by becoming track athletes, Jim a proficient high hurdler and Tom a world-class sprinter. The Swifts of Atlanta distinguished themselves in business, law, and various civic duties. Charles's father, William Tyre Swift (1812–90), was a deacon in the Baptist Church, a promoter of Houston Female College, a judge of the inferior court, and a treasurer for Houston County. In 1857, he built a dignified house now known as the "Swift House" on a street that bears his name. Literary as well as business talent graced the Swift family. One of Dickey's alleged ancestors, who left Yorkshire, England, for Dublin early in the seventeenth century, was the writer and dean of Saint Patrick's Cathedral, Jonathan Swift (1667–1715). Dickey liked to stress his connection with this literary Swift and also to imitate his scatalogical wit, reactionary views, irascible temperament, and flights of fancy. Allied to the British, Dickey also claimed kinship to seven Swifts from Virginia and Massachusetts who fought the British during the Revolutionary War. Dickey's feelings for the British vacillated between affection and animosity. At the height of his critical acclaim in America, he was deeply disappointed that so many British critics dismissed his writing as stereotypically American. Under such circumstances he adopted the truculent anti-British attitudes more typical of the Scottish and Irish.

If Dickey needed precedents to explain his conflicted and combative nature, he could easily find them on his father's side of the family as well as his mother's. The Dickeys traced their origins to Richard Talbot, a Norman baron who came to England with William the Conqueror in 1066 A.D. Talbot fought at the Battle of Hastings, and his banner displayed the motto "Forte et Fidele"—Brave and Faithful—ideals Dickey always felt obliged to salute. A family genealogy records that Baron Richard de Talbot, an owner of large estates in England, was the common ancestor of the lords of Malahide and the earls of Shrewsbury, and married the great-granddaughter of William the Conqueror. One Richard de Talbot "the Chevalier" obtained a castle near Dublin and the lordship of Malahide. Originally conferred by King Henry II, this baronial estate continued for seven hundred years in the male line of the Talbots.

The American Talbots descended from John Talbot, tenth earl of Shrewsbury, and Lady Frances Arundel, a member of a prominent English family dating back to 1200. Matthew Talbot traveled to Maryland in 1720, to Virginia's Prince George County in 1725, then to New London in Bedford County, Virginia, in the early 1740s. There he built a store and bartered wolf heads to the government for one hundred pounds of tobacco per head. An educated man, talented writer, and dedicated public servant, he earned many appointments, among them king's agent, high sheriff, commissioner, judge, and clerk of the church. He was known for his generosity, honesty, and manners. James Dickey may not have inherited all of his ancestor's virtues; nonetheless, he was so impressed by the Talbot line that he vowed to give the name Talbot to his first and only child by his second wife, whether it was a girl or a boy.

The Talbots moved closer to the Dickeys when one of Matthew's female descendents, Elizabeth, married Nathaniel Cox of Tennessee in the early 1800s. Cox's claim to fame was his mother, a sister of Pres. James Madison. Elizabeth and Nathaniel produced a great brood—thirteen children. One of them, Leonora, married Joseph Brison Smith in the mid-1800s, a man who helped found the first Atlanta building and loan association in April 1853. Joseph and Leonora gave birth to a daughter, Gertrude, who eventually married into the Dickey family. Before migrating to Atlanta, the Dickeys settled in Fannin County in the North Georgia hills, a place whose savage beauty always frightened and attracted Dickey. According to family legend, the Dickeys had been distillers in the Pennsylvania mountains who fled to Georgia in the 1790s when the federal government cracked down on the Whiskey Rebellion, a popular revolt against a whiskey tax. Dickey could not resist telling people that his relatives—including his brother Tom—were moonshiners, and in *Deliverance* suggested that his hillbilly characters have stills in the woods.

Out of a desire to identify with his father's rural ancestors, Dickey frequently told unsuspecting friends and interviewers that he had grown up in the mountains around Mineral Bluff, Georgia. Dickey had a right to be proud of and perplexed by his father's ancestors; the Dickey line was nearly as prestigious as the Swifts. One of the most famous Dickeys was George, an Irish immigrant who, in 1803, married Hannah Taylor, daughter of Joshua Taylor (a hero of the Battle of King's Mountain). Hannah was allegedly the niece of Zachary Taylor, the twelfth president of the United States. George's father, Robin Dickey, was probably the first Dickey to sail from Ireland and settle in America. Family lore contends that he settled in North Carolina in the mid-1700s and later died at the hands of Indians. Around 1841, George and Hannah Taylor Dickey traveled from Rutherford County, North Carolina, to Fannin County with about eight slaves. Some historians maintain that George got involved in the mica and soapstone mining business that gave Mineral Bluff its name, but this is unlikely since he died shortly after his arrival—on September 15, 1842. From her husband, Hannah inherited a small fortune. An 1860 census listed her as a "farmeress" with fifteen slaves (two adults and thirteen children) and assets of $13,815 in real estate and $1,500 in cash. She became the fourth largest landowner and the seventh wealthiest person in Fannin County.

George and Hannah's most famous son was John Brady Dickey. Born in 1817 in North Carolina, he migrated to Georgia with his parents, married Catherine Kilpatrick, and according to some accounts founded the town of Douglas in May 1858 (later that year the name was changed to Mineral Bluff). Locals also claimed John Brady as the first man from Fannin County to serve in the U.S. House of Representatives (the Directory of American Congress shows no John

Dickey on its list). He was, however, a Republican member of the State Constitutional Convention of Reconstruction after the Civil War. Among his many talents was the ability to sire children. He had nine and indicated his political loyalties, which were divided between South and North, by naming some after Southern heroes (Thomas Jefferson Dickey) and some after Northern heroes (William Tecumseh Sherman Dickey). John's family farmed the fertile land along Hot House Creek in Mineral Bluff and operated a grist mill and sawmill in the area. Because of the Dickey wealth and penchant for land speculation, a 1900 census listed John's wife Catherine (a widow at the age of seventy-nine) as a "capitalist."

James Dickey inherited a talent for making money from his immediate ancestors. Several of John Brady's sons became successful businessmen. Thomas Jefferson Dickey established himself as a contractor, builder, and sawmill owner in Mineral Bluff before moving to Atlanta. John Rucker Dickey, who also left home, founded the Atlanta Stove Works. As if to consecrate the ground from which the Atlanta Dickeys sprang, John Rucker (Dickey's great uncle) contributed money to build a church in Mineral Bluff. But when the townspeople refused to call it "the Dickey Church," he and his relatives locked its doors. Later, the benefactors relented and opened it for worship. The church became a favorite shrine for the Dickeys.

Gertrude married the poet's namesake, James Lafayette Dickey, in Atlanta on October 16, 1873. James was a well-to-do landowner and developer with large holdings along Hot House Creek near the Toccoa River in Fannin County. Gertrude and James left a sizeable estate to their three sons: James Lafayette Jr., who worked in the fire insurance business and who, according to the poet, donated the land on which the Georgia governor's mansion was built; Ervin John, who also worked in fire insurance; and Eugene, the poet's father. Born on January 26, 1888, Eugene was the youngest. Although he made Atlanta his home, he never forgot the rustic origins of his immediate predecessors. He encouraged a strong, if not bloodthirsty, competitive streak in his sons, and set the standard by excelling at football and track at Boys High School in Atlanta, at Georgia Tech, and finally at Mercer University, where he studied law and graduated in 1907. According to his son, he set the record for the 220-yard sprint at Georgia Tech.

Like his son, Eugene could be both generous and ruthless. One of his gifts, which Jim remembered well, was the guitar—some said it was a banjo—he gave to Walter, the mentally retarded son of Mary White, a caretaker who fed Eugene's fighting cocks on the farm he bought to raise them. Walter so impressed Jim that, in the 1950s, he planned to write a short story, "The Silk," about the gift of a silk shirt to "an idiot country boy"[19] who spends his time beating musical tunes on a lard can. Walter White later appeared in more memorable form as Lonnie in *Deliverance*, the genetically deformed banjo player who enthralls the canoers with his homespun talent. In the film version of the novel, the character based on Walter applies his finger-picking skills to "Dueling Banjoes," impressing millions of viewers as an Appalachian idiot savant.

As far as his legal profession was concerned, Eugene was a dilettante, unconcerned with success or salary, and therefore earned his son's scorn: "My father was a rather unsuccessful lawyer, a born loser. . . . He revered the profession of the law—not the letter of the law and the legalistic paraphernalia of the law, but the ethical qualities of the law."[20] Dickey's childhood friend Jim Coleman, who accompanied Dickey through grammar and high school and who later became a lawyer in Texas, never heard any Atlanta lawyers talk about Mr. Dickey's legal activities. The *Martindale-Hubble Law Directory* listed Eugene as a lawyer from around 1930 to his death in the 1970s, but gave him either a mediocre rating or no rating at all. In 1976, Dickey told an English class at the University of South Carolina that his father was a racist redneck and "linthead" who worked in a textile mill: "Daddy believed the way to settle trouble was with lynchings. His daddy, my granddaddy, believed it too." The purpose of Dickey's story was to emphasize his moral struggle as a young man: "It was *hard* for me as a college boy to rise above this kind of thinking."[21] The fact that his father's brothers were successful businessmen only increased Jim's disappointment with his father.

Eugene liked to consort with disreputable types in Atlanta and its outskirts. One of his friends was the notoriously unscrupulous businessman Tom West, who owned something called the BX Corporation, which purchased the delinquent taxes of poor blacks and then foreclosed on them when they couldn't make their payments. He acquired about nine hundred parcels of property in Atlanta in this way and became a "slum landlord" known for his strong-arm tactics with impoverished tenants. Eugene used his law office in the Peters Building to meet with people like West. His cockfighting friends, whom his wife called *Bettelsacks* ("riffraff"), also congregated there to drink Wild Turkey and discuss their sport. Jim remembered that his father *did* work occasionally as a criminal lawyer but mainly out of generosity to those poorer clients who could never pay him much. His impecunious law business, however, was not entirely without glamour. According to Jim, one of Eugene's early office secretaries was Margaret Mitchell. As it happened, Eugene Mitchell practiced law in an adjacent office in the Peters Building and sometimes visited the other Eugene for friendly talks.

Income from the SSS Company; commercial real estate holdings on Broad Street, College Park, and elsewhere in Atlanta; and securities investments allowed Eugene to take a laissez-faire attitude toward his career. Eugene's brother-in-law, Mitchell King, managed the real estate. Eugene left the house every day partly to get away from his wife and the servants. Dickey's childhood friends described him as a "mystery man" and a "lone wolf"—epithets often applied to his son as well. They never saw Eugene on any of their numerous visits. His grandchildren noted that he rarely spoke to their grandmother when he was in the house and slept in a different room. The children were brought up by their mother and her servants. Cowed by his wife's affluence and aristocratic airs, Eugene retreated to his own provenance among the farms and wooded hills of North Georgia, often with a shotgun to hunt squirrels and rabbits. Eugene never took his literary son hunting, but together they often traveled north to meet family and friends. "His real heart was in country people and country things and country ways, which my mother looked down on as being extremely low class and sorry. But my father loved sorry people,"[22] Dickey commented years later.

Eugene also went to the country to participate in the illegal activity of cockfighting. To the annoyance of his neighbors, who disliked being awakened at dawn by roosters, Eugene quartered some of them behind his West Wesley garage. The birds were so mean-spirited that Eugene instructed his grandchildren to keep away from them except during feeding. Occasionally a servant would pluck one of the less successful fighters, cut off its head, and let it run around the yard scattering blood. Jim Dickey had only to look out the window to discover one of his most enduring subjects: the convergence of civility and savagery. Most of Eugene's fighting birds, however, stayed outside Atlanta on a farm that ran from Bankhead Highway to the Nickajack River, a site Dickey later used for the sadoerotic events in his poem "May Day Sermon."

As a youth, Dickey took friends to his father's cock farm, swam in the river, hunted for Civil War relics, or just roamed like one of the Cherokees who'd once lived in the nearby woods. The farm was full of interesting animals and the sort of disreputable characters that populated his later poems and novels. As James Dickey's literary reputation grew, he shocked his audiences by pretending to embrace his father's violent passions rather than his mother's refinements. In a 1961 letter to the poet James Wright, he spoke of his "fanatically prideful North Georgia folk heritage" and attributed his "well-known aggressiveness" in all sports, including writing, to it: "In my early youth I was so fiercely competitive (very like the gamecocks that my father has spent his life raising) that most of the time I was fretting myself to death over whether I could gain ten pounds before next football season, whether I could keep from hurting my knee this year, whether I could pare .5 of a second off my time in the high hurdles."[23] He elaborated on his attachment to his father's gamecocks in an interview:

> I remember saying to my father, "Dad, why do you fight chickens?" I know my mother was telling me—my mother was a kind of religious fanatic who suggested that this was a disreputable business my old man was engaged in. When I was no more than nine or ten years old, I went to my father and said, "Dad, why are you doing this here chicken fighting stuff when you could be providing for the family a little better some other way than gambling on your chickens?" He said, "'Cause, I tell you, it's *inspiring*. Every man that ever lived would like to have the *guts* those chickens have." . . . My father also bred fighting dogs, bull terriers, those kinds of dogs. You don't like to see a dog get torn up by another dog, but a chicken is just something you can't like. You don't care what happens to them.[24]

As a boy Dickey did care. He abhorred the use of razor-sharp gaffs clamped to the chickens' heels. His father's preference for short-heel gaffs, which allowed the cock a better chance to prove its endurance and bravery, rather than long-heel gaffs and "slashers," was little consolation.

Dickey sometimes confided that he had once fainted when he saw a fighting cock drive a razar-sharp gaff through his father's hand. Because of his squeamishness, Eugene began calling him "Blood" and insisted on taking him to cockfights to overcome his fears of carnage. Generally Dickey refused to go, just as he refused to read his father's stacks of *Grit and Steel* cockfighting magazines that lay around the house. Asked if her brother showed any interest in the sport as a boy, Dickey's sister retorted, "Not in the least."[25] Even after Eugene hired one of the

South's top cockfighting managers, moved him and his family from Alabama to his farm, and spent most of his time overseeing the cockfighting stables, Jim would not alter his view of the sport.

In later life, to compensate for his pusillanimous beginnings, Dickey impersonated the machismo of his forebears. He celebrated his father as one of the South's preeminent cockfighters. "He had serious qualifications for being the grand old man of American cockfighting,"[26] Dickey boasted to an interviewer in 1973. Twice he told his friend Jim Mann that his father had won the World Cockfighting Championship in Miami during the Depression "and came back home with . . . $200,000 in cash in a brown paper bag, and dumped it out on the kitchen table."[27] In a more reliable version of the story, Dickey said: "He won the International Tournament in Orlando in, I believe, 1934, and won a lot of money. He won the top prize money, but he also won a great deal of money gambling on his own chickens. He and a bootlegger and numbers racketeer friend of his named Bob Hogg had a stable of chickens, and they went down there and won. They picked up all the marbles. Florida's the only state in the Union in which cockfighting is legal."[28] Shocked and repulsed as a boy, as a poet Dickey treated cockfights as a necessary rite of passage. After he took a job at the University of South Carolina in 1969, he quipped: "One of the few things my father approved really in my later days, was that I affiliated myself with a university whose mascot was the Fighting Gamecocks."[29] To prove his pride, Eugene supposedly gave his son several prize cocks, which Jim said he ate.

Eugene's love of gambling was not limited to cockfighting. He bet on football games and, if *The Entrance to the Honeycomb* and *The Casting* can be trusted, the ones in which Jim played. In the novel, Dickey's persona, Julian Glass, gets a tongue-lashing after doing poorly in a high school game. Julian has cost his father and his father's friends a considerable sum. Ignoring his son's injured head, Mr. Glass angrily denounces him by the locker room: "You clown. Throwin the ball around before the game like you knew what you was doin. God-*damn!* I just wanted to tell you. You can read all the god-damned books you want to, but by God you ain't never goin to get back on that field again, or any other field. Do you do this way at every game? What do you go out there for? . . . I didn't know you was makin a fool out of me. Do you know how many of my friends saw this game tonight? These three gentlemen did, and I told them your number. Well, all I got to say is that I wish to God I had told them somebody's else's!"[30] The mortified Julian goes to his locker and sobs, and in the shower suffers an ailment that Dickey sometimes suffered under stress: a bloody nose.

To his intimate companions, Dickey bemoaned the fact that he could never please his father, who favored sports over books. Dickey's attempts at fulfilling his father's athletic expectations continued unabated over the years. He felt obligated to succeed in all fields, and readily created legendary successes to make up for his failures. The spirit of his judgmental father was so strong that it interfered with his relationships with others, particularly women. Once when Dickey complained about his inability to satisfy his father, a lover snapped back, "Is he then the one who matters?"[31] Eugene, however, did not always fit the molds of tyrannical redneck or lackadaisical fool his son made for him. Although not overly bookish, he liked to read old-fashioned writers like Montaigne, Macaulay, and Carlyle. In *Self-Interviews* his son pointed out that he and his father established rapport by reading and debating almost all the famous cases in the multivolume *Classics of the Bar*: "He had a set of law books of famous cases from the trial of Jesus Christ up to the trial of Fatty Arbuckle. And I expect at one time or another, he read them all to me, or we read them to each other. His great heroes as lawyers were men with an oratorical flair. He was very fond of Clarence Darrow, and we read through the Scopes trial transcripts and also read about Sargent Prentice [sic], a lawyer from Mississippi who very eloquently defended some Mississippi boys on trial for murder in Tennessee [it was Kentucky]. That was perhaps his favorite case."[32] Although Dickey usually confused the cases and the testimony, to the end of his career he traced his love of grandiloquence to *Classics of the Bar*.

Dickey paid homage to his father's discussions of law and morality in *Deliverance*, where Lewis, Ed, Bobby, and Drew wrangle over the legal ramifications of killing the hillbilly rapist. Dickey commented: "A lot of that debate business in *Deliverance* was based on conversations I had with . . . [my father] when I was a little child."[33] Father and son may have discussed the law on their trips to Fannin County to visit the relatives Jim imagined were outlaws. They liked to wander through the two graveyards—one on a high ridge near Mineral Bluff called Hogback and the other in town—where their ancestors were buried. As an adult Dickey romanticized his attachment to this side of the family. He told a *Time* reporter in 1968: "My people are all hillbillies. I'm only second-generation city."[34] Hard at work on *Deliverance*, he mischievously implied that his kin resembled the backwoodsmen who torment the four Atlanta men on their canoe trip. In an interview conducted shortly before he died, he said, "I'm a real hillbilly of the most backwoods sort. I really don't talk like I'm talking now. . . . It took me a long time to get that [redneck inflection] out of my voice so that people could understand me who were not from up there."[35] Having achieved literary fame, Dickey pretended that his aunts, uncles, and grandparents had rolled out of the hills in jalopies with shotguns hanging in the cabs and beaten-up furniture piled behind them. But neither Dickey's ancestors nor his siblings were "hicks."

Born on July 2, 1912, Jim's sister, Maibelle, who was eleven years older than Jim, earned a reputation for beauty and charm in Atlanta when she was elected Queen of the May Festival as a ten-year-old E. Rivers student. Like her mother, she attended Washington Seminary. She did well in her classes, making the honor roll and graduating in 1930, about a decade after fellow alumna Margaret Mitchell. Allegedly founded by George Washington's relatives, the seminary—a neoclassical mansion surrounded by Corinthian columns—was a finishing school at the pinnacle of Atlanta's social register. According to Margaret Mitchell's biographer: "Although well into the 1930s the institution still genuflected to the conservative Baptist Puritan morality of its founders, snobbish social values competed with academic standards as the dominant characteristic of the student body."[36] Maibelle shared an English teacher with Mitchell, Miss Nora Belle, who encouraged both women in their writing. Like Mitchell, Maibelle also felt a tension between the orthodox mores of her school and her literary goals, which may have been one of the reasons why, as adults, the two women developed a friendship at teas and other social occasions.

As a young woman, Maibelle cut a dashing figure as she drove around Atlanta in her yellow 1930 Auburn sports car. She exuded charm, humor, and high spirits. She liked to dress fashionably. Members of All Saints Episcopal Church still recall the huge hats she wore, which sometimes blocked their view of the pulpit. While less ambitious than Mitchell, Maibelle possessed literary talents of her own. She wrote poetry, which she sometimes boasted was better than her brother's because it was intelligible and pleasing rather than obscure, violent, and sexual. By 1990, she had published over one hundred articles, mainly about gardening and ornithology, in such magazines as *National Wildlife*, *Horticulture*, *Organic Gardening*, *Flower & Garden*, and *The American Rose*. For these publications she received the highest honor granted by the Georgia Garden Club—a Certificate of Merit. An accredited American Rose Society judge, she was also an active member of the Atlanta Audubon Society and Georgia Ornithological Society. In the woods off Dalrymple Road in North Atlanta, she turned her property into a kind of nature sanctuary. Bird feeders and birdhouses hung near a dazzling array of roses. The subject of numerous magazine articles, her rose garden also inspired the garden in her brother's book *Bronwen, the Traw, and the Shape-Shifter*.

Relations between Maibelle and Jim were often contentious. Although she suffered a period of alcoholism, her brother's alcoholic shenanigans dismayed her, especially when they erupted after their mother's death in 1977. She despised the many lies he told the press about the Dickeys and the unflattering way he depicted her in poems. In "Power and Light" she appears as a grotesque crone "trailing ground-oil / Like a snail" from her rose gardens to her house. The poem insulted her further by portraying her husband, John Hodgins, as a lonely drunk fleeing the "sad way-station"[37] of his home to drink whiskey in his dark cellar.

Tom Dickey shared Maibelle's dismay about their brother's lies. When *Reader's Digest* journalist Sheldon Kelly visited 166 West Wesley, where both siblings were recuperating from divorces, Tom expressed gratitude that someone finally had the sense to question others in the Dickey family about Jim's stories. In a gentlemanly drawl, Tom said, "We have been described as poor but friendly rednecks, moonshiners, killers, *Deliverance* types. . . . Now look around you. This is where Jim was raised. This is Jim's house as much as it is my house. . . . James has alluded to the fact that we don't like Negroes. We have always had Negroes and we like Negroes and we have no reason not to like Negroes." To demonstrate his point, Tom asked an elderly black man in the living room how long he had been employed by the Dickeys. He said forty years. "See, Mr. Kelly," Tom resumed, "we've had . . . [him] forty years, and James doesn't think we like Negroes."[38] Kelly concluded that he had entered a Southern family drama worthy of Tennessee Williams.

Unlike Maibelle, Tom tended to attribute his brother's flaws to his genius and thereby excuse them. Born on February 5, 1925, two years after Jim, Tom became an outstanding athlete, a businessman (a real estate executive for Draper Owens in Atlanta and a shopping center owner), and an author of Civil War books. Jim once said, "My brother sort of dabbled in real estate as an occupation, but he didn't really have much of an occupation. He lived very largely on the family money from my mother's side."[39] The put-down revealed as much about Jim's sense of rivalry as it did about Tom's abilities. As a young man, Tom compensated for his mediocrity in the classroom by excelling on the track at the 440-yard dash. He also broad jumped; ran the 100-, 220-, and 880-yard dashes; and competed in the mile relay. A nervous disturbance affected his digestion—Jim would suffer similar problems in later life—and for that reason his parents sent him to the private Peacock's Academy. When the school closed, he transferred to Powers Ferry School, where a football coach discovered his speed and entered him in a 100-yard dash, which he won. At Marist School in Atlanta and Baylor School in Chattanooga, Tom continued to win. As an undergraduate at Louisiana State University (LSU), where he majored in physical education, his speed became legendary, as did some of his whimsical training methods (he once ran sprints through the rain with an umbrella). He became the third highest track scorer in the Southeastern Conference (SEC). In 1945, he won the SEC 100-yard dash in 9.8 seconds and the 220 in 21.8 seconds. He continued his triumphant ways at the SEC meet for the next two years.

Tom's career reached its zenith in 1948, when he qualified for the Olympic tryouts. Although he had switched to a longer distance—the 400-meter dash—because of a muscle pull earlier in the year, many believed he could still make the team. The nagging injury hampered his performance, however, and he was cut. A decade later, his brother wrote the poet James Wright: "My brother just missed the 1948 Olympic team by about six inches, give or take a few, in the 880 [sic]."[40] Like Jim's failure to become a pilot a few years earlier, the rejection resonated through Tom's life. Though he had garnered plenty of track trophies and though he continued to run, breaking a world record for a forty-seven-year-old man in the Atlanta Classic meet in June 1972 (he ran the 220-yard dash in 25 seconds), Tom never really overcame the disappointment. Decades after the Olympic tryouts, he supposedly confided to Jim, "When I stepped off that track at LSU at twenty-one years old, my life was over. I've never really been interested in much since."[41] His Olympic failure came at the age of twenty-three. With a master's in physical education from LSU, he wanted to be a track coach. Instead, he returned to Atlanta with his wife, Patsy, sold cars for a year, and then managed the family's real estate business. For Jim, who had invested so much enthusiasm in Tom's track career, Tom's life had lost its luster.

Tom's brooding on personal and public failures may have galvanized his interest in the Civil War. After giving up his track career, his relic-hunting became an obsession comparable to his father's cockfighting. He told a friend: "It all started when father would take Jim and me to a farm we owned on Nickajack Creek out off the Bankhead Highway. This was the location of Johnston's river line on the Confederate left. We'd collect minié-balls, belt buckles and other stuff by just picking it up off the ground. When we were kids—this was in the 1930s—there wasn't much interest in the Civil War and nobody thought much about it. I collected a shoe box full of relics which I kept at home."[42] (Jim remembered these early expeditions as well as his brother's later, more scientific ones in the poem "Hunting Civil War Relics at Nimblewill Creek.")

Tom became an avid collector during the 1950s, when battlefield relics were still plentiful. By 1967, as a *Time* article attested, Tom had a national reputation. Within another decade, as relics dwindled and the National Park Service guarded the remaining ones more fiercely, Tom had acquired over ten tons of shells. With Sydney Kirksis he wrote two distinguished books on munitions: *Field Artillery Projectiles of the Civil War* and *Heavy Artillery Projectiles of the Civil War*. In 1980, he published a third and final volume, *Field Artillery Projectiles of the American Civil War*. These books became the standard reference guides for collectors and historians. While living at his parents' house after divorcing his wife, Patsy, he sometimes lined the driveway with artillery shells from his excavations, impressing but also frightening the neighbors. His expertise with projectiles was so renowned that NASA consulted him about rocketry. He provided artifacts to many Civil War parks and prominent museums, including the Smithsonian, and traveled around the world giving lectures. In 1996, the Atlanta History Center exhibited his Civil War ordinance collection, which was the most extensive one of its kind in the United States.

For two brothers as gifted and competitive as Tom and Jim Dickey, sibling antagonism was almost inevitable. Jim viewed his brother as a competitor from the start. Much of Jim's contentious behavior can be traced to his relationship with Tom. Al Braselton, who befriended both men while working in Atlanta advertising during the 1950s and 1960s, once wrote: "Jim was the apple of his mother's eye until Tom Swift Dickey was born. Tom soon took his mother's attention from his older brother and Jim, until then a fairly dutiful, sensitive child, got his first taste of competition. He lost. He never regained the number one child slot."[43] In infancy, Tom was the loud, boisterous one. When he wanted something, he screamed for it. He enjoyed dancing and shouting on tables, a practice his mother, a slack disciplinarian, allowed. Jim was more reserved, and as a result didn't command his mother's attention the way Tom did. It was not until Jim became an English professor and well-known writer that he routinely hoisted himself up on tables to attract attention.

As he grew, Tom became the natural star of playground sports. Jim vied with him for his parents' praise, but usually came up short. In high school and college, Tom was the one whose athletic feats made newspaper headlines. When his mother used her influence to keep Tom at home during the war, Jim did his best to accept her efforts on his brother's behalf. In a letter written during basic training, Jim admonished his mother: "Do everything you can to keep Tom out of the army, but if he has to go, don't worry. It's a cinch."[44] A year later, on January 16, 1944, Jim coached Tom on getting a deferment, and on June 29 he congratulated his mother on successfully helping Tom get turned down by the draft board. Still, the fact that his mother had interceded on Tom's behalf galled him. His brother stayed in the South to become a track hero while he risked his life in the air war over the Pacific.

Jim's later accomplishments, real and imagined, were due in part to this fraternal dueling and preferential treatment. "If it had not been for Tom," Braselton speculated, "Jim might have been one of those Byron-quoting . . . failed Southern talkers that come from breeding romantic sons of strong mothers in a heady atmosphere of wysteria, bourbon, and a kind of smothering gentility."[45] As in John Cheever's revenge story "Goodbye, My Brother," where the author's alter ego nearly kills his brother with a piece of driftwood, Jim Dickey cultivated a taste for imaginary violence that was diametrically opposed to his quiet, sensitive nature. As he got older, he usurped Tom's role as the aggressive, undisciplined child, while Tom grew gentler and quieter. Competing with other athletes, soldiers, businessmen, professors, and writers for the number-one rank, Jim demanded adulation from friends and lovers with the vehemence that his younger brother had once displayed before his mother.

The sibling competition emerged most visibly in high school athletics, principally in track and field, where Tom dominated. In the rougher sport of football, Jim had the advantage because he was bigger and stronger. At times Jim found this one-upmanship intolerable and demeaned his brother's running as a "sissy sport." The fame and fortune Jim eventually gained as a writer signified a victory over Tom, but the athletic rivalry persisted. As poetry consultant to the Library of Congress in the late 1960s, Jim insisted on a footrace with his brother, who was visiting his home in Leesburg, Virginia. Out of shape, overweight, and groggy from too much alcohol, Jim not only lost; he nearly collapsed from the exertion. When Al Braselton learned of the nearly disastrous race, he remarked that his friend abided by the motto: "I'd rather be dead than number two."[46] Those who competed with James Dickey and won usually did so at a price, as Braselton knew all too well.

As a writer, Dickey exposed his competitiveness by attacking most of his peers and claiming he was completely original. Asked whether Dylan Thomas, T. S. Eliot, Wallace Stevens, or some other major writer had influenced his poetry, he usually denied it, just as he denied he was born into a talented, literary family. As late as 1986, he contended: "I was not introduced to poetry by anybody in my family, or any teacher or acquaintance. . . . I've always had the feeling that nobody really understands poetry but me, because I came to it of my own free will and by a very devious and sometimes painful route. I feel that it's something I've earned."[47] Dickey's mother had, in fact, begun reciting poetry to her son when he was one or one-and-a-half years old. According to Patsy Dickey, Jim revealed his affinity for poetry as a child by recalling the poems verbatim.

To achieve originality and stardom Dickey believed, with some justification, that he needed to rebel against his immediate family. Throughout his life he held that an inherited income had compromised his parents' and siblings' ambitions. Like Joyce's Stephen Dedalus and his mythical precursor, the Greek Daedalus who designed labyrinths and wings to escape them, James Dickey planned to fly over the parochial confinements of home and region in order to forge a separate identity. Not surprisingly, rites of passage and the myths based on them fascinated him when he began to write. His protagonists, like Joyce's, resemble legendary heroes who depart from comfortable homes, undergo difficult initiations and frightening trials, and return home emboldened with their new knowledge and new ability. Musing several months before he died, he said, "I was very independent minded, very early, and I wanted to do everything myself. I saw the way that my sister and brother were going, and they were so dependent on the family, especially my mother. And I just didn't want that."[48] Dickey's heroes fare forth on similar quests for independence.

Like most mothers, Maibelle Dickey worried and to a certain extent resented her son's efforts to achieve self-reliance. She hoped Jim would stay in Atlanta and become a wealthy businessman like her father, Charles Swift, rather than a poet and novelist writing about gruesome subjects as he roamed from one underpaid job to another. Eugene Dickey also had career plans for his son, most of them involving sports (Jim said baseball and boxing were high on his father's list). Tom was the one, however, who would choose sports and business and win his father's approval. Eugene respected books, but not a son who wanted to write them. The idea of his son writing poetry offended his traditional views of masculinity, and after choosing poetry as a profession Jim became a relative outcast in the Dickey family. In the popular imagination, poets were paupers and fops. Having absorbed some his family's prejudices, Dickey did everything he could to line his pockets with gold and prove to the world he was a literary Tarzan.

II.

THE INVISIBLE STUDENT

2. "A Good Old Scout" (1929-1936)

Like many writers, James Dickey gave few hints of future literary greatness in elementary school and high school. At first he had no desire to go to school. While his young friends in Buckhead signed up for Miss Bloodworth's private kindergarten at the intersection of Peachtree Road and Peachtree Battle Avenue, he resisted. After his sixth birthday, when enrollment in E. Rivers Grammar School across the street from the kindergarten became inevitable, he still had little desire to attend school. He preferred playing with neighborhood friends or having books read to him at home. His reluctance to join institutions—whether churches, social clubs, or elementary schools—remained constant throughout his life.

Entering E. Rivers's two-story granite building in the fall of 1929, Jim showed none of the swagger associated with him in later years. The principal—a gray, stout, tough-looking woman named Mrs. Osterhout—imposed a regime of stern discipline over her three hundred students. Jim's teachers, all of whom were women, followed Osterhout's example, often slapping disorderly students on the hand with a ruler. Shy and self-conscious, Jim rarely spoke in class. Here he rubbed shoulders with a diverse group of students. Some, like Dickey, were the scions of wealthy Buckhead families. Others were the offspring of hardscrabble families who lived in shacks in the Peachtree Creek section of town. Embarrassed by his luxurious upbringing, Dickey tried to identify with the less fortunate ones, just as his father identified with lower-class clients and kin.

Dickey began elementary school only months before the devastating stock market crash of 1929. The Dickeys' SSS fortune only made Jim's self-consciousness more acute. The E. Rivers boys who played tackle football would sometimes cry when they fell to the ground—not because they were bruised, but because they had torn their pants. They knew their parents, who could not afford new clothes, would punish them at home. Dickey, by contrast, never had any financial reasons to cry. He wore fashionable clothes—usually knickers and sports shirts—and he had servants to wash or repair those sullied by rough play. Later, when he played on sports teams, his parents bought him the best apparel and equipment. His friends were quietly envious.

During the Depression years, many families around E. Rivers did not own cars. Most students walked to school, even if the distance was a mile or more. Dickey, on the other hand, enjoyed a chauffeured ride in one of his family's cars. This convenience provoked one of Dickey's first dissimulations and one of his first rifts with his parents. He told the chauffeur—probably Andrew James Burney—to stop the car a block or two from school so he could walk the remaining distance. His father and brother could understand such dissembling, but his mother and sister, who were proud of the family fortune, were irked by his poor-boy act. When Dickey's sister recounted the story to Sheldon Kelly, she did so with scorn. Tom, however, pointed out, "Jim was doing this so he could at least play with his pals. His pals would beat up on rich boys."[1] As for Dickey's mother, she felt little compunction about displaying and distributing her wealth. To Jim's friends she would say, "No mun, no fun," and give them money for candy or entertainment. Every year she presented both Tom's and Jim's teachers with a five-dollar gold piece—an extravagant gift at the time. Elizabeth Sutton, an E. Rivers teacher whose sister taught Jim in third grade, recalled how the fortunate recipients fell all over Mrs. Dickey with gratitude. While the coins were intended as tokens of appreciation, Jim was embarrassed by his mother's largesse.

In the 1970s, with an annual income of several hundred thousand dollars, Dickey got a more public opportunity to evince solidarity for the impoverished when he worked on the short documentary film *One Third of a Nation*, which focused on Depression-era families in Beaufort, South Carolina. "How bad *was* it, living here, fifty years ago?" Dickey asked at the start of his screenplay. His answers came in a monologue in which he reminisced and offered asides about photographs of indigent locals and their homes. His purpose was similar to James Agee's in *Let Us Now Praise Famous Men*, a book about Depression-era sharecroppers that Dickey adored. Dickey's sympathy for the poor families, like Agee's, led to virtual identification:

> It's hard to think about the Depression without wondering what would happen if we had another one. (Pause) If we would prove as tough, as brave, as resilient the second time around. As energetic. As bewildered. In fact, it's hard to remember that these were our parents and grandparents, alive at that time . . . in this place. Only fifty years ago . . . , but already it's easy to forget that these were *people*, not actors. . . . People who listened to rain on the tin roofs over them . . . or felt the shriveled chinaberries under their feet . . . who lay in bed at night trying to figure out what to do . . . how to eat . . . how to live through the next day (Long pause) . . . how not to die.[2]

Dickey and his parents and grandparents never suffered such nocturnal worries. It was easy to forget that his subjects were not actors because, in Dickey's case, he *was* acting the role of a Depression survivor.

Dickey's desire to fit in required more subtle camouflage as he grew older. By the age of ten, according to his sister-in-law, Patsy, he took desperate measures to hide the intelligence he feared might earn him the epithets "sissy" or "bookworm." When questioned by his teachers, he sometimes feigned ignorance: "During grade school and high school, beginning with the fourth grade, he contrived to make errors so he would not stand out among other students."[3] Only a perceptive few detected the astute literary mind forming behind the mask. One teacher remarked to Dickey, after reading a published story during a lesson, "You could have written that."[4] His best friend at the time, Richard Lamb, realized his talent only belatedly—at the age of twelve when he read a story that Mrs.

Dickey had kept from Jim's second-grade class. One of the only people who knew much about Jim's budding aspirations was his mother, who continued to serve as mentor and confidante for the next decade. Because Dickey also disguised his early gift as an adult, most believed that he never put pen to paper until World War II. In fact, he wrote his first book at the age of five. Bound with string and only a few pages long, his manuscript dealt with personal hygiene—specifically toothbrushing. To give the book a printed look, he cut out a picture of a child from a magazine for the cover and the words "You and Yourself" for a title. Inside, opposite his signature, he pasted a picture of Forhan's toothpaste, a woman, and a toothbrush. He also drew a calendar to keep track of his daily toothbrushing. As if premonitory of the advertising work he would do in the late 1950s, the young Dickey laid out the pages like a toothpaste ad. Years later, after the success of the film *Deliverance*, he revealed his boyish pride in his good teeth by boasting to friends that Colgate had asked him to perform in its ads.

Dickey's second book was similarly self-involved and prophetic. At the age of six he authored *The Life of James Dickey*, in which he characterized himself as a fighter pilot. He illustrated his five-page autobiography with crayon drawings of airplanes. Dickey's fantasy of himself as a combat pilot became so deeply ingrained that during the postwar years he repeatedly lied about having been one. Much of his later poetry, fiction, and pseudoautobiography can be traced to this seminal *Life of James Dickey*. It can also be traced to his awareness of the rapid developments in aviation after the Wright brothers began testing planes at Kitty Hawk in the early 1900s. During Dickey's childhood, "barnstorming" stunt pilots became a regular feature at country fairs (in his 1965 essay "Barnstorming for Poetry," he would compare his frequent flights and carnival-like performances on the poetry circuit to the stunts of these pilots). In the year Dickey was born, two army lieutenants in a Fokker monoplane traversed the United States for the first time. On May 9, 1926, Lt. Comdr. Richard Byrd flew across the North Pole. A year later Charles Lindbergh flew *The Spirit of St. Louis* from Long Island to Paris (one of Dickey's earliest memories was of watching a parade for Lindbergh pass his grandmother's house on Peachtree Street in October 1927). Atlanta had joined the flying frenzy when it procured Asa Candler's Hapeville Speedway in 1925 to build an airport; by 1928, regular flights had commenced. Doug Davis, one of Atlanta's pioneer aviators, who directed an aviation school and flying service at Candler Field, plunged to his death on September 3, 1934. Daring flights and tragic crashes riveted Dickey's youthful as well as adult imagination.

The quiet, unassuming boy, who may have been daydreaming of piloting planes in the classroom, came alive on the E. Rivers playground in dodgeball, football, baseball, running, and marble games (he fondly recalled his marble playing in Frank Cahill's reminiscences of grammar school in his 1987 novel *Alnilam*). During recess at E. Rivers, Dickey befriended one of the school's superior football players, Jack Emerson, idolized him (Emerson later starred at North Fulton and Clemson), and berated himself for not being as good. Emerson's relaxed, humorous manner always reminded Dickey of Bob Hope. In *Deliverance* he may have commemorated his happy-go-lucky friend by giving his last name to Ed Gentry's advertising partner, Thad Emerson.

Dickey enjoyed other sports as well. Partly because it was so cheap, roller-skating was one of the most popular ways children entertained themselves during the Depression. Dickey and his cohorts liked to skate down Buckhead's long hills: "It was sort of like a skiing slope. . . . You could really get to flying. You could get hurt, too. You'd fall, and we didn't have all those knee pads [that contemporary roller-blade skaters wear]."[5] Dickey imparted his love for roller-skating to Frank Cahill as well:

> Alone, he had skated the streets of south Atlanta, swinging from one leg to the other along many streets, through rich and poor neighborhoods, past communities, stores, unknown schools with their frazzled poplars and empty playgrounds and the brick chimneys of their power plants. . . . Toward the northwest part of the city the land steepened into little hills, and around his steady and driving sweep larger houses and grounds arose, and through these he would move, afternoon by afternoon, his feet planted in long splaying strides out-angled, split, dealt like cards from a hand. Sometimes, in these northern suburbs, he would be completely alone, and trees on some streets closing almost over him in spring, he would power through that freshness in what might have been the strong swings and balances of a powerful sleep. That was best.[6]

The years before high school and World War II were as idyllic for Dickey as they were for Cahill. In the early 1970s, after a heart attack killed his childhood hero Jack Emerson, Dickey wrote his friend Jim Coleman:

> [Our lives] will never be what they were when we were boys, and as I think back on those times I am filled with an enormous nostalgia for the decent fellows we were in those days, though God knows, as boys we were certainly not any angels. But I remember the long afternoons when we used to go skating down on Rivers Road, the afternoons always organized by Jack Emerson, when we played football until we could hardly see the ball in the air any longer, and the rest. That is not the worst way to grow up, and I remember Jack and you and Richard Lamb and Dick Harris, and the others, before we got into the *organized* phase of sports at North Fulton, with a great deal of affection. . . . When the war came along, all those days went with them, and all we can do now is remember.[7]

Only through writing would Dickey redeem his fallen Atlanta paradise.

Dickey's relations with girls in elementary school were relatively idyllic as well. At E. Rivers, a pretty girl named Virginia Kirkland, with whom he played marbles and dodgeball, gave him his first intimations of sexual bliss when she revealed her underwear during a game of skin-the-cat on the monkey bars. As their friendship grew, he became bolder in his advances, but usually refrained from physical contact. During class parties organized by their "homeroom mother" at his friend Tom Lewis's house, they liked to play risqué games like spin-the-bottle and post office. At these carefully chaperoned affairs, Dickey would call Kirkland out for a "special delivery letter," which was supposed to be

a kiss. Usually he just chased her around the room a few times, a ploy he repeated with other women as an adult. Thirty-five years later, the impression
Kirkland had made on Dickey's adolescent imagination was still vivid. After receiving a stirring letter from Kirkland about her recent marital troubles, in
which she also referred to elementary school parties and special delivery letters,
Dickey responded: "You have a very special place in my mind, for . . . the sight
of you and some other girls—but especially you, playing on the old jungle gym
in that kindergarten across the street from E. Rivers school, with your shirt
tucked up like bloomers, was the first really sexual vision I ever had, in the mortal life. I felt something come over me like the sun coming out from behind a
cloud, and have never really been the same since. No wonder I called you out for
a Special Delivery Letter!" Dickey ended with the hope that they could renew
their innocent liaison: "I'd like to get together with you face to face after all
these years, if you will promise to tuck up your shirt again and swing upside down
from the bar. I mean the *exercise* bar."[8] Since Dickey was drinking heavily at the
time, he needed to specify which "bar" he meant.

Along with many other E. Rivers boys, Dickey also harbored amorous feelings
for an attractive, athletic girl named Peggy Stewart. Like several of the women
he wrote about when he became a poet, she saw her high spirits dashed as an
adult when the Hollywood actor she married committed suicide. Dickey flirted
with the lovely Beverly Adams as well. In the class picture for the 1936 E. Rivers
yearbook, Adams and Stewart sit side by side as if perched on the same romantic pedestal. He also had a crush on Angelique de Golian, who came from a
wealthy, cultured Atlanta family, and he wrote a poem about her in the 1950s,
"The Entrance into Jerusalem," in which he compared her opulent house to the
holy city and himself to a supplicating Christ. His attachment to her and to
other young girls, as the poem's religious imagery suggests, was more subliminal
than sexual.

After graduating from E. Rivers, Dickey continued to spend time with some
of these girls at Margaret Bryan's ballroom dancing lessons. Like others who
danced with him, Virginia Kirkland was surprised at how the shy boy was meta-
morphosing into the brash teenager. Within a few years, Dickey was telling his
old sweetheart how he no longer dated Atlanta girls, how he rode his motorcycle through the North Georgia hills, how he only dated tough mountain girls.
When Dickey was not dreaming of beatific girls with angelic names or of apocryphal motorcycle trips to their rural counterparts, he was more than likely involved in sports. His father took him to Atlanta Crackers baseball games and
track and football events at Georgia Tech (Tech had compiled a perfect record
and won a national football championship in 1928). At one track meet, the
family dog was left behind in the car, tore all the knobs off the doors, and
chewed up the upholstered seats. Dickey's penchant for writing about violent
dogs, such as Buck in his screenplay of *The Call of the Wild* and Zack in *Alnilam*,
may have originated from such scenes.

When Jim was about eleven, Eugene gave his sons their biggest athletic boost
by purchasing some collegiate-style high-jump and pole-vault equipment for the
backyard. The Dickey boys spread sawdust on the ground to cushion their falls
and invited their friends to compete. Lester Hardwick, one of Tom Dickey's

classmates who often practiced there, recalled how Tom spurred Jim's competitive instincts. Jim fashioned a vaulting pole from bamboo, wrapped it with electrician's tape, and began practicing obsessively behind his house. In a pattern that would repeat itself throughout his life, his eagerness to triumph led to an accident. As if prefiguring the broken bones of his most famous character, Lewis Medlock in *Deliverance*, and the olfactory troubles of Frank Cahill in *Alnilam*, he took a big leap and crashed, shattering his nose. For the rest of his life he had little or no sense of smell.

George Montgomery, whose grandfather's house abutted the Dickeys' backyard, also practiced on the newfangled equipment. "Here we emulated the great track stars of the day we had seen on the news reels in the local Buckhead Theater,"[9] Montgomery remembered. Hoping to dominate his friends and Tom, Jim became a bodybuilding zealot. As he later recalled in his poem "The Other," he chopped logs with a heavy axe in order to transform his "rack-ribbed" body into a godlike one. He also tied a rope between two trees for hand-over-hand exercises to enlarge his biceps. In 1935, he ordered a brochure from the York Bar Bell Company, "The Road to Super Strength." He was fascinated with the way Charles Atlas had evolved from a weakling into a world-class muscle man, and fashioned the main characters of his novels—Lewis Medlock, Frank Cahill, and Muldrow in *To the White Sea*—out of his adolescent fantasies of Herculean strength.

Dickey learned about current sports heroes from his family's black chauffeur, Andrew Burney, as well as from news reels, magazines, and bodybuilding pamphlets. Burney told stories about training the promising heavyweight William "Young" Stribling from Macon, Georgia (Stribling's career had been cut short by a fatal motorcyle accident in 1933). As Dickey got older, the world of violent sports, motorcycles, and early deaths had an almost sexual attraction for him. In many of his most famous poems, like "Cherrylog Road" and "May Day Sermon," sex, death, and motorcycles appear in a compelling alliance. Fascinated by Burney and his tales, Dickey accompanied him to their backyard playhouse for lessons on the punching bag. Over the decades his interest in boxing never diminished.

Richard Lamb was another regular visitor at the backyard sports complex and also went with the Dickey boys on chauffeured rides to the Georgia Tech track meets and football games. Other participants in neighborhood games were the Roper brothers, who lived on Habersham Road not far from 166 West Wesley. The Ropers and Dickeys played army in trenches and dugouts they excavated to resemble those on World War I battlefields. Their enthusiasm for such games may have influenced their more serious commitments to the army a decade later. Besides leaping bars, running footballs, and storming trenches, Albert Roper, known as "Roper Roper," achieved neighborhood fame with his tree houses. To demonstrate his Tarzan-like agility around the age of nine, Dickey followed Roper up the high trees to see what he was doing. "It was a point of honor with Albert to build in the highest tree he could find. And on the slenderest part of it,"[10] Dickey said. Thirty years later Dickey used his frightening tree-climbing experiences as the basis of his poem "In the Tree House at Night" and characteristically appropriated his hero's abilities:

Each nail that sustains us I set here;
Each nail in the house is now steadied
By my dead brother's huge, freckled hand.
Through the years, he has pointed his hammer
Up into these limbs, and told us

That we must ascend, and all lie here.

High in the pine tree with his spiritual and real brothers, Eugene and Tom ("one dead, / The other asleep from much living"),[11] Dickey experiences a joyous epiphany, which he communicates in lines echoing Yeats and Roethke.

Many of Dickey's ecstatic moments came inside the Buckhead Theater as well as inside Roper's tree houses. With Jack Emerson, Richard Lamb, George Montgomery, and other friends he watched dozens of B-grade movies. Their parents took them to the theater at one o'clock on Saturdays for two cowboy movies, two serials, and one or two comedies. They relished the popular cowboy stars like Buck Jones, Tim McCoy, Ken Maynard, Tom Mix, and Hopalong Cassidy. It was the "greatest babysitting you ever had,"[12] Lamb reflected. It was also affordable for those hit hard by the Depression; four hours at the cinema only cost a dime. When the weather was warm, other pleasures were to be had at Buckhead's Wender and Roberts's Drug Store. Here the boys slaked their appetites on ice-cream cones, Cokes, sodas, or one of the store's famous ham sandwiches. Thirty years later, Dickey memorialized these outings in "Looking for the Buckhead Boys":

First of all, going home, I must go
To Wender and Roberts's Drug Store, for driving through I saw it
Shining   renewed   renewed
In chromium, but still there.
It's one of the places the Buckhead Boys used to be, before
Beer turned teen-ager.

Alcohol, he suggests with a pun, is an "ager," an agent that corrupts. As a teenager Dickey rarely drank. Tom Mix and Hopalong Cassidy, who inveighed against drinking and smoking, were his heroes.

As Dickey approached his teenage years, he felt restless in his Buckhead home, where his mother and her servants hovered over him like guardian angels. He also felt confined in the sleepy suburb of Buckhead itself and enjoyed making forays with Richard Lamb to watch stage shows at the Capital Theater or movies at Loew's Grand Theater (where *Gone with the Wind* premiered in 1939) or one of the other half-dozen theaters in downtown Atlanta. His friend Lester Hardwick noticed his growing discontent with life at West Wesley in his acerbic humor, which was usually laced with sexual innuendo, and practical jokes. Tom Lewis heard him complain about the fancy meals at home. To escape the surfeit of roast beef, steak, chicken, and sumptuous desserts, which most people craved during the Depression, Dickey went to Lewis's house nearby to make peanut-butter-and-jelly sandwiches. If these visits signaled his modest tastes, Dickey still struck Lewis as vainglorious. He often caught Jim staring at himself in their big wall mirror, preening like a dandy about to attend a banquet or ball.

In 1936, the year Jim Dickey graduated from E. Rivers, only a few of his friends noticed the fissures opening in his personality. By keeping his literary interests and psychological divisions largely to himself, he impressed most of his friends as a normal, happy-go-lucky boy. Only later would he flaunt his different personae and project them into his poetry and fiction. In the section of his school annual, *The Rivers Overflow*, where a rhyming couplet defines every student, Jim Dickey is judged "A good old scout, / Everyone's happy when he's about."[13] His classmates, it seemed, had glimpsed his love of adventure. They also recognized his talent for advertising. In a picture of the *Overflow*'s advertising staff, Dickey stands above the rest on a back step. His hair is blond and tousled. He looks tall for his age, but his chest looks thin, undeveloped, as he tilts his head and smiles. He seems pensive, aloof, enigmatic. The image of the big, boisterous James Dickey is hard to detect in the boy's demeanor.

3. An Athlete's Masks (1936–1941)

Jim Dickey entered North Fulton High School in September 1936, still determined to maintain the image of a mediocre student whose principal concern was sports. To a reporter for the *Buckhead Atlanta* newspaper, he said of his high school years: "I was very undistinguished academically. I made grades that were just good enough to allow me to participate in sports. Football was the big thing in those days."[1] His high school transcript supports his claims. His cumulative average after five years was 78.57, a C plus. Mediocre to a fault, he never attained a yearly grade point average below 76 or above 82. Although he was reading voraciously, he felt little need to bring his extracurricular knowledge to bear on his course work. His attitude toward his studies remained lackadaisical. As his alter ego Julian Glass explains in a draft of *The Entrance to the Honeycomb*: "Studiousness indicated an unfitness for manly pursuits."[2] For Dickey, scholars and sportsmen were different breeds, and in high school he desperately wanted to belong to the latter group.

North Fulton High School, a Georgian–Classical Revival–style building with towering Ionic pillars on its main façade, had been built in the early 1930s to serve the swelling community of Buckhead. By the time Dickey graduated in 1941, it was the largest high school in the county system, with 1,270 students and 44 teachers, and known all over Georgia for its athletic and academic achievements. Despite its reputation, North Fulton failed to stimulate and accurately assess Dickey's gifts. (During his first year, his numerical scores proved that even in English he refused to apply his talents. He scored in the low eighties in English; in algebra, Latin, and general science his scores were lower. Over the next few years, his highest grades—a 91 and 95—came in spelling). His feelings for his teachers generally wavered between indifference and antipathy. As his Conduct grades attest, he treated many of his classes as opportunities for mischief. Demerits were regularly dispensed, and he received his fair share. The only teacher he admired, and who admired him in return, was Miss Yeargan in English, although later he scoffed at her by recalling that her most memorable scholarly contribution was an article about Virginia Woolf's dog. Forced to choose between "scientific," "classical," and "general" academic programs, Dickey chose the scientific because he believed it held the most promise for his future. His poor performances in Mr. Orea's math class typified his attitude toward the program. Once, Dickey failed to solve some problems at the black-board with his best high school friend, Bill Barnwell. Orea hollered at the two boys: "You get dumber every day."[3] Disgusted with Dickey's nonchalance, Orea told him to sit at the back of the room and read a magazine if he wasn't going to pay attention. For the rest of the term that's what Dickey did.

Dickey's antics in math class underwent a sea change in his poem "Mangham," which he collected in *Buckdancer's Choice*. Dickey wrote in his book *Self-Interviews:* "I had a teacher at North Fulton High School named Mr. Mangham, a gray, undistinguished man but an extremely good mathematics teacher. What happens, though, when you're an extremely good mathematics teacher and nobody cares about learning mathematics? We had a class in which Mr. Mangham would teach trigonometry assiduously every day, and we would more or less go through the motions of learning it. But this was all changed when he had a stroke one day in the classroom; he died a week later."[4] In the poem, Dickey imagines Mangham leaving the classroom to get ice for his stricken face and heroically finishing his class. When Dickey became a teacher, he acted similarly. Afflicted with jaundice and pulmonary fibrosis during his fi-nal years, he risked his life to keep teaching. But at North Fulton he showed lit-tle respect for his teachers. In fact, Dickey never studied under a teacher named Mangham and never took trigonometry. He took Algebra and then Geometry 1, failing the latter course before retaking it. At the end of "Mangham," Dickey ad-mits that he ought to wear a dunce cap decorated with moons and stars, and sit in a corner on a high stool. In Mr. Orea's class he suffered the punishment of a dunce without the exotic garb.

Like the men in the film version of *Deliverance*, Dickey and his Atlanta friends were united more by their passion for football than for books. He and Lamb spent long afternoons devouring sports magazines, especially the well-known *Street & Smith*, which published news about college teams at the end of summer. They memorized statistics, debated strengths and weaknesses of teams, and made their predictions for the fall season. Just as he'd announced his desire to be a fighter pilot in his adolescent "novel," Dickey made it clear to Lamb that he wanted to be a football star. As he got more involved in high school sports and in "running with the boys," he and Lamb spent less time together. He also drifted away from Tom Lewis. Like the Lewis character in *Deliverance*, Tom Lewis loved to hunt, fish, and hike. When Lewis invited Dickey into the woods, however, Dickey showed little interest in such rugged activities. One of the only times he accompanied Lewis on a *Deliverance*-like trip was when they lashed Lewis's kayak, which he had built himself and recently patched, to Dickey's car and drove to a bridge over the Chattahoochee River. Dickey launched the kayak, and Lewis drove downriver to wait, just as another Lewis—Lewis King—would do in two decades. At his post downriver, Tom Lewis waited and waited, wondering if his friend had drowned. Several hours later, Dickey walked up to him on the riverbank and explained that he had hit some rocks, scraped off the new patch, and sunk the kayak. The event foreshadowed his later canoe trips with Al Braselton and Lewis King, and the more cataclysmic events in *Deliverance*.

When Dickey decided he wanted to devote more time to pursuing girls, Bill Barnwell replaced Lamb as his closest friend. Barnwell was not an athlete, but exuded the sort of *joie de vivre* Dickey admired. Barnwell also liked poetry. For the two young romantics, Robert Frost was the "king of poets." His later denials notwithstanding, Dickey "worshipped Frost"[5] at the time. Fifty years after they graduated, Barnwell could still recite lines from Dickey's favorite Frost poems. Poe was a great favorite, too, as the melodramatic subjects and anapestic rhythms of Dickey's later work suggest. In his accounts of his literary origins in *Self-Interviews*, Dickey mentions neither Frost nor Poe, just as he mentions nothing about his boyhood infatuation with Roy Rockwood's *Bomba the Jungle Boy*, Lester Chadwick's *Baseball Joe*, and the Hardy Boys mysteries. According to Dickey, it was Byron and John Drinkwater's biography of Byron, *The Pilgrim of Eternity*, that commanded his greatest admiration. Amused by Byron's reputation as a *poète maudit*, for years he liked to tell stories about Byron keeping a tame bear in his retinue, drinking burgundy out of human skulls with college friends, having sex with his half-sister, and dining with a motley assortment of jockeys, gamesters, boxers, parsons, and poets. Dickey's memory of Drinkwater's biography, however, was colored by subsequent biographies he read. *The Pilgrim of Eternity* either glosses over or dismisses nearly all the reports of Byron's bisexual and incestuous philandering. What emerges from the biography is a portrait of a tempestuous poet at odds with his mother and the cant-ridden, aristocratic class into which he was born.

For better or worse, Byron became one of Dickey's enduring idols. In 1974, he told a writer for the *Washington Post*: "If I had my chance to sup with the gods, I'd choose him."[6] In 1981, after emulating Byron's profligate lifestyle for years, Dickey told another reporter he wanted to write a movie script based on Byron's life and give the leading role to Burt Reynolds.[7] He also claimed that Byron was "the kind of man that I've always attached a particular kind of personal value to. The guy who is an enormous phony, but who makes the public take him on his own terms, the terms of his persona. And underneath it all [he] is an extremely practical, hard-headed, and utterly honest person."[8] For Dickey, Byron was another model of the supreme poseur who was also a disciplined artist keenly aware of the facts he was transposing.

Drinkwater's biography, whose title came from a line by Shelley, may have inspired Dickey to read the poetry of Byron's fellow pilgrim. If he enjoyed Byron for his sarcastic wit and picaresque escapades, he enjoyed Shelley for his visionary flights and romantic idealism—traits that he found in the early Frost, another admirer of Shelley. *Alnilam*, whose first title was *The Romantic*, acknowledges Shelley's early influence through numerous allusions to the poet and his poetry. The popular genre of pulp fiction, whose roots were in the gothic romanticism of Poe, Byron, Shelley, and their peers, also appealed to Dickey. As a youth he had plenty of pulp magazines from which to choose. In the three decades spanning the two world wars, nearly 160 different pulp titles appeared. Their melodramatic style and subject matter drew on the horrors of the wars, the rise of organized crime, and the relaxed sexual mores of the 1920s. They featured Prohibition-era speakeasies, tough-talking bootleggers, gangsters with tommy guns, and hard-drinking detectives. Dickey's appetite for pulp magazines was insatiable. He read *The All-Story*, which published Edgar Rice Burroughs's *Tarzan of the Apes* series; *Amazing Stories*, which featured science fiction by Burroughs and H. G. Wells; *Dime Mystery Magazine*, *Terror Tales*, *Strange Tales*, *Horror Stories*, and *Weird Tales*, which trafficked in all sorts of titillating grotesquerie. Sex and sadism were particularly prized by the editors of *Horror Stories* and *Terror Tales*. With keen anticipation, Dickey followed the heroes as they searched misty graveyards and cavernous pits for necrophiliacs, witches, apelike madmen, and homicidal perverts. Usually the hero rescued a damsel mauled by a sex-obsessed brute. The plots of Dickey's future novels and poems, which so often explore nightmarish otherworlds replete with gruesome sex and violence, owe a large debt to these stories.

In the September 1935 issue of *Horror Stories*, readers could sample "Satan's Lash," a story of religious fanaticism and flagellation accompanied by a drawing of a black-coated man whipping a buxom beauty manacled to a chair. On the cover of the April/May issue in 1936, a robed man hurls a screaming woman clad only in a bra and short slip into a blazing furnace. In *Alnilam* Dickey probably alludes to this picture, which he mistakenly attributes to *Terror Tales*, when Frank Cahill's wife inspects her son Joel's pulp library and tells her husband, "This here's called *Terror Tales*. . . . On the front of it, it's got . . . a picture of a woman, and it looks like there's these two big muscled-up men with black masks, and it looks like they're fixin' to put her in a furnace."[9] Mrs. Cahill also describes in gory detail several other magazine covers that advertise stories by Arthur Leo Zagat. Zagat, who produced some twenty-five stories for *Dime Mystery Magazine*, *Terror Tales*, and *Horror Stories*, was a master of sadomasochistic melodrama, ornamenting his tales with such phrases as "choking fetor," "lambent gloom," and "virulent torchglow"[10] and titles like "The Corpse Factory," "Dr. Midnight—Surgeon from Hell," and "Girl for the Torture God." In *Alnilam*, Dickey bestowed his early taste for such pulps on Joel.

Dickey's fascination with sadomasochistic pulp fiction began as a reaction to what Al Braselton called "the cosseted gentility of the child raised in the petticoats of the last bastion of English matriarchy, the Old South."[11] Testosterone astir, Dickey was at war with himself and the matriarchal culture that he found entrenched in his household. He adopted the old-fashioned Southern ideal of womanhood even while wanting to violate it. His breeding and the breeding of the girls he dated in high school made normal sexual relations verboten. Most Atlanta belles resisted premarital sex. "They were well trained to do nothing," Bill Barnwell said. "If you got a kiss you were lucky."[12] In the pulps Dickey could entertain fantasies of imposing his sexual desires on lovely damsels and also rescuing them when others did the same. These stories, satanic one moment and sentimental the next, permanently shaped his feelings about sex and women.

Masked detectives clambered through pulps like *The Shadow* and *Dark Sider* in the 1930s. Dickey also felt a special affinity for *The Phantom Detective*, a magazine started in 1933. The Phantom was a rich playboy bored with his privileged life and eager for adventure. An early issue explained that he "felt stifled by the smugness of the people around him and the sort of lives they led. He tried big-game hunting, deep-sea fishing, polo, other sports. All these eventually lost their appeal. He was bored—desperately, terribly bored."[13] As a diversion, he solved crimes that baffled the police. The Phantom was a master shape-shifter, whose disguises were so convincing that even the daughter of his adopted father misconstrued his true identity for twenty years. Dickey's disguises and lies would prove similarly deceptive to his audiences, including his family.

Dickey gravitated toward another pulp, *Secret Agent X—The Man of a Thousand Faces* (he would make Joseph Campbell's famous study of mythology, *The Hero with a Thousand Faces*, the basis for the mythical plot in *Deliverance*). Dickey also adored *The Spider*, which began publication in 1933 and which regularly featured stories by Zagat. In daily life the crime-busting Spider was Richard Wentworth, an heir to a family fortune, a college football and track star, a combat pilot in the First World War, a bon vivant who cut a wide swath through the New York debutante scene after the war, a scholar who abandoned a promising law career to follow his whims, and finally a vigilante who roamed the crime-ridden streets in disguise, leaving a red spider stamped on his victims' temples. Finding his privileged life similarly boring, Dickey also sought escape in athletics, war, hunting, philandering, and role-playing.

According to Dickey's son Chris, who often listened to his father retell his favorite pulp stories, the *Doc Savage* magazine also gave him images to emulate. Each month a new pulp novella appeared in which the bronze, muscle-bound, brainy Doc Savage commandeered missions to destroy purveyors of evil in exotic locales. Savage and his crew tramped through jungles in Asia to destroy gigantic, human-eating falcons; they battled fabulously wealthy foes in an ancient Mayan kingdom; they plunged deep into the Earth to neutralize a survivor of a lost supercivilization who kills with the touch of a finger. Doc Savage undoubtedly supplied one prototype for the intelligent, muscular, half-savage Lewis Medlock in *Deliverance*. As one villain named Watches puts it in a March 1935 issue: "That bird Savage is a wizard! They say he knows all about electricity and chemistry and psychology and engineering and them things. They say he's a mental marvel. On top of that, he's supposed to be able to bend horseshoes in his hands. . . . He's what the newspapers call a big-time adventurer. He's supposed to travel around over the world, helping people out of trouble and punishing wrong-doers."[14] Dickey may have commemorated this bizarre character, who possessed an array of watches that doubled as weapons, when he himself lined his arms with watches during the last decades of his life.

Dickey's love of the mythic and fantastic also drew him to science fiction stories by Edgar Rice Burroughs. He pored over Burroughs's stories about flights to Mars, imitated them in his juvenilia, and, as he neared the end of high school, read Burroughs's new science fiction series about Carson Napier, who made interplanetary flights to Venus. To satisfy his fantasies of terrestrial as opposed to extraterrestrial flights, Dickey could read about combat pilots dogfighting over Europe and Asia in *Dare-Devil Aces*, *RAF Aces*, *Sky Bird*, *War Birds*, and other war pulps. While stationed at an air force base in Waco, Texas, during the Korean War, he and a friend went to a local store that specialized in old pulp magazines, and Dickey afterward wrote his wife: "To our immense delight the shelves were groaning with numbers of 'War Birds,' 'Doc Savage,' 'Flying Aces,' and 'The Secret Six' which we remembered from our boyhoods. We bought a couple of them . . . and have been roaring with laughter ever since."[15] As a youth, Dickey also sampled magazines like *Western Tales*, *Round-Up*, *West*, *Nickel Western*, or *Western Story* and adored the Westerns by Zane Grey, especially *The Thundering Herd* and *The Border Legion*. The Darwinian lens through which Grey filtered his knowledge of Indians, buffalo hunters, soldiers, and their natural habitat in the West made Grey's stories irresistible and influential.

Of all the adventure heroes in Dickey's youthful reading, the one to have the most impact was Tarzan. Dickey alludes to Tarzan numerous times in *Deliverance*, and sometimes in jest signed his letters "Bolgani," drawing a comparison between himself and the monstrous gorilla in *Tarzan of the Apes*. The story of Tarzan appealed to Dickey because it traced another journey from a wealthy, aristocratic home to a savage wilderness and then a return to civilization. Tarzan's real parents are the English lord and lady Greystoke, who die on a visit to Africa. Having learned to live by the "kill-or-be-killed" ethic of the wilderness, Tarzan returns and ends up in a city (Baltimore), where he finally realizes his true identity. In these Tarzan books, Dickey found his aristocratic and savage attitudes amplified, and in his later poems and novels drew on the books' mythic plots.

On the track and football field behind North Fulton High School, Dickey struggled to become the pulp fiction superman of his fantasies. Despite its fledgling status, football at North Fulton was particularly competitive. Coach "Beef" Tucker commanded the team with a bulk so massive that, as one student noted, "If you were walking down the hall . . . you had to make an effort to go around him."[16] With Assistant Coach Kelly by his side, the domineering "Beef" shaped a winning squad. By the end of the 1939 season, the team had compiled twenty-two consecutive victories and won the North Georgia Interscholastic Conference Championship. Among his compatriots, Dickey was proficient, but not outstanding. In *Self-Interviews*, where he speaks of the "absolutely formative" nature of high school experience and how terrible it is to fail in athletics, he confessed with rare candor: "I was sort of neutral in high school, poised between success and failure."[17] He made the football squad in 1938, 1939, 1940, and 1941, but spent much of his time on the bench as a substitute quarterback for Richard Gray, or as a second-string wingback. (As the "single wing," he had the job of a modern-day wide receiver and running back.) If Dickey got the ball, he surprised some players and infuriated others by zigzagging up the field or running laterally to avoid direct contact. According to fellow player John Jarrell, Dickey acquitted himself satisfactorily as a blocker and tackler in the days when players had to serve on both offensive and defensive teams, but Dickey also earned a reputation for being self-conscious, thin-skinned, and literary. Although he posed as "one of the guys" by talking and acting tough, he was not always convincing.

Dickey so desperately wanted to become a football star that he arranged his high school schedule around the sport. He should have graduated in 1940, but he deliberately failed to attain the required seventeen units (credits) so that he could spend a fifth year perfecting his football skills. Richard Lamb, who knew of his friend's ploy, suspected he accomplished it by not signing up for ROTC his junior and senior years. The first two years of ROTC were mandatory and provided one-quarter-unit per course. His military ambitions still dormant, Dickey submitted reluctantly to ROTC's drills, parades, and military science courses. He preferred a football to a military uniform.

By immersing himself in football, Dickey was staking out territory where he, and not his brother, Tom, could dominate. Then as now, campus track stars shone less brightly than football stars. It was in track, however, that Dickey had considerable talent. His coach, Robert Lowrance, had built a cinder track around the football field at North Fulton, and Dickey was part of the formidable team that ran on it. At the start of his first season, Dickey impressed the coach with his strength and agility. Lowrance recalled: "I squatted beside the hurdle and watched him barely clear the cross-piece and slap his forward foot as close to the hurdle as possible, then stride on to the next one. Jim was 'doing it right.' His championships testify to that. Although slightly tall for the low hurdles, Jim was a strong, intelligent athlete, and he adapted his stride to a conquering length and pace."[18] Managing only a second-string position on the football team, Dickey broke records on the track team. By April 1941, he had the fastest time in the 220 low hurdles (26.6 seconds) in North Fulton's history.

The 1940 team on which Dickey ran surpassed all previous teams. It won the North Fulton Relay and nearly all of its other meets. Dickey's moment of glory, which he commemorated in the title essay of his 1983 book *Night Hurdling*, came in the 1940 North Georgia Interscholastic Conference (NGIC) track meet. In the trials, he lost to a hurdler from Canton, Georgia, because of a bad start. His opponent, by contrast, had set a new NGIC record. In the final race that night, Dickey sensed that he and the Canton boy were dead even:

The finish-line crowd was coming at us like a hurricane. I concentrated on staying low over the hurdles and made really good moves on the next three. I began to edge him by inches, and by the next two hurdles I thought that if I didn't hit the next two I'd make it. I also said to myself, *don't* play it safe. Go low over the last stick, and then give it everything you've got up the final straight.

But I did hit the last hurdle. I hit it with the inner ankle of my left foot, tearing the flesh to the bone, as I found out later, and the injury left a scar which I still have. However, my frenzied momentum was such that I won by a yard, careening wildly into the crowd after the tape broke around my neck. I smashed into the spectators and bowled over a little boy, hitting straight into his nose with my knee.[19]

As everyone crowded around to congratulate the new record holder, Dickey bent over the boy, whose nose was bleeding, wiped away the blood, and kissed him. Whether true or false, what he called "the best moment I ever had out of sports"[20]—with its melodramatic nosebleeds (a recurrent motif in his fiction), bodily wounds, and sentimental attitudes toward men and boys—belied the different forces in Jim Dickey's teenage personality that he was struggling to compartmentalize. He was the victorious jock and wounded, sensitive young man who kissed the suffering boy. As an adult, because of his reputation for rough-and-tumble machismo, he often surprised men and boys by kissing them.

In another short essay published in *Night Hurdling*, "Starting from Buckhead," Dickey also tried to bring into focus the impulses that in high school had threatened to split him apart. He joked about being more of an aesthete than an athlete. It was the beauty of an athlete's movement that excited him rather than the pomp of victory. He enjoyed watching the javelin's graceful arc, the broad jumper's leap, the receiver's run before the football spiraled through the air. "Although I was collecting splinters [as a bench-sitter]," he pointed out, "I was also collecting a set of rudimentary aesthetic responses."[21] These pleasures, however, did little to assuage his disappointments on the track or football field. He grew irritable if he could not compete with the best and tended to blame his failings on the coaches. He complained: "I was always running on a team that needed me to do a lot of other stuff too. Run the 100 and the 220, the broad jump, and throw the shot, the discus, run on the relays. I stayed all tired out."[22] One way to overcome his frustrations was to identify with winning athletes. "My best races were run," he recalled, "not by myself but by my chosen Self in the person of a Georgia Tech quarter-miler named Charlie Belcher, with whom I identified in all seasons."[23] He also identified with Bobby Pair, "the Tech High Flash." Both of these runners contributed to the image of the flashing sprinter that haunts Frank Cahill in *Alnilam*.

Dickey unleashed many of his anxieties about conforming to the stereotype of the all-American football star in *The Entrance to the Honeycomb* and *The Casting*. His spokesman, Julian, feels more comfortable on the track team than the football team, but track does not have the same prestige so he continues to try to prove himself on the gridiron. Julian admits that his efforts are in vain: "I seldom hit my receiver; when I did it was always with a feeling of complete astonishment, which vanished almost immediately when I recalled that the pass had no significant context, that the game had not yet begun. I was absolutely worthless to the team: I was not fast enough to run with the ball; my will in opposition to another's was easily overcome; I had no 'drive' and was too timid to tackle or block with much effect. I knew these things even before the coaches discovered them, but being a member of the team carried a prestige I would not otherwise have had, [and] my father thought it a good solution to what he considered my excessive introspection."[24] Julian's goal, like the teenage Dickey's, is to detach himself from his mother's aestheticism and attach himself more firmly to his father's ideals of tough-minded competition. *The Casting*'s title, as Dickey revealed in a notebook from the early 1950s, was taken from an anthropological study, *The Native Tribes of Central Australia*, and referred to an initiation ceremony in which: "The young man steps out from the centre of the group and throws his boomerang high up in the direction of the spot at which his mother was supposed to have lived . . . to symbolize the idea that the young man is entering upon manhood and thus is passing out of the control of the women and into the ranks of men."[25] In *The Casting* and its later incarnation, *Entrance to the Honeycomb*, Dickey traces his own painful initiation into the violent world represented by Julian's father, who is modeled on Eugene Dickey.

In the drafts of his first novel, Dickey tried to explain why he felt obligated to embrace violent experiences. A crucial scene in the novel depicts Julian's father sadistically attacking his daughter, Ann, for a minor act of insurbordination (she refuses to change schools). Sadism, incest, and voyeurism mingle in a vignette shaped by Dickey's reading of pulp fiction and the Marquis de Sade, but also by Dickey's repugnance for his father's obsession with violent sports, whether cock-fighting or football. Like Dickey as a child, Julian is ensconced with an encyclo-pedia (*The Book of Knowledge*). His father interrupts his reading and forces him to participate in the cruel punishment of his sister, who has been stripped and bound with tape to a couch. Julian says of his father:

> He walked back to the closet, and from a shelf took down a thin limber cane, which I had never seen before, then went back to the couch, where Ann lay making a roaring sound entirely strange to me and humping fren-ziedly up and down on the narrow plush of the sofa. He flicked the cane against his hand, and took a wide stance at the side of the couch, facing the fireplace. "No, no," Ann squealed, "Please don't, Father, please." He brought the cane down with a trembling sound across the full of her strain-ing buttocks. She gasped unbelievingly, then shrieked like a horse. Her but-tocks dimpled as they drew involuntarily together against the pain. He whipped her very hard, very patiently, like a man beating a carpet or flail-ing grain, breaking off in the middle to immobilize her by placing the great leather bolster from his chair beneath her stomach and passing the tape across the backs of her knees, so that she was bent a little forward at the waist. Thin lines leapt out across her tight skin, crossed and recrossed.[26]

In his later novels and poems Dickey would rework this sort of flagellation in less overtly pornographic ways.

After his World War II service, Dickey often complained of feeling "cast" in glass and numb to cruelty, which may have been one reason he chose Glass as his persona and *The Casting* as a possible title. Like Dickey, Julian also "casts" many masks for himself. "Work into the thing Julian's (as mine) . . . fondness for masks: the consequent tension between 'putting the mask over' and the anxiety of its success,"[27] he advised himself in a notebook. Julian's voyeurism promises to turn his introspective gaze outward, which is what Dickey's father hoped to ac-complish by bringing his son to cockfights. In fact, as a teenager Dickey devel-oped a taste for voyeurism and sadoeroticism. In a scene that Dickey reworked in his poem "The Fiend," Julian climbs a tree by a boardinghouse to watch his girlfriend undress:

> For a time I closed my eyes, opening them periodically to look toward the window; on the last of these times, as I lifted the lids, the tree gained quite coolly and unpredictably a startling efflorescence; in the nimbused glow the undersides of the leaves above me turned pale, and shone an unstable gold. . . . I stood up and parted the leaves. Twenty feet away, Laverne, her blouse off, moved to the window and pulled down the rusty shade. It was torn raggedly, however, and obstructed my view of only part of the room.

She moved in and out of my line of sight, disrobing slowly, chewing gum. Having removed her slip, she took a quilted robe from the closet, curled it loosely around her, and lay back on the bed to read a bright covered magazine.

Julian also watches one of Laverne's other boyfriends, Taz, beat her in her boardinghouse room, which spurs his own fantasy of taking a whip and "sweeping it over the wet tight back of the girl, her nude hips, her burning erected nipples, and her shaven sex" while she "shudders, moaning gratefully."[28] Julian demonstrates his newly acquired sadism more ferociously when he impales his girlfriend's cocker spaniel with a harpoonlike spike and drives both dog and spike into her father's desk.

Latent homosexual urges are partly responsible for Julian's complicated attitudes toward women. On a walk through the family garden, Julian's sister announces in a sarcastic tone that she knows about her brother's sexual confusion: "There are certain little boys who don't like girls, darling; they don't become breathless at the thought of girls; they don't like to be with girls, except to talk. But they sometimes marry girls. . . . And if you want that Herlong fellow [his football friend] you're with so much, why then you just bring him right along, or keep him where you've got him; if you like, he can move in with us; we'll make a chauffeur out of him; but the point is, you can *have* him."[29] Although Julian dismisses his sister's accusation with a laugh, he often feels effeminate and cannot consummate sex with the woman he intends to marry. Jack Herlong, the quarterback he tries so hard to emulate, calls him "Julie." For years Dickey struggled with similar worries about his masculinity and sexual leanings, and did everything he could to prove to his cockfighting, football-loving father—and to everyone else—that he was an all-American heterosexual superman. His desires for intimate companionship with men, however, were often stronger than those he felt for women.

While craving thrills and courting mischief in his last years of high school, Dickey was not the maniacal daredevil of some of his stories. He was relatively well mannered. Bill Barnwell, who played Huck Finn to his Tom Sawyer, vouched for his innocence: He didn't get into fistfights like the rougher boys, he didn't race cars along Northside Drive as Barnwell and Ed Van Valkenberg did, he didn't visit the infamous pool hall much, he didn't drink except on rare occasions, and, although he could be aggressive with girls, he didn't get too far in his romantic gropings. Much of his free time was spent reading and listening to music, especially old boogie-woogie blues, late 1920s Dixieland jazz, and hillbilly music. Hank Williams's rendition of "Birmingham Jail" was a special favorite. In high school Dickey could read music, and in the company of Barnwell or another friend, Dick Hardwick, he played a little piano, saxophone, and trumpet.

Dickey's later poems like "Cherrylog Road" and "May Day Sermon" offer an older man's erotic gloss on what, during his teenage years, was quite tame. He chased girls—friends nicknamed him "Flash Dickey" because of the speed at which he did so—but most of them remained elusive. Barnwell, who often double-dated with his friend, was amused by Dickey's tactics. Perhaps thinking of the trapped women in *Terror Tales* or *Horror Stories*, Dickey sometimes locked all the doors in his car to prevent a date's quick escape. Once one of his locked-in girlfriends implored, "Jim if you just stop all this I'll fix you the finest breakfast you ever had in your life."[30] Dickey decided to forgo one pleasure for another. On another occasion he pushed a girl up against a refrigerator in her parents' house for some intemperate kissing. When one of her parents walked in, the quick-thinking Dickey explained, "I was just getting something out of the refrigerator!"[31] "Necking" and "petting" were the only acceptable forms of romantic intercourse at the time.

During high school, Dickey was infatuated with a number of girls inside and outside Atlanta. One was Peg Roney, who lived in Winter Park, Florida, where her father taught French at a local college. "She just visited Atlanta occasionally," Dickey said, "and I would take her out. She was interested in poetry and things of that nature, and was very witty and sharp, as well as being rather pretty. . . . She liked things that most other people didn't even know anything about. She read a lot of history. . . . She knew all about the Lincoln murder conspiracy." Dickey enjoyed women who would talk to him about arcane subjects like poetry as well as submit to his amorous advances. He pursued Daisy Eastman, who lived in the neighborhood and whom he described as "extremely unconventional, very strong, with a pretty face" and an interest in literature. She married in high school, and within a decade, according to Dickey, "she committed suicide by eating lawn fertilizer."[32] In Dickey's romantic pantheon, she became another of his doomed beauties.

Although Dickey preferred unconventional women with an intellectual bent, his tastes were eclectic. While he vacationed off the Georgia coast during the summer of 1941, a sweet-tempered girl named Ellen Gayle England professed her love to him almost every day by letter. As their romance flourished, she promised not to romantically disappoint him like Peg Roney. While not with England or other girlfriends, Dickey tried to pick up strangers around town with a flirtatious line or two. His flattery and boyish exuberance, as in later life, were disarming. Courting strangers, however, had its risks. When he was about seventeen, he asked a girl he met in a store for a date and then asked Barnwell, who had his own date, to drive with him to the girl's house outside Atlanta. The car they normally used for such outings was Eugene Dickey's Ford, which they sarcastically dubbed "the shit wagon" because of the odor that permeated its interior from Eugene's fighting cocks. Around eight o'clock, after spending more than an hour trying to find her house, they knocked on her door. Her father answered and brought them into a dilapidated living room, which had a shotgun hanging over a blazing potbellied stove. Staring at them as if they were kidnappers, he barked, "Get my daughter back here at eleven o'clock!"[33] Frightened by the old cracker, they replied, "Yessir." Rather than risk getting lost again, Dickey drove around the block a few times, parked, and returned the girl at the appointed hour.

A decade later, Dickey began to write a story about a drunken, violent father, Robert Carson, and his daughter, Elise. In the story Carson orders his daughter to return from a date at midnight, but she slips in at three in the morning: "Before he knew it, he had lashed out at her. He heard his palm smack her face solidly; then he stepped back, almost sorry." Elise responds: "God-damn you. If you ever touch me again, I'll kill you." The story ends forebodingly with the sadistic father lowering the shades and cursing, "You little bitch. . . . You're going to come out of this room singing a different tune. I can god-damned well tell you that."[34] Dickey's frightening date with the redneck's daughter may have influenced the Carson story as well as the poem "Cherrylog Road," in which his persona is:

> Praying for Doris Holbrook
> To come from her father's farm
>
> And to get back there
> With no trace of me on her face
> To be seen by her red-haired father
> Who would change, in the squalling barn,
> Her back's pale skin with a strop,
> Then lay for me
>
> In a bootlegger's roasting car
> With a string-triggered 12-gauge shotgun
> To blast the breath from the air.[35]

Dickey's numerous variations on this theme recall the sadoerotic melodramas in his favorite pulps, but also the fears he experienced on teenage dates.

Dickey conducted less threatening trysts with Mary Ann Robinson, a woman he remembered as being attractive, reclusive, and secretive. He always felt a need to protect her, perhaps because he saw his own reclusiveness and vulnerability mirrored in her. Like Daisy Eastman, she committed suicide as an adult. In his elegiac poem "The Leap," she appears as Jane MacNaughton, an athletic tomboy on "the passionless playground" at E. Rivers, a rebellious high school girl at "the annual dance / Of the dancing class we all hated," and ultimately a victim of a bad marriage who "leapt to her death from a window / Of a downtown hotel." The poem moves toward an unexpected climax when Dickey assigns blame to men like himself who use their quick wits to catch women, only to betray them. "I examine my hands,"[36] he says at the end, as if brooding on his guilt.

In his late teens, Dickey grew increasingly impatient with Southern courtship rituals that offered titillation and little else. Because of his aggressiveness, women usually refused his requests for a second date. Joining one of the half-dozen fraternities at North Fulton High School might have helped his prospects, but Dickey resisted. The Greek system (there were also about eight sororities) was the center of the high school social scene. Fraternity boys, who were called "jellies," customarily "jellied around" with the "pinks," the sorority girls who wore pink angora sweaters. If parents left for a weekend, the "jells" and "pinks" often turned their homes into havens for eager partiers. Dickey occasionally partied with his fellow socialites or attended their weekend dances at the Biltmore, Brookhaven, or Druid Hills Country Clubs in Atlanta. According to Dickey's friend Betsy Fancher, on these occasions:

The "jells" came, shined and polished, in tuxedos they actually owned, and dutifully jotted their names on the little gold tasselled no-break cards the "pinks" wore on their wrists. . . . The pinks wore bare-shouldered satin ball gowns with crinoline petticoats under their hoopskirts and long, white kid gloves on their arms. They had three dates in an evening, one for dinner—a formal affair at linen-draped banquet tables served by white-coated waiters—one for the dance, in mirrored ballrooms garlanded with smilax, and at 2 A.M. a breakfast at the Crossroads for a very special date. To the music of Bill Clarke or the Auburn Knights, the "jells" danced the dances they had learned at Margaret Bryan's Dancing School—the fox trot, the waltz, the tango and, this they hadn't learned at Margaret's, the jitterbug, wild, foot-stomping dances to "A-Train" or the "One O'clock Jump" with the crowd circling around the dancers, clapping and cheering. The stag-line was long and eager and the "pinks" with a squeeze of the hand and a look that promised everything—almost—would welcome each comer. For a minute or two each "jell" was special.

The dance ended with the strains of "Goodnight Ladies," and the "pinks" and the "jells" reassembled for breakfast, where, in the afterglow, over steaming cups of coffee, the issue was decided. The entire evening was a prelude to a kiss, a lingering kiss amid crushed crinoline and gardenias, and it was then, if a jell's intentions were not entirely dishonorable, that he surrendered his fraternity pin.

In later years Dickey told Fancher that he considered this period "a magic time." In high school he often scorned its pettiness.

His romanticization of the underside of Buckhead life came as a reaction against the sort of Little Lord Fauntleroy lifestyle approved by his mother and many of his peers. He wanted to give the sorority belles something more memorable than a fraternity pin, and he wanted something more substantial than a peck on the cheek in return. Because of his sexual urgency and because of his passion for poetry, Dickey felt like a pariah. Fancher observed: "The progeny of Atlanta's Northside—the pinks and jells—were not expected to write poetry. . . . I don't think Dickey had begun to write then, but he had discovered Byron, and that was enough."[37] In fact, Dickey *had* been writing—fiction if not poetry—and discovering other poets besides Byron.

Searching for models to guide the Byronic rebel germinating in his soul, Dickey looked to dangerous characters like Ed Van Valkenberg—"a tremendous battler" and "almost a gangster,"[38] as he later recalled—who lifted weights, drank, and rode a motorcycle. In the rough draft of *Entrance to the Honeycomb*, Dickey paid homage to his dubious high school idol in the character Ed Van, whom Julian Glass admires. In "May Day Sermon" and "Cherrylog Road" he pretended to be Van Valkenberg astride a motorcycle. Another rakish, motorcycle-riding friend was Walter Armistead. Because Armistead loved music, especially the drums, he and Dickey listened obsessively to records of Gene Krupa playing with the Goodman band. Dickey wrote about his music-loving friend in an elegy titled "Walter Armistead," although here the drumming is done with an axe on a tree and the music is played on a harp.

Years after graduating from North Fulton, Dickey loved to reminisce about being a carefree high-school rebel gunning his motorcyle through the North Georgia hills, his hair fluttering in the wind and a girlfriend clutching his back. In his poems, he straddles motorcycles the way D. H. Lawrence's characters straddle horses, and usually with similar intent—to whisk nubile girls away from their repressive families so that they may sample the joys of sex. From Van Valkenberg and Armistead, who resembled Evel Knieval more than Lawrence's horse-riding deliverers, Dickey learned how to operate a motorcycle, but he never owned or drove one in high school. And although he sometimes bragged about driving his car at breakneck speeds as a bootlegger, the closest Dickey got to racing cars was in the stands of the Lakewood Amusement Park in South Atlanta, where he occasionally watched stock car races.

The rough crowd in Buckhead congregated at the pool hall owned by Red Dorough, an Atlanta man who made a fortune in real estate. In "Looking for the Buckhead Boys," Dickey describes it as an infernal pit embodying the essence of Buckhead masculinity. It was a place so dirty that one needed courage to use its toilet:

> I could tell you where every spittoon
> Ought to be standing. Charlie Gates used to say one of these days
> I'm gonna get myself the reputation of being
> The bravest man in Buckhead. I'm going in Tyree's toilet
> And pull down my pants and take a shit.

The pool hall, at least in Dickey's retrospective gaze, was a preferable alternative to the ballrooms full of smilax and crinoline petticoats. But as usual Dickey distorted his original feelings, just as he distorted the names of his original Buckhead acquaintances. (The character in the poem named Mr. Hamby is George Murray, owner of the hardware store; Charlie Gates is Charles Cates, the captain of the second-string football team; Dick Shea is Dick Gray, the quarterback who also ran track; Punchy Henderson is Jack "Punchy" Emerson, Dickey's football idol; Tommy Nichols is Martin Nicholes, another track and football teammate; the name Tyree's Pool Hall comes from James Tyree, a hard-hitting tackle on the North Fulton squad.) Although Dickey eulogized these Buckhead boys as old friends in the poem, he was not that close to them, and for the most part he stayed away from the mirky pool hall.

Dickey searched for other alternatives to the stilted refinements of Atlanta on an island off the coast of Georgia. Each summer the Dickey family rented a beach house for at least a month on Saint Simons Island. Jim invited friends like Tom Roper, Richard Lamb, and Bill Barnwell to join him on his vacations. Together the boys played in the ocean, went to movies, and bowled at the local alley. In his poem "At Darien Bridge," which recalls some chained convicts he saw working by a road near Saint Simons, Dickey identifies with the criminals and their hope for a miracle to deliver them. He also expresses his desire for deliverance in "The Shark's Parlor," a poem inspired by an ambitious fishing trip he took with Bill Barnwell. Normally he used a hand line with his father, but on one occasion he and Barnwell rowed a wooden boat into a channel, fastened meat to large hooks on long steel leaders, attached them to bottles that acted as corks, and threw the tackle overboard. To make their bait more appetizing, they dumped blood and gobbets of raw meat in the water. They soon saw a big fin slicing the water in their direction. Or so they thought. According to Barnwell, they "got the hell out of there."[39] This youthful encounter with what was probably an imaginary shark provided one source for Dickey's poem "The Shark's Parlor."

In the poem, the fictional place is Cumberland Island (about ten miles south of Saint Simons Island), Dickey's friend is Payton Ford, and the shark is definitely illusory. In the beach cottage the narrator and his friend "dreamed of the great fin circling / Under the bedroom floor." Afterward, they procure from a local slaughterhouse a "bucket of entrails and blood," tie a line to the porch pillar, bait their hook with a collie pup killed on the road, and then toss the blood and "the two-gallon jug stoppered and sealed / With wax   and a ten-foot chain leader   [with] a drop-forged shark hook" into the ocean in front of their house. When the shark strikes, "Payton took off without a word," just as Barnwell and Dickey fled from their own phantom shark. During the ensuing tug-of-war in which a crowd somehow pulls the shark through the house, the Dickeys' "vacation paradise" is shattered: "With one deep-water move   he unwove the rugs in a moment, throwing pints / Of blood over everything we owned   knocked the buck teeth out of my picture / His odd head full of crushed jelly-glass splinters and radio tubes   thrashing / Among the pages of fan magazines   all the movie stars drenched in sea-blood."[40] Dickey's alter ego fears the shark, for sure, but like the motorcyclist in "Cherrylog Road," who is "wild to be destruction forever,"[41] he also welcomes the apocalypse visited on the tranquil summer cottage and identifies with the hammerhead shark by hammering his own head against the wall to free his memories.

During his penultimate high school year, Dickey saw his ambivalence toward his aristocratic background played out in one of the most popular films of all time. To much fanfare, Gone with the Wind premiered in Atlanta at Loew's Grand Theater on December 15, 1939. To celebrate the event, the city decked itself in all its Confederate finery. The United Daughters of the Confederacy along with local dignitaries lit "the eternal flame of the Confederacy," the one gas lamp that survived Sherman's holocaust; the Junior League sponsored a lavish ball at City Auditorium; Loew's was decorated to resemble a columned manor house. The film, more than the novel, elegized the mythical Old South destroyed by the Civil War. In poems like "The Shark's Parlor," Dickey suggested that he wanted the confining mores of both Old and New South baptised in blood. Yet the South and its traditions held a lasting appeal for Dickey. Although he played the Lawrentian rebel, he soon became a devotee of the Victorian poet Ernest Dowson, who coined the phrase "gone with the wind" in his poem "Non Sum Qualis Eram Bonae Sub Regno Cynarae." Dowson wrote about being torn between two times and two women. Having tried to obliterate memories of his innocent beloved by drinking, dancing, and fornicating with prostitutes, he admitted that he could not keep her from returning in his dreams. In similar fashion, Dickey tried to eradicate vestiges of the Old South in his background, but they kept returning to haunt him.

The North Fulton High School Annual records that Dickey graduated in 1941 after having lettered on football and track teams in 1940 and 1941. With his wavy blond hair brushed stylishly back from his forehead, his photograph reveals a movie-star handsomeness. Unlike the other boys next to him, he smiles and proudly shows his teeth. Under the "Besetting Sin" category in the "Class Prophecy," the yearbook names "Rich's Beauty Saloon," and under "Hobby" it names "hair." His "Redeeming Virtue" is "modesty," which is probably ironic since he was well known for his egotism and vanity. His "Future Aim" is "Jeeter Lester, II." Jeeter Lester I was the poor, incompetent, racist "white trash" farmer in Erskine Caldwell's novel *Tobacco Road*—a perfect foil for the aristocratic Dickey. Other comments in the annual belie the frustrations beneath Dickey's photogenic mask. In the jocular "Last Will and Testament," in which the seniors "in an insane state of mind and unsound state of body" are supposed to leave their "most treasured possessions," the editors note: "Billy Barnwell and Jim (Flash) Dickey just hope to leave."[42] In subsequent years, Dickey inflated or deflated his high school record according to his moods. In 1982, he told a writer for the *Atlanta Journal* that at North Fulton he had been "an indifferent student, an indifferent athlete, [and] an indifferent swain."[43] At other times he pretended to be a motorcycling troubador with a slew of sexual conquests and a potential career in the NFL. One thing was certain: Upon graduating from North Fulton he wanted to improve his scholarly and athletic record before entering college. With this in mind he entered Darlington School in the fall of 1941.

4. Postgraduate Blues (1941–1942)

On May 25, 1981, nearly forty years after leaving Darlington School, Dickey registered a complaint with the current school president, James P. McCallie. Like any alumnus, Dickey received numerous solicitations for donations. He hoped that his protest—"both formal and extremely personal," as he put it— would convince the school to stop expressing "desires for money to one who has not the slightest intention of giving . . . any." In laying out the reasons for his rebuke, Dickey could not have been more blunt:

> Let me make myself quite plain on this matter. Anything pertaining to Darlington School, past, present or future, is thoroughly abhorrent to me. I was there one year, and a more disgusting combination of cant, hypocrisy, cruelty, class privilege and inanity I have never since encountered at any human institution. The school is such an insipid place that it really shouldn't call forth reactions as strong as the above, but when the functionaries of a place whose memory I so thoroughly detest come to me, quite literally, hat in hand, asking me for money to help *support* such a bastion of snobbery and privilege, such emotions do arise, perhaps unfortunately but quite authentically.
>
> I hope this note will serve to get me forever off your mailing list. And if possible, please expunge me also from your rolls, if that is possible, as I wish I could do with the recollection of the place that I have.
>
> You may print this if you like.[1]

President McCallie had been on the job about two years when this jeremiad arrived on his desk.

Compared to North Fulton High School, which Dickey remembered approvingly as "very democratic and populist,"[2] Darlington School was an affront to his conception of himself as one of the rough-and-tumble set that had struggled under financial duress during the Depression. That the younger Dickey was "an absolute aristocrat, on a par with kings,"[3] as an intimate friend and Darlington alumnus noted, made Dickey's later denunciation all the more ironic. In trying to expunge all records and recollections of his prep school days, he was also trying to expunge the memories of his privileged upbringing in Buckhead.

Like so many institutions in the South, Darlington School had been shaped by the Civil War. The school was conceived by John Paul Cooper, who lost his father in the first Battle of Manassas. Cooper had found a substitute father in Joseph James Darlington, a teacher and counselor at the private Proctor School in Rome, a town in northwest Georgia. After the Civil War, Cooper moved to Boston, where he married and started a successful business. Painfully aware of the need for a good school in Rome (there were no high schools in the city or in the county after the war), Cooper decided to return and build one. Out of respect for his earlier mentor, Cooper named his school Darlington. In 1905, he set about making plans and formulating a constitution, whose modern versions still emphasize two cardinal principles: "First, that no denominational, political, or private interests should limit or interfere with the usefulness of the School; second, that no private gain should ever be realized from the enterprise." A school catalogue specified: "It is not a school for the sons of wealthy parents merely; all classes are represented, and no special consideration is shown to any class or any pupil that is not given to all."[4] Dickey disputed this.

By the time Dickey arrived in the fall of 1941, Darlington had expanded from a makeshift classroom in the Rome Fire Department to a small campus accommodating two hundred boys. For the privilege of being a boarding student, Dickey paid a fair sum—$790. Carl Warren, a fellow football player who graduated in his 1942 Darlington class, heard that Dickey's parents sent him to Rome because he was frittering away his time with Atlanta girls and because he needed further preparation so he could go to a reputable college. There were, however, plenty of girls in Rome—at the high school, at Shorter College, and at Berry College—and Dickey took advantage of whatever romantic opportunities came his way. He went to dances, double-dated some of the town girls with his roommate, Wesley Coleman, and still visited girlfriends in Atlanta, which was only about sixty miles away.

Whatever the concerns of his parents, Dickey made more progress at Darlington with girls than with textbooks. His Atlanta friend George Montgomery, who was also a boarder at Darlington, recalled a conversation they had during track practice in the spring of 1942: "We were idly chatting on a cool-off walk around the track after a few laps when Jim turned and remarked to me that 'I got my first piece of tail this week-end.' It was a Monday, and he had just returned from a week-end in Atlanta. He never elaborated further, and although I was anxious to press him for details, the approach of the coach and others precluded any further pursuit of this subject. He smiled to himself when he told me, and the implication was that he was just citing a milestone in his life, nothing more."[5] Dickey's assertion may have been true. At North Fulton, his attempts at full-blown sexual experiences had been rebuffed. Although his sex life would not reach gargantuan proportions for another two decades, he was pleased it had begun.

According to Dickey, the main reason he attended Darlington was to hone his football skills so he could play at Clemson with his idols Jack Emerson and Tom McIlwain. Almost as an afterthought, he planned to strengthen his academic credentials. Darlington's reputation as a football stronghold was well known. In 1939, the Darlington Tigers led the Mid-South Association, and in 1940, the team was undefeated and scored a whopping 219 points to its opponents' 19. Most Georgia school systems, like Dickey's in Atlanta, only had eleven grades, but Darlington had twelve, and this gave it an advantage over opponents. Realizing that Darlington's team played at a high level, colleges regularly advised their applicants to get a year of further preparation there, and also gave scholarships for this purpose. About two-thirds of the players on the Darlington varsity team were "postgraduates." Clemson may have urged Dickey to go to Darlington, but whether or not it gave him a scholarship—as he always claimed—is questionable. If he *had* received one, he probably would have told his teammates. They remembered no mention of one. When his favorite Darlington teacher, Frank Bloodworth Rogers, heard Dickey's story of getting a Clemson scholarship, he was incredulous. Dickey "didn't play worth a darn,"[6] he said.

Darlington as well as Dickey had high hopes for his football development. His friend on the 1941 team, Carl Warren, said Dickey was "a highly touted football player . . . [who] played end position."[7] He also played wingback as he had at North Fulton. Tall, muscular, highly competitive, but rather slim, he acquitted himself adequately in some of the games, but miserably in others. "He was not a good football player,"[8] alleged R. Bryan Ellis, who won a coveted Darlington trophy as a guard during the year Dickey played on the team. Another teammate, Roland Paylor, recalled that Dickey played third-string wingback. Other teammates, such as Daniel Smith, remembered Dickey more favorably as an aggressive end who charged down the field with head low and legs high after catching a pass. The consensus, however, was that Dickey contributed little to the team. Other players made the 1941 season a successful one in which the team suffered only two defeats.

Dickey's disappointments on the football field were partly to blame for his tirade against the Darlington president. By his own admission, his performances were "dismal."[9] He blamed his athletic failures on a damaged hamstring, which hobbled him throughout the year. It even bothered him during the winter when he played touch football. Dickey had no more success on the track team during the spring. Musing as an old man, Dickey still winced at his failure to compete. He had been especially upset because his brother, Tom, had been triumphing on his track team. "I was hurt more than my brother was," he said. "My hamstrings are a little bit short for my body, and I had to warm up a good hour before I could run effectively. When you warm up to run high hurdles, you have to time it to where you finish your warm up right before the race. . . . I had a lot of times when I got caught over the sixth hurdle, and I could feel it [my hamstring] beginning to tighten. And I would consequently have to clear the hurdle higher, go up, so that I wouldn't hit the hurdle. But that cuts down on your time. You've got to be right down on every hurdle if you're going to run a good time." Dickey tried to make up for his difficulties with the hurdles by competing in other events: the 100-, 220-, and 440-yard dashes as well as the discus and javelin. Still his legs bothered him. His disabilities notwithstanding, Dickey boasted that he was "the mainstay of the track team."[10] He still could not accept defeat.

It should come as no surprise that the football section in the Darlington yearbook reveals almost nothing about Dickey. In the group picture, while most of his teammates smile under old-fashioned skull-cap helmets, Dickey stands in the far corner of the last row and scowls. Out of anger or indifference, he withheld a graduation photograph; his name appears in a special section titled "Seniors Without Pictures." In a 1973 *Playboy* interview, Dickey tried to finesse the disappointment that was so obvious to his teammates by saying that during this pre-Clemson period he was still an unbookish football star: "In those days, poetry was the furthest thing from my mind."[11] Poetry, in fact, was securely on his mind, and mainly because of the inspiring teaching of Frank Rogers, a graduate of the University of North Carolina. A few months before he died, Dickey admitted that Rogers had been a formative influence: "He was a lover of Browning. I don't think I've read any Browning since those days, or very little. Also, 'The Rubáiyát [of Omar Khayyám' by Edward FitzGerald]. He used to read it to us in class. And then I could get something from that."[12] With its melodramatic flourishes and doleful rhetoric, Victorian poetry commanded Dickey's attention at Darlington as it did later at Clemson and in the Philippines during World War II.

A Victorian gloom hung over Dickey during his postgraduate year. Speaking for all Dickey's Darlington teachers, Rogers declared, "He broke our hearts." Rogers used to watch him trudging alone, head hung low, between the main buildings, his dormitory, the dining hall, and the classrooms. "Nobody could get close to him,"[13] Rogers observed. Headmaster Ernest Wright, a College of William and Mary and University of Virginia graduate who also taught English, tried to help, but to no avail. Wright encouraged his literary bent, but Dickey continued to wallow in a slough of despond. Rogers attributed Dickey's depression to several things. He believed Dickey's parents had forced him to go to Darlington in order to separate him from troublemakers in Atlanta. He also heard that Dickey's home life was in turmoil. Dickey must have told other students or Rogers himself that his parents were in the midst of a bitter divorce (they were not). To the end of his life, Rogers believed that Dickey was upset because of the divorce.

Darlington was known to be a haven for troublemakers from Atlanta. This may have been why Dickey made Joel Mitchell, in a preliminary draft of *Alnilam*, a graduate of Darlington with a "romantic link with Hitler."[14] Rogers, however, never witnessed any outward hostility from Dickey. His prize student was consistently quiet and polite in class. Dickey should have been cheered by his academic improvement at Darlington. Under Rogers's tutelage, he finally excelled in English. Rogers taught Special English, a year-long college preparatory course, to about thirty students. Most of the exercises were intended to train students to write critically about traditional texts. Dickey applied his previously concealed literary talents to his papers and gained for them the recognition they deserved. His began to earn As. Dickey also won his first literary prize—the Society of Colonial Daughters' "Patriotic Essay Medal"—for a tale about a thrifty Italian immigrant who buys defense bonds. Given his excellence in English and his relatively poor performance in the sciences and math, his decision to enroll as an engineering major at Clemson A & M College in the fall of 1942 must have baffled his teachers, but that is what he did.

5. A Cadet's Rites of Passage (Fall 1942)

If Dickey needed to prove he could play football with the best, Clemson was the place to go. In 1939, led by the all-American Banks McFadden, the football team beat Boston College at the Cotton Bowl on New Year's Day. Although Dickey entered Clemson three years after this victory, he often referred to it to indicate the quality of football he played. Throwing humility and truth to the winds, he boasted to Paul O'Neil, who wrote a nine-page profile for the July 1966 issue of *Life* magazine, that he contemplated a possible professional career in football after leaving Clemson. O'Neil wrote: "The Southern Conference muscleman . . . would very conceivably have drifted into pro football as a quarterback, ball carrier or safety man. He had both the requisite size and the requisite speed when he was a prize freshman back at Clemson. . . . He went to Clemson to play football and, as a freshman, made the transition from wingback to T quarterback so smoothly that the coaching staff sent him long, cozy letters all through his subsequent war years of service."[1] A reporter for the *Washington Post* added fodder to the myth of Dickey-the-potential-NFL-player when he wrote in 1974 that Dickey had been "a star football halfback for Clemson (of pro caliber)."[2] Professional football, however, was never a possibility for Dickey. Even a starting position on the freshman team—never mind the varsity team— was questionable. In the end, as at Darlington, he typically found himself on the bench at the start of the games.

One of the reasons Dickey revered George Plimpton in later life was because Plimpton, who probably had less football ability than Dickey, actually played with an NFL team—the Detroit Lions—in order to write his book *Paper Lion*. After seeing the film made from the book, Dickey wrote Plimpton a complimentary letter in which he described an experience at Clemson similar to the one at the end of the film in which the quarterback stumbles with an open field before him: "I played four games for the freshman team at Clemson as quarterback in the T-formation, a system just then gaining credence in college football. I had exactly the same thing happen to me against the University of Georiga, and can still see that wide open field, all those receding stripes I could have crossed, spreading out before my eye after I fell, at that immobile time, almost at eye-level with the stripes."[3] Despite his laughable failures with the pro team, Plimpton ignited Dickey's belief that he too could have played in the NFL.

At Clemson, Dickey also took steps toward realizing his boyhood dream of becoming a combat pilot. At the time Clemson was a military college that considered its program superior to the one at its peer institution in South Carolina, The Citadel—and with good reason, since it often beat its rival in military competitions. Dickey liked to say that Clemson "was the poor man's South Carolina military college. The Citadel was the rich man's military college."[4] No poor man himself, Dickey at Clemson continued to disguise his affluence and literary propensities. He signed up for the most popular major—engineering—which attracted 55 percent of the 931 entering freshmen. Because of World War II, the country needed engineers to design and maintain the many machines churning out equipment for battle. Despite Dickey's teenage vagaries, he had a strong patriotic streak, as his award-winning essay at Darlington attested. Clemson president R. F. Poole no doubt stirred his patriotism when he addressed the freshman class in late August 1942: "You are entering college at a time when practically the entire world is at war. Our nation will not perish if we prepare adequately for its defense."[5] Dickey took heed. America's plunge into war had been made inevitable on December 7, 1941, when Dickey was finishing his first semester at Darlington. Japan had attacked Pearl Harbor, and the next day Congress had declared war on Japan. Three days later Germany and Italy had declared war on America. Like millions of other young men, Dickey began preparing for his country's defense.

Having taken ROTC at North Fulton and Darlington, Dickey was no stranger to military training. Clemson's program, however, proved to be both painful and humiliating. In the late summer heat of western South Carolina, like the rest of the entering class he donned his woolen uniform and braced himself for the hazing that would follow. For a handsome teenager whose hobby, according to his high school annual, was getting his hair done at Rich's Beauty Saloon, the first order of business was a shock to his vanity. In becoming a "rat"—the name given to all freshmen—Dickey had to have his golden locks shorn to the scalp. Entrepreneurial upperclassmen set up "barbershops" around the main entrances to the campus, cornered incoming freshmen, and then assaulted them with scissors and hand-operated clippers. If the "rat" resisted, the "barbers" could beat him or disfigure his hair. The haircut had further ramifications. The cadets were expected to grow their hair back quickly, as if such things could be willed, so that they could part it by the time of the big Thursday football game in a month. If they failed to do this, the "rats" would get scalped again. To encourage the eventual part, the boys constantly brushed and smeared vaseline or Octagon soap on their hair. Proud of his blond hair (his later attempts to disguise his thinning hair were legendary), Dickey resented but submitted to his shearing.

Assigned to Company E-2, Second Barracks, Dickey often commiserated with his two roommates, Mason (Mickey) Dorsey and Chris Hollinsworth. He felt homesick, even though in high school he couldn't wait to leave Buckhead. Several days after arriving at Clemson, he wrote his parents:

Well, now I'm safely installed in the great institution of Clemson. I would have written sooner, but they had me running around like the proverbial chicken with his head cut off. I've got everything I need now, except money to buy my books with. I don't know just yet how much I'll need, but I'll write it in my next letter.

I have really been busy these two or three days, and it seems as though I've been here for months instead of just a couple of days. There are a lot of country hicks around here, but most of them are pretty nice fellows.

I am working as hard as I can on everything I have to do, and I think I can make a success of most of my endeavors up here. We haven't started classes yet, but probably will within the next couple of days.

This place is kind of tough to take for one who loves home as much as I do, but I'll get along o.k.

I went out for football yesterday, and did pretty well considering it was my first day. I am one of the littlest ones on the team, so you can see what I'm up against. The coach, "Rock" Norman, seems to take an interest in me, and has me playing quarterback. He may change me later, though. It's pretty hot out there, but it is no harder than North Fulton or Darlington, so far. There are plenty of tough freshmen on this team. We play the Citadel freshmen, N.C. State, Duke, N. Carolina, and there's a surprise— Georgia freshmen. I am the only one on the team that can kick and pass worth a damn, and also, I think the fastest (but not the biggest). There is a fellow named "Hoockie" Morgan who is pretty fast, too. Most all the football players here have nicknames. They call me "Peachtree" (because I'm from Atlanta, I guess).[6]

Surrounded by country hicks and mammoth football players, Dickey survived as best he could.

In a few days, his survival skills would be put to a rigorous test. After orientation week, when only officers and a few upperclassmen inhabited the campus, the freshmen met all the other returning students. They now became "gofers" as well as "rats." When commanded, they had to haul the arriving students' trunks from the parade ground to the barracks. The new students expected the "rats" to know their names, which was impossible; and as the "rats" spelled their names with the help of their superiors, they received one stroke of a paddle for every letter they pronounced. The "rats" memorized the names of all upperclassmen as quickly as possible. If they forgot a name, the second spelling lesson was more painful than the first. As Dickey quickly learned, the inability to name a superior was not the only occasion for paddling. If a freshmen did a sloppy job cleaning his "rat sergeant's" room, he could expect to be beaten. If he dawdled when an upperclassman ordered him to fetch a package of cigarettes, clothes from the cleaner, or any other item, he could expect the same. To ensure the "rats" were appropriately cheerful about their duties, "pep meetings" were held after supper. At these meetings, upperclassmen called out "rat" names alphabetically. As the new cadets processed down the barracks hall, bending over by each door, the upperclassmen paddled them. Those "rats" who missed their punishments got a double dose the next day. If parents complained about their sons being mistreated, the president of the college might conduct a mass inspection after morning chapel at which all the "rats" were forced to pull down their pants. The president inquired whether any cadet wanted to lodge a formal complaint. Knowing the consequences, even the most severely bludgeoned kept quiet.

If Dickey assumed he would get preferential treatment because he was bigger than most of his superiors and a member of the football team, he was proven painfully wrong. Because he *was* bigger, the upperclassmen felt he needed *more* punishment to bring him down to size. The sophomores, for whom hazing was a recent memory, were particularly zealous. Detecting a real or imagined violation, they grabbed anything—broom handles, boards, dustpans, paddles, straightened coat hangers, swords—and beat Dickey on the rear. His roommate Mickey Dorsey, who slept in the bunk above him, remembered that Dickey was sometimes so sore that he could not sit in a chair. He had to do his homework standing by his desk. Dickey's concern for survival, which became a dominant theme in his work, began in earnest in this hostile environment.

During Dickey's short stay at Clemson, many of the cadets expressed their resentment toward hazing. Some of the honor societies attempted to phase out paddling in initiation ceremonies. A college-wide poll indicated that most cadets did not support paddling, and on October 1, 1942, the college newspaper, *The Tiger*, urged the administration to prohibit it. Despite these protests, the paddlings continued. Dickey's attitude toward hazing, at least in hindsight, was ambiguous. Like the English poet Swinburne, who acquired a lifelong devotion to flagellation during similar hazings at Eton, and like Dickey's hero, T. E. Lawrence, whose taste for sadomasochistic practices developed in the British army, Dickey may have been secretly drawn to hazing. Unlike his literary precursors, however, the older Dickey preferred administering the punishment to receiving it. Paddling women aroused him sexually, gave him a feeling of authority, and no doubt fulfilled his need to avenge former humiliations. In *Deliverance* he may have been remembering assaults on his own backside by those he called "hicks" when he came to write the harrowing scene of Bobby's sodomy. Dickey set the rape in the Chattooga woods only miles away from rustic Clemson.

To the end of his life Dickey claimed that football players like himself were exempt from punishment and that he had never witnessed a paddling at Clemson. The paddlers "didn't bother us—not me, anyway," Dickey said. "The football boys . . . were too tough. The guy that played end on the freshman team, my best friend then, was a boy named James Huff, or Junior, or Junes. If they'd tried to haze him, he would have torn them to pieces. He was such a tough guy."[7] Plenty of football players, however, suffered paddlings and other forms of hazing. Dickey's denials regarding Clemson hazing belied his ambivalence toward sadomasochistic behavior. A decade after leaving the college, he wrote in a notebook: "There is a novel in my Clemson experience, short as it was."[8] In 1952, he took modest steps toward the novel by first working on "Sennacherib," a short story dealing with flagellation. One character recounts a beating uncannily similar to the sort Dickey received at Clemson: "He beat the living fire out of me. I couldn't sit on my butt again for two weeks. At first I called him everything I could think of, but after two or three times I didn't."[9] Dickey never wrote his Clemson novel, but transferred the violent rites of cadets to the sadomasochistic scenes in his other writings.

An incident recorded by a 1940 graduate, Ellis Mellette, in his memoir *Old*

Clemson College—It Was a Hell of a Place may have contributed to Dickey's portrait of Muldrow in *To the White Sea*. Mellette writes about a similarly sadistic Muldrow at Clemson:

> A typical question and stock answer before paddling was, "Are you going to sink that upper classman ———?" "Hell no, soft shit won't sink."
> At another meeting, I was asked something like this, "Who is that ugly junior over there?"
> After hesitation, Muldrow, the indicated junior said, "You mean Rat Mellette, you haven't learned my name yet?"
> "Oh yes, your name is dull mower," I replied.
> "Bend over, I am going to mow your grassy ass, Rat Mellette, and you need not tell me how pretty I am."
> "Pretty hell, pretty ugly."
> After a few licks, I said, "I just now see your handsomeness. It's coming through in a wonderful way. Sun blindness kept me from seeing it."[10]

In *To the White Sea*, Dickey's Muldrow is similarly preoccupied with excrement—he hides in the Tokyo sewer—and he is also a "dull mower," a sadistic aviator who mows down bodies as he travels through enemy territory in Japan.

The brutalized "rats" got their revenge against the Clemson system in other ways besides those allowed during the controlled mutiny of "Rat Day." On the parade ground they sometimes altered march songs with sarcastic verses, shouted obscene versions of their superiors' names, or deliberately made mistakes while drilling. They pelted buildings with rocks and bricks, set off firecrackers in the barracks, lit brush fires in the surrounding woods, short-sheeted beds, smeared peanut butter on door handles, flipped beds while their occupants slept, or sprayed their enemies with fire hoses. This sort of insurrection from within occurs at the end of Dickey's long novel *Alnilam*, where cadets at a military base upset a graduation ceremony by playing bumper cars with their planes. At Clemson, however, cadet Dickey only imagined rebelling. As at E. Rivers, North Fulton, and Darlington, but with more at stake now, he worked hard to conform to the status quo. To his roommate, Mickey Dorsey, he confided his determination to enter the air corps and become a pilot. About his literary aspirations he remained silent.

While not cleaning his rifle, drilling, and serving upperclassmen, Dickey worked at his courses. The teachers tried to be as hard-boiled as everyone else since the academic regimen was also designed to toughen the cadets through punishment. The teachers gave few As. In such engineering "shop" courses as Forge and Foundry, Dickey felt wholly inadequate to the assignments. In a mid-September letter to his mother, he tried to mask some of his disillusionment: "I'm doing pretty well in my books, except for a few things. I am working hard to become a successful engineer, though sometimes I wish I was just going to be a 'helluva' engineer at [Georgia] Tech, and drinking liquor and belonging to a fraternity and having dates all the time in the old home town. When I have thoughts like these, it is really a strain on the old will power not to pull out of this hell hole in South Carolina. It's all for the best, though, and when all of the

Atlanta gigoloes are 'A-1 in the army,' little Jimmy will be thumbing his nose and having the last, and longest, laugh (I hope)."[11] Dickey tried to assure his mother, who hoped her two sons would avoid the draft, that he would remain in college for the duration of the war. Within a few months, his patriotic dreams of piloting would overcome his pacifism, and he would enlist. His journey toward war was a direct rebuke to his mother, which he acknowledged in his later novels and poems by making his main characters renounce mothers and maternal women in their quests for "consequential" experience.

Although life at Clemson was grueling and frequently darkened by reports of cadets captured or killed in the war, Dickey's time there was not an unremitting hell. He went to films and dances. He dated occasionally. In mid-September, he reported to his mother that he had just seen a wonderful thriller, *Desperate Journey*, with Errol Flynn and Ronald Reagan. The movie, which told the story of fliers shot down and struggling to escape from Germany, added impetus to Dickey's urge to become a combat pilot. There were other pleasant diversions. On November 20, right before the big Furman football game, Ray Herbeck and his band played at the annual autumn ball. Professors and cadets sang and joked in a traditional blackface minstrel show like the one Dickey commemorated in his poem "Buckdancer's Choice." In November, the cadets submitted pictures of girls for a beauty contest organized by the college magazine, *Taps*. Dickey's old-fashioned devotion to beauty contests, which remained intact until he died, and his eagerness to tell stories about dating beauty queens like Miss New Mexico, derived in part from his semester at Clemson.

While his father approved of Dickey's military exercises and engineering courses, his mother must have realized that they did not suit him. As the lachrymose letters he wrote his parents suggest, Clemson was not turning Jim into his father's ideal of a tough, stoical soldier. In a September 12 letter in which he addressed his mother "Dearest, dearest Mom," he sounded downright sappy: "Mom, I wish you would do me a favor. Give Pop a big hug and kiss for me. I was just listening to the radio, and Pete Cassel sang 'That Silver-Haired Daddy of Mine': and tears came into my eyes. Mom, I know that you would be the last person in the world to say such a thing, but I feel that I have been such a disappointment to everyone. I wish sometimes I could just pass out of the picture, but then I think of *my* wonderful family, and that gives me strength to go on." He signed off by saying, "I love you very, very much. Your devoted son. Jim." In her reply, Dickey's mother was equally sentimental: "Could any son write a sweeter tribute to his Mother? Bless you, my darling, for loving me like this and telling me so."[12] Where was the head-ripping machismo of his companion James Huff? Homesickness was reducing Jim to a whimpering child. In another letter declaring his love for his mother, he proclaimed: "About once or twice a day that terrible sick feeling comes over me, and I feel as if I will die if I don't see my folks pretty soon. . . . My ideal existence is to live for ever and ever at our home, and see you all every day." He signed off flirtatiously: "Goodbye, sweetheart, and write soon. Don't forget I love you more than anything in this world."[13] Because he so rarely included lovable women in his novels and because he could be so callous toward women in his private life, his tender sentiments for his mother seem out of character. But it was precisely these oedipal feelings for his mother that compromised his relations with other women.

At Clemson the main way Dickey sought to dispel any traces of femininity and mother worship was on the football field. Clemson's football program became legendary because of Frank Howard, who had started at Clemson in 1931 as a track coach and football trainer before becoming head football coach in 1940. Over the next thirty years, he assembled some of the most formidable teams in the nation. While Howard coached the varsity, "Rock" Norman coached the freshmen. Under Norman's tutelage, Dickey claimed to be "the first T quarterback in the South." He attributed this honor to the fact that the varsity needed to practice against such a quarterback to prepare for a rematch with Boston College: "The freshman team coach was ordered to put in a T formation just so the varsity would get used to defending against it, and I was the quarterback. And I drove them crazy too. . . . [The defense would] go right by me, and I'd just be standing there holding the ball. I'd have faked the hand-off to somebody, and they'd just go by on both sides, and I'd straighten up and just fire it out . . . or run with it."[14] Although too ill to read his poem "The Bee" at Frank Howard's eighty-fifth birthday on April 8, 1994, Dickey nevertheless instructed a Clemson professor to repeat his story about being the first T quarterback in the South.

Dickey's fortunes on the gridiron varied. At 6'1" and 190 pounds, he played safety on defense as well as wingback and quarterback on offense, but never well enough to be a consistent starter. On October 4, 1942, he wrote his father about being demoted from the first string to the third string for loafing. Earlier he complained of a hurt ankle. To his father, he highlighted the grim combativeness of Clemson practices, such as the one in which he tried to tackle a runner and got bulldozed in the process:

> After that, I was feeling pretty bad, and when we knocked off, I didn't feel much like talking. I felt like hell, in fact. Back in the barracks, some of the fellows in my company said they were proud of me and they were sure I would make the team. I've never seen such a swell bunch of fellows. There's something about this college stuff that gets me. I understand now something I never did before. After all those boys were so nice to me, we went to a pep meeting, and I stood there and sang the college songs with tears rolling down my face. It's a feeling impossible to describe, but I know that win or lose, this is the only school for me. When I heard those 3,000 cadets yelling and band playing, I realized that it's not the individual that matters, but the school. Every player on the team is but a means to an end, to win for the school.[15]

A few weeks earlier Dickey had told his mother that Clemson was a "hell hole." Now he pitched his comments differently, emphasizing the sort of patriotic bravado his father admired.

Dickey's NFL fantasies were given little support by his actual record as a Clemson freshman. His team played four games, and won two of them. During the abbreviated season, the "Baby Tigers" scored four touchdowns, kicked two extra points, and tallied no field goals. Their last game with Duke was canceled because of the austerities of war. After a modest 7–0 victory in the first game against a team called the P.C. Anklets, the Baby Tigers encountered a stronger team from Daniel Field (an air corps base in Macon). One of Clemson's interior linemen, Arnold Levine, recalled: "This team had quite a few 'name' college players and one or two who [later] played in the NFL . . . Jim acquitted himself quite well. I can recall his Dad standing behind our bench rooting him on, which I thought quite admirable, coming from a long distance to watch his son."[16] On October 15, the college newspaper, *The Tiger*, reported: "Quarterback Brasington played safety man and was a constant threat to the [Daniel Field] soldiers with his punt returns taken on the dead run. Dickey, who subbed for Brasington, also gave a fine account of himself."[17] Clemson won the game by a score of 6–0. At the start of the next game against the University of South Carolina, Dickey sat on the bench (USC won 19–6). For the season finale against the University of Georgia, he had the dubious honor of starting and watching his team get routed 33–7.

In a 1958 letter to the poet James Wright, Dickey lay some of the groundwork for the football myth he constructed from his Clemson experience. Counting on Wright to broadcast the news around the literary community, which he did, Dickey declared:

> I was a scholarship boy (hired hand) at Clemson in 1942, and before that had played four years of high-school football, basketball, and track. All this proves, I guess, that there is no royal road to poetry, though I must say that the other American poets I have met have not had similar backgrounds. Anyway, I played on the freshman team at Clemson until after the varsity played two or three games. After that, the Southern Conference passed the Freshman Rule, which allowed Freshmen to play with the varsity, this being at the beginning of the war and the draft. I finished the season with the varsity, and started the last five games, and was on the second All-Southern team. I played wing-back on Frank Howard's (the coach's) old straight-away power-type single wing, and did mostly blocking, though I got to run on a reverse every now and then, and catch an occasional pass. I was pretty fast for an 195-pounder, though, and tried my best to make them as good a back as I could, although I was too long-striding to be shifty, and too big to miss on a tackle. I could make a linebacker live hard, though, and I scored three touchdowns and was actually leading ground-gainer against Boston College, whom we played in Fenway Park, and who had an All-American back named Mike Holovak, whom we stopped cold that day, though we lost the game.[18]

In reality, Dickey never played on the high school basketball team, never earned All-Southern Conference honors at Clemson, and never played on the varsity team under Frank Howard.

In addition to football, Dickey also fabricated a respectable basketball career for himself at Clemson. "I played on the freshman team," he once said. "We had a good bunch. We could beat the varsity. I played forward on the right side. I didn't shoot very much. I was more of a play-maker."[19] A November 5 article in *The Tiger* reveals that Rock Norman doubled as a basketball coach, but that football players were not trying out yet for the team. Norman planned to cut the varsity basketball squad on November 15 and then begin practicing for the winter season. It is highly unlikely that Dickey played in any games or even tried out for the team before fall classes ended on December 18. After finishing the term, Dickey left Clemson and never returned. Perhaps the fact that he had played one sport under Rock Norman allowed him to imagine he played another.

Self-aggrandizing in letters and interviews about his football and basketball prowess, Dickey was surprisingly modest in his poems. He inevitably cast himself as the middle-aged, out-of-shape ex-ballplayer trying to recapture an athletic past that was marked more by hope than by glory. In the poems he appears as an earnest young man trying but only partially succeeding to live up to the ideals of fatherlike coaches. Sports are rites of passage in which he learns the Darwinian lesson that the fittest survive and dominate, while the weaker lose and perish. In this grim, naturalistic world, he confesses that he is a struggler rather than a conquerer, that his failures accelerate his competitive drive, and that his dreams of heroism are born of disappointments.

"The Bee," which Dickey wrote in the mid-1960s and dedicated "To the football coaches of Clemson College, 1942," demonstrates these themes in a dramatic way. Superimposed on a scene where Dickey-the-father chases his son, who has been frightened by a bee, toward "the sheer / Murder of California traffic," is his former father-son relationship with Rock Norman. The poem moves from a suspenseful description of the bee incident that took place at an archery range near San Fernando Valley State College in the 1960s to an interior dialogue in which Dickey plays both father-coach and aspiring son. His empathy with all winners and losers is so intense that, as in much of his writing, all the characters—even the offending bee—become personae for his protean sensibility. To save his son from the bee, he also needs wings—the beelike wings of a Clemson wingback. In his pep talk to himself, he says: "Old wingback, come / To life. If your knee action is high / Enough, the fat may fall in time   God damn / You, Dickey, *dig.*" In this psychodrama, Dickey struggles to conjure up his former coach and self from middle-aged sloth. He plays the role of Rock Norman (here disguised as "Shag Norton") to lampoon what he "badly did / At Clemson" and to spur his chase for his son. As he transforms himself from a cumbersome, middle-aged father into something resembling a fleet-footed wingback, Dickey leaps and wrestles his son to the ground before a car hits him. The end of the poem contains a touching scene where father and son sit together as on a football bench "while the first string takes back / Over, far away." Facing death only minutes before, Dickey now pays homage to his dead coaches who made his heroic sprint to the highway possible, whispering: "Coach Norton, I am your boy."[20] While the obeisance smacks of the sort of sentimentality evident in Dickey's Clemson letters to his parents, other parts of the poem smack of exaggeration (at the Litigo Canyon archery range, his son Kevin had seen one pickup truck on the narrow mountain road, and his father had taken only a few steps to prevent him from moving toward it). Most of the poem, however, skillfully finagles the "life-as-football" analogy.

In 1968, Dickey wrote a less successful poem, "In the Pocket," which is interesting only because it gives another candid portrait of Jim-Dickey-the-football-player. Commissioned by the NFL—perhaps in the belief that Dickey once had a chance to play for the league—the poem depicts its author on the verge of getting sacked. Dickey assumes none of the panache or skill of a quarterback like Joe Namath or Bart Starr. From the pocketlike space formed by blockers, he seems to focus on social and political breakdowns (it was 1968, after all) more than possible pass receivers. The world is "breaking / In breaking down / And out breaking / Across."[21] His "friends," as he politely calls his receivers, are either too far away or too ineffectual to catch his passes. Dickey again berates himself like an old coach. In a related poem, "For the Death of Vince Lombardi," which the NFL commissioned in 1971, Dickey analyzes his need for pretending to be a superstar. Wavering between arrogance and humility, he turns the Green Bay Packers and their prominent coach into his personae, but humbly says to Lombardi:

> I never played for you.   You'd have thrown
> Me off the team on my best day—
> No guts, maybe   not enough speed,
> Yet running in my mind
> As Paul Hornung, I made it here
> With the others, springing down railroad tracks,
> Hurdling bushes and backyard Cyclone
> Fences, through city after city, to stand, at last, around you
> Exhausted,   exalted, pale.

Implicit in the description of imaginary leaps to Lombardi's funeral is Dickey's acknowledgment that he was a better hurdler (he is "hurdling bushes") than a wingback or quarterback. But it is precisely because of his mediocrity as a football player that he and all other armchair athletes nurse NFL fantasies. If Dickey indicts his propensity for lying, he also indicts Lombardi, who was famous for his "winning-is-all" philosophy, for ruining him and other American men like him. He compares Lombardi to General Patton and asks: "Did you discover the worst / In us: aggression   meanness   deception   delight in giving / Pain to others, for money?   Did you make of us, indeed, / Figments   over-specialized, brutal ghosts / Who could have been real / Men in a better sense?"[22] What is surprising about this interrogation is its implicit avowal of Dickey's less appealing traits—aggression, meanness, deception, sadism, avarice—and his attack on the athletic and military values that had been literally beaten into him at places like Clemson.

At Clemson, Dickey continued to cultivate the stock image of the big, brawny, brainless football jock, and for years afterward professed he had been "a numbskull football player" devoid of any interest in "mathematics, English, history, economics, and whatever else."[23] Already an eclectic reader, he declared: "At Clemson the only book I read was the play book. . . . It was almost like a bible . . . , but it wasn't very hard to learn . . . , just straight ahead brute force football, or as they said at Clemson, 'three yards and a cloud of dirt.'"[24] He maintained that all his friends were football players. Dickey failed to distinguish himself scholastically, but some of his teachers caught glimpses of his intelligence and imagination. His favorite, Prof. Claud Green, saved some of his English papers because of their promise. Because Dickey was embarrassed by his less-than-noteworthy performances in the classroom, he later concocted all sorts of bizarre stories about his true interests at Clemson. In a 1970 *Playboy* interview, he told Geoffrey Norman that he had wanted to be a veternarian and therefore took courses in animal husbandry. (In a 1972 commencement address at Francis Marion College, he repeated his claim.) Dickey, in fact, marched with the other cadets to the same drummer: He studied engineering and then decided to enlist. The pressure to enlist was strong. One of the most popular teachers, Major Farr, addressed the cadets before he himself left for military duty in early December 1942: "Clemson men, the time has come when we must think and act not as individuals or as separate states, but as a nation. Firm, constructive, hopeful, Christian leadership is what the world now needs. We must stand ready to fight and die if necessary to uphold the ideals upon which our nation was founded. This is the only way by which German aggression and Japanese imperialism can be destroyed."[25] Dickey responded to the call. On December 3, the day Major Farr's speech appeared in the college newspaper, he decided to leave Clemson and follow his commander and his many peers to war.

III.

JOURNEY TO WAR

6. The Failed Pilot (1943–1944)

The Second World War shaped Dickey's life like no other event. He once said: "I remember almost every day that I was in the war, and I think almost everything that I've done is influenced, at least to some degree, either directly or indirectly, most probably directly, by the fact that I was in the war."[1] Along with thousands of other American teenagers, Dickey entered the war with no clear sense of direction. Engineering and football, he realized at Clemson, were not his forte. Like his alter egos in *Deliverance*, he wanted to abandon his hemmed-in life and plunge into a new realm of risk and adventure. Military training at various bases in the United States gave him his first opportunity to venture beyond the pale of the Southeast. As he traveled, however, he felt a contradictory urge to return home. Dickey never completely resolved these tensions and later expressed them in the cyclical plots of his poems and novels.

Like many veterans, when Dickey returned from the war, he routinely enchanted audiences with his tales of heroic combat. He assumed the role of a battle-scarred pilot who had flown one hundred combat missions over the Philippines and Japan. An editor friend from Doubleday, Herman Gollob, heard one of Dickey's many yarns at a dinner party given by William Styron on Martha's Vineyard in the summer of 1971. Styron had invited the well-known *New York Times* reporter James Reston to his house. In a manner Dickey found insufferably pompous, Reston puffed on his pipe and attacked America's involvement in the Vietnam War. Smiling menacingly, Dickey questioned Reston about his knowledge of combat. Discovering that the reporter had little first-hand experience of war, Dickey delivered account after graphic account of his bombing missions over the Philippines and Korea. After hearing these vivid and disturbing testaments, Reston fell silent, convinced he was in the presence of a pilot who had flown dozens of missions in two wars.

Like Hemingway and Faulkner after the First World War and Mailer after the Second, Dickey transformed his military experience into a tantalizing myth. He had always wanted to be a pilot, so when pilots were in demand near the beginning of the war, he jumped at the chance to enroll in flight training. But as Japan's and Germany's air forces dwindled, the demand for pilots decreased. Earning one's wings became more competitive. Like many other trainees, Dickey failed some of his preflight tests and was reclassified. His pilot fantasy, however, was too firmly entrenched to make way for reality. For most of his life he repudiated the circumstances that led to his demotion, insisting to almost everyone, including his family, that he had occupied the pilot's seat when he flew.

Having taken ROTC at Clemson from September 5 to December 2, 1942, Dickey first enlisted in the Reserve Corps of the army for the duration of the war plus six months. On January 5, 1943, opting for more-active involvement, he requested an appointment in the Army Air Corps. Since he needed a recommendation, he asked W. Gilbert Mill, his Clemson trigonometry teacher, to write one. Mill obliged, saying of Dickey: "I have found him to be trustworthy, industrious, courteous, neat and above the average in technical ability. His physical qualifications are excellent and as far as I know he is in good health. In my opinion he would be successful in any endeavor requiring coordination, stamina and courage."[2] In response to his application, Maj. Henry Konigemark informed Dickey that the War Department had specific quotas regulating the number of aviation cadets. As a result, he couldn't guarantee Dickey a place. Undeterred, Private Dickey boarded a train for Miami Beach, where he joined the 584th Technical School Squadron for basic training. In a letter he wrote his parents on February 24, 1943, he reassured them that his journey to war had begun auspiciously. He had met a young Atlanta woman on the train (she became one of Dickey's bevy of female correspondents during the war) and several Clemson friends in Miami. Although his official crew cut made him "look like several varieties of hell" and reveille at 5:20 A.M. curtailed his nightlife (soon he would be waking at 4:30 A.M.), he had grown used to such hardships. He told his parents to send his love to Virginia Lee in Atlanta and joked that his enlistment ensured an Allied victory. Miami, he said, "is the prettiest [place] I've ever seen (except the Jews)."[3] The fact that he was training for a war waged in part to protect the Jews had little effect on the genteel anti-Semitism he had inherited from his parents.

By the time Dickey began his training, the Allies had made substantial gains against the Japanese and Germans. Having inundated the Pacific Islands like a tidal wave, Japanese troops had begun to suffer defeats, principally at Midway, Guadalcanal, and New Guinea. In late 1942 and early 1943, the American navy and army initiated their "leap-frogging" strategy, bypassing Japanese strongholds to build air and naval bases on the islands so that they could cut off Japanese supply routes. The Army Air Corps played a role in these activities by protecting Allied ships as they transported troops and supplies, repelling Japanese aircraft from Allied bases, and bombing enemy fortifications.

Compared to soldiers in the Pacific, Dickey had it easy in Florida. As a new member of the 412th Training Group, Flight E-1, he lodged in the Sands Hotel on Miami Beach. For amusement he and his buddies visited the Miami nightclubs and dog tracks. In March, however, he began basic training. As anyone who has undergone it will attest, "basic" strained body and mind to the breaking point. Singing old songs like "Yankee Doodle Dandy" and "It's a Grand Old Flag," Dickey marched with his Enfield rifle and gas mask, crawled on his stomach over the beach sand, jumped to his feet, dove back to the sand, and repeated this robotic routine until he was exhausted. His ability to execute his tasks over the next few months would determine whether he would become a pilot, radar observer, navigator, or bombardier. Initially, he worked hard at his drills and remained optimistic about his chance of becoming a pilot. Despite his weariness, he kept up a lively, cheerful correspondence with his brother, Tom, his father, and especially his mother. In the letters to his "dearest, dearest Mom," he portrayed himself as a patriotic defender of his homeland. "I don't want the town and territory I love so much devastated and blown to bits,"[4] he declared in a March 11 letter. Perhaps thinking of his mother's Confederate ancestors subjugated during the Civil War, he vowed never to let the Japanese or Germans rape and pillage his folks.

To his parents Dickey explained that his main regret during his first months in the army was that he hadn't left Clemson earlier: "I hope they don't send me back to Clemson. I hate that place, and hope to hell I never see it as long as I live again."[5] His enthusiasm for the army, however, soon declined. He informed his mother in the middle of March that he had failed his physical exam because of high blood pressure. He believed it was the result of nervousness, and his anxiety was made worse by the awareness that a second failure would scuttle his air corps plans. "Nothing ever happens the way I want it to," he wrote despondently on March 16. "I knew almost from the beginning I was no good, and that something would happen to thwart my plans. It's always been that way, and it always will. I'll never even see an airplane. I shouldn't have been enthused about flying. From now on I don't give a damn for anything or anybody. Except you and Tom and Pop."[6] He considered going to Officer Candidate School if he failed his physical again. In the meantime, life continued with target practice, at which he excelled, and KP duty, which he likened to cesspool cleaning. To break the monotony he and Clemson football friend Roger Kibbett, who had fortuitously appeared in his unit, swam and tried to pick up girls at the beach. Although his mother regularly sent him checks, establishing a policy she would continue over the next few decades, Dickey tried to keep his pleasures simple and inexpensive because of his twenty-one-dollar-a-month salary.

On March 23, Dickey sent good news to his mother: He had passed his physical even though his blood pressure remained high. He decided that shooting his Enfield rifle at the rifle range had caused the surge in his blood pressure (he would fear guns for the rest of his life). The depressing prospect of "washing out" had subsided for the moment. He happily announced he had acquired a new girlfriend, Jean (he confessed to his mother that she was a Yankee, but not a Jew). Despite his new attachment, he looked forward to moving to his next post, which might be in Ohio, and to joining the aviation cadets, partly because his salary would increase to seventy-five dollars per month. When orders for his transfer didn't materialize, he grudgingly returned to guard duty. His mood sank when he rebroke a finger he had broken at Clemson. Finally, on March 28, he received orders assigning him to High Point, North Carolina.

Having completed basic on April 3, Dickey traveled to what in military parlance was called the "College Training Detachment" at High Point College near Greensboro, North Carolina. During the war the federal government helped colleges suffering financially from a depleted student body by paying them to educate soldiers. Dickey was in the first group of aviation cadets to attend High Point. According to his description, the college sounded like another vacation spot with "plenty of girls, good food, and the cleanest air that I've seen anywhere." In this refreshing environment, he studied physics, math, and other technical subjects needed for flying. He wrote home ecstatically: "Some people the army starts on the downward path, but with me it is doing more good than I could ever possibly tell you. When I come back to you, I'll be a much better Jim than when I left."[7] Assuring his mother that he was not a profligate son—profligacy would grow more appealing after the war—he returned to his books.

Dickey was, in fact, doing very well. The army's discipline had harnessed some of his wayward energies. By April 12, he had attained the student rank of lieutenant in the College Training Detachment of the Air Cadet Corps. He was the fourth-ranking "officer" for a group of over two hundred men. His grades were high. He was competing on a softball team, running on the local track, and playing basketball (he told his mother he was high scorer in some of the games). In charge of a flight group known as Flight A, he was proud that his cadets regularly won dress parade. He was certain of his future success in flight training. Dickey, however, was in no rush to go overseas as a fighter pilot. In mid-May, after a slump in his classroom performance, he told his mother he might have to stay at High Point an extra month, which was fine by him: "I'm not any more anxious to go over and get shot at than you are to have me go."[8] He assured her that he had plenty of girlfriends at the college to keep his mind off the war.

During the final weeks of May, Dickey improved in his classes in code, navigation, Civil Air Regulations, English, geometry, physics, algebra, and history. He raised his average in his most difficult course, physics, to an 87. He prided himself on graduating to Flight E, an elite group composed of forty cadets from which officers were chosen. At this stage in his training he tackled "field problems"—simulations of battles to test combat skills. He explained to his father: "It's just like actual war, except we don't shoot each other. It is also quite a bit like the 'cowboys and Indians' . . . I used to play in the back yard."[9] On June 7, he began flying Piper Cubs and other small planes.

Some of Dickey's new confidence about his future as a pilot came from an odd source—a writing assignment for his English class. He wrote his mother on May 31: "Something wonderful has happened. I know I am good for something. . . . *I can write*. Always before I have had some doubt as to my ability, but not anymore. The English teacher here says my themes are the best he's ever read."[10] If Dickey could succeed at writing, he believed he could succeed at flying. His essay "The Rebel Soul," however, was neither about a pilot nor about flying, but about Bix Beiderbecke, the 1920s jazz cornetist, pianist, and composer. Dickey identified with this talented musician and elevated him into a pantheon that included Napoleon, Beethoven, Byron, and Shelley. Beiderbecke typified the romantic genius who transcended ordinary restrictions and paid a price for his transgressions. He was one of those "who by the very nature of their own being, and by their particular talents, are destined to be singled out from the many and live brilliant but strangely distorted and out-of-focus lives."[11] In this tragic artist Dickey found a model that foreshadowed his own career, which was beginning to gain momentum in the form of prose pieces he mailed to his parents.

Inside as well as outside his English class, Dickey established himself as the sort of romantic he wrote about in his Beiderbecke essay. He periodically launched into extemporaneous flights of fancy, endearing himself to his fellow cadets as well as to his English teacher. Everyone recognized his talent as a storyteller. Among the cadets, Dickey got to know Frank Spain (who later appeared as a character in *Alnilam*), Winston Smith, Joseph Doyle, and Watson Smooth. One of his closest friends, Andrew Harbelis, also lent his name to a character in

Alnilam and its unfinished sequel, *Crux*. Dickey and Harbelis shared a passion for the undergraduate girls at High Point and frequently met to gossip about the officers who ruled over them, like the corps commander Johnny Schmidt and Deputy Commander Oliver Snow. Their friendship, with its intimation of con-spiratorial rebelliousness, resembled Joel Cahill's *Alnilam* group in miniature. Although Dickey modeled *Alnilam*'s fictitious flight training base after a base in Camden, South Carolina, in the novel Dickey located it—like High Point—in North Carolina.

With Harbelis, Dickey spoke candidly about his wish to be a writer and his plan to get a job in advertising, a business he deemed compatible with writing. Having witnessed his storytelling abilities, Harbelis encouraged him. Their friendship, however, grew more from athletic interests than literary ones. In this area, as in others later in his life, Dickey assumed the role of master. He gave Harbelis lessons in proper running style before they jogged five miles across the North Carolina countryside. Having tried hard to blend with his peers in high school, Dickey was beginning to assert himself in a more dictatorial role. When officers at High Point warned Harbelis and the other cadets that, at least while visiting other bases, they should refrain from flaunting their privileged status (aviation cadets enjoyed more fashionable uniforms and higher pay), Dickey opted to draw attention to his status and even tried to set himself apart from his immediate peers by wearing leggings.

In a retrospective account of High Point, Dickey remembered almost nothing about his technical training, his rising military status, or his new dedication to writing:

> I was mainly active in a social life, and girls. They had some very nice girls there. . . . That's when I began to get into sex. It was rather late in the day, but that's when it really began to dawn on me. . . . I remember this red-headed girl, who was probably a nymphomaniac of some degree, but I love red hair. . . . She was so ardent that it was frightening to me. Those timid high school kisses were nothing compared to this gal. She was after you. She wanted to do the deed, the act of darkness. I was sure I was quite ca-pable, [but] certainly not up to her intensity. . . . I thought, my God, are they all like this? I never saw any other girl act like this. It was quite enough for me, maybe too much.[12]

Although he had admitted to losing his virginity at Darlington, his more mem-orable introduction to sex came at High Point.

As early as June 1943, Dickey's writing, which he saw as a way to enhance his love life, began to take precedence over his commitment to flying. In his letters he expressed doubts about his future in the Army Air Corps. On June 7, he told his parents he no longer cared whether or not he earned his wings. He also glumly noted that he quit football at Clemson to become a pilot only to please them. The cause of his sudden melancholy was ill health, but he soon had other reasons to feel depressed. After passing his first flight test on June 8, he nearly failed a subsequent one. A failing grade was 70 or below, and Dickey had only managed a 72. He had received average grades in taxiing, taking off, and flying in a holding pattern, but he had scored below average in all other aspects of flying. Because of this temporary setback, he told his parents he considered abandoning the air corps and returning to Atlanta.

When Dickey traveled to Nashville on June 19 for classification, his spirits continued their downward spiral. He wrote his mother on June 23 that the camp "compared favorably with most of our Georgia prison camps" and was "the most inefficiently run army camp"[13] he had ever seen. He and his fellow cadets lived in primitive barracks (Dickey served as barracks chief in one of them), and over the next few weeks they had to take innumerable technical, physical, and psychological tests to decide whether they should become pilots, navigators, or bombardiers. The tests measured alertness, coordination, memory, reflexes, and manual dexterity. In late June, worn out by the daily interrogations, Dickey told his parents he no longer cared about his final assignment. By Independence Day, his optimism had returned. "I am almost certain to be a pilot,"[14] he told his mother, while assuring her that he probably would never see combat.

During his first two weeks in Nashville, Dickey could not leave the five-acre compound where he was stationed. Living in such a confined space irked him, especially when he discovered that many of his fellow trainees were Jewish. He complained to his mother: "There are a good many Jews in this outfit, always getting the easy details and going on sick call for athlete's foot. Very disgusting."[15] Even when Dickey boasted that he had shed some of his provincial biases in an August letter, it was obvious that he had a long way to go: "I've learned how to get along with all kinds of people. Jews, Greeks, Wops, all kinds. (One of my Jew friends just walked by muttering, 'Another day, another dollar fifty.') What a life!"[16] In another letter, written after watching Gene Kelly and Judy Garland in the musical *For Me and My Gal*, he called Garland an "obnoxious kike."[17] His attitude toward African Americans also showed little improvement. "I got another nigger hair cut. *You should see this one*,"[18] he wrote on January 26, 1944. The fact that he sent all these slurs to his mother belies her tacit complicity.

Maibelle Dickey, however, did not approve of all her son's cynical views, especially those regarding marriage. At the young age of twenty, Jim Dickey was already arguing with his parents—and himself—about marriage. He often took the position that marriage was a form of incarceration not unlike military service. At a dance following his initial restrictions in Nashville, he met a woman named Jane Davis who convinced him that marriage might not be imprisoning after all. Although she had a humdrum job at Nashville's National Life & Accident Insurance Company, he found her more enchanting than his other girlfriends. During the rest of the 1943 summer, Davis wrote Dickey nearly every day, sometimes referring to him as a "Greek God."[19] Before long, however, she took umbrage at his Dionysian ways. In a letter written on March 21, 1944, she expressed mild shock at hearing that he and a friend had recently consumed forty bottles of beer. She warned Dickey that she had no intention of marrying him. Nevertheless, she was anxious to see him and on May 23 invited him back to Nashville to continue their romance. Dickey later said of Davis: "She was a sweet girl who wanted to get married to just about anybody, just for the sake of getting married."[20] In fact, Dickey was the one who wanted to marry her for the sake of marrying. About half a year after his introductory dance, he proposed to her. In a May 25 letter, Davis again voiced her opposition to his unconventional religious and marital views. Even though she found his status in the air corps glamorous, she planned to marry another soldier when he returned from the war. In his retrospective imagination, Dickey erased the disappointment of being rejected by pretending that he was the one who rejected her. He also continued to court other women such as Peg Roney.

Looking back on his weeks in Nashville, Dickey downplayed the desperation aroused by his military tests: "As it turned out, almost anybody who could pass the physical, the eye exam, was classified as a pilot, because they needed them mighty bad. And the navigators, I'm sure there were very few that were qualified, because they were guys that wore glasses, or scored relatively well in mathematics."[21] In fact, the need for pilots was waning, but after passing his grueling exams Dickey left Nashville as a bona fide pilot trainee on July 28, 1943. With fresh resolve, he entered Preflight Training at Maxwell Field in Montgomery, Alabama.

"Prepare for combat" was the motto of the Southeastern Army Air Forces Training Command, and that's precisely what Dickey prepared for day after day at Maxwell. The course work was demanding; it included aerial navigation, Morse code, aircraft identification, math, physics, and physical training. Dickey studied hard and achieved perfect scores on a number of his tests. To the end of his life he could name all the different kinds of World War II aircraft he had memorized at Maxwell. His confidence about flying one of these planes without an instructor, however, continued to waver. So far he had accumulated only a smattering of flying experience. When his mother informed him that two of his friends had recently died in flying accidents, Dickey replied that he would probably wash out of flight training before he ever flew solo. Deaths on the base added to his fears; he told his father two or three cadets died of heat exhaustion on the obstacle course. On the same course, the accident-prone Dickey suffered a deep cut to his hand. Despite these setbacks, his superiors made him athletic representative for his squadron of five hundred men. Maxwell Field trained thousands of cadets, so it was with a special feeling of authority that he took control of the basketball and track teams. Dickey's basketball team had a chance to win the base championship, or so he maintained. His good grades assured his graduation from Preflight Training, and on September 30, he left Maxwell Field to begin Primary Flight Training at Camden, South Carolina. If he passed his tests at Camden, which involved sixty-three hours of flying (mainly in PT-17 Stearman airplanes), he would go on to Basic Flight Training and Advanced Flight Training.

At Camden, Dickey felt a sense of camaraderie with the other trainees and with the instructors, too. His best friend was Gene Griner from Savannah (he may have borrowed his name for the backwoods garage owners in *Deliverance*). He also befriended a young man named Philip Root, who later corresponded with him about their days in South Carolina. When Root read a newspaper synopsis of *Alnilam* in 1982, he was sure that its plot derived from a specific accident at Camden. The cadet who crashed was named Peck, which may explain why Dickey changed the name of the training base from Camden to Peckover. Root reminded Dickey in his letter that Peck had done a high-speed stall into trees while hedgehopping on a solo flight. The doctors were still picking glass splinters from his face two or three days later when he died. Dickey knew the difficulty of flying Stearmans all too well. Years later, in court because of a lawsuit over his book *Puella*, he spoke with rare truthfulness about his experiences during Primary Flight Training: "I was held back a class. They had some sort of jam-up on the Basic Schools that were there, and my flying was not suitable to the Air Force at that time, so I was eliminated from Pilot Training; but, I was determined to stay in aircraft."[22] He was not alone in his failure; all his roommates and his friend Griner had washed out, too.

In a letter to his brother, Tom, written on October 28, 1943, Dickey supplied specific details about his first solo flight. Allegedly writing left-handed because of a broken thumb (his penmanship was not that different from previous letters), he confessed:

I was flying with my instructor Saturday and we came in and landed and taxied up to where you parked the planes and my instructor got out and I started to, but he said "Oh no you don't, you ??—?-@@*!. You have been trying to kill me for three weeks now, and so you can take it up yourself and bust your own ass."

"No, NO," I said, "You can't do this to me," but he was gone by then, so I taxied out to the line and took off. I made the shakiest takeoff ever seen around these parts, and circled the field. I was shaking so bad the plane was vibrating like Pop's '34 [Ford] on the road to What-cha-know Joe's [Joseph Underwood took care of his father's fighting cocks in North Georgia]. I was afraid the engine would fall out, so I cut the motor and came in. I made the prettiest landing I ever made—the plane only bounced 30 ft. in the air four times. By the time I had it on the ground and was congratulating myself I noticed a very peculiar thing—one of the wings was dragging in the dirt. The plane went 'round and 'round and finally stopped, but not before I banged my thumb up against the instrument panel. When I got out I expected St. Peter to greet me at the Pearly Gates, but it was only the mechanics with a hose to clean the *shit* out of the cockpit.[23]

Dickey's sarcastic tone and obvious exaggerations deflected some of the embarrassment he felt about his nearly disastrous solo flight. He had lasted only five minutes in the air, and during his landing he had panicked. Fearing his parents would worry about his safety, Dickey never divulged the specifics of his accident to them. On November 12, he merely informed his mother that he had failed his first check ride and went on to express renewed confidence in his ability to fly. In his many later attempts to assuage his wounded pride, he denied his failures at Camden and, in their place, invented tales of valiantly piloting airplanes.

Courage, rites of passage, heroic quests, and compensatory lies became Dickey's literary fixations, and understandably so. His journeys to military bases around the South had all the trappings of a heroic quest. At Camden, he had botched his first major trial. Thirty years later he would reinterpret the event that led to his washing out in "Two Poems of Flight-Sleep." In the first section, entitled "Army Air Corps, Flight Training, 1943," he attributes his loss of control on his solo flight to a death wish and a dream "of letting go" of "The cold   the war   the Cadet Program and my peanut-faced / Instructor and his maps." With the truthfulness he paradoxically reserved for his poetry and fiction, he admits: "I would have to become / A legend, curled up out of sight with all the Western World / Coming at me under the floor-mat." The real Dickey, as the poem suggests, is curled up in a fetal position, afraid that the world is rising to destroy his out-of-control plane and his legend, too. His denial of any eyewitnesses—"No one ever lived to prove he thought he saw / An aircraft with no pilot showing"—is pure wish fulfillment. His superiors witnessed the mishap and punished him accordingly. Of his near fatal landing, Dickey avers: "I was in / Death's baby machine, that led to the fighters and bombers, / But training, here in the lone purple, / For something else."[24] One of the working titles for *Alnilam*—*Death's Baby Machine*—refers to Dickey's ambivalent fear of death, a fear that reduces him to a trembling infant in the cockpit and that, in the end, sends him to "the washing machine." The "something else" he was training for was writing, which depended more on high-flying fantasies than on aviation skills.

While in poems and novels Dickey bore witness to his trauma at Camden, in conversation he dismissed his old fears and failings to stress the bliss of flying alone:

> I liked flying solo. . . . You just make one circuit, and come back around and land. But when you see there's not anybody in the front seat of the airplane, there's not anybody in the airplane but you, it gives you quite a turn. But you just go through it mechanically, just do what they told you to do, and you don't have any trouble. The only trouble is in the landing. The Stearman has very close-together landing gear. And a lot of them would not be able to get both wheels down on the ground at the same time, and they would tip up on one wing and do what's called a ground loop, where the tip of the wing would hit the ground and the plane would spin around. You didn't hurt anybody, but it was very bad marks against you if you did that. I never did it myself, but a lot of them did.

Regarding the grades he earned for his solo test flight, he said they were "good, very good, almost textbook."[25] He continued to deny his gyrations in the dirt by the Camden runway until he died.

Dickey's impression of Camden as a wintry wasteland haunted him until it reached its final expression in *Alnilam*. He always remembered the fleece-lined pants the aviators wore and made much of the warm sheep wool in his novel. He said about Camden: "It was cold, my God, it was cold. The instructors were all bundled up, and walked out there like a bunch of zombies."[26] In the novel he projected his feelings of desolation onto the landscape. Because family and friends expected him to succeed as a pilot, he now distanced himself geographically and philosophically from them. As his gloom deepened, he increasingly relied on books for escape and solace. When Dickey left Camden on January 6, 1944, his view of his home ground as a provincial backwater solidified. Although he could still play the adoring son, he frequently expressed indifference and disdain toward his parents and wrote fewer letters to them. He no longer wanted to return to 166 West Wesley and take care of his parents "always and always." He was bound for adventures on distant shores that he hoped someday to turn into memorable poems and novels.

Before traveling to Boca Raton to train for his new position as a radar observer, Dickey went to Buckingham Field in Fort Myers, Florida, where from January 7 to March 12, 1944, he studied the art of aerial gunnery. His course included the operation, maintenance, and firing of small arms, thirty- and fifty-calibre machine guns, air-to-air gunnery, and ground-to-ground gunnery. The debacle at Camden had made him morose. At first he had to live in a tent; only later did he move into barracks, which weren't much more comfortable than the tents. He found shooting from B-17s at targets towed by B-26s and AT-6s nerve-racking. To learn the inner workings of machine guns, he spent tedious hours taking them apart and reassembling them. Putting together the guns blindfolded after instructors tossed in extra parts as decoys irritated him, as did shooting skeet from turrets on moving trucks and tramping into the marshy, snake-ridden Everglades to shoot at targets from six hundred yards.

At gunnery school, Dickey's rebelliousness and literariness went hand in hand. Having grown increasingly antagonistic toward army discipline, he surprised one of his fellow gunnery trainees, Irvin Dahmen, by boldly gate-crashing a dance that was off-limits to cadets. His main pastimes now were girl chasing and reading. On February 25, 1944, he instructed his mother to cash some war bonds he had purchased and with the money buy Hemingway's *A Farewell to Arms* and *The Sun Also Rises*, Dreiser's *An American Tragedy*, Farrell's *Studs Lonigan*, Joyce's *Ulysses*, and Van Tilburg Clark's *The Ox-Bow Incident*. He told her to buy poetry by Conrad Aiken, Jesse Stuart, and James Thomson. This list of requested books was the first of many he sent his mother during the war. Dahmen, who bunked nearby, remembered him spending hours on *Ulysses* and *Studs Lonigan*. Like so many of his later friends, Dahmen was astounded by Dickey's literary stamina.

That Hemingway should figure so prominently in his list is unsurprising. *The Sun Also Rises* focuses on a character, Jake Barnes, who has suffered a mysterious war wound that complicates his sex life. Frederic Henry in *A Farewell to Arms* has been broken by wars and other calamities. Having suffered recent wounds to both ego and body, Dickey could identify with the stoicism, cynicism, and hedonism of Hemingway's protagonists. He also identified with Hemingway's contradictory desires to bid farewell to the army and to win glory in combat. After the war, Dickey would imitate Hemingway in both art and life. The fact that he was reading one of the most complicated novels ever written—*Ulysses*—was a sign of his new literary seriousness. In his later poems and novels he would adopt Joyce's unsqueamish preoccupation with the body and the "nightmare of history," as Stephen Dedalus calls it in *Ulysses*. He would also obsessively use Joyce's "mythical method" to shape public and private experiences into narratives with universal significance. The gloomy Victorian poet James Thomson, whose most famous poem was "City of Dreadful Night," also captivated Dickey. Thomson dedicated his poem to exposing "the bitter old and wrinkled truth /

Stripped naked of all vesture that beguiles, / False dreams, false hopes, false masks and modes of youth." He speculated that his most sympathetic reader would be "someone desolate, Fate-smitten, / Whose faith and hope are dead, and who would die."[27] This appealed to Dickey because he too was shucking off the false dreams and hopes of his Atlanta boyhood and staring bitterly at the naked truths of adulthood. That he soon substituted new dreams and new masks for the "wrinkled truth" did not decrease Thomson's relevance. In *Alnilam*, he had Joel Cahill assume Thomson's cryptic initials, B.V., and he had Joel's apostles recite bits of Thomson's poetry.

Dickey's discomfort increased when, in late February, he cut a finger on the jeep range. On February 25, he wrote his brother, Tom, about wanting to flee the army's drudgery and pain. He glumly admitted that he might fail at radar school and become a gunner. His memories of gunnery school supplied some of the animus for his rancorous protagonist in *To the White Sea*; Muldrow is a gunner who trained at Buckingham Field in Fort Myers. Years after his dismal training period in Florida, Dickey remembered his two months at the base with characteristic license. "I liked to shoot things," he said. "I was delighted with gunner's school; I had real good scores."[28] For Dickey, as for the Greeks, Mnemosyne was mother of the Muses, and sponsored imaginative rather than historical reconstruction.

To learn the techniques needed to become a night fighter radar observer, or RO as he was soon called, on March 12 Dickey left Fort Myers for Boca Raton, Florida, a city that literally meant "mouth of the rat." He knew he would be indoctrinated in "some sort of secret program,"[29] but had only a hazy notion of what it comprised. Radar must have reminded him of the futuristic weapons wielded by Doc Savage and the other pulp magazine warriors he'd once adored. In military circles, radar was considered so potentially advantageous that it had to be kept top-secret. Prompted by the success of British night fighters in North Africa, the American air corps had initiated its first serious training program in radar only about a year and a half before Dickey arrived in Boca Raton. When four night fighter squadrons were formed, the British RAF sent instructors to give guidance. For Dickey, radar lived up to its mystique: "It was like some weird miracle. It seemed beyond science to turn some dials and to see something come up on the screen and represent its relationship to you and to your aircraft."[30] Because it had the power to conjure up images and to represent the world and the mind's relationship to it, before long Dickey used radar as a metaphor for the poetic imagination. In *Alnilam*, the "secret program" of radar is as much a clandestine art as poetry.

On the base that had once been a lavish club, Dickey continued to feel oppressed. His new trials were legion. In a physical education course, other soldiers sprayed him with tear gas so he could practice using a gas mask. He climbed into a pressure chamber in order to test his body functions at simulated altitudes of thirty thousand feet. Barbed wire surrounded the school, and security guards searched the men as they entered and exited the classrooms. "We were taken in under guard and we couldn't take any materials out," he remembered. "Everything was kept under lock and key, and everything that we did was under surveillance. . . . It was top secret, sure enough. In fact, radar itself was a word that was not allowed to be used. . . . We were not called radar observers; we were radio observers."[31] One cadet got into trouble when he wrote a letter in his note-book to his girlfriend and tore it out to mail; he was suspected of copying down secrets to send to the enemy. Sequestered in soundproof rooms, the cadets were not allowed to take home any writing for fear that information might get into the hands of spies. Dickey's radar classes could only strengthen the memory for which he later became famous.

While at work on *Alnilam* in the 1970s and 1980s, Dickey developed a passion for navigation. He bought expensive sextants and even took a correspondence course to improve his skills. At Boca Raton, however, he only grudgingly applied himself to the course work in navigation by radar and dead reckoning, the practice of interception techniques, and the maintenance of radar and radio equipment. The training could be frightening. During the day, the cadets simulated night flying by blacking out the windows in their planes. They flew blind, just as the blind Frank Cahill and the bats do in *Alnilam*. Because radar technology was in its infancy, the screen the cadets depended on for their bearings was primitive and difficult to read. Learning how to intercept an enemy was tricky. Dickey explained:

> When the other aircraft took evasive action, and you had to chase them just by means of the electronics, that was tough. There were two types of radar that the United States used then. One was called 540 SCR. Signal Corps Radio 540. . . . It has a time baseline that's in the middle of the scope. It's a round scope. . . . You judge the distance of the aircraft by where he is on this in relation to the bottom of it. The target will appear just as a sort of triangle. If one wing of the triangle is farther over that way, the target is to your starboard. If it's farther over that way, it's on the other side. It's very very difficult because the scope is jumping and glittering all the time, and you can just barely make out the target.[32]

The radar observer was called "the brain of the plane" for good reason. Without him, the pilot could not track and shoot down enemy aircraft.

On May 7, Dickey's instructors awarded him a certificate for mastering all the equipment in a P-70's rear cockpit. On May 21, he was officially classified as an "Aircraft Observer, Radar Observer Night Fighter" and given a temporary appointment as a second lieutenant or flight officer by the Headquarters of the Army Air Forces Eastern Technical Training Command. His accomplishments, however, did little to dispel his growing antagonism toward the military. He told his brother, Tom, what he would tell his son Chris twenty-five years later: "Boy, don't let anybody convince you that you should join the army. Go to college and get an education, so you'll be fit for something in later life."[33] Dickey's disillusionment with the army lifted only when he learned that his new destination would be California.

Dickey celebrated in Fort Lauderdale and Miami and then boarded the train for Hammer Field in Fresno, a place he would soon call "the best post in the Army."[34] The long, comfortable trip west by Pullman could not have been more propitious. On D day, June 6, 1944, four days before arriving at Hammer Field, he met Gwendolyn Leege, a stunningly beautiful and intelligent woman with whom he fell deeply in love. Years later Leege remembered: "We met by miraculous chance one night aboard the silver streamliner 'City of San Francisco' en route to Chicago."[35] In a reminiscence that Gwen sent Dickey in 1996, a year before he died, she said she was taking the train from Los Angeles back to Bryn Mawr for the fall semester. The train stopped at an obscure station in California, she rushed to the exit to glimpse the exuberant, boarding flyers, and she collided with Dickey, who flirtatiously remarked that she had a face like a rose. Dickey's letter to his parents postmarked June 11, 1944, refers to the fortuitous meeting (Leege, in fact, was returning home to California after her spring term): "I met some real nice girls in Chicago and we had a fine time all the way out. One lives in San Francisco and I am going down to see her this week-end."[36] This was Gwen.

Dickey was infatuated with Gwen, whom he later compared to Grace Kelly, and Gwen was infatuated with the handsome man in uniform who, she said, was as "beautiful as Apollo."[37] Leege talked all night to Dickey about life, literature, and philosophy. Despite his qualms about wealthy, well-bred girls, Dickey was intrigued by Leege's background and broad knowledge of German and Spanish literature and philosophy. Of Leege's family, Dickey said: "Her mother was German [and a nurse for the Germans during World War I]. I believe her father had been Dutch-German."[38] After her first husband, a biologist, had died, Leege's mother had married into the wealthy Stien family, and Gwen had grown up, like Dickey, accustomed to privilege. Dickey assured his mother that she would like Leege's mother simply because she was German.

At first smitten with Gwen, Dickey had reservations after spending a week on her family's country estate in Marin County, just outside San Francisco. He enjoyed going to San Francisco's Chinatown, zoo, aquarium, nightclubs, and bars with Gwen, but he complained that she grew shrewish when he didn't give her what she wanted. Dickey was not about to satisfy all her lavish demands. He favored a more economical approach, both with his money and with his love. On July 22 he confided to his mother: "I am in love with Gwen, but I don't think anything will ever come of it, because she is inclined to be a little snotty . . . when she doesn't have everything she wants (which is plenty) and who wants a wife like that? . . . Anyway, love and marriage are different in a lot more than name. I have an infinite capacity for one and absolutely none for the other." Once again he asked his mother to get involved in his love life: "Mom, send Gwen one of those pictures like I gave Jackie and Betty Fitts and Jane Davis. . . . I'm sure she'll swoon over it."[39] The fact that he solicited his mother's help a few months later in his romance with his Atlanta girlfriend, Peg Roney (he told her to assure Roney on the phone that he loved her), betrayed a cooling in his relations with Gwen. Not long afterward, he asked his mother to send one of his beach pictures to another girlfriend, Virginia Grimm, who lived in San Francisco. During Maibelle's liaison work on his behalf, he told his mother: "[I love the other women] not one millionth as much as I love you."[40]

One of Leege's expectations may have involved fidelity—an expectation Dickey was not prepared to fulfill. His new girlfriend would not be the first woman to try to curb his amorous whims. The couple would get engaged in an informal way (without a ring, he later stipulated), but they soon abandoned the agreement. Even while "provisionally engaged" and visiting Leege nearly every weekend in the summer of 1944, Dickey argued with his mother about his suitability for marriage. Having declared his unstinting love for Maibelle, he concluded that he should remain a bachelor. He also argued with his father about his libertarian morality, which was evolving toward its mature form in Fresno. While courting Leege, he enjoyed the favors of several other women. As he explained: "My big sexual endeavor . . . was with a woman who was about 26, and a widow. She was a nymphomaniac. . . . She had unashamed tornadoes in her blood. She was like the High Point girl, except much more experienced. She was a sex nut. But I always had a feeling that she was a little bit older than [the sort of women] I wanted to be hanging around with."[41]

Years after his California sojourn, Dickey declared that of all the girls he had known before his first wife, Maxine, he had come closest to marrying Gwen. He appreciated the boost she gave to his literary education: "She introduced me to some experimental writers and also to something for which I will always be grateful, the Gotham Book Mart in New York City. When I got back from the Pacific, I went to New York to see her, and we visited the Gotham Book Mart. There were all the books I had heard about all those years and had never seen copies of. I had some money and mustering-out pay, so I bought a lot of them and began to read. I had a vague notion then that I might try to write a poem myself one day."[42] Dickey had already confessed to Leege his deep yearning to be a poet, and at Hammer Field as well as in the Pacific he had taken steps, albeit tentative ones, toward a writing career.

Despite his gratitude to Leege for her tutelary influence, he could also be condescending when he remembered her: "She knew literature pretty well, especially poetry, and she was multilingual, which was an interesting thing about her. But she was a rich man's woman. She could never have survived the scruffy life I lived as a student. She did not influence my *Weltanschauung*. She was not that deep a person, but she was very decorative and pretty. . . . She was not made for the nitty gritty of life, of getting in there and shoving with the rest of 'em like Maxine."[43] Dickey's snub came in part from his memory of Leege's superior knowledge of literature in 1944. At the time he was envious of her college education. He had also been hurt when Leege rebuffed his marriage proposals. Despite his criticism, Dickey carried on a lengthy correspondence with Leege while stationed in the Pacific and continued to write to her until he died.

As a flight officer in Hammer Field's 450th Base Unit, Dickey had plenty to keep his mind off romantic entanglements. It was here that pilots and radar observers paired up, developed friendships, and practiced night-fighting techniques. As Dickey explained: "All the new pilots and all the new intercept officers, or radar observers . . . [gathered] in one big room, and we went around from one group to another, talking to each other. You'd team up. I fell in with a fellow named Bradley, who came from Kentucky. He was a nice, quiet-spoken, kind of stocky guy. . . . I was convinced, just by talking to him, that he would be quite a good pilot to team up with. And I was never sorry, because I flew with him all through combat."[44] Earl Bradley was several years older than Dickey, married, and had a son. Because the subject of marriage aroused such turbulent feelings in Dickey, it touched off several heated arguments with his pilot. For the most part, however, they maintained a respectful alliance.

At Hammer Field, pilots took an intense three-month course that covered instrument flying on the ground, high- and low-altitude night flying, interception tactics, evasive maneuvers, coordination with ground control, navigation, and night-vision. The twenty-seven-year-old Dr. Iannone, who was Hammer Field's flight surgeon as well as its eye specialist, taught the night-vision class. He adored his aviator students, calling them the "cream of American youth,"[45] a compliment Dickey repaid by making him the doctor at Peckover Field who treats and befriends Joel Cahill. In the novel, Dr. Iannone distinguishes himself from the other characters by being avuncular and wise. He sits down with Joel's father at the end and tries to explain how the cadets' wild-eyed fanaticism makes them attractive as well as dangerous. "You've got to remember that these are kids," he says. "They may be pilot trainees, but they're still kids. If it weren't for the war they'd be in college, most of them. Fraternities. Societies, some of them 'secret.' Skull and Bones. Porcellian. This bunch [the Alnilam cabal] is in a way the equivalent of that."[46] The real Dr. Iannone regarded his dedicated students just as sympathetically.

During their fourth month in Fresno, the pilot trainees and radar observers practiced aerial gunnery at nearby Hayward Field. They flew P-70s, P-70Bs, AT-23As, and P-70-As, but their main focus was on the P-61 Black Widows, which were designed by Northrop Aircraft specifically for night fighting. The Black Widow was highly prized for its maneuverability, its reliable performance above altitudes of thirty-five thousand feet, its state-of-the-art radar interception equipment, and its 20-mm cannon and four .50-cal. machine guns. The P-61B Black Widow had been upgraded with night binoculars, which allowed the pilot to see five times as far at night as a pilot without the scope. The plane also had a radar scope so the pilot could oversee how the radar observer was tracking an enemy plane. Northrop Aircraft had been fine-tuning its night fighter planes over several years, and with the Black Widow it had produced its masterpiece.

Dickey enjoyed working in the Black Widows, just as he enjoyed his new status as a flight officer and its attendant privileges at the officers' club. He especially liked his new uniform, partly because of its effect on the local girls. In his romantic as well as his military pursuits, he was flourishing. He excelled in his three-month radar course. On October 5, he sent home the good news that he had been enthroned in the position of instructor. Teaching radar was hardly taxing. He worked two out of every four days, earned a substantial salary ($250 per month, as opposed to his $125-per-month salary in the Pacific), and found plenty of time for reading poetry and dating. Living quarters were posh by army standards. He had a private, air-conditioned room. Like many of the characters in his novels and poems, he kept fit and well tanned by swimming in the local pool. "The officer's pool is right across the street, full of pretty nurses,"[47] he told his mother after a date with a nurse named Nan Ross. An ID card issued on September 18, 1944, contained a photograph of Dickey with the sort of movie-star looks that made him irresistible to California women. Blond, blue-eyed, and over six feet tall, he looked debonair in his flight officer's uniform. Having overcome his aversion to training bases, Dickey made it known that he was content to sit out the war.

Recalling their time together at Hammer Field, Bradley said, "Jim was not too keen on going overseas. . . . Jim enjoyed Hammer Field. He was single and the California girls loved men in uniform, especially flying officers."[48] Dickey felt that his radar instruction fulfilled whatever obligations he had to his country's war effort. In contrast, his pilot agonized guiltily over the fact that some of his students, who were now retraining to be night fighters, had already experienced combat as day pilots overseas. One of Bradley's first disputes with Dickey erupted when he expressed his desire to fly in combat. Dickey scoffed at him. Only a fool would want to exchange California's dolce vita for the carnage of war. Dickey wrote his parents on October 5:

My pilot . . . has been to see the colonel three times already requesting overseas [duty]. He is scared to death of the Japs, but wants to say he's been to combat so his little son (aged 18 mo.) won't have to be ashamed when the other kids in school (all theoretical) ask him what their father did in the war. Funny, but things like that never bother me in the slightest. Finally I told Bradley (my pilot) if he wanted to go to combat that bad he could get him another R.O. and he was plenty burned up, but he didn't dare say anything derogggatory [sic] for fear I would rip him to shreds (literally) which I could do with no trouble whatsoever.[49]

In later life, it was Dickey and not Bradley who sought to impress his children and everyone else with tales of illustrious overseas combat.

Having recently read Hemingway's *A Farewell to Arms*, Dickey may have adopted the attitude of its main character, Frederic Henry, who wants to make "a separate peace" and abandon the war. Like Hemingway's disillusioned hedonist, Dickey was all for enjoying life as best he could on the fringes of a war-torn world. His array of California girlfriends also gave him sufficient reason to stay. A letter evaluating a list of novelists compiled by *Life* magazine (Hemingway, Willa Cather, John Dos Passos, Sinclair Lewis, Thomas Wolfe, Ellen Glasgow, Theodore Dreiser, John Steinbeck, Kenneth Roberts, William Faulkner, Marjorie Rawlings), which Dickey sent his parents in August, also showed why he wanted to remain in the United States. His schedule at Hammer Field gave him plenty of time for reading. Rather than plunge into combat, he told his parents he wanted to go back to college. He had narrowed his choices to Louisiana State University, the University of Virginia, Harvard, or Oxford. He was through with engineering and Clemson football; he wanted to be a literary scholar and a writer.

Years after the war, Dickey claimed that he went overseas because he wanted to be promoted to first lieutenant. In a typical inversion that made him appear more bellicose than he ever was, he explained, "The commanding officer . . . said, 'We're going to hold you all back as instructors.' Now I said, 'I don't want to instruct; I want to go and fight.' 'No, no,' he said, 'we want Bradley to instruct the pilots. But what we really want is you. You're the best man we've got. We want you to be instructor and we'll make you head R.O. here in a little while.' And I said, 'Well, I'll try it but I had my heart set; I want to go over there. I want to fight. I want to go do what I was trained to do—not instruct.' But I instructed . . . and I gave it my best shot."[50] In real life, Dickey did not strain against the military reins in order to fight; he strained against them in order to stay at Hammer Field.

Dickey dramatized the debate he had with his pilot and with himself in *Alnilam*, but switched roles so that Dickey-the-navigator took Bradley's hawkish position and Bradley-the-pilot took Dickey's pacifist position. The combat pilot named Faulstick, who follows Dickey's example by embellishing his war record, articulates some of his creator's misgivings: "What on earth am I doing, doing what I'm doing? I didn't have any great desire to be a pilot. . . . It was just something they told me I could do if I wanted to, because they had this program, and they said I was eligible." Faulstick's interlocutor, a navigator named Whitehall, favors active engagement out of a sense of responsibility: "After I finished navigation at San Luis Obispo, I stayed and instructed for one class. We had only three boys to wash out; I did my best to keep them, but they were better off somewhere else than in long-range aircraft. . . . When the others went, though, when they graduated and went on to combat, I knew that there was no way in the world I could stay in California and send other people out." Later Whitehall contradicts his earlier pro-war sentiments and speaks more for Dickey, the fun-loving navigator who wants to stay in California. He says pilots are dumb, like truck drivers and taxi drivers, for wanting to engage in combat: "Navigation is for the aristocrats, the smart people, the intellectuals of the wild blue yonder. If you'd'a had the sense, if you'd'a qualified, you'd be in navigation; right now you'd be maybe on the beach in California or Florida, flying . . . in nice warm AT-9s, instead of in this dump in the pine barrens, freezing your ass off in an open cockpit."[51] In fact, neither Dickey nor Bradley had any power over their destiny. Their commanders gave the orders to stay or fight.

The quarrel between Dickey and his pilot echoed the quarrel Dickey was having with his father. Dickey found his pilot's ideals reflected in his father's Southern values. A good ol' boy, after all, was supposed to serve God, country, and the fairer sex with chivalric devotion. He was supposed to be honorable, truthful, and faithful. He was supposed to be a good soldier. Eugene Dickey had implied as much in his correspondence; so on October 16, Dickey said he wanted to be free of all such shams. Having doubted traditional values since his early teenage years, he announced that he had been "a somewhat apathetic atheist"[52] for almost a decade. Since his father was also an atheist, rather than attacking his father Dickey may have been trying to get sympathy from him. In any case, Dickey's skirmish had all the flair of a young man's Oedipal rebuke. He remained devoted to his mother, who hoped her son would stay out of the war, though tension threatened that relationship as well since it was his mother who subscribed to the South's traditional social and religious principles more ardently than did his father. Realizing his rebellious remarks had disturbed her, on October 20 he wrote consolingly that his hedonistic and atheistic theories were only theories. He said he wanted to embrace Judeo-Christian morality, but his current environment militated against it. His roommate, Bob Davis, had died the previous night when his plane exploded on impact in the Sierra Mountains.

Such accidents proved that existence was precarious and precious, and God absent or inscrutable. Like the existentialists he would soon endorse, he felt that all life—and all women—should be passionately embraced rather than abjured by a worn-out ethical code.

If the words of God and father and his air corps commander left him cold, it was partly because his new allegiance was to poetry. Despite his later denials, at Hammer Field Dickey struggled to give shape to his tumultuous feelings and ideas in poems. He boasted to his mother that he had earned the grand sum of three dollars by publishing a poem in a small monthly magazine desperate for submissions. A woman he had met in California, Jane Kirksey, was trying to find a publisher for some of his other poems, which had been written, like so many of Robert Frost's poems, in the pastoral form. To give his mother an example of his budding talent, he included "Rain in Darkness" in one of his letters, and to ward off her critical misgivings he announced that "the unknowing godfather of this unworthy piece"[53] was Robert Bridges's "London Snow" (he also asked her to keep the poem away from his father, who would probably mock it). Bridges, the English poet laureate best known for publishing his friend Gerard Manley Hopkins, was an unlikely model for Dickey. His "London Snow," which describes the quiet beauty of a snowfall, was geographically remote from both Atlanta and Fresno. Perhaps because he was feeling increasingly alienated from his home city and the military, Dickey found the poem strangely moving.

While Dickey avidly read and imitated fin-de-siècle Victorians, he also absorbed the modernist free verse of poets like T. S. Eliot. He bought Eliot's *Four Quartets* in California, but unlike Eliot he continued to revel in archaic diction, conventional meter, and predictable rhyme. Over the following years Dickey learned valuable lessons from Eliot, but never entirely warmed to him. In a letter written to the critic John Simon in 1979, he vociferously stated his objections to the *Four Quartets*: "Like Auden, Eliot is a profoundly unreligious man, interested in the paradoxes and intellectual problematics of theology more than anything else; his pose of humbleness is frightfully false, as it is quite clear that what he called his religion is an emotion compounded of fear and the kind of snobbery that has always been his personal characteristic and stigma. The grave, owlish, pontificating tone is very ennervating to me."[54] Dickey's own fears and poses did little to bring him any closer to Eliot over the years.

Putting his ideological differences with his parents temporarily behind him, Dickey left Fresno in late November and traveled home for a two-week vacation. He basked in the conviviality of family and friends, regaling them with stories of his military adventures and listening intently to accounts of Tom's track victories. After he returned to the West Coast in early December, he felt homesick. Having signed a certificate on December 7 promising that he would "divulge to no one by word of mouth, by writing or by any other means, information concerning my probable or actual overseas destination,"[55] he promptly wrote his father that he was about to leave California and would probably end up in the Philippines. He prepared for his trip by getting inoculations against smallpox, tetanus, yellow fever, cholera, plague, and influenza. He wrote a last letter home on Christmas Day in which he asked his parents to send Wilfred Owen's *Collected Poems*, Siegfried Sassoon's *The Old Huntsman*, and

Roy Campbell's poems. These "war poets," whom he read carefully, confirmed his sense of the futility and horror of combat. Even though he assured his mother that he had the safest pilot in the air corps, he worried about what lay ahead in the Pacific. With mounting anticipation, he picked up his goggles, gloves, helmet, oxygen mask, shoes, suit, trousers, headset, microphone, flashlight, flyer's bag, and flying glasses, packed them in his duffel bag, and headed for the port.

7. The Brain of the Plane (1945)

Having gathered at Camp Stoneman with hordes of other soldiers waiting to embark, Dickey spent the last morning of 1944 lugging his equipment onto a troopship and getting settled in his new quarters. The USS *General A. E. Anderson*, a mammoth vessel over six hundred feet long built specifically for transporting about ten thousand soldiers, eased from Port Pittsburg in San Francisco Bay at one o'clock that afternoon, passed beneath the Golden Gate Bridge, and began its slow, zigzagging course toward the Pacific's war-ravaged islands. Throughout his life, Dickey would reimagine his momentous journey as a heroic one to an infernal "otherworld." The daily routine on the USS *Anderson*, however, was more monotonous than mythical. Stacked like cordwood in their hammocklike bunks, the men rose early for a six-thirty breakfast and gobbled it in fifteen minutes while standing. Their second and last meal came at three-thirty in the afternoon. Because of long lines, using the toilet and shower (only two showers were allowed each week) required planning and patience. To pass the time, the soldiers played cards, checkers, chess, and cribbage, and gambled. Others listened to the radio (many tuned to the Rose Bowl game on New Year's Day) or gossiped about women they'd left in the States.

Used to the sweet life of Fresno, Dickey was irked by the cramped quarters and constant inconveniences. Surrounded by an unrelenting horizon of water, he spent as much time as possible reading in his bunk. Even though soldiers swarmed over the ship, Dickey once told a journalist: "I was lonely . . . so I read a lot. Then I started writing poetry to relieve my own loneliness."[1] Confusion often broke the tedium. On New Year's Day, there was an "abandon ship drill" during which everyone milled around not knowing what to do. Dickey found some consolation in learning that the ship was less likely to be torpedoed since it was sailing alone rather than in a convoy. Accustomed to Army Air Corps routines, he was intrigued by the novel practices of the navy. At dusk the boatswain's mate blew a whistle and shouted: "Now hear this; now hear this. The smoking lamp is out on all weather decks." In the morning, the same man whistled and shouted: "Now hear this; now hear this. The smoking lamp is lit on all weather decks." This strange lingo soon lost its luster, as did the mate's commands: "Army deck cleaning detail, man your brooms! Clean and sweep down fore and aft!"[2] Dickey swept and scrubbed with his army cohorts, while the navy men chiseled rust from the ship in preparation for painting.

By January 5, the USS *Anderson* had passed Hawaii, and the men, including Dickey, loitered on deck to watch flying fish leap and glide up to one hundred yards. The fish propelled themselves out of the waves rolling away from the hull, flicked their tails in new waves, and propelled themselves once more over the water. Dickey was so fascinated by their aerodynamics that he started his unfinished novel *Crux* with such a scene. The narrator comments: "On a troop-ship there was nothing else to do except try to make sense out of whatever you could see; to watch it, and think about it. He believed, he could not help believing, that their fins must be something like feathers, though the membranes did not flutter, or do anything to keep them up. He wished he could see their faces, especially when they left the water, and when they were ready to fall. It would not be bad, either, to see them while they were in flight, two inches airborne, free, all in formation."[3] For the narrator the flying fish are premonitory of the flying airmen on the Pacific Islands. "I amused myself between [Thomas] Hardy and [Robinson] Jeffers and the flying fish,"[4] Dickey said about his transpacific trip. Since both Hardy and Jeffers envisaged the world as a Darwinian arena of predatory violence governed by instinct and fate, Dickey must have found in their poems confirmation of his gloomy thoughts on his way to war.

Dickey's boredom temporarily lifted at nine o'clock on Sunday morning, January 7, when the *Anderson* crossed the equator, and the men participated in a ceremony initiating them into "the Realm of King Neptune." There was further excitement on January 12 when the ship's gun crew sighted a large iron ball floating in the water. Believing it to be a mine, they tried to detonate it with a few rounds from their guns. Dickey took more interest in the sighting of land on January 13; the small island in the Solomons called Ulawa was the first sign of terra firma he had seen since leaving San Francisco. Soon afterward the ship passed Guadalcanal, the recent location of a ferocious battle. Then at seven o'clock on the morning of January 15, Dickey watched his ship slow to a standstill in the port of Finschhafen, New Guinea. Having survived two weeks of stifling heat and restless nights, all he wanted to do was head for shore.

Unfortunately, orders to disembark were not forthcoming. The men waited until 11:00 A.M. before hearing from an Australian officer, who approached the *Anderson* in a skiff, that they were supposed to disembark at Hollandia, a port city to the west. They completed their diversion by 5:30 P.M. the next day, anchoring among fifty other ships about one hundred yards from shore. Dickey must have thought he had sailed into a South Sea paradise. Mountains rose almost vertically from the blue-green harbor. Lush vines straggled up the cliffs toward giant mahogany trees. The gorgeous scenery tantalized him. Day after day he waited in sweltering quarters for orders to go ashore. As one of Dickey's fellow radar observers noted in his diary on January 17: "Another day has passed and we are still aboard this ship. They don't know if we belong here or not. Just like the army! We played cards and ate 'K' rations that we swiped from other soldiers."[5] Finally the *Anderson* pulled closer to the beach.

After nearly a week of claustrophobic tedium, on January 21 Dickey finally climbed down nets thrown over the side of the ship and boarded a personnel landing craft, which cruised about ten miles up an inlet before stopping on a beach at Sentani. Here trucks transported the men to a "transient camp" where they pitched tents, washed clothes, changed their dollars into Dutch guilders, and examined the airstrip, where wrecked Japanese planes, already ransacked by souvenir hunters, littered the ground. The tropical vegetation, the ocean, and Lake Sentani, which some of the men compared to Lake Tahoe, made their new home eminently liveable. One event, however, struck Dickey as ominous. A daredevil pilot—not unlike Donald Armstrong in Dickey's poem "The Performance"—had run out of fuel while trying to fly his P-61 over Mount Cyclops, crashed in the jungle, and faced court-martial after hobbling with a broken leg down the mountain.

At eleven o'clock on January 23, Dickey climbed into a plane bound for Finschhafen, where the quarters were as hospitable as those at Sentani. The days were slow, the monotony broken only by movies shown at night, mail from friends in the States, a weekly allowance of three beers, and small chores like washing clothes. Rain and wind blew through the tents, offering brief respite from the equatorial heat. Some of the men traveled to a beach of black sand and swam in the muddy water. Many just lay in their beds and whiled away the hours by reading or sleeping. Trained for a more active life, they grew irritable when orders for their next move failed to arrive. Dickey and his pilot visited the personnel tent every day to inquire about their destination. Bradley remembered:

> All we had to do was sit and wait for orders. The war had long since moved on except for a small contingent of Japs who had been by-passed and apparently were abandoned. They were trying to raise gardens and do whatever they could to keep alive. We let some of the pilots go up and strafe these poor souls every day just to give them something to do while we waited. There must have been one hundred thousand people there awaiting orders. We went down to the huge tent serving as the headquarters to beg to get out of that place. I'll never forget that it was so hot that no one wore shirts and when meal time came, we put on a shirt and left it unbuttoned with the shirt tail out. There was a captain standing at the opening to the tent telling everyone to put his shirt tail in. I wondered how bad that officer had goofed up to get an assignment like that.[6]

The sultry doldrums only intensified Dickey's desire to retire to his tent with a book. One of his new discoveries was the poet and novelist Frederic Prokosch. Gorgeous stylists like Prokosch cast a spell on the young soldier desperate to remove himself from his present environment.

Looking for something to do, some of the men started hammering their newly acquired Dutch guilders into rings. Dickey remembered this ring making in his poem "The Wedding," which he published in his first book, *Into the Stone and Other Poems.* In "The Wedding" the men make "moon-glowing, center-bored rings"[7] for wives in America they can only imagine. Finally, on Saturday, February 3, Dickey and his cohorts awoke at three in the morning to prepare for a flight by C-47 transport plane to Biak Island off the western tip of New Guinea. Here, by coincidence, Dickey met the commander of the 418th Night Fighter Squadron, Maj. Carroll Smith, who was on his way to Nadzab before returning to America. Smith was one of the preeminent night fighter pilots in the Pacific theater. Flying his Black Widow *Time's A-Wastin'*, he accomplished the unprecedented feat of shooting down four Japanese aircraft in one night.

Imitation being the sincerest form of flattery, Dickey probably had Smith in mind when he told his postwar audiences about his escapades as an ace night fighter pilot. Over drinks at the Biak officers' bar, the decorated commander talked to Dickey and the other replacements about the squadron they would soon join. On February 6, Dickey boasted to his parents that he was now a member of the "hottest" squadron in the world, a squadron that had racked up more victories than all the others in the Pacific combined.

Before he flew any missions, heroic or otherwise, Dickey flew north to Peleliu, a small island in the Palau chain that had been wrested from the Japanese by the navy and marines. As Dickey got closer to the front, his anticipation of danger quickened. It was on Peleliu's Bloody Nose Ridge that Americans had used some of the first flamethrowers to incinerate Japanese soldiers hiding in caves. The island base, with its white sand drifting like snow, its swaying palms, its flowers growing neatly around a walled-in flag, its efficient showers, and its mess hall stocked with fresh turkey and ice cream, could not have contrasted more sharply with the blackened caves. Peleliu gave Dickey yet another example of the conjunction of beauty and horror that he would dramatize in his later writing.

Dickey's island-hopping continued on February 5 when he and the other replacement crews flew three hours to Leyte in the Philippines, an island that Allied troops had been fighting for since October 1944. The main campaign had finished around Christmas, but mopping-up operations continued into February. On Leyte's Tacloban airstrip (the site of MacArthur's well-publicized return to the Philippines after his retreat to Australia), even the pilot Stanley Logan, who had been in good spirits so far, found conditions abysmal. Tired, hungry, thirsty, and eager to find a toilet, the men found themselves waiting once again. As they stood outside the orderly room tent, a siren erupted, and a lone Japanese plane dropped a bomb on the runway. They were almost too numb to care. Finally a truck took them to the transient area, where they ate and tried to sleep without netting among swarms of mosquitos. Dickey always remembered the airstrip on the beach with its carcasses of American planes scattered among submerged landing barges and ships. Of Tacloban, he said, "It was very traumatic. That was the first time I knew I was really in a war. Boy, it looked like a war. It looked like every set you ever saw for a war in the movies except much worse. There were all kinds of planes on the beach that had bellied in, and all that sort of thing. You could go look at them and there was blood all over the cockpit."[8] In his passage to war, Tacloban had all the revelatory force of a bloody rite of initiation, which is why he wrote one of his first themes at Vanderbilt on his experience there.

After their wretched night, Dickey and the others scrambled to find a plane to take them to the island of Mindoro, but only managed to get a ride to Luzon, the northernmost island in the Philippines. From there they flew south over Corregidor, which in two weeks would be the site of a number of suicidal battles by the Japanese. Looking through the plane's window, Dickey could see Manila burning to the east. For the next several weeks, as Japanese soldiers butchered, tortured, and raped tens of thousands of their Filipino civilian prisoners, the Allies bombed and bombarded and shot their way from building to building to rout the enemy from the capital of the Philippines. Dickey did not participate in the combat. He landed in the town of San Jose on Mindoro during the evening hours of February 6 and helped set up camp on a small hill by an old Catholic cemetery.

On February 7, Dickey took his first orientation flight, logging one hour and ten minutes of "combat time." According to Dickey, the flight set him apart from the others:

> When I had hardly stepped off the truck, they said, "We need an R.O. for a mission." I said, "I'll take it." And they handed me a simple map and said, "MacArthur's made another landing in southern Manila and we want cover there. Keep the airplanes south of them." I got to fly cover for the landing. And I said, "Bradley, let's go." And Bradley, for some reason, was taken up with doing something else. They said, "We need them bad; we gotta go now." One of the pilots in the outfit named Carl Tidrick said, "Are you qualified? I mean, are you ready to go?" And I said, "Let's go. Get in the truck." So we went up there. I navigated her by the radar and we hit the target. . . . We didn't run into any enemy action there, but we did the mission and came back at dawn. I remember we were flying kind of low and there was a Filipino guy driving caribou along the beach and I said, "Man, this is a new world. This is going to be something else." So we came back and Tidrick and I had breakfast and I was the only guy of the replacements that had flown a mission and everyone was crowding around wanting to know what I did, and how I was, and whether it was dangerous. Did you draw any fire? And so on and so on. It was very heady. I was automatically thrust in a sort of lead position among the replacements and I took over the best I could without being ostentatious about it and tried to set the tone for what we did.[9]

On this mission, Dickey claimed (wrongly) to have used a silk map for the first and only time, even though silk maps and silk identification notes were usually kept in escape kits. To memorialize his dubious mission, he made the map that Muldrow carries through Japan in *To the White Sea* a silk one.

Dickey's immediate ascent to the lead position among the replacements was mainly fantasy. He didn't assume the role of lead RO until July 1945, when Bradley became operations officer on Okinawa. Harold Whittern, a pilot Dickey wrote about in his Vanderbilt poem "Whittern and the Kite," recalled that Dickey's first mission was for the purpose of orientation, not combat cover. It was Whittern's job to send up the new crews. Perhaps disappointed that his initial flight over Mindoro was not more heroic, Dickey got his revenge on Whittern by depicting him as a sickly hanger-on in his poem. In reality, Whittern remained with the squadron until the spring to earn his captain bars. In the poem: "Whittern, malarial, his final mission bland / On the yellow sheets, squints from his beaked shade / Up past soft-writhing tents and limed clay flats" to watch a kite. Due to a recent bout with malaria, Whittern was pale, haggard, and thin when he met Dickey, but he wasn't lying in a tent watching kites (he had flown kites at Finschhafen). Dickey was the one who grew sick of the bland routine on Mindoro, and he later projected his malaise onto Whittern.

Whittern became such a powerful symbol of Dickey's own boredom in the Philippines that in the early 1950s he contemplated writing a play involving Whittern and another pilot, Gilbert Eissman. The fragments of the play that exist in Dickey's journal cast Whittern and Eissman as friends (Whittern actually despised his fellow pilot, whose flying was so shoddy that Carroll Smith once grounded him). Perhaps because Whittern had contracted dengue fever before his malaria, Dickey situates him in the hospital, but his thoughts belong to Dickey. Whittern asks, "Why doesn't fever make you have pretty dreams? All I can think about is the house where I used to live that burned down and my kid brother that died of meningitis." It was Dickey's brother Eugene who had died. In the play, Whittern is about to return to America and wears a "tropical uniform, full of medals, and a polished leather jacket with the insignia of the outfit on it."[10] In Whittern, Dickey found a vessel for his own discontent, nostalgia, and hope. Whittern had been promoted to captain shortly before returning to the States on June 7; Dickey wished he could go home, too, and with the same rank as Whittern. Part of the play takes place in a tent where someone (like the actual Whittern during orientation) explains to the replacement crews how the squadron operates. For the duration of his time overseas, Dickey shared a tent with fellow replacements George Kamajian and Stanley Logan. Bradley and other officers rotated in and out, making a foursome. According to Kamajian, "We were never really close friends. Each had different interests and developed close associates of our own."[11] Dickey remained aloof; as on the USS *Anderson* he spent most of his free time reading. "All I do is read Shakespeare and Louis Untermeyer's *Modern American Poetry / Modern British Anthology* and write letters and exercise,"[12] he told his mother on April 1, 1945. Since he flew at night, during the day he had plenty of time for literature.

Throughout the first half of February, Dickey and his pilot flew local patrols and convoy covers in a plane that Bradley had christened *Millie*, after his wife. When Bradley's marriage unraveled, he allowed Dickey to rename it *The Flaming Terrapin* after a Roy Campbell poem. Campbell's books—*The Flaming Terrapin*, *Adamastor*, *The Georgiad*—were some of Dickey's favorites at the time. The title poem of the first possessed the grandiloquence that Dickey admired in Campbell: "For when the winds have ceased their ghostly speech / And the long waves roll moaning from the beach, / The Flaming Terrapin that towed the Ark / Rears up his hump of thunder on the dark."[13] The flaming, thundering beast guiding precious cargo through danger to safety became an emblem for his missions. The title he chose for the plane may also have contained a humorous admission of rookie clumsiness. According to some of the night fighters, Bradley and Dickey didn't work well together. By his own admission, Bradley found Dickey to be a difficult partner. Tensions between them eased in the spring without entirely vanishing.

While not flying or working on their planes, Dickey's fellow aviators censored squadron mail or drove jeeps to the beach for swimming. Sometimes they socialized with nurses, and, as Dickey indicates in his poem "The Enclosure," fantasized about making love to them. Food was always a topic for heated discussion, mainly because of the lackluster menu. Breakfast might consist of powdered eggs, coffee, baked bread or buns; lunch of bully beef (Dickey sarcastically called it "Crème de Bully Beef" because the meat was tough as rubber), canned vegetables, powdered mashed potatoes; dinner of canned chicken or the ubiquitous Spam. Allotments of K-rations provided some variety with bacon, salmon (known as gold fish), cheese, jelly, candy, biscuits, and cigarettes. On occasion, the squadron cook treated them to fresh pork, chicken, hamburgers, or roast beef. Some of the men altered their diet by killing wild chickens that roamed around San Jose or by attending wild boar roasts organized by the locals. The squadron doctor also doled out two ounces of whiskey to each aviator after every mission. Dickey's love of whiskey no doubt originated here, although at the time, rather than rush to consumption, he and his pilot instructed the doctor to save their jiggers until they had accumulated a whole bottle. Sometimes Dickey traded his portion for food or souvenirs.

Dickey's attitude toward athletics and his athletic companions had changed drastically since high school and college. Earlier he had gone to great lengths to mask his love of literature; now he posed as an intellectual with aesthetic preoccupations that elevated him above the rest. He occasionally boxed and played in the popular volleyball and softball games, but for the most part he lay on his cot and read. When he talked to his squadron mates about literature, he did so in a way that offset his second-class status as a radar observer. Since pilots generally considered themselves a superior breed, Dickey needed a way to counter their pretensions with his own. Like the characters in his novels, he needed a distinguishing mystique. This he found in his rapidly growing knowledge of books. He cultivated a habit of memorizing his favorite passages, a habit that would stay with him until he died. His tent mates sometimes heard him reciting poems to himself. A letter home warning his family to stay away from the books he had left in Atlanta underscored his bibliophilia. Dickey's bookishness struck many in the squadron as odd, as did his conversation, which he peppered with highfalutin phrases culled from his reading. Many were hesitant to talk to him for fear of incomprehension or humiliation. Stigmatized as a pariah, he often became the butt of gossip and jokes. Why did this large man who boasted of an illustrious football career in high school and college spend so much time poring over poetry?

George Kamajian's appraisal of Dickey was typical. Harking back to flight training days, he said:

My earliest recollection of Jim Dickey was after teaming up with our pilots at Hammer Air Force Base. He impressed me as a typical Southerner, with the usual Yankee prejudices. Even then he was reciting poetry and trying to impress us with his physical prowess by relating his numerous sports achievements while in college. These were repeated and magnified during each encounter. He was a male "primper," always well groomed and "on the town," having more "dates" than others. After the War, he planned to go back to college, write books and cash in on a trunk of Southern paper money stored in his family's attic, because "the South will rise again," and all Confederate money would be valuable again.[14]

On Mindoro, his primping aroused contemptuous bemusement. After seven- or eight-hour stints in their planes, most of the night fighters went to sleep and woke at about 11 A.M., shaved, and quickly organized themselves for the day. Dickey, by contrast, hung his mirror on a palm tree or pole for an hour of shaving and preening. Every blemish had to be addressed; every blond hair had to be set right. In a camp where personal hygiene was usually treated with perfunctory efficiency, Dickey's grooming habits were considered narcissistic and bizarre. He regularly lifted self-made barbells in front of his mirror, flexing his biceps so he, as well as others in the squadron, could admire them (on March 27, he proudly wrote his father that his bicep had grown to nearly fifteen inches in circumference and his weight had stabilized at 187 pounds). In a September 1945 letter to his mother, he proposed a way to make his chest muscles even more noticeable to the men around him: "Mom, see if you can find out how much it will cost me to have all the hair taken off my chest, and who does it. That is one thing I'm really looking forward to. I'd willingly pay my whole 'fortune' for that. Of course you needn't tell them that. What's the use of having a good build if you look like an ape?"[15] According to his son Chris, his father shaved his chest most of his life to look like a professional bodybuilder.

Those in the squadron who did scrutinize Dickey realized that he didn't have the broad-shouldered, well-muscled physique of most top football players and speculated that he was lifting weights to make his stories more credible. In the novel he worked on after the war, The Entrance to the Honeycomb, his characters expressed his obsession with well-conditioned masculine bodies. Julian, whose narcissism borders on homophilia, admits: "Before the long mirror of my room, I lifted the barbell to my chest and paused. . . . After four years, I had what anyone would have to call a good build . . . ; the shoulders had filled out 'massively,' as the magazines I read had proclaimed they would; the latissimus muscles were full and winglike, and the pectorals, running now with clean sweat, were tempered and like those on a breast-plate of armor."[16] Dickey's best-known paean to well-muscled masculinity comes in Deliverance when Ed gazes at Lewis's naked body— which happens to be a mirror image of Dickey's—in the river.

Throughout his career Dickey wondered and worried about his love of the male body. In Deliverance he dramatized his debate with himself in the conflict between Ed's Platonic homophilia and the hillbilly's homosexual rapacity. Because Dickey cultivated the mystique of an avid womanizer, gay literary friends like Richard Howard found Dickey's interest in homosexuality and his friendliness toward gay men surprising and charming. Other friends found Dickey's attitude toward homosexuality divided and disturbing. He propositioned men (sometimes crudely and in jest), he claimed to have had sex with men (partly to shock), and he discussed homosexuality as if it might deliver him into a new region of risk and inspiration (he romanticized the breaking of all taboos in such a way). To dispel the suspicion that only effeminate homosexuals loved poetry—a suspicion not uncommon in the military during the 1940s— Dickey sheltered his sexual ambiguities behind the mask of a lady's man, and continued to flex his literary as well as his physical muscles to the men in his squadron.

Dickey glamorized his war experience by saying that he discovered his poetic talents by writing letters home to girlfriends. He also told his family and friends that he had married a young Australian woman on a trip to Sydney, Australia, just after the war ended. When he returned home a conquering hero bedecked with medals, he expected her to be at his side, a prize trophy won in a foreign land. Unfortunately, she died just before they planned to leave the Pacific. Bradley, for one, was skeptical:

> I never thought of Jim as a womanizer, although he was good looking enough to sweep them off their feet. I could talk about his reticence to en-gage in any involvement with the opposite sex when we made our first trip to Manila after it was taken. The Filipinos were ecstatic at our arrival, and women who had been abused for years by the Japanese almost threw them-selves at us. Little boys would tug at our pants legs saying "Pompom, GI, my mother, she's very good?" As far as I know he never took advantage of the availability even when a little girl whose husband had been killed came to his room while he was taking a nap. She almost crawled into bed with him—he got mad as hell.[17]

On this visit to Manila, which occurred in late May 1945, Bradley and a group of friends had told one of the young prostitutes sitting with them on the balcony of their small hotel that Dickey wanted to sleep with her. As Dickey remem-bered the incident: "There was a little tiny Filipino girl, a teen-aged girl I picked up, and I had no sexual desires at all. I just wanted company. Bradley and I took her to dinner and . . . I paid a hundred dollars for ice cream made out of caribou milk."[18] Dickey said nothing about his angry response to her forwardness and the laughter of the others as she scampered from his room.

In letters home Dickey often expressed his desire to fly to Sydney during the late spring of 1945 for a rest leave. In April, he told his brother with typical gusto: "I hope I will be able to go down to Sydney within a couple of months. They say the girls down there are really eager to fuck Americans."[19] Shortly af-terward, he admitted: "We can't go to Sydney any more, because it's too far."[20] His invented marriage claim grew from his need to re-create himself as a swash-buckling heterosexual war hero. Early poems like "The Enclosure," which de-scribes visits to brothels during the war, were intended to bolster Dickey's reputation as a lady's man. His actual comments about women to his squadron mates were usually scatalogical and derogatory rather than romantic. "To test whether you really love a woman," he once told Stanley Logan, "you have to imagine her on the pot taking a shit."[21] Most of the young soldiers found such comments offensive.

Dickey bewildered his squadron mates in other ways as well. If he demon-strated a fondness for the beautiful male body by manicuring his face and toning his biceps, he also spurned military rules as well as common etiquette by paying little attention to his uniform, which in the Philippines consisted of khaki shorts and a T-shirt. He liked to walk around camp barefoot (for this reason he was given the nickname Jake). He rarely washed his filthy clothes. His T-shirt and underwear were consistently gray or brown. Kamajian commented: "Although Dickey showered thoroughly every day, he always used the same dirty towel to dry himself and wore the same undershorts and undershirt without having them washed for weeks at a time. We had available laundries (self-wash) or [Filipino] house boys, [of] which he chose not to avail himself."[22] His clothes were what Yeats called an "antithetical mask"—a disguise for his clean, shapely body.

If refusing to wash his clothes was a tactic to ensure his isolation in the squadron, it often worked; the other men kept out of smelling distance. Periodically he conceded to normal standards of hygiene by soaping his underwear while he wore it in the shower. According to another night fighter, Darrell Campbell, on one occasion some of the volleyball players, who welcomed his talent but not his aroma, decided to clean him: "He wore the same T shirt to every game. It finally became rather odoriferous and offensive to the rest of us. One day several of his buddies grabbed him, took him to the shower room, scrubbed him down with G.I. soap and forced him to don a clean T-shirt."[23] Dickey suggested to Campbell that his dirty shirt brought him good luck in the volleyball games. Campbell and the other players still disapproved. So did his tent mates, who also complained of the disheveled heap of books, equipment, and soiled clothes around his bed.

Despite reservations about his eccentric habits, the men respected Dickey's intelligence. He could analyze personal problems with acuity. He also impressed them with his ability to locate regional accents. Once he approached a colonel after listening to him speak and asked him about life in Pennsylvania. The colonel was dumbfounded by his clairvoyance. Dickey's attentiveness to accent, dialect, and other aspects of voice benefited his later writing, especially when he created characters from different regions in America. In addition, it contributed to his endless impersonations of movie stars like Marlon Brando, comedians like Jonathan Winters, and politicians like Jimmy Carter. Despite his squabbles with his pilot, Dickey was also a clever navigator. His most impressive accomplishment, according to Bradley, was in planning and executing a bombing raid on a munitions plant in far-off China. Charles Lindbergh had come to the South Pacific to show fighter pilots how to extend their range by adjusting propeller speeds. On June 12, pilot William Sellers, who was now the 418th's commander, had flown an 840-mile round-trip to Aguiguican to test the maximum range of the P-61. To receive a China-Burma-Indian ribbon as well as extra points (aviators could return home after accumulating a certain number of points), Bradley and Dickey decided to attempt the long flight to Shanghai. Bradley remembered:

Jim and I flew over Shanghai one time. We were getting our daily briefing in preparation for the night's activity when some one lamented the fact that they couldn't seem to hit a munitions factory on the Yangtze River in Shanghai. Jim said that he thought he could work out the mathematics and that we could hit it at night with our radar. The next day we proposed it and we, he and I, made a stab at it. We had two one thousand pound bombs . . . and two 300 gallon belly tanks. I felt somewhat unimportant because Shanghai didn't even turn out their lights as we approached. It looked like a major U.S. city at night. We went up the Yangtze River a few miles with no fire on us and we turned around and dropped both bombs . . . at the same time. We were only 5000 feet and the explosion almost upset the plane. We had instantaneous fuses, but then they started shooting from an island in the river. It looked like fireflies. I told Jim to look down and I told him that they were shooting at us. He said: "Let's get the Hell out of here," which we did. We did not hit the target. We should have been more successful if we had used our usual method of strafing and bombing at low level but intelligence told us that there were barrage balloons there.[24]

Luckily, the antiaircraft guns missed, and the shock waves from the bombs (the mission report mentioned only one one-thousand-pound bomb) were weak enough for the plane to stabilize. This close call, which occurred on August 5, was undoubtedly one source for Dickey's many (false) stories about crashing into the South China Sea and being rescued by a submarine. With the help of Lindbergh's advice and Dickey's navigational savvy, Bradley flew the plane safely back to Mindoro. On future missions as well, they never crashed and never received any serious hits from enemy guns.

Dickey began reinventing his war experience almost as soon as he arrived in the Philippines. In February, he told his parents that he and his pilot were flying four hours every night. To emphasize the ghastliness of his surroundings, he told them that a kamikaze bomber had crashed into an ammunition boat near their base and that the squadron had found another kamikaze pilot shackled to the rudder controls of a downed plane. He said kamikazes were ramming American B-29s over Japan. Much of this, according to others in the squadron, was exaggerated or simply false. Crews flew about four hours every *other* night, and often less. There had been a kamikaze attack on the boat carrying the 418th's water echelon to Mindoro, but that had happened around Christmas in 1944, before Dickey arrived. Dickey's stories home, like the ones he told his squadron mates, were designed to impress. To make his parents even prouder, he told them he planned to get the Air Medal, the Distinguished Flying Cross, and several other medals.

What Dickey's letters usually kept secret was his reluctance to fly into combat. His fear was certainly in evidence on February 16 when the crews learned that they would cover Manila during one of the battles to retake the city. Their job was to draw Japanese antiaircraft fire and thereby expose enemy positions to American attack. Dickey judged the mission to be suicidal; he didn't want to participate. Before one of these frightening missions Dickey tried to translate his sense of doom into poetry. In a bizarre fragment, "Prelude to Combat," he recorded a vision not unlike the one that gave him the idea for *Alnilam*. Staring at the propellers and wings of his plane, he sees nothing but images of death: "Through the whirled, light-rinsing blades / Shift the shades of rotting men. / Upon the tapered way, the curve-ended shell / Which lifts us and our sharp-voiced pebbles of destruction / Dance young carrion spectres of Teuton dead."[25]

In this danse macabre, friend and foe join hands. The Germanic Dickey was no doubt imagining himself among the "Teuton dead."

By contrast, the other crews in the 418th were enthusiastic or took these missions in stride. Logan remembered: "Most of us were eager for the potential action. George [Kamajian] and I flew night artillery spotting [missions] near Taytay, east of Manila, during the battle of Manila and worked directly with army artillery by radio to pinpoint Jap artillery locations and the impact locations of U.S. return fire. We flew at about 6,000' altitude and were warned to back off occasionally when firing of U.S. 155 mm guns with a trajectory of 15,000' was about to commence. We spotted the first identified launching of Jap rocket missiles in the area."[26] With time Dickey's trepidation lessened, and flights over liberated Manila became routine. Herbert Vaughn recorded in his journal on February 18: "Our day began very early today. Twelve fifteen A.M. to be exact. We flew cover over Manila for an hour and a half. The entire flight lasted three hours [and] a half. We could see scattered artillery fire. We could see different fires in the southern part of Manila. Also could see Jap motor convoys moving along the road. Every time we would go over they would stop and turn out their lights. We weren't allowed to fire on anything."[27] Dickey's high-altitude views of Manila were the same.

In a March 2 letter to his brother, Dickey tried to describe the sort of gloomy wasteland that surrounded him. Manila was "a wreck."[28] San Jose on Mindoro was not much better. The Philippines seemed even more infernal after two popular arrivals—a pilot, John Agan, and his radar observer, Hubert Hutchinson—were killed when a plane hit a fuel truck on the runway. In between missions, which in March consisted of thirty-nine hours of convoy cover and patrols, Dickey often grew bored in the muggy heat of the camp. Some of the men amused themselves by dynamiting fish so they would have something fresh to eat. Or they walked into the hills to visit local Filipinos, who offered them the foul-tasting *tuba*—a kind of whiskey made from palm leaves—in their palm leaf huts. A whole day might be spent searching for a lightbulb. To relieve the tedium and terror of war, Dickey visited a sandy beach to swim, tinkered with differential equations in one of his calculus books (a practice he quickly abandoned), crafted a ring for his brother from a silver dollar, and wrote his father about buying a cock he named Max, which supposedly won five fights before being killed in the ring.

Dickey had plenty of time to listen to records, which played on the loudspeakers, and watch sports newsreels and films, which appeared almost every night. He especially remembered *Meet Me in St. Louis* with Judy Garland, and *The Picture of Dorian Gray* with George Sanders and Hurd Hatfield. Oscar Wilde, the original author of *The Picture of Dorian Gray*, would be a lifelong favorite, not least because of his endorsement of lying. The squadron screened *Rhapsody in Blue* repeatedly, as well as *The Princess and the Pirate, Saratoga Trunk, The Doughgirls, Kismet, National Barn Dance, Girl Crazy, Falcon and the Co-eds, The Heavenly Body, The Falcon Goes to Hollywood,* and *The Adventures of Mark Twain.* Occasionally the newsreels, which tended to glamorize the war, elicited outrage from Dickey. In a stilted poem he wrote at the time, "To the Newsreels, Radios and Magazines," he argued for a more truthful rendering of combat:

By what foul means entice you from
This boy with riven leg such smile
And hearty upward movement of the thumb?
Whom do you wish to beguile?

Think you that we be fools?
Can you intend that this butchered lad
May stem the flood of rancor that fills
His guts? Or think aught of humanity but bad?

. . . .
Who do you think you deceive?[29]

In his own deceptive war reporting, Dickey vowed to play up rather than gloss over the horrors of combat.

During the spring of 1945, Dickey was hard at work composing poems and reading Louis Untermeyer's poetry anthology and Shakespeare's sonnets. He paid particular attention to Untermeyer's selection of Ernest Dowson's delicate, antiquated lyrics, and tried to imitate them in his own poems. He liked Dowson so much that on May 29 he asked his mother to find his Dowson collection at home, copy out several poems, and send them to him (she complied). He also asked her to send a biography of Dowson by Mark Longaker, and grew furious when she suggested that she might return the book to the store after buying it. To show Dowson's beneficial effects on his style, he sent her one of his imitations:

I having found in you more than dreams
more sunlight than pride or wine
huddles in the heart, now sanction,
before diaphonous memories bequeath us
to nothingness effete—

the sun winking
the slow radiance
fading
dissolving the lean shadows—
all glorious things
in utter loveliness stand
held in an instant fleeting to darkness

It was Dowson's sentimental melancholia and his gift for phrasemaking that made him attractive. "It's funny," Dickey remarked after the war, "that a minor 1890s versifier could have been such a phrase-maker such as everybody and his brother could have picked up on. 'Gone with the wind' comes from Ernest Dowson. 'Wine and woman and song' and 'days of wine and roses' come from him. 'Faithful . . . in my fashion' comes from him."[30] During the war, nostalgia for wine, women, and song gripped Dickey's emerging poetic sensibility.

Few would have expected Dickey to feel kinship with the sickly, hashish-smoking aesthete who had read Latin poetry at Oxford, dissipated the rest of his short life in seedy taverns near the London docks and Paris markets, and written a few quaint poems about girls he dared not touch. Dickey seemed surprised by his Dowson infatuation, and in his sonnet "Dedication, To Ernest Dowson," which began a pamphlet of poems he wrote in the Philippines, he tried to analyze the other poet's spell on him:

No mighty invocation, this, O weary singer
Who had no thundrous [sic] tongue to hurl
Defiance at Time, only one song to linger
After you, treader backward from the world
Toward oblivion, what then, have you left us
We who lift our lyres to Milton's praise
In smoky halls, why in lowered tones discuss
One who only sang of listless days,
Of weakened waters, of virginal devotion
And unrequited love; a young French girl.—
Why this, O weary, why this forward seeking motion
And the quiet-frenzied nostalgia in one loose curl?
This, Ernest, in thy song shares memory
Who ever lost his love, who lost her not like thee?[31]

Admitting differences with the Victorian versifier, Dickey also admits he shares Dowson's idealization of purity, which leads, paradoxically, to decadence. He may have been thinking of his asexual love for Gwen Leege, and how his yearning for her overshadowed his desire for other, more sexually inclined women. The poem also evinces a nostalgia for the archaic diction of poets like Milton. Dickey's later scorn of Milton as one of the great "stuffed goats" of English departments derived from a need to dispel Milton's early influence.

Dickey's *Poetical Remains*, as he humbly called his pamphlet, was little more than juvenilia. Awash with sentimental pining and sententious philosophizing, the poems are interesting mainly for the light they throw on Dickey's emotional state during the war: his homesickness, his sorrow over lost loves, his disillusionment with the military, his morbid cynicism about life, and his interest in "easeful Death" and other forms of oblivion. A poem titled "Dirge" typifies his angry brooding:

So much have I been lined, tagged, asked questions to
Preceded by one, followed by another, that I am past
Sickness or indignation, and apathetically acquiesce.
                    In much
The same manner shall I die, shoved unquestioningly into line
Awaiting my turn.
                    Through dull eyes, I have seen, however
That life is no better or worse than war; the only difference being

That life makes no pretense of heroics over death, is not methodical
And takes longer.

To the jaded poet, life, war, and death all seem to partake of the same mechanical futility. Before long, Dickey renounced Dowson's hackneyed diction and aimed for a vivid, visceral way of addressing the war.

To gain practice in a more down-to-earth style of writing, in March 1945 Dickey volunteered to replace Philip Porter as the squadron historian. Until late May, Dickey kept track of the 418th's activities and also typed orders for various citations and awards bestowed by Gen. George Kenney, who commanded the Far East Air Forces. As might be expected, Dickey's prose in the squadron history has an elegance and gothic tinge absent in chapters by his predecessors, although there is little remarkable about his accounts of combat missions and camp life until March 16, when a calamity occurred that resonated in Dickey's imagination for the rest of his life. He wrote: "A most unexpected and tragic occurrence befell the Squadron when 2nd Lt. DONALD H. ARMSTRONG . . . and his [radar] observer F/O JAMES J. LALLY . . . high-speed-stalled close to the ground over the Jap strip at Saint Jose [sic], Panay, and crashed northwest of the field." Dickey tells of second lieutenant Spencer Porter witnessing the crash and directing their commanding officer, Sellers, to the position of the wrecked plane: "[The plane] was found to be almost completely demolished except for a small portion of the crew nacelle. The entire Squadron awaited apprehensively the guerilla radio operating near San Jose, for the plane had gone down between Japanese and Filipino-held positions. Finally the guerillas informed us that Armstrong had been killed and Lally, badly injured, was in the hands of the enemy. There has been no further news to date."[32] The accident happened on a daylight flight back to Mindoro after the squadron had flown night cover for a convoy making its way to Panay, an island about one hundred miles southeast of their base. Relieved by day fighters, Armstrong decided to buzz the runway on Panay. One of the only eyewitness reports of the accident came from Herbert Vaughn, Porter's radar operator, who had been flying alongside Armstrong on his way back to Mindoro. In his diary he recorded how both crews had flown over Panay to look at some bombed Japanese airplanes: "Both planes went down to buzz and get a better look. Lt. Armstrong and F/O Lally made a sharp turn and crashed into a bunch of coconut trees. We circled and saw that the plane didn't burn. We could see that it was torn all to pieces and could see no sign of life. I don't know if they landed in Jap or Guerilla territory as they are fighting around there."[33] As it turned out, they had landed in Japanese territory.

Although Dickey remained aloof from many of the other night fighters, he identified with Armstrong's offbeat ways and usually insisted that Armstrong was his best friend in the squadron. "He was an enthusiast,"[34] Dickey said, like Lewis Medlock. He was particularly saddened by Armstrong's death because only a few nights before, Armstrong had invited him to watch the film Laura. To Dickey, the gesture proved that Armstrong cared for him. Others in the squadron remembered Armstrong as a kind of free-spirited "nut" whose marital turmoil in the States contributed to his erratic behavior. If he planned to strafe the Panay airstrip, he did so without orders, since that job was usually delegated to day fighters. In any case, the strip was insignificant; only a small enemy force inhabited the area. Harold Whittern, who was still with the 418th at the time, had a different explanation for Armstrong's decision to land on Panay. Armstrong, he said, had an attack of diarrhea in the air, tried unsuccessfully to relieve himself out the plane's window, and then decided to land: "He called control tower giving his reasons for landing. He was totally unaware that it was held by Japanese."[35] He didn't live long enough to find out whether the strip was safe.

After the war Dickey repeatedly transformed his original report of Armstrong's and Lally's plane crash, all the while pretending that he was repeating the facts. In 1984, he told an interviewer that Armstrong was "making a raid on the islands south of us called Panay. . . . He misjudged the distance. He hit the ground and tore up the airplane. He and an observer were taken out and kept prisoner for a night and beheaded the next morning. The Filipino guerilla forces on the island radioed almost a blow-by-blow description of the whole proceedings. We knew almost exactly what happened."[36] On September 19, 1945, six months after the actual crash, Spencer Porter and Herbert Vaughn returned to Panay on a fact-finding mission. The Army Air Corps wanted to declare the two men officially dead. At first failing to uncover any new information, in the town of Iloilo Vaughn and Porter finally located American intelligence reports based on interrogations of the captured Japanese who had participated in or witnessed the executions. Vaughn said that the reports "described how they [the Japanese] found the crashed airplane with the pilot dead. Lally was hurt but alive. They took him to their camp but would only doctor his wounds when told to do so by an officer."[37] The Japanese then beheaded Lally.

According to Darrel Campbell, who was also privy to the reports, the Japanese suspected Lally of being a member of a secret intelligence outfit: "When the Japanese became aware that the Americans were invading Panay, they decided to execute however many prisoners they were holding. According to their records, they dug a long trench, bound all of the prisoners, blindfolded them, forced them to kneel on the edge of the trench, & then beheaded them one by one with a Samurai sword."[38] George Kamajian recalled grislier details of Lally's and Armstrong's fate: "Their remains" had been "buried to their shoulders" and their "heads had been used for bayonet practice."[39] Besides Armstrong and Lally, the 418th lost no crews to crashes or executions during Dickey's tenure with the squadron. Because of its uniqueness, the incident came to symbolize for Dickey all the horrors of war. Crashed planes and severed heads recurred with ghastly frequency in much of his subsequent writing.

Dickey began mythologizing Armstrong and their friendship as early as June 1946, when he wrote about the dead pilot for an introductory Composition and Literature class at Vanderbilt. In his short essay "Tacloban," which describes his February 5 stopover on Leyte during his trip to Mindoro, the two men take a wistful, taciturn stroll through the debris on the beach:

> After awhile Armstrong lit a cigarette. The smoke curved up and back into the plane. He sat on an old barracks bag, his feet propped on the door, mo-

tionless, elbows on his knees, his long, thin hand holding a cigarette. I had seen him like that . . . many times all the way through flying school and at bars in the States trying to pick up girls and be gay with them after his wife had left him, but this time there was a difference. He looked out toward the ships, and I watched him, thinking that he was the best friend I had, and while we were sitting there it started to rain, softly at first and then more fiercely until we could not see the ocean any longer. But we sat quietly and did not speak.[40]

The dark, rain-soaked, wreckage-strewn landscape in which weary comrades commune without speaking owes much of its atmosphere and style to Hemingway's A Farewell to Arms. And like Hemingway, Dickey re-creates the facts. The stopover on Leyte had been hot, humid, and mosquito ridden. Hot sun and short tempers, however, did not fit the sort of lugubrious mood Dickey wanted to create. While the two men may have walked on the darkening beach after dropping off their equipment in the transient camp, other details in Dickey's account are inventions. They had not been together "all the way through flying school"; they had met at Hammer Field, where Armstrong was flying planes and Dickey was teaching radar. In addition, fellow aviators at Hammer Field said it was Armstrong who moved out on his wife and not vice versa. What is significant about the early vignette is not its truthfulness, but its revelation of Armstrong's melancholy (he seems disillusioned with both love and war) and Dickey's sentimental adoration of him. The affection seems largely one-sided. Armstrong simply gazes at the ships while Dickey gazes at him.

Another of Dickey's early literary treatments of the incident was his unpublished short story from the 1950s, "The Eye of the Fire," in which Armstrong and Lally appear as Beaumont and Laster. Here Dickey abides by the facts: the pilot is killed in the plane crash and his radar observer is beheaded after being captured. Later the story turns into a revenge fantasy not unlike the beginning of To the White Sea. Dickey's persona, Nettles, drops two napalm bombs on the school building where he suspects Laster was interrogated and tortured. The most famous account of Armstrong and Lally came in Dickey's poem "The Performance," published in 1959. But in this retelling, Armstrong rather than Lally is beheaded, and Dickey celebrates Armstrong as a Christ-like hero. In his introduction to the poem in Self-Interviews, Dickey adds to Armstrong's mystique by claiming that he was the sort of night fighter who switched on his automatic pilot and slept while returning from missions. Other pilots in the squadron dismissed this claim as "hog-wash" and also dismissed Dickey's claim that "almost every word of 'The Performance' is literally true."[41] They never saw Armstrong practicing "The back somersault" or "the stand on his hands,"[42] which the poem recalls, and rarely saw Dickey and Armstrong together. (Dickey was the one who did the handstands; on one occasion he hurt his right foot doing them.) Reiterating a common perception in the 418th, Vaughn said: "Dickey was a loner + to my knowledge did not have any close friends."[43] Only in his imagination was Armstrong his "best friend in the squadron."[44]

Why was Armstrong so important to Dickey? And why did Dickey turn the pilot into a mythical hero executed by sadistic enemies when in fact his own recklessness caused his death? Dickey idolized Armstrong because Armstrong was a risk-taking, fun-loving man who had succeeded where Dickey had failed; he had become a pilot. In Dickey's imagination, he resembled one of Hemingway's risk-taking, pleasure-seeking heroes who died tragically. As Dickey knew from his days at Hammer Field, Armstrong was prone to romantic tumult: He had vicious fights with his wife, moved out of their apartment, drank a lot, and started picking up women at local bars. Armstrong provided Dickey with a mirror in which he could see himself in larger-than-life proportions. He provided Dickey with a model for his stories about himself as a cavalier night fighter pilot. He also provided a model for Dickey's fictional enthusiasts—from Medlock to Joel Cahill to Muldrow—whose hubris precipitates catastrophes.

Much of "The Performance," in fact, draws attention to the way Dickey revises Armstrong's life by reenvisioning it. In the first scene, the narrator turns from the actualities around him and stares into the blinding sun so that he can envision the pilot as he wants:

> The last time I saw Donald Armstrong
> He was staggering oddly off into the sun,
> Going down, of the Philippine Islands.
> I let the shovel fall, and put that hand
> Above my eyes, and moved some way to one side
> That his body might pass through the sun. . . . [45]

By the end of the poem Dickey has transformed the historical Armstrong into an archetypal being who dies, reduces his executioners to penitential tears, and rises again "in kingly, round-shouldered attendance." The poem typifies the "mythical method" that made Dickey's early work so powerful. With incantatory rhythms and apocalyptic conceits he absorbed from Dylan Thomas, Dickey creates a moving elegy that admits to its ahistorical methods. Meddling with historical facts, however, had its risks (at Kenyon College in January 1981, Dickey even maintained that he had witnessed the beheading of Armstrong). When Stanley Logan heard Dickey read "The Performance" near his home in New Mexico, he was appalled by the way he had treated the incident because he identified so closely with Armstrong and Lally. Logan, who had followed the military investigation of his dead squadron mates, recalled that the war crimes trial of Lally's executioners was the first of its kind. Logan wanted Dickey to write more about the criminal treatment of Lally and less about his visionary apotheosis. For his part, Dickey was aware of his dubious enterprise. With his shovel in hand at the beginning of the poem, he intimates that his methods are culpable, that he—like the Japanese executioners—has violated Armstrong by burying him in his grandiose style.

If Logan had heard the other poem that Dickey wrote about Armstrong and Lally, "Between Two Prisoners," he would have been doubly incensed because here Dickey equates the Japanese executioners with the prisoners and bestows on both parties a mantle of saintliness. As in "The Performance," he abandons any attempt at historical accuracy, and projects his own poetic preoccupations onto the doomed night fighters so that they become indistinguishable from himself. His principal goal is to explain how his own poetic imagination grew during his prisonlike experience in the Philippines, and he uses Armstrong and Lally as convenient vehicles. Contrary to what the poem claims, the two men were not imprisoned in a schoolhouse, they never saw poetic visions of angels inscribed on the blackboard, and they never communicated "in a foreign tongue, / All things which cannot be said" (Eliot's flame-tongued saints do that in the *Four Quartets*). Dickey creates a semblance of historical truth in statements like: "I watched the small guard be hanged / A year later, to the day, / In a closed horse stall in Manila."[46] His "watching," however, is imaginary rather than actual. A year after Armstrong's and Lally's deaths, the war was over, and Dickey was in America preparing to go to Vanderbilt.

The deaths of Dickey's fellow aviators may have set off a new round of anxieties about his own mortality. Adjutant General Golembieski sent a disturbing message to the squadron from the War Department in Washington on April 6: "Request Flt Off [Flight Officer] Dickey be given a new final type physical exam with particular attn to chest. . . . Exam will include report of stereoscopic Xrays of chest, report of exam by chest consultant and report of comparison of all available chest Xray films preferably over period of more than six months."[47] Since his mother had heart trouble, Dickey may have worried that he was similarly afflicted. According to Darrell Campbell: "Jim was always worried that some sort of medical dilemma might befall him."[48] With his tent mates he repeatedly talked about his brother's death, as if fearing he might contract a similarly fatal disease. In the spring of 1945, he was relieved when his X rays turned up nothing unusual in his chest.

With death always hovering near, the proper attitude toward life became a topic of strident debate between Dickey and his pilot. As Dickey watched Bradley lose weight from worrying about his broken marriage, Dickey once again declared his opposition to the institution. He also aired his opinions in letters to his mother: "I don't think I will ever get married. I have developed a genuine horror of it that I frankly believe I will never overcome. Love is one thing, but habit and seeing your loved one deteriorate and fade with the passing years and not be able to do anything about it, to raise a family of squealing troublesome children, which I am certain I shall care absolutely nothing about, and fall into the ruinous decay of married life, is another. To court public opinion and conventionality are [sic] not enough temptation to lead me to such a life." Dickey told his mother he planned to pursue "the joys of single bliss forever!!!!!"[49] On the same day he wrote his mother he sent a letter to his brother about making love to a Red Cross worker in New Guinea the previous week. Dickey kept up what he called his "monthly tirade against the joys of wedded bliss"[50] throughout the spring. On April 2, he concluded that marriage was suitable only for drudges: "All the married mediocrities drone 'You'll see, there's nothing like it.' To which I can only reply (silently) 'You poor damned fools!!' "[51] Men who married sought shelter from life's rich possibilities, he fumed, and were "moral cowards." "If I ever form any lasting attachment for a woman," he added, "it must be someone who would not only live with me openly sans ceremony, but insist upon

it. . . . At any rate, I'll not wed any female mountebank who trades in her carefully hoarded virtue for a lifetime of security: a sorry bargain, at best."[52] Four days
later his mood changed. Now he confided: "I find myself debating the merits of
this girl or that girl, and am finally and always driven back to the only yardstick
I ever had, my own mother."[53] He considered Jane Davis a possibility, but he
leaned more toward the honey-haired Peg Roney. He admired her athleticism
(she played tennis and rode horses), her artistic interests (in 1941, she acted in
plays), her wit, and her beauty. Roney had been elusive, so Dickey repeatedly
asked his mother to call her and urge her to write him. Despite these requests,
Dickey concluded in his letter to his mother: "I do not think I could ever love
any girl more than I love you."[54] His maternal yardstick would determine that all
marriage candidates came up short.

At the end of March, Dickey and the other night fighters started flying pro-
tective cover for a big task force that was about to bombard and invade Legaspi
on the northern island of Luzon. In April, combat flying was minimal, as it was
in May and June. During lulls between missions in early spring, the men organized a trap-building competition to purge their camp of vermin once and for all.
A six-foot iguana had slithered over Dickey while he napped on his cot (George
Kamajian eventually killed it), but rats were the principal menace. When not
designing rat traps, Dickey nursed his literary ambitions by writing imitations of
Shelley and Shakespeare, participated in simulated combat—what they called
"war games"—each Friday, prepared for the rainy season by building a wooden
floor to his tent, and helped construct what he called in the squadron history "a
grade 'A' boozing place"[55] for the officers. The local brew—sixty-five-proof
Manila whiskey—was the drink of choice, although other brands were available.
Dickey, surprisingly, showed little inclination to drink. In a letter he sent his
mother about the party to open the officers' club, he said: "Almost everyone in
the squadron but me drinks like mad. I just can't see it, though. Anyone ruined
by liquor must really be a weakling."[56] Although his drinking habits changed after the war, his condemnation of drinkers "ruined by liquor" remained constant.

In late April, Dickey received the good news that he might be made second
lieutenant (he had failed to make the rank the first time). A memo sent to the
commanding general of the eighty-fifth Fighter Wing on May 5 was full of praise
for his integrity and professional ability. According to the memo, Dickey had
amassed a total of twenty-six combat missions and fifty-nine hours and forty-five
minutes of combat time in the Pacific. A form revealed that he had received no
wounds. Heartened by his imminent appointment, Dickey was ecstatic when he
heard on May 8 that the Allies had declared victory in Europe. Nevertheless,
the Pacific war persisted. Dickey wrote his brother on May 19 that his squadron
was now bombing Formosa. Captain Sellers had made the long trip, and so had
Dickey and Bradley. These exhausting missions only increased Dickey's fears of
getting shot down and captured. Having heard that a downed pilot from another
squadron had been captured and burned alive, on May 23 he assured his brother:
"Everything you hear about the Nips is true. They are really brutal. I wish we
could kill them all."[57] His attitude changed little after the war, and in *To the
White Sea* he unleashed a character on the Japanese who also wanted to "kill

them all." His fears of getting wounded materialized on May 27, but under friendly circumstances. While most of the officers enjoyed a rowdy beer fest in the club, Dickey and several others returning from Manila in a C-47 careened off the Mindoro runway at ninety miles per hour and ended in a ditch. He wrote his father on May 28 that he had "pretty well smashed" his left hand, while others had been "cut up pretty bad."[58] Although Herbert Vaughn contradicted this account in his diary (he wrote: "No one was hurt but the plane was ruined"),[59] Dickey did suffer a minor cut. In his poem "The War Wound," which he included in *Buckdancer's Choice*, he referred to his small, moonlike scar with embarrassment: "I lie with it well under cover, / The war of the millions."[60] He "lied" about it in other ways as well. In his autobiographical *Self-Interviews* he boasted: "I was given the Purple Heart for it because it was suffered in action. . . . I was sitting in the co-pilot's seat and when I reached up to protect myself, my hand was cut on the instrument panel."[61] None of his military records acknowledge his Purple Heart or his service as a copilot.

Dickey's attitude toward the war vacillated as unpredictably as his attitude toward marriage. Sometimes he cowered, retreating to his cot to find escape in books. At other times he seemed to enjoy the war, partly because he believed his feats in the air surpassed those of his brother on the track. He wrote his mother in June: "It sure seems funny for Tom to be worried about how far he throws his left arm down the track and running the 100 one tenth of a second faster when I have seen airplanes going 500 m.p.h. crash into each other and guys all shot to hell, and guts hanging out and dead Japs lying rotten in the sun."[62] Dickey had more reason to believe he was outdistancing his brother when, on June 5, his promotion to second lieutenant was officially approved. He also learned, on June 9, that the squadron would soon prepare for departure to another island. To make sure he had enough to read at his new base, he asked his mother to buy and mail four dozen books ranging from philosophy, psychology, music, mythology, poetry, and biography to boxing. When he became a famous writer, his detractors liked to lampoon him as a philistine. Early as well as late in his career, nothing could have been further from the truth. The letter he wrote his mother on June 30 looked like an acquisitions order from a librarian. He asked for Freud's *General Introduction to Psychoanalysis*, Durant's *The Story of Philosophy*, Goepp's *Great Works of Music*, Bullfinch's *Mythology*, O'Neill's *The Complete Greek Drama*, Guerney's *A Treasury of Russian Literature*, Ross's *Fundamentals of Boxing*, and Darwin's *Origin of Species* and *Descent of Man*. He asked for poetry books by Auden, C. Day Lewis, Trumbull Stickney, Kenneth Patchen, Richard Aldington, Dylan Thomas, Robert Penn Warren, R.P. Blackmur, Stephen Spender, Randall Jarrell. Soon he told his mother to send Faulkner's *The Marble Faun*, *As I Lay Dying*, *Idyll in the Desert*, *The Sound and the Fury*, and *Salmagundi*. Earlier in the spring he had confessed to his mother that he had "no other interest (as a profession) than writing" and that "if there were more money in poetry" he would "quite naturally"[63] turn to it. His appetite for books was insatiable as he lay the groundwork for his writing career.

As missions grew longer and more stressful, Dickey's animosity intensified toward the war, toward civilians at home commenting on the war, and toward life in general. He despised the jingoism of propaganda films and those on the sidelines paying lip service to the patriotic deeds of the soldiers. They were "not fit to shake the hand of any of the men on Iwo, Leyte, or any of the rest of the Pacific deathtraps," he said. As for those Americans who wanted to keep fighting the Japanese even after their surrender was all but a certainty, Dickey said his comrades in the Pacific hated them more than the Japanese. At times, however, he sounded like the sort of "Hollywood patriot" he ridiculed. "Do not think I am working myself into a paroxysm of patriotic fervor and losing myself in a lather of words," he told his father on June 5; then, reversing himself, he proclaimed: "America is the hope of the world. There has never been anything like us and never will again. And when we fight for America, there is something bigger than a country, bigger than men banded together against each other. And that is the freedom of the individual. Men have struggled toward it for many thousands of years. . . . This war is a thing surpassing the Crusades, and the Saracen wars, and all the great religious wars and political wars and social wars ever waged. On its outcome will hinge the entire future of civilization."[64] Dickey mimicked one of the oratorical lawyers from *Classics of the Bar* because he knew his father would approve.

As Dickey reevaluated his past, at times he appeared to be moving toward scholarly monasticism. Among his renunciations would be women, track, and football. In this sour, ascetic mood, he indicated that all he wanted was solitude to read and think. On June 13, he told his brother: "I'll let you be the athlete of the family. I never was much good anyway."[65] In a letter he wrote his mother on June 18, he stridently proclaimed his disgust with his past:

> When I get home I am through having a good time. Peg [Roney] and all the rest of them can go to hell. I'm never going to run again or play football or anything else like that. I have been fooling myself long enough. I am going to school and just study for the rest of my life and work hard. I despise work and I hate to study but after this I will go crazy if I don't do something. I never did have a very good time anyway. I don't get any enjoyment from drinking and I never got anything but despair from anything I ever really wanted to do.
>
> I realize that I have made everybody at home very unhappy by my actions in the past, and this makes me feel pretty bad. I am truly sorry, but it is just the way I am. I wish I was some other way, but I am not. I am just different from other people, I guess.
>
> I don't care much for fame now. I guess I wore it all out wishing for it before. It doesn't matter. All I want is for people to leave me alone.[66]

At the end of this dyspeptic letter he told his mother that Tom was worth fifty Jims. In a letter a few months later, however, he mocked Tom's major in physical education at LSU and his goal of coaching a high school track team. In his pursuit of a writing career, he hoped to prove he was worth fifty Toms.

During June, Dickey had other matters beside books and his future writing career on his mind. He prepared to leave Mindoro for the island of Okinawa, which had witnessed gruesome fighting since April and which would not be declared secure until June 21. The Allies had chosen Okinawa as a base from which to launch air and sea attacks on Japan. Shortly before flying to Okinawa, some of the night fighters landed on Tinian, the island near Guam from which huge B-29s had been firebombing Japanese industrial plants since the end of 1944. Tinian would be the base from which Muldrow and his fellow firebombers depart at the beginning of *To the White Sea*. Although Dickey and his pilot never landed on Tinian, they flew to Saipan, which was close, and undoubtedly heard stories about the large B-29s roaring into the air with their devastating bombs.

On July 4, Dickey participated in a less deadly assignment by flying cover for the initial landings on Borneo, southwest of Mindoro. Eight crews flew from Sanga Sanga, aiding the invasion convoy of two hundred warships, naval bombardments, and landings. Five days later Dickey and his pilot touched down on Okinawa and proceeded to their assigned campsite twelve miles from the beach. Strewn over the ground from a recent battle were helmets, canteens, rifles, and gas masks. Track vehicles and trucks had pressed decomposing Japanese bodies into the mud. Once the debris had been cleared, the ground echelon set up tents, and everyone gathered for an unappetizing meal of Spam and bully beef. Dickey recalled the dugouts and caves nearby: "It was just absolute chaos, absolutely. There was a place up in back of our area which was all coral caves and where the Marines and infantry had just gone . . . with flamethrowers. There were Japanese guys sitting up there in what must have been a machine-gun emplacement just incinerated. Just black."[67] A soldier named Easy returned from the caves with a handful of gold teeth he had knocked from a corpse with the butt of his carbine.

The first night on Okinawa was nightmarish. According to Bradley, who had temporarily replaced Sellers as the squadron commander: "At the south end of the island, near Naha, the fighting was still going on and the Japs were being pushed into the sea. We did not take the north end of the island until much later and the Japs were sneaking through the American lines to make their way to what they considered refuge. On their way up they would often try to steal food from the camps. . . . There was a full moon, and there were a lot of bushes with a steep precipice just beyond the edge of the camp. About midnight a shot rang out just two tents away. Before I could get my pants on, everyone was shooting at what they thought they saw in the bushes. It was a sleepless night."[68] One soldier discovered he had pitched his tent on a rotting body flattened by trucks. If Dickey needed gothic subjects for his writing, there were plenty here. One of the first papers he wrote at Vanderbilt described the carnage of Okinawa.

To make the situation on the island worse, forty-mile-an-hour winds soon assailed the campsite and toppled the soldiers' tents. The inclement weather and ghastly locale exacerbated Dickey's ill-temper. In his letters home he fired salvos at his parents, as if hoping they would join him in his misery. "If I was religious I could not stand this life here. Don't ever talk to me again about 'God's justice,' "[69] he told his devout mother. On July 28, Dickey and Bradley left their hellish surroundings on their first "night intruder" bombing and strafing mission over Japan. The squadron's target was Kanoya on the southern coast of Kyushu. According to Dickey, these missions were the result of a new policy conceived by Commander Sellers, whom he called "an alcoholic guy . . . ambitious for himself and for the squadron." Dickey added: "A lot of people in the squadron didn't like that because they were used to things being the way they were under Carroll Smith. But Sellers wanted us to go out. He wanted us to take it to them. I was not at all averse to that. . . . In fact, I wanted to do it. I took every mission I could find, with Bradley or with anybody else. If they wanted to fly I went with them. I had twice as much time as any R.O. in the outfit."[70] In fact, Sellers was not an alcoholic, no major shift in strategy had occurred, few in the 418th complained about the intruder work besides Dickey, and Dickey did not compile twice as much flight time as the other ROs. Only a slight change occurred, for which Dickey was partly responsible. Because Sellers wanted to keep Japanese planes on the ground rather than risk fatalities in dogfights, Bradley and Dickey delivered a plan to the one-star general at Okinawa's wing headquarters. The general approved it. As a result, the 418th regularly circled Japanese airfields and strafed targets on the way home.

In July, Dickey had a relatively easy schedule; he was in the air for only twenty-two hours. He flew routine convoy covers and patrols as well as intruder missions to Kyushu. In early August, as he and his squadron mates scrounged lumber to build two houses over the rain-soaked mud and fretted about numerous Japanese planes flying over their camp at night, they did so with the conviction that the war would soon end. Rumors of a Japanese surrender increased after President Truman, Winston Churchill, and other military leaders met at Potsdam on July 26 and issued an ultimatum: Japan must agree to a unilateral surrender or face complete destruction. Fearing the zealous militarists surrounding him, the Japanese premier, Suzuki, refused to respond. On the morning of August 6, 1945, Col. Paul Tibbets flew the *Enola Gay* over Hiroshima, a city known for its shipbuilding factories, electrical works, and other industries. His bombardier dropped the first atomic device—a uranium bomb named "Little Boy." The ensuing inferno killed about seventy thousand civilians and soldiers, wounded about eighty thousand more, and incinerated about 80 percent of the city's buildings. Thousands later died from radiation. With dread mixed with relief, the 418th listened to news about the blast on the radio. Years after the cataclysmic event, Dickey said, "I remember coming in from a mission and somebody telling me that the United States had just dropped a bomb on Japan that was the equivalent of twenty thousand tons of TNT. We thought it was just some sort of extra powerful type of dynamite. We didn't know. Everybody was mystified by it. I don't think we knew it was an atomic bomb for several days."[71] Dickey and his fellow aviators gazed in disbelief at the newspaper pictures of Hiroshima's charred rubble.

Despite this lethal blow, the war continued. On August 7, the 418th registered a rare "kill." As Vaughn noted in his diary, one of their pilots "reported that he had shot down a Jap plane as it was about to land at Kumamoto. That was the first plane that our squadron has gotten in eight months."[72] Dickey's stories of knocking planes from the sky like the Red Baron were just that—stories. Three days after the bomb fell on Hiroshima, a plutonium bomb named "Fat Man," which had also been flown from Tinian, fell on Nagasaki, killing about thirty-five thousand and wounding thousands more. As Nagasaki burned,

Dickey recalled, "We were all up that night. They told us not to go over there, on the west side [of Kyushu]. We just thought maybe the third fleet was up there and they were afraid of us tangling with some of their night fighters or something. But really they were keeping us away because they dropped the atomic bomb on Nagasaki."[73] The 418th had been bombing the city of Kumamoto, about sixty miles from Nagasaki, and on the night of August 9, some of the men decided to go back to see if they could still see the fires. According to Bradley, "Jim and I were over Fuchu the night after Nagasaki was bombed and we were very careful not to go into any clouds in the area. I couldn't at that time believe that it would have been that dangerous."[74] Dickey could see smoke over Nagasaki from the plane. In a 1978 interview with a veterans' newsletter, for the sake of drama Dickey placed himself closer to the original blast: "I was flying above Nagasaki when they dropped the second Atomic bomb. Nobody knew exactly what had been going on. . . . We didn't know that the secret of the universe was involved."[75] Dickey gave his imaginary flights over conflagrations more permanent form in his novels—in Joel Cahill's disastrous flight over a fire at his air corps base and in Muldrow's similarly disastrous flight over the fires of Tokyo. In fact, Dickey kept his distance from all such infernos.

Dickey may have had another reason for associating plane crashes and enormous fires. Close to the time of the nuclear explosions in Hiroshima and Nagasaki, he and his pilot nearly collided with a Japanese plane on one of their routine missions. The near miss had more to do with an argument between Dickey and his pilot than with burning cities. Such embarrassing events always evoked colorful exaggerations from Dickey. As Dickey told it, he and Bradley had an opportunity to shoot down two enemy planes:

Bradley told me that he had a visual on the aircraft. They were in . . . night formation and they had wing lights on. They were not showing any IFF [Identification: Friend or Foe]. So they were either allies or they were Japanese, and we were going to fire. . . . I had run a real good interception on them, real good, the best I ever did. Bradley said, "I got them; I got them." But he didn't want to fire the gun because it might mess it up and we were way out, a thousand miles from home base. We didn't want anything happening. So we navigated with the air-to-air radar, which you have to do in a special way. And so Bradley had miscalculated the closure rate and he went right in between them. Next thing, I looked around and they were behind us and they could've shot us right out of the sky. . . . Bradley screwed it up. We could have had two kills right there; they were sitting right there. Minimum range, attack position, everything, and he just went right through them. . . . Bradley panicked. . . . He took evasive action. . . . I regret that to this day.[76]

After the near miss, Dickey expressed his disgust to Robert Herzberger and other squadron members. The memory still rankled decades later when he incorporated the incident in Crux.

Stanley Logan, who had flown on the same mission and spoken to Dickey right after they landed, recalled a very different sequence of events: "After Dickey picked up a radar blip, he kept telling Bradley to 'throttle back' again and again as he recognized a continuously high overtaking speed. Because they didn't cooperate well, Bradley discounted the commands ('You're crazy; they can't be going that slow!') and was slow in throttling back. They had slowed to 100 mph or less when they overtook and flew between two Jap biplanes, assumed later to be Jap air cadets up for night training."[77] The "enemies," Logan said, were unarmed. Bradley was similarly dismissive of Dickey's version of the botched dogfight:

> I looked down below me to the right and saw a single plane with running lights on. I was sure that it was a Black Cat [a top secret B-24 used for Allied night work], but we went in on it anyway. The plane turned out its lights but Jim had locked onto it. He kept telling me that we were closing too fast—I had my throttles all the way back and had dropped flaps but just as I got a good visual we whizzed by him just a few inches below him, it seemed, and instantly the tail warning device went off, set off by the plane that we had just shot past. The plane was a very slow biplane with floats that couldn't have been traveling over 90 miles an hour. I took some evasive action but when we turned back to pick him up again we couldn't do it so we finished our mission and came home. I was so sure that the plane would be a Black Cat that I possibly waited too long for a more perfect visual. I did see the exhaust earlier and he would have been a sitting duck had I fired—I guess I was too cautious because some Allied planes had been attacked by our own planes and I didn't want to make that mistake.[78]

The impetuous Dickey, at least in hindsight, wanted to register a "kill," whether his target was a friendly aircraft or an innocuous trainer.

The mission report filed with the squadron clarifies some of the details that Dickey embellished. On August 8, Bradley and Dickey had strafed and bombed Kumamoto, with "nil observed results." While flying over Shiraiwa Yama they saw two enemy aircraft flying at four thousand feet: "Upon obtaining visual, pilot immediately closed in with throttles clear closed and overshot as he held fire in attempt to identify the planes. As pilot passed the bogeys, he recognized them as biplanes. Upon completing first pass, P-61 sighted another bogey passing head-on off his port wing. Pilot then started to make 360 degree turn to second pass on the bogeys, but discovered another plane, believed to be an enemy night fighter, was on his tail. P-61 took 20 minutes of evasive action and the bogeys were gone when P-61 shook enemy plane off tail."[79] In the official report, Dickey's plane was more pursued than pursuing. His imagination, however, refused to accept the unflattering truths of officialdom.

During the last few days of the war, Dickey practiced some small-scale fire-bombing that would lead to one of his most controversial poems. Up until then, Dickey's grandiose claims notwithstanding, he and his squad mates had done little bombing of any kind. Most of the bombing was done by B-24s, which were flying from a strip not far from Dickey's base, and by the B-29 "Superforts," which in the spring and summer were flying from Tinian and adjacent islands. It was Gen. Curtis LeMay who had decided in the late winter of 1945 to load B-29s with oil and napalm incendiaries, and to alter conventional policy by attacking Japanese cities at night. The firebombing raids were devastating. On the night of March 9–10, 334 B-29s lifted off from airfields in Tinian and other islands in the Marianas and flew to Tokyo. The napalm bombs and subsequent fires killed more than eighty-three thousand people and wounded forty-one thousand others. A quarter of the buildings in Tokyo—nearly 267,000—went up in flames. One million civilians were left homeless. During March, LeMay ordered four more night raids on the cities of Nagoya, Osaka, and Kobe. Between June and August, he ordered sixteen more on fifty smaller industrial towns. Dickey bore witness to the holocaust created by the bombs dropped on Tokyo in *To the White Sea*.

In his poem "The Firebombing"—famous partly because it elicited a vociferous attack from the writer Robert Bly—Dickey pretended to be one of the pilots who took part in LeMay's devastating raids. Even though his pilot persona departed from Okinawa, which is in the Ryukyu and not the Mariana Islands, his detractors took his narrative to be largely autobiographical. Dickey encouraged them by presenting his account as a confession: "One is cool and enthralled in the cockpit, / Turned blue by the power of beauty, / In a pale treasure-hole of soft light / Deep in aesthetic contemplation, / Seeing the ponds catch fire."[80] Bly and like-minded critics in the 1960s condemned Dickey for shamelessly committing and glamorizing atrocities.

When interviewed about his poem, Dickey spoke of "the sense of power one has as a pilot of an aircrew dropping bombs," a "sensation [that] is humanly reprehensible" in hindsight but, in the context of war, is necessary. He intended his poem to express "the guilt at the inability to feel guilty because you have not only proved yourself a patriot but something of a hero. You've been given medals for doing this. Your country has honored you—but there are those doubts that stay with you. You feel as a family man what all those unseen, forever unseen, people felt that you dropped those bombs on. You did it. The detachment one senses when dropping the bombs is the worst evil of all—yet it doesn't seem so at the time."[81] If Dickey felt little guilt, one reason was that he never participated in the sort of massive firebombings the poem describes. His denials aside, his poem is full of the empathy that makes guilt possible. He depicts the Japanese "homeowners" who get bombed as no different from his American neighbors in California, where he wrote the poem. He is keenly aware of Japanese suffering, as his graphic images of their plight attest. His pilot-narrator, like so many of his characters, is a projection rather than a mirror image of his actual self.

Dickey's response to the firebombing of Japanese cities, which killed more civilians than the atomic bombs, was complex. In a biographical statement he sent to *Contemporary Authors* on April 11, 1983, he repeated his desire to take responsibility for the firebombing by claiming—falsely—that he had dropped napalm on the Japanese as a fighter pilot. To the end of his life he maintained: "We carried two thousand-pound bombs and three-hundred gallon gasoline tanks full of napalm. We carried as much payload as a B-25, but we had to put them on wing shackles . . . instead of having them in the bomb-bay. . . . We did a lot of bombing, firebombing, napalm, phosphorous."[82] His pilot confirmed that during the four-day period after the bombing of Nagasaki and before the Japanese surrender, "We . . . used fire bombs twice . . . on the Japanese. These flights were mainly for us to learn some of the techniques involved so we could pass the information along. The war ended before we ever got into full swing."[83] In preparation for the "scorched-earth" policy of the invasion of Japan, Dickey and Bradley tested their firebombing capabilities on the port city of Fuchu. The mission reports substantiate Bradley's claims. A report filed on August 11, two days after the atomic bomb fell on Nagasaki, reveals that Bradley and Dickey, along with three other crews, dropped eight one-thousand-pound "demos," which were firebombs.

As Bradley explained, they bombed "civilian" targets because the Japanese had moved many of their manufacturing operations from factories into homes or other shelters in rural areas:

> Because of this we stopped bombing factories; everything was open for at-tack. Many people lived on boats along a river front. These boats were pro-duction lines also. It was efficient in that the boats could be moved to different locations as the need dictated. The sad part of this was that the families lived in the houses and boats. Jim and I would usually announce our departure from an area by strafing these boats, so it seemed natural that we would do the same with the napalm, which we did on these two trial missions. I always maintained a detached state of mind when we did things like this, but Jim . . . placed himself, mentally, into the scene . . . [and] imagined what it must have been like to have been on those boats or in those houses when they were attacked. . . . All I remember were huge fires behind us as we sped away at low altitude. These happened just before daylight—we had some light, enough to get fairly low, but not as low as the dayfighters because of the visibility problem. At that time . . . [the Japanese] were saving their planes, gas, and everything else as a final de-fense so we were not challenged on these two missions except perhaps from small arm fire.[84]

The bombs they dropped near Fuchu on these two occasions burned one-hundred-yard swaths. They dropped no phosphorus bombs (only the igniting devices in the bombs were made of phosphorus).

In his story "The Eye of the Fire," Dickey collapsed these two firebombing missions into one: "The mission was an important one; if successful it would do much to establish the P-61 as an offensive weapon. . . . His [Nettles's] ship and White's were equipped for the first time with napalm bombs: three-hundred-gallon drop tanks which, upon impact, would scatter jellied gasoline over a wide area, to cling, burning, to whatever it struck." Nettles, who resembles Dickey, describes how he and his pilot, White, who resembles Bradley, fly at night to a group of small houses in a seaport that supposedly contain ammunition. They drop their bombs, but Nettles reflects: "He was not at all certain that he had hit the right group of huts."[85] After the war, when Dickey claimed that he had participated in the massive firebombings of Japanese cities, his squadron mates reacted with incredulity. In his fantasies he seemed determined to play the role of Dr. Strangelove raining bombs on the enemy so that he could confess enigmatically that he had little guilt to confess.

It was not until 10:00 P.M. on August 14 that Dickey and the rest of the 418th heard that the beleaguered Japanese emperor had accepted the Potsdam terms. The squadron history recalls:

> On the night of 14 August the 418th was torn away from "Two Girls and a Sailor" by a most unprecedented demonstration of fire from practically every gun on the island. At first everyone ran for cover, thinking the Nips were making final kamikaze charges on all installations on Okinawa. Soon, however, rumors swept across the island that the Japs had sued for peace. Everyone became violently excited with every news report on the radio or with liquor laid away against VJ Day. As each outfit heard a fresh rumor, there were new outbursts of hilarity and fireworks until there was a greater display of ack ack in the sky than there had been for any Nip bomb raid. The celebration came to a sudden halt when the island commander ordered a red alert as a safety precaution against wild shooting and falling flak.[86]

Despite sporadic fighting, the war had finally come to an end.

Several days after the emperor's surrender, Dickey received instructions regarding the imminent invasion and occupation of Japan. Yen were distributed, and the commanding officer, Gen. Ennis Whitehead, circulated a letter that mingled contempt for the Japanese with calls for forgiveness and civility. Dickey found it hard to forgive, then and later: "We hated the Japanese so much. They beheaded Armstrong and Lally, tortured them and beheaded them in the Philippines. We hated them. Boy, I would have done anything against the Japanese. If there were any creatures on this earth that I would want to drop an atomic bomb on, it would have been them. And it still would. I've never forgotten it."[87] Behind many of the hostile antagonists in his novels and poems are Dickey's wartime enemies, the Japanese.

On August 28, after delivering a lengthy lecture on what to expect over the next few months, Maj. Sellers told his squadron they would settle in the Tokyo area between September 1 and 15. He also declared that the lackadaisical lifestyle of the Mindoro and Okinawa camps would soon change. The men would have to obey military dress codes and salute officers. Officers would inspect them to make sure clean uniforms and clean shaves were the rule rather than the exception. Calisthenics and close order drills would be mandatory. Used to a more relaxed regimen, Dickey found the new rules a nuisance. He made no attempt to hide his antipathy when, on August 31, he told his mother he would rather fight than put up with all the new peacetime army's "crap."

To lay the groundwork for the invasion of Japan, Gen. MacArthur and Adm. Nimitz sent an advance group to Atsugi Airfield near Tokyo, where Dickey would shortly be stationed. Ships from the American and British Fleets entered

Tokyo Bay, and on September 2, 1945, MacArthur, the Japanese foreign minister, and representatives from eight Allied countries signed the surrender agreement on the battleship *Missouri*. As was his style, MacArthur made a dramatic broadcast to Americans from the ship: "Today the guns are silent. A great tragedy has ended. A great victory has been won." With the horrendous destructiveness of nuclear warfare so recently displayed, he warned that "the survival of civilization" was in the balance: "If we do not devise some greater and more equitable system, Armageddon will be at our door."[88] The Pandora's box of the nuclear age had been opened, and, like MacArthur, Dickey viewed it with both trepidation and relief. In his 1978 interview with the journal *Vetletter*, Dickey acknowledged that he and many of his compatriots owed their lives to the atomic bombs dropped on Japan. Yet, like millions of others, Dickey feared the possibility of nuclear annihilation. In *Deliverance*, he projected those fears onto Lewis Medlock, who builds a well-stocked bomb shelter to survive a nuclear holocaust.

Impatient with the new regulations, Dickey had more-pressing concerns in September when a typhoon with 70-mile-per-hour winds struck Okinawa. On September 17, he woke in the middle of the night to find that the typhoon's wind, having changed direction and accelerated, had blown down many of the tents, including the parachute, supply, order room, and part of the mess hall tent. The only relief from the daily chore of nailing down equipment and cleaning up debris came on September 22 in the form of an officers' dance, which two hundred nurses attended. The inclement weather taxed the equanimity of even the most patient air crews, as did the crowded living quarters and the declining quality of food. As another typhoon advanced in mid-October, winds gusted up to 120 miles per hour, leveling all rather than just some of the tents. A Quanset hut was uprooted and bent into an L shape. Only Maj. Sellers's shack remained intact. To escape the typhoon's fury, some of the men hid in sacred burial tombs in the hills, tossing urns filled with ashes out the narrow doorways to create more space. Because the tombs were holy sites, the Okinawans vehemently protested. Dickey later told a man editing Conrad Aiken's letters that he had escaped into the tombs on October 7 with a first edition of Aiken's collected poems (his mother had mailed him a copy). He supposedly brought the book home after the war and, years later, gave it to Aiken when he met him in Savannah, Georgia.

Dickey and most of the other men, in fact, found protection in less controversial, if less comfortable, settings. They stayed in their aircraft. In mid-October Dickey wrote his father that the wind had blown so hard that it was almost impossible to stand: "Finally we went down to the airstrip and spent the night in B-25s."[89] One of the benefits of the typhoon, Dickey later pointed out, was the multitude of "armed service edition" books blown from a destroyed service library at ISCOM—Island Command. For the bibliophile, this was paradise regained from pandemonium. Dickey said that he recovered from the rain-sodden mud a copy of Yeats's collected poems; the famous textbook by Cleanth Brooks and Robert Penn Warren, *Understanding Poetry*; J. B. Priestley's *Midnight on the Desert*; and novels by Melville, Faulkner, Wolfe, Agee, and Maugham (some, but not all, of these were armed service editions). The typhoon undoubtedly scattered books, but probably rendered them unreadable as well (in his various tellings, Dickey usually changed the date of the storm and titles of the books). Although Dickey's claim about the Pacific typhoon educating him had all the rugged glamor of Ishmael's declaration in *Moby Dick* that a whaling ship had been his Harvard and Yale, Dickey's mother was the more likely source of his growing library.

If the effect of the typhoon on Dickey's scholarship was questionable, there was nothing uncertain about its effect on the planes. They were battered. The crews worked for a week repairing them before flying, on October 25, to Atsugi Air Base in Japan, about ten miles from Yokohama. Here Dickey and his squad mates stayed in large, cold, rickety wooden barracks formerly occupied by kamikaze pilots. The air inside was stifling. The oil stoves, which they used for heat, were dangerous and smoky. One of the barracks burned down in a matter of minutes. The toilets were little better than primitive latrines. While beds were too small to accommodate taller men like Dickey, the officers did enjoy certain privileges, like personal valets. American cooks supervised the Japanese cooks, ensuring that the food was better than usual. Dickey was glad to have fresh eggs, fresh fruit, fresh vegetables, and meats like ham, steak, and lamb. The men made their quarters more accommodating by installing Ping-Pong and pool tables. From his new domicile, Dickey could see Mount Fujiyama's snow-glazed summit, although the constant rains usually obliterated it.

Newly released from combat, the soldiers tried to acquaint themselves with their enemy's territory. As tourists, they visited sites in Tokyo like the Dai-itchi Hotel, the Palace, the Imperial Hotel, and the open street markets. They fraternized with the Japanese girls, who, like the rest of the population, had been ordered by Emperor Hirohito to treat the invaders as royal guests. Some visited Japanese families in their homes, toured a plane assembly plant that was partly underground, warmed their cold bodies in hot tubs, and explored miles of tunnels the Japanese had wired with lights and stocked with food to survive the Allied bombardments. Dickey made note of many such places for his later poems and for his novel *To the White Sea*.

As October waned and many of the enlisted men, including Dickey's pilot and commander, returned to the States, Dickey once again slumped into a melancholic funk. In November he complained to his father: "I am pretty well shot as far as nerves go."[90] Upon receiving his orders to return home, he was anxious to leave Japan. Thoughts of his future, however, depressed him. He was particularly disheartened to learn that Peg Roney, the Atlanta girl he contemplated marrying, had chosen a navy pilot. Dickey told his mother that he might marry Gwen Leege. Because she was "really loaded down with dough," as he put it, he wouldn't have to worry about being a destitute student. Then, with Hamlet-like vacillation, he said: "I probably won't do any of this. All the nice things I imagine for myself always seem to remain exclusively in my mind. But I'll have to see how everything works out when I get back."[91] He vented his frustrations by accusing his mother of not sending more books. In the absence of typhoons, he depended on her largesse, and refused to accept her argument that a paper shortage made some of his desired books hard to find and expensive.

Used to the tropical Philippines, Dickey began to think of Japan as a gigantic refrigerator, a fit locale for his coldhearted enemies. On November 9, the temperature hovered around thirty-one degrees during the day and sank to twenty-three degrees at night. The men had to drain water from their jeep radiators to prevent them from freezing. The cold dried the muddy roads. Dust blew relentlessly and stuck to the men, making them look ghostly. To keep warm at night, some wore their flying suits to bed. It got so cold in mid-November that many of the men couldn't sleep. Near the end of November, GI gas stoves helped dispel the cold, but these were hard to control. Dickey woke on December 4 to find the ground white with frost and ice. On December 18, it snowed for the first time at the Atsugi base. For Dickey, Japan's snowy desolation reached its most haunting expression in *To the White Sea*, where it represented, among other things, the cold-blooded, predator-prey relationship between all creatures.

Dickey no doubt read the front-page story in the December 6 *Stars and Stripes* about the Japanese sergeant who had used a sharp sword to behead two American airmen on Cebu Island on March 26. The revelation came in one of the war crimes trials proceeding in Manila. The Japanese executioner, Takeo Kawaii, described the atrocity with chilling sangfroid: "I was sitting on a bench in the normal school yard . . . watching Sgt. Maj. Higashi . . . execute a prisoner in a very unskillful manner. My captain, Tsurayama, said: 'Go over and give him a hand.' . . . I had a dull sword, so I borrowed the sword of Lt. Seijiro Sakai . . . because I thought it brutal to kill a prisoner with a dull sword. Then . . . I replaced Higashi and he made the American sit near a foxhole with his hands behind him. I stood behind him, lopped off his head with one stroke, and he fell into the hole."[92] Kawaii argued with his commander against beheading the second airman to no avail. The fact that the airmen were kept in a Cebu schoolhouse by their executioners must have given Dickey the idea to place Lally and Armstrong in a schoolhouse in "Between Two Prisoners." Proximity of time and place probably touched off Dickey's associations; the beheading reported in the *Stars and Stripes* occurred ten days after Armstrong's fateful crash on an island almost adjacent to Cebu. Dickey could read about further Japanese crimes and punishments the next day under the *Stars and Stripes* headline: " 'Bataan Butcher' Must Hang." The article told of the conviction and sentencing of the first Japanese war criminal, Gen. Yamashita, for condoning sixty thousand atrocities during the Bataan death march. The trial occurred in Manila, and although the Japanese general appealed to both the American and Philippine Supreme Courts, he was eventually hanged on February 23, 1946. Fifteen years later, these accounts of war trials, or those like them, helped shape Dickey's poems about Armstrong and Lally.

Having scoffed at his pilot's eagerness for combat, once the war was over, Dickey was pleased to take some of the credit for defeating Japan. "Well, it has been quite a war and I am sure glad I was in it," he told his mother. "I don't think I would have felt quite right about it if I hadn't come overseas."[93] He was also pleased by the decorations he received on October 27, 1945: an Air Medal for operational flight missions from January 31 to August 11, an Asiatic theater ribbon, a Philippines liberation ribbon, several Overseas Service Bars, a Battle

Star for the Southern Philippines Campaign, a Battle Star for the air offensive in the Japanese Campaign, an American theater ribbon, and a World War II Victory Medal. His Report of Separation indicated that he earned a total of five Bronze Battle Stars for his role in air offensives over the Philippines, Japan, and Borneo.

Although Dickey impressed some of his colleagues as a sloppy, aloof intellectual "with his nose forever in a book,"[94] he made a better impression on others. On December 15, 1945, 1st Lt. Paul Fridley wrote to the commanding general about Dickey's eight-hour missions during the Borneo campaign. Fridley praised Dickey and his pilot for flying out of Sanga Sanga to provide cover for the invasion forces off Balikpapan when other crews refused to go up because of bad weather. With regard to "intruder work against the Japanese homeland," Dickey's missions were laudable "because they involved low level strafing and bombing at night over unfamiliar terrain." Friendly fire, apparently, was a constant threat. "Many times, because of lack of fuel, it was necessary to land at the home base on Okinawa during red alerts and air raids; and therefore he was fired upon several times by friendly ack-ack and night fighters, who were too eager to check for proper identification."[95] According to Fridley, during twelve months of overseas duty and eight months of combat, Dickey never received a rest leave. He now deserved one.

Later in life Dickey would provide friends with similarly inflated data and cajole them into writing letters on his behalf, usually to encourage prominent magazines such as the *Atlantic Monthly, Poetry,* and *Harper's* to publish his poems; college administrations to give him honorary degrees; or prize committees to grant him awards. Could Dickey have pressured Fridley into writing such a flattering recommendation to the general? At least one of his comrades, Stanley Logan, thought so: "I don't know why Fridley wrote the alleged letter unless it was a blanket letter covering a number of crews. Many of us endured the long gruelling missions to Borneo. I never heard of any night fighter pilot who 're-fused to go up because of bad weather.' We cut our eye teeth on such weather. This sounds like more B.S. Similarly with Kyushu missions. Following the friendly fire incident that Maj. Smith related in January, before we joined the squadron, the only incident of friendly fire that I knew about was when Frumer (an R.O.) bailed out over a naval unit near Okinawa they made the mistake of flying over unannounced."[96] Logan pointed out that most of the flyers never received rest leave.

However he procured Fridley's testimonial, Dickey got approval from army headquarters in Atsugi for a six-day leave. He and Herbert Vaughn packed their clothes early on Christmas Day while the others slept, then drove their jeep four hours through little villages covered with snow to the Fuji-View Hotel at the foot of Mount Fujiyama. They relaxed in the hotel's steam heat, bath, and soft beds; dallied with two Red Cross women (one of whom they knew from New Guinea); consumed sandwiches and coffee all day in the snack bar; and at night dined by candlelight on steak, French fries, and ice cream. Two days after they arrived, it began to snow. Feeling adventurous, Dickey experimented with skis, which for a Southerner unused to snow was probably more dangerous than flying combat missions. Dickey also rowed on the lake, attended a Japanese stage show, sampled a sukiyaki dinner with hot sake in a Japanese home, and watched a kimono demonstration before driving back to Atsugi on the last day of December. Decades later he planned to end *Crux* the way he ended his war year: at a Mount Fujiyama hotel.

Having begun his journey to war on New Year's Eve, Dickey began his return to civilian life on the following New Year's Eve. For the rest of his life, the plot that gripped his imagination most consistently was that of the circular journey in which beginnings and ends coincide. After his heroes survive traumatic ordeals, they compulsively return home. Gazing at the mountain beyond his hotel, as his poem "A View of Fujiyama after the War" bears out, he felt the tremors of war in the tremors of earth (in the form of a slight earthquake); he also felt a survivor's sense of blissful release. The volcanic mountain, beautiful in its dormancy, was a fit symbol for Dickey's sense of transcendence and tranquility. "Overcome by the enemy's peace," he pledges to "live at the heart / Of his saved, shaken life,"[97] and write from a conviction of hard-won triumph.

Dickey's return to the States on the USS *Sea Devil*, which commenced on January 10, 1946, took approximately the same time as his voyage to the Philippines—about two weeks—and he passed the time in approximately the same way—by reading books. He told the poet Frederick Turner years later that he devoted many happy hours to J. B. Priestley's book on time theory, *Midnight on the Desert*. He also thought about his future: "I still couldn't get used to the idea that I was going to live. I didn't have any plans. I sort of thought about going back and playing [foot]ball again, but I didn't really want to do that. I thought that maybe I could go to another school and further my literary interests. I had no idea that I would be a writer. That was too ambitious for me."[98] But his writerly ambitions had incubated and hatched in the heat of the Pacific Islands. He docked in Seattle on January 23, and made his way back to Atlanta and from there to Vanderbilt to become a writer.

A form filled out by air crew personnel in the U.S. outlined Dickey's war service. His official aeronautical rating and crew position were listed as "radar observer," his total combat hours 119.10, and total combat missions thirty-eight (any assigned flights in a combat zone, with the exception of training flights and DC-3 supply flights, were considered combat flights). Another form, titled "Separation Qualification Record," issued by Fort McPherson just south of Atlanta on March 1, 1946, confirmed these numbers. A brief account of his service appeared under the heading "Summary of Military Occupations": "[James Lafayette Dickey] flew long range night strafing and bombing missions. Acted as bomber escort on night missions and provided cover for landing forces and convoy attacks. Tracked and bombed seaborne and land targets by means of synchronized radar methods, using designated radar bombing equipment. Operated and performed first echelon maintenance on radio and radar sets and equipment. Completed 38 combat missions. Total flying time 403 hours, of which 120 were combat hours."[99] Upon these bare bones Dickey fleshed out his myth of piloting, dogfighting, firebombing, and crashing in P-61 Black Widows. Apprised of his inventions, some of his squadron mates wondered if he had simply forgotten his activities in the war. Since he carried a Photostat of his discharge papers in his wallet for the rest of his life, he obviously had not.

Dickey's exaggerations would be accepted readily by a postwar audience eager to believe that American soldiers had acted daringly in vanquishing an evil empire. Like the character played by William Holden in a World War II movie he loved, *The Bridge on the River Kwai,* Dickey prevaricated about his status as a combat pilot to impress men and women alike. Like his movie resemblance, he admitted the facts were fictions only when pressed by authorities who knew or suspected the truth. Only the well-informed knew the extent to which Dickey embellished. As his career as a poet and novelist flourished, his military tales flourished in tandem, becoming so ingrained that even a well-known Dickey scholar like Richard Calhoun could affirm in a standard critical study: "Dickey was in the Air Force from 1942 to 1946, heavily involved in combat, flying nearly one hundred combat missions in the Pacific campaign in the Philippines, at Okinawa, and participating in the firebombings of major Japanese cities."[100] Asked to give specifics of his military record as a pilot, as John Kelly did while writing *Night Fighters of the Sea,* Dickey pretended to be too busy to answer. On the same day he refused Kelly, August 4, 1982, he requested from Prosper Rufur, one of his old night fighter cohorts, a copy of the squadron history for use in his burgeoning novel, *Alnilam.* He told Rufur, who was in charge of squadron records, that he had refrained from attending squadron reunions in the past, but might go to an upcoming one in Orlando. Partly out of fear of having his invented war record questioned, he never went to a reunion.

Dickey was as deeply ambivalent about his military service as he was about his lies. In the early 1950s, he proposed to write a short story that evinced some of his feelings regarding the Army Air Corps. The narrator would visit a deserted air base where he had once trained and say: "I was glad to see it standing deserted, for I had always hated military life, with the really profound hatred of uninterrupted irritation and interference, though I had nothing better, or other, to do."[101] He expressed his ambivalence no better than when he told his friend Ernest Suarez, who watched a group of ROTC students jog across the University of South Carolina campus several weeks before he died: "There's nothing that attracts and horrifies me more than people marching and chanting. The rhythm is extraordinary; it makes you want to be part of it, to get up and join them. But for all that we know they're the next Hitler Youth."[102] Despite his harsh remarks, Dickey always acknowledged that his World War II experience was the catalyst for his literary career. The war purged many of the superficial values of his Atlanta upbringing, made him more aware of the fragility of human life, and convinced him of the subversive and ultimately redemptive powers of the imagination.

About a decade after he left Japan, Dickey hailed his decision to become a writer to the novelist Andrew Lytle: "To be of the same variety, the same profession, or calling, as the writers I like (or love) is quite sufficient compensation for my life. I have never valued life greatly, since I was in the war so young. It seemed then that most of the things I had been told about human life were false, constructions, rationalizations only, which would not stand up against any kind of forceful reality. But the artist is after another kind of reality: the underlying, the typical, the profound, the symbolic, the substructure of reality, the hidden anatomy."[103] In becoming a writer, Dickey substituted "symbolic" fictions, which revealed the truth of his feelings and ideas, for the "false constructions" of his youth as well as for the "realities" he found arrayed against him. He began to live more consistently in an "invented world," a "supreme fiction"—as Wallace Stevens would say—of his own making, and he convinced others to do the same.

IV.

BECOMING A POET

8. Vanderbilt University (1946–1950)

When Dickey left America for the war, he was a dabbler in verse. When he returned, he was a committed poet. "My values had changed, everything about me had changed, because of the war experience,"[1] he once said in an interview. He considered transferring from Clemson to universities in Georgia, but he felt that he needed distance from his home state. Most importantly, he wanted to attend a college with a strong literary reputation. While in the Philippines he had asked a Special Services officer and Harvard graduate, Henry Howe, for help gaining admission to Harvard. In the end, he decided that Harvard was too remote, and that Vanderbilt University in Nashville, Tennessee, was best suited to his needs. Vanderbilt had been an epicenter of the Southern renaissance and still had a strong English Department, even though such luminaries as John Crowe Ransom, Allen Tate, and Robert Penn Warren no longer taught there. Having filled out the requisite forms and received a favorable response, Dickey excitedly prepared to renew his college career.

Before traveling to Nashville for the 1946 summer term, Dickey visited family and friends in Atlanta. Everyone noticed that he had changed. For starters, to prove he had been a pilot he wore an expensive sheepskin flight jacket that had not been issued by the Army Air Corps. Unlike some veterans traumatized by combat, Dickey made no attempt to keep quiet about his recent experiences. Instead, he sensationalized them in one far-fetched story after another. He had traveled to "the heart of darkness"; now he wanted to convince everyone that, like Kurtz in Joseph Conrad's novel, he had been tempted by savagery. He made a blowgun from aluminum tubing, sharpened segments of coat hangers into darts, and practiced his aim at targets around his West Wesley home. He would continue to shoot blowguns for the rest of his life.

When not dwelling on the barbarism he had left in the Pacific, Dickey considered how best to savor the joys of civilization. In February, he dated an Atlanta woman named Jackie who admired his poems. During the spring, he also pursued a Sweet Briar art student named Alice Dulaney, and wrote love letters to Beth DePenning, who was working for an eye surgeon at the University of Oregon Medical School. In his ongoing debate about marriage, for the moment he decided that he favored it. Peg Roney, unfortunately, remained steadfast in her wedding plans, so Dickey turned his attention to Gwen Leege, who was about to graduate from Bryn Mawr. Shortly after Christmas, Leege had written Dickey a twelve-page letter in which she declared her unstinting love for him and her desire to bear him four fair-haired boys. When she traveled to Atlanta in February, Dickey proposed that they marry in June, but Leege hesitated to make a commitment. Disgruntled, Dickey accused her—as he had done in California—of being coldhearted and materialistic. Why wouldn't she marry a jobless veteran who was about to begin college? In conversations and letters after their argument, Leege protested that she was not as Dickey had depicted her. She couldn't grant Dickey's wish for a June wedding because she already had plans to return to her family in Marin County and then to travel in Europe. She asked Dickey to wait for her, and in a letter written on March 5 she reassured him that their commitment to each other would ultimately triumph over the various delays and obstacles. Dickey was skeptical.

On February 27, Leege suggested that she spend part of her spring vacation (March 28–April 7) with Dickey at a fishing village somewhere between Atlanta and Bryn Mawr. Because of the mores of the time, she looked for a chaperone. When the designated chaperone proved unavailable, on April 5 she took a train to Atlanta instead. Once again, they mulled over their marriage prospects. As in later life with other women, Dickey could not resist spinning fanciful scenarios of connubial bliss. "Let's have six children," he said, adding, "but we must have one daughter." Leege greeted these overtures with a combination of maternal solicitude and stern practicality. She reminded Dickey, "You've lost years in the war. There's so much ahead of you. You're too young to marry."[2] Dickey partially agreed, but grew disconsolate over her rejection.

In a letter Leege wrote a week after her three-day visit, she thanked Dickey for his hospitality in Atlanta, for introducing her to friends, and for the Rilke poem he'd sent her. She apologized for treating him badly in their discussions of the practical aspects of marriage. Proud of her Teutonic heritage and knowledge of German literature, Leege must have denigrated Dickey's Anglophilia; she promised to read the English books he prized so dearly. In another letter, she warned him jokingly that if they married he would have to tolerate her endless nagging and traveling. Her final months at Bryn Mawr and her distress about marrying Dickey brought her anxieties to a fever pitch. In March, she explained to Dickey that she had gone to the infirmary with bad nerves, which she tried to placate with sleeping pills, vitamin pills, and counseling.

Suffering from a sinus infection and worries about her final exams, Leege also feared that she might lose Dickey to another woman when he went to Vanderbilt. She wanted to take a job in Europe for ten months after graduation, but could their love withstand such a long separation? She suspected that Dickey would resent such a hiatus, especially since the war had already separated them for a year. On May 16, she wrote Dickey that she loved him for his impractical desires, but nevertheless wanted him to accept them as such. (Later, Dickey insisted that Leege was impractical.) During one of their last meetings, on June 4 at Bryn Mawr, Leege repeated her reservations about a hasty marriage. She wanted to see the European countries whose literatures she had studied so assiduously. After finishing her degree as a German major with a minor in Spanish, Leege went to Germany to teach for the Allied forces. Dickey accompanied her to the pier to bid her farewell, and when her boat, the *John Ericsson*, eased into the harbor, he shouted that she was sailing to enemy territory.

Leege later settled in Zurich, Switzerland, where she married a businessman. She always treasured what she called her "unique love" for Dickey, stipulating it was not "a jumping-into-bed kind of love."[3] In retrospect, Dickey decided that marrying Leege would have been foolhardy. Even Dickey's mother, who consistently argued for marriage, thanked Leege for urging her son to return to college as a bachelor. Nevertheless, Dickey cherished their youthful romance. He visited Leege in Switzerland and the United States, and during his last decade told her that he wanted his daughter, Bronwen, to follow her to Bryn Mawr (she would go to Duke). In drafts of *The Entrance to the Honeycomb* and *The Casting*, he also preserved Leege's capacity for intense, platonic intimacy in the character Sara, who loves her boyfriend, Julian Glass, without ever getting around to sex or marriage.

Putting his marriage plans on hold for the time being, Dickey joined hundreds of other veterans eager to renew their studies at Vanderbilt. The university, as he knew, had established a reputation for ideological ferment. During its first decades after opening in 1875, the university had groped from one religious dispute to another. In a final power struggle between Methodist sponsors and secular administrators in 1914, it had decided to divorce itself from its Methodist roots. The next controversy—the one that made Vanderbilt attractive to Dickey—involved a broad-based cultural attack on the North carried out in poems, novels, political manifestoes, economic essays, history books, sociological studies, religious critiques, and every other genre. Dickey wrote: "Vanderbilt is a school where you can't be interested in literature without being made aware of the Vanderbilt literary tradition and the great days of the late twenties, the days of the Fugitives and *The Fugitive* magazine and of the manifestoes, such as *I'll Take My Stand*."[4] The Fugitives, so called because of their outcast status amid the sentimentalism of the Old South and the commercialism of the New South, were writers who had taken a stand for Southern agrarianism.

Several of the Fugitives, who had once gathered in the house of the affable, eccentric Sidney Hirsch to discuss literature and politics, had a profound effect on Dickey's career. John Crowe Ransom's poems and New Criticism provided standards for Dickey's early poems. Although as a mature writer Dickey renounced Ransom's stylistic example, he espoused Ransom's opposition to science, technology, and industry his entire life. (After departing Nashville for Ohio, Ransom published some of Dickey's early poems in the *Kenyon Review*.) Walter Clyde Curry, who became an eminent Shakespeare and Chaucer scholar, taught Dickey medieval and renaissance literature (Curry also provided him with a model for the sort of dry, scholarly exactitude he vowed to reject). Dickey kept his distance from the novelist Donald Davidson, who had attended Hirsch's soirees as an undergraduate and who later became a professor in the Vanderbilt English Department, but Dickey declared an affinity for some of his sociological views. Allen Tate, who had joined the Fugitve group as a student around 1921, was instrumental in securing a Sewanee Fellowship for Dickey so he could travel and write poetry in Europe in the early 1950s. Tate's own poetry encouraged Dickey to explore rituals of redemption in a highly wrought, rhetorical style. Robert Penn Warren, who began submitting his undergraduate poems to the Fugitives in 1923, became one of Dickey's closest writer friends in later years. They shared a preoccupation with gothic deeds and nature's savage beauty, and in the 1970s Warren acted as a catalyst for Dickey's experiments in looser poetic forms.

Most of the contributors to *I'll Take My Stand*, including Andrew Lytle, who in a few years would serve as Dickey's mentor, based their theories on two unshakeable assumptions: the perniciousness of Northern ideas and the inferiority of blacks. Although they tended to avoid racist jeremiads in *I'll Take My Stand*, periodically their anger overwhelmed their good manners. The Vanderbilt historian Frank Owsley, for instance, spoke of "the half savage blacks" freed after the Civil War, arguing that some "could still remember the taste of human flesh and the bulk of them [were] hardly three generations removed from cannibalism."[5] Davidson refrained from condemning blacks as savage cannibals in his essay, but his racism was implicit and later erupted in cantankerous defenses of segregation and of organizations akin to the Ku Klux Klan. Only Robert Penn Warren confronted the issue of race directly, and his "progressive" views so offended Davidson and the others that he was asked to revise his essay. In the end he argued that blacks should remain on small farms where they were less of a "problem."[6]

Like any community decimated by war, these proud Southerners, who were also well-read critics and highly accomplished writers, rankled under the victor's yoke. Some of the writers, like Allen Tate, suggested that a second Civil War might be necessary to win back their old ethos. "How may the Southerner take hold of his Tradition? The answer is, by violence,"[7] he said. The Agrarian manifestoes seemed prophetic during the Depression, when capitalist America had collapsed and destroyed the financial stability of millions. During the prosperity that followed World War II, their principles appeared quaint and full of the perverse abstractions they supposedly opposed. Nevertheless, as the historian Paul Conkin said of the Fugitive-Agrarian group at Vanderbilt from 1915 to 1930, their "discussions eventually made up the most important single chapter in a now widely recognized renaissance of literature in the South and stimulated the most extended twentieth-century debate about the cultural identity of the South and about the economic and social institutions appropriate for such a South."[8] Proud of his Southern heritage and determined to add something to it, Dickey accepted many of his predecessors' ideas, rejected others, but never officially joined their ranks.

Dickey's novel *Deliverance* is, among other things, an argument with the pastoral idealism of the Vanderbilt Agrarians. Sympathetic to the Agrarians' condemnation of big-city capitalism, Dickey scoffed at their idealization of the farming life. Although Ed Gentry echoes the old Southern "gentry's" complaints about commercialism, when he leaves the city for the country, he comments:

There is always something wrong with people in the country. . . . You'd think that farming was a healthy life, with fresh air and fresh food and plenty of exercise, but I never saw a farmer who didn't have something wrong with him, and most of the time obviously wrong; I never saw one who was physically powerful, either. Certainly there were none like Lewis. The work with the hands must be fantastically dangerous, in all that fresh air and sunshine, I thought: the catching of an arm in a tractor part somewhere off in the middle of a field where nothing happened but that the sun blazed back more fiercely down the open mouth of one's screams. And so many snakebites deep in the woods as one stepped over a rotten log, so many domestic animals suddenly turning and crushing one against the splintering side of a barn stall. I wanted none of it, and I didn't want to be around where it happened either.[9]

In Dickey's pastoral Eden, Satanic snakes—like the sadistic hillbillies Ed soon meets—disabuse all erstwhile Agrarians of their utopian dreams.

At Vanderbilt, one of the books that helped clarify Dickey's conception of himself as a Southerner was W. J. Cash's *Mind of the South*. Published in 1941, Cash's monumental study supplied Dickey with an image of the South quite different from the Agrarian one. Cash remarked: "*I'll Take My Stand* was, like their earlier prose works in general, essentially a determined reassertion of the validity of the legend of the Old South, an attempt to revive and fully restore the identification of that Old South with Cloud-Cuckoo Town, or at any rate to render it as a Theocritean idyll."[10] Cash traced what he considered to be the genuine "mind of the South" to the frontier spirit established by Irish and Scottish emigrants rather than to an Anglican Arcadia. The English aristocrats, he said, stayed on their comfortable estates in England while the more adventurous lower classes, who had little to lose, built the first colonies in America. These pioneers were given "to cunning, to hoggery and callousness, to brutal unscrupulousness and downright scoundrelism. In practice, on any frontier . . . there invariably arises the schemer—the creator and manipulator of fictitious values, the adept in spurring on the already overheated imaginations of his fellows."[11] The "basic Southerner," according to Cash's class-conscious view, was not the Agrarian squire, but the backwoodsman who followed "the savage ideal" of his half-wild ancestors in seventeenth- and eighteenth-century Europe. Dickey's lineage and temperament connected him to both classes, but his World War II experience made him increasingly wary of civilized ideals. To survive and to thrive, Dickey needed more of the frontiersman's cunning than the squire's chivalry.

Dickey modeled much of his public persona on a figure Cash called "the Southern pioneer," who exhibited "a kind of mounting exultancy, which issued in a tendency to frisk and cavort, to posture, to play the slashing hell of a fellow—a notable expansion of the ego testifying at once to his rising individualism and the burgeoning of the romantic and hedonistic spirit. . . . To stand on his head in a bar, to toss down a pint of raw whisky at a gulp, to fiddle and dance all night, to bite off the nose or gouge out the eye of a favorite enemy, to fight harder and love harder than the next man, to be known eventually far and wide as a hell of a fellow—such would be his focus."[12] At the advent of the twentieth century, according to Cash's psychohistory, a fissure between antebellum hedonism and a new puritan ethic opened in the Southern mind. "On the one hand, the sense of the clandestine became always more distinctly a necessary ingredient of the highest enjoyment; and on the other, the sense of sin and the need for absolution in more or less orgiastic religion always more pressing."[13] Refusing to sacrifice the pleasure principle to the puritanical reality principle, Dickey attained great notoriety for his various indulgences. His poems like "May Day Sermon" are full of orgiastic religious rhetoric, but also manifest a desire for confession and absolution. In his life and art, Dickey displayed the contradictions Cash spelled out in his anatomy of the Southern mind: its code of honor and its outbreaks of sadism, its "Cult of Southern Womanhood" and its misogyny, its ideal of agrarianism and its obsession with commercial success.

Dickey also found a useful map of his Southernness in Donald Davidson's *The Attack on Leviathan*. He particularly liked the way Davidson analyzed Northern industrialism and defended Southern regionalism. "I had always thought that such an attitude would almost have to be chauvinistic," Dickey said in *Self-Interviews*. "After all, I thought, I'm not so much a Southerner or an American as a citizen of the world and a human being, which is sort of a nice way to look at it. However, it's not really true."[14] Davidson's 1938 book attacked the North's industrial-military-capitalist complex as a leviathan whose imperialistic aim was to gobble up the Agrarian institutions of the South and replace them with science, diluted religion, and "equality for the Negro—a full equality that ultimately will go far beyond suffrage reforms and the destruction of such discrimination as now appear in Jim Crow laws and bi-racial school arrangements."[15] Dickey's relationship with Davidson was marked by a young poet's anxieties about being overwhelmed by an older writer's dogmatic ideas. One of Dickey's closest graduate student friends, Bill Pratt, recalled: "He deliberately avoided taking Donald Davidson's course in Creative Writing, he told me, and stuck to literature, though he knew he was shrinking from Davidson's high reputation and probable influence on a fledgling poet, and it obviously pleased him that Donald Davidson had recognized him once, even spoke to him in passing through Calhoun Hall, but called him 'Mr. Hickey.' "[16] According to another student, Thomas Daniel Young—the future biographer of Ransom—Davidson felt equally ambivalent about Dickey; he admired Dickey's writerly talents while disapproving of his personal habits.

In later life Dickey sought to establish a closer association with Davidson. He boasted to numerous interviewers that he had audited some of Davidson's classes. In the journal *Contemporary Literature*, he stated frankly, "Donald Davidson was my teacher."[17] In 1996, he repeated the claim in the magazine *Reckon*. By this time, after his own fashion, Dickey had become a Fugitive, too—an outcast among the writers and critics who controlled literary reputations and prize committees in the liberal North. As early as 1957, Dickey tried to draw closer to the old Fugitive Davidson:

> A friend has lent me a new copy of *Still Rebels, Still Yankees*, and I have read it with a great deal of interest. I thought I should write to you and tell you what immense admiration I have for your book. It has gone a long way toward providing an account of the South I was born in, and would like to believe in.
>
> Thank you again for the very great pleasure your book has given me. It makes me sorrier than ever that I was not able to participate in your classes when I was at Vanderbilt.
>
> P.S. I like particularly the review of Cash![18]

Still Rebels, Still Yankees was an apologia for Southern traditions that gathered together Davidson's essays on poetry, fiction, and the South. In his review of *The Mind of the South*, he blasted Cash for writing a book for dumb Yankees. On the subject of race he was predictably rebarbative: "It is not possible to absorb the Negro into white society in full and equal status without tearing that society to pieces and completely, perhaps convulsively, changing it."[19] Dickey admired Davidson's Confederate stand, even though he had stubbornly shunned the professor as an undergraduate.

When Dickey entered Vanderbilt, the campus was anything but an Agrarian paradise. Construction and all the machines implementing it surrounded him at every turn. According to Harvie Branscomb, who had left Duke Divinity School to become Vanderbilt's chancellor in 1946, the university was dilapidated and undersized:

> It was surrounded by privately owned, deteriorating property and thus was increasingly isolated on its own meager acreage. It was virtually a campus without permanent dorms—only old Kissam for men [where Dickey lived] and an inadequate McTyeire for women. The only dining hall was in Kissam, with aluminum trays and poor service. [It was] . . . an impossibly provincial campus, with half the students from Nashville, two-thirds from Tennessee. Vanderbilt was no longer a pacesetter for the South, for it had almost no impact on the South. Three of its professional schools—Law, Religion, Engineering—had woefully inadequate facilities. The School of Social Work, an illegitimate child, had no permanent facilities at all. Faculty salaries were low, fringe benefits few, and in spite of the rules too many faculty members were not yet members of the retirement system.[20]

The university was also strictly segregated; admissions policies forbade blacks from applying. Racist sentiments were so strong that when the football team played Yale in 1948, some Vanderbilt alumni argued that their all-white team should refuse to play colleges like Yale that suited up blacks. Over the decade-and-a-half of his chancellorship, Branscomb tried to ween Vanderbilt from its provincialism and bigotry, and to a certain extent he succeeded.

Calhoun Winton, a fellow student who became one of Dickey's lifelong friends, recalled that Vanderbilt at the time was "a somewhat dingy collection of redbrick buildings, crowded helterskelter onto a hillside in residential Nashville. Summers were hot and humid, and in the winter black coal dust poured from nearby chimneys and smokestacks. . . . Vanderbilt was an urban university, and though the oaks and hackberry trees provided some green relief, it was not a prepossessing place. One went there for an education; that was why Dickey joined hundreds of other veterans in the long registration lines."[21] The quality of education at Vanderbilt, according to Winton, was on a par with that of Duke, Chapel Hill, and Tulane.

Despite the university's relatively low fees, Dickey claimed that he depended on the GI bill and an athletic scholarship for his survival. A manager of the football team living in Kissam Hall suspected that Dickey had ample funds from another source. His expensive clothes set him apart. Although he never garnered an athletic scholarship, he did receive the GI bill stipend (about seventy-five dollars per month), and with this he paid his tuition. As usual, his mother helped pay his other bills with checks from home. Much of his extra money went to buy books. With easy access to bookstores, Dickey quickly built a substantial library of poetry and literary criticism. He liked to advise friends about what books to buy and read. Once he admonished Winton to buy Wallace Stevens's *The Man with the Blue Guitar*. When his friend complied, Dickey grabbed the volume from his hands in the Vanderbilt bookstore and declaimed the famous lines of the title poem: "Things as they are / Are *changed* upon the blue guitar."[22] Dickey knew Stevens's dictum well, and at Vanderbilt he continued to change "things as they are" in the stories he told about his past.

Socially, Vanderbilt in the late 1940s resembled many other universities. Students joined sororities and fraternities in droves. Dickey's distaste for fraternities had altered little since high school. According to Winton: "The social side of college—fraternity beer busts, gym dances, cheerleader tryouts—he simply ignored."[23] To Dickey's relief, his Clemson credits allowed him to skip many of the initiatory activities of the freshman class. Having recently survived the life-and-death struggles of war, he had even less tolerance for the callow social affairs of freshmen. The all-male Calumet Club, which had been established in 1906 to cultivate the literary spirit of the university and which had been a breeding ground for young Fugitives, also failed to arouse Dickey's interest, as did the poetry students who congregated around the undergraduate literary magazine, the *Gadfly*. *Gadfly* editor Bertrand Goldgar, who later became a prominent professor and scholar of eighteenth-century literature, remembered Dickey as a distant figure striding across campus in his air corps flight jacket. Despite his independent ways, Dickey respected the journal enough to publish in it. In a 1948 issue, his last two undergraduate poems, "Sea Island" and "King Crab and Rattler," appeared behind a *Gadfly* cover illustration of a horse kicking backwards as if to repel all bystanders.

In 1948, the year Dickey graduated, the Vanderbilt English Department employed only four full professors, two associate professors, and one assistant professor. In his first English course, Composition and Literature, Dickey set out to impress his professor, William Hunter, with his newly acquired book learning and writing skills. Dickey recalled with a dash of hauteur: "For our first writing exercise the little girls, recent high school graduates, were writing themes on 'What the American Flag Means to Me' or 'My First Day on the Campus of Vanderbilt University' or 'What I Did with My Summer Vacation'; I wrote about the invasion of Okinawa. After reading my paper to the class, Hunter called me up after class and told me that Vanderbilt had a tradition of trying to encourage writers. He said, 'I think your essay is really very promising, even remarkable. So from now on I'll give the class theme assignments, but you just write whatever you want to write.' "[24] Taking Hunter at his word, Dickey wrote poetry—imitations of Kenneth Patchen and George Barker as well as a sonnet sequence—a reminiscence of Donald Armstrong, a surrealistic play, and a critical essay. If Hunter thought Dickey was exceptional at the beginning of the course, by the end he had reservations. He gave Dickey a B, the same grade he earned in his first-semester algebra class.

Regarding his football career at Vanderbilt, Dickey either said that he never played or that he started to practice under the legendary coach Red Sanders, only to learn in late July that his previous athletic experience at Clemson disqualified him: "I was ineligible to play football and basketball at Vanderbilt. . . . The Southeastern Conference, which Clemson was affiliated with at the time, passed a rule that you were ineligible to play at any other school when you returned from the war, to keep the coaches from stealing each other's players."[25] In fact, no rule precluded the eligibility of transfer students like Dickey; they could play football on whatever college team accepted them. Since Dickey had played only one season of football at Clemson and had not received a degree from that college, he could have played for at least three years and maybe four at Vanderbilt. Other players on the football and track teams corroborated this. Dickey had actually asked his father in a letter he had sent from Okinawa during the war: "How about giving me the particulars on the eligibility ruling? Do they still have the one-year rule or can't transfers play at all? I'd sure like to know."[26] If his father sent the right ruling, Dickey chose to ignore it.

To play football at Vanderbilt, Dickey had to make the team. The equipment manager from 1946 to 1948, Bedford Calhoun, recalled issuing Dickey a practice uniform that came back dirty—a sign that he was scrimmaging. But Calhoun never issued him a game uniform. Another manager, James Martin, who served the team from 1945 to 1949, also remembered Dickey at practices. According to Martin, Dickey stayed with the team for several months, but when he realized that he would never play in a game, he quit. Dickey had told Martin that he had every intention of becoming a varsity football player. Competition with the other returning veterans, whose average age was about twenty-six and whose skills were better than his, ultimately proved too tough. Although Dickey implied that eligibility rules prevented him from playing basketball as well, Martin, who was also the basketball manager, said that Dickey never tried out for the team.

Dickey may have entertained hopes of football stardom because of Vanderbilt's weak record before the war. In 1939, the team won only a single major victory. To rectify the dismal situation, the university hired Henry R. "Red" Sanders in 1939 and a year later decided to give twenty football grants annually. By 1941, Sanders had turned the program around and won the Southeastern Conference "coach of the year" award. Play was suspended during the war. In 1946, Sanders resuscitated Vanderbilt football and recruited some of the best football players in the country for his 1946, 1947, and 1948 teams. By 1948, when many of the war veterans were seniors, Vanderbilt was ranked twelfth in the nation by the Associated Press poll. Away from football for nearly four years, Dickey had virtually no chance to play on Sanders's top-ranked teams. He could have practiced in the spring of 1947 to improve his chances for the following fall, but he wisely decided to run the hurdles on the track team instead.

His first summer session at Vanderbilt over, Dickey returned to Atlanta for a month's vacation and then headed back to school for the fall term. He signed up for College Algebra (which he failed in the fall but aced in the spring), Elementary Biology, Elementary Spanish, American Government and Politics, Survey of English Literature, and Intermediate Spanish. His professors gave him mainly Bs, although in his English course he received an A. He also signed up for another composition and literature class, Writing 101, with the wife of Monroe Spears, who was helping out with classes overloaded with returning students. Nearly half a century later, Monroe Spears recalled:

> When Betty [his wife] started to grade her first batch of themes from that class—she had assigned "Head by Scopas," by Edward Donaghue, in *Understanding Fiction*—she brought me one she said she was troubled about: it was so much better written and so much more sophisticated than the others that she wondered if it could have been copied. I read it and assured her that there was no reason to suspect plagiarism: there were a few small flaws that would mark it as non-professional, but most importantly, it was a far better essay than anything the student could have found in print. A most extraordinary student, I said, and I'd like to meet him. So Betty introduced us, and Dickey took several of my classes.[27]

Just as the older Fugitive writers had invited undergraduates like Tate and Warren to their soirees, Monroe Spears "adopted" Dickey as a protégé.

Unlike most of Dickey's early mentors, Spears became a lifelong advocate of his work. Dickey reciprocated, never swerving from his contention that Spears was one of the most remarkable intellectuals he had ever met. On April 24, 1981, he wrote a moving tribute addressed "To Posterity":

> Dear Sir—if so I may address all the millions who compose you now and the billions who will compose you—I should like, as one assured of your continuous and deepening attention, to place, for my works in poetry, in the novel, in literary criticism, in advertising, in film-making, in speech writing, in political controversy, in interviews, in private conversations and dreams and reveries, to the entire credit of Monroe K. Spears: to his early influence when he was my first real teacher—and incomparably the best—and to his continuing presence in everything my mind conceives. In the parlance of the football field, it was Monroe Spears who threw the key block for me: who opened up the whole field upon which all kinds of running were possible. I would wish for every writer to have such an angelic blocker ahead of him, but there is only one Monroe.[28]

More than any other professor, Spears convinced Dickey that a literary career was a worthy pursuit: "The fact that a man of this enormous critical acuteness could devote himself to literature instead of engineering, medicine or something sanctioned by the scientific orthodoxy in this country, was inspiring to me."[29] As his commitment to football waned, he chose Spears to "block" for him in his substitute enterprise.

At first Spears did his best to temper his student's romantic excess. Dickey recalled: "Spears got me interested in the eighteenth century, his specialty. He also helped me to be much less apocalyptic, which was probably good at that time, and he introduced into my feverish mind the notions of measure, form, and wit. He had me read an awful lot of eighteenth century works, and I got interested in the idea of writing verse satire and still would like to, except that I don't have the touch."[30] Dickey tried his hand at heroic couplets, Pope's favorite form, but realizing that his strength lay in the visionary mode of Blake and Coleridge, he returned to his more expansive, romantic way of writing. Spears was struck by the difference between the boldness and authority of Dickey's writing and his outward demeanor, which remained—at least in his teacher's presence—unassuming and mild. Was Dickey simply donning the mask of humble apprentice? Spears said: "In class his behavior was impeccable: he was quiet, but willing to talk when called on or when comments were appropriate. He was considerate of other students and never intimidated or embarrassed them by showing off his obviously superior abilities. Our significant discussions took place, however, not in class but at odd times in my office, usually with Dickey standing or leaning in the door. (I always invited him to sit down, but he seemed more comfortable standing, I suppose through diffidence and fear of imposing.) He would, however, sit down when he brought me his poems to read." Spears sympathized with Dickey's attempts to make sense of the "exotic and beautiful Pacific Islands filled with violence, brutality, and sudden death,"[31] but found most of his poetry too obscure.

It was the intellectually precise Spears who encouraged Dickey's already formidable ability to refashion the truth in his writing. Examining some of Dickey's poems, Spears once asked his student why he didn't make his narrative more dramatic. Dickey replied: "Because it didn't happen that way." Spears supposedly retorted: "Well, what difference does that make? It would be so much better if you did it that way." If Dickey was looking for a surrogate father to replace the one he sometimes shrugged off as a lackluster philistine, he found one in Spears. "My parents were very much against lying in any form," he later admitted, but Spears had proven that "lying, with luck sublimely, is what the creative man does." Another of his aesthetic guides was Picasso, an artist he would soon meet in France: "Picasso once said something to the effect that art is a lie which makes us see the truth, or which makes truth better than it is. . . . And this is what the poet wants to do; this should be his sovereign privilege, because the province of a poem is the poet's, and in it he is God."[32] The view that the poet was an unacknowledged legislator comparable to God was an old one. Spears helped liberate Dickey from a dependence on fact in his poems, but Dickey took it upon himself to act as a God-like prevaricator in his day-to-day discourse.

For the war veteran struggling to articulate his views of life, literature, and the general scheme of things, Vanderbilt's philosophy courses proved helpful. Dickey minored in philosophy both as an undergraduate and as a graduate student. One of the first courses he took was Prof. Eugene Bugg's Introduction to Reflective Thinking. Vanderbilt friend Kelsie Harder recalled: "Jim always topped the class, usually obtaining perfect scores, while the rest of us did our usual guessing and stayed within passing range. At the time, I thought of Jim as the most intelligent person I had ever seen. Professor Bugg gave only one A in his rather large classes, and Jim always got it."[33] The future novelist Madison Jones, who took the same class, almost caught up to Dickey on one exam with a 96. Unfortunately, Dickey got a 100.

Respected for his braininess, Dickey was also known for his machismo. By 1949, according to Harder:

> Jim was well known among the English majors . . . as a hotshot combat pilot in the South Pacific, a great football player who transferred from Clemson (he never played at Vanderbilt, and even then I suspected that he was not what he said he was at Clemson, for I was a sports freak and kept up with "great" players), an outstanding student (which he was), a womanizer (it was rumored that he was married; among the stories that circulated among us about him was that he removed the door handle on the passenger side of the car so that the woman could not escape when he made his moves—few of us had cars, but he did have one), and the best poet on the campus, a campus steeped in the Fugitive tradition. . . . John Crowe Ransom, Robert Penn Warren, Cleanth Brooks, and Allen Tate were our gods.[34]

To cultivate his heroic mystique, Dickey kept facts about his life to a minimum and fictions to a maximum.

Another student in the class—the tall, shapely, dark-haired, green-eyed Margarite McEachern—remembered the more sinister side of Dickey's brilliance. An intelligent English major who had also just returned from war service, she dated Madison Jones before Dickey convinced her that he was the more suitable man. In 1968, she wrote Dickey about the nihilism he had once espoused, but congratulated him on having found "the good life" that the sometimes tedious Dr. Bugg had once expounded. Dickey replied a month later that he had found "the good life" twenty years before in her arms: "In other words, you represent for me the sad, intelligent last gasp of adolescence, in this case after a long war. Which is to say that in a sense you were indispensable to me and you remain so wherever you are."[35] Margarite replied from Geneva on February 10, 1969, that she cherished her memories of listening to Rachmaninoff's *Paganini* and talking about Lorca and Rimbaud with Dickey. She had marveled at his ability to quote his favorite passages. Poetry and romance, as for the troubadours, always mingled in Dickey's "last gasp of adolescence"—a gasp he tried to stretch out over a lifetime.

During Dickey's heady years at Vanderbilt, the English majors often met for impromptu discussions at Ireland's, nicknamed "Butch's," a restaurant-bar near the library that was run by an aging Vanderbilt football star and that specialized in Dickey's favorite steak and biscuits. Sometimes Dickey met his friends for literary chats at the university snack bar, or in dorm rooms, or in the library smoking room, where the bolder students also drank whiskey and attempted to have sex with dates before the librarian discovered them. Dickey was forever enlisting friends in his quest for dates. Bill Pratt realized from the start that the unabashed sentiment Dickey strutted before women was partly calculated, partly sincere. Most girls found his initial charm irresistible, but then grew dismayed by his aggressive demands for sex. As in high school, his behavior assured a high turnover rate. Nevertheless, he never seemed at a loss for girlfriends, quickly replacing one with another. He dated business majors and English majors, girls who worked in the city, and girls who attended the local finishing school. Some of his dates, like Anne Locke, inspired him to write poems. Others, like Louise Brown, a dentist's receptionist, motivated him to take notes for future short stories. One, who worked for American Airlines at the Nashville airport, became his wife.

The woman who elicited his most intense romantic and poetic efforts during his first year at Vanderbilt was Anne Locke, a graduate student in English from East Tennessee. Quiet, with long blonde hair, she enjoyed reading and talking about books and worked in the library. She had majored in English and minored in philosophy at the University of Tennessee, and now pursued the same courses for a master's at Vanderbilt. One early December afternoon in 1946, while studying at a long table on the second floor of the library, she looked up to see a tall, handsome student with blond hair brushed high on his head. He sat down beside her, studied fitfully for a few minutes, and then, after some preliminary remarks, proposed leaving the library. Soon both were walking across the street to the drugstore for a seventy-nine-cent dinner. Among the plain, cafeteria-style tables and slot machines, they had such a good talk that they agreed to meet in the library the following day. For the next five months they studied and ate dinner together every day. On Saturday nights they usually broke from their scholarly routine to watch a movie or go to a dance in downtown Nashville. Sometimes they splurged by dining at the Hermitage Suite Hotel or other fancy restaurants.

Locke enjoyed Dickey's mischievousness. He acted crudely at times, picking up his dinner meat with his fingers to make a point, but she took it in stride. She was particularly impressed by Dickey's devotion to his courses and by his ability to recall so much of what he had read. He seemed aloof in an endearing way. When it came to sex, Locke abided by the traditional Southern restraints, and Dickey respected them just as he had done with Gwen Leege. With Locke he played the Southern gentleman rather than the bawdy cavalier. He loved to give her gifts: first a bracelet that she kept her whole life, then poems he wrote to her every month. The poetry books by Frederic Prokosch, Robinson Jeffers, George Barker, and James Joyce that he gave her reflected his own interests at the time. He also enthralled her—as he did everyone else—with his war stories. Since he was often clad in his flight jacket, she had no reason to doubt him when he said he had been a decorated combat pilot whose tail gunner had died when their plane was shot down in the China Sea. To make his sad tale more plausible, he gave her a picture of himself standing with other night fighters by a P-61 Black Widow.

Even if Dickey and Locke had wanted to make their liaison more erotically satisfying, they had little opportunity to do so. In Kissam Hall such trysts were forbidden (the penalty for breaking the rules was expulsion), and Locke rented a room from landlords who upheld the university policies. For five months Dickey insisted on nothing more than literary conversation, a long walk home, and an innocent kiss at the door. One afternoon early in 1947, however, he decided he wanted to consummate his relationship. He chased her around her room so fervently that he ended up breaking a coffee table and then had to make a quick escape when a landlord returned. Angry about being rebuffed, Dickey decided to end his platonic affair. While visiting some friends with Locke on a Sunday in April, he suddenly announced that he wanted to leave. As they walked home, he told Locke that they were not intended for each other and should stop dating. Crushed, she walked to her apartment and wept.

A few years after the breakup, Locke returned to her room one day to find Dickey gathering up the books he had once given her as presents. Both laughed about the contretemps, and in the end Locke persuaded him to leave some of the books as keepsakes. Among the books were six poems he had composed for her in longhand—one for each month they were together and a final one to signal his leave-taking. The first, "Poem for Anne in the Twelfth Month," is indicative of Dickey's romantic ardor:

> The adorned peacock phrases, words
> Of snow and star no longer my possession,
> Nor rifling Time's aisles for a dusty charter
> Or words or water crystals flashing like swords
> Falling from the clouds my lips
> Commemorate my love your beauty
> Nor blaze the glass-and-iron forest with your name.
>
> No. Our place arises between blood-pulses
> Where the dove and skeleton intertwined
> Grow from the clock's face and lock the hands at Love—
> Or when a glance plunges myrtle through my veins
> And your hand curls summer in a grip of azure
> Or through your pillowed hair I watch
> The sun bleed grace upon the windless sea.[36]

The diction, which paradoxically expresses an impatience with florid "peacock phrases" and a desire for sensual contact, is reminiscent of the ornate obscurities of Dylan Thomas, Allen Tate, and Hart Crane.

Most of the other poems Dickey wrote for Locke were similarly gorgeous and opaque. How much they communicated to his girlfriend about his love is questionable. He seemed more preoccupied with his laborious poetry, his experiences in the war, and his invention of masks than with her. In another poem set at Sea Island off the Georgia coast, which he slipped into Prokosch's *Chosen Poems* as a gift for Locke, he began inauspiciously:

> Although there are no formulae, strict as March,
> the spliced quadratic or passionately unalterable
> square-root, to augur the error of the human
> equation, here the wind and water shiver
> their voluble thunder against the basalt cliffs,
> the worn seagull whirls in his vacuum of simple
> conceit, sustained by food rather than freedom.[37]

In stanzas that echo Lowell's "Quaker Graveyard in Nantucket" (a poem that had appeared about two years before in the *Partisan Review)* and Allen Tate's "Ode to the Confederate Dead," Dickey ponders his own war experiences. He mentions poets of World War I and World War II (Alun Lewis, Edward Thomas,

Sidney Keyes), and tries to lift himself from his nihilistic mood with a flourish of moral righteousness:

O nations, humans, O immaculate dead
newly living, for Christ's pity arise from desert,
converse in tolerance, walk in humility,
Honor the simple, the ungreat.
In years to come, turn the blind masquer from your door.[38]

In his relationship with Locke, he had shown both his Christian virtues and self-aggrandizing masks.

The last poem Dickey wrote for Locke in April 1947 reveals some of the impulses behind his contradictions. Three times in the four stanzas of his "Baroque Poem" he uses a refrain to express feelings of unreality, of having no identifiable self. Confined to his room and listening to "the young / Who cough their stories" outside, he says: "I, no more real than my enclosure / Devise my eye to irrigate my love / For where the slates slew down my roof / The sky tilts back its shingle with no sign."[39] Much of the poem traces the dismantling of a self in a cosmos emptied of traditional signs of deity. In the godless void, Dickey suggests, he has the license to play God, to devise stories about himself, to deliberately make his girlfriend cry with pain or love. Not entirely aware of Dickey's machinations, the real Locke remembered her college boyfriend with bittersweet fondness. With her he let down his guard partway, dispelling some of the aura of the "mystery man" or "lone wolf" that others noticed. Nevertheless, she was glad her association with Dickey never evolved beyond dating.

During the spring of 1947, Dickey cast aside his literary masks to run hurdles on the track team. At the time, the team resembled one of the "amateur" club sports that Donald Davidson supported (Davidson proposed abolishing all intercollegiate athletics at Vanderbilt). No scholarships were given to track athletes. The team was a hodgepodge of regular track members and football players. In his forty-first year at Vanderbilt, Coach Bill Anderson would call up football players like Bill Fuqua and John North before important meets, have them compete, and then let them return to spring football practice. The aging coach issued his first call for track candidates in early February 1947. Dickey was among the thirty-four to respond. Due to bad weather, the team had only two weeks of practice at Dudley Field before their first meet. Despite the fact that no lettermen returned, the 1947 team performed surprisingly well. Although the "thinclads," as they were called, failed to place in the Florida relays in Gainesville on March 29, they beat Tennessee Tech, Southwestern, and Kentucky (hampered by injuries, they lost to the University of Mississippi). Dickey's performances were on a par with the team's record. He sometimes won the high hurdles, but not consistently. He did well at the prestigious Cotton Carnival meet at the end of the season in Memphis. A teammate who traveled to Memphis, "Flicky" Ford, remembered Dickey running the hurdles in 15.1 seconds. Near the end of his life, Dickey tried to set the record straight: "My best was at the Cotton Carnival at Memphis, where I won, though not in the best time."[40] He had the potential to do better, but, as he explained: "My heart really wasn't into sports anymore. I just did it because I wanted to get out and get some exercise."[41]

Impressed by Dickey's graceful form, Coach Anderson constantly complained about his lack of speed. For his part, Dickey resented the coach's insistence on quarter-mile time trials every afternoon. Despite their differences, Dickey and the coach remained friends. Anderson had an eccentric habit of toting an umbrella wherever he went, and on road trips he bestowed it on a team member as an honor. At the start of their first road trip in 1947, he honored Dickey with the token umbrella. On these trips Dickey entertained his teammates by telling funny stories and jokes, by playing the piano with more verve than skill, and by singing. Dickey remembered his track friends Charlie Hoover, Tony Corcoran, Lee Nally, Bill Fuqua, and "Flicky" Ford with special affection, but always alleged that his best friend was John North, the captain of the team, who was also a superb football player. He claimed to go out drinking with North on road trips while others slept in the hotel. On one such excursion in Montgomery, Alabama, Dickey and North supposedly stumbled on some attractive women they wanted to seduce. According to Dickey, "I said, 'Listen John, you're married. What are you doing talking about that?' He said, 'Yeah, I sure am married, but I ain't dead.' "[42] In Dickey's imagination, North joined Donald Armstrong, James Huff, and Ed Van Valkenberg as the sort of swashbuckling hero he wanted to emulate. In fact, North remembered almost nothing about Dickey and maintained that they never spoke about their war service (Dickey said North had been a marine). North's post-Vanderbilt career in football may have galvanized Dickey's fantasies of intimacy. After excelling under Red Sanders, North was drafted by the Baltimore Colts; later coached college football at Tennessee Tech, the University of Kentucky, and LSU; and in 1965, began coaching a series of NFL teams (the Detroit Lions, the New Orleans Saints, the Atlanta Falcons). This was the sort of person whose friendship Dickey valued.

At the beginning of the 1948 track season, Coach Anderson again delivered his dire prophesy to the college newspaper, the *Vanderbilt Hustler*. If he couldn't get better athletes (he often recruited from the local Boy Scout troops), he predicted that the season would be a complete failure. Neither Dickey nor Anderson felt especially proud of their 1948 record. The team won its meets with Tennessee Tech, where Dickey came in first in the high hurdles, and Western Kentucky, but lost to Ole Miss and the University of Kentucky. At the Tennessee Intercollegiate Athletic Conference Championship in Sewanee, the "thinclads" placed second.

All Dickey needed to magnify his track record (he abandoned the team after the 1948 season) was a little distance from it. In 1958, he wrote James Wright: "I finished college on a track scholarship . . . and in 1947 set a high hurdles record for the South in the Cotton Carnival Meet at Memphis. I think the record is still standing, though I am not sure."[43] To most interviewers he confined his hurdling record to Tennessee. To the unsuspicious, he also contended that he had met famous writers on his road trips. He told a bookseller in Oxford, Mississippi, Richard Howorth, that he met his town's most distinguished writer, William Faulkner, after being beaten in the high hurdles by someone named

"Hairline" Harper at Ole Miss in 1947: "A distinguished gentleman was in the stands and mentioned, as I climbed up the boards to watch the rest of the meet in dejection, that 'you made a good try, son.' It was Mr. Faulkner. I remember that William Faulkner was the last person to address me as son."[44] Dickey regaled others with stories of meeting Faulkner, although in these he usually played the insubordinate upstart rebuking the master for his writerly flaws. On later trips to Mississippi when he socialized with Faulkner's niece, Mrs. Dean Wells, Dickey had the wisdom to keep quiet about his make-believe encounters.

During the 1947–48 academic year, Dickey tested his mettle in the classroom as well as on the track. He took numerous literature courses—American Literature, Nineteenth-Century Literature, Shakespeare, British Novel—as well as courses in General Astronomy, United States History, Introduction to Art, Materials of Music, Classical Drama, Social Philosophy, and Logic. In the Art, Drama, and Shakespeare classes he earned As and Bs. He received comparable grades in his other classes, except in Logic, where he only managed a gentlemanly C. By emphasizing electives, Vanderbilt encouraged its students to explore many different disciplines to improve their general knowledge. Having been introduced to astronomy in flight school for the purpose of aerial navigation, Dickey reacquainted himself with the subject at Vanderbilt, garnering As in all three of his courses. He spent time at the observatory, which had been built in 1875 and run by Edward E. Barnard, a man famous for discovering numerous comets. By the 1940s, the torch had been passed to Carl Seyfert. As a department of one, Seyfert directed the observatory, taught all the astronomy courses, and imparted a love of stargazing to Dickey. "Through him I got a feeling of intimacy with the cosmos," Dickey recalled. In high school, his curiosity about extraterrestrial realms had been spurred primarily by science fiction pulp novels. Later, as his poems and novels attest, he gravitated toward idiosyncratic rituals (like obsessively determining the latitude and longitude of his South Carolina home with a sextant) to rejuvenate his youthful awe of the heavens. With Seyfert, who was fond of quoting Edwin Arlington Robinson's line "The world is a hell of a place, but the universe is a fine thing,"[45] Dickey sought refuge in the marvels of space. His claim that he took every astronomy course at Vanderbilt was another example of his powers of exaggeration, but it also signaled the high regard he had for the subject and for Seyfert.

In his poems, which began appearing in the 1947 *Gadfly*, Dickey examined the mundane rituals that parodied the sort of inspiring rituals he associated with stargazing. His first, "Christmas Shopping, 1947," juxtaposed the crass commercialism of the holiday period, which he had learned from the Vanderbilt Agrarians to despise, with the biblical significance of Christ and the romantic consolations of nature. If a star once guided the Magi through a desert to find God, now shoppers made a mockery of the sacred event in their journeys to the supermarket:

Wingless, wayworn, aging beneath a perpetual
folded sun, despair unsounded in the eye's drum,
these wheel in lax processional

past the cold counter and listless stall;
desire in rayon, in cellophane the dream.
Outside, the day, the frozen intercourse of streets;
glass placid, grave glitter of guilt and gift
bear single witness to the bartered birth. . . .

Because nature provided an escape from such tawdriness, Dickey ended with images "of chestnut waters / linked back with autumn floating leaves, / the flow of stallions over cloud-white hills."[46] His Christian rhetoric and tangled syntax once again betrayed the influence of Allen Tate and Hart Crane.

In later years Dickey was one of the harshest critics of his early poems. He once said: "If I was handed that stuff in class today I'd say to the student, 'You have no chance, no chance as a poet at all.' "[47] In 1978, he reflected more philosophically: "These are the poems of a returned veteran, one who has been through the Inferno and the Purgatorio but not the Paradiso—there was none—of the Second World War. They are the writings of a veteran desperately behind the position he should have been in: behind because of the war and the convulsions of history. But in the South Pacific he had caught intimations of a new kind of life, different from the college football field from which he had come, and from suburbia. Words had happened, although clumsily, to the returned veteran, wandering about the campus of Vanderbilt in a filthy flight jacket."[48] Only gradually would he redeem the inferno and purgatory of his war experience and create a poetic *paradiso*.

Dickey may have wandered around campus worrying about his clumsy attempts to be a writer, but in class he didn't strike his friends as clumsy at all. To Bill White, a fellow undergraduate and later a fellow graduate student, Dickey's intellect soared above the rest. He was especially loquacious in Dr. Curry's English 450 class—a prerequisite for all English majors. Since his Fugitive days, Curry had become a leading medievalist, whose book *Chaucer and the Mediaeval Sciences* was hailed as a towering work of historical scholarship. He had also become the chairman of the English Department in the 1940s and 1950s. Curry selected the top four students from his class of forty or fifty to give special presentations. Quoting Italian from the original text, Dickey delivered a lecture on Dante's *Divine Comedy* that astonished the class.

Because the war had slowed his education, Dickey kept enrolling in summer school so he could graduate as soon as possible. In 1948, he took courses in Modern Poetry and Fiction, Twentieth-Century American History, and Southern Literature, receiving all As and Bs. During his senior year, 1948–49, he did even better. In History of Philosophy, Modern Drama and Theatre, Modern and Contemporary Art, Renaissance Art, General Astronomy, General Anthropology, Cultural Anthropology, and the Comprehensive Course in English Literature, he got nothing but As. As a senior, he paid particular attention to the anthropology courses taught by Professors Charles Brown and Emilio Willems. For Willems, Dickey wrote a long paper on the primitive rituals of the Murngrin tribe that lived in an isolated region of Australia. Anthropology, like astronomy, convinced Dickey that primitive, intuitive, and mythical ways of engaging with the world had as much or more merit than the "lax processionals" of contemporary "Christian" society. Dickey once remarked of his Cultural Anthropology course:

> That was a good course, but mainly what I remember from it is what I read myself. When I was a junior, I was given a stack permit [in the library] . . . I remember I read through a whole row of anthropology books. I read Malinowski, Radin, Robert Lowie, Clark Wissler on the American Indians, Franz Boas, W. H. R. Rivers, Freud. I read everything that was on that row. Radcliffe-Brown. I read the Cambridge anthropologists, the mythologists. I read Cornford. I read Jane Harrison. *Themis* was wonderful! Fascinating! I didn't have to read systematically, but I read because I thought that this would give me some kind of long-standing basis for the mythological interpretation of things.[49]

From Malinowski, Radcliffe-Brown, and Rivers, he learned about the mythologizing of "totem" animals, which he appropriated later in his poetry and fiction. He also read Jung on the collective unconscious, James Frazer's *The Golden Bough*, Stanley Edgar Hyman's *The Tangled Bank*, and Joseph Campbell's *The Hero with a Thousand Faces*. Like other poets from T. S. Eliot to Robert Bly, Dickey learned from the psychologists, anthropologists, and mythologists that his own psyche contained a reservoir of timeless compulsions and conceptions. By tapping what was archetypal in himself, he could connect with others by raising his experience to the universal level of myth. He also studied primitive rituals (and the myths based on them) designed to deliver individuals or groups from infertility into more fertile lives. Their influence can be traced in almost all of his books.

From his History of Philosophy class he also gained a deep respect for "the mythological interpretation of things." His notebooks teem with notes on the polytheistic views of early Greek philosophers. In one class he wrote of early Greek culture: "Little distinction [was made] between animate & inanimate objects. Man was at home in the world of nature—much of Christian thought is opposite this."[50] In his subsequent writings, Dickey, who wanted to be similarly at home in the natural universe, usually opposed Christian divisions with Greek unities. He also studied orphic mystery cults and learned that for the ancients all nature was instilled with "anima" or spirit, and that a sympathetic unity existed between human spirits and natural ones, as Orpheus proved with his lyre. These animistic perspectives guided much of Dickey's future nature writing. Having studied pre-Socratic theories about the elemental composition of the cosmos, Dickey showed his bias against modern science by repeatedly depicting the world in his poetry and prose as if it were composed of 4 elements—earth, air, water, fire—rather than the usual 103. His class notes also evince an early interest in Heraclitus's theory of creative contraries, a theme that runs throughout his work.

Science merged with mysticism in these early Greek philosophers in a way that suited Dickey's poetic outlook. He took notes on Anaxagoras's belief that a spiritual mind or "nous" set the elements in motion, and found in Plato and Aristotle corroboration for the orphic belief that a soul or "anima" inspired all things. The titles of Dickey's later collections of poems—*The Early Motion, The Middle Motion, The Whole Motion*—as well as his many poems about animals bear the impress of these early philosophies. If God and spirit were prime movers, Dickey celebrated their animated "motions" with his own poetic ones. His respect for pagan metaphysics was matched by his respect for pagan ethics. From a lecture on Aristippus, Dickey gleaned an endorsement of hedonism. "Pleasure is the natural sought-after state of man," he wrote in his notebook. "Moral good is in pleasure of moment—immediacy & intensity are only criteria of good."[51] In his ongoing argument with the Christian morality inherited from his parents, the epicurean Greeks gave him plenty of ammunition.

Dickey's philosophy notebook reveals a mind fascinated by its subjects. In neat, well-ordered pages, he sketched a detailed outline of Western thought—from the Greek philosophers like Plato and Plotinus, to Augustine, Philo Judeas, Aquinas, Duns Scotus, William of Occam, Bacon, Bruno, Hobbes, Descartes, Spinoza, Leibnitz, Locke, Berkeley, Hume, and Kant. As for Coleridge and other Romantics enchanted by the imagination's power and those experiences that periodically overwhelmed it, Kant held particular importance for Dickey. Of Kant's treatise on aesthetics, *The Critique of Judgment*, Dickey wrote significantly: "Beauty distinguished from sublime is feeling of peace, harmony in consequence of the perfect agreement between understanding + imagination—Sublime agitates, disturbs us, transports us—disagreement between understanding + imagination—discord between reason (which conceives infinite) + imagination (whose limits are fixed)—Man has a feeling of grandeur because he himself is grand through reason."[52] For Kant all overwhelming events, from the creation of the universe to the eruption of a volcano, aroused feelings of sublimity when the mind proved its superiority by reducing the events to concepts. Dickey constantly sought out overwhelming experiences in his life and writing to test the powers of his imagination and reason. Because he sometimes appeared ridiculous in doing so, he admitted that he walked the "razor's edge between sublimity and absurdity."[53] Tumbling over the edge, however, never convinced him to abandon his pursuit of the sublime.

Drawn to Kant's transcendentalist views of the mind, especially his belief that—as Dickey wrote in his notebook—"we cannot know thing-in-itself—the phenomenal world is one of our own making," Dickey also gravitated toward the more down-to-earth views of John Dewey and Henri Bergson. "Thinking is biological," Dickey wrote in a notebook section on Dewey. Regarding Bergson's famous approval of intuition, he noted: "Feeling is an organ of knowledge: the agnostic, pragmatist + intuitionist all distrust the ability of the intellect to achieve intellectual truth. . . . Intellectual knowledge is static + dead—Reality is like a flowing stream; thought is frozen portion of reality, like ice in a stream. . . . Intuitive knowledge is immediate + absolute." Throughout his life Dickey remained loyal to Kant's conception of the intellect as a shaper of reality and a conduit of the sublime, as well as Bergson's trust in intuition. Another note states: "The art of living consists in keeping the intuition + the intellect together."[54] His writing depended on the creative clash of both faculties.

Beside these rarefied concepts in his notebook are more worldly notes on politics. Regarding Hegel and fascism: "Political Doctrine of fascism—based on an organic + historical concept of state, which gives state a life over that of citizens: subordinate individual to state—society is end + individual is means." By this definition, the allegations that Dickey was a fascist ring hollow. If anything, he was a staunch individualist who made sacrifices to the state only grudgingly. Much of Dickey's mature thought on politics and on almost every other topic can be found in seminal form in his Vanderbilt philosophy notebooks. Comments like "Adventure is what saves civilization from staleness, boredom, orthodoxy" could have been spoken by Lewis in *Deliverance* or by any of Dickey's other major characters. In a section on Santayana, his summary of the Catholic philosopher's iconoclastic remarks—"We know external world by animal faith. *This world is* the kingdom of heaven"—could serve as an epigraph for Dickey's poem "The Heaven of Animals." A final, underlined note on Bergson's theories of creative evolution—"*To exist is to change, to change is to mature, to mature is* to go on creating oneself endlessly"[55]—encapsulated Dickey's belief, which he followed to a fault, that he should keep creating new personae and evolving stylistically until he died.

In his evolution as a Vanderbilt student, Dickey had decided that becoming a husband was part of the maturing process he desired. In his poem "The War Bride," which he gave to Anne Locke, he suggested that she might make a suitable wife. A year later he directed his attention toward Mary Domingos. A mutual friend had introduced them at the student center during the spring of 1948. Domingos was a business administration major from Texas, and on their first evening together Dickey's formidable intellect and wit charmed her. As with many dates, he infused his book talk with offbeat humor and crude sexual overtures. One moment he seemed to be a scholarly Prince Charming, the next a priapic Don Juan. When Dickey called for a second date, Domingos acquiesced only because she thought she could persuade him to moderate his sexual advances. He drove to her aunt's Nashville house, where she was living, but so offended her aunt that she advised her niece to stay away from him. For the time being, Domingos ignored her. Once again Dickey kept trying to make love to her even though she resisted. After his unsuccessful night, Dickey called for a third date, but Domingos refused to see him. She never met him again, although in 1971 she remembered his aggressive dating tactics when she heard he had pressured Wesleyan College in Georgia, a school Domingos had attended before Vanderbilt, to grant him an honorary degree. In an October 19, 1970, letter to Wesleyan's President Strickland, Dickey had agreed to read at the college for thirty-five hundred dollars and declared that even though he had been offered many honorary degrees, he had turned them all down: "But I *would* like to have the first—and only, for I intend to accept only one—degree conferred to me by a college in my native state."[56] In the end Dickey used similar tactics to obtain degrees from many colleges inside and outside his home state.

Dickey never satisfactorily resolved his quandaries about women and marriage. The homesickness he occasionally felt overseas augmented his desire to have a home of his own, but the idea of domestic responsibilities repelled him. His latent conservatism drew him toward marriage while his wanderlust propelled him in the opposite direction. Dickey's debate came to a sudden, albeit momentary, resolution on November 4, 1948, when, as a twenty-five-year-old undergraduate, he married Maxine Webster Syerson. In retrospect, his decision seemed impulsive, but he must have known intuitively that Maxine was the sort of woman he could depend on and who could tolerate his prodigal ways. Like his mother, she was an attracitve Southern woman—she looked somewhat like Elizabeth Taylor—but she resembled his father in important ways, too. Although he said, "My wife was just a poor country girl from a little bitty town up above Memphis, Union City, Tennessee,"[57] it was Maxine's mother, Maxine Webster, who had grown up in Union City. Maxine had grown up with her mother in Nashville and with an aunt in Birmingham, Alabama. She was gracious, fun-loving, and capable of running the practical business of a household. A working woman, she seemed more mature than many of the college girls Dickey dated, even though she was younger than Dickey by several years. Dickey once confided that he portrayed Maxine as Martha in *Deliverance*, about whom the narrator says: "She was a good wife and a good companion, a little tough, but with a toughness that got things done." Martha's efficiency was evident in her "practical approach to sex,"[58] but also in her ability to keep house while Ed explored the woods of North Georgia. Dickey spoke like Ed when he said of Maxine: "She was just romantic enough. But that was not the whole thing with her. The whole thing with her was efficiency."[59] If she had been more romantic and less efficient, he implied, she would never have survived the marriage as long as she did.

Dickey met his future wife in a fortuitous way. He had been dating his math professor at Vanderbilt—a woman named Smith—and to avoid an unseemly incident Smith introduced him to Maxine. According to Dickey:

> [Smith] lived out near the airport. And she got the idea that it didn't look any too well for her to be hanging around with a student, especially one with a dubious reputation. And she said if I would give up my quest of her favors she would put me onto two very pretty girls at the airport that she knew who worked for the airlines. One of them was witty and a wonderful companion and good company and the other one had a knock-out figure. "So which one do you want to meet first?" I said: "I'll take the one with the figure." And that was Maxine. She was . . . the local Miss American Airlines; and she did have a good figure. She was a little stocky, but she was really very feminine and very womanly and practical. [She] presented sort of a peasant wisdom. . . . She would do anything for the family. As soon as we married she started scheming—in fact, before we married she was scheming—where we were going to live, how much we were going to pull, could we have a car . . . ? And I remember, she would work two weeks and then she would get four days off that we would spend together.[60]

Maxine had already been married and divorced. Dickey recalled that she had married a bellhop who later went into the navy. According to Chris Dickey, a more reliable source, Maxine's first husband was a small-town jeweler. When Dickey met her, she was single, lonely, and living in a modest residential hotel in downtown Nashville with her mother.

Family legend made Maxine's mother out to be a "flapper" who had squandered an auspicious marriage prospect for a disastrous one. An heir to the Jack Daniel's whiskey fortune had supposedly courted her before she met Val Syerson, a Danish immigrant, at Yellowstone Park. Val had first talked to her after she sang "Pistol Packin' Momma Don't You Two-Time Me" to an audience gathered around a campfire. Val got her pregnant, "two-timed" her, and left for another woman several weeks after his daughter was born. On July 26, 1926, Maxine's birth date, Val was living in Clearwater, Florida. Later, when Maxine's mother got a job as a secretary for Tennessee's attorney general, she met a prominent lawyer, Nathaniel Tipton, who was in the same office. They married in the late 1950s and also moved to Clearwater, Florida.

Clad in an attractive blue uniform, Maxine worked as a reservation receptionist selling tickets for American Airlines in a downtown office. Dickey's friends never heard she was "Miss American Airlines," but Calhoun Winton attested: "She was a young woman of great beauty and considerable wit, but not much formal education—nothing beyond a convent high school."[61] Winton had known her slightly when she attended Saint Cecilia School; but because public high school students didn't associate with parochial students, his knowledge of her was meager. Maxine, in fact, was not a Catholic; her mother probably sent her to Saint Cecilia's to keep her out of trouble. Since she had developed few literary interests in convent school, while they were dating Dickey brought her to some of his classes. Several of Dickey's intellectual schoolmates were bewildered by his choice of a bride. What was the Vanderbilt poet who flirted with nihilism and hedonism doing with a woman educated by nuns?

Maxine's good looks, practicality, and friendliness allowed her to fly occasionally for American Airlines as a stewardess, and this was one of the reasons she appealed to Dickey. She supplemented her modest salary by working part-time at a country music station. He declared: "I couldn't have thought of marrying anybody til I met somebody who could bring some money into the family."[62] For the student trying to disguise his affluence and make his own way, it was important to give the impression that he and his wife were financially independent. Another benefit of Maxine's job was American Airlines' policy of offering free flights. A year after they married, the Dickeys flew to Quebec on a honeymoon, compliments of her employer. They stayed in a château and took a pleasant cruise down the Saint Lawrence River past Montreal to Toronto.

Despite their apparent differences, Jim and Maxine shared a number of shared interests. Maxine enjoyed reading books about art and music. Occasionally they played tennis and swam. In the first poem he wrote for her, Dickey depicted her waking up naked beside him in bed, then reimagined her at the beach striding toward him over the waves like the woman in Botticelli's "Birth of Venus":

Body the color of the sands;
Eyes like the sea at morning
A stillness of motion over depth;
You came before me, poem about to be spoken,
Half-revealed, the foam at your ankles,

The drift of the sea-burst about you,
Behind you the sun and ceaseless waver of water.[63]

If Maxine was down-to-earth, in this imitation of Ezra Pound's lyricism she appears with all the luster of a goddess rising out of the Mediterranean.

Along with other classic virtues, Dickey attributed to Maxine a love of bows and arrows: "She was pretty good at archery. In fact, she was the one who got me into archery. . . . She loved to shoot arrows."[64] Since Maxine had been married before and since Dickey pretended to have been married before, they decided to forgo a traditional ceremony. About his wedding he said: "We were married above a feed store in Rossville, Georgia. We weren't even married by the fellow who was supposed to do the wedding ceremony. He was a substitute minister, and we didn't have any witnesses. There's always been a question in my mind about whether we were really married or not."[65] Dickey's new status seemed more certain when Mrs. Valdemar Syerson issued an official announcement of her daughter's nuptials on Thursday, November 4, 1948, from her home at 3511 Wilbur Foster Road, Nashville. The ostensible reason for the feed store ceremony was its convenient location. Dickey claimed that he wanted to formalize his attachment to Maxine on a trip to Atlanta before introducing her to his family, and Rossville, just south of Chattanooga, was on the way. His mother, for whom conventions were important, was nonplussed, but nevertheless approved out of affection for Maxine. Maibelle's comment on meeting her new daughter-in-law was: "Jim, that girl doesn't need any make-up. That girl's just naturally beautiful!"[66] Or so Dickey said.

In the late 1960s, rushing from one love affair to another, Dickey still claimed that "the most fortunate event" of his life had been his marriage. Maxine deserved such a compliment, he said, because she had urged him to pursue his aspirations as a writer:

The first night we were married we went out of Chattanooga down Highway 41 to a dingy little night club to celebrate the nuptials. We didn't know each other very well. We sat there, had a couple of drinks, and started talking about the future. I hadn't given it any thought at all. I was a senior in college. . . . I thought I would try to finish up and then go to graduate school if I could swing it financially. And Maxine said, "Now, I don't want you to pay so much attention to studying all the time. I want you to do your own work." I thought, "Lord, what hath God wrought? That's just what she should have said!" I think my whole career is the direct result of her saying that and taking that attitude about my writing.[67]

Throughout their tumultuous life together Maxine took charge of domestic chores, often acting as her husband's secretary, publicity agent, and business manager. "He has an old-fashioned attitude about women," a friend admitted. "He said to a girl he knew once that he wouldn't want his wife to work. He'd want her working for him."[68] For all his talk of survival and survivalists, Dickey never would have survived without Maxine. He owed much of his literary success to Maxine's unstinting devotion to his career. For Dickey, writing a check, obtaining an airplane ticket, or buying groceries were difficult tasks. Having given up her airlines job, Maxine trained herself to manage her husband's career and did so with admirable efficiency.

Maxine began her duties as housekeeper after she and her husband moved into an off-campus apartment in South Nashville, not far from Belmont Avenue and David Lipscomb College. To make traveling around Nashville and to and from his classes easier, they bought a secondhand car (a "flivver"). Often accompanying the Dickeys on their downtown jaunts were the Wintons. Maxine had become a close friend of Calhoun's wife, Liz, and together the couples visited the Gerst Brewery for Bock beer and the Willow Plunge swimming pool to escape the summer heat. Dickey commemorated these swimming trips in *Alnilam* by giving the name Willow Plunge to Frank Cahill's Atlanta amusement park, which featured a big pool. The Dickeys and Wintons also attended movies together. Maxine was an avid moviegoer, and in the first few months of their marriage Dickey spent more time in theaters than he had in the entire time he had been at Vanderbilt. They regularly went to the foreign film series at Nashville's all-black Fisk College (here they watched *The Heiress*, based on Henry James's *Washington Square*, and *Torment*, an early Ingmar Bergman film, among many others). They also enjoyed more popular films like *King Kong*.

Dickey and his young wife were deeply in love at first. Within a few years, however, Dickey made only halfhearted attempts at keeping his extramarital adventures a secret. "She was very well aware of his propensity to philander and knew there was nothing much she could do about it, but [she] also knew that he wouldn't leave her,"[69] a friend commented. Maxine was not so thick-skinned that her husband's infidelities bounced off her without bruising. "She certainly didn't go on about it that much," Calhoun Winton remembered, but Maxine was "no doubt not happy about it."[70] As the affairs mounted during the years after Vanderbilt, Maxine sometimes threatened to leave her husband, but never did. Daunted by the prospect of returning to the workplace by herself, she increasingly relied on alcohol to anesthetize the wounds of her marriage. A conventional Southerner, she was prepared for a man to leave home for other women—her father had done so—but nothing could entirely eradicate her anguish.

Dickey's career as a Byronic Don Juan was still in its infancy in the late 1940s. He was more concerned with graduating and getting a job. On June 5, 1949, he accomplished the former with a record few would have predicted before the war. He earned magna cum laude honors with an impressive 2.67 grade point average out of a possible 3.0. He was ranked fourteenth in a class of 446. The college newspaper announced on April 29, 1949, that he had been elected to Phi Beta Kappa, an honor he flaunted for years by hanging his Phi Beta Kappa key near his belt. Realizing an additional degree would help him secure a better academic job, four days after his graduation he enrolled as a master's student in English with a minor in philosophy.

One of the incentives for Dickey's abrupt immersion in graduate studies was the worsening international situation. By 1949, most Americans believed that their next foe would probably be Russia. Veterans at Vanderbilt worried that World War III might begin at any moment. The Russians had established the

Berlin Blockade on June 24, 1948, and the massive American and British airlift was still going on when Dickey signed up for the master's program (Stalin ended the blockade on May 12, 1949). After his tour in the Pacific, Dickey had joined the reserves to earn extra money, but he had little desire to fight in another war. By pursuing a higher degree he could avoid military service, at least temporarily. For many veterans, Winton recalled, "Graduate school looked like an attractive alternative [to the military]. . . . The Vanderbilt Graduate School back then was small [there were about twenty master's students in English], but intelligently and humanely administered by Dean Philip Davidson. Course requirements were not onerous, though they included a thesis."[71] Writing a thesis was certainly preferable to being shot at in a plane.

During the first 1949 summer quarter, Dickey took a seminar in Romantic Prose and Poetry given by Claude Finney, and Contemporary Philosophy taught by Eugene Bugg. Both professors bored Dickey, but he earned As in their classes. Over the next year he took courses in nineteenth-century literature, a seminar in American literature, a course on Milton, and a course in aesthetics. Except for Bugg's aesthetics course, in which he studied ideas about sublimity and beauty relevant to his poetry writing, Dickey received all As. From Bugg he could only eke out a B. His favorite professor continued to be Monroe Spears, who taught a seminar on Restoration and eighteenth-century literature. No easy grader, Spears regularly frightened graduate students from his class by announcing that only As and Bs would receive credit. Still relatively new to the Vanderbilt English Department, Spears was a war veteran and Princeton graduate who liked to pose as a dandy by wearing a camel hair topcoat to class, puffing at a cigarette in a long, black holder, and jumping up to gaze out the window as if searching for ideas in the heavens. He dashed around the classroom, leapt toward the blackboard to write down a sudden thought, and stared fixedly at students when they spoke, quizzing them about their remarks with utter seriousness. He kept the students' attention, just as his most famous student would do in similar classrooms and with similar dramatic gestures a few years later. "By the end of the term I would expect you graduate students to be able to distinguish the couplets of John Dryden from those of Alexander Pope, without reference to their content,"[72] he proclaimed in one class. In his own poetry classes, Dickey paid homage to his early professor by making his creative writing students practice traditional forms for an entire semester. As a student, Dickey avidly absorbed the poems favored by his professor. After one of Spears's classes, Calhoun Winton got his first chance to talk to Dickey about his poetic tastes. Suspecting Dickey was masking a keen intellect behind his T-shirt and khaki trousers, Winton nevertheless reacted with surprise when his new friend leaned over and said: "Cal, have you ever thought about physical *decay?*"[73] Dickey proceeded to discuss bone imagery in the poetry of Donne and Dryden with great panache.

Compared to Spears, Richmond Croom Beatty, who taught a year-long seminar in American literature, was one of the gray old men. Approaching retirement, he had spent his whole academic career at Vanderbilt. Dickey had little respect for his tedious lectures on Irving, Poe, Hawthorne, Melville, and Whitman. Beatty assigned readings from an anthology he coedited, and in class allowed little time for discussion. Jane Pepperdine, who went on to a distinguished academic career at Agnes Scott College, was a fellow student who often commiserated with Dickey. Winton reacted to the aging professor similarly: "Beatty impressed a graduate student as a serious, even somber teacher, seated almost immobile at his desk in the front of the classroom, speaking in a cracked tobacco-scarred voice."[74] To add some levity to these solemn occasions, Winton and Dickey traded notes lampooning the idiosyncrasies of their professor, fellow students, and assigned authors. They pursued their literary fun outside class as well, often with a game they called "Who's the Best Poet?" Dickey or Winton would choose a Best Poet, debate their candidate, and try to determine the poet's best and worst lines. Dickey played this game zealously for the rest of his life, sometimes submitting his own name for the top spot.

Dickey's snickering in Beatty's class arose from impatience with his teaching methods rather than disrespect for his scholarship. Eventually he asked Beatty to direct his master's thesis—*Symbol and Image in the Shorter Poems of Herman Melville*. Although he later regretted his choice of supervisor and subject, at the time he diligently applied himself to a New Critical analysis of the poems. Dickey declared in his thesis, "It is a sad fact that Melville never wrote a poem which is good all the way through,"[75] but he nevertheless sympathized with Melville's iconoclastic vision of the world. In his most enduring work, Dickey argued, Melville rejected the Christian concept of a benevolent God and expressed "an overwhelming dread of penetrating the mystery of whiteness, of 'striking through the mask,' lest it prove not mask but essence, not veil but composition: not God, even a malevolent one, but a 'colorless, all color of Atheism.' "[76] In his own writings, Dickey envisioned the universe in similar terms, but concluded that behind the mask was an original mysterious source that was inspiring rather than depressing.

A discussion of Melville's *The Confidence-Man* sheds light on Dickey's own preoccupation with masks and role-playing: "[In the novel] the chief masquer (Melville subtitled the work 'a masquerade') is the confidence man, 'a portmanteau character who wears a variety of masks, shifting from one to the other with his light-fingered dexterity almost before the very eyes of the passengers.' When he first appears he is dressed in 'cream-colored clothing,' and is wearing 'a high white fur hat.' From his attire, symbolic of the 'natural mask' of the world or of an assumed mask behind which one's activities go undetected and where any sort of deviltry may be practiced in perfect freedom (it is notable that there occurs nowhere in Melville's writings an explicit rendering of the cleavage between the two), the confidence man shifts through a dazzling array of disguises and identities."[77] In Melville's writings, Dickey found memorable characters who imitated the protean creativity of God or the devil (Melville—like Blake—did not always distinguish between the two) by manufacturing "a dazzling array of disguises and identities." Dickey aspired to the same godly and devilish inventiveness.

If nothing else, Dickey's year as a graduate student (his thesis was approved by Professors Beatty and Purdy on May 19, 1950) allowed him more time to read and collect books. Behind his many masks was the devout bookworm. One of his sacred haunts was Zibart's, a well-known bookstore that stocked about seven thousand books at 719 Church Street. Here, from the time of the Fugitives, the literary community congregated. The bookstore encouraged students through advertisements in the *Gadfly* to "Come In and Browse." Dickey needed little persuasion. Carl Zibart grew especially fond of his young patron during their chats about contemporary writers. Dickey would visit his store every two or three weeks and leave with a stack of about a dozen books. Because Dickey claimed he was at Vanderbilt on a football scholarship, Zibart later said: "I thought it was very unusual for a football player to show so much interest in books."[78] Zibart was so impressed by Dickey's bibliophilia that he gave him a part-time job over a Christmas holiday. Years later Dickey told Zibart that it was his first job.

At the Dickeys' apartment for beer parties, fellow student Bill White was struck by the lack of furniture and all the books stacked in columns or simply dumped in mounds on the floor. When leaving his chair became a strain during the months before he died, Dickey resorted to the same methods of arranging his books for easy access. Dickey once said: "The little money I had I spent on books usually. I lived a Spartan life in Vanderbilt."[79] To White, Dickey approached books with the same tenacity with which he approached the high hurdles, which was a good thing since he sometimes had to leap over the books on his apartment floor. White witnessed Dickey's athleticism in a more visceral way when they Indian-wrestled, locking right arms and right legs and trying to throw each other. The competitive Dickey usually won. At times Dickey's manic book buying exasperated Maxine. She contended that he could get many of the books at no expense in the library. Careless about money and domestic amenities, Dickey ignored Maxine's creature comforts and kept buying books. Shocked by the way Dickey treated Maxine later in their marriage, White had inklings of Dickey's indifference in the 1940s.

One of Dickey's closest graduate student friends at Vanderbilt, John Hall, also witnessed the divisions in Dickey's marriage and recognized their source—the divisions in Dickey himself. Hall had gotten to know Dickey on the Vanderbilt track team. Both ran the 220 high hurdles, often competing against each other in practice. Their friendship developed when they and their wives decided to rent a house on Cherokee Road. As with the Wintons and Pratts, the Dickeys and Halls regularly partied and watched films at a local drive-in theater. Hall shared his friend's keen interest in literary theories like the New Criticism as well his desire to mock them. On the way home from watching lowbrow films like *Tarzan of the Apes* or *Flash Gordon*, he and Dickey liked to deploy all the New Critical jargon about symbols, ambiguities, and ironies to criticize the films. Dickey would recollect these films and some of the high-spirited camaraderie of these trips in *Deliverance*. For Ed, Lewis is "like Johnny Weissmuller in the old Tarzan movies."[80] Ed and Lewis banter sardonically about establishing a Tarzan-like "kingdom of sensibility" in North Georgia, just as Dickey and Hall bantered about the films. The two Vanderbilt students also resembled the *Deliverance* characters in the way they periodically abandoned their wives in pursuit of adventure. Their wives, according to Hall, became good friends partly to commiserate with each other over their husbands' infidelities. Despite the resulting anguish, Maxine usually remained cheerful, and for the most part the two couples enjoyed each other's company.

For one of their parties, the Halls and Dickeys decided to splurge and make Moscow Mules, a potent drink composed of ginger beer and vodka (and so called because it was poured into copper cups with a kicking mule engraved on the bottom). Acting as bartender for the night, Dickey mixed the proportions in a special sterling silver cocktail shaker. To his surprise, the ginger beer exploded when he shook it. Realizing they had no money to buy more alcohol, they sopped up the spilled drink, cleaned it with a makeshift filter, and drank it as if nothing had happened. For Dickey this episode became symbolic of his early financial hardship, and he recounted it many times, inserting different characters and locales willy-nilly.

Even in the late 1940s, Hall found it hard to separate Dickey's facts from his fictions. On one of their drives through the Tennessee countryside, Dickey pointed to a billboard advertising 666 Tonic and told Hall that his family had made their money from that tonic (Dickey incorporated a similar incident into *Deliverance*). Unaware of his friend's slight distortion, Hall *was* aware that Dickey liked to disguise his love of books by acting like a redneck. Books, Dickey sometimes sneered, were a "load of crap." He vowed never to join the professorial crowd of "harmless drudges." Devoting years to a Ph.D., he averred, only proved you were a "chickenshit grind." "Scholars" should not be "old, learned, respectable bald heads" shuffling and coughing in ink, as in Yeats's poem; they "should have balls."[81] Hall recalled a time when Dickey, feeling more doggedly anti-academic than usual, made fifty dollars by writing a jingle for Lay's potato chips. Having proved his abilities (or at least having claimed he had), when Dickey tired of academia five years later, he again resorted to writing advertising copy, and within a few years was working on the Lay's potato chips account.

Although both men were intellectuals—Hall would go on to get his Ph.D. in English from Vanderbilt in 1957 and, after a Fulbright in Greece, develop an expertise in archaeology and anthropology—they stood firm in their contempt for academic pettiness. Dickey found in Hall a kindred soul and, later in life, expressed his solidarity by appropriating some of Hall's experiences as his own. Hall once told Dickey about taking a high school girlfriend into the middle of a junkyard in his hometown of Helena, Arkansas, and making love to her in a dilapidated car. He explained that this modus operandi helped them evade her stern, disapproving father, who happened to be a farmer. The story so gripped Dickey that he used it in one of his most famous poems, "Cherrylog Road," transforming the farmer's daughter into Doris Holbrook and the Arkansas junkyard into a Georgia junkyard. In his hilarious introductions to the poem he consistently made the narrator's sexual forays his own. Hall once had the dubious privilege of sitting in an audience when Dickey introduced and read the poem under the false pretense that it was autobiographical.

Probably the most important literary friendship Dickey forged during his postgraduate year was with Bill Pratt. Hard at work with Donald Davidson on a master's thesis concerning Faulkner's *The Sound and the Fury*, Pratt was closer to the Fugitive-Agrarian tradition than Dickey, but looked up to his friend as a guide to contemporary poetry. Dickey was glad to oblige. "Besides Donald Davidson," Pratt once remarked, "the person from whom I learned the most at Vanderbilt was not a teacher but another student, James Dickey. Ours was a true literary friendship, the first and most important in my life, and through him I became acquainted with a number of poets and critics I would not have encountered on my own for some time."[82] In addition to discussing literature, Dickey and Pratt traded anecdotes about sports (Pratt excelled at tennis, the sport Dickey hoped to master) and family. With Pratt, Dickey was uncharacteristically open about the tensions in his family. He often talked about his brother, Tom, and about his parents' great pride in Tom's athletic success. Tom, Dickey said, had become a coach at LSU (actually he was only a student), and this made his parents, particularly his father, exceedingly happy. Dickey was proud of his brother, too, but he complained to Pratt that his father favored Tom and disapproved of Dickey's interest in poetry. He was convinced that if he had done better on the football field or on the track, his father would have treated him with more respect.

With Pratt as his audience, Dickey demonstrated his admiration for T. S. Eliot, Robert Lowell, Richard Wilbur, and Randall Jarrell by delivering moving recitations of their poems. He also relished Jarrell's devastatingly incisive reviews, and often read them aloud. The judgmental style for which Dickey became notorious in later reviews was already evident in a paper he wrote on August 14, 1947, for Professor West's English 202 class. Titled "The Fitful Gleam," the paper took a scalpel to the corpse of William Collins's poetry. In a burst of sarcasm, he compared Collins's mind and method of composition to "a trapped monkey who is unwilling to relinquish his hold on a handful of rice in a narrow-necked gourd even at the price of his freedom."[83] With Pratt, Dickey also liked to read from Stephen Spender's autobiographical *World within World,* which recounted how he had met Auden at Oxford in the 1920s and how Auden had treated him as a "mere neophyte who needed to learn that 'Art is born of humiliation.' "[84] For Auden and Spender, this master-servant relationship had homosexual overtones, as did some of Dickey's domineering literary relationships later in his career. As for the current masters, Dickey boasted to Pratt that he would someday outdo Lowell, who had won a Pulitzer Prize in 1946 for *Lord Weary's Castle,* and Wilbur, who in 1947 had published *Beautiful Changes* to high acclaim.

One of Dickey's most memorable celebrations with Pratt came in 1950 when the *Sewanee Review* accepted his poem "The Shark at the Window." Pratt was awed, especially when Dickey triumphantly presented the twenty-five-dollar check he had received from the editor. To celebrate his first major publication, Dickey and Maxine took Pratt and his young wife, Anne, to Zanini's, one of their favorite Italian restaurants in Nashville. After the initial euphoria, Dickey had to wait a year for his poem to appear. In diction reminiscent of his favorite early poets—Hart Crane, Allen Tate, and Dylan Thomas—"The Shark at the Window" explored some of the family tensions he discussed with Pratt. The poem's ostensible subject was his brother's wedding in Anderson, Indiana, and what he called the "very strong family feelings" evoked by the occasion. His fraternal feelings, he slyly admitted, were "mixed up in my mind—and in the poem—with a trip that my brother and I had made to Florida where we stopped by Marineland and stood and stared in fascination at a huge shark through one of those port-holes where you're level with the fish. It was the first shark I'd ever seen that close."[85] In the poem he implied that his brother and the shark were one:

> Brother in the window welcome,
> Welcome brother at the seatrap
> Glass. Near ghost, your lacquered
> Shade drops off and waits—
> Aqueous, breath clouded, seeming.
> Our centers meet.[86]

In the other two sections of the poem Dickey compared the aquarium to his mother's womb and suggested that he and his brother had been born into a frightening, sharklike world.

By the end of the obscure poem, Dickey also implied that he and his brother wanted to return to the "pearled and helical" womb because the shark was actually their "old man." Dickey envisioned his father in the "mouth, the slatted / Gills, the absolute and unknown terror" of the fish. He next imagined his brother returning to the womb (which he now compared to a conch shell) by making love to his wife. He commanded: "In the shell of the bridal / Chamber, in the still sump of midnight, / Know without fear // This with her." Focusing on the sexually suggestive image of the conch in the aquarium, he identified it as a sanctuary to "tremble into":

> It was fear first pressed
> Us through that pearled and helical threshold where
> No adumbrations pass.
>
> Expecting the dark, we found the shapen cupping
> Resplendent with the light we made.[87]

What the convoluted poem implied was that Jim and Tom shared fears of birth, sex, and a sharklike father. It also implied that the two brothers feared they had inherited their father's sharklike ways.

By the time he wrote "Shark at the Window," Dickey knew his future sister-in-law well, but in the poem she appeared, literally, as a shell. He had first met Patsy when she was visiting Tom in Atlanta around 1946. He picked her up, sat her on his lap in a book-lined sunroom, and said: "Let's take a look at this!"[88] Patsy later recalled: "I was blown over backwards by him and would have physically fallen had I not been propped up on his knee like a dummy." Examining his future sister-in-law, Dickey told his brother: "She's bright, Tom. It's good. We need some new blood in the family." From that point on Patsy both feared and adored her brother-in-law. He presented himself as a savage warrior as well as a charismatic intellectual. One of the first stories he told Patsy was of being shot out of the sky by the Japanese on a night mission. As his plane plunged toward the ocean, he threw a dingy out of the plane and parachuted into the water. His pilot was not so lucky; he died in the crash. Finding the dingy, he lay in it until an American submarine came to his rescue. Dickey told his story with such conviction that

Patsy, as well as other family members, believed it. Because of his charm and talent, Patsy worried that she might fall in love with Jim and, as she put it, "cause a breach of the blood."[89] She remained close to Jim even though she knew all too well that he was capable of sharklike rapacity.

Ensconced in an advertising job in the late 1950s, Dickey often pined for his Vanderbilt years as a lost dream world. He began a letter to Pratt in 1959 with a quotation from Joyce's dream epic *Finnegans Wake:* " 'Years dreams return . . .' said Mr. Earwicker, and I return often to those curious dream-like years when we were at Vanderbilt together, with . . . Anne Locke living in that elevated rathole, Davidson softly intoning ballads, and Finney showing us all about the circles (I think it was circles) of Proclus and holding forth on *The Enneads* of Plotinus (which, incidentally, are pretty good)."[90] Dickey's intense concentration on his studies made his four years at Vanderbilt seem even more dreamlike. He once said of college: "[The] main things I remember about Vanderbilt besides the track were the dormitory room and the class rooms."[91] He also remembered most of the books he read.

In one of their conversations about their future careers, Pratt, who was writing poetry at the time, sketched out his plan: "Jim called me a 'pure idealist' because I was determined to stick it out until I could earn a proper teaching position and he was just as determined to make it on his own as a writer."[92] Dickey, however, was open to compromise. One day Professor Curry called him into his office and asked: "Would you like to teach in Texas when you finish your degree?" Apprised of the details, Dickey agreed to go to Rice Institute. Unlike future academics, who usually needed a Ph.D. and scholarly publications before they could even consider entering the job market, Dickey got an offer and took it. His chairman, he said, "just slotted me in there and I went down there and started in at the lowest possible rung of the college teaching ladder."[93] As a freshman English instructor, Dickey quickly realized that in order to climb the academic rungs he would need another degree. Nevertheless, he remained loyal to poetry.

V.

A KING IN THE CLASSROOM

9. Rice Institute (1950)

William Marsh Rice Institute, as it was called in honor of its founder—an eccentric Texas millionaire suspected of being chloroformed to death on Madison Avenue—had established a reputation primarily as a technical college since opening in 1912. At the start, its small campus clung to Houston's South Main Street, but under the post–World War II direction of president William V. Houston, it had expanded rapidly. During Dickey's brief tenure in its English Department in the early 1950s, it remained all-white, tuition-free, and mainly a training facility for engineers and architects. Glad to have a job, Dickey had reservations about leaving Vanderbilt for Houston in the summer of 1950. At Vanderbilt he had stretched his literary wings among friends and mentors; at Rice he would be neither a reputable scholar nor a well-known poet. The paltry salary confirmed his sense of being at the bottom of the heap. He earned "twenty seven twenty," he recalled acrimoniously, "and I don't mean twenty-seven thousand. I mean two thousand, seven hundred and twenty. And nothing in the summertime."[1] Records show that his salary was slightly more substantial—he started at thirty-three hundred dollars—but for someone with Dickey's background and ambitions, the sum was humiliating.

Having found a college apartment at 4811 Mount Vernon, Dickey moved his family south, and in Houston's muggy heat began preparing for fall classes. Unlike most beginning teachers, Dickey felt little trepidation about crossing the threshold to confront his students for the first time. From the start, the classroom was a stage on which he could perform and also learn. "Bernard Shaw was quite right," he once said, thinking of Rice. "If you ever want to learn a subject, teach it. . . . I learned more grammar and syntax from teaching those engineering students. They don't take any easy answers. Boy, I had to know it before I could teach it. I was about two pages ahead of the workbook. Sometimes they were two pages ahead of me. But we got along fine. I loved those kids. They were so hungry for anything literary. . . . They were so responsive. Boy, we drilled on that grammar. . . . I'd sit up there in the office hour after hour working on their papers."[2] The situation was not optimal. The students felt overworked (they took five classes and attended class six days a week), and their professor felt overworked and uninspired by much of the material he had to teach.

Dickey taught English 100—English Composition, Study of Fundamental Literary Forms (a required freshman course); English 200—Outlines of the History of English Literature, which concentrated on major writers from the Middle Ages to the present; and a writing course for science students. No matter what the subject, how ennervating the preparation, or how monotonous the grading—sometimes he had one hundred papers at one time—Dickey enthroned himself in the classroom as if he were its king. A colleague, Edward Lewis, recalled:

"I would see him in a lecture room in the chemistry building sitting on a chair on top of the chemistry demonstration bench and lecturing down to the students whose chairs were only on the floor."[3] The gas jets, looping faucets, and other scientific paraphernalia served as props for his soliloquies on proper grammar and other literary subjects. Dickey followed this regal style of teaching at numerous universities during the 1950s and 1960s.

One student, a math major named Joseph Bloxsom, took English 100 with Dickey his freshman year. Like the eight or nine other students in the class, Bloxsom was enchanted, bewildered, and somewhat frightened by Dickey's style of lecturing. Perched on the lab table, Dickey often gazed out the window—just as Monroe Spears had done at Vanderbilt—and let his imagination fly. His impromptu lectures were full of bizarre and amusing non sequiturs. He regularly talked about himself—about his aversion to making beds in a boarding school where officials punished untidy boys and about his plan to get a job in advertising so that he could retire early and write. At times he gave his informal lectures in the Rice swimming pool, and only allowed women to attend. Like so many of his audiences, the Rice students didn't know what to believe.

According to another student, Pat Moore, Dickey also addressed his classes with his feet on the floor. The first time she met him, he seemed utterly conventional in his saddle oxfords, argyle socks, khaki pants, blazer, and tie. After he returned her first paper, however, she began to realize that he was not a typical, genteel, 1950s English professor. "Come see me in my office this afternoon, Miss Moore," he told her. When she approached his office, which was in the library behind a glass-windowed door, he told her to come in and shut the door. "You're a damned good writer, you know, but, goddamn, have you read some bad stuff. Did you bring your theme?" he said. As she looked through her papers, he mused: "You have a beautiful mouth, Miss Moore. Anybody ever told you that? It's probably the most beautiful mouth I've ever seen." Moore took her professor's comments as innocent flattery, and continued to meet him every week to discuss her themes. Playing the role of Pygmalion to her Galatea, he advised her to read certain books, write in certain ways, and date certain boys. He sometimes lamented meeting her in his Fondren Library office; he would rather be discussing sex and books over martinis in a darkened lounge. "That's one of the things wrong with marriage," he complained. "Don't get married too young, Miss Moore. If I take Maxine to a lounge, we sit and talk about the insurance that's coming due or dental bills. I want to hold somebody's hand and talk about literature and writing." Then, without warning, Dickey asked: "Have you ever thought it would be interesting to have sex while your hands were tied? Or maybe chained against a wall?"[4] Moore took his question as an expression of boyish mischievousness, which it partly was, although she must have had second thoughts when he read from the novel he was writing—*The Entrance to the Honeycomb*—which had numerous sadoerotic scenes.

At Rice, Dickey yearned for a job more conducive to his literary and financial needs. He even pined for the military, alleging he had more free time and more money as a radar operator than as an English professor. To earn a few extra dollars, he published book reviews in the *Houston Post*. He earned some pocket money when the distinguished journal *Poetry* began publishing some of his poems. His first appearance in a book came when *Soundings: Writings from the Rice Institute* published his poem "Utterance I" in 1953. Dismissive of the scholarship that furthered academic careers, Dickey in general kept to himself and worked on his poetry, fiction, and journals. Once asked about his Rice colleagues, he responded tersely: "I didn't have any." He was not, however, wholly bereft. He sometimes met Edward Lewis at track meets to watch the hurdlers (Dickey liked to pull up his trousers and show Lewis his hurdling scars from North Fulton and Vanderbilt). He attended football games at Kyle Field with another professor, Ed Phillips, who later involved Dickey in a faculty performance of Gilbert and Sullivan's *Trial by Jury*. Dickey told Phillips about being a successful Clemson halfback and Black Widow pilot. He told the same stories to Pat Moore, who believed he had to leave Rice early to fly bombing missions over Korea. Dickey also associated with James Young, a new professor deeply committed to poetry and active in a local acting group, The Players. Like Dickey, he came from a university with a prominent literary reputation. At Stanford, Young had studied with one of the most eminent poets and critics of the time, Yvor Winters. Dickey listened intently to Young's stories about Winters's curmudgeonly relations with Hart Crane, Allen Tate, and other distinguished writers. Dickey was also intrigued by what he believed to be Young's bisexuality. Years later he made a point of saying: "He was a married homosexual. His wife . . . was actually quite comfortable with that. She loved him very much, but she understood and they had a child together and all that. He was queer, but very bright and an intelligent guy and a nice person."[5] At Rice, Young became Dickey's favorite colleague.

Despite his heavy course load, Dickey made progress with his poetry. He took some pride in being asked to give his first formal poetry reading in Houston, although the circumstances were hardly propitious:

> I was sponsored by a ladies' church group and I gave the reading in the parish room or one of the Sunday School rooms in the bottom of the Baptist church. It was in our neighborhood in Houston, and the lady introduced me. They'd never had any speakers before in this group, except religious speakers, people with messages, good words and uplifting speeches, homilies, that sort of thing. So at that time I was on a kind of death and disease kick and was writing about nothing but cancer. . . . And then I read other poems about people dying of leukemia. It was the most gruesome kind of depressing subject matter you could imagine. So I finished. There were about four or five, maybe ten people in the audience of ladies obligated to come, including my wife with a couple friends of hers. And when I finished there was a polite spattering of applause, very light indeed and short, believe me, and the lady that had introduced me got up and said, rather uncertainly, after I had given all this death and destruction, disease, "Ladies, I'm sure we all want to thank Mr. Dickey for that nice message."[6]

Already a lord of misrule, in five years Dickey would shock another group of elderly ladies in Florida, but with severer consequences.

To preserve his scattered literary thoughts at Rice, Dickey began writing in four bound ledgers. He said: "I went out on the grassy part of campus and opened a brand new notebooklike ledger because I once heard Thomas Wolfe wrote in those. I had bought one figuring what worked for him might work for me."[7] He filled his ledgers with notes on myths, especially those involving kings and regicide; decadence and renaissance; war, exile, and repatriation. He analyzed dreams, fantasies, and fairy tales as expressions of the unconscious. (In one notebook he said he wanted to unite fact and fantasy in short stories "so that the reader may go, with a little effort, *wholly* one way or the other into reality or pure dream.")[8] He commented on the *Kenyon, Sewanee, Partisan,* and *Hudson* reviews; scrutinized books on philosophy, mythology, music, psychology, history, and literary criticism; sketched out "A Folk Singer of the Thirties" and "Approaching Prayer," which a decade later appeared in book form; and roughed out scenes for *The Entrance to the Honeycomb* and many other projects.

Dickey offered a glimpse of the tensions he felt at Rice in a journal entry: "I wonder if the discipline of writing can hold me together. . . . I feel constantly that I am at the edge of hysteria." What held him together, he explained, was his dedication to "fantasy, daydream, re-creation of the world deliberately and/or compulsively on '[my] terms.' "[9] Dickey coped with his demanding students and judgmental colleagues by adopting personae and playing roles. He admitted: "I find that when I cut myself from the outside world and concentrate on literary matters . . . I am a great deal more satisfied with myself than at other times. At these other times, talking to people, walking the streets of a city when I could be working, I tend to assume a Byronic attitude toward myself and others which is more a defense mechanism than anything else."[10] His playacting helped him survive.

The poems Dickey wrote at Rice, like those he wrote at Vanderbilt, sounded like a medley of Crane, Lowell, Ransom, and Tate. "For a Ballet" typified the formalism that he struggled to master:

> The Knight danced onto the captive stage
> Hung round with chains and rosemary,
> Circled the lights of the Spider's House,
> Clanked and called his Lady.
>
> Her strains of gauze snared thick his heart,
> His gold greaves fixed in their raptures;
> The drinking light from underneath
> Devilled her claiming features.

Ransom could have written this unflattering portrait of a spidery, cannibalistic lady ensnaring her aristocratic lover. In a similar effort, "The Crusader's Dream," Dickey again strives for archaic effects:

> I flashed my blade, I crowed with ire,
> The Samite Warrior slew;
> I sank to the sand with a giddy phrase
> And rose with the ringing dew.

The Snake slid glistening round the Tree
Where the Hanging Man was slain;
I wiped my blade on golden . . . weeds . . .
And slew my brother Cain.[11]

The images of flashing blades, soldiers, and snakes find more credible settings in Dickey's later work. Here they appear as allegorical figures borrowed from Robert Lowell's *Land of Unlikeness* poems.

Dickey's notebook poems have little to recommend them, yet they gave him enough confidence to decry similar defects in other formalist poets writing at the time. With only two poems published in national journals by 1952, Dickey began to blaze his own trail and, as he did so, push aside other poets who were ahead of him. "Surely I can write the couplet with more success than Lowell,"[12] Dickey declared. About another rival, Richard Wilbur, he said: "[He is] not a very good poet. He is skillful; he is gracious, graceful, charming. He means well. 'But where's the bloody horse?' All his poems are metaphoric 'examples.' In essence very mechanical." With more venom he deplored the decorative triviality of James Merrill and Anthony Hecht. John Berryman's poetry stood above the fray, but Dickey complained: "It [too] is full of tricks, 'craft,' and purely mechanical effects. He literally has nothing to work with but 'the art of poetry.'" After reading Randall Jarrell's *The Seven-League Crutches,* he dispatched another volley: "It is like nothing so much as listening to a garrulous, self-pitying, thoroughly untalented . . . old woman tell the same tiresome, sentimental story of her tiresome, sentimental life over and over."[13] Having learned how to wield his critical weapons from Jarrell, Dickey turned them against him.

During the 1950s, Dickey tried hard to perfect what he called the well-engineered, "rational" poem, but what he really admired was the "immediate" poem full of spontaneous associations and visionary flights. Because his allegiances were divided, he decided to sign some of his more "unconventional" poems with a pseudonym, "Virgil Shawker" (no doubt to rhyme with "shocker"), and to sign his formal poems with his own name. He listed the models for the "Shawker" poems as "[St.-John] Perse, [Dylan] Thomas, W. S. Graham, Herbert Read, Hart Crane," and the models for the formal poems as "[Robert] Lowell, [Paul] Valéry, [Robert] Bridges, the metaphysicals, W. S. Merwin."[14] To explain his goals, he used a fable of a beast and a net. In his more formal poems he would net the beast; in his other poems he would let the beast run free.

10. The Korean Distraction (1951–1952)

Dickey soon found himself struggling in a net of a different sort. A little over a month after he finished his master's degree at Vanderbilt, seventy thousand troops from North Korea swarmed into South Korea, breaching the thirty-eighth parallel that partitioned the country into a Russian-dominated north and an American-dominated south. Dickey's old commander, Gen. MacArthur, took charge of the United Nations forces mustering for war. On September 15, marines landed at Inchon, recaptured Seoul, and began the northward offensive. In two months, two hundred thousand Chinese troops took up positions to block MacArthur's advance. As a result, MacArthur wanted to invade China, even if it meant risking another world war. Other United Nations countries like England preferred a more limited strategy, especially now that Russia had atomic weapons and an alliance with China. France had already committed half its army to put down the Viet Minh revolt in Indochina. Because of MacArthur's stubborn brinkmanship, in mid-April 1951, President Truman relieved him of his command. America, however, remained committed to Korea, and once again Dickey found himself preparing for war.

Dickey liked to tell audiences after the Korean Conflict that he had resumed his distinguished career as a bomber pilot. In 1971, he reported to his boyhood friend James Coleman, who was working as a lawyer in Texas: "I was stationed in Waco after I came back from Korea for a few months."[1] Around the same time he informed his University of South Carolina student Jim Mann that he had dropped napalm over Korea. To his close friend Willie Morris, who had asked for information about piloting planes for a novel he was writing, Dickey responded on January 10, 1972:

> In answer to your question about fighter missions in Korea . . . my MOS [military occupational specialty] was that of an instrument man, and I never saw the light of day outside the cockpit. We were what was originally called night fighters, but in Korea was called all-weather fighters. The general intention of a night-fighter group is that it "scrambles" and is vectored in by radar on the enemy bent on doing our position damage. All this worked out fine in World War II. But in Korea the enemy had nothing up at night, and we mainly spent our time banging up and down those ridges doing what is called "night ground support." It was really not much of a war for the kind of thing we did. Most of the fellows with me were re-tread, like myself, and were just concerned with preserving their lives, putting in their time, and waiting out their orders to go home when the time came for them to be rotated.[2]

Dickey's facts in this apocryphal tale served his feelings. In 1951, he had little desire to reunite with radar observers and pilots he had known only superficially in the Pacific.

Dickey did, indeed, return to what was now called the air force, but he never went to Korea. He worked as a radar instructor on several military bases in the South. Dickey regarded his recall as a distraction from his literary career, which had already been frustrated by World War II. He had little desire to immerse himself in the technical aspects of radar observation and navigation all over again: "I had hoped never to be in another plane again. It [the Korean War] was a dreadful time for me, as it was for many others. I surely think the air force learned its lesson through us, though. It really must have been a nightmare for the regular air force personnel because none of us retreads had any enthusiasm. Everybody just wanted to put his time in and get the hell out."[3] Dickey had only himself to blame, since he had voluntarily signed up for the active reserves.

While on Okinawa during World War II he had written his father proudly about being recommended for a reserve commission: "That means I will be on active duty two weeks out of the year, will be called first in any national emergency at probably a captain or major. . . . It will not inconvenience me too much, and I think it will be a very good thing."[4]

On January 25, 1951, shortly after Dickey's first term at Rice, Maj. Gen. Thomas assigned Dickey to a twenty-one-month tour of duty, from March 10, 1951, to December 9, 1952. Dickey bided his time until mid-March, when the headquarters of the Fourteenth Air Force at Georgia's Robins Air Force Base (AFB) instructed him to travel to McGuire AFB in Trenton, New Jersey, as a "radar observer on fly status." First, however, he had to report to Maxwell AFB in Montgomery, Alabama, for "reindoctrination." In the letter he wrote Maxine on March 16, he said he relished his new uniforms, but disliked his temporary job in Maxwell's Records Processing Department. Dickey soon found relief from his dull job in friendly chats with the young African-American writer Albert Murray. Murray, who would rise to the rank of major in the air force, had been on leave from the English Department and ROTC program at the Tuskeegee Normal and Industrial Institute, a black college founded in Alabama by Booker T. Washington. Murray recalled meeting Dickey in the Processing Department: "I spoke to him because I was surprised to find an Air Force Lieutenant reading the sort of literary publications I saw on his desk . . . Kenyon, Paris Review, Southern Review, stuff like Ransom, Blackmur, Eliot, Pound, . . . Randall Jarrell. . . . He in turn was also surprised and pleased to find another Air Force officer type who not only had literary interests but was also in personal contact with some of the New York people."[5] The two writers began a literary friendship that remained cordial over the following decades.

Taking advantage of the leisurely pace of life at Maxwell Field, Dickey read Kenneth Burke's A Grammar of Motives, Kafka's diaries, and many other books. Still considering alternative careers, Dickey wrote Maxine, who was visiting her mother in Nashville: "I have decided one thing: that no matter what the air force offers me, no matter how little I can earn 'on the outside,' or no matter what, I will not (or could not) make a career out of this life. The life of an officer in the Air Force is essentially a surrender: a surrender to the 'good deal,' a surrender to an indolent, unthinking life, a surrender to expedience, a surrender to the officer's club, and a surrender of all I want most to do. Even now I can feel the insidious and delightful pull away from my work in the genial and innocent 'Let's go up to the club and have a brew,' and 'Let's see what's going on up at the PX.' "[6] The air force life was seductive, but Dickey decided that it was for lotos-eaters and not for committed writers like himself.

Dickey's next orders directed him to Keesler Air Force Base on the Gulf Coast just west of Biloxi, Mississippi. Near the end of April he traveled to Biloxi for a twenty-four-day refresher course in night fighter radar observation and navigation. Like most bases, Keesler resembled a small town. Divided into about sixty-five blocks, it had a theater, chapel, library, bowling alley, baseball field, boxing arena, post office, gym, swimming pool, and numerous service shops. Still without Maxine, Dickey found a motel cabin in a town called Pass Christian, where he roomed with two friends. For the next month he learned about new developments in radar interception and navigation with the hope of getting a job as an instructor. Dickey expressed his loneliness in his love letters to Maxine. "Most wonderful of all wives," he began one letter, "Hail! I couldn't decide whether to make this THE IRONIC LETTER: ('Such hospitality in the Air Force!') the FUNNY LETTER: ('Well, here I am in the Air Force again, Sugar Lamb') or just the letter that tells you that you are the most loved woman in the world tonight and all the rest of the nights in which I participate."[7] To Maxine he harped on his status as an intellectual pariah in the air force. While his colleagues discussed Buicks and radio shows, he lugged books around the base, reading them any place he could, even in airplanes. He scorned the mediocrity of his peers and sneered at their jibes about his bookishness, which allowed them "to nourish their fantastically protected ignorance."[8] It astonished him, he wrote Maxine, that the other men could "conduct themselves on the plane of imbecility these people here do. All of them I have met are simply idiots."[9]

Many of Dickey's letters were about Maxine's pregnancy and imminent motherhood. Because Maxine's childhood had been so painful after her father had abandoned the family, Dickey wrote: "What a wonderful *loved* childhood our little one is going to have both because it should have one and to make up for *your* childhood."[10] He assured her that he was, at heart, a family man. He also consoled her about the weight she was gaining and sent her money to buy presents for herself. His tone, however, often sounded condescending: "For the first two and a half years of our marriage you have made wonderful progress in many directions. Best of all, you have been truly moved by a least one poem ('The River-Merchant's Wife' [by Ezra Pound]) and by many paintings, and for the right reasons, I think. The rest is simply learning, 'feeling,' analyzing, insisting upon getting things into some kind of significant relationship to yourself and love."[11] Assuming the role of Pygmalion again, Dickey in one letter told Maxine that he hoped they could read James Joyce's highly esoteric book *Finnegans Wake* together; to that end, he patiently spent a paragraph deciphering the meaning of the main character's name, Anna Livia Plurabelle. Maxine started with Joyce's *Dubliners* and *A Portrait of the Artist as a Young Man*. Understanding them made her feel intelligent. *"You made me boy!"*[12] she happily exclaimed. When Chris was born, Dickey vowed to "make his head" as well, but his son would not be as malleable.

Maxine joined her husband during the summer of 1951 in a garage apartment in a suburb of Biloxi called Gulfport. Although it was expensive, Dickey maintained both base and off-base quarters (the military paid for his room at the Base Bachelor Officer Quarters). Maxine enjoyed the Gulf Coast's balmy climate and gambling establishments. Shortly before she arrived, Dickey had described the Gulf Coast near Biloxi to her: "There are dice tables, card houses, whorehouses, damn near everything or anything you might or might not want to see. Ah, the lusts of the flesh! All the field personnel are pretty lustful, but all I want, ever, is to see and be near you."[13] Dickey often pointed out that he had no friends at Keesler, while Maxine had many. He was not entirely alone, however, especially after Albert Murray hailed him one day from the chow line. In order to talk further about writing, Dickey invited Murray to his apartment. As trains rumbled on the nearby tracks, they discussed Theodore Roethke (a poet Murray had met), Louis Armstrong, Shirley Jackson, and other Southern writers. Murray told Dickey about a letter he had just received from his old college friend and mentor, Ralph Ellison, who was finishing *Invisible Man* in New York. He also talked about his correspondence with Jackson. They did not discuss civil rights and race relations, although perhaps they should have, considering what happened after Dickey drove Murray back to Keesler's bachelor's quarters. Dickey recalled: "We [Maxine and I] were asked to leave [the apartment] by our landlord because of asking a black to visit us, but later reconciled these differences with said landlord."[14] Before long Dickey took a public stand against such segregationist attitudes, even though he often shocked audiences by echoing them. It wasn't until a 1972 National Institute of Arts and Letters meeting that Murray learned of the trouble he had caused at the Gulfport apartment. Dickey told Murray that the landlord had prohibited him from socializing with "a nigger."[15]

After Maxine left Gulfport near the beginning of August, Dickey complained in a letter: "It is so *boring* here. . . . The swimming pool is boring, the club is boring, Gulfport is boring, the movies are boring, the Gold Coast is *very* boring, and I am bored without you to bother me about things all the time."[16] Dickey spent his time reading periodicals like the *Hudson Review,* the *Kenyon Review,* and *Partisan Review,* writing poems, playing basketball in the Mississippi heat, and learning to swear in Polish from his roommate. A schedule he devised at the time offered a glimpse of his literary ambitions:

1. Thirty lines of poetry a day; either on one poem complete or part of another.
2. Two pages of the novel a day.
3. At least twenty pages of poetry read *carefully* every day.
4. Fifty pages of prose a day.
5. Exercise.

In addition to reading such poets as W. S. Merwin, Vernon Watkins, Robert Graves, and Wallace Stevens, Dickey plowed ahead with *The Entrance to the Honeycomb.* Later in life he satisfied what he called his Germanic predilection for schedules by drawing up ones that accounted for every half-hour of his day.

In between his literary activities, Dickey labored at deciphering aviation manuals. It was a large leap, and a jolting one, from correcting freshman essays at Rice. He had to learn how to do such things as: "Connect up on the circuit Demonstration Trainer a simple power supply circuit with a vacuum tube voltage regulator in its output circuit. Use a varistat to change the AC input voltage to the power supply circuit. Arrange for changing the load on the power supply circuit by using different values of load resistance."[17] Joseph Sokolewicz, Dickey's roommate and a former night fighter, remembered how hard they studied the advances in radar technology. They had to master airborne radar that picked up airborne targets on a cathode tube and learn how to gauge where the target was, how far away it was, whether it was to the right or left, below or above. They had to figure out how to correct the relation of their plane to its target in terms of distance, azimuth, and elevation, and how to instruct the pilot to make steering corrections. On July 24, 1951, having satisfied the requirements for his Technical Instructor course, Dickey received a USAF Air Training Command certificate. Records show that by the end of August he had logged about forty-six hours in C-47 and B-25 aircraft in Keesler's 3380th Technical Training Wing. Orders to leave Keesler for James Connally AFB in Waco, Texas, came on August 8, 1951. Dickey traveled with Sokolewicz to his new base and then spent his short rest leave with Maxine at the Memorial Apartment Hotel in Nashville. Maxine was about to deliver their baby, and Dickey did what he could to make her comfortable in the summer heat before returning to Waco, where he worked as a radar instructor for the 3565th Training Wing.

Dickey approached the impending birth of his child with an oratorical flourish. He wrote Maxine "of our great and quiet joy and anticipation and of the fearful responsibility we have taken on, and of the even more fearful and great responsibility the child has to us, and to itself, in that it is a human being, half animal murderer, part saint, sometime Antichrist, pardoner and the fruit and consummation of our love and the living knowledge of the guilt we all lie down in, that we may permit another to rise above us."[18] Around this time Dickey wrote "The Son," a poem describing what he called "the parricidal vision of the loin." To fulfill all these roles—from saint to Antichrist to parricidal son to jock (in an October letter Dickey said he couldn't wait to buy his child his first jock-strap)—was a tall order for any child, and reflected the roles Dickey assumed for himself. On August 28, he dispatched another grandiloquent letter to Maxine: "I shall come to you soon, fresh in your sacramental blood and the warmth of a great room, and watch your small lips curl and try in that inarticulate music Beethoven heard when he saw the storm break over his pure deafness, and we shall then meet, and what speech we shall have together is already in whatever richness you have been allowed to proceed, cautiously and cruelly, from, and has been in my head from the time I was myself conceived, to lie wrecked and new and unsheltered save by love on that cast and lone shell of time the tremendous unceasing wind that blows us full of breath filled that night, and this night of all my love, and my litten and hallowed wife."[19] While Maxine focused on her waters breaking and her cervix dilating, her husband took flight in a peroration on mystical communication.

In his poem "Utterance I," Dickey imagined his wife calmly delivering their baby in the hospital. Dickey did not attend the birth of his son, Chris, on August 31, 1951, but soon made arrangements for his new family to be together. In mid-September he went to Atlanta to speak to his parents about taking care of Maxine and Chris at the end of the month. When Maxine was installed at West Wesley, Dickey visited for three days in mid-October, and upon returning to Waco found a house not far from the base and within walking distance to a supermarket and drive-in movie theater. Around this time he took a job on the flight line (he had been editing aviation manuals and teaching in a classroom) that required six or seven hours of flying per week. Typically the radar instructors accompanied about five aviation cadets in a B-25 bomber. Dickey's schedule was not as strenuous as he feared, which may explain why he remembered his time in Waco fondly. He enjoyed the ample facilities—especially the library and gym—and decided "to tackle the three toughest novelists in the twentieth century simultaneously"[20] by reading Joyce's *Finnegans Wake*, Proust's *Remembrance*

THE KOREAN DISTRACTION (1951–1952) / 165

of *Things Past*, and Thomas Mann's *Joseph in Egypt* tetralogy. He was also reading less demanding books like *The Catcher in the Rye* and William Carlos Williams's autobiography.

For recreation, Dickey often played tennis and drank with ex–night fighter Avery Miller. George Kamajian, Dickey's tent mate in the Philippines, also made Dickey's Texas sojourn more pleasant, at least at first. Kamajian had come to Connally after taking the same refresher course in radar at Keesler. When Maxine relocated in Waco with Chris, the Dickeys invited George and his wife, Alice, to their house for dinner. The Kamajians reciprocated. This polite exchange continued until one night George reminisced too candidly about their time together in the Philippines. He mentioned some of Dickey's odd habits, like walking barefoot around camp and never cleaning his bunk. Having established a more sanitized version of his year as a crack fighter pilot, Dickey recoiled from such unsavory details. Although Kamajian was just teasing, Dickey never invited him or his wife for dinner again.

At Connally, Dickey again shared a room with Joseph Sokolewicz. Perhaps because they did not have a common history, their families socialized without interruption. Sokolewicz's wife was drawn to Maxine because her daughter Stephanie was born the same day as Chris. Dickey intended to portray his roommate in a short story, "The Grotto," which was supposed to be a Hemingwayesque account of two young recallees who become friends as they wait for their children to be born. The character based on Sokolewicz admiringly calls Dickey's alter ego "Wolfgang Amadeus." Wolfgang is a "Nietzscheite or existentialist"[21] who, despite his Austro-Germanic sympathies, listens to the Sokolewicz character talk about Poland's history and patriots. Sokolewicz, in fact, regularly conversed with his well-read roommate over Camembert cheese. Having read such writers as Robinson Jeffers and Norman Mailer, Sokolewicz could act as a literate sounding board for Dickey. As early as 1951, Dickey broached the plots of *Deliverance* and *Alnilam* in their conversations. He spoke excitedly about a novel that would document the trials of several characters returning to the Southern wilderness with bows and arrows, and around the same time he jotted down lines in his notebook for a poem to be called "The Deliverer"—the first title for *Deliverance*. He also outlined a story about a girl who allows a cat to lick her nipples before throwing it in the face of a voyeuristic boy. He later used the idea in the *Deliverance* scene where Ed catches a glimpse of a model's naked breast when he picks up a cat to be used in an underwear advertisement.

During the early 1950s, Dickey filled his notebooks with plans for short stories and novels. In February 1952, he laid the groundwork for a story about the "sexual reaction to low-level fire-bombing" to be called "The Fire Music" (it later became "The Eye of the Fire"). He mapped out a story that would dramatize a twelve-year-old boy's frightening encounter with a naked woman in a shower while vacationing with his wealthy family on an island off the Georgia coast. Four years later Dickey changed the gender of the person in the shower and the genre when he wrote "The Father's Body." Dickey also hoped to write a story about a small boy's horror at seeing a porpoise on his first fishing trip with his incommunicative father. The story evolved into "The Shark's Parlor." In most of these sketches Dickey focused on gothic events that both shocked and titillated. He wanted to write about "(Maibelle's abortion) her furious screaming that she will not be able to perpetuate herself, that her image has been marred"; a long trip from Florida to New Orleans by a married man who seduces a girl in a hotel without saying anything about his wife and child; a young Jewish veteran in New York who has an interview with his stockbroker father about a job and feels the "frustration . . . of many who have, in the violence of war, found a sense of solidarity which is dispelled by the (old, familiar) civilian world returned to"; "an old ('perpetually young') poet (Cummings) whose forte is 'fresh' love poetry, and who must constantly reconstruct the past";[22] a young man who dates his high school idol and finds she is demoralized by the affair. For Dickey, life and art were permeable; one infused the other. His ambivalence toward his father inspired the fishing story; his awareness that his sexual encounters with women were privately uplifting but socially taboo influenced the shower and hotel stories; his difficulty blending into civilian life after World War II informed the stockbroker story; his attempts to constantly reconstruct his past gave rise to the Cummings story. He also planned to write a story about the inability of his wife's grandmother to "do anything about young, disorganized and essential and destructive love which here involves her granddaughter (Mrs. Webster)."[23] Here, in fictitious form, he proposed to confess the pain and anger that his romantic conduct caused his wife and mother-in-law.

In his letters to Maxine, Dickey implored her to tolerate his free-spirited ways. On October 5, shortly before visiting her, Dickey delivered an impassioned apologia concerning his ideas on marriage and love:

> I don't want us to be bound in by the *ordinary* ways of loving and affection that you, frequently, and I, sometimes, are hamstrung by. The standards of loving of . . . your mother and my mother and father and Val and all the other petty and sometimes admirable people we know are not by a damn sight enough or good enough for us. If we could shake the million meaningless jealousies and envies out of the movies and radio programs and the other sources that we sneer and laugh at and are influenced and wrongly live by, we would then begin to know what each other is for, and we are together for, and why that togetherness is such a marvelous and un-ordinary thing. My god, the good thing about us is that we are never alone, as I have sometimes been utterly alone in the inmost bowels and veins of the most "luscious blonde," and that we are together a refuge against the tremendous cold hate and indifference [sic] of all humane beings for their companions. . . . I want to *come back to you* from other people and find you the same, always, but I don't want to wear you around my neck and feel you grow intolerable with heaviness. All this by way of attempting to define the kind of relationship we should have, and the kind I want. Love, if anything, is a freedom of choice; slavery is death to it. . . . Don't take from your mother or anyone we know or don't know the kind of deadening middle-class morality that insists that one "act in this way," or says that "if he loves you, he wouldn't, . . ." or " . . . if you have any self-respect, you won't, etc" all of which are perfectly meaningless when parroted by dissatisfied

and ignorant and wretched people. Begin to think for yourself. Get out of the ridiculously small personality that the inconsequential people you have known all your life have tried to build for you. The earth is opening like a tremendous flower. It is not a thing you can put in a window-seat. Be in it, and live in it, and take from it what you most love and want to live by.[24]

His planned short story recounting a seduction in New Orleans, which he later retold in the "Summer" section of his poem "False Youth: Two Seasons," had a basis in fact. During the summer of 1951, he spent a weekend in New Orleans with a woman (he gave her his grandmother's name, Huntley, in the poem). "It was one of the happiest times I ever had in my life,"[25] he recalled. In his letter to Maxine he attempted to justify his affair without going into any of the details. He promised to always come back to her after loving others, and he kept his promise. For her part, Maxine stuck with her man, although her devotion came at a high emotional and physical price.

Most of Dickey's embryonic stories issued from what Freud called "the family romance." One particularly intriguing plot involved a father loosely based on Dickey's father and his paternal grandfather, James L. Dickey Sr., who owned trotting horses and a racing track where the Atlanta federal prison now sits. The mother, like Dickey's, has artistic tastes (she is a landscape painter). The main conflict arises from an oedipal rift between father and son. According to Dickey's notes: "Child and father unable to come together. Child identifies father with Reddy [a boy who loves cockfighting] and then with rooster. When rooster loses to Reddy's, he picks him up, weeping, and carries him off with gaffs (stolen from Reddy's father's gaff box), talks to him; cock puts gaff through hand. Kills cock with stone. End: 'And you love me, you love me,' he cried, striking again and again, 'you *love* me.' "[26] The attack on the rooster amounts to a displaced attack by the son on the father. The scene of the gaff puncturing the boy's hand was one Dickey claimed to have witnessed, but in life the gaff had pierced his father's hand, not his.

At Connally, Dickey continued to explore the creative possibilities of lying. He wrote in his journal: "Ern Malley a good forebear as a hoaxer."[27] While in the Pacific, he had heard about the poet Ern Malley, a fictitious character invented by two Australian poets, Harold Stewart and James Macauley. Claiming that Malley had died of Graves' disease, the two poets convinced the editor of *Angry Penguins* to publish a special issue and later a book of Malley's poems. In a 1985 letter to a New Zealand poet, Kendrick Smithyman, Dickey said that he had devoured the Australian journal during the war. In September 1951, he told Maxine: "I learned a great deal I didn't know about the workings of the imagination from rereading the poems [in *Angry Penguins*] and the comments on them."[28] Dickey was so enchanted by the hoax that he borrowed the line "Do not speak of secret matters in a field full of little hills" from the epigraph to Malley's book and attributed it to Joel Cahill in *Alnilam*. Stewart and Macauley were two more confidence men who proved how gullible audiences could be. In the novel he worked on at the time, *The Entrance to the Honeycomb*, Dickey began his first extensive investigation of his own need to counterfeit his life.

With Julian Glass as his spokesman, Dickey also explored his appetite for sadoeroticism. A chilling entry in his notebook reads: "I sometimes think (that)
the only way to teach a woman both the essence + particularities of love is to
take her first to bed with a jar of [V]aseline + strap and work on her with both.
That way she will learn, with no diversion, no unnecessary and unhappy com-
plication, what cruelty love entails, and what respect it deserves."[29] It should
come as no surprise that Dickey was sampling the writings of the Marquis de
Sade in the early 1950s, but it is ironic that he should choose one of the pioneers
of contemporary feminism, Simone de Beauvoir, as his guide. Beauvoir's *The
Marquis de Sade: A Study*, which Dickey bought in 1953, brushes aside all talk of
Sade's villainy or heroism and instead dwells on the way he "forces us to re-
examine thoroughly the basic problem which haunts our age in different forms:
the true relation between man and man."[30] Sade is important, Beauvoir contends, because of his insights into the sinister and criminal side of eros. In
Beauvoir's portrait of Sade as a maladjusted eighteenth-century aristocrat who
held to the conventions of his class with one hand while flailing at them with
the other, Dickey found traits with which to identify. Both men found their
surest access to power in fantasies and lies. Both were husbands, fathers, and
heirs to wealth who rebelled against conventional comforts. Beauvoir might be
speaking of Dickey when she says of Sade:

> He wished to be not only a public figure, whose acts are ordained by con-
> vention and routine, but a live human being as well. There was only one
> place where he could assert himself as such, and that was not the bed in
> which he was received only too submissively by a prudish wife, but in the
> brothel where he bought the right to unleash his fantasies. And there was
> one dream common to most young aristocrats of the time. Scions of a de-
> clining class which had once possessed concrete power, but which no
> longer retained any real hold on the world, they tried to revive symboli-
> cally, in the privacy of the bedchamber the status for which they were nos-
> talgic, that of the lone and sovereign feudal despot.[31]

Dickey also found fulfillment for his sadoerotic fantasies in *The Memoirs of Dolly
Morton*, the nineteenth-century pornographic novel about a Virginia plantation-
owner who gets pleasure from whipping women, whether free—like his aboli-
tionist mistress from the North—or slave.[32] Because of the Civil War, the
slave-owning Mr. Randolph expresses the same sort of desperate nostalgia as the
Marquis de Sade. Through their sadoerotic acts, Dickey and many of the characters in his poems and novels also seek to resurrect the former privileges of "the
lone and sovereign feudal despot."

Much of Dickey's writing in the early 1950s took overt or covert aim at the
reigning puritanism in America. He became fascinated with Thomas Mann's
novel *Doctor Faustus*, which contended that the artist must sell his soul to the
devil in order to be truely original. Mann's exemplar, Adrian Leverkuhn, is a
morbid, aristocratic nihilist not unlike Sade, whose monstrous obsessions and
appetites contribute to his genius. Aligning himself with the demons of concu-
piscence rather than the angels of propriety, Dickey was drawn to Dr. Faustus's

principles. He yearned for a more European openness to the varieties of sexual experience. He defined his poetry as "the Extreme: open, free, athletic, Baudelarian—the Extreme Decadent,"[33] and in it he planned to decry the hypocrisy of American women who "never [agreed to] the whole-souled submission to sex one might expect of a people so . . . obsessed by it." The root of his complaints lay in his marriage. "Maxine," he wrote in his notebook, "has no notion of the depths of sexual desire in me.—Or the direction these take. It is not pre-eminently physical; Lawrence was wrong. For me really to love a woman, love her completely, she would have to enter into that part of my world."[34] That part of his world was the one ruled by his fantasies.

Dickey's imagination flourished in the unlikely setting of the air force base. Not only did he sketch the plots for dozens of stories, he also conceived of at least a dozen novels. He entertained the ambitious, if unworkable, scheme of composing a tetralogy: one novel would focus on old people in Florida, another on an aging historian, another on the historian's attempt to resurrect Assyrian civilization in his imagination, and another on the aftermath of World War II. In 1953, he completed *The Entrance to the Honeycomb*, the 151-page novel that expressed his romantic and athletic frustrations as well as his sadoerotic fantasies through Julian Glass. He submitted the manuscript to Lee Barker, an editor at Doubleday. Dickey explained to Rice colleague Willard Thorp on December 26: "Doubleday and I corresponded vigorously about the book, but ended looking at each other like two stags (deer) must look into (or for) each others' eyes when their horns are locked and they are tired of fighting. There's just no way to *laugh* in such a situation, with neither of you satisfied, or willing to back down, so I withdrew the book in favor of another I'm about half-way through the first draft of; it is immensely and excitingly better than the old *Honeycomb*, which I am saving to rob of its few good passages for use in later stuff."[35] Dickey did ransack *The Entrance to the Honeycomb*, recycling the labyrinth scenes in *Alnilam* and the sadoerotic and voyeuristic scenes in poems like "Cherrylog Road" and "The Fiend." In 1953, he had already started *Alnilam*, and Doubleday would indeed publish it, but not until 1987.

Behind much of Dickey's early writing was a need to confess as well as conceal his pent-up sexual interests. Homosexuality and sadism recurred in many guises. In a story synopsis dealing most ostensibly with his present situation—the characters are air force recallees—a seedy figure named Haynes tires of his wife and child, has an affair with a woman in his house, and then lends the house to an ex–javelin thrower named Dahmen. About the adulterer, Dahmen, Dickey writes: "[He] takes the girl out [to Haynes's house] and beats the hell out of her. Haynes hears her screaming; then D pushes her out the door into the wind off the lake."[36] Near the end, Haynes kills a coral snake in a symbolic attempt to rid himself of the sexual compulsions that drive him to violence and grief. In another notebook entry, Dickey declares in a Dahmen-like mood: "I would deliberately beat sex down like a snake; it has controlled me too long."[37] Throughout his life Dickey struggled with his sexual demons, sometimes submitting to them, at other times sublimating them.

In other stories Dickey planned to investigate other sexual taboos. In one, Dickey imagines "a (timid) man, rejected from military service, who gets himself a job . . . as archivist of the war photographs and letters" in a small town. Like Dickey he is a scholar and writer intrigued by homosexual experience; he tries "to understand warfare [through] letters from one homosexual soldier to his buddy." In a more risqué scenario, Dickey construes a "short novel about the disruption of the 'friendship' of two 'happy' lesbians by a dissolute 'sexual athlete.' "[38] The athlete's dissolution includes masochism; the lesbians beat him and walk on his body. In a similarly bizarre story, a young American man abuses his homosexual lover, a famous poet resembling Auden, by pulling his hair, slapping him, and eventually destroying his talent. On vacation, the American demonstrates his sadism by killing a Frenchman, an act he deems "no worse than killing a dog,"[39] but then gets enmeshed in a legal system he doesn't understand. In *Deliverance* Dickey gave a more credible shape to these themes of murder, homosexuality, and foreign codes of justice. A married man's perilous affairs, a track and football athlete's sadism, a rich young man's departure from and return to his home city with new values, a journey to Europe on a grant—these were some of the subjects, which had obvious parallels in Dickey's life, that he tried to turn into fiction. What is intriguing is the way his personae feel guilt about their destructive behavior but fail, for one reason or another, to expiate their guilt or alter their behavior. Like Dante's sinners, they seem doomed to reenact their crimes without ever passing through the cleansing fires of purgatory. As far as bringing these germinal plots to fruition, Dickey seemed as stymied as his characters. He conceived of stories with Southern abandon, but wrote almost none of them.

Despite his discontent with all civilized constraints, at Connally AFB Dickey again tried to order his free time with a rigorous Jay Gatsby–like schedule:

I.	12:00–6:00	Write
	12:00–1:30	My poetry (conscious) craft
	1:30–1:45	Loosen up: "image bank": 2 pages
	1:45–2:30	Cyril Swift
	2:30–5:00	Novel
	5:00–6:00	Stories
II.	6:00–6:30 or 6: 45	Exercise
	7:00–8:00	Eat—Family
III.	8:00–9:00	Analyze poems: reconstruct them: notes
	9:00–10:00	Analyze novel: notes, or stories: notes
	10:00–10:30	Read philosophy (any form)
	10:30–11:00	Outline books on prosody: notes
	11:00	Bed[40]

The blockbuster success of Dickey's first published novel, *Deliverance*, is less miraculous in the context of his early fiction writing.

During the fall of 1951, Dickey spent little time instructing radar operation in the air. In December, he got busier, logging twenty-four hours of day flying and six hours of night flying. In January he flew forty-six hours during the day and seven hours at night. For his service, on January 23, 1952, the air force promoted him to first lieutenant. On April 19, for reasons unexplained by his military records, his superiors suspended him from flying status. Four days later they re-voked the suspension and allowed him to resume flying. As spring turned to summer, his hours of instruction in the B-25K training aircraft tapered off, and soon the two thousand graduating radar observers left Texas for Korea, Japan, and Alaska. During his last few months at Connally, Dickey worked in the scheduling department planning training flights, a position suited to one so given to drawing up schedules. In Korea, MacArthur's replacement, Gen. Ridgway, had won peace and begun armistice negotiations on July 10, 1951. Outbreaks of fighting, however, continued until a final agreement was reached on March 5, 1953. Dickey's contribution to the war effort ended when he left Connally on August 7, 1952. Records reveal that he survived his second tour of duty in good form; he weighed 198 pounds and had suffered no wounds (he would suffer a mishap several months later, in December, when he broke his hand and hurt his shoulder in a car accident). Outwardly robust, inwardly Dickey was anxious about his impending return to Rice. He wrote Maxine two weeks before leaving the base: "I sort of dread getting back to grading those god-damned freshman themes."[41] He felt like an exile returning to an unwelcome home.

11. Return to Academe (1952–1954)

When the Dickeys moved back to the university apartments on Mount Vernon Street in August 1952, their section of the building had changed with the ar-rivals of four new professors: Bud Rorschach in physics, Arlen Brown in math, Edmund Peckham in history, and James Simms in engineering. Of the four, Peckham got to know Dickey the best, partly because he had a fifteen-month-old daughter and a three-and-a-half-year-old son, who sometimes played with Chris. With Peckham, Dickey trotted out his favorite stories and added some new ones. He convinced his friend that he had been a pilot who had just re-turned from flying combat missions over Korea. He spoke of the traumatic death of his first wife in Australia shortly after World War II and bragged that he was the privileged scion of an Atlanta family that had inherited Coca-Cola money. Dickey regaled other colleagues with similar yarns. According to George Garrett, who taught at Rice after Dickey left, Dickey claimed that "he was a really top-flight tennis player" who, "except for his war wound . . . , would have [been a star] . . . on the Jack Kramer tennis tour."[1] Dickey also trumpeted his football achievements, convincing Rice friends that he had given up a career in professional football to pursue literature.

An English professor, Wilfred Dowden, also leant a receptive ear to Dickey's exuberant lies. Dowden had served in the navy, so the war often came up in con-versation. Because Dickey perceived Dowden as "one of [chairman] McKillop's minions"[2] and because Dickey detested the English Department chairman, he often lampooned and hoodwinked Dowden. He once said that he had frantically dodged a swarm of Japanese planes while dogfighting over the Pacific and that, during the maneuver, his tail gunner had watched pieces of fuselage fly off as enemy machine-gun bullets raked their plane. By pressing the throttle into high-speed overdrive, Dickey had escaped and, to the amazement of his fellow night fighters, fallen asleep right after landing the plane. When he woke, a friend told him to check his plane—his engine had melted during the flight home into an amorphous chunk of steel. (Dickey reworked an incident at Hammer Field when tape on Donald Armstrong's plane unraveled during a training flight, and another pilot flying beside him—George Aubill—convinced Armstrong that his plane was disintegrating.) Dowden accepted the fiction as fact.

Dickey entertained his classes at Rice with similar flights of fancy. To the students' delight, he resumed his habit of holding court from a chair perched on a table. Unlike the other professors, he renounced neck ties, sported an open shirt, and even wore shorts to class. He also liked to teach outdoors. A colleague, George Williams, kept his office window open—there was no air-conditioning in those days—and after eavesdropping on one of Dickey's classes decided that it was one of the most effective jobs of teaching he had ever witnessed. Dickey loved to rile up his students. One freshman in a 1953 class recalled Dickey blurting out: "This is a class of engineers, isn't it?" The students shuffled their books nervously. Dickey continued: "That's what I thought. Well, I'm a modern poet. Now we know what we're up against."[3] His flirtatiousness with the women, his macho posing with the men, and his lenient grading made him one of the most popular teachers in the department.

While he may have resented the introductory classes that all English professors had to teach, Dickey generally kept quiet about his dissatisfactions at Rice. He struck Dowden as an enthusiastic worker, even if he did flout the rules. While Dowden took periodic breaks from his library carrel, he noticed that Dickey remained utterly absorbed in his work for hours. Dickey did find time from his strenuous labors, however, to rekindle his friendship with Pat Moore and other students. Before Dickey's military recall, Moore and her classmates had donated money to buy him a silver keychain engraved with his initials. Upon returning, Dickey contacted Moore, who had a job in the library, and again acted as her unofficial supervisor. He urged her to read French books (he said he'd read nearly everything that was any good in English) and inquired about her dating life. "Anything between you and Henry?" he'd whisper on their picnics at Galveston Beach with Maxine, Chris, James Young, and student editor Henry Delaune. As for his own interest in student women, he told her: "I couldn't ever have an affair with a student, you know. It would ruin my career. I would never teach again." He sometimes shocked Moore with his sadoerotic remarks. "You *are* going to be Phi Beta Kappa, aren't you?" he once asked. "I'll turn you over my knee and spank you if you aren't."[4] Before long, Dickey surmounted his fears about having affairs with students.

Despite Dickey's success with students and absorption in his work, academic life proved just as disappointing as army life. His salary—always a major concern—was depressingly meager. During the 1952 academic year, he alleged that his wife had to work as a receptionist at a local radio station to help pay the bills. Rather than small payments from journals for his poems, he was collecting rejection slips. His main source of agony, however, was the department chair, who demanded that he publish traditional scholarship. Dickey said: "I felt a sense of entrapment in the academic world at a very low level from which I could not possibly rise without a Ph.D. The Ph.D. was something the people at Rice were insisting on, especially the head of the English Department, Dr. Alan McKillop, who was a very un-understanding person in this regard and whom I have had an extremely strong enmity toward ever since. He didn't *mind* my writing, but he didn't want me around unless I became a reputable scholar. The fact that I had been through two wars, had tried desperately to get educated, and was trying my best to develop as a writer under almost overwhelmingly adverse conditions concerned him not at all."⁵ As the 169-book-long reading lists and myriad notes in his ledgers prove, Dickey was educating himself more thoroughly than most doctoral programs. He wanted to be treated as if he had a Ph.D.

To break from academe or at least bolster his status at Rice, Dickey concluded that he had to publish a successful novel. To this end, during the summer of 1953, he sequestered himself in his parents' Atlanta home and vowed to work eight hours a day on the final draft of *The Entrance to the Honeycomb.* He would be free of his squalling son, who was almost two, and would be able to resume his old life with parents and servants doting on him. Maxine agreed to tolerate the isolation for one summer and dutifully took Chris to live with her mother in Nashville. She found the separation a terrible strain. "Darling," she wrote on July 2, "I don't like this widowhood at all—I love you and miss you so much—I would even welcome your *nasty little habits!* When are you coming to see us?"⁶ She looked forward to reuniting on Saint Simons Island during the last week in August and spending two weeks together in Atlanta before returning to Houston. Because they were trying to save money, Dickey approved of their new arrangement. In Atlanta Dickey pretended to be lonely, but in fact slipped back into his routine of swimming at the Venetian with friends, playing tennis (he entered an Atlanta tournament, but was beaten in the second round), reading at home with his family, and going to movies.

Dickey's completion of his novel by summer's end did little to mitigate his situation at Rice. He knew it was a Rice policy to terminate contracts of young professors who failed to earn their Ph.D.s. According to one of his new friends at Rice, Dickey's feud with McKillop escalated when Yale offered him a temporary poet-in-residence position and Rice denied him leave to take it. Since Dickey had published only a handful of poems and book reviews, it is more than likely that the Yale job was a figment of wishful thinking. During this frustrating time, he commiserated with a student, David Dowler, from Cambridge, England. Dowler, he said, "was a very bitter, acerbic English guy [who] . . . hated America and hated Rice and hated Houston and naturally he and I became very close friends." Something of a snob, Dowler railed against the ignorance of Americans. "They asked me at Cambridge to come over to a place like this? My God, they don't know what the first folio [of Shakespeare] is!" he would say. Dowler shared Dickey's scorn of American Ph.D.s and loved to tell the story of how, after McKillop instituted a Ph.D. program at Rice, a middle-aged ex-librarian submitted her thesis on Milton and the visual arts. Dickey, Dowler, and the rest of the English Club at Rice attended a lecture based on her thesis. When the chairman asked if there were any responses to the paper she'd read, Dowler raised his hand: "I think she should change the title of her dissertation."

McKillop asked: "What should it be?" Dowler said sarcastically, "She should change it from *Milton and the Visual Arts* to *What Milton Might Have Seen in London . . . if He Hadn't Been Blind.*"[7] Dickey and Dowler had a good laugh.

Dickey also commiserated with a visiting Malory scholar from Princeton, Willard Thorp, who also disliked Rice. Together they gossiped about Edmund Wilson's sex life and other literary and extraliterary matters. Another disgruntled colleague and close friend was Lester Mansfield. According to Dickey, he was a "rebellious spirit . . . , a strange, shadowy character . . . , a silver-haired sort of sanguine, thin fellow . . . who was raised in France. . . . He was the one who introduced me to the martini. As he would say . . . , 'This is one of the things the French have learned from Americans, Jim. This is called a martini and it's really, as they say over there, the only drink.' "[8] Dickey concurred, and before long was drinking pitchers of them. In addition to cocktails, Mansfield also helped cultivate Dickey's knowledge of existentialism. Mansfield wrote down many of his thoughts on the French philosophical movement for a Rice lecture he gave on October 11, 1953, and published in an October 1954 issue of *The Rice Institute Pamphlet*. Mansfield made it clear that existentialism derived from a particular moment in history—World War II—and a particular experience—Sartre's work with the French Resistance. What Mansfield wrote about Sartre's belief in unconditional freedom jibed with Dickey's beliefs: "At any moment we can choose to be something else. Since human liberty is always intact, human character is never a reality, but merely a possibility. The only reality is human action. The key to our behavior is not to be found in the past but in the future, for whatever we do, the character we seek to found is always in some way future to our project to found it. This is why Sartre says of his own characters that each one 'after having done anything whatsoever, can do anything whatsoever.' " Mansfield explained that existentialism was an optimistic form of humanism because "it declares that man is the fabricator of his own destiny and that he is free to make of it what he will."[9] Dickey admired the way Sartre rooted his doctrine of freedom in the nitty-gritty experiences of war and liberation. Dickey's experiences in the war had convinced him of his own freedom to repudiate conventions and fabricate his destiny. It also convinced him that he could re-create his past as he saw fit.

In his conversations with Mansfield, Dickey confided his plans for *Deliverance* and how he hoped to depict the struggle for freedom in a warlike environment, where God and traditional Judeo-Christian values no longer pertained. An early draft of the novel shows that Dickey planned to use an epigraph from Sartre about freedom. He also considered using a title for the novel—*Trouble Deaf Heaven*—suggested by Mansfield. The phrase fit the existentialist conviction that heaven was "deaf" to human misery because it and God did not exist. The phrase came from Shakespeare's twenty-ninth sonnet, which Mansfield quoted to Dickey:

When, in disgrace with Fortune and men's eyes,
I all alone beweep my outcast state,
And trouble deaf heaven with my bootless cries,
And look upon myself and curse my fate. . . .

Dickey was so excited about Mansfield's proposed title that he made him sign a permission statement allowing him the right to use it.

Trying to contain his anger over his "outcast state" at Rice, Dickey persevered in his low-level instructorship. Occasionally he received auspicious signs from literary journals, such as the flattering letter John Crowe Ransom sent from the *Kenyon Review* about some poems he'd submitted. Afterward Dickey commented: "I am fairly launched. I am on the right road to writing like I should. I am breaking through."[10] McKillop, however, remained indifferent to his breakthroughs and hostile toward his teaching of poetry. Dickey later told a story about Dylan Thomas's death to illustrate McKillop's attitudes. When Thomas died on November 9, 1953, Dickey changed his course plan to pay homage to the great Welshman: "The only thing I did . . . that got me into any trouble there was when Dylan Thomas died I cancelled the regular instruction for the day and just taught the whole period on Dylan Thomas and read some of his things. I was called on the carpet for doing this."[11] Over the years Dickey would pay homage to Thomas in other ways, principally by emulating Thomas's poetic style and outrageous lifestyle.

Dickey may have been rebuked only once for violating official Rice policy, but colleagues complained about his other breaches of protocol. Many found his philandering deplorable. One of his favorite pastimes was sunbathing with or near faculty wives. To make himself more noticeable, he wore the tightest and briefest bathing suit he could find. Posing on the grass, his chest muscles bare from shaving, he propositioned whoever happened his way. Maxine tried to ignore her husband's ostentatiousness, but it was not easy. Years later, when Dickey flew to Rice from the West Coast for a reading, Wilfred Dowden got an inkling of the pain behind Maxine's stoic grace. He picked her up at the airport (she had flown in from the East Coast) and drove her to Rice. On the way, she said: "You know, Will, I'm the last of the poet's wives who could stick it out."[12] Many at Rice wondered why Maxine chose to do so.

By the end of 1953, Dickey gave up hope of a future at Rice. Just before Christmas, he told Willard Thorp: "I had a long talk with McKillop . . . at his suggestion. I told him that there was not much chance of my ever taking a degree, as I have not yet learned how to support my family on ninety dollars a month; he had no further comment than that I should get a Fulbright. The general import of the conversation seemed to me to be, 'We don't care *what* you do, but *we* certainly can't be expected to keep you, improperly qualified as you are.' Against which I kept silently and redly thinking, though I never said, 'Asking me to teach freshman English is like asking Rembrandt to draw Dick Tracy.' "[13] In early 1954, his salary still woefully below his expectations, Dickey seethed at his assigned course load: Argumentation and Public Speaking, Outlines of the History of English Literature, and two sections of English Composition: Study of Fundamental Literary Forms. Hoping for more-advanced classes and more money to teach them, in January he wrote Robert Highfill in the English Department at Mercer College, his father's alma mater. He informed Highfill of his three air medals, his Distinguished Flying Cross, his academic record at Vanderbilt, and his father's achievements on the Mercer football team. He half apologized for not having a doctorate: "Because of my excessively long military service, together with family duties, I have been unable to pursue work toward the advanced degree which most schools seem to require. Aside from this, however, my commitments to my own writing tend to minimize the interest I might otherwise have in scholarly research."[14] He did "have a novel [probably an early draft of *Alnilam*], now about half completed, spoken for by Doubleday," which he hoped would make up for his lack of a doctorate. Highfill had nothing to offer.

On January 8, 1954, as editor of the *Sewanee Review*, Monroe Spears invited his former student to submit some poems for the fellowship that his journal sponsored with financial help from The Rockefeller Foundation. Hoping that this would be his ticket out of Houston, Dickey mailed his poems to Spears with the explanation: "The money would make it possible for me to complete work on a great number of poems now only floating around . . . and on my second novel (some Texas people are interested in the first one, now completed), which I have about half the notes for."[15] The Sewanee judges—among them Allen Tate and Andrew Lytle—showed more sympathy for Dickey's plight than did the colleges he petitioned for jobs. On March 29, Spears informed him by telegram that he had won a fellowship. Soon afterward, Tate and Lytle sent congratulations (they also gave fellowships to Madison Jones and John Edward Hardy). The fellowship was worth thirty-five hundred dollars (in his recollections Dickey increased the amount to seventy-five hundred dollars, which was closer to what he actually spent in Europe). To Lytle he confessed that he was dazed and thrilled: "Allen Tate writes (Spears tells me): 'Dickey seems to me to be one of the most original young poets I have read since the war.' All this good fortune is a pretty terrible burden on the vanity of one who has not, until now, had much contact with people whose opinion on literary matters he respects."[16] On May 2, Dickey sent his thanks to Tate. The fellowship not only freed him from Rice; it allowed him to follow the distinguished transatlantic paths of other expatriate writers like Henry James, Eliot, Pound, Hemingway, and Fitzgerald.

Lytle's interest in Dickey's literary career came at a time when Dickey yearned for encouragement from an older, recognized writer. By 1954, the ex–Vanderbilt Fugitive had established a reputation as one of the South's premier men of letters. He had published a biography (*Bedford Forrest and his Critter Company*), two novels (*The Long Night* and *A Name for Evil*), a historical novel about De Soto (*At the Moon's Inn*), and numerous short stories, essays, and reviews. In many respects an old-fashioned Southern gentleman, Lytle responded to his eager apprentice with paternal solicitude. In his first letter, sent on March 21, 1954 (although he got Dickey's name wrong—he began "My Dear Dickie"), he expressed real admiration for "The Shark at the Window," which he had already read in the *Sewanee Review*, and for the poems Dickey submitted for the fellowship. "I feel that you are the real thing," he said. "Your imagination is the freshest, and the feeling it evokes, passionate response to the complexities of experience, give that promise of what I feel poetry is, or should be." Lytle, however, had reservations. He told Dickey that his poems tended to be too private and too puzzling. He also inveighed against Dickey's high-speed novel writing: "You've got to take that as an art, too, or it will undo you."[17] Lytle's evenhanded judgments began the first important literary correspondence of Dickey's life.

Lytle's letters released all of Dickey's bottled-up aspirations. On March 23, he praised Lytle for giving him the most intelligent and most sympathetic criticism he had ever received. "With your letters," Dickey responded breathlessly, "there is always the sensation of some hampered vital organ in me, just under my breast-bone, cut suddenly and softly and quite without hesitation free; I must have got my ideas about art filled up with this wonderful release of free breathing, alive beyond any state of being I have ever been granted."[18] Many of their letters concerned the poems Dickey worked on, such as "The Sprinter's Mother" and "Fathers and Sons." They also concerned "the fictive art," as Lytle called it, quoting Henry James, and such topics as aesthetic distance, plot tempo, dramatization of characters, point of view, symbolism, and style. With regard to Dickey's novels, Lytle advised: "I think you may find a controlling image at the post of observation invaluable as the restrictive guide."[19] Years later, Dickey always maintained that each of his three published novels originated from one "controlling image." For the masterly Lytle, Dickey had nothing but the highest esteem. *The Long Night*, he exclaimed, was "the best novel ever to come out of the South, Faulkner's not excluded." The short story "Alchemy" was "the best fiction on an historical subject I have ever read: the most imaginative, the deepest, and the most moving."[20] So that his paeans would have maximum force, Dickey took great care in scripting his letters to Lytle; he took notes, composed several drafts, and typed out the final copies.

Lytle accepted Dickey's effusions with appropriate modesty. Like a wise father advising an overly earnest son, he urged Dickey not to worry too much about the expectations of the Sewanee Fellowship judges: "You've already justified the prize. Just go ahead and make the most of the time. There are no strings attached to this money, even if you don't write a line."[21] Spears was similarly paternal, and must have smiled at the florid rhetoric of Dickey's thank-you letter: "I wish that, by making the appropriate passes over this paper, I could cause to appear the most effective rhetoric summonable, the sincerest, the deepest, and widest-moving, to let you know how favored I consider myself, how proud and grateful I am. I cannot, however."[22] With prize in hand, Dickey said farewell to the detested McKillop. He had already decided not to return to Rice after his year abroad.

In the months before embarking for Europe, Dickey kept up a steady correspondence with Lytle. Some of the letters divulged plans for the future *Alnilam*, whose gestation Lytle was already supervising:

We've kicked around my own book (the one taking place now) so much, and your advice has been so valuable, that I feel I should tell you a little [more] about it. The problem is to show a middle-aged fellow, a mild, truculent, inconsequentially mistrustful man, at a Primary Training Air Force Base during the early part of the last war, having come on hearing that his son has been killed. He has been divorced from the boy's mother for years, and consequently hasn't had much contact with his son. Partly out of frustration and boredom, wishing to browbeat the authorities, partly on impulse, and partly out of curiosity, he questions the personnel of the base, and the townspeople who have known his son, and learns himself, partly at least, from what he finds out from them. I started out, as nearly as I can remember, with a sound in my head of the engines being pre-flighted, before dawn, when I was in flying school. In a couple of days the outline of the plot came to me, and I sat down and sketched it out.[23]

Later Dickey offered a different origin for *Alnilam;* he said it began with the ghostly image of a man created by two propellors spinning one in front of the other. He also said Joel was modeled after his son Chris, but Chris wasn't born when Dickey first worked out the plot. The truculent, recently divorced father was partly based on Dickey's father (at Darlington he had circulated the story about his parents' divorce). Dickey said little about his actual father to Lytle, although it was apparent that in Lytle he had found the sort of paternal figure he had always wanted.

The adulation flowed both ways in the early letters between Dickey and Lytle. Obviously smitten by Dickey's attentiveness and applause (Dickey had been offering copious suggestions regarding Lytle's novel in progress, *The Velvet Horn*), Lytle expostulated on his feelings of "communion": "It is as if two consciousness[es] existed in the dynamic stasis of two brimming bowls, held in the perfect poise of a timeless state, seemingly spaces apart, when all along there has been this invisible movement of time and space bringing them to the slight jar which has set the bowls to flowing into each other, and there is such an indistinguishable identity between the exchanging liquids that in spite of the flowing the bowls still tremble upon the full-lipped brims." Lytle went on in this suggestive way about "exchanging liquids" and "full-lipped brims" to speculate about "the anima, that image of the feminine in each man,"[24] which he found in Dickey's poem "Anniversary," and which he found and cherished in Dickey himself.

In April, Dickey began packing up his Houston apartment in preparation for his return to Atlanta. While Chris sat on the packing barrels shooting at his parents with his cowboy pistol, his father tried to organize what he called a Robinson Crusoe–like salvage operation. Although Maxine had refused to let her husband abandon his family again for a summer of writing, the prospect of the family being together for a year in Europe may have softened her resolve. Around June 4, Dickey drove his wife and son to Nashville's James Robertson Hotel. A few days later he was back at his parents' home at 166 West Wesley. His mother, who was vacationing in Coral Sands, Florida, sent a provocative postcard of a blonde in a bikini to stress what her son was missing. Dickey's plan was to stay in Atlanta and write. He also looked forward to meeting Lytle, who usually visited an Atlanta friend, Whittier Wright, during the summer. Lytle wanted to reserve a hotel room so that he could spend two uninterrupted days with Dickey. Dickey, instead, insisted that he stay at West Wesley.

On June 12, Lytle flew into the Atlanta airport and for the rest of the day, in the quiet rooms of the Dickeys' home, he traded manuscripts with his protégé and spoke fervently about literature. After dinner, they continued their discussion until it was almost time for Dickey to drive the older writer, flagging from the combined effect of numerous drinks and nonstop conversation, to the airport for a flight to a Utah writers' conference. Although Dickey showed few signs of fatigue in Lytle's presence, the next night he slept sixteen hours. Several days later, Dickey wrote Lytle with the adoration of a disciple: "You are the greatest man I have ever known, and the only great one. . . . The fact that we were once together for a few hours would itself suffice to justify my life."[25] According to Dickey, only Rilke had comparable imaginative gifts; Faulkner and Robert Penn Warren and all the other Southern writers would remain forever in Lytle's shadow. Lytle was similarly moved by their meeting. A day after parting, he again used images of ecstatic communion to describe their friendship. "Our farewell, like any true climax, was both an ending and a beginning," he wrote. "It was you who gave it what each had wanted; it was I who was lost in the humors of fatigue and drink. Those humors were burned away into the essential communion—by you. I don't have to say more to be understood; indeed I don't have to say what is understood."[26] Like many young writers whose fathers express little interest in their sons' seemingly futile literary efforts, Dickey was starved for Lytle's encouragement. Both men, in fact, discussed what to do about Eugene Dickey's indifference and decided that a letter from Lytle might help.

Lytle dutifully wrote Eugene the day after he left West Wesley, combining gratitude for Eugene's hospitality and praise for his son:

> As you know, I think your son is wonderful. He's already a fine poet, a gentle sensibility, and a man. He's going to make literary history, if he has luck which he has already shown he has. But luck can't be bolted and haltered. There's nothing harder to be than a good poet. Few read the poets; poetry greases no belly, but it defines the very best of being, and a society finally gets its image in posterity from the artists, whose imaginations fix it, so that what is dead stays forever alive.
>
> Generally neglect, misunderstanding and small change is the joy the world gives its artists, but then praise and understanding from any but your peers enslaves—so it is just as well. I tell you this because I know you know what a fine boy he is, but that you might like to know what somebody else in the calling thinks, too.[27]

The skeptical Eugene must have taken heart at such an eloquent endorsement. Jim, as Lytle now called him, responded with thanks: "He [Eugene] has no understanding of what I do, but now I think he does, a little."[28] Lytle told Dickey he would write every week and hoped that Dickey would reciprocate:

> I can't tell you what you mean to me. I think I don't have to. The things you say flow through me like an everlasting stream. I suppose from now on we will be writing for each other. You are my one perfect reader. . . . How wonderful it would have been, if you could have come along with me [to Utah]. I've had a strenuous time and I didn't sleep much on the plane. . . . You are a part of me now forever. Your strength of heart and mind and body, which I surmised, but which I know—after being with you and after you opened up with no reticences—it was like coming on an oasis—this strength I need, for I don't have too much. . . . Those few hours we were

together, it was like putting lips to the spring, tasting and then having them snatched away, when you could have plunged deep—and in the plunge not get enough.[29]

Shortly afterward, Dickey gushed in kind: "There will be no powers to intrude and destroy what is between us, Andrew, for our courses have run far and deep enough together to be proof against anything."[30] Their intense affection, however, was destined to suffer diminution.

On June 17, Dickey wrote Maxine, who was still in Nashville, about his euphoria over Lytle's visit and also about the possibility of a teaching job at the University of Florida, which Lytle had encouraged Dickey to pursue after his Sewanee Fellowship. Lytle, he explained to Maxine, was nothing less than a literary saint: "He is so generous, so perceptive, so sympathetic, and so kind that I was left time and again absolutely unable to say what I wish I had been able to say." Lytle had paid him the ultimate compliment by comparing him to Shakespeare and contending that he was superior to the Bard. At least that was Dickey's interpretation: "Once I quoted some lines from Shakespeare, and he leaned forward and tapped me on the knee and said, gravely, 'But don't you see how much better your lines . . . are? Can you feel that?'" Such compliments, which a more modest poet would laugh at as absurd hyperbole, left Dickey speechless. He told Maxine that at the airport before departing for Utah, Lytle had embraced him: "He reached out and took my hand and put his other arm around my neck, the way fathers sometimes do with grown sons. Both of us were strongly moved."[31]

As surrogate father, Lytle during the summer of 1954 listened to Dickey's many complaints about his actual father and family. Dickey informed Lytle of his brother Tom's failing business and his many unpayable debts, and unfairly deflected blame from Tom to his wife's spending habits. Rivalry with Tom inspired these snubs, but Dickey also hoped to appeal to Lytle's prejudices against the business world. "Business," Dickey contended, adopting the Agrarian stance of his mentor, was guilty of a "systematic denial of human values, for which it can substitute only accumulation, and its gray, hopeless world." Dickey added: "There is nothing worse for an artist than to have to make his living in the commercial world. Because of his preoccupation with his real work he is almost certain to be a failure at his job; the two realms cannot help interfering with each other in the most savage and debilitating ways. Yet how many American artists have had to do this! I think of poor Crane, writing advertising-copy, and of Poe, of Phelps Putnam, and Faulkner. The university is about the only refuge there is."[32] What he failed to tell Lytle was that money was almost as important to him as artistic freedom and that, to solve his dilemma, he had already contemplated getting a job in advertising. In the end, he hoped his writing would become a highly remunerative business.

After Lytle's visit, Dickey spent his free time as he had the previous summer—by reading (he was particularly moved by Forster's *The Longest Journey*), writing, and visiting the fleshpots of the city. On June 24, he took boyish pleasure in writing Maxine that he was swimming as much as possible at the Venetian and The Driving Club: "I bought a bathing suit I like better than any that I have ever had, though some said that it makes me look like Rocky (Marciano). It is a ($2.25) pair of basketball trunks with elastic around the top. Maroon, with a gold stripe down the legs, and around the ham. Very comfortable, and I can swim and dive like mad." Hoping to arouse her jealousy, he then tried to disperse it: "I thought you might be delighted to hear that I haven't yet taken to wearing my new bathing suit, and consequently haven't succeeded in 'whowing' . . . any of the local debs. I just mention this to set your mind at ease. . . . I love you more than you, I, or anyone will ever be able to say, or even know, but only feel."[33] Such abstract love made for impassioned prose, but it did little to assuage Maxine's disappointment about having to spend another summer apart from her husband.

With Rice permanently behind him, Dickey relaxed with old high school teammates, watched boxing matches, and flirted with former girlfriends. What he gained from these activities was a conviction that he had outgrown his Atlanta friends. From his Olympian perspective, even new friends like Lytle seemed somewhat paltry. Dickey conceded to Maxine that he was lucky to know such a talented gentleman as Lytle—"He is awareness, imagination, and sympathy themselves"—but he also felt it was a little sad "that Andrew Lytle seems so much to depend on me."[34] Now that he had his Sewanee Fellowship, he looked forward to leaving Atlanta, mentors, and, indeed, America for the magnificence of Europe.

12. Travels in Europe (1954–1955)

In June and July, the Dickeys prepared for the trip they would later regard as a watershed event. "Afterward," Chris Dickey said, "we would measure every event in our family's life as 'before we went to Europe' and 'after we went to Europe.' As little as I was, I had this sense that our trip had changed everything."[1] The trip was momentous for many reasons: It brought Dickey face to face with the treasures of Western culture, it gave him new perspectives on America, it introduced him to foreign writers, and it invigorated his marriage after the depressing jobs at Rice and Waco. With tickets and suitcases in hand, the Dickeys left Atlanta for New York on the evening of July 26. Dickey had hoped to visit Lytle at Harvard, but decided an extra excursion would be too hard on Chris. He hoped instead that Lytle could meet them in New York.

Dickey celebrated the beginning of his fellowship with a week-long visit to Calhoun Winton, who lived in Princeton, New Jersey. The Dickeys and Wintons went to a Swedish smorgasbord, swam at the beach, and met Bill Dix, a Rice librarian who now headed the Princeton library. One night they dined with Allen Tate and his wife, the novelist Caroline Gordon, and while Chris slept in Tate's study, they talked until two in the morning. They returned for more conviviality the next evening. Before they left, Gordon, who had just returned from a year in Italy with Tate, kindly typed out addresses of hotels and restaurants in Florence and Rome. Realizing Dickey needed employment when he returned from Europe, Tate offered to secure a job for him at the University of Minnesota. A proud Maxine wrote her mother: "I feel we are in the big league now and Jim is sure holding his own."[2] Two days later, on August 4, they boarded the *Queen Elizabeth*, settled into their cabin on the C deck, and set off for England.

Dickey had such a good time eating, drinking, swimming, and playing Ping-Pong (he won top prize in a tournament) that he didn't want to get off the boat when it docked on August 9. For starters, the weather was dismal. London had experienced little summer in 1954, and in the usual rain and fog that descended on its streets, Dickey fell ill. When his health improved, he started to make forays from London's Prince's Lodge Hotel. Fascinated by the ancient city he had read about but never seen, he noted the contrast between hallowed English traditions and brash TV shows and nightclubs. He sent Lytle observations calculated to please him: "One thing I have noticed here is that the customs, the ceremonies seem to be losing their efficacy, their vital power of suggesting a mystical and perhaps holy relationship between the body of the sovereign, the land, and the people. There is a terrible air of 'going through the motions'; the people seem even a little rootless, wanting comfort and conveniences more than anything else. They don't realize what they are giving up, but maybe it is too late in the day . . . for these things to be preserved. I believe the old England is finished, or soon will be, though the last of its glory is magnificent, especially in the autumn, as it is beginning to be here."[3] Just as he waxed nostalgic about the feudal South to Lytle, Dickey lamented the passing of the aristocratic England of hierarchy and ceremony that had been idealized by Southern Agrarians and by their mentor T. S. Eliot, now a prominent British citizen. In his poetry Dickey also bowed to the trappings of empire, kingship, and ceremony, even though he expressed indifference or impatience with them in his day-to-day life.

Because Allen Tate recommended that he visit Stephen Spender, who was editing the magazine *Encounter*, Dickey brought "The Maze" and several other poems to his editorial office on the afternoon of August 24. Dickey had admired Spender's poetry and prose ever since he'd started reading it during World War II. On meeting him, however, he decided that Spender was a "nice fellow, in a sort of misty, homosexual way," but "vague about everything."[4] Spender and Dickey spent several afternoons talking about the British literary scene; about James Agee, who was suffering from alcoholism and a heart attack (he would die on May 16, 1955); and about the possibility of *Encounter* publishing Dickey's poems. On August 24, Spender rejected them. Because of this disappointment, Dickey could remember little about his talk with Spender besides "that professional shy-fellow condescending to me, talking about 'compression' and 'the need to clarify.' "[5] Spender's snub continued to rankle. A few years later Dickey referred to Spender as "that detestable fake" and relished an account of how one of his favorite poets, the belligerent South African Roy Campbell, had "hobbled on-stage [at a poetry reading] and flattened grovelling Stephen Spender with a looping overhand right to the side of the head."[6] The aptness of Spender's critique of Dickey's obscure, long-winded poems no doubt made it more infuriating.

Along with Spender, Dickey intended to meet Eliot, but as he nonchalantly recalled: "I never did get around to it."[7] Dickey's sister-in-law, Patsy, had originally proposed that the two poets get together. While modeling in Atlanta, she had met Mrs. James Gussow and at Gussow's house made the mistake of expressing her dislike for Eliot before finding out that Gussow was Eliot's niece. Embarrassed, she made amends by suggesting that her brother-in-law go see Eliot in London. On August 2, 1954, Gussow wrote Eliot to make arrangements. Because Dickey admired Eliot's poetry as well as his politics at the time, he looked forward to the meeting, but he also may have felt intimidated by Eliot's stature. Six years before, Eliot had won the Nobel Prize as well as Britain's Order of Merit. Intellectuals around the world deferred to him as the pope of English letters.

In a story he told an English class in the fall of 1976, Dickey revealed his former reverence for Eliot even while playing fast and loose with the facts. He said he had lunched with Eliot in New York after World War II when *Murder in the Cathedral* was playing on Broadway. "I sat awed," Dickey claimed. "When I looked at the menu, I drew a blank. Eliot ordered for me."[8] He told one colleague that Eliot brought attention to their common background. "You're a Southerner," Eliot said at the lunch. "I'm from Saint Louis, so I'm partly Southern. The Civil War is something from which your country will never recover."[9] During the 1940s and 1950s, Eliot did fill Dickey with awe, but the two poets never conversed in New York. Dickey had hoped for the sort of lunch he described to his students and colleagues, but Valerie Fletcher, Eliot's Faber secretary and future wife, explained to Dickey on May 4, 1955, that her boss would not be able to meet him in New York. He had been in New York, but was due to sail for England on June 15.

Dickey wanted to meet Eliot in America because he had failed to call him in London at the beginning of his Sewanee Fellowship. After receiving Gussow's letter in August 1954, Eliot expected Dickey to contact him when he arrived in London. All fall Eliot waited to hear from Dickey. On December 19, he wrote his Atlanta niece: "The primary reason for [my] delay [in writing you] was that I supposed that I should be hearing from your friend James Dickey. I am sorry that I have never heard from him or his wife, and that I have not met what seemed to be such an excellent sample of Atlanta society. Did he never come to England? Or was he too busy elsewhere or in other ways? Or was he too shy to present the introduction? Anyway, if you are in touch with their relatives I trust that you will tell them that I had been expecting him."[10] Mrs. Gussow was irritated by this news; she had gone out of her way to organize the meeting. In the letter that finally reached the Dickeys in Cap d'Antibes, she urged Dickey to send a formal apology and make up the excuse that he had avoided Eliot out of a concern for the older poet's poor health. Dickey, in fact, had heard of Eliot's illness from Gussow's sister, Theodora, who lived in London.

Taking Mrs. Gussow's advice to heart, Dickey sent an apology on January 23, 1955, in which he expressed his hope to visit Eliot when he returned to London. Eliot dutifully wrote back; Dickey got the letter in Florence in mid-March. Now it was Eliot's turn to apologize for not making contact: Due to the recurrence of his illness, his correspondence had slowed to a trickle. He would not be able to welcome Dickey in London because of his trip to New York, but said: "I hope that after what Mrs. Gussow has told me about you that there will be some future occasion to meet on one side of the water or the other."[11] As it turned out, Dickey and Eliot crossed the Atlantic at exactly the same time in 1955. They never met.

Dickey quickly adapted to England's left-lane driving and innumerable roundabouts in a newly purchased British car, a Hillman Minx, and soon felt confident enough to drive to Cambridge, about sixty miles north of London, to visit David Dowler, who had returned home from Rice. On the second day in Cambridge, Dickey fell sick again, this time with what he called "a kind of dysentery which seems ordered to go with the British weather."[12] Their unheated, damp, sparsely decorated room in Cambridge made him feel worse. As Dickey struggled to recuperate, Dowler introduced him to the pastoral splendors and nightlife of the ancient university town. Together they went punting on the river Cam (Dowler poled), played darts and drank beer in pubs, and visited the university's resplendent gardens. Determined to show the Dickeys more of England, Dowler drove them to Windsor Castle, Eton College, Portsmouth (to see Lord Nelson's flagship), and Hampshire, where his mother lived. Because of all the traveling, Dickey decided to scrap his original plan of driving to Ireland, the ancestral ground of his maternal grandmother, and Scotland, the home of other ancestors. Instead, he returned to London to celebrate his son's third birthday on August 31 and then drove his family south to Dover, a trip he memorialized in his long poem "Dover: Believing in Kings." On September 2, the Dickeys boarded a ferry for Dunkerque, spent the night in the French town of Arras, and the next day headed for Paris, where Dickey's Rice colleague, Lester Mansfield, met them below the Eiffel Tower. While standing in line for tickets to go up in the elevator, the Dickeys saw a man jump from the top of the tower and land not far from where they stood. Two American soldiers, who had been waiting in line, rushed to the man, who was already dead. Mansfield did his best to calm Dickey's nerves, and soon led him to a hotel room on Saint Germain in the Latin Quarter.

In Paris the Dickeys did what most tourists do; they visited Montmarte, the Arc de Triomphe, the Champs Elysées, the Luxembourg Gardens, the museums, the zoo, the cafés. They especially liked the restaurants. So that she could duplicate some of Paris's culinary wonders in America, Maxine started compiling recipes from the French chefs. While the wife of their hotel manager took care of Chris, Jim and Maxine also sampled the city's fabled nightlife. They watched scantily clad women perform at the Follies and attended a lesbian nightclub where gay men put on an extravagant floor show. If Dickey had expected the city to satisfy all his hedonistic and aesthetic desires, he quickly grew disillusioned. Another illness soured his mood. His main complaint about the city, however, was that it was too expensive and too dangerous. Matters grew worse when a thief cut open the convertible roof on his Hillman Minx with a knife. He had to wait two-and-a-half hours at a police station for an interpreter to file an official report and six days to have the roof repaired at a cost of fifty dollars.

Dickey tried to articulate his jaundiced view of Paris to Andrew Lytle on September 25: "Paris in some ways is as great a city as I have always heard it was, but I missed something there: perhaps it is the lack of personal discipline everywhere evident. I am not used to so much personal freedom: in dress, in language, in taste, sex, and so on."[13] The libertarian Dickey seemed shocked by all the liberties paraded before him. Years later, considering the non-English-speaking cultures that influenced his lifestyle and writing, Dickey always pointed to the French. In Paris he said he got a chance to listen to one of his favorite writers, Albert Camus, whose views on freedom and tradition were diametrically opposed to Lytle's. He attended a lecture Camus gave at the Sorbonne on how people create their own destiny. What most impressed Dickey about the Frenchman's existential views was a comment he made about religion: "In the front row was this long-haired guy wearing a black turtleneck, beard and a large cross on a chain around his neck. 'What must I do to start a new religion?' the guy asked Camus. Camus thought about it and said: 'Get yourself crucified and rise from the dead.'"[14] Some of Dickey's characters, like Joel Cahill and Muldrow, came close to following Camus's advice, and for a similar reason—they wanted the reverence accorded to divinities.

Although other expatriates had found London and Paris conducive to their artistic temperaments, Dickey felt alien in both places. In London, aesthetic tastes rather than the language kept him at bay. As for Paris, he told Lytle, it was "a great city for writers; that is, for the kind of writers who need other writers around, who need the 'literary life,' who need to discuss and drink together, and the rest of it. I had a sample of that, but my writing felt too lonely there; I knew none of the latest writers, and had a good deal of trouble understanding what was going on."[15] Dickey's French was not good enough for him to talk to the local writers or read their work. To improve his command of the language and its literature, Dickey bought piles of books at Paris's many bookstores, read as often as he could with a dictionary at hand, and attended the theater, where he knew enough vocabulary to enjoy the plays of Jean Vilar and Henri Pichette. If nothing else, French theater stimulated his ambition to be a playwright—an ambition he periodically resuscitated over the years. Gradually his French improved.

Ill at ease in the Parisian culture he had often romanticized, Dickey decided to move south. He picked up the family laundry sent from London, where he had forgotten it, and drove toward the Mediterranean: "We came down on the Côte d'Azur, the Riviera, and we motored up and down looking for a suitable place. We tried several places like St. Tropez and St. Raphael, and we couldn't find anything that we liked. So we ended up on Cap d'Antibes, which is about five miles from Cannes, ten or eleven miles from Nice. It was a pretty good location. It was right near the Villa America, where Gerald Murphy had his house with Scott Fitzgerald. [It was] the setting of the opening part of *Tender Is the Night*, and we used to go swimming down on the beach that Gerald Murphy had made."[16] In Provence, the temporary residence of so many past writers and artists, the Dickeys on September 24 found "a big house with a tremendous yard full of red flowers and cactus plants, lizards and little birds, with a great yawning silence surrounding it."[17] The yard had a rope swing for Chris and a small pool with two fat goldfish, which he tried to catch with a string attached to a stick. Although Maxine had reservations about the villa—it was a long way from stores and it was not well insulated—they signed a lease that allowed them to stay from October 1, 1954, to June 1955. Because it was the off-season, the villa's rent had dropped from $250 to $75 per month. Dickey adored the local flora and fauna, "the grids of the vineyards laid subtly up the uneven hills, the poplars lining the roads, the Rhone leaning furiously on its banks, straight for miles." In this earthly paradise, he concentrated on his poetry with a new intensity. He wrote Lytle: "I know now, though dimly, what I want from poetry: emotional depth: spontaneous, immediate: that the poem should strike the reader down through the more obvious levels of his being into the hidden and essential ones, and stay there, giving up its meanings as the reader's life does, not all at once. I want a poetry both human and imaginative: 'forcer le plus réel à exister.' But there is all that to do yet, of course."[18] He assured Lytle that he would make the Sewanee judges proud by the end of his year abroad.

Dickey welcomed the artistic community of Provence. He reported to Lytle that he had met Picasso several times in Vallauris, a nearby mountain town: "He is a fine old man, small, rather peasant-like, gentle, with many children and relatives, most of the former, I believe, illegitimate."[19] Picasso's earthy fecundity was more to his liking than Spender's aloofness. Picasso had a ceramics workshop nearby, and according to Dickey he gave Chris a small ceramic bull made in its kilns. (On January 12, 1955, Maxine reported in a letter to her mother that they had gone to Picasso's ceramic shop and *bought* some souvenirs.) Picasso's many children had not diminished his appetite for child's play. Maxine told her mother that while attending a Picasso show in an Antibes museum, Picasso had walked up to Chris, rubbed his head, complimented him, and introduced him to his grown son and granddaughter. The Dickeys saw Picasso again on October 2 when they went to Cannes to see a movie. Attracted to Chris, Picasso asked if he could sketch him. His parents agreed, but when Dickey reached for the sketch, Picasso indicated that he wanted to keep it.

Dickey also claimed that he met Picasso in the local bookstore where he bought poetry books and practiced his French. The owner, Monsieur Aldon, a veteran who had been captured by the Germans during World War II, corrected Dickey's halting sentences as they swapped war stories. One day, as Dickey recalled: "Picasso came in the store with his entourage, his son Claude and some of the other people he had following him. And he bought something there, and went away, and I said to Monsieur Aldon: 'Picasso!' And he thought I was asking him if he had any art books of Picasso. I said: 'Non, non, cet homme, c'est Picasso lui-même!' 'Picasso lui-même, Mon Dieu! Il a acheté un livre de cuisine!' He bought a cookbook!"[20] Dickey also indicated that he was on friendly terms with Matisse. After returning from Europe, he told an *Atlanta Constitution* reporter that he had attended Matisse's funeral. Maxine's letters to her mother, which are more reliable than her husband's recollections, only mention visiting a Dominican chapel in Vence decorated by Matisse. Also living in the vicinity was the renowned writer Nikos Kazantzakis, whose novels and poems Dickey admired. Several people encouraged Dickey to call on him, but, as with Eliot, he was either too shy or too busy to bother.

In Antibes Dickey set himself the task of learning French well enough to appreciate the poets he already knew in translation. Maxine facilitated his efforts, as she usually did, by tending house. By November, Dickey had mastered French well enough to write Bill Pratt: "If you don't know French, learn it, by all means. The French writers have been a revelation to me. They cut loose down the imagination like Mel Patton on the 220: none of this niggling around, making tiny surprises. How good it is to hear someone speak out with something to say, instead of mealing about getting up something from a rose-garden and the Kenyon Summer Writers Conference!"[21] Among the French poets, he especially admired René Char, Paul Éluard, Henri Pichette, Antonin Artaud, Pierre-Jean Jouve, and Michel Leiris. Years later, when asked about the early influences on his work, he usually mentioned Thomas, Barker, Eliot, Hopkins, and Roethke, only to add: "But the poets that have influenced me in my fashion from the time I really started publishing books were foreign-language poets, mainly the French: Jules Supervielle, Pierre Reverdy, André Frénaud, René Guy Cadou, and other writers of the contemporary French scene. . . . I discovered them when I used to sit in cafés in France in 1954."[22] Dickey's interest in French poetry was insatiable, as the dozens of book titles in his notebooks attest.

In Provence Dickey had time for family outings as well as for books. In early November he drove the family to the ski resort at Valberg. Despite the scarcity of snow, Dickey once again tried to ski. He took other excursions with his family to visit cafés in Cannes. When the sun came out, he hiked with Chris up to the lighthouse and sailors' chapel on top of the large hill behind their villa. The view of the Mediterranean from the summit was breathtaking. He told Lytle he could see "the whole coast from Cannes to Menon, a huge half-opened wing preparing some hesitant and marvelling flight toward something never to be disclosed, blue with age and hope and decision and inaction, under the intense frost of the mountains opposite. There is nothing so calm, nothing so full of immediate and contemplative beauty."[23] He frequented the beaches, snorkeled while Maxine and Chris followed him in a pedal boat, ogled the practically naked women in their bikinis, and soon convinced Maxine to buy one.

With few American friends, Maxine asked her mother, who had just become the new attorney general's secretary in Nashville, to come to Europe for a visit. She wrote on October 26: "If it wasn't for Jim, I would start home tomorrow. The United States is the most comfortable, best place in the world. It's fine to see all these places but to do it right, you need lots more money to spend than we have."[24] Dickey contacted his own mother periodically to ask for financial assistance. As Maxine explained in a letter on June 3, 1955, Maibelle had provided a five-hundred-dollar monthly allowance throughout their stay in Europe. Maibelle also sent an additional twenty-five hundred dollars to cover various expenses. When they wanted to get a more comfortable villa in early November, Maibelle came to the rescue with an extra one thousand dollars that she planned to deduct from the ten thousand dollars she was saving for their future house purchase. She sympathized with what she called Maxine's "Shot-to-Hell-Budget-Blues."[25] Several weeks before they sailed home, the Dickeys asked Maibelle for and quickly received an extra thousand dollars to pay for their boat tickets. The plea Dickey sent to his mother from Salzburg on May 24, 1955, was typical: "Though we have set aside the money to ship the car back, though we have cut every corner we can . . . , our money keeps flying, or melting, or running, or just disappearing. We might still be able to make it home on what we have now, but, planning for the worst (which one must do in Europe), it would be better if we had a final $500, on which we would resolve to sink or swim."[26] In the end, the Dickeys would spend eight thousand dollars—more than twice the amount allocated by the Sewanee Fellowship—during their trip overseas. The extra cash from Maibelle, however, did little to allay Maxine's homesickness.

With the advent of winter, the Dickeys found the cold unbearable. Maxine and Chris came down with sinus infections. Jim's cousin, Eugenia, visited from the States, and even though Maibelle sent extra money for her entertainment, her constant complaining about the villa exasperated everyone. Dickey struggled with the coal-and-wood-burning furnace to keep the family warm:

> What we didn't realize was that those French families that own those villas down in the resort place don't expect to live in them, and they don't expect for the madame to be cooking in the kitchen either. The kitchen was very primitive. We didn't even have a refrigerator. We had an icebox. Chris and I would go down and get a big chunk of ice in the washtub everyday, bring it back and put it in the icebox. It began to get cold . . . and then the *mistral* began to blow. . . . I was feeding [the furnace] all the time, and chopping up wood and throwing in pine cones and sticks and everything else I could find. I was spending most of the time trying to keep my family warm. And I couldn't write.[27]

In January 1955, the Dickeys decided to search for a more hospitable area. Since their French landlords expected them to stay until June, they negotiated a release from their contract, and on January 15, Dickey drove his Hillman Minx along the Italian Riviera through Genoa, Pisa, and on to Florence.

After the slow, tortuous trip through foggy mountains with cliffs rising on the left and dropping on the right, the Dickeys were heartened by the mild, sunny weather of Florence. They quickly located a modern *pensione* that served delectable pastas, salads, wines, cheeses, and fruits. Most important, the rooms were warm. Taking advantage of the sunshine, the Dickeys set off on sight-seeing tours. They visited the famous cathedral, the Duomo, where Dickey and Maxine wept at the organ music. They went to the church of Santa Croce, which held the tombs of Galileo and Michelangelo, as well as the Uffizi Gallery. They also enjoyed socializing with local Americans like the dapper Memphis man Henry Fonda (unrelated to the actor), who owned plantations in Mississippi and Arkansas. They met a young architect on a fellowship, Herb Oppenheimer, and his wife, Judy. Although both Maxine and Jim objected to Herb's Jewishness (Maxine wrote her mother on February 28, 1955: "Yes he is a Jew . . . and he is the vilest one we've ever known"),[28] they occasionally went to parties with Herb and his wife.

To ensure that he made progress with his poetry, Dickey set himself a schedule of four hours of writing and four hours of sight-seeing per day. On January 28, he wrote Bill Pratt about his recent move: "We hated to leave Provence; I had grown quite to love the place, the terraced hills, and the whole soft crumbling-and-held-together-with-vines look and air of it, but France, for our shekels, was *trop cher,* and too cold, too, despite the work I did on the *chauffage* every day, which, if translated into heroic action, would have slain a thousand Medusas, tracked and strangled the Minotaur, and lifted Prometheus's peak out from under him. Italy is better for us, though the majesty of it is hard to assimilate through the poverty of most of the people: you feel like you ought to be attending meetings and speaking wildly against the conditions rather than standing mutely in the Uffizzi [sic], looking up at the da Vinci's and Botticelli's. But these latter are unbelievably beautiful, nonetheless; I have not been to any meetings."[29] Dickey paid attention to social conditions and their political solutions, but not to the detriment of his main commitment, which was to writing.

Among all the glorious artifacts, Michelangelo's "David" and Cellini's "Perseus" struck Dickey as the most riveting (he went to see the statue of David every Sunday). He wrote Lytle: "Sweet mother of the Muses, what a form! *There is heroic statuary.* He has the . . . look that, somehow, fits the hero, a face somewhere between an unconcerned woman's and a gilded and lazy god's, a torso like a young bull, full of balance and cruelty."[30] Such artwork appealed to Dickey's mythic imagination as well as his obsessions with heroes and beheadings. In between walks around Florence, he labored on a mythical poem about Perseus and the Medusa, which was going to be his magnum opus and personal "farewell to arms." He also tinkered with another ambitious poem-in-progress, "The Vision of the Sprinter." In a letter to Monroe Spears, who had just taken his poem "The Confrontation of the Hero" for the summer issue of the *Sewanee Review,* he explained his desire to use myth for the sake of universality: "I wanted for a long time to work at the intersection of the classic myths and everyday life: to try to discover in what ways the ageless patterns contained in the myths are played out, perhaps unknown to the players, among the real things and situations of life."[31] On his way to mastering what Eliot had called the "mythical method," Dickey tended to clot his poems with rhetoric that made more sound than sense. At the end of "The Confrontation of the Hero," a poem about the Philippines in which Dickey imagines a heavenly warrior resurrecting a corpse, he writes:

He placed his armor on the stair of light
And bent to take my yellowed head,
His muscles gliding naked in the mirror
Of the air, his face warm as a man's
Who shall hold at his breast the look
To freeze his peaceful cities to the stone
Lamp of every room, though over plotted graves
He bear it in trembling gentleness, till it be richened
With the stars between the ships of all the bays,
And nail it to the ground in secret weeping.

Dickey still needed to harness classic myth and classic clarity to his apocalyptic horses.

In Florence Dickey had more-mundane matters to worry about than mythic poems. His job anxieties swelled when Maxine thought she might be pregnant. Maxine wrote her mother on March 21: "Of course we are very ready for another baby and Chris talks about wanting a little sister all the time. In fact he wants twins. But it would have been hard on me to travel as much as we have planned."[32] Although the pregnancy turned out to be a false alarm, Dickey continued to write letters to U.S. colleges for a job. He contacted thirty-five in all. When he met Allen Tate's friend Professor Ames in Florence, he quizzed him about the job possibilities at the University of Minnesota. By mid-March he'd received rejections from the University of Minnesota, Alabama, Sewanee, Emory and Henry, Davidson, and Rollins. With no job in sight, he asked his sister-in-law to help find a position in Atlanta television. He also considered looking for a job in an Atlanta public relations firm. In desperation he implored Lytle to send word about his prospects at the University of Florida. On February 7, 1955, Lytle told him to contact Jacob Wise, head of the freshman English program. Dickey wrote Wise, but heard nothing.

In search of warmer weather, the Dickeys headed south to Naples on April 11, and stayed for a week at a *pensione* facing the sea. They next drove to Rome, where Dickey hoped to remain until mid-May. They went to the Roman Forum, the Coliseum, Saint Peter's Square (the pope blessed them), the circus, movie theaters, and museums. On Easter Sunday, they sat at a café on the Via Veneto to watch an extravagant Easter Parade and bask in the sun. Intoxicated by Rome's pomp and ceremony, Dickey found the festive spirit in unlikely spots outside the city as well. He took side trips to Naples, Capri, and Pompeii, the ancient Roman city that had been wracked by an earthquake in 63 A.D. and buried with cinders and ash when Mount Vesuvius erupted around 79 A.D. In Pompeii he visited the ancient Roman whorehouse, the only building in Pompeii that still had a roof. An engraved penis on a wall pointed the way to cubicles the size of horizontal telephone booths where the Romans bought sex with tickets. The guide shone his flashlight on frescoes of different sexual positions. "They were some of the weirdest looking contortions you could possibly imagine,"[33] Dickey recalled. As Dickey stood enthralled, the guide recounted how some of the brothel-goers died in medias res when Vesuvius choked them with ash. "In the Lupanar at Pompeii," a poem collected in *Drowning with Others*, revealed Dickey's ambivalence about such open displays of sex. (Drawn almost against his will down the old chariot ruts, past the flower sellers and cindery produce market, to the prisonlike cells where Romans vented their lust, he concludes that "the marvel of lust" can "Become more than it believed, / And almost always is less."[34])

During his three-week residence in Rome, Dickey met the poet Richard Wilbur for the first time. In his rented apartment Wilbur was working hard to finish a book of poetry; he was also drinking lots of wine, eating pasta, playing tennis, and staying up late with visiting writers like Dickey. The frenetic pace soon caught up to him, and he collapsed beneath the hot Italian sun. His local doctor attributed the sudden blackout to a mild heart attack and hinted that Wilbur might never climb stairs, play tennis, or exercise in any strenuous way again. Fortunately, a more levelheaded American doctor traced Wilbur's problems to a stomach spasm caused by too many beer chasers after tennis matches. To help their new friend, the Dickeys took care of the Wilburs' children, entertaining them at zoos and picnics. Although Dickey had scoffed at Wilbur's "mechanical" verse in private, meeting the poet softened his critical barbs. In a few months he wrote Wilbur to ask permission to use his verse "as a kind of stick to beat other poets with"[35] in a review he was writing.

Dickey also got to know one of Wilbur's close poet friends, William Jay Smith, who had taken an apartment on the Via Princiana with his wife, the poet Barbara Howes. They often gathered for drinks and literary conversation with Dickey at the nearby Hotel Eden. Around Smith and Wilbur, Dickey was modest and reserved. Because they had published several books and because Dickey had published only a few poems and reviews, he looked up to them as elder literary statesmen. In their discussions, however, Smith realized that Dickey had clearly defined aesthetic opinions. With regard to Ransom, Tate, and Warren, Dickey proclaimed his independence. Another Southerner with a formalist bent, Smith advised Dickey to master the forms that the Fugitives had used; then he could pursue free verse as recklessly as he wanted. Unswayed by such advice, Dickey vowed to go his own way.

While in Rome, Dickey received an auspicious letter from Lytle about a job at the University of Florida. On April 14, Jacob Wise wrote that he was confident a position would open for Dickey. Dickey would have to teach introductory freshman and sophomore courses, but he would be able to team teach an upper-level creative writing course with Lytle. According to Maxine, after hearing from Wise: "Jim was so nervous + happy, he developed an upset stomach + we were up all last night with him vomiting, but he is fine today."[36] Dickey's constitution, which he pretended was forged out of wrought iron, quailed before the possibility of either good or bad news. Ecstatic about the prospect of being so close to his mentor, Dickey nevertheless resented the salary when a formal job offer arrived on June 14. It was thirty-eight hundred dollars, only a slight improvement over his thirty-three-hundred-dollar salary at Rice. Lytle was glad to hear of the job, too, although he warned Dickey that Wise was not appreciative of poetic talent and took a mechanical approach to teaching. Nevertheless, Dickey wrote Wise a letter of acceptance. "Teaching is my chosen profession," he said. "I believe in it, and I believe in my own powers to contribute something of permanent value, to human beings, through its exercise."[37] Despite the vagaries of his academic fortunes, Dickey remained loyal to this credo.

Dickey bid farewell to Rome in mid-May and drove his family through the spring countryside back to Florence, where he enjoyed meeting the often hilarious poet Peter Viereck. After a week in Florence, the Dickeys continued on to Venice, where from May 18 to May 22 they visited Harry's Bar as well as the more traditional sites. They next drove to Cortina, a ski town in the Italian Dolomites; Salzburg, Austria, which was crowded with American soldiers; and Innsbruck, where they experienced a slight earthquake. Chris remembered that his father was so terrified of the mountain roads that he was sick for several days. Finally, on May 26, they arrived in Zurich, where Dickey hoped to locate his former girlfriend Gwen Leege.

Around 1960, Dickey recalled his failure to find Gwen in an unpublished poem, "To Gweno, With a Guitar." Since he had not seen Gwen in about a decade, he could only imagine what she was like. In the unflattering poem she capers in "the abandoned dance fat women dream, alone":

You would be larger, now, and loving more
     All Nimble sounds of the ear,
All winds and strings of the same light on the earth.
     For heavying girls, all love depends upon
     The weight that drives them slowly to the ground.
You would be larger, now, and loving more.

This I thought, beside the lake at Zurich,
     The day I searched for you,
Following a letter with an old address.
     I never found you, in the one bright day I had there,
     But walked, in sun and moon, and looked at water
Which I thought, beside the lake at Zurich.[38]

In the end, Dickey's persona sends Gwen a guitar as a gift and hopes she will use it to conjure up their romantic past.

When the Dickeys arrived in Paris on June 1 after passing through Lucerne, Interlaken, and Bern, the city was cold and rainy, but in full springtime bloom. Dickey wanted to make the most of his last weeks in Europe, as he told Pratt:

> Paris is jumping, as it has always been except during the Resistance, and we are jumping with it, in our small way: into and out of huge panoramic shows of Picasso and Jacques Villon, night clubs, student dives, book shops, movies . . . , and sometimes just standing on the corner of Boul' Mich' and St. Germain and jumping up and down, to keep from stopping, even for a minute. My God, the *money* you can spend in this place really can haunt you. It must be more expensive here than in Hell (the American's hell must certainly involve a lot of *wasted* money, and the knowledge thereof). We are hanging on, though, trying to wing the best punches our poor few dollars of the Sewanee's money will buy for us, where they will do the most good.[39]

Knowing that he would miss the freedom and excitement of travel, Dickey nevertheless looked forward to a more comfortable routine in the States. Living out of suitcases for so long had been trying, especially for Maxine. On June 7, she wrote a heartfelt letter to her mother in which she admitted that she couldn't have lasted in Europe without her mother's supportive letters. To give her spirits a boost, Maxine got her hair fashionably streaked, as she had done during her previous stay in Paris, and went to see Notre Dame and the zoo with Chris. On June 16, their wanderings over, they boarded a boat train to Le Havre. Early on June 17, with regret mixed with anticipation, Dickey set sail from France on the SS *United States* and after a rough voyage saw the Statue of Liberty loom above the New York harbor on June 21.

Among its many beneficial effects, Europe invigorated Dickey's commitment to poetry. He no longer filled his notebooks with plot sketches for short stories and novels he would never write. Rather, he tried to systematize his ideas about poetry and bring his poems to publishable completion. Like many twentieth-century poets, Dickey discovered new perspectives in foreign sources. Upon returning to America, he began translating French poets, especially the surrealists, in earnest. He learned helpful lessons about representing multiperspective views of his subjects from artists like Picasso. As for James, Eliot, Pound, and Joyce, Europe presented Dickey with a panoramic view of a Western culture in need of renewal after its many wars. He now had a clearer idea of the monuments he wanted to emulate.

13. Uncle Ez and the Pen Women Scandal (1955–1956)

Having breathed the expatriate air of Europe and felt his literary lungs quicken, Dickey was intent on meeting one of the most famous American expatriates—Ezra Pound—who was living in the United States. Bill Pratt had promised to escort Dickey to Saint Elizabeth's Hospital and introduce him to Pound when Dickey traveled south from New York. A mental hospital was an unusual home for one of the world's premier poets, but Pound was an unusual poet. He had been confined to the asylum after being judged mentally unfit to stand trial for delivering treasonous broadcasts over Fascist radio in Italy. Nevertheless, admirers still flocked to this Faustian genius to hear him pronounce on whatever topic preoccupied him. After all, he had been the pioneer of modernism; the friend of James Joyce, T. S. Eliot, Ernest Hemingway, William Carlos Williams, Ford Madox Ford; and the avuncular guide for two generations of twentieth-century writers. Pratt, who was doing research for his Vanderbilt Ph.D. on Eliot, Pound, and Henry James, remembered an excited, glamorously dressed Dickey at the Washington, D.C., airport:

> In June of 1955, with Maxine and Chris, [Jim] . . . got off the plane in a new Italian silk suit, which my wife particularly noticed. We then told them we had booked a motel near where we were living in Falls Church, but after Jim consulted with Maxine, he said they thought it was too expensive and so they would make their own reservation for a place to stay, since we had a one-bedroom apartment and couldn't invite them to stay with us. I had asked Ezra Pound, whom I met in May—after writing to Winifred Overholser, the head psychiatrist at St. Elizabeth's, and receiving permission to visit him—if I could bring Jim to see him. Pound said fine, and Jim was delighted with the opportunity of meeting Pound. So we drove out to St. Elizabeth's together . . . on a Sunday afternoon when I would have been off duty with the Navy Judge Advocate General's Office where I worked, and talked with Pound on the lawn of the hospital for an hour or so.[1]

Compared to the smelly hospital where deranged patients paced and mumbled, the scene on the lawn was almost bucolic. Just back from Italy—Pound's adopted country—and beset with mixed feelings about his repatriation, Dickey established immediate rapport with Pound, whose ambivalence toward America was legendary.

Normally Pound discoursed on his old literary friends in London and his various political and economic schemes to save the world. During these fragmentary rambles, he inevitably offered his pet theories about avaricious Jews conspiring to wreck civilization or Negroes adulterating American culture. When Pratt brought up the Fugitive writers of his alma mater, Pound offered a typical riposte: they were "a talented bunch" organized by a Jew (Sidney Hirsch was Jewish). As if to mollify Pratt, an admirer of the Fugitives, he added: "The individual Jew is often a cultural activator, but collectively they have to be watched."[2] Sometimes given to anti-Semitic and anti-Fugitive broadsides of his own, Dickey spent most of his time simply sitting on the lawn and listening to the bumptious oracle.

When Pound asked about his trip to Europe, Dickey summarized what he had done and mentioned the Sewanee Fellowship that had made it possible. He also mentioned his Vanderbilt idol, Monroe Spears, who was editing the *Sewanee Review*. Feigning truculence, Pound asserted that if Spears was a poor editor, Dickey and Pratt should have him either replaced or shot. Since Dickey had visited Paris, they talked about French writers. Pound singled out Jean Cocteau as a writer he had once championed, although he admitted that he no longer kept up with the French literary scene. Afterward, Dickey spoke exuberantly to Pratt about "Il miglior fabbro" ("the better maker"), as he liked to call Pound, echoing Eliot's phrase for him in the dedication of *The Waste Land*. According to Pratt, "Jim considered it the high point of his year . . . and thanked me many times for the privilege. . . . We both remembered the occasion afterwards whenever we met."[3]

Near the end of his life, puzzling over the significance of his tête-à-tête with Pound, Dickey sought to overhaul the general image of Pound-the-Fascist-monster:

He was awful sweet. . . . He was no more crazy than I am. He was like an older American person, like maybe your grandfather or a slightly eccentric uncle, who would say things like: "My son, you're not going to get this in the history books, but whatever happens, this is the truth of it. Nobody's going to tell you this, but I can tell you this is the truth of it." You felt that he felt that he was talking as a source all the time, [revealing] the real truth of the matter.

He was very funny. He was a great big fellow. He was as tall as I was. I thought he was a little mouse of scrolls. . . . And his wife, Dorothy Shakespear, was there, and very beautiful. The day I went out there with Pratt . . . , they were holding court. He had sort of a lawn chair, and his wife was passing out sandwiches and apples to the people. I just sat there and listened to him talk. People were wandering around under the trees, and a young lady detached herself and came over to our group, and said: "Good afternoon, Mr. Pound." He didn't say anything, and I didn't say anything. Nobody said anything. So she stood there, and said a couple more things, and then went on her way.

After she was out of earshot, I said, cautiously: "Mr. Pound, does that lady live here?" He said: "No, son, I think she's the cause of somebody else living here. Last time I said good afternoon to her, she monologued for two hours, and we're not going to give her another chance."

But mainly what he talked about was . . . the old days [in England]— D. H. Lawrence and Ford Madox Ford— . . . and France—Joyce and Hemingway. . . . There was a young soldier who was about to ship out overseas, and he asked him if he could give any sort of instant advice about being a writer. And he said: "Just keep your eye on the objects, son; just keep looking at the objects."[4]

Dickey no doubt was thinking of his own poetic beginnings as a soldier, and the advice that could have benefited him at the time.

Dickey often used an old Russian proverb to distinguish himself from Pound and his friend T. S. Eliot: "The fox knows many things, but the hedgehog [sometimes he said groundhog] knows one big thing. Eliot and Pound are the foxes, you see, and I'm the hedgehog." Dickey liked to exaggerate both his friendship and differences with Pound. In 1968, he told a reporter for the *Colorado Daily*: "In Washington University I have a two or three hundred letter correspondence with Pound [only about fifteen letters and postcards exist in the archive]. I went down often to see him in St. Elizabeth's Hospital in Washington D.C. . . . But I never saw any evidence of insanity in him at all."[5] In 1973, he told the publisher John Logue that Pound had sent him "300 or 400 letters."[6] Although he claimed that the racist ideologue John Kasper had been at Pound's side at Saint Elizabeth's, Dickey chose to accentuate Pound's grandfatherly charm rather than his fascism. Pound, he said, had given him encouragement: "I once sent him some poems that had appeared in a poetry magazine and he said it was the best thing he'd read in a poetry magazine since 1912."[7] No record of Pound's adulation exists.

According to Pound, who presided over his makeshift "Ezuversity" at Saint Elizabeth's, artists were either "serious characters," like himself, or they were forgettable dilettantes. Pound told Pratt: "We liked your friend Dickey. He seems to be a serious character."[8] Flattered by this encomium, Dickey exchanged letters with Pound until the late 1950s. Pound's overbearing sermonizing on political, economic, racial, and ethnic matters taxed Dickey's patience, but he blamed the demise of their correspondence on simple inertia: "It wasn't based on any altercation or any falling out. . . . It just sort of faded out."[9] In his first letters to Pound, Dickey complained about returning from the life of a European troubadour to that of a freshman English teacher. He also informed Pound: "My wife and I are collaborating on a kind of project (she works, and I goad) to knit you a sweater, or I guess it will be a kind of sweater, though at the present stage it knows more what it is trying to be than we do."[10] Dickey wondered if Pound would like an outline of his head—the one carved by the sculptor Gaudier-Brzeska—knitted into the fabric. Pound replied in his inimitable style: "May I suggest that Madame make it WITHOUT sleeves / That will both simplify her labours [and] fit the need of the beneficiary. . . . at any rate fer XrizaChe don't make it short. . . . OMIT fancy adornments / trouble enuf to git the garment constructed."[11]

Playfully rebuking Pound in a letter he began with "Dear Uncle" (usually he began with "Cher Maitre"), Dickey insisted: "We *will* put on the Gaudier head, which we have been at some pains to work out, on sheets of grocery paper, with rulers, pins, and a good many revisions."[12]

While he tried to solve the intricacies of the sweater design, Dickey also wondered whether he should help get Pound released from Saint Elizabeth's. A number of famous writers, including Hemingway and Eliot, had tried. Dickey told Pratt in a letter that imitated some of Pound's wit and misspellings: "I wish the possibility of springing the tough old bastard eggzisted, too, but I don't see much chance of it. If Hemingway can't get him out, I sure can't. But I keep thinking I ought to try. Anyway, I'm going to have Maxine get to work on the sweater as soon as we can get enough money to buy the wool. Maybe he and his wife can both get in it, and the ghost of Gaudier-Brzeska will lift them out over Washington and take them where Kung [Confucius] is setting down the rules for modern poetry and morals under some bo-tree or other. . . ."[13] In the end, Robert Frost, Archibald MacLeish, and James Laughlin were instrumental in convincing the government to let Pound return to Italy.

For the time being, Dickey had to concentrate on his teaching duties at the University of Florida. Dickey at first relished the opportunity to serve as Lytle's creative writing assistant, and Lytle continued to treat him as a gifted son. As promised, Lytle found a house for the Dickeys not far from his own. After a few weeks in temporary quarters, the Dickeys moved to 1720 NW Seventh Place, within walking distance to the university. Dickey reported to Bill Pratt:

> Here, we have all been sick, I most of all. But none of this happened until after we had gone down to Florida and got more or less squared away down there. It is a huge high-schoolish University I am in, and a little forbidding, with its kindly old gentlemen running the English department and asking me if I have read Walter Pater, and if I thought Edna Millay and Emily Dickinson were representative modern poets. But we have a nice little house there, with a low rent (comparatively: $70) and several very good friends. The salary is pretty good, and they tell me that "we don't insist on you writers working summers," which naturally pleases me a good deal. All in all, it oughtn't to be a bad place, at least for a while.[14]

At the start Dickey had little reason to complain. His teaching load was light: "I taught one class and I assisted . . . [Lytle] with his night seminar, which was held in the library."[15] Still, he felt bound to the same treadmill that had exhausted him at Rice. Once again he struggled to find time for his own writing in between grading dozens of freshman composition papers. Convinced he was on the verge of a poetic breakthrough, he treated his classes as irritating distractions. One of his students, Lucy Trowbridge, commented: "He was not much as a teacher. . . . He was inclined to overdo the analyzing of a story. He went very slowly and methodically through every line of the story. This would have been fine if it had been a poem. (It was definitely a snore experience.) It was hard for him to step into the shoes of Andrew Lytle. Most of the students in the class had also taken creative writing with Andrew. I was quite surprised that he was so dull as a teacher since in private life he was anything but dull, a true eccentric with a large ego. He thought no woman could resist him. He had a very attractive wife but I gathered he didn't take faithfulness to her very seriously. They gave wonderful parties with delicious Virginia ham and southern biscuits [and] . . . there was a great deal of liquor served."[16] Galvanized by these boozy occasions, Dickey inevitably made passes at Trowbridge, who was married, and at other female guests. He found Trowbridge particularly attractive because she was tall, and he fancifully bragged to friends that they could really "rattle a bed." Convinced that most women found Tarzan-like physiques irresistible, Dickey diligently bronzed and toned his body by lifting weights in the Florida sun. An acquaintance, Dick Vowles, remembered him pumping barbells in slight attire as housewives in the neighborhood watched in amusement. To keep in shape he also played tennis with Lucy Trowbridge's husband, Clinton, another graduate student in the writing program. Trowbridge recalled that Dickey was such "a fierce competitor [that] he would grimace when he turned his back, hardly able to contain his fury at losing a point."[17] When losing, he slammed the ball as hard as he could against the fence and unleashed a welter of profanity.

At the University of Florida, Dickey felt like a minotaur trapped in a labyrinth. In 1955, the English Department had a byzantine, two-tier structure. Freshmen and sophomores took English in the lower level, and juniors, seniors, and graduate students took courses in the upper level. Lower-level courses were part of a Basic Studies program that included social science, mathematics, physical science, and biology. The Basic Studies English course for freshmen had three divisions: writing lab, classroom, and lecture. Overseeing the budget and its complicated implementation was the chairman, Jacob Wise, who kept his distance from the lower-level instructors. Even as Lytle's assistant, Dickey was entrenched in the Basic Studies English course known as C-3.

According to Gordon Bigelow, an English professor in the program, Dickey despised the complex hierarchy of Basic Studies. He also despised Jacob Wise for condoning the bureaucracy. Despite Dickey's well-known view of the department, Bigelow and his colleagues were stunned one April night during the spring semester when Dickey abruptly left Gainesville. As if to spite his tormentors, he left a stack of blue books in his office that needed grading. Bigelow and his colleagues, who were already overworked, quickly had to reorganize their complicated schedules to teach Dickey's classes. Lytle felt especially betrayed, since he had pressed the chairman to hire Dickey in the first place. Usually well-mannered to a fault, Lytle swore revenge after Dickey's unannounced departure. He told a graduate student, John Lyons, that "Dickey would never have another academic appointment if he had any say in the matter."[18] In other conversations, the ever-courteous Lytle rebuked Dickey for being "discourteous." Dickey had betrayed the code of conduct that Lytle expected of all Southern gentlemen. For his part, Dickey felt Lytle had betrayed him. He wrote Maxine after leaving the university: "I should suggest that Andrew . . . back up a little of that big talk about 'dying' for people, fighting duels, and so on, with a little action, at least once in a while. . . . He wants to take credit for these attitudes without ever having to prove any of them in action, and that is too bad."[19] On the same day he wrote Maxine, April 8, he telegraphed his formal resignation to the university.

Still retaining some paternal feelings for his prodigal son, Lytle persuaded the irate chairman not to sue Dickey for breach of contract. In his subsequent correspondence with Dickey, Lytle did his best to sound friendly. In one letter he even supported Dickey's decision to leave teaching; he simply couldn't accept the way Dickey had carried it out, especially since he maintained that neither Wise nor the administration had been vindictive toward Dickey. Dickey also hoped to preserve at least an appearance of friendship. But in private he dismissed Lytle's interpretation of the incident as ludicrous. "I sincerely and genuinely love Andrew," he wrote Maxine on April 20, 1956. "And yet he is *such* a fake, and *so* pretentious. All you can do is laugh hopelessly and helplessly, and not take him seriously." Dickey never forgot Lytle's failure to stick up for him at the University of Florida. Several years later, he got back at Lytle by mistreating one of his daughters while she was visiting his home. According to Madison Jones, Lytle said with disgust: "Dickey was playing with my daughter and got her all worked up!"[20] Dickey infuriated Lytle in a more public way in 1977. Having been invited to Washington, D.C., to read a poem at one of President Carter's inaugural ceremonies, Dickey blasted Lytle, although not by name, in the pages of *Newsweek* for allegedly mistreating Maxine around the time of his departure from Florida.

Why did Dickey leave Gainesville with such dispatch? The ostensible reason was a poetry reading and discussion in which Dickey offended a local group of elderly writers known as "the Pen Women." One of his Florida colleagues said: "Bad language was the crux of the matter, or the beginning of it. Jim caused a scandal by using four letter words in his presentation to the ladies."[21] Dickey had read some fairly innocuous poems by other writers like Auden as well as one of his own poems. In Dickey's dubious account of the event that he published in *Self-Interviews*, he wrote:

> I wanted to do something about sensual experience that had not yet been done. So I wrote a poem called "The Father's Body" about a child's recognition of the physical differences between himself and his father. As a result of writing this poem and reading it at the insistence of a group of ladies at the University of Florida, I got into a certain amount of trouble which I resolved by simply walking out. I told Andrew Lytle that I had no further interest in teaching at the University of Florida—which indeed I did not, and I haven't seen him to this day—and I told the authorities there that I had no intention of apologizing for my supposed transgression. So I left the University and went to New York to become a businessman of whatever kind it's possible to become at the age of thirty-three.[22]

Who could blame Dickey for sticking to his poetic principles when attacked by a group of blue-haired ladies, whose tastes were frozen in another century?

John Edwardson, a friend in the Agronomy Department who invited Maxine to dinner shortly after her husband quit, recalled the incident much differently. He said Maxine was deeply upset by her husband's precipitous departure and spoke to them about the circumstances that had led up to it. From Maxine's conversation, Edwardson concluded: "He used his published poems except a description of some poem he was working on ['The Father's Body']. This exception came about in response to a question from a Pen Woman who asked what he was working on at the time. This work involved a to-be-completed description of some thoughts and actions of a young man. . . . Some members of the Pen Women complained about Dickey's language to the President of the University, J. Wayne Reitz. Dr. Reitz was not noted for brains or backbone. Dickey apologized to the Pen Women after learning that he had offended them, or at least some of them, but he was fired."[23] The four-letter words Dickey used in his commentary on the "The Father's Body" roused the ladies' puritanical hackles. The poem itself was relatively innocuous and, in any case, probably too obscure to be understood by them—or anyone—on a first or even a second or third reading.

On the most literal level, the action in "The Father's Body" is simple: a son gets into a shower with his father, envisions his sexual future by looking at his father's body, and then the father gets out of the shower and sings. The mundane scene, however, is deliberately clouded from the start. The father stands "in the rising lamp of steam / [And] turns his fatted shoulders on." The son stands beside him with "The ink-cut and thumb-ball whorl of planks / About him like the depth in a cloud / Of wire, dancing powerfully." When the son joins his father in the shower, they coalesce in steamy vapor:

> They ride there, in beginning.
> He takes a long drink of velocity
> Shucking his face.
> It keeps wearing out there,
> Its pointedness keeps running down,
> So that his closed eyes pelt back at it, and see,
> Uncontrollably, a wood
>
> Where nothing pours. Grass comes gently
> Down into being, in a ring.

The shower's warm water baptises and purges the boy's body. Eyes closed to the real world, he journeys in spirit to a visionary Eden, where his father appears as God the Father and sadistically "binds on the glittering chains" to extract his son's Adam-like rib. As in the Genesis story, his father makes from the rib an Eve-like mate. Boy and girl "are laid together," Dickey writes with a heavy-handed sexual pun, and soon marry. But the image of the Father-God hovers over them, hindering his son's urge toward consummation:

> He parts the girl's terrible legs; he shouts
> Out silence; his waist points
> And holds and points, empowered
> Unbearably: withheld: withheld . . .

In Dickey's free-flow of associations, the son is now Christ "stretched on the nails / Of the inward stars of noon." Like *The Entrance to the Honeycomb*, the poem dramatizes bouts of sexual confusion and impotence rather than sexual accomplishments. Finally, the actual father "snaps the water off" and "Breastward in the spring dream of seed, / In the bestial completion of sunlight / Hid up and down, branchingly sings."[24] With his singing, the father brings the steamy biblical vision to an end.

The poem owes much of its diction and chaotic mythopoesis to Dylan Thomas, who was always ferreting sexual connotations from biblical stories like those in Genesis. If the Pen Women had been more astute critics, they would have complained about the poem's derivative obscurity rather than its obscenity. Dickey used no overtly obscene language in the poem, only highfalutin rhetoric and hackneyed puns. Although Lytle had warned Dickey not to participate in any event sponsored by the officious Pen Women (Lytle had sensibly declined a similar invitation), Dickey ignored the warning and, perhaps out of frustration and anger over the group's confusion, as much as a desire to shock, used graphic language to bring his message home. Lytle told Kelsie Harder, who was working on his doctorate at the University of Florida in the early 1950s, that Dickey had made "a disgusting speech." Others heard that he had inserted the word "fuck" into his *explication de texte*. Harder, however, suspected that there was more to Dickey's sudden departure from Gainesville than profanity: "Dickey may have had difficulty with Lytle, or he may have been angry about something and took it out on the Pen Women."[25] Another old Vanderbilt classmate, Thomas Daniel Young, agreed. He speculated that Lytle had irritated Dickey by confronting him about his improprieties.

After the Pen Women complained to the university president, some faculty members felt that Reitz, who was a liberal, open-minded man, would simply reprimand Dickey. Not long before the crisis, a student's parents had complained about a history teacher reciting some of Andrew Jackson's unseemly language in the classroom. Reitz had judiciously dispatched the matter. Unfortunately, in Dickey's case Reitz bowed to the reactionary sentiments of the time. On a campus where blacks and homosexuals were unwelcome and where liberals were suspected by McCarthyites of being closet Communists, rowdy poets were viewed with similar suspicion. Reitz wrote Wise in the English Department to register his dismay about Dickey. The chairman now felt he had an excuse to discipline Dickey for a number of real or alleged offenses. He chastised Dickey and told him to apologize to the president. According to Edwardson, Dickey complied. Unsatisfied with Dickey's acts of contrition, the university refused to renew his contract for the 1956–57 academic year.

Dickey may have been secretly content with the outcome. Close friends believed that he wanted an excuse to flee the oppressive English Department and its poor students. Lucy Trowbridge said his sudden departure "was his own doing. . . . He'd had it with the academic life at that time. I'm sure he felt it stultifying and not conducive to his type of creativity. It probably was. Some of the students from rural parts could barely talk. There were no entrance requirements."[26] Piecing together the incident afterward, colleague and friend Smith Kirkpatrick concluded that Dickey had reacted as he often did when cornered: he bristled and ran. Kirkpatrick had glimpsed the overly sensitive, easily hurt side of Dickey and knew from the start that his blustering, extroverted manner was a mask. Once while lunching with Kirkpatrick after conducting a press conference, Dickey ate nothing, downed martini after martini, and at one point looked his colleague in the eye and said: "You wouldn't know it, but I'm really scared."[27] Kirkpatrick had to restrain himself from laughing, so convinced was he that Dickey's strutting was a way of deflecting attention from his fears. Dickey confirmed Kirkpatrick's analysis in the early 1970s before a reading at the University of Florida. In Dickey's room, Kirkpatrick watched Maxine hand her already-tipsy husband a tall beer and then offer him another in the car to quell his fears about confronting the audience. Alcohol was Dickey's antidote to stage fright, or so Kirkpatrick decided. When Dickey climbed on stage to read, he was his usual boisterous, charismatic self. During the aftermath of the Pen Women incident, Maxine again had to act as her husband's guardian. She stayed behind to deliver the embarrassing news to the English Department chair that her husband would not finish the term.

As Maxine knitted a sweater for Pound during the early months of 1956, Dickey sent reports to Pound about his battle with the Pen Women. He told Pound that the incident had occurred in February: "I lectured, I mean 'lectured,' to the American Pen Women's Society so furiously (and, I guess, controversially) that their National President wrote to the president of *this* place and demanded that I be kicked out. I haven't been, yet, but the U. of Florida may martyr me still. I rather hope so, though it may just be possible that I am doing one or two people some good here."[28] After Dickey sent the sweater to "Uncle Ezra" in mid-August 1956, Pound thanked him and applauded his martyristic stand in Gainesville, lumping the Pen Women together with Jews and blacks. He urged Dickey to take further action: "If yu are sighing for action . . . , god knows we need a super ku klu klux."[29] In Pound's bigoted vision, Dickey was a potential lieutenant in his crusade against cultural undesirables.

Dickey responded to Pound's jeremiad courteously and inquisitively. He complimented Pound on his new "Rock-Drill Cantos," mentioned his correspondence with Pound's old friend the English poet Basil Bunting, and asked Pound to recommend books on economic reform. On June 6, 1957, over a year after the incident with the Pen Women, Pound poured out more vitriolic rhetoric: "If Pen Women mean P.E.N club wimmen / yu have been ditched by one dirty jew gang."[30] In his last postcard to Dickey, sent on November 7, 1958, after he had been freed from Saint Elizabeth's, Pound again combined compliments about the sweater with racist and ethnic slurs: "Grey sweater resisting alpine blasts and Agassian geog/formations. send some nooz of the real south, and how it feels to have so many dem/ cong/men. yrz E.P."[31] All Southerners, Pound implied, should be white supremacists like himself.

To a certain extent, Dickey identified with and imitated Pound's Dr. Jekyll and Mr. Hyde personality. Bill Pratt thought his identification with Pound was so close that he may have appropriated the story of Pound's dismissal from Wabash College and applied it to his own situation at the University of Florida. Pound had also been fired by a philistine college administration for what it judged to be scandalous behavior. As a low-level instructor of Romance languages at Wabash College, Pound had offered his bed to a girl stranded from a burlesque show in Crawfordsville, Indiana. Even though nothing illicit transpired, Pound's old-fashioned landladies, like Dickey's Pen Women, complained to the college. Was Dickey simply recycling Pound's story? In a conversation with Pratt, Lytle also contended that Dickey's account was partly fabrication. According to Lytle, Dickey left because he wasn't making enough money. Dickey's meager salary was certainly a factor. On March 11, 1956, Dickey wrote William Jay Smith, who was still living in Europe, a long letter pining for their halcyon days in Rome and excoriating the "God Damned place" in which he labored: "What existence Gainesville has is not valuable to anyone, that I can see, and certainly not to us. There is nothing here for me but the genteel poverty of the University teacher, and the possibility, in twenty years, of its being a little more genteel. 'Here lies one whose name was writ on fifty-seven thousand freshman papers.' So we're thinking about chucking it, and trying to get into something where they'll give a man a salary he can ride, where the world is pushy, crass, and rich, and poets are eaten up with the disease of money."[32] Dickey was only half kidding. His altercation with the Pen Women had already occurred, yet he attributed his leave-taking to poor pay.

Three years later Dickey told James Wright that the scandal over "The Father's Body" was insignificant compared to his low pay: "[The] trouble at the Univ. of Florida . . . was trivial, really, but I made a stand on it, and would have got thrown out for impertinence (or something) had I not left of my own accord first. I feel I have gained a kind of revenge over my self-righteous tormentors . . . for I [as an advertising copywriter] now earn more than the whole English Department at the U. of Florida, and can snap my fingers (really *snap* them: you know: good and loud) at the money troubles that used to drive me off my nut."[33] To Al Braselton he also emphasized the financial reasons for leaving the University of Florida:

> We were poor. I remember we'd been there a while and it was sort of obvious that we were long overdue to have a party. All the other members of the faculty had had some kind of gathering at their homes. We were so poor that we had to have a party with one bottle of bourbon. That was all we had for the party along with some little snacks and dip. We cleaned up the little back porch area and patio and invited some other teachers over. Right before they got there, I dropped the bottle of bourbon and it broke. We sopped [it] up [with] towels, filtered out the glass, and saved a little over half a bottle of bourbon and gave everybody a light drink. I decided I was going to quit starving for literature. So I got a job with McCann Erickson in advertising.[34]

Although the bottle-dropping incident happened at Vanderbilt, Dickey airlifted it to Florida to make his point.

Hurt pride as well as unwarranted fears of poverty provoked Dickey's decision to leave Florida. His mother still sent SSS money when he needed it, but Dickey wanted to make his own fortune. Sensitive to the fact that he didn't have a Ph.D., he deeply resented slights from his academic colleagues. When Jacob Wise criticized him for the way he taught *Huckleberry Finn*, he was furious. He found academic politics tedious and the pressure to publish scholarly essays onerous. He told Pratt a year after leaving Florida that quitting his teaching job was his only option: "One always has the dwindling suspicion and hope that one can really 'do something about it': get things (students and teachers) off their rear end, and heading in the direction of things that matter. And you *can* do enough of this to make teaching a vastly exciting and profitable venture. But there is no chance of moving the vast and sluggish mass of the academic mind, or rendering any permanent good except to individuals. I suppose, now that I think of it, that that is what the whole thing is about, anyway."[35] At the University of Florida, Dickey had confronted a sluggish behemoth and had fled rather than suffer an Ahabian fate.

VI.

INTO THE STONE: THE ADVERTISING YEARS

14. Coca-Cola and Jingle Jim (1956–1959)

Dickey's plunge into New York advertising in early April 1956 resembled one of the risky actions of his fictional heroes. About getting his job he told Jim Mann: "I met a guy, somewhere along the line. He said if you ever think about going into the ad business let me know."[1] To Bill Pratt he claimed that he knocked on the door of New York's biggest advertising firm and announced he was a writer. At first rebuffed, he replied, "Just give me a chance," and immediately produced the jingle "Enjoy your thirst with Coca-Cola."[2] Astonished by such compositional speed, the firm offered him a job on the spot. Dickey's entrance into the advertising business, however, was not so sui generis. He made a desperate call to his sister-in-law shortly after learning he would be fired from the University of Florida. "You've got to help me get a job!" he exclaimed. Patsy Dickey responded: "What about advertising?"[3] He said he was interested, so she contacted Thad Horton, her neighbor on Dean Drive who was acting manager of McCann-Erickson's Atlanta office, and Dickey immediately flew to Atlanta for an interview.

Horton and Dickey had many things in common. Horton had grown up in Atlanta and graduated from Darlington School, studied English and philosophy in college, served in the war as a B-29 pilot, and had a passion for sports, which had led to his position as sports director of Atlanta's WSB radio and television station. It was through this latter position that he got a job in Coca-Cola advertising, first working as a copywriter for D'Arcy, the agency that originally handled the Coca-Cola account, and then for McCann-Erickson in Atlanta, when they took over the account on April 1, 1956. Like most veteran aviators, the two men spoke of their war experiences. Impressed by Horton's status as a pilot, Dickey admitted, as he rarely did, that he had always hoped to be one but had served as a navigator. Dickey also told Horton that he had never known another person named Thad (in *Deliverance* he gave Horton's first name to Thad Emerson, Ed Gentry's advertising partner). When Dickey laid out a dozen sample ads he had written, Horton said, with some uncertainty, "Jim, this is very interesting stuff. Why don't you go home this weekend, and then on Monday bring back what you consider your five best and your five worst. And be prepared to explain why you've made the choice."[4] On Monday, Dickey passed the test and got a copywriting job. For the next three months he studied the art of Coca-Cola ad writing at McCann-Erickson's office at 50 Rockefeller Plaza in New York.

In New York, Dickey stayed briefly at the New Western Hotel, a site engrained in his memory mainly because of William Faulkner. A decade later, while reading at Kent State University, Dickey told Peter Makuck, who was writing his Ph.D. thesis on Faulkner, that Faulkner had been his usual laconic self when they met at the hotel. To goad him from silence, Dickey said that any-body who drank a fifth of bourbon could write the sort of long-winded, preten-tious prose for which he was famous. With a few more carefully aimed insults, Dickey reduced the great Southern writer to what he deemed his proper stature. In a more sober reminiscence (Dickey was swigging king-size beers at Kent State), Dickey admitted: "I looked across the dining room [of the New Western Hotel] . . . and there was William Faulkner. I didn't say anything to him, but it was him. It was the one time I ever saw him."[5] If Dickey did see Faulkner, he was probably too shy to introduce himself. Or perhaps he spurned Faulkner because he saw his own weakness for garrulous prose, gothic melodrama, and strong drink magnified in him.

Despite the later prestige of the ad firm and its main client, when Dickey joined McCann-Erickson The Coca-Cola Company was in trouble. Robert Woodruff, who had controlled the company since the early 1920s, was in his six-ties, and many of the other executives were aging, too. The company had grown complacent, self-satisfied, antiquated. Many employees feared that the company would stagnate without radical initiatives, and that arch-rival Pepsi would carve out a larger portion of the soft drink market. America was changing, the Cola Wars were heating up, and Coke had to adapt to survive. Soda fountains—the traditional place for drinking Coke—were becoming less popular. Big supermar-kets were edging out local grocery stores, where Cokes were usually sold; and Americans were taking more Pepsi home to drink by their new television sets.

Dickey began his training by writing ads for magazines, but soon switched to radio and television, where he learned to "time out" ads for thirty-second or sixty-second slots. His goal was to get dealers to feature large Cokes at fountains and later to sell cases of Coke at gas stations. Among those who gave Dickey as-signments in April were Neal Gilliatt, an account supervisor; Carl Everett, a bottle sales executive; Barry Dillow, a fountain account executive; and Dave Lippincott, the copy chief. In mid-April, when Gilliat and Dillow visited Thad Horton in the Atlanta office, they both complimented his work. In May, Dickey's principal job was to develop commercials for the fifteen-minute "Coke Time," which featured Eddie Fisher, whom Dickey described as a "very nice, tired-looking, pocked Jewish boy who talks a good deal in the jive lingo of 'The Wild One.'"[6] Fred Robbins was the show's pitchman for Coca-Cola, and he was the one Dickey regularly consulted. Despite their best efforts, neither Robbins, Dickey, Fisher, nor Coca-Cola could save the show, which aired three times a week during prime time. Its Nielsen ratings were abysmal, and Coca-Cola soon withdrew its sponsorship. In retrospect, Dickey said, "I enjoyed working on 'Coke Time.' . . . There was so much money. You never saw so much money. [As] a poor starving college freshman teacher, I could not believe it. . . . At Florida, I was making $3,600 and they asked me what I wanted to start at McCann, and I said, 'I want twice what I'm getting. I want $600 a month— $7,200.'"[7] If this is what he asked for, he got more: the offer from the Radio-Television director at McCann was $8,600.

Despite his new affluence, Dickey remained ambivalent about New York. His ad writing was ephemeral, and he felt like a stranger in the city's steel-and-glass canyons. He wrote Pratt:

As you can see, I've gone for the big money, and they are giving (some of) it to me. There is considerable pressure here, for the account is a big one (Coca-Cola), and the writing done for it must be what *everybody* wants. What everybody wants is a kind of calculated banality-trying-to-raise-itself-to-the-level-of-pre-poetry-about-soft-drinks; once a man trained on language (poetry, say) gets on to what they want him to do, there's nothing to it at all: the only thing one must be careful about is giving them the impression that it is as easy as it is; then you would not seem to be *earning* the money! The life is fast, hard, full of organized pressures, but not heartbreaking, for your heart is not in it. How could it be to anyone who has read Pound's line "The sharp song with the sun's radiance under it"? How could one possibly care when one of the "wheels" in this business is dissatisfied with you when you say "It's time for a Coke," and ecstatic over you when you say, "Enjoy your thirst, with Coke"?[8]

Dickey hoped that with bonuses and profit sharing his salary would soar to eighteen- or twenty-thousand dollars a year.

In the heart of Donald Davidson's capitalist Leviathan, Dickey had to combat headaches and loneliness in order to write poetry at the end of his long days. Maxine stayed in Gainesville to pack their belongings for the move to Atlanta. Newly settled at the Winslow Hotel on Madison Avenue and Fifty-fifth Street, in a room he complained was no bigger than a telephone booth, Dickey labored on "The First Morning of Cancer," an ambitious poem full of visionary flights fueled more by masturbatory fantasies than by worries about cancer. Reminiscing on his advertising days in a 1979 *TV Guide*, Dickey lamented "not only [New York's] increasingly cold and Northern-made air but also a basic difference in values." His values were Southern and Agrarian, or so he implied. Although some of his colleagues expressed interest in his poetry writing, he felt he was *of* them but not *with* them, as he later said of Ed Gentry and his advertising colleagues in *Deliverance*. One fellow McCann worker he admired was art director Edward Lewis Wallant, who wrote a successful novel, *The Pawnbroker*. Dickey was also trying to combine two careers, but felt torn "selling his soul to the devil all day in commercial cubicles and trying to buy it back at night in the accusing silence of home, hotel room, or wherever."[9] He tried to master the formulae of advertising as quickly as possible so he could reserve energy for his poetry.

He was not, however, spending all his nights in solitary communion with his muse. He was also fraternizing with New York women and local artists: "My main friends were down in the Village. Grouped around Oscar Williams were some poets and painters that I used to go out with at night and on weekends. . . . One boy was named . . . David Johnson from a little town in Tennessee or Kentucky. He was a strange and good fellow, dedicated to French poetry. . . . [I associated with some] very enthusiastic, art people who centered around Selden Rodman, who was trying to effect a revolt against abstract expressionism in favor of representational art. . . . Oscar Williams was extremely kind to me. He had a little bitty . . . apartment with a terrace on Water Street. . . . He called me up and invited me to come down there."[10] In his letters to Maxine, Dickey provided few details of his nocturnal escapades.

A friendly, fun-loving man, and one of the best-known poetry anthologists at the time, Oscar Williams had many literary connections. Dickey said:

> He introduced me around to some other people. Clement Greenberg, the art critic, was one of them. He had a bust of Gene Durwood [Williams's wife] made and he dedicated it at a party of poets and painters and writers that he knew down at that little place on Water Street. On the terrace they had a little ceremony for that and that's where I met Clem Greenberg. . . . Anatole Broyard, the guy who passed as a white, was there. And some other people. Edwin Honig was there and one mysterious millionaire who wrote poetry named Hy Sobiloff. He was friendly to poetry and I think financed some of the more indigent poets and wrote a terrible book of poems that I think he probably paid to have published, called *Dinosaurs with Violins*.[11]

Because Williams had gotten to know Dylan Thomas in New York in the early 1950s, Thomas became a frequent topic of discussion. After Dickey gave a poetry reading at a party, Williams was convinced that he had met another Dylan and before long asked him to introduce a poem in his anthology, *101 of the Greatest Poems of the English Language*.

Dickey also socialized with poets Bruce Hooton, David Ignatow, and the beautiful Claire McAllister. He dined with one of Allen Tate's ex-mistresses, who lived in his hotel, and also with the Criterion Books editor Sidney Phillips, who expressed interest in publishing a book of Dickey's poems. Ignatow, who would go on to become a highly regarded American poet, was also working in advertising. He and Dickey spent several evenings discussing their poems as well as French poets they revered, like Arthur Rimbaud and Paul Éluard. They also shared a passion for Hart Crane, partly because Crane had tried to cultivate his poetic talents while working for the New York advertising firm J. Walter Thompson. After Dickey left New York, Ignatow carried on a brief correspondence in which he documented his sleepless nights, tense days, fitful loves, marital crises, and ennervating jobs. The friendship, however, dwindled when Dickey published a mixed review of Ignatow's second book, *The Gentle Weight Lifter*, in 1956.

Among the women Dickey courted in New York, Claire McAllister was one of his favorites. In the letters she wrote Dickey following his return to Atlanta, she addressed him as a golden-haired prince or a Southern knight. Remembering their conversations, she said, was like drinking champagne. Years later he referred to her as a member "of the then-bohemian Greenwich Village bunch [who] were important to me as a bulwark against Coca-Cola."[12] He reviewed one of her books favorably and in 1981 tried to find her a publisher for a new book. Dickey's principal companion, however, was Violetta Brown, a young woman who had grown up in Bill Pratt's hometown. Pratt had encouraged Dickey to call her in New York. According to Pratt: "Jim took pleasure in sharing women with others, and once he outraged Maxine by hinting that she and I might have an affair—nothing came of it, of course, since neither Maxine nor I would have dreamed of anything more than friendship. Later, he bragged about having an affair with Violetta Brown in New York [it was never consummated], knowing she was from Shawnee, Oklahoma, and that I had dated her once; it was part of his sense of friendship that we should have women to share, though it never appealed to me."[13] If Maxine had or threatened to have affairs, Dickey quickly dropped his libertarian idealism and grew enraged. With Maxine miles away, however, he played the libertine to his heart's content.

A graduate of Smith College, Brown shared Dickey's interest in poetry and philosophy. She wrote poetry herself, some serious and some light, and usually showed the latter to Dickey. She wrote prose for *Vogue* magazine, hobnobbed with fashion people at The Stork Club, and worked on New York fashion shows. Dickey liked to call her his "New York glamour girl." Fascinated by the *Vogue* crowd, he depended on Brown as a guide. Because Dickey gave little thought to his appearance among her fashionable friends, he was often considered a country bumpkin. At parties he appeared with short white socks exposing his hairy legs, cheap pants, and rumpled shirts, while the other men came well-groomed in knee-high socks and tailored suits. "My friends didn't know what to make of him," Brown said. "I thought he was fascinating and I would whisk him away. I didn't want him to get embarrassed." Romantically unattached at the time, Brown fell under the spell of Dickey's intelligence and creativity. She had always wanted to meet New York's writers and intellectuals. In that realm Dickey could act as her guide. Smitten by this attractive, literary twenty-seven-year-old, Dickey began spending his nights with her.

As with Gwen Leege, Dickey engaged Brown in epic conversations centered on books. Brown recalled, "We both lived on a completely imaginary plane, talking philosophy, walking around New York at dreadful hours just observing things. We were fearless." One night in May they attended about eight different parties. They started at the top of the social pyramid in a posh apartment on East End Avenue where the footmen wore white gloves and the hosts served caviar and champagne. Before long they moved to a party given by Allen Ginsberg. It was the first time Dickey spoke to him. Dickey rarely had a good word for Ginsberg afterward, but at the party Ginsberg and his other guests—Norman Mailer, Stephen Spender, and Jack Kerouac among them—greeted Dickey like a hero. They knew his work and respected it. By the end of their night of revelry, Brown and Dickey were stepping over drunks in the Bowery. Oscar Williams accompanied them on many of these party runs, and on this particular occasion he calmed Brown's fears by saying of the drunks: "They all want to get in my anthologies, so we're safe."[14] They proceeded to Williams's apartment on the tip of Manhattan for a breakfast at dawn.

Dickey and Brown frequented Greenwich Village and the White Horse Tavern, a pub where Dylan Thomas had held court several years before. Or they visited the Bronx Zoo, made famous in literary circles by Marianne Moore's many poems about its animals. Believing Dickey's story about befriending the reclusive Samuel Beckett while on his Sewanee Fellowship in Paris, Brown eagerly accompanied him to a special production of *Waiting for Godot* on May 15 and a by-invitation-only reception afterward. On these excursions, Dickey spoke rhapsodically of Paris, but denigrated Maxine for not being able to keep up with his intellectual friends there and elsewhere. He wanted to return to Europe with an intelligent woman like Brown. Although he rarely talked about advertising, Brown sensed that he was restless and unhappy at McCann and that he wanted to resume his life as an expatriate writer.

Meanwhile, Dickey complained about his dull social life in his letters to Maxine. In mid-May he told Maxine that his "bachelor" existence had become busier, but divulged few details. He typically ended his letters with amorous flourishes. On June 1, he declared: "I love you. My heart goes out of me at night and stands in the great wings over the house where we live. Take care of yourself, and of Chris."[15] To Brown, Dickey never mentioned his wife or his son. One day in June, not long before his return to Atlanta, Dickey indicated that he wanted to consummate his affair, which had been platonic, and elope to Paris with Brown. On a park bench near her Sutton Place apartment, according to Brown, "Jim first pulled out a picture of a woman from his wallet, tore it up, and threw it in the East River. Next he took out a picture of a boy, tore it up, and threw it in the East River. He then said, 'That's my wife and my son.' It was a powerful scene. You see, his wife and child were in his way."[16] Having grown up in a straitlaced Oklahoma family, Brown was flabbergasted by the revelation that Dickey was married and by the cruelty Dickey directed toward his family. Brown rushed to her apartment and for days refused to answer the phone. Finally Dickey reached her at her *Vogue* office and said: "I want you to come to my room. I won't touch you. I have something for you."[17] He had been working out his own romantic angst in a five-page poem about a stag pursuing and finally killing a doe. When she went to the Winslow Hotel, Brown noticed that he had scattered blood on the poem and that he was washing his cut hand in the sink. Around this time, after finishing a letter to Maxine with "Love, love, love," Dickey tried the same melodramatic gesture on his wife, writing "signed in blood"[18] in parentheses by his name. Brown was as shocked and bewildered by Dickey's self-mutilation as she had been when he tore up the photographs and suggested eloping with her. Dickey continued to surprise her by writing more poems to her after she married Bill Dodge. The letters that accompanied them were calculated to offend; they usually mocked her husband for winning an Olympic medal in bobsledding.

Like many women, Brown had been charmed by Dickey. He seemed boyishly vulnerable and awkward in New York society, and his fantasies of European adventure were contagious to a girl from Shawnee, Oklahoma. His other fantasies, however, disturbed her. "There was an undercurrent of violence in him," she remembered. Usually gentle and even shy, he once distressed her by confessing his most intimate sadoerotic desires during a nocturnal chat. On a later occasion, after a doctor had treated her for a severe arm injury, for no apparent reason he grabbed and squeezed her badly bruised arm. "He had a look in his eye," she recalled. "It was not an act when he reached for my arm, nor an act when he was fantasizing."[19] Brown witnessed his cruel side fifteen years later when she became head editor of *Frontiers*, a magazine published by the Academy of Natural Sciences in Philadelphia. Brown wanted to publish some of his writing, but on the phone he made bitter and false accusations about how terrible it was for her to support her husband by working. She decided not to proceed with her request for a submission and told him to stop corresponding with her.

Among the other women Dickey pursued in New York was the poet Carolyn Kizer, whom he met while perusing books at the Gotham Book Mart. He told James Wright that his first encounter with Kizer was unpromising:

A big blond gal picked me up in a book store (I don't mean this to sound like Jack Kerouac, but that's actually what happened). It turns out that she is (or was, rather . . .) or aspired to be a poet. She came from Seattle. Her name was Kizer, I think (or maybe it was Kayser). . . . We had a couple of drinks and hung around together for a day or two . . . It happens that [she] . . . is a big patroness of the arts out there in Seattle, has pots of money, and knows all the artists (Graves, Tobey, et al) there are in that section of the world. Do you or did you know her? She's a very odd character, believe me. She used to talk about David Wagoner (an entire mediocrity) as some marvellous, mystical type of genius, which is enough right there to make you suspicious that something odd is going on, either in the blond's mind, or between her and Wagoner.[20]

Relations between Kizer and Dickey grew more amicable in a few years when he served as writer-in-residence at Reed College, not far from Seattle.

While Dickey mingled with Greenwich Village bohemians and honed his advertising skills at McCann, Maxine, whom he now called "Chubbin" and "Miss Chubby of 1956," took care of Chris and settled her husband's unfinished business in Florida. She was pleased that the family income had doubled; in fact, she had encouraged her husband to find a more lucrative job to better support the family. When Dickey informed her that McCann would transfer him to Atlanta soon, with her usual efficiency and the help of his brother, Tom, who worked in real estate, she found a house in Buckhead. In late April, Maxine's mother arrived from Nashville to help with the move from Gainesville to 2930 Westminster Circle off Howell Mill Road, a short drive to 166 West Wesley. The suburban ranch house was by no means grand; it had three bedrooms, a couple of baths, a small dining room, a kitchen, and a living room. Surrounded by other low-lying brick houses with the obligatory carports and barbecue grills, it appeared "tacky" to some of Dickey's advertising colleagues. Following established precedent, Dickey approached his mother for financial help, and she provided much of the down payment. After a nomadic decade, Maxine was thrilled to finally have a home of her own. Chris liked the jungle of brush and trees around a nearby cul-de-sac, where he could find snakes, turtles, and salamanders. Dickey was especially cheered to know that his many books would have a permanent resting place, and, following a home-decorating plan he applied to all his other houses, he had them shelved on nearly every wall.

Dickey claimed that he left New York early—he had planned to stay for six months—because of "Coke Time"'s declining fortunes: "It was evident that Coke was going to cancel the show. The only thing to do was to send the radio/TV commitment to Atlanta and portion out the radio/TV budget among the local bottlers, of which there were 3,500 [in another account he said there were 2,600]. So I took charge of that."[21] Dickey made it sound like he would direct the Atlanta operation himself; in fact he took a job as a copywriter for an art director and a number of executives. His three-month training period over, Dickey rejoined Maxine and Chris during the summer of 1956 and began commuting to McCann's office at 836 West Peachtree Street across from the Biltmore Hotel. In his new quarters, decorator designed with rosewood paneling and walnut desks to impress Coca-Cola, Dickey and his cohorts acted as liaisons between the New York office, which created all the advertising slogans and strategies, and The Coca-Cola Company. Another agency, Marschalk and Pratt, soon merged with McCann in order to service smaller local accounts with companies like First National Bank, Cox Broadcasting, and SSS (Dickey was especially busy with the radio and television advertising for the bank). In 1956, only about a dozen people worked at McCann's Atlanta office, but by the time Dickey left in 1959, it had doubled in size and become one of the fastest-growing agencies in the Southeast.

Most of Dickey's assignments involved radio commercials. Dickey adapted ideas sent from New York for the use of local Coca-Cola bottlers all around the country. Because there were about 1,150 (not 3,500 or 2,600) independent bottlers, his boss, Mark Bollmann, said: "Jim had a very busy job. He had to churn out the ads. We all thought he was working on his poetry, but he got the commercials out."[22] It was a logistical feat to tailor advertisements for dozens of different cities. As Dickey once pointed out in an interview: "Coke was in a real pricing war with Pepsi and had given autonomy in pricing to all of its local bottlers across the country. So we were turning out spots for little towns in Louisiana and Minnesota and Arkansas and California frantically. Our secretaries had a terrific workload; I don't know why they didn't commit suicide."[23] A Chicago bottler might want an ad for a free six-pack for every six-pack purchased. A Los Angeles bottler might want an ad for free tickets to Disneyland for every case purchased. Dickey was in charge of supplying the copy.

Dickey soon felt overwhelmed, especially since he was trying to reserve office time for his literary endeavors. The burden of having to invent so many separate ads, he complained to his boss, was backbreaking. Once when an account executive demanded to know where the TV ads for Des Moines were, Dickey shot back: "They're in my head, and you'll get them when I get them out and on paper!" He also began reciting his old complaints about low pay:

All I had was two or three people. So I told them it was too much to handle. I wasn't getting paid enough to do all of this. It was impossible to do. They said to keep working with it and see what you can do. So I figured out a way to adapt one locality's commercials to another one's by changing the prices and doing various small things [to the original]. . . . I put up for awhile at my part of the agency Darwin's advice to the animals: "Adapt or Die!" So we were adapting right and left . . . ! I was going all day long. I also did commercials for the local television shows that Coke sponsored. I did all that stuff. And it was tough. I was very busy. I was enjoying it. I enjoyed the challenge of it. Every time I had a minute to spare, which was not often, I would stick a poem in the typewriter where I had been typing

Coca-Cola ads. I worked on "The Lifeguard." I wrote "The Lifeguard" under those conditions. It took me almost a year.[24]

Dickey considered hanging a sign over his door with the inscription that Dante placed over the gates to his inferno—"Abandon all hope, ye who enter here"—but thought his Darwinian pun on "adapt" was more appropriate.

If colleagues knocked on his office door, Dickey usually cleared his desk of poems and poetry books and began typing ads. With one young colleague, Inman Mays, he was not so deceptive. With a degree in journalism from the University of Georgia, Mays had signed on as a trainee during the summer of 1957. As "Traffic Operator," he took Dickey's assignments, collected them at the end of the day, and delivered them to account executives and clients. He liked talking to Dickey about literature. Sometimes when Mays entered his office, Dickey seemed to be working on a jigsaw puzzle; he moved around bits of paper with one word written on each. In fact, he was practicing a new way of composing poems by juxtaposing different words to see what associations they might trigger. He used this method throughout his career, often filling up the back sides of manuscripts with columns of individual words.

From the start, Mays realized Dickey was different. While most admen at the agency kept their doors open, Dickey always kept his firmly shut:

> He didn't act like someone who knew or cared a whit about normally accepted office protocol. On the rare occasions when he would emerge from behind his closed door, he would walk about the office twirling his gold Phi Beta Kappa key on a pocket chain, stopping to chat with secretaries about the most intimate aspects of their personal lives, interrupting AEs [account executives] to talk about sports and doing everything possible not to think about business or advertising. If Dickey happened to spy a stranger in the visitor's lobby—an ad salesperson, a client, or prospective client, he would walk up, introduce himself and say, "Who are you and why are you here?" After the startled visitor would reply, Jim would say, "I'm the writer, creative director and resident wordsmith. Call me direct when you need anything really creative."[25]

Because of his presumptuousness, account executives tried to keep potential clients away from Dickey. McCann's office manager advised Mays to keep his distance as well. Ignoring his superiors, Mays spent as much time as possible discussing books with Dickey.

Even though Dickey boasted that his New York colleagues had nicknamed him "Jingle Jim" because of his flair for coining catch phrases, Mays was convinced that he had invented the title as a kind of self-advertisement. Dickey showed his disdain for his copywriting job almost from the start. He refused to go to meetings or work overtime. He constantly tried to outfox the executives in order to spend time on his poetry: "If they said, 'Alright, today we need ten television commercials and five radio commercials and two print ads; this is your assignment for the day,' he'd say, 'OK.' He'd shut the door and within an hour he'd have it all done. Then he'd spend the rest of the time working on his own work—his correspondence, his poems. But of course they didn't know that. They figured: 'That'll keep him busy all day.' But he was so smart and so fast, he could get it done."[26]

To his business cohorts, Dickey did not always appear to be a master of efficiency. Howard Hyle, who worked as Coca-Cola's sales promotion manager under advertising manager Delony Sledge, frequently visited the McCann offices to discuss ad campaigns. The problem with Dickey, he said, was that "he saw everything he did as a challenge to demonstrate his uniqueness. Everything he did had to be the best. He was going to spend all the time to do it. The executives wanted competent copy in volume. . . . He certainly didn't belong in the business world."[27] Hyle, whose father had been a maverick inventor, sympathized with Dickey, but thought he belonged in an artist's studio rather than a conference room. Another McCann friend, Mike McDonald, who had transferred from New York to Atlanta in 1958, remembered Dickey as "far down the food chain as far as directing ads for Coke" and "far removed from creating jingles." He would go to Dickey's office and say: "Jim, we've got 150 more requests we have to take care of." Jim would respond slowly: "Don't worry. Everything is going to be just fine. Surely we'll get to them in good time."[28] McDonald enjoyed Dickey's humor, blasé attitude, and mischievous spirit.

Dickey struck many of his office mates the way he'd struck many of his schoolmates at North Fulton High School—as an introspective maverick who kept to himself except when pursuing women. An account executive, Doug Smith, found him "unique, and a little strange,"[29] and never believed all his stories about being a combat pilot. The secretaries, on the other hand, were amused by Dickey's eccentricities. One woman who worked in the Art Department saw Dickey doing push-ups by his desk. She also heard that he pursued his muscle building in the bathroom, where he did chin-ups on the bar over the toilet stall (at home Dickey did similar exercises on a chinning bar with ski boots on his feet to add extra weight). At office parties, Dickey's flamboyance did not always amuse. Thad Horton recalled: "At one Christmas party he was the scourge of the place. He made the women indignant by trying to 'make' them. By that time I had lost confidence in him as a working colleague."[30] Horton tried to remain cordial, and years later—in 1973—when he became a priest and then headmaster and admissions director of Storm King School in Cornwall-on-Hudson, New York, he even made Dickey a member of the school's board of visitors.

Dickey did strike up new friendships at McCann. With the art director, Jonis Gold, he partied and practiced with his bow and arrows and blowgun. Gold, who was Jewish, and his wife, who was half-Chinese, felt like pariahs in Atlanta society, but they felt that Dickey was even more of a pariah: "He didn't have . . . [a business] mind. He was not clever and facile enough with [advertising] ideas, not good at marketing. He was just making a living grinding out bottler ads. He was just a guy on the line. There was no glory in the job."[31] Because of his love of books, Inman Mays was Dickey's closest friend. Together they would browse secondhand bookshops on Peachtree Street during lunch breaks. On paydays, Dickey diverged from his bookish routine by going to the Rendezvous Room at the Biltmore for two double martinis and a bowl of soup.

Dickey tried only halfheartedly to resume the life he had lived as a youth in Atlanta. He looked up former friends and kept athletically fit, but he was a changed man. Rather than play football or run track, he played tennis and hunted snakes with homemade blowguns in the small creek behind his house. Sometimes he just shot the darts at trees. (When they landed in nearby yards, neighbors called the police.) His other new sport was archery. Maxine had bought him a bow in Gainesville, and in Buckhead one of Tom and Patsy Dickey's neighbors, Dave Sanders, reintroduced him to the sport. Sanders "was sort of a party boy,"[32] Dickey said, for whom archery was an obsession. Sanders taught Dickey about the best equipment and took him to the best ranges around Atlanta. Sanders also had literary interests, which made him more companionable. In some ways he served as a model for the excesses Dickey himself pursued in the years to come—he was an alcoholic, a womanizer who treated his wife miserably, and a merry prankster who liked to do things like serve Dickey weak tea foaming with soap suds and pretend it was beer. Sanders was partly responsible for the increasing acrimony between Dickey and Maxine. He invited Dickey to his house on Friday evenings; and as Dickey spent more time drinking there, Maxine became increasingly indignant. She would call and ask him to come home. When he did, it was late, he was drunk, and a fight would ensue. She implored him not to spend so much time drinking away from home; he ignored her pleas.

During the early fall of 1956, Sanders took Dickey to the wooded Cherokee Bowmen Club range in Smyrna, Georgia. In an essay titled "Air-Slash," Dickey recalled that on this first trip he "had only the most rudimentary notion of how to aim. I had an all-fiberglass bow, a backyard bow of not much account, five or six unmatched—and doubtless crooked—wooden arrows, hardly more than toys; in fact if I saw one of these now I would probably wonder it didn't have a rubber suction cup on the end of it." Because he knew little about shooting, he watched Sanders fire an arrow at a round black-and-white target partially blocked by a branch. Lifting his bow, Sanders purportedly uttered a Zen aphorism ("One shot—one life"), drew his tournament bow (a Long Drake), and hit the black section of the target, scoring three points. It was now Dickey's turn: "I had a notion then, already, that I would never again find such an exact challenge. . . . It came to me that the challenge here was stillness, and, possibly at the center of that high-tension immobility, a feeling of disregard, almost of nonchalance." Dickey surmised that the feeling resembled the sort of lordly equanimity experienced by "James Joyce's version of the true artist,"[33] who is so aloof that he can pare his fingernails while overlooking his re-creation of the Creation in his art.

Dickey's aesthetic stance did not improve his accuracy: "My shot fishtailed badly and buried-up, as they say, in the lower part of the gully, well below the target bale, but I already knew that I would have to save some money and get myself a real bow, and some matched aluminum arrows. Then I would come back."[34] Over the next months, partly to relieve stress, Dickey practiced alone at the range, losing dozens of arrows. He also took a keen interest in Eugen Herrigel's stress-relieving cult classic, *Zen in the Art of Archery*, which Sanders had recommended. Dickey admired the book so much that when he reentered academe in the 1960s he regularly read it to students. He also urged the actors on the film site of *Deliverance* to read it in hopes of bettering their archery skills. With or without the aid of Zen Buddhism (Herrigel advocated years of arduous spiritual training), Dickey began entering tournaments with the ambition if not the dexterity of a great archer.

Atlanta friends wondered whether Dickey paid homage to Sanders by making him a character in *Deliverance*. Was he Lewis Medlock, the expert archer, or Ed Gentry, who can also shoot a bow and arrow? Or was he the wisecracking party boy, Bobby? Al Braselton, who most closely resembled Drew Ballinger in the novel, pointed out that Sanders and Bobby shared a similar sense of humor and an aversion to camping trips: "Dave was a strange duck. . . . He was the last man you wanted to be out in the woods with. He went with us one time and made nothing but sarcastic remarks."[35] Bobby was sarcastic as well, at least until his traumatic encounter with the hillbilly. Dickey, however, denied Sanders served as any sort of fictional model. The novel's characters, he contended, were based on Lewis King, Al Braselton, and himself. Evidence suggests that Sanders played a larger role. Without Sanders's archery instruction, a central component of the novel would be missing. In the first draft of *Deliverance*, Dickey commemorated his friend in the character of Shaw Sanders, an advertising man whom Ed contacts after his canoe trip.

The fact that archery in Georgia during the late 1950s was a small, cliquish sport made it appealing to Dickey. As Medlock would say, it had a "mystique." Primitive and unregulated, bow-and-arrow hunting resembled Eugene Dickey's cockfighting and returned Dickey to his father's terrain in the Georgia hinterland. Once ambivalent about his father's rural activities, he now warmed to them. Entrenched in his city job, he better understood why his father wanted to escape Atlanta. Dickey became a proficient archer and soon joined the Cherokee Bowmen Club on hunting trips to the Piedmont National Wildlife Refuge in Juliette, Georgia, about forty miles southeast of Atlanta. Or he went to the military training camp in Dahlonega, about forty miles north of Atlanta and not far from Springer Mountain—the site of one of Dickey's best-known poems about bow hunting. Proficiency, however, was never enough for Dickey; he embellished his respectable skills with stories of winning major championships, shooting rapacious hillbillies, and killing deer, foxes, and wild boar. To the end of his life he claimed that he won a state tournament in Red Oak, Georgia. Although he was never a champion archer, he liked to mingle with champions like Bud Adair, who made Dickey a magnificent bow with an uncommonly heavy handle section and a special arrow rest. Dickey was so proud of the gift that he gave Ed Gentry a similar bow in *Deliverance*.

Bow hunting became a dominant theme in many of Dickey's major works. To Glenn Helgeland, the editor of *Archery World* magazine and one of Dickey's hunting companions, Dickey explained his attitudes toward the sport: "I like hunting, not only in practice, but in theory. I like to be out there with the wild animals in the situation they understand the best, which is that of life and death. I would much rather be out stalking a deer with a boy than giving one a lump of sugar in the zoo. Because he has you in *his* condition: his condition as a wild animal. Any animal senses that the condition he lives in from day to day is the condition of life and death. Animals understand that things are trying to kill them. And men should be in that kind of deep relationship with animals at least occasionally to find out where the human race came from."[36] On his forays into the wilderness with his bow, Dickey could shed his everyday attire—as he literally does in "Springer Mountain"—and get into a more primitive relation with the world.

Dickey's days at McCann filled him with the sort of malaise he read about in existentialist writers like Camus and Sartre. Work, he decided, "was very much like the myth of Sisyphus, pushing the stone up the hill only to have it roll back down."[37] The title of his poetry book-in-progress, *Into the Stone*, underscored his petrifying routines in the ad business and the way he had to burrow and dissemble in his stonelike office in order to write. Regarding his work "for Coca-Cola, and for the American Way of Life," he lamented to Bill Pratt at the end of May 1957:

> Business is the death of the spirit, the death of every good impulse, the death of time, and the death of life. Yet, yet. . . . *there is money in it!* And *that* means I can support my family, raise Chris half-way decently, and take care of any and all succeeding off-spring. . . . That is much. Only, I have to live like a schizophrenic, bowing and scraping before the Powers, and being the friendly young businessman with good ideas though with vague bohemian (that is to say, "literary") leanings, and, at night and early in the morning, the poet himself, in T-shirt and Bermuda shorts, payed [sic] for in blood money and the slaughter of useful ideals, putting desperately down The Truth.[38]

The world, he believed with cynical conviction, was a lie masquerading as the truth. Poetry, on the other hand, was a lie revealing the truth.

To alleviate his feelings of estrangement from the literary community, Dickey kept up a hectic correspondence with other writers. He contacted Pound's protégé, the English poet Basil Bunting; Ben Belitt, a poet and a translator of Pablo Neruda teaching at Bennington College; Allen Seager, a novelist and future biographer of Theodore Roethke; Ann Stanford, a poet he would meet at San Fernando Valley State in California (she informed him of Kenneth Rexroth's "Beat" poetry renaissance on the West Coast); and Jon Silkin, an English poet he especially admired. Like so many poets of his generation, he also paid homage to William Carlos Williams, one of the pioneers of twentieth-century poetry. In the fall of 1957, he wrote a fan letter to the ailing Williams in Rutherford, New Jersey. Typing the letter in his McCann office, he complained about the business distractions that tore him from his poetry, but admitted that Williams had written under more taxing circumstances. Most of the letter was an attempt to express solidarity with Williams's imagistic free verse:

> One of the faults, and I guess, the occasional beauties of being a recognized poet, one of the best we in this country can put on the street, is that you become a kind of rallying-place for cries like this one. It is, I hope, a cry of

homage more than of anything else, and I hope it dins in your ears with at least as much force as the others coming in over the brain-waves of poets every day. I would like to thank you for a lifetime of devotion to the language I love, and for bringing to it the resources of a beautiful and responsible human being. This is all we can do about our situation as human beings. . . . I can walk out with my son, for instance, and sit on the ground in the sunlight. I can feel my body die (I am 34 now, which is when I guess all this begins. Or perhaps it never begins and never ends). I know the supreme importance of the moment, and have a certain conviction that I may be able to feel more of it, to keep prolonging it, if I write about it. I do, and sometimes I am in awe of my efforts. Sometimes they are good poems, for the experience, or more than the experience is in them. That is the essential of poetry to me. All the infinitely detailed commentaries about the technical properties of verse are somewhat beside the point, to me. Anyway, your own verse has the hardness (I realize you have heard all this a thousand times before, but I would like you to know that the feelings are renewed in me), the vividness of such moments as I have with my little boy. This is understanding life and experience, because the feelings themselves *are* the understanding, if you can get them into words.[39]

If Williams had seen any of Dickey's poems, he would have realized that Dickey's dense, surrealistic style diverged markedly from the sort of plain American speech that he advocated.

Dickey's flattering, sentimental remarks inspired an unexpected response from Williams. Having suffered crippling strokes and having been hounded by anti-Communist McCarthyites at the beginning of the 1950s, Williams by 1957 was a frail and often bitter man. As a partial rebuke to Dickey's kind words, he told a story of a Ukrainian woman who had recently visited him. The Ukrainian woman had been captured by Russians and through a difficult process had escaped to America. Because Williams had spoken tolerantly of a well-known group of Communist sympathizers in Hollywood, the woman attacked his naïveté. "It was as if I had stabbed her through the heart," he told Dickey. "She wanted to warn me not to do it again." The chastened Williams now chastised Dickey for being too tolerant and too mild: "Your letter by its mildness and talk of your small son for some reason makes me think of that [Ukrainian] woman. We are all too tolerant, too mild. The poems I write are a violent reaction against our undemonstrability. . . . Take care of yourself, at least you wrote."[40] Dickey must have chortled at the old man's conception of him as a mild lamb. In his response, Dickey tried to be polite: "Thank you for your comments on 'gentleness' and the rest, though, certainly, it is the first time anyone had ever noticed this in me, or in anything I have ever done. This may be because, at the age of thirty-three [he was actually thirty-four, as he had stated in his previous letter], I feel it important to admit to myself the things I really care about, and to try to say something about them."[41] Although Dickey implied that he had followed Williams's example by quitting his teaching job (Williams had chosen a medical career over an academic one), Williams's reprimand undoubtedly rankled. In most of his later comments about Williams, Dickey made sure to use his advice against him by being demonstrably intolerant. He repeatedly dismissed Williams as a poet without an iota of talent.

If he had begun his advertising career by making at least visual contact with Faulkner, Dickey soon made verbal contact with another major Southern writer, Flannery O'Connor, whose preoccupations with myth, ritual, and grotesquerie resembled his own. O'Connor resided at Andalusia, her family farm in Milledgeville, Georgia, where she suffered from lupus erythematosus. Dickey told a reporter for an Atlanta paper that before O'Connor died in 1964, at the age of thirty-nine, he had made about half-a-dozen visits to Andalusia, sometimes bringing his son, Chris, to admire O'Connor's menagerie: "She was my first writer friend. . . . Really, she was the only writer friend I had for a while."[42] A mutual friend, Edith Ivey, arranged Dickey's first visit to O'Connor's home in early March 1958. In a letter to the novelist John Hawkes, written on July 27, O'Connor appeared pleased by the visit. She said that Dickey had shown Chris the farm ponies and had admiringly discussed Hawkes's novels with her. Impressed by her literary acumen, Dickey gained confidence from her interest in his poetry. On one visit O'Connor gave him Donald Davie's *Articulate Energy*, a critical book that argued for orderly syntax in poetry rather than the fragmentary syntax of modernists like Pound and Eliot. Davie's book may have persuaded Dickey to keep his syntactical experiments to a minimum before opting for a fragmentary style in the 1970s and 1980s. Although friendly toward O'Connor, when asked to lecture on her work at the first Flannery O'Connor Writer's Forum at Georgia College—her alma mater—in April 1988, Dickey made it clear that she was no longer "a great favorite." He still liked her short stories, but her novels lacked "staying power," as did her lackluster criticism and nonfiction: "She has a very narrow compass and a very limited subject matter. . . . Sort of grotesquerie combined with religious preoccupations."[43] Dickey could have been thinking of his own themes when he spoke of O'Connor's.

At about this time Dickey formed a much more influential friendship with James Wright. On the surface, the two poets were opposites. Wright had grown up in the small factory town of Martin's Ferry, Ohio. His father, a die setter for the Hazel Atlas Glass Company, and his mother, a descendant of mountain folk, had suffered terribly during the Depression. Wright tended to be self-belittling and neurasthenic (he had suffered a nervous breakdown as a teenager). He was a Northerner and a liberal like his close friend Robert Bly. A number of similarities, however, brought Wright and Dickey together. As teenagers, both had revered Byron. Both had served in occupied Japan (Wright was an army typist), and both had attended college on the GI Bill. At Kenyon College, Wright had studied under the old Vanderbilt Fugitive John Crowe Ransom, but had already begun to rebel against Ransom's New Critical principles. As their poetic styles evolved, both shared a taste for what Dickey called "country surrealism"—an idiosyncratic blending of nature, domesticity, and fantasy. Like Dickey, Wright was a man divided against himself, and like Dickey he blamed some of his conflicts on his family's involvement in the Civil War. He wrote Dickey:

You see, I was born and raised in southern Ohio, just across the river from West Va. Both grandparents and their own forebears are southerners.

Since I like my own relatives, and some of them very deeply, I feel very profoundly involved in the Civil War in a peculiarly terrible way. You see, my great grandparents were in W. Va. about the time it seceded from Va., after Va. seceded from the Union. . . . It is just possible, and in fact I have often suspected, that many of my forebears on both sides of the family . . . fought on *both* sides in the War between the States: this is not merely a melodramatic fantasy of mine, either, because I have not merely seen (in my childhood) but *lived* and *felt*, in my childhood experience with relatives and *inside myself* during the last few years, this sense of murderous and despairing violence between *immediate close kin*, that lies underneath the Civil War, close to the surface, and somehow gives it its really *tragic* horror.[44]

In early 1958, the poets began an impassioned correspondence in which Dickey complained about the advertising business and Wright complained about his painful marriage. In one of his letters Dickey railed: "I abominate advertising. When I think of all the hours I have racked my brains and run my mind through one meat-grinder after another in search of new ways to say, 'For God's sake, you idiots, drink Coca-Cola. Well, all right, *don't* drink it! But *buy* it!' When I think of all *those* hours, I try not to think any more, for, whom the gods would destroy, they first make mad. Oddly enough, as much fulminating as I do against it, I love teaching. But I could not earn a living in it."[45] After a particularly long series of meetings to discuss marketing strategies for Coke, he wrote: "Ten days of meetings of this kind, full of this jargoning, Kiwanis-type verbiage, and I am ready to turn slowly into a wild, really wild animal. Tell me, James Wright, what is life, real life, with real human beings in it, really like? I have forgotten."[46] If this was hell, he would imagine its opposite in "A Heaven of Animals," although there, too, the "really wild animals" were unreal.

Dickey also carried on a steady correspondence with Donald Hall, who had already established himself as a poet and a first-rate editor at the *Paris Review*. In addition, Dickey exchanged letters with the brilliant young English poet Geoffrey Hill. Since Hall had befriended Hill at Oxford in the early 1950s, Dickey and Hall discussed schemes for getting Hill published more widely in the States. Dickey felt particularly close to Hill because of their common stylistic goals. Both aimed for a powerful rhetoric that derived from Romantic visionaries like Blake and Coleridge, contemporary Romantics like Dylan Thomas and George Barker, and Fugitives like Tate. "I think Hill is a sure winner," Dickey wrote Hall on April 2, 1957, "and I am sorry to hear him sound so discouraged over his rejections. . . . He is one of the few English-speaking poets I have read recently who have any imaginative daring." In the same letter, Dickey promised to send some of Hill's new poems to the *Sewanee Review* and perhaps to the *Yale Review* and the *Kenyon Review*. He assumed Hall, who was publishing Hill in the *Paris Review*, would send other poems to *Partisan Review*, *Poetry*, and the *Hudson Review*.

On March 25, 1957, Hill wrote from the University of Leeds in England thanking Dickey for trying to place his poems in America. With the letter he included about half-a-dozen new poems that eventually appeared in his first book, *For the Unfallen*. Despite their common likes and dislikes, Dickey and Hill had many things beside an ocean separating them. Hill had grown up during World War II in a lower-middle-class family in the small market town of Bromsgrove, Worcestershire. His parents had left school at the age of thirteen. His father and grandfather were police constables, his mother's people nail makers. While Dickey had been throwing a football and jumping hurdles, Hill, a child prodigy, had been writing some of his best poems. His poetry from the start was profoundly historical and political, often addressing past wars and holocausts and the way language glossed over their horrors. Dickey admired Hill's early poems such as "Genesis," but felt Hill's subsequent poems lacked mythic resonance, clarity, and sensuality. They were too disjointed, too intellectual. As in his other literary alliances, Dickey jousted with Hill without losing his fundamental respect for him.

From the start, the epistolary exchanges between Dickey and Hall were also marked by thrusts and counterthrusts. Hall's schooling—he had been educated at Exeter, Harvard, and Oxford—aroused Dickey's envy, and to a certain extent so did Hall's Audenesque facility with language. A Connecticut Yankee who was liberal in his politics and eclectic in his literary tastes, Hall championed formalist poets like Richard Wilbur and Robert Lowell as well as their opponents like Robert Bly. As a foil to Hall, Dickey posed as a hot-headed rebel from Dixie about to mount a Confederate battle charge:

> I am glad you like Thom Gunn personally, which undoubtedly I should too, if I knew him, and that you defend his work against the likes of me. I still don't think he's much good, being much too tenuous and propositional and generality-forming and stiffly proper, and totally without the *feel* of significant experience on any of his stuff. This is somewhat the case, too, with Richard Wilbur, whom you have made the best of all possible cases for (a better one, really, than he deserves), and James Merrill, that chocolate-frosting of a poet, and Anthony Hecht, with his tiresome and empty "elegance," and William Merwin, a prettified interior decorator with no subject and perfect manners and plenty of time to write. I'm sorry, here, to shovel so much earth (which, of course, you don't really think I've succeeded in doing) onto writers you have defended, expounded, praised, and promoted. I don't include your own work among theirs, and like what of it I have seen.[47]

Dickey heaped as much dirt as he could on the poems that Hall, Robert Pack, and Louis Simpson had just published in an influential anthology, *New Poets of England and America*.

Dickey particularly resented Hall's promotion of the Wilbur-Merrill-Hecht-Merwin "garden school" of poetry and what he called its "well-meaning, mannered management of nothing." He preferred the bardic afflatus of Theodore Roethke and Richard Eberhart. In his duels with Hall, he also tried to win sympathy for himself as an academic martyr and outlaw. He resented being excluded from Hall's anthology of "academic poets" just as he resented being driven from academe by the sort of well-mannered old ladies who might appreciate a Wilbur or a Merrill. "How *can* you talk as if the blarsted university were a *good* place for him [the poet]?"[48] he asked Hall with Poundian scorn. His distaste for universities, however, was not strong enough to prevent him from actively seeking new appointments and getting friends like Hall and Wright to help him. He applied unsuccessfully to the University of Richmond around 1954, and considered reapplying in April 1957. Late in 1957, Monroe Spears suggested that Dickey apply to Vanderbilt as well as Miami University in Ohio, where Spears had friends. Two years later Dickey wrote the poet Theodore Weiss to see if Weiss could get him a job at Bard College.

With Hall, Dickey pretended to be a blacklisted victim of the sort of anti-communist witch-hunters ransacking the universities in the 1950s. He stitched a well-embroidered tale of his academic misfortunes:

Yes, I have taught: at Vanderbilt, where I went to school, as a football "fellow," and then as a god-damned graduate student and teaching assistant. I taught at Rice, in Houston, and for a year I was Andrew Lytle's assistant at the University of Florida, in "The Creative Writing Program." I was booted from Florida for a controversial talk I made to a group of spiritual thieves called the "Pen Women's Society" or something to that effect. You can read the offending poem in last December's *Poetry*, if you like. I am more or less black-listed in teaching, and perhaps it's as well. I worked as a professional fisherman for a while, and coached track at a small college, and as groundskeeper worked in the mornings, before the boys got out of class.

It was Tom Dickey who considered becoming a track coach. As far as keeping the grounds, he may have been thinking of his family servant Andrew Burney. With regard to professional fishing, most of his angling experiences had been confined to a hand line on Saint Simons Island. In his fictitious epistle, Dickey also claimed (falsely) that Pound had written him complimentary letters about his recent magazine publications. Dickey ended his letter with more bluster: "I am a tall blond tennis-looking man, still in pretty good shape. I still think I could fight three or four pretty fair rounds, though not ten. . . . You must let me abuse you, and give you a hard time, for really I would not, except that you stand up to it so well."[49] Hall may have believed Dickey's Hemingwayesque lies—he had no intimate knowledge to disprove them—but unlike some of Dickey's other friends, he was not the sort who would hang from the rafters as Dickey's punching bag.

The combination of anger and despair Dickey expressed to Hall derived in part from the fact that Hall was rejecting his poems at the *Paris Review* as being too dense and disheveled. In a letter written to Hall on October 9, 1957, that contained a poem for possible publication, Dickey went to extremes to wring pity from his obstinate foe: "I have been very ill, and almost dead, the doctors tell me, of Asiatic flu and compounded other sicknesses."[50] Then he made a pitch for his poem, "Mindoro," which Hall ultimately accepted and finally printed in 1960. The acceptance, it seemed, brought Dickey back from the dead, although, as he lugubriously told Hall on November 16, he was still shaken: "For days I lay as though walking slowly into a long slender shadow, frightening at first, but then incredibly mild and shady, with a soft flicker to it, as though a place I knew and remembered and liked. I could have knelt down in relief, but felt that walking was part of the reason I was there, going so slowly along I remained in the same place for hours at a time, in absolute silence."[51]

Despite his revivified state, the advertising business continued to cast a pall over Dickey's life. He had told Pound a year after taking the job at McCann what his business colleagues knew only too well: "I am now making a living by half-successfully disguising myself as a 'business man,' coming downtown to work in an office from nine to five each day, and banging away at lunch hour and evenings at poems and a few reviews."[52] While his work as a copywriter progressed in fits and starts, his poetry moved forward more promisingly. Leading journals such as the *Sewanee Review*, the *Hudson Review*, the *Yale Review*, *Poetry*, *Partisan Review*, and the *Beloit Poetry Journal* were accepting his poems. Howard Moss, the poetry editor of the *New Yorker*, had asked to see more poems after sending back "Sleeping Out at Easter" and other submissions in 1958. In 1959, Dickey was thrilled when Moss accepted "Orpheus Before Hades." Years later Moss told one of Dickey's students, Franklin Ashley, who visited his editorial office, "The most exciting moment I ever had as an editor was when I discovered James Dickey. His poems came to me unsolicited over the transom."[53] Dickey could finally claim that he had made it as a poet when Moss, one of the finest and most influential poetry editors in the country, began regularly publishing him.

Each time Dickey toyed with the idea of returning to an academic post, his advertising salary persuaded him to do otherwise. At the beginning of 1958, he reported to Hall: "I got a big raise in pay, and I am afraid that I am more or less totally committed to advertising now: a thing I have been increasingly afraid of for the last two years. I wanted to get back into teaching, but I am afraid that is impossible now."[54] In addition, the persona of the long-suffering, exiled poet— like Pound in a Pisan prison, Eliot in a London bank, or Wallace Stevens in a Hartford insurance company—appealed to Dickey's histrionic streak. He liked to have literary friends commiserating with him and conspiring to liberate him. Even though he chafed against McCann's golden shackles, he also realized that his business schedule forced him to organize his life in a way that benefited his poetry. He told Hall: "Certainly I would write more if I had nothing but that to do. . . . When I had the Sewanee fellowship, though, I didn't really work as much, or as well, as I am doing now. Somehow, when one has all the time one needs, it seems rather a duty to *live* than to write. Especially in Europe. Here, there is very little living to be done, and so I am driven back on writing. I have two or three hundred poems . . . in progress, and have never really been so *full* of working on poems."[55] Free from the distractions of travel, by April 1958 Dickey had nearly finished the manuscript of *Into the Stone*.

Dickey also involved Wright in his ambiguous job search. When Wright assured Dickey that there were jobs available for writers without Ph.D.s, Dickey growled:

Part of the source of my very real bitterness against the Universities is that people like [Philip] Booth and Lou Coxe and Wilbur and Tony Hecht all have good jobs teaching where they like, and *what* they like, and nobody ever asked me, who am a better poet and a better teacher and a better human being than any of them (*Don't laugh*: it's true. I know them all, and what I say is so). True enough, I was Andrew Lytle's assistant in the Creative Writing Program at the University of Florida, but I was only so in addition to carrying a full load of freshmen and with the same salary as the freshman instructors got. And that did not suit me, any more than it would have suited you, or Lytle himself, who taught two hours a week to my fourteen, and salted away seven thousand five hundred dollars a year for doing almost nothing. Well, I now have an income of almost twenty thousand a year [it was actually about ten thousand dollars], but I still feel I was *had* by the teaching profession, and did no good in it at all, except in the minds and hearts of a few people.[56]

Jealous of those poets whose careers had accelerated more quickly than his own, Dickey bristled at what he believed to be their unfair advantages.

Dickey had friends closer to home to console him in his plight. At the Biltmore Hotel he occasionally ate lunch with his former schoolmate George Montgomery, who was similarly divided between literary interests (he later wrote novels like *The Eye of the Eagle*) and his business career at the Atlanta Coca-Cola Bottling Company. In the spring of 1958, Dickey also befriended the young poet Larry Rubin, who was completing a two-year stint as an English instructor at Georgia Tech. He often asked Rubin for help on his poems over lunch on Wednesdays or snacks on Sunday nights at Dickey's house. With Rubin, Dickey was serious, well behaved, and scholarly. Inman Mays also became a regular guest at the Dickey house. A bachelor, he appreciated Maxine's hospitality and good cooking, and was amazed by the maternal way she handled Jim's life:

Maxine not only functioned as wife and mother, she also acted as Jim's amanuensis, business manager, agent and resident public relations counselor. She ran the household, cooked and took care of the children, like any suburban housewife and relieved Jim of any and all worries about mundane domestic concerns, which allowed him to spend all his free time away from the office writing poetry. Maxine typed his manuscripts and correspondence and performed various other secretarial duties, such as opening all daily mail addressed to Jim, extracting any checks that might have arrived, then reporting to Jim who wrote what in regard to various ongoing literary matters. . . . Maxine ran a very tight ship as far as the Dickey domestic enterprise was concerned. She handled all family finances, and kept Jim on a strict budget, allowing him $1.00 daily for lunch money. Except on paydays, when she would always arrive at the office to collect Jim's check and join us for lunch. Somehow Jim managed to squirrel away enough cash which he would use to buy books, books and more books, like some obsessed bibliophile.[57]

Because Mays and Maxine got along so well, Dickey playfully accused them of having an affair. Mays's friendship, however, remained platonic.

Dickey needed his Atlanta friends to bolster him in skirmishes with his Northern peers. After publishing a mixed review of *New Poets of England and America* in the April–June issue of the *Sewanee Review*, Dickey drew salvos from Hall, Wright, and others. How could Dickey dismiss all his poems with only two words, "ploddingly 'sincere'"?[58] Wright bitterly asked. Dickey not only lacked generosity; he acted like a mean-spirited professor, which sparked off Wright's blast: "I have never greeted a student by telling her to go fuck herself and shove her hideous poems up her ass because they have blotched my soul and insulted the names of Homer, Dante, and Shakespeare. . . . If the versifier (like myself, as you well know) fails to achieve a poem, I don't see why the critic has to kick him in the balls." Along with his letter Wright enclosed a more formal, but still angry, reply to Dickey's critique that he planned to publish in the *Sewanee Review*. In it he upbraided Dickey for his "pugnacious refusal to rationalize his strong likes and dislikes" and his "obsessive spraying of venomous hatred"[59] at worthy poets.

Dickey responded with a mixture of contempt and disarming courtesy. Wright, he said, was guilty of "a pathetic exhibition of aggrieved, adolescent whimpering and 'stricken' self-righteousness." He felt sorry for Wright, but he would not tolerate a blasphemous letter in his house: "Such language addressed to the home of a total stranger must be taken either as the doing of a hopeless crank . . . or of someone who realizes the implications of his actions, and is prepared to be held responsible for them: i.e. to resolve the differences in personal action, rather than in print. If you persist, you have my word that this will be the case."[60] A decade later Dickey made similar challenges to Wright's closest literary friend, Robert Bly.

The day after receiving Dickey's threats, Wright responded with a self-effacing apology. He told Dickey: "[Your letter's] firm courtesy startled me into an inexcusably belated realization of the extraordinarily ugly thing I had done." He promised to withdraw the rebuttal from the *Sewanee Review*. Contrite, he now agreed with Dickey's contention that "under the influence of God knows what powerful, self-protective compulsion, [I] . . . have evidently invented a dreadful, irresponsible, arrogant fellow named James Dickey who thinks of you as a person congenitally unable to tell the truth." Wright confessed he had been paranoid, hysterical, stupid, adolescent, and cowardly: "Mr. Dickey, I am ashamed and humiliated. Even *this* letter is one long adolescent whine. I would take it as a very great, though of course undeserved, personal kindness if you were to accept my apology for insulting your family and you."[61] The childish spat came to an end and prepared the way for a twenty-year friendship.

During the winter of 1958, Dickey lectured Wright about making enemies: "Ezra Pound, who wrote me once about some poems of mine he had seen, once told me that a man must be judged *by the quality of his enemies*. I don't think much of the *quality* of my enemies, but perhaps I can make up for that by their quantity. I sure have a lot of them, as well as a few loyal people."[62] To the end of his life Dickey decried the quality—though not the quantity—of his enemies. With Wright and with other potential enemies, however, Dickey usually tried to make amends. Skirmishing was a game to be played with scrupulous meanness, but afterward the combatants should lay down their arms and fraternize. Because Wright had quit when the fight had hardly begun, forever afterward Dickey suspected him of being a whining coward. On July 23, he tried to cheer up his battered, self-deprecating opponent: "You are entirely too hard on yourself. . . . As far as I can tell, you have a very great deal more ability than you seem to want to allow yourself to think. Your beginning has been a good one. The only point I would make about it is that I think it should be beginning to show a direction. You seem to write very easily (which God knows I do not), and there is a very real danger in facility. You must watch out for the more sentimental and easy kinds of saleable sincerity, and for a too-easy solution to poems. I expect you will do well as a poet, and as a teacher, also."[63] Dickey revised this ambivalent assessment of his friend's poetry very little over the years.

Dickey felt genuine empathy and affection for Wright. He also realized that he could bully Wright into believing almost anything. After Dickey had attacked him for inventing a dreadful James Dickey and Wright had confessed: "I suppose you are as unquestionably honest as anyone I ever knew,"[64] Dickey started passing along details of his invented life. Awed by his "Southern Antagonist," as Wright now called Dickey, Wright acted as an unofficial publicity agent, circulating Dickey's Hemingwayesque myths among his literary friends. Following a Michigan-Minnesota football game in Ann Arbor he attended with Donald Hall, Wright told Dickey: "We spoke of you, by the way, and Don, who also loves sports, was delighted to hear that you had made all-Southern backfield after playing with one of the great teams of the South [Clemson]."[65] Dickey felt compunction about the success of his lies. In an apologetic tone, he told Wright: "Humility is not my forte: I much more easily run to arrogance and insolence, but I do want to come off that for a moment and tell you how grateful I am for your letters, but most of all, for being the kind of person you must be: striving continually for honesty in your writing, but most of all in your life. In the world I live in, there is no one else like that. I aspire to be the same way, but I really am not. But I know what that kind of honesty and that kind of life must be, and I admire it."[66] Acknowledging his deficiencies, Dickey also bragged to Wright of his bow-and-arrow skills (he said he had just killed a big deer on a hunt and later claimed he had killed a fox, from which he was having a hat made). A month later, on March 23, 1959, Dickey gave a more truthful account of his deer hunt to Donald Hall: "Last fall I bought a bow and some broad-head arrows and went up to North Georgia to hunt. I was actually so inept that I shot at a buck at about thirty yards and the arrow rattled around in his antlers. He seemed, literally, to be playing with the thing, before he took off through the bushes."[67] Dickey's hunting companions denied that he ever killed a deer or fox in his life.

In one of his typically garrulous letters, Wright sent Dickey greetings from a University of Minnesota colleague—and one of the few poets Dickey praised in his *Sewanee* essay—John Berryman. Dickey had called the birth sequence in Berryman's *Homage to Mistress Bradstreet* "the most daring and successful rendering of human experience ever to appear in American poetry."[68] Berryman returned the compliments by singling Dickey out as "one of the most brilliant and serious writers on poetry to appear in a long, long time."[69] Dickey had told Berryman as early as May 9, 1958, that *Homage to Mistress Bradstreet* deserved every major prize given for poetry in America. The two poets grew closer when they realized that they shared a passion for the work of the neglected poet Robert Bhain Campbell. Campbell had been one of Berryman's closest friends from 1939 until his death more than a decade later of a gruesome cancer. Dickey told Berryman about discovering Campbell's work on the remainder counter of a department store in Waco, Texas. He had been struck by a statement by Campbell about how he wanted to "read all the books of criticism, rebore the blocks, and get ready to run steadily for five years."[70] Mixing fact with fiction, Dickey said that he had felt the same way after returning from the war in Korea. He asked Berryman to send photographs of Campbell and later wrote a poem "For Robert Bhain Campbell."

Despite his morbid complaints about being isolated from the literary world, at McCann-Erickson Dickey forged most of the literary connections crucial to his early career. During the summer of 1958, Wright pointed him toward a fellow Minnesotan who would also play a significant role in his rise to eminence: "You would surely be interested in the appearance of a new magazine called *The Fifties*. The editor, Mr. Robert Bly, whom I have never met but some of whose poems appear in the [Hall, Pack, Simpson] Meridian Anthology, sent me a copy."[71] After reading a translation of a poem by Georg Trakl in *The Fifties*, Wright sent Bly two dollars and instructed him to mail a copy of the magazine to Dickey. Bly, as it turned out, had already done so.

As a poet and editor, Bly had a definite poetic agenda: to dethrone the reigning New Critical orthodoxy and in its place substitute surrealist free verse. Form and meter, Bly argued, were passé. A more archetypal and mythic poetry was needed and one more in tune with the unconscious mind. To find models for the kind of poetry he favored, Bly searched the literatures of other nations. As a result, his magazine was filled with translations. With as much zany wit as critical perspicacity, Bly railed in *The Fifties* against the "Madame Tussaud's Wax Museum" of academic poets. When Bly wrote Dickey about his disenchantment with the reigning orthodoxy shortly after *New Poets of England and America* appeared, Dickey responded: "Let's do it; let's do the rebellion."[72] Dickey signed his letter "Fletcher Christian," after the character in *Mutiny on the Bounty* who led the insurrection. In a decade, Dickey would redirect his rebellion from the academic establishment toward Captain Bly himself.

With Bly, Dickey followed his usual courting ritual: he quickly instigated a feud and almost as quickly became best friends. While they shared several important aesthetic principles, Bly's dogmatism irritated Dickey. Their skirmishing began when Bly rejected a poem Dickey submitted to *The Fifties* in the summer of 1958. The poem's archetypal images of sea, sun, and grass, he argued, did not have "enough rebellion or contrast." Its mood was too pastoral, so Bly advised Dickey to "cut out everything but the images."[73] Dickey responded by mocking Bly's principles as old-fashioned—a reversion to the Imagism of Pound, Hilda Doolittle, Richard Aldington, and others at the beginning of the century. Bly countered that Dickey had missed his point. He wanted deep images resonant with unconscious significance and mythic feeling rather than the "simple pictures"[74] of the Imagists. Non-English and especially Spanish poetry, he told Dickey, must lead British and American poetry out of its current doldrums.

Before long, Dickey came around to Bly's point of view and joined his fight against the all-too-realistic Confessional school of Robert Lowell and W. D. Snodgrass as well as the all-too-academic school of Wilbur, Hecht, and Merrill. What Bly wrote Dickey about the Confessionals on May 5, 1959, could have been uttered by Dickey himself: "Robert Lowell's new book, *Life Studies,* which I bought finally last night, and read, is only self-confession, and does not become poetry at all." Dickey also shared an aversion to what Bly called "the poison of John Hollander and the 'poetry is all a game' group." To give an example of the sort of surreal imagism he hoped to legitimize, Bly sent Dickey the lines: "Horses the color of ashes / Are plunging in the snow that is falling beneath the sea."[75] Dickey was already using similar hallucinatory scenes in much of his poetry. In urging Dickey to keep his eye fixed on real as well as unreal images, Bly helped Dickey cut the verbiage from his early poems. Bly also confirmed Dickey's belief that by translating foreign poems he could reinvigorate his own. In the summer of 1959, Dickey translated the French poets Yves Bonnefoy and Lucien Becker and continued to translate poets for the rest of his life.

Bly soon joined the group trying to liberate Dickey from his advertising job. Because sales of king-size Coke fell after an initial rise, one of Dickey's tasks—at least as he saw it—was to reverse the downward trend. To this end he supposedly wrote a jingle that the McGuire Sisters recorded for TV and radio. He told Wright that he had come up with the rhyme: "King Size Coke has more for you, / King Size Coke has more for you! / Get value . . . life . . . refreshment, too."[76] In the mid-1970s, while on a promotional tour for his coffee-table book *Jericho,* he also claimed responsibility for the slogan: "Everything goes better when Coke is there with you." His boss didn't think much of it, but Dickey asserted that his advertising agency later transformed it into "Things go better with Coke."[77] Since jingles were created in New York, Dickey's contentions are highly unlikely. An ad he wrote for the *Ed Murphy Weather Show* in Syracuse, New York, typified his jobs at the time: "Know one of my favorite occupations these days? Sitting in the shade! Try it! Pick yourself a nice big tree . . . put a camp stool under it . . . and relax! Perfect! No . . . not quite perfect. I need . . . this! A king-size bottle of ice-cold Coca-Cola: so good in taste . . . and *in* such good taste, it's the best-loved sparkling drink in all the world! Ah! Coke puts you at your best! No question about it! Makes the shade shadier . . . the sun friendlier . . . puts a bright little life in everything you do! Tell you what: see your dealer . . . today . . . and bring home a big new supply of delicious Coca-Cola in big new king-size bottles! Then you'll be ready to enjoy Coke in the shade . . . in the sun . . . indoors . . . outdoors . . . in short, *any*where you want the bright, bracing sparkle that only Coke can give! Get Coke in big king-size today! Great for a king-size thirst! Perfect for entertaining!" He inserted at the bottom of a similar vignette he sent to Wright: "How would you like to do *this* kind of thing for a living?"[78] He preferred posing for photographs in ads where white-uniformed waitresses served him a cold glass of Coke.

Moronic as they seemed, Dickey's television scenarios prepared the way for his more ambitious screenwriting efforts in the future. His acting career also got a boost at this time, and from a familiar source. Because McCann handled the SSS account, some of the executives decided to deviate from their normal medium—radio—and make a television ad. Mark Bollmann, Jonis Gold, and Dickey went to Jacksonville, Florida, with a camera crew and a script written by and for Dickey. Since the SSS Tonic was supposed to fortify the blood, the plan was for Dickey to breathe heavily as he trudged up and down a sand dune, and then, with a haggard look on his face, take a swig of tonic and exclaim: "You can feel better fast with SSS Tonic!" Dickey's debut before the cameras was disappointing. Tonic sales failed to rise, and McCann returned to selling the product on the radio.

As he toiled away at McCann during the hot months of 1958, Dickey considered almost everything he tried to do a failure. His poetry writing as well as his copywriting, he told Wright, had all been for nought: "Of all the stuff that I've brought out, *none* is good. Since I have been publishing since 1951, this is almost ten years of very hard labor for nothing. I have had the usual 'honors' and fellowships, and been offered others I couldn't take, but I have never believed in that kind of thing, and go back patiently reading my poems after they are published, finding in their unfashionable sprawl only a kind of conventional groping after the allegorical, and a perfectly amazing clumsiness which is what passes with me for honesty." Yet, looking around him, Dickey found all his rivals publishing bad work as well. "Richard Wilbur, so perfectly self-assured and so perfectly empty of any ability to move me as a human being, or the stone-cold, pedantic, dry, patient, academic stuff of Yvor Winters" were dead ends. "What we must have, Jim Wright," he exhorted, "is a poetry that *gives us life:* some act of the imagination: the live imagination as it leaps instinctively toward its inevitable (and perhaps God-ordained) forms: something that restores our sense of continuity with tragic life, or joyous life, or dying life."[79] D. H. Lawrence had been a clumsy craftsman, he argued, but more valuable than all the crafty formalists because he responded to life with his whole nervous system. Dickey found flashes of this responsiveness in Berryman, Roethke, Eberhart, W. S. Graham, Saint-John Perse, René Char, Alain Borne, Jules Supervielle, and a few other continental writers. His own ability to respond to life, Dickey said, had been rekindled by Wright: "Let me say once and for all I appreciate everything you have sent, said, thought of, done, explained, not thought-of, believed, felt, and brought me since I have 'known' you. There is no one in my entire experience like James Wright: no one so unfailingly honest, so talented, so human. . . . You are always bothering about my thinking you are gushing 'hysterically' about something or other: you just listen to me gush a little. . . . For once in my life I don't have to fence with somebody, don't have to fight, don't have to crush somebody's arguments, don't have to lie, don't have to do anything but say exactly what I feel."[80]

Dickey sympathized with Wright's vacillation between naïveté and toughness, and identified with the criminals, madmen, and other outcasts that populated his poems because in the ad business Dickey also felt like a victim, an outcast. He told Wright: "If I can just hang on and write a few more poems like

Dover ["Dover: Believing in Kings"] . . . and if the book comes out, I will for the first time in my life really *believe* I have some chance against the personal difficulties that have plagued me, perhaps forever: those, and the old spectre of suicide, which, along with drunkenness, seems the especial curse of my family." Book publication would help quell his myriad doubts and demons. "Despite my air of assurance in literary matters," he admitted, "I am really a pathetically unsure, groping person." To help ensure future publications, he implored Wright "to drop Rago [the editor of *Poetry*, in which "Dover" appeared] a note telling him you liked the poem." He allowed that this was perhaps "a shameless kind of log-rolling,"[81] but he implied that it would keep him psychologically and professionally stable. Wright was one of many friends Dickey prodded into rolling logs for him in editorial offices. Wright's support, in this case, may have done some good. On September 19, 1958, Henry Rago awarded *Poetry*'s one-hundred-dollar Union League Civic and Arts Foundation Prize to Dickey for "Dover: Believing in Kings."

Dickey cherished Wright's friendship because it supposedly freed him from the need to lie, but lying remained a staple of his correspondence. To demonstrate his "preference for criminals and insane people," which he felt solidified his bond with Wright, Dickey wrote in August 1958: "I was out at the Atlanta Federal Pen the other day playing tennis with one of the inmates. After a set or two, we went over and sat down on a pathetic little green bench and leaned back on the Great Gray Wall, and another prisoner brought us some lemonade. I said to my opponent, 'Dawkins, are you "going straight" after they let you out?' He thought a moment, and answered with surprising dignity, 'No, I don't think so. I consider myself a criminal.'"[82] The idea of playing a few sets of tennis and sipping lemonade with a hardened criminal was typical of Dickey's many prison fantasies. However ludicrous, it pointed to a truth about Dickey's psyche. He too wanted to accept his status as an imprisoned outcast with dignity.

Dickey and Wright often traded notes about their afflicted psyches and how to cure them. Wright was convinced that Dickey's craving for alcohol was similar to his own, and that it could be regulated by therapy. Out of his belief that his drinking was partly a function of manic depression, he counseled Dickey: "Will you let me suggest that, if you get depressed and haunted, you get an appointment w/ a psychiatrist for a chat?"[83] Dickey's attitude toward psychiatrists was similar to that of the Austrian poet Rilke, whose work he greatly admired: he believed scrupulous analysis would destroy his "angels" and rob him of poetic inspiration. He never swerved from his bias. Alcohol was his substitute cure. According to Al Braselton: "He was subject to black depressions. . . . He used alcohol to get him out of depressions. He said, 'Drinking is an artificial joy, but an artificial joy is better than no joy at all.' He used it . . . as a drug." Braselton, who became an alcoholic shortly after meeting Dickey, watched Dickey's drinking gain momentum in the 1960s until it became chronic. He commented: "To drink is to live a manic-depressive life. There's no question about it. You're either drunk or hungover. In the latter stages, Jim was either drunk or hungover."[84] A family predisposition increased Dickey's risk of alcoholism, but so did his poetics. Like Hart Crane, Dylan Thomas, and many of Dickey's contemporaries, he aspired to visionary ecstasy rather than meticulous reason, to magnificent up-heaval rather than calm decorum, to sublimity and what Robert Lowell called "pathological enthusiasm" rather than carefully controlled beauty. Dickey and Wright often discussed the pros and cons of their "enthusiasms" (from *en-theos*, the god within), knowing full well that traditionally "enthusiasm" was linked to impassioned religious states and aesthetic concepts of the sublime. Wright once said: "I am guilty, not for enthusiasm, but for feeling guilty about enthusiasm."[85] Dickey agreed and made "enthusiasm" a distinguishing trait of characters such as Lewis Medlock and Joel Cahill.

Flattered by Wright's concern for his mental health, Dickey soon questioned his sincerity. Monroe Spears as editor of the *Sewanee Review* had proposed let-ting Dickey and Wright argue their differences in the journal's "correspondence" section. In order to "lift the very important practice of poetry-reviewing out of its present maddening cocktail-party-atmosphere, and restore to it the anger and the fire which it has simply *got* to have,"[86] Wright now believed that he and Dickey should renew their feud in print. Dickey had neither the time nor the in-clination. "Besides," he added ingratiatingly, "I am beginning to think highly of you as a human being, and don't want to risk whatever may be in the future for us as friends by getting out on the duelling-ground with you. Believe me, that is what it would be, very shortly. So perhaps Bly or somebody else will oblige you. Anyhow, good luck."[87] Dickey tried to pacify Wright by talking about family matters. Since Wright's wife had just given birth to a son a month before, Dickey responded with an account of his own son's birth (Kevin Dickey had been born in Crawford Long Hospital in Atlanta after a long, difficult labor on August 18, 1958). He also implored Wright to forget the tiring, pointless brouhaha caused by his review of *New Poets of England and America*. Wright soon acquiesced.

Following his son's birth, Dickey entered into a new literary feud. His antag-onist was now Philip Booth, who on July 8 had protested Dickey's unfair treat-ment of his poems in the *New Poets* review. Dickey's criticism had, indeed, been damning: "Booth's is an American Georgian poetry, thinly descriptive, replete with easy answers, vacant, amiably bucolic. . . . He has a strain of complacent sentimentality which I find very much not to my liking. It may be that he will turn out well. . . . As far as I am concerned, however, his beginning does not in-dicate this as a strong possibility."[88] A respected poet, Booth was stung by these remarks. After releasing his critical arrows, Dickey, in characteristic fashion, tried to win over his prey. In 1959, he sent Booth eight poems recently published in *Poetry*, including "The Performance," "Landfall," and "Below the Light-house," and hoped a civil dialogue would follow. Booth was not so easily molli-fied; in a letter written on July 24, 1959, he deftly targeted Dickey's weakness for rhetoric and complained of all the references to kingliness and light breaking out of wombs and salt-crusted heads. Despite their sparring, Booth warmed to his Southern opponent, wrote Dickey about his wife, who had grown up in Georgia, and expressed hope that they could meet on one of his trips south to see his in-laws.

While Dickey continued to fend off poets angered by his harsh reviews, he and Wright resumed their friendly prattle. Having traded obligatory pictures, they traded insights about Robert Bly, who was mentoring Wright; about Pablo Neruda, the Chilean poet whose earthy surrealism they relished; and about many French poets. Dickey promised Wright he would order from a Parisian bookseller some books by Lucien Becker, who "was the best young poet writing in French today."[89] They also took up the case of Richard Hugo, vowing to find a publisher for Hugo's first book after Wesleyan University Press and the University of Minnesota Press rejected it. A poet of the gritty Northwest outback, Hugo worked as a writer for Boeing in Seattle as well as an editor for *Poetry Northwest*, a journal he helped start with Carolyn Kizer in Seattle. Dickey admired Hugo's craftsmanlike poems that used run-down towns in the Northwest as objective correlatives for his struggles to survive tough times. He also sympathized with Hugo's difficulties adjusting to civilian life after flying thirty-five missions as a bombardier during World War II. Like Dickey, Hugo in his poems mingled escapist fantasies with gruesome realities and gravitated toward such traditionally male concerns as sports, women, bars, battles, and the outdoors. Hugo tended to look up to Dickey as a more sophisticated version of himself.

In the late 1950s, Hugo was finishing years of psychoanalysis, and like Wright he often lectured Dickey about his problems and their solutions: "Let people joke all they want to about the psychoanalyst. When you're sick, and I mean really sick, and frightened of the world, and drinking yourself to death, and realize you're sick, and know that help is available and don't go because of superstition, or whatever reason, then you are a ten carat horse's ass. And don't let anybody tell you that sickness is necessary for good writing—that is horseshit. Emotion is necessary—but when you are well, you have a hell of a lot more emotion to throw into your work than when you're not."[90] Although he liked the harsh beauty in the poems that resulted from Hugo's mended spirits, Dickey was not about to follow Hugo to the psychiatrist's couch to mend his own.

Hugo's background opened a gulf that Dickey found hard to cross. Having been abandoned by his parents and raised by grandparents who in his recollections were consistently cruel, Hugo liked to play Jackie Gleason's role of a hard-luck Ralph Kramden. Hugo had done poorly in college, poorly in the war, and poorly in marriage. Dickey understood the reasons for Hugo's tragicomic poses and heroic reinventions, even though he sometimes sneered at his gripes about growing up in misery during the Depression. For his part, Hugo could be light-hearted about his need to dissemble. In one of his first letters to Dickey, he revealed:

I first knew I was going to be a writer when I heard Miss Akin read Tennyson's THE ROCK aloud in the 8th grade (7th?). I then changed my name from Hogan (real father) to Hugo (step father), because Hogan was not a writer's name, and Hugo was. I lied about the legality—said, yes, I had been to court—gave a vivid description of the courtroom proceedings, and have been Hugo ever since—except of course, come wartime, my little trick caught up with me, as the Government is stuffy, and after volunteering for the AAF, I actually did go to court and have my name changed. And it wasn't a bit dramatic, the way I'd described to the grammar school class. I often wonder—did crafty old Miss Akin really know I was lying?[91]

Unlike some of Dickey's more credulous friends, Hugo had inklings from the start that Dickey was a fellow liar. Hugo wrote Dickey a series of questions that betray his skepticism: "Jim [Wright] talked about you several times during his last visit [to Seattle]. Am I right? You were an all-conference player at Clemson . . . ? Are you really an ex all conf footballer? If so, you must be formidable! That is a wicked conference. I am too cowardly to play football." Hugo preferred the less combative sports of baseball and softball. In the same letter he gave Dickey advice about his poems: "Keep off the subject a little more—be dishonest—all this is advice to myself too."[92] Dickey, of course, had been giving himself similar advice about poetic dishonesty for a decade.

During the fall of 1958, Dickey regularly solicited suggestions from friends about where to publish his first book. Wright preferred Grove: "For the sake of your book . . . and for the sake of human civilization, or what is left of it, in this country, *please* don't turn it over to Scribner's to be published in (or, rather, flushed down the gaping maw of) that idiotic 3-layer package-deal of theirs."[93] On November 7, Donald Hall announced that he was on the editorial board of Wesleyan University Press, which had initiated an ambitious new poetry series. He told Dickey to send him *Into the Stone*. John Hall Wheelock, who had retired as a Scribner's editor in 1956 but who still controlled the poetry series, also wanted to see his book. Wheelock had admired Dickey's poems ever since reading "The Swimmer" in the 1957 *Partisan Review*. Howard Moss, who had published his own poetry with Scribner's, recommended Dickey to Wheelock. Sidney Phillips at Criterion Books had considered *Into the Stone* for publication, but on July 24, 1958, he forwarded the manuscript to Wheelock. At first Dickey grumbled about his book's peregrinations. He disapproved of Scribner's format; he had no intention of sharing book space with two other poets. Also, the financial benefits of such a lineup were puny. Wheelock explained: "Each poet receives about 13 cents on every copy sold."[94] When Dickey withdrew his manuscript from Scribner's, Wheelock said he understood, but added: "Should you at any time wish to submit a book for *Poets of Today*, I should always welcome an opportunity of giving it most interested consideration."[95] To keep the Scribner's door ajar, Dickey wrote back in January 1959 that the *Poets of Today* format and Wheelock's introductory essays pleased him; he might consider sending his manuscript back in the future. First, however, he wanted to contact other publishers.

Dickey's publishing frustrations continued into 1959. Envious of Wright, who was about to receive a doctorate at the University of Washington and whose book *Saint Judas* had been accepted by Wesleyan, Dickey chose him as a convenient whipping boy. Because Wright had failed to respond with sufficient alacrity to one of Dickey's letters—he was preparing to defend his Ph.D. dissertation on Charles Dickens—Dickey snarled: "I want to take you to task for not writing that letter 'within five days' of which you speak in the last card I have from you. What Ph.D. dissertation was ever worth the friendship of James Dickey. I jest, but only half way. You call yourself my friend, you had better be prepared to make huge, immense sacrifices . . . I have very few friends, and care to have only those few. As for the rest, I stand, somewhat self-consciously dramatically, alone. . . . I am tired of writing acceptable poems, or acceptable letters. I am thirty-five years old, and hope to god I never open my mouth again, except to say something essential."[96] To accentuate his lonely, beleaguered condition, he told Wright that he was the only man of letters in Atlanta and bemoaned Donald Hall's lukewarm response to *Into the Stone*. The pompous rebuke came at a particularly delicate time for Wright. He had just suffered a nervous breakdown in Seattle while agonizing over his thesis.

As usual, Dickey used one hand to browbeat and the other to beg for pity. Hall, in fact, had written on January 19, 1959: "I would like to have this book for Wesleyan,"[97] but stipulated that he would have to wait for the other two board members (William Meredith and Norman Holmes Pearson) to vote. When Dickey realized that Wright was about as low as he could go, his tone changed. He asked whether he could send Wright money: "How much do you think it would take to keep you going, and help avoid the deepest (I mean really the very blackest) pits of despair? Tell me, and I'll send you what I can. I was poor so very long myself, worrying about every available dime, that I don't want to have to think about your having to go through the same thing, day after day and without any relief in sight. So let me know if and how much I can help you. I would be honored to be able to do so."[98] Wright turned down Dickey's charitable offer.

Despite *Into the Stone*'s recent setbacks, Dickey hoped Malcolm Cowley at Viking would take his manuscript and told friends that Cowley wanted to award him the Lamont Prize. Macmillan, Doubleday, Grove, and Wesleyan also remained possible publishers. On October 3, 1958, Dickey told William Jay Smith: "I don't under any conditions want to dive headforemost into that wretched, handsome 'Package' format that Scribner's keeps grinding out."[99] On May 1, 1959, he changed his mind. Concluding that he could do no better than Scribner's, he returned his manuscript to Wheelock. In three weeks, Wheelock informed Dickey that he would include *Into the Stone* among eight finalists if a number of difficult poems were cut ("Dover: Believing in Kings," "The Red Bow," "The Work of Art," "Confrontation of the Hero," "First Morning of Cancer," "The Ground of Killing," "The Anniversary," "Genesis," and "The Swimmer"). On May 27, Dickey did his best to strengthen his position with Wheelock: "I have had three offers [for *Into the Stone*] which seem to indicate that these publishers would be willing to take my manuscript virtually sight-unseen. I hope it is apparent that I would most like to appear with you, especially in view of your own personal kindness to me. At the same time, I don't want to alienate the other people, and wind up by missing four opportunities instead of one, should Scribner's decide against me. I realize I can't legitimately ask you for a definite commitment now, since there are other people involved, all of whom, I am sure, are equally deserving of attention. But if you could give me some indication of *possibilities* I would rest more easily at night, and know better what to do and how to feel."[100] Fearing he might lose his prize poet to another publisher, Wheelock accepted the book on May 27, 1959. In mid-August, Dickey signed a contract assuring him a 10-percent royalty that had to be divided equally by the three poets in the book.

Around the time of Scribner's acceptance, Robert Bly invited Dickey to participate in a new series of poetry readings he was organizing for New York

University. Bly planned to join Wright, Dickey, and possibly Geoffrey Hill, who would be replacing Donald Hall at the University of Michigan during the 1959–60 academic year. The payment Bly proposed was miniscule—thirty-five to fifty dollars—but Dickey found the idea of a New York venue enticing. When Dickey agreed to read, Bly reserved a room for him at the Earle Hotel and invited him to a small party at his 123 West Eleventh Street apartment. In New York, besides conferring with Wheelock about the Scribner's volume, Dickey wanted to reunite with friends he made during his first months with McCann. He told Wright: "I have some good beatnik friends down in the Village, so we can get with them Saturday night if you like. Or we can do whatever you and Bly like, so long as there is plenty of excitement in it."[101] Dickey's "beatnik friends" were not the official Beats, but those like Dave Johnson who joined the three-some in Bly's apartment. There was, indeed, plenty of excitement when Bly, Wright, and Dickey gathered for the first time (Hill, in the end, stayed in Michigan) to read at Three Washington Square North on Friday evening, November 13, 1959. The next night at Bly's apartment, the poets drank, read poems, gossiped, told jokes, and roared with laughter. Joining in the high-spirited camaraderie was Bly's friend Louis Simpson, who was as astonished by Dickey as the others. Reciting famous and obscure poems from memory, Dickey convinced them that Mnemosyne had blessed him with her genius. Bly recalled that Dickey was "radiant, full of boyish energy and mischief" and that he fit Jung's profile of the "aeternus puer"—the "eternal boy."[102]

Beside himself with joyous recollections of their New York experience, Dickey told Wright two weeks later:

> Nothing I could ever write would do justice to the feeling of absolute *rightness* I had about everything we did in New York. Hart Crane and Lorca were leaning from the windows saying "Yes! Yes! That's it! You're home, now!" And we were. I could hear the voices over my head in the middle of the night when I fell on my knees on some street in the Village when Bly was walking me home and prayed for everything. After he left me I tried to sleep, but it was no good and I got up and dressed and walked around all night, praying in the middles of some more streets and singing and weeping and wringing my hands for joy. In the morning I did come in and slept a little, and then packed and left the hotel and went to Bly's apartment. You were gone, of course, as you had to be, and I left a note and began to drift by easy stages, each more painful than the last, out to the airport.[103]

Although Dickey's New York rapture may not have been mania or "pathological enthusiasm," it came close. He sounded like one of the Beat hipsters in Allen Ginsberg's *Howl*, "who wept at the romance of the streets" in New York and "bared their brains to Heaven under the El and saw Mohammedan angels staggering on tenement roofs illuminated."

Delivered from the dreary halls of advertising to the enchanting literary capital of America, Dickey felt especially indebted to Bly, who had been responsible for the NYU reading. He told Wright: "I love Bly. He is one of the most marvelous men I have ever seen, and yet a human being like all of us, too. But *what* a human being!"[104] Wright was equally effusive: "I could never really tell . . . in a thousand years—how much it meant to me to be with you and Bly last week. . . . I feel changed—perhaps restored, saved. I think I can go on now."[105] In a decade, Dickey's assessment of Bly's all-too-human qualities would turn from paean to pillory. He would remain on friendly terms with Wright, but denigrate Wright's dependence on Bly: "I felt that Robert Bly was gaining too much power of Jim [Wright] at that time—this was certainly disastrous for him—and probably said so more than once."[106] Latent poetic and political differences soon divided the dynamic triumvirate.

In addition to communing ecstatically with Lorca and Crane, on November 14, the Saturday after the reading, Dickey spoke to Wheelock, who had invited him to a midday dinner at his home. Dickey wrote in his florid thank-you note: "You must believe me when I say that you have completely removed from me the possibility of my ever thanking you adequately, for the right words do not exist, nor does any way I might ever put them together, even if they did. Just let me say that I have never spent another such afternoon, and that I will be happy about it for the rest of my life."[107] Among his less joyful duties in New York was his visit to the McCann offices to announce that he had quit his job in Atlanta. Dickey's sudden departure resembled previous ones from Rice and Florida: it was precipitated by dissatisfactions and quarrels that he sometimes denied. He told Mark Pendergrast, who wrote a history of The Coca-Cola Company, that he "didn't mind writing for Coke. It was the easiest thing in the world. My wrestling match was with my poetry." He boasted of advances in the company; he had been promoted to senior writer, then director of the radio-TV advertising division. Dickey laid the blame for his abrupt leave-taking on the office manager, Mark Bollmann, who supposedly introduced Dickey in late 1959 at a presentation to the First National Bank with the line: "And Jim's hobby is writing poetry and he frequently writes for the *New Yorker*." Recoiling in disgust, Dickey decided on the spot: "That ties it. Hobby, my ass! This *job* is my hobby; the poetry is my real work."[108] He quit McCann-Erickson in early October 1959.

Rather than write full time or teach, Dickey merely moved to another advertising agency: Liller, Neal, Battle, and Lindsey. He noted some of the reasons for switching agencies in his application to Liller, Neal: "My chief interest is in developing campaigns; the nature of my present job makes this difficult, since I can do this kind of work only after having tended to a truly vast amount of routine but necessary detail concerned with getting out the radio-television commercials called for by the shows sponsored in various localities by Coca-Cola Bottlers. This fact, coupled with the near-certainty that I shall soon be asked by the agency to fill a position in New York, prompts my present decision to seek out an Atlanta-oriented agency."[109] Dickey wanted to stay on his home turf and he wanted more-creative work, but he also wanted a less demanding job that would allow him more time to write poetry.

Although Dickey smarted from Bollmann's unintentional insult, he had actually done well at McCann, at least as far as his poetry was concerned. He had won several significant literary prizes and would win another on January 7, 1960, when Saul Bellow, Alfred Kazin, and Louise Bogan gave him a three-hundred-dollar Longview Foundation Award for his poem "The Vegetable King," which had appeared in the spring 1959 *Sewanee Review*. Indicative of his growing literary stature was a request for a recording of his poems from Richard Eberhart, poetry consultant at the Library of Congress. Nevertheless, Dickey resented wasting his talent on advertising. With morose sarcasm he predicted to Hall: "On my tomb someone will put, 'Here lies one who wrote 50,000 TV commercials for Coca-Cola, fifty reviews of forgotten books of poetry, and (maybe!) one poem.'"[110] His new post at Liller, Neal, he admitted to Wright, was temporary and strictly mercenary: "All of this, except for the money, is just so much horse-shit, of course, but unless I can get a respectable teaching job (*not* an instructorship!) I am stuck with it, I guess. And the money *is* good!"[111] So he continued to sell his soul to Mammon during the day, and buy it back at night by writing poems.

Dickey must have envied the poet James Merrill, whose father, a founder of the Merrill Lynch investment firm, had provided him with enough money to write and travel as he wished. Because Merrill's mother lived in Atlanta and knew the Dickey family, he often called on Dickey when he was in town. Merrill missed Dickey on a trip in June 1959, but arranged to see him in early October, about the time Dickey switched jobs. Dickey's jealousy of Merrill's immense wealth was partly responsible for his somewhat condescending tone in a letter he sent Wright: "He is an awfully nice boy [Dickey was only three years older] who, because of his family situation, has never really had a chance to be himself. He showed me some new poems that are real good. He seemed to appreciate sincerely the things I said about him in the *Sewanee*, though I was afraid he would be angry or hurt. But he was neither. We had a very nice couple of days together."[112] Although Merrill liked Dickey as a person and as a poet, he also had reservations. In a letter he wrote Dickey on October 12, he praised Dickey's poems "The Landfall," "The Performance," "Into the Stone," and "The Enclosure," but criticized the many overused, hyperbolic adjectives such as "incredible" and "remarkable." Merrill, like Booth, urged Dickey to rein in his rhetorical steeds. Now it was Dickey's turn to be graceful under fire. "Almost everything you say I agree with,"[113] Dickey responded. In the company of the well-mannered, cosmopolitan, gay Merrill, Dickey tended to be on his best behavior, even though in his reviews he savaged Merrill's poems for their empty charm. Merrill represented a lifestyle that Dickey could have inherited—his sister and brother lived off the family fortune—but that he had partly rejected. To earn his own salary he took the job as copy chief at Liller, Neal, Battle, and Lindsey—a job that led indirectly to the most important events behind *Deliverance*.

15. Potato Chips and Canoe Trips (1959–1961)

By 1946, six years after its founding, Liller, Neal, and Battle had garnered more than thirty accounts from clients throughout the Southeast (it produced ads for a variety of products from Hanna baseball bats to Mis' Julie's Pie Crust). In 1958, shortly before Dickey joined the firm, Liller, Neal, and Battle merged with Dan Lindsey and Company, an advertising firm located in Richmond, Virginia. The conglomerate employed eighty workers in their Atlanta, Richmond, and New York offices, and grossed about eight million dollars a year. To accommodate its expanding workforce, it moved from Atlanta's Walton Building to 1371 Peachtree Street, not far from Dickey's grandmother's house. Dickey gave himself various titles for his new post and provided various reasons for why he took them. To some he said he was an account executive with a salary of fifteen thousand dollars or more. To others he said he was a creative director. An actual account executive, Richard Hodges, confirmed that Dickey became a copy chief: "He took the copy from all the writers, edited it, [and] tried to make it better." Hodges added: "I don't think he was ever really comfortable with us."[1] While Dickey appreciated his new status and new income (his salary was ten thousand dollars), his attitude toward advertising remained the same.

In his new job Dickey worked primarily on Armour Fertilizer and Lay's potato chips accounts, but his clients also included the Bowater company and some local banks. Dickey was full of imaginative schemes to sell his clients' humdrum products. One of his colleagues, Paul Robertson, remembered how Dickey brought several of his children's books on prehistoric animals into the office and proposed putting small plastic dinosaurs in bags of Lay's potato chips. The dinosaurs proved a successful marketing ploy—one in a series that made Lay's the most prominent potato chip company in America. Dickey spearheaded other ad campaigns as well. RC Cola in the late 1950s had decided to introduce a new drink, Bev-rich, to compete with Kool-Aid. Since Liller, Neal had the RC Cola account, a special team worked on ways to draw Kool-Aid customers to Bev-rich. Jack Burton, an account executive at the agency who supervised Dickey's work, remembered Dickey writing almost all the Bev-rich ads and inventing cartoon characters for them. According to Burton, Dickey's ideas were occasionally too extravagant, but his ads sold the product.

To his old night-fighting cohort Thomas Hart, who later became vice president of Bowater North American Corporation, Dickey provided details of the sort of work that filled his days:

> I developed the advertising, including the logo of the twisted "board" that showed it to be "smooth on both sides," and which was supposed to be used extensively with the product that Bowater's was putting into the field to compete with Masonite, which as you know has only one smooth side, the other being a grid. At any rate, I paid several visits to the huge plant that Bowater's was then building in Rock Hill to produce the Board. I engaged

in endless planning sessions with the sales manager . . . about the possible markets, prospected volume sales, and various other strategies we hoped to initiate and implement. But at the time I left the agency, the mill—conceived as a twenty-four hour, incessant or perhaps interminable operation—had not worked, was not working, and seemed not able to be made to work. And there my association with Bowater's ended.[2]

No wonder Dickey's sense of futility resumed at Liller, Neal. Again he found himself pushing a rock—or a Bowater's board or bag of potato chips—up a hill like Sisyphus and watching it slide back to the bottom.

Years after leaving the ad business, Dickey liked to glamorize his role as "a hustler" who maneuvered his way to the top: "I was a player. I enjoyed it. If I had nine lives, I would like to spend one of them in business. You can dominate it easily. And there is so much money. You've got to love poetry to turn something like that down in American life in order to go back to something as unlucrative as poetry."[3] In other interviews he described the business world as "fascinating" and "exciting." Dickey may have enjoyed getting acquainted with the new people and the new routines at Liller, Neal, but his poetry took precedence over his job. Early in 1960, he revealed his unhappiness to Robert Bly, who responded on February 6 with a solicitous letter: "I am worried about your working in that damned advertising, shaving sandpaper. If you don't like teaching, work for the USIS [United States Information Service]. Six weeks in Washington and you'd be off to some mad place, with a good house, a salary around $10,000 I think plus expenses, and a work that I would think would be very interesting, and give you at least as much time, and more strength, than ad work. Carol's [Bly's wife's] uncle is Deputy Director, as they say, of the USIS, so if you are really interested, he's your man. Carol's brother is USIS's man in Brazil now, and from what he says, likes it."[4] Bly spoke to his brother-in-law, Malcolm McLean, on Dickey's behalf. MacLean contacted Dickey and laid out the pros and cons of a USIS job. While interested, Dickey wanted to know more about the pay, the working schedule, and the job location.

The idea of beginning a new career in another country appealed to Dickey, as he made plain to James Wright in March:

It is the usual dreary story [at Liller, Neal] of having no time to write letters, or anything else, but only time for pouring out the endless line of cynical, creeping-Jesus type of slop for the "markets," those mythical places where all good advertising men go when they die, as though to their appointed Hell. I am fed up with "business," its money and its stratagems, its people and its methods, its aims and its rewards. Bob [Bly] says he thinks he can get me into the United States Information Service in some foreign country, and if he can I am going, regardless of where I may have to work. I can feel the best of myself leak away day by day, and nobody but me caring if and whether it goes. But *I* care. And I'll just be God-damned if I'm going to put the rest of my life into something as hopelessly corrupt and damned as this is. . . . If you knew how much I would give to be able to sit down and work—*uninterruptedly*—on a poem for at least an hour, you would know how much I have *got* to get out of the business world. Success is ruining me. And that's the truth. I had rather be poor. The only trouble is, if I were poor I'd *still* have to do *something* for a living, and whatever I did would take as much as or more time than this does.[5]

Dickey implored Wright to find him a job at the University of Minnesota. Even the snowy North would be preferable to Atlanta advertising.

Dickey also hoped that the Ford Foundation's Program for Poets and Fiction Writers would deliver him from advertising. In his application for a grant for the fall of 1960, he qualified his complaints about advertising by admitting: "I have, because of it, learned to write in short, intense bursts of activity, and have finished more poetry than might be thought likely under such conditions." With a grant, he argued, he could prolong his "intense bursts" to work on novels and plays:

I now have serious doubts as to whether I shall ever complete even the one novel I began, three years ago, at the University of Florida. This is perhaps no great loss. But the idea of giving up the plans I have for a play, or rather a cycle of them, is a good deal more difficult to face. . . . The project I have in mind is a cycle of four plays, partly in verse and partly in prose, about the life which the dead lead after death, both among themselves and among the living. The cycle begins with the last days of the protagonist's life and culminates in his rebirth in another personality, the result of a choice which his experiences during the four plays leads him to make.[6]

Dickey again wanted to explore the effects of his brother's death on him as well as his compulsion to be "reborn" from the death-in-life of advertising.

Dickey had jotted down notes and lines of dialogue for one of these plays (about pilots Whittern and Eissman) in the early 1950s and inserted them among notes for what would become *Alnilam*, which was also about the death and rebirth of a hero. Just as contemporary French poets guided some of his stylistic experiments in poetry, French playwrights could serve the same purpose for his drama. In his Ford Foundation application he mentioned Giraudoux, Audiberti, Anouilh, and Vilar as the playwrights he wanted to emulate. To give the fellowship judges a better idea of his modus operandi, he singled out Henri Pichette's *Nuclea* and *Les Epiphanies*, two plays he had seen in Paris while on his Sewanee Fellowship, as models. Because of his admiration for French drama, he proposed returning to France to study with Jean Vilar at the Théâtre National Populaire. If that was impossible, he wanted to apprentice himself to Jules Irving at the Actor's Workshop in San Francisco or with Rachmael ben Avram at the Company of the Golden Hind in Berkeley. From these dramatists Dickey hoped to gain technical knowledge of the theater. To the Ford Foundation he cloaked his ambitious schemes in self-deprecating modesty. He vowed to "release what poetic abilities I have into the channels most likely to enable them to make a real contribution to the American theatre, and to help bring into it a realm of imagination and suggestiveness as yet foreign to our writing for the stage. I do not really know if I am capable of making such a contribution, or anything like it, but I do know that I have a good many ideas that seem to *me* worth trying."[7] Dickey's lack of playwriting experience must have turned the Ford Foundation against his proposal. Although Dickey rarely spoke of his desire to be a prominent American playwright, he never entirely renounced it. In the 1960s, he considered writing a play "about an old, blind poet whose children, possibly rich, try to persuade him, through an elaborate masquerade, that he is receiving the Nobel prize."[8] At the end of his life Dickey expressed gratitude to the writers, directors, and actors from Theatre West who adapted poems of his like "May Day Sermon" and "Bronwen, the Traw, and the Shape-Shifter" for the stage. At last he could claim success in a genre he had always planned to explore.

Disappointed by his failure to win a grant, Dickey returned to his ad work with a combination of stoicism, despair, and anger. He later vented his frustrations in the portrait of the Emerson-Gentry advertising firm in *Deliverance*. To the poet Dana Gioia he said unequivocally of Liller, Neal: "These are the offices described in the beginning chapter of *Deliverance*."[9] McCann-Erickson and Burke Dowling Adams, however, were also models, and he told Atlanta designer D. F. Cox: "Your studio, the old Cox, Kjelsen and Parker one, was the inspiration—if so it may be called—for the office where Ed Gentry works in *Deliverance*."[10] One thing is certain: Ed Gentry speaks for Dickey when he calls his ad work a living death: "The feeling of the inconsequence of whatever I would do, of anything I would pick up or think about or turn to see was at that moment being set in the very bone marrow. . . . I was really frightened, this time, and I knew that if I managed to get up, through the enormous weight of lassitude, I would still move to the water cooler, or speak to Jack Waskow or Thad, with a sense of being someone else, some poor fool who lives as unobserved and impotent as a ghost going through the only motions it has."[11] To dispel these feelings of impotent desperation Dickey sometimes spoke to Jack Burton, the probable model for Jack Waskow. An avid fisherman and canoer, Burton also felt somewhat stifled at Liller, Neal, which he said favored conventional as opposed to creative approaches to advertising.

For his secret yearnings and frustrations, Dickey found his most receptive audience in Al Braselton, the son-in-law of Bill Neal, one of the company's partners. Braselton realized from the start that Dickey never really understood or liked business: "He would encourage me to talk about how business works and I would explain things to him from time to time. But he never got into business that well. He was a fairly good copywriter, and he had a certain amount of integrity about him. He would hold out for a better thing. He played the game, but I knew that something secret was going on in there such that he wasn't spending his days worrying about whether or not the Armour Fertilizer account was successful." Having had a long-standing fascination with writers—he had studied literature at Darlington School and at Emory—Braselton was immediately drawn to his colleague, who posed as a football star and combat pilot, but who also published poems in the *New Yorker*. About his first encounters with Dickey at the ad firm, Braselton made the unsettling comment: "He rolled like a juggernaut, and the hypnotism of the man could be overwhelming. . . . I felt about Dickey the same way that Joseph Goebbels [the Nazi propaganda minister] felt about Hitler when he first met him." Braselton's attitudes toward Dickey, to say the least, were complicated. Awed by Dickey's powerful intellect, Braselton was also frightened by it. Having cruised with ease through the 1950s, Braselton was ready to be delivered into a more adventurous lifestyle even while recognizing the risks: "When I first met Dickey I was pursuing the American dream. I was heir-apparent to a prominent Atlanta business, a member of Atlanta's elite, tennis at the Driving Club, summer at Sea Island, a Junior League wife and two children in the best private schools. . . . Dickey was my Zorba and the dance he taught me was a marvelous *Valse Macabre*."[12] Dickey was also his Mephistopheles. The Faustian consequences of his friendship with Dickey were divorce, alcoholism, bankruptcy, a son's suicide, and his own near suicide.

The first time Braselton met his new master socially was at a cocktail party Dickey gave in his house. Mingling with the guests, Braselton met Lewis King, who was talking about trout fishing with the passion and expertise of Ernest Hemingway. Dickey had gotten to know King at the Bobby Jones–Bitsy Grant tennis courts in Atlanta, where he had asked King to play. Dickey often asked the better players for matches, impressing the aficionados with his chutzpah rather than his racket control, which was mediocre. By the time of the party, Dickey and King had solidified their friendship at numerous business lunches. Like Dickey's brother, Tom, King had inherited family real estate in Atlanta that he managed. King, however, was hardly a conventional businessman. He had begun an engineering degree at Georgia Tech, switched to industrial management, worked for a North Carolina bank after graduating, and returned to Atlanta to take care of his father's business. He was a voracious reader, often consuming three novels a week. Like Lewis Medlock in *Deliverance*, Lewis King was also an expert woodsman. Cowed by King's superior talents on the tennis courts and in the woods, in his company Dickey strutted his accomplishments as a fighter pilot, football player, and archer. King soon learned that despite his air of self-assurance, Dickey had little experience as an outdoorsman; he knew almost nothing about camping and always worried about getting lost in the woods. He pretended to be a top-notch bow hunter, but never shot anything on their hunting trips. He exhibited a childlike enjoyment of nature rather than a Thoreau-like knowledge of its flora and fauna. King, on the other hand, was as comfortable and crafty in the wilderness as a Native American, and for that reason he became Dickey's and Braselton's guide to the North Georgia wilderness.

One Saturday, after a few sets of tennis, Braselton stopped by Dickey's house on Westminster Circle and talked to Maxine. He described her as "a beautiful woman with facial lines and a classic Sophia Loren style. High prominent cheek bones and full lips. Beautiful eyes. She was a little on the plump side but she greeted me with that marvelous Southern falsetta." As Braselton spent more time at the Dickey house, he noticed, as others had before him, that Dickey's bond with Maxine was strained by the amount of work he expected her to do. Demanding carte blanche for his writing and his recreation, he assumed she would do everything else, from mowing the lawn to handling the family's finances. He once told Braselton: "I'm the world's oldest living adolescent. . . . If you're weighed down by obligations, how can you write a poem and really throw yourself into it? You just can't do this if you're worrying about how to pay the bills."[13] Maxine, it occurred to Braselton, fulfilled the role of both mother and wife to her gifted husband, and she did so with surprising grace.

Listening to Dickey's stories of love affairs, which Maxine also heard and did her best to ignore, Braselton began to realize that his friend "had a strange ambivalence toward sex." He told Braselton a story about visiting Paris for the first time on his Sewanee Fellowship and meeting a friend who ran an escort service. "When you go into Paris," he said, "you know deep down in your heart that no matter what vice you may have, it's going to be satisfied." His Parisian friend arranged for Dickey and a woman to meet at a café. At the designated time and place, Dickey drank a glass of wine with the woman and learned that she was the wife of an Eastern European businessman. He told Braselton: "I went out with her and we went to a store, a very fine jewelry store and we bought a string of pearls, and I helped her select the pearls she wanted. Later on we went back to her suite in the hotel and she cooked a meal and we made love."[14] When Dickey visited Paris, he knew few people there besides Lester Mansfield, who was a French professor with nothing to do with escort services. The apocryphal story alerted Braselton to his friend's odd mix of sentimental romanticism and lust.

Because Dickey played a tutelary Ezra Pound to his younger friend, advertising colleagues decided that he was leading Braselton astray. Dickey's superiors had grown wary of him because, as Braselton said: "He was working more and more on his poetry and less and less on advertising. As a matter of fact, we'd try to go in and work real hard on getting the copy out and sit for the rest of the day and talk about literature." Their topics included James Agee, Erskine Caldwell, Fitzgerald, Hemingway, Valéry, Supervielle, Roethke, Neruda, and Dickey's own writings. The two admen especially revered Rilke, who believed that poetry should change one's life. Braselton reflected: "To my social friends in Atlanta, Dickey was an unmitigated disaster, the iceberg for my business and social 'Titanic.'" But Braselton was intoxicated by Dickey's message. "Grab it, Al, risk it. Don't be content with the half-life of sliding through that greased chute of upper middle class America,"[15] Dickey would say.

On one of Braselton's early visits to Westminster Circle, Dickey began an informal tutorial that would stretch over many years: "Here, Al, this is my poetry book when I took the class under Robert Penn Warren and he had written a book that's got all my thoughts in it. This is Eliot's *Quartets*. Here's a complete book of Eliot's poetry. Here's a couple of other books I want you to read. I think you'll find this very interesting. We've waded through a lot of literature to get to the good stuff and I don't think you ought to have to wade through it. I'll just tell you what I think is good." Although Dickey had never studied under Warren, Braselton was taken in by his authoritative tone. To repay Dickey, Braselton gave him guitar lessons: "The first thing I ever played for Dickey was 'Wildwood Flower' [a classic Southern folk song], which was done with a . . . country rhythm called 'Carter Family Lick.' He looked up as if he had been shot. He pointed his finger at me and said, 'I'm gonna learn how to do that.' I said, 'I'll show you how to do that if you'll teach me about literature.' He said, 'You got a deal there, buddy.'" (Dickey transformed this incident in *Deliverance* by having Drew Ballinger play "Wildwood Flower" with the Appalachian boy Lonnie at the beginning of the canoe trip.)

According to Braselton, shortly after agreeing to teach each other:

We went down to a place and had lunch and we were coming back and he said, "I want to get a guitar." And I said, "Here's what you do. We'll go down to the pawn shops and we'll find you a Martin guitar, which is the best guitar you can buy. There are a lot of them, and they are a little bit more expensive than. . . ." He looked in a music store, and it was sort of a striking thing because buying guitars for me at that time was a major purchase. But he said, "I'm going to buy that guitar." So we walked into this music store and he said, "I want that guitar right there." Very to the point, no guile. . . . "How much is it?" The clerk pulled it off the wall. Jim never even played it, didn't know what it sounded like. . . . We tuned it up and it sounded terrible. It was a Framus, a German-made guitar, not a very good guitar. . . . I taught him a little bit about how to play. He was terrible. He had no musical ability at all, no feel, no sense of rhythm, and to this day [in the mid-1970s] (although technically he's a better guitar player; he can play faster runs and stuff) he still doesn't have any natural rhythm.[16]

Despite his poor ear, Dickey later made great claims for the guitar's influence on his poetry: "If somebody were to ask me what the strongest influence on the rhythm of my poetry is, whether it's the English Prosodic tradition or the pulse of the folk guitar, I would say . . . that the guitar is more important."[17] In fact, Dickey had already absorbed from "the English Prosodic tradition" the anapestic rhythm that shaped much of his best work. Just as he denied the importance of traditional prosody for his poetry, he denied the influence of Braselton on his guitar playing. He told Joyce Pair, the editor of the *James Dickey Newsletter*, that it was not Braselton but his father who had taught him the rudiments of guitar playing. He also told her that while teaching on the West Coast in the 1960s, he used to fill in for the lead guitar player in the popular Brazos Valley Boys, *Billboard Magazine*'s number-one Country Western band fourteen years in a row (their leader, Hank Thompson, was inducted into the Country Music Hall of Fame in 1989). Eugene Dickey, however, never played the guitar or any other instrument, and Dickey never played with the Brazos Valley Boys or any other professional group.

As Braselton, Dickey, and King grew friendlier, they met regularly to discuss books, business, archery, and other sports at such restaurants as the Lion's Head (later renamed Clarence Fosters), Mamma Mia's, the Red Dog Saloon, or the Rendezvous Lounge. Over beers or stronger drinks, like the characters at the beginning of *Deliverance*, they also discussed hunting and canoeing trips into North Georgia. At the time Dickey was trying to convert King and Braselton to bow-and-arrow hunting, and King was working equally hard to convert Dickey to rifle hunting. King was amenable to Dickey's arguments. He quickly became a competent bowman, but Dickey showed no sign of taking up guns. To explain his fear he once told a reporter that he had almost killed one of his sons with a shotgun: "It was your typical climbing-through-the-fence accident. . . . I shucked the shells out on the ground, went immediately home, and sold the gun.

I haven't touched one since."[18] What Dickey told a *Playboy* interviewer was closer to the truth. In the war he had "seen too many of them fired at men in earnest."[19] As for Braselton, according to Dickey, "Al was . . . more like Bobby in *Deliverance*. He was a good-time boy";[20] he had little interest in hunting with gun or bow and arrow.

During the summers of 1960 and 1961 the three men took the canoe trips that coalesced over the next decade into the one disastrous trip recorded in *Deliverance*. They canoed together only about four times and chose relatively safe sections of the Chestatee, Coosawattee, Toccoa, and Chattahoochee Rivers. On one occasion they brought Dave Sanders, and on another a journalist from *Time*, Roger Williams. They never ventured down the Chattooga, where the film of *Deliverance* was shot. The one time they drove to the Chattooga, the water was too high and turbulent from recent rains. Preparations for the canoe trips resembled those Dickey described in his novel. King supplied the maps, which the three men had scrutinized during their lunches. They drove to the river in two cars, left one car downriver, then drove the other to a bridge where they set off in canoes. On their first trip down the Toccoa and on subsequent trips, King went ahead to fly-fish while Dickey and Braselton, who knew little about canoeing or fishing, followed. (Dickey altered this procedure in the novel so that Lewis Medlock could rescue the other two men from the rapacious hillbillies.) Paddling down the Toccoa, both Braselton and Dickey felt they had entered paradise. The river passed through cool woods and pastures of Bermuda grass. Snakes slithered from banks into the current; birds flew overhead; cows stopped drinking from the river to stare at them. An ecstatic Dickey shouted to Braselton: "Man, this is livin', ain't it? Ain't this great?"[21] Within about fifteen minutes, however, they took their first spill and lost most of their cargo to the rapids. They turned over two more times, and found it impossible to navigate a bend in the river, even though they tried three times. Afterward they tied their possessions—most important among them the cooler stocked with beer and whiskey—to the canoe's thwarts. Understandably worried, King periodically abandoned his trout fishing and retreated upriver to make sure his friends hadn't drowned.

The canoe trips did not always proceed through bucolic landscapes. Paddling down the Coosawattee, the men were sickened by chicken offal dumped by a processing plant. Braselton recalled: "It was the strangest thing to look down and see the rocks covered with feathers. Just sitting there rippling . . . really a horrible thing. And lying between the rocks were chicken heads . . . staring up at you."[22] In *Deliverance* Ed recoils from similar pollution: "I pulled my paddle out of the water; a white feather was stuck to the end of it. I shook it off and peered into the river. Off to the right and getting ready to go by under water was a vague choked whiteness. It was a log completely covered with chicken feathers, with all the feather-hairs weaving and wavering in a perfect physical representation of nausea." Among the chicken guts, Ed discovers "a chicken head with its glazed eye half-open, looking right at me and through me."[23] The severed head foreshadows Drew's death, and in the novel's mythical dimension it corresponds to the head of the slain Orpheus drifting down the river toward Lesbos.

Dickey was so disgusted by this ecological ugliness that he first wrote about it in his poem "On the Coosawattee." Here he describes the feathers and heads turning the river into an infernal Styx:

All morning we floated on feathers
Among the drawn heads which appeared
Everywhere, from under the logs

Of feathers, from upstream behind us,
Lounging back to us from ahead,
Until we believed ourselves doomed
And the planet corrupted forever. . . .

At the end of the poem he tells how "Braselton and I clung and fought / With our own canoe / That flung us in the rapids," and how, after being thrown into the turbulent water, they

crawled upon shore and were found in the afternoon
By Lucas Gentry and his hunting dog, asleep
On a vast, gentle stone.
At a touch we woke, and followed the strange woods boy
Up the bluff, looking down on the roaring river's
Last day in its bed.[24]

When the poem appeared in the New Yorker in 1962, its distortion of the facts irritated King (it was his and not Braselton's canoe). Journalistic objectivity, however, was not the goal of the fabulist Dickey.

A lover of rivers, Dickey sometimes contended that the fictitious Cahulawassee, modeled principally on the Coosawattee, was the main character in Deliverance. One of the most beautiful rivers in North Georgia, the Coosawattee begins in the North Georgia town of Ellijay (the model for Aintry in the novel), where the Cartecay and Ellijay Rivers converge and flow southwest toward Rome. The dam referred to in Deliverance was an actual one begun in 1962 to stop the river from flooding cities and farms along its banks. By the fall of 1974, the 452-foot-high dam was completed, creating a long lake behind what used to be the Coosawattee Gorge. While plans were being finalized for the dam, Dickey and his two friends decided to canoe the river before it disappeared. On the first page of Deliverance, Lewis says: "When they take another survey and rework this map . . . all this in here will be blue. The dam at Aintry has already been started, and when it's finished next spring the river will back up fast. The whole valley will be under water. But right now it's wild. And I mean wild; it looks like something up in Alaska." Like Adam contemplating the loss of paradise, Ed imagines "the nighttime rising of dammed water bringing a new lake up with its choice lots, its marinas and beer cans."[25] The four Atlantans in the novel want to explore the pristine wilderness while it lasts.

Dressed in blue jeans, T-shirts, and tennis shoes (they wore no helmets or life jackets), Dickey, Braselton, and King set off for a valedictory trip down the Coosawattee. Dickey brought his nylon flight suit since it dried quickly in the sun (in *Deliverance* Lewis convinces Ed to take a "flying suit . . . because nylon dries out quick").[26] Following their accustomed pattern, they parked one car downstream where they planned to stop and another by a bridge upstream. On their way to the river, they stumbled through beer cans and condoms. Struck by "the strange forlorn sexuality of these country places,"[27] Dickey may have begun formulating the redneck sexual scene in *Deliverance*. With tents, cooking gear, bows, and broadhead arrows battened down, they launched their canoes, shot the rapids without any spills, and later, spotting a convenient sandbar, beached their canoes to set up camp. King had caught some trout, which they fried on a fire for dinner. The ambience of fresh air, woods, and stars made for an idyllic scene. That night, however, something unexpected happened. Braselton recounted:

> We were tired, sunburned and chafed, from the day's canoeing on the river and a little drunk. We had put up two tents, small two man pup tents. [Dickey] was already in one of them and he was drunk and hollering for me to get in there with him. [He] looked at me sort of funny. . . . "Come on, get in this tent with me. Are you afraid? Get in this tent with me." Well, I sat down on a log and smoked a cigarette and watched the embers of the campfire. I *was* afraid to get in that tent with him. So, I just waited until he quit hollering. It wasn't long. He'd had a lot to drink and soon he was asleep. Lucky for me it didn't rain because I slept outside that night. I wasn't taking any chances. Now, I don't believe he would have done anything . . . like a homosexual advance. But I didn't want to be put in a position of having to fight him off. He's a big son-of-a-bitch and strong as a bull.[28]

Dickey got up very early the next morning and left the campsite just as Ed does on the first morning of the canoe trip in *Deliverance*.

In the novel the homosexual assault on Bobby by a hillbilly sets the other events in motion with the inevitability of a classic tragedy. The assault was imaginary, but was affected by Dickey's complicated friendship with Braselton. In reality, the most frightening encounter for Dickey occurred when he met the local Gentry family. To his cosmopolitan perspective, they represented both the noble and ignoble aspects of a backwoods existence. To stress his and, by extension, Ed's identification with their savage ways, Dickey appropriated the ironic name Gentry for his narrator. The actual Gentrys bore no resemblance to the landed gentry and little resemblance to Ed Gentry in *Deliverance*.

The Gentrys on the Coosawattee and, for that matter, almost all the other mountain residents encountered on Dickey's canoe trips were helpful rather than rapacious. Braselton noted: "We never ran into any sadistic mountaineers. They were always friendly toward us. I remember one time a man and his son gave us a helping hand when we really needed it. I had hurt my ankle and was having a tough time walking and these people had taken us back to our car in a jeep. I remember the jeep had a bad clutch and it took a lot of grinding of gears and careful driving over those logging trails to get us out of there. But they did it. And they wouldn't accept any money for it either."[29] Dickey paid a back-handed compliment to their helpers by having Lewis Medlock tell a story of a backwoods father who instructs his son to go into the forest and find Lewis's lost hunting partner, which he does without question or complaint. Lewis praises this example of dependability, woods smarts, and "the kind of life that *guarantees* it."[30] But in *Deliverance* he also turns the father and son with the Jeep into the irascible Griners.

On the second day of their canoe trip, King got the car, drove the other two back up the river for more canoeing, and then drove downstream, where he planned to fish on foot. On a logging road six or seven miles below where he'd dropped off Dickey and Braselton, King consulted one of his topographical maps. Suddenly a man and a boy appeared. Seeing the maps, they assumed King was an officer from the Revenue Service who wanted to interrogate them about hidden stills and unpaid taxes on bootleg liquor. King assured the father, Ira Gentry, that he was simply a fisherman waiting for two friends to arrive in a ca-noe. To verify King's claim, Ira told his son, Lucas, to take King to the river and wait for the others. Although suspicious, the Gentrys were never overtly aggres-sive. But since Lucas had a gun, King feared he might use it if the other two ca-noers failed to arrive in a timely fashion.

Meanwhile, Dickey and Braselton had crashed their canoe in some rapids. Wedged against rocks by the canoe, Braselton at one point thought he might drown. According to Braselton:

It was a rather brutal trip, some heavy white water and then it was followed by shallows, where you almost had to walk the [canoe] . . . through the rocks. . . . And it was getting late, and we were exhausted. I finally said, "We've just got to get out of here. We can't wait to find Lewis." Lewis was somewhere downstream, but we didn't know how far. So we kept going un-til we couldn't go any farther. Jim said, "Let's get off the river and try to find some civilization." At that time the place was being logged. People were taking out timber and it was rather desolate, I remember. We took some logging trails and tried to get out. We walked and walked until it seemed like hours, and they were like a maze; they twisted and turned and we ended up about where we started. Anyway, we both went to sleep on a sandbar, very nice and warm for a change. There were palisades on both sides of the river, steep rock-face cliffs . . . and it was cold in the shade. . . . And in case Lewis came across us, we tied a handkerchief and stuck it on a stick, hoping maybe Lewis would keep coming upstream until he found us.

Well, he didn't come. And we woke up aching, sore and stiff, but we knew we had to keep going. So we got into the canoe and went on down the river. We kept going and kept going and finally we were discovered by Lewis, who was up on the high palisade and by a boy named Lucas Gentry, we later came to find out. Lucas was about fourteen, a fairly nice looking boy, quiet country boy in overalls. He had a single shot .22 rifle with him. And a dog. And Lewis came down (he had been trout fishing), and Lucas said, "Ya'll lost?" And we said, "Yeah, we'd like to get out of here." And Lewis said, "Well, there's an easier way to where we want to go." . . . So he took us on this rather circuitous route, I thought. And finally we came to a clearing. There was one of these old, unpainted country houses with a tin roof and a big back porch. There could have been 20 people in there looking out on you and you'd never see them. . . . All of a sudden the father of Lucas, named Ira Gentry, came out and he was one of these country people of indeterminate age. He's lost his teeth, but his hair is still black. Maybe a fairly young person when Lucas was born. He came out, with that sort of reserved friendliness that country people have: "Hey, how you doing. Good to see you. What ya'll doing up here? Oh, you're going down the river. Well, come on in here." He gave us a drink of the most delicious well water I've ever tasted. Out of one of those galvanized dippers.[31]

Before making their way to the ramshackle house, Lucas helped them haul their canoe and other gear to the car.

Resting on the porch, the three tired men noticed tall stalks of sugarcane around the yard. Sensing their curiosity, Ira cut a few segments of cane with his bowie knife and offered them to his guests, who dutifully chewed the sweet, pulpy fiber (Dickey brought some home for his son Chris). Lucas kept holding his single-shot .22 rifle as if Dickey and his partners might at any moment reveal their true identity as revenue officers. Ira drawled: "Wal, I guess you was wondering why I had Lucas here take y'all out from down there. I didn't want none of y'all to get into my bidness up that crick there. Now I used to be in the chicken bidness, but that went to hell and now I'm back in our original industry."[32] He smiled through a mouth of rotten teeth. Dickey and the others laughed nervously. Having acknowledged his true "bidness," Ira now brought out some jars of moonshine.

Glad to be off the river, Dickey tried to relax. Ira asked: "Where y'all boys from?" They replied, "Atlanta," so Ira shot back: "She-ut, we kill people like you up here." He chortled to indicate he was only half-serious, but his comment frightened Dickey. The conversation grew increasingly unnerving:

[Ira said:] "Ya'll got a lot of niggers down there in Atlanta, hadn't you?" And we said, "Well, as a matter of fact, we do." We were extremely polite. And he said, "Well, you know, we aint's never had none of much of them up here. We did have one come up here. The railroad brought him up. He was a pretty nice fellow, I must say; he never did bother nobody, just stayed down there on the railroad, down in a shack by the railroad. He was doing all right up here, nobody was bothering him much. But he just started acting up and we just had to get the sheriff to kill him." Of course, that sort of chilled our blood. He offered us some white whiskey, but I don't remember tasting it.[33]

As soon as they could, the three Atlantans bid the Gentrys farewell and walked to their car.

From these modest events Dickey constructed his tale of sodomy, murder, and suicide on the Cahulawassee River. Dickey mulled over his story line with King, especially the question of a fourth character and the encounter with the locals. At a party King had talked to Patsy Dickey about his idea for a plot based on their Coosawattee experience, and Dickey had called King the next day to see if he planned to use it in his own writing. King said he probably would not. Over the following years, King periodically advised Dickey on the novel that became *Deliverance*. He urged Dickey to focus on the way sophisticated men from Atlanta armed with primitive weapons (bows and arrows) clash with primitive men from the hills who have sophisticated weapons (rifles). Two city men based on Dickey and Braselton should canoe downriver until they meet their third friend, based on King, who is being held at gunpoint by a mountain boy. After one of the approaching men shoots an arrow into the boy's back, the moral quandary begins. Should the three men explain what happened to a local sheriff and submit themselves to what in all probability would be a prejudiced jury? Or should they concoct an alibi and do everything possible to avoid going to court? However Dickey chose to solve the dilemma, King thought the father should know who killed his son and stalk the Atlanta men in an attempt to get bloody revenge. Dickey borrowed some of King's suggestions and rejected the rest.

Although Braselton's friendship with Dickey was never sexual, homosexuality was a frequent topic of their conversations. Braselton said: "He told me one time that fear of homosexuality prevented American males from displaying their love for one another. Hell, Frenchmen and Russians and Italians hug and kiss one another. There's nothing queer about that. There's no *sexual* feeling. It's affection, brotherhood if you will."[34] Practicing what he preached, Dickey often called Braselton "Little Brother" and openly showed his brotherly affections and disaffections. Dickey admitted to Braselton, however, that his love for men had gone beyond hugging and kissing. Over Easter weekend in 1968, while vacationing by Lake Sydney Lanier in North Georgia, Dickey said: "You know, Al, I don't think there's any substitute for women. In all their infinite variety." Braselton asked what he meant. Dickey responded: "Well, I've tried men." "Men?" Braselton asked. Dickey replied: "Yeah, I tried it one time, just to see what it was like. . . . It was no good. Sex with men is no good. A very poor substitute for women. Very poor. I don't recommend it."[35] From this and other conversations, Braselton concluded that Dickey's homosexual experience had occurred during his military service.

For Dickey, homosexuality was a natural expression of the innate affection between men or between men and boys. After one of his groggy lunches in the late 1950s, Dickey picked up a handsome young boy, took him to his office at McCann-Erickson, and closed the door. A startled Inman Mays happened to walk in on them. Dickey quickly explained: "I'm going to teach this boy how to write poetry."[36] From that point on, Mays suspected Dickey's heterosexual boasts had a homosexual root. Many other men, including his son Chris, witnessed or glimpsed his sexual ambiguity. In the 1970s Dickey repeated to his mistress Mary

Cantwell what he'd told Braselton. During a discussion of homosexuality he said: "I tried it once. Didn't do nothin' for me."[37] To the end of his life, Dickey mulled over the origins and divagations of his sexuality. In their Easter conversation, Dickey suggested to Braselton that the main reason he sought sexual gratification from others was because his wife was frigid: "You know, Maxine doesn't like sex. She never did. It may be due to using it to get what she wants materially. . . . Southern women . . . use sex to get security. And once you view something as a necessary evil, you get the impression that maybe it's not so much fun after all. Anyway, I *do* like sex. And I go on these various readings [in] various places, Iowa State or Montana or someplace, and I'm always looking for that certain pale intellectual girl. And sure enough I end up sleeping with her that night. . . . When you're out there by yourself, you need a bedwarmer."[38] Even though he deemed sex with women preferable to sex with men, Dickey tended to view women as subsidiary—as bed warmers—and men as preferable companions.

As Braselton realized, Dickey's problems with Maxine provided one of the strongest motivations for the male outing in *Deliverance*. Like the journeys toward self-realization advocated several decades later by the men's movement, Dickey's canoe trip is essentially an attempt to escape the monotony of marriage in order to rediscover buried reservoirs of masculine energy. He confessed to Braselton at Lake Lanier that the only reason he stayed with Maxine, who had little inkling of his deepest thoughts and impulses, was for the sake of their two sons. Braselton found other reasons for their strained compatibility in the marital dynamics of *Deliverance*. The male characters want to be delivered from their humdrum marriages, but they also want to return to the security of a family. They want to be independent of as well as dependent on their wives. Braselton found this marital tug-of-war, which had replaced an earlier mother-son tug-of-war, particularly true of Dickey's relationship with Maxine, in which he played the role of prodigal son and she the role of scolding mother: "In a way you can see this in the fact that *Deliverance* was basically deliverance from women. The whole plot of *Deliverance*, even the homosexual rape . . . [shows that] women are not necessary. We've escaped them all. We've gotten away from that GOD-DAMNED BIG MOTHER CITY, where the grass is cut, and women dominate. Where apron strings are so prevalent, and children are underfoot."[39] Dickey's ambivalence toward women, Braselton concluded, derived from his dependence on them.

Years after sleeping outside the tent and watching Dickey vanish into the early morning fog with his bow and arrows, Braselton recognized the incident in the novel as well as in the poem "Fog Envelops the Animals." In both cases, the narrator undergoes a joyous purge. "I stood with fog eating me alive," Ed says in *Deliverance*. In his two-piece suit of long underwear, he blends with the fog and becomes "as invisible as a tree."[40] In the poem "The Heaven of Animals," which he wrote shortly after his experience in the woods with Braselton, Dickey describes his ideal world as a free-for-all where predator and prey fulfill their roles without any guilt. Like Yeats's Leda, who cannot push away "the feathered glory" of a camouflaged and rapacious Zeus, Dickey's victims accept and even enjoy their plights. "Fog Envelops the Animals" depicts a kindred situation. "In a white suit," Dickey's persona merges with the fog and drifts through the woods "Bourne by the river of heaven."[41] In his perfect camouflage, he can strike his prey with unimpeachable freedom.

In these "natural" scenes Dickey construes a realm beyond normal conceptions of good and evil, where predatory violence and predatory sex flourish, where the superego vanishes and the id roams unimpeded. *Deliverance* suggests that a violent, sexual, and guiltless union between predator and prey was one of Dickey's central fantasies. The book teases out parallels between arrow and phallus and snake. The mountain man's rape of Bobby and Lewis's murder of the mountain man are similar acts foreshadowed by the snakes in Dickey's Georgian Eden. Ed's rites of passage culminate when he can step into Lewis's shoes as well as the mountain man's, when his civilized and savage selves merge, and when homosexual rapist and homicidal archer become one. The arrow Ed aims at a man he believes to be one of the rapists on the cliff might as well be an arrow from a homosexual Cupid: "We were closed together, and the feeling of a peculiar kind of intimacy increased." The arrow's penetration imitates phallic penetration; afterwards Ed and the slain man separate like two lovers. "His brain and mine unlocked and fell apart, and in a way I was sorry to see it go," Ed says. Reveling in his new power as a Nietzschean king of the jungle, Ed shows that he and the hillbilly "lock" once again when he assumes the role of stalker and murderer. Because Bobby has failed to follow instructions, Ed takes the hillbilly's rifle and aims it at Bobby. His identification with his adversary is so strong that he hears the dead man say: "Do it; he's right there." When he attacks Bobby verbally, he focuses on the same part of Bobby's anatomy that the hillbilly has attacked.[42]

The actual encounter with the Gentrys that triggered the homosexual rape in the novel did not involve sex; it had more to do with a story about racist murder. Why, then, did Dickey turn a North Georgia sheriff's murder of a black man from Atlanta into a redneck's rape of a white man from Atlanta? And why did Dickey make the Atlanta men the murderers of the hillbillies? Dickey may have shied away from racial issues because, at about the time of his frightening encounter with the Gentrys, he confronted his racial attitudes head-on in an essay commissioned by Louis Rubin for a book on Southern culture. Dickey called his essay "Notes on the Decline of Outrage," and in it he spoke for the white Southerner who beheld the dismantling of the old racial order with a combination of sadness, anger, confusion, and relief. Dickey admitted that he had one foot planted securely in the Agrarian Old South and the other in the New South of commerce and industry, that he was torn between reactionary and progressive ideals. He published his divided statement about racial justice in 1961; in *Deliverance*, which he began composing shortly afterward, he explored other aspects of his Southern heritage.

In between canoe trips and ads for potato chips, Dickey worked diligently at his poems. In February 1960, galley proofs for *Into the Stone* arrived. On March 9, he returned to New York to give a poetry reading at the YM-YWHA Poetry Center with two poets he didn't know. Allotted two twelve-minute slots in which to read, he groused to James Wright: "The other two writers were crappy, if I do say so myself (they were Paul Carroll from Chicago and a nice housewifely lady named [Mona] van Duyn). So, seeing I had nothing to lose, I cut loose with some new poems, and I think the place really rocked."[43] Van Duyn, who later became one of the nation's first poet laureates, shared Dickey's estimation of Carroll, but was thrilled by Dickey's poetry: "Dickey, I thought, was absolutely sensational, and I beat my hands to a pulp with applause after his section of the reading."[44] Shortly after Carroll died and two months before he himself died, Dickey recalled his first meeting with Carroll very differently in a letter to Carroll's wife: "It was my first New York audience, and when I looked out and saw Norman Mailer in the first row and my venerable (new) editor at Scribner's, John Hall Wheelock, I felt that I was in the right place, and when I talked to Paul, a few minutes before the reading, I knew I was."[45] Dickey's subsequent friendship with Carroll and with Van Duyn, too, gave his memories of the Y a rosier tint.

Dickey also "rocked" with Robert Bly in New York. He told Wright, whom he missed: "Bob and I and some other people sat around a bottle of wine in New York and wrote a 'collective poem,' each contributing one line, and so on and on. We called the result 'Lobster,' and when we read back through it, it was surprisingly like the verse of some of Bob's contributors in *The Sixties*."[46] Before long, Dickey would accuse Bly's poetry of being similarly random. For the same reason he criticized John Ashbery, Frank O'Hara, and some of the other "New York Poets" who were imitating the avant garde methods of local abstract-expressionist painters. In deciding on "Lobster" as the title for the zany poem, Dickey may have remembered a drunken episode from Hendrik Marsman's long poem *The Zodiac*, in which the drunken poet-narrator invents a new constellation he calls "Lobster." Dickey's alter ego composes another "Lobster" in a rendition of *The Zodiac* he published in 1976.

Scribner's brought out *Into the Stone* on August 23, 1960, when Dickey was at the relatively late poetic age of thirty-seven. Among the many laudatory announcements, Wright's review in *Poetry* was especially pleasing. In it he praised Dickey for bringing "three great gifts" to life's crucial experiences: first, "an unpredictably joyous imagination, which is able to transfigure the most elemental facts of the universe and to embody the transfiguration in an unforgettable phrase . . . ; secondly, a delicate sense of music, which sometimes takes shape most beautifully in the skillful use and variation of refrains . . . ; and, finally, a humane quality which is very hard to characterize, but which I should call, inadequately, a kind of courageous tenderness."[47] Having complained about Scribner's triple-decker format, Dickey took heart when most of the reviewers rated his section of the book superior to the others. They praised his anapestic drumbeat, which he derived from Dylan Thomas and altered to prevent monotony. They applauded his sacramental vision of the world, which he also shared with Thomas. Dickey's decision to take John Wheelock's advice and divide the book thematically into four sections—"Family," "War," "Death, and Others," and "Love"—may have been a ploy to make the book more popular. Many poetry anthologies have been divided in such a way to appeal to readers who look to verse for advice on favorite subjects. Dickey went only so far in fulfilling standard expectations. His stance was deliberately apocalyptic; he wrote again and again about transfiguring the ordinary world into a miraculous one. As for Blake and other Romantics, imaginative energy was his god. Because this god revealed itself in the ecstasy and fertility of sex, Dickey tended to look at life like Freud—in terms of a binary conflict between Eros and Thanatos, the life force and the death force. Following the example of such modernists as Eliot and Pound, he frequently dramatized the cycle of his destructive and creative moods in terms of fertility myths. As a worldly mystic, as some critics called him, Dickey wrote of the struggle to recapture a sacred sense of awe at the mystery of creation and re-creation. "When we write poetry," he said later in life, "we try to emulate the Creator. We have the illusion of something in common with God. Sometimes we can sustain that for a second or two—that our process of creation is like His."[48] The artist's task, as Joyce announced in *A Portrait of the Artist as a Young Man*, was to re-create the Creation in all its glorious and inglorious multiplicity.

The poem that begins *Into the Stone*, "Sleeping Out at Easter," typifies Dickey's ritual and mythic approach to the world. Significantly, the narrator does not go to church on Easter Sunday to pay homage to the resurrection of the crucified Christ. Like Wallace Stevens's persona in "Sunday Morning," he conducts his own service on his own turf and in his own way. Having camped out in an army blanket, he groggily wakes on Easter morning believing that he is ritually reenacting Christ's resurrection and, in turn, all renewals of life from death. In *Self-Interviews*, Dickey admitted: "In the spring I *did* sleep out in a sleeping bag in a little pine grove behind my suburban house when I was in the advertising business in Atlanta. But I didn't wake up feeling that I was Christ. That's something I made up."[49] Dickey scores his feeling of renewal in a litany of end-stopped lines that echo Roethke's and Thomas's verse:

All dark is now no more.
This forest is drawing a light.
All Presences change into trees.
One eye opens slowly without me.
My sight is the same as the sun's,
For this is the grave of the king,
Where the earth turns, waking a choir.

Like many of his poems, Dickey's "Sleeping Out at Easter" draws on the Bible in a typological way so that God creating the universe in Genesis resembles Christ rising from the grave at Easter, and both resemble Dickey waking in his sleeping bag.

Grasping "the source of all song at the root," Dickey sings his worldly hymn, which is as sacred as it is profane. As with most fertility myths and fertility rituals, Dickey's poem hails sexual congress as the fundamental agent of creation. What is unusual and comic in "Sleeping Out at Easter," but typical of Dickey's unconventional attitudes, is his portrait of marriage. His persona has proved his fertility—he has produced a son—so he shifts his attention to poetic and visionary fertility, especially as they relate to masturbation. Dickey loved to shock audiences by extolling onanism, arguing that—like writing—it depended on the power of solitary fantasies. As for Joyce, for Dickey the Easter rising is also a phallic one: "The Word rises out of the darkness / Where my right hand, buried beneath me, / Hoveringly tingles."[50] Dickey "tingles" because he is "grasping" his "root." Soon afterward he tells himself to "*Put down those seeds in your hand.*" The etymological root of *semen* is "seed," and it is related to *sema,* a verbal sign. These "seeds" for Dickey are words and sperm, which he disseminates like a fertility god. His wife, characteristically, waits in the house as he pursues his writerly and erotic goals by himself.

Dickey had learned about fertility rituals from Eliot's *Waste Land,* George Frazer's *Golden Bough,* and the many anthropological studies he devoured at Vanderbilt. In one of his most anthologized poems, "The Vegetable King," which he called his "answer to Eliot's use of the Osiris myth," he achieved one of his most successful fusions of personal and mythic experience. According to the myth, Dickey explains: "The living victim was dismembered, thrown into a river or lake, and was supposed to be gathered together and resurrected when the crops came up in the spring."[51] As in the companion poem, "Sleeping Out at Easter," Dickey's persona ritualistically separates himself from his family and enters a meditative dark night of the soul in order to commune with a creator. According to Dickey's view, God and Christ and Osiris are all personifications of the earth that resurrects its vegetation from winter deadness. In a dream he only half believes, Dickey joins all "the gods . . . / Mismade inspiringly" in order to undergo "the acclaimed rebirth / Of the ruined, calm world, in spring." He wakes slowly from his dream world, in which he entertains divine and heroic fantasies of himself, because he prefers living in his imagination to plodding through his everyday routines. Coming back to his family, who welcome him with trepidation, the reborn poet offers "Magnificent pardon, and dread, impending crime."[52] Like Christ at the Second Coming, he is saintly as well as apocalyptic, gentle as well as ruthless. He forgives "mother, son, and wife" for their worldly concerns (his mother, after all, wanted him to remain in advertising, and his son and wife depended on his business job for their welfare). But he also damns them like the born-again zealot who returns to captivity after seeing the promised land.

In most of his descents to mythic underworlds, Dickey imagines confronting his dead brother, Eugene, and somehow works in his fantasy that Eugene sacrificed himself so that he could be born. This fantasy precipitates his fall in "The Underground Stream." In "The String" his six-year-old son Chris reminds him of Eugene, who died at that age, and how he himself was "brought to life / To replace the incredible child / Who built on this string in a fever" (in reality, Eugene never performed string tricks). In his many poems about the Second World War, Dickey tends to treat war in the same allegorical way—as a conflict between death and new life. *Into the Stone* also reveals Dickey's preoccupation with the way a fundamentally unheroic suburban man re-creates himself in the form of a hero. Through rites of passage, Dickey's lovers, soldiers, and athletes struggle to attain their imagined ideals. In "The Other," Dickey's double portrays himself as a "rack-ribbed child" with a "chicken-chested form" who transforms himself into a muscular sort of folk hero or god. The "other" is "a brother or king-sized shadow," an Orpheus figure with a great harp who attends the speaker's ordeals and inspires him to develop "the breast of a statue" and become "Like Apollo / With armor-cast shoulders."[53] It turns out that the "other" is another avatar of Dickey's dead brother, a "body-building angel" who teaches Dickey to affirm life with heroic zest. Dickey's brother was weak, ill, and mortal; therefore Dickey must be strong, robust, and divine. He must fashion an image of himself from his opposite—his other, his brother. In the "Love" section of *Into the Stone*, Dickey explores the ideal of the sexually faithful husband, which in life he usually betrayed. How can he remain faithful to an actual woman, he wonders in these poems, if each new woman represents a possible ideal? Again, his conundrums involve the imagination and its romantic images. Out of his quests and questionings, Dickey produced a book that yoked his personal experiences to mythic archetypes in a startling, powerful way that few other books at the time could rival.

By the time *Into the Stone* was published, Dickey had already completed most of his next book, *Drowning with Others*, and he had started collecting poems for a third. His immediate plan was to send the new manuscript, which Maxine was typing, to Harcourt Brace, Houghton Mifflin, Wesleyan, or Farrar, Straus. With Dickey's poems appearing in the *New Yorker* (he had signed one of the magazine's coveted "first-reading" contracts in November 1959, which paid a bonus and $1.90 per line), reviews in the *Sewanee Review*, a book in the Scribner's series, two more books in progress, and invitations to read his poems at colleges and high schools, Atlantans began to take notice. The journalist and short story writer Betsy Fancher was one of the first to publicize his growing literary reputation and one of the first reviewers to glimpse the demonic forces that would create the legend of James Dickey. Having just returned to Atlanta as a young widow to write a book column for the *Atlanta Journal-Constitution* and to conduct a daily talk show for WAGA radio, she called Dickey at his advertising office to arrange an interview. She remembered him replying: "I'm really terribly pushed but you can follow me around the tennis court at Bitsy Grant Saturday at ten." Trying to ignore his condescending tone, she agreed, only to be offended again because he failed to appear. This time she showed her anger: "I called him and told him he was a monumental Son of a Bitch, and he laughed and asked me for lunch. We spent three hours over lobster and caviar at Remonds, talking about Agee's *Let Us Now Praise Famous Men* (his favorite book), T. S. Eliot, whom he didn't like (I did) and George Barker who had influenced him and whom I had never heard of, and dozens of others. It took all we had between us to pay the bill and after that we met for lunch at a swing at Piedmont Park and ate sandwiches, but the talk was just as good."[54] They also talked about the schizoid life Dickey had chosen to live as a businessman-poet. Later, Fancher admitted that Dickey had conveniently forgotten his wallet, so she was the one who paid the bulk of the lunch bill. She also recalled that Dickey never admitted he was married. Assuming his romantic designs on her were innocent, she was shocked when he drunkenly entered her apartment one night after their lunch interview. She pushed him toward the door and told him to leave.

Dickey got a chance to show off his reputation for raising hackles when Louis Rubin invited him to Hollins College to read poems and debate Randall Jarrell. Dickey had always relished Jarrell's devastatingly insightful criticism and dismissed his poetry. Face-to-face with the prestigious poet-critic in November 1960, Dickey was prepared for a fight. He wrote James Wright:

After the readings, which were received with an enthusiasm which actually frightened me, Jarrell and I sat for two and a half hours arguing in front of the several hundred students and guests, and let me tell you it was exhausting! We agreed on almost nothing (and I *mean* nothing!) and we cut and slashed and parried with deliberate and desperate urgency. The audience was violently partisan, and seemed to me more or less equally divided; there was wild applause after each bit of repartee (by Jarrell) and each bit of raving (by me), and at one point I thought I actually detected the wonderful sound of "Go! Go! Go!" as we went at it hotly: the sound of a crowd cheering for the home team to score in the last quarter, or the sound of a good, knowledgeable and enthusiastic crowd at a jazz festival, when one of the musicians (for some reason I think of tenor sax players) goes from technical virtuosity into inspiration, or art. It was a great experience for me. God knows what I said, but I certainly said it, I am sure. After it was over we fell into each other's arms (literally!) and there was more applause and we then went out and got drunk and promised each other we wouldn't be influenced by the other's work, swore undying fealty to poetry, and so back home![55]

The two men undoubtedly argued, but Jarrell was a teetotaler. Dickey's rhapsodic summary of the occasion has the patina of his many other stories about fierce battles that end with sentimental displays of friendship.

To take a break from his stressful job and literary jousts, in November Dickey joined his archery club, the Cherokee Bowmen, for a hunting excursion in the Blue Ridge mountains. He shot no deer (the others did), but he told Wright that he shot a fox and three fat grouse. To Donald Hall he made larger claims: "My friends Don Yearwood and Bud Adair and I killed a 450 lb boar (or hog, as we North Georgians call them). . . . We put nine arrows in him and I climbed at least seven trees before we finished him off. Because of the dogs it was hard to get a good shot; for a long time we hit him in every place but the two or three right ones. No one could get into his lungs until finally Bud and I hit him from opposite sides at about the same time. He didn't know which way to charge, and before he made up his mind he fell over."[56] One of the best U.S. tournament archers in his class, Yearwood led Dickey's club on the hunt with his friend Bud Adair, who worked as a Delta pilot. Yearwood recalled that he shot the first four arrows at the boar, which was indeed 450 pounds, and the club hunters shot an additional twenty-one arrows into the animal before it crashed to the swampy earth. Yearwood had no recollection of Dickey's contribution to the boar's demise. In the poem "Approaching Prayer," collected in *Helmets*, Dickey commemorated the hunt when he wrote of a man like himself finding in his attic "the head of a boar / I once helped to kill with two arrows."[57] Like a tribal shaman, Dickey's persona puts on his father's sweater and gamecock spurs as well as the boar's head over his head so that he can envision both predator and prey, dead father and living son. Boastful of killing in his letters, in his poem he took a more sympathetic view of the dead boar.

After about a year with Liller, Neal, Dickey again decided to jump to a new agency—Burke Dowling Adams (BDA). A contemporary of E. B. White's at

Cornell, Mr. Burke Dowling Adams had literary interests, admired good writing, and was therefore well-disposed toward Dickey. For his part, Dickey respected Adams's successful business career. Adams had started a small agency in Montclair, New Jersey, that handled the Cunard account. Around 1945, when the founder and president of Delta Airlines promised to give Adams his company's account if he moved to Atlanta, Adams sold his New Jersey accounts and moved south. Delta soon comprised about 80 percent of his business. Starting out as a small Louisiana crop-dusting outfit with the slogan "We haul, y'all," Delta had grown into one of the nation's leading carriers in Atlanta. Just a few years before Dickey joined BDA, Delta had obtained cross-country routes and had started offering two-hundred to three-hundred-dollar package vacations to Miami, Chicago, New York, and other U.S. cities. According to George Bailey, one of Dickey's new colleagues in charge of promoting Delta's "million dollar dream vacations," the airlines led the field in package deals.

As he did at Liller, Neal, Dickey suggested to his new boss that he could lever the lucrative SSS account away from McCann-Erickson/Marshalk, since his family still played a significant role in the company. Adams wanted SSS business and counted on Dickey to get it for him (in the end Dickey did not deliver). At first Dickey ingratiated himself with Adams. He wrote some light verse for Adams's son, Michael, on his birthday, and the family framed it. He attended Adams's parties and talked to his boss about literature. But Dickey's thirty or so colleagues at 1750 Peachtree soon realized what others had realized: poetry and not advertising was his true calling.

In his new position as creative director, Dickey was in charge of copy and art departments as well as campaigns for the principal accounts. Or so he told Dana Gioia for an article about poets in business: "In a way this suited me fine; I had some good people working under me, and Delta had just been awarded the East-West transcontinental route, and it was up to me to make as much of this as I could, publicly."[58] Dickey's notebooks from the time give evidence of his work for Delta. One draft of an ad reads: "A New Dimension in Travel: Country Club comfort . . . at the speed of sound." He also came up with the poetic jingle: "The sound . . . the feel . . . the sheer magnificence . . . / (Magnificent comfort and speed) of the BIG jets—the Delta jets! / How the Air Loves them!— / The Air was made for them—the Big jets—the Delta Jets / As quiet as a Dream (of Candles) the Big jets / The Big Jets' Gentle Swiftness." In a less ambitious encomium to air travel, he wrote of the jets: "We *know* you, we *like* you!"[59] BDA used few if any of his lines.

When Glen Verrill came to work for BDA shortly after Dickey left, he heard others laugh at Dickey's nickname "Jingle Jim," since he so rarely came up with workable slogans. Behind his closed door, Dickey edited the slogans of others as quickly as possible and then returned to his poetry. Uncowed by office policies prohibiting employees from doing personal work on company time, he sometimes read his poems to secretaries. Jody Brown, an account executive who began work at BDA in 1959 and who later became an assistant vice president, regularly talked to Dickey, since their offices were opposite each other on the second floor. Dickey rarely wanted to discuss advertising; his only concern was poetry. Brown never saw any advertising copy issue from Dickey's office. A copywriter, Bill Cromartie, who also began work after Dickey left BDA, heard similar stories. "Gosh, he never wrote a single Delta ad, only poetry!"[60] Cromartie's colleagues said.

Some of Dickey's friends at BDA sympathized with his attempt to juggle two careers. Comer Jennings, who invited Dickey to lecture at the Woodruff Arts Center in the late 1960s, often took Dickey out to lunch. Convinced he had little money, Jennings felt sorry for Dickey and always paid the bill. A fellow copywriter, Joseph Parris, also listened sympathetically to Dickey's struggles. He remembered Dickey saying that advertising was the most boring job he could imagine, that he could hardly stay awake in it. Nick Halliday, BDA's print production manager, noted the results of Dickey's discontent. He remembered only one of Dickey's slogans being printed in an ad; it was for a cardboard fan with a wood stick for Atlanta's C&S bank.

Indifferent to his low standing as a businessman, Dickey set aside as many office hours as possible to finish *Drowning with Others*. In March 1961, he felt confident enough about his new collection to send a first draft to Hall for his editorial evaluation. Hall sent a favorable response on March 30, but in late May he bewildered and infuriated Dickey by rejecting the manuscript. Hall explained: "Part of the Board was in favor of your manuscript at this time, and the rest of the Board only felt that it wasn't quite as good as they had expected."[61] The board would meet again in October. Hall asked Dickey to beef up the manuscript with some new poems and resubmit it in August so that it could be circulated among the readers before the fall meeting. Hall tried to assure Dickey that the manuscript would be accepted. The main problem was that Wesleyan had decided to accept only two books each year, and these two crowded out Dickey's *Drowning with Others*. One of the books was James Wright's third collection, which he was calling *Amenities of Stone*.

Dickey learned, to his surprise, that his formalist peers John Hollander and Richard Wilbur had urged acceptance of his book, while the poet Norman Holmes Pearson had voiced reservations. With regard to Wilbur, he told Hall: "He and I are so radically different as writers, that it was hard for me to think, before I sent the book in, that he would like what I do. He must be a very generous man, as well as the best critic of poetry I have ever read, or certainly one of the two or three best. He is so beautifully willing to meet the writer on his own ground that he makes my comments seem mean and niggling, which they often are."[62] After Dickey established his reputation as a poet, critics often pitted his romanticism against Wilbur's classicism. Dickey, however, never forgot the support of his rival. Many years later in New York, when Wilbur gave a reading at a luncheon meeting of the National Institute of Arts and Letters, Dickey showed his appreciation by calling for encores. Piling into a taxi with James Merrill and Wilbur, Dickey remained effusive. "Dick, you are the best there is," he intoned. Wilbur later told Merrill that he was embarrassed by Dickey's praise. Merrill responded: "I think he meant every word of it—that he was wholly sincere."[63]

Because of Wilbur's and Hollander's support and the unexpected withdrawal of Wright's manuscript, Wesleyan finally accepted *Drowning with Others*. One morning, Hall remembered, his phone rang at seven in the morning: "It was

Willard Lockwood . . . saying that Jim Wright had withdrawn his book. Wesleyan was about to go to press; there was no time for the committee to meet again. Would it be all right to substitute the runner-up book, which was James Dickey's? I called Dickey in Atlanta, then and there, seven-thirty in the morning, and asked, 'Has your book been taken by another publisher? Can we still have it?' He said to go right ahead. So Wesleyan published James Dickey because James Wright withdrew his book."[64] Dickey hoped he would never have to be runner-up again.

With his poetry career gaining momentum, Dickey's advertising career became even more of a distracting nuisance. In April 1961, Dickey received some good news from the Guggenheim Foundation. The previous year he had requested $11,600 to travel in France and Italy, arguing that since his first book was largely written in France, his second book would benefit from "the same environmental and artistic influences."[65] Although he had virtually finished his second book by April 1961, the Guggenheim Foundation had no way of knowing and granted him a $5,000 fellowship. His escape from advertising assured, he became even more nonchalant about his job. "When I got the first and main part of the new campaign for Delta done, I left,"[66] he told Dana Gioia. On July 10, 1961, he wrote James Wright in a burst of excitement: "I have done it at last. Five minutes ago I quit my job as 'Atlanta's fastest-rising young businessman' (a term used by my present agency to its own purposes). . . . I am OUT, thank God! I simply could not do it any longer, and now that the break has come, 'everything I look upon is blest.' I feel like overhauling the poetic engine, grinding the valves, re-boring the block, and getting set to run like hell on the poetic Road to Glory (or elsewhere) for the rest of my life, God willing."[67] Dickey claimed that Wright was the first person—Maxine notwithstanding—to hear of his decision to quit. Having finally broken free from advertising's shackles, he celebrated by loading his bows and arrows into his MG and driving to the archery range.

Five days later he divulged the specifics of his leave-taking to Donald Hall: "After five and a half years of working in these dark Satanic mills of American business I am out at last. After consulting my finances, savings, and so on, I found that my family and I could pretty well get along until March—when we take the Guggenheim—without my having to work. So, after considerable preparation, which included just sitting in my effusively decorated office and looking at the walls in pure joy, I walked in and told my elegant, fatherly employer, Mr. Burke Dowling Adams (better known in the trade as 'BDA') that I was leaving. There followed such a scene as was never before enacted, comparable only to Priam's weeping over the body of Hector. I was ungrateful, the agency had spent a lot of money on me, and so on. Well, I have spent a lot of time on them: time I won't get back. Anyway, I am out now, and feel in possession of myself for the first time in a long, long while."[68] In fact, Adams had fired Dickey. Initially unaware of the extent to which Dickey wrote poems and personal letters at his desk, as Dickey's reputation for insubordination spread, Adams finally concluded that he "just never worked."[69] At the beginning of summer in 1961, Dickey pushed Adams's tolerance to the limit by taking a one-week vacation without his or anyone else's permission. While Dickey was away, a suspicious

Adams asked Joseph Parris if he had seen Dickey. Parris responded that he had not, and Adams decided that Dickey was absent without leave. At 9:05 on the morning Dickey returned (some believed he had gone to New York), Adams called him into his office, reprimanded him, and told him he was no longer wanted at Burke Dowling Adams. Glen Verrill saw the office papers confirming Dickey's expulsion. Other colleagues who learned of Dickey's firing were not surprised. They knew Adams would sooner or later put an end to Dickey's lackadaisical habits.

Dickey offset his failure as a businessman by inventing stories about his recent successes. A month after being fired, he trumpeted his accomplishments in archery tournaments. He told Wright on August 30: "I lost the state championship this year, but did pretty well in the Southeastern, a much bigger tournament in which I was a fairly close third."[70] Others who shot with Dickey at tournaments denied he was ever so successful. To the end of his life he maintained that he had won Atlanta's Young Man on the Go Award solely for his ad work at BDA. He told Geoffrey Norman in a *Playboy* interview and Dew James in a *Florence Morning News* interview that his prestige at the agency was such that Adams had raised his salary to $50,000 (his salary was about $20,000). While he wanted adulation, he also wanted pity, and sued for it by harping on his return to poverty. He told interviewers that he had to support his family on $35 weekly unemployment checks. On August 30, he asked Wright to badger Bly about his $150 advance for *The Suspect in Poetry*. "I am no longer a member of 'the affluent society,' "[71] he said. (Near the end of 1960, Bly had proposed that his Sixties Press publish Dickey's essays and reviews as a book.) He was so financially strapped, he later recalled: "For a couple of months, before I took up a Guggenheim Fellowship . . . I lived . . . by giving guitar lessons, and moonlighting (with dark glasses at night, yet!) at a coffee house in the hippie-and-dope section of town called The Fourteenth Gate."[72] Dickey was never so destitute, never gave guitar lessons, and never moonlighted in Atlanta coffeehouses.

When Sheldon Kelly asked Tom and Maibelle Dickey about their brother's postadvertising poverty, they adamantly denied it. "Jim was never a starving poet," Kelly reported them as saying. "When he left the advertising agency . . . , he went down and signed up for unemployment almost as a joke. . . . And he may have collected a check, but Maibelle had specific numbers . . . of the cost of keeping the James Dickey family [flourishing] and she [Dickey's mother] wrote checks and she kept the James Dickey family going. He didn't need the money. The unemployment checks—that was tip money."[73] Around this time, Dickey confided to Al Braselton that he was banking five thousand dollars in annual dividends from his SSS stock. That was an exaggeration, too, but with his savings, his mother's patronage, his investments, and his literary earnings he was far from impoverished.

Although Maxine supported her husband's decision to pursue his writing full time, Dickey's parents disapproved of his sudden exodus from advertising. How could he throw away such a lucrative career for such a notoriously impecunious one as poetry writing? Thinking back on his decision, Dickey said: "I had this notoriety in Atlanta business, 'The Young Man on the Go' and all of that. They couldn't see how I could step down from that to living as a poet. . . . It was all right with my mother because it was what I wanted to do, but my father had a hard time understanding it. . . . My father was very proud that I'd distinguished myself in the real world [of advertising]. When I told him I was leaving my job as creative director . . . and taking a fellowship to go and write poetry in Europe, he was somewhat nonplussed. He thought it was a bad trade."[74] Dickey's mother was not as supportive as he claimed. Other friends were startled by his decision as well. Betsy Fancher said: "He was then 39 and leaving advertising seemed to me the highest form of recklessness. He had a wife and two sons to support, and he was used to the good life."[75] Poet friends like Hall, Wright, and Bly reacted differently. Wright called his decision "an occasion of great and unmistakable heroism, of genuine *character*, perhaps *virtue* in the real, old-fashioned sense."[76] The others echoed these sentiments.

Dickey may have abandoned advertising, but he never forgot its lessons. He applied the marketing strategies he learned while selling Coca-Cola, potato chips, and Delta vacation packages to sell his poetry, fiction, criticism, and—perhaps most importantly—himself. Some of his later detractors, like Neal Bowers, the author of *James Dickey: The Poet as Pitchman*, argued that much of Dickey's success depended on his advertising abilities. In the 1960s, Dickey's career surely benefited from the way he promoted it, but in the 1970s, he seemed to duplicate the mistakes he once made in advertising offices; the images he concocted for himself no longer sold. His career began to suffer for another reason that can be traced to his advertising years. Advertisers in the late 1950s and early 1960s were deeply entrenched in the drinking culture. Business lunches often included three or four stiff martinis. Dickey drank in moderation as an aviator, a Vanderbilt student, and a college professor in Texas and Florida. At McCann-Erickson in New York, Violetta Dodge never saw him drink to excess. During his frustrating years in Atlanta agencies, his consumption of alcohol increased. His Friday night binges at Dave Sanders's house became routine. Queried about the escalation of his drinking in the 1960s and 1970s, Dickey sometimes explained that it was a promotional strategy. If he wasn't drunk and acting outrageously, his audiences would never "buy" his poetry. He told a *Philadelphia Inquirer* writer, Maralyn Lois Polak, that behind his drunken-bard mask was a "mild-mannered, agreeable, colorless and uninteresting [man]." He added: "I have to get drunk all the time to make myself colorful. . . . Just like Dylan Thomas. And believe me, I'm not averse to it."[77] Dickey characteristically said nothing about the detrimental effects of addiction.

It has often been said that alcoholism is the occupational hazard of writers, that it is an epidemic among writers, that only bartenders have a higher incidence of alcoholism. For Dickey, writing and drinking were twin forms of exhibitionism. Prone to solitude and silence, he drank to make himself more sociable; alcohol eased the transition from his writing study to the stage on which he was expected to perform. As on his canoe trips, alcohol fueled his reckless joy. He needed alcohol to overcome his fears of the dramatic and dangerous experiences that became his subjects. Alcohol also incited the fantasies so important to his writing. It gave him inspiration. If his self-esteem in the ad office dipped, if his confidence at his typewriter wavered, alcohol was a soothing elixir. If he felt guilty about his sexual misdeeds with women, booze was his

Lethe. If he worried about his homosexual curiosity or his bouts of impotence with women, a few stiff drinks made him bolder and more forgetful. Above all, drunkenness conferred upon Dickey the mantle of the fatally addicted genius, the Dionysian hero with a tragic flaw, the doomed Romantic whose plight evinced pity, shock, and awe. As with so many writers, alcoholism enabled Dickey at the beginning of his career, and disabled him at the end. As he sank into daily drinking in the 1970s, his effectiveness as a writer dwindled. But in the summer of 1961, with Wesleyan showing interest in *Drowning with Others*, Donald Hall accepting poems for a Penguin anthology, an editor publishing his work in *Best Poems of 1960*, and the Guggenheim Fellowship funding a trip to Europe, Dickey's career was full of halcyon prospects.

VII.

BARNSTORMING FOR POETRY

16. Return to Europe (1961-1962)

In early September of 1961, the board at Wesleyan University Press accepted *Drowning with Others* "enthusiastically and without dissent." Dickey was ecstatic, and especially grateful to Donald Hall for championing his book. "I can't really tell you how much I owe you," he told Hall. "It should be a kind of feeling that can communicate itself by some metaphysical means through the air between Georgia and Michigan; I hope you sense it, for the air is full of it."[1] To repay Hall, Dickey promised to send him the ears and tail of a black bear he planned to shoot on his next hunt. Although the gift of bear appendages never arrived, Hall began his editorial work on *Drowning with Others* in mid-September. Known for his stylistic perfectionism, Hall suggested cutting entire poems and revising others. Dickey submitted to the proposed revisions willingly. On September 14, he addressed Hall as if he were *il miglior fabbro*: "I rely completely on your sense of how the book ought to go. Not only that, but I *depend* on you to get the book into the best shape possible. My arrangement was only provisional at best. . . . I give you complete *carte blanche* to rearrange the poems as you and the other editors (but mostly you) see fit."[2] Hall conscientiously reshuffled the poems into their final order. He also tried to help Dickey find a teaching job at the University of Michigan by giving him instructions about writing a résumé and going to the Modern Language Association meeting for interviews. Welcoming Hall's editorial help, Dickey was less amenable to his academic advice. His humiliating experiences at Rice and the University of Florida still rankled: "Whoever I end up teaching with will have to *want* me and make active efforts to get me. I had rather teach in a small school, or even a high-school, where I was genuinely wanted than in a Yale or Harvard where I was just tolerated and made to feel suspect and 'grateful' all the time."[3] To stress his misfit status, he continued to cultivate his Daniel Boone image by writing Hall about shooting deer, wild boar, and bear.

Dickey supplemented his income during the period before his Guggenheim, which officially funded the year from February 1, 1962, to January 31, 1963, by directing a poetry workshop in Atlanta. Among its regular participants were Landrum Guy, George Mason, Van K. Brock, Mary Ann Coleman, Mickey Rubin, Patricia Wilcox, and Rosemary Daniell. The workshop was an offshoot of an adult education course at Emory University taught by Brock. When Brock retired as workshop director, he decided against asking Dickey to replace him because he disliked Dickey. Patricia Wilcox, who would go on to publish two books of poetry and found the Iris Press, was the one who asked Dickey to lead the group. She had met him at a tea party arranged by the wife of a well-known Emory philosophy professor, Charles Hartshorne. Out of nervousness, Wilcox plied herself with a martini and then, over tea, quietly listened to Dickey talk

about poetry with his usual passion. Wilcox, who was also a philosophy professor's wife, was not prepared for what followed. Dickey offered her a ride home,
flexed his bicep with Tarzan-like brazenness in the car, and said: "Feel this muscle. See how strong I am!" Relaxing with his arm behind her, he next declared:
"I'm looking forward to the day when all boys and girls can make love freely at
any time and anywhere. I'm looking forward to the time when this puritanical
thing is over."[4]

In the workshops he conducted, Dickey continued to perplex Wilcox with his
shifting moods. Sometimes he acted like an innocent Adam, at other times a
jaded warrior. He could be wise, gauche, silly, insightful, and bumptious in rapid
succession. He sometimes led the workshop as if it were a business meeting.
Amused, Wilcox, Mason, and Rubin tittered in the back of the room. Dickey
tolerated their insolence for a time, and then, white-lipped with fury, he reduced
Wilcox to tears. When not acting like an advertising executive, Dickey posed as
a seasoned combat pilot. Wilcox grew impatient with what she called his "bla-
tantly assertive masculine dominance" and his "killer's capacity to inspire terror."[5] Nevertheless, she was grateful for the way he encouraged the group with
helpful comments on the poems.

Despite the moments of insubordination, Dickey was fond of his workshop.
He wrote a poem "To Landrum Guy, Beginning to Write at Sixty," which applauded the eccentric, genteel, and at times curmudgeonly man's late start as a
poet. Dickey admired Wilcox as well, although in her presence he usually fluc-
tuated between flirtatiousness and condescension. Toying with her Phi Beta
Kappa key, which she hung around her neck, he once complimented her intelligence with a goofy smile. At a big party in her Rosedale Road home, he complimented her again, this time for her sloppiness. According to Wilcox: "Here,
again, his clairvoyance zapped a 'fault' and dubbed it a virtue. At the same time
he chided me for flirting, warning that he might throw me down on the bed right
then and there if I weren't careful. After this party we thought he must have
made good on this threat with one of the many dazzled females at the party because somehow the bed's side rail had gotten bent. This accident prompted me
to consider writing a verse satire, 'To James Dickey, Beginning to Break Beds at
Forty.'" Earlier Wilcox had taken Dickey into the bedroom to show off her two
young sons, who were sleeping. Dickey commented on their beautiful faces, but
said that he and Wilcox could have produced much more beautiful children. He
fixed her with a quirky stare and declared that Jack, her philosopher husband,
was of course the archetypal enemy of the poet (Plato had begun the battle by
prohibiting poets from his republic of philosopher-kings). His tone was ironic,
but Wilcox never knew how to take his quip.

Like the other members of the poetry group, Wilcox met Maxine and admired her stoic dignity and grace: "I got the impression at the time that . . .
Maxine took care of him and his work in a rather maternal—and, one suspects,
long-suffering—manner, given his extramarital enjoyment of other women."
Dickey treated the Atlanta workshop much as he had treated his classes at Rice
and the University of Florida. He mixed perspicacity with buffoonery. He played
the roles of clown, king, scholar, critic, huntsman, Don Juan, war hero, adman,

and football jock. He regaled the other poets with stories of foxhunting in the North Georgia mountains and once displayed bloody arrows to convince them that he was telling the truth. (Some of the blood may have been the result of Lewis King piercing a road-killed fox with an arrow and putting it in Dickey's car as a joke; King denied Dickey ever killed a fox.) Wilcox later reflected: "One felt he always projected varieties of himself, as though he were an actor hidden in his dressing room when not revealing himself in these various on-stage roles. This imparted a somewhat off-putting unreality to his general behavior and was perhaps one reason our set tended to mock him on occasion. To me, however, this signaled danger at getting too close to Jim."[6] The poets in the group were as intrigued as they were suspicious of their shape-shifting teacher.

Among the various workshop participants, Rosemary Daniell went on to achieve the most notoriety as a poet and prose writer. At the time, according to Wilcox, Daniell was "a resonantly Southern young matron with the easy-going, opulent sensuality and earthy wit of her type."[7] She was just finding her voice as a writer. Having met Dickey at a poetry reading in an Atlanta art gallery, Daniell had fallen under his spell. She later admitted: "Dickey was the first live poet I had heard read from his works, and I was transported, caught up in a near-religious thrall, hardly able to believe that language . . . could convey such beauty, such emotion."[8] Naive about the literary world and awed by Dickey's charisma, she looked to him as to a father for guidance. In her memoir, *Fatal Flowers*, in which Dickey appears as "The Great Southern Poet," Daniell recalled: "When our instructor [Brock] reverently told us that the great man had agreed, for two dollars a head, since he [Dickey] was living on unemployment payments, to meet each week with our workshop, I felt as though I was in a dream. Though I tossed and turned that night, fearing hellfire, though I filled my journal with new and disturbing doubts . . . , I had already found, without knowing it, a new god to replace the old. Yes, his spirit had grabbed me. Now I would sit at his feet."[9] If Dickey was a god, for Daniell he was more like Pan or Mammon than Jehovah. He insisted that all the poets in the workshop pay him before he read any of their poems. According to Daniell: "He carefully counted the money before commenting, just as he later called a college or university where he would be reading to make sure his check was ready. (By then I assumed that that was in case he did anything obnoxious that might make the school have second thoughts.)"[10] Dickey's gaucheness did little to subdue Daniell's infatuation.

Obviously on the prowl, Dickey quickly made Daniell the target of his seductions. He was unduly attentive to her poetry, telling her that it would soon be better than his. Mary Ann Coleman dropped out of the workshop because of his favoritism and wrote Dickey a letter of protest. To garner Daniell's sympathies, Dickey in private assailed her with complaints about his shrewish wife and stories about his arduous struggle to write. Understanding her ambition as well as her vulnerability, he whispered to her in his dark car after class, "Keep working with me, baby, and you'll be a great writer," and then slipped his hand down the back of her panty girdle.[11] The possibility of an adulterous relationship—she was married—frightened and thrilled Daniell. "Jim had a way of drawing people in,"

Daniell said with the benefit of hindsight, "of masking the violence of his intent or content in a wash of oft-repeated, much-honed stories, told with the skill of a natural, if often sloshed, raconteur."[12] In Daniell's case, the stories worked.

From her intimate conversations with Dickey, Daniell learned that he had grown up in the North Georgia hills "without a pot to piss in." When his mother inherited her family's tonic fortune, he had moved to a mansion in suburban Atlanta. At the age of twelve he had nearly died when a water moccasin bit him. Luckily he had slit the fang marks with a pocketknife and sucked out the poison (this fantasy later became the basis for the allegorical poem "The Poisoned Man"). He detailed his sexual conquests of Japanese and Filipino women during the war, and boasted of the many Japanese fighter planes he had shot down. He said he had narrowly escaped his plane after it crashed and exploded in Borneo. When Dickey spoke of Maxine and the afflictions he suffered in his marriage, Daniell confessed: "My sympathy made me so weak that I stood helplessly at a drunken class party as he unzipped the back of my dress, moving his hand up and down my bare backbone. . . . He whispered in my ear that he would call me at eight A.M. on Monday, that he had to see me naked. 'Are you brave enough for it, woman?' he murmured, implying an act of moral courage." Their tryst occurred at a friend's apartment:

> He sat back in a stuffed chair and had me serve him a double dry martini, then stripped the green ribbon from my hair and made me kneel at his feet. We would have intercourse without my diaphragm, he instructed, because he liked it better that way, and because he wanted me to have his "chile," which I would raise as my own. Then, after he left for his teaching position . . . , I would send him a postcard in code, letting him know whether or not our lovemaking had taken. If I did become pregnant, I was never to tell Paul [her husband] the true paternity; he would send me a box of candy for the baby each Christmas. . . . By making me the mother of his child, he would simply be making me worthy of his love.[13]

Not until the women's movement gathered momentum in the late 1960s did Daniell realize how absurdly submissive she was to the patriarchal Dickey. In 1962 she merely swooned.

Daniell gradually recognized that Dickey often acted like her father, who had been an alcoholic, and that his grandiose blather was a product of the bottle. But growing up with her alcoholic father made it easier for her to accommodate Dickey's excesses. Daniell also recognized that she was entrapped in a situation hallowed by Southern tradition. She was the credulous belle sitting at the feet of the chivalric, yarn-spinning good ol' boy. Custom forebade her to question or rebuke. Years later she tried to put her affair in perspective: "When it comes to his macho image, a certain kind of Southern man has, or pretends to have, a hard time separating fact from fantasy. And woe betide the woman who breaks the charm—and *her* charm—by acting skeptical during the telling. The fun comes in the gullibility of the listener, in the widening mascaraed lashes, the open little-girl mouth. Southern men, I was learning, meant Southern lies, especially lies about personal intention, marital status, genealogy, money, and achievement. Sentimentality, about himself, even his fantasies of himself, is the hall-mark of the grass-roots Southern-male mind."[14] Reading this dissection of his love affair and his personality in *Fatal Flowers*, Dickey was predictably incensed.

Dickey considered his philandering and fictionalizing harmless play, but Daniell began to pay a price for going along with it. Her marriage foundered be-cause her husband discovered her infidelities. Despite her promise not to see Dickey again, she wrote him a seven-page letter about her poetry and the work-shop on February 4, 1963. During the summer of 1964, after Dickey had re-turned to Atlanta, Daniell received a phone call from someone she was sure was Dickey (he disguised his voice, as he often did on the phone). In a threatening tone he said: "I'm coming over to get you."[15] Although nobody came, she was so frightened that she told her sons to lock the doors of her house. In 1967, Daniell met Dickey face-to-face to discuss an *Atlanta* magazine article to be entitled "Surrealist of the South" (in the interview Dickey expressed his love for his fam-ily, but added: "Illicit love is more important. For it gives the continual renewal of the spirit that can't be found in daily life").[16] Around this time, Dickey sought to renew his spirit in a steamy tryst with Daniell in New York's Gotham Hotel. She dressed for the occasion in a red leatherette minidress with a motorcyle belt, red high-heeled sandals, gold lamé hose, and gardenia perfume. About to appear on *The Today Show*, Dickey was in a festive mood. He practiced his Marlon Brando impersonation and, as they rode up the elevator, nibbled her ear.

Daniell had proposed in the cab to the hotel that Dickey divorce Maxine and marry her. Dickey was amused as a father might be by a wily daughter. "Yew jes' save your pennies, bebe, so yew kin come visit Daddy!" he retorted. He wasn't amused, however, when she came to his room fifteen minutes late the following night. As she remembered it: "He lurched from the bed and slapped me across the cheek. 'Thuh doctor says I'm dyin' of di'bee-tees!'—it was the first I had heard of it—'and hyah yew are, runnin' around with other men!' I burst into tears, grabbing my purse to leave as he pushed me down to the wrinkled sheets— 'A li'l spirit, jes' whut I lak!'—struggling with the intricacies of the nude body suit I had put on beneath my princess dress. . . . My lover, I was beginning to learn, liked not only reluctance, but humiliation, even fear. I knew his passion for hunting deer in North Georgia with razor-tipped arrows; now I recalled how he had told me in his other, literary voice—that 'the deer love to be hunted.'" The next morning Dickey kissed his doelike mistress theatrically, then waved good-bye as the television people whisked him away to their studio. "I felt like a whore,"[17] Daniell concluded.

Her humiliation and anger notwithstanding, Daniell continued to seek out Dickey. One morning in 1968, after he had guzzled three beers at a student hang-out near Georgia Tech called the Yellow Jacket, he told her in all seriousness: "I was thinking of running for president, but I decided against it."[18] His recent as-sociations with Eugene McCarthy and other politicians in Washington had fanned his presidential ambitions. She tried to bring him back to reality by talk-ing about her troubled son, but he showed no interest. Daniell crossed paths with Dickey again at an Atlanta 2000 Conference in November 1977. Dickey was scheduled to appear with the African-American writer Pearl Cleage and Daniell, but *after* them. Claude Terry, who was in charge of an environmental task force at the conference, heard a drunken Dickey angrily decry the "nigger woman and damn pornographer"[19] who preceded him. Daniell laughed off Dickey's comments and went ahead with her reading. Cleage refused to read because the Capitol City Club, which had organized a reception for the writers, did not admit African-Americans. After Daniell finished her reading, many in the audience left their seats to stretch. Daniell assured Dickey that they would return for his reading. "That's not why they're leaving,"[20] he remarked sarcastically, implying that her feminist poetry had driven them from the room. To show his disgust, he flopped down in his chair and soon began snoring.

In 1961, near the end of his tenure as Daniell's workshop director, Dickey invited Robert Bly to spend Thanksgiving in Atlanta. On their drive to the family home at West Wesley, Dickey spoke about literary matters with his usual verve. In the house, he slumped into his chair and said: "This is how I am when I have to spend time with my family."[21] He hardly said another word until he left the house and began describing his father's fighting cocks and where his father used to go for cockfights. Dickey said that he had fighting cocks, as well, and recently had bought one that was superior to the others. He told Bly that it was against the law to let cocks fight in the Atlanta area, but, like his father, he no longer cared about the law. Continuing to boast about his newest acquisition, Dickey fetched his bird from its pen and threw it into the ring with the others. To Bly's amazement and Dickey's chagrin, the highly touted fighter turned and ran. If Bly needed reasons to doubt Dickey's stories, he now had one.

During Bly's stay, Dickey arranged a cocktail party to which he invited numerous Atlanta friends. At the party Bly captured everyone's attention with a dramatic reading of Neruda's famous poem "Walking Around." Bly's passion for Neruda and the Austrian surrealist Georg Trakl was so strong that Dickey remarked in a letter to Donald Hall: "His wife is going to have a baby, and won't *that* be something! He'll be raised on the mother's milk of Neruda and Trakl!"[22] Bly may have chosen the particular poem because of its relevance to Dickey's recent complaints (Dickey was also a great fan of Neruda). In "Walking Around," Neruda hopes for an escape from the same sort of domestic and commercial situation that Dickey found so numbing. Dickey was not to be upstaged by Bly. In a conversation with Bly and Braselton, he quoted from memory a long passage from André Gide's *Journal*. Wondering if he was bluffing, Bly located the book in the G section of Dickey's vast library, opened it to the relevant passage, and confirmed Dickey's accuracy. An incredulous Braselton took the book from Bly and made a similar check. Like so many others who listened to Dickey recite the authors he revered, his two friends concluded that he had a photographic memory.

Soon after Bly's visit, the Dickeys began preparing for their return to Europe. Long trips always conjured up morbid fears in Dickey, so on February 5, 1962, three days after his thirty-ninth birthday, Dickey prayed with his family for a safe journey. On the first day they traveled to Charlottesville, where Dickey lectured on Hart Crane at the Rushton Seminars with R. W. B. Lewis. Dickey enjoyed meeting Lewis. Besides similar literary interests, Dickey and Lewis shared a military background (Lewis had served in an intelligence outfit in Italy that retrieved downed pilots and escaped prisoners in German-occupied territory). The seminars in Virginia served as a foundation for a lifelong friendship. When Lewis became a Yale English professor and Pulitzer Prize–winning biographer of Edith Wharton, he often socialized with Dickey at the National Institute of Arts and Letters, at Dickey's birthday symposiums in South Carolina, and at Yale.

As on their previous journey to Europe, the Dickeys stayed in New York before embarking. Using the Bristol Hotel as headquarters, they visited the Wintons and Wheelocks. Dickey also had the honor of introducing the poet e. e. cummings at the Poetry Center (cummings died later that year in New York). He set aside his disdain for the highly irregular way cummings scattered punctuation and words over the page, and chatted with him about Hart Crane and other writers. Before boarding the luxury liner, SS *France,* Dickey also got together with James Merrill, who hoped that they could reunite in Athens, Greece. Bidding farewell to his assorted friends, on February 13 Dickey watched the New York skyline recede behind the gray waters of Long Island Sound. The cold, stormy weather on the Atlantic made many of the passengers and most of the Dickeys seasick. Seemingly immune to the rough seas, Dickey took advantage of the abundant good food and wine. He also socialized with the other passengers, including James Jones, whose World War II novel *From Here to Eternity* had appeared in 1951. Five days after leaving New York, the *France* docked at Southampton, England, and the next day it crossed the English Channel, depositing the Dickeys in Le Havre, France, where Allied troops had invaded during World War II.

Although the Joyces and Pounds and Hemingways had left Paris decades earlier, for Dickey the city was still a vital literary center. His favorite bookshop was one Lester Mansfield had introduced him to on his previous trip: Le Pont Traversé—"The Crossbridge"—on a little back street off Saint Germain. Here he spent hours practicing his French with the owner, Marcel Béalu, an old poet who knew many of the local writers (Dickey later translated some of Béalu's poetry and submitted it to *The Sixties*). Dickey caught up on news about his favorite older poets and learned what new poets to read, while Maxine, who had the flu, took the children to cartoon movies and the Jardin des Plantes zoo. Nevertheless, the Dickeys felt the same disillusionment with Paris that had afflicted them on their last visits. Staying in the same hotel near the Place Saint Michel, they didn't recognize anyone. Because of troubles in Algeria, bombings and assassinations were commonplace in the city. Gendarmes strolled through the popular tourist sites with machine guns. Two days after arriving in Paris, the strain of travel precipitated a violent quarrel between Dickey and Maxine. Matters were made worse when Chris contracted a bad cold and Kevin got sick as well.

To make traveling easier, the Dickeys bought a car—a big, rambling VW bus for twenty-five hundred dollars—and drove to Antibes to escape the expensive, inhospitable city. Here, too, everything had changed. "You cannot go back,"[23] Dickey gloomily concluded, and continued his search for a suitable residence in Aix-en-Provence and Cannes before negotiating the rain-slicked roads along the Italian coast and heading inland to Florence on February 28. At first disappointed to find their former *pensione* under new management, they finally tracked down Signora Carmaratta at her new location. As the weather improved, so did Chris and Kevin's health, but then Dickey got a cold. Nonetheless, he felt well enough to visit the Uffizi Gallery on March 3, as well as the other museums, churches, and public squares he adored. He went to see the statue of Perseus and Medusa and Michelangelo's "Giuliano de' Medici," and even touched Botticelli's "The Birth of Venus." Dickey pointed out the splendors of Florence to his two sons, who were ten and three. In mid-March he packed them into the VW bus for a trip to Rome.

Their stops along the way—at Siena, Perugia, Assisi, Gubbio, and Losanna—were fraught with disasters or near disasters. On March 14, Perugia was so cold that the water in the fountains froze. As the Dickeys were on the way to Assisi, snow forced them to abandon their car. Upon reaching Gubbio on March 17, Dickey decided to abandon the car again and take a ski lift to a restaurant on a mountain peak. The ride over the snow in the open, oil-drumlike gondolas was frightening, especially for Kevin and Chris. Following a meal of spaghetti Bolognese at the high-altitude restaurant, Maxine boarded the ski lift, Chris got in a separate car behind her, and Kevin, who was supposed to accompany his father, jumped into a car but failed to shut the door. Worried that his three-year-old son might tumble to the valley below in a sudden wind gust, Dickey pushed aside the ticket collector, who refused to stop the lift, sprinted toward Kevin, and leapt from the cliff just as the car climbed into the air. Even though he had consumed a bottle of Chianti with Maxine at lunch, he somehow landed beside his son. "After that moment of stupid risk and ferocious bravery at Gubbio," Chris recounted, "all our luck, our travels, our time together seemed better than ever, at least for as long as that spring and summer lasted."[24]

The Dickeys' next stop was a quiet, friendly *pensione* near the Piazza del Popolo and the Borghese Gardens in Rome. As in 1955, the Dickeys looked forward to the ceremonies preceding Easter. They visited the Vatican Museum, toured the pope's private chapel, and watched the pope's consecration of a new cardinal. The Catholic Church, anachronistic as it was for Dickey, enchanted him with its majestic architecture and rituals. When a messenger on March 25 brought an invitation for a special meeting with the pope, Dickey accepted without hesitation. He also brought his family to the Forum, where he took mordant pleasure in standing on the spot where Julius Caesar had been stabbed to death. Always curious about the sex lives of celebrities, Dickey avidly collected local gossip about the torrid affair between the actors Elizabeth Taylor and Richard Burton, who were in Rome filming *Cleopatra*. He also sought out the expatriate literary community, socializing with the well-known critic and poet R. P. Blackmur and the future *Newsweek* writer Walter Clemons, who played the piano in a nightclub called Bricktop's. Dickey maintained that one night at the club he saw the two shadowy figures of Burton and Taylor together in a corner.

The Dickeys left Rome for Naples and Sorrento, and on a rainy April 6 drove up a winding road to the fishing village of Positano, which Richard Wilbur had recommended on their last trip to Europe. They wandered the streets past old, black-skirted women, who sat on the steps of light green and light blue houses, and entertained the vague notion of settling there, even though their original plan was to travel to the tip of the Italian boot and take a ferry to Sicily, which promised to be cheaper than the mainland. With Maxine's uncanny ability to locate bargain-rate living quarters and the help of a local *pensione* owner, they found a small house in the working-class section of town. It had a living room, kitchen, downstairs bathroom, and a large upstairs bedroom with a balcony. The reasonable rent—seventy-two dollars per month—as well as the splendid view of the Mediterranean from the balcony convinced them to sign a lease for several months. Although Dickey continued to complain to friends of the dire state of his finances, with a recent check from his parents he hired the sixteen-year-old daughter of their landlords, Laura, as a full-time maid, babysitter, and cook for the duration of their stay. To requisition more funds from his parents, Dickey pretended that his family was near starvation. On June 9, he wrote his father: "We are paying for food like mad, and at one point were eating one (slim) meal a day."[25] They had no shortage of food in their new home at 13 Via Boscariello, Positano.

From the cliff on which the town perched, Dickey liked to watch the fishermen—some had fingers blown off from fishing with dynamite after World War II—mending their nets and lugging them down stone steps to the shore. He also watched a rugged, tanned, long-haired man with tattoos named Casey Deiss and his red-haired friend climb the cliffs, which Dickey estimated to be seven hundred feet high. Dickey was amazed that they didn't use ropes or pitons. "Here come Jesus and Judas,"[26] he liked to say when they approached. The beach below, like many others in that part of the Mediterranean, was composed mainly of small pebbles that the multicolored fishing boats spewed with oil. The local pollution, however, did little to dampen the Dickeys' enthusiasm for the beach; they picnicked, swam, and went skin-diving. At night they were regulars at the pizzeria-nightclub Buca di Bacco ("The Cave of Bacchus"). Some of the locals even invited Dickey to give a poetry reading, which was a great success and followed by a number of wild parties. "It was the most intense period of our life as a family and probably in . . . [my father's] life as a poet,"[27] Chris recalled.

Some of Dickey's celebratory mood derived from a job offer he had received from Reed College in Oregon. Reed poet and English professor Kenneth Hanson explained on April 19 that Dickey's responsibilities would be minimal. He would only have to teach one class of fifteen to twenty students for three hours each week. Hanson urged Dickey to teach a creative writing class one semester and a modern poetry class the next. Dickey ultimately agreed and kept to this alternating format most of his teaching life. The salary was a fraction of his advertising salary—$5,000 with a $400 travel allowance—but if Dickey wanted to teach an additional class each term, he could earn $7,500. Shortly after Hanson's offer arrived, Reed president Richard Sullivan informed Dickey that Donald Justice had agreed to teach in the 1962 fall semester so that Dickey could continue his Guggenheim travels until the end of the year. Dickey could begin in the winter of 1963 and finish his residency at the end of the 1963–64 academic year. Sullivan promised a more generous stipend than Hanson: $3,750 for the first term and $8,000 for the following year. He would have a dual rank—assistant professor and poet-in-residence—and teach the two courses Hanson had described. Dickey warmed to the idea of being a poet-in-residence, and for the rest of his life claimed that he was the first to hold the post at Reed.

Three months of traveling over sea and land convinced Dickey he needed to settle in one place, get in shape, and resume writing. In Positano, he jogged up the hundreds of stairs from the beach and honed his muscles with isometric exercises. Or he simply walked the streets, which smelled pungently of wisteria and sea salt. He had promised James Merrill to visit him in Athens, but a one-way ticket on a car ferry to Greece cost $200. On April 16, he wrote Merrill: "Prices are so terribly much higher than they were when we were here before, and our money has just *fled*, especially in Paris, Florence, and Rome, all places we wanted to see once more. We couldn't swing the trip to Greece, though we very much wanted to. But what with the cost of shipping the Volks bus across and all the sea-travel expenses we couldn't do it to save our lives [the original round-trip boat fare to Europe had cost $1,855]. So we came down here to Positano where we have rented a small (very small) villa so that I can dig in and try to make some money to keep us over here until September. I'm really going to have to hump it, too."[28] Merrill, who routinely went to Greece to write, replied on April 26 that he was sorry the Dickeys wouldn't be able to visit him. He also congratulated Dickey on his new book, *Drowning with Others*, which Wesleyan had published on February 15, singling out "Between Two Prisoners" and "The Owl King" for particular praise.

Because *Deliverance* became a bestseller, Dickey could not resist mythologizing its inception in Positano. He said he had eaten a large Italian meal and gone to his room for a nap:

> I was lying in bed in the full of the spring afternoon sun, and, characteristically, I suppose, I began to think of America, and of the part of it that means the most to me, the mountains and rivers of northern Georgia. I had been canoeing and bow-hunting many times there, and I lay in the sun of Italy with some of the feeling of fear and promise that those trips had always raised in me. Why this strange, familiar sensation? I wondered. Every time I think about that wild country I have it. And then a possible answer occurred to me. A man is vulnerable in that kind of terrain; he is unprotected by any of the laws of what we are pleased to call civilization. A snake can bite him, for example, and, if he gets a lethal dosage, he will almost certainly die before medical aid could reach him, or he it. Almost anything could happen to him, or be done to him. And he as well could do pretty much whatever he wished, or felt compelled to do, or had to do. Considering the increasing violence of life in America, the emphasis on it in the public and private mind as well as the very real *fact* of it, I thought I might find a way to make this sense of isolation, fear, and promise that the wilderness engenders into some kind of dramatic situation which would bring all these elements together in an action.[29]

To another interviewer, Dickey elaborated: "I had never written any stories or novels or anything like that before, but it occurred to me that it might just work out fine. So I got up from bed, reluctantly, because I was so sleepy, and I made a few notes—I'd say half a page in longhand—and went back to sleep contented. And that was the beginning. I mean I knew the whole story in five minutes . . . or maybe even one minute."[30] The general plot may have struck the drowsy bard like a revelation, the way the entire "Kubla Khan" had appeared to Coleridge in an opium dream, but the novel's gestation was more complicated than Dickey implied.

Dickey also liked to say that the plot for *Deliverance* originated from the single image of a man with a rifle gazing down at a river from a cliff. As he wondered what the man was doing there, the novel suddenly came to him. The formative image was inspired in part by Casey and his friend on the Positano cliff, as was the rock-climbing scene near the novel's end. The proximity of the novelist John Steinbeck, who had an apartment near the Buca di Bacco, also may have contributed to Dickey's renewed interest in fiction. Steinbeck, who was in Positano for two weeks, sometimes talked to Dickey about books and events in America. The mythical and emotional lineaments of *Deliverance*—its "deep structure"—however, originated from an array of sources scattered over several decades: from Dickey's reading of Zane Grey, Edgar Rice Burroughs, and similar adventure writers in childhood; from his cockfighting trips to North Georgia with his father as a teenager; from his confrontations with violence, homosexuality, and death on the Pacific Islands during World War II; from his reading of Melville, Twain, Conrad, Joyce, Eliot, Hemingway, Paul Bowles (he cited Bowles's *The Sheltering Sky* as one model), and other novelists during and after the war; from his intensive study of anthropology, psychology, and mythology; from his frustrations in marriage and the advertising business; and from his canoe trips with King and Braselton. Even Milton, the poet he loved to ridicule as a stuffed goat, provided a model. When the four canoers plummet down waterfalls near the end, according to Dickey, they do so in imitation of Satan hurtling through Chaos in *Paradise Lost*.

Like Coleridge, whose explanation of "Kubla Khan"'s genesis was probably more fancy than fact, Dickey donned the mantle of the romantic genius in his claims about conceiving *Deliverance* in a few minutes. To a reporter for Charleston's *News and Courier* he repeated his claim: "It's the first plot I ever came up with."[31] In fact, by the time he gave this interview in 1979, he had made notes for dozens of stories and novels in his journals, written several unpublished stories and one unpublished novel, and composed a good deal of *Alnilam*. He had already discussed the general idea for *Deliverance* with Joseph Sokolewicz during the Korean War, and around 1960 he had confided to Inman Mays that he was writing a novel about what happened when three or four average Atlanta businessmen met some violent redneck mountain men in the wilds of North Georgia.

Dickey loved Positano and found he could work well upstairs in their small house while the children played downstairs. Several events, however, spoiled his paradisiacal writing conditions. First, Kevin took a bad fall while descending the hundreds of steps to the beach. He needed medical attention for a badly cut lip and nose. In early June, Kevin also succumbed to a mysterious infection that a local doctor thought was in his stomach or throat. Dehydrated and feverish, he responded poorly to the doctor's medicines. Partly because of doctors' bills—Chris and Maxine also got sick—Dickey continued to worry about finances. He pestered Robert Bly about paying him for recent poems he had sent *The Sixties*, including translations of poems by André Frénaud, Salvatore Quasimodo, and

Giuseppe Ungaretti, and on June 30 he blasted Bly for denigrating the *New Yorker*:

> About the *New Yorker:* I know well your feelings about it. Now know mine: The *New Yorker* has sustained life in my family for well over a year now; they have lent or given me money when I needed it most, and they have printed the best things I have written. I don't share your contempt for money (that is, for other people's earning money); I am not that pure. Don't talk to me about "kissing their rump": that kind of talk you can get away with with other people; not with me. You're not all that good a friend of mine; nobody is. . . . I am interested in letting you know just what bounds there are in my regard for you; they are wide, necessarily; if you understand that they do not include remarks of the kind you see fit to make on occasion. I'm sorry, truly, if I seem like an ill-tempered son-of-a-bitch, which I may well be and definitely am a good deal of the time.[32]

Dickey tried to assuage the sting of his harangue by saying that he hoped to see Bly again in New York. He even hoped Bly could somehow join him in Venice. Bly, who knew how much money Dickey had been making in advertising, must have laughed at Dickey's claim that the *New Yorker* had been sustaining his family for over a year. From early 1960 to June 30, 1962, Dickey had published nine poems in the magazine.

Sloughing off his monetary worries, Dickey took his family on numerous side trips away from Positano. On a visit to Pompeii on April 26, he joined the English writer of children's books Mary Norton, who was vacationing in Positano with her granddaughter, Charlotte. In late June, he drove to Naples and Rome before meandering through Tuscany to Venice, where, with the help of his parents' checks, he could afford to put his family up at the expensive San Marco Hotel and buy a new guitar. These indulgences convinced him, once again, that he was all but destitute. "We've been camping ever since we left Venice, occasionally checking into a cheap hotel to take a bath,"[33] he wrote Bly on June 30. They did do some camping, first at Innsbruck on July 4, but they never roughed it to the extent Dickey suggested.

Dickey had every reason to feel gratified by the progress he had made in Positano. He had mapped out the novel he was calling *The Deliverer*, and he had completed many of the poems he would publish in *Helmets*. To James Wright he summed up his sojourn by the sea with Hemingwayesque lyricism:

> My family and I have [had] . . . a wild, soaring release from the endless nightmare of business, with its "inexorable sadness of pencils." We lived for several months in a little fishing village on the South Coast of the Salerno Peninsula in Italy, where everything was stairs up and down and the sun coming into your brain and turning it as blue and vast as the sea. It was beautiful there, and I used to go out with the night fishers and dive for squid all night, and come back and walk through the little town at daylight, still drunk with the black part of the water, the cold, deep part, and then go to bed and get up in the afternoon, write a little, have a drink

with . . . the hairdresser who is also an octopus-fisher, and then go down to the docks again to wait for Nicola's boat, and get everything ready to go again. It was great, but when tourists began to come in, we left, and have been travelling and camping ever since, round Rome and Florence, then Cortina up in the mountains, then Innsbruck and Salzburg, where I bought the greatest guitar ever made, and for just thirty-four dollars, then to Munich and Augsburg, and finally to Paris.[34]

Dickey's nostalgia for Positano made anything—even all-night squid fishing—possible.

In July the Dickeys headed for Zurich to rendezvous with Gwen Leege Walti and her husband. Dickey looked forward to visiting his old love in her palatial house. Maxine, by contrast, hoped to avoid her. On March 6, 1962, Gwen had written Dickey in Florence, welcoming him to Europe with a mild rebuke for what he had said in 1946 about her return to the country of the enemy. Celebrating their reunion in a restaurant overlooking Zurich, they put their romantic peccadillos behind them. Even Maxine, according to her husband, enjoyed the occasion: "[When] we put the . . . luggage back up on the bus, getting ready to leave, my wife turned to me and said, 'Jim, I wish you had an ex-fiancée in every city in Europe!' I said, 'Alas, darling, this is the only one and we are leaving her!'"[35] Following an exchange of gifts (Dickey gave Gwen and her husband, Rudi, signed copies of his two poetry books), the Waltis wished them "bon voyage." In a letter written three weeks later, Gwen characterized the Dickeys' visit in her usual flowery prose, denying that words could do justice to it and praising each of the Dickeys for their dignity and grace.

About two weeks after leaving Zurich, Dickey received what turned out to be one of the most significant letters of his career. Having just read Dickey's poem "Springer Mountain" in the summer 1962 issue of the *Virginia Quarterly Review* (Dickey heard on April 11 that the journal had awarded him the second-place Balch Prize for the poem), Theron Raines contacted him about serving as his literary agent. Raines admired the way Dickey combined narrative and lyric modes in his descriptions of a bow-and-arrow hunter who conjures up an image of a deer—he cannot find a real one to shoot—and, in order to commune more intimately with his imaginary deer, strips off his four sweaters, dungarees, and even his boots and socks. Somewhat like King Lear, Dickey's persona goes to exorbitant lengths to expose the bare, forked animal beneath his civilized vestments. In the letter he asked the *Virginia Quarterly* editors to forward, Raines wondered if Dickey had given any thought to writing a novel. Dickey quickly responded to Raines about *The Deliverer*. Because he thought Dickey was a worthy prospect for the literary agency he had recently started, Raines wrote again on August 10: "I would be much interested in reading your book or any portion of it whenever you have something ready to show."[36] Dickey kept the offer in mind.

Dickey told different stories about the way "Springer Mountain" found him an agent and publisher for his novel. In the mid-1970s he explained to a San Francisco interviewer: "The people who work for publishing houses are like sharks; they're constantly maneuvering to find out where the meat is; they read the literary magazines, they're constantly just under the surface of the water, maneuvering around. So I published a suite of poems in the *Virginia Quarterly Review*, and they read the contributors' items, trying always to get a line on some new guy who might write 'em a bestseller. And they read that James Dickey, author of the prize-winning poem 'Springer Mountain' is now living in Italy working on a novel." According to Dickey, one of Houghton Mifflin's sharkish editors said: " 'This novel you call *Deliverance*, I managed to decipher it. Let's talk about a modest advance.' So we agreed on $5,000, which was modest indeed but seemed large at the time."[37] In fact, there was only one poem in his *Virginia Quarterly* "suite," and the contributors' notes said nothing about his novel. Dickey did not garner any sort of contract or advance for *The Deliverer* until he traveled to New York for several poetry events in late January 1964. At that time he signed an option agreement stipulating that he would give Houghton Mifflin first offer of publication rights after he finished revising his manuscript. For the option Houghton Mifflin paid a measley $250. (This was certainly better than the royalties Dickey collected for *Into the Stone* in 1962; Scribner's had sold only thirty-nine copies and sent him a check for $5.13.) Embarrassed by the option agreement, Dickey redressed the low fee with suitable exaggerations.

Because a charter plane full of Atlanta tourists crashed while taking off from Paris's Orly Airport near the end of spring (106 Atlantans died), Dickey reassured friends that he was still alive and busy contacting expatriate poets and editors in Paris. On July 24, he asked Wesleyan University Press to send him the address of John Ashbery, who was then living in Paris and writing art criticism for *Art News* and the European edition of the *Herald Tribune*. Although Ashbery's poetry was more abstract than Dickey's, they shared a publisher (Wesleyan had published *The Tennis Court Oath* in 1962) and a passion for avant-garde French poets like Pierre Reverdy. Before he could visit Ashbery at 16 rue d'Assas, however, Dickey had to leave for England. On August 2, he had better luck with Patrick Bowles, the Paris editor of the *Paris Review*. He dined with Bowles, and then wrote Bly that the *Paris Review* might serve as a clearinghouse for Bly's many translations. Despite his love for French poetry, Dickey continued to feel ill-at-ease among Parisian poets. He wasn't "beatniky enough,"[38] he told James Wright in July. Maxine also felt out of place. She explored the Eiffel Tower (which scared her as well as her husband), the Louvre, and the Luxembourg Gardens, but was tired of sight-seeing. In early August, having met Les Mansfield and his girlfriend, Malou, for drinks and gone to a nightclub, Maxine wrote in her diary: "I can't wait to leave."[39] On August 5, the Dickeys drove through Flanders to Calais and boarded a ferry for England. The next day they unpacked their bags in a hotel in Earl's Court, where they decided to stay until September 6. Maxine shopped at Harrods and took the children to movies. Dickey returned to his poetry and revisited local poets like Stephen Spender, who had invited him to read on the BBC Third Programme. On one of his walks along Regent Street he passed a newspaper stand and saw a headline announcing the death of Marilyn Monroe (she had died on August 5). He liked to tell people afterward that he suddenly remembered a couplet from Alexander's Pope's "Epistle II: To a Lady" about those "Who purchase pain with all that joy can give / And die of nothing but a rage to live." In a 1989 commencement address at Oglethorpe University, he said the couplet was "the perfect expression of Marilyn Monroe's meaning, her existence and her death, and the pleasure oriented, excessive and sterile culture that created her and destroyed her."[40] Dickey also found the couplet relevant to his own excesses and paradoxes.

Happier news arrived on August 7 in a letter from Donald Hall about the poetry manuscript Dickey wanted to call *Springer Mountain*. Somewhat startled to hear that Dickey had enough poems for another book so soon after the publication of *Drowning with Others*, Hall nevertheless admired the new work. With regard to his trip through England, Hall encouraged Dickey to see their mutual friend Geoffrey Hill. Dickey worried about meeting the poet he so esteemed, but Hall assured Dickey that Hill, despite his quirks, was a gentle soul, and he passed along his address in Leeds. During the latter part of August, the Dickeys drove southwest from London to Winchester, Stonehenge, and Lyme Regis and then north through Wales to Leeds, where on August 17 they visited Hill. Dickey marveled at Hill's house and grounds and wondered why he suffered so amid such grandeur. Several days later, Dickey wrote Robert Bly: "My God, what a strange one! What a talent for making himself unhappy in public! But we got on well together despite everything, and had a wonderful time. Remind me to tell you, some time, of our visit to the Jewish hospital to get his stomach x-rayed!"[41] To ascertain what was ailing Hill's stomach, Dickey had gone to a local hospital where Hill had supposedly said about being x-rayed: "I really don't like these kinds of things, but I must confess I do get some sort of dreadful masochistic pleasure out of it."[42] Maxine concurred with her husband's assessment of Hill. After dining with him and his wife, Nancy, she commented tersely in her diary: "Geoffrey a pill."[43]

Dickey and Hill got into a fierce argument, but then Hill implored him to extend his stay. Dickey wrote Hall:

> We did stay another day, and disagreed violently, and agreed even *more* violently (and when Geoffrey agrees with anyone, the sun comes out all over England, a thing which, as you know, it rarely does). He showed me some new stuff he has done with his *wonderful* (by which I mean incredible, stupendous, Ezekiel-saw-the-wheel-in-the-air stuff, and I mean, as the Bible says, in the *middle* of the air . . .). His worst tendency is to go cold and dead and academic, making poems which are just exercises and complicated explanations of what he's talking about, and which have no *reality* to them, no urgency, no nothing but the trimmed bones of discourse. Wait'll you see these *new* ones! My God![44]

Hill had published *For the Unfallen* in 1958, and was now working on a series of baroque meditations on historical atrocities—from the Wars of the Roses to the Nazi Holocaust—that he would include in his next book, *King Log*. Because Dickey judged Hill to be one of the most important post–World War II English poets, he did his best to excuse his rebarbative ways.

On August 19, the Dickeys left the industrial city of Leeds for the rolling, green mountains of the Lake Country, then turned north to Scotland, where they visited Sterling Castle, Oban, Inverness, and Edinburgh. They passed by Loch Ness, where Dickey, hoping to see the fabled monster, was disappointed by his family's unwillingness to camp by the shore. On August 26, they returned to London. Dickey went on a last book-buying spree with Les Mansfield, who had arrived from Paris, and also paid a poetically significant visit to the Regent's Park Zoo. Maxine commented in her August 30 diary entry: "Black panther didn't like Jim. Cheetahs didn't like boys." Chris had first noticed the panther, who had dropped a bloody piece of meat in his cage. Dickey caught the panther's gaze, walked back and forth, and was amazed that the animal followed his every move. A crowd gathered to watch the strange tête-à-tête. Dickey's mesmerizing encounter with the panther became the source for one of his favorite perform-ance poems, "Encounter in the Cage Country." In *Self-Interviews* Dickey gave a discombobulated account of the poem's origin, claiming that he had broken away from his family for the day because he couldn't stand any more sight-seeing: "I went to a pub and started drinking and talking to whoever came in. I left the pub in the middle of the afternoon. I had a check from *The New Yorker* or *The Atlantic* [*Monthly*] in my pocket, and I got the 'buying fever.' . . . I went into a surplus house and bought a pair of American dark glasses, the California type. I started walking around London, and I thought someone would mistake me for Marcello Mastroianni. I'd been drinking for five hours, or I'd've had no such il-lusions!" Dickey found himself in the London Zoo among ostriches, elephants, and rhinoceroses: "Finally I went into the cat house, or perhaps I should say the 'feline enclosure.' I walked over to the lion's cage and tried to relate to him. But he wouldn't give me the time of day. So I walked down past the ocelots, jaguars, and tigers, until I came to the black leopard's cage. . . . He dropped the meat he was chewing and came over to the edge of the cage as though to say to me, 'Where have you been? Did you bring it?' . . . To this day I don't know what he saw in me, whether it was my dark glasses, the way I dressed, the fact that I was an American, or my *soul*. But it was instant recognition on his part. He was ter-ribly interested and very patient with me."[45] The trip to the zoo was a family out-ing (Kevin and Chris rode camels there) rather than a solitary one where the drunken poet communed with a bestial alter ego.

Early in September, the Dickeys boarded the SS *France* in Southampton and embarked for the States. His arrival in New York on September 12 may have re-minded Dickey of Robert Frost's triumphant return from England in 1915. Both were about the same age, both had published two books, and both had estab-lished reputations as gifted poets while they were abroad. A month after his re-turn Dickey heard from his publisher, Willard Lockwood, that *Drowning with Others* had been nominated for a National Book Award. More good news came in mid-November from the English poet and editor Michael Hamburger, who recommended that Longmans publish the book. Frost's close friend Louis Untermeyer recommended *Drowning with Others* to the Pulitzer Prize Committee. Partly because his anthologies had played such a significant role in introducing Dickey to poetry, Untermeyer's praise came as an especially wel-come surprise, even though Dickey received it several years after it was submitted to the Pulitzer judges: "This, a thoroughly 'seasoned' book, is far and away above most of the books of poetry published during the year. It is as imaginative as it is ingenious; it is penetrating without being pretentious; it is, as Robert Frost maintained that poetry should be, both playful and profound. Technically Dickey owes little, if anything, to anyone. Scorning intellectual obfuscations, his thoughts are cleanly shaped and clearly communicated. He is not only one of the best of the so-called younger poets but unquestionably the best of the Wesleyan crop."[46] Although *Drowning with Others* failed to win any of the major awards, the fact that it came close gave Dickey's confidence a quantum boost.

Technically, Dickey owed a great deal to a great many, but he had absorbed his influences and alchemized them into something new and strange and enchanting. Because he saw himself as a redeemer or "deliverer," and often acted accordingly, he repeatedly explored such themes as salvation, apocalypse, and communion with others (especially animals). One of the most successful poems in the collection, "The Lifeguard," showed how Dylan Thomas continued to act as a beneficial model. Dickey may have been recalling "The Boat House" on the southern coast of Wales where Thomas lived near the end of his life, as well as Thomas's conception of the poet as a latter-day Christ redeeming a fallen world. Dickey wrote in *Self-Interviews* that the poem also grew from personal life-saving experiences: "I did once help dive for a drowned man in a lake where there was public swimming, and I remember going down ten or twelve feet where everything is blacked out. We didn't have any lights and all we could do was to *grope* around for the body. My fingertips *did* turn into stone, and it *was* awfully cold. There was very little chance that I or anyone else could find the body under those conditions. . . . I was the father of two young boys in those years and was acutely conscious of the protection motif in the human situation."[47] Dickey often posed as a lifeguard, telling friends that during high school he had worked at Atlanta's Venetian swimming pool. He told others, like Chancellor Francis Borkowski of Appalachian State University, that he had also lifeguarded in Florida. To his sons (perhaps because Kevin *did* work as a lifeguard) he was more specific; he asserted that in college he had lifeguarded near his father-in-law's apartment in Clearwater, Florida. His best high school friend, Bill Barnwell, and his college friends, however, remembered no such lifeguarding jobs.

In "The Lifeguard," Dickey represents himself as a failed lifeguard who, following the pattern of his other heroes, compensates for his failure by imagining success. At first he assumes the persona of a Christ-like savior:

I rise and go out through the boats.
I set my broad sole upon silver,
On the skin of the sky, on the moonlight,
Stepping outward from earth onto water
In quest of the miracle

This village of children believed
That I could perform as I dived
For one who had sunk from my sight.

The moonlit fantasy of walking on water to save the child, in the end, comes to nothing. Haunted by the loss of the child and his inability to perform a miracle for his young audience, the lifeguard imagines the voice of the dead child calling from the lake, and even imagines holding the child by his grave:

> I call softly out, and the child's
> Voice answers through blinding water.
> Patiently, slowly,
>
> He rises, dilating to break
> The surface of stone with his forehead.

The pathos in "The Lifeguard" issues from the sad realization that the Orpheus-like poet can only accomplish his miraculous feats in his imagination—with his voice and vision. As in so many of Thomas's poems, death denies the poet's childlike hopes. In this case, the fantasy of rescuing a drowning child merely produces "a child / Of water, water, water."[48]

With his own children, Dickey often played the role of savior, whether it involved jumping onto ski-lift cars or buying gifts for them when they fell ill. In *Drowning with Others*, Dickey also drew on his hunting experiences to illustrate the paradoxical relation between actual failures and imaginary successes. In "The Salt Marsh," which depicts the fields of tall marsh grass on the Georgia coast where he sometimes hunted, Dickey presents himself, not as a self-assured bowman slaying his quarry at will, but as a lost suburbanite struggling to grow accustomed to nature's terrors. In "Listening to Foxhounds," he constructs a fable based on fox-hunting methods in Appalachia, where the hounds chase the fox while their masters sit around the campfire drinking whiskey. Dickey often "hunted" in a similar fashion. Rather than tramp through snake-infested bogs and thorny brush for elusive game, he preferred telling grandiose hunting stories with a few friends over drinks by a fire. Dickey knew where his strengths lay. His mythical narratives redressed his shortcomings in language that was both vivid and marvelous, and in doing so he spoke for all who inevitably fell short of their heroic aspirations.

If his years in advertising were hell and purgatory rolled into one, Dickey imagined paradise as a wilderness playground where species hunted freely and their prey always rose from the dead. In his Liller, Neal office he wrote one of his most anthologized poems, "The Heaven of Animals," to describe this perfected natural state. His secretary supposedly typed the poem and, assuming it was advertising copy, asked: "What is it? What company does it go to?" Dickey said it was a poem, not an ad. "It is?" the secretary responded. "Yes it is, I hope," Dickey said. "What are we going to sell with it?" the secretary queried. Dickey said: "God. . . . We're going to sell God." The secretary was still befuddled: "Does this go to a religious magazine or something?" "No," Dickey said, "I'm going to publish it in *The New Yorker*."[49] Dickey was probably being more truthful when he traced the original idea for "Heaven of Animals" to Walt Disney's *The African Lion*, which he said he'd watched so many times that his children had stopped going to the movie theater with him. One scene of a leopard leaping from a tree and killing a wildebeest especially gripped him. The animals in Dickey's Eden, however, resemble the angels in Milton's heaven more than any animals in a Disney movie; they are spirits that fight, maul each other, but mend their wounds immediately: "They fall, they are torn, / They rise, they walk again."[50] In this imaginary arena, life is neither brutal nor short; it is a joyously ferocious game with no harmful consequences. To his friends' amusement or dismay, Dickey often treated his own life in the same way.

Some critics hailed Dickey in *Drowning with Others* as a leader of the "new mysticism," which prompted Dickey's quip that he didn't know anything about the old mysticism, so how could he lead the new? If Dickey was a mystic, his mysticism involved envisioning an ideal environment where he could live more naturally, where he could be at one with the animals, which for him were as much *anima* or "soul" as beast. Like Marianne Moore, who also wrote obsessively of animals, he wanted to create "imaginary gardens with real toads in them." "A Birth" begins: "Inventing a story with grass, / I find a young horse inside it."[51] The horse, Dickey insists, is real, even though it is imaginary. In "The Owl King," a poem sparked by the phrase *Le roi des hiboux* (the king of the owls) by the French poet Loys Masson, Dickey tells another fable where reality and imagination merge. He identifies with his three characters—the father who sings mysteriously and ecstatically in the dark woods, the owl king who wills his night vision "When all but my seeing had failed,"[52] and the blind child who learns to sing and see like both father and owl. Although the poem does not allude specifically to the way Dickey became a poet during World War II after being wrenched from his home, washed out as a pilot, and introduced to the dangerous art of night flying, all three characters suffer losses before inventing their poetic voices and visions. All three journey through the dark like night fighters.

The best poems in *Drowning with Others* are those in which Dickey grounds fantasy convincingly in fact. If he soars too far toward fantasy, as in "Dover: Believing in Kings" or in the title poem, "Drowning with Others," the rhetoric gets out of hand. As Philip Booth remarked, light seems to blaze from every stone, souls breathe from every mouth, the dead rise from every grave, kings walk on every wave, and awkward lines like "The sun flashed once / Or hand-shieldedly twice" hamper the lyrical flow. For the most part, however, *Drowning with Others* deserved all the critical approbation it got. Dickey had an uncanny ability for universalizing his private experiences and emotions in narratives that offered startling insights into their own genesis. His metaphors and rhythms were spellbinding even as they articulated the way poetic rhetoric grew out of its opposition to reality.

Following the laudatory reception of his second book, Dickey gave more poetry readings. Late in 1962, he appeared at the Georgia Writers' Conference, Washington University, Miami University, and the Western College for Women. Bill Pratt arranged the Miami reading for December 5 and got embroiled in the sort of financial negotiations that preceded many of Dickey's future readings. Dickey declared: "I don't believe I [can] come to speak . . . for less than a hundred and fifty or two hundred dollars. Or certainly not less than a hundred. You can understand how we travelling minstrels must strive to keep the prices up."[53] Pratt agreed to requisition the higher fee. In the end Dickey read for $150 and charmed his audience, as he so often did over the next decades. He was glad to see his Vanderbilt friend again and to meet Peter Taylor, the novelist and short story writer. Pratt had invited Taylor to read at Miami University on the same day and had driven Dickey to the Simpson Guest House on campus to introduce him to Taylor. Both writers admired each other's work, and remained loyal but distant friends for the rest of their lives.

Eugenia Buchanan, who taught at Western College and helped organize Dickey's reading there, sent a glowing report of it to his sister, Maibelle. Hinting at the provincial attitude of Dickey's siblings and parents toward his poetry as well as their disappointment over his departure from advertising, Buchanan urged them to be more supportive. He might not become a rich man as a professor and poet, she suggested, but he would enrich the world with his books. Dickey, of course, wanted to do both. In the early 1960s, his first reading contracts at the New Yorker, which were consistently renewed, helped supplement his income, and Dickey was not afraid to squeeze the magazine to his advantage. In December 1963, he argued for a substantial cost-of-living adjustment; the magazine consented to a new contract bonus. The sales of Drowning with Others also helped; its 500 hardback and 1,750 paperback copies sold out by the end of 1963. Determined to meet his family's financial expectations, before long Dickey was making more money than any other poet on the reading circuit.

17. A Southerner in Oregon (1963-1964)

Near the end of 1962, after closing the Westminster Circle house and packing luggage into both their cars, the Dickeys took to the road again. This time their destination was the West Coast. Dickey drove with Chris in the MG, which had been in storage during the European trip, and Maxine took Kevin in the VW bus. They followed a southern route toward Arizona, New Mexico, and Los Angeles before heading north along the Pacific to Reed College. The Dickeys arrived in Portland around January 7, 1963, "loaded down with guitars, manuscripts, broken toys and archery equipment" and, as he told James Wright, settled into "a rambling old barn of a place which we rented from a Political Science teacher on sabbatical."[1] The "old barn," which was located at 3807 Harold, belonged to Professor Goldschmidt, who leased it for the duration of the spring semester. During the summer the Dickeys moved into another big house in Milwaukie, a suburb in South Portland on the Willamette River.

Donald Justice had informed Dickey several months before his arrival that Reed was a unique college: its students were impressionable, young, enthusiastic, and nonconformist. Any student who walked around campus in a suit and tie would be branded an eccentric. He advised Dickey to get together with Donald MacRae, one of his friendliest colleagues, and promised to leave his mimeographed class notes to help Dickey construct syllabi for his classes, which would begin on January 14. He warned Dickey not to expect much from his creative writing students; his had been amateurish and rather pretentious. Dickey would later agree with Justice's assessment of nonconformism at Reed, but he would be pleasantly surprised by his students' abilities.

Reed was, as Justice pointed out, an offbeat institution. It recruited no students for extracurricular activities like football and discouraged athletic competition of any kind. No intercollegiate sports teams existed. On Saturday mornings someone might announce over the public address system an informal, six-man-on-a-side football game against a local Bible school. While the colleges Dickey had been familiar with—Clemson, Vanderbilt, the University of Florida—flaunted their athletic programs, from its beginning in 1910, Reed did the opposite. As for its academic regimen, it favored small classes and tutorials. It made all juniors take a full day's qualifying exam before entering the final year. In order to graduate, every senior had to write and defend a thesis, which comprised about one-quarter of the year's credits and workload. To promote knowledge for knowledge's sake, little emphasis was placed on grades. The registrar kept track of grades, but usually did not release them until graduation unless a student asked an advisor for special permission to see them. Although most colleges at the time denied men access to women's dormitories, Reed students could come and go as they pleased. Sororities and fraternities were outlawed, but there were plenty of less formal places to socialize. The burgeoning social and sexual freedoms of the sixties—without the drugs and violence—were everywhere in evidence. Dickey found the relaxed social atmosphere intoxicating. He needed no encouragement to mingle with students. Other professors stayed home; he frequently attended student parties and reciprocated by inviting students to his home.

During the decade before Dickey arrived at Reed, the college had suffered because of its reputation as an academic gadfly. The House of Representatives' Un-American Activities Committee had targeted Reed in 1954 because three professors were suspected of Communist activities. The Reed president suspended one of the professors, who was teaching summer school. Furious over this high-handed action, faculty, students, and alumni demanded that President Ballantine reverse his decision. Rather than comply, he, along with several trustees, resigned. For the conservatives in the nation and at the college, Reed had become too "red." Alumni contributions dwindled. The local political establishment mocked Reed as "that commie school on the edge of town."[2] In the early 1960s, Reed could only enroll about six hundred students. Dickey remembered Reed in terms of a single, defining image: "a Jewish boy with a beard [in] a black turtle-neck sweater, a guitar over his shoulder, and his back pocket stuffed with anarchist pamphlets"[3] standing outside the commons.

As soon as he settled into his new house, Dickey began preparing his courses and getting his two books, *The Suspect in Poetry* and *Springer Mountain*, into publishable form. He also returned to his novel. On January 28, 1963, he wrote Theron Raines, who was now acting as his agent, that he hoped to produce a bestseller that could be turned into a blockbuster movie. "We should make some money off this," he speculated, "for it is A-Number-One-Idea, or IDEAL, for the movies."[4] He planned to finish a first draft quickly and send it to Raines for comment. Raines advised his client to take his time. Dickey sent progress reports to other friends as well. He told Donald Hall that he was "filling some old boxes with notes for a new novel, a strange kind of thriller called *The Deliverer*, some of which is to come out in various magazines, and the movie rights . . . are beginning to be dickered for, even though I haven't actually written a word of the book as it will finally be! I have a high-powered agent in New York (for prose fiction, though I've never written any!) who evidently can sell stuff by prose synopses. Talk about monkeys on backs! What a burden on the poor writer! Especially since I am clumsy at prose."[5] The ease with which Dickey composed varied. Sometimes he said the pages were rolling off the typewriter as fast as he could type them; at other times he said writing the novel was like working in a wooden jacket.

In mid-January Dickey met with his creative writing and modern poetry classes—he had decided to take on the extra course—and quickly impressed his students as a friendly, relaxed teacher who occasionally made inflammatory remarks. Because he had a knack for interacting with undergraduates, he shocked them when he posed as a redneck from the benighted South. Many of the professors, who tended to be as progressive as the students, had similar reactions to Dickey. One of the first clashes occurred at Dickey's fortieth birthday party on February 2, which the English Department chair, Don MacRae, had organized. MacRae invited a number of professors and visitors, including the iconoclastic literary critic Leslie Fiedler, whose son, Kurt, attended Reed. Dickey introduced himself in his best Southern drawl: "You don't know me, but I'm James Dickey, the poet." Fiedler nodded and said nothing. Dickey then added: "Do you not believe in the sanctity of the family?" Fiedler nodded again. Determined to provoke the reserved critic, Dickey asked: "Do you not believe that it is a sin for a man to spill his seed on the ground?"[6] Fiedler nodded once more, but refused to acknowledge Dickey's unexpected questions. Finally deigning to respond, Fiedler matched Dickey's bluster with his own, and to the amusement of their fellow partiers, the conversational sparring culminated in a bout of shadow boxing.

An English professor at the party, Roger Porter, had difficulty distinguishing between Dickey's poses and positions. In his company Dickey was normally low-key and affable, but Dickey also played the primitive hunter and daredevil warrior. He took Porter to a local archery range to demonstrate his prowess with eighty- and ninety-pound bows, and bragged about hair-raising dogfights as a combat pilot and adventures as a priapic motorcyclist in North Georgia. Porter knew about Dickey's friendship with Carolyn Kizer, whose father was on the board of trustees at Reed, and knew he liked to flirt with female students; he also knew that Dickey was not a rampant womanizer, at least not in the same class as the poet Galway Kinnell, who came to Reed after Dickey. Dickey's fanny patting and flattering irked some of those who witnessed it, but in general it was dismissed as innocent horseplay.

Dickey's racial comments were a different matter. Ever since the Supreme Court banned segregation in public schools on May 17, 1954, many Northerners condemned the South for erecting obstacles to full integration. In 1957, when the governor of Arkansas mobilized the state militia to prevent a group of black students from entering a Little Rock high school, President Eisenhower dispatched federal troops to ensure their safe entry. Twenty thousand soldiers invaded the University of Mississippi in October 1962 to quell riots that broke out when the first black student tried to enroll. In August 1963, Martin Luther King Jr. galvanized the Civil Rights movement with his "I Have a Dream" speech at the Lincoln Memorial. The mere fact that Dickey was a white Southerner aroused the suspicions of many Reed students and colleagues. Richard Hugo, who visited Dickey soon after he arrived in Portland, had tried to prepare Dickey and his family for this reaction: "One thing I fear you may run into out here is a grass-roots, northwest liberalism that will stand ready to condemn you. We are so liberal we can't stand a southern accent. I hope you don't run into it, but if you do I hope you can ignore it. I think it's more attributable to the geographic isolation of the area, than to any real feeling about other regions. Nobody notices us here, so we grow paranoid. However, you'll find plenty of big people who will accept you for yourselves."[7] Normally Dickey did little to antagonize the northwesterners, but when he did they were slow to forget.

Having published his mixed feelings about racial justice in "Notes on the Decline of Outrage," Dickey continued to give mixed signals about race in public. Rather than apologize for the sins of his ancestors, he often flaunted them in order to shock. In one class he boorishly remarked: "Don't you agree that niggers smell worse than we do?"[8] To defend himself against those who complained, he claimed he just wanted to test their assumptions. When one student queried him about the Freedom Riders—the group of thirteen blacks and whites who exposed segregation in Southern bus terminals in 1961—Dickey gave a cryptic reply: "If there were a race war, I know which side I'd be on."[9] The normally argumentative students fell silent, too stunned to respond. Some students, like Richard Pincus, explained Dickey's unpopular political views by saying that he simply didn't share the local sense of outrage. As Dickey implied in "The Decline of Outrage," he had once been outraged because of integration, not because of segregation. With regard to the Vietnam War, which the Kennedy administration had been perpetrating with troops and materiel, Dickey could be just as inflammatory, although in private he admitted the war was an unconscionable waste of life.

No wonder Dickey baffled the idealistic students and professors at Reed. One moment he sounded like a liberal-minded "dove"; the next he donned the plumage of a Jim Crow or war hawk. To Vern Rutsula, a professor at nearby Lewis and Clark College who had done a creative writing thesis in poetry at Reed in the mid-1950s, Dickey seemed a jumble of paradoxes. Rutsula was never quite sure whether an Appalachian hillbilly or an Oxford don would emerge when they socialized, since Dickey routinely alternated his accent between Southern redneck and English aristocrat. At parties, if not discussing books and music, Dickey frequently assumed the stances of famous boxers, especially Rocky Marciano and Archie Moore, and quizzed the others about his identity. A boxing fan, Rutsula won Dickey's approval by always identifying his impersonations correctly. At one party Dickey tried to provoke an actual fight by denigrating Kenneth Hanson's poetry to his face. With students he tended to be gentler. On the rare occasions he assigned grades, he proved to be a "soft touch." Paul Warshow, who did an independent study with Dickey, made the frank admission—rare for a student—that he didn't really deserve the A that Dickey gave him. Dickey liked Warshow and also liked his father, whose essays on horror comics and movies he had read. Sometimes Dickey lavished inordinate praise on Warshow's poetry. Warshow remembered him pointing to one line in an otherwise lackluster poem and saying: "That is one of the great lines in English poetry."[10] Jim Rawley, the son of the actress who played Fletcher Christian's Polynesian wife in *Mutiny on the Bounty*, received similar outlandish praise. As Rawley's creative writing thesis director during the 1963–64 academic year, Dickey exclaimed about one of his poems: "There are things in here I wouldn't trade for some epics." To establish common ground with Rawley he spoke of all the rejections he had reaped from editors like John Crowe Ransom at the *Kenyon Review*. Rawley never received a harsh word from Dickey, and even got his permission to use his name when he submitted poems to magazines. "However formidable he may have been in some circumstances," Rawley recalled, "he wasn't a bully to his students."[11] Unfortunately, Rawley's examining committee judged his old-fashioned poems more severely than did Dickey.

To another student, Martha Holden, Dickey proved that he was perfectly capable of bullying. As a freshman in 1963, she was thrilled to be allowed to study with him. Only upperclassmen could enroll in his writing course, but Dickey held a contest at the beginning of the term so that a freshman could sign up for an independent study course. He read a poem and asked the freshmen to name its author; Holden correctly identified the poet as Rilke. During their one- or two-hour meetings, Dickey was invariably polite, full of empathy for her poems, and quick to offer insightful suggestions for revision. He encouraged her with heartfelt praise. Reading her best lines, he would say: "I wish I had written that line." He even helped her select poems to send to an intercollegiate poetry anthology. On a visit with a German friend to Dickey's house in Atlanta, she watched her kindly professor metamorphose before her eyes. As they drank and chatted on a couch, Dickey slapped Holden's thigh and, with Maxine, Chris, and Kevin in the room, asked in a loud Southern drawl: "How would you like to go in for some long-term fuckin?" Raised in a proper New England family, Holden felt like a rabbit before a cobra. The boys sat in silence, pretending that they had heard nothing. Maxine feigned indifference. To break the silence, Dickey repeated his scurrilous question. Holden continued to sit on the couch, dumbfounded.

To forget the outburst, Holden and the Dickeys drank a good deal that night. Holden slipped into bed downstairs and woke up with a hangover, only to find Dickey walking into her room. Without warning, he began fondling her breasts, and in her groggy state she had difficulty resisting his advances. Again she felt like a rabbit staring into the eyes of a cobra. Before Dickey imposed himself any further, Holden's German friend, who was in a cast and on crutches because of an accident prior to the trip, came to her rescue by telling Dickey that breakfast was ready. At breakfast, which was several rounds of Bloody Marys, Dickey appeared slightly repentant and began discussing his novel, in which another Martha appears as Ed Gentry's wife. Perhaps thinking of the way the *Deliverance* men return to their wives after their adventures, Maxine declared sarcastically: "Martha, you can have him if you want, but he will always come back to me."[12]

This was one of Maxine's trademark lines, and she uttered it without realizing that Holden and her friend only wanted to gather their belongings and leave the house as quickly as possible. Deeply embittered, Holden later surmised that Dickey was one of those lost, hollow men who attempt to fill their inner voids with alcohol and the he-man fantasies that alcohol induces. She believed that his attempt to connect with men, women, animals, stars, and the rest of the cosmos through his writing paralleled his search for functional selves.

Other Reed students witnessed Dickey's unpredictable oscillations between civility and savagery. Dugan Barr, who had been raised in northern California by parents sympathetic to the Civil Rights movement, had inherited a prejudice against Southern whites. One night after playing his guitar at a faculty dinner with fellow students Ken Kipnis and Ruth Meyer, he felt a hand grip his shoulder. A Southern voice boomed: "Son, you sure can play that guitar!"[13] Looking up, he realized he was face-to-face with the sort of man he had learned to despise. After the initial shock, Barr warmed to Dickey. Dickey reciprocated. He admired Barr's talents as a guitar player as well as a home brewer (Barr fermented beer in a garbage pail), and took advantage of both. Over guitars and beers, they regularly talked about books and politics. Although he never heard Dickey make overtly racist remarks in their discussions of the Civil Rights movement, Barr recognized that Dickey was still struggling to overcome his prejudices.

Ken Kipnis was also surprised by how quickly his friendship with Dickey grew. At first he shared Barr's reservations about Dickey's Southern machismo, especially after viewing Dickey's arsenal of razor-tipped hunting arrows. An activist in the Civil Rights movement, Kipnis approached Dickey with trepidation before traveling to Mississippi to work for the voter registration campaign during the summer of 1964. Would Dickey rebuke him for being a fuzzy-headed do-gooder? Dickey merely warned: "Be careful; there are a lot of dangerous people down there."[14] Dickey's advice was prescient. A few days before Kipnis arrived in Mississippi, three Civil Rights workers—James Chaney, Michael Schwerner, and Andrew Goodman—were killed. In addition to the murders, "The Mississippi Summer Project" incited eighty beatings, thirty-five shootings, thirty-five church bombings, and thirty house bombings. Despite their differing opinions about the South, Dickey was consistently generous to Kipnis. Meeting in Chicago in 1966, Dickey reaffirmed his friendship by helping Kipnis buy a new guitar to replace one that had recently been stolen.

Dickey liked to say that Reed was a "school for eccentric Jewish geniuses. No ordinary Jewish [student] need apply!"[15] One of the "Jewish geniuses" he befriended was John Ullman, a chemistry major who later earned a doctorate in microbiology from the University of Washington, founded a company in Seattle called Traditional Arts Service to represent local folk artists, and, partly as a joke, became minister number 10,256 in the Universal Life Church (in 1969, Dickey expressed his bewilderment that Ullman, who had often discussed his Jewishness, had become a Christian minister). During the fall of 1963, Ullman took Dickey's poetry class, which was a relief from the rigors of organic chemistry and other science courses. The class had about ten students, no textbooks, and no lectures. Dickey sat face-to-face with the students at a fold-out table, and usually divided his time between dramatic readings and discussions of famous poems he had xeroxed. Carried away by his sonorous voice, he often slammed his hand on the table and exclaimed: "How did that grab you!"[16] Because some students wanted less inspiration and more analysis, Dickey responded by assigning scholarly and analytical topics for papers (Ullman wrote one paper on the relation between blues music and poetry).

Dickey admired Ullman so much that he offered a free room in his house to him and his wife, Irene, in exchange for baby-sitting. The couple declined the offer but continued to dine with the Dickeys. On one of these occasions, Dickey surprised the two students by reading his new poem "The Firebombing." The poem offended Irene, who had grown up in Shanghai, where her Korean father and Japanese mother owned a sweater factory before moving to a city near Hiroshima and Nagasaki. John said: "Look, Jim, you were trying to firebomb Irene!"[17] Dickey laughed off the accusation without explaining that he had done almost no firebombing and that he and his pilot had dropped a more traditional bomb on a factory in Shanghai that produced munitions rather than sweaters.

As with his other students, Dickey liked to shock Ullman, who belonged to a Ralph Nader–like citizen's group in Oregon that picketed a local supermarket for refusing to hire black clerks, exposed bigoted landlords who turned away black renters, and tutored underprivileged blacks in Portland. Once Dickey quipped to Ullman about the black novelist James Baldwin: "I know James Baldwin. I think I'll invite him out here, dress him in livery, and make him stand on the lawn in front of my house."[18] Dickey upset students in a similar way by treating Kennedy's assassination on November 22, 1963, in a blasé manner; he remarked that there was nothing they could do about the president's murder so they might as well have class. Many wanted to return to their rooms to grieve. Several months later, two professors at Columbia University, Erwin Giles and Paul Schwaber, asked Dickey to submit a poem about Kennedy's presidency and death. There is no record that he complied. Despite his apparent sangfroid, Dickey was not as indifferent as some suspected. Even though Kennedy was a Northerner, Dickey identified with the president's fondness for football, heroic war service, rambunctious sexuality, literary flair, youthful charisma, and hunger for power. Jim Rawley recalled that in private Dickey was visibly shaken after the shooting in Dallas. He put his arm around Rawley and said: "This is the time the mouths are struck silent."[19]

Although Dickey boasted to Donald Hall and others that he was playing his guitar in coffeehouses and giving guitar lessons in Portland, in fact his student friends were playing in coffeehouses and giving *him* lessons. Barr and his two Reed friends Ken Kipnis and David Casseres often took Dickey to a coffeehouse in downtown Portland called the Way Out to listen to local musicians. Of the various students Dickey befriended, Kipnis, a philosophy major, helped Dickey's guitar playing the most. A New Yorker, Kipnis spent his vacations studying with the local folk guitarists in Washington Square, including Gary Davis, whom he invited to Portland. Kipnis's roommate, Jon Westling, had advised Dickey to get lessons from Kipnis, and soon Dickey was paying Kipnis five dollars an hour to learn his fingerpicking blues technique. Kipnis rated Dickey's guitar playing poor, but Dickey worked so hard that he finally became proficient. Among the dozens of songs Kipnis taught him, Elizabeth Cotten's "Freight Train" became a standard piece on Dickey's poetry tours. Another song they practiced was "Buckdancer's Choice," which inspired the title poem for his 1966 National Book Award–winning collection.

It was Ullman who introduced Dickey to local musicians Mike Russo and Ron Brentano. Dugan Barr had piqued Dickey's interest in the duo with a tape of their music, which included "Dueling Banjos"—the eventual signature tune for the *Deliverance* soundtrack. Dickey began attending their concerts and jam sessions around Portland. A native New Yorker, Brentano had come to Portland in 1959 to study art and play guitar and banjo. He soon teamed up with the talented six- and twelve-string guitar player Russo. Their repertoire—bluegrass, ballads, blues, spirituals, Southern mountain laments, ragtime country music—made them among the most sought-after musicians on college campuses and at Northwest music festivals in the 1960s. They also played regularly at Portland's Thirteenth Avenue Gallery, run by the entrepreneurial bohemian Paul Hebb. It was at the Gallery that Dickey often listened to them.

In his early twenties when he met Dickey, Brentano remembered the heyday of Portland folk music with great relish:

> Musical opportunities were everywhere, and James Dickey came along at just the right time to provide encouragement and appreciation. I think James loved the music more than anything. Of course a lot of what and how we played was influenced by southern folk music traditions and, I'm sure, close to James's southern roots. And when the music started, James absolutely beamed, and that's how I'll always remember James—grinning and laughing like we were performing the most magical show on earth. I don't remember anyone ever enjoying himself more. But James especially admired Mike's guitar playing and [liked] participating in some rather unconventional, unorganized all night jam sessions. I can't say there were ever any formal music lessons. "Just keep playing till you get it right," that's the way we all learned. And believe me, James would stay up all night playing if he could, and he often did![20]

The local photographer, poet, and journalist Wes Taft often joined Dickey at these uproarious soirees at Russo's or Brentano's house. Taft was Brentano's oldest friend. Insisting that Taft play an instrument even though he had no special skill, Brentano rigged up a "washtub bass" with a broom handle and nylon cord that could be tightened and loosened according to the desired pitch. Taft plucked, Dickey strummed and grinned, and Brentano and Russo led, picking their way deftly through their favorite tunes—the lively "Buckdancer's Choice" and "Dueling Banjos." Seven years later Dickey did everything he could to make Warner Brothers hire Brentano and Russo for the *Deliverance* soundtrack. Because of union regulations, his efforts came to nothing. In 1993, Dickey contacted Russo to play the music for the soundtrack of *To the White Sea*, but again in vain. Disappointed by Hollywood's rejections, both Russo and Brentano took secret pride in having introduced Dickey to "Dueling Banjos," which bucked current musical trends by becoming one of the most identifiable tunes in America after *Deliverance* premiered in 1972.

His fondness for Portland's music scene notwithstanding, Dickey told close friends that he wanted to return to the South, where he felt less of an outcast. He wrote Gwen Walti in Zurich that he was determined to live and die among his Southern ancestors and that he had applied for a job at Washington and Lee in Virginia. On February 21, 1963, Walti wrote a three-page, single-spaced letter encouraging him to return to his home ground, despite its racial strife. Walti planned to talk to Dickey about this and other matters when she visited her ailing mother in San Francisco in late March. Struggling with her romantic feelings for Dickey, Walti couldn't decide what to do. On March 26, she wrote Dickey from San Francisco to cancel her visit to Portland. Then she changed her mind again, bought a plane ticket, and canceled it. On April 21, disgruntled and forlorn, she informed Dickey that she would be flying directly from San Francisco to New York and then on to Zurich. Why hadn't Dickey contacted her? she wondered. Was he or Maxine angry at her? She told Dickey of her mother's bad nerves and cancerous tumor (Walti's mother would die of cancer on July 9, 1964). She implied that her mother had worried about the resurgence of her love for Dickey. Gwen also fretted about it and about hurting Maxine by arousing her jealousy as she had done in Zurich.

Dickey was so busy during the winter and spring of 1963 that he had little time for rekindling old romances. Among other things, he had numerous poetry readings to organize for himself and others. On January 10, he tentatively invited Donald Hall to Reed. Returning the favor, Hall invited Dickey to Michigan. According to Hall's plan, Dickey would read at Michigan State in East Lansing on March 11, then at the University of Michigan in Ann Arbor on March 13. He might also read at Western Michigan University in Kalamazoo, where one of Hall's friends, John Woods, could act as his host and drive him to Hall's house in Ann Arbor. In mid-March, Dickey followed the itinerary drawn up by Hall, gave his various readings, and met Woods, who escorted him to Ann Arbor. On March 12, Dickey shook hands for the first time with the editor and friend he had been corresponding with for six years. Hall had expected Dickey to be flamboyant, but was surprised by some of the directions his flamboyance took. On the night of March 12, Dickey accompanied Woods to the guest room, where the Halls had two twin beds. Like others before and after him, Woods was baffled—and amused—by what appeared to be Dickey's homosexual advance. Dickey asked: "Are you homosexual?" Woods blurted: "No!" Dickey said, "Too bad,"[21] and went to sleep.

Dickey's reading at the University of Michigan was a great success, and both Hall and Dickey enjoyed their time together. Despite his outward show of support for Dickey—on March 23 Hall complimented his new poetry manuscript, which would become *Helmets*—Hall may have suspected that his alliance with Robert Bly would compromise his friendship with Dickey. Dickey had recently chastised Hall for following Bly's precepts too closely: "His [Bly's] way of writing is as constricting as it is releasing: no narrative and so no real interest in 'what comes next,' in the sense of a story, no associations but rather fortuitous ones, no real rhythmic structure. Jim Wright has written his whole third book this way, largely at Bob's prompting; he (Jim) seems to me diminished thereby; I love some of his early stuff; I can't love any of this; it is too arbitrary and drifting."[22]

Dickey assured Hall that it didn't matter if he passed along his denigrating re-marks to Bly; they argued all the time anyway. Within a decade Dickey was fol-lowing at least some of Bly's stylistic principles by forgoing narrative, logical associations, and rhythmic structure in his poems. He was also blasting Hall as a "no talent" and Bly as a political imbecile.

For the time being, relations among the three men remained reasonably civil. Dickey wrote Hall a recommendation for a Guggenheim Fellowship, which Hall got in 1963. Dickey also lined up a number of readings for Hall in the Northwest, beginning with an evening on April 8 at Reed. Complaining that Donald Justice had emptied the college's coffers by inviting his mediocre friends to read and treating them like royalty, in the end Dickey mustered two hundred dollars. Hall flew to Oregon, bearing the blue pajamas that Dickey had left in Michigan (in turn, Hall left his bedroom slippers and a handkerchief at the Dickeys' house, which Dickey then returned). Dickey invited Carolyn Kizer, with whom he had just read at Victoria College in British Columbia, to join the festivities surrounding Hall's reading. In Portland, the threesome drank, dis-cussed books, and drove around in Dickey's blue MG. On one of the MG rides, Hall listened in amused disbelief to Dickey's story about his marriage to an Australian woman during World War II: "A very romantic story, where he met this girl and they fell in love and were married and had a brief honeymoon and then he went off to the combat missions, where he was a pilot of course, and she died back in Australia. Also, I remember asking him, as we drove along in his MG, 'What was the best thing you did in the war, Jim?' I believe he was making it up when he answered me that the best thing he had done in the war was to shoot down two Japanese troop transports, unarmed, 'just flying along there, fat and slow, waiting to be slaughtered.' He knew I was a standard American aca-demic liberal with pacifist tendencies. . . . He just said it to be shocking."[23] Hall suspected that Dickey treated people the way he treated the truth, so he asked: "Don't you think loyalty's a great quality?" Dickey retorted: "No, I think it's a terrible quality. I think it's the worst quality there is."[24]

Out of his own sense of loyalty, Hall continued to do everything he could to improve Dickey's literary and financial situation at Wesleyan. In May, he argued with Willard Lockwood about the best title for his next book, pointing out that *Helmets* was more distinct than *Springer Mountain*. Since Dickey sided with Lockwood in this debate, Hall had to convince Dickey as well. In late May, Dickey came around to Hall's point of view and retitled the manuscript. Hall also badgered Lockwood into extending the normal eighty-page limit on poetry books at the press. With a few additional poems, Hall contended that *Helmets* had a good chance of winning the Pulitzer Prize or National Book Award. Lockwood relented; in the end *Helmets* contained ninety-three pages. Because Dickey grumbled about the puny checks he received from Wesleyan, claiming that he had earned only $150 on *Drowning with Others* by May 25, 1963, Hall also made an effort to improve his royalty agreement with the press.

In order to make Dickey more visible in the poetry world, Hall offered Dickey his editorial position at the *Paris Review*, which he planned to relinquish during the summer. Dickey responded: "I can pretty much say that I would probably ac-cept it if advised to do so by my literary executor, Mr. Donald Hall (now don't forget that part of things, for God's sake)."[25] Out of gratitude for his editorial help, in 1963 Dickey had asked Hall to oversee his literary estate if he should die. At about the same time he also implored Hall, who considered leaving Wesleyan's editorial board, to remain so that they could continue working together. In his new role as executor, Hall now advised Dickey *not* to become an editor of the *Paris Review* because the salary would be miniscule and the workload enormous. Dickey said he could still be tempted if an annual stipend of $500 could be extracted from George Plimpton's wealthy backers. Plimpton's dolce vita and a foothold in the New York literary scene, he told Hall, were hard to resist, but in the end he decided he was too busy for the job.

Apprised of his paltry salary increase at Reed from $8,000 to $8,050, Dickey became even more determined to make other colleges pay high prices for his readings. One of the first invitations came on February 21 from Robert Heilman, chairman of the English Department at the University of Washington. Dickey eagerly accepted, and looked forward to meeting his idol, Theodore Roethke, who taught at the university. In Seattle on April 17, 1963, Carolyn Kizer introduced Dickey to Roethke on a tennis court (Roethke had once been a coach and was still a formidable player). They got more of a chance to grow acquainted over lunch with James Wright and at a party Kizer gave before Dickey's reading. Despite his worshipful opinion of Roethke's poems, Roethke-the-man disappointed Dickey:

> I saw only a sad fat man who talked continually of joy. . . . Like everyone else who knew him even faintly, I was pressed into service in the cause of his ego, which reeled and tottered pathetically at all hours and under all circumstances, and required not only props, but the *right* props. What did I think of Robert Lowell, Randall Jarrell, and "the Eastern literary gang"? What did I think of the "gutless Limey reviewers" in the [the] *Times Literary Supplement?* . . . I was identified in his mind only as the man who had said . . . that he was the greatest poet then writing in English. He kept getting another drink and bringing me one and starting the conversation over from that point, leading . . . into a detailed and meticulously quoted list of what other poets and critics had said about him.[26]

According to Dickey, when Roethke gave the prefatory remarks at the reading that evening, Roethke began by restating Dickey's praise for his own poetry. He then talked about himself for another ten minutes before beckoning Dickey to the podium.

On another occasion, while driving through Seattle with Roethke, Dickey must have thought he was conversing with his double. Roethke bragged about sparring with a famous heavyweight boxer, then rebuked Dickey for suspecting he was a liar. Dickey reflected: "I would have found Roethke's lies a good deal more memorable if they had had some of the qualities of his best poems, and had not been simply the productions of the grown-up baby that he resembled physically." In his encounter with another fabulist, Dickey implied that he was the more skillful liar. Nevertheless, he expressed more sympathy than antipathy: "None of his lies—of being a nationally ranked tennis player, of having an 'in' with the Detroit 'Purple Gang,' of having all kinds of high-powered business in-terests and hundreds of women in love with him—would ever have shriven him completely, but these lures and ruses and deceptions did enable him to exist, though painfully, and to write; they were the paraphernalia of the wounded artist who cannot survive without them."[27] Dickey needed the same fictive para-phernalia.

In later years Dickey continued to belittle Roethke's personal failings. He once said: "Theodore Roethke is the only person I have ever seen do what the comic alcoholic is supposed to do—have liquor around in different places. He's the only one I ever saw actually do that. He and I had been driving around on some errands . . . [in Seattle], and he parked the car in the garage. He said, 'Would you like a drink?' I said, 'Sure, I'll have one with you. Why don't we go in the house?' He said, 'Why wait?' and he reached behind an old tire in the garage, and there was a bottle of whiskey, half-empty."[28] Roethke's "comic" al-coholism made Dickey's own love of the bottle seem less serious. At Reed, Dickey was drinking every night. On Sunday evenings, when about half-a-dozen students gathered at his house for dinner, the group regularly polished off two "fifths" of bourbon while they watched the TV show *Bonanza* (with the volume turned down so Dickey could ad-lib risqué dialogue). Earlier in the day, Dickey usually played Ping-Pong and drank gin fizzes with other friends. By 1963, Dickey had already begun promising family and friends that he would quit drink-ing. On the wagon, he grew irritable and inevitably relapsed, conforming to the cycle that he found so pathetically funny in poets like Roethke.

Roethke and Dickey never saw each other again. In the summer of 1963, Roethke died of a heart attack while swimming in a Seattle pool; he was only fifty-five. Dickey's reaction was puzzling. Richard Pincus remarked to Dickey at the time: "The booze finally got him" (Pincus had visited Roethke several months before and discovered bottles everywhere, even in a birdhouse). Dickey replied: "They found him in the shallow end. That makes it worse, somehow. I don't want to be found in the shallow end."[29] According to Pincus, Dickey meant that he wanted to be considered a "deeper" poet than Roethke at the end of his life.

Because of his infatuation with Roethke, Dickey inflated his friendship with him. To an interviewer in 1984, he claimed: "Theodore Roethke was a good friend of mine. The last year of his life I saw a good deal of him. He was obsessed with the idea that he wanted to become a business tycoon, or a gangster over-lord."[30] To his University of Wisconsin students in 1966, he also spoke of Roethke's gangster persona and the obstacle it had posed to their friendship. David Keller, a Ph.D. student in Dickey's class, heard his apocryphal story about inviting Roethke to Reed. Roethke had promised to come, but warned Dickey that if he were manic he might hurt Dickey's children. Dickey had responded: "If you did, I'd have to kill you." Roethke acknowledged that Dickey was enough of "a Southerner and a son-of-a-bitch"[31] to do it. Dickey also liked to claim that, while drinking in a bar on a trip to one of the mental institutions that treated Roethke for manic depression, he gave Roethke the title for his last book, which won a National Book Award. In 1981, Dickey told the journalist William Childress: "As I recall, the manuscript was then going by the title of *Dance On*,

Dance On, Dance On, and I told Ted that the poems were some of his best, but that he really should call the book *The Far Field*. . . . At the time he seemed to dissent, and then died."[32] Dickey had a talent for coming up with appropriate titles for his friends' books, so his story may be less fanciful than it sounds.

While in Seattle for his reading, Dickey also spoke with Richard Hugo, who wrote an appreciative letter two days later. He compared Dickey's reading to others he had attended by Dylan Thomas, Robert Lowell, Delmore Schwartz, Robert Creeley, Donald Hall, W. S. Merwin, and Roethke: "Your reading was the best I've heard at the UW for years. It isn't simply your way of reading, but a sort of animal intelligence that comes through. The audience knows it has seen and heard somebody a little extra-human."[33] Dickey was glad to be cast as "extra-human," and soon began flexing his poetic muscles as Hugo's mentor. For his part, Hugo grudgingly played the acolyte. Alluding to a particularly difficult assignment, Hugo responded: "I wish, sincerely wish you hadn't told me to write those rough diction poems like 'Digging Is an Art,' because I have to go back a bit to gray times to get the poem to fit the language and while I did write one of the best poems I've ever written as a result of your advice, I have been weeping a great deal in the process."[34] If Hugo sincerely regretted Dickey's advice, he showed no signs of steering clear of it in his poetry. His whole oeuvre was founded on the marriage of rough diction and gray periods in his life.

Because they had talked about their love of the outdoors, Hugo, in mid-July, tried to interest Dickey in a camping trip to the Cispus River area northeast of Portland. He promised good fishing. With regard to cooking au naturel, he wrote: "I'm sure if we bring food, utensils etc. we can improvise like the good Indians we are."[35] Chief Laughing Cloud—Hugo's self-designated name—would act as guide. A week later, Hugo wrote again, but without any laughter: "Barbara [his wife] has been gone for 8 days. I've discovered that I am old and no longer attractive to young girls in taverns—was I ever? I lost all my fishing tackle Saturday when my basket tore loose from the strap. I fell down a rock cliff and cut my hands. I caught no fish. Reed Whittemore just rejected a bunch of poems with a cold note. I'm MISERABLE."[36] This litany of woes failed to bring any consoling words from Dickey, so Hugo wrote again about a possible fishing trip with Dickey and included details about his poetry book *A Run of Jacks*, which had sold only 514 copies. Hugo's penchant for misery led Dickey to comment later: "He was a poor, benighted, kicked-around guy. . . . You felt so sorry for him you wanted to hit him. Add to his sorrows, because he's going to add to them anyway."[37] Impatient with Hugo's whining, Dickey tried to support his poetry all he could.

According to his article "The Grass Mountain Kid," Dickey first got the idea for camping in the Northwest in a cocktail bar and then took his family in their VW bus to a place near Alsea, on the west slope of the Cascades. When he finally went camping with Hugo, he made sure to bring a cocktail bar with him. David Wagoner, one of Roethke's former students who taught at the University of Washington, organized the trip. Along with Hugo and his wife, Wagoner, Dickey, and their two wives spent a few days near Mount Ranier in log cabins owned by the grandmother of Wagoner's wife. Showing little interest in roughing it, they quaffed drinks, ate ham, and talked about poetry. Dickey hoped to hunt for deer with a bow and arrow in the surrounding woods, but the grand-mother had prohibited it. The comical high point of the trip was when the poets tried communicating with the bullfrogs by the lake. To immortalize the occasion, Wagoner wrote a poem, "The Poets Agree to Be Quiet by the Swamp," in which they remain silent until: "They stick their elbows out into the evening, / Stoop, and begin the ancient croaking."[38]

During the summer, Dickey redoubled his efforts to finish the novel about his more arduous trips into the Georgia woods. Sidestepping his agent, he contacted Scribner's, and told them he planned to send them the novel. On June 10, 1963, Donald Hutter wrote that he was happy Dickey planned to give Scribner's the first look at *The Deliverer*. As he applied himself to his novel, Dickey also con-tacted the man behind "the deliverer," Lewis King, as well as his other canoeing partner, Al Braselton, who in a letter written on June 21 sounded the low note that would resonate through the first section of the book:

I am 28 today with so many ambitions yet unfulfilled and no hope of really doing anything worthwhile. You know, it's funny when you reach this time of your life, the zenith at which your whole existence has been aiming, all the years of education and apprenticeship; happily married with a fine fam-ily; and you realize that this, brother, is all there is to it. I don't want to sound like I'm whining, but it is depressing to really take a good look and realize that you've been going at 10% speed, loafing through life, and that the most you can hope for in your career is to be immortalized as the cre-ator of the yellow stain campaign for some toothpaste or some such.[39]

Still toiling at Liller, Neal, Battle and Lindsey, Braselton was looking for the sort of deliverance from inconsequence that became Dickey's central theme.

Fleshing out his mythical plot on paper, Dickey tried out versions of the ac-tual events on various friends. He told John Ullman that the original idea for the novel had come on a trip to North Georgia with his son Chris. They had met two old, rifle-toting hillbillies engaged in moonshining. "Who are you?" one asked with a belligerent twang. He replied: "Jim Dickey. You remember me. We played football together. I was the Crabapple Cannonball." One hillbilly looked him over carefully, and then said: "Ohhhhh yes. I do remember you, Jim. And a damn good thing I do, because otherwise we would have shot both of you."[40] Ullman had no reason to doubt the veracity of Dickey's tale. Dickey may also have discussed *The Deliverer* with local novelist Don Berry, who had a cult fol-lowing among Oregon students in the 1960s because of *Trask* (1960), *Moontrap* (1962), and *To Build a Ship* (1963). In his novels Berry had demonstrated the sort of mystic reverence for nature and clashes between mountaineers and city folk that Dickey was evincing in his novel. If Dickey felt out of place at Reed, Berry could sympathize. He had enrolled in 1949 and had lived with several Reed students—poets Gary Snyder, Philip Whalen, Lew Welch—who later be-came associated with the Beat movement. Dickey and Berry often met at bars and parties to talk about Reed and books.

To initiate his new friend into the treats of the Oregon hinterland, Berry in-vited Dickey to a party in Portland where he served deer, elk, and bear meat that he had shot with his rifle. According to Berry, the evening ended in calamity when an older woman friend of his took such a disliking to Dickey's guest— Carolyn Kizer—that she stooped to the floor and bit Kizer on the ankle. Wes Taft, one of Berry's close friends, remembered the incident differently: "A Latino sculptor of some note, Manuel Izquierdo (whose dashing good looks and political bent would have made him a fitting companion for Tina Modotti) found himself at a party with other artists and literati in Portland's West Hills. Manuel, a man of short stature and equally truncated fuse, did not suffer patronizing poets gladly. Mid-way through a grandiose pronouncement by Ms. Kizer, Manuel strode up to confront her, and finding his nose on an equal plane with her bosom, buried his face in her décolletage and . . . *blew!* This astonishing act galvanized and stupefied Ms. Kizer, who retired to a corner, leaving Izquierdo grinning like a triumphant matador."[41] His faulty memory aside, Berry provided Dickey with another example of the kind of person he was writing about in *The Deliverer*—the sophisticated urban man drawn to the primitive ways of the wilderness.

By the fall of 1963, Dickey was ready to show his novel to a publisher. On December 20, 1963, Dickey wrote Donald Hall: "A mysterious man, a senior editor for Houghton Mifflin, turned up out here and absconded, over my weak protests, with the pre-pre-*pre* first draft of my novel, shoving various monies into my hands. He thinks it's wonderful—though this may be because he can't read it in its present state; nobody could—and so I may have to go to work trying to make something of it, after all, though I know nothing whatever about writing novels."[42] The "mysterious" editor from Boston was Robert Lescher. Lescher had come to Portland on a scouting trip to discover prospective authors for Houghton Mifflin. He had stopped at a writers' conference in Indiana before moving on to Chicago, Las Vegas, Los Angeles, and San Francisco. In Chicago he had met editor Henry Rago, who had showed him the August issue of *Poetry*, containing three of Dickey's poems and a contributor's note that announced Dickey was at work on a novel called *The Deliverer*. An admirer of Dickey's poetry and critical prose, Lescher sent Dickey a letter in mid-September proposing they get together on October 21.

When Lescher arrived in Portland, Dickey drove his MG to Lescher's hotel and gave his future editor his first ride in a sports car. In his roomy house, where seagulls regularly flew by the study window and ring-necked pheasants promenaded on the lawn, Dickey convinced Lescher to have a number of drinks. Feeling tipsy from the three before dinner, Lescher faced two bottles of white Mersault beside a delicious chicken dinner made by Maxine. Normally a light drinker, Lescher tried not to act besotted. The dinner conversation meandered from topic to topic until his host suddenly blurted out: "I got myself the beginning of a novel upstairs!" Lescher remarked as casually as he could: "It's called *The Deliverer*." Dickey reared back: "You son of a bitch. How do you know that?" To which Lescher responded: "It's my job to know that." They stared at each other for a moment, and then Dickey asked: "Want to read it?" "Of course I want to read it,"[43] Lescher answered. To make sure his guest was worthy of the task, Dickey proposed that they play Ping-Pong.

A proficient player, Lescher took a severe drubbing from Dickey, and afterward concluded: "[Dickey was] conceivably as fiercely competitive as any man I've ever met."[44] Woozy from alcohol and almost asthmatic from two arduous matches, Lescher gladly left the game room for Dickey's study, a small room with a chair in disrepair and numerous shelves heaped with books. Dickey tipped Lescher into the chair and fetched his manuscript. Gazing at all the well-thumbed volumes of French poetry, Lescher, like others getting acquainted with Dickey, had a hard time reconciling the images of the macho pilot-hunter-jock with the cosmopolitan poet-professor-novelist. When Dickey finally pressed *The Deliverer* into his hands, Lescher was too dazed to concentrate on the manuscript, which was a palimpsest of lines typed between lines, words scratched out and scratched in, and comments scrawled in the margins. Lescher asked if he could take it back to his Boston office and circulate it among his colleagues. He promised to respond as soon as possible. Dickey consented.

According to Dickey's version of the evening in Portland, Lescher promptly digested the manuscript after Ping-Pong and was so overwhelmed by the novel's power that he immediately offered a substantial advance: "He took it upstairs and read it. He said, 'We want this. We'll give you an advance.' I said, 'How much?' He said, 'We'll give you five thousand dollars.' Well, I never saw that much in my life."[45] Unfortunately, a three-figure option didn't materialize for another few months, and a four-figure advance didn't occur for another few years. What Lescher saw was the ninety-page novella that Dickey had already sent Scribner's. It began in a style reminiscent of John Updike's imagistic prose ("Build up many details, à la Updike," Dickey wrote in one of his margins) and the fragmentary, free-associational technique pioneered by Joyce in *Ulysses*: "Unrolling. Green, tan, and the little letters and names of landmarks, concentric waverings and contour notations. A beer stein from each of us on the four corners, and the river is running in an uncertain black line from right to left, going down, from northeast to southwest across the top of the state. Lewis's hand has now a pencil and marks out a light X somewhere in the mountains, bled white of green; now moves, now down following across, slowly down the river crossing the state through the green woods. Images, confused, many rivers and pictures of rivers, all of them map-green. Huck Finn, and the boats of the Nile. What water? Where? Which one?"[46] In this first draft, in which the river was called the Cohutta and the bar restaurant The Hornet's Nest, Dickey eschewed normal grammar in order to present images as they impinged on Ed's consciousness. Later he settled for a more traditional narrative.

In 1963, the names and occupations of Dickey's characters were still in a state of flux. At the beginning of the story, Lewis Medlock is Lewis Queen (an obvious double entendre on Lewis King); near the end of the manuscript he becomes the more allegorical Lewis Followill to suggest that his three friends will follow him. The Drew Ballinger character is Drew Davis, a lawyer who works in his father's firm (Al Braselton worked in his father-in-law's advertising firm and, like Gary Davis, played the guitar). Drew also appears as Dale Davis and, in another draft, Al Brasington. About the main characters' names, Dickey once told a reporter for the *Florence Morning News*: "The name Medlock is . . . appropriated from a feed store front in a small town. The name of Drew Ballenger [sic] in the novel resulted from the juxtaposition of the names of two fellows . . . [I knew when] growing up in Buckhead—Bill Ballenger and Drew Davidson."[47] Drew Ballinger also sounded a little like Al Braselton.

For the director of the advertising agency at the novel's beginning, Dickey chose the name Haddon Burke, an obvious echo of the Burke who directed Burke Dowling Adams. The names of Bobby Trippe and Ed Gentry remain fixed in the early drafts, but Bobby shares some of Al Braselton's attributes. It is Bobby and not Drew who plays the guitar around the campfire in the first draft. With regard to the original Ed, he is fiercer than the lethargic, melancholic Ed in the final novel. His relationship with the model for the Kitt n' Britches ad is full of menacing sexuality. In a note Dickey says he wants to express Ed's "desire to go straight to the center of her, straight up between her legs with no intervention or delay, no knowing of her, no conversation, no seeing her again. . . . He wavers for a second in the light, like the man about to shoot the Arab in Camus's *L'Étranger,* thinking she might be the one to restore all that was being taken away." In the first draft Ed seeks his deliverance in something akin to a murderous rape. As alienated as Camus's protagonist, Ed also resembles Julian Glass in Dickey's previous novel *The Entrance to the Honeycomb.* He describes his life among family, friends, and colleagues as if he too were encased in glass: "Lately I had felt like a ghost that can come near those he has loved in life but can't touch them, and can do nothing but watch things happen to them as though he did not exist." Like Camus's characters, Ed is trying to figure out how to break through his entrapments into a more engagé lifestyle. In one draft of the novel, which Dickey finished in 1969, an epigraph from Camus's compatriot Sartre summarizes Ed's dilemma: "If we are to believe in an enterprise we need in the first place to be pitched into it; we have to ask ourselves what is the best method of bringing it to a successful conclusion; we must not ask ourselves what its object is." Perhaps because of the skewed logic of the statement (how can one think about a project's conclusion without thinking about its object?), Dickey decided to drop the epigraph from the published book. Although the biblical epigraph that he included in the first draft was more relevant to Ed's situation— "Who will deliver me from the body of this death?"[48]—he decided to expunge that as well.

Dickey also bowdlerized his story to make it less offensive. The original version begins scatalogically and ends sadistically. On the second page, Ed tries to convince Bobby that the Cohutta is not as ferocious as the Colorado River: "It won't be anything like that; it'll just be good fast water. A lot of fun, and we can shake this day-to-day crap for a little while. My God, we're all turning to shit, and time's passing." The Joycean scatalogy segues into a Joycean interior monologue, in which Ed is "Thinking: rivers, and the middle-class turning to shit all day and in their off-time. What to stop it? What is worth doing? Lewis is rich, and likes the woods, fishing with expensive equipment, knowledgeable, with violent enthusiasms and nothing much to do except look after property his suicided father left him and collect the rents, and try to *live.*"[49] Some of Lewis Queen's characteristics match those of Lewis King (Queen, like King, manages real estate bequeathed by a father who committed suicide), but are exaggerated for dramatic effect.

The way Dickey based his Georgia river journey on the archetypal structure of a mythical adventure also echoed Joyce, whose paean to "many rivers" reached its zenith in the figure of Anna Livia Plurabelle in *Finnegans Wake*, a book from which Dickey liked to quote. Dickey paid further homage to Joyce by including an epilogue about Martha's fantasy life that imitated, in diminutive fashion, Molly's monologue at the end of *Ulysses:* "And Martha's imagination, her fantasy, increased boldly. We found out, without going to a psychiatrist, that what she really wanted was punishment; she wanted to be whipped, and she wanted to deserve it. She wanted it at a particular time and place—all history was open to us—and for a particular thing. She wanted it to change her, to exorcise the demons that she would get back before the next time. I read history books a good deal, and my good dependable Martha became a Carthaginian slave girl, a Spanish heretic, an English queen, an American slave." Molly Bloom, at the end of *Ulysses*, also vents her sexual fantasies candidly; but the sadomasochistic fantasies owe more to Dickey's *Entrance to the Honeycomb*, in which Julian reads *The Carthaginians* at his uncle's house, and to Dickey's own sexual tastes. In the original draft, the sodomy scene is more graphic than in later ones; Bobby has to strip completely and kneel across a log: "The older man shucked his suspenders away from his shoulders and over his repulsive waist down to his knees. His penis stood up out of a mucky tangle of belly hair. 'Now you just reach on back and spread them fat little cheeks,' he said, and knelt down behind Bobby. . . . The white-haired man worked steadily on Bobby, held still with the sweat streaming out of his hair down his face, and then slowly pulled back. His sexual organs and lower belly were rich with blood." Recoiling from the mountain man, Ed recoils from Bobby as well: "I remembered how unmanly he looked, crouched over the log, how soft, how willing to let anything be done to him."[50] Ed concludes that if he had been sodomized, he would not have cried so loudly.

In *The Deliverer*, as the postscript indicates, the river journey is more ostensibly a journey through history. The Griner brother with whom Lewis bargains at the garage about driving the cars downriver is an emblem of the viciousness inherent in Confederate soldiers and their Southern kin. Thinking of past wars and lynchings, Ed says: "I was sure that the biggest Confederate heroes of the ranks were like this man." Drew's death fits into this context of Southern violence by resembling Kennedy's assasination in Texas. Ed sees "the eaten-away pinkish matter of his brain lolling backward, loosening,"[51] and has good reason to assume a bullet is the cause of the head wound. The murder of Drew's assassin is also less ambiguous. On the clifftop, Ed reveals that he has killed an honorary deputy sheriff—the man has a license in his pocket—while in *Deliverance*, readers are left guessing his real identity. Over the next seven years, the manuscript doubled and then tripled in size as Dickey made his characters and their actions more complex.

Along with teaching his two classes and tinkering with his novel, during the fall of 1963 Dickey also worked on book reviews, essays, and poems. He put the final touches on what would become one of his manifestoes, "The Energized Man," which he delivered at the Oregon State Poetry Association banquet on October 12. In his lecture he called for a poetry of responsiveness and affirmation different from the gloomy, anger-and-guilt-laced confessional poetry written by Lowell, Sexton, Snodgrass, and Plath. He echoed Ed's call in *The Deliverer* for a life of consequence, and told his audience: "Let me leave you with that image: the energized man standing against the forces, the vast, sluggish forces of habit, mechanization and mental torpor."[52] Ed also takes a stand against such negative forces, even though he ends, like many of the Confessional poets, amid unnerving guilt and terror.

While blasting Lowell as "Lord Dreary"—a pun on his book *Lord Weary's Castle*—Dickey was more consistently gracious toward James Merrill, whose reputation was still in the ascendant. He hoped Merrill could give a reading at Reed in November, and on September 15 invited him to the "big sort of Faulknerian, decaying mansion type of place"[53] they rented on 1200 SE Lava Drive. To entice Merrill west, he told him how much he admired his new book, *Water Street:* "This is beginning to be what I have always wanted for you; you've got it in your hands; you've done it; you're doing it."[54] He also thanked Merrill for sending his recently completed opera about the Brontës. The ever-cordial Merrill responded enthusiastically and visited the Dickeys in late November.

Dickey also reached out to another poet, Henry Taylor, who was young enough not to stir his competitive animus. Taylor, who had been studying at the University of Virginia under George Garrett, had written Dickey a fan letter earlier in June with an unusual proposal. Garrett had conceived of an anthology of poems and stories about a mysterious girl wearing a raincoat to be called, appropriately, *The Girl in the Black Raincoat*. Taylor asked Dickey to submit something (Annie Dillard, Leslie Fiedler, John Updike, Reynolds Price, W. D. Snodgrass, and numerous others were also contacted). Dickey did not respond until he heard again from Taylor on October 5. This time Taylor enclosed a parody of Dickey, "Mr. James Dickey in Orbit," along with a more flattering imitation, "The Horse Show at Midnight," which became the title poem for his first poetry book. Dickey said he appreciated the poems, but never contributed to the anthology about the girl in the raincoat.

At Reed, Dickey remained as prolific as ever. On December 20, 1963, he told Donald Hall, who was in England on his Guggenheim Fellowship, that he had finished yet another collection of poems for Wesleyan, which he wanted to call *The Common Grave, Slave Quarters,* or *Buckdancer's Choice*. Confirming the confidence he had in his new work, the nation's most prestigious colleges bombarded him with invitations to read. In November, Harvard included him in a series that Robert Lowell had recently commenced. Literary agents beckoned. On December 19, Armitage Watkins wrote that he wanted to represent him. Arthur Gregor at Macmillan discussed the possibility of publishing another collection of his critical articles after *The Suspect in Poetry*. Prominent magazine editors like Henry Rago at *Poetry*, who accepted "The Firebombing" on December 19, 1963, applauded his current poems. Dickey's fame also translated into job offers. On October 9, Paul Cundiff, the English Department chair at the University of Delaware, urged Dickey to apply for their writer-in-residence position. In December, Milton Orowitz asked if he would consider a visiting professorship at California State College in Los Angeles with a thirteen-thousand-dollar salary. In late January 1964, Walter Hardy at the State University College of New York

(Geneseo) offered him a visiting position with a comparable salary. Another college trying to entice him away from Reed was San Fernando Valley State in Northridge, California.

The new year had hardly begun when Dickey decided to leave Reed on a "barnstorming for poetry" trip. An organization called the Midwest Poetry Circuit had signed him up for nearly a dozen readings in Indiana, Illinois, Minnesota, and Wisconsin. Between February 6 and March 1 he read at Carroll College, University of Wisconsin, Lake Forest College, MacMurray College, Lawrence College, Ripon College, Notre Dame, Rockford College, Beloit College, Miami University, Western College for Women, Depauw University, Wabash College, Saint John's University, University of Minnesota, and Macalester College. Working out the logistics of such trips proved almost as taxing as taking them. A typical request came from Winifred Van Etten of Cornell College in Iowa: "May Cornell have Mr. James Dickey for February 21, at four o'clock? We have checked transportation and find bus and train impossible. But Mr. Dickey could leave Beloit by air at 10:30 P.M., reach Chicago at 11:05, stay the night in Chicago, leave Chicago at 7:25 A.M., and arrive in Cedar Rapids at 9:09 A.M. We would meet him in Cedar Rapids and bring him to Mount Vernon."[55] Such itineraries showed little concern for the amenities of sleep and meals.

Dickey demonstrated his typical negotiating tactics with the Poetry Center at New York's Young Men's and Young Women's Hebrew Association (YM-YWHA), which asked Dickey to read and participate in a symposium on "The State of American Poetry Today" in early February. On January 21, 1964, he informed the Y that he almost never read for under $125. The Y generously granted him $200. Sensing it had deeper pockets than he had expected, he asked for more, only to receive an apologetic reply pointing out that he was already getting more than anybody else at the symposium, and in any case, the Y had no additional funds. Dickey rarely refused a final offer, even if it was substantially lower than his request. On his birthday, February 2, he joined a motley group of poets—Gregory Corso, Jack Gilbert, Howard Nemerov, and Theodore Weiss—on a panel moderated by John Simon.

In New York, Dickey startled Simon in his customary way—by flitting between Southern redneck and sophisticated writer. Simon, who soon became one of Dickey's close friends, blamed his erratic behavior on alcohol, noting that Dickey acted in one of three ways: sober and charming, drunk and obnoxious, or sober and ornery. Alcohol or the lack of it seemed to rule his temperament. Dickey's assessment of Simon was less complicated. He relished Simon's notoriously caustic criticism of books, films, and plays: "He's a wonderful critic. I don't always agree with him, but John Simon knows the most and he cares the most. He's incorruptible."[56] Simon's enemies, as Dickey often said of his own, were a measure of the courage and honesty of his judgments.

At "The State of Poetry" symposium, Simon found Dickey sober, subdued, and gracious. Some of his fellow panelists were the opposite. Gregory Corso, who had originally refused to participate, was especially belligerent. According to Simon, Nemerov had to act as a "wild animal trainer" to keep Corso in line.

Dickey tried to tame Corso's outbursts, too, by emphasizing that the different panelists were all trying to do the same thing by writing poetry. Corso rejected this gesture of goodwill and attacked Dickey for being a former businessman. How could Dickey call himself a poet when he looked like an ex-football-playing advertising executive? With some justification, Corso felt like an outsider. Gilbert had recently won the Yale Younger Poets competition; Weiss, Nemerov, and Dickey taught at well-respected colleges and published at well-known presses. Having shuffled between foster homes, mental institutions, and prisons, Corso despised the "establishment" they represented. He had developed as a poet under the aegis of the rebellious Allen Ginsberg, and during the symposium he raised the issue of privilege repeatedly. He wanted to know how much money the other poets made and ridiculed them as rich academics. His blustering nearly got him ejected from the Y. Gilbert, who also liked to inveigh against academic poets, directed his ire at Nemerov, whose formal poetry was anathema. But he also blasted Corso. After the symposium Simon declared: "My conclusion was the state of poetry . . . was war."[57]

Dickey used his free time in New York to socialize and conduct business. Before appearing at the Y he joined Nemerov, whom he would invite to Reed in late April, for a visit to the poet, scholar, and publisher Stanley Burnshaw. Burnshaw had written Dickey for the first time near the beginning of 1964. Without any forewarning, Dickey rang the doorbell at Burnshaw's Seventy-Five Central Park West apartment and said: "I'm Jim Dickey and this is my friend Howard Nemerov. May we come in?"[58] Their hour-long talk was so invigorating that Dickey and Burnshaw made arrangements to see each other again after the symposium. Having founded the Dryden Press in 1939 and directed it until 1958, when it merged with Henry Holt, Burnshaw considered publishing Dickey's poetry. Four months after Dickey appeared at his door, Burnshaw spoke to his colleagues at Holt about the possibility. Although Dickey remained with Wesleyan for the time being, he appreciated Burnshaw's interest, continued to correspond with him, and periodically visited him in New York or on Martha's Vineyard.

Dickey also spoke to Bob Lescher about his revised manuscript of *The Deliverer*, which he was now calling *Deliverance*, and about signing an option with Houghton Mifflin. It was probably on this occasion that Dickey met Houghton Mifflin's editor-in-chief, Paul Brooks. According to Dickey, after a drink of whiskey, Brooks announced with some anxiety: "Well, Jim, everybody here likes the book, and we think we're going to have a big success with it, but some of us frankly were a little bit worried to the effect that it might possibly be true—an eyewitness account of something you participated in." Dickey replied: "Well, yeah, some of it is true. Yeah." His anxiety mounting, Brooks asked: "Were you ever in any situation where somebody was killed like that? Or two people or three people were killed?" Dickey said he had not been in such a situation. Brooks, who was a knowledgeable outdoorsman and conservationist, said: "I'd like to see some of the southern Appalachian Mountain river country. Suppose I came down next August, and you and I got a canoe. You could take me up there and show it to me." Dickey agreed with a wry twinkle: "Yeah, Paul, I'd be very happy to, if you like. Come down next August. Just let me know when you're coming, and I'll get a canoe, and I can show you where everything happened."[59] Brooks and his Houghton Mifflin cohorts again began quavering.

Dickey's favorite line about the actuality of the sodomy and murder scenes in his novel was that he could not comment because the statute of limitations had not yet expired in Georgia; he was still vulnerable to prosecution. Brooks's questions and responses, however, were figments of Dickey's imagination. Brooks admired neither Dickey nor his novel, made no attempt to get to know the author, felt the rape scene was disgusting, denounced the murder of the hillbilly stalker on the cliff as ridiculous, and, in the end, was surprised the book sold as well as it did.[60] Brooks's negative appraisal of Dickey and his novel was probably one reason for the meager option of $250.

Because of his travels to New York and other points around the country, Dickey often left his classes teacherless. When Dickey cavalierly told his students to write an epic poem during one of his long absences, colleagues and students protested. Carolyn Kizer proposed a solution; she could act as Dickey's substitute and in the process strengthen her résumé, earn some money, and get out of Seattle. She told Dickey that everyone assumed she was married to a millionaire and didn't need any money. But she did need money. Dickey was receptive to her proposal and soon made her the object of his seductions. On his February trip to New York they enjoyed an impassioned tryst, which later troubled Kizer more than it did Dickey. On February 21, 1964, Kizer wrote that she was struggling to articulate her complex feelings. She thanked him for teaching her how to love people in a new way and promised to keep at the head of her bed the white flower he had brought her. Nonetheless, she thought their brief fling was terribly wrong. Deeply affected by Dickey's charm and sexual bravado, she continued to write him amorous letters.

As with Kizer, Dickey continued to fan the flames of his romance with Gwen Walti. Concerned about her effect on his marriage, Walti asked in a letter from Zurich, dated January 31, 1964, whether Maxine objected to their correspondence. Maxine did resent his old girlfriend's letters, just as she resented those from his new girlfriends. On February 3 Maxine sent a "Happy Birthday" letter to Harvard, where Dickey was due to read, in which she gave her husband some maternal advice: "It seems NY really was good to you. Did you see Carolyn K. again? She is a fool and don't pay any attention to her." Maxine included news of the family—a trip to the Portland Zoo with the boys, an upcoming dinner party at a friend's house, her mother's planned visit from Clearwater, Florida—and ended with an emotional proclamation: "We love you and miss you so awful much. I don't see how we can stand a whole month without you. It will be exciting for you though and the money too. Do take real good care of yourself and know that we think about you every minute." In her postscript, she added: "I do love you Jim."[61]

Dickey's carousing was not without complications. On February 20, a letter arrived from a distraught, ill mistress in Saint Louis, who wrote in anger that her drunken husband had threatened to kill her when he discovered her love for Dickey. She regretted the fact that Dickey could not be her lover, but wanted to keep exchanging letters, so advised Dickey to write her with a non-Portland postmark. Dickey had met the Saint Louis woman, who wrote poetry and taught

English at Washington University, during a reading trip to her university in mid-1963. At the time she was the frustrated wife of an Episcopal minister and the mother of several children. Invited to a party for Dickey at the house of Mona Van Duyn and her husband, Jarvis Thurston, she arrived without her husband and before long was kissing Dickey while others danced to jazz on the record player. Late in the night, Dickey leaned over to Van Duyn and said: "It's all set up. All you have to do is leave the door unlocked. . . . She says she's desperate. She's going to come as soon as her husband and kids are asleep. And you won't have anything further to do with it." Van Duyn protested that she didn't want to get involved, but in the end she complied. At breakfast the next morning, she asked Dickey what had happened. Dickey said: "She came. But she scared me to death. I was sound asleep."[62] He wrote a poem about the unrequited visit, published it in the August 1963 issue of *Poetry,* and asked Van Duyn to point it out to his lover, which she refused to do. (Another local poet, Donald Finkel, passed along the message.)

News of Dickey's affairs and one-night stands trickled back to Maxine, who was predictably hurt and furious. She had threatened divorce in Atlanta and continued to do so at Reed. Her accusations about her husband's "whores" resonated through the house, as did Dickey's denials. Confused and upset by the quarrels, Kevin and Chris watched their parents try to dissolve their animosity in alcohol. In fact, Dickey was not quite the Byronic conquistador to which he aspired. For Dickey what mattered more than the consummation of an affair was the presumption among others that it had been consummated. His salacious stories on his reading tours contributed to his image, as did his boasts at home. "I must have fucked a thousand women,"[63] Dickey exclaimed one night to his fourteen-year-old son, Chris. About to go to sleep, Chris wondered why his father would say such a thing.

At the end of his winter reading tour, Dickey spent a joyous weekend talking and drinking with Bly and Wright in Minneapolis. "The occasion," he told Wright, "was one of those that come along so rarely that you feel sometimes that times of that kind are impossible, really, or just happen in the best of dreams or reveries."[64] They walked on the frozen Mississippi River and visited Allen Tate, who still taught at the University of Minnesota and who was acting as Dickey's host. Bly's objections to Tate may have encouraged Dickey to act objectionably toward his former mentor. He remained drunk and surly for most of his stay and failed to leave any sort of note when he left early one morning. Relations cooled even further after Dickey encouraged one of his students in 1965 to write Tate for help on a term paper. The paper was about Dickey himself. The student, Judy Stangler, asked Tate to provide biographical information about Dickey's childhood, education, military experience, advertising work, marriage, and family that might throw light on his poetry. Apart from the vainglorious nature of the assignment, the student must have been unaware that Tate's New Critical principles militated against such a biographical approach. Tate scribbled in the upper left-hand corner of the letter that it was the most preposterous request he had ever received and blamed it on Dickey.

It was around the time of his reunion with Bly and Wright that Dickey spoke of his sense of being encased in a glass coffin. The two poets, Bly recalled, were sitting in a tall building overlooking Chicago when Dickey said in perfect seriousness: "You see that glass [in the window]. I feel like I've been looking through it a long time, and now it's getting closer and closer, and pretty soon it's going to close around me."[65] The confession startled Bly. Dickey expanded on his remark in a letter to Wright:

> During most of life I have the sense of strangulation, of a kind of strangulation and compression of a ghost which is myself, where everything is seen through a thickening pane of glass that is really the deadening of the senses that comes with aging. I also have, rarely, the sense of breathing deeply, suddenly becoming a full-blooded human body, and being able to reach out and take up things and hold them, touch them, with exquisite and meaningful intimacy. That is the kind of thing, the kind of time that I live for. It is because poetry helps or even perhaps causes such states that I care for it; it can, as Lawrence says somewhere, help you "not be a dead man in life." It is the sense of that deadness that is most frightening to me, and it is also the sense that such deadness can't *really* be got around or done away with by liquor, sex, or other stimuli that both scares me and stimulates me. Whatever *does* militate against the deadness has got to come from deep within; one has to be able to sit still and *receive*, so that the flow of a river becomes something so inexplicable, haunting and uplifting that it is past all telling, the air-spines in an ice cube of a rare and delicate essence, fragile and *there*. This is where I am going—or want to go—in poetry.[66]

Having resuscitated the goodwill of Bly and Wright, Dickey attempted to do the same with Richard Hugo, who had been dispatching bearish letters to him from Potenza, Italy. On February 10, Hugo wrote: "Not only have you not written, you didn't even thank me for the poem I sent dedicated to you and Maxine. Shithead. Try to be responsive." Hugo then turned to his book *Death of the Kapowsin Tavern*, which had just been accepted by Harcourt Brace, and Bly, who had just ruffled a lot of gray hairs by attacking a number of older poets in a *Choice* magazine article: "What a wild character [Bly is], but for all his carelessness and inaccuracies he does have a real value. Who else blurts out the way he does, hitting a few points that no one else would dare hit?"[67] Dickey sympathized with this view, so long as he wasn't one of Bly's targets.

Friendly overtures helped assuage their spats, but Dickey's need to compete continually strained his relations with Bly, Wright, and Hugo. In 1964, it must have been obvious to his friends that Dickey was pulling ahead of the pack. Dickey's stature was such that libraries already expressed interest in buying, or at least procuring, his papers. On February 21, 1964, the deputy administrator of manuscripts at Syracuse University, Martin Bush, announced that he wanted to start a Dickey archive. The librarian Lawrence Thompson wrote Dickey on March 28 to see if he might donate his papers to the University of Kentucky. Like Syracuse, Kentucky refused to pay, but Thompson pointed out that a donation would allow a large tax write-off. On March 13, Mona Van Duyn at Washington University also asked Dickey about his manuscripts. A week later Dickey told Van Duyn that he had bales of letters and manuscripts because he could never bear to throw away anything. Nonetheless, he was unsure about establishing his archive in St. Louis. In a letter sent on April 26, he claimed to have received offers from five or six schools and asked Van Duyn to urge Washington University to make a payment that would also guarantee tax relief. On April 29, William Matheson, chief of the Rare Book Department, named a fee. Much to Dickey's delight, a bidding war ensued. On May 1, Martin Bush from Syracuse argued that if Dickey were paying $1,500 in income tax, donating his papers to Syracuse would eliminate all income tax over a five-year period. He estimated Dickey's manuscripts were worth from $5,000 to $10,000. Tempted by this offer, in the end Dickey decided to sell his papers to Washington University.

Having taken over a 50-percent salary cut when he left advertising to teach at Reed, Dickey continued to look for ways to pad his income. Shortly after *Helmets* was published on February 27, 1964, he again tried to pry more money from Wesleyan University Press. Winning the Georgia Association Literary Achievement Award in March convinced him that he deserved a bonus. Without fully appreciating Dickey's discontent, on March 18 Lockwood congratulated Dickey on selling over two thousand copies of *Drowning with Others*, and jokingly suggested awarding him "The Used-Coke-Bottle-Cap Award" for the feat. Perhaps remembering the fees paid by Coca-Cola, Dickey responded to Lockwood's jest with acrimony. He threatened to leave Wesleyan if they refused him a larger advance—$500—for his next poetry book. Lockwood agreed to consider an advance of $250, but no more: "We can't offer you much in the way of instant money. We can only offer to continue to do right by you and your books, to be energetic and loyal in promoting and disseminating them—whether you write the great American novel or not."[68] Energetic loyalty was fine, but Dickey wanted the sort of money a commercial publisher could provide.

Because of what he deemed Lockwood's tightfistedness, Dickey approached Ken McCormick, the legendary editor at Doubleday. McCormick expressed interest in considering his next book of poems, but would make no offer before seeing a manuscript. Dickey also tried Donald Hutter at Scribner's. On April 13, 1964, Hutter repeated what he had said about *The Deliverer* a year before: he needed a manuscript in hand before he could discuss a contract. His attempts to jump to a new publisher stymied for the moment, Dickey decided to stay with Wesleyan. The additional money, he now reasoned, would only boost his income taxes. It was tax-paying season, and he complained to his mother that the greedy IRS was robbing him. His mother wrote back: "Your Mama really feels for you having to pay all that lovely money to the Income Tax Department,— $1,000—WOW! That's a bit much. . . . When you hassle with the U.S. government you always wind up the loser and spitting mad. Stay away from that hi [sic] income bracket. It's murder!"[69] A day after his income taxes were due, Dickey sat on a panel at Portland State College's Fine Arts Festival and, surprisingly, argued against the government giving money to artists. Artists should earn their living like everyone else, he told the audience, ignoring the grants and family subsidies that had helped his career.

A constant monitor of her son's financial well-being, Maibelle sent Dickey money whenever he needed it. In June 1964, his MG needing repairs, she dispatched a check for $125. "Here comes help!" she wrote, adding one of her trademark jingles: "Don't cuss, phone us."[70] Nearly every letter Maibelle wrote her son eventually circled around to the subject of money. Despite her largesse, she refused to think of herself as her son's benefactor. When a family friend, Thomas Rypert, and his wife were killed during the mid-1960s in a plane crash on Saint Simons Island, Maibelle wrote: "This is what happens so often when a person inherits too much money—(Ho hum, not one of the Dickey problems)."[71] Her son's reckless behavior, she implied, had little to do with the family money given him over the years. After all, unlike her two other children, Jim had broken away from Atlanta and the family's business. In the notoriously unpredictable, nomadic world of poetry, he continued to line up jobs.

In 1963, Dickey had visited San Fernando Valley State with the hope of convincing its English Department to hire him. He had endeared himself to Ann Stanford, the poet-in-residence, and to her husband, an engineer who had talked to him about designing the tree house in the Swiss Family Robinson section of Disneyland. He had also won over the English professors with a witty, energetic poetry reading. On February 25, 1964, Chairman Charles Kaplan offered Dickey a job for the 1964–65 academic year. He had been so enthralled by Dickey's reading that he deemed his offer a pure formality. If Dickey accepted, he could teach "English 308, Verse-writing," and another course of his choice. Two months later, on April 21, 1964, the English Department at the University of Wisconsin in Madison offered Dickey $5,000 for an eight-week semester as its writer-in-residence. The teaching load would be relatively light—only two one-and-a-half-hour creative writing classes per week. Dickey agreed to teach at San Fernando Valley State from the fall of 1964 to the end of 1965, and at the University of Wisconsin during the winter semester of 1966 from February 1 to April 1. The chair, Helen White, was delighted. With his teaching schedule set for the next two years, Dickey made plans to leave Reed at the end of the spring.

Before moving to Valley State, Dickey planned to teach a poetry workshop from June 15–19 at San Francisco State College and, while in the Bay area, reunite with Gwen Walti, who would be visiting her ill mother. Walti had written Dickey another of her romantic epistles on May 1. Afraid that Dickey was still smarting from her rejection of marriage in 1946, she apologized profusely for the pain she had inflicted. At the time, she was determined to strike out on her own, she said, and have Dickey do the same. She spoke of the long talks with Dickey's mother she had had in which both women agreed that he should return to college unburdened by the responsibilities of marriage. Destiny, she felt, would keep them together in spirit if not in flesh. Whether by fate or by choice, their romance kept flickering.

In a lecture delivered three years after leaving Reed, Dickey joked about the college's "terrible and wonderful" atmosphere, where "everybody had a beard except one or two of the girls": "Most of the kids there were awfully poor. The girls all had long stringy black hair and burning eyes and ate nothing but yeast (*that* year), and the fellows all played the guitar and wore Mexican rope-soled sandals. But the sense of exploration, of *quest:* the sense of intellectual excitement was breathtaking! A lot of the students lived on horse-meat (which was delicious, the way they cooked it, though don't ask me how they cooked it). They talked all night every night, and to be with them would either make a teacher cut his throat at his own academic 'invincible apathy' or make him resolve to raise himself to their level of passionate and intelligent involvement."[72] Because his values had the stamp of another generation and another region, Dickey viewed Reed as a jocular bystander. Nevertheless, he felt sad about leaving his first writer-in-residence position. According to Jim Rawley, he "wept, in a barely-holding-back-the-tears-way, when he made his farewell speech at the end of the year."[73] To express his gratitude to his students and colleagues, he gave a valedictory poetry reading on May 3. If his students had tweaked his Southern conscience, they had also helped him in unforeseen ways. Kipnis and his friends had expanded his skill and repertoire on the guitar tenfold, and, in the process, introduced him to musicians and music that directly benefited his two most successful books—*Buckdancer's Choice* and *Deliverance* (Kipnis was still sending Dickey taped guitar lessons in 1966). Other students had made other contributions. To fulfill her thesis requirement, Richard Pincus's wife, Monica Moseley Pincus, printed a special edition of Dickey's long poems "The Firebombing" and "Reincarnation," which in a few decades was worth hundreds of dollars. She had worked with Dickey and one of Dickey's Reed friends, the world-famous calligrapher Lloyd Reynolds, to produce an exquisitely crafted book.

Among these vital, ambitious students with whom he often discussed his writing projects, Dickey made progress on *Deliverance,* completed *The Suspect in Poetry* and *Buckdancer's Choice,* and published *Helmets.* Many of America's finest poets and critics greeted the new poems in *Helmets* with rave reviews. James Merrill told Dickey that he was astonished by the book: "I can't think of anyone since Rilke who has given one such a sense of encountering pure vision—in an idiom simple as light, that transforms everything it touches. . . . I am such an indoor type myself that rock + stream + wilderness have become, as settings, more exotic than Paris or the Boar's Head. Well, thank you—more than I can say. I'm real proud to know you."[74] Merrill invited Dickey to his home in Stonington, Connecticut, and was as pleased as Dickey by the news that *Helmets* had been chosen as a finalist for the National Book Award.

In *Helmets* Dickey returned to old subjects with a fresh perspective. He wrote about World War II as a foot soldier traipsing through the carnage rather than as an aviator flying above it. His determination to shift perspectives had characterized his visionary mode from the start, but in *Helmets* he took new liberties. In the first poem, "The Dusk of Horses," he tried to describe the world as seen through the eyes of horses:

Right under their noses, the green
Of the field is paling away
Because of something fallen from the sky.

They see this, and put down
Their long heads deeper in grass
That only just escapes reflecting them

As the dream of a millpond would.
The color green flees over the grass
Like an insect, following the red sun over

The next hill.

Under the setting sun, the horses go to their stalls and continue reinventing the world with the sort of apocalyptic sensibility that Dickey esteemed.

In the book's second poem, "Fence Wire," Dickey again presents himself as a magical shape-shifter; he assumes the persona of a winter hawk, a robin, a boy, and a farmer. Poem after poem celebrates the way an altered apprehension of the world can transform it into a "new heaven and new earth." His poems about hunting typify his attitude; in them he yearns for visionary transformations rather than slain animals. In "Winter Trout" he shoots an arrow at a fish and misses, in "Springer Mountain" he gives up his bow-and-arrow hunt, and in "Chenille" he gets lost as he pursues his quarry. In each case, Dickey wants to commune with animal spirits like a shaman. The animals are totemic—they represent instinctual grace and a deliverance from human perplexities—and when Dickey lays down his weapons, he does so with the reverence of an initiate who desires to learn from his masters how to enter a more animated and more imaginative consciousness.

The new poems about soldiering and hunting record Dickey's efforts to break through the anaesthetic, artificial enclosures—the glass coffins—that surrounded him. Like the Romantics, symbolists, and modernists, he bestowed a sacred mantle upon the imagination and its ability to liberate the individual from the death-in-life of everyday routines. In *Helmets* he found his holy grails in unusual places—horse farms, chenille bedspreads, scarred faces, submerged army trucks, Okinawa battlefields—and communicated his sacramental vision with the metaphorical and rhythmical vigor that characterized his earlier books. Despite the general praise for the book, which it richly deserved, it failed to win the National Book Award. Looking for someone to blame, Dickey pointed a finger at Allen Tate, who had been one of the judges. He told Bly that he had heard rumors that Tate had been "loud in denunciation of Dickey's character and his influence"[75] ever since his drunken visit to Minneapolis.

In a two-car caravan, on June 10 the Dickeys left Portland and headed south to San Francisco before continuing east to Atlanta. Although Maxine had complained bitterly about splitting up the family for the summer, Dickey again insisted on the arrangement. While his wife and children stayed with his mother-in-law in Florida, he hoped to make progress revising *Deliverance*. His first order of summer business, however, was the publication of another poetry book. On May 11, 1964, Dickey had told Donald Hall that he would submit *Buckdancer's Choice* to one of the six other publishers that wanted it if Wesleyan did not honor all his demands. Angry about the way Wesleyan had handled the marketing of *Helmets* on his recent Midwest poetry tour, he said: "If this sounds highhanded please forgive me; it is just that I seem to be a salable item this year, and must make whatever hay I can from these conditions, which are perhaps not likely to be repeated."[76] Dickey requested that Wesleyan evaluate his manuscript in June and publish it in February 1965.

Reminding Hall that he was the best editor he had ever had and still his literary executor, Dickey pressed his case. Hall was adamant about slowing the flow of Dickey's books and also wanted Dickey to stop complaining about Wesleyan. *Helmets* was selling well; it had sold over one thousand copies by late May, and *Drowning with Others* had passed the two thousand mark. By saturating the market, Hall argued, Dickey might suffer from overexposure. Why couldn't he sit on his poems the way Robert Frost had and surprise readers when he finally released them? Why did he have to be so mercenary? Dickey brushed Hall's warnings aside: "Nothing could matter to me less than the deliberate hoarding and juggling with poems, the strategic employment of them in the interests of my 'career.' That has no fascination for me. And it shouldn't have for you, either: not for a man of your gifts. That kind of thing should not even occur to you. We are not in the gold market, after all, but are trying to get something said. And if it's said it should be heard."[77] If Hall objected to bringing out *Buckdancer's Choice* so soon after *Helmets*, Dickey would make good on his threat to take the book elsewhere, which he might do anyway if Wesleyan failed to give him a larger advance.

Dickey's decision to release the manuscript of *Buckdancer's Choice* as soon as possible was not entirely his own. On April 22, 1964, Willard Lockwood had advised him to send it to Hall. Still irritated by Dickey's pushiness, Hall read the new collection in early June and expressed the sort of reservations he had had after first encountering Dickey's poems at the *Paris Review:* "I think you get too long-winded pretty frequently. . . . As it stands, it is distinctly poorer than *Drowning with Others* and *Helmets*. I'm sure you know it. I want Wesleyan to accept it, and then you and me to edit it like crazy. I think you would be very foolish to insist on publication next February. . . . If you allow yourself to print a book which isn't quite as good [as previous books] . . . people will be reading funeral rites over you."[78] Although he admired poems like "Shark's Parlor," Hall recommended that Dickey cut many of the others.

In a few weeks Dickey and Hall reached a compromise. Dickey retreated from his demand for February publication, and Hall gave a more balanced appraisal of the book's contents. Agreeing that the book needed pruning, Dickey again entrusted it to Hall: "It seemed the best thing simply to put in everything I have published since *Helmets*, and let you help decide what will make up the final version. That has worked well in the past, and from every indication it will also work well again: there's no reason for it not to."[79] Dickey's main support at Wesleyan during this trying time came from an unlikely source, Denise Levertov, who was on the editorial board. The letter she wrote Dickey on July 16, 1964, was part commendation and part warning. As one of the readers of *Buckdancer's Choice*, she thought the manuscript was terrific: "Let me beg you not to let Don Hall persuade you that poems should be dropped, altered etc. In *his* report he revealed that he thinks himself your mentor, which is absurd, to my mind, as the handful of decent poems he has written can not compare with yours, + as for his critical judgment, no one who apparently thinks Robert Bly is a major poet—Bly who at best is an agreeable, semi-naive, most minor one—can be taken seriously."[80] Levertov hoped that Dickey would free himself from Hall and edit the book himself.

Although many judged *Buckdancer's Choice* to be Dickey's best book, some—notably Bly—read his funeral rites as Hall predicted. Up until the mid-1960s, Bly and Dickey had argued like friends. Bly published *The Suspect in Poetry* early in the summer of 1964, and while in England in late July, he prepared to lecture on Dickey and his poetry for the BBC. Like Hall, who was in England at the time, Bly must have realized that Dickey was using him as a de facto publicity agent. To Bly's request for biographical information for his radio broadcast, Dickey responded with customary self-aggrandizement:

> In answer to your questions: yes, I played football for Clemson in 1941 or 1942. I was a freshman and played two regular freshman games, but after that the Southern Conference passed the Freshman rule (everybody was beginning to get drafted) and I moved up to the varsity and started the last six of their eight games. I was honorable mention for all-Southern, which was supposed to be pretty fair for a freshman. I played wingback under the old single wing formation, not much used any more except by the University of Tennessee, though the pro "shotgun" formation is a variation of it. When I got back from the war I went to Vanderbilt, but was declared ineligible for football and so couldn't play there. I had played in three basketball games also at Clemson, and so was also ineligible for that. But I did run track all three years I was an undergraduate at Vanderbilt. I ran the sprints and hurdles and broadjumped. My best race was the 120-yard high hurdles at the Cotton Carnival invitational meet at Memphis in 1947, but I won pretty regularly in Southeastern Conference meets for three years. My best time in the hundred was 9.7 (done only once, but I was fairly consistent under 10) and for the 220, 20.9 (on a straightaway). My best broad jump was around 24'5". Yes, I was field archery champion of Georgia. My best field round was about 450.[81]

Dickey tried to make this wildly exaggerated self-portrait convincing by filling it with precise—and poetically irrelevant—details.

Bly's talk undoubtedly had something to do with the summer publication of *The Suspect in Poetry*. Seemingly oblivious to his far-fetched distortions of facts, Dickey in his introduction to the book complained about the way poets prevaricated: "This air of falseness, of the Suspect in poetry, is one cause of the fatal and much-deplored rift between poet and audience in our time. Very subtly, the feeling of basic honesty . . . has evaporated from our poetry; there is no longer a sense of communion involved: that communion upon which all meaningful communication in the arts depends. 'The poets lie too much' has grown from a still small voice into a thundering accusation, though it has been with us at least since Plato."[82] Assuming the high ground, Dickey fired his critical guns at most of the major poetic camps. Randall Jarrell's formalist poetry, he said, was "dull beyond all dullness of stupefaction or petrifaction . . . , untalentedly sentimental, self-indulgent, and insensitive." Yvor Winters's classical school dehumanized experience in overly moral and rational poems. Allen Ginsberg's *Howl*, which helped launch the Beats, was simply "the skin of Rimbaud's *Une Saison en Enfer* thrown over the conventional maunderings of one type of American adolescent, who has discovered that machine civilization has no interest in his having read Blake." An anthology like Donald Allen's *The New American Poetry*, which featured Beat poets like Ginsberg, amounted to a lot of "low-grade whale-fat." The Beat guru Kenneth Patchen wrote "tiresome, obvious, self-important, sprawling, sentimental, witless, preachy, tasteless, useless poems and books." Thom Gunn, who tried to marry Winters's classicism to Beatnik subjects, was a "fashionable, rote versifier" with an offensively "pedantic, pontifical manner." The radical innovations of Charles Olson's "projective verse" were a hoax. James Merrill, Anthony Hecht, and the "School of Charm" were superfluous. Confessional poets like Anne Sexton, who wrote about "the pathetic and disgusting aspects of bodily experience," created "little more than a kind of terribly serious and determinedly outspoken soap-opera." Dickey also took aim at honors bestowed by the poetry establishment, such as the Lamont Poetry Prize ("surely the most infallible badge of accepted-and-forgotten mediocrity our culture can bestow") and the Yale Younger Poets Prize ("if you feel in the mood for a sad, unbelieving laugh, look at Yale's list all the way back to the beginning, and *read* a few of the books"). Dickey left only a few poets unscathed: Geoffrey Hill, Philip Larkin, W. S. Graham, and Jon Silkin among the British; John Berryman, Howard Nemerov, and Theodore Roethke among the Americans. Having damned the multitudes, Dickey felt obliged to offer his prescription for exemplary verse. The good poet, he proposed, must be "master of a superior secret," and this secret "dwells . . . in the development of personality, with its unique weight of experience and memory, as a writing instrument, and in the ability to give literary influence a new dimension which has the quality of this personality as informing principle."[83] This distinctive, secret personality or persona helped poets of "the second birth" approach experience with a unique vision and voice.

His critical assault of the poetry world completed, Dickey turned his attention to his novel, which had grown to 151 pages at Reed. On March 5, 1964, Lescher had complimented Dickey on the way he had fleshed out his characters, but still insisted that the story needed "a greater economy of prose." Disappointed that Lescher had not given more-practical suggestions on how to revise (Lescher had merely recommended that he read Percy Lubbock's *The Craft of Fiction*), Dickey was further disappointed when Lescher left Houghton Mifflin in March to become a literary agent for Brandt & Brandt in New York. Despite the fact that Theron Raines was already acting as his agent, Dickey wanted Lescher to represent him as well as edit his novel. Lescher agreed and soon plied Dickey with possible projects besides his novel: a short history of American poetry for Dutton and a major biography of Ezra Pound for McGraw Hill. Dickey declined both, and suggested that Richard Ellmann write the Pound biography.

Over the previous months Dickey had contacted numerous editors about his novel as well as his poetry. On July 13, Lescher warned Dickey not to negotiate with half-a-dozen publishers at the same time. Nevertheless, Dickey continued to act on his own behalf. By mid-April 1965, Lescher had received about nine queries from different editors about publishing *Deliverance*. Exasperated with Dickey's tactics, he wrote sternly: "I think publishers' interest is a great thing, but I'm frankly concerned about the way you're leading these people on. Wouldn't it be better simply to say that you're working on a novel, under option to Houghton Mifflin, and that you don't know what your poetry plans are until a decision on the novel is made? What you've been saying, in fact, to virtually each of these editors, is that you'd love to be published by them, that if Houghton Mifflin doesn't pay enough, you'd love to have these projects go to them. I think this kind of response takes an awful lot of people—eight out of the nine—up the garden path."[84] Dickey tried to take the gentle reprimand gracefully. He didn't want to drive away his editor, at least not yet.

On May 7, 1965, Paul Brooks asked Lescher for a progress report, and indicated that he wanted to publish *Deliverance* in 1966. Lescher assured Brooks that Dickey would revise the novel over the 1965 summer and mail the final draft around September. Then, in July 1965, Lescher's relationship with Dickey suffered a crisis. Lescher had arranged a number of meetings for Dickey with magazine editors in New York (the editor of *Holiday* was one) who were interested in articles or stories by Dickey. According to Lescher: "I went to tremendous trouble to make some appointments for him that I thought would be fruitful. And the day came when he was to be there, and I began receiving phone calls from the editors who had essentially gone out of their way . . . to meet with him. . . . Dickey had apparently come into town and shacked up with somebody for a couple of days and probably had been on a binge and just didn't make any of his appointments."[85] Lescher severed all ties with his client shortly afterward. Dickey tried to persuade Lescher to reconsider. On July 30, Lescher wrote: "I'm sorry to say that I still feel we ought not to continue to represent you. I don't think we can effectively represent any author who has a penchant for operating on his own."[86] On the same day Lescher sent the same message to Brooks: he could not work with a literary vigilante.

Following the feud, Dickey told Brooks that he had split with Lescher because Lescher was never around to close important deals. He called Theron Raines and explained that he had left Lescher because Lescher had complained about not getting a commission on a short screenplay he had agreed to write for a West Coast aerospace company. Raines, who had trained as a navigator in World War II and studied at Oxford, appealed to Dickey's ideal of the soldier-scholar-businessman; now he wanted Raines to be his full-time agent. Lescher, however, was not completely through with Dickey. Between his 1969 separation and 1971 divorce from his wife, writer-editor Mary Cantwell, Lescher learned that Dickey was having an affair with her. Dickey's partnership with Raines was a happier one. It flourished from its official inception in the mid-1960s until Dickey died.

Free of Lescher, Dickey decided in mid-August 1965 to send his novel in its current unrevised form to Brooks. "For God's sake don't lose it, for it's the only copy,"[87] he implored. Brooks did not want to be the editor of *Deliverance*, and, according to Dickey, berated his narrative at a breakfast meeting in New York. "The climb up the cliff is too long. You could do that in a page,"[88] Brooks purportedly said, citing one example of Dickey's verbosity. On September 28, 1965, Brooks told Dickey that Jacques de Spoelberch would take charge of the manuscript. Spoelberch wrote Dickey the next day, complimenting *Deliverance* as "a powerful and gripping piece of writing . . . as potentially stunning as *Heart of Darkness*."[89] Dickey responded quickly to Spoelberch with a plea for help with revisions and a warning that the book would not be finished until, at the earliest, March 1966. He added: "It's going to be a wonderful book, the only question being whether or not I'm the one to write it. I know very little of the writing of novels, and I'm going to have to lean so heavily on you that you're in danger of being driven right down into the ground, like the cat in the Tom and Jerry cartoons when the mouse hits him over the head with a sledge-hammer." Spoelberch wrote back with encouragement and clues to pronouncing his name: "As for my unpronounceable name, think of a spool of thread and a bear with a de before it, and you not only have the name licked but also correctly pronounced."[90] Dickey's next letter, written two months later, began "Dear Mr. Spool-Bear."

Still smarting from his turbulent break with Lescher and tense discussions with Brooks, Dickey welcomed his witty, intelligent new editor. Somewhat like Dickey, Spoelberch was a man of many talents who felt slightly put off by the WASPish Saint Mark's–Harvard clique at Houghton Mifflin. Born a viscount in a Belgian aristocratic family, he had been a baseball prodigy (he had tried out for the Philadelphia Phillies at the age of sixteen before major knee surgery had ended his prospects) and a professional drummer. He had also been an outstanding student at Princeton, nearly winning a Rhodes Scholarship. At Houghton Mifflin in his early twenties, he proved himself a versatile editor who could work with French poets, sports writers, or American poets like Galway Kinnell. Spoelberch and Dickey quickly established the rapport needed for the arduous shaping of *Deliverance*.

During the summer of 1964, Dickey spent more time talking to the real people behind his novel than to its editors. With Al Braselton, who had recently left his father-in-law's advertising firm for a job in General Electric's Computer Department, and Lewis King, who still handled his family's real estate, Dickey renewed his conversations about books, guitars, canoes, bows and arrows, and writing. King suggested that they go off on another canoe trip to North Georgia "with vintage wine and blazing fires,"[91] and promised to teach Dickey the fine art of fly-fishing. Dickey wrote Maxine on August 8: "Lewis is proposing another of his wild canoeing trips, this time down 'a real tough one,' the Chattooga, but I'm putting him off. My novel has scared me off all such projects!"[92] Dickey preferred shooting arrows with Lewis in the relative safety of the Sequoia archery range to shooting rapids and waterfalls on the Chattooga.

His family sequestered in Florida, Dickey had a good time in Atlanta and made little progress with his writing. In a letter to Donald Hall reviewing his summer, he said: "I spent most of the evenings playing the guitar in some dark dive in Atlanta where I was known, for some reason I could never fathom, only as 'Clem.' It was a kind of coffee-house, and thank god there were no poets reading there. I also almost got killed again in a canoeing accident in North Georgia on the greatest river in the world, the Chattooga (*not* the Chattahoochee or the Chattanooga), swam a good bit, read some things I'd always wanted to read, and geared up for the next struggle, which was (and is) California."[93] Dickey undoubtedly coined the nickname "Clem" because of his term at Clemson; he had no jobs playing guitar in Atlanta coffeehouses, and, despite Lewis King's entreaties, he refused to canoe on the Chattooga. In his letter to Hall, as in his novel, Dickey assumed the personae of Lewis King and Lewis Medlock. Even though the novel was far from completion, he had already spoken with King about using the Chattooga as a possible film site for *Deliverance*. On October 23, 1964, King sent Dickey a scouting report: "I checked out that stretch of river between Ga. and South Carolina . . . and if anyone ever considers making a movie from the Story, believe me, that's the place to shoot it. It's got the cliff and everything. It's much colder and clearer than the Coosawatee [sic], and has huge, (some as big as a small house) boulders in the river bed. There is more diversity than the Coosawatee, but it has that same generally sinister quality, only with a lot more grandure [sic]."[94] Six years later, as a technical adviser for John Boorman, King reiterated his recommendation, and the film, indeed, was made on the Chattooga. But before Dickey could think seriously about film sites, he had to finish his novel, and he also had to move his family to a new location on the West Coast. The drive from Atlanta to California, as it turned out, was as adventurous as the canoe trip in *Deliverance*.

18. California Sojourn (1964–1965)

On the way to San Fernando Valley State, Dickey kept stopping to get the brakes checked in his MG. His car was overheating, but none of the garage mechanics could discover the problem. According to Dickey: "Just as we were dragging into Winslow, Arizona, there was a loud cracking noise forward, smoke poured up from the front wheels, and the brake pedal went all the way to the floor while the speed held." Remembering the advice of a high school friend, Dickey geared down and then experienced a conflagration. "Surrounded by more blue-black smoke than Satan when he fell or was pushed from the crystal battlements of Milton's heaven, we coasted to a standstill in a filling station that seemed fated to be there like the number a roulette ball stops on, or like Pandemonium."[1] Dickey left the MG in Winslow for repair, piled into the Buick station wagon that Maxine had been driving, and several months later returned to find his car impounded, the owner of the filling station dead, and his assets frozen in probate. A woman at the garage wanted to charge Dickey a hefty sum for storing the MG. Dickey vehemently protested and told her to call the sheriff. "Hi, Betty. How are you doing?"[2] the sheriff said as he ambled toward them. Dickey confronted the man with all the animosity he could muster, but to little effect. Maxine intervened, paid the fee, and resolved the crisis. Dickey may have drawn on his altercation at the garage in *Deliverance* when he wrote about the

Griners' garage and, at the end of the novel, the sheriff's friendliness toward the locals and coolness toward the outsiders.

Dickey and his family arrived in Northridge, California, at the end of August, and moved into a cedar-sided bungalow across from a big discount store on Balboa Boulevard. Dickey was probably thinking of this busy six-lane road in his poem "The Bee," when he imagined his son Kevin chased into "the sheer / Murder of California traffic."[3] Their new location on Balboa Boulevard became the setting for another intimate family poem, "The Night Pool." The Dickeys spent much of their free time in their new swimming pool, *senza pantaloni* ("without pants"), as Dickey liked to say in remembrance of his flirtatious comments to his Positano maid. Maxine often swam naked at night so that nobody would notice the weight she had gained from drinking (in the dark Dickey usually refrained from insulting her with remarks like "Hath [thou] seen the white whale?").[4] Maxine took "The Night Pool," in which Dickey expresses his love for a woman he is with in a swimming pool, as a kind of tribute, and was upset in 1968 by his admission that the other woman was not Maxine.

San Fernando Valley State College was, as Dickey put it, "one of those California schools that yesterday was a potato patch and today has twenty thousand students."[5] In fact, when the original 165 acres were purchased north of Los Angeles in the mid-1950s, orange, eucalyptus, and walnut trees grew on the land, and banana squash had been harvested where the ground-breaking ceremony occurred. The new college, which specialized in education courses, enrolled 1,475 students. By the fall of 1964, enrollment had jumped to around 11,000. According to Robert ApRoberts, one of Dickey's friends in the English Department, morale was high at the time: "State support was very generous, buildings multiplied, the library mushroomed, and there were funds for lectures by such notables as André Maurois, Malcolm Muggeridge, Anaïs Nin and Derek Walcott."[6] Paul Bowles arrived to teach in 1966, just after Dickey left. Another of Dickey's colleagues, Harry Finestone, said: "The expectation that San Fernando Valley State College would be transformed into a vigorous, new, highly research-oriented college . . . seemed a real expectation, and it attracted the kind of people who wanted to do that."[7] As a visiting writer-in-residence, Dickey was a privileged anomaly. He enjoyed half the normal teaching load, no research expectations, and no obligation to attend faculty meetings or serve on committees.

Dickey at first thrived in the relaxed atmosphere at Valley State, which reminded him of his days at Hammer Field in Fresno. He continued to thrill his students by lecturing from a chair perched precariously on top of a desk and by interspersing literary aperçus with stories about shooting Japanese planes as a combat pilot and wild boar as a bow-and-arrow hunter. Before long, however, he had misgivings about his new home: "[At Reed] I longed for the sight of a football player or a dumb co-ed. [So I] went to California and all they had were football players and dumb co-eds. And [there] I longed for the anarchist and the girl who eats nothing but yeast!"[8] To a certain extent, Dickey continued to be viewed as an outcast. As Valley State developed a reputation for revolt second only to Berkeley's, Dickey's alleged political views met with suspicion and, at times, denunciation. "On news of his being hired, one irate colleague declared that we had hired a fascist," one of Dickey's friendlier colleagues, Richard Blakeslee, recalled. Some professors derisively called Dickey "the Southerner-in-residence." Dickey liked Blakeslee partly because he knew his friend would not try to pin him down on political issues (during his entire sixteen months in Northridge Dickey never voiced a political opinion in Blakeslee's company). The two men talked about sports over a few drinks—Blakeslee had a passion for bowling and table tennis—or played guitar together. They both loved folk music, and Dickey showed off his new proficiency. In turn, Dickey admired Blakeslee's approach to poetry. When Blakeslee published an article on Stephen Spender's "The Express" in *College English*, Dickey surprised him by declaring loudly that "it was the best article on poetry he had seen in many years."[9] Blakeslee had argued that the poem described a train rather than the rise of the proletariat, the creative process, or a girl's first sexual experience, as his students had suggested.

Other colleagues were not so tolerant of Dickey's homespun attitudes. Finestone, a fellow Atlantan, disdained his good ol' boy and bad ol' boy roles. Sober, Dickey exuded charm and vitality; drunk, he flaunted his "retrograde politics." "Unlike Jim," Finestone recalled, "Maxine was always publicly charming and seemed always to put his needs first, in a way no woman her age would do today."[10] Maxine, at least at social occasions, showed few signs of anger or pain over her husband's roving eye or excessive drinking. She no doubt approved of her husband playing the teetotaler at his birthday party in 1965. While his friends drank heavily, Dickey made the dramatic pronouncement that he had given up alcohol and cited a poem as the reason. Once when drunk he had composed what he believed was one of the greatest poems of all time only to discover the next morning that it was gibberish. His birthday party pledge was one of many renunciations.

If he downplayed his drinking among colleagues, Dickey played up his womanizing. To some in the English Department, such as Marvin Klotz, John Clendenning, and Henry Van Slooten, Dickey more than earned his reputation as a philanderer. Respectful of Van Slooten's passion for the rugged outdoors, Dickey tested their friendship by attempting to seduce his beautiful wife (Mrs. Van Slooten became so distraught that she told her husband she never wanted to see Dickey again). Clendenning reported: "There was a dark rumor that he was having a torrid affair with the wife of one of our colleagues in the department."[11] Dickey's "torrid affair" was with an attractive, slim, intelligent woman married to an English professor. The fact that he was a poet and married to an attractive woman must have aroused Dickey's competitive impulses. Dickey challenged him to an arm-wrestling match during one of their first meetings, beat him handily, and later proved his dominance at the Ping-Pong table. Dickey next competed with the young man for his wife. Maxine, whose graciousness the other poet admired, exhorted him to put a stop to what was happening. Somewhat otherworldly—he had been raised in India by Lutheran missionary parents—at first he had no idea that he was being cuckolded. He ignored colleagues who apprised him of the affair. Finally realizing what was happening, he suffered a nervous breakdown and entered therapy. The rumor that Dickey had fathered an illegitimate child probably originated from the other poet's wife, who in a fit of verbal anger told her husband that their child was Dickey's. When Dickey got wind of the accusation, he scolded his mistress for making such a cruel and false allegation. In the end, Dickey's unfortunate colleague separated from his wife and got a divorce.

The cuckolded poet may have been slow to act because of Dickey's widely recognized penchant for inventing rumors and stories. He boasted at Valley State that the New Yorker was offering him sumptuous gifts for his poems. His stock was so high at the magazine that its financial managers had honored his request for a Corvette (Dickey's "first read" contract at the New Yorker included bonuses, but not Corvettes). His politically active colleagues, who demanded to know his views on civil rights and the racial situation in the South, found his statements just as perplexing. A tall, handsome man named Calvin Israel, whose wife taught at the college, once discussed the topic of miscegenation with Dickey at a party. Dickey, who occasionally spoke out against mixed-race marriages, did so with the Israels. Accusing them of not being suitably outraged by the results of such marriages—mulatto children—Dickey suddenly vanished into the night.

Dickey appeared disdainful of the liberal academics who surrounded him. At a dinner party given by department chairman Charles Kaplan for the Clendennings and Dickeys during the summer of 1965, Dickey abruptly left the table for the family room and turned on the television to watch a sports program. After a while, Kaplan found him asleep. Someone asked Maxine how she managed to cope with such an unruly husband. She replied: "Oh, I don't mind this. At least I know he's not with some woman."[12] Maxine's breezy indifference belied her anguish. Her husband, she confided to some, was often impotent, but that reflected on her sexuality as much as his. She must have realized that his gallivanting about was one way to prove that he was not consistently impotent. The emotional stress took its toll. In Northridge she suffered temporary blindness, which she attributed to the pressures of managing her children and difficult husband, and she kept drinking.

Perhaps because he found the California girls so irresistible, Dickey joked about becoming a polygamist. He wanted to sire a vast brood, he told an interviewer for a college journal, but conceded that this was unlikely: "I would like to have had eight or ten children, but what I hope is that my boys will be more productive than I am or I have been, because what I really hope to be is a patriarch. I'd like to have hundreds and hundreds of them running around. Population explosion be damned! Let those others be sacrificed; my brood will be indispensable."[13] Comments like these were designed to aggravate Maxine and others as well. One English professor, Wallace Graves, grew increasingly critical of Dickey: "As for Maxine, people generally felt sorry for her as a two-timed, neglected wife whose breeding demanded that she remain loyal to a brash and sometimes arrogant man. She made every effort to befriend other faculty wives, and to run a tight ship at home." It was obvious to all that Maxine had lost her grip on her husband. Graves heard of affairs besides the one with the young poet's wife; the most shocking involved a student who had to go to Tijuana to get an abortion. One of Graves's female students commented after Maxine's untimely death: "She died of Southern poetry."[14] Graves agreed.

Dickey tended to dramatize his controversial fantasies in public as well as in private, and sooner or later they appeared in his poetry and fiction. Around the time he debated mixed marriages with the Israels, he mulled over his patriarchal ideas about race and sex in his controversial poem "Slave Quarters." In it he traced the journey of a man—ostensibly Dickey—to a ruined mansion on an island off the Georgia coast (Dickey once revealed that he had seen the ruins as a boy while visiting Saint Simons Island). Dickey identified with the original slave owner, no doubt because his own ancestors had owned slaves, but he also identified with the compromised slave. If he portrayed himself as divided between two races the way Norman Mailer did in "The White Negro," an essay published in 1957, Dickey went one step further by imagining himself divided between two genders. Dickey's slave owner "seeks the other color of his body"; he wants to connect with the African woman in his psyche as well as the slave on his plantation. In Dickey's psychomachia, she represents primitive passion ensnared by Caucasian conscience. Dickey's white master achieves a complicated emancipation by freeing both himself (his repressed libido) and his slave through sex.

In his commentary on the poem, Dickey said he intended to expose the hypocrisy of the antebellum South and its Sir Walter Scott–like chivalry. Beginning as a protest against what Dickey called the Southerner's stultifying "pseudo-English, phony gentility," the poem plunges quickly into murky issues of race and gender. If "the South was essentially a matriarchy"[15] in which Southern women found sex degrading, as Dickey contended in *Self-Interviews*, the poem exonerates the white master even while agonizing over the consequences of his fornications. The master declares:

My body has a color not yet freed:
In that ruined house let me throw
Obsessive gentility off:
Let Africa rise upon me like a man
Whose instincts are delivered from their chains. . . .

The poem ends with a series of unanswered questions: How should the present white Southerner accept the guilt of his slave-holding ancestors? If Africa represents an "Eden / . . . of sexual treasure,"[16] how should he reclaim the African within him? What should he feel toward the actual child—the mulatto slave boy—he has produced? At Valley State, Dickey exonerated white patriarchs and asked similar questions about their mixed-race offspring (these may have been prompted by curiosity about the African-American Dickeys, who took their name from their masters and could have experienced the sort of interbreeding "Slave Quarters" describes). In the poem, his persona's sexual politics seem both progressive and regressive. The slave owner wants to deliver himself and others from sexual and racial bondage, but he remains bound to racial myths and stereotypes. He associates Africa and African slaves with "primitive vital functions." Imagining possible careers for the mulatto boy, he comes up with prizefighter, prisoner, waiter, and parking-lot attendant. Why not teacher, businessman, writer, and civil rights leader?

A year before finishing "Slave Quarters" (it appeared in the *New Yorker* in August 1965), Dickey sketched out a poem, "In Fannin County," about the territory where his father's slave-owning predecessors had lived. Again he planned to describe the attempt to reclaim a more primitive, natural, Edenic past from a contemporary wasteland. In this case, however, the recuperation of Eden depended on the absence rather than the presence of African-Americans. He hoped to depict "industry moving out, empty chicken house, land reverting, foxes on the roads—dead hosiery mills, 'no niggers.'"[17] According to Dickey's mythical view of the South, were Africans spoilers or redeemers, satans or saviors? Were Southern women, past and present, seductive Eves or repressive matriarchs? Dickey vacillated. He seemed to speak for opposed factions, and as a result he left his audiences bewildered, appalled, or applauding.

Because Robert Bly charged that poems like "Slave Quarters" provided ample evidence of Dickey's racism, Dickey became more defensive and more cautious—at least some of the time—in his proclamations about African-Americans. He liked to refer to his essay "Notes on the Decline of Outrage" to prove his liberal sentiments. To Ernest Suarez, who wrote a book blaming Bly and other like-minded critics for undermining Dickey's reputation, he said: "Martin Luther King quoted from the end of that essay ['Notes'] in his speeches—that for white southerners 'it can be a greater thing than the South has ever done' to discover that blacks are our 'unknown brothers.' That was written back in the 1950s, which as far as the Civil Rights movement was concerned was practically prehistory. I took an awful lot of flak for that. I didn't get a job I wanted with an advertising agency in Atlanta because the people were so rabidly pro-Southern and antiblack. I came out for black citizens and said that if it took repudiating part of my so-called Southern heritage in order for blacks to have an equal chance, I would do it—and I advised other people to do it also." He went on to tell Suarez the story of how his teacher, the Fugitive Donald Davidson—"one of the most humane, sensitive, and caring persons I ever knew"—became so consumed with racist notions that "he ended up allying himself with all these 'white citizens' councils and the most dubious kinds of redneck racist groups."[18] Dickey was no doubt sincere in his self-defense and his eschewal of those like Davidson, but as usual he exaggerated. Davidson was never his teacher, and "The Decline of Outrage" evinced an ambivalent acceptance rather than an outright endorsement of the Civil Rights movement. He wrote the essay during the final months of 1959—not exactly the movement's "prehistory" (the landmark *Brown v. Board of Education* case, the Montgomery bus boycott, and the Little Rock confrontation had already occurred). Moreover, Louis Rubin published the essay in 1961; Dickey left Burke Dowling Adams in July of that year, having already decided never to return to advertising.

Since Dickey scorned the concept of Southern matriarchy in deed and word, Wallace Graves and other members of the English Department found it ironic that he so often wrote his mother. Graves remembered Dickey mailing letters to her nearly every day and charging the postage to the department. Noting Dickey's Oedipal bond—and his denial of it—Graves surmised that homosexual impulses lurked behind Dickey's masculine façade, and that Dickey considered homosexuality something new and titillating (Dickey himself attributed homo-sexuality to the Oedipal complex). Robert Peters, a young professor of Victorian literature at the University of California, Riverside, who became a prolific poet and critic, detected more-overt signs of Dickey's sexual ambiguity. Peters, who became openly gay in the 1970s, had recently bought *Helmets* and convinced his department to pay Dickey $150 to read at Riverside. Peters met him at the air-port on December 1, 1964, deposited him at the motel, and asked Dickey if he would look at an elegiac sequence of poems he had written about his son, who had died from meningitis. Later in the evening Dickey gave one of the best read-ings Peters ever attended. Peters recalled the reception that followed in Prof. Herbert Lindenberger's home:

> Dickey had little to say, particularly seeming to avoid any faculty wives anxious to gush over him. He appeared at the party with guitar in hand and sat on a couch, drinking Scotch and water, holding the guitar, trying out various chords and finger arrangements, insulating himself against the need to say anything of any consequence to anyone there. He motioned for me to sit beside him on the couch. . . . I felt sexual attraction between us, and came to believe that his legendary womanizing was a diversion from a powerful latent homosexuality in him. If these impulses were there, I have no evidence whatsoever that he ever acted on them, insulating himself via image of football star, southern gentleman, and Civil War weapons and paraphernalia lover. I felt his love also during later public readings, particularly one at the University of Utah where I was teaching for the summer. Women seemed disposable; friendships with males were important. . . .
>
> "Walk with me to the car," he eventually said, suddenly getting off the couch. "I'll thank the host and leave. It's a good drive back to Northridge."
>
> We exited, with the Lindenbergers accompanying us. After putting the guitar in its case in the back seat, he opened the front door ready to get in behind the wheel. He drew me towards him, his hands on my shoulders. "I did read your manuscript today," he said. Then he kissed me on the lips. "You don't know how original you are." He climbed into the car and drove away. I was high for days afterwards, and since he was the first professional poet to see my work, and was so encouraging, I made my commitment to pursue poetry, believing that I might find publishers for it.[19]

Dickey was generous to Peters again in the late 1960s when Peters's marriage collapsed and he was jailed—mistakenly—on burglary charges.

With Dickey's sexual posturing in mind, Graves wrote a hilarious satire based on Dickey for the *Kenyon Review*. For his mock interview with the poet "Harrison Byrd," Graves assumed the pseudonym "Jack Swing" and discussed Byrd's recent departure from an advertising agency, where he worked on the Dr. Pepper account. Image, Byrd concludes, is everything. He tells Swing: "Poets to-day have plumb forgot something as old as history: you got to develop the Image, then you got to *advertise* it." Byrd has worked hard to conform to the image of the big, beer-swilling bard: "I'm naturally big, you see. I always was tall, come from tall folks, and at the agency I started drinking beer, a lot of beer, and whiskey, too. And a lot of Dr. Pepper. So, besides being tall, I started getting fat. I looked around and said, who's tall and fat, and the image of Dylan Thomas popped into my head. Dylan wasn't so tall, you understand, but he was fat, man, he was fat and shaggy. And then there was Theodore Roethke. He was plenty fat, too, man; he walked like a bear." Because the bearish Roethke played tennis, Byrd struts around campus with his tennis gear (Dickey often walked around Valley State in a V-necked sweater, cradling a tennis racket). To seduce women and make them buy his poetry books, Byrd plays the role of the gentle, soft-spoken outcast at parties. He advises others to do the same:

Part of the big, shaggy image is making the women think you're as neurotic as they are. I'll bet I could lay 90 per cent of all the women at these gatherings, just using my withdrawal system. . . . At least once during the party, make a kind of impulsive lunge for the woman. Even if you hate women. It's important that it be impulsive, like everything else you do, like the urge comes from the subconscious, comes from the part of your soul that you just can't control, the part that's in touch with God, or the Devil. . . . Even if you're a faggot, as queer as a three-dollar bill, make a lunge for that woman—they're the ones that buy the books. The best advice I can give any young lyric poet is never, never do anything that looks like you're in complete control.

The implication is that Byrd/Dickey is always in control, deliberately foisting a false but convincing image on a gullible public.

The real Dickey makes a cameo appearance in Graves's spoof: "Another thing I found out when I surveyed the market: lots better if you're a war hero like, say, Jim Dickey or Howie Nemerov. They were both flyers in World War II, I think, if I remember correct. . . . Always, and I mean always, mention the war service. . . . Poetry audiences . . . like to see the big man up there who took his knocks in the war. They like a hero. I don't mean dwell on it, but make sure your introducer gets it in. You know—'50 missions over the Japs dropping bombs,' or something like that. And, if it doesn't get mentioned then, make sure you say it during the reading." To appeal to the antiwar sentiments of the 1960s, Byrd says that the soldier-poet should pretend he was shell-shocked and confess that he made a youthful mistake by joining the military. Regarding women poets, Byrd sounds a lot like Dickey on Anne Sexton or Sylvia Plath: "I feel for them. Most of them have voices about as heroic as a castrated rabbit." Asked to name a few promising women poets, he can only quote a line he attributes to Roethke about "Sapphos, decked out like female impersonators, leaning over the podium, dugs a-droop, moaning, barking like sea-lionesses."[20] Byrd ends his cynical, offbeat tirade with more misogynist harangues and more advice about focusing on prizes, especially the Nobel Prize. Like most satirists, Graves dissected his subject's motives and behavior with a scalpel and exaggerated what he found. The result was as humorous as it was harsh.

Part of the fictitious interview with Byrd was based on stories Graves had heard about Dickey's reading tours. Soon after beginning his classes at Valley State, Dickey suspended them so that he could go on a "barnstorming" tour. He first went to Dartmouth in mid-October 1964, where he drank with his host, the poet-in-residence Richard Eberhart, and entertained students (including the future publisher David Godine) with folk tunes on his guitar. As if stepping into his belligerent Harrison Byrd role, he also threatened to beat up the kindly Eberhart if he were not allowed to read before the poet Richard Murphy, who was visiting from his native Ireland. Like many subsequent hosts, Eberhart learned that an inebriated Dickey never liked to play second fiddle. Dickey next read at the YMHA in New York on October 25, and then flew west for the Ohio poetry circuit. Like a political candidate stumping on the campaign trail, he shuttled to a new town or city almost every day. He performed at Cleveland State and Oberlin College on October 29, Kenyon College on October 30, The College of Wooster on October 31, Kent State and Fenn College on November 1, Ohio University on November 2, Denison University and Ohio Wesleyan on November 3, Miami University on November 4, Wabash College on November 5, Earlham College on November 6, Antioch University on November 7. After the whistle-stop tour in the Midwest, he traveled to the University of Rochester on November 9 and to UCLA on November 20. While each campus was different, Dickey's routine was essentially the same. He dined, drank, read, partied, chased women, and scrambled to get to his next destination.

Dickey described the harrowing and intoxicating bustle of his reading tours in his essay "Barnstorming for Poetry," which the *New York Times Book Review* printed on January 3, 1965. To accommodate the expectant crowds at all the campuses, he said he created a public persona vastly different from the mild-mannered, agreeable, colorless man he left at home. His guitar, which he carried everywhere, was a prop for the role of modern-day troubador. Almost everything he did while barnstorming was part of an elaborate ritual. He reflected on his histrionic roles as if they were acted out by another person:

A strange madness took hold of him when he discovered at the first reading that everything he said was noted and commented upon. Too, he *thinks* he heard a bearded student mutter something discontented about "lack of fire" (or was it lack of flair?), and at that moment the image of his great predecessor, the only predecessor, Dylan Thomas, blazed up humiliatingly in the front of his mind. The result of this was that he deliberately drank twice as much liquor as he is accustomed to at the party after the reading, waved his arms wildly about, said anything and everything that came into his head, insulted somebody—merciful heavens, who on earth was it?—and had a terrible hangover the next day.

Yet he has in some obscure way been a good deal better satisfied with himself, has drunk very nearly as much at all the six or eight schools following that one, and is now looking forward to acquiring the courage to get drunk *before* the reading. He is exhausted and exalted as he has never been, and now, standing in the center of a new reality—in this case a cold, sleepless room—he looks at these things for the last time, picks up his bag and manuscripts and his symbolic guitar, and goes out into the white darkness.

At the conclusion of his road trip, the Maileresque showman returns home and admits that he "is still bothered by the difference between his touring self and his usual self. He has definitely been another person on this trip: more excitable and emotional, more harried, more impulsive. Yet he knows that these qualities will die out upon his arrival home and he is more than a little glad of it; they are too wearing, too hard on the nerves. He might live more vividly in this condition, but he cannot write in it. He must calm down and work."[21] Dickey could play Harrison Byrd only so long before returning to the serious task of writing.

Like Dylan Thomas on his own bibulous tours of the United States a decade before, while barnstorming Dickey acted the enfant terrible, drinking and fornicating from college to college. Part of Dickey, as "Barnstorming" made clear, recoiled from the Dionysian Thomas whom he emulated. In the mid-1960s he told an interviewer: "Thomas's influence on poetry for the so-called spoken word is, in my opinion, absolutely disastrous. I think he is one of the worst readers that I have ever heard, because he brings in that awful theatricality which is the last thing in the world one would want in a poetry reading—some kind of a performance by an actor."[22] As with Roethke, Thomas reminded Dickey too painfully of his own alcoholic antics.

His hectic autumn tour over, Dickey began work on a film version of "Barnstorming." He told friends like Robert Bly that MGM wanted to make a film based on his article; his Hollywood agent was negotiating a lucrative contract and the director would be Jeffrey Hayden. Dickey worked on a step outline in mid-January 1965 and in 1969 resuscitated the project with director Larry Klingman, who helped make the documentary about Dickey, *Lord Let Me Die, but Not Die Out*. Learning in late-November 1964 that Donald Hall was about to become a literary adviser for Harper and Row, Dickey turned his attention to *Buckdancer's Choice*, which he began revising with a new sense of urgency. Hall hoped that Dickey would follow him from Wesleyan and offered an enticement: "It is time for a collected or selected poems, which will win you a number of rubber medals like Pulitzer and NBA, but WUP can't do it because its format is limited to 80 pp. . . . But if you do want to leave Wesleyan, will you come to me? I am sure I can get you a very good deal."[23] Dickey wrote back that he planned to leave Wesleyan after the publication of *Buckdancer's Choice*, but might go to Knopf rather than Harper and Row. Despite their future plans, in late 1964 and early 1965 Hall and Dickey kept working on *Buckdancer's Choice* for Wesleyan. Dickey then learned to his surprise that the poet Denise Levertov was also editing his book. He wrote Hall that he was not overly distressed—he respected her judgment—but he expected Wesleyan to consult him when it deviated from its usual editorial arrangements. He had worked well with Hall and did not want to jeopardize their close association. Dickey soon realized that he had nothing to fear from Levertov. She believed that Dickey's book was ready to go to press and argued against Lockwood's proposal to cut some 31 pages from the 111-page manuscript.

Because Lockwood instructed Hall and Levertov to keep cutting, they drew up a hit list of expendable poems: the first section of "Shark's Parlor," "Them, Crying," "Mary Sheffield," "The War Wound," "The Celebration," "Reincarnation 1," and "The Fiend." Levertov added others to the list, she and Hall argued over them, and Hall mailed Dickey the suggested cuts on February 3, 1965. Three weeks later Levertov wrote Dickey a letter of explanation and apology, which ended up making the cutting process more difficult. She had been angry, she said, because Hall had compared Dickey's book to Bly's *The Light Around the Body,* which Levertov felt was abysmal. Hall had judged Bly's book to be superior (eventually it, too, won a National Book Award). Levertov wanted Dickey to know that she had stood up for *Buckdancer's Choice.* She also wanted to explain how she had become his editor:

> As I had written and spoken so excitedly for it [I thought] perhaps I would be co-editor, especially as I had liked best just the poems Don hadn't. I accepted for one reason alone: to protect the Mss from probable depredations by Don—i.e., he had indicated that in his opinion you were in dire *need* of an editor, and that yr other books had been dependent on his taste in getting them into shape, and that he in fact was yr mentor—all of which, in view of his judgement in regard to Bob Bly's work and his dismissal of the Poems of the Air as inferior to the rest of the MS . . . seemed not only crazy but downright dangerous. Even before that I had told Don that I couldn't understand why any poet shd *let* his book be edited by anyone else; but if you and WUP thought you *had* to have editors, then after my defense and championing of the Ms I felt it was my responsibility to see it thru.

Levertov advised Dickey to step in and take control of editorial matters. In the margins of her letter she wrote in longhand: *"Don't* let Don Hall PATRONISE you, PLEASE!"[24] Despite his fury over these revelations, Dickey continued to work with Hall on shortening the book to fit Wesleyan's prescribed length.

Dickey's response to what he considered Hall's betrayal took several forms. He dropped him as his literary executor and reassigned the job to Levertov. When he reviewed Hall's new book of poems, *A Roof of Tiger Lilies,* in the autumn issue of the *American Scholar,* even though he had sent Hall a letter early in 1965 praising it, he unsheathed a dagger: "Hall seems too often to write a poem simply because, as a poet, he is expected to do so: to write *some* poem. He obviously enjoys the act of writing, but he does not seem particularly responsive as a human being, and this frequently results in a kind of attenuation, a pleasant skilled inconsequentiality, and the production of poems that even while they are being written are being herded peacefully toward the abyss marked Oblivion."[25] In later years Dickey spurned Hall more thoroughly by denying he had ever been his editor. "I think he was one of the editors at Wesleyan," Dickey said with deliberate amnesia, "but Wilbur did more than he did." Wilbur, in fact, had almost nothing to do with Dickey's early books. With the denial came the insults that had become routine: "Don Hall . . . is another untalented writer. . . . He doesn't have the beginning of an aptitude. . . . He's just a professional sort of a literary man . . . and he hangs around with Bly."[26] Dickey could never forgive Hall for championing Bly. Trading tit for tat, Hall dismissed his opponent with equal vigor. With regard to the last two decades of Dickey's career, he contended: "The fall of James Dickey has absolutely nothing to do with literary politics. It has entirely to do with his bad writing. I think the bad writing started a lot earlier than other people do. I love *Drowning with Others*, and I think after that he goes downhill—though there are still some good poems in the next two Wesleyan books. When I first read his poems [at the *Paris Review*], before he was publishing, he ran on and on, and was too rhetorical—and eventually he got back into the same old habits. I think that maybe *Puella* is a lot worse than that, but I dislike the 'May Day Sermon' and 'Falling.'"[27] Hall and Dickey had worked fruitfully together at Wesleyan; when they parted company, their buried resentments erupted with vitriolic candor.

Dickey's friendship with Levertov followed a similar pattern. Discovering she was an editor on the Wesleyan board, he curried favor by sending her one of the three hundred copies of Monica Moseley's *Two Poems of the Air* in the summer of 1964. Even though one of the poems was "The Firebombing," the antiwar activist Levertov praised the poems and said the chapbook was one of the most beautifully crafted books she had ever seen. She also complimented Dickey on the stand he had taken against Robert Lowell and looked forward to meeting him at Colgate University, where they were supposed to read together with Norman Mailer and Philip Roth. When Dickey passed on the mantle of literary executor to Levertov, she at first expressed gratitude. On May 3, 1965, her only stipulation was that she be allowed to review their agreement in twenty years. On May 21, 1966, she asked Dickey to release her as executor. If Dickey should die—he was always entertaining the possibility—managing his estate would take too much time away from her poetry. She also said: "The problem of sorting out my love of your poems from my distrust of your political (+ some of your literary) views undoubtedly enters in my request for a release." She promised to send Dickey "some information on the pacifist position and the war in Viet Nam."[28] What she sent had little effect on Dickey's views regarding the escalating Vietnam War. Soon he was villifying her as another untalented poet.

While finishing his work on *Buckdancer's Choice*, Dickey tried to line up more poetry readings. He traveled to Beloit College on February 20, Miami University on February 21, DePauw College on February 24, University of California (San Diego) on March 9, Stanford on April 1, and Pitzer College on April 26. Dickey rarely turned down an offer, whether from a college or a publisher. In March, he even agreed to write a poem, "The Christmas Towns," for Hallmark cards, which paid him one hundred dollars to use it in their 1966 edition of *American Christmas*. Like Robert Frost before him, he was determined to become a successful entrepreneur of poetry.

Dickey's reading at Pitzer College in Claremont, California, met with such a favorable response that he was asked to be the commencement speaker on June 6. The address would be the first of many he would give at graduation exercises. Playing to the antiestablishment mood of the times, he spoke of carrying a poetry book into his advertising office in the late 1950s and touching it every so often to remember the world he truly valued. The act, he suggested, was as subversive as carrying a bomb. He also discussed one of his heroes who had also written poetry in ennervating circumstances, the Welsh poet Alun Lewis, who had died in Burma near the end of World War II. Dickey quoted a statement Lewis made while in the inferno of jungle warfare—"My life belongs to the world. I will do what I can"[29]—a line Dickey later used to end his inauguration poem for Pres. Jimmy Carter. He implored the Pitzer students to develop self-protective strategies, just as he had done in war and business, to prevent the forces of indifference, coarseness, and apathy from destroying them.

The spring term over at Valley State, Dickey decided to return to Atlanta to write without interruption while his family stayed in Northridge. He especially wanted to finish another draft of *Deliverance*. Maxine disliked the separation as she had done before, and Dickey again wrote her forlorn letters. On June 16, 1965, he declared:

> I love you, and I can't sleep without you close to me. The only solution has been to stay up late, out with Inman or Worley or Al and Lewis, but that isn't really a very good solution; it would be much better—infinitely better—to have you, my one true earthly lifelong woman, with me and near me, bitching and loving. The only consolation is the rapid mounting-up of the bank balance that this way of operating helps. . . . The terror about money is the worst, most destructive psychological force in our society, and we have got it licked, and with a few more thousand can bury it forever. That leaves only death to worry about, and I worry about that less and less.

To prove that the family finances were in order, Dickey tallied up his recent earnings: "According to my latest count, we are somewhat upwards of $11,700, which is a pretty good place to be. Don't forget to get the bank interest added onto the Great Little Book at the end of this month. That'll bring us up to around $11,800, and the $250 for the last two essays—on Smart and Hopkins—will set us on the grand peak of $12,000. Then Bill Hale's $500 plus the $1,500 I hope to net from the Milwaukee venture will put us up to $14,000! We are really going good, and it is a vastly comforting thought to me that Chris's college education is already in the bank, and most of Kevin's, too."[30] Dickey was ecstatic about Bill Hale's acceptance of his nine-page screenplay, *The Celebration*, which was based on John F. Kennedy's book *A Nation of Immigrants*. He had worked with Mel Sloan on a script that celebrated the "new year" of America's democratic spirit (perhaps with a glance at Kennedy's "New Frontier") by focusing on various ethnic and racial groups. A Chinese dragon festival in San Francisco, a Zuni Pueblo ritual in the Southwest, an animal blessing in Los Angeles, an eagle dance by New Mexican Indians, a rodeo, and an Italian carnival were some of the scenes Dickey chose for his celebration of American diversity. The film was finally made and sold to the U.S. Information Agency for distribution in other countries.

To make sure his bank account kept expanding, Dickey taught a poetry seminar, Major Developments in Modern Poetry, for about an hour each morning from June 21 to July 16 at the University of Wisconsin, Milwaukee. Concerned about his separation from his family, in Milwaukee he wrote a moving letter to his son Chris, who was almost fourteen: "I want most to tell you, just simply to tell you, how much I love you, my dear, irreplaceable oldest boy, and how proud I am of you. I want to say, too, what I think you and I ought to do about insuring your future as one of the great ones: one of the great human beings, which you have a chance to be." Dickey had decided that there were two ways to live: one by simply "being" (the beatnik way) and the other by actively "doing." He counseled his son to find a happy medium between the two. Dickey then expressed how odd it was for him—a perpetual adolescent—to be a father: "My God, what a strange role being a father is. A *Father!*" Nevertheless, he had plenty of fatherly advice: "Love, really, is all we as a family have. When your petty side wants to gripe, wants to be lazy, wants to talk back to your mother, that great, troubled, lovely woman, think about it a little. And then maybe you won't want quite so much to nag at Kevin, to be insolent to your mother, to shut yourself away from us like the Wounded Fawn of romantic eighteenth century novels."[31] He ended the letter more like a coach than a scold by telling Chris that the family was like a team pitted against Time, Death, and Separation; the family must play hard together today because tomorrow its foes might triumph.

Dickey had been accepted for a July 20–August 8 residency at Yaddo, the famous artists' colony in upstate New York. Philip Roth, Alfred Kazin, W. D. Snodgrass, and the composer Karel Husa would also be guests. In Dickey's stories about his brief stay, he claimed to have shared a room—in some stories it was a bathroom—with Philip Roth, whose novel *Portnoy's Complaint* would vie with *Deliverance* for the number-one ranking on bestseller lists in 1970. To his friend Charles Gaines, who asked for a recommendation to a similar writer's colony, Dickey revealed: "I myself have only been in one such place. This was Yaddo, up at Saratoga Springs, New York, where I roomed with Phil Roth during the time he was first drafting *Portnoy*. He used to come in the place where I worked a couple or three times a day while I was sitting around not working but playing the guitar, and read me what he had written that morning, doubling up with laughter, and assuring me that, if I were Jewish, I would think it twice as funny as I did, which in point of fact I didn't think it was: that is, I didn't think it was funny, especially, even though I am a redneck Southerner."[32] About their fabled meeting at Yaddo, Roth had no recollection. Yaddo's files had no record of Dickey's 1964 stay, either.

During Valley State's fall semester in 1965, Dickey again left teaching behind to barnstorm for poetry. From October 22 to November 7, he read at the University of Chicago, Connecticut College, Syracuse University, Oberlin College, College of Wooster, Kent State, Ohio University, Denison College, Ohio Wesleyan University, Miami University, Wabash College, Earlham College, Antioch University, and the University of Rochester. Before taking up his residence at the University of Wisconsin, he reflected with his usual blend of flippancy and sincerity about what he was abandoning: "One of the nicest things about Valley State is that it's confirmed me in my lifelong propensity as a fanny watcher. There are some very nice things going on at the campus every time classes change. As to writing students, I've had some very good ones."[33] He predicted that he had taught at least five and possibly ten students who would make names for themselves. Three decades later he revised his assessment. Only one student, the elderly Helen Sorrells, had published any decent poetry. Of his other students, Dickey said: "I don't remember their writing being particularly good."[34]

If he failed to produce any gifted poets at Valley State, Dickey certainly succeeded at getting his students fired up about poetry. Sorrells spoke for the majority when she extolled Dickey as her best teacher. Another student, Bill Cole, quit the seminary and his plans to become a priest, fell in love with a girl, and devoted himself to writing, so inspired was he by Dickey's class. Two other students, William Ford and David Widener, enrolled in the University of Iowa writing program. Robin Johnson also became a published poet. Perhaps because of their proximity to Hollywood, a number of Dickey's students went on to successful careers in film. Dickey's favorite, Michael Allin, wrote scripts for *Enter the Dragon* (1973), *Flash Gordon* (1980), and *Hotel Paradise* (1995). Allin's friend Andy Wallace had introduced him to Dickey over Easter vacation in 1964. Allin (who wrote poetry at the time) subsequently audited Dickey's creative writing class and took his twentieth-century poetry class. Dickey was such an unpredictable and entertaining teacher that Allin attended every class, even when sick. Over the next three decades, Allin and Dickey kept up a running conversation about books and films. In 1998, Allin published his first book, *Zarafa*—an intriguing, deftly crafted account of the first giraffe transported from Africa to France—and paid homage to Dickey in an introductory chapter.

Dickey also discussed screenwriting projects with Andy Wallace, another poetry student at Valley State. Wallace and several of his friends regularly visited Dickey's home to drink, talk about books and movies, and run footraces (although Dickey boasted that he had been called the Crabapple Cannonball at Clemson because of his speed, Wallace beat him). Wallace later proved himself in Hollywood, composing scripts for *Combat*, *Zandy's Bride*, and Ronald Reagan's *Death Valley Days*. Dickey liked to play the guitar and discuss movies with David Gyler, whose father was an established movie and television writer (Gyler became a successful producer and screenwriter, with *Myra Breckinridge* and *The Black Bird* among his credits). For Dickey, Gyler typified the sort of free-spirited student he regularly taught. Rather than turn in a final class project, according to Dickey, Gyler took LSD and claimed that his paper topic was beyond words. Dickey instructed him to take more LSD and submit the paper the following week. Once he had finished, Gyler told his professor that his paper contained the secret of the universe. Back at his office Dickey opened the manila envelope and read the one line that Gyler had written: "The banana is large, but the banana skin is larger."[35] The story sounds apocryphal, but for Dickey it captured the spirit of the times in California.

19. A Frozen Berkeley (Spring 1966)

At the start of the 1965 fall term, Harry Finestone and Henry Van Slooten tried to convince the administration to create a permanent position for Dickey at Valley State. On December 27, 1965, the college president offered Dickey $14,472 for the 1967–68 year. Dickey was tempted, but first he had to go to the

University of Wisconsin in Madison. Having discussed accommodations in the cold north with the poet William Meredith, who had held a similar visiting position, Dickey instructed the new English Department chair, Walter Rideout, to reserve an apartment in the Claridge Hotel. He made only one request: "Please make sure I have a big bed, for I am a monstrous big fellow, and I thrash; what's more, I *need* to thrash."[1] Dickey took up residence at 333 West Washington Avenue in January 1966, several days before he was due to teach his English 305 writing class. He had ordered Shapiro and Beum's *A Prosody Handbook* for his students to consult (there were no assigned texts). One of his students, Roberta Greiffer, recalled the first class. As a nineteen-year-old undergraduate, she took precautions against being immediately overwhelmed by Dickey and the fifteen or so graduate students pursuing master's and Ph.D. degrees: "I always chose a seat in a remote corner of the room and never uttered a sound. . . . Mr. Dickey, a large man to begin with, towered over the small classroom. He announced in the very first session that anyone who wished to enroll in his workshop could do so; there were no prerequisites. His usual mode of operation was to assign a poem of a particular type—sonnet, villanelle, etc. For the following week's discussion, he would mimeograph many of the students' poems—minus the author's name. The poems appeared to be discussed in ascending order of effectiveness, from the 'worst' to the 'best.' My assignments, when selected, were usually among the first discussed." Toward the end of the semester, when one of her poems made it to the top of the stack, Dickey commented: "Anyone who can write a poem like this is a poet."[2] The praise inspired Greiffer to continue writing poetry for the rest of her life.

At first cowed by his reputation and tough standards, Greiffer and the other students soon relaxed. Dickey usually doled out suggestions for improving poems in a soft-spoken, unpretentious manner. He often continued class discussions over beers in local taverns on State Street, a gambit some of his students relished. Other students, like David Keller, regretted that he didn't do more teaching, that he treated the workshop that met twice a week in the afternoon as a stage for reading what interested him—such as Borges's short stories. Dickey seemed to be in Madison to have a good time; Keller saw him at numerous parties, usually wearing a sweatshirt and carrying a guitar. He usually came with an undergraduate woman and proceeded to proposition other women with the line: "It's lonely sleeping alone." If he got a response, his second line would be: "Now don't you laugh at an old man. Sweetheart, do you live in an apartment or a dormitory?"[3] According to Keller, about one in a dozen women went to bed with him.

Among his colleagues, Dickey was similarly whimsical and flirtatious. Rideout was one of the first to get to know Dickey. He took Dickey to lunch the day he arrived in the department office, and they immediately struck up an easygoing friendship. They talked about Sherwood Anderson, one of Rideout's specialties, and a new anthology called *American Poetry* that Rideout had edited with Gay Allen and Jim Robinson. Dickey had high praise for the collection, partly because the editors included five of his poems and no poems by Robert Bly. "Bly will undoubtedly write you a letter telling you how corrupt you are,"[4] Dickey warned. At one point during their first lunch, Dickey turned to Rideout and said in his best Georgian accent: "Mistah Rahdout, Madison is a FROzen BERKley."[5] Over the next two months Dickey would try to thaw the northern climate with his Southern flamboyance.

At the end of the first week of classes, Rideout got another chance to converse with Dickey at a cocktail party he and his wife organized to welcome Dickey to the English Department. Dickey puzzled many at this occasion by drinking nothing stronger than orange juice. "Either . . . the stories of his drinking are exaggerated, or he's just getting over a big night before," Rideout thought at the time. He concluded: "The latter was obviously the case, for at another party . . . he was putting our heavy drinkers to shame."[6] At the other gathering—a dinner party hosted by a senior professor, George Rodman—Dickey drank numerous glasses of scotch and moved on to martinis. Rodman remembered: "As the guests were going into the dining room, Dickey saw the partially depleted pitcher of martinis on the mantle, picked it up and drained it. Needless to say, we were somewhat apprehensive about conversation, particularly since one of the guests was Professor Helen White, who was near the end of her career, and of her life, at the time. The dinner went off without incident, except when Dickey got into an argument with the wife of the Associate Chairman of the Department and expressed his views with considerable vehemence."[7] Despite his occasional pretenses as a teetotaler, Dickey performed other alcoholic feats at Madison parties as well.

Without Maxine by his side—she remained in Northridge to take care of Kevin and Chris—Dickey tended to give free rein to his appetites. Lawrence Dembo, a future editor of the journal Contemporary Literature, witnessed several of Dickey's bacchanalian outbursts. Not long after Dickey's arrival, Dembo was supposed to have dinner with him and introduce him at an informal party in his honor. At the restaurant, Dickey showed little interest in food. He kept waving off the waiter with an empty glass and demanding more drinks, even after consuming eight martinis. For a reason unknown to his host, Dickey implored Dembo to leave with him for New York. Finally Dembo convinced the inebriated Dickey to attend the party: "Dickey began well enough. He entered the room like a Greek god, swooping down on the women, but being generally congenial to all who approached him. After half an hour of this kind of treatment, nobody could deny that James Dickey was a jolly good fellow. He was, however, becoming increasingly restless when he abruptly announced that he wanted to call a lady in California. He took out a telephone credit card and told the host not to worry about the bill. Then he called the operator and gave her the number. Apparently it was garbled or invalid for she wouldn't accept it, the consequence being that Dickey launched into a tirade that shook the house like an earthquake, silenced all conversation, and made a shambles of the party."[8] Dembo admired Dickey's poetry, usually enjoyed his company, and attributed his grandstanding to his growing addiction to alcohol.

Dembo reached his judgment of Dickey as a poseur after listening to a story he told about a fellow combat pilot so charged with adrenaline that, failing to find enemy aircraft to shoot down, he went hunting the skies for friendlies. Because of Dickey's increasing fame, local newspaper reporters lapped up and regurgitated many of the exaggerations that made Dembo and his colleagues laugh or flinch. Robert Cromie reported in the *Chicago Tribune* that Dickey "at the age of 19 . . . was flying night-fighters in New Guinea, a skill he later used in Korea"[9] (at nineteen Dickey was in Darlington prep school). To Leslie Cross of the *Milwaukee Journal Sentinel*, Dickey claimed he had been a combat pilot who "came home as a captain."[10] At the University of Wisconsin, Dickey cultivated his legend as a Herculean Don Juan by lifting weights, as he had done on other campuses, so that faculty wives could ogle him. His ruckus over the California woman at the party was just one of many efforts to publicize his philandering.

The woman Dickey tried to phone at the party may have been Robin Jarecki, with whom he was indeed having an affair. Dickey said at the end of his life: "There'll never be another like her, and as an old man, I want to die thinking about that face." Dickey had met his California Beatrice in Rome in 1962. She had asked him questions about Ezra Pound while he cashed a check at an American Express office. Dickey recalled: "I turned around and she was talking to some other people. She was a tall girl with one heavy braid of hair. . . . I just looked at her and I said, 'My God. Look at that. What a woman. Wonderful. Superhuman.' . . . And I said, 'Are you American?' And she said, 'Yes, I come from California.' And I didn't see her anymore in Europe at all. I just had that one glimpse of her. It was like a vision." Jarecki's beauty, intelligence, and bohemian spirit enchanted many men. On September 1, 1965, after Dickey published "Slave Quarters" in the *New Yorker*, Jarecki wrote a letter to him in care of the magazine. She praised Dickey as one of the outstanding poets of his generation and wondered if he was the same person she had talked to in Rome. Dickey responded that he most definitely was and phoned her. Since Jarecki lived in Los Angeles and Dickey in Northridge, they decided to get together: "We met at a place that she knew about down on the strip called 'The Cock and Bull.' I walked in there and she was there. And I thought 'This is my destiny. This is what I was made for.'"[11] Considering the way Dickey distorted facts, the name of their trysting place seemed appropriate.

According to Dickey, three things attracted Jarecki to him: his archery, his guitar playing, and his knowledge of French literature. An avid traveler and writer herself, Jarecki fell under the spell of his troubador image. He often took her to the Litigo Canyon archery range, where she followed him from target to target. Or he visited her in her Los Angeles home, not far from the advertising agency where she worked, to read and discuss books. Dickey said: "She had some books in French, but she was reading the same ones in English. I would read them in the original and she was very impressed by that."[12] Dickey's knowledge of French may have been one of the reasons Jarecki decided to call him Bosie, the nickname of Oscar Wilde's lover, Lord Alfred Douglas. Because Douglas knew French, Wilde had him translate his play *Salome* from French to English. The name was also ironic: full of youthful charm and energy, Dickey was nevertheless the older man in his affair with Jarecki. The fact that Wilde's homosexual adultery with Douglas led to a great scandal also made "Bosie" appropriate; the whiff of Wildean scandal always titillated Dickey.

Once set up in the Claridge Hotel, Dickey invited Jarecki to come live with him. Ignoring her other commitments—she took night classes in literature at UCLA and worked as a waitress while not doing ad work—she joined him. So great was Dickey's passion for Jarecki that he seriously considered divorcing Maxine and marrying her, at least up until Jarecki's illness. For reasons she could not understand, in Madison she began to lose partial feeling in her hands and feet. Even with the heat on, she suffered constant chills. Dickey grew increasingly worried and suggested that she return to California for proper medical care. Through correspondence with her mother and her best friend Ruth Feld, who worked at UCLA, Dickey learned that her ailment became more debilitating over the following months. Dickey never saw her again. She died in California on April 28, 1967, and was buried in Glendale at Forest Lawn, a cemetery famous for its replicas of Michelangelo's statues.

Devastated by the loss of his favorite lover, Dickey worked on a long poem, "The Indian Maiden," whose title came from a bawdy song he often sang to his son Chris. In the poem he planned to commemorate what he called Jarecki's "authentic sexuality and authentic tenderness."[13] Her beauty haunted him. "The only reason I married Deborah [Dodson]," he said of the woman he married after Maxine's death in 1976, "was that she looked something like Robin. The first time I saw Deborah on campus I said, 'My God, Robin's resurrected. Come back from the grave to haunt me.' She didn't know what I was talking about. But she did later."[14] Refusing to serve as Robin's reincarnation, Deborah Dodson in a fit of jealousy destroyed the rough draft of "The Indian Maiden."

As Dickey transformed Jarecki into a goddess and muse, he inevitably fictionalized her life and death, just as he had done with his apocryphal Australian wife. He told most people that Jarecki had died of multiple sclerosis. He confided to his son Chris that she had died of a brain tumor. In fact, Jarecki died of Guillain-Barré syndrome, a rare inflammatory disorder of the peripheral nerves outside the brain and spinal column that causes extreme weakness, loss of sensation, and paralysis. Most people recover from the disease; only 5 percent die from it. Jarecki's family—she had three siblings—believed that her two jobs and night classes had exacerbated her fatal illness. No doubt worrying that others would see his adulterous affair as contributing to Robin's stress and fatal illness, Dickey invented other illnesses for which he could not be blamed.

Dickey unleashed his grief and guilt over Jarecki's death in a number of poems, among them "Exchanges," which he delivered at Harvard's 1970 Phi Beta Kappa ceremony. In the poem Dickey communed with his dead lover as well as the nineteenth-century poet Joseph Trumbull Stickney through a series of "exchanges" that interspersed Stickney's lines about the Pacific coast with Dickey's memories of Jarecki. On a cliff between the Los Angeles smog and the ocean's oil slick, Dickey recalled playing ballads of "moon and murder / And Appalachian love" for her. Anguish over her loss incited his wish for the "pure death" of the moon. Because he had attended the Apollo moon shot in Florida two years after Jarecki's death, he used the astronauts' flight to the Sea of Tranquility as an example of the transcendence he craved, but concluded: "Nothing for me / Was solved."[15] His sense of loss remained intractable.

In the *paysage moralisé* of "Exchanges," Dickey sang of the paradoxical innocence he'd recaptured with Jarecki. He did the same in *Sorties*, a book he published while Maxine was alive: "Robin Jarecki and I . . . were like children who had discovered sex and literature together, I at the age of forty three, she at twenty-nine. I think of this as true glory, at least for me. . . . What matters is that Robin and I tried to make some kind of life, which was really outside of life. We tried to make something with the tools that we were allowed, and they were pitiful indeed. . . . My God, to hold that big sweaty body in my arms again!"[16] Like so many women Dickey pursued, Jarecki evoked intimations of an unfettered adolescence, an Eden of delights beyond the worries and disillusionments of marriage and middle age.

Dickey's affair with Jarecki bore more poetic fruit in the form of "Adultery," which the *Nation* published in the middle of his Madison residence. The poem contrasts the pain and tawdriness of an extramarital affair with the way it reinvigorates the two lovers. Much about their adulterous sex is unappealing. The narrator points to "Me with my grim techniques / Or you who have sealed your womb / With a ring of convulsive rubber." Surrounded by tacky pictures in a cheap hotel, the woman's masochistic cries of pleasure resemble those uttered by the young woman who is whipped by a sadistic father in "May Day Sermon." In "Adultery," the narrator's paramour pleads: "Please don't / Oh God, Please don't any more I can't bear [it]." The affair is inconsequential, as Dickey tirelessly suggests with the double entendres "come" and "die": "Nothing can come / Of this nothing can come // Of us"; "Although we come together, / Nothing will come of us"; "We have all been in rooms / We cannot die in"; "One could never die here // Never die never die." The diction as well as the sex is tedious. When Dickey's persona addresses his lover in the final stanza— "We have done it again   we are / Still living. Sit up and smile, / God bless you. Guilt is magical"[17]—his pep talk is unconvincing.

Guilt brought on by adultery is magical, Dickey implies, because it delivers the jaded spirit into a new realm "beyond good and evil." It is magical because it helps the flagging poet write new poems that will atone for his guilty behavior. For Dickey, guilt was also magical because he so rarely felt it. Speaking to Chris about Jarecki the year she died, he expressed no remorse for the pain that his affair had inflicted on the Dickey and Jarecki families. Chris remembered: "I thought how strange it was that he would sit there and show me a picture of his mistress [as if] . . . we were just two men." Chris wanted to say: "Excuse me, you know I'm your sixteen year old son and where does my mother fit into all this. I don't quite get this, Dad."[18] In pursuit of the magical properties of guilt, Dickey conducted numerous affairs in Madison. He boasted to a number of people that he went to bed with Anne Sexton at this time—an odd claim from someone who so thoroughly reviled Sexton's poetry. Whatever the attraction, Sexton wrote Dickey mildly seductive letters, and he responded in kind, even while continuing to lampoon her as "Rag-time Annie" because of her poems on menstruation. At times Sexton seemed to want to win over her staunch enemy. In the late fall of 1965 at Syracuse University, she decided to use what she called her "female con"[19] on him. Dickey recalled: "I had given a reading and then gone to bed, staying clear of the almost obligatory party that follows such affairs. I was stopping at the home of the college president, Dr. Piskor, and Anne woke me up over the phone to see if we could not meet for at least a little while. I got up and she came by, in a big black coat that looked like it had come from a gorilla, and we walked up and down the suburban road a few times, during which, as I remember, she told me about various episodes of her childhood."[20] On their nocturnal stroll Dickey propositioned her, but apparently Sexton's "female con" did not yet include sleeping with one of her most ferocious critics.

In letters written after their conversation in the cold Syracuse night, Dickey professed that Sexton had "opened a new tenderness" in him. He hoped that "a good strong man-woman response" would continue between them. For her part, Sexton had heard so much malicious gossip about Dickey that she had construed an image of him as Norman Mailer in Batman's clothes with two poison rings on his toes. In Syracuse, Dickey had done nothing to disabuse her; he told her he was so full of violence that he wanted to kill someone or something. Dickey must have perceived cracks in Sexton's resistance as early as December 12, 1965, when she implied that she might prefer a sexual to an epistolary relationship: "I'll tell you this, and in truth, I fear a letter relationship. When you met me you asked me 'Do you sleep around?' or something like that. My answer was negative, as I recall . . . but I'll tell you this . . . I once made the mistake of believing in a letter-relationship—I 'wrote around.'"[21] Later in December, Sexton told Dickey that she still refused to have a "*mad passionate* affair" with him. She wanted a friend rather than a lover, but cautioned: "I cannot promise that I am geared to your kind of self. I think maybe I am. But I cannot promise. I do not know you well enough yet. I *can* promise that I will not hurt or presume upon the self you offer to me. I can tell you this as a friend who trusts—I trust that you do not lie to me. I trust what I met of you. I trust the (and now I must hesitate or . . . will get into trouble) . . . but never mind . . . say it, Anne, —the poet in you."[22] This tentative, stumbling profession of faith in her untrustworthy seducer must have amused Dickey.

One night around the end of February 1966, a drunken, lonely, nervous Dickey called Sexton at her Weston, Massachusetts, home and insisted that she declare her love for him. Sexton complied and got in trouble with her husband, who overheard the conversation. Sexton reprimanded Dickey the next day and warned that a sexual affair with him would release her demons: "I'm ready to love you as a dear friend & fellow-poet—to be gentle with each other & tender. I have that. Isn't it enough? Or will you throw it away because I can't be all woman—all whore—all that your momentary desire might wish to call forth?" She ended by saying "my soul loves you."[23] Feeling contrite, Dickey apologized for his late-night phone call: "It must be shocking and saddening and bewildering to hear your wife tell another man over the phone that she loves him not one but fifteen times. . . . It's just one of the sadnesses of husbands that things like this sometimes happen to them. I hope I haven't done any permanent damage to your marriage; I can't believe I have, really. But I *am sorry*, and I hope that, if you won't forgive me, you will at least not fret anymore about it."[24] Sexton was prepared to let bygones be bygones, especially since she sometimes indulged in the same emotional outpourings to friends. She assured Dickey that his call had not ruined her marriage, but added: "It's tough enough to be married to me without the bonus phone calls that insist on love and god knows what. You do. For, as I recall, you said you got kind of an excitement out of them. . . .

If you have to hurt someone then leave *me* alone. I can't take it. I don't need it. If sex and or pain is in the cards—then deal me out."[25] Sadoeroticism—whether emotional or physical—was not for her.

Sexton suggested that they renew their civil dialogue over cocktails and dinner in Baltimore around April 20, 1966, when Dickey would be in the vicinity of her Goucher College reading. Despite a pledge to treat her as a friend, Dickey slipped back into the role of Sexton-basher. Sexton retreated with justifiable hurt and anger. One of those who later heard rumors of an affair between Sexton and Dickey was the poet and editor Peter Davison. Curious about its validity, he discussed it with Diane Middlebrook, Sexton's biographer, who replied that Sexton had numerous affairs, but had passed over Dickey.[26] Nevertheless, Dickey bragged to friends like Phyllis and Hubert Shuptrine that he had been successful in his seduction. Even to his son Chris he remained coy about his relations with her. Surmising that Sexton had been another unstable woman his father had pursued out of a desire to "play at madness," Chris asked him shortly before he died whether he'd slept with her. His father replied: "Well, you'd have to ask her."[27] Chris pointed out that Sexton had been dead for over two decades.

While Dickey carried on like a romantic minstrel in Wisconsin, Maxine took Chris and Kevin to horse shows, movies, and school events in California. The long separation was hard on her as well as on the children. For support, she kept in close touch with her mother, who was becoming increasingly leery of her prodigal son-in-law. Dickey missed his family, too, even though he had his girlfriends, students, and various writing projects to alleviate feelings of isolation. One of his new projects was an anthology of twentieth-century French poetry, which he started editing with the Irish poet John Montague two weeks after he arrived (it was never published). Dickey's main diversion, which he happily accepted, was the publicity surrounding his National Book Award for *Buckdancer's Choice*. In March, journalists from all over Wisconsin and the United States called to learn more about the poet and the book that had garnered the prestigious prize. Wisconsin's lieutenant governor sent congratulations. Dickey celebrated his success, after a fashion, with his family in California. Chris, Kevin, Maxine, and Michael Allin opened a bottle of champagne and relayed their congratulations over the phone. "Whatever you do, save that cork,"[28] Dickey said on hearing the pop of the distant bottle.

Dickey won his one-thousand-dollar award against stiff competition. Auden's *About the House*, Elizabeth Bishop's *Questions of Travel*, Richard Eberhart's *Selected Poems: 1930–1965*, Irving Feldman's *The Pripet Marshes*, Randall Jarrell's *The Lost World*, and Louis Simpson's *Selected Poems* had also been nominated. The judges—Ben Bellitt, Phyllis McGinley, and Elder Olson—knew that Dickey's other books, which were just as deserving of major awards, had earned none. On March 15, 1966, Dickey joined fellow prizewinners Katherine Anne Porter, Janet Flanner, and Arthur Schlesinger Jr. at a gala ceremony in New York's Philharmonic Hall. In his acceptance speech he joked about his family's perception of him: "Last year's description of the poet—graciously contributed by my fourteen-year-old son—was 'decadent.' This year's . . . is 'insufferable,' coming this time not from the son but from the wife, who is certainly in a position to know." He then delivered a short paean to the sort of memory and imagination that could transfigure private affairs, fantasies, wishes, daydreams, and virtual selves into significant poems. "And really," he affirmed, "that is why you have asked me here tonight: why you have called me up: not so much to honor but to recognize one human being's story, the events and meanings of his life, [which] . . . through the medium of his art, has at last succeeded in getting outside of himself and has come to rest in others."[29]

After the ceremony, Dickey mingled with the literary hoi poloi at a champagne dinner. Among the more famous guests were Robert Lowell and Elizabeth Hardwick. If Dickey believed he had ratified his friendship with Lowell during his visit to New York several months before (Dickey had written him: "I have seldom got on so well with another writer"),[30] he was mistaken. At the celebrations Lowell snubbed Dickey out of loyalty to Elizabeth Bishop. In subsequent correspondence Lowell explained that he had wanted Bishop's book to win and mocked Dickey as a poet who read his poems better than he wrote them. From Dickey's point of view, the National Book Award indicated that he had surpassed Lowell and all his confessional epigones. He gleefully told Al Braselton: "I'm catching up with them. I'm passing old Lowell now."[31] A compulsive ranker of poets himself, Lowell still reserved the number-one slot for himself.

As far as literary awards were concerned, 1966 was Dickey's annus mirabilis. He won the Melville Cane Award from the Poetry Society of America, a National Institute of Arts and Letters Award, and one of the highest honors bestowed on an American poet—the poetry consultantship at the Library of Congress. These various honors boosted sales of Buckdancer's Choice from 1,810 to 3,752 in the four months following March 15. Dickey never again won a major American literary award. Unlike his peers—Lowell, Berryman, Warren, Wilbur, Merrill, Bishop, Howard, Ashbery, Ammons, Justice, Wright, Levine, Merwin, Kinnell—he never received a Pulitzer Prize. He never won a Bollingen Award, a National Book Critic's Circle Award, a MacArthur Award, or another National Book Award. In Madison, however, Dickey's star was unassailable. Rideout spoke for many at the University of Wisconsin: "We are delighted at the decision of the judges because we think Mr. Dickey's poetry fully deserves the national recognition that the award implies. Incidentally, we are pleased here at Wisconsin that so fine a poet as Jim Dickey is also so fine a teacher of poetry." For the university's publicity agents, Dickey pretended to be unimpressed by the status conferred on him by the National Book Award: "I think it's fine. It has some merit on the logistical side. Awards are fine for calling attention to poems and poets. . . . But if anyone enters into the writing of poetry for the purpose of awards, it is a misconstruction of the nature of poetry and of the communication-in-depth which real poetry necessarily must aspire to be."[32] There were, of course, many "logistical" benefits to the award, among them a more permanent appointment at the University of Wisconsin. (Rideout supported the idea, but his colleagues decided to stick with their current system of two-month residencies.)

Most book reviewers showered praise on Buckdancer's Choice. Charles Monaghan in Commonweal called it the finest volume of poetry published in the

1960s and the best since Lowell's *Life Studies*. Monaghan and many other critics agreed that Lowell and Dickey now stood alone on the summit of America's Parnassus. The book attracted several negative reviews as well, the most stentorian coming from Robert Bly. On November 21, 1966, Bly hinted he was about to attack Dickey in a note with a royalty check for *The Suspect in Poetry*, which had sold out: "I doubt that I will be East this winter, and I'm not sure that we are really friends anymore, as we once were. I've reviewed *Buckdancer's Choice* for the new *Sixties*, but, judging by the anger you felt over a chance remark I made about that book in a letter to you, I doubt if you will like this review either. However, as critics, we must put down what we see."[33] Bly knew that his review would enrage Dickey, as did James Wright, who tried to convince Bly not to publish it.

Dickey was unprepared for the severity of "The Collapse of James Dickey," which appeared in the spring 1967 issue of *The Sixties*. Bly's first evaluation of Dickey's poetry in 1965, "Beasts and Angels," had been complimentary. Bly had discovered little that was offensive in what he later condemned as Dickey's rampant militarism. He praised Dickey's war poems as a refreshing antidote to others that cast the poet as a sensitive aesthete crushed by the machinery of combat: "Dickey, who was a fighter pilot in both World War II and the Korean War, a first-rate pilot, an ace in World War II . . . violates the conventional idea of the poet as an incompetent boob." He applauded "the tremendous physical energy" contained by Dickey's poems: "In his best poems something subterranean and preconscious is always present. He is like a big moose adapted somehow to living beneath the water in some calm inland lake. The moose is constantly rising to the surface and breaking water so he can see his own huge horns in the sunlight, and giving a fixed and strange smile to the frightened bourgeoisie out fishing."[34] At first Dickey appreciated Bly's insightfulness; later he dismissed the fanciful critique as ridiculous: "If you want to play that game it's a lot of fun . . . , but I don't think such analogies can be pursued without a certain danger of misrepresenting everybody concerned."[35]

Some of the reasons for Bly's attack surfaced in his first essay's references to the regional differences that separated the two poets: "James Dickey embodies more of the South in his poems than any southern poet ever has. Not only does his content remind us of the South, but the style seems southern: it is quite plainly rhetoric, and a ghastly rhetoric is the worst weakness in these poems."[36] Perhaps the crucial issue dividing Bly from Dickey in 1967 was not so much Southern rhetoric as the Vietnam War. Ever since Kennedy had attempted to prop up President Diem's South Vietnamese regime in the early 1960s, intellectuals and average Americans alike had vehemently opposed the war. Would South Vietnam and its neighboring countries drop like dominoes if the Communists encroached from the north? In August of 1964, when President Johnson decided to bomb North Vietnam after alleging its ships torpedoed American destroyers in the Gulf of Tonkin, the debate over the war grew more rancorous. As the Pentagon dragged the country deeper into the bloody quagmire, Bly protested and expected fellow writers to do the same. Dickey felt the pressure to take a stand when Bly organized "American Writers Against the

Vietnam War" in 1966. Bly staged several of his protest readings in Milwaukee and at Wisconsin State University in Oshkosh. Because Dickey refused to participate, he drew criticism. To a journalist from the *Wisconsin Review* who questioned him about his reluctance to get involved, Dickey said: "I disapprove thoroughly of that kind of use of poetry. I don't share Bob's views on Vietnam either, and I wouldn't have participated if he had asked me. But mainly I think that poetry is very badly served by being used as a medium for propaganda." Dickey's view of Vietnam, as he explained to the journalist, had been shaped by World War II. If Johnson appeased the North Vietnamese the way Neville Chamberlain appeased Hitler, Southeast Asia would collapse: "I have seen the results of appeasement, and I know how many lives were lost when Hitler was not stopped at Munich."[37] Therefore, Dickey reasoned, America should fight.

Traveling from campus to campus in 1966, Dickey often satirized Bly's liberal politics. Bly, who was just as popular on the poetry circuit, heard about the insults and wrote a letter to complain: "I was at Knox College [Illinois] recently after you were there [on May 7], and found that you had a pet phrase for me: 'a stupid farmer from Minnesota.' . . . What surprised me most was the gung-ho sermons you have been giving around the country in favor of the Vietnam War. I had expected some strange things from you but I hadn't expected you to turn into Kipling."[38] Dickey tried to make amends by saying that he had also complimented Bly's poetic vitality even while deploring his politics:

> As to the Viet Nam thing: you are mistaken in what you say, and mistaken in the willful and irresponsible and self-seeking way that seems entirely characteristic of you. I have been on no "platform" "in favor of the Viet Nam war." Platforms and propaganda poetry seem rather more in your line: have you in all truth not been doing some such lately? Come on now, confess it. No, I have been on no platforms. If someone comes to me and asks my private opinion as a citizen (emphatically *not* as "a poet"!) I try to point out the dangers of appeasement, as exactly as I can make them out. This is as honest as I can be about the thing, for it is what I really do think, though I don't like killing people any more than you do, and possibly less. You seem to think that it is somehow dishonest to be honest if such honesty is not in agreement with yours, and, again, I can't buy it. If you want to run with the rest of the herd on this matter, that is all right with me. But you can also, as Sam Goldwyn once said, include me out. I am no politician nor statesman, and would not presume to tell the government what to do, nor would I make propaganda or public capital out of any such.[39]

Considering the political statements made by Pound, Eliot, Yeats, Frost, and Stevens, to mention only a few poets given to undemocratic creeds, Dickey had some justification in steering clear of politics.

Dickey's argument did little to mollify Bly. Bly began "The Collapse of James Dickey" with staccato candor: "*Buckdancer's Choice* has received a lot of attention from reviewers, but curiously no one has talked about the content. I thought the content of the book repulsive. The subject of the poems is power, and the tone of the book is gloating—a gloating about power over others." Bly cited "Slave Quarters" as an example of Dickey's racism: "The poet feels that the old South treated the Negro pretty much all right. He accepts in fact all the Southern prejudices, and by adding artistic decoration to them tries to make them charming. . . . I consider this poem one of the most repulsive poems ever written in American literature. . . . It is pure kitch [sic], a *Saturday Evening Post* cover, retouched by the Marquis de Sade." In "The Firebombing," he argued: "As objects of sadism, the Negro women have been replaced by the civilian population of Asia." In "The Fiend," the voyeur's malignance toward the defenseless woman was a "sadistic business." Considering the attitudes inherent in these poems, Bly was not surprised that "when Mr. Dickey visits college campuses for readings, he makes clear his wholehearted support of the Vietnam war." As if Bly had not pulverized Dickey enough, he attempted a final knock-out blow by calling him "a huge blubbery poet, pulling out Southern language in long strings, like taffy, a toady to the government, supporting all movements toward Empire, a sort of Georgia cracker Kipling."[40] According to Bly, Dickey had evolved from a poet writing sensitive mythical poems about nature to a remorseless brute who cared only about making more money than his peers and who took a sadistic relish in Parnassian power. Although Dickey's reactions to the Vietnam War and to the military were not consistently jingoistic, and although his attitudes toward the Old South were deeply ambivalent, Bly's broadside typecast Dickey in the literary establishment for decades.

Dickey, unfortunately, was his worst advocate. Rather than tone down his retrograde opinions, he often played up his roles as sexist, racist, and militarist to bait and enrage his critics. He could not resist making a commotion, especially in the liberal groves of academe. Some of his outspokenness was due to alcohol, some of it to his impatience with overly refined academics, and some of it to the fact that he *did* harbor animosity toward women, minorities, Northerners, and poetic rivals. No rabid martinet, he nevertheless had a penchant for sadoeroticism. He was sincere when he told Geoffrey Norman in a 1973 *Playboy* interview: "Nobody can love peace like somebody who has been in a war. I love it. There isn't any machine or dial to measure this by, but I can categorically guarantee that I'm no lover of war, killing, pain, and suffering. The things high-speed metal can do to human flesh and bone are so horrendous that once you've seen one battle fatality or fatal aircraft accident, you are never quite the same afterward. You learn just how mortal you really are and how vulnerable your body really is."[41] In his fantastic tales of love and war, however, Dickey had given Bly plenty of evidence to the contrary. Apart from boasting about his kills as an "ace" combat pilot, he had once told Bly that he had been married to a "gook" in the Philippines who enjoyed being whipped. He would beat her mercilessly, he said, only to watch her crawl back for more punishment.[42]

About Bly and his pacifist friends, Dickey told Al Braselton, in a frightened and depressed voice: "They'd forgive my success if I'd march with Lowell in Washington. Hell, what do I know about the Vietnam War? My wars were the Second World War and Korea. A writer must write about subjects that interest him. The Vietnam War is a tragedy, but it doesn't interest me at all as far as my work is concerned. In Russia they censor those who attack the state; in the U.S., the literary establishment attacks those who don't attack the state."[43] Dickey, in fact, occasionally made statements supporting the peace movement. Asked by his Doubleday editor, Ken McCormick, for a signed comment to be auctioned at a Publishers for Peace rally in the fall of 1970, Dickey produced the following note: "Dear Friend and Fellow Peace Lover: . . . No one wants to die, in a war or in any other way, but many have died and are dying . . . ; more will die. Let us hope and work for peace in any way it is possible to do."[44] Dickey vacillated between bellicose and pacifist sentiments, and, to the anger of his peers, refused to take a consistent stand.

Considering their argumentative temperaments, the friendship between Bly and Dickey was doomed from the start. Their regional differences, which erupted in a kind of verbal Civil War after "The Collapse of James Dickey," made a lasting union impossible. Bly thought "of Northerners as trying to tell the truth, be honest with friends, and Southerners as being evasive, formal but not forthright, mannerly without being honest."[45] Obviously a generalization, Bly's statement pointed to his irreconcilable differences with Dickey. Unwilling to make peace, the two poets sniped at each other for the next three decades until, shortly before Dickey's death in 1997, Bly considered visiting his ailing archrival to offer an apology. It had been arrogant to appoint himself as Dickey's scourge, he had concluded, and also mean-spirited to violate Dickey's Southern code of trust. Mulling over the plan with his wife, he decided that his desire for reconciliation was sentimental and would only paper over disagreements that persisted. He never made the trip. His rancor having evaporated over the years, Bly felt mainly pity for his old enemy, and speculated that Dickey's sadistic fantasies—whether directed toward women, blacks, Jews, or "gooks"—were neurological in origin and probably the result of a childhood trauma.[46]

Reviewing *Buckdancer's Choice*, Bly must have had in mind Dickey's statement in Chicago about the glass window encasing him and deadening his sensitivity to the world. Many, but certainly not all, of the poems in *Buckdancer's Choice* contain confessions of numbness and isolation. Dickey's personae repeatedly undertake a meditative *via negativa* in order to pass through anesthetizing enclosures to fantasy worlds of sensual—and usually forbidden—delights. In his poems about firebombing, peeping, and fornicating, Dickey seems to be attacking as much as reveling in his own visionary sensibility. He registers his ambivalence toward his imagination in "The Firebombing" by branding it "The honored aesthetic evil." In the poem Bly berated so harshly, Dickey identifies with the pilot, but mainly to admit that he too is glassed in and glassed off from mundane experience. The pilot is a "technical-minded stranger with my hands / . . . in a glass treasure-hole of blue light." A "Cloud flickers / At my glassed-off forehead,"[47] he says. If he feels any elation over the fireworks displays he engenders on the ground, it is overshadowed by his recognition that the consequences of his acts will never break through his glassed-in cockpit. His poem attempts to atone for the fact, which is so common in modern, technological warfare, that the perpetrators of violence are aesthetically detached from their victims.

Bly pounced on the poems in which Dickey sought to transcend pain, guilt, and death, as if he were attacking Dickey's romanticism as much as his personality. Dickey did imagine sloughing off his humanity in order to become something Satanic, purely libidinal, even murderous. In "Reincarnation" he contemplates exchanging his human body for that of a diamond-back rattlesnake "waiting—all the time a symbol of evil— / Not for food, but for the first man to walk by the gentle river." In "The Fiend" he abandons his routine self and takes on the persona of a knife-wielding Peeping Tom who ogles his victim from behind a window. For the voyeur, the glass barrier stimulates rather than curtails his fantasies: "He will casually follow her in   like a door-to-door salesman / The godlike movement of trees stiffening with him   the light / Of a hundred favored windows   gone wrong somewhere in his glasses / Where his knocked-off panama hat was   in his painfully vanishing hair."[48] Dickey masked his misgivings over similar fantasies by joking: "The best fan letter I ever got was from a police lieutenant who read 'The Fiend' in the *Partisan Review*, and he wrote to me and said, 'I've always had a sneaking sympathy with you guys. Please don't answer. I'm not going to sign this, and I won't give you any return address, but I'm a member of the New York City Police Department.'"[49] Other versions of the story posit that a member of New York's Special Vice Investigation Squad (Dickey may have meant the Vice Enforcement Division) wrote him the fan letter. No such letter exists in Dickey's massive archive.

In a poem like "Pursuit from Under," Dickey again explores the guilt aroused by his sadistic impulses, tracing his propensity for violent fantasies to his cock-fighting father and his father's North Georgia ancestors. His dream vision of his father's cock farm associates his father with a killer whale that pursues an innocent seal. Admitting that he has both whale and seal within him, Dickey's narrator struggles to keep his whalelike father beneath "the flawing glass" of ice. A similar poem, "Gamecock," associates Dickey's father with one of his murderous roosters, but because his father is sequestered behind a hospital's "blue windows,"[50] he again maintains his aesthetic distance from evil. Although Bly was right to claim that imagined violence attracted Dickey, real violence haunted and repelled him. Dickey approached the destructive compulsions in himself and others the way a scientist might a virus. He studied them—sometimes with fascination, sometimes with horror—behind a glass lens. The triumph of the poems arose from the profoundly engaging way he redeemed his flaws.

Buckdancer's Choice took risks in poetic form as well as subject matter. In poems like "The Fiend" and "The Shark's Parlor" Dickey experimented with what he called his "block format" or "shimmering walls of words." He stretched his lines from margin to margin to make them look like prose, and also split them into word clusters surrounded by spaces. If he had hoped to lull readers with the anapestic flow of his early poems, now he wanted to jolt them with short linguistic bursts. Even in poems whose lines didn't fill the whole page, such as "The Firebombing," he deployed this new technique of spacing phrases. While many of the poems still followed a mythic story line and were divided into regular stanzas, they had a looser, more improvisatory feel. Critics who overlooked his stylistic brinkmanship, which allowed his voice to become even more expansive and enchanting, missed both Dickey's complexity and artistry. Dramatizing the conflicts that tore at his psyche, Dickey achieved—in Robert Frost's memorable words—"a momentary stay against confusion"—but in a distinctly new way. He confessed his demons in order to purge them, and did so in some of the most ambitious and stirring poems of his generation.

Dickey had a chance to flee the barriers of ice and glass he associated with the North and his own aesthetic temperament, and visit a more familiar Southern setting as soon as he finished his term at Madison's "frozen Berkeley." Rather than return to his family in California (he visited them on May 28), he went on another barnstorming tour. On April 5, he traveled to the now nonmilitary Clemson for the first time since his student days. His reading in the chemistry auditorium drew an audience of about five hundred, which included former teachers, classmates, football teammates, and his lifelong friend, William Hunter. Dickey read magnificently and basked in the applause accorded his homecoming. He read to similar adoring crowds at North Carolina Wesleyan College, UNC Charlotte, UNC Greensboro, Davidson, Duke, East Carolina, University of Georgia, Huntington College, and North Carolina State in Raleigh. His visit to Duke was especially happy because he met the poet Jim Applewhite, who was a graduate student. In the Applewhites' humble abode, Dickey charmed his hosts as they all crowded around a small Sears TV to watch the Master's golf tournament. On April 12, Applewhite got to know Dickey better while driving him to East Carolina University in his grandfather's large black Buick. Because the recaps on the old tires started to peel off and flap against the fender, Applewhite had to cut them off with a hunting knife. Afterward Dickey liked to remind him of the way they had beat out a new prosody with the dilapidated tires.

Dickey gave so many readings in so many different places during 1966 that Bill Thompson, his agent at Lordly and Dame in charge of booking the events, began calling his client "the pied piper" or "my wandering poet." During the spring he also read at Greenville College, North Central College, Smith, the Trenton City Museum, Bennington, Iowa State, Rhode Island College, Mankato State, the College of Saint Teresa, Wiess College, Towson State, Boston College, and Rice. Dickey usually made two hundred dollars per reading, although colleges were beginning to pay him as much as five hundred dollars. He usually traveled alone, but sometimes his family joined him. On these occasions, such as the reading at Rice when Chris, Michael Allin, Kevin, and Maxine were in the audience, he seemed determined to shake them off his trail. Chris said: "I remember sitting next to my mother and watching her as he read 'Adultery.' . . . She was very neutral. I was crushed. I couldn't . . . believe it."[51] Watching his father drunkenly clasp the podium, divulge his adulterous affairs, and steer the audience with comments like "Isn't that good!" Chris felt both embarrassment and disgust. As she listened to her husband flout their marriage in public, Maxine could hardly contain the pain beneath her stoic mask.

Dickey flustered as well as infatuated his audiences. At a University of Utah writer's conference from June 13 to June 18 (he was joined by poet William Stafford and novelists Virginia Sorensen and Alec Waugh), he shocked some of the conference goers when, as he recalled, he "fell in with the most depraved [Mormon] girl that ever existed. . . ."[52] To his chagrin, she followed him to the

University of Wisconsin in Milwaukee, where he delivered the opening remarks at the Summer Arts Festival and taught a poetry workshop from June 20 to July 16. Because he cut such a wide romantic swath through Milwaukee and because he said he had been a bombardier, one of his students, Wayne Cody, dubbed him "the Blond Bomber." The girls he left in his wake were either brokenhearted, dazed, or thrilled by their flings with the great poet. Dickey had a similarly ambiguous effect on some of the local literati. At a German professor's party, Dickey at first enthralled the guests by arguing, as he often did, that the Earth was the only planet in the universe that contained sentient life. The discussion turning to politics, Dickey abruptly segued into his Southern drawl and asked: "Did anyone ever stop to think that maybe the Blacks *are* inferior?" According to Cody, who attended the party: "You could have heard a pin drop and then the floodgates opened and Dickey was awash in Political Correctness (tho' it wasn't called that then). So he went back to playing his guitar, strumming it in the corner, which he didn't play very well."[53] Dickey displayed the more charming half of his Southern personality on a visit to Cody's mother in Milwaukee. He was amiable and polite, even declining to seduce Cody's lovely, buxom sister despite his inclination to do so.

Offers and awards continued to come Dickey's way as a consequence of his National Book Award. The National Institute of Arts and Letters welcomed him as a member on May 25. On June 29, the National Book Award Committee asked him to judge next year's contest. In June, Michael di Capua, an editor at Farrar, Straus & Giroux, asked him to contribute to a book commemorating Randall Jarrell, which was being organized by Robert Lowell, Peter Taylor, and Robert Penn Warren (he never did). On June 14, Helen Eustis, an associate editor at *Redbook* magazine, promised Dickey $1,250 for an article on how best to introduce children to poetry. Another big magazine, *McCall's*, proposed to interview him in New York. Dickey's reputation got its most substantial boost from *Life* magazine's feature-length article "The Unlikeliest Poet," on July 22, 1966. Dickey must have heard the crowds cheer when the author, Paul O'Neil, proclaimed that Dickey was not only a decorated poet but a former NFL-class football player and seasoned combat pilot. Leading the cheers were members of his family. His mother wrote on July 29: "If we lived to be a hundred years old the Dickey family can never be as thrilled again as we were when we opened Life Magazine and saw James Dickey standing there in all his glory—big, bold, and handsome! (and I might add, full of snobble). Gosh, we were proud!"[54] Maibelle, Patsy, and Tom Dickey all sent congratulations. None of them drew attention to the fact that much of the article was self-aggrandizing fiction.

With so much traveling, Dickey struggled to make time for his poetry and novel. On June 29, 1966, Paul Brooks urged him to finish *Deliverance* as soon as possible. To capitalize on Dickey's National Book Award publicity, Brooks wanted the manuscript by the end of the summer so that the final editorial review could be completed by early fall. The book could then be published in the spring of 1967. Dickey argued against such a schedule: the formal contract he signed with Houghton Mifflin on September 2, 1966, set a December 31, 1967, deadline for the final draft. His advance of $5,000 would come in two installments: $2,000 on signing the contract and $3,000 on delivering the manuscript (the publisher also offered generous royalties: 10 percent on the first five thousand copies sold, 12.5 percent on the next five thousand copies, and 15 percent on all copies sold thereafter). Dickey, however, made little progress with *Deliverance* after receiving his portion of the first $2,000 because from 1966 to 1968 he served in America's most prestigious poetry-related post: poetry consultant at the Library of Congress.

VIII.

IN POETRY'S CATBIRD SEAT

20. First Term (1966–1967)

As poetry consultant at the Library of Congress, Dickey was as determined as ever to set himself apart from the pack. He had no desire to emulate the staid gentility that characterized the position. His colleagues-to-be recognized this on the warm September day in 1966 when a maroon Corvette Sting Ray, which Dickey had bought in Northridge to replace his MG, pulled into the library parking lot, its 427-cubic-inch engine thundering. At a press conference in the Poetry Room on September 9, 1966, Dickey intimated how he would conduct himself as the nation's premier ambassador for poetry. First of all, he had no intention of being a paper-shuffling desk clerk; he would leave the library as much as possible to disseminate the joys of poetry to the populace. Unlike former consultants, he would not compile bibliographies of other poets. To the assembled librarians and journalists, he held forth on LSD (he said he had tried the drug but found it disappointing), Allen Ginsberg ("Surely the most inept and ludicrous writer on the scene"), Norman Mailer (he "has integrity enough to be crazy and advance crazy ideas"), Robert Frost ("He's a writer I never have cared for much"), and Theodore Roethke ("immensely superior to any other poet we have had in this country"). He continued in the same oratorical vein about the presidency, sports cars, Madison Avenue, Vietnam, and the Watts riots.[1] After the press conference, Dickey submitted to a private interview with LeRoy Aarons, a writer for the *Washington Post*. The article in the next day's *Post*, titled "Ex-Adman Dickey: Don't Just Wait for Oblivion," began with a mission statement by Dickey calculated to make people sit up and furrow their brows. "I want to get every guy to sit down and have a beer with his soul," he declared. The "ex-college football star, ex-ad man, ex–World War II bomber pilot,"[2] as Aarons described Dickey, planned to bring a draft of fresh air—or beer—to the consultant's office.

The poetry consultantship was, indeed, an old post in need of renovation. The idea for a chair of poetry had originated in the minds of Herbert Putnam, who became librarian of Congress in 1899 under President McKinley, and Archer Milton Huntington, a wealthy philanthropist who befriended Putnam during his thirty-year term at the library. At first rather nebulously conceived, the chair received more-precise definition in 1939 from Archibald MacLeish. As the new librarian of Congress, MacLeish stipulated that the poetry consultant should first "bring to the Library of Congress a practicing poet able and willing to answer the inquiries about American and English poetry which occasional readers may bring in, and to have general supervision of the collection in a non-technical way; and, secondly [he or she should] offer to practicing poets a place where for a period of a year or two a man [or woman] may have time and access to the Library for the purposes of his work."[3] MacLeish chose

Allen Tate to serve under him. Two decades later Stephen Spender, who had once rejected Dickey's poems as an editor, and the new librarian of Congress, L. Quincy Mumford, chose Dickey for the chair. If Spender had lingering reservations about his suitability, Dickey dispelled them during a reading that galvanized everyone at the library's Coolidge Auditorium on November 8, 1965.

Thrilled by the honor, Dickey also saw it as a chance to put down roots again in the South. He told one interviewer that he was tired of wandering, that he had taken so many writer-in-residence jobs that he had started to feel like "a poetical bum."[4] Before he could take the reins from Spender, however, Dickey had to release himself from a commitment he had made to Hollins College for the 1966–67 academic year (he had accepted an offer from Hollins over the one from Valley State). With the help of Roy Basler, a Lincoln scholar who directed the library's Reference Department and Whittall Fund, Dickey prevailed on English Department chair Louis Rubin to annul his contract. (Rubin may have been relieved by this turn of events; he was so worried about Dickey's womanizing that in July 1965, he warned Dickey that the Hollins administration would fire him if he fraternized with students.) His new job, as defined by L. Quincy Mumford, would be to advise the librarian, the director of the Reference Department, and the General Reference and Bibliography Division on literary matters relating to the Library of Congress. Dickey agreed to his duties and to Quincy's offer of a fifteen-thousand-dollar salary.

As for accommodations, Dickey decided to live in the country rather than on another busy thoroughfare like Balboa Boulevard. In August, while house hunting in Leesburg, Virginia, a small town about thirty-five miles northwest of the capital, Dickey found a stately, furnished, antebellum house at 47 King Street. With his family's approval, he signed a lease on August 20. According to local lore, Robert E. Lee had withdrawn to the brick mansion after the critical second Battle of Manassas. Dickey told people that Lee had recuperated there from broken wrists after a horse had thrown him. Most of the Dickeys insisted that the rooms were haunted. Often they heard footsteps clattering up and down the stairs, and ballroom music emanating from the attic, where Dickey kept some of his ten thousand books. Dickey's friend from the University of Florida, James Bexley, once saw someone standing in the bathroom doorway while he showered. Patsy Dickey heard a ghost playing harpsichord music in one of the rooms. With or without such spooks, the Dickeys' new domicile had an aura of formality and dignity that reminded them of the Old South. It had a large entrance hallway, twin drawing rooms, a library, a formal dining room, a modern kitchen with pantry and bar, eight bedrooms, a sitting room, a servants' room, three baths, a study, and an ancient boxwood hedge stretching from its fortresslike walls. Here Maxine took up her duties as gardener, housekeeper, chauffeur, personal secretary, and mother, while her husband reapplied himself to his books and commuted to D.C.

On September 6, Dickey began his first week at the Library of Congress. He worked on the third floor in a comfortable, book-lined room with leather sofas and windows. From his office, which was sometimes affectionately called "poetry's cat-bird seat," he enjoyed panoramic views of the Capitol. He met Phyllis Armstrong, who was in charge of his office, and Nancy Galbraith, her assistant.

Although the elderly Armstrong struck him as stiff, distant, and somewhat forbidding, he admired her efficiency. She told Dickey where to be at what time and made sure he kept to his schedule. With Galbraith, Dickey felt more rapport, perhaps because, like Gwen Walti, she had graduated from Bryn Mawr (as an English major). In her midthirties, she was more relaxed and friendlier than Armstrong. She respected Dickey greatly, and Dickey reciprocated. He especially endeared himself to Galbraith by proposing to begin a new custom of gift giving in the office. At the end of his tenure as consultant he bought expensive gold watches for both his assistants. Engraved on the back of Galbraith's watch were the boyishly presumptuous words: "Nancy loves James Dickey."

While Armstrong acted as Dickey's secretary, composing memos and compiling schedules, Galbraith did most of the actual typing. His activities and correspondents were legion. Requests to give lectures, edit books, and write recommendations inundated the office. Dickey deflected many of these requests, but it was harder to ignore the dozens of poets who called for meetings or sent poems. Emotional appeals for Dickey's help usually got a quick response. Dickey began a correspondence with someone he must have thought was his double—a former football player, soldier, advertising man, and bow-and-arrow hunter—who now wrote poems in an Indiana federal penitentiary. Other letters caught his attention as well. On May 24, 1967, a high-strung poetry student with whom he had had a brief affair at San Fernando Valley State complained to him of her hurt romantic pride. Dickey had revisited the old campus two days earlier to give a reading, but acted self-consciously with her, perhaps because of Wallace Graves's satire in the *Kenyon Review* (the interview with Harrison Byrd so galled Dickey that for years he maintained—falsely: "[Graves] tried to carry on an affair with my wife, with only moderate success").[5] If the Valley State woman had expected Dickey to act like the philandering Byrd, she was disappointed. He was so unnerved by her presence that his hand shook and he almost dropped his pen while autographing a book for her. Over the next few years, she wrote Dickey in harrowing detail about her marital troubles and struggles to write poetry. Her stream-of-consciousness letters grew longer and more agonized even though they elicited little sympathy from Dickey. By 1981, her adoration seemed so intemperate that Dickey's second wife wrote her a letter demanding that she put an end to her correspondence. While bothersome, she and others like her were thematically important to Dickey; they encouraged him to examine in his poetry and fiction the power of charismatic personalities.

More-reasonable writers and writers' groups constantly jockeyed for Dickey's attention as well. He served as guest-of-honor speaker at a dinner at the International Inn for "Upward Bound" students on September 15, 1966. Four days later he participated in a subscription kickoff luncheon for the Washington Performing Arts Society. On September 28, he dined with President Johnson at a White House luncheon honoring the Republic of Senegal's president, Leopold Senghor. The next day he met Senghor again at a Women's National Press Club gathering. Dickey's life swirled with such engagements. Many old and new friends, such as Willie Morris, Carolyn Kizer, Calhoun Winton, John Barth, and a hunting companion named Terry Miller came to his office. He also attended many of the library's prestigious lectures sponsored by the Whittall Fund: Karl

Shapiro discussing Randall Jarrell, Allen Curnow lecturing on New Zealand poets, Herman Wouk reading his fiction, and Yevtushenko ("the great bogus poet of the Soviet Union,"[6] as Dickey called him in a letter to Stanley Burnshaw) performing his poetry. In addition, Dickey recorded interviews for TV, whooped it up at parties given by Library of Congress friends, and continued to read at elementary schools, middle schools, high schools, and colleges around the country.

Even for a man of Dickey's robust constitution, the reading schedules organized by Bill Thompson and the library's assistants were grueling. He seemed to be perpetually dashing to catch planes, buses, trains, and cars. During October and November 1966, he traveled to Seattle University, Gonzaga University, Simmons College, Kent State, City College of New York, The Poetry Center at the New York Y, Seton Hall, and the Nassau County public schools. Between January and June 1967, he read or lectured at the International Poetry Forum in Pittsburgh, Castleton State, Temple University, Art Alliance Philadelphia, the State University of New York (Stony Brook), Montclair State College, St. Norbert College, Exeter Academy, Towson State, Hollins College Arts Festival, Harvard, Western Reserve University, the Women's National Democratic Club, National Secretaries Association, Loyola University, Okaloosa-Walton Community College, Brooklyn College, Coe College, Texas Christian, and Wayne State. Rightly proud of his poetry's success in the literary marketplace, Dickey earned around $500 for individual readings in the fall of 1966; by the spring of 1967, his fee had increased by several hundred dollars. Occasionally he earned as much as $1,300 if he stayed at a college for several days and conducted workshops. Magazines paid substantial fees as well. Dickey's friend, Bill Emerson, who edited the *Saturday Evening Post*, paid $1,000 for the poem "Dark Ones" on November 23, 1966. Two weeks later Howard Moss at the *New Yorker* renewed his first-reading agreement, which provided 25 percent more than the magazine's going rate of $2.30 per line, a possible additional payment for cost-of-living increases, and a signing bonus of $400. Another indication of his growing popularity was Arthur Klein's proposal in May 1967 to record his poetry on a Spoken Arts album. Dickey was beginning to realize his dream of growing rich on poetry.

To get the highest price for his services, Dickey frequently irritated his hosts with his bargaining tactics. When Princeton, in the summer of 1967, asked him to read for $250, he flatly refused. His contact person, Edmund Keeley, responded that Auden had recently read at Princeton for $500, which was the largest fee that the university had ever paid for a reading. Dickey said he would read for what they paid Auden. Inviting him to deliver the Phi Beta Kappa address at Miami University in the spring of 1967, Bill Pratt was taken aback by Dickey's deference to the "mysterious shadowy figure hovering around me at all times of the day and night"—his agent Bill Thompson at Lordly and Dame. To take the sting out of his financial demands, Dickey resorted to flattery: "But, dear Bill, dear Old Friend, do know that I think of you as my Exemplary Man, and I am as proud of you, of your critical acumen, your translations, and your integrity as if you were a kind of virgilian companion."[7] Perhaps to prick Dickey's newly acquired celebrity status, in a letter confirming the Phi Beta Kappa date Pratt included the aside: "Stephen Spender was with us last week . . . and you'd be amused to hear his anecdotes about . . . sitting next to Maxine while you read a poem about adultery in a motel room, and being amazed that she didn't bat an eye."[8] After Pratt introduced Dickey at his March 21 reading in Ohio, Dickey got a measure of revenge with what became a standard backhanded compliment. He quipped: "I hope you're around to speak at my funeral."[9] To perpetuate the friendly sparring, Dickey read "The Sheep Child" (a poem about Georgia farm boys copulating with sheep), which startled the bright-eyed Phi Beta Kappa students just as much as "Adultery" had startled Spender.

One of Dickey's more hilarious escapades was with Henry Taylor in mid-April 1967. Taylor had invited him to read at Roanoke College in Virginia. Since Taylor still had a home in a small town a stone's throw from Leesburg, he had recently spent a good deal of time with the Dickeys. An adept horseman, Taylor sometimes invited Dickey's sons, who had taken riding lessons on the West Coast, to his family's horse farm (Dickey himself never rode out of fear of horses). Taylor, who adored Maxine, also invited the Dickeys to dinner on occasion. Reciprocating Taylor's hospitality, Dickey spoke to Roanoke College's morning assembly, visited some classes, read his poetry, and appeared with Taylor on the local TV station's *Panorama* show.[10] Before the TV cameras, however, Dickey grew increasingly agitated. Their interviewer, Mrs. Kathy Thornton, had found a married pair of actors to read a poem by Taylor ("Remembering Kevin McKenzie") and a poem by Dickey ("The Escape"). The woman read Taylor's poem in a juvenile tone, and her husband, who had an audible cleft palate, struggled with "The Escape." Afterward, on their way to a taxi cab, Taylor qualified his apology: "It's another first for James Dickey. You're the first man to have his poetry read on television by an actor with a hare lip."[11] Dickey laughed, and laughed again at the nearly unintelligible messages emitted by the cab's dispatch radio. At subsequent reunions the two poets invariably acted out their cab ride, imitating the voices crackling with static on the radio.

Taylor next escorted Dickey to nearby Hollins College. Louis Rubin, Taylor's former thesis supervisor, had told him that Howard Nemerov would be reading at Hollins. In order to protect the undergraduate girls, however, Rubin had warned Taylor: "Don't bring that son of a bitch over here." Taylor could understand Rubin's concern; he had often heard Dickey approach coeds with the crude line: "Hi, honey; fuckin' anybody regular?"[12] Brushing Rubin's injunction aside, another Hollins poet, Julia Randall, invited both Dickey and Taylor to a party at her house after Nemerov's reading. Dickey, as it turned out, did little to upset Rubin or anyone else. He spent much of the evening talking cordially to Nemerov. His one indiscretion was committed in the presence of Richard Dillard, who left a gathering in the kitchen to find Dickey in the living room gnawing an entire brick of cheddar cheese.

In his first annual report to the library, Dickey attributed his hectic reading schedule to his belief that "the essence of poetic communication is personal contact between poem and reader, between poet and reader or listener." To enhance "poetic communication," Dickey relied on his guitar, punctuating his readings with lively renditions of folk songs like "Freight Train," "Candy Man," "Apple Blossom Special," and "Handsome Molly." Dickey's audiences usually cheered, and Dickey urged them to relay their cheers in letters to his boss. Because he wanted his poetry to change people's lives, he said he had "accepted almost every offer to speak . . . whether or not it entailed payment."[13] On some occasions, however, Dickey refused. One such refusal catapulted him into a battle that lasted for months and culminated in an attempt to impeach him as poetry consultant.

In the fall of 1966, when the president of the National League of American Pen Women invited Dickey to read and talk about his poetry for only fifty dollars, he saw a chance to avenge his debacle with the Florida Pen Women. His reply was swift. Would the president of the Pen Women expect to pay a doctor with peanuts? he asked. He demanded seven hundred dollars. The woman, who was also a member of the Poetry Society of New Hampshire, complained to her friend Raymond Swain, the president of the Poetry Society. Swain wrote Dickey a vindictive letter and also wrote his two state senators, inquiring how someone like Dickey could be chosen for such an esteemed post as poetry consultant. The letters passed to Mumford, who defended Dickey. The matter could have ended there, but Dickey wrote Swain on December 12, 1966, defending his and any poet's right to demand high wages. He tried to trap Swain in a self-contradiction: "You evidently care for poetry, do not want it held cheaply, as in the case of some organization—Pen Women or whomever—tacitly assuming that, since poetry is not worth much, neither is a poet's time, and he may therefore be asked to read, lecture, or appear as a luncheon speaker when the local bank president isn't available for a pittance, or, as I seem to remember in this case, for nothing at all." If Swain and his friend valued poetry, they should agree to pay someone like Dickey to deliver it (Swain's friend *had* agreed to pay, but not enough). Dickey concurred with Swain's charge that he was a "literary snob": "Yes indeed: I not only affirm it; I insist on it: I believe in values, and I will uphold them now and from now on. Since we live by money, value ought to be paid for, and should not be given away save by the decision of the person involved." Dickey finished with a denunciation and a threat: "Your pompous letter, impugning my motives and questioning my character, is plainly intended as an insult. If you insist on this course of action, I shall take the matter up with you on a personal basis when I come to your part of the country in a month or so. Believe me, it would be wiser to let it drop."[14] Swain may have thought he was about to fight a duel.

The curmudgeonly Swain would not retreat. On December 16, he fired back a letter expressing contempt for Dickey's sarcasm. Although he allowed that Dickey could be as avaricious a poet as he wanted, he still thought it was wrong for the poetry consultant to write insulting letters to his friends. A subtext of his complaint, which he didn't immediately reveal, was his conviction that Dickey was a pornographic poet. He had been deeply offended by Dickey's poem "The Sheep Child" in the August 1966 issue of the *Atlantic Monthly*. How could the nation's most visible poet write about "Farm boys wild to couple / With anything   with soft-wooded trees / With mounds of earth   mounds / Of pinestraw" and leeringly dwell on "this thing that's only half / Sheep   like a woolly baby / Pickled in alcohol"?[15] According to Swain, Dickey advocated incest. (In fact, the poem had nothing to do with incest; Dickey had used a legend about sex with animals to dramatize the origin of sexual taboos and to show how a fear of breaking taboos drove men toward civilized institutions like marriage.)

Dickey's review of Lawrance Thompson's *Robert Frost: The Early Years*, which had appeared in the November *Atlantic Monthly* as "Robert Frost, Man and Myth," added fuel to Swain's fire. Dickey had begun the review by treating the mythical Robert Frost—the "kindly, forbearing, energetic, hardworking, good-neighborly" Yankee gentleman—as an invention worthy of Hollywood. According to Dickey, fear, confusion, pain, terror, and hubris had compelled Frost to create an artificial self. He concluded: "The *persona* of the Frost Story was made year by year, poem by poem, of elements of the actual life Frost lived, reinterpreted by the exigencies of the *persona*."[16] Dickey's insights applied equally to his own persona, personality, and poetry, as some of the responses to Dickey's review indicated. Although he could hardly damn Frost for lying about his life, he made it plain that he disliked both Frost's actual life and his persona. Dickey later claimed that Frost was little more than a "sententious, holding-forth old bore who expected every hero-worshipping adenoidal little twerp of a student poet to hang on his every word. . . . If it were thought that anything I wrote was influenced by Robert Frost, I would take that particular work of mine, shred it and flush it down the toilet, hoping not to clog the pipes."[17]

Swain held tenaciously to the myth of Frost-the-benevolent-grandfatherly-poet-of-New Hampshire. After "May Day Sermon" appeared in the April 1967 *Atlantic Monthly*, which Swain now scorned as an oracle of the devil, he became nearly apoplectic with moral outrage. The poem, he concluded in July, was nothing but a diseased individual's vomit. In the poem, as in many of Robert Lowell's early poems, Dickey had created a complicated allegory in which Jehovah—because of his self-righteous fulminations and cruel punishments—merges with Lucifer. Dickey's satanic Jehovah is played by the farmer, Eve by the farmer's daughter, and Christ by the motorcyclist who delivers the daughter from the horror of her father's vengeance and into the bliss of sex. What undoubtedly provoked Swain and his cohorts was the poem's sexual violence—and the enjoyment of it—by the various characters. The Baptist preacher who supposedly narrates the "sermon" lavishes her frenzied rhetoric on sadomasochistic scenes. The poem begins with the farmer whipping his daughter in a barn:

On the red clay floor of Hell   she screaming   her father screaming
Scripture   CHAPter and verse   beating it into her with a weeping
Willow branch   the animals stomping   she prancing and climbing
Her hair   beasts shifting from foot to foot about the stormed
Steel of the anvil . . .   each May you hear her father scream like God
And King James as he flails   cuds richen   bulls chew themselves white-
    faced
Deeper into their feed bags, and he cries something the Lord   cries
Words! Words! Ah, when they leap   when they are let out of the Bible's

Black box   they whistle   they grab the nearest girls and do her hair up
For her lover in root-breaking chains   and she knows she was born to
    hang
In the middle of Gilmer County . . .   the quartermoon on the outhouse
    begins to shine
With the quartermoonlight of this night   as she falls and rises,
Chained to a sapling like a tractor   WHIPPED for the wind in the willow
Tree   WHIPPED for Bathsheba and David   WHIPPED for the woman taken
Anywhere   anytime   WHIPPED for the virgin sighing   bleeding
From her body   for the sap and green of the year   for her own good
And evil.

The sadism is sacrificial; it is part of a rite of passage that invigorates the woman
and assures spring's renewal. According to the preacher, the whipped girl, whose
cross is a maypole as well as a post in a barn, is "drunk with pain."[18] Unlike the
participants in Dickey's fertility ritual, Swain found little to celebrate.

On June 12, 1967, Swain informed Mumford that he and 420 members of the
New Hampshire Poetry Society had written letters to their congressmen protesting Dickey's appointment at the library. He had received copies of Mumford's
letters to Senators Norris Cotton and Herman Talmadge exonerating Dickey;
now he wanted action. No longer would he and his Poetry Society tolerate
Dickey's poems. Holding up his beloved Robert Frost as a model, Swain maintained that Dickey had degraded the poetry consultantship and decried the fact
that the U.S. mail circulated smut like "May Day Sermon." In his best oratorical manner, he contended that both the Greek and Roman Empires had collapsed because the arts had collapsed, and Dickey might be responsible for a
similar catastrophe. From Dickey's perspective, Swain was another William
Tecumseh Sherman in an ongoing Civil War against all things Southern. He
had struggled to understand "the *southernness* of being a southerner," he told the
poet Miller Williams, and "['May Day Sermon'] is both the longest and the best
thing I have ever done."[19] Many of Dickey's more astute readers agreed.

On July 26, Swain lobbed another shell, this time at Mumford. He told the librarian that Senators Mundt and Cotton, who had expressed their disgust for
"May Day Sermon," were about to set up a commission to investigate obscene
materials and punish those responsible for disseminating them. Asked to serve
on the commission, Swain planned to call the librarian as a witness and force
him to justify why he had appointed Dickey as poetry consultant, why he had re-
tained Dickey after others had pointed out that he was a pornographer, and why
he had continued to defend him and his obscene writing. Swain bragged that his
condemnation of Dickey published in the July *Atlantic Monthly* had incited over
two thousand supportive responses. Even Boston's Cardinal Cushing had sent
his prayers and blessings. With Cushing and God on his side, Swain must have
felt certain that he could get Dickey expelled from the Library of Congress.

Swain was not alone in denouncing Dickey's recent contributions to the
Atlantic Monthly. The gothic sex and violence in his poems had offended many.
Loyal readers delivered tirades similar to Swain's against the magazine and can-
celed their subscriptions. To a certain extent Dickey enjoyed the fray, especially

when friends weighed in with their support. One of his most adamant supporters was the *Atlantic Monthly*'s editor, Robert Manning, who had paid nine hundred dollars for "May Day Sermon" and had hailed its publication as a milestone for both the magazine and for literature. Dickey actively solicited other testimonials. On May 8, 1967, after receiving compliments from Edward Dwelle at Davidson College, he wrote his new fan: "If you could manage to say some of the same things [about "May Day Sermon"] to Bob Manning, the editor of the *Atlantic*, it would do us a power of good, for both editor and poet are taking a heavy beating from the umbrellas of little old ladies and the candlesticks of preachers."[20] Dickey also asked better-known writers such as Jean Burden and L. E. Sissman to write Manning (their letters soon appeared in the magazine). Since editors of other journals also published his controversial poems, Dickey directed his supporters to write them as well.

As allies and enemies traded salvos outside the library walls, inside the library Dickey earned almost everyone's respect. His colleagues approved of his innovations, especially the reading format he developed for two participants instead of one. Dickey himself said about it: "This arrangement not only offers the audience twice as many poets as before, but the added advantage of hearing each discuss his own work, the work of the other poet, and any and all questions arising between them."[21] Dickey also initiated videotaping sessions for the double readings, which were stored in the library's archive. For his first session, which occurred in the Coolidge Auditorium on December 5, 1966, Louis Simpson and James Wright shared the stage. In 1965, Dickey had met Simpson at Stanford, where Simpson taught, and also at San Fernando Valley State, which Simpson visited at about the same time. Otherwise, the two poets had had little contact during the 1960s, partly because Simpson disdained what he assumed were Dickey's pro-Vietnam views. At the library reading, they found common ground. After both poets read for twenty minutes, Dickey moderated a discussion in which all three agreed that English departments were bastions of ignorance. The following day, WETA, an educational TV station in the Washington area, videotaped the two poets and broadcast the reading several weeks later. Successive writers followed the same format.

Dickey's travel schedule for the winter and spring of 1967 outpaced his busy fall schedule. Because he had agreed to join Louis Kronenberger, Dudley Fitts, and Peter Davison as judges for the Saint Botolph's Arts Award, he flew to Boston about two weeks after giving the keynote reading at the MLA conference in New York (on January 12, he voted for Howard Nemerov to receive the Saint Botolph's award). In mid-January he and his son Chris boarded a plane for a visit with the poet Laurence Lieberman on Saint Thomas in the Virgin Islands. Lieberman had published a laudatory review of *Helmets* in 1965 (Dickey called it one of the most understanding appraisals of his work that he had ever read), and had met Dickey for the first time at the MLA conference. Lieberman's review had appeared in the *Antioch Review*, whose editor, Judson Jerome, had recently helped the dean of Antioch College establish The College of the Virgin Islands. As the new college's first English professor, Lieberman accepted the job of building a department and invited Dickey to read to the professors and students in January. For almost a week Dickey and Lieberman sampled the local

Caribbean cuisine, drank, and chatted about books. An expert underwater swimmer and speargun fisherman, Lieberman introduced Dickey and his son to the sport. Both Dickey and Lieberman felt refreshed by their time together on Saint Thomas. In the many letters written afterward, Lieberman discussed articles he was writing or planning to write about Dickey's poetry, and by 1968 he had published his insightful study *The Achievement of James Dickey* in the Scott Foresman Modern Poets Series.

On his return to the cold streets of Washington, Dickey plunged into his consultant duties once again. He commented on some poems from Al Braselton, finished correcting the proofs of what would become his most substantial collection, *Poems 1957–67*, and also supervised several dual readings. On March 6, Donald Hall and William Stafford read together. Considering their rancorous past, Hall had a hard time understanding why Dickey had invited him. Was Dickey merely being sentimental about their former collaborations? Hall remembered their time at the library well: "He took Bill [Stafford] and Maxine and me out to dinner and he got terribly drunk. He had a bunch of Manhattans without ice, and then champagne, and when we were all finished he got another bottle of champagne, drank a good bit of it, and stuck the bottle in his pocket while we walked from the restaurant. [At the Library] we stood back stage waiting to come forward through the curtains—this was recorded on television—and just before the curtain went up he said to Bill and me, 'Isn't this a wonderful thing to do for your country?' . . . He seemed absolutely straight when he said it."[22] Stafford must have been just as puzzled as Hall. A conscientious objector during World War II, Stafford was a long-standing pacifist and critic of his country. Politics aside, Dickey simply admired his poetry. When Stafford became poetry consultant a few years later, Dickey wrote: "Please understand that I think you are truly the best of us all, Bill. You have got what old high school football coaches call the real natural *lich*. You are in a right relationship to the earthly life."[23] Stafford, who had liked Dickey's poetry since first reading it in 1963, returned his affection.

A day or two after saying good-bye to Hall and Stafford, Dickey traveled to New York to meet his fellow National Book Award judges, Auden and Nemerov, and to attend the award ceremonies in Philharmonic Hall. Pleased that the prize was going to his old friend James Merrill for *Nights and Days*, Dickey also was gratified by Merrill's acknowledgment in his acceptance speech: "I would be hard put to name three other poets whose critical intelligence I have admired more on previous occasions. Their faith in my work comes as a most pleasurable shock. Of the three, I believe only Mr. Dickey has written anything about me—a stern and tonic paragraph still vivid after seven years. It did me a world of good."[24] Merrill may have uttered these words tongue-in-cheek, since as a friend of the Dickey family he probably knew that they had inherited their wealth from a tonic company.

Dickey's meeting with Auden kindled a number of stories that revealed Dickey's complicated attitudes toward the elderly poet and his adopted city. In one he spoke of helping Auden get a taxi back to his house at Seventy-seven Saint Mark's Place:

Auden lived in Greenwich Village at the time and he was afraid to go home. The Village had changed a lot since he had moved there. The neighborhood had gone black. So I took him home in a taxi and he asked me to go up with him and see him safely into his apartment. Auden was an old man. This was just a few years before his death and he was very frail. We were trying to get into the apartment, but he had five locks and his hand was shaking with age and, I guess, fear. Sure enough, while he was fumbling around, we heard a voice in the dark, "Hey, honky, you got a match?" We were in the dark, too, but I knew they could see us or had seen us. Auden grabbed my arm in fear. I figured I'd better meet this head on, so I stepped out into the streetlight and drew myself up as tall as possible, ready for anything and said, "Yeah, I got a match, nigger. You want to come and get it?" That was the last we heard from that bunch. They knew they were talking to a Southerner, by God.[25]

Dickey liked to flirt with and help homosexual writers like Auden, especially those in New York's literary establishment. He also liked to play the Southern redneck in the city, but as Mary Cantwell revealed, *he* was the one afraid of being mugged at night. He insisted that she, who was petite, walk in front of him like a bodyguard shielding him from possible danger. In other versions of his Auden story, Dickey always portrayed New York as a dangerous place that only he, the indomitable Southerner, could subdue. With his University of South Carolina friend Ward Briggs, he shifted the time to 1970 when he and Auden served with Mrs. Robert Hayden on the Pulitzer Prize committee. Instead of Hayden, who was married to the black poet Robert Hayden, he substituted Anne Sexton, spoke of conspiring with Auden to outvote her lunatic candidate for the prize, and claimed that Auden invited him to a gay bar. He declined the offer, he claimed, and waited on the street corner with the frail Auden, who was in his pink bedroom slippers. Before a cab pulled up, a black man approached. Dickey said he fended off the "nigger" with a menacing threat: "He knew that a Southern white man will stand up to him. He knew that in our culture we can if necessary kill one of them and not a jury will convict us."[26] If Dickey ever did come to Auden's aid in such a *Deliverance*-like situation, Auden rarely if ever acknowledged it. Although he met Auden three or four times at the Library of Congress and in New York, Dickey established little rapport with him. Queried about Dickey, Auden usually responded that he had nothing to say.

Dickey did have several frightening experiences when he revisited the Virgin Islands two weeks after his trip to New York. Having enjoyed his first stay with Lieberman so much, he took his family to Saint Thomas for the last week of March 1967. Again he swam and partied, but this time with what seemed to be fateful consequences. During a spear-hunting dive for sharks and barracudas, Lieberman shot a large grouper and followed it a good distance away from Dickey, who remained in the shallows. Surfacing with his prize, Lieberman noticed that Dickey's face had turned white with fear. "I thought I had lost you,"[27] he said, convinced that a shark had dragged his friend out to sea. Dickey feared he would lose Lieberman, his family, and his own life as well when two of

Lieberman's friends took them for an all-day cruise on their large yacht. On the boat Dickey drank in moderation, but the skipper did not, and Dickey soon realized, with night falling and storm clouds approaching, that the skipper could not see well enough to steer the yacht to port. Since the skipper was the only one who knew the dangerous stretch of water around Saint Thomas, he had to mumble instructions about locating the treacherous reefs while Dickey and Lieberman navigated. As they gingerly turned the steering wheel and operated the throttle, the two poets waited for the sound of coral scraping the boat's hull, knowing that such a collision would send the yacht to the bottom.

Relieved to get back to Saint Thomas safely, Dickey was also glad to return in a few days to the safety of his Washington office. Heartening news awaited him. Mark Schorer, the novelist, critic, and Sinclair Lewis biographer, had asked Dickey to teach at Berkeley. James Hart, the chairman of the English Department, followed up with a generous offer of $16,000 for the 1968–69 academic year. Perhaps worrying about fitting in at such a politically radical campus, on May 8 Dickey told Hart that only a substantial salary increase could tempt him back to the West Coast. With his usual horse-trading skills, he contended: "The other offers I have had are in the $30,000 class, and Berkeley would have to offer a salary predicated on this figure. . . . If you can manage the sum of $20,000 for two semesters, it would make my participation in your programs much more likely."[28] (Loyola University had also expressed interest in hiring Dickey, but not for $30,000.) Berkeley declined to make a higher offer, so for the time being Dickey stayed put.

Dickey's attractiveness as a job candidate increased after the publication of *Poems 1957–67*, which collected his first four books as well as two dozen new poems. To mark this watershed volume, Wesleyan held a party in New York on April 25, 1967. In a decade Dickey had written a body of work that exceeded in quantity and quality the lifetime outputs of all but a handful of twentieth-century poets. Geoffrey Wolff, the book editor of the *Washington Post*, observed in a review with the misleading title "Poet on a Motorcycle": "It is unusual for a man only 43 years old to have produced enough poems to assemble . . . the kind of collection that generally summarizes a life's work." Wolff praised the "even quality" of the poems and their "deeply serious" themes. Dickey, he pointed out, was "one of the few poets alive whose books are widely bought and, presumably, read." What accounted for this phenomenon? "Part of this success, but only a small part," he conceded, "can be written off as the achievement of a man who knows how to sell a product: he labored for a good many years in the vineyards of the advertising racket."[29] The main reason for his success was the irresistible way he married common experiences and fresh, exotic language, inviting the ordinary reader to participate in his accounts of war, love, death, nature, and machines. Compared to most poetry books, the sales were phenomenal: Wesleyan sold 5,153 copies by the end of August 1967.

One of the longest and most startling of the new poems was "Falling," whose lines, broken into word clusters by spaces, stretched from margin to margin. The "walls of words" presented a rhapsodic, slow-motion account of a stewardess's fall to earth. Although Dickey would deny it, his eccentric spacing owed something to the idea of a "breath unit"—the number of words spoken naturally in a single breath—that had been formulated by two poetic schools he regularly derided: Charles Olson's Black Mountain poets and Allen Ginsberg's Beats:

> she sheds the jacket
> With its silver sad impotent wings   sheds the bat's guiding tailpiece
> Of her skirt   the lightning-charged clinging of her blouse   the intimate
> Inner flying-garment of her slip in which she rides like the holy ghost
> Of a virgin   sheds the long windsocks of her stockings   absurd
> Brassiere   then feels the girdle required by regulations squirming
> Off her: no longer monobuttocked   she feels the girdle flutter   shake
> In her hand   and float   upward   her clothes rising off her ascending
> Into cloud   and fights away from her head the last sharp dangerous shoe
> Like a dumb bird   and now will drop in   SOON   now will drop
>
> In like this   the greatest thing that ever came to Kansas.[30]

As Dickey describes it, the stewardess's striptease in midair is a "last superhuman act" that arouses the reproductive energies in the boys, girls, and fields of Kansas.

The idea for the narrative, Dickey revealed, derived in part from Flannery O'Connor, who sometimes found ideas for short stories in newspaper articles. Dickey had read in the *New York Times* an account of a stewardess who had fallen out of an airplane. To stymie the fact checkers, he conveniently left out dates, names, and places from the quotation that he used as an epigraph. In an interview Dickey recalled that the stewardess "was a French girl who had come to this country to live. And she was a bit too old for a stewardess, something like twenty-eight or twenty-nine, so she wasn't with the major airlines. . . . This girl had been undergoing psychoanalysis for several years [this was untrue] and—this is the thing that caps the climax—her main fantasy, her obsessional nightmare, was that she was a bird."[31] In Dickey's poem, however, she became more fertility goddess than bird, and by the end of the poem, she flew without any plumage.

Dickey had gleaned the facts, which he later mythologized, from two articles in the *New York Times*. The first appeared on Saturday, October 21, 1962, the second on October 22. The articles told how Françoise de Morière, a stewardess on an Allegheny flight from Washington to Providence with stops at Philadelphia and Hartford, had been sucked from the airplane when the rear emergency door suddenly opened. Problems with the door had developed near Philadelphia. Because wind whistled around it, crew members stuffed a pillowcase into the crack. As the plane approached Bradley airport in Hartford around 8:50 P.M., Morière began to announce landing preparations. A sudden decompression at an altitude of four thousand feet broke open the door. "Ladies and gentlemen, we . . ." were Morière's last words. When the passengers looked back, they saw the door flapping on its hinges. Two men grabbed another stewardess, who had been in the lavatory, and prevented her from falling out the door. Morière's body was found twenty miles southwest of Bradley Field. She had fallen into a rocky meadow on the outskirts of the sparsely populated town of Farmington, Connecticut. State police reported that several people in the vicinity had heard a scream for thirty seconds, then silence.

Four-and-a-half years after the accident, Dickey found out much more about the stewardess from one of her closest friends, Andrew Sherwood, a portrait photographer living in Paris. On February 23, 1967, Sherwood wrote a seventeen-page letter in response to a copy of "Falling" sent to him by his mother. He informed Dickey that since the accident he had been unable to visit his friend's grave or mention her death to anyone. Now he poured out the details of her life. Françoise-Marie-Gabrielle Chabiel de Morière, he said, was descended from an ancient Poitou family of *petite noblesse* dating back to Charlemagne. As a girl she vacationed at her family's châteaux and lived the sort of life her aristocratic lineage allowed. During the austerities of World War II, she changed into a somber, frail, sensitive child. Studying in the intensely competitive Académie Julian to become a fabric or interior designer, she suffered a nervous breakdown. For the next three years she shuttled from sanitarium to sanitarium and rarely spoke. On one occasion she ran around her parents' garden, flapping her arms and screeching like a bird (that was her only memory of her silent period). Subjected to numerous psychiatrists, she grew to loathe them. Despite Dickey's claim about her having been in psychoanalysis, she had vehemently refused to enter analysis later in her troubled life. Her identification with the bird was simply a childhood memory.

As Morière recovered from her illness, she painted, played the piano, taught small children, and got a succession of jobs as governess, cosmetics salesperson, and eventually stewardess. Because of her age and false teeth, the major airlines rejected her applications. Allegheny Airlines finally hired her and flew her between Hartford, New York, and Washington, D.C. In New York she often dined with her friend Sherwood. She also dated and sometimes traveled with a businessman she had once worked for at Lord & Taylor's. The man fell in love with her and proposed, but Morière dreaded the idea of marriage so much that she considered retreating to a Dominican convent in São Paulo. The businessman, who had taken a job in Denmark, promised to arrive in New York around October 19, 1962, and whisk her off to Europe and marriage. On the night of October 20 she fell, unceremoniously, through the cold Connecticut air.

In "Falling," Dickey imagines Morière preparing for a marriage with the soil rather than with a man. On her prolonged descent through the warm air above Kansas (Morière's favorite place name, oddly enough, was Wichita, Kansas), she strips off her girdle, stockings, bra, and all her other clothes. As Yeats had done in his own poem about high-altitude sex, "Leda and the Swan," Dickey relied on his sexual and mythical fantasies for the poem's material. He knew little about the actual stewardess (in fact, Morière was so slim that she never wore a girdle). Sherwood informed Dickey that his voluptuous American sex goddess differed markedly from the prim, short-haired, narrow-hipped, flat-breasted Morière, but the elegy for her death still moved him to tears. To show his appreciation, he had his mother send Dickey the original of one of two drawings that Morière had made for him, and he invited Dickey to visit him in Paris. On May 7, 1967, Dickey thanked him and said he had hung Morière's artwork in his office.

When "Falling" appeared in the *New Yorker,* it generated more mail than any other poem Howard Moss had published. Some of Dickey's more ardent supporters seemed determined—sometimes jokingly—to confer upon him other laurels beside poetic ones. On May 19, 1967, his rambunctious friend, the poet J. Edgar Simmons, responded to a *New Republic* article titled "How to Remove LBJ in 1968" with a plan to replace Johnson with Dickey. Because he believed Dickey would make an ideal third-party candidate (in the article Doris Kearns and Sanford Levinson had proposed organizing a third party), Simmons decided to start a "James Dickey-for-President" campaign. Although this endorsement was in jest, Dickey sometimes spoke to friends as if he did, indeed, harbor presidential ambitions. Simmons took more concrete steps to honor Dickey by inviting him to read at the University of Texas in El Paso on May 12, 1967, and by arranging for the city's mayor, Judson Williams, to proclaim May 12 "James Dickey Day" (Dickey was also made honorary mayor for the day). Dickey later recalled that he received "an ornate key to the city and a date with the current Miss El Paso, a dark, humorous, diffident girl half my age with great propriety of manner and a large store of information about beauty contest competitions."[32] After his reading, Dickey climbed a hill overlooking the valley with Miss El Paso and, as they gazed at the city lights, listened to her describe the fine points of runway turns and competitive smiles at beauty pageants.

As spring eased into summer, Dickey made plans to leave the Library of Congress. According to the annual report, with Dickey at the helm the Poetry Office had bustled with activity during the 1966–67 fiscal year. Important acquisitions had been made, chief among them a series of taped readings by Randall Jarrell. In all, 18,383 pieces of typewritten documents had been produced, 1,997 reference telephone calls handled, 731 visitors received, and twenty-three separate performances staged at the Coolidge Auditorium. As the library's chief cultural representative, Dickey had done a prodigious job on the reading circuit and had enriched himself in the process. Always eager to hear about her son's financial successes, Dickey's mother wrote him at the end of his first term: "Hello there, busiest man in the world! Still flying around filling up the old money-bag with goodies? Can't think of a pleasanter thing to do!"[33] In a few weeks she sent him a Father's Day check to add to the bag.

Technically on vacation in the summer of 1967, Dickey still had to handle letters and meetings associated with the consultantship. On November 2, 1966, Mumford had invited him to serve a second term, but Dickey had no job for the fall of 1968, so he was heartened on June 30 by Georgia Tech's offer of nine thousand dollars to teach as the Franklin Foundation Distinguished Lecturer in the Humanities. The course load for the fall quarter would be light—a three-hour seminar once a week with about eighteen students. He was especially glad to hear from Georgia Tech because his former colleague Wilfred Dowden had told him two months before that Rice wanted to rehire him. The idea of returning to Rice was repugnant.

Dickey's summer, however, was not all work. He often socialized with his new Washington friends and invited old friends to his home. He threw a big party for his brother, Tom, who was visiting from Atlanta. Inman Mays was there, as were Henry Taylor and the managing director of the Kennedy Center, Roger Stevens. In another show of sibling rivalry, Tom and Jim wrestled on the living room floor until one in the morning. It may have been on this occasion that a quite drunk Jim challenged Tom to a footrace and nearly passed out from the exertion. On

August 9, Dickey had drinks and dinner with a less competitive man, Eugene McCarthy, of whom he was growing increasingly fond. The author Elizabeth Janeway had suggested in early May that the two men get together. McCarthy, she declared, greatly admired Dickey's poetry and frequently quoted from it. With or without Janeway's prodding, McCarthy visited the library to talk to Dickey about poetry and politics. Unlike most politicians, McCarthy wrote poetry and published it. Dickey dismissed it as amateurish, but admired McCarthy's aspirations and, because McCarthy was a powerful politician, exaggerated their intimacy:

> When I was in Washington, as consultant in poetry to the Library of Congress, Eugene McCarthy became my closest friend. I felt he was a political leader that this country hardly deserved because he had a tremendous commitment to the life of the mind—especially to poetry. . . . I became devoted to him: his cause seemed right because he wanted to end the Vietnam War and was a positive politician. He didn't just condemn, but said we have to go forward—that we're going to upgrade the whole national sensibility so that people can live more and have more of themselves. I loved the man. I think he stood for the right things. I wish he had become president.[34]

Dickey first learned of McCarthy's decision to run for the 1968 Democratic presidential nomination at a party Dickey gave for John Updike and Peter Taylor in November 1967. Dickey soon began telling people that he was writing McCarthy's campaign speeches. According to McCarthy, this collaborative arrangement never existed.

Dickey did give political advice to McCarthy, however, just as he later gave advice to another poet-politician, Jimmy Carter. Dickey told both politicians the same thing: they needed to state their goals with more passion, more conviction, more clarity. He wanted McCarthy, who was often wistful and contemplative, to live up to his model of "The Energized Man." The friendship between McCarthy and Dickey, which remained intact for several decades, depended on the open-mindedness of both men. McCarthy was a pacifist during the Vietnam War and deeply sympathetic to Dickey's rivals—Robert Bly, who shared political ideals and a home state with McCarthy, and Robert Lowell, who traveled with McCarthy during his 1968 campaign. In some ways McCarthy and Dickey could not have been more different.

Northern politician and Southern poet were, in fact, suspicious of each other's views. In candid moments Dickey rated McCarthy's political savvy about as high as his poetry. "He could have been president," he said, "but it's a good thing for this country that he wasn't. He was not of presidential calibre."[35] To Al Braselton, Dickey was more forthright: he hoped McCarthy would quit the race because "Gene don't know a God-damn thing about being President."[36] For Dickey, whose politics were often linked with the unpopular war policies of Lyndon Johnson, McCarthy was a convenient ally, even as a failed presidential candidate. McCarthy sometimes questioned Dickey's motives for befriending him, just as he questioned the violence that so often surfaced in his poems. In the poem "James Dickey," which McCarthy published in his 1968 collection

Other Things and the Aardvark, he mounted an inquisition of his friend in the agonized voice of Robert Lowell: "Why do you shout of things, not thought / or if thought, not spoken?" In the following barrage of questions, McCarthy struggled to understand Dickey's violent imagination, tacitly alluding to "The Firebombing," "Falling," "May Day Sermon," "The Sheep Child," and other poems "of man, / animal, earth, machine." The last two stanzas almost sounded accusatory, as if McCarthy were siding with Raymond Swain:

> What is your license to drag us
> to the May-day barn scourging,
> we who would rather stand off and listen,
> to hold us, while lasers of light
> from roof board holes
> thin slice our souls?
>
> What is your writ to whisper us
> back to dusty shelves
> where man and his animal
> face their beginning and ending
> in a clouded jar of alcohol?

For McCarthy, who was more comfortable with the classical writer's acceptance of limits and laws, Dickey was a gothic romantic who preferred sensing to thinking, passion to reason, mystic silence to articulate discourse, boundless appetite to reasonable restraint.

McCarthy's eclectic enthusiasm for poetry and Dickey's eclectic enthusiasm for political power made for a diplomatic truce between the two men that sometimes broke down. To their mutual friend, Elizabeth Janeway, Dickey expressed his impatience and anger over McCarthy's political incompetence:

> History casts the man in a role in which he could have been at least influential, and probably crucial, and he did nothing with it, or about it, at all. Just to sit down and talk to him is to have the whole unspeakably frustrating thing of his candidacy and the rest of it happen all over again. I am very glad indeed that I do not have to go through that but one time in a life time. McCarthy has got a way of sliding off an issue with a remark that he thinks of as enigmatic, a remark that may have a great deal of wisdom in it, and may not, and even as he says it you think, privately, that it doesn't. This is such a stock in trade of his that it is almost impossible to talk to him directly, and if American politicians cannot talk directly they cannot talk to the people, and if they cannot talk to the people they cannot do anything at all in politics. People want simple answers, even if the answers turn out to be, in action, more complicated than they are; at least in a campaign they must *seem* simple. For example, Gene's great appeal to the young and to the liberals was that he was against the prolongation of the Vietnam war. If you talked to him during those days, you could see that he had no really well conceived plan of *doing* anything about it; it was just

the fact that he was registered in the public-mind as a man who had stood up and spoken out against the continuation of the war. He was fairly direct about *that*, and that is what got all the kids and the liberals and the others kind of like myself, who believed in him, to working for him and helping him. But the final thing that defeated Gene was his personality; he wants to say and not to say, and above all not to be held accountable *really*.[37]

Lunching together at The Assembly or talking in the Poetry Room, Dickey and McCarthy built a friendship that often teetered on mutual distrust.

Rather than take a vacation from his frenetic social life so that he could write and be with his family during the summer of 1967, Dickey embarked on another busy round of writers' conferences and teaching assignments. To use one of his favorite metaphors for the poet, he resembled an engine without a governor. From June 5 to June 30, he read and taught at a conference held on the Star Lake campus of the State University at Potsdam, New York. The conference was organized by SUNY English professor Kelsie Harder, a friend from Dickey's Vanderbilt days who had followed his former classmate's career with interest. Harder had asked Dickey to join Archibald MacLeish, Anaïs Nin, Paul Engle, and Richard Poirier, and had also persuaded Krishna Vaid, who would soon become a leading Anglo-Indian novelist, to serve as on-site director. His offer to Dickey was generous—twelve hundred dollars to give one poetry reading and several lectures and workshops. With his wife and four-month-old baby, Harder met Dickey and Poirier at the airport in Watertown, New York. Since Harder had befriended Andrew Lytle while completing his doctoral work at the University of Florida, he knew of Dickey's capacity for immoderate behavior. Nevertheless, he was surprised when Dickey clomped off the plane in a new pair of midcalf, high-heeled, alligator-skin cowboy boots and announced: "Well, Kelsie, I am a legend in my own time." He accompanied his boast with a good deal of backslapping, which left both Harder and his other guest, Poirier, cold. Harder recalled: "We loaded up and began the trip to Star Lake. Jim was doing all the talking; Dick [Poirier] was silent; my wife was holding the baby. We had not gone ten miles when I glanced at Dickey's hand sliding down on the right breast of my wife. She moved aside. Nothing was said, and Jim kept up his patter."[38] Harder could smell the alcohol on Dickey's breath.

The Potsdam campus was idyllic. Small, well-furnished cabins nestled among trees by the lake. From the pavilion, which held lecture halls and classrooms, participants could see the gray-blue Appalachian mountains in the distance. Dickey quickly took to the rustic surroundings and casual atmosphere of the conference. He compensated for his rude advances on Harder's wife by giving marvelous readings and lectures. Before each of his talks, however, he insisted that Harder bring him a bottle of Jack Daniel's. He guzzled between sentences and nearly finished the bottle by the time the lecture ended. Before long, Larry Lieberman, who had been finishing *The Achievement of James Dickey* at Yaddo, arrived with Holly Delevan, a Saratoga musician and singer. The three partied together, usually with Dickey playing the guitar as Delevan sang. In his private cabin Dickey acted as a Dionysian Master of the Revels. Lieberman recalled in a letter to Dickey: "I think back to the cabin where we . . . sat and where all that loveliness flowed between us, and I know I'll be able to close my eyes and recall it instantly. . . . As you say, that is the way people can live all the time, and should. Your poetry, your music, just plain you—have a way of bringing people together, giving them a world of rich experience to share before they hardly know each other: I've never seen anything like it."[39] Others at the conference, such as camp director Chip Hunter, were not so sanguine about the merrymaking.

While the young people at the parties puffed on joints, Dickey drank. The only time he didn't drink was late at night when he struggled to revise *Deliverance*. To calm his nerves, around one or two o'clock in the morning he took long walks around the campus. To Harder he complained of furies swirling through his head. "Jim was bordering on alcoholism or already there," Harder concluded: "Still, I never saw him . . . drunk." Alcohol seemed to improve his performances at the lecture podium and in workshops, but made him truculent in conversation. According to Harder: "The only really sour note was Jim's calling Krishna a nigger. I don't know what brought that matter on, but I had to settle Krishna down, for he was really angry, raising hell, as I would say. Apparently, Jim apologized, for later Krishna would attend readings and conferences at which Dickey was present and would talk with Dickey."[40] Vaid decided that Dickey's Dr. Jekyll was a courtly gentleman full of sophisticated conversation about literature, his Mr. Hyde a cruel, vulgar, drunken, racist, and sexist redneck. Like John Woods, Robert Peters, and others, Vaid also concluded that beneath Dickey's machismo lurked powerful homosexual impulses. Some of the gay students at the conference told Vaid that Dickey brought out the gay side in them. Harder also heard stories of Dickey pursuing boys. A colleague who was gay told Vaid that he sensed Dickey's sexual ambivalence. Vaid agreed, although he wasn't sure whether Dickey made homosexual gestures to startle people or whether he had a genuine passion for men. Dickey seemed to thrive on remaining a mystery.

In one of their marital quarrels following Star Lake, Maxine told her husband of a secret tryst she had had with Harder at the Georgetown Inn. Unbeknownst to Dickey, before the end of the Star Lake conference Harder called Maxine on a trip to Washington, D.C., where he worked as a part-time consultant at the Department of Education. Seeking revenge for the way Dickey had treated his wife on the ride to Star Lake, Harder spent the night with Maxine at the Georgetown Inn after getting drunk on martinis at dinner. Years later, Dickey admitted to his friend Ernest Suarez that Maxine had once had an affair with an insurance salesman. "This was the one and only time she did anything,"[41] Dickey said. He never mentioned Harder, but at the time he was furious at both Maxine and Harder for their carousing. According to Harder: "Jim sent word through Krishna Vaid that I was no Southern gentleman, and that he did not want ever to see me again."[42] Considering his own adulterous affairs (in July he again took up with his "soulless" Mormon girlfriend at another University of Utah writers' conference), Dickey's invocation of Southern gentility was laughable.

21. Second Term (1967–1968)

His summer barnstorming over, Dickey returned to an avalanche of offers and proposals on his Library of Congress desk. Dickey also had to answer correspondence regarding his problems with Robert Bly. Hoping to placate Dickey before he read Bly's essay in *The Sixties*, James Wright had written on August 22, 1967, that he was greatly dismayed by the attack. Several days later, Dickey told Wright that he had read Bly's review and thought that it was more welcome than worrisome. It had amused him and convinced him that critics who had wrongly enlisted him as one of Bly's "Deep Image" disciples would now recognize their differences. "The article does not harm me," Dickey assured Wright. "I am already far past it, working on new things. But it will surely hurt Bob, even if nobody else ever reads it, for the writing of such a thing, and that amount of deliberate falsification, the venom and personal malice that went into it, are sure to fester badly."[1]

By the end of the summer of 1967, the feud between Bly and Dickey had entered a new arena. Dickey wanted to include some of the reviews from *The Suspect in Poetry* in his new collection of criticism, *Babel to Byzantium*. Because Bly's Sixties Press had published *The Suspect in Poetry*, he had to obtain permission from Bly. Bly refused to give it. Although Bly and Dickey had never signed a written contract for *The Suspect in Poetry*, there had been a legally binding verbal agreement. Dickey's editor at Farrar, Straus & Giroux, Michael di Capua, feared Bly would have an unbeatable case against his company if they went ahead and published without his consent. To complicate matters, in September Bly announced his intention to reprint *Suspect* himself; he had recently secured a grant that would help cover the cost. *Babel to Byzantium*, he argued, would infringe on his market. Therefore, he demanded a $1,500 permission fee. He ended his September 23 letter to Di Capua with a caustic ultimatum: "This business is dragging on too long. If the matter is not settled in ten days . . . I must require that you black out in your catalog all mention of *The Suspect in Poetry*, and material taken from it, and remove all such material from the body of the collected Dickey criticism you are preparing."[2] Such a purge would reduce Dickey's new book to a skeleton.

Di Capua believed that they had two choices. Dickey could pay Bly the permission fee, or he could hire a lawyer to wrest his articles from Bly's grip. Dickey thought of a third alternative: he could bargain. Rather than $1,500, he offered Bly $150. Bly retorted: "$1500 may be a trifle high, but $150 is absurd."[3] Aggravated by Bly's maneuvering, Dickey was confident that his opponent would soon relent. On December 20, Bly told Roger Straus that "the matter seems to be drawing to a conclusion by itself." In his defense, Bly contended that the issue was not financial so much as moral, and chastised the larger publisher for failing to help out a "smaller literary publisher who takes the initial risk on certain work which is, in its first publication at least, unpopular." Dickey's paltry offer of $150 was unacceptable: "I prefer that the material simply be taken outright, if that's what they want to do. As the Spanish say, 'A leap from the hedge is better than a mumbled prayer.'"[4] On the same day, he wrote Dickey: "I prefer nothing to such an offer. Why didn't you offer $4.25. . . . Legally, you may be able to pirate it, but it will be, literarily and morally, a pirated edition."[5] Straus responded on January 5 that he had no counterproverb for Bly and that he rejected his accusation that Farrar, Straus & Giroux was a "big" publisher. They were relatively small, and because they had to survive on slim budgets, they had proceeded on Dickey's assurance that there were no permissions claims on the material Bly had published (Straus told Bly that Dickey had never said a word about his essays being previously published after he submitted them). The altercation over *Babel to Byzantium* showed signs of ending when Theron Raines pointed out that Dickey owned his reviews as long as he did not legally transfer his assignment of copyright to the Sixties Press when he got permissions from the various magazines where his reviews had first appeared. A lawyer, Shirley Fingerhood, examined Bly's letters to Farrar, Straus & Giroux and on January 5, 1968, concluded that Dickey and his publisher should not be concerned about Bly's legal threats. Relieved by her assessment, Dickey was irritated that he had to pay for it.

The legal tussle with Bly hardly depleted Dickey's resources. In late September and early October, Dickey read at Bryn Mawr, the University of Missouri, the University of Arkansas, Lindenwood College, Indiana University, and in Atlanta, usually earning one thousand dollars for each appearance. One of his most memorable campus performances in the fall was at Harvard, where he reunited with the other poet Bly had recently excoriated, Robert Lowell. The poet Richard Tillinghast was responsible for bringing the two poets together on October 25. A graduate student in English at the time, Tillinghast was a fellow Southerner and great admirer of Dickey's poetry, who had first spoken to Dickey as an undergraduate at Sewanee around 1960 (Monroe Spears had introduced them). Tillinghast remembered Dickey as friendly, supportive, and unpretentious. At Harvard, Tillinghast noticed a drastic change. Dickey's comments to Robert Shaw in an interview for Harvard's the *Crimson* were typical: "Nowadays if you want to f—— somebody, you *do*, if he or she is willing. You just do it for whatever there can be for both of you. This is why *The Scarlet Letter* is so quaint to us—all that agitation about fornication." He told the story about a member of the New York Police Department commenting on "The Fiend," and added: "You can read all the sex manuals in the world, about married love, manipulation. . . . You come to the conclusion that society wants you to have a certain kind of sexual life and sexual response. But that may or may not be the one that you *do* have. The man in 'The Fiend' is a voyeur—as I say, don't knock it if you ain't tried it. I thought of the fiend as one who had come to a tacit understanding with himself that he needed this, no matter what it led to—ridicule, disgrace or even electrocution. The sex instinct is that strong."[6] Dickey had come to a similar tacit understanding about his own sexual proclivities.

On the way from the airport to Cambridge, Dickey insisted that Tillinghast stop at a bar. As Dickey got drunker, Tillinghast became apprehensive about the lunch he had arranged with Lowell. Peter Davison, another one of the lunch guests, had argued in the October 1967 issue of the *Atlantic Monthly* that of all the poets in America, only Lowell and Dickey deserved the title "major." Tillinghast had good reason to suspect that lunch might turn into a Parnassian heavyweight bout. Lowell had annoyed Dickey with his letter explaining why he had avoided him at the National Book Awards ceremony. Late in 1966, he had also judged Dickey in a slightly condescending way by drawing attention to his repetitive symbols: "Reading you again, I see you have many fine symbols, somewhat the same, but usually more made up and nightmarish than Williams: shark, killer whale, fire-bomber, voyeur. You are awfully good at these things, and awfully good at getting almost invariably a curious, dazed wondering state, around it often the southern air, behind it often death, the wounds of the body, sex—all those deep things that imprison and keep us going."[7] Lowell appreciated Dickey's work, but the comparison with Williams, whom Dickey deplored, amounted to damnation by faint praise.

Dickey was not one to act as Lowell's punching bag. With Lowell in mind, he once said: "People are worn out listening to somebody else's weeping and sackcloth-and-ashes attitudes, breastbeating, and gnashing of teeth, frustration, and tearing of hair and personal grievances. . . . No poet should be so egotistical as to ask the reader to fasten onto his own personality and his own confessions."[8] In a letter to James Wright that referred to Davison's article, Dickey allowed that he and Lowell shared some similarities in temperament, but that Dickey struggled heroically against psychological turmoil while Lowell submitted to it:

> I have had to fight with all my strength against . . . [self-destruction and despair], but the results are sure worth it, believe me. It is better to be happy than to be Rimbaud or Baudelaire, and I mean by my example to show that a far greater poetry can be written out of a simple sense of joy than out of all the self-analysing self-accusation and misery-mongering in the world. Cal Lowell has never been able to understand this, and as a result the two kinds of poems we write are going to decide, one way or the other, what American poetry is going to do in the next years. It may be that Cal will win, but he will not win totally. There will be others who will repudiate his vision and go with mine, or with something like mine.[9]

Often complaining that journalists misrepresented him as Lowell's opponent in a battle for the summit of Parnassus, Dickey viewed himself in exactly those terms.

After Davison's article appeared, Dickey was even more convinced that he had to depose Lowell. The New York literati, he decided, were firmly under Lowell's command. Attempting once again to rally his troops, he asked Wright and many others to send supportive letters to the *Atlantic Monthly*. On November 1, Davison sent Dickey a copy of Stanley Burnshaw's letter, which touted Dickey over Lowell even while pooh-poohing the term "major." Davison commented that he knew the term "major" was silly; he had used it to arouse the attention of academics. Other fans rallied to Dickey's side as well. One commented on November 2: "It's good to have the War in the open—a declared war—not a cold war. I reckon it must infuriate Cal Lowell to have the declaration appear in his own Boston backyard."[10] A student of modern and ancient wars, Lowell probably welcomed the rebel yells in his backyard, certain that he would triumph.

At the lunch for Lowell and Dickey, the friction was palpable. Tillinghast later wrote:

> We met at Chez Dreyfus on Church Street in Cambridge. Dickey and I had been drinking beer since breakfast, and had just come from my writing class, where he had put in a splendid guest appearance. Lowell was not supposed to be drinking, as alcohol was incompatible with the lithium pills he took for his [manic-depressive] illness. He made an exception (not unusual) for the occasion; food was soon forgotten, vodka flowed. Sparring between the two poets was in evidence, some of it good-natured, some of it not. Dickey, who at that time hunted with bow and arrow, pulled up his shirt under the disapproving eye of our French waiter and showed us a large bandage on his back. Then he started telling us about a recent trip to the West Virginia wilderness. It was a good story. Having stopped to drink from a mountain stream, he had looked up just in time to see a huge bear reared up on its hindlegs, making straight for him. Just as the bear had attacked, raking his back and shoulder with razor-sharp claws, Dickey got off an arrow that killed the bear. "But the bear wasn't dead, Jim," Lowell interrupted, himself suddenly bearlike, clearing his way with his gesturing hands, laughing as he always did at the remark he was about to make— "When you got back to your office, the bear was sitting at your desk. It was Robert Bly."[11]

Lowell, who often played a complex fantasy game in which he took on the roles of different bears, was not taken in by Dickey's Hemingwayesque tall tale.

Dickey's bear story was yet another of his "creative lies." He had gone bow hunting with Terry Miller in West Virginia from October 16 to 19, and according to Kevin Dickey, who accompanied them, his father had shot nothing—not even a squirrel. Dickey's story, like so many of his others, had a grain of truth— or at least what Dickey supposed to be the truth. On another recent hunting trip to Miller's farm, which was close to the West Virginia border, Dickey was convinced he had seen a black bear. According to Miller:

> That particular day he went up the . . . hill behind my house and onto a piece of land not too far from my house, a pretty wild place. And he came back to the house about 9 A.M. and he was excited as can be. . . . He was actually frightened. He thought he had seen a bear. Now there are bear up there, although I had never . . . seen one. . . . But bears are very shy, very afraid of men, and the odds are he didn't see a bear. I went back to where he was because he . . . was afraid to shoot the bear without somebody there to help. . . . That is a relatively safe thing to do even if you are alone, because if you get the bear in the kill zone with an arrow they almost inevitably go off and die. But even a black bear will attack in rare instances. . . . We went back up there and there was a herd of black angus

in the woods. . . . And I'm sure that's what he saw obscured by the brush. . . . If you don't feel at home in the woods, which he didn't quite, that would look like a bear.[12]

Miller, an expert woodsman and bow hunter, found the tracks of the Black Angus in the dirt, but never had the heart to tell Dickey that his bears were simply cows.

Miller had never seen a bear in his thirty-six years of hunting in Virginia and West Virginia, although hunters killed bears in the area. Nonetheless, he understood how Dickey mistook a Black Angus for a black bear. Dickey started drinking beer at six in the morning as Miller prepared bacon and eggs for their prehunt breakfast. Miller realized that for Dickey the imagined hunt took precedence over the actual hunt. Dickey was as theatrical with Miller as he was with Lowell. Before a hunt he liked to meet Miller at Washington's National Airport in camouflage fatigues with a big floppy camouflage hat and his bow racked with arrows. Having just left his computer job in a business suit, Miller would be as startled as the bystanders in the airport. In preparation for deer and bears, Dickey smeared camouflage paint on his face. At night, quaffing beers in Miller's house, Dickey again demonstrated his penchant for imaginary pursuits when he bragged of piloting night fighters out of England and shooting down enemy planes. Miller taught Dickey how to shoot from tree stands and stalk his quarry through brush, but for all his braggadocio Dickey never shot any animals on his numerous hunts with Miller. In a candid moment with his friend Jim Whitehead, Dickey said he had only shot one animal in his entire life—a possum—and that may have been fanciful, too.

Entertaining an audience at a national poetry convention in Oklahoma with tales of growing up in the jack pine hill country of North Georgia and playing quarterback on the Vanderbilt football team, Dickey fleshed out more details of his fanciful bear hunt: "I was working up a creek bed in West Virginia last October, hunting deer . . . with a bow and arrow. I came around a bend and here was this bear. A black bear . . . , big rascal. Weighted 305 pounds. Maybe 35 feet from me. I tried at first to talk him out of anything rash, then I saw he was going to come for me. I let him have an arrow in the chest, then another in his neck. Then I scrambled. He was still coming. As I went up the creek bank, he clawed my back—peeled that hunting jacket off like paper. Took 64 stitches to patch up. I put a third arrow in his eye when he poked his head up over the brush. That one stopped him."[13] Not all the journalists at Central State College doubted the inebriated Dickey; his story appeared in the Daily Oklahoman on June 18, 1968.

Those close to Dickey knew that his drinking was now chronic and beyond his control. Having sailed to France on September 9 to study in Rennes with the Exeter Academy boys-abroad program, Chris Dickey worried about his father's condition. "Your letter of a few weeks back frightened me. It sounded too typical of too many poets. Have you really stopped drinking?"[14] he asked on October 30. Despite their differences, father and son had many things to draw them together—among them a love of literature and film. Chris told his father that he was reading Hemingway and Fitzgerald, working on a film, and writing (he hoped to someday make a career as a film director). Proud of his father's accomplishments, Chris also felt dwarfed by him, especially as he brooded on his own mortality: "I feel always so close to death now, riding my Mobylette. . . . If I am killed then I will have left nothing but the hollow yet great fact that I am your son and what greatness you have will be a part of me, and when you are remembered then I shall be forgotten."[15] Chris's premature balding at age sixteen only exacerbated his existential anxieties. "I had spent so much of my life being scared," he said in his memoir *Summer of Deliverance*, "that I just couldn't be scared any more. So I gave myself twenty years to live."[16] By accepting an early death at thirty-five, he believed that he would be immune to lesser fears in the interim.

Relations between father and son became more troublesome when Dickey told Chris not to apply early to colleges. Chris wanted to apply to UVA, Harvard, UNC–Chapel Hill, Dartmouth, and William and Mary, but his father wanted him to transfer to Exeter after finishing the foreign study program in France. He thought Exeter would guarantee Chris a place at Harvard and Harvard would give him a reasonable chance at becoming a Rhodes scholar. (To the end of his life Dickey regretted that neither of his sons had been elected Rhodes scholars.) The Vietnam War was another source of tension. Chris explained: "On the one hand he wanted me to have my war. On the other hand he didn't want me to get drafted. And he didn't want me to go to Canada, but he didn't want me to get killed, and there was a big confusion."[17] Dickey expressed his antimilitary sentiments in a letter to Chris on November 7: "If you think you dislike Exeter, wait until you get in the service, which is really a form of going to prison. It really *is*, you know. So think a little more about *that* part of it."[18] Chris had tried to allay his father's worries: "Do not worry about Vietnam. If I am put into the army it shall be as an officer and, anyway, most of what I want to do will be begun and can be continued in the army—yes, even there. I won't be killed. I have no doubt that I will die young, but it will not be too soon."[19] How Chris knew he would "die young," but not "too soon," must have puzzled his father. Luckily, Chris's number in the draft lottery kept him out of Vietnam.

As soon as Dickey received these lucubrations from his son, he wrote Chris a three-page, single-spaced response designed to console. He had suffered hair loss and existential fears, too, as a teenager. He wisely decreed: "The troubles that you speak about are very real ones for you now, but they are not so serious as you think." He advised Chris to turn his despair and loneliness "into that essential creative state of being which the artist, above all men, knows. When loneliness becomes creative rather than destructive, the artist is alive, and in his element. Out of that, anything can come. Real creative work is not done by committees; it is done in the dark night of the soul, in the labyrinth of being, in fear and trembling and the solitary exaltation beside which Heaven itself is pale and commonplace."[20] To appease Chris, he promised to abide by Chris's college plans, but he still urged his son to attend Exeter for a year to prepare for Harvard. Dickey had hated his year at prep school, but he had liked Exeter when he read there in late February 1967. He had brought Chris along to introduce him to the school. Among other things, he introduced Chris to the comforts and discomforts of too much drink. Chris, who was only fifteen, got so drunk with his father that he felt the ceiling spin over his bed. Chris never enrolled in a prep school, although Dickey later maintained to friends like Gordon Lish that Chris had gone to Exeter. To be closer to the exciting political scene in Washington, Chris abandoned the Exeter program in Rennes, applied to Washington and Lee University and UVA, was accepted by both, and went to UVA.

If Dickey could be emotionally sincere in private, in public he continued to disguise his actual feelings and thoughts in elaborate and often hilarious fictions. At readings he often spent more time introducing his poems with pseudoautobiographies than reading them. On November 8, 1967, he told an audience at Washington University during his introduction to "Cherrylog Road":

> In North Georgia, when I was in Crab Apple High School, I played football and was known as the Crab Apple Cannonball. A girl named Doris [Holbrook] had the next locker to me in school . . . ; the erotic possibilities of adjoining high school lockers have never been fully explored in literature.
>
> Doris and I got on well, but her father took an unreasoning dislike to me. Maybe he thought I made too much noise blasting around on my red Harley Davidson. He told me to stay away from his house. He was said to have killed two or three people so I took him at his word.
>
> But Doris and I used to meet in an old junkyard full of mice, beetles and kudzu vine. Somehow it seemed very important to get to the middle of it. So I'd climb through a couple of bootlegger's 1934 Fords and we'd meet in the spacious back seat of an old Pierce-Arrow. I don't know what that grandmotherly car was doing in that company, but there it was with its back-seat telephone still intact.
>
> One day I wrote about it as "That wild stock-car race in the parking lot of the dead." . . . Isn't that good?
>
> Anyway . . . The New Yorker accepted it as "very original, your first variation on the Romeo and Juliet theme, no doubt." When it was published, 17 women wrote in from different parts of the country to tell me that they remembered that junkyard well. I wrote them all back and told them that the junkyard was not in Louisiana, or Virginia, or . . . Missouri, but Georgia. I never did hear from Doris, though. I guess she just isn't the kind who reads The New Yorker.[21]

The poem was not based on Romeo and Juliet but, as Dickey admitted in more truthful moments, on Eastern concepts of reincarnation and the Egyptian myth of Osiris in which Isis brings her dead husband back to life by reassembling his scattered body parts, most importantly his phallus. As usual, Dickey substituted modern characters for ancient ones. In early drafts of the poem, Doris had the maiden name of Al Braselton's mother-in-law: Charlotte Holbrook. Dickey liked the name Charlotte Holbrook because of its sound, but he also used it because of its connection to the sort of authority figure he wanted to escape. Charlotte Holbrook was the wife of Bill Neal, one of Dickey's advertising bosses. Out of deference to Neal, who was upset by Dickey's use of his wife's name, Dickey changed the first name to Doris.

At the Library of Congress, Dickey's tandem readings continued through the fall of 1967, only now they included fiction writers as well as poets. Ben Belitt, the poet and translator of Neruda, and John Frederick Nims, the poet and current editor of *Poetry*, began the fall series on October 23. Peter Taylor and John Updike initiated the fiction readings on November 13. Dickey worried about the possible friction between these two writers, and rightly so. Updike remembered: "Jim was very anxious that it go well, so anxious that he drank more than he ate at dinner, and rambled on stage."[22] The post-reading discussion grew contentious. Dickey pronounced Taylor the winner in a letter to Taylor's wife, Eleanor: "The difference between Peter's work, which is absolutely unique, and John's, which is like the writing of the perennial A-student in the creative writing class, is very large, and was certainly noted on that occasion, as the history that now goes forward from us will also surely note it."[23] Out of earshot, Dickey accused Updike of being superficially stylish, unoriginal, and too negative. Judging a Northerner like Updike and a Southerner like Taylor, Dickey made his regional bias plain.

In the Washington, D.C., apartment he had rented to entertain visiting writers, Dickey threw a party for Taylor and Updike. All guests, including the two sparring writers, were thrilled because he also invited Eugene and Abigail McCarthy. Dickey's library colleague John Broderick recalled: "Only days earlier Gene McCarthy had expressed his intention of challenging Lyndon Johnson in the primaries, so it was a heady time for those present. The point is that Jim and Gene McCarthy were already good friends by then and continued to be so, each one deriving some glamour from the other."[24] To make the occasion more glamorous Dickey insisted that it was *at* his party that McCarthy announced his candidacy. If Dickey had reservations about Updike's prose, he had none about him as a person. He let Updike spend the night in his apartment. According to Updike: "I had to get up early to catch a plane and he very graciously drove me to Dulles, after giving me an enchanting little concert of guitar music, sitting there on the sofa in his pajamas."[25] Updike was on his way to one of Dickey's favorite spots, the Virgin Islands. It may have been before his flight that Updike explained his long battle with psoriasis, which he tried to ameliorate on sunbathing trips to the Caribbean. Dickey used the information about psoriasis in his portrayal of Joel Cahill's similar skin ailment in *Alnilam*. He made use of this most talented of American writers in other ways as well. He asked him to compose blurbs for his poetry books, and to the end of Dickey's life Updike generously complied. He asked Taylor for favors as well: to set up a reading at the University of Virginia, where he taught, and to encourage the university's admissions department to look favorably on his son's application.

As 1967 ended, Dickey tried to finish several projects that still dangled in limbo. Jacques de Spoelberch reminded him in early November that he needed to finish the revisions of *Deliverance*. Spoelberch still wondered if Dickey could ever work his material into a full-length novel. If he could not, he said: "I am sure that you will be able to make it a truly good short piece."[26] Rather than tackle *Deliverance*, Dickey put the finishing touches on *Babel to Byzantium* and continued to travel. On November 17, he read at the Poetry Day benefit for

Poetry magazine in Chicago with William Alfred and James Merrill. On November 30, he lectured at York University in Toronto on "The University, the New Student, and the New Literature," using the occasion to mock the popular antihero in contemporary poetry and fiction: "No longer is the hero . . . the *engagé* man of Sartre's and Camus' novels, or the 'metaphysical adventurer' of Malraux's, or the doomed specialist of war or bullfighting, sticking to his code, as in Hemingway. Now, the protagonist of the novel—and of a good deal of poetry, such as Robert Lowell's or Philip Larkin's—is bewildered."[27] He also sneered at overly political 1960s students who listened to the Beatles and Bob Dylan, pinned a poster of Allen Ginsberg dressed up as Uncle Sam over their beds, experimented with drugs, and read Beat literature. He contended that such poetic gurus as Ginsberg, Ferlinghetti, Bly, and Olson were charlatans. As he made clear in the lecture he gave at the library shortly after returning from Toronto, Dickey was not strictly opposed to charlatans; in "Metaphor as Pure Adventure" he once again endorsed the poet's right to re-create himself as a fictitious being: "I remember how tremendously excited I was when I first formulated to myself the proposition that the poet is not to be limited by the literal truth: that he is not trying to *tell* the truth: he is trying to *make* it."[28] For Dickey the metaphor-making poet was a kind of handmaiden to God who re-created the original Creation in miraculous ways. What he objected to in his adversaries was their brand of re-creation.

At the end of 1967, Dickey mulled over job possibilities for 1968 and the future. Jack Guilds, who chaired the English Department at the University of South Carolina (USC), had recently invited Dickey to his campus for interviews and meetings. Dickey wooed his hosts, especially Guilds's wife, Carolee. Initially dismayed by her husband's request that she prepare yet another English Department party for a visiting professor—it meant making flower arrangements, washing crystal, polishing silver, cleaning linen, buying food—she had a premonition that her guest would be someone special. Her excitement mounted until the moment Maxine and Jim appeared at her door. Pretty, soft-voiced, and congenial, Maxine showed the same guarded smile as her mother when Carolee, who had Grace Kelly looks, greeted them. Dickey walked into Carolee's house, which stood on Lake Katherine opposite from where the Dickeys would eventually live, as if emulating the Great Gatsby. He had on a white linen suit, blue cotton shirt, and an exquisite tie. He filled the house with his presence. Carolee later said that she had traveled through three continents, twenty-seven countries, and thirty-nine states, and had met many learned men at consulates, universities, and churches: "Yet immediately I felt someone truly different had arrived." Dickey seemed to be "a divine phenomenon."[29] After he took the job of writer-in-residence at USC, Carolee became one of his close friends, frequently seeing him at parties or whenever Dickey knocked on her door. They grew even closer when she taught Kevin in the fifth grade at Heathwood Hall, an Episcopal school in Columbia. Although Dickey was usually on his best behavior with Carolee, who was as devoutly religious as she was gracious and beautiful, Maxine remained suspicious.

It was mainly because of his Vanderbilt friend Calhoun Winton that Dickey went to USC. Winton, who taught in the English Department, gave an auspicious account of Columbia, the university's tenure regulations, the two-course load for the writer-in-residence job, and the contract. By academic standards, the salary of $25,000 was extremely generous, as was the $600 moving allowance. On December 19, 1967, Dickey wrote the university: "I accept with honor and pride the offer which came in your letter of December 12."[30] At last he had a permanent, or at least tenurable, job.

With one contract settled, he now tried to improve his first-read contract with the *New Yorker*. Because Howard Moss refused to publish many of Dickey's new poems—a foreshadowing of a more comprehensive rejection in the years to come—Moss had decided to cut the *New Yorker's* signing bonus to $200, half the usual amount. Dickey filed a complaint on December 15. Other money issues rankled as well. On the same day he wrote Moss, he complained to William Matheson in the Rare Book Department of Washington University about the measly $600 promised for a recent shipment of his papers. Dickey wanted $1,000, and threatened to divert his remaining papers to another institution if he couldn't get it: "Since I am going permanently to the University of South Carolina it is likely that I will henceforth consign my papers to that Institution's Library."[31] Matheson refused to budge, reminding Dickey that he had just paid $2,350 in cash for a recent shipment. Dickey kept sending papers to Saint Louis into the early 1970s, but by 1974, the library had to curtail its purchases because of a shortage of funds. As a result, Dickey let the University of South Carolina store his papers in its Special Collections library.

At the beginning of one of the most volatile years in American history, 1968, Dickey became more politically engaged than usual. It was hard for anyone to stand passively on the sidelines. North Vietnam's Tet Offensive in January and the My Lai massacre in March revealed how deeply America had sunk into the morass of Vietnam. The bloody year grew bloodier when assassins shot Martin Luther King, Jr., in April and Robert Kennedy in June. Antigovernment violence reached a peak at the Democratic convention in Chicago, when Chicago police battled rioters in the streets with tear gas and nightsticks. The United States reeled through "a psychedelic breakdown," as one of Dickey's friends, Anne Rivers Siddons, put it. Unwilling to countenance another term, President Johnson withdrew from the campaign. As McCarthy's antiwar message attracted more and more voters in the early primaries, Dickey did what he could to support his campaign. In the end, George McGovern became the Democratic nominee, Nixon became president, and the breakdown continued.

In Washington, at the focal point of the political maelstrom, Dickey bustled with activity at the library. On January 8, despite a pesky flu bug, he attended a lecture on Carl Sandburg by the esteemed Columbia professor, critic, and poet Mark Van Doren. Two days later he talked to students at Woodrow Wilson High School about creativity. Back at the library on January 15, he entertained Rod Serling, the feisty former boxer, paratrooper, and creator of *The Twilight Zone*. Dickey also began spending time with someone who would become one of his closest literary friends—the young Southern editor of *Harper's*, Willie Morris. A Rhodes scholar and writer from Mississippi, Morris had taken over *Harper's* at the tender age of thirty-two. As editor-in-chief, he had shaken off the magazine's image of docile respectability and made it more responsive to the turbulent sixties. Morris was the sort of bibulous, prank-loving Southern raconteur with whom Dickey could feel at ease. In trying to sum up his endearing and sometimes obstreperous friend, Morris said: "Jimbo Dickey may be the most complicated person I ever knew, which is why I love the old son of a bitch. In his deep heart's core he was a truly great poet. It was his complexity that made him write poems. Jimbo was a sufferer. He suffered through the war in the South Pacific. He reminded me a great deal of James Jones. He was a highly tortured and suffering soul who had this incredible persona, overpowering almost. . . . My deepest intuition tells me that he had to have his incredible persona to sustain his work. He was one-half actor, but his deepest part was an artist."[32] As a Southerner, Morris felt a sympathy for Dickey's Rabelaisian ways.

Another Southern writer who got to know Dickey at this time was Dave Smith. After reading *The Achievement of James Dickey* and some reviews of Dickey's poetry in the *Hudson Review*, Smith asked Larry Lieberman for more articles about Dickey, which he supplied. On January 27, 1968, in his first letter to Dickey, Smith apologized for reading Dickey's mail in the Rare Book room of the Washington University library (Smith lived in Saint Louis at the time), and explained that he was doing research for his M.A. thesis at Southern Illinois University: "I guess after I read Poems '57–'67, and these scraps and manuscripts, I found myself thinking how much alike we were (without your skill, hard work, experience etc.). I mean I was once an athlete and my life has seen its rough spots (family-death). I even spent two years coaching three sports at a high school in Yorktown, VA. You seem to be the type of person who appreciates the immeasurable sweat left on those many practice fields. . . . I bet you remember the first gun you had and the first time you shot something." Having grown up in Tidewater Virginia, Smith could identify with Dickey's Southernness. Many Northern writers—Robert Bly among them—left him cold: "I think this is because my personality is oriented to the formal and I attribute this to my Southern background. . . . I know of no place that could have taught me more about dignity and humanity and . . . morality. I wouldn't trade Faulkner for a dozen Whitmans and Hemingways."[33] Dickey responded to his new admirer: "Heavens! Thank you a very great deal for your long letter of January 27. I have seldom had the benefit of such enthusiasm about my work or indeed about existence itself."[34] The fact that Dickey loathed guns, scoffed at Faulkner, admired Hemingway (with reservations), and felt no compulsion as a Southerner to uphold traditional principles of morality and dignity did not prevent him from welcoming Smith's admiration. To a certain extent Smith found in Dickey a literary father. In March 1968, Smith got a chance to meet the poet with whom he would be so closely linked over the following decades when Lieberman introduced them at Dickey's reading at the University of Illinois in Urbana.

In March Dickey also met Reynolds Price and John Cheever at one of the library's dual readings. Price, a Southerner like Morris who had also studied at Oxford on a Rhodes Scholarship, was amused by Dickey's peculiar sense of morality; he conducted an unabashed interrogation of the two writers' masturbation habits backstage before the introduction. Price had first met Dickey on the day of Evelyn Waugh's death, April 10, 1966—a fact Dickey mentioned on every subsequent meeting. Around Price, whose writing he encouraged, Dickey delighted in the sort of comical, unexpected behavior for which Waugh was famous. In 1969, at a party given by Peter Taylor to celebrate an honorary degree bestowed on Eudora Welty by Washington and Lee University, Dickey first delivered an uncannily accurate imitation of Marlon Brando and then picked up Price, who weighed 175 pounds, and carried him across the room to an armchair. Full of gay flirtatiousness, he said: "I've never done so but if I were ever to sleep with a man, I'd want it to be either you or Ned Rorem."[35] Price didn't think that Dickey was a repressed homosexual, but he was nevertheless surprised that a man who normally posed as a womanizer would say such a thing.

Over their three decades of friendship, Price often wondered whether Dickey's innumerable readings, punch-and-cookies receptions, and drunken nights in hotels hadn't "jarred some fragile internal gyrostabilizer that would never again steady itself."[36] If Dickey harbored similar worries, he showed no signs of giving his gyrostabilizer a rest in 1968. He set forth on his most ambitious poetry-reading tour yet. At the request of the Department of State, he agreed to act as a poetic ambassador to New Zealand, Australia, and Japan. On March 5, he flew to New Zealand, lectured and read poems at Wellington's Victoria University, and spoke at length—primarily about Vietnam—with the American diplomats and their staff. He then flew to Auckland to meet the New Zealand poet Allen Curnow, who had befriended Dickey the year before while staying in Washington, D.C., with Milton Starr, an old Vanderbilt Fugitive, and reading in the Whittall series at the library. In Curnow's Aukland house, overlooking a harbor full of sailboats, Dickey drank and chatted about the health hazards of itinerant poets. Exhausted by his long plane flight, he nevertheless projected his usual robust, masculine athleticism to a local newspaper reporter and mustered enough energy to regale the reporter with stories about his feats as a hunter, folk singer, weight lifter, star college athlete, and decorated pilot (he said he had shot down five enemy planes in World War II and the Korean War). The *New Zealand Herald* announced his visit with the headline "Poet Built Like a Rugby Forward."

Dickey next went to Sydney, Australia, for a twenty-four-hour stopover made at the request of the American consul. Grace Perry, a doctor who edited *Poetry Australia*, greeted him at the Kingsford Smith International Airport and took him on a tour of Sydney's suburbs before going to a party at her house on Bilgola Beach. One of Perry's friends, the poet and psychiatrist Dr. Craig Powell, accompanied them on the tour and later wrote:

Strange as it seemed then, he insisted on being driven through all the suburbs on the southeastern shore of Sydney Harbor. During the drive he became more and more despondent, then finally revealed that he had visited Sydney during the Second World War. He was a USAF fighter pilot stationed in New Guinea at the time. During his leave in Sydney he had one of those abrupt wartime romances with an Australian girl, and married her.

386 / JAMES DICKEY

A few weeks after he returned to his unit, he was informed by her family that she had died suddenly of septicaemia. This was the first time he had been back to Sydney since then.

By the time he arrived at the party he was very morose indeed. The poet Bruce Beaver and I sat with him on the front verandah of the house, which overlooked a magnificent ocean beach. It could have been the quality of the conversation, the splendor of the surf under moonlight or the steady supply of liquor, but Dickey became gradually more animated. He began to talk about John Keats, whom he admired enormously as a poet and as a person. He told of Keats' journey through the lake district in England, where he encountered Samuel Taylor Coleridge. Keats was then only 24, but already suffering from advanced tuberculosis. At the end of the meeting he clasped Coleridge's hand and left. Coleridge said to a friend who was with him, "There is death in that hand."

Soon he was talking about music, especially the mountain music of the Ozarks and the Appalachians. By now he was glittering with enthusiasm, and he went to his baggage and produced a guitar. He began to play and sing American folk songs, Bible-belt Baptist hymns, with such panache that he soon had everyone singing with him. I can vividly remember doing a solo of "What A Friend We Have In Jesus" (I was the only one present who knew all the words) while Dickey accompanied me and murmured, "Ah, thet's purty!" He must have had quite a bit to drink by then, because by no stretch of the imagination could my singing voice be described as "purty."

The singing continued as the moon shimmered on the surf. The party finally breaking up, Bruce Beaver grasped Dickey's hand and exclaimed: "Jim, there's *life* in that hand!"[37]

Dickey developed a special fondness for Beaver, who was imitating the "split-line" technique he had used in poems like "The Shark's Parlor." Dickey wrote him several months later:

> Surely that was a great evening at Grace's and though the dreadful travel hysteria was on me with all its long claws, the (guitar) picking didn't seem to suffer unduly. . . . I have been trying to figure out a way to get back down to Australia, for ever since I was married to an Australian girl from Adelaide when we were both eighteen or nineteen (she died shortly after this) and since the special feeling that American servicemen in the Pacific had about Australia in those days, the feeling was perhaps more intense in me than in most of them. I have regarded Australia if not quite as a second home, then as something like the Great Good Place to which I would return if I were very good.[38]

If his Australian friends had known that at the age of nineteen Dickey was still in an American high school, they would probably have attributed his apocryphal story about the dead Australian wife to his "dreadful travel hysteria." In any case, Dickey's tale, which echoes the death of Frederic Henry's young lover in *A Farewell to Arms*, enhanced his image as a swashbuckling former combat pilot. Beaver wrote back that he was deeply moved by the sad news of his first visit to Australia. When Dickey told the poet Tom Shapcott, whom he met in Adelaide, that his young wife had leapt to her death in the Gap (a well-known suicide zone at the end of the suburban Watsons Bay tramline in Sydney), Shapcott was similarly consolatory.

Following his interview with Carol Buck for *Poetry Australia,* in which he was equally fanciful about his life and accomplishments, Dickey flew to Adelaide and on March 10 gave the formal address opening the city's week-long, biennial literary festival. Seven hundred and fifty writers from all over the world attended, and many turned out for Dickey's address and reading. One of the first American poets to read in the five-year history of the festival, Dickey beguiled and sometimes shocked the crowds who gathered at the world-renowned Yaldara vineyards and winery in the Barossa Valley outside Adelaide and at the more official venues at the University of Adelaide and Elder Park. "You should have seen the faces in the audience when I read 'The Sheep-Child,'" Dickey said later, alluding to the many sheep farms in Australia and New Zealand. He also read "The Firebombing," "Falling," and "Hunting Civil War Relics at Nimblewill Creek." Although Dickey's poems had been published in *Poetry Australia* and a few other little magazines, only a small number of Australians knew his work. His duties completed at the festival, Dickey went on an American-style barnstorming tour of the country, reading at factories, high schools, technical schools, and Rotary Clubs. He next took a plane to Hong Kong, which he called an "Oriental Las Vegas,"[39] and to Japan, where the State Department had scheduled a final week of readings and lectures. Having revisited Japan so many times in his war poems, he must have been surprised by the clean, prosperous capital that confronted him on March 17.

Dickey's schedule called for appearances at the American Cultural Center in Shin-Osaka on March 18 (his most vivid memory of Osaka was of its hundred-mile-an-hour train), conferences with professors and graduate students in Kyoto on March 19, and readings and discussions at the Tokyo American Cultural Center on March 20. During these occasions, Dickey usually avoided poems that recalled the war. At the U.S. Information Agency in Tokyo, however, several of his Japanese listeners brought up the subject. The American poet Stephen Sandy, who was teaching on a Fulbright Fellowship at Tokyo University, attended the affair. He remembered Dickey entering the small lecture hall with a doyenne of Tokyo's literary demimonde named Ruth Witt-Diamant, who resembled both a grande dame and a Zen novice. Dickey gave a standard reading of anthology pieces like "Cherrylog Road" and "Buckdancer's Choice," talked about his background in advertising and football, and made some apologetic comments about all the prose he was writing. Someone asked him to read a few poems about the war. He obliged. Questions followed, and in his answers Dickey expressed his pleasure at the Japanese attentiveness to his poetry.

A Japanese man asked in fluent English whether the poems in *Helmets,* which he believed celebrated war, death, violence, and destruction, were consistent with an intelligent person's definition of art. Dickey responded calmly that he would defend the right of the poet to address any subject whatsoever. The polite audience grew agitated. Next, a surly woman asked if Dickey was aware that the firebombings of Tokyo, in which she presumed he had participated, had killed more civilians than the rest of the war, including the atomic bombs dropped on Nagasaki and Hiroshima. Dickey gave the woman a wide-eyed stare, shrugged his shoulders, and, raising his arm as with a football, passed the question on to Witt-Diamant, who suggested everyone adjourn to the reception. Dickey had no intention of apologizing for acts he considered legitimate during the war or of telling the woman that he had never firebombed Tokyo. He had already confessed in "The Firebombing" to the mixture of vengeance, guilt, glory, and indifference that he felt over his "demo" firebombing raids. That was enough.

Over coffee, soft drinks, and cookies, some of the Japanese apologized for the rude questions. Dickey, like the firebombing pilot in his poem, remained aloof; he merely smiled and sipped his coffee. After his book signing, however, he seemed anxious and asked Sandy: "Do you know where we can get something to drink? I mean to *drink?*" Sandy mentioned the bar in Dickey's hotel, the New Japan, a rather decrepit building that normally housed visiting sumo wrestlers. Dickey suggested that they first try the basement restaurant below them. Discovering that its bar only served Oriental liquor, which he found distasteful, he guided Sandy to a nearby bar that served Kentucky bourbon and soup. Dickey proceeded to drain four or five bowls of corn soup and numerous bourbons-on-the-rocks. Their conversation veered from Dickey's poetry tour toward more delicate topics:

> Soon he wanted to know what kind of sexual experiences I had had in Japan. I tried to convey in general and diffident terms my brief life in Tokyo. Now he wanted to know if I had had homosexual experiences with the Japanese; he had heard that the idea of homosexuality was more acceptable to Orientals than to Westerners. They were more permissive, and some were forward with foreigners. It was an opportunity not to be missed.
>
> The conversation turned, over another round of drinks, to more general subjects: how I liked Tokyo, how long I had been there, the Japanese, what sorts I had met. A friendly but persistent grilling. He had backed off but came back to sex. For someone who had been in Tokyo for six months, I must have had intimate relations with *someone* Japanese, male or female. Was he right? He was. And what about men?
>
> I was surprised. Perhaps he had been reading one of those books in hotel lobby gift shops. He was working on a novel, I was to understand. Then he wanted to know if I had had anal intercourse in Japan. Taken aback, I assured him I had not. Sexual mores and relations between the sexes were the same in Japan, I tried to explain, yet different. If he wanted to see interesting sights, I could take him to some amusing places in Sanchome.
>
> It got to be about 10 P.M. Jim asked me to take him out on the town. I offered to, but it had been growing apparent that he was not going anywhere but bed. I was expected at a party in Shinjuku and looked forward to taking him, but he pled exhaustion and jet lag. I walked him, holding his arm, back next door to the New Japan lobby. A bell-hop took over and

he disappeared into an elevator. I went down to the subway to catch the Marounchi line train and get to my friends.[40]

Next morning at eight-thirty, as they had agreed, Sandy brought a sheaf of his poems to discuss with Dickey over breakfast at the Hotel New Japan. Dickey was nowhere in sight, and the front desk clerk could not rouse him. Sandy waited half an hour, left his poems at the desk, and departed.

Like so many others, Sandy assumed that Dickey had been a combat pilot involved in the extensive firebombing of Japan. During the question-and-answer period after his reading, why had he acquiesced so calmly to his alleged role in killing the Japanese? And why had he grilled Sandy about homosexuality at the restaurant? The novel Dickey had alluded to was, of course, *Deliverance*. The crucial scene involved unsolicited anal intercourse. Was Dickey soliciting a similar experience, albeit obliquely, from Sandy? Was he trying to find out where he might have such homosexual experiences in Tokyo? Was he simply trying to fluster Sandy by exploring taboo subjects, as he liked to do? Or was he simply picking the brain of a fellow writer, hoping to get information he could use to make the homosexual scene in *Deliverance* more credible? The different sides of Dickey's personality were all at work. Thinking back on his few days in Tokyo years later, Dickey could remember the name of only one poet he met there, and it was not Sandy: "I ran into a British poet, a homosexual poet, who was a spelunker, a cave explorer. . . . He wore make-up and everything, but I liked him very much." Returning in the 1980s to give a graduation address to a University of Maryland program in Japan, Dickey supposedly looked for the poet, but couldn't find him.

Dickey flew home on March 23. Rather than rest, he continued to tour at a breakneck pace, giving readings in early April at the Women's National Democratic Club, Rhode Island School of Design, Saint Bonaventure College, Lafayette College, North Shore Community College, Lycoming College, and on April 13 at the University of South Florida in Tampa. In late April, he traveled to London, where he discussed the state of contemporary British and American poetry with M. L. Rosenthal, Donald Davie, and A. Alvarez at an American embassy conference and, with George MacBeth, broadcast some of his poems on the BBC's Third Programme. He was in a triumphant mood when he returned to the United States to read at Princeton on May 1 (there he met his poet friend Theodore Weiss, who had published some of his early poems at *Quarterly Review of Literature*). The next day he attended a New York publication party organized by Farrar, Straus & Giroux for his book *Babel to Byzantium*. Among the writers at the Gotham Book Mart to help launch his book were Robert Lowell and Marianne Moore. Moore was one of the few living women poets Dickey praised in *Babel to Byzantium* (he declared that if he had to choose someone to "construct a Heaven for us, out of the things we already have,"[41] he would choose Moore). Inman Mays, who also came to the party, followed Dickey upstairs to a darkly lit room where Moore sat in a thronelike chair, a long white dress flowing over her spare frame, her trademark black, tricornered hat perched on her white hair. "Miss Moore, this is Inman Mays, an old friend," Dickey said. She asked: "Does he follow the Yankees?"[42] Aware of Moore's devotion to the Brooklyn

Dodgers, Dickey replied that Mays did not follow the Yankees. Relieved, Moore engaged them in amiable conversation. Dickey also talked with Stanley Burnshaw. Because of their admiration for each other's work, Burnshaw proposed dedicating his scholarly book about poetics, *The Seamless Web,* to Dickey. Dickey suggested that Burnshaw select one of his older friends (in 1991 Dickey got his name on the book by writing an admiring introduction to a new edition).

In general, Dickey's *Babel to Byzantium* was well received. Ralph J. Mills wrote in the *Chicago Sun-Times:* "James Dickey's critical book is the most perceptive one we have had on contemporary poetry since Randall Jarrell's *Poetry and the Age* appeared well over a decade ago."[43] Thomas Lask praised it in the *New York Times.* Some critics, however, faulted Dickey for his conservative tastes and deliberate contentiousness. Lawrence Lipton wrote: "He writes condescendingly or downright insultingly about such radical and revolutionary American poets as the late Kenneth Patchen, Allen Ginsberg, Robert Duncan, and Charles Olson." Lipton put on brass knuckles for an ad hominem assault: "James Dickey as a poet is a mediocre academic hack who accepted an appointment by a President of the United States to serve a term as Librarian of Congress, an offer which any first rate poet, even among academic poets, would regard as an insult to his integrity as a poet."[44] Since many of the best American poets had served as poetry consultants, Lipton's rebuke was obviously misguided, but it showed the sort of animosity Dickey was arousing from liberal critics in the late 1960s.

Dickey brought his extraordinarily busy two years as poetry consultant to an end with a final flurry of activities. He visited Hotchkiss School in Connecticut after the Gotham Book Mart party, judged the first Roethke Poetry Prize with Carolyn Kizer (the prize went to Dickey's friend Howard Nemerov for *The Blue Swallows*), and read at D.C. Teachers' College, Bethany College, Northern Virginia Community College, and Bucks County Community College. On May 6 he also gave a farewell reading at the Library of Congress, and with his family attended an evening reception honoring him in the Whittall Pavilion. His colleagues used the occasion to thank him for his indefatigable service to poetry and the library. Although his poems and conduct had stirred controversy outside the library, inside he was considered one of the most effective consultants ever. William McGuire stated in his history of the consultantship: "Dickey's expansive and gregarious manner earned him many friends around the Library. No Consultant, other than Frost perhaps, had been so well-liked and well-acquainted."[45]

Shortly after he finished his library term, Dickey decided to reflect on his accomplishments, past and present, in an oral autobiography. Two Miami University students, James and Barbara Reiss, had proposed the project. Using as a model Edith Heal's collaboration with William Carlos Williams, *I Wanted to Write a Poem* (1958), which also began as a master's thesis, Barbara contacted a number of well-known poets, including Robert Lowell and Richard Wilbur, about conducting a series of "self-interviews" for her own master's. Lowell and Wilbur declined to participate, so Barbara decided to focus on Dickey. Both Reisses had first spoken to Dickey at his Phi Beta Kappa reading at Miami University on March 21, 1967, where he had captivated them with his poems and annoyed them with his flirtatious comments about Barbara's "delicate bones."[46] On June

6, 1968, the day after Robert Kennedy was shot, they drove to Leesburg with their daughter and tape recorders for a week of interviews.

Acting the ebullient host, Dickey greeted the Reisses warmly and gave them a tour of his house, pointing out the living room where they would work (James never forgot its "1890s garish, velvety, whorehouse red upholstery")[47] as well as the large, blue, Chagall-like watercolor hanging in the kitchen with a French poem superimposed on its surface (the painting had been composed by the Allegheny stewardess he had memorialized in "Falling"). Dickey introduced them to Maxine, who kindly made sandwiches during work breaks and cooked dinner for the Reisses as well as for James Reiss's parents, who sometimes visited after baby-sitting their granddaughter. Maxine's mother, Mrs. Tipton, who worked as Dickey's secretary, also joined them for dinner.

Because he was busy cleaning out his poetry consultant's office and making arrangements for his move to South Carolina, Dickey at first promised to talk about his life and writing for only a day or two. As his enthusiasm for the interviewing increased, he agreed to sit for five full days. Each morning at nine o'clock they gathered in his cool living room among the ceramic owls, hunting bows, guitars, review books, and fin-de-siècle chaise longues. Thunderball, the family's Australian sheep dog, slept at Dickey's feet. Returning from school, Chris and Kevin often listened to their father's stories. Dickey sat astride an ottoman, glanced at the Reisses' outline, and sometimes spoke into the tape recorder nonstop for ninety minutes. His remembrance of things past seemed Proustian in its comprehensiveness.

Although the twenty-seven-year-old James Reiss drank a good deal, he was surprised by Dickey's capacity for alcohol. Before they sat down in the morning to tape, Dickey downed several Bloody Marys or martinis. If they went to Dickey's club for lunch, he retrieved a bottle from his locker and drank it with his meal. One night, the Reisses witnessed the sort of tantrums Dickey's drinking unleashed when he delivered a scathing denunciation of his son Chris and refused to attend his graduation ceremony at Loudon County High School. To calm his nerves Dickey continued to drink, withdrawing to his "owl's nest" with a pint-size tumbler of straight Scotch. Since the constant drinking made Dickey more energetic and talkative, the Reisses did nothing to discourage it. He rarely looked fatigued, even though he stayed up late into the night working on poems, played his guitars vigorously between taping sessions, periodically rushed off to the archery range, and forever jumped up to answer phone calls, most of them— he told the Reisses—from important politicians in Washington who requested his advice on campaign issues.

Wowed by his charisma and relatively unfamiliar with his life, the Reisses accepted Dickey's reminiscences as fact, but harbored reservations about his character. Following a particularly vitriolic row between Dickey and Maxine on the way to dinner at the Knife and Fork in Washington, according to James Reiss: "Dickey was feeling expansive after cocktails. In a rare burst of enthusiasm for anyone but himself he told me that he would see to it that the University of South Carolina, where he would commence teaching in the fall, would invite me down for a poetry reading [he never did]. Naturally, I was ecstatic—which offset my anxiety when the check came and I had to pay in cash. B[arbara] and

I bought the movie tickets, too, and I remember squeaking by with two or three dollars to spare."[48] They saw *2001: A Space Odyssey*, which had just premiered. At the beginning of the film, as the apes pranced around the large, black monolith, Dickey shouted: "That's my world! That's what I write about!"[49] During their week in Leesburg, the Reisses witnessed plenty of Dickey's shifts between savagery and civility.

The taping sessions completed, Barbara produced transcripts that she and her husband revised. Dickey was professional and punctual, authorizing their corrections and offering his own. On December 5, 1968, the Reisses wrote Ken McCormick to see if Doubleday might consider their manuscript for publication. McCormick soon issued a contract. Relations between the editors and their publisher grew tense during the summer of 1969 because of an argument over a title. Barbara had proposed *Listening to James Dickey: A Literary Autobiography of the Poet in Mid-Career*. Obviously too unwieldy, it was rejected by Doubleday for the simpler *Monologues*. According to Dickey, the final title, *Self-Interviews*, came about in a fortuitous way at the Apollo moon shot in July 1969, where he and Norman Mailer were supposed to interview each other. Rather than follow the original plan, he told Mailer: "Why don't you interview yourself?"[50] In the ensuing discussion, Mailer, who had created a minor uproar in 1959 with *Advertisements for Myself*, suggested that Dickey call his new book *Self-Interviews*. On July 28, 1969, McCormick wrote Dickey that he was delighted with Mailer's title. James Reiss, on the other hand, felt it was immodest and deceptive, since the Reisses had been the ones interviewing Dickey. If critics thought Dickey had spent hours talking to himself about his life, Reiss predicted that the book would be attacked as narcissistic. Reiss's bitterness intensified when he heard that Doubleday wanted to keep the Reisses' name off the book jacket. He wrote his agent on August 6, 1969, the day Theron Raines informed him of Doubleday's slight: "I was shocked and disappointed with our phone conversation today. Once again, Barbara and I want to make it absolutely clear to Doubleday that our names *must* be on the cover and the title-page, along with Jim's name. We realize that the Reiss name may not be a super-saleable commodity, but we feel that due credit can be expressed only by Doubleday's placing our names on the cover."[51] Reiss also complained to Dickey about the publisher's slight. Dickey wrote back on August 22 that he'd assumed their names would be on the cover.

Dickey had little intention of sharing a book jacket with relative unknowns like the Reisses. In an August 3 letter to his publisher, he claimed to have lost his contracts for the book and laid out a strategy for selling the book with his name and his many kudos. In the genre of self-advertising autobiography, he wanted to out-Mailer Mailer:

It would not be a bad thing at all if the book were controversial; I intend some of my remarks to incite this kind of reaction. Let us make some bold claims for me. I will leave these claims to you, but if we can stir up the Lowells and *The New York Review of Books* people to a violent attack, we can then rally our forces and as the result of the interplay the book will sell rapidly. Controversy is the very name of the game in the case of writers and their opinions. . . . I believe a good many people will be shaken up by this book, and shaken up in far deeper ways than people are shaken up by the deliberate shaking-efforts of people like Norman Mailer. I believe that the tremors from this particular shock will be deep indeed, and will cause a certain revaluation of poetry, and, yes, of existence in this time and place.[52]

Dickey spoke to the Reisses about pitching the book against the establishment as well, and in the introduction they tried to arouse attention by calling their book a radical hybrid of autobiography, criticism, and literary interview: "Obviously this book departs drastically from the quietist tradition of New Criticism and perhaps—if we may make claims for our own creation—signals in a still newer criticism in which the poet's own words about his life and poetry matter, at least as much as any biographer or critic's words about him." The editors highlighted the "frankness and honest . . . , unpremeditated reliability" of this "new genre," and commended their subject as "a man unafraid to speak the truth." Dickey resisted calling his exercise in self-revelation an autobiography, and also told the Reisses "that this would be the only work resembling a biography that he would ever authorize."[53] Little did they know that Dickey was doing what he did best when speaking about himself—telling engaging lies based precariously on facts.

Embittered by the publisher's decisions regarding the title and credits, James Reiss tried to remain friendly toward Dickey. Asked by Dickey to write the *Atlantic* in support of his poem "The Buckhead Boys," whose profanity had incited angry protests, Reiss complied and told Dickey that he had urged a dozen others to do the same. Despite his amiable gestures, Reiss could do nothing to persuade Dickey or Doubleday to alter the book cover. Only in the second printing did Doubleday try to make amends by printing the Reisses' names on the spine. Reprinted in paperback by Louisiana State University Press in 1984, the book again failed to include the Reisses on the cover. The haggling between editors and publisher notwithstanding, *Self-Interviews* sold remarkably well for a book about a poet's work. By October 30, 1970, 4,395 copies had sold; by January 1971, 8,500. The book went into several printings, and the Reisses discovered that its appeal was widespread enough for it to be pirated in China. Nevertheless, the Reisses felt their subject had used and discarded them. Correspondence dwindled. James Reiss saw Dickey at Miami University in the mid-1970s and at the West Side Y in New York in 1983, but never again.

In mid-June 1968, Dickey heard from Dave Smith, who also wanted to explore his life and writings. Smith asked about enrolling in Dickey's USC classes (he eventually entered the Ph.D. program at Ohio University) and about writing Dickey's biography. To explain his interest in Dickey's life, he said: "I think it was through you and the interest I took in your background that I became aware of what I wanted to do with my life."[54] Dickey had no intention of encouraging other biographical projects, but he was glad to teach Smith at USC and act as his mentor in the meantime. When Smith got drafted into the military, Dickey called to commiserate, since he knew that Smith worried about going to Vietnam. Smith wrote about his quandary in a testimonial letter praising Dickey's poem "Victory," which he sent to the *Atlantic Monthly* on August 8.

"Victory," Smith argued, appealed to those like himself "who do not condone the atrocities, the stupidity, the dishonor of such as Vietnam, but [who] . . . cannot turn their backs on their country for they believe too much is at stake: not merely the country, but their own moral selves . . . . Telling it like it is is very popular just now and no one does it better than Dickey. He gives us war as it really was and IS for one man, as he actually experienced it. . . . He does not embellish the truth, but publishes it."[55] Dickey must have been flattered to know his poems were so believable.

Throughout the summer of 1968, as America's cities reeled with political turmoil, Dickey kept busy with numerous literary jobs. He began the initial jury work with Louis Simpson and Howard Nemerov for the 1969 Pulitzer Prize in poetry. From June 17 to 23, he gave readings and workshops for a conference organized by the Poetry Society of Oklahoma. From July 21 to August 2, he taught at a University of Colorado conference at Boulder, where he was delighted to see his former Rice student Pat Moore and a Canadian girlfriend whom he called "Miss Hannah," a pseudonym he later applied to Frank and Joel Cahill's girlfriend in *Alnilam*. (When Moore went to Dickey's dorm room to escort him to a conference function, she was startled to find them together.)[56] To take a break from his arduous teaching and reading schedule, Dickey considered going to the exotic-sounding Bohemian Grove, a lavish summer camp for celebrities and artists that Jack London had helped establish in Sonoma County, about seventy-five miles north of San Francisco. Instead, he took a vacation with his family in his old childhood haunt, Saint Simons Island, from August 4 to 10, and then supervised the family's relocation to South Carolina.

Dickey soon heard from Robert Manning that his review article on Roethke, "The Greatest American Poet," which would appear in the November *Atlantic Monthly*, might run into legal trouble. Manning admired the article, but worried that Dickey's tough rebuke of Roethke's wife, Beatrice, might be libelous. He planned to consult his lawyers before publishing it. If Manning's cautionary letter on August 23 aroused anxiety, Dickey found consolation in a letter Allen Seager's wife, Joan, sent about a month later. She agreed with Dickey's assertion that Beatrice had abetted Roethke's infantile behavior and obstructed a truthful biography. If Beatrice sued Dickey, Joan would certainly be a strong witness for his defense. As expected, Dickey's allegations infuriated Beatrice, but she aired her gripes in letters rather than in court.

Although Dickey in later years sometimes belittled the importance of the poetry consultant and its later incarnation, the poet laureate, he felt that he had made a significant contribution as America's official poetry ambassador between 1966 and 1968. With regard to improving the state of poetry, he stated in his final report that his trips to the Pacific and to England were his outstanding achievements. He had enjoyed being at the hub of poetic as well as political power in Washington, D.C. The simple act of writing condolences allowed him access to dignitaries in the U.S. and abroad. As consultant, he took it upon himself to write a moving tribute for the poet laureate of Great Britain, John Masefield, who died on January 3, 1968. He also cabled congratulations to the new laureate, C. Day Lewis, on January 3, 1968. On April 5, 1968, Dickey wrote an official condolence to Mrs. Martin Luther King, Jr: "I pray, with you and your husband, who is still praying, that the great work may not falter, but go on." For all his less charitable remarks about African-Americans, Dickey could compose stirring rhetoric for a fallen civil rights leader. On June 7, 1968, he wrote another prominent woman grieving for a slain husband, Mrs. Robert F. Kennedy: "Sincerest condolences. I am as speechless as the rest. I hope you will understand the depth of feeling that underlies the dumbness of the man of words."[57] At the Library of Congress, Dickey was more "acknowledged" than—in Shelley's famous definition of poets—most of the "unacknowledged legislators of the world."

nes Dickey's mother,
ibelle Dickey.

nes Dickey papers MSS745,
cial Collections Department,
bert W. Woodruff Library,
ory University.

nes Dickey's father,
gene.

oto by Petrie Studio. James
key papers MSS745, Special
llections Department, Robert
Woodruff Library, Emory
iversity.

The Dickey house at 166
West Wesley Road in
Atlanta.

Photo by Bill Barnwell.

James Dickey, twenty-two
months old.

*Courtesy of Maibelle Dickey
Hodgins.*

James Dickey on bicycle, 1930.

Courtesy of Maibelle Dickey Hodgins. James Dickey papers MSS745, Special Collections Department, Robert W. Woodruff Library, Emory University.

James Dickey's sister, Maibelle, 1946.

James Dickey papers MSS745, Special Collections Department, Robert W. Woodruff Library, Emory University.

James Dickey (middle) running the high hurdles
at North Fulton High School, 1940.

Photo by Declan Haun. James Dickey papers MSS745,
Special Collections Department, Robert W. Woodruff
Library, Emory University.

nes Dickey and his pilot, Earl Bradley, by a P-61 Black Widow, 1945.

*nes Dickey papers MSS745, Special Collections Department, Robert W. Woodruff Library,
nory University.*

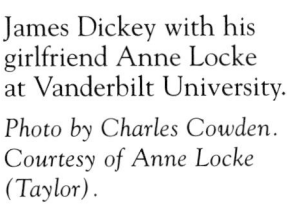

James Dickey with his
girlfriend Anne Locke
at Vanderbilt University.

*Photo by Charles Cowden.
Courtesy of Anne Locke
(Taylor).*

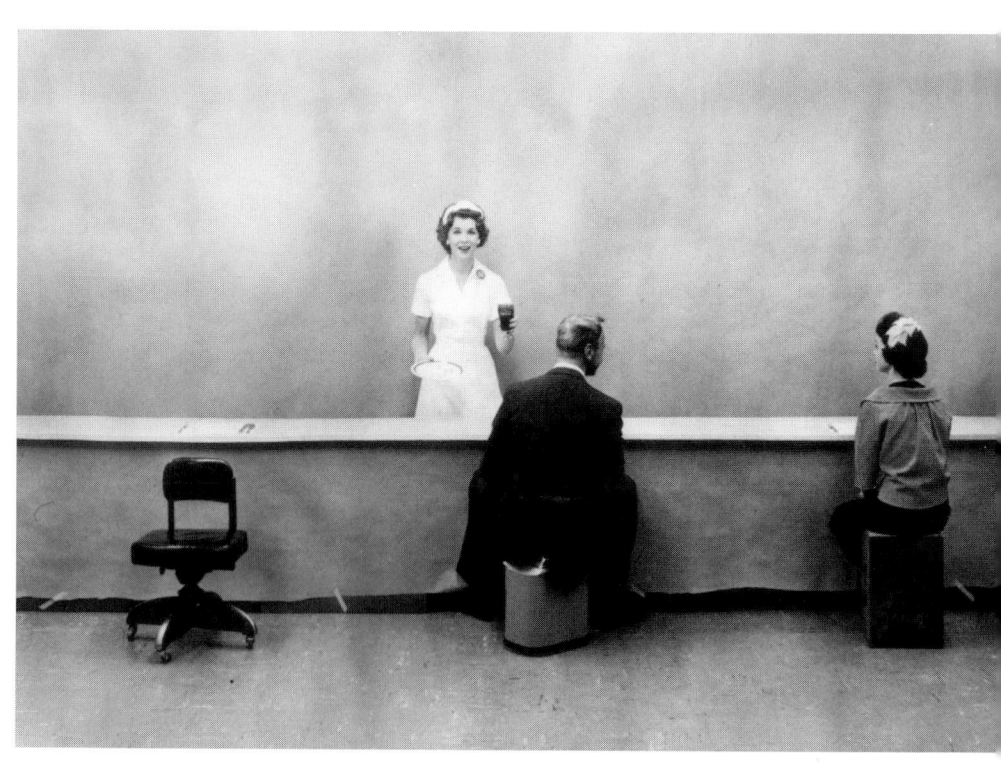

As an employee of McCann-Erickson, James Dickey posed in a Coca-Cola advertisement, 1958.
Photo by Jerome Drown. James Dickey papers MSS745, Special Collections Department, Rober
W. Woodruff Library, Emory University.

(Clockwise) James Dickey, Maxine, Chris, and Kevin, having just arrived in New York
in September 1962 after traveling in Europe on their father's Guggenheim fellowship.
From UPI. James Dickey papers MSS745, Special Collections Department, Robert W. Woodruff
Library, Emory University.

James Dickey's friends Al Braselton (foreground) and Lewis King (background) preparing to go on one of the canoe trips that would later appear in *Deliverance*, ca. 1960.

Photo by Joan King.

Dickey hunting in camouflage gear in North Virginia, ca. 1967.

Photo by Terry Miller.

James Dickey playing the role of Sheriff Bullard on filmsite of Deliverance with his son Chris, ca. 1971.

Photo by John R. Hamilton. James Dickey papers MSS745, Special Collections Department, Robert W. Woodruff Library, Emory University.

mes Dickey playing the guitar at West Virginia University in June 1969.

oto by Lloyd Davis. James Dickey papers MSS745, Special Collections epartment, Robert W. Woodruff Library, Emory University.

James Dickey with William Styron at the University
of South Carolina in 1974.

Courtesy of The Gamecock. *James Dickey papers MSS745,
Special Collections Department, Robert W. Woodruff
Library, Emory University.*

James Dickey with Robert Lowell at the University
of South Carolina in 1974.

Photo by Janet Lee Burnet, from the collection of David Havird.

James and Deborah Dickey in Atlanta soon after their marriage, ca. 1977.
Photo by Al Braselton.

mes Dickey with his daughter, Bronwen, 1987.

oto by Joe Jackson: The State. James Dickey papers MSS745, Special Collections Department, bert W. Woodruff Library, Emory University.

James Dickey with his University of South Carolina friends. *From left to right:* Matthew Bruccoli, Ben Franklin, James Dickey, Don Greiner, Ward Briggs, in 1995.

Photo by Mitchell West. Courtesy of University of South Carolina.

James Dickey with a raven on his shoulder in the
Edgar Allan Poe Museum, Richmond, Virginia, 1994.

*Photo by Pierre Courtois. Courtesy of The Library of
Virginia. James Dickey papers MSS745, Special Collections
Department, Robert W. Woodruff Library, Emory
University.*

James Dickey, 1985.
Photo by Paul O'Mara.

IX.

TENURE IN SOUTH CAROLINA

22. "A Starry Place Between the Antlers" (1968)

After years of scurrying between rented homes and apartments, Dickey looked forward to putting down roots again in the South. Maxine shared his anticipation. She told Malie Bruton, a reporter for the Columbia newspaper *The State*: "This will be the first time since Jim was in advertising that we've been in one place very long. . . . All that traveling has been a little wearing—especially on the furniture. Now I'll be able to do something like collecting paintings, in which I'm quite interested." She also said that her husband, who for years had sacrificed his writing to the rigors of touring, hoped to spend more time in his study. When Maxine revealed that she would be stationed in Columbia all fall while her husband taught at Georgia Tech, Bruton asked her about the liabilities of being married to a roving poet. Diplomatic and loyal to a fault, she replied: "I don't think being the wife of a poet can be so different from being the wife of anybody else. . . . I think the main difference in my particular case . . . is that Jim is so happy as a poet and teacher, and that makes our home so happy. It's a way of life that we both like very much." And her children's feelings about their minstrel father? "I don't think the boys have any special feeling about their father's profession . . . except that, as I do, they enjoy the interesting guests it brings to the house." She added: "[Chris] has no plans to be a poet, though. At the moment he's interested in politics—he's for Eugene McCarthy—and photography."[1] She spoke less about Kevin, whose main interests were basketball and oceanography, perhaps because he was unhappy about his new hometown. Maxine gave few hints that her husband's prodigal "roving" brought anything but happiness to the family.

Dickey's family, in fact, had hoped to move back to California. California's reputation as an academic haven for radical students, however, had convinced Dickey to find a job elsewhere. He wanted to go to a university steeped in the Southern past; the University of South Carolina was such a place. Founded in the first decade of the nineteenth century, it had sent students to the Civil War and served as a Confederate hospital in 1862. General Sherman had spared it when he burned the rest of Columbia, but it had suffered economic hardship during Reconstruction and had struggled through forced integration (professors resigned and students chose other colleges when the first black student enrolled in 1873). Over the succeeding decades, USC had worked hard to become a first-rate university, and by the time Dickey joined its faculty it had gone a long way toward attaining that goal.

To better familiarize himself with USC, where he was to begin teaching in January 1969, Dickey traveled to Columbia to give the commencement address on June 1, 1968. He geared his speech to both the conservative and radical elements in his audience of one thousand graduates assembled on the university's historic Horseshoe. At times he sounded like an old-fashioned Agrarian, at other times a 1960s rebel. He lamented the decline of ethics and religion in modern capitalist society, denigrated advancements in science that saved lives but failed to make them worth living, and warned against specialized careers that turned people into "prisoners and beneficiaries of a kind of half-benevolent, half-indifferent economic concentration camp." He also reminded his audience: "Even the attempts to escape or drop out of [society] . . . , to flee from it in hippie beads, by means of bohemian communes, drugs, or by any other means, are still made possible by the system itself."[2] Arguing that good manners should govern all revolts against the status quo, Dickey expressed both his and, he hoped, his Southern audience's divided sentiments.

Used to rubbing shoulders with presidents and presidential candidates in Washington, Dickey was anything but obsequious in his job negotiations with USC president Tom Jones. Jones, according to Dickey, had to convince him that the job was worthy of his talents:

> The president of the college was full of good sly half-naive cracker honesty. When I asked him what incentive might cause me to wish to live in South Carolina, I brought in, as though a matter of general knowledge, the opinion that the state is a depressed area economically, perennially snake-bit as to its money crop. The turpentine from the pine trees had lost its money when sail gave way to steam, I said, having looked this up in a John Gunther *Inside U.S.A.*, thirty years out of date. Indigo had not done well either, killed off by the advent of aniline dyes; even the indigo *snake* is on the endangered list. And the rice they used to raise in South Carolina, which had to be cultivated under water by hand, could not compete with the highland rice of Arkansas and Texas, and furthermore, Sea Island—or long staple—cotton had been blitzed by the boll weevil during the Depression, and improvements in textile machinery had made it even less valuable, into the bad bargain. So now, as far as I knew, South Carolina was soybeans, illiteracy, and maybe even pellagra and hookworm, and my chief mental image of it was of a dilapidated outhouse and a rusty '34 Ford with a number 13 painted on it, both covered by kudzu. Why should I become part of such an environment? President Tom Jones looked at me with sincere friendliness and said, If you like two things, you would like to live in South Carolina. What two things? I asked suspiciously. Flowers and birds, he replied. Talk on, I said.[3]

It's doubtful that Dickey subjected President Jones to such a detailed geography report (and it was Maibelle Dickey who had a special passion for flowers and birds). For Jim Dickey, the city's *symbolic* location mattered most. "The best thing about Columbia," he wrote after moving there, "is its meridional aspect: the way it balances Appalachia and the Atlantic . . . the deer of the mountains and those of the sea . . . : that is my balance, and it is right for me: the starry place between the antlers."[4] Midway between the rustic folkways of the mountains and the cosmopolitan amenities of cities like Charleston, Columbia embodied Dickey's bifurcated loyalties. As if to remind himself precisely where he was and who he was, he soon began his elaborate ritual to determine the longitude and latitude of his new home. Using a radiolike box known as a "time cube" to synchronize two digital watches, which he usually wore on different wrists, as well as a host of other paraphernalia—sextant, chronometer, sight-reduction table, circular slide-rule, artificial horizon—Dickey determined his position in the universal scheme of things. The outcome of his calculations was always the same: 34°, 00.2 north and 80°, 58.5 west.

While Maxine, Mrs. Tipton, and the boys settled into Columbia, Dickey prepared to teach a semester at Georgia Tech. Frank Beckum, the chairman of the Franklin Foundation Lecture Series, had arranged for Dickey to stay in a furnished efficiency at Burge Apartments at sixty dollars per month (Dickey dubbed it his "Casa Cucaracha"). A. J. Walker, the chair of the English Department, made sure he had an office and classroom when he arrived on September 23. James Young, his close friend from Rice who now taught at Georgia Tech, gave advice about what to expect from students. To reintroduce him to his home city, the Atlanta Constitution offered the following portrait: "James Dickey is a big, blond man, who looks as if he could wrestle the life from a python. And he is so big on college campuses these days that the University of South Carolina recruited him like a prize yeoman who could play tackle on Saturday after plowing all week."[5] This Viking yeoman footballer got along well with the brainy engineering students who attended his weekly three-hour poetry class, English 381, in the campus's Aerospace Building. Larry Rubin, who taught at Georgia Tech, sat in on one of Dickey's classes: "Jim was fantastic. He held the class in the palm of his hand with his wit and enthusiasm and his incredible ability to make poetry come alive. He even quoted from Paradise Lost with verve and panache!"[6] Believing knowledge should be acquired entertainingly and at a leisurely pace, Dickey often invited his students to Harry's Bar and Grill on Spring Street. There he serenaded them with guitar music in between beers and remarks about poetry.

Dickey remembered his time at and around Georgia Tech with pleasure: "I never had such good students in my life. Those engineers were starved for this kind of thing. And they wrote poetry all day and all night."[7] Having begun his college career as an engineer, Dickey felt immediate rapport with the Tech students. They, in turn, appreciated his relaxed teaching style. One of his students, Marshall MacFarlane, said: "When I learned that a great American poet was teaching a course, I jumped at the chance for a change from the tedium and discipline of my engineering studies. . . . Jim was a friendly and helpful teacher, never critical, always interested in the student's view, no matter how naive or impractical. He was eager to be part of the class, and his crackling personality was a real contrast to the typical Tech professors, who usually had more pencils and pens than personality." Like the other students, MacFarlane relished Dickey's mischievous humor: "I last saw Jim just before Christmas, as the term was winding down. He didn't have a car at the time, so I had agreed to meet him at the faculty apartments where he stayed, and I drove us both to a local pub, where the class met one last time to say farewell. On the drive back to campus, after a few drinks, I told Jim how much I liked Atlanta, and how I wished I could stay and live there. I asked Jim if he agreed with my perceptions of the city, and if he could be comfortable there. He chuckled and said, 'All there is to do in Atlanta is drink and screw!' We both had a laugh at the comment, and I drove on. Then, after a few minutes of silence, Jim said quietly: 'There's more to life than drinking and screwing for a man with a purpose.'"[8] Because of a misprint in a student newspaper that seemed to pertain to Dickey's womanizing, some Georgia Tech students referred to their teacher as "poet-in-residence." Dickey suggested that a different man existed behind his bacchanalian persona.

In Atlanta, with his light teaching and lecturing responsibilities—he had to give three public lectures, two in October and one in November—Dickey returned with renewed vigor to *Deliverance*. Theron Raines had kindled his flagging interest in the novel during a visit at the beginning of the year. On September 22, Dickey told his agent that he had finished a fifty-page section of the penultimate draft. He proclaimed excitedly: "Let's make a million. . . . And what a movie it will make! Every night I put in a new cast, each better than the last!"[9] A note Jacques de Spoelberch wrote on October 7, 1968, boosted his confidence: "You *are* on the right track and I'm certain the best thing is for you to let everything out in this draft. There is no question in my mind but that first person narration is the best, in fact the only vehicle for your story. Everyone here agrees with me on that score. Again, write Ed's climb up the cliff exactly as you see and feel it; personally I didn't think there were too many details in earlier drafts, but if we suspect that there are too many in the final draft, we can always polish down slightly."[10] Dickey sent another ninety-four pages of revised manuscript to Houghton Mifflin in December. The day after Christmas, Spoelberch responded encouragingly; the new section had finally convinced him that Dickey had the makings of a novel rather than just a novella.

Dickey could have made more progress with *Deliverance* if he had not been sidetracked by offers he was unable to refuse. Shortly after the term at Georgia Tech began, he left his classes and novel to do something that even by Dickey's standards was extraordinary. On October 9, he flew to Florida to observe a rocket launch. *Life* magazine had asked him to write a poem about the Apollo 7 mission, the first manned flight of an Apollo spacecraft. He accepted the job with alacrity, commenting to a *Time* reporter: "Americans have sunk into the sloth of more and more comfort and convenience. . . . Many want to give up and see life as essentially miserable. I see life as hardly explored yet. These space guys are showing that miracles can still happen. I was born believing in great efforts."[11] In a few years Dickey would tell people that he himself had planned to fly rockets. "I could have been an astronaut had I been inches shorter,"[12] he informed some students in Johnson City, Tennessee.

Philip Kunhardt, one of *Life*'s assistant managing editors, had the challenging assignment of organizing Dickey's meetings with the astronauts and chaperoning Dickey around Cape Kennedy. Kunhardt did not come unprepared for his mission. He had grown accustomed to the vagaries of temperamental writers. He had hired Norman Mailer, among many others, to write for *Life*. Dickey, however, gave him pause when he strode from the plane in the Orlando airport in cowboy boots with a guitar dangling from his fist. They talked amicably enough as they drove to Cape Kennedy; but after they checked into their motel rooms and got ready to visit the astronauts, Dickey's manner changed. He started drinking at an alarming rate and grew more and more bellicose. Kunhardt rightly feared that a drunken Dickey swaggering in cowboy boots and cowboy hat would infuriate the immaculately groomed and rigidly controlled astronauts. Kunhardt considered leaving him behind and conducting the interviews himself.

Astronaut Walter Schirra had already told Kunhardt that Dickey would not be allowed to come to the first dinner in the crew quarters. Kunhardt and his associate, George Hunt, were the only ones who had permission to attend. Nevertheless, Dickey persuaded his *Life* cohorts to bring him. At dinner with Schirra, Walter Cunningham, and Donn Eisele, Dickey spent most of his time talking to Schirra. At one point he gave Schirra his camera, insisting that he smuggle it on board the spacecraft and take pictures of the Earth with it. Schirra humored him politely and resisted. Kunhardt remembered: "It was Wally Schirra who made an extra effort over Jim, devoting a good deal of time to him, driving him around + keeping him from causing disturbance. I guess Wally was cool enough to do this for, although on the 11th he would fly, he had already piloted Mercury and Gemini flights + was a pretty cool character anyway."[13] Realizing Dickey could use some fresh air, Schirra kindly took him outside for a drive in his car. Perhaps because of his friendliness, Dickey singled out Schirra as the most promising of the astronauts and the one who should command a rocket to the moon.

On the morning of October 11, Dickey and Kunhardt watched Apollo 7 break from its scaffolding and arc into space. Awestruck by the explosive liftoff, Dickey found it difficult to compose a poem. The assignment was also deliberately vague. According to Kunhardt: "His assignment was to turn his considerable poetic talents to our exploration of space. Even though what he wrote ran after Apollo 8, it wasn't meant to be about any particular mission."[14] Dickey never wrote a poem about Apollo 7; he wrote a poem about the Apollo 8 mission, the first manned voyage around the moon by astronauts Lovell, Borman, and Anders. Before he wrote the moon flight poem, however, he dashed off three pages of prose about encountering the Apollo 7 astronauts in the small dining and living room area of their quarters. *Life* cut Dickey's story down to a few paragraphs and on November 1, 1968, published them alongside photographs of the astronauts.

Dickey began his reminiscence with the unlikely account of a man lugging an elk head into the astronauts' quarters and placing it in a chair. "If you were near enough to the elk," he said, "you could see the astronauts in tiny replicas of themselves, in the animal eye. One was saying his greatest ambition was to learn to play the guitar. Another was showing a poem he had written. . . . Another had just come in from hunting doves. His name was Schirra and the elk head was for him."[15] The astronauts and NASA staff were amazed and offended by this. "[In] no way do I recall an elk head or dove hunting just prior to the flight of Apollo 7,"[16] Schirra insisted. Cunningham, who had no tolerance for Dickey's drunken shenanigans, repudiated Dickey's description of the crew quarters as well. His talk with Dickey, he said, was a waste of precious time. He also objected to the way Dickey had concentrated on Schirra. Since the mission depended on teamwork, each crew member was equally important. Although

Dickey maintained that Cunningham got chummy enough to show him some of his poems ("they were not so bad,"[17] he allowed), and although Dickey said he liked all the astronauts, the feelings were not reciprocated. Of the seven or eight people in the crew quarters, all but Schirra responded to his antics with contempt.

In his *Life* article, Dickey projected his own interests—guitar-playing, poetry writing, hunting—onto the astronauts. The severed-head motif, which Dickey associated with his fellow night fighter Donald Armstrong, may have appeared because it reminded him of his failures as a pilot. The visionary eye, as in his poem about Armstrong, redeemed such failures. In the elk's eye, Dickey saw replicas of the astronauts as well as replicas of himself. "In a sense they [the astronauts] are all poets, expanders of consciousness beyond its known limits," Dickey announced. Like the characters in *Deliverance*, a book Dickey discussed with Schirra before the flight, Dickey's astronauts are figments of his own personality, sallying forth on a mythical journey "up from the meadows and rivers and mountains and the beds of wives into the universal cavern, into the mathematical abyss, to find us—and return, to tell us what we will be."[18] As Dickey soared with the astronauts into what Kant had called "the mathematical sublime," earthly facts gave way to archetypal fictions.

Submitting his short piece about Apollo 7 on October 13, Dickey applied his new journalism penchant for merging facts with fictions. His efforts once again drew fire. "It was absolute junk," Kunhardt said. When he called Dickey to tell him so, Dickey was furious. "Do you know who you are talking to?" he bellowed into the phone. "You are talking to James Dickey!"[19] Unfazed, Kunhardt repeated his judgment and insisted that Dickey send another version. To help with revisions (Kunhardt had suffered a heart attack five weeks after the Apollo 7 launch), Kunhardt dispatched his colleague Ed Kern to Columbia. Kern had orders to stay as long as it took to get an acceptable poem from Dickey. Irritated by what he considered editorial high-handedness, Dickey greeted him coolly and suggested that no one should censor his work, not even *Life*. His gruffness soon vanished, as it so often did in the presence of opponents. He asked the Anglo-American Kern about his background, and was intrigued to learn that Kern's father had been a Rhodes scholar who so loved Oxford that he raised his son there. As tensions eased, Kern explained as judiciously as he could that *Life* needed a shorter, tighter poem. Dickey accepted this, got out his guitar, and began to entertain his guest with American folk songs. For several hours Kern basked in the ambience of Dickey's music and conversation, then flew back to New York.

"For the First Manned Moon Orbit," as he later called it, was one of the first occasional poems Dickey wrote about a significant national event. He liked to joke to friends like Inman Mays: "NASA had to spend billions and send a man into outer space to inspire me to write that poem."[20] Dickey was deservedly proud of getting it inserted into a ten-page spread in *Life* along with photographs of rockets, astronauts, earthscapes, and moonscapes. Few poets enjoyed such international visibility. His poem made its way into other venues as well. On August 27, 1969, independent filmmaker Carol Connor told Dickey that she was composing *Anthem for Apollo* from NASA videotapes of the moon shot, choir singing, astronauts reading from Genesis, and a rendition of "For the First Manned Moon Orbit."

In the grand, metaphysical style he chose for his Apollo poem, Dickey struggled to unite thoughts of divinity with the particulars of the mission, such as when "The radio, and the one voice / Of earth" went silent as the rocket orbited the far side of the moon. He indulged in verbal play to communicate the ineffable mystery that the astronauts beheld in space: "it is something // Else: nothing is something / Something I am trying / To say O God." In *The Whole Motion: Collected Poems 1945–1992*, where the poem appears as the first section of "Apollo," these rather sententious phrases precede two half pages and one full page of total blackness. The literal blackout corresponds to the communications blackout the astronauts experienced while flying around the dark side of the moon; it also accentuates the final burst of visionary rhetoric describing the astronauts' return to "the blue planet." Although Dickey had renounced Robert Frost by this time, his astronauts express the same sentiments as Frost's youthful persona in "Birches," who wants "to get away from earth awhile," soar "*Toward* heaven," and, after gaining a new perspective of Earth's magnificence, "come back to it and begin over." "Earth's the right place for love," Frost declares. Dickey agrees. His astronauts are "shaking with / The only love" as they return to Earth. What the astronauts see and learn is what the visionary Dickey has seen and learned already; they "behold / The blue planet steeped in its dream / Of reality."[21] Set against the black abyss of space, the real lives and loves of earthlings are miniscule, invisible, dreamlike.

In the stories he told about his visit to Cape Kennedy, Dickey was determined to put himself on an equal footing with his subjects partly because he had long possessed the sort of perspective they gained from space travel. His whole weltanschauung was based on it. He was also jealous of the astronauts, who were, after all, successful pilots. (Dickey's compulsion to offend pilots by posing as an outlandish poet was nothing new; he had behaved similarly as a member of the 418th Night Fighter Squadron.) He told Al Braselton:

> I've been covering the Apollo program for *Life*. You cannot imagine what it's like to see one of those big Saturns fire. It's as bright as the sun, the earth trembles and people fall down and weep and pray like [those at] a holy roller's meeting. Somehow before you see one for yourself you have the idea that a launch is just another one of those machine-controlled, scientific pseudo-miracles that we have become so accustomed to in this decade, but for me its sheer awesomeness created a sense of wonder in me like Blake confronting God. Of course, knowing the astronauts personally, Schirra, Anders, Borman, and roaring around drunk with them in their matching red Corvettes added a human dimension.

Used to Dickey's exaggerations, Braselton shot back skeptically: "I heard you got drunk and showed your ass to the astronauts." Dickey conceded: "Yea, by God I did. I'll always remember their names and . . . I was sure as shit gonna make sure that they remembered mine."[22] Of the three astronauts who flew the Apollo 8 mission, only Borman recalled meeting Dickey at a Bohemian Grove gathering.

The two surviving Apollo 7 astronauts, Schirra and Cunningham (Eisele died in 1987), remembered Dickey only reluctantly.

In his journal, Dickey wrote about the events in Florida with a combination of chagrin and braggadocio:

> I think with terrible sadness of the evening spent with the astronauts a couple of nights before Walter Schirra's lift-off. I was drunk out of my mind, and could not focus on anything that happened, but simply sat in a corner in a drunken stupor attempting conversation with one or another nice young fellow who drifted by doubtless out of a sense of duty, or of some kind of obscure loyalty to the *Life* people I was with. That opportunity will not come to me again, that is certain. And yet if I had been cold sober, what would I have done? Would I have been an eager-eyed middle-aged fellow, terribly receptive to all their personalities, and so on? No; if I had it to do again, I would be a drunken poet among the astronauts. And, by God, I was a drunken poet.[23]

Dickey's association with Time/Life had evolved during the late 1960s until he became a regular visitor and partier at its New York offices. Peter Bird Martin, the senior editor of *Time*'s press, cinema, theater, and show business sections, took note of Dickey when "The Eye-Beaters" appeared in a November 1968 *Harper's*. What appealed most to Martin about the poem, which described blind children beating their eyes to create lightninglike illusions, was the way Dickey summarized the action in the margins (Dickey's model was "Rime of the Ancient Mariner"). Martin called the Morgue—*Time*'s editorial reference library—and discovered that the magazine had never written a story about Dickey. Martin obtained permission for an article from managing editor Henry Grunwald, and appointed Larry Du Bois to go to Columbia in November and write a story. The following month *Time* published "The Poet as Journalist," which quoted Dickey on the resemblance between poetry and journalism, the heroism of astronauts, his own humble origins ("My people are all hillbillies," he said), his musical and athletic prowess as a young man, his one hundred missions as a firebombing "combat flier" during World War II, his dependence on "welfare checks" after quitting his advertising job, and his enchantment with the NFL. Like George Plimpton, who played briefly with the Detroit Lions so that he could write *Paper Lion*, Dickey said he wanted to try his hand at participatory journalism. (As poetry consultant he had told the *Vanderbilt Alumnus* that he planned to enter the 1968 Olympics' two-man canoe race with Plimpton.) On the other hand, he felt he should resist such athletic temptations for the sake of poetry. Du Bois reported: "Now, at 45, back in the South as Professor of English at the University of South Carolina, the former football star is having difficulty deciding whether to accept an offer to train with an N.F.L. team to write about his experiences."[24] No record exists of such an offer. Envious of Plimpton's chutzpah, in 1968 he made it his own, only to later deny that he had ever entertained such an impractical scheme.

Dickey relished the adulatory story in *Time*'s December 13 issue because it accorded so well with his heroic fantasies. He sent his congratulations to Martin and began attending Time's "closing parties," which took place on Friday nights around dinnertime while Martin and his staff typed their articles and evaluated the final copy. Since Time provided its editors with alcohol as well as expense accounts to buy it, drinks flowed. Dickey added substantially to the conviviality of the parties. Since he was working on Deliverance, he recounted scenes from the novel, recited his characters' lines, and tried to persuade everyone that he was Lewis and that he had killed someone on a North Georgia canoe trip. When he wanted his listeners to believe a particularly outlandish anecdote, he would stare at them, ears close to his head, teeth bared, a ferocious glint in his eye, and slowly articulate his lines. His charisma usually overwhelmed all skepticism. Sometimes Dickey would stay sufficiently sober to go out to dinner with the Time people; at other times he fell asleep on Martin's office couch.

Dickey frequently spoke to a less sympathetic and less gullible Time employee, Stefan Kanfer, the cinema critic and later the senior editor of the book review section. Kanfer liked to talk to Dickey about Eliot, Faulkner, Hemingway, and other writers, but disliked Dickey-the-"verbal-novelist" who would boastfully recount machine-gunning Japanese planes in fierce dogfights over the Pacific. "It was better than fuckin! It was better than fuckin!" Dickey exclaimed on one occasion. Kanfer responded matter-of-factly: "No it wasn't Jim. I know what it was like." If not about the war, Dickey's tales were simply about sex. He liked to blurt out accounts of his latest conquests as soon as he breezed into Kanfer's office. "I just woke up next to a drunken glamour girl!"[25] he once said. Kanfer realized that Dickey wanted everyone to adore him. Kanfer also realized that Dickey was embarrassed by Maxine, who didn't fit into New York's swashbuckling literary scene (he told the Time editors that Maxine was a nurse like Martha in Deliverance), and that his yarns in the Time offices arose partly from his desire to disassociate himself from Maxine.

Because Kanfer didn't drink, he always had plenty of alcohol for Dickey. Arriving in a less-than-sober state, Dickey proceeded to drink large quantities from the three or four bottles of Scotch, gin, or bourbon that Time allotted Kanfer each week. While enjoying the free drinks, Dickey was equally intent on ingratiating himself so that Time would give good exposure to his books. Dickey was gratified when Kanfer, after reading the galleys of Deliverance, assured him that the novel would be a big hit and, on April 20, 1970, when Kanfer published a generally laudatory review of the novel in Time. Along with the review was a profile, "Everyone's Notion of a Poet," which paraded all the myths of Dickey the football star, fighter pilot, and advertising executive. The article also offered glimpses of Dickey at the "closing parties": "James Dickey is everyone's notion of a poet: part Proteus, part Puck. People marvel at how much liquor he can hold, but he wonders why he can't drink as much as Hart Crane. Others are awestruck that he writes poems, criticism and fiction. He frets that he cannot paint."[26] Amused by Dickey's alcoholic performances, Kanfer and some of his colleagues at Time also found them exhausting and, when alcohol aroused Dickey's competitiveness, irritating. During an especially strenuous argument with Kanfer, Dickey slurred in his best Southern drawl: "You are one tough little Jewboy."

Kanfer concluded that Dickey was a "brute cavalier"[27] whose inherited biases erupted when he got drunk and angry. In different moods, Dickey could be exceedingly gracious, as when he wrote a generous blurb for a book Kanfer wrote. He did the same for other Time-Life writers he attacked, like Philip Kunhardt and Lance Morrow, as a gesture of reconciliation.

While courting Time-Life editors during the fall of 1968, Dickey also courted future publishers. Since Richard Wilbur had been instrumental in beginning the Wesleyan poetry series, Dickey wrote him a long letter on September 16 explaining why he wanted to find a new publisher. Among those he considered were Doubleday, Atheneum, Farrar, Straus & Giroux, and Houghton Mifflin. At issue were Wesleyan's inadequate advances, advertisements, and promotions. Confiding to Wilbur that his new book, *Eye-Beaters,* was his best yet, Dickey explained that he needed a larger publisher to distribute the book more effectively:

> Some of these other publishers are talking of advertising the book as they would a best-selling (hopefully bestselling *to be,* I mean) novel, and that has a strong appeal, I must say. There is no question but that they can do it, and if I change to one of them I will demand an advance that will make them *have* to do it, in order to get their money back. Maybe these are crass commercial considerations, but if there's one thing I've learned both from business life and writing, it is that it's not a question of whether your book is going to compete in the market-place or not: it *is* going to compete. The point is whether it is going to compete successfully or not. This can be an awfully paid-attention-to book, or it can just be another poetry book, though by a more or less "established" writer. And there is no doubt at all in my mind that publicity, and the money spent on it, will inevitably have something to do with this.[28]

Dickey finished his assessment of Wesleyan's poor marketing capabilities by asking Wilbur what he would do if he were in his situation.

Two days later Wilbur recounted his experiences with Harcourt Brace, which he once considered abandoning in favor of Farrar, Straus & Giroux. He questioned Dickey's analysis of big publishers and their ability to promote his new book, pointing out that the poets with real mass appeal were those like Ginsberg and Ferlinghetti, who were handled by small publishers like City Lights: "I frankly do not believe that any commercial publisher would be so uncommercial as consistently to give bestseller promotions to anyone's books of verse; that would lose money, and commercial publishers don't like to lose money."[29] Proud of the series he still helped direct, Wilbur urged Dickey to stay with Wesleyan.

Paying only scant attention to Wilbur's advice, Dickey began a series of aggressive negotiations with Willard Lockwood. If Wesleyan wanted to keep him on its list, he argued, then Lockwood would have to pay a much higher advance for his books. In late October, Lockwood capitulated: "I propose that we offer you an advance of $1,500 for each of the [next] two books, one-third payable on contract and the balance on publication."[30] This was three times more than the largest advance he had ever paid for a poetry book, but Lockwood conceded that Dickey's sales—thirty-five thousand books during the 1960s—merited it. On

October 9, 1968, Ken McCormick at Doubleday offered $25,000 for Dickey's next two poetry books. Michael di Capua, who also looked forward to future collaborations with Dickey, reported on October 29 that Farrar, Straus & Giroux could never come close to matching Doubleday's offer. Neither could Houghton Mifflin. So in early December Dickey severed his bonds with Wesleyan and moved to Doubleday. He would never again have such a fruitful decade as a poet.

One of the books McCormick soon hoped to publish was *The Indian Maiden*, the long poem-in-progress that Dickey had started after Robin Jarecki's death. In October 1968, Dickey had contacted James Laughlin about the possibility of his publishing house, New Directions, buying the book. He gave an indication of its contents when he said it might be too risqué for Grove Press (Grove was famous for publishing controversial books). To circumvent the obscenity laws, Laughlin concluded that he would have to bring out a limited edition (in the end no part of the poem was ever published). Dickey entertained other publishing ventures besides those with McCormick and Laughlin. In early November, the creative director of NFL Properties, Dave Boss, asked Dickey to write a book of verse about football. He proposed as a working title *The Violent Green Plain*. To whet Dickey's appetite, Boss invited him to the Super Bowl and promised to get a special pass so he could stand on the field with his camera. With so many other books in the works, Dickey let the football season lapse before turning down Boss's offer. Boss now made a more modest proposal. Could Dickey write a poem on football for a special issue of *Life* commemorating the NFL's fiftieth anniversary? Boss promised to pay one thousand dollars for the poem, which would be published in October 1969. Dickey wrote back that he now had time for a football poem and composed "In the Pocket" in a matter of weeks. On March 16, he sent the poem to Boss with an explanatory note: "It is supposed to be a kind of rapid fire stream of action interior monologue about the sense impressions and thoughts of an NFL—or indeed, any—T formation quarterback as he tries to find his receiver before the imposing linemen break through on him." He also informed Boss that the poem was "about men, fate, destiny, life, death, and probably a lot of other things too."[31] Boss was thrilled with the result. Among more serious editors and critics, Dickey's topical poems about Apollo missions, football, and other sports did little to bolster his reputation.

Dickey finished his eventful term at Georgia Tech in the late fall of 1968, and joined his family in the suburban ranch house they had bought on Lelia's Court overlooking Lake Katherine, which had once served as a reservoir for nearby Fort Jackson. Visitors usually noticed a canoe pulled up on the grass, an archery target in the nearby pine trees, the basketball hoop where Kevin practiced, and Dickey's barbells. Maxine had decorated the house with furnishings she had admired for years in magazines and architecture books: deep orange-and-blue custom-made sofas, Wassily chairs by Walter Gropius, Barcelona chairs by Mies van der Rohe. Dickey's library, which allegedly contained twenty thousand volumes, took up much of the wall space. One of the more unusual artifacts was a murky blue oil painting of a mountain scene by William F. Buckley. Buckley had first shown it to Maxine on an airplane flight. She had offered to buy it, but Buckley generously signed it and gave it to her. Expensive guitars lay on the floor beneath racks of high-powered, state-of-the-art bows. Two dogs, a dachshund named Gretchen and the Australian sheep dog, Thunderball, roamed over the carpet. A blue Toyota Land Rover, a Corvette, a Jaguar, and a new green Cadillac, which Dickey referred to slightingly as his wife's "Jew canoe," soon occupied the driveway.

Local papers heralded Dickey's arrival in Columbia. The managing editor of the *Columbia Record*, Robert McHugh, wrote: "A native Southerner, in some respects Dickey qualifies for the ultimate accolade that one Southern male can bestow upon another—'Good Old Boy.' The genuine 'Good Boy' is inherently well-mannered, puts others at ease, cherishes his family, enjoys the outdoors, works hard at his job, whatever it may be; is tolerant of the faults of others and is not so pure that he isn't above a certain degree of mischief himself. Dickey appears to qualify in all of these respects. If he misses the mark at all, it is because of his urbanity and his occupation."[32] Good ol' boy or not, as at all his other academic posts Dickey quickly gained renown at USC as one of the most unconventional and popular teachers on campus. He taught his standard fare: one course in creative writing and another in modern poetry. He divided English 601—Verse Composition—into two semesters. During the fall he made students write formal verse, and in the spring he made them work on poems inspired by dreams, fantasies, and lies. Following old precedents, he spiced his lectures with ribald anecdotes while enthroned on a desk or table. About such lofty teaching methods, he told one class: "I learned this while teaching at Oxford."[33] Always fascinated by Oxford and Rhodes scholars (he said that the conspiratorial cadets in *Alnilam* were based on Rhodes scholars), he had neither studied nor taught at Oxford himself.

Dickey told an interviewer in Columbia:

A lot of American poets and other writers complain about teaching or having to teach, but I'm one of the ones who *should* be a teacher. Because I *do* enjoy it so much. I like the interplay of the minds, you know? I like to see what the students say, and how they respond to different poets and so on. I think it's very good. There sometimes will come along a student that you don't have the secret for. You can't be all things to all people or all students, but most of them, they're very eager to know whatever it is you want to tell them. And if you like the telling of it, and you like the subject itself, it's a very fortunate way to earn a living, as a writer. I don't feel that they consume my time unnecessarily, in any way. And if I want to curtail my activity with them, I do.[34]

Despite his passion for teaching, along with many other writing professors Dickey maintained that "poetry" was unteachable. He began one class: "Notice the title of this course. . . . It ain't 'POETRY.' You can't teach anybody 'PO-ETRY.' . . . But you sure as hell can teach verse composition. . . . That's why, when I ask you to rhyme, or put so many feet in a line, to construct a couplet—a verse—you'd best damned sure know your basics and demonstrate control of your craft. There's no excuse for sloppy work." Dickey combined rigorous standards with a freewheeling teaching style. As one student, George Redman, put it: "JD is one of the best writing teachers I've encountered, but not . . . in the sense of the 60s touchy-feely school of crammed classrooms, joints, wine and groupies. He's the kind of person who would join you for a beer, let you pay for the bills, and still, if your work didn't stand up on its own legs, hand you the F you deserved."[35] His sudden shifts from good ol' boy to poetic taskmaster evoked surprise as well as respect.

Primed with alcohol, which he regularly began consuming in the morning now, or cold sober, Dickey turned his afternoon classes into riotous affairs. During one, a red-haired student with an open silk shirt and chest glittering with jewelry asked him to explain the difference between the Victorian period and the twentieth century. "I'll tell you, my red fox!" Dickey shouted as he leapt from his desk, eyes wide and saliva frothing on his lips. "I'll tell you what happened to Matthew Arnold and all them fuckin' Victorians! . . . They, and Matthew Arnold, and their whole fuckin' society stepped on a huge SKATE-BOARD!" He made a swishing noise. "And that skateboard was DARWIN!"[36] Dickey's seriousness about teaching was evident in his assignments if not in his asides. His verse composition class stressed using free association and fantasy to provide material for poems and, as the semester progressed, he assigned increasingly difficult forms, moving from epigrams, epitaphs, haiku, couplets, quatrains, ballads, sonnets, and villanelles to sestinas. Students handed in ditto masters of their work, which would then be mimeographed, circulated, and "workshopped." Dickey sometimes treated the verse class like his modern poetry class, resorting to lectures on major and minor poets. According to one of his first students, Jim Mann: "[For] major poets, he'd bring all the books that he had, biographies and critical books and original books, and he would give you a rundown on the biographical facts, and then he'd tell you what he thought of the work, and what other people thought. He'd read from other critics, but he'd also give you his own opinion. What you saw was a literary sensibility with a completeness that almost no other teacher you had would be capable of showing to you. Since it's the sensibility of the greatest moment, for me it was a wonderful exposure to literary life, to literary opinions."[37] After receiving a Ph.D. in 1975, Mann was so enthralled by Dickey's teaching that he continued to audit his courses. Over the next two decades, in between publicizing his Vandalism art movement and teaching in Brazil, Argentina, and France, Mann attended between five and six hundred of Dickey's classes.

Among the other students in Dickey's first class were Franklin Ashley, who later compiled a James Dickey bibliography, and Karen Lindsay, the granddaughter of the eminent poet Vachel Lindsay. With his students, whom he invited to bars and parties at his house, Dickey was both engaging and aloof. Mann observed: "Unlike most teachers he had students pursuing him all of the time. He sort of tried to fend them off. He was curious in the sense that he gave it his all while he was in class, and he seemed interested in individual students, but his behavior there was of a piece with his behavior in life. . . . He paid attention to them while they were there, and when they weren't, he didn't think about them." Dickey's compartmentalized approach sometimes perplexed and upset Mann, as it did other devoted students. When he finally left the university, Mann wrote Dickey numerous letters but never received a response. Mann liked to tell a story he'd heard from Bill Emerson, who also taught at USC, about

Dickey going to a doctor for an EKG and the doctor finding it blank: "[Emerson] didn't mean that Jim was heartless in the sense of cruel, but . . . [that] his affections for other people were more abstract than they were concrete."[38] Distance did not necessarily make his heart grow fonder.

In class, Dickey awed students with his quick, razorlike assessments of their poems. An older student who wrote a creative Ph.D. dissertation under him, Elizabeth Adams, once wrote: "He was a sharp sword cutting out the carelessness, idiocy, and plain bad writing we brought to class. It was a glorious quest in his classes, even when he was hung-over or slightly under the weather and his head fell with an alarming bang on his desk over and over again mid-lecture, with him miraculously awakening after each bang and, not missing a beat, continuing exactly where he had left off."[39] Adams later became one of Dickey's close Columbia friends. At their first lunch, he flirted and teased her with a marriage proposal. They grew closer on the tennis courts, where she always won, a fact that did not prevent him from insisting that he had once played in the U.S. clay court championships.

Dickey's quick judgments of student work were usually gentle, but they could also sting. In one class he picked out a line from a student poem and read it with a grimace: "And do raise their voices in loud amens." He asked mockingly: "Why 'do raise'? Why not just 'raise'?" He grew more vehement: "That word 'do' has no business in there! It is kapok! It makes the reader think the person who wrote this is full of shit! . . . Will you people ever learn to write poetry?"[40] Dickey's friend George Garrett, who taught at USC from 1969 to 1973, remarked: "About half of the people responded very favorably and well. About half of them professed at least to have been injured by the experience. It was one of those things where either you got on the bus or you weren't on it. Everybody, even the closest of the students, the friends that he had, had a story about somebody in the class that had been singled out and injured in some way." Garrett also noticed that Dickey rarely deviated from his teaching routine: "He did the same last class every year which appeared in his organization totally spontaneous." Before he reached the end of his final class he suddenly told his students, "I've taught you all that I can," and cited a passage from Eugen Herrigel's *Zen in the Art of Archery* about masters imparting wisdom to their apprentices. Then he rushed from the room. The students whispered: "He's right on the button this year."[41] Some lampooned Dickey or squirmed under his sharp criticism; others found his emotional openness wholly endearing. The women whose bottoms he liked to pinch or pat rarely complained. Hovering in the background, Maxine controlled him as best she could and rebuked him if he misbehaved.

Dickey hailed his new teaching position as an unmitigated boon. Privately, he offered more sober appraisals. To his son Chris he wrote on March 16, 1969, two months after his first class:

> The students here are pretty good, though a little docile for my taste; it may be that I have had too much exposure to you ever to be satisfied with anyone less intellectually and imaginatively aggressive. However I have one or two promising young writers, including Vachel Lindsay's granddaughter, and at least one very good scholar in the modern poetry class. It

is enjoyable to talk to them, and to put them onto books and writers that previously they had no notion about. It is very nice, also, for *me* to reread these people, to read new material on them, and gradually to work up to some kind of personal relationship with these writers which is higher than the one I had, say, last year. All in all, the University of South Carolina situation is working out for us much better than I ever . . . hoped it would, and we are gradually establishing a kind of life rhythm here that is what we have been working toward all these years.[42]

Preoccupied with teaching and writing, Dickey paid little attention to the bureaucratic workings of the USC English Department. Because he was one of the leading writers of his time, some of his colleagues expressed disappointment that he did not do more to recruit and cultivate talented students. Lowell had acted as a magnet for brilliant students such as Sylvia Plath, Anne Sexton, and George Starbuck. John Berryman had taught Philip Levine and Donald Justice. Roethke had taught Richard Hugo, James Wright, and David Wagoner. John Kimmey, who initiated an MFA in Creative Writing as the graduate director in the 1980s, spoke for many when he said of Dickey:

He supported the program but never was involved in its planning and never did much to develop it, never attending a meeting or helping us get more faculty and funds. What is more he never attracted any very promising students. That was one of the most disappointing aspects of his tenure for me, his failure to draw poets to the university who would make a name for themselves. This is not to say he wasn't a good teacher. He was superb, not only a mesmerizer but also excellent at presenting the basics of poetic composition. And he did turn out students who published. However, he didn't help any I know of get published in major magazines or presses and never did as much as he could have to help a number of them get jobs. In one instance he refused to write a letter for one who did a dissertation under him and who published in *Poetry* and who ended up in a junior college. Then there was the case of a woman who got a poem in *The Paris Review* and when she told him he dismissed it and she was crestfallen.[43]

In 1975 his student Susan Ludvigson had asked Dickey if he wanted to see the poem; he said he would wait until it was published, and not long afterward Ludvigson quit the program.

Dickey did not go out of his way to make friends in the English Department, but he did develop several close ties that remained intact over the following tumultuous years. Matthew Bruccoli, a publisher, bibliographer, and acclaimed biographer of Fitzgerald, Hemingway, John O'Hara, and James Gould Cozzens, became Dickey's literary executor and one of his staunchest advocates. Having arrived from Ohio State during the summer of 1969, Bruccoli met Dickey by chance in the English Department. Later, at a party Bruccoli and his wife, Arlyn, gave at their house, Maxine approached him and said: "I'm going to need a friend and I want you to be that friend." It was through Bruccoli's close friendship with Maxine that he got to know Dickey.

Busy setting up the Center for Editions of American Authors, Bruccoli often dropped by Dickey's house on Sunday afternoons. He revered Dickey's knowledge of books: "James Dickey had the most retentive literary mind I've ever encountered. Drunk or sober, when he talked about literature, I paid attention. Anybody who didn't was a fool. It turned out that we liked many of the same prose writers. Jim would always . . . astonish me by having read some obscure novel that I had read, and I was secretly rather vain about my knowledge of this novel that other people didn't know about. And of course Jim not only knew about it, but he could talk about it with total recall."[44] Because Bruccoli had his own publishing firm, Bruccoli Clark, he and Dickey frequently discussed projects for possible publication. One of the first to materialize was a deluxe limited edition of "Exchanges," Dickey's Harvard Phi Beta Kappa poem. Many others followed. Bruccoli and Dickey also talked about boxers by the hour and occasionally watched middleweight bouts on closed circuit TV at places like the Fairgrounds or Township. Bruccoli was amazed at how easily Dickey shifted from his encyclopedic discourses on books to his redneck conversations about boxing with the rough clientele.

Don Greiner, a scholar of contemporary fiction who eventually became a USC provost, was another of Dickey's early friends. Greiner had begun teaching at USC in 1967, and had first met Dickey when Calhoun Winton introduced them in the spring of 1968. He became more intimately acquainted at a cocktail party that he and his wife, Ellen, held in April 1969. Dickey insisted on pressing his hand on Ellen's stomach for nearly an hour—she was nine months' pregnant with her second child—while discussing the mysteries of birth. Later, drinking beer on the porch with Don, Dickey said: "That's some wife you got." Greiner agreed. To disconcert his host, he added: "I just fucked her back in the house." Greiner tried to deflect the comment with a witty rejoinder: "Well, you're doing better than I have during the last six weeks."[45] Dickey laughed and asked what Greiner was reading. Greiner said he was rereading *Three Soldiers* by John Dos Passos for a class. Dickey began discussing it in meticulous detail. Over the following years Greiner witnessed many more examples of Dickey's baffling oscillations between crude reveler and bookish companion.

Another colleague Dickey befriended was Bernie Dunlap, a Columbia native who had studied at Oxford as a Rhodes scholar and taught at Harvard before returning to Columbia. His first encounter with Dickey was not propitious. Dickey, Maxine, and the Wintons had "crashed" one of his parties. Standing by a bookshelf, Dickey looked down at his host, who was about eight inches shorter, and asked aggressively: "So what are you like?" Dunlap snapped back: "Trumbull Stickney." He could not have chosen a better answer. The two men quickly warmed to each other as they quoted their favorite passages from Stickney's poems. Before he moved on to other guests, Dickey asked: "How old are you?" Dunlap replied that he was thirty-three. Dickey answered: "My God, if I were thirty-three . . . . What I would do!" Dunlap responded: "If I were forty-six, what I would have done!" Both enjoyed the hard-edged banter, although Dunlap later conceded that "being Jim's best friend was a full-time occupation." Over the next two decades, Dunlap consoled him during crises, drove him to football games, and did his best to tolerate his "monstrously egocentric"[46] behavior.

Dickey's new reading fee betrayed his desire to stay in Columbia. Tired of shuttling from one campus to another, he demanded two thousand dollars for a one-hour performance and lashed out at those who expected him to read for anything less. To a woman from the Hollins Alumnae Club of Atlanta who had asked him to speak at a fund-raising dinner for free, he wrote that, as much as he liked Hollins girls, he could no longer honor such requests: "I have now been speaking and reading almost continuously for five years and believe me my dear young lady an offer for dinner, yet another public appearance, a cocktail party, and no money, can hardly be calculated to appeal to me from the standpoint of novelty. You must understand that being away from one's family, that travelling, that being among strangers are exhausting conditions, and that public adulation is more exhausting than any of these. My nominal fee is $2,000 for an hour's public exposure and, though this may be exorbitant, it is the only conceivable conducement, after so many others, that would make me consider anybody's proposal for such further exposure."[47] Instead of maintaining his usual reading schedule, in early 1969 Dickey turned inward—at least for the moment—worked on several books, and developed an obsession with an imaginary illness that would inform his writing for the rest of his life. On February 5 he told his friend Stanley Burnshaw, who had invited him to go to Israel: "I'm not only awfully busy now, but my diabetes has taken a bad turn—mainly through too much drinking to try to calm down from the excitement of so much writing, I think—and I've been advised not to stray too far away from doctors familiar with 'the case.'"[48] Dickey got interested in diabetes because he associated it with blindness, drinking, and the prophetic insight of seers. His son Kevin, who became a doctor, denied that he ever suffered from the disease.

Dickey made himself into a full-fledged diabetic partly to write a poem about the subject early in 1969. In the poem "Diabetes," which appeared in the June issue of Poetry, Dickey worried as much about alcoholism as diabetes since diabetics were not supposed to drink. "I thirsted like a prince / Then like a king / Then like an empire   like a world / On fire," he wrote. Because "firewater" inspired his prophetic "tongue / Of flame" and helped regulate it, he refused to give up drinking. The doctor in the poem wisely recommended "needles [of insulin,] moderation / And exercise." But wisdom and tranquility were not Dickey's goals; they blunted his imagination. So he concluded, "Companion, open that beer,"[49] opting for the prophet's blindness and fiery tongue, even though he knew that drinking might result in alcoholic or diabetic death. Doctors could save his life, he implied, but not make it worth living.

In 1969, Dickey consulted a number of real doctors about his possible diabetes. One doctor hinted that he might have the disease, so Dickey got a second opinion. In July, he informed Burnshaw: "I've just been to yet another doctor . . . [and] he tells me I have no symptoms of diabetes at all. Fancy that! . . . His 'explanation' was that the California doctor examined me when I was twenty pounds or so over my present weight, and such conditions sometimes . . . bring out 'diabetes-like' symptoms."[50] With others, Dickey was less forthright. On May 22, 1970, he wrote his Princeton friend Willard Thorp: "I have just been informed that . . . I am a diabetic."[51] He told Thorp that his doctor had described two kinds of diabetic writers: those like H. G. Wells who took care of themselves and lived into their eighties, and those like Brendan Behan and Dylan Thomas, who were careless and died young. Like his persona in "Diabetes," he said he was drinking a little forbidden bourbon to decide which literary camp he would ultimately join. In mid-June 1970, he sent a more auspicious diagnosis to his friend, the poet Richard Howard: "My own diabetes seems to be all right, or at least it hasn't found a way to bother me yet other than mentally. But that is a plenty bad way, as you may know. Christ, the damn curious disease has made such a hypochondriac of me that I can hardly walk to the door without feeling some new pain, probably having to do with a sugar and a regulatory system I had no notion, four years ago, that I even had."[52] Rather than confront his drinking problem head-on, like so many alcoholics Dickey denied it and diverted his attention to other ailments that didn't exist.

Dickey's phantom illness did little to slow his writing. To James Bexley, he exclaimed: "I have never been so absolutely fanatical about writing as I am at the present time; there doesn't seem to be any end to what I can think up these days; some of it is crazy, some of it is rather classical in form, some of it is like nothing ever heard or seen by God or man before."[53] Having abandoned the relatively tight, mythically shaped narrative poems that had made him famous, Dickey explored a looser style that allowed his rhetorical voice more freedom. He devoted much of the spring to finishing The Eye-Beaters, Blood, Victory, Madness, Buckhead and Mercy, an alliterative title indicative of his new, free-flowing style. The Victorian Jesuit Gerard Manley Hopkins, whom he often discussed in his USC classes, was one model for the poetry's ornate wordplay, wrenched syntax, clanging consonants, alternating line lengths, and oratorical "Ah"s and "O"s. Although Dickey emulated the linguistic fervor of Hopkins's paeans to God and His Creation, the good Jesuit would have been confounded by Dickey's subjects—the whorehouse in "Mercy," Tyree's excremental toilet in "Looking for the Buckhead Boys," the beer-drinking diabetic in "Diabetes," the whiskey-guzzling cancer patient in "The Cancer Match," the snake-tattooed soldier in "Victory," the beheaded dog in "Madness," the children punching their eyes in "The Eye-Beaters." If Dickey harbored doubts about his stylistic experiments, he kept them from his publisher Ken McCormick. He said of his new book: "We have a market such as no American poet has ever had before. . . . We have a great book, I am quite sure. With the two long poems I am now working on, it will be an even greater one, but it is great right now."[54] On May 23, his confidence in the poems soared to new heights. He told McCormick: "We have a chance to do something unparalleled in American publishing, and simply sweep the boards or, as my little boy says, pick up all the marbles."[55] The Pulitzer and Bollingen Awards, he was sure, would fall in his lap once he published Eye-Beaters. McCormick eagerly read the manuscript in the early summer, and while not quite as exultant as Dickey, he responded with enthusiasm on June 16. When the book appeared, few critics echoed Dickey's and McCormick's optimism.

To distract himself from his poetic labors, Dickey reserved as much time as possible for his guitar playing. In February, he asked his Portland friend, John Ullman, to send tapes of Ron Brentano and Ry Cooder so he would have new guitar music to practice. To satisfy his craving for the biggest and best, he asked Roy Noble of Custom Guitars in California to make him a twelve-string Doc Watson–style guitar. Noble began in March, and in mid-May sent him a $580 guitar. On July 31, Dickey congratulated Noble on his handiwork; it was the best guitar he had ever played. He had to have another one, which Noble duly supplied in October for $588.15. The new guitar, however, only whetted his appetite for another, which he soon ordered. Like sextants and bows, guitars became Dickey's toys, and he took a boyish delight in collecting them.

Dickey left his typewriters, which he had installed around his house so he could work on different projects simultaneously, to read at the University of Alabama mainly because a friend from his Leesburg days, the young poet James Seay, taught there. Seay picked up Dickey at the Tuscaloosa airport, and on the way to the motel listened to Dickey's stories about preflight training at Maxwell Field in Montgomery. Dickey described "war games" in which bombers tried to hit soldiers on the ground with sacks of flour. One of the first planes to fly over hit him, he said, so he had to join the other "losers" in the "dead and wounded" area. Seay told Dickey that his reminiscence would make a good poem, especially if he used the flour to suggest rising and resurrection. Seay even gave him a phrase: "self-rising flour." As soon as he got to his motel, Dickey started writing the poem that would become "Haunting the Maneuvers." At the reading that night he told Seay: "I'll be indebted to you for the rest of my life. But what kind of flour was it? Self-rising flour?"[56] In the final poem, which he published in Strength of Fields, he changed the location from Alabama to Louisiana and stressed the absurdity of the war game, but preserved the phrase "self-rising."

In Washington, D.C., Dickey had regularly neglected his family for his many duties inside and outside the library. Now he tried to get more directly involved. One of the ways he did so was by meddling in Chris's love life. Chris had entered the University of Virginia in the fall of 1968. During his second semester, while Chris dated another student, Page Allen, his father wrote Page:

> You ask about Chris, and I can only say that he is the most perplexing and rewarding son that any human being ever had the difficulty and glory of trying to raise. But I can say this much; he seems to be taking hold at Virginia very well. His grades are good, and he is hatching a good many projects of his own which will, I don't doubt, have a strong effect on the University. He is a born agitator, which is all right; but he must develope [sic] the will to get the practical details of agitation into the game. Otherwise he is just talking and not doing. Chris is a brilliant boy, but is impatient of details, and details are the name of the game in politics, or in literature, or in love. I don't know what lies in store for you and Chris; maybe everything, maybe nothing. But I do know that Chris needs a real woman to stand with him and, if necessary, to give it right back to him. In some ways his maturity is frightening, and the maturity of the woman to match his must be available. Chris has never been tolerant of girls that desolve [sic] into tears and throw themselves on the floor kicking their feet like children. This is not to say that you are likely to do this, but if you feel

so inclined do it with someone else and not Chris. He needs a steady hand, a good companion and an equal. He is not an easy person to live with; but then, neither have I ever been. I demand a lot of myself, and a lot of Chris; and he demands, in turn, a lot of those whom he associates with. Virginia girls, some of them, are likely to be delicate flowers, full of the Old South and fainting spells and tantrums. With such a girl Chris would be inclined simply to walk away, or to use the reverse side of a hair brush where he was convinced it would do them the most good. But probably he would walk away, and seek out someone who would match him rather than solicit his distainful [sic] protection.[57]

In his advice about Chris, Dickey may have been recalling his own early vacillations between the sophisticated, tempestuous Gwen Leege and the tough, down-to-earth Maxine. He implied that Page Allen needed to be another Maxine to handle his son.

On March 16, Dickey wrote Chris another of his long, rambling letters, but mentioned nothing about Allen. He concentrated on Chris's career and what they might do together to augment it. For starters, he hoped they could get together in July at Cape Kennedy to cover the moon shot. William F. Buckley planned to rent a motel to accommodate a number of guests, including the Dickeys. Worried about Chris living in Washington, D.C. (Chris hoped to get a job as a photographer for *National Geographic*), his father offered to pay gas expenses so he could commute from a safe suburb. The city, Dickey said, was a "shakey place" because of all the crime. He encouraged Chris in his journalism plans, but wanted to know exactly what they were (in the end Chris didn't work for *National Geographic*). To avoid any hard feelings, he wanted Chris to know that he bore "the greatest love in the world, and the greatest admiration"[58] for him.

Dickey also hoped that some of his *Time* friends could help his son get started in journalism. To demonstrate his influence at the magazine, he told Chris about a recent meeting with *Time* writer Larry Du Bois: "It looks now as though *Time* will do the cover story on me sometime next winter, if all goes well."[59] If Dickey wanted to convince *Time* of his suitability for its cover when he visited New York earlier in the year, he went about it in an odd way. At a lunch hosted by Peter Martin at a posh restaurant, the Ginger Man, Dickey drank and caroused as usual. Martin had arranged the lunch mainly to introduce one of his friends, William F. Buckley, to his other two friends, Dickey and Willie Morris. Martin also invited colleagues Stefan Kanfer and Ted Kalem. Although Dickey and Buckley had corresponded in the past, they hardly knew each other. (Ideologically, they shared certain conservative positions; Dickey once told Buckley: "I don't know your specific position on *all* things, but you may be sure that on the main thrust of life and ideas, we are pretty close.")[60] According to Martin, the lunch was a fiasco:

At one point, Jim loudly said to Willie (in a spirit of heavy-handed fun, and in his heaviest deep-South accent, and to stir up a bit of action, and to emphasize the fact that two Southern Crackers were having lunch in a

New York bistro), "There seem to be a lot of Jew-boys in this restaurant." And Willie answered, in a higher-pitched version of the same voice, "There sure are. I wonder, can any of them fight?" Our table was quite close to the bar, and he might have gotten some response—which, as host, I surely didn't want. Bill Buckley was obviously embarrassed (which may have been one of the points of the game) . . . so I intervened and told them that I had been to a Southern School, knew Southern-boy games when I saw them, and told them to stop playing. They did, for a while, but then raised their voices in a mock quarrel and Jim announced, loudly, "Let's step outside and settle this," scraping his chair on the floor and starting to get up. I again told them to cool it, and after that Jim's energy flagged, and the broadside humor stopped.[61]

Buckley, who was not averse to pranks, sat in stunned silence before the uproarious Southerners.

Dickey's routine in the Ginger Man lost its comic edge. In a drawl made thick by numerous martinis, he snarled: "If there's anything I can't stand in the world it's a Southern Black."[62] Buckley cringed and dropped his head. Perhaps sensing that his remarks were unappreciated, Dickey announced halfway through his meal that he had to go see his publisher, Doubleday. Without further ado, he got up and walked out the door. If Dickey had broached the possibility of a *Time* cover story before his abrupt exit, Martin would have disregarded it with a laugh. Martin remarked: "I'm sure *Time* never had any plan to put Dickey on the cover; this sounds like one of Dickey's dream desires (of which he had plenty), but the only way he would have got on the cover would have been through a smash success of *Deliverance*, the movie, and although it succeeded it didn't succeed that well. . . . I was then senior editor of the Press section . . . as well as the Cinema, Theater and Show Business Sections, and all cover stories in those areas would have had to be 'sold' to me by one of the writers, and I would then have had to re-sell it to Managing Editor Henry Grunwald. This didn't happen."[63] Despite the futility of his cover story dream—a dream kept alive by Larry Du Bois—Dickey refused to relinquish it. On March 4, 1971, he wrote Ken McCormick: "Peter Bird Martin, Managing Editor of Time, wants me to get together with him and Kurt Vonnegut on March 9th . . . for I think he means to do a cover story on the both of us."[64] Martin, who was not the managing editor, had written Dickey on February 25 about introducing the two writers, and brought them together at New York's Pavilion restaurant without ever discussing a plan for a cover story.

At Doubleday, Dickey may have spoken with one of Morris's close friends, editor Herman Gollob, who would later serve as an important advocate for *Alnilam*. A Texan, Gollob admired Dickey's literary sophistication and his rambunctious Southern wit. He often accompanied Dickey to New York bars, and remembered how Dickey aggravated almost everyone with his sexual clutching and flirting. Gollob, who was Jewish, found his preoccupation with Jewishness bothersome and tried to ignore it (Dickey insisted on calling him "the Texas Jew"). Despite his slurs, which he expressed jokingly, Dickey wanted to make sure that Gollob believed that he and his friends like William F. Buckley were not anti-Semitic. Once he told Gollob flatly: "You don't like William F. Buckley because you think he's anti-Semitic. Well, he's not."[65] He then delivered a half-hour sermon on why Buckley was not anti-Semitic.

At a time when some of Dickey's idols, like Ezra Pound, were renouncing their anti-Semitism, Dickey continued to make sardonic remarks about Jews. Dickey knew of Pound's recantation because James Laughlin had written him about it in the fall of 1968. Depressed about his many blunders, Pound had taken a vow of virtual silence. In letters he wrote the novelist Fred Exley in 1969, Dickey showed no signs of taking such a vow. He spoke contemptuously of New York Jews and the way they conspired to control the literary establishment, especially the awards meted out to writers. The fact that Dickey regularly served on many of the prestigious prize committees, such as those awarding Pulitzers and National Book Awards, did little to diminish his theory of conspiring Jews. In fact, when he wrote Exley, he was serving on the Advisory Committee for Rockefeller Fellowships, and promised to do all he could to obtain a fellowship for Exley.

In mid-March, Dickey met Morris for a less inflammatory talk than the one at the Ginger Man, although it, too, culminated in rowdiness. Morris, who was in the middle of a painful divorce, called Dickey and asked if they could meet at the Saint Moritz bar. Dickey replied: "Will, I am deeply honored that you have called up in your mental suffering, to talk to your buddy Jimbo." Dickey already considered himself one of Morris's closest friends; the only other person to call him "Will" was William Styron. At the bar they drank martinis and ruminated about human suffering, Dickey dwelling on his months in the South Pacific as a fighter pilot and Morris on his divorce and difficult job at *Harper's*. Before long they began quoting Yeats and Tennyson. As if secretly alluding to his tall tales about the war, Dickey told Morris never to forget that the historic function of writers was to be entertainers. As their voices grew louder and Dickey recited his own poetry, the maître d' walked toward them and said: "I want you gentlemen out of here." Feigning incredulity, Dickey blurted: "Pardon me?" The maître d' repeated his command: "I want you gentlemen out of here." Undaunted, Dickey retorted: "Do you know that you are talking to one of the greatest poets in America and the editor of *Harper's?*" Unimpressed, the maître d' pointed toward the door and shouted: "Out!"[66] The two writers obeyed.

In his March 16 letter to Chris, Dickey said Morris blamed his marital problems on his wife's psychoanalyst. Always suspicious of "head-shrinkers," Dickey sympathized with Morris's belief that the therapist had little more acumen than a medieval sorcerer: "Together, in the bar of the Saint Moritz, he and I composed a letter, half horrific and half serial comic, to this man, in which Willie poured out all his grievances in a flood of vindicative [sic] which would make *Portnoy's Complaint* seem like the complaint of a kindergarten student. It was really amazing how much invective I could come up with to visit on someone I had never even met, but who, to me, represents one of the worst and most foul of the Twentieth Century scientific elements, as it impinges on the consciousness of a vulnerable human being."[67] When Dickey's second wife badly needed counseling, his prejudice would have damaging effects. Friendly consolation in a bar was all the psychotherapy anyone needed, according to Dickey, who would soon be providing more of it in May 1971 after Morris was fired from *Harper's*.

During the spring of 1969, Dickey consented to read at the University of Tennessee, The Academy of American Poets, Davidson College, Armstrong State College, and Sweet Briar College, but at times his contempt for those who induced him to leave home proved uncontrollable. Aware that his alcoholic behavior deeply offended some of his hosts, he complained to journalists like Lee Simowitz at the *Atlanta Journal* that too much attention was being paid to his life. His furies, of course, attracted journalists even while intending to drive them and everyone else away. This *sturm und drang* was most noticeable when he read at Sweet Briar in western Virginia on May 2, 1969. As usual, a bibulous Dickey enthralled his audience, which included almost the entire student body of five hundred. His host, William Smart, applauded with the rest, although he had seen Dickey read before and realized that every ad-lib remark, every story, every joke was part of a well-rehearsed repertoire. Dickey paused, as usual, to savor his line "the parking lot of the dead" in "Cherrylog Road," commenting: "My, I like that line." The audience laughed. The tone of the reading changed abruptly, however, when Henry Taylor, who had driven to Sweet Briar, asked Dickey to read a certain poem. Dickey lashed out with unexpected crudity, accusing Taylor of being one of "the biggest fucking imitators of his work" and ordering him to go "shit in his pants."[68] Stunned by the rebuke, Smart and others in the audience—never mind Taylor—fell silent. For the rest of the night Smart watched Dickey turn his charm on and off like a faucet.

Earlier in the day Dickey had laughed and played the guitar on Smart's front porch for the three young children of Paul and Celia Mathews, who had traveled from Pennsylvania to hear Dickey read. Smart had invited Paul and Celia to a dinner party because Paul had recently introduced Smart to Dickey's poetry. Unbeknownst to Smart, Dickey had prowled the campus for women, and took the liberty of inviting a female professor and a student. Smart surmised that Dickey intended to bring at least one of them back to his hotel that night. Fortunately, Peter and Eleanor Taylor joined them at dinner; in their presence Dickey was polite. In fact, he dazzled everyone with his recitations of poems by Ernest Dowson and A. E. Housman. Eleanor had known only one other poet who could recite poems like Dickey, and that was Robert Frost. Unlike Frost, Dickey drank steadily and, as soon as the Taylors left, reverted to his adolescent locker-room talk. "Now that the grown-ups have left," he slurred mischievously, "we can pull our pants down and whip our dicks out." Realizing the evening was quickly slipping into chaos, Smart proposed driving Dickey to his hotel. Dickey agreed; he couldn't wait to leave the "bunch of wimps" at the dinner. From the backseat he kept up a steady barrage of invective. "Slow down, pilot,"[69] he growled when Smart, eager to get rid of his guest, accelerated to fifty miles per hour. At the door of his hotel room, Dickey prodded Smart's chest with his finger and threatened to fight. Smart quickly returned to his car.

Humiliated and angered by Dickey's conduct, Smart still planned to go ahead with a picnic he had arranged for the following day. His wife and guests convinced him to cancel. His wife recounted how Dickey had followed her to the kitchen during dinner and propositioned her. She said she had kicked Dickey in the shins. Smart heard a similar story from Celia Mathews: Dickey had prodded her to ditch her husband for the night and follow him back to his hotel.

Disgusted by what had happened, Smart phoned Dickey the next morning and told him he could find his way to the airport by himself.

In hindsight, Smart attributed some of Dickey's outbursts to the low fee Sweet Briar paid him. Dickey had asked for two thousand dollars; Smart could only requisition eight hundred dollars from the college. Dickey also resented that his nemesis, Robert Bly, had preceded him at Sweet Briar by only a few weeks. Once he had scandalized a host, Dickey tended to be remorseful and better behaved, which was the case at most of his other college readings in the spring. The most significant of these was at a writers' conference at West Virginia University in June. The director having refused to greet Dickey at the airport, English professor Lloyd Davis drove him to the campus. If Dickey worried about his drunken outbursts at Sweet Briar, he channeled his angst into stories about his diabetes and insulin injections (he also told Davis a far-fetched story about his close friendship with guitar great Rev. Gary Davis). Those like the conference director who had expected Dickey to upset his audience were pleasantly surprised. Dickey gave a rousing performance and socialized cordially at a reception where, among other things, he expressed his fears that the astronauts on the upcoming Apollo 11 mission might sink in the moon's dust until they suffocated.

Over the next few days Dickey found relief from his demons by falling in love with a writing student in his workshop named Marie Tyler McGraw. McGraw, whose life was in turmoil, had just moved back to Morgantown after teaching three years at a black college, West Virginia State. Her politician husband had lost his job, and her marriage was in disarray. To make himself more appealing to McGraw, whose roots were in West Virginia, Dickey led her to believe that he came from a "working-class, rural, hardscrabble, Anglo-ethnic background." He waxed nostalgic about "the good ol' country girls" of his youth and their uninhibited ways. He made his Georgia-cracker persona more credible by periodically uttering bitter remarks about "niggers" and Jews. "I'm a Southerner," he once said. "I never got anything out of those New York Jews. I don't have to kiss up to them." He owed a lot, of course, to "New York Jews" like Howard Moss. He told McGraw a story about getting together with Styron on Martha's Vineyard to talk about what "those niggers" had said in a collection of responses to *The Confessions of Nat Turner.* McGraw observed: "His social conscience was not highly developed in the sixties and seventies."[70] Liberal in her political views and artistic tastes (she was debating whether to go to Woodstock at the time), McGraw ignored Dickey's obnoxious remarks and basked in his attention. With a job, two daughters, and a tottering marriage, she needed romantic solace, which Dickey happily supplied. Charmed by the noble sound of their names—Marie Antoinette and James Lafayette—she also shared Dickey's passion for country music and sang with him as he played the guitar. Because she had little tolerance for heavy drinkers, Dickey moderated his consumption in her company. If he griped about Maxine—her obesity, her spendthrift shopping habits, her philistine ways—she tried to redirect the conversation. She enjoyed the fantasy of amorous bliss that Dickey spun around her. He proposed to marry her many times. Only later, as a historian of American culture, did she think of

Dickey as a "Faux Bubba," a false good ol' boy, who manipulated her with sentimental lies.

Unable or unwilling to differentiate between delusion and reality, Dickey seemed better able to control the mood swings that incapacitated some of his peers. Intrigued by the bipolar illnesses of Lowell, Jarrell, Roethke, Berryman, Plath, Sexton, and others, he also scorned those poets who blazed like meteors and burned out just as quickly. "My father was a kind of dilettante of madness. I don't think my father was mad at all. . . . He was playing with madness a lot of the time,"[71] his son Chris contended. Asked why there was so much scandal and violence in his writings, Dickey bluntly stated: "Because I'm a coward. I can do things in what I write that I can't do as a person."[72] If he periodically acted the mad, bad, alcoholic artist on road trips, he only occasionally exhibited the sort of violence associated with mania at USC. Returning home, he tried to make amends for the sins he had committed abroad. On May 21, for instance, he implored Smart to forgive and forget: "Write it off to exhaustion, alcohol, and to the terrible kind of traffic and travel hysteria that sets in [on these occasions]."[73] He was similarly contrite in a letter to Elizabeth Janeway, a writer and officer in the Author's League. Dickey had attended a party at her house after his Academy of American Poets reading in New York on March 24, 1969, and offended some of the guests with his usual combination of biting insults and crude insinuations. One of the people he attacked was Janeway's friend Senator Hartke, whom Dickey had known in Washington. He lectured Hartke on the faults of the president and Congress. Politicians were all alike, he said; they had no concern for other people; they were all out for themselves. Trying to be gentlemanly, Hartke said he was sorry Dickey felt that way about his government. He attributed Dickey's tirade to too much whiskey. On May 22, Dickey wrote one of his typical apologies to Janeway: "It is just that the Demon of the Perverse gets on my shoulders every now and then, and in that case it seemed to have been in your very gracious house. . . . The monster appears . . . usually with a bottle, and I hardly know what to do with him myself, and never know how to explain him."[74] Dickey was alluding to Poe's story "The Imp of the Perverse," and blaming his disruptiveness on what Poe called the tendency to do wrong simply for the sake of doing wrong. Dickey's imp, like Poe's, usually resided in a bottle.

23. To the Moon and Hollywood (1969)

The year 1969 was one of great expectations, as Dickey revised *Deliverance*, prepared the poems soon to appear in *The Eye-Beaters*, flirted with Hollywood filmmakers, and once again fixated on the quest for the moon. Dining and singing with William F. Buckley on February 27, 1969, at Buckley's parents' house in Camden, South Carolina, Dickey made plans for attending the historic Apollo 11 moon shot, which was scheduled for July. Buckley was charmed by Dickey's "enormous presence,"[1] which seemed to emanate as much from his intellect as from his natural vigor. Buckley had made reservations at the Beach Park Motel in Cocoa Beach, Florida, for a group of literary people and friends, including Dr. and Mrs. John Converse—the former Mrs. Gary "Rocky" Cooper, a woman Dickey socialized with in New York. In July, Dickey joined Michael Allin (as a graduate present Dickey had promised Allin—and then forgotten to deliver—a pass to the launch) and the rest of his family in Florida. Along with one million others, Dickey rose with keen anticipation on July 16 to watch Apollo 11 blast off for the moon. Former President Lyndon Johnson waited expectantly, as did Vice President Spiro Agnew. Diplomats, literati, surfers, hippies, movie stars, scientists, and ordinary citizens gathered to behold the historic flight. Standing next to Mrs. Converse in an area cordoned off for VIPs, Dickey marveled at the 363-foot-tall rocket, perched like a huge white candle against the brightening dawn. According to schedule, the Saturn V rocket ignited at 9:32 A.M. A flock of sea birds flapped from the water near the launchpad. The blaze and tremors were so powerful that people covered their eyes and fell to the ground. In a matter of seconds the rocket thundered through the warm morning air and disappeared. As Rocky Converse, an avid photographer, snapped pictures with her camera, Dickey muttered in annoyance: "For God's sake, just look at it!"[2] Asked by a reporter for his reaction, Buckley said he beheld the launch in awestruck silence. Dickey said the same thing; he doubted he could find words commensurate with such an event.

Several years later, speaking to Buckley on *Firing Line* about the significance of Apollo 11, Dickey was less ready to condemn representations of the moon shot: "I think one of the most important things that came of the business of men going out from the earth and . . . orbiting the moon or landing on the moon, is that they brought back these photographs showing the earth against its background of eternal blackness: the void. We realize that we don't have infinite resources, and we can't plunder and exploit just at will any more."[3] Images of the small, vulnerable "blue planet" drifting through the abyss afforded a message that was as ecological as it was mystical. Like so many of the heroes in Dickey's poems and novels, the astronauts had to leave Earth before they could truly find it.

Faithful to his belief that writing depended on fantasy more than fact, Dickey wrote his poem about Armstrong's and Aldrin's strolls on the moon before they actually occurred (*Life* published "The Moon Ground" on July 4, 1969). Because he too wanted to go to the moon, as his son Chris indicated in a ferocious argument with Buckley's wife about the possibility of NASA replacing Armstrong with his father, Dickey assumed the persona of an astronaut and, in his medley of folksy and philosophical voices, made the astronaut sound like himself. "Buddy, / We have brought the gods," Dickey writes, pretending to speak for one of the two men on the lunar surface. The "gods" are the gods of technology in the spacecraft that bears an ancient god's name—Apollo. In his attempt to depict the "godliness" of the first human encounter with the moon's "magic ground," Dickey teeters between sublimity and bathos. Michael Collins, who orbited the moon in the command ship, sounds more like Dickey's friend Robert Penn Warren reflecting on time than an actual astronaut. As the speaker worries that his moon rocks might carry a "moon-plague" back to Earth, his sentiments for "the blue planet" and for his fellow astronauts reach a lachrymose climax:

"O brother! Earth-faced god! APOLLO! My eyes blind / With unreachable tears   my breath goes all over / Me and cannot escape."[4] Fortunately, he remembers that he is on the moon to pick up stones and not to pontificate about time or weep about the Earth's fate. Although Dickey deployed a new stylistic design for his poem—he centered the lines so that they seemed to hang from an invisible pole in the middle of the page—he sometimes lapsed into his old penchant for grandiloquence.

In addition to reading "The Moon Ground" at the Time-Life offices in mid-July—he was supposed to read the very day Armstrong and Aldrin walked on the moon—Dickey officiated at an awards ceremony for a Time-Life poetry contest. Hal Crowther, a former Columbia journalism student working as an intern under Peter Martin, had organized the contest for the company's weekly newspaper *F.Y.I.*; its advisor, Tom Flaherty, had convinced Dickey to judge the contest. Among the three thousand poems submitted by company employees, Dickey chose one by Susan Mitchell for first prize. A Columbia graduate student and *Time* copy editor, Mitchell had never had a poem celebrated in such a way by a major poet. According to Crowther, who was in the audience when Dickey read and spoke about the winning poems: "Joy reigned through Dickey's reading of Susan's poem. I wanted these New Yorkers to hear a true poet read in the drawl they associate with George Wallace and Lester Maddox. Dickey was superb, but I noticed that his bottle of Jack Daniel's was half empty. The whiskey was below the label when he said something sexually explicit—menacing, actually—to the prizewinner."[5] Before the awards speech, Dickey had shaken hands with Mitchell and exclaimed in a resonant Southern accent: "Miss Mitchell, you're a wonderful, wonderful poet."[6] During his awards speech Dickey repeated his testimonial.

Dickey kept gulping whiskey, and as the alcohol disappeared, so did Dickey's Southern charm. When an editor thanked Dickey for awarding his poem an honorable mention, Dickey looked at him with steely eyes and snapped: "Your poem was shit." Another prizewinner flirted with Dickey, and he berated her for being insincere. Mitchell recalled:

His conversation began to move on five different tracks, switching back and forth, somehow managing to make progress on all of them. Track 1 was my poem and his praise for it. Track 2 was a film that he wanted to make. He never mentioned a title, but I suspect it was the beginnings of *Deliverance*. Track 3 was his obsession with King Kong. He was passionate about King Kong films. Track 4 was sexual, after his fashion. "Have you ever had a brutal beating?" he asked me. This eventually moved up a notch to, "Would you want a brutal beating?" Track 5 was his interest in poems he had written to honor the astronauts. He was supposed to record them at Channel Five later that afternoon. Dickey kept switching back and forth between these different tracks just as one would in a poem with several narratives.[7]

Mitchell was more intrigued than horrified. She tried to keep her poise, although Crowther watched her face grow ashen after Dickey suggested the sadoerotic beating. Years later, having established a career as a distinguished poet (her second book of poems, *Rapture*, received the first Kingsley Tufts Poetry Award and was a National Book Award finalist), she echoed many other young poets when she said that Dickey, in his unconventional way, had given her the courage to believe in herself as a poet.

As senior editors and executives retreated from the melee in the reception room, the increasingly combative Dickey prodded the bigger men to fight. He kept pushing the 6'3", 260-pound ex-football player Crowther until he agreed. At twenty-two, Crowther thought of Dickey as an "old man" who would be too weak to wrestle. Sensing Crowther's reluctance, Dickey emptied his bottle of Jack Daniel's and seized his younger opponent in a headlock, squeezing Crowther's head so fiercely that he nearly passed out. Dickey convinced other muscular partiers to arm wrestle on the floor, usually beating them. Fearing Dickey might hurt himself or someone else, Crowther coaxed him toward the elevator, where he slurred to a black copy girl: "I see this elevator has been ineffectively segregated."[8] At the network building where he was supposed to record his moon poem, he kept up his insulting diatribe. Deeply mortified, Crowther left his charge as quickly as possible. Over his shoulder he could see Dickey pushing back people who rushed out to meet him and shouting that he didn't want to be touched by any Jews. Crowther wondered if booze was entirely to blame for Dickey's malevolent conduct. Later he doubted it was. In the early 1980s, during a visit to Columbia, Crowther heard Dickey say that he derived something akin to sexual pleasure from feeling his son's body contort with frustration and pain when they wrestled. Although he loved his son (he must have been referring to Kevin), he admitted that he always wanted to dominate. As for his abusiveness surrounding the awards ceremony at Time-Life, Dickey said he remembered none of it.

Dickey got a chance to read "The Moon Ground" on a more sober occasion and to the astronauts themselves when the president of Marquette University invited him to a black-tie dinner honoring the Apollo 11 crew. Marquette was celebrating the three hundredth anniversary of their eponymous hero's exploration of the Mississippi River by presenting the first Père Marquette Discovery Award Medals to the astronauts. On November 8, 1969, the day Dickey read his poem in Milwaukee, thousands of people lined the city's streets to throw confetti and cheer the astronauts' motorcade. At the dinner, Aldrin compared their journey to Marquette's. Perhaps because of their flagging spirits—the astronauts were tired from their thirty-seven-day world tour—Dickey got little opportunity to talk to them, but he did read his poem, introducing it by pointing out that he had finished it before the astronauts had finished their flight. "I'm sure it will come as a surprise to the crew of Apollo 11 that this is what they thought,"[9] he said to a chorus of laughs. As at his previous encounters with Apollo astronauts, Dickey made little impression on the men he so admired. Reflecting on the event, Neil Armstrong recalled Dickey's distinctive accent, but nothing more about him.

A summer of traveling, drinking, and writing sapped Dickey's formidable energy. Near the end of August, he told Herman Wouk, who had hoped to accompany him to the Bohemian Grove, that he "was absolutely prostrated and devastated by the exigencies of the past few months."[10] In another halfhearted attempt to cut back on his readings and make the few he performed more profitable, he raised his fee to three thousand dollars per hour. His helter-skelter life had made him more quarrelsome, especially with those poets he considered potential rivals. When a jobless Galway Kinnell, who shared many of Robert Bly's poetic and political ideals, asked Dickey to arrange a reading for him at USC, Dickey replied gruffly: "Stop hanging around with Bly. He's a loser, and he'll make one out of you if you let him. He'd like nothing better."[11] To the editor of the *Tennessee Poetry Journal*, Stephen Mooney, who asked Dickey to contribute to a special issue of essays on Bly by Southern writers, Dickey replied testily: "Dear Mr. Mooney: You asked me my opinion of Mr. Bly's work. I authorize a one-word statement, and that is—Pitiful."[12] In the same journal Louis Simpson claimed that Bly was a poet from whom greatness could be expected. Simpson would soon become one of Dickey's principal targets. Dickey blasted Donald Hall as well. In a letter to Jim Applewhite, who had been involved in a recent altercation with Hall, Dickey growled: "I knew Don for a long time—he was one of my first editors—and I have never seen a person decline so badly as he has done. But then there was nothing much to decline from, so maybe his present low state is not so much of a surprise after all."[13] Hall's poetic "decline" was really a development away from an early Audenesque formalism toward a freer, more surrealistic style advocated by his close friend Bly.

As Dickey's life became more frenzied during the tumultuous sixties, he never wholly relinquished his pose as a well-mannered man of letters. He played up his conservative values to Eric Fiedler, who asked Dickey to act on behalf of another poet arrested for marijuana possession, car theft, and burglary: "I am, God save the mark, rather a clean-liver, and take a very dim view indeed of drugs, drug users, and drug peddlers. This stamps me, I guess, very much as a square; that, I am very happy to be."[14] If he attacked all poetic rabble-rousers from Bly to Ginsberg to Olson, he simultaneously aligned himself with poets known for their formal mastery and personal civility. In late July, as a judge on the Pulitzer Prize committee, he sent a flattering letter to Richard Wilbur, who perhaps more than any other poet represented gentlemanly decorum in verse and manner: "I have just received your new book as part of the material for judging the next Pulitzer Prizes (I expect this part of it should be kept quiet). But I just wanted to tell you how good it is; it is the kind of writing that I have always wanted for you."[15] He continued in this vein by denigrating a harsh review of Wilbur's poetry in the *Washington Post*. Recently Dickey had written with brotherly affection about "the really extraordinary closeness I have come to feel for you personally, though I have only seen you twice. I don't know exactly how to account for this, but it is there. I won't go on and on about it, but just register it. . . . I feel closer to you, *personally*, than to any other poet alive."[16] In the journal entries published in *Sorties* in 1970, the Janus-faced Dickey was not so complimentary. With regard to Wilbur's habitual use of poetic form, he said: "That is the wrong way to get a poem to behave."[17] Despite his kind words to formalists like Wilbur, Nemerov, Merrill, and Richard Howard (whom Dickey chose for the Pulitzer Prize), Dickey was as ambivalent toward formal conventions in poetry as in life.

Preoccupied with stylistic innovations that would do justice to his restless imagination and his restless times, Dickey returned to Hart Crane as a possible model, no doubt because Crane could be formal and frenzied at once. Crane's word wizardry enthralled Dickey, as did his self-destructive lifestyle (Crane eventually leapt from a ship and drowned). Crane was a largely self-taught genius whose alcoholism and reckless libido, like Dickey's, often got him in trouble. His love affairs were mostly homosexual, which seemed to increase rather than diminish Dickey's interest in him. Near the end of the 1969 summer, Dickey plunged into a new biography of Crane by John Unterecker, a Columbia University professor, and in mid-September wrote the author: "I was absolutely enraptured by the book, and hope to read it many times during the next years. I have not been so caught up in a poet's—or a human being's—life since my initial fascination with John Keats. Crane was a marvelous, that is to say miraculous, human being. . . . My own life, in some ways so much like Crane's and in some others utterly unlike it, is uncommonly enriched and broadened by the enormous and intelligent work you have done."[18] Dickey endorsed Crane's weltanschauung, and sympathized with his arduous struggle to write more affirmative poems than those in the bleak Waste Land mode made fashionable by T. S. Eliot. Dickey also sympathized with Crane's personal struggle between Apollonian and Dionysian polarities of order and ecstasy, reason and passion. Dickey told many friends and students over the years that Unterecker's Voyager: A Life of Hart Crane was his favorite biography, although sometimes he reserved those laurels for Philip Horton's earlier Crane biography.

In the journal Dickey kept at the time, a more qualified view of Crane emerged. While Dickey acknowledged that Crane's highly wrought figurative language might guide his current attempts to get beyond his "anecdote poems,"[19] what bothered him about Crane was his artificiality, his aestheticism. What also bothered him was his self-destructiveness. Dickey admitted that he had emulated Crane's bacchanalian excesses: "I have been drunk, more or less, for about the last twenty five years. Everything I remember is colored at least to some extent by alcohol." Even so, he impugned his and Crane's alcoholism: "I am sick of the petty wildness and the phony ecstasy of drinking." He also claimed to be sick of Crane-like licentiousness: "Which one of us does not want to be delivered from sex?" At one point, comparing Crane's superhuman capacity for alcohol to his own, he conceded: "I am not really a very good madman. I guess I will last longer that way. Or I hope so, at any rate."[20] Dickey did last longer, although his Dionysian ways in the end hastened his demise.

Pondering Crane's life, Dickey considered taking up the cudgels against Louis Simpson, who had criticized both Crane and the Unterecker biography in a recent review. Dickey wrote in his journal that he "would surely win without as much trouble as might be gone to, were the opponent better."[21] To friends he pilloried Simpson's condescending remarks about Unterecker's book. He wrote Peter Neumeyer that Simpson's review had been "appallingly bad" and "appallingly arrogant in its badness," adding: "When a man of Simpson's ordinariness of mind talks about Crane and his supposed inability to get his ideas straight . . . one simply wants to kick Simpson's ass." Crane, according to

Dickey, "had one of the most vivid, incisive, volatile and above all *original* minds that have ever been concerned with poetry."[22] If Crane's ideas had been disorderly, so be it.

In his search for signposts to guide his new poetic style, Dickey consulted another volatile, original, self-destructive poet, Winfield Townley Scott, who had committed suicide in 1968. Dickey pored over his posthumously published notebooks and also corresponded with Scott Donaldson, who was writing Scott's biography. What Dickey found particularly relevant to his current aesthetic dilemmas was a distinction Scott had made between "plain language" and "magic language." His tirades against Frost notwithstanding, Dickey, like Scott, was attracted to the "plain" Robert Frosts and Edwin Arlington Robinsons as well as the "magic" Hart Cranes and Dylan Thomases. For the time being, Dickey vowed to follow the latter. He never renounced plain speech entirely, however, even though his phrasing and syntax became more idiosyncratic. What he avoided was the narrative story line that had given his poems fluidity, archetypal resonance, and popular appeal.

During the fall of 1969, Dickey juggled his USC teaching and his usual array of projects, chief among them a film about his life and writing sponsored by the Encyclopedia Britannica. The director, Stanley Croner, had asked him to help organize the cast, which he was glad to do; he dispatched a letter to Robert Lowell, asking him to meet in New York on November 21 for a "short conversation—for the benefit of the Generations to Come."[23] Wary of Lowell's current poetic tastes and antiwar activism, Dickey nevertheless wanted someone of Lowell's stature to give his film credibility (he contacted Norman Mailer and several other writers, too). Lowell was amenable: "I guess if the thing can be done painlessly and freely—without rehearsing, redoing, standing around in the studio while something else is on. These things are death, they fill the swill pail with chafed flesh and nerve. Still, you are one I would find it exciting and amusing to do something with."[24] Similarly excited by the prospect of a tête-à-tête, Dickey told Lowell on October 29 that they could get "everything straightened out: everything, that is, like Love, Fate, Poetry, Time, Art, and all the rest of those things."[25] They might even become genuine friends. His misgivings about Dickey as a sly opportunist and ferocious competitor aside, Lowell ranked him with Berryman and Bishop as one of the best poets writing. Grateful that Lowell had agreed "to emerge, out of [the] busyness and loneliness of a great writer on to a fragment of time," Dickey expressed his high hopes for the collaboration. "I would be willing to bet," he said, "the future will not ever let die, completely [our moment on film]." Regarding Lowell's brief compliments, Dickey was deeply moved: "As for the things you say about my own work, I am grateful beyond the ability to say I'm grateful. It—the note—will be with me for the rest of whatever there is."[26] Dickey's overblown comments were a measure of his insecurity before the more critically acclaimed Lowell as well as part of an attempt to win over a rival.

The Encyclopedia Britannica's schedule called for filming to begin in Columbia shortly after the crew arrived from Los Angeles on November 5. Dickey would read poetry at the Russell House, shoot at the archery range with

Calhoun Winton, mingle with his family at home, write in his studio, teach students at the university, play his guitar over breakfast, and then get in a plane bound for Atlanta. Next the crew would film him reading at De Kalb Community College, hunting Civil War relics with his brother, talking with Lewis King and Al Braselton about *Deliverance*, and touring familiar sites in Buckhead. The crew would follow Dickey to Cape Cod Community College in Hyannis, Massachusetts, and, while on the Cape, film Dickey on an early morning bow hunt for deer. The following stop would be New York for literary conversations with Lowell, Norman Mailer, William F. Buckley, Willie Morris, or John Simon (in the end only Lowell appeared in the film). The crew intended to return to Los Angeles on November 25.

The filmmakers remained generally faithful to their original plan, and Dickey performed admirably in his various roles and settings. But because he worried that Croner and his partners might somehow produce an unflattering portrait, he asked some friends in Beverly Hills—Ann and Delbert Mann—to see if they could get a sneak preview of the film and report back to him. Dickey informed his appointed detectives: "Stan is one of these secretive Hollywood geniuses who doesn't communicate with the *subject* of the film very much."[27] On the same day, March 19, 1970, he tried a more confrontational approach by asking Steven Larner, who helped produce the film: "When do I get to *see* the damn thing?"[28] In late March, Dickey's Hollywood friend, Larry Klingman, wrote that Croner was showing a forty-five-minute cut of the film. Croner wanted to get feedback from his peers before showing it to the company officials. When Dickey finally got a chance to view the film in the spring of 1970, he at first approved of the way Croner had cut twenty-five hours of footage down to forty minutes of film. To Ken McCormick at Doubleday, however, he expressed misgivings. He wished Croner had included more of the original scenes, such as those of hunting Civil War relics with his brother, Tom. Dickey must have been bothered by some of the unflattering scenes, too, and the modest fee of twenty-five hundred dollars for his services.

In *Lord, Let Me Die, but Not Die Out*, Croner presents Dickey as a folksy literary man full of provocative opinions. At the start, Dickey appears at a USC party, drinking from a plastic cup and sounding off to students about pornographic movies, fantasies, and the similarities between Hitler, Sophocles, Eliot, Crane, and Thomas (Dickey argues that they all followed irrational principles). Later he plays the guitar, types in his bow-lined study, and discourses on the divine seizure sometimes experienced during poetic composition. He says that poets will sell their grandmothers down the river, contract syphilis, and become alcoholics in their pursuit of poetic ecstasy. At the Columbia airport, Maxine maternally tucks plane tickets and schedules into his jacket pockets and quips: "I think I better go with you." Dickey agrees: "I want you to go with me; I don't like those other girls." He then lugs his bow with its rack of arrows onto the plane. In Atlanta, the city fetes him royally. Mayor Ivan Allen proclaims the day—November 14, 1969—Atlanta Poets' Day, and De Kalb Community College makes special arrangements for their own Poetry Day. To the De Kalb students Dickey talks about his tragic—yet affirmative—view of life, reads "Looking for the Buckhead Boys," discusses poetics, and later flies to Cape Cod.

In the North, Dickey's tone shifts dramatically. He makes derisive comments calculated to enrage Robert Lowell, the man he will shortly meet. He calls John Milton, one of the most important influences on Lowell's early poetry, a "great stuffed goat" who "has nothing to say about the world." "Who cares about *Paradise Lost*, really?" he asks before blaming the poem for turning him away from poetry as a teenager. Students at Cape Cod Community College pose hard questions that Dickey tries to sidestep as he swigs from a tall can of Schlitz. What do you think about the "liberated woman"? one asks. Dickey replies that he is not a woman, turns the question back on the questioner, and sneers at liberated women for wrangling endlessly with their husbands about doing simple household chores. If he is concerned about the extinction of animal species, why does he hunt? another asks. Dickey answers that his hunting poses no real threat to the animals. The film segues to Dickey in camouflage gear and camouflage paint, stalking deer on Cape Cod.

With Lowell in a study above his New York apartment, Dickey talks about his reasons for writing and his ideal audience. He claims he writes so that others can "break through the glass wall we all live behind" and glimpse an apocalyptic "new heaven and new earth." He introduces Lowell to "The Legend of the Happy Swimming Pool." Lowell puffs on a cigarette and looks bored as Dickey recounts a dream he has had several times: He is walking down an unfamiliar street in his old Buckhead neighborhood and suddenly arrives at a swimming pool surrounded with lovely, expectant girls who ask him where he has been. Regretting the years it has taken him to get to this suburban Eden, now he regrets the bliss he experiences there because he knows it is fleeting. As if suddenly recognizing the relevance of *Paradise Lost*, he tells Lowell: "I fear the end of the happy dream." His visit to Lowell over, Dickey gets into a New York taxi cab with his bow and arrows.

Dickey judged the film a great success partly because it brought him closer to Lowell. Dickey's envy of the other poet's reputation, at least for the moment, evaporated in a burst of extravagant praise. On December 10, he reminisced about their meeting: "I cannot even begin to tell you what a great day it was for me. I don't much care about the movie, nor the movie folks, one way or the other, the main thing was that we had a chance to sit down and talk, and drink, and the rest. I wouldn't have missed it for anything, believe me." He lavished compliments on Lowell's wife, Elizabeth Hardwick, their child Harriet, and their New York apartment. "It surely must be obvious to you that I like you very much indeed," he reminded his new chum. Overwhelmed by Lowell's kindly presence before the cameras, Dickey made a typically flamboyant request; he asked Lowell to be his literary executor. Lowell, who agreed, must not have known about his distinguished predecessors (James Merrill and Howard Nemerov would soon join the group). Dickey was delighted by their new bond: "I hope you won't have to edit my papers, and all that melancholy job, but it is a source of great consolation to me that you will do it if you have to."[29] Since Lowell could be as fanciful as Dickey, especially when manic, he may have agreed to the job of executor in the same high-spirited mood in which it was offered.

Later in December, during a two-week teaching stint as Washington University's Fannie Hurst Resident, Dickey turned his attention to family matters—his son Chris's wedding in Boston. Chris had dated Susan Tuckerman while she was a student at Foxcroft, a girls' school among the horse farms near Middleburg, Virginia. She had graduated, and her parents had sent her to summer school in Switzerland (partly to get her away from Chris), but after her return in late July she had gotten pregnant and decided to marry. In late January 1970, Dickey reported to his poet friend Ann Stanford: "Chris is *very* happily married, to a lovely Boston girl, and everything seems fine in their house."[30] Although he agreed to help support them, Dickey was actually furious that Chris had married. According to Chris: "The first time that Susan and I went together to Columbia, when she was still pregnant, he could not bring himself to sit at the same table with us at dinner. 'You have thrown away your youth,' he said between his teeth with a ferociousness, and at the same time a tone of despair, that I had never heard."[31] Chris and Susan soon had a baby boy, James Tuckerman, whom Dickey grew to adore. He later wrote the children's book *Tucky the Hunter* for his grandson, who in the book appears as a comical and fanciful hunter like himself.

Before the end of 1969, Dickey returned to New York to see Willie Morris and Marshall Frady, a biographer and journalist who had published a long article about Ronald Reagan and other Californians in that month's *Harper's*. Morris liked to tell a story about a taxi ride during which three Southerners joked about a new uprising of the Confederacy:

> We were talking in the back seat of one of those New York City cabs that have a bullet-proof window which separates the driver from his passengers and a little aperture where you put the money. Jim Dickey and I were talking about . . . the power of writing. And we had a cab driver, Mr. Lebowitz from the Bronx . . . [who] leaned through the aperture in the bullet-proof glass and said, "You gentlemen aren't from around here, are you?" We said, "No, we're not." And then Mr. Lebowitz proceeded, I must say, to just dump all over our black brethren. He just said some of the worst things I've ever heard. He went on and on. Finally, Professor James Dickey leaned through the aperture and said, "Mr. Lebowitz, if there's anything I can't stand it's an amateur bigot." Jim said, "We had the finest fighting men in the field in the history of warfare. Only our machines failed us. We only had one ball bearings factory in the whole Confederacy. It was in Richmond, Virginia, and late in the war it produced sixty-three ball bearings. In the latter stages of the Civil War the poor old Confederacy was so distraught that they used them ball bearings for bullets. Sixty-three dead Lebowitzes." At this point, Mr. Lebowitz, knowing nothing about the power of writing or the power of poets, put his head down to this bullet proof aperture and said, "Well, what are you gentlemen doing up here now?" Dickey said, "We came up to buy a ball bearing factory."[32]

Morris, who shared Dickey's mischievous penchant for embroidering events, in this case did Dickey a disservice. Dickey, in fact, never got in the cab. Larry King, a contributing editor of *Harper's* at the time, was the third passenger.

Dickey had decided to walk to the Empire restaurant, where they all were to have dinner. As Frady remembered, when the driver realized his passengers were Southern, he growled: "Why don't you take all these spades you sent us back down where they came from?" Frady was the one who rejoined sarcastically: "If there's anything I can't stand, it's an amateur bigot." And it was Morris who surmised that the South could have whipped the North if it had possessed more ball-bearing factories. Because of traffic in the snowy streets, Dickey got to the restaurant first. Invigorated by his thirty-block trek, he spoke excitedly about Frady's article in *Harper's*, quoting phrases and lines verbatim. The men drank and talked at their table until all the other customers left. Frady, who had brought a collection of Dickey's poetry, returned Dickey's compliments with a spirited rendition of the long poem "May Day Sermon." Everyone in the restaurant, even the staff, huddled close to hear Dickey's electrifying tale of a farmer whipping his daughter for her lustful tryst with a motorcyclist. Dickey sat across from Frady, cheering him on: "Yea, listen to that! Isn't that great! Yea!"[33] When the poem ended, the staff persuaded the group to return to the snow-clogged streets.

Another friend Dickey regularly visited in New York was the poet, critic, and translator Richard Howard. Dickey had gotten to know Howard in the late 1960s, when Howard was working on his highly esteemed book about contemporary poets, *Alone with America*. Howard's essay on Dickey evinced a keen understanding and appreciation for his poetry. Upon receiving a draft of the essay, Dickey proposed getting together in New York. During their first and many subsequent meetings, Howard realized that Dickey was both Dionysian rabble-rouser and Apollonian philosophe. Howard enjoyed his exuberant friend and in a letter called him his favorite American poet. Nonetheless, having witnessed alcoholism in his own family, Howard found socializing with Dickey trying. In Howard's presence, if not talking about writers, Dickey gave free rein to his outrageous fantasies, impersonated Marlon Brando and other celebrities, and became increasingly unmanageable. On March 8, 1967, when Howard attended Atheneum's dinner party honoring James Merrill in the wine room of Pierre's Restaurant, Dickey was at his saturnalian worst. Merrill pointed out in his toast that many of the poets at the party could be divided into Ms and Hs—Moss, Meredith, Merrill, Merwin, and Howard, Hecht, Hollander—and leaned over to Howard and said: "Yes, and D for drunk."[34] Despite Dickey's bibulous frolicking, Howard became a loyal advocate of his work. To consecrate their bond in the 1970s, Dickey appointed Howard his literary executor, a position Howard gracefully accepted and later, like his forebears, gracefully declined.

Because of Dickey's reputation for bedding numerous women, Howard was surprised that Dickey relished the company of his gay friends. While visiting Howard he liked to discuss the gay lifestyle and flirt with Howard's lover, as well as some of the gay Ms at the Atheneum party. In January 1970, Dickey wrote Howard's lover with typical flattery that he would never have a better reader than him. Like many others, Howard noticed Dickey's preoccupation with homosexuality in *Deliverance*, which he agreed to review after Dickey pressed him to do so. Howard also noticed that Maxine, whose charm and humor he admired, discounted many of her husband's heterosexual boasts as so much palaver.[35]

Dickey's friendship with Howard grew closer as a result of the 1970 Pulitzer Prize. On January 2, Dickey reported to the Pulitzer administration that he, Auden, and Mrs. Charles Hayden had voted unanimously to give the prize to Howard's *Untitled Subjects*, a series of allusive, highly crafted dramatic monologues influenced by Browning and his Victorian culture. In a letter to Howard a decade later, in which he proposed nominating Howard for a new honor—admission to the National Institute of Arts and Letters—Dickey explained that Auden had wanted to give the Pulitzer to "someone who will continue, who will persevere and keep on adding." Dickey had assured Auden that Howard would do this: "Auden never made a better choice, and neither did I."[36] Educated at Columbia University and the Sorbonne, Howard didn't think he was Dickey's kind of poet. The Pulitzer Prize was doubly surprising because of the surreptitious way Howard found out about it. The good news had come via John Hollander, a Yale friend, who in turn had heard it from John Simon at a party. Neither Howard, who considered Simon an enemy, nor Hollander could understand how Simon knew of the award, which was supposed to be kept secret. Had Dickey leaked the information to Simon before the official announcement? Dickey went to great lengths to convince Howard otherwise and to assure him that Simon could do nothing to jeopardize the Pulitzer committee's decision: "I don't think anything John Simon could do, even if he wanted to, or was careless enough to, would make any difference."[37] In the end, Howard collected the prize without incident.

As the 1960s tumbled into the 1970s, Dickey's self-destructive ways increased proportionally with his fame. Asked by a writer for the *Atlanta Journal-Constitution* to offer his prophesies for the new decade, he revealed his own as well as his country's needs: "I think the major concern of people in this decade—especially among the young people—is going to be the discovery and the reconstructing of a new system of values. It may possibly be the all-encompassing thing and will go beyond the 1970s. People have been very much mixed up on values during the 1960s. They no longer think the American dream through acquisition is the answer. The pleasure principle is going bankrupt. This business of sitting out in the suburbs and having a new car every year . . . ; people aren't satisfied with just that anymore. And a cruise to Nassau is pleasant, but it's not the answer to anything."[38] Dickey believed that religion might exert a new appeal. To control his increasingly chaotic life, by the end of the decade he professed he was a Catholic.

Dickey began his campaign to bring order to his life in 1970 by drawing up another schedule. He vowed to wake at 6:00 A.M. and work on short poems before and after breakfast, and at nine o'clock run three-and-a-half miles around Lake Katherine. (Dickey bragged to a skeptical Norman Mailer that he completed the long lap in twenty-five minutes.) At 10:00 he would play the guitar for an hour; at 11:00 work on two long poems; at 12:30 eat lunch; at 1:30 lift weights and stretch on cables to strengthen his arms for archery; at 2:30 practice the guitar again; at 3:30 work on his novel *Alnilam*; at 5:30 practice more guitar; at 6:30 shave and get ready for supper; at 8:30 prepare for class; at 9:30 dictate letters; at 10:30 read books for pleasure; and at 11:30 go to bed. Despite his avowals to reporters and friends, his attempts to be another well-scheduled Ben Franklin were always short-lived.

Dickey needed to husband his energy for an array of different enterprises in early 1970. He was involved peripherally in Croner's Encyclopedia Britannica film and also Len Richmond's short 16-mm film based on "May Day Sermon." On January 9, Dickey wrote Richmond: "I am a little frightened, considering the nature of the material as I wrote it down, that the poem, as set to film, might have elements in it which would be shocking to whatever audience. . . . Could you give me a brief synopsis of how the sequence runs, what you show, and so on?"[39] Would the punishment of the farmer's daughter in the barn make the film pornographic? Since Richmond was not immediately forthcoming, Dickey again played the sleuth. He asked Larry Klingman to check on Richmond: "I'd like to know something about him [Richmond], because he wants to do some other things of mine for underground film houses."[40] As it turned out, there was little in the *May Day Sermon* film to arouse concern. Richmond assured Dickey that it was safe enough for TV, and went on to make films based on "Falling" and "The Sheep Child."

Taking a break from teaching and film work, Dickey traveled to New York in early February for a Doubleday party celebrating the publication of his poetry book *The Eye-Beaters, Blood, Victory, Madness, Buckhead and Mercy*. Doubleday had invited a host of prominent writers (George Plimpton, Norman Mailer, John Simon, Richard Howard) and editors (Willie Morris, Jacques de Spoelberch, Steven Kanfer, Peter Bird Martin, Philip Kunhardt) to its bookshop at Fifty-third Street and Fifth Avenue. At the party on February 12, Dickey also got a chance to renew contact with Gary Cooper's former wife, who had been enchanted by the excerpt of *Deliverance* she had just read in the *Atlantic*. He also socialized with Peter Farb, his old biology lab partner from Vanderbilt; Stewart Richardson, a Doubleday editor who would work closely with Dickey during the 1970s; and Don Anderson, an associate editor at *Sports Illustrated*, who had asked Dickey to write an article on white-water canoeing in North Georgia. On the evening of the party Dickey and Richardson dined at the Ginger Man to discuss the publication of a collection of journal entries he was tentatively calling *Assertions*. Dickey may have told Richardson to make sure *Eye-Beaters* was nominated for the National Book Award. Later in the year, learning that a clerical mistake had delayed the book's nomination, he angrily wrote Richardson: "The way the juries are shaping up, I stand a very good chance of being the first double winner in the history of the award, and we don't want to miss this because of an oversight by some secretary."[41] *Deliverance*, he hoped, would win the other National Book Award. With so much success in the offing, Dickey wanted to talk to Doubleday about his next novel, *Alnilam*, which he hoped to finish in the next three to five years.

To promote *Eye-Beaters*, which he was calling his strongest collection to date, Dickey urged friends like Richard Howard to review it in prestigious journals. Howard agreed to do so in the *Nation*, and must have sent Dickey a draft because on June 17, 1970, Dickey wrote him a note of thanks: "It seems to me one of the most favorable and penetrating things yet written on anything I have done."[42]

The review, however, never appeared. Those that did appear were less than con-gratulatory. Robert Shaw, who had recently interviewed Dickey at Harvard, crit-icized the book in *Poetry* for its bathos and obscurity. He felt Dickey's new expansiveness was a mistake and that his "split-line" technique amounted to lit-tle more than a "chronic stutter." He admired some of the poems, like "Pine," for their Hopkins-like music, but in general he believed the volume suffered from too many "long-winded, loquacious poems, springing from a milieu of tall tales, yarns, leisurely long-summer-evening-front-porch stories."[43] In the *New York Times Book Review*, Herbert Leibowitz recognized the book as a new departure for Dickey, but in the wrong direction. Dickey's new voice, he complained, was fragmentary, maudlin, overblown, and childlishly petulant. The book indicated that Dickey was stuck in a "poetic backwater."[44] Both reviewers implied that Dickey was writing out of his persona as a boozy raconteur. As if to spite them, Dickey wrote his entire next book, *The Zodiac*, in the voice of a drunken bard. He was undoubtedly emboldened by the popular success of *Eye-Beaters*. The book went through three printings in 1970 and sold nearly twenty thousand copies—an astonishing number for a book of poetry.

Some of Dickey's friends rallied around his new work. James Wright com-pared Dickey's talent to Beethoven's. On March 5, he wrote: "[*Eye-Beaters*] is my favorite book among your single collections. I don't know how to say why, but I don't care."[45] On March 16, Dickey invoked Picasso in his response: "I am *so* happy that you like the new book, for it is really not very much like any of the others. . . . It seems to me that the great lesson of Picasso is that he never al-lowed himself to be trapped in a single style, as so many of your young and not-so-young American poets have done. Anyway, I wanted to move out of what had already been successful for me. . . . You have convinced me that I have made at least part of the right move, though while I was writing the book I was quite prepared to have critics say that this book was 'disappointing,' that it 'repre-sented a retrogression,' and so on."[46] Pleased with Wright's faithful support, Dickey invited him to the March publication party for *Deliverance*.

The title poem of *Eye-Beaters* was not all that different in style and theme from some of Dickey's earlier poems; it was written in his "wall-of-words" format and dealt with blindness and vision in a compelling narrative. He had heard the story that inspired his poem from Mary Bookwalter, a woman he'd met on a reading trip. Dickey's blind children who masochistically beat their eyes to pro-duce visions are "retrogressive" in the sense that they commune with prehistoric ancestors—the godlike cave painters—who inhabit the dark caves of their own psyches: "There, quiet children stand watching / A man striped and heavy with pigment, lift his hand with color coming / From him. Bestial, working like God, he moves on stone he is drawing / A half-cloud of beasts on the wall. They crane closer, helping, beating / Harder, light blazing inward from their fists   and see   see leap / From the shocked head-nerves, great herds of deer on the hacked glory plain / Of the cave wall: antelope   elk: blind children strike for the middle / Of the brain, where the race is young." As Dickey admits, the eye-beaters are essentially his own creations and reflect his own poetic biases and yearnings; they hope to create another "Heaven of Animals" in their minds. He could be talking about any number of his fantasies when he says: "Yes, indeed I know it is not / So   I am trying to make it   make something   make them make me / Re-invent the vision of the race." Regarding the children's self-flagellation, therapists and doctors try to prevent it by binding the children's hands. Dickey argues against the doctors' restraints: "*Hold on to your fantasy; it is all that can save / A man with good eyes in this place. Hold on, though doctors keep telling / You to back off   to be what you came as*." Dickey concludes the poem with a valediction: "Therapist, farewell at the living end. Give me my spear."[47] Devoted to the notion that redemptive vision arises from bodily sacrifice and from what Rimbaud called a "dérèglement de tous les sens," Dickey spurns all those who prescribe healthyminded regimens. In "Diabetes" he made the same argument.

Dickey flew back to New York two weeks after the *Eye-Beaters* party to attend the National Book Awards ceremony in Lincoln Center. He had been asked to make a ten-minute statement at a press conference in the Biltmore Hotel, but looked forward with greater anticipation to another meeting with Robert Lowell and their mutual friend Peter Farb. For Dickey the ceremony turned into a melee with detractors, both his and Lowell's. As judge of a Hallmark cards poetry contest in mid-March, Dickey gave the organizer, Edgar Sheldon, some inkling of what happened in New York; Kenneth Rexroth, who was also a Hallmark judge, "rose up and called Robert Lowell a Fascist. Shortly thereafter, when the ceremonies were over and everyone was standing around talking, he made a point of coming up to me and calling me a Nazi. . . . I damn near threw him down the stairs."[48] Accepting the National Book Award for Elizabeth Bishop, Lowell had read Bishop's "Visits to St. Elizabeths," and when he came to the line "This is a Jew in a newspaper hat / that dances weeping down the ward," Rexroth shouted, "Fascist!" Although Lowell in his manic phases identified with Fascist leaders like Mussolini (in his poem "Crossing the Alps" he says of Mussolini: "He was one of us / only, pure prose"), and although Dickey evinced a fascination with the Nazis, Rexroth's remarks were more inflammatory than substantive. Sometimes touched off by envy, sometimes by political assumptions, such attacks would only increase during the years following the success of *Deliverance*.

X.

DELIVERANCE

24. A Bestseller (1970)

Through all of 1969, Dickey had labored on *Deliverance*. By June, he had reached page 255 in his revisions. With about twenty more pages to go, he was having problems making the book cohere and would call Jacques de Spoelberch at three in the morning with requests that he get more involved. Spoelberch would respond as calmly as he could that the novel depended on Dickey's poetic prose and fine ear for Southern dialect, and that as an editor he could not write it; he could only help shape it. Dickey troubled his editor again when Spoelberch visited Columbia on June 30 for several days of intense revising. Dickey had invited Theron Raines as an ally in what he expected to be a combative session. Spoelberch's position was a delicate one. On one side were Dickey and Raines, on the other Paul Brooks and Richard McAdoo, the new editor-in-chief at Houghton Mifflin. Spoelberch felt Dickey needed to cut about eight thousand words from the current draft and modify several important scenes. Dickey resisted further amputations. On May 23, he wrote Spoelberch: "If anything happened to me between now and the time I was able to revise it, I hope you would go ahead and print it just as it stands in this draft we now have."[1] Spoelberch wanted his writer to stay alive and keep cutting.

Spoelberch assured Dickey on June 18 that the Houghton editors considered *Deliverance* "an enormously powerful and provocative tour de force,"[2] but he also said that he had consulted a mountain climber who had determined that the chronology and distances in Ed Gentry's rock-climbing scene were wrong. Spoelberch also demanded that he excise Ed's "Portnoy-like" ejaculation on the cliff and the epilogue about Ed's sadomasochistic marriage. Raines agreed. Dickey willingly cut the cliff episode, but in a letter to Spoelberch he defended the sadistic whipping of Martha: "I wanted to implant in the reader's mind a couple of things. First, that the narrator without his knowing it, has been a monster all his life, a born killer as well as an 'ordinary suburbanite,' and this one chance episode which *gave* him a chance to energize this hidden part of his personality has, in a sense, freed him of it. His monstrousness may now take other forms: ones that are imaginary and harmless. That's why I've added the final sexual scene with the wife."[3] In the end, Dickey conceded that the scene was unnecessary.

Spoelberch also worried about the rape scene: "The sexual molestation of Bobby should be made slightly less graphic and . . . the many references to sexual parts should be deleted; for the sexual overtones that run through the narrative are readily apparent anyway and will have stronger impact for being less explicit." Spoelberch's other criticisms concerned style: "The main problem still is over-writing; you tend to editorialize a bit heavy-handedly at times or to pile on unnecessary images. You are also too devoted to sequences of multiple adjectives and the use of certain words . . . , the latter bringing you perilously close to a kind of superficial mysticism."⁴ During Spoelberch's visit to Columbia, the collaboration of writer, agent, and editor was not always easy, but for the most part it was productive. Maxine acted as benevolent host, mixing tumblers of bourbon and soda for her husband and providing her guests with lunches and dinners.

On August 5, 1969, Dickey sent Spoelberch fifteen pages of proposed corrections to his manuscript, which dealt with everything from names to the color of the map Lewis unrolls in the bar. The next day he mailed another long list of corrections and addressed his editor's concern about the four life jackets in the canoe at the end of the trip. If Drew had drowned wearing his life jacket, the survivors should only have three. This detail needed fixing (in the final draft Ed explains the extra life jacket by telling the inquisitive sheriff that they carried extra ones). And what about the possibility of the sheriff taking a motorboat up the river to look for evidence of the canoeing accident? Clearly the river was too rough for a motorboat, Dickey replied. The minutiae taken care of, Dickey wanted to hand deliver his completed manuscript to the Houghton editors in Boston, but morbid thoughts assailed him once again. Fearing that he might "vanish without a trace—or, maybe [more] to the point—without a trace of the manuscript,"⁵ Dickey mailed it.

On August 23, Dickey answered Spoelberch's additional questions about the height of the cliff (175 feet) and the distance of the river from Atlanta (175 miles), and asked his editor to check an almanac for the appropriate phase of the moon on September 15 and 16, the days Ed climbs the cliff and hunts his stalker. Dickey wanted the moon to be not quite full, and planned to shift the novel's mid-September dates to make this possible. He told Spoelberch that he had submitted the book manuscript to Robie Macauley, the fiction editor at *Playboy*, to see if he might publish an excerpt. He had also written John Guest, an editor at Longmans, Green and Co. in England, who was interested in publishing the novel in Britain. (In the end, Hamish Hamilton bought the English rights, offering a five-thousand-pound advance for *Deliverance*, *Eye-Beaters*, and Dickey's next book of poetry.)

Dickey could not resist getting involved in every aspect of his novel's production. In August, he bickered with Louise Noble at Houghton about the cover design. He wanted an eye looking through a bow sight. Noble rejected the eye image in favor of a bow and arrow, so Dickey sent photographs of archers and their archery gear to help the cover designer. As if laying out an advertisement in his McCann-Erickson office, he told Noble: "I had also conceived of the jacket in black and the design and title and author's name in the same orange as the peep-sight and the eye, and the whole thing on paper of relatively rough stock (*not* slick paper): something simple and mysterious."⁶ Author and artist reached a compromise, deciding to stress the visionary as opposed to the murderous element in the story. A blue eye peering through a ring of leaves on a green background adorned the book jacket.

Convinced that his novel would be a sure-fire seller in Hollywood, Dickey was in an exultant mood when Warner Brothers offered a contract for movie rights on November 19, 1969. They would pay $25,000 for the first draft of the screenplay (due January 15, 1971), $15,000 for the second draft and its revisions, and $10,000 if they made a feature-length movie. Theron Raines had negotiated the contract and continued to negotiate favorable contracts for the novel's foreign rights. Before long the novel appeared in Turkey, Greece, Holland, Italy, Spain, Germany, France, Sweden, Japan, and other countries as well. Always concerned with the reception of his work, during the latter part of 1969 Dickey stepped up his prepublication publicity campaign. His usual strategy was to flatter a critic while denying he ever flattered and then request, or simply hope, that the critic would supply a glowing blurb or review. In May, he had told Mark Schorer, after reading his book *The World We Imagine*, that Schorer was the best critic alive; shortly afterward Schorer got requests to provide blurbs for both *Deliverance* and *Eye-Beaters*. On January 3, 1970, Schorer obliged, calling *Deliverance* one of the most absorbing novels he had ever read. In mid-December Dickey wrote the prominent critic and cofounder of *Partisan Review*, Philip Rahv, about Rahv's book *Literature and the Sixth Sense:* "I'm not a natural writer of fan mail. But certain things should be attended to. . . . You are the best literary critic I have ever read, and, I can tell you, I have read a lot of them."[7] Dickey wrote a similar letter to Wallace Stegner, a novelist in the Stanford English Department: "This is an impulse letter, pure and simple. I have just finished *All the Little Live Things*, and this reading prompted what is probably the only fan letter I have ever written."[8] His approbation often reached ludicrous extremes. He wrote Ellen Lane, a college student in Rock Hill, South Carolina, who had sent him an appreciative letter: "The things you say about my writing mean more to me than the words of all literary critics in New York, Chicago, London, and the rest. . . . I would rather have a letter from Ellen Lane than hear from Ezra Pound, T. S. Eliot, Edmund Wilson, and all the rest of them combined. . . . Meanwhile, let me know what your life is like. . . . And send along a picture, because you are very important to me."[9]

Readers got a glimpse of what to expect from *Deliverance* in an excerpt, "Two Days in September," which appeared in the February 1970 *Atlantic Monthly*. Lewis King and Al Braselton were more eager than most to see how their experiences had been transformed. When a mutual friend, Pegram Harrison, brought a copy of the magazine to lunch, King and Braselton read it as they ate. Harrison asked which of the two had been sodomized. "Not me; I'm Lewis," King replied. Braselton chimed in: "Not me either; I'm the guitar player."[10] For the rest of their lives Braselton and King would fend off similar questions about the incidents informing *Deliverance*.

The excerpt of the novel captivated many besides King and Braselton. John Logue, the managing editor of *Southern Living*, sent compliments, as did Scott Donaldson. Because of the excerpt's controversial nature, Dickey advised Logue to relay his feelings to Manning. He lobbied Donaldson, too: "If you like it *that* much, please write Bob Manning . . . and tell him what you told me, for he took a great chance."[11] Grateful for Donaldson's praise, Dickey invited him to the New York *Deliverance* party. The gathering on March 23 in New York's Saint Regis Sheraton would be one of the grandest ever arranged for Dickey, but in typical fashion he wanted to make it even grander by supplying his own touch of theater. So Dickey conferred privately with King and Braselton, instructing them to tell the New York intelligentsia that all the crucial scenes in *Deliverance* had actually happened on their canoe trips. Braselton and King went along with the ruse up to a point. Braselton later wrote: "Why in hell does Jim want us to tell these people that *Deliverance* was true? Is it as he says just a put-on for these New York intellectual types or is it that Jim is beginning to believe his own lies?"[12] To a reporter for the *Atlanta Journal-Constitution* who asked him a week before the party whether the characters and events were true, Dickey pretended to be circumspect: "Well, I can't say that. I'd rather not. There's come a big flap on it in various quarters as to whether the thing is really true, whether this actually happened, and I really can't say."[13] A week earlier he had bluntly confessed to a journalist for *Family Weekly*, who had asked a similar question: "I have never been able to understand what 'truth' is in relation to fiction."[14] He did not want to distinguish between the two at the party, either.

After Dickey told Rocky Converse about the real *Deliverance* characters, she walked up to Braselton and said: "I thought you were dead." Slightly hungover, Braselton refused to acknowledge this grim news. She repeated: "You were the one that was killed, weren't you?" Still startled by his presumed death, Braselton agreed that he was the model for Drew Ballinger. Converse turned to Braselton's wife: "Well, I offer my condolences to the widow." A nostalgic, inebriated Dickey approached Braselton and King with cheerier news: "This is our book. You helped me write this book. You all helped me write it. If you hadn't taught me how to play the guitar, Al; if we hadn't done those trips, if Lewis hadn't had the canoes, it never would have been done. It's our book and I want you to share with me. I want you to help me write the screenplay."[15] He expressed the same sort of gratitude to Spoelberch: "All of this I owe in a very large measure to you, who worked with me so patiently and diligently and intelligently on the book. I am not inclined to gush; it is not my way, but if a writer ever had the right editor for him on the right book, it was you working with me on *Deliverance*, and now, look what has come of it!"[16] Dickey's appreciation was genuine, although with Braselton and King his collaborating went only as far as canoeing. Maxine, who was at the party, also showed her affection for her husband's two friends by presenting them with small gold canoes engraved with the publication date of *Deliverance*.

The next day, the Braseltons met various Dickeys—Maxine, Chris, Tom, Patsy, Jim—at the Algonquin Hotel, the site of many illustrious literary gatherings. The Dickey entourage then moved to the Time-Life building for more drinking. As Braselton recalled, his several days in New York marked the beginning of his alcoholism. He and Dickey consumed Bloody Marys in the morning and martinis and brandy at lunch, and drank all afternoon and evening until they went to bed. While Braselton soon admitted he had a drinking problem, Dickey denied he drank at all. In March, when asked by a writer for the *Atlanta Journal-Constitution* whether he drank a lot, he said, "No. I'm a diabetic, so I can't," and added that he was nothing like the self-destructive "to-hell-with-tomorrow types"[17] Thomas Wolfe and James Agee.

In between parties, Dickey attended publicity events for *Deliverance*. A preliminary interview had been scheduled for the morning of March 23 to prepare him for a July 22 appearance on the *Dick Cavett Show*. On March 24, the *Casper Citron Show* recorded an interview in the Algonquin Hotel. On the same day

Bill Mazer spoke to him in the Steer Palace Restaurant. On March 25, John Barkham from the *Saturday Review* discussed *Deliverance* at the Plaza Hotel, and on March 26, Mike Wallace interviewed him for CBS Radio. A few days later he flew to Atlanta for a series of radio shows, press club luncheons, and book-signing parties. In mid-April he traveled to Washington, D.C., Birmingham, and Richmond. He appeared with Barbara Walters on *The Today Show* on May 26 and again on July 20, and on *The David Frost Show* in September. At first the publicity work thrilled Dickey, but before long he grew impatient with its grueling demands. His appearance at a Book and Author Dinner in Richmond typified his irritability. Outraged by the way another speaker at the dinner, Erich Segal, courted the audience by running down the aisle like a costumed actor and upbraiding films and books for their obscenities, Dickey punched the backstage curtain and, unable to find an opening, lifted the curtain over his head and stumbled toward the microphone. He rebuked critics who tried to second-guess his intentions in *Deliverance*. Taking a swipe at the stagey, ingratiating Segal, who had crooned that "love" was the four-letter word he preferred, Dickey implied that the only four-letter word in his book was "fuck."[18] He then left the building, bypassing the book-signing tables.

Dickey's bumptious publicity campaign helped sell *Deliverance*, but it was the writing itself that made the book so irresistible. With a poet's sense of language, Dickey had written a classic American adventure story that was also an intriguing murder mystery. Although Lewis Medlock's murder of the mountain man who sodomizes Bobby Trippe is indubitable, the death of Drew Ballinger and Ed Gentry's murder of the mountain man on the cliff are shrouded in uncertainty. Was Drew really shot, or did he commit suicide? Did Ed kill Drew's killer? Is the mountain man Ed shoots really the man who ran off after threatening to make Ed perform fellatio? Confronted with such horrifying doubts and convinced that the truth might convict them, the three survivors lie to survive.

The drama of *Deliverance* arises from the conflict between Lewis, Ed, and Bobby, who vote to bury the corpse of the shot rapist and concoct a story for the police, and Drew, who cannot accept prevarication. Overwhelmed by the nightmare he has entered, Drew makes it worse by trying to avoid it. He topples from his canoe and causes the second canoe to crash, Lewis to break his leg, and Ed to climb the cliff in his hunt for the supposed stalker. *Deliverance* culminates in a power struggle between the forces for truth and the forces for deception. Deputy Queen, whose brother-in-law never returns from his hunting trip, assumes that the canoers murdered him; he therefore insists that Sheriff Bullard and his officers do everything possible to uncover the facts. Ed lies about capsizing at Griffin's Shoot, and signs a statement asserting that Drew died and Lewis broke his leg on that part of the river. Queen ferociously objects: "He's lyin'. He's lyin' thu his teeth. He's done somethin', up yonder. He's done kilt my brother-in-law."[19] The lies prevail.

At the end of *Deliverance*, Ed could be speaking for the way Dickey visualized and wrote the novel: "As I went through some of the story that Bobby and I had rehearsed on the river, I made it a point to try to visualize the things I was saying as though they had really happened. I could see us searching for Drew, though we never had. I saw these things happen at the place near the yellow tree, and for me they were happening as I talked; it was hard to realize that they had not taken place in the actual world; as I saw him [the officer] taking them into account, they became part of a world, the believed world, the world of recorded events, of history." This survivalist's sense of triumph comes not in the wilderness, but in Ed's imagination as he mingles with law-abiding and law-enforcing citizens. Although Ed worries that the FBI with its powerful IBM computers and "the whole vast, inexorable web of modern communications" will eventually demolish his version of the truth, he is confident that his "version was strong." He says: "I had made it and tried it out against the world, and it had held. It had become so strong in my mind that I had trouble getting back through it to the truth." After the dammed-up river buries the evidence of their crimes, Ed says: "My lies seemed better, more and more like truth."[20] Physical strength ultimately proves less important than imaginative strength. The strong, Tarzan-like Lewis has fallen while Ed, the imaginative advertising designer, has saved his two comrades from the mountain men, from legal prosecution, and from prison.

Burt Reynolds, who played Lewis in the film version of the novel, was among the many whose gullibility Dickey tested with the "facts" of *Deliverance*. Reynolds recalled: "One night Dickey and I were walking along in the parking lot and he said, 'You know it really happened.' I said, 'You mean the story?' He said, 'Yep, but don't tell any of the others. You're the only one that could handle it.' I said okay. Fade out. Five years later, Jon Voight and I are talking one night, and I said, 'Do you know what Dickey told me one night?' Jon said, 'I don't know what he told you but he told me it actually happened.' I found out later he told Ronny Cox it had actually happened, [and] he told Ned Beatty [the same]."[21] Dickey also told Hugh Blackburn, the archery consultant who trained Voight and Reynolds to shoot arrows for the film, that the murder, rape, and canoeing accidents had all happened. When John Boorman visited Columbia before filming, Dickey said in a solemn tone: "John, I want to tell you something that I have never told another living soul. Everything that happened to me in *Deliverance* happened to me in real life."[22] Even as late as 1995, when asked by a writer for the *North Georgia Journal* whether he had experienced the events in *Deliverance*, he replied with a devious twinkle: "I can't say. The statute of limitations hasn't expired yet."[23]

As his novel and his discussions about it made clear, Dickey wanted to be thought of as a Hemingwayesque hero who had triumphed over the most barbaric elements in life. In March 1972, two years after *Deliverance* was published, he pointed toward the insecurities that motivated his posturing in an interview with David Arnett:

> I think that we all yearn to be something other than what we are. I'm really very dissatisfied with what I am. This is the whole secret of Lewis, because he despises himself. Lewis is no more or less than an intellectual and physical counterpart of Charles Atlas, who was once a skinny, 97-pound weakling, but now can be proud of himself, because he's put all this time in on his body. He is a victim of a crushing inferiority complex, so that he spends enormous amounts of time on himself, making himself im-

pressive intellectually—physically first, and then hopefully intellectually—with all his theories and mystiques, so that he can make other people feel inferior.[24]

Tracing Ed's ascent into Lewis's commanding role, Dickey was really tracing his own aspirations. The fact that he was not the omnipotent and omniscient superman of his fantasies only gave him more reason to entertain those fantasies.

If Dickey was Lewis and Ed, he was also Drew, Bobby, and the mountain men rolled into one. Dickey explained his contradictory intentions to novelist Fred Exley three weeks after the book's publication: "I intended to show a man who, in defending his own life and the lives of people who depend on him, becomes both a hero and a criminal: intended to show, in fact, that there is no real line of demarcation between these two types, some or even most of the time."[25] For a decade he had been using his poetry to examine his civilized and savage, heroic and criminal impulses. Now he projected them onto a larger canvas. He told an English professor at Appalachian State: "The four main characters are *more or less* based on people I knew—and still know. But it would probably be even more true to say that they are all aspects of myself. For example, I was an art director like Ed, a kind of survival nut and archer like Lewis, a guitarist like Drew, and a weakling like Bobby."[26] Drew in many ways resembles the younger, more innocent Dickey—the boy who developed a respect for the law by listening to his father recite famous court speeches. Ed describes Drew as a "straightforward quiet fellow," which is how Dickey's early teachers and friends described him. In the novel Drew is a young husband "devoted to his family, particularly to his little boy" and a sales supervisor "for a big soft-drink company [Coca-Cola]." With regard to the guitar, Drew, like Dickey, was a belated student who "without having any talent . . . played mighty well, through sheer devotion [and who] . . . went in for all the really hard finger-picking stuff; Reverend Gary Davis, Dave Van Ronk, Merle Travis, Doc Watson." Ed says of Drew: "You were the best of us. . . . The only decent one."[27] Through Ed's eulogy Dickey glances wistfully at his own prelapsarian innocence.

Although Dickey once implied that he modeled Bobby after Al Braselton and Dave Sanders, his own personality went into the mixture as well. Bobby first appears in *Deliverance* as Lewis's foil: "He had smooth thin hair and a high pink complexion. . . . He was pleasantly cynical and gave me the impression that he shared some kind of understanding with me that neither of us was to take Lewis too seriously." While Dickey was writing his novel, his hair was also thinning, his complexion (when healthy) pink, his mood often cynical and wry. If he romanticized Lewis-types, he also cut them down to size, especially when they were his rivals. Bobby represented the sociable, sneering pitchman in Dickey (Bobby sells mutual funds) who enjoyed parties and business deals. Ed says: "Bobby, particularly, seemed to enjoy the life he was in. . . . He was very social and would not have been displeased if someone had called him a born salesman."[28] Not much bothered Bobby. As Dickey once told an Englishman writing an essay on his work, Bobby was the type who could shrug off the rape in the woods: "Much as he disliked what happened to him, [Bobby] would get over it easily enough; Bobby is a lubricous sort of man; being buggered would not mean

all that much to him."[29] Some readers perceived in Bobby the stereotypical homosexual—a weak, effeminate misfit unfamiliar with the rough ways of the
woods who doesn't fight back and whose occasional outbursts of anger seem unmanly. One of his tirades reminds Ed of "the rage of a weak king."[30] Like Bobby,
Dickey was overweight, occasionally bad-tempered, awkward in a canoe, and,
according to Lewis King, sometimes "terrified of the woods."[31] He was also more
intrigued than repulsed by homosexuality.

In *Deliverance* Dickey treats buggery as a rite of passage, and no doubt that's
how he viewed his own homosexual encounter—or at least the imagined version of the encounter—that took place earlier in his life. Like the remembered
act of sodomy in "The Sheep Child" that drives the Georgia boys toward marriage, Dickey's homosexual experience had the paradoxical effect of convincing
him that heterosexuality was preferable. He occasionally hinted to friends that
homosexual experiences were necessary rites in the heterosexual development
of men. About the time *Deliverance* was published, he took his student Ben
Greer to an archery range in the woods, talked about the homosexual writer
André Gide, and asked Greer if he thought a particular boy was handsome.
Greer waffled. Dickey ceremoniously put Greer between himself and the target
and said he would shoot over him because he wanted Greer to hear the sound of
a broadhead arrow. Frightened, Greer stood where he was told, and Dickey shot
two arrows over his head. "By the way," he remarked all of a sudden, "ain't nothing that says you can't have it both ways."[32] With other men Dickey performed
similar rites and made similar comments about the way men arrived at their—
albeit ambiguous—heterosexual orientation.

The description of Bobby as "a weak king" punningly suggests that he is a
weaker version of Lewis King as well as of those mythic kings who might oversee such rites that transform boys into men. Dickey's envy of King and his competitive desire to usurp the "strong king's" throne is a subtext of *Deliverance*.
Dickey genuinely admired King's abilities with a canoe, fly rod, and tennis
racket and learned a great deal from him. He especially respected the way King
dedicated himself to mastering new skills. But he was also somewhat frightened
by King's fanatical devotion to the out-of-doors, especially when it came to canoeing down rivers like the Chattooga. In *Deliverance* the religious fanatic in
Lewis Medlock attracts and scares Ed. Both Ed and Dickey resemble Ishmael in
the way they only reluctantly follow their zealous, charismatic Ahabs.

Dickey scored some of Ed's and some of his own mixed feelings about women
and sex into the love scene at the beginning of *Deliverance*. Making love to his
wife, Ed ignores her and imagines the scantily clad Kitt'n Britches model hired
to make an underwear ad for his firm. Martha simply serves as a launching pad
for his fantasies: "The girl from the studio threw back her hair and clasped her
breast, and in the center of Martha's heaving and expertly working back, the
gold eye shone, not with the practicality of sex, so necessary to its survival, but
the promise of it that promised other things, another life, deliverance." The gold
eye—the organ of visionary delight—contains romantic promises that never
materialize. Dickey tracks Ed's disillusionment through a series of significant
"touches." After Ed "stepped over and touched" the model in the studio, he is
overcome with desire. Touching Martha in bed is not so arousing. As Ed leaves

his women behind and passes the boundary where "suburbia ended and the red-neck South began," he says: "An inhuman coldness touched me." He encounters the Southern outback more palpably when a predatory owl lands on his tent and he repeatedly "touched the cold reptilian nail of one talon below the leg-scales." The reality of the redneck South is most vividly apparent when the mountain man cuts Ed with his knife before the rape scene. Ed reflects: "I had never felt such brutality and carelessness of touch, or such disregard for another person's body."[33] What Ed—like Dickey—wants to touch, commune with, and be delivered by is a fantasy of feminine beauty. The alternative, Dickey would agree with Tennyson, is "Nature, red in tooth and claw." Actual women, as their dearth in the novel attests, provide little consolation. But after witnessing the homosexual brutality in the woods, the men have only one alternative—to return to their women in the city.

Among *Deliverance*'s many forebears, Conrad's *Heart of Darkness* was the most influential. Dickey's novel resembles Conrad's in many ways, especially in its double-edged appraisal of civilization and savagery. To Conrad's narrator, Marlow, London is not all that different from Kurtz's Inner Station in the African wilderness, where he carries on his nefarious ivory trade. Ed thinks that Atlanta is a commercial hell and that the North Georgia wilderness is a savage hell. At the start of *Deliverance*, Ed is as beguiled by the unknown land on Lewis's map as Marlow is by the mysterious spaces on his childhood map of Africa. Lewis laments that the river on his map will soon be filled in by a lake; Marlow laments that his map "had got filled . . . with rivers and lakes and names. It had ceased to be a blank space of delightful mystery—a white patch for a boy to dream gloriously over. It had become a place of darkness. But there was in it one river especially, a mighty big river, that you could see on the map, resembling an immense snake. . . . And as I looked at the map of it in a shop-window, it fascinated me as a snake would a bird." Both the Thames and Congo Rivers are serpentine; they tempt decent people into "the dark places of the earth." The Cahulawasee River has the same effect on the decent men from Atlanta. What Ed and Marlow realize on their river journeys is that civilized folk cannot bear much reality, that legal and religious institutions shelter them from painful truths, and that they need comforting lies to survive. On his return to "the sepulchral city"[34] of Brussels, Marlow lies to Kurtz's intended bride about Kurtz's final romantic thoughts of her. He judges her too weak to accept the facts. For the same reasons, Ed lies about Drew's actual death to his wife in Atlanta.

At Vanderbilt Dickey learned to regard his childhood journeys between city and country, and his even more disturbing journeys between home and college, military base and war zone, as rites of passage. He also learned that myth is often the linguistic equivalent—the spoken or written story—that rites enact. He admitted to David Arnett that *Deliverance* grew from his study of ritual and myth at Vanderbilt, and had a specific origin: "If there's any literary or mythological precedent for *Deliverance*, it comes from a review I read in *The Kenyon Review* in the summer '49 issue, when I was a senior in college. It was an enormously impressive thing to me, and it's been in my mind ever since. It's a review by Stanley Edgar Hyman on a number of books on myths and rituals, and he quotes Van Gennep's 'rites de passage' on myths and rituals, and cites 'a separation from the world, a penetration to some source of power, and a life-enhancing return.'"[35] The book Hyman examined at the beginning and end of his review, and which became so central to Dickey's purposes in *Deliverance*, was Joseph Campbell's *The Hero with a Thousand Faces*. According to Hyman, Campbell practiced a kind of *allegoresis*; he interpreted all myths so that they conformed with a three-stage "adventure of the soul" in a "monomyth." Campbell, who began his career with a scholarly guide to James Joyce's *Finnegans Wake*, took his term "monomyth" from Joyce's book, which was an immense compendium of myths. All myths of the heroic quest, according to Joyce and Campbell, articulated the difficult process of the child forsaking the influences of parents, whether benevolent or oppressive; descending into the shadowy underworld of frightening and exhilarating experience; and returning to civilized society to disseminate the lessons learned from the journey. Dickey took Campbell's ideas about the mythical hero's departure, initiation, and return and used them to universalize his own experiences in *Deliverance*. As a result, his canoe trip resonates with the heroic journeys of other mythic figures like Osiris, Odysseus, Orpheus, Lucifer, Aeneas, and Christ. Deeply traditional, his novel is also modern in the way it self-consciously reflects on its own status as a fiction, myth, or lie. It is a story in which the narrator continually debates whether he should tell a story or tell the truth. The last instance of this is when Ed lies to Drew's wife about the death of her husband: "As we drove home I wondered if it would have been any better if I'd been able to tell the truth. Would it be easier for her if I could tell her that Drew was lying in a wild stretch of the Cahulawassee with part of his head bashed in either by a bullet or a rock?"[36] Like Dickey, Ed opts to tell a story.

The novel is also modern in the way it undercuts the mythic paradigm of the life-enhancing return. There is no happy end; there are no traditional heroes. Dickey supplants the Edenic myth of innocent relations between males, which critics like Leslie Fiedler have found in such American classics as *Huckleberry Finn* and *Moby Dick*, with unsavory adult realities. The violent powers of the river and those who live by it overwhelm the insouciant voyagers. Although James Wright insisted to Dickey that "*Deliverance* is another poetic recreation of *Huck Finn*,"[37] in *Deliverance* the boyish men do not remain boyish. They become as barbaric as the men they confront. Dickey's ending leaves us with ambiguities and questions rather than tidy resolutions. Lewis may be a tragic hero or a foolish zealot, Ed a clever survivor or a misguided vigilante. Homosexuality is represented as appealing and repugnant, heterosexuality as consoling and boring. Does Lewis take voyeuristic pleasure in seeing his friend buggered? He could have fired his fatal arrow earlier, but waits. Is the Kitt'n Britches model a stimulating or tiresome fantasy girl? At the end Ed confesses: "I still loved the way she looked, but her gold-halved eye had lost its fascination. Its place was in the night river, in the land of impossibility."[38] If "guilt is magical," as Dickey liked to say, Ed's dallying with the model no longer possesses much guilt. To find guilt he must remember events on the river.

Dickey ends his novel with a subdued, anticlimactic sentence: "One big marina is already built on the south end of the lake, and my wife's younger brother says that the area is beginning to catch on, especially with the new generation, the one just getting out of high school."[39] Dickey expresses no enthusiasm for this new generation of superficial pleasure seekers. Questioned in 1995 about Carter's Lake, which was formed when the Coosawattee River was dammed, Dickey was similarly glum. The hydroelectric power, flood control, and recreation were pale substitutes for his original canoe trips: "I will probably never get into another canoe. But I remember those days when I paddled the Coosawattee with great favor. 'Progress,' so called, can be a dreadful thing."[40] In the novel, Dickey refuses to say whether the mythic river, on which boys became men through violent rites and crimes, was preferable to the artificial lake. His heroic tale ends quietly with the simple fact that the turbulent past has been buried.

Most reviewers praised *Deliverance* as a gripping story by an author still getting used to the novel form. Evan Connell in the *New York Times* quibbled with the first-person narrative technique, but conceded that Dickey had fashioned an exemplary drama. Stefan Kanfer in *Time* found the story compelling throughout, despite the one or two episodes that taxed credibility. Princeton's offer to purchase the manuscript drafts of the novel gave some indication of the critical respect for *Deliverance*. (On April 13, 1970, Willard Thorp congratulated Dickey on writing a classic and broached the idea of selling the manuscripts to Princeton.) Not all the reviews, however, were laudatory. Benjamin DeMott panned the book in the *Saturday Review* for its gratuitous, sophomoric, "shoot 'em up" violence. A number of women wrote hostile reviews, which Dickey greeted with denials and a humorous story. He wrote Catharine Meyer at *Harper's*: "When the people at Houghton Mifflin first persuaded me to finish the novel . . . the only possibility they expressed doubt about was the reaction to the book by women. These doubts appear, now, to have been unfounded, for as many women are buying the book as men are, and perhaps a few more. I was at first a little at a loss to explain why this should be, until some lady at an autographing party told me that women want to know what men do and what happens to them when they go off by themselves."[41] A year later, Dickey was not so flippant. Convinced that his detractors had torpedoed his book's chance to win a major award (he complained to his friend Marcia Cavell: "*Deliverance* missed winning the National Book Award . . . by one vote"), Dickey was particularly disturbed by comments made about the book's endorsement of machismo. Citing a review by Hilton Kramer, he declared: "I don't understand what he means by machismo, at least as it applies to this book. The character who professes to possess this mysterious quality, Lewis, is put out of action, and the self-effacing Ed Gentry must perform all the tasks that Lewis has spent hours and months and years in preparing himself to do."[42] At the same time he tried to exonerate his novel, he indulged in the sort of women baiting that made him so vulnerable to attack. To Joyce Carol Oates, who admired *Deliverance* and sent Dickey an autographed book of her poems as a gift, he wrote: "Despite all the Anne Sextons and the Adrienne Riches . . . there has been very little real womanly sensibility in American poetry. Many are called but few—well, very few women can or do write like women."[43] In this instance, he praised Oates for writing like a woman. Later, he drawled to an *Esquire* reporter: "Joyce Carol Oates? Oh, she is one a these female intellectuals, we have so many of 'em, don't we, these ov'ly intense American intellectu'l *females*, such as Mary McCarthy. This sort of writin' is so unsavuh'bly negative."[44] Dickey's old-fashioned concepts of womanhood were those that feminists most wanted to deconstruct.

The accusation that Dickey applauded hairy-chested, macho stereotypes in *Deliverance* was misguided. The novel, in fact, endorses almost nothing except tight-lipped endurance. The book focuses on men, but the focus is withering rather than celebratory. Women are marginalized, but Dickey allows one woman—Drew's wife—to deliver a judgment that encapsulates much of the novel's message: "Nobody can do anything. Nobody can ever do anything. It's all so useless. Everything is useless. It always has been."[45] She articulates the despairing existentialist point of view that the novel began with and returns to at the end. If Dickey's personae wait for some godlike Godot to resolve their uncertainties and transport them into a happier state, they are disappointed. Their deliverer never arrives. As in the darker writings of Camus, Sartre, and Beckett, the characters at the end are survivors rather than celebrants of their Sisyphean routines.

Despite the feminist critiques and Dickey's sarcastic responses to them, some women revered *Deliverance*. The future Nobel laureate Toni Morrison wrote Dickey that *Deliverance* was an unrivaled American classic that she regarded as highly as the novels by Marquez and Kafka. The poet Diane Wakoski praised the novel as an allegory particularly relevant to the early 1970s because it explored the myth that men belonged to nature and, without bitterness or cynicism, exploded it. Male critics offered allegorical interpretations as well. A history professor, Tom Fiddick, at the University of Evansville in Indiana claimed that the four Atlanta canoers represented John F. Kennedy's New Frontier administration. The murderous events in North Georgia paralleled America's war in Vietnam, and the lies told by Dickey's characters recalled the disinformation concocted by Kennedy's men about the war. According to Fiddick, Drew played the role of Kennedy, assassinated by a bullet from a mysterious Communist. (Dickey, indeed, had originally intended Drew's head wound to resemble Kennedy's.) If all readers interpreted *Deliverance* as did Fiddick, drawing parallels between the Vietnamese Communists and Georgia hillfolk, the book would have aroused more controversy than it did. As it was, some North Georgia residents accused Dickey of demeaning them. Robert Linn, writing on May 24, 1970, from the small town of Calhoun, Georgia, decried the way the novel distorted the relations between country and city folk. Linn admitted that mountain people were often wary of the city, but was offended by the suggestion that all mountaineers were bent on sodomy. On November 27, 1970, the North Carolina poet and editor Jonathan Williams, who had gotten to know Dickey in Atlanta during the late 1950s, wrote an even more scathing rebuke of *Deliverance* and sent it to *Esquire* after the magazine ran an article about the novel. Years later, Georgia governor Zell Miller, who grew up in northeast Georgia, placed *Deliverance* near the top of his list of most hated books. In the wake of comparable rebukes, Dickey began telling friends that he stayed away from his old canoeing haunts for fear of getting lynched.

Conservative groups were also dismayed. In early June, Dickey learned from the *Atlantic Monthly*, which had become a dartboard for those who reviled

Dickey, that an English teacher in Fortuna, California, named James Vince had been punished for using the magazine's excerpt of *Deliverance* in the classroom. The situation, as relayed by Vince to Robert Manning on June 10, 1970, was desperate. Friends had warned him to leave the city for safety. Because he had taught Dickey's work, community members were blaming him and his sympathetic colleagues for the school's drug problem, protests, lax dress code, ineffective teachers, and other faults. On June 10, Dickey rushed to his defense: "*Deliverance* is not a work of pornography, as some of your townspeople seem to feel it is. It deals with one of the most frighteningly manifest aspects of our society—violence."[46] Many of *Deliverance*'s less sophisticated critics failed to distinguish between an acknowledgement and an endorsement of violence and pornography. Because Dickey wrote about such things, they assumed he advocated them. Ed, in fact, despises graphic pornography and resorts to violence only to protect himself and his friends.

Dickey's frustration with his critics turned to anger when he learned that in some parts of the country local citizens had banned and burned his novel. An English teacher, Bruce Severy, in a North Dakota high school reported to Dickey that his administration had gathered up all copies assigned to the eleventh grade and incinerated them on November, 15, 1973. Apparently the school board hadn't even read the book; they based their condemnation on rumors that the book contained scenes of animal intercourse, although they called it "annual intercourse." According to the school officials, the intercourse—whether annual or anal or animal—was not a proper subject for course books. On a reading trip to Brown University that coincided with the book burning, Dickey met with Ben Weiser at the campus radio station to talk about the events in Drake, North Dakota. "It seems to me that Hitler has risen from the grave," he sneered. "He surfaced not in Berlin but in North Dakota." He told Weiser that he deplored "those who exploit the relaxation of censorship laws to put the most prurient and self-serving pornography in an obvious sense before the public," and he deplored with equal vehemence those philistines who "attempt to make themselves self-righteous by attacking the smut mongers and the artists . . . without discrimination."[47] Dickey planned to go to Drake with Kurt Vonnegut, whose books had also been committed to the flames, to make a public protest. He also wanted to help the English teacher who had assigned his novel, since the school board threatened to fire him.

The attacks on *Deliverance* did not end in North Dakota. Fearing the corruption of his teenage son, in 1974 a Maryland resident initiated a campaign to ban the book in the Montgomery County school system. Since the novel was on a required reading list for sixteen-year-old students, he filed a reevaluation request with the Department of Education to get it dropped. He also wrote a chastising letter to Dickey. A decade later, the furor continued. Complaints came from parents of students at Catholic Bishop Gibbons High School near Notre Dame. Having collected letters from other parents whose children had read the novel and seen the film, they sent them to Dickey along with their own denunciation on January 19, 1983. Attempts to ban *Deliverance* were even made after Dickey's death. In 1998, the parent of a student at Connecticut's Sheehan High School, who found the homosexual rape scene pornographic, appealed to the superintendent of schools to remove the book from the seniors' reading list. Irritated by such simpleminded reactions, Dickey's daughter from his second marriage took up the fight for the novel, perhaps finding some consolation in the fact that her father's book was still being read.

One of Dickey's principal worries following his novel's publicaton was that his success as a fiction writer would overshadow his reputation as a poet. He wrote McCormick at Doubleday on April 8, 1970, to assure him that he was selling as many copies of *Eye-Beaters* as *Deliverance*. Dickey said he hoped to push sales of his poetry book over the ten thousand mark as soon as possible. He would help his cause by reading poems from *Eye-Beaters* at Young Harris College on April 2 and at Oklahoma State University on April 4. In late May, sales did top ten thousand, but his poetry book was no match for his novel. Having exaggerated once to McCormick, he exaggerated again: "We're moving up toward a hundred thousand copies [of *Deliverance*] now. . . . But I do want you to know that I am battling hard to keep our book [*Eye-Beaters*] from being swamped by the attention being paid to *Deliverance*, just as I have always fought to keep poetry itself from being ignored in the attention paid to the novel."[48] Since Houghton Mifflin had published fifty thousand copies of the novel by March 23, Dickey could not resist doubling the figure of possible sales.

Dickey's competitiveness was as vigorous among novelists as it was among poets. His main opponents in fiction, he decided, were those vying for the top position on the bestseller lists. Determined to push *Deliverance* into the number-one slot, he studied lists around the country for signs of openings. Because Erich Segal's *Love Story* was the main obstacle, he leapt at opportunities to ridicule it. In late May, he wrote Christopher Sinclair Stevenson at Hamish Hamilton, the English publisher of *Deliverance*, that Segal's novel was "a very light-weight, women's-magazine type of soap opera, and everybody who is going to read it has already read it. It may take us a few more weeks or months to overtake it, but we shall surely do so."[49] *Deliverance*, however, never bumped *Love Story* from the top slot. In some cities Dickey's novel surpassed such competitors as Mario Puzo's *The Godfather* and John Fowles's *The French Lieutenant's Woman*, but on most of the bestseller lists, such as those at *Time* and the *New York Times*, it climbed to number three in early June and then subsided.

The success of *Deliverance* only made Dickey's claims for his novel and for himself more grandiose. Usually he played up his penurious career as a poet and his total lack of experience as a fiction writer to make his "first" novel seem more miraculous. What he told George Stevens, a director at the American Film Institute in Beverly Hills, about *Deliverance* on April 8 was typical. He was bewildered by the popular success because he was "used to seeing his work come out in small circulation literary magazines."[50] Why he considered the *New Yorker*, *Harper's*, and the the *Atlantic Monthly*, where he sometimes earned $1,000 per poem, "small circulation literary magazines" he didn't say. As spring turned to summer, Dickey had more reason to feign bewilderment. By July 21, his novel had sold 67,000 hardback copies. Jacques de Spoelberch predicted that the novel would sell about 750 copies per week for the rest of the summer and remain on the bestseller lists into the Christmas season. The paperback, to be released by Dell in April 1971, would initiate a new round of sales. By the eighth printing in June 1973, about 1,800,000 copies of *Deliverance* had sold. Needless to say, Dickey reaped a financial windfall. In 1970, he earned about $20,000 on the paperback rights and $17,500 from the Literary Guild rights. In 1971, royalties amounted to $45,000. Future editions brought in more royalties.

To some of his friends Dickey spoke freely of his burgeoning bank account. He told Peter Neumeyer: "This noveleering is a strange business, particularly to one who has been publishing in the literary quarterlies for twenty years at fifty cents a line. It's a whole new ball game, as they say, but I must play in it as hard and as well as I can, for it promises to make my family well off—even rich—for the rest of our lives; yes, and for my children's lives, too."[51] If worthy causes solicited contributions, however, Dickey relapsed into his pretense of destitution. During the summer of 1970, he told John Ullman, who had asked for a donation to help preserve a folk music archive in Seattle:

> About the funds required for the preservation of the folk archives up there, I can't help you. My family situation is such that I am supporting two or three other families beside myself. My son Chris is now married and has given me, of all things, a grandchild [Chris and his wife, Susan, had given birth to James Bayard Tuckerman Dickey on June 9, 1970]. I must get him through college and perhaps through a year or two of graduate school. My brother and his family are also fallen upon hard times, and of course my mother and my father have always been destitute. So I don't have money for projects like yours, which would indeed be the first of all projects if I had the dough to put into them.[52]

His solicitude for his impoverished parents, his brother's family, and Chris's family sounded noble. To anyone who knew about his parents' wealth, his brother's real estate business, and his grandson's college education eighteen years in the future, Dickey's claims were laughable.

With *Eye-Beaters* and *Deliverance* successfully launched, Dickey turned to other projects. On April 8, he agreed to serve as a judge on the prestigious Bollingen Award committee, staunchly supporting Mona Van Duyn's *To See, To Take*, which won. In May, he applied himself to his Harvard Phi Beta Kappa address, pointing out to friends that Emerson had delivered his "American Scholar" essay on the same occasion. Dickey planned to read "Exchanges," his poem inspired by Robin Jarecki and Trumbull Stickney. In May, Dickey also worked on a short article about adultery for Mary Cantwell, the managing editor of *Mademoiselle*. Since Dickey extolled adultery as revitalizing, on May 19 Cantwell asked him to acknowledge its cruelty. Dickey complied with the addendum: "Adultery is terrifying and beautiful, unutterably delightful and unspeakably awful, and the eternal sad thing about it is that, in the name of preserving your own self-image and sexual adventurousness, you are also in danger of destroying—or at least seriously injuring those people to whom you owe all your better instincts of the *other* kind: plodding easy-goingness, small pleasures that are admittedly small, years of give-and-take. These are valuable and necessary, but so are chance-taking and craziness and breaking-out."[53] *Mademoiselle* never published the article, but published others by Dickey—an appraisal of W. N. P. Barbellion's *Journal of a Disappointed Man*, a chapter from *Self-Interviews*, and a short piece on female sexuality.

The letters that Dickey wrote Cantwell in the early 1970s indicated that he might like to make her a partner in his adulterous adventures. Although Cantwell wrote Theron Raines on June 9, 1970, that she wanted to meet Dickey, she was suspicious of him. Her husband, Bob Lescher, whom she divorced in February 1971, had spoken to her years before about Dickey's conduct. Shrugging off warnings from numerous friends, in November 1970 Cantwell agreed to have dinner with Dickey on one of his weekend trips to New York. In a blue, paisley-lined suit, a paisley tie, and long hair carefully brushed over his bald spots, Dickey guided her to the dining room of his hotel and abruptly asked: "Mary, you evah been screwed till ya screamed?" Before Cantwell could mumble a response, Dickey reflected: "Ah'm a womanizer. Ah just love them tight-assed little girls." Wanting to prove she was no willow before such bluster, Cantwell sat down to a dinner of steak tartare. Showing little appetite for food, Dickey proposed that they retire to his room, where he had a couple of six-packs on his windowsill. Cantwell balked, and, after Dickey dropped some guitar picks on the table, she nervously told a long, involved tale about listening to *fadista* singers in Portugal. Dickey's sexual bravado cooled. He began quoting Matthew Arnold, Gerard Manley Hopkins, and Stevie Smith, and ended with a friendly declaration: "Mah Mary. . . . You know what I like about you? You're mah equal. Mary Cantwell, we're gonna be one long thing." Accompanying Cantwell to the lobby door, Dickey admitted: "It's just as well you didn't come upstairs. I wouldn't have been much good to you."[54] Cantwell assured him that she would have been happy to just sleep beside him, put her arms around his neck, and kiss him.

About a month later, his macho persona rehabilitated, Dickey called Cantwell and threatened to take down her pantyhose and spank her. He wanted to see her again in New York and sent her a ticket to a panel discussion on film writing he was chairing. In her memoir *Speaking with Strangers*, where Dickey appears as "the balding man," she confided that his dirty talk had her "as mesmerized as a mongoose faced by a snake." She consulted her psychiatrist about her tumultuous feelings, and he advised her to stay away from Dickey. Cantwell, instead, decided to let Dickey purge her of the sexual longing she still felt for her ex-husband. Following the dinner party for the film panelists, she led him to her bedroom, put on her sexiest nightgown, and welcomed Dickey into her bed. Without his clothes, Dickey once again lost his sexual bravado. As Cantwell reached to embrace him, he said almost shyly: "Well, this is me." The next morning he was surprised that Cantwell appeared so chipper. "You don't feel any shame at all, do you?"[55] Although Dickey was only the second man to share her bed, she welcomed the relief from loneliness.

Over the next few years, Cantwell looked forward to her meetings with Dickey at his hotel or at her apartment. To be in the company of a "genius," as she believed he was, boosted her self-esteem, which had been crushed by the collapse of her marriage to Lescher. He read her articles and gave her books. Like many before her, she recognized Dickey's pretensions and the flaws that necessitated them, but forgave them. His brilliance and boyish charm were suitable compensation. She later wrote: "Alcohol had taken its toll of the balding man, and although he was never impotent, he was demanding. Neither the athlete his publicity claimed nor the sexual Goliath his reputation promised, he was more myth than male. That may not have been true when he was young. 'The first time I ever had a girl, mah Mary, I couldn't wait and neither could she. So I took her on the kitchen table, only a room away from where her parents were sitting. Oh, mah Mary, I wish you'd known me then.' But by the time we met he needed fantasy. I was Scheherazade . . . , a teller of tales of Great Danes [having sex with women] and girls' reform schools and female warders and whippings and frightened virgins on all fours, urged onways by his murmured 'That's good, mah Mary, that's real good.'"[56] At about the same time, another lover, Paula Goff, was asked to tell similar stories to facilitate Dickey's lovemaking (Dickey enshrined these stories near the end of *Alnilam*). As with Goff, Dickey's affair with Cantwell had a sadomasochistic element. But unlike Goff, she justified Dickey's indignities by viewing them as punishment for failing as a wife and mother.

The lies and insults Dickey directed toward Maxine were harder to justify. Speaking to Maxine on the phone in Cantwell's presence, he made up stories about his activities in New York, just as he made up stories for Cantwell about how she was his only lover. "Fat!" he would say about Maxine. "She's got the sex appeal of a walrus." Then he would make snide remarks about her feminine hygiene. As with his other women, Dickey constantly engaged Cantwell in make-believe and role-playing. He said he had World War II nightmares; Cantwell pretended to console him like a mother. "Mah Mary," he once said, "I think we're kinder to each other than either of us has ever been to anyone else."[57] His moods zigzagged like quicksilver. When he flirted with an old girlfriend at a dinner party and Cantwell rebuked him, Dickey threw a tantrum and threatened to leave with the other woman. Cantwell occasionally considered leaving Dickey, not only because of his womanizing but because of his racist and ethnic slurs. One of his favorite jests was: "Well, I'll be a nigger aviator." Because Cantwell praised her first husband, who was Jewish, Dickey said: "But I don't see how you could have done it." She asked: "Done what?" He responded: "Marry a *Jew*." On another occasion, while waiting with her two daughters in the living room before a dinner date, Dickey said: "You kids don't look like you have any kike blood in you at all."[58] Fearing the comment would spoil her love affair, the girls hesitated to reveal it to their mother. Feeling cowardly for not reprimanding Dickey for his bigoted remarks, Cantwell chose tolerance over loneliness.

Once on the heels of a fight Cantwell accused Dickey of lying. He responded: "Yes, I lied. But what has truth to do with me? I'm an artist. I *make* the truth." Unlike some of his friends, Cantwell usually knew when he was "making" the truth, such as when he told her he had won the Congressional Medal of Honor and when he told her he had played guitar with an Australian Aborigine who had a wind instrument called a didgeridoo. His endorsement of lying notwithstanding, Cantwell believed his claim that he intended to marry her after Maxine died in 1976. They often discussed their future together. Cantwell was ambivalent: she wanted him to propose, but because she knew he was an alcoholic, she thought an affair was more prudent. Meeting at intervals would allow her to overlook his failings and appreciate his virtues. Her experience with Dickey in the 1970s, as she surely knew, was not unique: "He had performed so constantly, had so consciously constructed a public image, that he had erased his self. Maybe he had no self. Maybe to live he had to kill it. Maybe, too, his best work was behind him, so his next work, the one that would keep him busy for the rest of his life, was to create the legend he wanted to leave after himself. For all his weight and height and boasts and booming voice, and the way he V'd his thin, pale eyebrows over his round blue eyes and drew back his lips over his tall, narrow teeth when he feigned anger, he was as insubstantial as the jack o'lantern he sometimes resembled."[59] Dickey, of course, was not *simply* a blustery will-o'-the-wisp or histrionic jack o'lantern. If he had been, Cantwell would have disposed of him.

In 1970, Dickey once again tried to cut back on the performances that augmented his "public image." His first round of promotional readings and book signings for *Deliverance* was an ennervating distraction, so in mid-April he told his booking agent at Lordly and Dame, Bill Thompson, that he was retreating to his study. Angry that his agent had signed him up to read in El Paso for $1,250, he declared: "I am no longer able to spare the time for readings, and don't expect to do any more [he said nothing of his reading at Vanderbilt in twelve days]. . . . I don't need the money. I have an almost unbelievable amount coming in from the novel, the film, the paperback people . . . , and I no longer wish to take the energy that travel necessitates for the thousand or so dollars that each reading gives. Tell everyone—no readings or ask for $5,000, which might interest me, although I could not guarantee I would go even at that figure. The point of the fact is that I am sick to death of all this traveling."[60] He had had enough plane flights, taxi rides, poetry readings, cocktail parties, and strange hotel rooms. Exactly three months later, in a less exclamatory tone, he explained to Thompson: "I can almost categorically state that I will never again go on as intensive a schedule of readings as I have done in the past. No; that is over. Selected readings at a very high price, yes. But junketing all over the map for just *any*thing; no."[61] In future letters about readings he argued that if Al Capp, a lowly cartoonist, could get $3,500 to speak, then he, an award-winning poet and best-selling novelist, should get much more.

Some of Dickey's students and colleagues noticed a new swagger in Dickey's manner after the success of *Deliverance*. He began wearing to class a cowboy hat and blue jean jacket, upon which his daughter-in-law had sewn a large eagle and the large letters POETRY. He sometimes strummed his guitar while he lectured, bragged about his lucrative film and paperback contracts, and flirted drunkenly with the girls. Tim Gautreaux, who went on to become a successful fiction writer, was disappointed by Dickey's lackadaisical teaching. Ben Greer, who took his verse composition class in 1970, thought Dickey had become a different man. "He completely crushed me," Greer recalled, by sneering at one of Greer's poems as "lousy doggerel." In 1991, after they attended a football game together, Greer told his former teacher: "You are the real reason I became a novelist." "Why?" Dickey asked. Greer answered that it was because Dickey had judged his student poetry to be the worst he had seen in all his years as a teacher.[62] For the student who in a few years produced the superb novel

Slammer—a novel Dickey imitated in his own writing—this judgment was hardly deserved.

Paula Goff reacted differently to Dickey's teaching in 1970. She found his assignments and advice helpful. Goff had met Dickey in the spring of 1969 before ever setting foot in one of his classes. She had first read about Dickey's arrival in the local newspaper and dreamed of meeting "The Unknown Man." When Goff gleefully announced to her husband that a living, breathing poet was coming to town, he responded: "Oh no." During the fall of 1969, while the Encyclopedia Britannica filmed the class partying at Dickey's house, Goff sat at his feet as he played the guitar. According to Goff: "He suddenly reached out and put his hand on my head and said one of those very shocking things that The Unknown Man said [in dreams], that I had written down the previous April. . . . From then on, I followed him."[63] What he said was: "Let's go out and fuck all night"—something not captured on the Encyclopedia Britannica film.

Fifteen years later, reflecting on their prophesied meeting, Goff wrote in the USC literary magazine: "The world was never the same for me thereafter. It was one thing to dream of Robert Kennedy's assassination before it happened; his death was a world-shaking event. But there I was, a suburban housewife and mother gone back to school to learn to be a teacher; my own world was shaking. I had glimpsed the pattern that underlies life not only on a grand scale but also on my own level. I had to know more."[64] Dickey provided more corroborating evidence that dreams predicted and even governed life. Goff's dreams of Dickey, which he often fulfilled, became so common that she gave them a special name, her "connections," and gradually filled several filing cabinets with her dream poems.

Goff was looking for a mentor and found one in Dickey. Until 1969, she had lived a relatively sheltered life. Born Paula Culclasure in 1938, she had grown up in Olympia, a mill village on the south side of Columbia. She had graduated from a local high school in 1956, married, given birth to three children in quick succession, entered USC in 1965, and earned her B.A. in 1970 and M.A. in 1974. Dickey not only inspired many of her poems, he laid the groundwork that made it possible for her to win USC awards for both her teaching and poetry writing.

After all the students had left one class, Dickey asked Goff if she was in love with him. She said she was. They would have to decide what to do about it, he declared. With that in mind, they got together for lunch. Dickey decided they should consummate their love on a reading trip, and instructed Goff to join him at Wesleyan College in Macon, Georgia, on January 4, 1971. Responsibilities at home prevented her from going. "Somebody was supposed to be in Macon, if I'm not mistaken,"[65] Dickey scolded with a rhyme when he returned. For a while he distanced himself from her, but soon they began drinking together at a bar called the Stage Door at Five Points. They also saw each other farther afield: in Saginaw for the Roethke awards in May 1971, and in New York, Knoxville, New Orleans, and other cities where Dickey had appointments.

Goff's affair with Dickey lasted until 1976, the year Maxine died and Dickey remarried. Goff was Dickey's "soul mate," as his friends in Columbia put it. She revered Dickey partly because he resembled her father, an intelligent man who had managed a local textile mill where her mother had also worked. Dickey loved her for her down-home innocence, her talent as a poet, and her unswerving devotion to him. She impressed Dickey as an earth mother and moon goddess rolled into one. She claimed to have telepathic and clairvoyant powers. Wracked by anxiety, she experienced seizures. No all-American beauty, as she herself acknowledged, she was a soulful Galatea that Dickey could shape like Pygmalion. In his fantasies, she exuded sensuality and in real life submitted to his sadoerotic demands. Before meeting Dickey, Goff had never had a drink, never been in a plane, and never had much contact with famous writers. The change Dickey implemented was both painful and thrilling.

Maxine, at first, liked Paula. She invited her to parties, introducing her as "Jim's star student." When she discovered the affair, her attitude turned vitriolic. Because the USC classicist and Homer translator Ennis Rees admired both Dickey and Goff (he awarded her the Academy of American Poets' Fanny Fay Wood Prize for a sestina in 1970), he invited them to his annual Christmas parties. Here Maxine sometimes squared off with Goff, throwing a drink in her face, hitting her with a handbag, or simply warning her to stay away from her husband. Similar battles erupted on Goff's turf. Her husband tolerated her liaison with her "magic man" at first, but then kicked her out of the house. Later, she did the same to him. Matters were disastrously resolved in a few years by a man who burst into a local bar where Goff's husband was drinking and shot him in the head. He died shortly afterward. On the road with Dickey at the time, Goff was distraught. She began drinking heavily, and, her guilt and despair unassuaged, she tore up some of Dickey's books in a symbolic rejection of him. Her love for Dickey and his literary life, however, was not so easily exorcised. She later collected the tattered pages for a collage to be called "Orpheus in Jericho" (one of the torn books was Dickey's *Jericho*) and returned to him.

Goff's and Jericho's fate were not dissimilar. Reflecting on her association with Dickey shortly before he died, she said: "I paid the price for what I wanted most in the world. I was the best I could be when I was around him, [but the affair] . . . did cause me the loss of my house that I'd lived in for thirty-one years . . . , and two heart attacks, and I'm left with seizures to the point that I'm on disability. I still seem to have enjoyed my life. I'm not holding this against him. It was great fun. I just wish he thought of me as more than a functionary."[66] In a fit of pique, Dickey had called her nothing more than a "functionary" because of her job as his assistant, which she held off and on during the 1970s, '80s, and '90s. Dickey normally thought of her in more endearing terms and treated her kindly. On a trip to New York he bought her new clothes when she suffered a terrible episode of menstrual bleeding. Later he bought her son a sailboat.

Among Dickey's many duties in 1970, the one that gave him the most pleasure was organizing the USC literary festival, which he scheduled for April 30–May 2. Guests included John Barth, John Simon, Richard Lippold, and Ned Rorem. Dickey grew particularly fond of Rorem, a well-known musical composer and diarist whom he had first met at a literary party in New York. Ingratiating and self-deprecating but also playing the bumpkin, Dickey introduced him first: "Now I don't know about his music, but if you ain't read his *Paris Diary*, you ain't read anything."[67] At the conference Rorem played music, conferred with students, and partied at Dickey's house. Wearing a cowboy hat, Dickey flirted with the gay Rorem and on later trips to New York continued to do so. He once said that he would sleep with Rorem if he were gay. Rorem contended, however, that Dickey did not have a strong physical or sentimental need to have homosexual experiences. "He was not a closet queen"[68] nipping off to the gay baths in New York. Rorem would have heard about such escapades if they had occurred.

Dickey's friendship with Rorem developed over the years through correspondence and visits. A few weeks after the conference, Dickey wrote him: "We have been having one of those boring student strikes down here, and I am very happy that our conference was able to take place in comparative peaceful suroundings. If we had waited another week, we would have all had to wear gas masks, for the police have been gassing the campus regularly."[69] Dickey wanted to meet again and dreamed up bizarre collaborations for that purpose. In New York on December 12, 1974, he proposed that Rorem "illustrate" one of his books with what he called "sonic backgrounds" to his poems. Rorem wasn't quite sure what to make of the idea—Dickey was quite drunk at the time—and soon let it drop.

As spring turned to summer, honors and invitations kept landing in Dickey's mailbox. The prestigious American Academy of Arts and Sciences made him a Fellow on May 13. At about the same time, the nominating committee for the National Medal for Literature welcomed him as a member. He was asked to speak with Buzz Aldrin at a black-tie banquet honoring the Apollo 11 astronauts in New York's Waldorf Astoria Hotel on June 1. Despite his repeated efforts to cut back on travel, he continued to barnstorm for *Deliverance*. On June 5, he visited Chicago for a series of televised interviews on Robert Cromie's "Book Beat," *The Tim Conway Show*, and Kup's TV show. He also got together with *Playboy*'s fiction editor, Robie Macauley, for an interview. Jacques de Spoelberch, who accompanied Dickey, found him on the brink of alcoholic frenzy. Before the Bob Cromie show they went to a bar and consumed about twenty-five drinks between them, Dickey downing fifteen bourbons and Spoelberch ten stingers. Dickey, who weighed about 240 pounds at the time, wanted to arm wrestle Spoelberch, who was sixty pounds lighter, at the bar and inside their rooms. Spoelberch was convinced that Dickey had other intentions as well: "I'm pretty sure he was interested in some homosexual sex. . . . He drank so much and when he drank he came on to whatever was there—man or woman. . . . I rather quickly sensed that, like many many artists, there were feminine and masculine components in him. And [they were] very strong."[70] Spoelberch was relieved when his drinking partner trundled off to the Cromie show.

Dickey traveled to Boston for more promotions, and on June 17 he went to the twelve-day Hollins Conference on Creative Writing and Cinema. R. H. W. Dillard and George Garrett had lined up an illustrious poetry staff including Richard Wilbur, William Jay Smith, James Seay, Henry Taylor, James Whitehead, and Dickey. Along with the poets at Hollins's bucolic campus in southwest Virginia were about fifty movie producers, publishers, critics, agents, novelists, and English professors. Fiction writers Larry McMurtry, Sylvia Wilkinson, Jesse Hill Ford, R. V. Cassill, David Slavitt, and Ralph Ellison attended (Whitehead remembered Ellison and an inebriated Dickey doing Shirley Temple impersonations at a party, and even dancing like Shirley Temple).

Movie producer Samuel Goldwyn, Jr., was there, as were O. B. Hardison, director of the Folger Shakespeare Library, and Louis Rubin. The distinguished guests lectured, gave seminars, and directed workshops. The conference participants could attend classes on horror films, Westerns, Soviet cinema, avant-garde cinema, young New York filmmakers, African-American films, and Shakespearean films. Some of the 250 students even got academic credit for going to the classes and films. Chris Dickey, who was studying filmmaking in an interdisciplinary program at the University of Virginia, was one of the many who attended.

Dickey arrived at the Hollins Conference in grand style. As Dillard recalled, he had a good-looking blonde woman by his side and told people she was a professional prostitute named "the Miami Hurricane." (Dickey was embarrassed when a large photograph of him with the blonde woman appeared along with Annie Dillard's article in the November 1970 *Hollins College Bulletin*.) He tried to seduce many of the women, even Dillard's wife, Annie. Perched on a sofa beside her, he showed her pictures of his family and lavished praise on his "beautiful boys."[71] Before long, he was fondling her leg and moving his hand up her dress toward her thighs. Dickey offended others besides the Dillards. In a room that included the writer Fred Chappell, Dickey announced in a stentorian voice: "Mah tennis game is more important than Veet Nam."[72] Drinking like Dylan Thomas, Dickey echoed his predecessor's remark about World War II: "I think a squirrel stumbling at least of equal importance as Hitler's invasions."[73]

William Smart, who had recently witnessed Dickey's drunken conduct at Sweet Briar, witnessed more of it at Hollins. Dickey, he recalled, organized—or said he organized—his own version of *The Dating Game* in which Hollins girls competed for a week vacation with him by performing fellatio. Dickey's sexual pranks were legion at the conference. At one point he picked out a "sacrificial virgin," who was supposed to offer herself to him during the night he read. As the evening progressed, the designated woman grew increasingly nervous, while Dickey grew increasingly excited. Unable to bear the anxiety any longer, the young woman told Dickey that she had to go up to her room to prepare herself for the promised consummation; he would have to wait in the parking lot. According to Hal Crowther, who knew the "sacrificial" woman, she said: "Let me run up and get a nightie, Jim." Beneath her dormitory window he called abjectly: "Ciiiindy . . . Ciiindy."[74] Because she failed to materialize, soon the night watchman guided Dickey from the dorm. In a version of the story told by George Garrett, thirty girls opened their windows and mooned Dickey. "Good Night Mr. Dickey!"[75] they shouted in unison.

On June 29, Dickey wrote Garrett that the conference had been "relaxing, easy-going, and no sweat at all." It had given him time "to recuperate from a particularly harrassing schedule."[76] He was less sanguine in a letter to James Whitehead: "I think that is about the last one of those occasions that I will submit to, though these affairs have a certain baleful charm, a kind of exotic limbo in which the writer attempts to realize all those fleshly dreams that he has conjured up while sitting at the typewriters turning out things he wishes were better. I guess occasions like Hollins are supposed to be the 'reward' that American writers feel is reserved for them. Yet their fascination has a detrimental effect on them, which can indeed prove fatal." He was reminded of some advice Allen

Tate had given him about the poet's peregrinations, and passed it along to Whitehead. Tate had warned: "Don't do what I did, Dickey. I have spent my life making myself into some kind of poetical bum."[77] Hard as it is to imagine Tate, the chivalrous Southern gentleman, admitting to bumhood, Dickey frequently did, and in poems like "Bums, On Waking" (*Helmets*) he attributed his indelicate behavior to the sort of drinking he did on his travels.

Having talked up the film of *Deliverance* at Hollins, Dickey renewed his efforts to make the film a reality. The producer, Barry Beckerman, wanted Dickey to fly to California to discuss directors, actors, film sites, shooting schedules, and related matters. Too busy to join his producer, Dickey addressed his concerns in letters. With regard to the screenplay, he told Beckerman that he would write one draft by himself and modify it later with the director's help. Dickey had strong misgivings about Roman Polanski directing *Deliverance*, even though he was one of Warner Brothers' top choices. He listed his objections to Beckerman: "One is that he is not an American, much less a southerner, and might have some trouble understanding some of the nuances. . . . The other is that, because of what happened to his wife [Sharon Tate, one of the victims of the Manson family massacre], he might possibly suffer some kind of psychological trauma in making a movie which deals so obviously with violence and bloodshed."[78] Dickey's worries about Polanski's sensitivity to violence were unfounded; Polanski soon made an extremely bloody version of Shakespeare's *Macbeth*. Even in his jokes Dickey expressed reservations about Polanski. To George Stevens, he said: "I made it clear to my Hollywood contacts that I would not welcome being invited to any parties at his house [the site of the massacre]."[79] The better choice, according to Dickey, was Sam Peckinpah, and on May 26 Peckinpah assured Dickey that he was eager to direct *Deliverance*.

Looking ahead to the soundtrack, Dickey wrote Mike Russo in Portland about recording music for the film. In August, Russo agreed to play the introductory guitar music, the guitar/banjo "duel" between Drew and the Appalachian boy, and the later solos. Dickey also contacted Ron Brentano, who was equally enthusiastic. Even as late as November 1970, Dickey was convinced that Warner Brothers would sign up the Portland musicians. On November 2, he wrote Wes Taft: "We will try to use both Russo and Brentano, not only because they would be the best instrumentalists for the film, but as a kind of tribute of my own to the old days in the Pacific Northwest, never to come again."[80] Dickey may have contemplated using the renowned Doc Watson on the soundtrack as well. On August 21, G. Alex Bernhardt, an ex-marine night-fighter pilot who knew Watson, flew Dickey in his private plane to Watson's North Carolina home. To play the guitar with such legendary musicians as Doc and his son Merle was a rare treat. Warner Brothers, however, had its own plans for the soundtrack.

In early September, Dickey took a longer flight on *Deliverance* business. To launch the publication of the British edition of the novel, he, Maxine, and Kevin traveled to London for the week of September 8–15. As usual, Dickey looked forward to buying books and talking to poets. He wanted to see Vernon Scannell, D. J. Enright, Robert Conquest, and, above all, Geoffrey Hill. On September 9, still somewhat jet-lagged, he read his poetry and sections of his novel at a party honoring *Deliverance* at the Institute of Contemporary Arts in London. If he had regrets about his London trip, chief among them was missing Hill. He wrote Hill shortly afterward about how much he admired the sensuous, brooding rhetoric in *King Log*, Hill's latest collection. "I don't think there is another poet writing in English that is as good as you are. Surely there are none writing in England."[81] In a decade Dickey would change his mind, telling his friend David Bottoms that Hill's poetry had become "a complete mystery."[82]

When Dickey became *Esquire's* poetry editor in 1970, Hill was one of the first poets he solicited. On June 2 in New York, Dickey had spoken to Gordon Lish, an *Esquire* editor and also a successful fiction writer, about becoming the magazine's poetry editor. Later in June, Dickey signed a contract. The guidelines for his job were somewhat restrictive, and the annual salary was a meagre two thousand dollars. Dickey was supposed to accept poems around sixteen lines or less and submit only five poems per issue to senior editors like Harold Hayes, who would make the final selection. To celebrate his new editorship, *Esquire* threw a party for him on December 7 at the Esquire Exhibit Hall at 448 Madison Avenue. Before the festivities began, Dickey visited Lish in his office and, with a new girlfriend, Amy Burk, waited in the Exhibit Hall. As Lish recalled, many of the *Esquire* editors were Southerners who disapproved of Dickey. Harold Hayes, the editor-in-chief from North Carolina, was especially antagonistic. The *Esquire* staff gave Dickey a subdued welcome and left the party early. Dickey's flamboyance, which repelled the other editors, attracted Lish, and they became regular drinking partners. On his New York jaunts, Dickey regaled Lish with tales about his girlfriends (he claimed to have had an illegitimate child by Amy Burk), his wife (Maxine had formerly worked as a hooker and taxi driver in New Orleans), his sons (Chris had gone to Exeter, and Kevin was a layabout), and his own background (he had grown up in poverty and become a combat pilot). After Dickey met Lish's newborn son at a 1971 dinner at the Saint Moritz and playfully threw him into the air like a beach ball, Dickey pretended to be the boy's godfather, even though no religious ceremony ever took place.

The most elaborate ruse Dickey imposed on Lish involved Amy Burk, the sister-in-law of Raymond Carver, whose short stories Lish was editing and publishing. Burk met Dickey for the first time at the *Esquire* party and soon began an affair. At the time she was a single mother acting in Brendan Behan's *Borstal Boy* on Broadway. Dickey told her he wanted her to play the Kitt'n Britches model in *Deliverance* and convinced her to fly to Los Angeles for an interview at Warner Brothers. In 1971, she moved to Los Angeles because of the possibility of the *Deliverance* job and another job in a stage production of *Othello*. Neither materialized, so she got other acting jobs in commercials and small theaters. Dickey lavished attention on Burk, buying her fancy clothes and expensive meals. He also adored her young daughter, and devised an intricate scheme to provide her with money. He told Lish that after he had fathered the child, Maxine had refused to send child support. He implored Lish to act as an intermediary, passing his messages and money to another intermediary who, in turn, would pass them along to Burk. Lish believed Dickey was telling the truth and went along with the byzantine scheme.

Unlike Goff, Cantwell, and many of his other mistresses, Burk had only fond memories of her affair with Dickey. Having suggested that she play the Kitt'n Britches model, he tended to act as Ed did in the novel, treating her as a fantasy woman. Around 1974, he nearly recited Ed's lines about pornographic films when, on a lark, they decided to see the film *Deep Throat*. Repulsed by the early sex scene, he jumped from his seat and shouted: "This is an outrage!"[83] He railed against the way such pornography destroyed the beauty of sex, grabbed Burk from her seat, hustled her up the theater aisle, unleashed a similar tirade to the ticket seller, and demanded a refund.

Dickey acted in a similar way with Geoffrey Norman, who conducted an interview and wrote a story for *Playboy* during the fall of 1970. Norman wanted to have a *Deliverance* experience, so Dickey organized a canoe trip with Lewis King and Al Braselton on the Chattahoochee River. Dickey brought beer, bows, and broadhead arrows, and they spilled several times just like his characters in the novel. After playing guitars and reciting poetry at King's house, Dickey and Braselton picked up some women. Braselton remembered how surprised and innocent his friend seemed in the presence of overt sex:

> That same trip Jim and I met some women and I . . . had access to a friend's apartment; so we took these women over to this apartment with the idea of having a little fun. Well, we sat over there and began to drink; and at that time I drank a lot, too. Jim usually was a little ahead of me, but I enjoyed drinking and so did these girls. So we sat there and drank until it came time to get amorous. And we began to get amorous. I went back in the bedroom, and my girl and I took off our clothes and as a matter of fact, I really didn't care whether anybody saw me or not. It was kind of a little curtain. We could look out through there and see them, but they couldn't see us at the time because it was dark back there. So Jim sat there and talked to this girl, and I made love. I remember after that he said, "You know, that's remarkable. It's so marvelous that she will let you do that right there." . . . If he were as cynical as some people think he is, he wouldn't have thought that was marvelous. . . . And he kept going on about it.[84]

As *Esquire*'s poetry editor, Dickey said he wanted to make literary history by publishing a variety of known and unknown poets. To Willie Morris he announced grandiosely: "I plan to blow everybody's mind. My general notion is to get established poets to write the kind of poetry that they are *not* identified with, and to solicit poetry from poets who are not known as poets."[85] One of the nonpoets he solicited was Morris himself. He also asked Monroe Spears and his nonpoet friends at *Time* to submit poems. Among the established poets, he contacted James Wright, Robert Penn Warren, Wendell Berry, and Charles Simic. Hill sent the book-length *Mercian Hymns*, which Dickey greeted with a combination of puzzlement and adulation. In the end *Mercian Hymns* appeared elsewhere.

The day after the *Esquire* party, Dickey dined with Ken McCormick and discussed, among other things, his new novel, which he was calling either *The Field of Dogs* or *Death's Baby Machine*. Two weeks before their dinner, Dickey had notified McCormick of a recent feud with Houghton over his plan to bring the novel to Doubleday: "Houghton Mifflin is pretty well shook by this, as you can imagine, but I was not at all happy with the way the advertising for the book [*Deliverance*] was handled."[86] He also told McCormick that he had resisted Spoelberch's attempt to rush him into a hundred-thousand-dollar advance contract for his new novel. Spoelberch had urged his bosses to present Dickey with a contract soon, but no money had been discussed. By December 22, 1970, Dickey was in close touch with Stewart Richardson at Doubleday about the book that would mushroom over the next two decades into *Alnilam*.

25. Making the Movie (1971)

Considering his lack of screenwriting experience, the speed with which Dickey completed the screenplay for *Deliverance* was remarkable. He told John Logue that he had written only a few documentary films prior to tackling *Deliverance*. One, he claimed, was about aircraft carriers. The other was *Celebration*, the short film loosely based on John F. Kennedy's *A Nation of Immigrants*. Inexperience proved to be a goad rather than a liability. From the start he decided to write a script as detailed and artful as the novel. To achieve this goal he tossed aside the model scripts sent by Warner Brothers and studied James Agee's screenplays. On August 6, 1970, he sent his first draft to John Calley with the explanation:

It may be that I have gone into too much detail in places; I can't of course know what you will think of this. I read through the scripts that Barry Beckerman sent along [*A Clockwork Orange* was one], and it seemed to me that they were pretty thin. I had much rather try to do a James Agee–type script, and perhaps put in too much rather than too little. Anyway, you will tell me what you think. This is, as the agreement has it, a first draft. Doubtless there will be some changes suggested, perhaps by you and almost certainly by whatever director we select. Nevertheless, this screenplay is essentially what I want to do, and when I thought I had come up with a good shot or camera angle, I said so. This is for the director to accept or reject, as he sees fit. As you will notice, I have changed the ending and several other of the parts to include material that is not in the novel. But I have stuck pretty closely with the story, for I think that any changes we make should be in the interests of making a better film of our material, and not simply to change for the sake of changing.[1]

Dickey later admitted that he had been naive in believing a director would follow his copious instructions: "I left almost nothing to the actors—to whatever actors there would be—to the director, to the cinematographer, to the sound technicians, or even to the safety crew on the river. I had Platonic, ideal working conditions, and no one to tell me what I had done wrong. I had a thousand ideas I thought not only workable but positively inspired for every scene, every camera angle, every movement, every transition, every fortissimo or diminu- endo of sound, every change of chord in music, every birdcall."[2] According to his "Platonic" script, the film would open with a black screen and sustain the blackness long enough for the audience to wonder whether something was wrong with the projector. The sound of running water would begin and suddenly stop. A quick burst of loud twelve-string guitar music like "Buckdancer's Choice" would break the silence and also come to an abrupt end. Slowly the camera would focus on a scarred tabletop where mysterious hands unrolled a map weighed down by steins of light and dark beer. One hand would hover ceremoniously over the map before pointing to a single river. At that moment "DELIVERANCE" would appear across the screen, followed by credits. In subsequent shots the camera would reveal Lewis, Bobby, Drew, and Ed sitting in a bar decorated in a gay-nineties style, with paintings of reclining nudes in the background. Lewis would banter about the pros and cons of his canoeing plans. The first ten or fifteen minutes of the film would dwell on the "well-financed boredom" of the Emerson-Gentry advertising firm. The camera would move from the Kitt'n Britches model to Ed's plain-looking wife, who would announce: "Sex is not romance. It's practice."[3] One of the final Atlanta scenes would show Ed organizing his knives and arrows for the trip. The rest of the movie would fol- low the calamities on the river depicted in the novel.

The day before he mailed his screenplay to Calley, Dickey received a disturb- ing letter from the Writers Guild of America informing him that Warner Brothers had terminated his contract because he had failed to apply for guild membership. Dickey quickly filled out and mailed the required forms, but took this sudden rebuke as an omen of future troubles. He told the young poet William Heyen, who had just invited him to read at the State University College at Brockport, New York: "I expect there will be a great deal of agony connected with the making of the film, but when has the artist ever had any- thing else?"[4] Brooding on his script's future, Dickey was relieved on August 20 when Warner Brothers approved it. Once again his Hollywood prospects seemed boundless. He told friends that Warner Brothers had chosen *Deliverance* to be one of their two major widescreen films for 1970. To Henry Abrahams he could hardly contain his glee: "John Calley, production chief at Warners, says that in his fifteen years at the studio he has never been so besieged with directors and actors to do a single film. . . . Not to seem immodest, I don't blame these people at all."[5] At the end of the summer Warner Brothers had narrowed the shortlist of directors to one—Polanski—and Dickey to another—Peckinpah. Dickey wanted Peckinpah because he admired his treatment of violence in civilized set- tings and was particularly enamored of his recent film *The Wild Bunch*. He must have recognized the uncanny resemblance between Peckinpah's gang of doomed gunslingers and his own doomed adventurers in *Deliverance*. Dickey welcomed Peckinpah as a kindred artist who shared his nostalgia for a primitive past, ob- session with violence, and anxiety about masculine romanticism.

By early September 1970, Dickey knew that Peckinpah's bid to direct *Deliverance* was in trouble. Peckinpah wrote a rancorous letter on September 3 about his battles with Warner Brothers, informing Dickey that he was suing the company and that, in any case, John Calley had told him twice over the past three months that he was close to signing a deal with Polanski. He desperately wanted to direct *Deliverance*, but he doubted Calley would make an offer. Warner Brothers, Dickey assured Peckinpah in a letter, had made no firm deal with Polanski and as far as he was concerned Peckinpah was still the top choice. He instructed Peckinpah, who was living in London, to contact him at Old Saint James House on Park Place when he was in the city to celebrate Hamish Hamilton's publication of *Deliverance*. On Peckinpah's turf, Dickey repeated his support, but he could not speak for Warner Brothers. Near the end of their long conversation, the director said to the poet: "Well, if we don't do your movie, Jim, we'll do something together." Dickey agreed. Peckinpah continued: "Remember all the time, when we get together again, we do the same thing, you with your words on the page and me with my pictures up on the screen. We try to give them images that they can't forget." Dickey replied: "Amen, I'll go with that." Because Peckinpah's recent film *The Ballad of Cable Hogue* had failed at the box office, and because of his litigation, Fred Weintraub and Ted Ashley at Warner Brothers made it clear that they wanted nothing to do with Peckinpah. In December, Peckinpah accepted defeat and began expressing reservations about Dickey's screenplay, which he felt was more of a treatment. If a film were made from the script, he pointed out, it would run about four hours. He told Dickey that he was going ahead with his film *Siege* (it became *Straw Dogs*). In later years, out of admiration for the film Peckinpah made instead of *Deliverance*, Dickey romanticized his association with Peckinpah. "I was sort of an unofficial adviser on *Straw Dogs*," he said. "We had a lot of correspondence on that."[6] Dickey kept his correspondence with Peckinpah, but no letters suggest he worked on *Straw Dogs*.

When Dickey heard that Warner Brothers was considering John Boorman as the director for *Deliverance*, he was initially ecstatic. On October 12, 1970, he wrote Larry Du Bois at *Time*: "When Calley told me that Boorman wanted to do the film I immediately got in touch with him, and he said he had read the book already three times and would break with MGM, where he is now halfway through a film . . . in order to do *Deliverance*."[7] To Larry Lieberman, who had invited Dickey to the University of Illinois for a reading in early November 1970, he expanded on his reasons for endorsing Boorman. Polanski, he claimed, was essentially a mood director who did not handle action well. Boorman excelled at action that had a philosophical dimension, which was what he wanted. Dickey especially liked Boorman's film *Hell in the Pacific*, in which a Japanese soldier and an American soldier fight to the death on a Philippine island. The film reminded him of his World War II experiences, which *Deliverance* recapitulated in different form. Dickey was convinced that Boorman would not only turn his story into a gut-wrenching drama; he would give it the existentialist inflection he had intended.

Boorman had mixed feelings about taking on *Deliverance*, even though its theme of heroic quest, which characterized many of his films, attracted him. For the Englishman, North Georgia was alien territory. Besides, he had hoped to continue working on one of his favorite projects, a film version of Tolkein's *The

Lord of the Rings. Financial reasons, however, pushed him toward *Deliverance*. Because his last film, *Leo the Last*, had been a commercial flop, he needed a hit to stabilize his reputation. He thought Dickey's screenplay might do the job. Boorman contacted Dickey and arranged for a visit to Columbia so that he, his production manager Charles Orme, and Dickey could talk about the screenplay and filming. Orme and Boorman flew from London to the United States on October 28, 1970. For the next few days, Boorman joined Dickey at his Lake Katherine home while Orme remained at a Columbia hotel to work on the screenplay.

Dickey and his director enjoyed each other's company, drinking and telling stories late into the night. They had much to share. Although ten years younger than Dickey, Boorman had vivid memories of the war that Dickey had allegorized in *Deliverance*. He had grown up in the midst of World War II–ravaged England, a situation comically recalled in his film *Hope and Glory*. From an early age he was steeped in the urban man's painful awareness of savage violence. Like Dickey, Boorman tended to conceive of his private experience in mythical terms: as a departure from parents and home, an initiation into a violent world of battles and contests, and a return to civilization. Working with a director conversant with the writings of Eliot, Joyce, and Jung was a privilege. Nonetheless, Boorman disagreed with the way Dickey had remythologized the heroic quest in *Deliverance*: "Philosophically, we had little in common. Dickey's beliefs are not unlike Hemingway's, especially the idea that one attains manhood through some initiatory act of violence. For me, the contrary is true: violence doesn't make you a better person—instead, it degrades you."[8] Boorman may have been responding more to Dickey's personal conduct than to his message in *Deliverance*, since the book makes clear that Ed's initiation into violent manhood *is* degrading and wounding. Ed returns to civilization not as a triumphant hero but as a haunted suburbanite.

Boorman knew that collaborating with Dickey would be difficult. In Columbia, Dickey was almost always drunk, overexcited, and reluctant to work. He acted as if his script were engraved in stone and recoiled from the director's proposed alterations. Because Boorman insisted on revising the dialogue, the opening section, and the last scenes, Dickey soon concluded that Boorman was an incompetent meddler: "[Boorman] didn't know anything about the woods. He didn't know anything about the rivers or canoeing or hunting. . . . He was one of these Hollywood people or movie-making people who pretend to know more than they actually do, and you could tell it immediately."[9] The real disagreement was over who controlled the script.

On October 31 Dickey took Boorman and Orme to northeast Georgia to look for film sites. Several advisers—Lewis King, Charlie Wiggin, and Claude Terry—had all come to the conclusion that the Chattooga and Tallulah Rivers would be perfect for the film's white-water scenes. Stretching only fifty miles between its origin in North Carolina and its end in Tugaloo Lake, the Chattooga covered a greater vertical drop in an average mile than the Colorado River. The final few miles—designated Section IV—were a series of boulder-strewn cataracts. An Emory biology professor and an avid member of the Georgia

Canoeing Association, Terry knew as much about canoeing rivers as King and
Wiggin. The threesome had considered the Little River in Alabama and the
Coosawattee in Georgia, but had rejected the former because it was too dry and
the latter because nearby trees had already been chainsawed in preparation for
the lake. They considered the Nantahala in North Carolina, but rated it too
tame. The Chattooga, which ran along the South Carolina–Georgia border, had
drawbacks too: it was relatively inaccessible, and it had dangerous rapids and
"hydraulics" that could drown capsized canoers in swirling underwater currents.

On their first foray into the Chattooga woods Dickey proved to be as theatrical as ever. Charles Orme recorded some of Dickey's melodramatic ploys in his
journal:

> From the highway we made our way down towards the Chattooga River by
> an old loggers' track. It ran through a forest of very tall trees, with very lit-
> tle foliage. Although set well apart, the trees were dense and seemed to
> reach up to, and obliterate, the sky. They were overpowering. No birds, no
> animals, only the sound of the breeze moaning through the tree trunks. It
> was in this ambience that Jim decided to go through a range of histrionic
> gestures recalling various episodes from his book. Jim would suddenly stop
> walking, throw his arms wide in apparent alarm, and hiss "Quiet! . . . did
> you hear that . . . ?" Everyone froze and looked at each other. It was a fine
> performance and Jim's impressive oratory and the way in which he moved
> arms and body to emphasize his points, was really most effective in the
> midst of this apparent wilderness. . . . I believe it was this little expedition
> Jim had in mind when he wrote in the book he gave me: "To Charles—
> who knows where the thing took place." We marched on. No soul in sight
> anywhere. At one stage, Kevin [Dickey] . . . moved alongside me and mur-
> mured words to the effect: "Don't pay too much attention to Dad. Hikers
> and naturalists come here quite often during the summer." Duly encour-
> aged, we finished our first exploration of the area . . . , returned to the
> highway and drove back to Lelia's Court.[10]

Boorman was particularly curious about the rape scene. Had a homosexual redneck ever assaulted Dickey? Had he ever had sex with a man? Dickey responded
with a denial couched in a qualification: "I have never made love to a man, but
if it gave me the slightest pleasure I would do so immediately."[11] With Al
Braselton, Dickey had simply denied that his one homosexual encounter had
been pleasurable.

To get a more intimate feel for the Chattooga and to better understand the logistics of making a film on its rushing waters, Boorman decided to paddle down
its less dangerous Section III in a raft. Dickey, King, Terry, and several others offered to accompany him in canoes. Recognizing another chance to demonstrate
the reality behind *Deliverance*, Dickey tried to show off his canoeing skills.
Unfortunately, in the first rapids he plunged over the canoe's gunnels.
Boorman's crew had to drag a shivering, gasping Dickey into their raft. A combination of fear, shame, alcohol deprivation, exertion, and cold water had precipitated in Dickey a mild seizure not unlike an asthmatic attack. Unable to live

up to the Thoreau-like image he had created for himself, he shivered and slumped in melancholic silence. Dickey mentioned little about his accident to friends. Instead, he repeated a story of an accident that nearly crippled Boorman: "I took him [Boorman] over into North Georgia . . . looking for locations, and damn near got him bit by a big copperhead. Now *that* would have been a touch of 'authenticity'! Imagine having an Englishman filming a novel about north Georgia *in* north Georgia, his veins full of north Georgia copperhead poison!"[12] In fact, Dickey was the one who usually acted like a foreigner in the Georgia woods. Realizing this, Boorman assured Dickey that he should feel no obligation to act out *Deliverance* on the Chattooga's potentially lethal waters; writing the book was heroic enough.

Shortly after their November trek to the Chattooga, Dickey sent Boorman a letter full of queries about his screenplay. Sensing Dickey's worries about directorial heavy-handedness, on December 10, 1970, Boorman wrote a six-page letter promising to consult Dickey about all revisions and to properly reward him for his services. He also told Dickey that Warner Brothers was not prepared to make the movie on the basis of the present script. They had to submit another draft that was the right length and in the right style, and it needed to have a budget, shooting schedule, breakdown, and cross plot. Boorman had set aside three months from mid-November to mid-February to complete these tasks. His letter lectured Dickey about the intricacies of filmmaking: "Let me say something about the relationship of scripts to films. In modern cinema the script is not a static document that is taken from the typewriter to the actors and director like holy tablets from the mountain. It is a blueprint, an indicator. Making a film is a dynamic process and the script must constantly change and evolve and respond to the pressures upon it."[13] Boorman belabored the point that Dickey was merely the preliminary architect. He, as the director, was the actual builder. Dickey agreed to consider his director's suggestions, but he insisted on writing the final version of the script. "I would like credit for the revision," he stipulated in late November, "because I have some kind of clause in the contract that I must do it, and, naturally, get paid for it. . . . Also, I would like exclusive credit for the script."[14] He also wanted a quick response to his demands.

Because they would be rewriting together, Boorman refused to grant Dickey "exclusive credit" as screenwriter. With regard to alterations, he told Dickey on December 10 that he wanted to replace the initial discussion over the map with a scene at an archery range where Lewis and Ed revealed their master-apprentice relationship. He also wanted to condense the activities in the bar and advertising firm, tone down the sex between Ed and his wife because he considered it potentially comical, and tinker with the sheriff's interaction with the surviving canoers. "I have made the sheriff slightly more sinister," he told Dickey, who had already announced his desire to play Sheriff Bullard, "and increased the suspicion that he might secretly know the truth—I was very nervous that after the high tension of the main story, the end might seem anti-climactic. I have therefore intensified the suspense element and kept the audience wondering until the latest possible moment."[15] Boorman had other worries about some of Dickey's details. Would the bodies of the buried hillbillies rise to the surface when the dam turned the river into a lake? In the final film, Boorman suggested such a resurrection with an image of a dead man's hand breaking the lake's surface. Could Bobby be made funnier and more sympathetic, the hillbillies introduced earlier, and the ambulance scene shortened? And would it be feasible near the end for Ed to vanish into the lake with the advertising model as in a dream?

It took only a few days for Dickey to respond to Boorman, who had moved from his home in Ireland to London. In general he concurred with the director's proposals. He admitted his script was too baggy. Perhaps in an attempt to prevent further excisions, he was downright obsequious: "I am lost in admiration for the *manner* in which you have done it [the cutting]. In other words, if we film the story as you have it, we will have the strange and magnificent movie that we *should* have: that I am convinced is *in* the story itself. As to the matter of listing the screen play credits as a collaboration of myself and you, that is quite all right with me, particularly since I have your assurance about the money part of it. There is no one else's name that I would more care to have bracketed with mine. You are the director that I want for the film; surely I must have made that clear by now. I met with Sam Peckinpah in London before I ever heard your name at all, and I figured I could do better. I *have*, in fact, done better, and we are going to make a hell of a movie. I will go with you right down the line on what you want to do. As you say in your letter, it is my novel, but it is *your* film."[16] Despite his compliments, Dickey had no intention of giving his director carte blanche with his script or sharing credits.

Dickey advised Boorman to open the film at one of two archery ranges he knew—Cub Run in Virginia or Litigo Canyon in California. Because Boorman wanted to start filming in the spring, Dickey suggested that they add some dialogue between Drew and Lewis to justify their illegal deer hunting before the fall season. Other anachronisms needed to be addressed. The Atlanta men talk about watching football games as they drive to the river, yet football, like deer hunting, is a fall sport. Dickey proposed the men refer to generic "ball games." Dickey, however, was not prepared to accept all Boorman's changes. He took exception to cutting Lewis's disquisition on survival, since surviving nuclear war was a pressing subject. He also disagreed with Boorman's final scene of Ed vanishing with the model. The girl from the advertising studio, according to Dickey, was expendable, and he refused to have "some kind of Disneyesque subliminal dream-imagery for the end of the film. . . . If you want to keep the girl, we should have whatever is to happen between [Ed and the model] happen in the office, rather than some kind of nude swimming scene. Personally I would like to *see* such a scene because I like naked girls, though naked men much less well, but it is not functional at all. It is far too Hollywoodish, and that is the last thing we want to do here. The scene should be in the office, and the girl should just be indicated as a pleasant part of the furniture."[17] If Boorman hoped to give women more visibility in the story, Dickey wanted to reduce them to bric-a-brac, even though he had proposed that his girlfriend Amy Burk or another friend, Milie Condon, play the role of the advertising model.

In a late-December letter to Boorman, Dickey expressed dismay about an apparent snub from Warner Brothers. Having learned that Calley would only accept a script from the director, Dickey asked Boorman why Calley hadn't communicated this proviso directly to him. And why hadn't Calley consulted him about the actors and the filming schedule? He told Boorman that everyone had urged him to take the money from Warner Brothers and refuse all further involvement. But he had rejected their advice because he wanted some control over the final product and he wanted to give his son Chris some valuable film experience. On January 9, Boorman tried to assuage Dickey's concerns. He promised to rework the final dream episode, and informed Dickey that he would fly to Los Angeles in late January to oversee casting, investigate film sites around Clayton in February, and spend all of March in Georgia preparing for the seven weeks of shooting that would commence in early April (the schedule was later changed). Dickey approved. "I'll swing with you, anyway *you* swing," he said at the beginning of the new year. Despite his determination to "swing," Dickey wrote Boorman a five-page, single-spaced letter expressing more reservations about Boorman's altered script. He reiterated the unimportance of the Kitt'n Britches model and stressed the need to show Ed's fading preoccupation with sex. Killing the hillbilly was "not to be seen as any kind of *substitute* sexual longing at all," Dickey said, "but is merely meant to show that a sense of unfulfillment which gravitated, under Ed's ordinary, day-to-day circumstances, to sex, as such things will, has actually found a much more powerful and positive medium than his erstwhile sexual preoccupation." The "more powerful and positive medium,"[18] Dickey argued, was violence.

With regard to the film's beginning and end, Dickey was adamant about preserving the story's mythical structure, its "circular movement": "What I really have in mind for the whole story, both in the novel and the film, is an updated version of Van Gennep's *Rites de Passage:* 'a separation from the world, a penetration to some source of power, and life-enhancing return.' This blueprint for 'the hero with a thousand faces' is a very powerful adjunct to this story. *Deliverance* illustrates this for our time just as surely as *The Odyssey* did for its, or any other work at any other time which employs this theme. For my money, it is the most powerful theme in all of literature, all of mythology, and, if you couple it with my *other* favorite theme, that of the hunted becoming the hunter, well, you really *have* something. It follows, though, that if we follow the *Rites de Passage,* we must in some measure show the *return,* and, as I say, I am for doing this, though we may very well do it very briefly indeed."[19] Dickey's later troubles with Boorman arose primarily from the director's disregard for the plot's mythic circularity.

For the moment, Dickey's faith in his director outweighed his doubts. To convince Boorman they were working with a winning story, he declared on January 18, 1971: "It now looks as though *Deliverance* is a solid bet to win both the National Book Award and Pulitzer Prize over here."[20] His novel would vanquish the competition: John Updike's *Bech: A Book,* Saul Bellow's *Mr. Sammler's Planet,* and Eudora Welty's *Losing Battles.* On leave from USC during the spring and summer of 1971, Dickey promised full support of his director and soon flew to Hollywood to attend casting conferences, confer with Warner Brothers executives, and revise the screenplay. Unfortunately, Dickey was as reluctant to work on the script in Hollywood as he had been in Columbia. Like his precursors

Faulkner and Fitzgerald, he drank in Hollywood until he was incapacitated. Because he had little respect for Hollywood types, he spent most of his time with Amy Burk. A frustrated Boorman remembered how he and Burk had to "pour" him onto the plane at the end of the futile trip. Their collaboration in a shambles, on the flight east Boorman said little to Dickey, who fell asleep. At one point Dickey suddenly woke and exclaimed: "John, if I weren't a Baptist and a famous poet, I'd divorce my wife and marry Amy Burk."[21] After this startling revelation, he fell back into an inebriated slumber.

Dickey's alcoholic behavior in Hollywood may have been partly the result of his losing so much control over his screenplay. He remembered imploring Boorman on the plane to preserve the mythic pattern of his story: "I said give me five minutes to show them [the four characters] being picked up in their apartments and homes in the suburbs so that when they come back the story would have a circular movement to it." Boorman said: "No, we've got 110 minutes on screen and I want to get them on the river sooner and I want to build up the music scene more."[22] Dickey also felt betrayed by Warner Brothers, who showed little respect for Dickey's screenwriting abilities. On a reading trip to the University of Arkansas in 1979, he took aim at those in Hollywood who had meddled with *Deliverance*: "Their sole mission in life was to suggest changes so they could get their names in the screen credits. . . . One of them suggested that instead of four men making that boat trip, we could have two guys and their wives; then we could get some sex out of it. The next guy said we should have one married couple and one guy with his girl friend; then we could get some *illicit* sex out of it. Another guy said the hillbillies should be Negroes so we could inject the race issue, and another said they should be drug-crazed hippies. The best one was the guy who suggested that we replace the hillbillies with Martians."[23] Dickey's sardonic recollections were more farce than fact, but they demonstrated his real frustration.

To Boorman, Dickey presented a bewildering and often unmanageable array of selves. Boorman understood that the conflicts between these different selves created the tension in *Deliverance*: "The four characters represent four facets of Dickey's personality; and, in a way, one might interpret the story as an attempt on his part to reunite these four fragments in one. Dickey was an athlete, an archer: that's the Lewis, vaguely fascistic side of his personality. He plays the guitar, he has, like Drew something of the artist and the moralist in him. And, like Bobby, he's also a bit of a coward: there are certain dangers he's afraid of, as is often true of men with imagination." Boorman also knew that he had worked for an Atlanta advertising firm like Ed. Coping with Dickey's embattled and combative personality proved difficult. (He admitted to Michel Ciment, who wrote a book about Boorman, that his film "was inspired as much by the time I spent with Dickey as by his novel.")[24] As for the actors who would give voice to Dickey's clashing personae, by late January 1971 Warner Brothers considered Jack Nicholson and Robert Redford the most likely candidates to play Lewis and Ed. They entertained other possibilities as well. According to Dickey, Charlton Heston, whom he had met on a talk show in late 1970, wanted to play Lewis. But Dickey felt audiences would confuse him with Moses or Ben Hur. Jimmy

Stewart, Warren Beatty, and Henry Fonda were also considered. Dickey explained the exquisite dilemma of choosing between eager stars to Ron Brentano at the end of the winter: "We wanted, or at least we were thinking about, Robert Redford for Lewis, but he wants the role of Ed to such an extent that he refuses to play Lewis. We want Jack Nicholson for Ed Gentry, the narrator, and he wants to do it, but he may be asking so much money that Warner Brothers won't pay him, in which case we will use Marlon Brando as Ed, and, probably, George C. Scott, as Lewis. Brando says he will be glad to play either Ed *or* Lewis, and I have to go to New York in a couple of days and confer with him on this."[25] Brando, as it turned out, was too expensive.

On April 28, Boorman wrote from the Warner Brothers offices in Burbank, California, that he had decided to cut all the introductory scenes from the film. He thought that critics would accuse the director of flaunting gratuitous sex if they kept Ed's lovemaking with Martha and his flirtation with the half-naked Kitt'n Britches model. He was also convinced that he could do all his character development on the river; he didn't need to introduce the four men in Atlanta. Dickey vehemently disagreed. Unable to resolve their differences, finally Boorman took complete charge of the screenplay, which partly explains why he claimed in an interview: "In fact, I wrote the script; it wasn't he who actually drafted it."[26] Angered by Boorman's emendations, Dickey reneged on his promise to share screenwriting credits. He and Theron Raines contacted the Screenplay Writers' Guild to make sure that only he would receive credit. Dickey argued his case on August 24, 1971. The Credit Arbitration Committee made a "determination" in Dickey's favor. On December 17, Warner Brothers notified Dickey that he would receive sole credit for the screenplay.

While Dickey's feud with Boorman escalated throughout the winter and spring of 1971, so did his feud with Robert Bly. Although Boorman waited to criticize the "vaguely fascistic side of his personality," Bly was already using such epithets in the 1960s. Dickey told James Wright in mid-January 1971 that he would have to confront Bly man-to-man or through his lawyers about these slanders: "One simply cannot allow someone to go about in public meeting after public meeting, at reading after reading on college after college calling one a racist, a fascist, a nazi, a nigger-hater, a toady of the government, and so on. This is quite clearly slanderous, and if you have any contact with Bob, you may tell him that I am not going to put up with it any longer." As with Bly's previous onslaughts, Dickey tried to pretend that he was above them: "It is not that all this is disturbing to *me*, but that the laws of this country are set against the kind of character assassination that he is bent on doing." Bly's barbs, however, had pierced Dickey's armor. He winced at Bly's accusation that at one reading he had declared: "Tell that nigger down in the front row to get me a mint julep or I won't read." Counting on Wright to defend him against such charges, Dickey feigned innocence: "Now can you imagine my possibly saying that, or anything remotely resembling it? I think Bob should be in a straight-jacket, and I am either going to put him there, or in jail, or in the poorhouse, or in the hospital."[27] Despite his denials, a drunk or sober Dickey was perfectly capable of such remarks.

To the poet Greg Kuzma, Dickey wrote a similar letter in which he blamed

Bly's false accusations on envy. A week later, on February 8, 1971, he complained to Bly directly:

> The most disturbing stories come to me from all over, from students, from teachers, from people who come to hear you read and talk to you. Now let me make my position very plain at the outset. I do not object to anything you want to say about my writings, or even any of the absurd interpretations that you insist on putting on them. What I object to is your campaign of bald-faced lies about me, my attitude toward minority groups, my politics, and things of that nature. I will stand behind anything I have ever gone on record as saying; that is, things that are facts. What I object to, and what I will do something about if it continues is your paranoic habit of fabricating stories about me and giving them out to audiences as though they were the truth. One boy called me, for example, from some place in Arizona or New Mexico, and told me that you had told an audience that you had *heard* me read, and say "tell that nigger down there in the first row to get me a mint julep or I won't read." You have never heard me read anywhere, since that time at NYU. Again, let me put this to you very, very directly. If I get one more report from anywhere that you have said anything of this nature, I am going to take you to court. If you have money for lawyers' fees, fine. I would very much like to get this on public record, in a court of law. After all, you leave behind you when you do these reprehensible, disgusting, and dishonest things, not only tapes of the various performances, but hundreds of witnesses at each college. It would not be difficult to gather all the evidence I need to make a case against you that would stand up in any court in this country, and I will do just that. Be guided by this as you may, but I will put you on the line against the laws of this land, if you continue this. And that's the truth.[28]

Dickey could have made a case against Bly, but Bly could have just as easily made a case against Dickey.

On February 25 Bly charged that Dickey was the one given to fabrications and slurs:

> Michael Harper came back from Urbana recently full of fantastic stories that Lawrence Lieberman had told him, and which Lieberman had said came directly from your lips. You had made them up out of whole cloth. The gist of these tale[s] was that I had rewritten a poem you had given me for the Sixties without your consent, that I had altered your prose without your consent, that I was a dishonest free-speech advocate, a lying editor, etc. None of these tales has a trace of truth. As you quite properly say in your letter to Jim Wright, this has got to stop.
>
> In my readings I have never called you a racist or anything remotely resembling that. I am not the originator of the mint-julep story, I am a listener. I heard that story in three separate parts of the country over the last months, and I have never said that I was present to hear it from you. On

the contrary, I don't know where it was supposed to have taken place. I don't know who originated that story, but I swear it was not me![29]

The war of words continued, complete with reconciliations, truces, and further hostilities, for the next two-and-a-half decades. In May 1972, after Bly sent Dickey a photograph of himself, Dickey was moved to nostalgia: "Whatever happened to my old friend? It's surely been a long time, so write at more length, whenever you have the time or the inclination, and let me know how things are with you these days, and with your family. I would look forward to hearing from you again, and, if our paths should cross, to getting together for a drink, or even dinner, for, as they say on the Sunday afternoon ball games, 'the clock is running.'"[30] As if recognizing the truth of some of Bly's accusations, Dickey wanted to forget and forgive, or simply forget. Could he not pacify or at least tone down his opponent with sentimentality and charm? Despite his friendly gestures to Bly, in letters, interviews, and conversations Dickey consistently berated him as a clownish poetaster who browbeat and brainwashed other poets like James Wright, Donald Hall, and Galway Kinnell.

Between salvos aimed at Bly, Dickey contended with Boorman. On April 8, 1971, he told Larry Du Bois that he was determined to employ only unknown actors and Georgia locals for his film: "My director, and I have managed to talk Warner Brothers out of filming the movie with *any* stars or actors that anybody has ever seen. We are going to make it like a wide-screen documentary, so that people that come into the theatre or the drive-in will have the illusion that they are actually watching these things happen, rather than watching them happen with Marlon Brando, Jack Nicholson, or whomever."[31] Actually, Boorman had just about finished selecting the final cast by early April, and it was not without a star—Jon Voight. For the lead role he wanted a less well-known actor, Burt Reynolds, who had surprised him by showing an appreciation for Dickey's writings. Assuring Boorman that he could speak with a Southern accent—he had grown up in Florida—Reynolds went to see the director at Warner Brothers in Los Angeles. The meeting, Reynolds recalled in his autobiography, *My Life,* proceeded awkwardly. Like Dickey, Reynolds was suspicious of an Englishman's ability to handle such an intensely Southern story. And why had Boorman chosen him to play Lewis? Was it simply because he did all his own stunts? Reynolds pressed the director to name films in which he had acted. Boorman allegedly dodged the questions and instead praised the way Reynolds had recently hosted Johnny Carson's *The Tonight Show:* "I have to have a guy who's in control of three men. Total control. And that night I watched you control five people. You're absolutely fearless, aren't you?" Reynolds answered self-mockingly: "No, I'm dumb. . . . I'm too dumb to be scared."[32] Boorman may have detected in Reynolds a man, like Lewis, at odds with his "dumb" persona.

Reynolds said that he accepted fifty thousand dollars for three months' work on *Deliverance,* a small amount by his standards. He knew, though, that the part was perfect for him and that, if he played it well, it might catapult him toward stardom. If Boorman was looking for an actor who resembled Dickey as much as

Lewis, he found one in Reynolds. Reynolds, like Dickey, had been born in Georgia (he had subsequently moved to Florida), and in high school had chosen football as a way to earn respect and woo girls. While the war delivered Dickey from college football and redirected him toward the arts, a knee injury did the same for Reynolds. As a sophomore he left college and football for an acting class at Florida's Palm Beach Junior College. After winning a scholarship to New York's Hyde Park Playhouse, he started acting on Broadway and in TV shows. In 1971, Reynolds was not in the same league as Heston, Brando, Nicholson, or Redford. He had appeared on the New York stage in *Mister Roberts* and *Look: We've Come Through*, played an Indian for two years in *Gunsmoke*, and acted in other television series like *Hawk* and *Dan August*. He had achieved modest success in the action thrillers *Operation CIA* (1965), *Shark* (1968), and *Skullduggery* (1969). The actor Boorman chose to play Ed—Jon Voight—was more than moderately successful; he had recently received an Oscar nomination for his performance in *Midnight Cowboy*. According to Reynolds, Boorman asked him if he would read with Voight to test their compatability. He agreed, and Voight, who had been hiding in an adjacent office, suddenly appeared. Reynolds claimed: "I started talking with him—in a southern accent—and we immediately got into an improvisation together, about going up to this river—which later turned out to be the improvisation over the opening credits. We did it first in that office."[33] The two actors also read from the script—at times hilariously—until Boorman was confident they could work together.

Reynolds remembered flying to Washington, D.C., with Voight to meet the actors who would play Drew and Bobby. Ronny Cox and Ned Beatty were at the Arena Theater performing in *The Pueblo Incident*. When the play finished, they went backstage to congratulate Cox and Beatty on being chosen as their *Deliverance* costars. As for the other actors, Boorman abided by the plan that Dickey favored by choosing residents of Clayton, Georgia. The doctors and nurses in the small hospital where Lewis receives treatment for a broken leg actually worked in the Clayton hospital. Along with the locals, Boorman cast members of his family and members of the actors' families. His son played Ed's son. Ned Beatty's wife played Ed's wife.

In early May 1971, Boorman gathered with actors and film crew at the Kingwood Inn and Country Club, a posh resort in the green, rolling hills near the center of Clayton, Georgia. The Dickeys, including Chris and his family, who were living in Charlottesville, stayed in A-frame chalets on the golf course. Others stayed at the Heart of Rabun motel in town. Boorman rented a large, one-thousand-dollar-a-month cottage where he showed movies, held Ping-Pong tournaments, hosted large dinners, and rigged up hi-fi equipment for parties. On May 7, Dickey arrived at the cottage and proceeded to evaluate the actors. "Do you really want to play Drew?" he asked Cox. Cox nervously replied that he did. Dickey slapped Cox's knee: "Good, because I want you to."[34] Dickey confronted the other actors with similar queries and confirmations. On May 8, Charles Orme escorted Dickey and Maxine to some of the film sites to see what obstacles lay ahead for them. Because of the rough terrain and rutted logging roads, it usually took over an hour to drive the canoe-laden Jeeps to the river. Kudzu, copperheads, ninety-degree temperatures, swarms of bugs, and waterfalls like Bull's

Sluice and Sockem Dog would test the men's endurance to the breaking point. Practicing canoeing skills on a quiet pond near the country club, even Reynolds admitted that he was unprepared for the Chattooga: "I got in one [canoe] with Ned Beatty and Jon Voight got in the other with Ronny Cox, and we paddled out in this quiet lagoon [sic]. John Boorman was standing on a hill with two propmen. We were out there a total of ten minutes and both canoes tipped over. And I remember as I was swimming to the shore I heard the prop guy say, 'We're going to be here a *long* time, a *long* time.'"[35] About the subsequent hiking, rock climbing, and bow-and-arrow training, Reynolds said: "It was like being plucked off the street and going to training camp with the navy S.E.A.L.S."[36] Reynolds was in fact working with a former member of the SEALs, Charlie Wiggin. According to Claude Terry, Reynolds developed a special bond with Wiggin, and to get into his Lewis Medlock persona he copied Wiggin rather than Lewis King. (The aggressive, athletic Wiggin had suffered a Medlock-like injury through similar adventurousness—he had blown off the inside of his hand while killing sharks with a shotgun probe.) In general, the crew and actors were glad to have such experts as Terry, Wiggin, King, and Payson Kennedy to help with the canoeing, but because of his stunt background Reynolds tended to presume mastery. Dickey noticed: "Reynolds didn't want to be an actor; he wanted to be a movie star."[37] He rarely accepted advice. If Terry and the other advisers tried to lend him a hand when he overturned his canoe on the Chattooga, which happened frequently, he grew furious. "We'll meet you down river,"[38] he would snarl, and struggle through the rapids on his own.

In addition to canoeing lessons, the actors needed archery lessons. They had neither the right archery equipment nor the right advisers to show them how to use what they had. In this area Dickey proved valuable. He called Hugh Blackburn, whom he had met in an Atlanta archery tournament around 1964. Living near Pensacola, Blackburn was a southeastern archery champion and Bear Archery's southeastern district manager. Thinking Dickey needed advice on filming an archery match, Blackburn was startled when he learned that Warner Brothers wanted his assistance on a major film. Dickey said: "You'd better get up here to Clayton. . . . We're in a hell of a shape. They've got some old wooden arrows they picked up in a dime store and I've got a bunch of bows here but . . . they can't shoot them."[39] Blackburn drove to Clayton and quickly ordered the proper bows, arrows, quivers, and fishing equipment from his company. Realizing that the actors and film crew knew nothing about stringing bows and nothing about using the correct terminology, he coached Voight with a $70 Kodiak Hunter bow and Reynolds with a $190 Takedown bow. Because of Voight's indifference to target practice, he got the two actors to bet a dollar a shot, which prompted them to take the shooting more seriously. Like Lewis King, Blackburn was sometimes disgruntled by the actors' blasé attitudes. Since Reynolds and Voight used expensive Razorhead hunting arrows rather than "field points" while shooting at targets on the riverbank, and since they fired the damaged arrows into the woods, Blackburn had to keep ordering new arrows. He also had to order numerous expensive bows because the actors at first failed to tie them to their canoes. During the scene when Ed shoots the mountain man on the cliff, the crew kept throwing away broken bows and using new ones. A bow lover like Blackburn found the wastefulness shameful, especially since Bear Archery was supplying all the equipment free.

Blackburn's experience with the two lead actors was typical; he found Voight meticulous, patient, and a good learner and Reynolds stubborn, prickly, and overconfident. Reynolds rarely waited for Blackburn to finish his instructions before trying to shoot. Reynolds exemplified his wilfulness in the trout-shooting scene. Boorman wanted Blackburn to do the shooting, but Reynolds staunchly refused. He shot arrow after arrow into a heavily stocked pool until he finally hit a fish (in *Summer of Deliverance* Chris Dickey says *he* was the one who shot the many arrows before skewering the trout). Reynolds later wrote that his ability with a bow depended not on Blackburn's lessons, but on Eugen Herrigel's *Zen in the Art of Archery*, which Dickey had insisted that he read. Zen helped him get into Lewis's character. In the initial scene on the Atlanta archery range, which was later cut, Reynolds claimed that he shot seven arrows into the bull's eye from forty yards when he was in character. "And *I* didn't release the arrow; *it* released me,"[40] he said, echoing one of Herrigel's Zen aphorisms. Out of character, he shot arrows wildly into the trees.

Blackburn discovered that there were more troubles on the film site than those relating to archery. Over breakfast he listened to Dickey denounce Boorman for eviscerating his novel. Blackburn sympathized with Dickey's predicament, but also saw that Dickey was becoming increasingly unmanageable. Instead of cereal or eggs, Dickey began his day with Heinekens, martinis, or a large glass of bourbon. As he drank, he became wistful and sententious. Blackburn remembered him waxing mystical about Yevgeny Yevtushenko, a poet he was translating: "I walked with him on the mountain. I communed with him. I still speak to him in wondrous ways. He talks to me about everything."[41] The drinking also made Dickey dangerous. He would ask: "How far is that hole on the putting green out there? . . . Could you hit it at 65 yards? Ninety yards?"[42] He was talking about arrows rather than golf balls, and started shooting at the greens, hoping the golfers stayed out of range.

Dickey sometimes conceded that he knew little about the spontaneous, trial-and-error way that films evolve. He felt he could help with the music and dialect and let Voight record his voice to improve Voight's Southern accent. The rest of the time he lumbered into rehearsals drunk and truculently proclaimed his opinions. Boorman recalled: "Sometimes he was jealous and hated me for, as he imagined, stealing his story from him. Then, another day, he'd congratulate me on one of my ideas and regret that it hadn't occurred to him when writing the book!"[43] According to Reynolds, Dickey regularly tried to take command with a bow and arrow over his shoulder and a double triple martini in his hand: "We'd be about to do a scene, and Voight would be pure concentration, he'd have everything all together, and just as we were about to shoot, Dickey would pull Voight over to one side and say, 'Yaw knowah that this actualla *happened*, don't you boay?' And Jon would go right out of his bird."[44] Reynolds was one of the most vocal critics of Dickey's meddlesome presence:

At night we would go to this great bar at the country club. At first no one but Jon, Ned, Ronny, and me were there. However, Dickey . . . started coming there every night too. Well, I just couldn't handle his act—his Jim Bowie knife on his belt, cowboy hat, and fringed jacket. He would corner Jon, Ned, and Ronny every night and tell them stories about the real people the novel was based on. However, he insisted on calling everyone by their names in the film. One night I was sitting way over at the other end of the bar, talking to my favorite cocktail waitress, and I heard: "Lewis! Lewis, I'm talking to you, boy."

The waitress whispered, "Mr. Dickey's calling you."

"He ain't calling me. My name's Burt," I said.

"Lewis, goddammit, I'm calling ya, boy. Come over here!"

I didn't move. I saw this mountain moving over toward me. Soon he was standing above me.

"Lewis, I'm talking to you, son. Now why aren't you answering me?"

I said, "Because I'm not Lewis. Tomorrow morning at six-thirty A.M. I'll be Lewis, but, goddammit, right now I'm Burt, so get your big ugly face out of my way. If you want Lewis, talk to him in the morning!"

It got real quiet. Then he knelt down close to me and said, "By God, that's exactly what Lewis would have said!"[45]

Reynolds understood how painful it must be for Dickey to stand by as Boorman manipulated his script. Nevertheless, he resented Dickey's proprietorial supervision. Reynolds told movie critic Judith Crist what he told many others: "He is a wonderful poet, a *wonderful* poet. And the kind of man that after he has four martinis you want to drop a grenade down his throat—he becomes a total ass."[46] In public Dickey usually glazed over his rough relations with the lead actor, but in private he mocked Reynolds's pretensions as a woodsman, his box of thirty toupees, and the lifters for his wolverine boots.[47]

Voight's problems with Dickey ran deeper. He disagreed with *Deliverance's* survivalist message, and he deplored Dickey's complaints about his acting. Under Boorman's supervision, Voight altered Dickey's lines to make them more plausible. About Dickey's interference, he told an *Esquire* writer:

How would *you* feel? You're the actor, and there is the writer looking over your shoulder all day saying, "Well, suh, that's not the moment I wrote," or even, "Well, suh, *today* you did pretty good work.". . . Man, suppose I looked over *his* f——ing shoulder when he wrote his f——ing book? It was worse than the goddamn proud father at the Little League game, rooting so hard his kid can't hit the ball! Christ! I mean, man, I'm working f——in' twelve hours a day at absolute one-hundred-percent capacity. I don't want somebody even saying that I was okay, because I was *not* okay, I was giving the *best I've got!* . . . Certain things in his script would have been pure *asshole-ism* to attempt! Just goddamn *literary!* And Dickey is there worrying over every f——ing moment. . . . We're trying to make a human document. And if some moment or other doesn't get Dickey a good review from Pauline Kael or somebody, well, I can't give a f—— about that.[48]

Although Voight and Dickey clashed, Dickey must have realized that Voight, like Ed, resembled an earlier version of himself. As a youth, Voight had been a gifted wrestler, golfer, and football player. He'd wanted to play football more than anything else, but teachers recognized his talents as a promising artist. Just as Dickey had renounced football for poetry at Vanderbilt, Voight hung up his cleats to concentrate on art and scene design at Catholic University. Voight's father, a golf pro at a fashionable country club in the wealthy New York suburb of Scarsdale, disapproved of his son's artistic bent, just as Eugene Dickey disapproved of his son's devotion to poetry. Rivalry with a brother, like Dickey's rivalry with Tom, contributed to what Voight called his "compulsiveness about winning."[49] Voight's performance in *Midnight Cowboy* should have satisfied his compulsion, but his two subsequent films, *Out of It* and *The Revolutionary*, had been judged mediocre. *Deliverance* gave him a chance to resume his winning ways.

Boorman tolerated Dickey for several days at rehearsals, but on May 10, the day the main shooting commenced, he decided that Dickey had to go. Boorman asked Orme to break the news to Dickey as tactfully as possible. On May 11, Orme explained the director's wishes over lunch. Dickey was understandably angry, but agreed to return to Columbia. When Claude Terry went to the Kingwood Inn for dinner, he was surprised by all the commotion at the table where Orme, Boorman, Beatty, Cox, Wiggin, and Dickey ate. Terry soon learned that it was Dickey's "going-away party." He was drinking hard. "Claude," he said, "they're fucking up my movie. They're letting that New York Jewboy Weissberg do Dueling Banjos. They're not letting my protégés do the music." He hoped Terry would sympathize. Terry remained silent. Dickey subsequently shouted: "God damn it, answer me!"[50] Terry answered tersely, and Dickey quieted.

Before he left on May 12, Dickey insisted on bidding the actors a ceremonious farewell. Boorman accompanied him to where the actors were rehearsing. He remembered Dickey declaiming with oratorical grandeur: "It appears my presence would be most efficacious by its absence."[51] He also remembered Reynolds not understanding "efficacious" and asking someone to explain. Reynolds wrote in his autobiography:

> One day midway through rehearsals, we were all on the floor of this wonderful old house, splayed out and thoroughly exhausted after a day on the water, and the door opened. A cold, foreboding shadow filled the room. Dickey followed it inside.
>
> "I understand that my presence would be more advantageous by my absence," he intoned.
>
> I looked around.
>
> "What the fuck did he just say?" I asked.
>
> "I think," Jon piped up, "Mr. Dickey is saying that he's going to go home and allow us the honor of taking care of his picture. He'll be back to play the sheriff, and we love him for it. At least I think that's what he said."
>
> "That's what I said," Dickey added.
>
> Before leaving, Dickey addressed each of us in character. He went to Ned first and whispered, "Bobby, save my picture. You're the only one I can trust." He said the same thing to Ronny. Then he went to Jon, who I heard respond, "I don't think . . . see, I . . . well, I'll try." I finally interrupted and

said, "Shut up, Jon, he's going to talk to me now." Then Dickey grabbed the back of my head with hands as big as hammocks and asked, "Are you Lewis now?"

"Yeah, I'm Lewis," I said.

"Lewis," he whispered. "Lewis, save my picture. You're the only one I can trust."

"Don't worry," I said. "I will."[52]

Boorman asked Dickey to return in a few weeks to play the sheriff. Dickey snarled: "You can go get yourself another boy."[53] Convinced that Boorman was wreaking havoc on his screenplay, he drove home, but in a few weeks, flanked by his family and somewhat chastened, he returned.

Shooting proceeded as planned, although it was slowed by the difficulty of getting good shots of the rapidly moving canoes. Trees and rocks often obstructed the view. To ensure that he had plenty of back-up footage, Boorman repeatedly filmed the two stunt doubles, Claude Terry and Payson Kennedy, running Bull's Sluice. They spent two days at Deliverance Rock on the upper part of Section IV. Here Boorman got so frustrated that he hurled his microphone into the river. (Terry and his partners retrieved it, gilded it, and presented it to him as a souvenir.) Voight's perfectionism also created delays. The impatient Reynolds shouted at Boorman: "Dammit, don't ask if he wants another one. He's going to say *yes* every time until you reach take one hundred. For chrissakes, let's get on down the river."[54] To expedite matters, Boorman filmed scenes in more accessible areas off location. The early conversation about football and pompom girls on the drive to the river actually occurred on the Atlanta archery range. The scene where the four men dig a pit with their hands to bury the dead rapist occurred by the eighteenth hole of the Kingwood Country Club golf course.

The filming taxed the muscles and minds of everyone involved. For the misty scene of Ed shakily aiming his arrow at the deer the morning after his night in the tent, the crew had to blow steam from dry ice scattered on the ground. The domesticated deer, which a local farmer loaned them, died after it had been tranquilized and propped in the woods like a statue. Pulling the arrow out of the rapist proved especially tricky. The crew inserted a flexible arrow into a plastic tube and bent it around the mountain man's chest. Reynolds had to carefully extricate the arrow to make it look real. It took four tries before he succeeded. Because of the treacherous locations on the Chattooga, often only four crew members—the cameraman, two technicians, and the director—accompanied the four actors. The crew used canoes or heavy-duty U.S. Navy rafts mounted with cameras to record the white-water scenes. Men in wet suits prevented the boats from careening down the river. Rapids, however, played havoc with the rafts, sometimes pitching soundmen, cameramen, and valuable equipment overboard. On the first day of filming, rocks ripped a hole in a raft. Assistant director Al Jennings had to return to Hollywood after he gashed and bruised his leg on a rock. A waterfall pulled Ned Beatty underwater. "After 30 seconds," Boorman said, "I sent the divers down after Ned. I don't know how long he was down. I was sure he was gone. Then all of a sudden he popped up about 50 yards downstream."[55] The crew thought that Ronny Cox and Jon Voight had drowned when their canoe crashed in some rough water. Nobody could see where they had gone. During a rafting lark, Chris Dickey got caught in a hydraulic and was battered against rocks before being pulled to shore on a rope.

One of the most frightening incidents occurred on the cliff. Boorman explained: "Jon [Voight] . . . was lowered down that 200-foot monster repeatedly. He climbed almost all of it, in sections, of course. We couldn't use a double, guy wires or any other aids because you could have seen them in the finished film if we did. So we'd just lower him down by a cable wrapped around and tied to a huge tree trunk, and then Jon would simply unhook himself and climb. There was a tremendous element of risk in it. At one point, Jon did slip and fall; fortunately, he was only about 15 to 20 feet from the base. But it was worth it. That cliff face has a marvelous veracity to it. And the final shot of Jon coming up over the top of it—we lowered him down about 20 feet for that one—turned out spectacularly."[56] No wonder the actors compared their work to military training.

Voight's triumphant moment in *Deliverance* came when he scaled the cliff and shot the mountain man he suspected of stalking his group. An expert rock-climbing double, Ralph Garrett, did some of the more dangerous climbing, and Voight used a safety cable at times, but Voight also grappled with the cliff at Tallulah Gorge unaided. Two months of filming had toned his muscles and dropped his weight by fifteen pounds. Still the challenge of the cliff was daunting. The journalist Joan Downs, who interviewed Voight for *Life*, reported that a misplaced stand-in caught him once when he fell. Supposed to plunge into the river with the stalker, whom he lowers down the cliff, he was lucky again. He just missed several submerged boulders as the current dragged him about fifty yards underwater. Fortunately, Voight did not have to climb at night, as Ed does in the novel. It would have been suicidal and nearly impossible to film. To capture a pitch-black and moonlit sky simultaneously, the cinematographer Vilmo Zsigmond used an ingenious "day-for-night" technique and had the color altered in the lab. To film the underwater scene in which the submerged Ed gets tangled with the rope tied to the dead mountain man, Boorman deployed simpler techniques; he dumped soil into a swimming pool in Clayton, strapped on oxygen tanks, and dove into the pool with a hand-held camera.

On June 25, Dickey watched Voight climb the cliff and was petrified. In a letter to Jacques de Spoelberch, he said that as he gazed across Tallulah Gorge, he wondered to himself: "Lord, Dickey, what kind of horrendous situation have you got all these people—director, cameraman, actors, so on—into? I am deathly afraid that somebody will get hurt on this film, because there is no doubt that it is the most dangerous one ever made."[57] He continued to coach Voight from a distance: "Come on, Jon. You can do it, baby. That's it. My God, what if he fell?"[58] Dickey's palms perspired as Voight ascended.

Awed and scared by the actors' daring exploits, Dickey was downright angry at his two sons for scampering near the cliffs. On one occasion Chris looked like he was going to fall as he carried film, makeup kits, and other equipment across a rickety rope bridge slung over a chasm. Kevin remembered that he nearly did fall as he edged out along the rope, jumped across a gap, and slipped: "I almost went down this ninety-foot precipice and obviously could have been seriously hurt or killed. I really didn't think all that much of it, but my parents had been watching with field glasses from the top of the Tallulah Gorge." To his father, who wrote up the incident in an article, "Delights of the Edge," the twelve-year-old Kevin exemplified the fear and ecstasy of living on the brink. According to Kevin, after he clambered up to Chris on the slippery rock, his father retrieved him: "He was just livid. [He] basically jerked me off the set, [and] said, 'You're coming with me. Do you realize you scared the hell out of me?'"[59] It was one thing to celebrate risky deeds in writing, another thing to witness them in person.

For the more dangerous canoeing scenes, Boorman relied on Terry and Kennedy as well as Garrett. The canoe crash that sends Reynolds hurtling through rapids and over a cataract posed the most danger. Tallulah Gorge, which had been dammed in the early 1900s by the Georgia Power Company, was the chosen site. Here the technicians strung a cable to the top of the gorge at about a fifty-degree angle and used it for lowering and raising canoes. They also rigged up a prebroken canoe with a cable-release system. The instant Reynolds's Gruman aluminum canoe hit the Old Town canvas-and-wood canoe, Voight released the cable so that the Old Town split. Boorman had to do several shots before he got it right. For the one of Reynolds breaking his leg in the waterfall, Terry and the others set up a platform in a pool, placed Reynolds's canoe on the platform, signaled for the dam to open, and then jerked the canoe forward with a rope so that Reynolds catapulted into the water rushing from the dam. Reynolds never careened down the entire waterfall, although the camera suggested that he had.

Boorman was leery of his lead actor doing the waterfall stunt himself. Only after filming a cloth dummy, ingloriously dubbed "No Balls," going over the falls did he accept Reynolds's offer to try it. "How are you going to do this, Burt?" Boorman asked nervously. Reynolds replied that he would imitate the dummy: "When I go over I'm going to go down there, turn left, hit the rock, I'll bounce over there, do a quick slide, and then flip into the water." With the control dam above the falls shut, the crew pounded a spike into a boulder to which they attached a rope. Reynolds wrapped the rope around his hand and waded into the river in his cutoff wet suit, army pants, and boots. Reynolds heard a sound like an approaching tornado. The surge of water tossed him down the falls as if, indeed, he were the dummy: "The first rock I hit cracked my tailbone like an egg. Somehow I made it to the surface and gulped some air before getting pulled again through the racing falls. I turned several flips, hit something, doubled up, landed on my neck, and entered the hydrofoil [sic] at the bottom where the falls plunge back into the river." According to Reynolds, the current pulled him about two hundred yards downriver; stripped off his boots, pants, and wetsuit; and jettisoned him at about 180 miles per hour from the water. He crawled from the river and then woke in a hospital X-ray room. When Reynolds asked how the stunt looked to the film crew, Boorman supposedly responded: "Like a dummy going over a waterfall."[60] The close-up of Reynolds's broken leg, however, was anything but dummylike. Remembering a similar accident in the film *Wages of Fear*, Reynolds said he bought a pork bone at a butcher shop, broke it in half, and tied it to his leg. Audiences later shuddered at the verisimilitude.

Reynolds's account of plunging down the waterfall was highly exaggerated.

He confused the high-speed boat that rides above water on struts—a hydrofoil—with the underwater waterfall—a hydraulic—that sucks bodies to the bottom and traps them there. He bruised rather than cracked his tailbone. According to Terry, who worked on the shot, Reynolds never even made it to the hydraulic, which was at the bottom of the waterfall. The crew pulled him to shore from an intermediary pool. The danger of the stunt invited hyperbole. Dickey could not help embellishing Reynolds's stunt as well. On July 26, the day it took place, Dickey told Stewart Richardson: "Burt himself told me that they waited to do this scene last in case he were to get killed. In other words, if Burt got his brains knocked out, we would still have our footage."[61] The footage, as later audiences attested, was thrilling.

According to Reynolds, the rape scene was fraught with as many difficulties as the canoe crash. At first Boorman had a difficult time finding someone who would pull down his pants and perform the rape; he also had a hard time finding someone who had two false front teeth that Ed could pull out at the top of the cliff. Reynolds knew just the man for the role, the daredevil Herbert "Cowboy" Coward, with whom he had done Wild West stunts years before at a tourist resort, Ghost Town in Maggie Valley, North Carolina. Soon after Reynolds contacted him, Coward drove up in a truck wearing bib overalls and ungainly shoes. He fit Boorman's image of the mountain man perfectly, but when asked to read from the script, he balked and complained that he had forgotten his glasses. Recalling that Coward was illiterate, Reynolds suggested that he read the lines for him. When Reynolds read, "Go over by the tree and pull down your pants," Coward improvised in a hillbilly accent: "Get over by that sa-a-a-plain and take your p-p-p-anties down." Boorman worried that Coward might object to the pay—just a little over three hundred dollars a week—and to playing the sidekick of a man who sodomized another man. Coward supposedly replied: "That's all right. I've done a lot w-w-w-worse things than that."[62] He got the job.

In his stories about Deliverance, Reynolds mixed up Cowboy Coward and Bill McKinney, the man who actually does the raping. A part-time tree surgeon who had played a villain in Clint Eastwood's The Outlaw Josey Wales, McKinney was hardly the monster of Reynolds's recollections. He found it hard to conceive of and act out the rape. He "couldn't relate to Bobby sexually," he told one reporter. To evoke the proper emotions, he tried to remember some of the mountain people he had known as a boy growing up in Tennessee: "There's a lot of degenerate stuff in these hill people. So when these guys [in the movie] get a little smart with me out in the woods, that's it. . . . That's what I'm just waiting for. And so I say to myself, all right you smart ———, now I'm really going to get you!"[63] McKinney's homosexual role irritated Reynolds. In My Life, Reynolds claimed that McKinney ran nude through sprinklers on the golf course, stared at Beatty in "an odd, unnerving way," and whispered to his victim: "I've always wanted to try that. Always have."[64] Some on the location seriously questioned the accuracy of Reynolds's recollections.

Tensions mounted before the filming of the rape scene. Chris Dickey sensed the general feeling of unease when he was called to act as a stand-in for Ned Beatty, crawl up the bank while being pursued by the rapist, and bend over a log as if to be sodomized. He felt humiliated, as did Beatty. That night Chris called his father and asked him why he had included the homosexual scene in his story. Dickey responded as he always did: "I had to put the moral weight of murder on the suburbanites."[65] Chris pointed out that audiences were going to come away from the film thinking of only one thing—the homosexual rape. His father disagreed. Chris, who knew that the locals were already complaining about the demeaning way they were portrayed, was scared enough to want to leave the film site. His personal embarrassment may have been compounded by the fact that his own parents had worried that he was vaguely homosexual. As a teenager, his mother had bought him a subscription to *Playboy* to prevent what they regarded as his potential deviance.

Like many who saw the film, Reynolds shuddered at McKinney's and Coward's portrayals of violent degenerates. Dickey had a similar reaction, and for once thought the alterations to his script, such as the memorable "Squeal like a piggy" lines, were improvements. "Bill McKinney is the best actor I ever saw," Dickey said. "He's not so much a physical villain as a symbol of mindless evil, the monsters that are walking among us. That's the most terrifying thing. Falling into the hands of a mad stranger who cares nothing about your life."[66] Reynolds responded so viscerally to the rape that he claimed McKinney had actually tried to sodomize Beatty: "Finally, I couldn't stand it anymore. I ran into the scene, dove on McKinney, and pulled him off. Boorman, hot on my tracks, helped hold him down. Ned, who was crying from both rage and fear, found a big stick and started beating him on the head. Half a dozen guys grabbed Ned and pulled him away. We separated the two of them and let things cool off."[67] About this gothic account Boorman said: "It's absolute nonsense. Bill McKinney is a fine actor and a marvelous man, and the scene was strictly professional and technical."[68] Chris Dickey, who was there, remembered that Reynolds had not been called to the site.

Near the end of filming, Voight quipped that he had spent so much time underwater from the constant spills that he felt like he was making a Jacques Cousteau documentary. On his way to Clayton to witness how his canoeing experiences were being dramatized, Al Braselton met Voight and his girlfriend, Marcheline, at a roadside bar and noticed how tired he looked. He spoke briefly about the character of Ed Gentry and abruptly excused himself to go to bed. Braselton checked into the Heart of Rabun Motel, where Tom Priestley, one of the film editors, was swimming laps in the pool. He asked if he were any kin to J. B. Priestley. "My father, sir" was his reply. Braselton told him of his association with Dickey, and Priestley invited him to the motel rooms that he used as a photo lab, explained the difficult process of developing film, and showed him the "rushes"—the unedited film that the director viewed the night after it was shot. On his return trips to Clayton, Dickey also spent time with Priestley, whose father's novels he adored. Watching rushes of Drew's drowned, mangled body in the rocks, both Braselton and Dickey were amazed and slightly repulsed by the way Ronny Cox could pull his shoulder out of joint and stretch his arm behind his back. Satisfied that his double, Drew, was performing admirably, Braselton returned to Atlanta.

Around July 6, Braselton drove back to Clayton with his wife to be with Dickey while he performed as Sheriff Bullard, a role Dickey insisted had been imposed on him. Boorman had supposedly said: "You've got to do it, Jim. It's your story, and we're in a bind. So you go down to wardrobe and get fitted up. We'll shoot it tomorrow. We'll show you what to do." Seeing a chance to wrest some control back from Boorman, Dickey responded: "Okay. Gimme back the script and let me build up the sheriff's part some." Boorman refused. "Consequently, I was only in two scenes,"[69] a crestfallen Dickey later recalled. His recollections notwithstanding, Dickey had asked for the sheriff's part long before filming began, and although Boorman was pleased that Dickey had returned, he was also worried. Just as Ed's wife had to nurse her wounded husband at the end of *Deliverance*, Boorman had to nurse Dickey through his performance. More pliable than before, he was drunk and too soft-spoken. With much coaxing and coaching, Boorman finally got Dickey to look appropriately sherifflike and speak his few lines to the three surviving canoers. In the end, both director and actor took pride in the languorous, powerful presence of Sheriff Bullard. Dickey relished his role and costume so much that he wanted to remain in character after the cameras stopped rolling. He said in a *Playboy* interview: "After we made that scene, I wore the uniform back to where we were staying and had dinner. Somebody said to me, 'Does your sheriff's outfit fit you OK?' I said, 'Yeah, I haven't had it off all day. In fact, ever since I've had it on, I've been going around collecting graft from every whorehouse in Rabun County. And that isn't all I got, either.'"[70]

On July 27, 1971, Dickey wrote a friend, Lilia Drinnon, in an exultant mood about the film, which he had viewed at Boorman's cottage in Clayton. He told Drinnon that he planned to fly to London in August to help Boorman edit the "rough cut." Then he would fly to New York for more editing and speak to distributors and public relations people. He hoped that the film would open simultaneously in London, New York, Los Angeles, and Atlanta in March of 1972: "I think the general consensus of opinion is that we will have the stars, the director, and the writer as well, in Atlanta, where the premiere is expected to be the biggest there since *Gone with the Wind*. . . . I think it is a film that is going to establish a new trend in acting, directing, in photography, and in just about everything else."[71] To realize these high expectations, Boorman spent weeks cutting and recutting his film. With Zsigmond in Los Angeles, he "desaturated" the color so that only whites, blacks, and greens appeared. "Desaturation not only lent the landscape a greater reality," he later commented, "but it gave the dreamlike, nightmarish quality I wanted."[72] On completing work in the Technicolor lab, Boorman screened his rough cut and flew to Ireland to take care of the final editing and sound mixing. Tom Priestley helped piece together the river scenes like fragments of a mosaic, and for his artful job he received an Academy Award nomination. The music had already been recorded in Georgia, but now it needed to be incorporated. One of the unusual features of *Deliverance* was the way the soundtrack had been recorded at the start of shooting to avoid another trip back to the States. In the end the permutations of "Dueling Banjos" were as haunting as the scenes they accompanied.

By September 1971, Boorman was in Ireland editing and working on publicity with a Frenchman named Pierre Rissient. Boorman assured Dickey that the audience's response to the preliminary screening had been enthusiastic.

Viewers even complimented Dickey's acting. Nevertheless, Boorman still worried that the ending (he had opted for images of exhumed graves, a church being moved, and a corpselike hand surfacing in the lake) failed to communicate Ed's sense of triumph. Since audiences would be drained by the gruesome events in the middle of the film, Boorman thought they would want an emotional lift at the end. Dickey sent advice: "What I want more than anything else is the sense, at the end, of a man with a secret victory."[73] This could be expressed in a slight smile of confidence on Voight's face, he suggested. Boorman promised to show Dickey his final version in the late fall, and also announced his plan to release the film in the United States in April 1972.

Viewing the edited film for the first time in early November 1971, Dickey forgot all his past squabbles with Boorman. To Eugene Patterson, a professor at Duke, he proclaimed: "*What* a film we have got! Some of the scenes are so horrifying that I cannot even look at the screen while they are taking place. And *I* wrote the screenplay! Anyway, I can guarantee that in all your movie-going days you have never seen [anything] as . . . disgusting and exciting as this. Or as puzzling, either. You come out of the theater not knowing where your sympathy indeed does lie, or if you would have done anything differently, if you had been any of these fellows. Warner Brothers says it is going to be one of the most controversial, one of the most attacked and defended pictures that they have ever had anything to do with."[74] Dickey saw the film as he saw many of his works—at the center of a whirlwind of dispute. To examine Boorman's final version Dickey flew to Los Angeles in mid-December and stayed for about four days at the Beverly Hills Hotel on Sunset Boulevard. Dickey's main concern was the schedule for the European and American premieres. Boorman was also concerned, especially when he learned that Warner Brothers had switched the film's release date from April 1972 to October 1972.

For the sake of promoting his film, Dickey tried to paper over his quarrels with crew and cast. This became more difficult after their conflicts surfaced in the *Atlanta Journal and Constitution Magazine* on July 25, 1971. Distressed by the article as well as by Dickey's suspicion that he had leaked the story to reporters, Boorman wrote: "I have been careful not to mention any differences that may have arisen between us. Some friction was inevitable in this kind of relationship. I myself feel that we are closer and stronger than we were at the beginning and that we've tried to be honest and considerate with each other. I think it's very important to stress that this film is a collaborative effort. I'm not the author of it, and it would be disastrous if a story circulated that we had major differences."[75] Dickey's response was less caustic than Boorman expected. He thought negative publicity was inevitable and might help rather than hinder the movie.

The attempt to muffle differences among author, actors, and director became even harder when a January 1972 *Esquire* article exposed Jon Voight's difficulties with Dickey on the film site. Voight wrote Dickey an apologetic letter, claiming that he had been misquoted or quoted out of context. Dickey's novel, he said, was a classic, and his performance in the film was superb. Just as eager to bury hatchets, Dickey replied with a letter praising Voight's acting: "I have seen you work, and seen the results of what you do, and there is no doubt in my mind that you are the finest young screen actor in the world. So much did you make the part your own that I cannot even think of the *novel*—nor the film—without thinking of you as Ed. You have my eternal gratitude for the chances you took on behalf of my story. When I saw that cliff, I could not even look at it without the sensation of already falling. I won't go on and on in this immoderate vein, but will close now with the great good hope that I will see you again some day, and tell you these things looking you straight in the eye, as such things should be done."[76] With characteristic aplomb, Dickey tried to win over his former antagonist.

All indications to the contrary, Dickey never forgot the way his screenplay was altered by Boorman, Voight, and everyone else involved in the film. Ten years later, he published his original draft of the script, quipping: "By the time the film begins to move into the actual production process, the writer has begun to feel like the pig in Randall Jarrell's parable of the Poet and the Critic. The filmmaker, like the Critic, like the judge of pork at the country fair, says to the pig-poet-novelist-screenwriter as he pokes him contemptuously in the ribs, 'Huh! What do *you* know about pork?' Though he *is*, unfortunately, pork, the novelist can in fact find little by the way of answer."[77] Dickey was particularly upset by Warner Brothers' handling of the soundtrack. He had led Mike Russo and Ron Brentano to believe that they would be hired. On July 5, he wrote Russo, who had sent him a tape of new music:

> I wanted you to know that I voluntarily left the set of my film so that two conditions could be carried out. One of these is that my son, Chris, would be retained as a cameraman and other functionary on the second unit for the remainder of the film. Boorman agreed to this, and has carried it out. The second consideration was that you and Ron would play the final, decisive music. John has not said anything to me about this beyond his promise that it would be carried out. I would like to know, from you, what provision has been made in this matter. I have no knowledge of whether John has sent you a copy of the final shooting script. But if he has, you will know that we have a sequence of visual images depicting the rising water over the valley of the Cahulawassee. This then modulates into a dream sequence in which Ed Gentry, the protagonist, played by Jon Voight, imagines himself as captured by the local sheriff—played, God help us, by me—and made to face up to the crimes he has committed. The music comes up very strong here, and I know that you and Ron will do us all credit with it.[78]

Dickey, of course, had not left the set "voluntarily." Since Eric Weissberg had visited Clayton and recorded the soundtrack in Atlanta before July 5, Boorman must have told Dickey early on that he had no intention of employing his Portland musician friends. Dickey entertained the possibility of Russo and Brentano recording the soundtrack in another "ideal" *Deliverance*. The version Boorman made, he said, was a bastard version: "[It] is not the film as I would have it. That version is still only in the wide screen of my head . . . ; it is still Platonic and possible; it is still in the making. And I like to think that someday, long after I have departed this and all other scenes, it will be made, with the full

implications of the story restored, the delineation of character as I have indicated it, the dialogue as I have written it, and the dramatic emphases as I have
placed them."[79] At his death, Dickey's film still remained a platonic ideal.

In between film work, Dickey had other endeavors to bring to fruition in
1971. As chair of the Bollingen Prize Committee, he had to oversee the final ad-
judication at Yale on January 9, 1971. By February, he had finished about half of
a new poetry book called *Slowly Toward Hercules*, a title inspired by a speech
Neil Armstrong made to Congress in which he declared: "The Earth is traveling
in the direction of the constellation Hercules to some unknown destination in
the cosmos."[80] (Later Dickey changed his title to *The Strength of Fields*.) He continued to give readings. Earnings from his many different activities made 1971
one of his most profitable years. Dickey grossed about $107,000 just from publi-
cation advances and royalties. His salary and reading fees brought his income to
about $200,000. He was making so much money that his lawyer, Kirkman
Finlay, proposed that he shift the bookkeeping burdens from Maxine to an accountant, Talcott Stith. Dickey's obvious pride about making money won few
friends in the literary world. "Money really buys life; it buys experience," he said
in an interview. "This business of penny-pinching and economizing and so on is
spiritually degrading to people."[81] Dickey's contract for his next novel only
added to his burgeoning coffers. To Ken McCormick he promoted his work-in-
progress as "a much more compelling novel than *Deliverance*, though not nearly
as fast-paced or exciting."[82] On July 27, 1971, Doubleday offered Dickey an advance of $150,000 to be paid in installments of $30,000 every year for four years.
The fifth installment would come on January 5, 1975, or on delivery of the manuscript. To secure this lucrative deal, Dickey had to extricate himself from
Houghton Mifflin. Like most publishers, Houghton had included in its first contract a clause stipulating that Dickey send them his next book. If Dickey decided
to publish his second novel elsewhere, the contract called for a payment of
$10,000. Spoelberch reported to Houghton's Richard McAdoo that Dickey
wanted to leave. On February 1, 1971, McAdoo wrote Theron Raines a testy letter demanding to know more about Dickey's plans. Because neither author nor
agent had registered any complaints about the handling of *Deliverance*, McAdoo
could not understand Dickey's desire to jump ship. He wanted a letter justifying
the decision, and he also wanted Dickey to pay $10,000 for breaking his con-
tract. Dickey consulted his lawyer, Kirkman Finlay, who wrote McAdoo on
August 13, 1971, rejecting Houghton Mifflin's demand for a $10,000 payment.

Dickey discussed the sort of principles that guided his dealings with his publishers on an August 25 episode of William F. Buckley's *Firing Line*. The ostensible subject was "the American spirit," which Dickey said was at a low ebb
because of too much moralizing: "We can't do the simplest thing, such as eating
an ice cream cone, without somebody telling us that we are really fascists."
Buckley, to a certain extent, agreed. Reflecting on the anti-American mood of
the Vietnam era, Buckley also regretted that so many intellectuals pilloried their
country. Why did they assign guilt to everyone but themselves? Before the cult
of "political correctness" took hold, Dickey and Buckley clasped hands in their
renunciation of it. Dickey advised everyone in the audience to go out and do
something simple and enjoyable after watching *Firing Line*. "Just do it," he said,

foreshadowing future Nike commercials. "But don't say that when you drink a Coca-Cola it means you're knuckling under to the American system that condoned the My Lai massacre."[83] Several people in the audience suggested that Dickey's libertarian "just do it" philosophy, which seemed at odds with his conservatism, was naive and dangerous. As the 1970s progressed, even Dickey's more sympathetic critics began to question his political and literary judgment. Only his most zealous advocates argued that his new work surpassed *Deliverance* and the poetry books that preceded it. The novel made him rich; but wealth, fame, and alcoholism slowly eroded the talent that had made his previous books so potent.

XI.

THE SECOND ACT

26. King of the Cats (1971–1972)

F. Scott Fitzgerald once claimed: "There are no second acts in American lives."[1] If Dickey's post-*Deliverance* period was his second act, it was frequently marred by tragicomic vauntings and collapses. In early October, he told a friend he was producing poetry and prose that would "make *Deliverance* [look] neat and pat."[2] Dickey sounded like James Joyce contemplating the hybrid language of his most ambitious book, *Finnegans Wake,* or Ezra Pound mapping out the linguistic palimpsests of *The Cantos:* "I want to make a new language based on English: one which will be infinitely more expressive than English, as it is written to-day . . . or, for that matter, more expressive than it has been when written at any other day."[3] Distractions such as the October 6–8 Playboy International Writers' Convocation slowed his progress. Geoffrey Norman had invited him to the Chicago Playboy Club, and Hugh Hefner had paid his expenses. Dickey had a chance to mingle with writers and directors like Sean O'Faolain, Alex Haley, Arthur C. Clarke, Studs Terkel, Ray Bradbury, Kenneth Tynan, and Roman Polanski. A perk of the conference was a Playboy Club Key-card honored at all the Playboy Clubs in the world. Although Dickey wrote one of *Playboy's* vice presidents, "I never had such a good *time* with other writers in my whole entire life,"[4] he found the panel discussions dull and refused to attend most of them.

Frustrated with his daunting works-in-progress, Dickey was pleased to greet Doubleday's publication of *Sorties* on December 10, 1971. As usual, he hoped the book would create a stir. Some of the essays, like the one on Theodore Roethke, had already done so. Many of the journal entries, which composed two-thirds of the book, were also deliberately inflammatory. In a classic rhetorical move, Dickey pretended to abjure any provocative intentions at the beginning: "Surely I am not likely to say anything scandalous or private . . . except maybe my opinions of various writers and personalities." In the next paragraph he launched into a defense of masturbation as "one of the most profound forms of self-communication and even self-communion." As he ranged over topics like homosexuality, race, fantasy, archery, guitars, advertising, lies, women, money, and perversion, he trampled on conventional opinions. In his appraisals of other writers, whether friend or foe, he was devastating. Norman Mailer was "the bell-wether of all intellectual cuteness and overintellectualization" and his *The Naked and the Dead,* compared to *All Quiet on the Western Front,* was "a vastly inferior book." Galway Kinnell was "a very boring writer." Richard Wilbur was "tiresome." Elizabeth Bishop was unreadable. Donald Hall was "bad, awfully bad, and funnily bad." Sylvia Plath, Anne Sexton, and everyone else in "the School of Gabby Agony" were "bad—awful." John Berryman was a "timid little academic who stays drunk all the time . . . in order to convince himself and others that he is inhabited by the true demon." (In a letter written to Berryman in response to his *77 Dream Songs*, Dickey had called it "the best poetry book" he'd read in ten years and Berryman "the best living poet in English.")[5] Joseph Heller's *Catch-22* was a "sophomoric and inept, trying-for-it piece of silliness." Mark Strand's poetry was "essentially silly, being a simple-minded kind of exercise in deliberate eccentricity." Ted Hughes wrote "the kind of stuff I throw away." Robert Lowell was "limited to a heavy, driving sort of paranoiac verse."

In *Sorties*, Dickey played both the curmudgeonly and the beneficent critic. If he damned one minute, he renounced those who damned the next. In his essay "The Self as Agent," he embraced poets who created masks and lied, and then, throwing logic to the winds, scoffed at them: "One feels so damn sorry for writers, the poor posers. People like Hemingway and Yeats spend their whole lives trying to make good a pose because they despise themselves. They put infinite time and energy into trying to make themselves come true, when they know that it's all a damn lie, anyway." Staring at himself in the mirror, Dickey pretended to see only the pitiful poses of his models. Only at rare moments did he strip off his own masks and reveal himself candidly. At one such moment he confessed: "I am not what I seem to the world to be; a fine-looking fellow in the prime of life, big enough and strong enough to do almost anything he wants to do. . . . I am a haunted artist like the others. I know what the monsters know, and shall know more, and more than any of them if I can survive myself for a little while longer." Because Dickey had such confidence in his disguises, he proclaimed that his life was "more unknowable than that of Lawrence of Arabia."[6] In *The Seven Pillars of Wisdom* and in conversation, T. E. Lawrence had so mythologized his military experiences that most of his admirers knew nothing about his failures, self-doubts, homosexuality, and sadomasochism. Dickey tried, almost as successfully, to hide similar weaknesses and inclinations.

Around the time he published *Sorties*, friends noticed that Dickey was trying even harder to pose as a Hemingway or Lawrence. According to Inman Mays: "Now, he projected an even more pronounced macho look, wearing a western leather-fringed jacket and a large safari fedora, along with a Navaho-type leather string tie with a silver and turquoise clasp. This was the he-man look Dickey presented to the public at poetry readings, literary seminars, TV interviews and other public appearances and doubtless enhanced the growing myth of Dickey the bare-chested bard, ex-football star, combat pilot and great white hunter."[7] If Dickey intended to win respect, he accomplished the opposite, as reviews of *Sorties* attested. Anatole Broyard in the *New York Times* mocked the book as the maunderings of a "countrified . . . hayseed."[8] A. L. Shaff in the *Minneapolis Star Tribune* blasted it as narcissistic and shoddy, and concluded: "I'd never buy the book if I could borrow it from a friend."[9] Writing for the *Los Angeles Times*, Jascha Kessler suspected that Dickey was "fabricating a [heroic] personality" to hide his sadistic "fantasies of self-gratification."[10]

The reviews were disheartening, especially since Dickey had entertained such high hopes for the book. He had spent three days in September 1971 editing *Sorties* with Stewart "Sandy" Richardson, and had written McCormick conspiratorially: "In the most strict possible confidence, I think we have put ourselves in a very good position to win a National Book Award. Sandy will tell you all about this."[11] He had declined to serve as a National Book Award judge in 1971 so that *Sorties* would be eligible. Unable to accept the book as a failure, seven years after its publication he told Sandra Greenberg in an interview: "It was a runner-up to, I think it was a biography of Mozart, in non-fiction for the National Book Award and the Pulitzer Prize."[12] He blamed his loss on Frederick Morgan, the *Hudson Review* editor who had been on the committee and supposedly voted against it.

As his books became more provocative and experimental in the 1970s, Dickey grew more desperate for awards. In 1971, discovering that *Eye-Beaters* had not made the final shortlist for the National Book Award, he took some consolation from the fact that Lowell's *Notebook* and Berryman's *Love and Fame* had failed to make the list as well. Nevertheless, he raged to his publisher: "The whole list is taken up with pip-squeaks."[13] He now hoped *Eye-Beaters* would win the Pulitzer. It did not. The only significant award he won in 1971 came from another country. In late November, Dickey flew to Paris with Maxine and Kevin to accept France's Prix Médicis for the best non-French novel of the year. Wearing a wide-brimmed Texas hat, he expressed his gratitude to the crowd gathered at the Cercle des Allies: "I hope that every person will find in my novel what he needs. Again thank you, and I hope that despite my hesitant French, you will understand the depth of the feeling from which these words come."[14] The Prix Médicis would be one of the last literary awards Dickey ever won.

His need for recognition intensifying, Dickey became more aggressive and wily in his pursuit of honorary degrees. The humiliation he had suffered at Rice Institute for not having a doctorate still festered. When Theodore Stern, the College of Charleston president, invited him to be the featured speaker at the Fine Arts Festival on March 19, 1971, Dickey sniffed at the meager fee of two hundred dollars, demanded thirty-five hundred dollars plus expenses, and asked for an honorary doctorate. "I have had a good many offered to me," he said, "but none of the schools seem to have the associations or the *locality* that I want in a matter of this kind."[15] Dickey's campaign for a degree succeeded, and the local newspaper claimed it was his first. A letter to Austin Briggs at Hamilton College proves that he had started supplicating for degrees as early as 1970: "I have held off accepting honorary degrees, but I would surely accept one from Ezra Pound's old college. . . . I am kind of touchy about this subject. I have turned down a good many degrees from schools that did not seem to me to have the proper literary associations yours does."[16] Like Wesleyan College in Georgia and the College of Charleston, in 1972 Hamilton submitted to Dickey's request. Moravian College followed suit a year later.

Dickey approached many other colleges over the next three decades. When Pitzer College president Robert Atwell asked Dickey to speak at the tenth anniversary commencement in 1975, Dickey wrote back in typical fashion that he would: "But I would like also the guarantee of an honorary degree."[17] In May 1975, contacted by the University of Michigan to recommend *Esquire* editor Arnold Gingrich for an honorary degree, Dickey made a pitch for himself: "I would also be pleased to accept an honorary degree from the University of Michigan where my experiences have always been pleasurable. I have five or six honorary degrees, but nothing would please me more than a degree from you."[18] His appeal went unheeded, so Dickey made another plea later in the year. While

Michigan balked, Northwestern and the University of Illinois acquiesced in 1975. Five or six degrees, however, were not enough, so in 1976 he wrote Jarvis Thurston: "Since I have been your writer-in-residence, and since you have my papers, it would not seem to me inappropriate for Washington University to award me an honorary degree in letters come graduation this spring. I have five of these to date, but would welcome none of them so much as I would welcome one from a school with which I have such pleasant, deep and personal association as I do with Washington University."[19] Dickey's attempts to lever degrees from colleges continued unabated. In 1980, he told writer Greg Gatenby, who was trying to lure him to Toronto's York University for a reading: "If I should be fortunate enough to be given an honorary doctorate, it would make my presence a certainty."[20] During the summer of 1981, he badgered James Kilroy, the English Department chair at Vanderbilt: "I cannot for the life of me understand why Vanderbilt, my old university, has not seen fit to confer an honorary degree on me. Though I realize that this may sound fatuous, it is a matter of some concern to me. I have six others, but in all the time since the first one Vanderbilt did not come forward."[21] Kilroy responded that Vanderbilt customarily refrained from giving honorary degrees. Three years later Dickey implored Scott Donaldson: "Why don't you in your distinguished professorship . . . get me an honorary degree from William and Mary?"[22] Despite the reluctance of many universities to grant Dickey's wishes, by 1993 he had acquired over a dozen doctorates.

As Maxine drank steadily to keep pace with her husband, her health and marriage deteriorated proportionally. In 1971, in the Robert E. Lee room of Charleston's Mills-Hyatt House, a reporter for the local News and Courier asked how the Dickeys had stayed together for twenty-three years. Dickey joked: "We simply don't want each other to find happiness with anyone else so we stay together for spite." About her subservience to her husband, Maxine conceded: "This is my role in life; I have no great ambitions of my own." Did she not embrace any of the goals of the women's movement? Dickey grinned mischievously: "Women are dying to be enslaved . . . , but only by the right man."[23] Before long, those who knew Maxine intimately witnessed the harmful consequences of her "role." Dickey demonstrated how debilitating his own drinking had become on November 10, 1971, at a Clemson reading. After checking his bags into his hotel, he called up Rock Norman, his freshman football coach, and invited him to his room. Gulping Jack Daniel's and rehashing old football stories with Norman, Dickey bragged that he could have been an all-American player. The fiction writer Barry Hannah, who taught at Clemson, joined the festivities, as did Richard Calhoun, who was responsible for guiding Dickey to the reading. Calhoun grew so concerned about Dickey's ability to perform that he called Dr. Bill Hunter, Dickey's former football teammate, to try to sober him. Hunter arrived from his clinic to find Dickey picking his guitar, clad only in his underwear, cowboy hat, and cowboy boots. Dickey regaled Hunter with dialogue from Deliverance, savoring the scene in which Reynolds shoots the hillbilly rapist with an arrow. Hunter snarled: "Dickey, you son of a bitch, you were paid a lot of money to talk to the students, and now you get off your ass and get over there."[24] A contrite Dickey admitted that his friend was right. He began crying and took the medicine and oxygen Hunter had brought.

At first Dickey cooperated with the two professors acting as chaperones. Each held one of Dickey's arms, but as soon as they left the hotel Dickey shook them off and headed for a store to buy a six-pack of beer. The audience waited expectantly in the auditorium. Finally, Dickey stumbled onto the stage and read two poems—"Cherrylog Road" and "Haunting the Maneuvers." Complaining the lights were glaring in his face, he abruptly stopped and fell onto the stage. Saddened by his friend's abject performance, Hunter blamed it on "the Celtic gene" that made him susceptible to alcohol. Dickey was a type of "high-functioning autistic,"[25] Hunter speculated, and alcohol facilitated his need to act out his fantasy of a good ol' Southern boy. Others in the audience were not so ready to explain and forgive. John Hopkins, who chaired the Speaker's Bureau, told Dickey how disappointed he was and asked him to fulfill his contractual agreement with Clemson at a later date. Once again, Dickey felt contrite. He promised to return.

In Washington, D.C., to read at the Corcoran Gallery of Art a few weeks later, Dickey gave no sign of altering his drunken routine. Phil Casey from the *Washington Post* interviewed him with Maxine at the Georgetown Inn. Glancing at the two bottles of Scotch on the table, Dickey told Casey of his fondness for whiskey, beer, and wine: "I can taste all right, but I have no sense of smell. Maxine can smell everything. She thinks the whole world stinks." The reporter asked about Dickey's earnings from poetry. Not to seem avaricious, Dickey explained the altruistic motives behind his many public appearances: "I sure don't need the dough. I want to improve the situation of poets and poetry generally. It's one of the few altruistic motives I've ever had. . . . Why should a Sammy Davis Jr. get $12,000 for a college appearance, or Al Capp get $3,000 or $3,500, and a poet only $150. There's no reason for that. The students would be better off with the poets and get more out of them." Dickey said nothing about the $1,500 he had recently earned for his two-poem reading at Clemson or the $3,500 fee he usually demanded. Digressing, he trotted out his favorite fables about being a college football and track star, a bomber pilot in the Philippines and Korea, and a pugilist. He told the reporter of breaking his nose several times in boxing matches. Maxine retorted: "I think it was mostly streetfighting."[26] With mock self-righteousness, Dickey confided that he hadn't been in a fistfight in five years.

Before going to the Corcoran, Dickey attended a dinner party in Georgetown hosted by Katie Loucheim, a sometime poet who served under President Johnson as the first female assistant secretary of state. Eugene McCarthy dined with the group as well. Dickey got so drunk that he could hardly stand for his reading. Inman Mays, now a manager of the *Washington Post's* promotion department, watched his friend fumble for his books, totter, and slur. Like others who witnessed Dickey's readings, Mays felt the alcoholic performance was partly a way to create drama. As the reading progressed, Dickey gradually sobered. Mays noticed that Maxine never acknowledged the pathos of the situation. She simply accepted her husband as he was.

During this heady time, Dickey did not always sober up for his classes at USC. One of his students in 1971, Pat Conroy, vowed: "If I become a writer, I cannot become like this man."[27] Conroy had been introduced to Dickey's poetry by a friend, Jim Belk, who was teaching at a USC extension college in Beaufort, South Carolina. Belk's rendition of "The Lifeguard" had dazzled Conroy, as did most of *Poems 1957–1967*, which he soon bought. After finishing his novel *The Water Is Wide*, Conroy wrote Dickey a complimentary letter and asked if he could study with him. Dickey said he could, so at the end of the 1971 summer Conroy enrolled in Dickey's American/British poetry class and his creative writing class. His contact with Dickey had an unexpected result; he left the two classes convinced that he should concentrate on prose. Dickey's comments on his poems, like those on Ben Greer's, were devastating. In fact, Conroy had kept at his fiction during, and sometimes even in, Dickey's classes. He explained in a 1980 letter thanking Dickey for a blurb for his novel *The Lords of Discipline*: "The Dave Murphy sequence which begins on page 289 of *The Great Santini* I wrote in your class one day after I re-read 'The Bee.'"[28] Dickey's stories of teaching Conroy were predictably different. In 1974, he told the *Atlanta Constitution* that Conroy had composed *Conrack* under his tutelage (Conroy had already finished the novel), just as he claimed that Larry McMurtry had written *The Last Picture Show* in his Rice class in the early 1950s.[29] In 1972, Conroy nevertheless heard Dickey claim that he had helped him write *all* of *Conrack* in his class. "I didn't know how to say: 'No, he's lying,'" Conroy said, so he let Dickey continue talking. Irritated by Dickey's need to take credit for his successes, Conroy adored his teacher: "He was as fabulous a teacher of poetry as ever lived. He inspired me beyond description." But the inspiration applied only to his writing. Dickey's boasts that he had bedded all the girls in his class left Conroy cold, as did his active recruitment of disciples. Conroy remembered his teacher's posturing all too well. During the last class of the semester, Dickey proclaimed: "Today I am going to an island off the coast of South Carolina. I'm only taking my bows and arrows. I will sleep in the swampy ground. There's a bear up on this island, a huge black bear, and I have an appointment with this bear. And only one of us, only one of us will survive, and I do not know which one." Dickey promised to smear his face with bear's blood if he managed to kill his prey. Conroy remarked: "I decided never to teach in college after my experience with Jim."[30] He would simply write.

Conroy glimpsed Dickey's competitive animus in less feral contexts than stories about bear hunts. Once while signing copies of *The Great Santini* in a Columbia department store, Conroy saw Maxine approach alone. She informed Conroy that her husband regarded his former student as a competitor and therefore refused to come. Dickey, however, was not always so aloof. He occasionally proposed that the two authors collaborate on screenplays. "All Hollywood will take notice,"[31] Dickey said at a dinner in Charleston, grabbing and shaking Conroy to emphasize his point. Although Conroy's novels were made into successful films, he did not share Dickey's fascination with Hollywood. Despite their differences, Conroy planned to pay homage to Dickey at the Academy Awards ceremony in early 1992 if the film made from his novel *The Prince of Tides* won an Oscar. Because it did not, he sent Dickey a letter instead:

> I write you only to praise you, Jim. I'm sorry I never talked in class, but I was listening and I emerged from your class a murderous critic of my own

work and a ferocious critic of others. I wanted all writing to affect me as yours did, even my own. But I wish I'd gotten to know you. I found myself shy around you and I still do. I could not figure out why the man who wrote "The May Day Sermon" would be interested in a single thing I had to say.

Again, all praise and homage and gratitude. Your teaching stays with me still. It lives inside me and sustains me. If I could, I'd be a better writer. But I promise you, I take my talent to its furthest edge. I learned to do that in your class and what I can't accomplish is due to a limitation of talent, not will.[32]

According to colleagues at USC, Dickey often scoffed at these impassioned letters. He probably did so out of an awareness of his former student's success, which contrasted sharply with Dickey's failures in the 1980s. About Dickey's post-*Deliverance* writing, Conroy himself asserted: "There was a decline that was precipitous."

Dickey's bid to become America's premier poet seemed more promising on January 7, 1972, the day John Berryman threw himself from a Minneapolis bridge. As with Randall Jarrell, Dickey wondered if his belittling criticism had contributed to Berryman's presuicide depression. He was saddened by the news of his ghastly death, but glad to have one less rival on Parnassus. Dickey's student Ben Greer witnessed his reaction firsthand. He had gone to Dickey's house for lunch. By the time the food arrived from La Petite Château, Greer and Dickey had consumed a good deal of alcohol. When the phone rang, Maxine answered. Greer could hear her say: "Oh no. My goodness. Let me get Jim." The caller next gave Dickey the news. "Oh no. Oh my God. Oh no, no. Maxine, here baby, you take this," he said. Dickey strutted back to his chair at the table. "Ben, John Berryman is dead," he announced. Assuming that the two poets had been close friends, Greer said he was sorry and asked how Berryman had died. Dickey said it had been a suicide and, with flawless delivery: "You know, Ben, the greatest American critics say the very first American poets are John Berryman, poor Cal Lowell, and *me*, James Dickey. Now John Berryman is dead by his own hands beneath a cold Yankee bridge. Cal Lowell is crackers."[33] He repeated what Yeats had told his sister the day after Swinburne died: "Now I'm king of the cats." Dickey had responded similarly to Mary Cantwell when Robert Lowell had suffered yet another manic-depressive breakdown.

To dramatize as well as assuage his guilt, Dickey made up various stories about his role in Berryman's fatal leap. At lunch with fiction writer Richard Bausch, Dickey regurgitated his favorite lines about his "disastrous generation of poets." On the subject of Berryman, he said he had talked to Berryman on the phone shortly before he killed himself. "I'm going to do it this time, Jim," Berryman allegedly had said. Dickey had responded: "You aren't going to do it this time any more than you did it the other twelve times." Leaning and leering across the table, Dickey added: "But he diiiid; he did!"[34] In devilish moods, Dickey told friends that he had actually *urged* Berryman to jump from the bridge. His mother-in-law, Mrs. Tipton, heard him say this. Al Braselton heard a similar story: "Soon after talking to him one night, John Berryman was so discouraged with Jim's assessments of his abilities, combined with hard drinking and depression, he committed suicide off that cold bridge."[35] Dickey was probably recycling the old hypothesis that Keats's harsh reviewers had precipitated his early death, substituting Berryman for Keats.

Nearly two years after Berryman's death, when John Haffenden wrote from England asking for letters, critical insights, and anecdotes for his biography of Berryman, Dickey replied: "Although I wish you every success with your project, his death is still too close to me to allow me to discuss it, or him or his work with anyone. I'm sure you can understand this, and will be guided accordingly."[36] The closeness of Berryman's death had little to do with Dickey's unwillingness to talk about it, and he was not averse to helping biographers. He wrote Ian Hamilton: "I have just read your biography of Robert Lowell with very great interest, for I knew Lowell fairly well and remember him with great esteem and affection. I also knew—and know—a good many of the other figures in your book, including Roethke, Berryman, Flannery O'Connor, Allen Tate, Robert Penn Warren, Elizabeth Hardwick and almost everybody except Jean Stafford and Lowell's various doctors. I am mildly surprised, with the enormous amount of research . . . you quite obviously did—that you didn't come here, for I have a good deal of material concerning Lowell, including a segment of a film featuring him and myself sitting and talking about things that concerned us at the time." Dickey pointed out a mistake in Hamilton's account of Roethke's death on a tennis court (it was in a swimming pool), thanked him for writing such a "useful and powerful book,"[37] but could not disguise his disgruntlement about being neglected.

Apart from his lampoon of Berryman in *Sorties*, Dickey had kept up a friendly correspondence with him during the two years before his suicide. On October 21, 1970, he asked Berryman to submit poems to *Esquire* and fondly remembered their earlier letters about the poet Robert Bhain Campbell. Hoping to get together, Dickey asked Berryman if he could arrange a double reading for them at the University of Minnesota. He said he usually refused to share the stage with other poets, but promised to make an exception with Berryman. In his reply, Berryman complimented *Deliverance* and Dickey's poems, and also agreed to submit something to *Esquire*. Early in 1971, Dickey resuscitated the idea of a dual reading: "If you get a decent reading somewhere, let the people know that I will be very happy to come up there and read with you, wherever it might turn out to be. I don't care at all about the fee. If I get what I usually get, I will split it with you. But we *should* get together, because, as they say on the pro football games on Sunday afternoon, the clock is running. I know all about the alcoholic situation, though my own condition is further compounded by diabetes. But we will last awhile, and we will write some poems. Yes, by God."[38] Dickey's admission of alcoholism was rare—much rarer than his false claims about diabetes.

Another renowned poet Dickey courted and castigated at this time was Yevtushenko. In late January 1972, the tall, gaunt, thirty-eight-year-old Russian arrived in Columbia to begin a five-week reading tour. Journalists flocked to him as to a pop idol or movie star. He attracted one of the largest poetry audiences in the Southeast; four thousand people gathered in the Carolina Coliseum to hear him read. Responsible for introducing him, Dickey deflected attention from Yevtushenko's athletic prowess, political views, and charm to emphasize his courage as a poet. But as Yevtushenko recited "Babi Yar," a poem that indicted anti-Semitism, and part of "In a Steelworker's Home," which endorsed pacifism, Dickey grew resentful. When Yevtushenko told students, who presented him with bouquets, that flowers were better than bullets, and flaunted a Jesus Christ Superstar T-shirt bought in Columbia, Dickey's resentment mounted. Nevertheless, Dickey joined Yevtushenko on January 28 at New York's Madison Square Garden, where he, Stanley Kunitz, and Richard Wilbur had been asked to read one of their own poems and one of Yevtushenko's. The evening turned into a cacophanous melee—part poetry reading, part political event, part rock concert. Eugene McCarthy read, as did Allen Ginsberg. A rock ensemble called the Bijou Singers contributed to the din, which Dickey found distressing because it muffled his poem. "As for all that rock 'n roll and the light show and all the rest, well, I don't know, but I'm willing to go along with it," he told a reporter for the *National Observer*. As in Columbia, the crowd of five thousand found the performance uplifting. "Who said that American people don't love poetry?" Yevtushenko said in his halting English. "Next time I come to United States I promise to fill *all* Madison Square Garden."[39] Dickey felt the audience had been bamboozled by the Russian's political diatribes against America. Because Yevtushenko had proclaimed himself "anti-anti-Semitic," Dickey pointed out that Russia's treatment of its Jews was far more reprehensible than America's. Dickey later recounted: "When Yevtushenko and I appeared together at Madison Square Garden, I spoke to him about the line of his that says, 'The stars in your flag, America, are bullet holes.' I said, 'Suppose I went to your country and got up at a poetry reading and said, "Russia, your flag is red because it is dipped in the blood of millions of Jews." He said, 'They would not like to hear that from *you*.' And I said I didn't like hearing the same thing from *him*."[40] Despite their disagreements, the two poets abided by the friendly Russian custom of swapping hats.

After the Madison Square Garden gala, Dickey encountered smaller, less partisan audiences at the Guggenheim, where he introduced James Wright, and at Choate, the Connecticut prep school his daughter would attend in the 1990s. At his various public readings, he replicated rather than renounced Yevtushenko's double-edged way of confronting audiences; he also mixed charisma with insults. To Carl Dolmetsch, the English Department chair at the College of William and Mary, who invited him to read in the spring of 1972, Dickey tried to explain some of the reasons for his baffling behavior. He indicated that as his fiftieth year approached he had to do everything possible to avoid boredom and overcome the negative criticism aimed at some of his recent books.[41] He had written in a 1970 letter to Richard Howard: "People do not understand, actually, the desperation that begins to settle on one at this time of life. Erotic experience comes to seem, not only the best of answers to the Void, but the *only* one. If people—wives, lovers—would grant us this very obvious fact and let us go our way and do our thing when the body and the mind most demand that it be done, things would be very much easier all around, and we would no longer live in the world of phoniness that we now inhabit."[42] Sexual boisterousness was only one way Dickey flouted taboos, dispelled boredom, and got attention. Insulting hosts and audiences, such as those at William and Mary, was another.

Dickey was better behaved on an NBC roundtable discussion of the Apollo moon flights in early May. Moderated by John Chancellor and Edwin Newman, the panel also included science-fiction writer Arthur C. Clarke, Apollo 14 astronaut Alan Shepard, and Norman Mailer. In his opening remarks, Mailer bemoaned the difficulty of writing about the Apollo 14 mission amid all the hyperbole surrounding Apollo 11, some of which he himself had created in *Of a Fire on the Moon*. After Alan Shepard hit a golf ball on the moon, he contended, the moon had lost its poetic mystery and become just another country club. Rather than chip golf balls, he, like Clarke, wanted the astronauts to engage in experiments to investigate "the psychic phenomena of the moon." Turning away from this psychobabble, Chancellor asked Dickey for his opinions, and he replied, as he had before, that it was the extraterrestrial perspectives of Earth that mattered. Photographs that revealed "the blue planet" hanging in the immense nothingness of space should inspire humans to treat nature and themselves with more loving kindness. Dickey declared that he didn't want to be part of a generation that lost the Earth while gaining the moon. He wanted Earth to keep its hallowed position in the cosmic order of things:

> I see myself, and the rest of human beings, existing by the result of some enormous cosmic mischance or mistake or, if you choose, you could call it something in the nature of a miracle. And I just don't believe it would happen again or ever has or ever will. We human beings drastically need to believe that we are not the only intelligences and the only sentient beings in the universe, because that puts maybe too great a burden of responsibility on us. Maybe, as Mr. T. S. Eliot once said, "humankind cannot bear very much reality." And the reality of being, in a sense, the consciousness of the universe, the entire universe, is a great deal to have to bear up under, and yet, it seems to me, that's our fate.[43]

But at the May 17 National Institute of Arts and Letters meeting Dickey showed how far his love for fellow inhabitants of "the blue planet" went. He was happy to greet writers Julien Green, W. S. Merwin, Walker Percy, Harrison Salisbury, and W. D. Snodgrass, who were also being inducted, as well as Ann Stanford and Peter Davison, who were receiving literary awards. To the black poet Michael Harper, who was also receiving an award, Dickey was less gracious.

Dickey displayed his condescension toward African-Americans again among his white audience at Dartmouth College the following week. On May 24, when the poet Robert Siegel welcomed him at the airport, Dickey drunkenly impersonated the "redneck abroad." With Siegel's friend, the poet Sydney Lea, he talked about the upcoming boxing match between Jerry Quarry and Muhammad Ali, whom he insisted on calling Cassius Clay. "Muhammad Ali" was "just nigger talk,"[44] he told Lea. According to Dickey, the white Quarry was going to whip the black Clay. Put off by Dickey's insolence, Lea bet him five hundred dollars that Ali would win the bout. Dickey accepted the bet gladly and shook hands to confirm it. The fight occurred a month later, on June 27 in Las Vegas, and Ali knocked out Quarry in seven rounds. Lea wrote Dickey a letter demanding his five hundred dollars, but never got a reply.

For several years Dickey had hoped for Ali's defeat in the ring. He had no tolerance for a loudmouthed black superstar who claimed to be a poet and who refused on religious grounds to serve in Vietnam. Before the notorious Atlanta match between Ali and Quarry on October 26, 1970, when Ali received racist death threats, Dickey had gone so far as to write Quarry an encouraging letter, addressing the boxer as if he were "the great white hope": "Until the last minute, before your fight with Clay, I was to come to Atlanta and interview you and cover the fight for *Harper's Magazine*. I got sick, though, and couldn't make it. . . . I sympathize as much as can be done with your bad luck in the Clay fight. . . . I will make a prediction. . . . You will be heavyweight champion, if you keep on. I very much believe that you could knock Cassius Clay's brains out, given a proper chance. Yes, and Joe Frazier's too."[45] In a letter to Willie Morris, who had asked him to write about the match, Dickey had blamed his inability to do so on a nervous breakdown, a short coma, the possibility of another breakdown, and weekly blood tests for his diabetes.

As if to counter charges of racism, Dickey agreed to go on record as opposing the World Boxing Association's decision in 1967 to strip Ali of his title and ability to fight. He signed a statement circulated by *Esquire* in the summer of 1969 supporting Ali's return to the ring. He wrote Harold Hayes at *Esquire*: "I *do* believe that Cassius Clay should be allowed to defend his title, particularly against Joe Frazier or Sonny Liston (who may be honest now), or even Jimmy Ellis or Jerry Quarry. And I also think Clay (none of that ridiculous Muslim stuff) is the champion, for there is only one way of dethroning a man who can still (physically) fight, and that is in the ring, not in the courts. The part of us that goes back to the flickering of cave-fires knows this, and no amount of legal hocus-pocus is going to change the fact that physical champions remain so as long as they *are* so."[46] Dickey stood up for Ali's physical rights even while mocking his religious and legal rights. While he espoused Walt Whitman's mystic vision of the "miracle" of "the blue planet" and the cosmos itself, his vestigial resentments usually undermined whatever attempts he made to affirm Whitman's enlightened democratic spirit.

At Dartmouth, Dickey stayed with Siegel and his family in the house on Webster Terrace normally occupied by Richard Eberhart, who was teaching in Florida. Siegel brought out his guitar, which Dickey played in the gazebo on the front lawn while telling stories about his days as a fighter pilot. He later tried to endear himself to Siegel's family by playing with their adopted pet raccoon. Pretending it was a hat, he put it on his head, whereupon it promptly defecated. Dickey got along well with Siegel, but was not as successful with others at Dartmouth. His histrionic behavior repelled those who gathered for afternoon tea among the stately interior balconies, burnished oak tables, and soft yellow lamps of the English Department's Sanborn House. Late, loud, and drunk, he stormed into the room sporting a wide hat, tan jacket, and cowboy boots. He surveyed the group of thirty eager faces for a place to sit, stomped to an empty chair at the end of the room, and slammed it on an antique French table, drawling that he hoped he wouldn't fall and break his "ass." Some of the tweed-jacketed professors looked up in silent horror. Too drunk to carry on a lengthy conversation, Dickey managed to utter a number of jocular profundities like: "I don't represent the generation gap—I am the generation gap!" Later he boomed: "I'm not a Southerner—I'm the Southerner!"[47] His listeners were convinced.

Following his Dartmouth trip, Dickey joined Maxine and Mrs. Tipton at Chris's UVA graduation. Peter and Eleanor Taylor invited the Dickeys to their house for a party and dinner. Among friends and family, Dickey felt little compulsion and had little opportunity to play the Southern cracker. Nevertheless, he drank and bantered with Peter about the "broads" they had met at the University of Utah writers' conference in 1967. Over supper on the Taylors' terrace, Dickey whispered to Eleanor: "Let's you and me run away together."[48] An hour later, Dickey whispered the same thing to the Taylors' friend Mary Washington Graham. Dickey's lighthearted entreaties amused the company, except for Maxine, who struck Eleanor as dejected and defeated by her husband's inveterate flirtations.

In July, before dashing off to the premieres of *Deliverance* in New York and Atlanta, Dickey vacationed with his family in a rented West Tisbury house on Martha's Vineyard. He looked forward to socializing with Stanley Burnshaw, who had invited him to his house in West Tisbury three years before. He also wanted to see Norman Mailer, who had asked Dickey to come to Bar Harbor, Maine, for some sailing. Dickey never saw Mailer, but he did spend many joyous hours with Burnshaw and Styron. According to Styron, who regularly played morning tennis with Dickey at the Vineyard Haven Yacht Club near his house:

> Jim was on a perpetual high, quite aware that he was on the verge of that rare happening: that of an author of an exceptional novel seeing an exceptional movie made of it. As everyone in the world knows, Jim loved the bottle—and so did I in those days—and I shudder to recall that we would hit the tennis court at 10 in the morning fortified by a pitcher of dry Martinis. After these disastrous games we'd sit on my front porch, and it was there that he told me about his life in the Air Force. He spoke of fear, and of the exquisite fragility and vulnerability of the men who flew those planes, and as he told me of these desperate matters I began to see how *Deliverance*, which I had so admired as a novel, was in a sense an allegory of fear and survival.[49]

Styron was awed by Dickey's rambunctious energy and joy. After publishing *Darkness Visible* in the 1990s, a haunting personal account of his struggle with depression, Styron reflected that Dickey's euphoria "certainly mimicked the mania of manic depression,"[50] but was not as ungovernable as the real illness.

While not batting a tennis ball, Dickey and Styron reminisced about their Southern backgrounds in a segregated society, common military experiences, and current attitudes toward racial tensions in the United States. Styron's *The Confessions of Nat Turner* had been a magnet for accusations of racism in 1967. Regarding similar charges hurled at Dickey, Styron commented: "I think that Jim had a strong streak of the professional Southerner in him. Which I don't find disagreeable at all if he carries it off pretty well. I don't think he's a racist at all. I never did. I think he may have had some conventional attitudes, generational attitudes about blacks, that a lot of people would misconstrue as racism, but really are just conditioned reflexes. I think blacks, as they sometimes are, are to-tally wrong about somebody like Jim being a racist."[51] Those blacks who wit-nessed the nastier displays of Dickey's "generational attitudes" and "conditioned reflexes" were not so forgiving of his "professional Southerner" role.

On Martha's Vineyard, Dickey sometimes visited Stanley Hart, who owned a bookstore near West Tisbury. At a party given by the Burnshaws, Hart had no-ticed Dickey crouching on the back lawn with his bow and arrows, running from shadow to shadow, stalking imaginary prey, and shooting at tree trunks and rab-bits. Dickey soon visited Hart's bookstore for drinks and literary talk. He also dropped hints that he would like a ride on Hart's boat, the *Red Cat*, a two-masted, gaff-rigged Gloucester schooner that had once served as a fishing vessel on the Grand Banks. One sunny day, Jim, Maxine, and Kevin Dickey joined Hart on his boat. Also included among the passengers were Rose Styron, New York attorney Jim Austin, and Columbia English professor Luciano Rebay. On their way from Edgartown Harbor to Woods Hole and Hadley's Harbor, as Hart steered and related a story to Dickey, who was drunk and lying with his head against the companionway, Rebay's wife shouted that the schooner was about to ram another boat. Within seconds the *Red Cat's* bowsprit punctured a cabin cruiser, nearly decapitating the wife of the boat's owner, who happened to be the president of Williams College. Hart backed up his schooner, shouted his name and address, told the man who was screaming at him that he was insured, and departed. Dickey hadn't moved during all the hubbub and soon fell asleep in the sun.

Before long a Coast Guard rescue boat pulled up to the *Red Cat*, and a man cried "Heave to" through a bullhorn. A crewman fastened ropes to the schooner. Hart was stunned when all of a sudden Dickey hollered: "Cut the fucking lines! Cut the fucking lines!" The young Coast Guardsman ignored him, so Dickey asked him if he would like a beer. He said he didn't drink on duty. "You don't drink on duty?" Dickey bellowed. "Well, boy, if you don't take a fucking beer, I'm throwing your ass overboard." Startled by Dickey's threats, the guardsman went below to the galley, where he remained until a larger boat—a cruiser-size Coast Guard warship—intercepted them near Chappaquiddick. As Dickey awoke from a second sleep, a crewman from the other boat arrested Hart and ordered him back to Woods Hole. At the Coast Guard headquarters, a polite and sober Dickey rounded up Maxine, with whom he had been squabbling earlier in the day, and Kevin, who was dismayed by the fiasco, and took a taxi to the ferry for Martha's Vineyard. Austin and Rebay stayed behind to help their troubled cap-tain, who was eventually charged with eight crimes, including kidnapping a fed-eral officer (a criminal defense lawyer got the eight charges reduced to one misdemeanor—leaving the scene of an accident). Dickey knew that he had dis-appointed Hart by refusing to stand by him at the Coast Guard headquarters and at the federal magistrate's office that evening. To make amends, he bought $684 worth of books at Hart's store and gave him a Southern planter's hat.[52]

Although Dickey's drinking on Martha's Vineyard and elsewhere was out of control, it was Maxine who needed care. She was beginning to pass blood. A combination of weight and alcohol made her clumsy. Walking out the door of Styron's house, she tripped and broke her ankle. These crises were merely har-

bingers of her gradual decline. Exacerbated by her husband's drinking and philandering, her use of alcohol eventually would kill her.

27. Premieres and Their Aftermath (1972–1973)

After drawn-out negotiations, Warner Brothers had decided to release
Deliverance at approximately the same time in Los Angeles, New York, and
Atlanta. The Atlanta screening would be held at the Memorial Arts Center
with a champagne reception and other appropriate fanfare on August 1, 1972.
The New York premiere would be at Loew's Tower East on July 30 and the Los
Angeles premiere at Cinerama Dome. The reaction to the film in New York
gave Dickey every reason to believe that it would be a blockbuster hit. To share
the triumphant moment, Maxine invited Inman Mays to join her and the rest of
the family at 3:00 P.M. at the cinema. Mays greeted them as they exited a taxi,
immediately noticing Dickey's leather-fringed jacket and large hunting hat with
a leopard-skin band. Giddy with drink and boyish élan, he strode down the side-
walk and introduced himself to the long line of ticket buyers. Used to cranks on
their streets, the New Yorkers tittered nervously or stared in disbelief as Dickey
hailed them: "Hello, I'm James Dickey, and you're going to see a great movie. I
wrote the novel, the screenplay and the music, and I also have a star role. . . .
Believe me, you're going to get your money's worth today."[1] Some in line realized that the real James Dickey was addressing them, laughed, and said they were
looking forward to the show.

Inside, Dickey was similarly irrepressible. At the moment of keenest suspense,
when Reynolds pulled back the arrow in his bow and aimed it at the rapist,
Dickey jumped up and hollered: "Kill the son of a bitch!"[2] Laughter and applause erupted around Dickey. After Reynolds let his arrow fly, Dickey interrupted the silence again: "Hot Damn!"[3] Some of the more reserved spectators
shuffled and murmured, trying to figure out who would be so gauche as to yell
during such a gruesome scene. When Dickey appeared in the final scenes as the
sheriff, again he jumped up and yelled: "That's the best damn piece of acting in
the whole movie!" The lights coming on, Dickey pulled his sheriff's hat from under his seat and propped it on his head. He welcomed the throng of admirers,
calling *Deliverance* his movie: "I did everything in this movie—wrote it, selected
the banjo music, acted in it . . . , everything but direct it, and I even did some of
that, too."[4] Mays followed Maxine out of the theater and joined them at the
Saint Moritz for drinks with Stewart Richardson. At the celebratory dinner in
the Saint Moritz dining room, Dickey continued his ebullient patter with
Robert Manning, Richard Howard, Theron Raines, and other literary friends.
Jon Voight, who was eating at a nearby table with his father, got up and spoke to
Dickey about the film. As they laughed and traded jokes about the difficulties of
filming, all their past conflicts seemed forgotten. But not everyone shared
Dickey's saturnalian mood. Chris Dickey told Richard Howard at the dinner
that he was ashamed and angry that his father had made such a spectacle of him-
self in the theater.

The day before the Atlanta premiere Dickey made an unusual visit to Al Braselton in the alcoholic section of the Peachtree Hospital. Having done all he could to ensure an Atlanta premiere for *Deliverance*, Braselton had suffered a series of crises. He knew that his drinking and extramarital affairs had destroyed his marriage, and had sought help at the hospital. Dickey strode from the elevator in his cowboy hat and fringed jacket and made his way through the haggard alcoholics with two enormous guitar cases and several books, *Crazy Sundays: F. Scott Fitzgerald in Hollywood*, *The Poems and Prose of Gerard Manley Hopkins*, and the Modern Library collection of Saki's stories, which he planned to give to Braselton. Dickey was sorry to the point of tears to see his friend in such depressing surroundings. He remarked tenderly: "Here you are, little brother, here you are. What are we going to do?" As they walked to a private room, Dickey wondered rhetorically: "How did it come to this—this bright gleaming hell?" Gazing at the phantomlike patients reclining in their chairs, Dickey tried to disassociate his friend from them. "You ain't no more an alcoholic than I am,"[5] he declared. Dickey played his new Martin guitar, but Braselton's hands were too unsteady to accompany on the other. Dickey read Hopkins's poems, and they laughed over Fitzgerald's drunken shenanigans in Hollywood, which both agreed they had duplicated in their own ways. Dickey was heartened when Braselton told him he could attend the premiere of *Deliverance*.

The next evening, Braselton shakily entered the Memorial Arts Center. Local and foreign dignitaries swarmed from limousines. Surrounded by fawning women and an attentive Gov. Jimmy Carter, Dickey was pleased beyond measure. Proud friends and relatives basked in the excitement that Dickey had brought to Atlanta. In the red plush and marble galleria, he stood out from the eighteen hundred well-dressed guests in his black, broad-brimmed hat, maroon blazer, blue trousers, and bright red leather shoes. The motley outfit seemed appropriate as he clowned with Carter for the cameras, jamming his ungainly hat on the governor's head. With the reporters he was also serious. Worried by Maxine's recent ailments, Dickey tried to be solicitous. He assured reporters like Betsy Fancher that his wife made possible such successes as *Deliverance* by taking care of all "the tedious and endless minutia of life." He extolled Maxine as the gravitational center of his existence: "No woman could ever make me leave my wife. I don't understand these men who marry casually, then put their wives aside like an old snot rag—not after you've been through all the problems of finances and raising children."[6] Wearing a free-flowing dress to cover the weight she had gained in recent years, Maxine looked regal, but in deference to her husband she took a back seat in the balcony with her mother and Polly Braselton.

Dickey was similarly generous toward Boorman, calling his film superior to the novel. Not all his grudges, however, were forgotten. According to Boorman, a radio journalist who questioned Burt Reynolds about his allegation that James Dickey had been "a pain in the ass"[7] to work with on *Deliverance* incited a brief skirmish. Reynolds replied that it was true, but that he judged Dickey to be one of the greatest poets in America. Standing nearby, Dickey shot back that Reynolds had no credibility as a judge of contemporary poetry. In a couple of months, on September 22, 1972, Dickey complained to Boorman that Reynolds was turning him into a demon and urged him to silence Reynolds for the sake of the movie's success. Over the next few years, Dickey matched Reynolds's tendency to mythologize with his own, alternately demonizing and glamorizing Reynolds. Dickey said he had mentored his struggling protégé and roomed with Reynolds on the film site of *Deliverance*.[8] He even convinced Gordon Lish that he had had a homosexual affair with Reynolds. Reynolds had expressed his affection for Dickey at a postfilming party by giving Dickey his wrist compass, although at other times Dickey said the gift was an underwater watch. To a reporter for the *Pittsburgher* Dickey claimed: "Burt got up to make an announcement. He said 'Ladies and gentlemen, I'd like to make a presentation to Jim Dickey.' Then he looked at me and said, 'If you wear this compass on your right hand, and your watch on your left, you'll be master of time and space.'"[9] Considering Reynolds's animosity toward Dickey, it is likely that Dickey was referring to a time before filming when Charles Orme gave him a Finnish compass and Dickey gave Orme an army-issue wrist compass. Dickey proffered another view of Reynolds in a 1996 letter to Saul Bellow: "If Burt Reynolds is not dumber than an ox, he is not any smarter than one, either, and insisted on playing Lewis as an over-bearing bully, when the whole point is that the others follow him because of his mystiques, which they think may supply some of the answers they seek."[10] In most of his comments about Dickey, Reynolds said he wanted to give him a hand grenade rather than a compass.

Dickey either scoffed at Reynolds or romanticized him because of his muscular, swashbuckling image. He liked to tell how Reynolds called him up in a supplicant mood while Dickey was adapting *The Call of the Wild* for TV. Reynolds allegedly thanked Dickey for making him famous in *Deliverance*, and begged for a role in *The Call of the Wild*. Dickey retorted that he could have a job if he could pull a dog sled. Along with pretending he had masterminded Reynolds's career, Dickey also assumed the role of Reynolds's guardian. In 1973, during the filming of *The Man Who Loved Cat Dancing* with Sarah Miles, Reynolds had been implicated in a highly publicized scandal at Gila Bend, Arizona. One night, after Miles visited Reynolds's room while he was getting a massage, her jealous business manager, David Whiting, beat her. Miles called Reynolds for help, but by the time he found her, Whiting had fled. Later Whiting was found dead. Although three autopsies concluded that Whiting had overdosed on pills, a gash on the back of his head aroused suspicions that Reynolds had murdered him out of loyalty to Miles. Reynolds testified under oath that he had never seen or touched Whiting. Dickey told friends that he had forced the lawyers bent on prosecuting Reynolds to let him go free.

Amid all the hoopla in Atlanta, Dickey took care of his real protégé, Al Braselton, who was struggling with tremors and memory loss brought on by alcoholic withdrawal. Unnerved by all the people and excitement at the premiere, Braselton wanted to return to the hospital. Dickey gave him an exuberant bear hug and told him he was to be a guest of honor. He could sit between Dickey and Gov. Carter to watch the film. When the lights dimmed, Dickey fidgeted manically, poking Braselton in the ribs, telegraphing scenes, and repeatedly exclaiming: "Hey, you're really going to like this!" As the film's dialogue and scenes got more lurid, a hush fell over the audience. Braselton nudged his friend: "Damn, Jim, this is pretty raw." Dickey responded: "I don't give a shit. This damn Memorial Arts Center ain't no place to see *Deliverance* for the first time. We ought to be out up Highway 85 [at a] drive-in with two cases of Pabst Blue Ribbon and two fat horny country girls." During the rape scene, the hospital's dose of tranquilizers could not calm Braselton's agitation. Perhaps remembering the night on the river when Dickey bellowed threateningly from his tent, Braselton fought for control. He tried to joke about it, leaning over to Carter and whispering: "This ain't no junior league movie, is it, Governor?" Carter agreed: "It's pretty rough. But it's good for Georgia." Trying to convince himself, Carter paused, and said again, "This is good for Georgia," adding less confidently, "I hope."[11] Braselton struggled to keep from laughing about Carter's worries.

After the film ended, Carter and Reynolds spoke to the audience about the film, and the Atlanta Film Festival presented *Deliverance* with the Golden Phoenix Award. Braselton went from the Arts Center to Atlanta's Biltmore Towers, where the Dickeys were staying, and noticed that in between parties Dickey had gone on a book-buying spree. The room was littered with astronomy books that Dickey planned to use in his book-length poem *The Zodiac* and his novel *Alnilam*. Determined to make his friend an active participant in the fun, Dickey again insisted that Braselton was no more an alcoholic than he. "You just don't want to quit drinking altogether,"[12] Dickey cajoled. As people gathered in Dickey's room, Braselton fought the temptation to drink whiskey. He succeeded, but with the Dickeys at dinner he drank wine and couldn't stop before downing six glasses.

Braselton later discovered that Dickey had slipped out for a night on the town after telling Maxine that he needed to see some Warner Brothers people. Someone at Warner Brothers had lined up an Atlanta call girl for Dickey, a woman nicknamed "the Mechanic" (her real name was Kathy). His comments about marital fidelity to Betsy Fancher notwithstanding, Dickey was eager to meet her. Braselton recalled: "I knew her very well. A lovely redhead of starlet beauty quality who had entertained a lot of the stars. . . . When Jim got to Kathy's apartment, he was surprised to be greeted by a lovely woman who was familiar with his poetry. He was very drunk, but this took him aback so they sat and talked for a while. Then Jim started some rough stuff. . . . [He] wanted to get into some sadomasochistic [sex]. . . . He wanted to whip her or beat her or something like that . . . and Kathy, who looked forward to going to bed with the great writer, got so mad at him that she threw him out."[13] The account might seem apocryphal except for the fact that Dickey had approached other women in the same way.

Dickey attended openings of *Deliverance* in other cities besides New York and Atlanta. "I can't wait to see it again,"[14] he told many a reporter. He rarely deviated from his routine of inviting friends to the theater and providing a running commentary. For the December 22 premiere in Columbia, South Carolina, one of his guests was George Garrett, who later expressed his gratitude:

He was extremely nice and gracious and generous about that. He really insisted that Susan and I go with Maxine and him in the limo to the premiere. And we all got in a big stretch limo in our tuxedos and went there.

Everybody from Columbia, South Carolina, was there in their tuxedos. There must've been a run on them all the way up to Spartanburg. We went in . . . and as soon as the film got underway Jim jumped up. We were sitting in the middle section, and we got him walking up and down all the aisles, throughout the entire movie, talking about it. He'd say, "You're gonna really like the next part when Lewis comes over the hill here." Then when he himself appeared on the screen, he lip-synched . . . the dialogue with the character. Then people gave him a great cheer.

Not satisfied with just one such performance, Dickey returned many times to the Columbia theater during the film's six-week run, flustering as many moviegoers in Columbia as he had in New York. The young English Department graduate who ran the cinema didn't know what to do. According to Garrett: "The story was that he called [Calhoun Winton] and said 'What can you do about this? These customers don't know who this guy is. He's wandering [around and] they think he's in off the street, telling them [about *Deliverance* and] shouting at the movie.'"[15] Garrett was amused by the spectacle. Dickey himself denied attending the theaters or pretended that they were too full to attend. He wrote Boorman on September 22: "You ask about the kind of response the official public opening of the film got in Atlanta. I didn't go, but my sister-in-law did, and she reports the occasion was absolutely dumbfounding. She couldn't get in until she demanded to see the theater manager, identified herself, and so got a seat on the back row." About the New York premiere, Dickey told Boorman: "One simply cannot get into the theater. In order to gain entrance, I had to get together with the theater manager, who at first thought I was a hold-up man."[16] Dickey's exaggerations had a purpose—to convince Boorman, who didn't need convincing, that the film was a smash hit.

Reviews in the *New Yorker*, *Time*, the *Washington Post*, and other prominent magazines and newspapers raved about the film's gut-churning drama. If there were reservations, they usually had to do with the banality of some of the dialogue, Boorman's refusal to introduce the characters in Atlanta, and the gratuitous nature of the violence. The critical haggling only increased public awareness of the film. Its extraordinary popularity had a ripple effect that touched many lives. It brought international fame to Dickey, made Burt Reynolds a star, and boosted Boorman's ebbing fortunes as a director. During its first week, the film reportedly grossed more than that week's intake from *The Godfather* and *Love Story* combined. *Variety* magazine stated that by November 8 it had grossed $2,186,140, a substantial sum for the time. Disappointed he wasn't making more of a percentage of ticket sales, Dickey protested that the $150,000 he had earned on the movie was unfair. By February 1973, Dickey told the *State* that *Deliverance* had grossed $6,500,000, and that it had placed third among the top fifty moneymakers of 1972. In 1973, the film's popular and critical success translated into three Academy Award nominations: for best director, best picture, and best film editing. Dickey, who watched the awards ceremony with friends, was convinced that *Deliverance* would win best picture, even though it was competing against *The Godfather*. Maxine was similarly convinced and stomped out of the room when *The Godfather* won. In 1972, the Writer's

Guild of America nominated Dickey for its annual screenwriter's award. Paperback sales of the novel soared; by October 1972, the novel had sold 1,070,000 copies.

Rather than rest on his cinematic laurels, Dickey wanted to plunge into new films with his son Chris and, somewhat surprisingly, Boorman. In a letter he sent Boorman in mid-September 1972, he referred to a plethora of film offers: "I have not made any commitments to any of these studios, and will not until I hear something of your personal and working situation. I have told the people I've talked to that I will work only with one director, which is yourself. I realize that you have projects of your own which do not and can not concern me. Nevertheless, any film projects that *I* either initiate or accede to will perforce concern you. So, it would be a good idea for you to give me some indication of your situation at the present time."[17] Boorman responded that he was flattered by Dickey's confidence in him. Nonetheless, because of his previous troubles with Dickey, he resisted any future collaborations.

The film's international success did not come without obstacles. As with the novel, there were charges of obscenity that needed to be addressed. Having learned of a plan by French censors to bowdlerize the rape scene, Boorman reassured Dickey that he was monitoring the situation and that: "We are assured of a great critical success. . . . The respected veteran French director Jean-Pierre Melville who is on the government censorship committee threatened to resign if one frame was cut. He says it is one of the best five films ever made. He is convening a special jury of distinguished critics, poets, directors and members of the Académie Française to award the film a special prize."[18] In London, matters were more problematic. The official film censor insisted on eliminating the sodomy scene. Boorman mustered influential support to dissuade the censor. Distressed by the news, Dickey contemplated calling the American embassy in London to enlist their help. In the end, both Boorman and Dickey were pleased by the highly favorable critical reception in England of the uncut film.

The most hostile reaction to the film came from the area around the film site itself. Many residents in Clayton and surrounding towns reacted to the film as they had reacted to the book. Daniel Roper summarized their views in the *North Georgia Journal:* "Unfortunately, the movie . . . portrayed the long-dwelling mountain families as dirty, backward, violent, and unfriendly. *Deliverance* did for them what *Jaws,* another well-known movie, would later do for sharks."[19] Aware that his film had made him even more of a persona non grata in North Georgia, Dickey complained: "I can't go over in those counties now. I'm afraid somebody is going to shoot me because they said I portrayed all mountain people as degenerate sodomists and it's given them a bad name."[20] One resident who had tried to get work on the film, Ralph Shaw, had already reproached Dickey in Clayton for the way he and others associated with *Deliverance* had condescended to the locals. Having canoed, fished, and played in the Chattooga as a boy, Shaw felt Dickey was a charlatan. Shaw's family had known and occasionally helped the Gentry family. Dickey's transformation of the Gentrys into sadistic rapists, Shaw felt, was reprehensible. And why did Dickey insist on dressing up and acting like a mountain man when he knew so little about the mountains and their inhabitants? On his own canoe trips, Shaw had always been happily surprised by the way mountain folk like the Gentrys suddenly appeared from the woods, shared their moonshine, and told stories around the campfire. *Deliverance*, he believed, had demonized these friendly rustics. To counter such charges, Dickey could have pointed out that not all his backwoodsmen were rapists; some of them possessed the virtues extolled by Shaw.

Because of the resentment felt toward Dickey and the "Hollywood types," those locals who participated in the film were sometimes scorned as collaborators. One of the Clayton residents who took the most flak was John Rickman. A wild boar hunter, a carpenter who helped build the Kingwood Country Club (Boorman admired his skills so much he asked him to come to Ireland to help construct his house), a successful entrepeneur, and an adviser for Walt Disney films, Rickman helped the film crew find suitable locations on the Chattooga. He also provided essential advice. Asked by Boorman to name the "lowest creature" he knew, he said "the pig" and volunteered his imitation pig squeal for the rape scene. His carpentry skills came in handy when Boorman needed props. Rickman built the flimsy bridge over the river on which the deformed boy—another Clayton resident, Billy Redden—stood and swung his banjo. Since he knew the townspeople so well, the casting director asked Rickman to find local actors. Rickman created some tension with Dickey by suggesting Jim Dillard for the role of sheriff, but gracefully withdrew his candidate because Dickey insisted that the role had been reserved for him. Because of his porcine sound effects in the rape scene, Rickman acknowledged that after the film's release: "It was open season on me."[21] Still, he remained convinced that *Deliverance* was beneficial to Rabun County since it showcased the area's natural splendor and began the Chattooga rafting and canoeing business.

With *Deliverance* circulating among the world's cinemas, Dickey could return to his writing. He told his friend Larry Gluck in September 1972: "I'm delighted it has finally been released, that I no longer have to be bothered with it, and can now get to work on something else, for it has surely taken up a great deal of time these past couple of years."[22] During the fall he tried to finish two poetry books—*Slowly Toward Hercules* and *The Zodiac*. He also returned to teaching, where he met one of his most devoted students, the poet David Havird. Havird joined Jim Mann and Mann's girlfriend, Janet Lee, as a "regular" at the Dickey house, partly because he got along so well with Maxine. Like Mann, Havird enrolled or audited nearly every class Dickey taught until he graduated in 1976.

Dickey was as vigorously ostentatious as ever in the classroom, but in other areas he became more perfunctory. As his fame increased and his drinking continued unabated, his letters became more formulaic. George Garrett, who had found Dickey accessible and friendly before *Deliverance*, noticed that in his interactions with USC colleagues he was more aloof. In the midst of all his success, he also seemed disappointed. According to Garrett, Dickey believed that "he was going to get out from under academia, that he would get jobs as a screenwriter, that he would continue to earn a lot of money." Dickey told Garrett that he had an agent handling his acting career and that he was waiting for offers, but the ones that came had little appeal: "He was offered one role . . . as some kind of demented farmer, and he didn't want to play the part. . . . He said, 'I had to turn that one down. I was gonna have to go barefoot and in overalls and chase chickens.' Then he said that Colgate toothpaste (because he had beautiful teeth) had been in touch with him, and they wanted a starter, and then more if they showed it more times. [He was offered] ten thousand dollars to do the Colgate toothpaste commercial. . . . He used to sit around and talk about . . . what a terribly important decision it was for him to make. Perhaps the fate of American poetry hung [in the balance], and if he did the wrong thing he would pull us all down, into the mire. If it was the right thing it would open up new and wonderful vistas for all of us. Obviously, we didn't get to see the commercial."[23] Dickey's vision of himself as a new Moses with Colgate-whitened teeth leading American poets to the promised land suffered other setbacks in the years to come.

Dickey's drinking contributed more than any other factor to the disturbing changes his friends perceived in him. Alcohol flowed in the Dickey household. Even Dickey's mother-in-law, who had moved to Columbia to be closer to her daughter, joined the libations. Garrett remembered that Mrs. Tipton "was a very polite Southern lady-drunk. She controlled it so well that you didn't know until she went over like a tree and fell. It happened again and again in the evening. You'd see this nice little lady, probably talking to some stranger, chatting along, and then suddenly going *wham!* Jim . . . would pick her up . . . like a trophy . . . , saying how awful it was to have a mother-in-law who was a drunk."[24]

Garrett did his best to remain on friendly terms with Dickey, who tended to view his new colleague as a rival. In 1969, Garrett had written Dickey at the behest of Calhoun Winton: "There has never been + I doubt ever will be any sort of *competition* between us. No jealousy at all. . . . Oh, *some* competition is inevitable. But it's the competition of teammates doing windsprints, running all out not for defeats + victories but for the sweaty, lung-burning, pure joy of it. . . . And therefore, in joy, I rejoice in your successes."[25] Dickey described the competition that would inevitably exist between them (Garrett had arrived in 1970 to teach fulltime at USC) in slightly different terms. He said they were like two gunfighters who, having ended up in the same town, should try not to kill each other.

As proof of his friendly sentiments, Garrett or his wife occasionally shuttled Kevin Dickey to and from the private Heathwood Hall Episcopal School, which Kevin attended from the fifth to the eighth grades before going to Dreher High School in 1972. Garrett recalled that Jim and Maxine "were drinking so much that by 8:25, the time to take the kids off to school, they'd be too drunk to drive. . . . The same would be true at 3:30 in the afternoon, and they didn't want to have an accident with their child . . . in the car." Kevin, who became an acolyte in the Episcopal Church (his mother attended Trinity Episcopal Church in Columbia and All Saints Episcopal Church in Pawley's Island) was grateful for the Garretts' help. In 1972, Garrett also helped out with Chris's schooling by encouraging his father to send him to Boston University for a degree in film studies. Thankful for Garrett's help, the Dickeys invited him to their parties: "We'd go out there some—it was right after *Deliverance*—and they never had any [food]. . . . Ten people would go out to his place and just drink all day. . . . Everyone would get hungry around one o'clock. Two of his ex-students ran a little gourmet restaurant. We would call them up and they would bring an entire meal for everybody, and we would sort of drunkenly swill it, and it was wild. This went on a long time."[26] As with other American writers like Hemingway, Fitzgerald, and Faulkner, Dickey's talent waned as his drinking waxed.

Maxine's alcoholism made taking care of her mother, husband, son, and house more difficult. To govern her ungovernable husband, Maxine often had to play the role of legal guardian as much as wife. To curb his extravagant spending habits, she took away his checking account and gave him an allowance. Even so, most of his USC friends noticed that he rarely carried cash. Once Garrett witnessed Dickey's clandestine attempt to get money without Maxine's permission. On meeting Maxine in the bank, Garrett said: "Oh, you just missed your husband here by about five minutes." Maxine asked: "What was he doing here at the bank?" When Maxine found out that her husband had just cashed a check, she was furious. She suspected he had opened a secret bank account. For several days, Maxine refused to give her husband his allowance "or anything [else] until he confessed about the secret bank account." Maxine's matriarchal discipline had some effect on her prodigal husband. "She really knew how to handle him and he seemed to be enjoying that,"[27] Garrett observed.

While Dickey never received his expected deliverance into the glamorous world of Hollywood, on his lucrative lecture and reading trips he tried to live like a movie star, always demanding first-class travel and the best hotel accommodations. His earnings, compared to those of most professors and writers, were remarkable. In 1972, he earned $120,268 from advances and royalties. His teaching salary, which would soon become the highest at USC, combined with his reading fees, pushed his gross income well above $200,000. His relations with Hollywood, in fact, were not as dismal as Garrett believed. On November 8, 1972, his agent, Theron Raines, negotiated a $150,000 deal for Dickey to write a screenplay based on Allen Seager's novel Amos Berry. The producer, Elliott Kastner, promised to secure a director and distribution contract by January 31, 1973. In November, Dickey traveled to Chris's home in Hamilton, Massachusetts, near Boston, to consult his son about collaborating on the project. Rather than work, however, Dickey spent a drunken night with John Updike, whom Chris invited from Ipswich, and spent the other nights drinking as well. Although Seager's agent, Armitage Watkins, and Seager's wife raised financial roadblocks, Dickey persisted with the film project. Near the end of 1975, he sent an outline for a screenplay to the Hollywood producer Charles Fries. Fries looked into buying the rights for the story, but never did.

Dickey hoped to end his busy year with a hunt. "It is likely that I will go on a grizzly hunt in the near future,"[28] he told the Allen Archery Company in a letter complaining about the puniness of the bows and arrows they had recently sent him. Instead, he joined Glenn Helgeland, the editor of Archery World, who had proposed taking Dickey to Bull Island off the coast of South Carolina for a deer hunt and making him the central figure in a magazine article. After nearly colliding with another car while telling stories in Columbia, Dickey allowed Helgeland to drive to the coast. Once there, he surprised Helgeland with his blasé attitude toward hunting. He had absolutely no desire to kill deer; he simply wanted to socialize, and for that purpose he had brought two six-packs of beer, a fifth of gin, and a fifth of George Dickel. Quickly depleting his supply on the boat and on the island, Dickey visited other camps to cadge drinks. While his fellow hunters roamed the island with bows and arrows, he guzzled, told stories, read poems, and played songs on his guitar like Leadbelly's "Gallows Pole." The only arrows Helgeland saw him shoot were aimed at a makeshift target.

As 1972 wound to a close, Dickey once again griped about the fatigue that came from his public life. Reading at Worcester State College in early November, he interrupted the applause by intoning dramatically: "I don't give many readings these days. . . . This may be my last one." Dickey seemed determined to retire to his hermitage: "I have made God knows how many appearances in the last 15 years to advance the cause of my craft . . . and whatever good they do has been done. Now what I have to do is sit down and write and I can't do it this way."[29] Having two years before told his booking agent at Lordly and Dame, Bill Thompson, that he wanted no more appointments, at the end of 1972 he temporarily broke off ties with him.

Dickey's hint of a permanent retirement to his "Cave of Making," as he liked to call his study, may have been inspired by Ezra Pound, who rarely spoke to anyone in his final years. On November 1, 1972, a week before his Worcester pronouncements, the eighty-seven-year-old Pound died in a Venice hospital. Journalists asked Dickey to comment, and he gladly obliged:

> The son of a bitch outlived them all. . . . Pound was a monolith, a great writer, a wonderful writer. We all know how wrong he was—about fascism—we all know that. But Pound did more for the human imagination, did more for the cause of imaginative delight and personal power, than anyone of our time. He was a curious and terrifying mixture of imaginative heroism and sick fear, but anyone who has truly submitted to what Ezra Pound had to give—and the emphasis is on the word give—cannot ever know his own inconsequentiality again. He believed in the primacy of the creative act, no matter what its form. . . . He is now with his great protégé—T. S. Eliot—and we all need to think that they are talking about poetry and will come back to us in some form thereby. He was sort of a fabulous grandfather to us all.[30]

To a certain extent, Dickey hoped to inherit Pound's mantle as "fabulous grandfather" for succeeding generations. Exhibiting a similar "terrifying mixture" of generosity and orneriness, experimental poetics and reactionary politics, he did become a Poundian grandfather for many younger poets, especially in the South.

On December 18, 1972, Dickey gave his old Atlanta friends a glimpse of the "terrifying mixture" of forces that controlled him. A group of men successful in their respective fields who took their name from Dickey's poem "Looking for the Buckhead Boys" decided to bestow their first award on the most distinguished "local boy" they could think of—Dickey. To that end, the Buckhead Boys invited him to make a short speech at their third annual reunion at Saccone's restaurant in Atlanta. On arrival he began drinking compulsively. Standing beside his high school pal, Bill Barnwell, he said: "Bill, you filled in a large part of my youth, but . . . let me go see my friends." In about five minutes, Dickey returned. "Well, did you see all your friends?" Barnwell asked. Dickey looked forlorn. Despite the youthful camaraderie evinced in "Looking for the Buckhead Boys," Dickey realized that he was even more of a loner than he had been at North Fulton. Some high school acquaintances were jealous of Dickey's success and snubbed him; others were put off by his unseemly behavior. Depressed by the unfriendliness of the group, Dickey asked Barnwell to get him another drink. As he got drunker, he uttered the inevitable slurs. "The niggers are coming; the niggers are coming,"[31] he chanted to Barnwell. By the time he was called to the podium to receive his award, he could barely rouse himself. He mumbled his speech until, unable to go on, he fell unconscious to the floor. The other Buckhead Boys were shocked, disappointed, and resentful. Some just shrugged their shoulders, remembering that Dickey at North Fulton had never been especially civil.

At the beginning of 1973, Dickey's indiscretions—in this case his boasts rather than his disorderliness—could have implicated him in a costly lawsuit. At issue was the authorship of "Dueling Banjos," the piece that had contributed to *Deliverance*'s huge success. Since Dickey had gone to court to win authorial credit for the screenplay, he should have known better than to take credit for composing the soundtrack. But take credit he did. Early in 1972, he told Ned Rorem: "I wrote the music for the film—a guitar-banjo duet—and you may be sure that *that* will be the *only* incursion into *your* domain."[32] Rorem, who knew something about Dickey's musical ability, must have laughed. Dickey made the same claim to Gordon Lish. On April 9, 1973, he repeated his boast to his *Jericho* collaborator, Hubert Shuptrine, this time adding that he had begun recording the music before approaching Eric Weissberg. He told Shuptrine that he didn't think New York Jews could play Southern bluegrass and repeated what Weissberg had supposedly said to disabuse him: "Mr. Dickey, we have an enclave up here in the Bronx of people who do nothing but play that kind of music; they're all Jewish—so we call it Jewgrass."[33] Several weeks later, he told a woman who worked at the University of Florida that he had written "Dueling Banjos" and that an impostor was now suing him for copyright infringement. Each summer from 1973 to 1975, when Dickey spoke at Don Greiner's house to a group of students being recruited by USC, he told them he had written the music for *Deliverance*. Even as late as 1993, he could not relinquish his fictitious authorship. He told a *Denver Post* reporter that while working out a bluegrass tune on his guitar he had improvised "Dueling Banjos."[34]

Hearing of the copyright lawsuit brought against Warner Brothers, Dickey temporarily moderated his claims. In a January 1973 interview with the USC newspaper, the *Gamecock*, he said: "I suggested the music, but it was Warner Brothers' responsibility to check out copyrights and that sort of thing. It was a big enough job for me to write the book and screenplay."[35] According to Dickey, the producers were at fault for neglecting to determine the original composer of "Dueling Banjos." Eric Weissberg, who knew the composer, partly agreed. Rospo Pallenberg had phoned him about recording the soundtrack in the winter of 1971, and didn't seem concerned about copyright assignments. He simply wanted Weissberg to audition with his partner. Weissberg contacted his guitar-playing friend Steven Mandel, and after they played in Mandell's New York apartment for half-an-hour, Pallenberg hired them.

Weissberg knew almost nothing about *Deliverance*, which may have been one reason that Dickey objected to him. When he arrived on the film site with Mandell, Boorman had just started filming the garage scene where Burt Reynolds and the other men try to get someone to drive their cars downriver. Boorman wanted the musicians to see the scene before playing the music for it. Mandel and Weissberg taught Billy Redden, who had no banjo skills, and Ronny Cox, who knew how to play the guitar moderately well, how to give a convincing impression of playing their instruments on film. The two musicians then drove to Atlanta for a weekend of recording with Tom Priestley at Master Sound studio. Boorman was delighted by the tapes and asked Weissberg and Mandell to record the entire soundtrack. Over two weekends, they recorded fourteen hours of "Dueling Banjos" in different styles and at different speeds. The tapes were then played through speakers on location so actors and crew could better understand how the music fit into the film.

Weissberg never met Dickey and never learned much about the film's plot. He returned to New York to resume his business as a musician. One day late in 1972, while he was recording music for a commercial, a friend asked if he had heard his record from the *Deliverance* soundtrack on the radio. Weissberg hadn't cut a record in ten years so he was dumbfounded. Eager to hear his music, he called Mary Martin at Warner Brothers Records. She, too, was puzzled, but promised to look into the matter. What she discovered was that Warner Brothers, without bothering to consult Weissberg, had released a 45-rpm recording of "Dueling Banjos." Over the next few weeks an incredulous Weissberg watched his record move up the charts. By February 5, 1973, the *Deliverance* soundtrack was number one on *Daily Variety*'s disk soundings list in Los Angeles. By March 11, the album was number two on *Billboard*'s list of top two hundred albums, and "Dueling Banjos" was number two on *Billboard*'s list of top one hundred pop songs (the song eventually became number one). Pleased to have a hit, Weissberg was uncomfortable with Warner Brothers' surreptitious conduct. Pallenberg never asked him about the history of the tune; he simply asked Weissberg to play it. Boorman and others at Warner Brothers assumed "Dueling Banjos" was a "traditional" tune whose composer was dead and anonymous. The record company also acted as if the musicians who played it for *Deliverance* were anonymous. Due to Warner Brothers' failure to acknowledge Weissberg on the first album, he had to consult a lawyer, A. Richard Gollub, to make certain his name appeared on the second batch of record labels.

"Dueling Banjos" did have a history, and Weissberg was well aware of it. Arthur Smith had composed the tune "Feudin' Banjos," originally copyrighting and recording it for MGM Records in 1955. Weissberg, who was studying the banjo at the time, used to attend concerts given by Smith, who played the four-string tenor banjo with his partner, Don Reno, who played the five-string banjo. In 1957, Carl Story and the Brewsters recorded another version of the tune for the Mercury Star Day label titled "Mocking Banjo," which combined a banjo and a mandolin. Premonitory of his troubles with Warner Brothers, Smith had to lodge a complaint with a copyright agency to receive proper credit and royalties from Mercury. Around 1962, a bluegrass group from the Ozarks, The Dillards, brought out their recording of "Dueling Banjos," and a year later Dickey heard Russo and Brentano play it in Portland.

Since the single of "Dueling Banjos" had soared up the charts, Weissberg proposed to his lawyer that he make a whole album of similar bluegrass music. His lawyer immediately called Joe Smith at Warner Brothers Records. Weissberg was in for another surprise. Smith said that an album had already been cut and distributed. Taking matters into their own hands, Warner Brothers had refashioned the album "New Dimensions in Banjo and Bluegrass" that Weissberg's band the Tarriers had made in 1962. They had scrubbed Weissberg's favorite piece on the first side and replaced it with "Dueling Banjos." To the music newspaper *Melody Maker,* Weissberg said: "I was a little annoyed that they did issue it without asking me. But in all modesty I think it's a good album, bearing in mind that it was made ten years ago."[36] Shortly after the album's release, Warner Brothers heard from Arthur Smith, who was furious over the multiple acts of piracy. By that time, Smith had apprised New York lawyer Joseph Santora of the theft. At first Santora was skeptical. Santora's wife, who was from North Carolina, quickly came to Smith's defense. "Next to God and Billy Graham, he [Arthur Smith] is number three in North Carolina,"[37] she said. Smith was a man of many talents and also a strict Baptist with rigid moral principles. Because Warner Brothers continued to deny that "Deuling Banjos" derived from Smith's composition, Santora was forced to sue on his client's behalf. After taking depositions, Santora knew that Weissberg, whom Warner Brothers claimed to be the composer, had not written the music.

Although Smith and Dickey never met (Dickey was not called to court), Smith tried to enlist his help in the case. He called Dickey three or four times, but Maxine usually intercepted the calls and told her husband to keep quiet. She wanted the lawyers to handle the case, and spoke to Smith threateningly in order to dissuade future calls. Afraid that Warner Brothers' lawyers would fend him off for five years and thereby annul the suit, Smith hoped Dickey could somehow expedite matters. In the end, Judge William Conner heard the case in the Southern District of New York Courthouse from February 3 to February 5, 1975. Santora, Stephen Ross, and Michael Perstein represented Smith's Combine Music Corporation, and Eugene Girden and John Keene represented Warner Brothers. In his opening statement Santora told the judge, who had contemplated removing himself from the case because he was tone deaf, that Warner Brothers had willfully stolen Arthur Smith's music for *Deliverance* and, discovering their copyright infringement, "relied entirely on their power, wealth and size, and in combination with others of equal size, to give ultimatums, to ask this man to give up his entire copyright or face the alternative of being dragged through court for three or four years and an expense of hundreds of thousands of dollars."[38] Santora told the court that he would prove with testimony and analysis that "Dueling Banjos" and "End of a Dream" (a slow version of the former tune) were unauthorized arrangements of Smith's "Feudin' Banjos."[39] Despite his defective ear, the judge soon realized that Warner Brothers had plagiarized, and urged the two parties to settle out of court. Recognizing the futility of their case, Warner Brothers agreed to pay Smith 75 percent of past royalties and 100 percent of future royalties from the record that contained "Dueling Banjos."

Accusing Smith and Warner Brothers of mustering their forces against him,

Dickey told USC friends that he had to take on an even more hectic reading schedule to raise money for his legal expenses. During the late winter and spring of 1973, he read at Catawba College, Santa Fe Community College, Washington and Lee, Appalachian State, Elon College, Atlantic Christian College, Tulane, St. Mark's, Morris Harvey College, and Seminole Junior College. Because of his late-night carousing on these visits, Dickey in his USC classes periodically closed his eyes, nodded off, and miraculously awakened to continue his lessons.

At his fiftieth birthday party on February 2, 1973, Dickey again displayed the megalomania at the root of his fantasies. Tom and Patsy Dickey drove to Columbia for the celebration, as did Al Braselton and a date. Chris and his wife also attended. The party was a happy reunion even though Braselton could drink nothing stronger than Tab. Braselton remembered:

We went to the party and had a good time and after[ward] we all went out to eat at a Chinese restaurant in Columbia, South Carolina. Jim was getting very drunk, terribly drunk. We had to wait in line and he got very upset about that. And he went up and told them who he was. "I'm James Dickey and I wrote *Deliverance*." "Well, we're so solly; we don't know who you are." And he got very upset about that. So we're standing there waiting in line, and there's a pretty woman waiting with another group. He walked up to her and said, "I wrote *Deliverance*." And it was downright embarrassing. Terribly embarrassing. And Chris and I were trying to do something with him. And finally Jim started saying things that didn't make any sense. So finally his brother, Tom, took him home. And we stayed.

The birthday party, which everyone had been enjoying just moments before, had suffered a typical denouement. Stung by his father's conduct, Chris told Braselton in earshot of his mother: "I don't know why my parents have stayed together. They're not suited to each other, and I think it's hurting my father." Maxine retorted, "You shut your God-damned mouth," and complained about having to support Chris financially. (She was writing checks for Chris's education, his family, and soon his film studies project—a documentary about Tom Dickey's Civil War relic-hunting, *War Under the Pinestraw*—that cost over three thousand dollars.) Undeterred by his mother's complaints, Chris continued: "That's the way I feel. I think it's hurting both of them, and I think it's particularly hurting my father."[40] Maxine fumed.

Braselton wondered why Jim and Maxine refused to take their son's advice. Their bond seemed an ugly parody of marriage now that both were such heavy drinkers. But he concluded that Maxine liked the privileges that her husband's fame and fortune allowed. And he reasoned that Dickey needed Maxine to organize his itineraries, purchase his plane tickets, screen negative mail and hostile reviews, and protect him from total debauchery. She made it possible for Jim to be "the world's oldest living adolescent."[41] Like Dickey's real mother, Maibelle, who had also spoiled him, Maxine was becoming increasingly dysfunctional. Despite her denials, she knew that divorce was preferable to the anguish and squalor of her marriage. After the birthday party, Maxine called Chris in Massachusetts and said that she was definitely getting a divorce. She could no longer tolerate his father's affairs and drunkenness. Chris convinced her to come to Hamilton for a vacation. He would go to Columbia, hire an accountant to pay the bills (his father still could not, or pretended he could not, write a check), make sure Kevin got to school, and try to convince his father to moderate his drinking. He bought plane tickets for himself and for his mother. Then his mother, as she had done so many times in the past, reconciled herself to her sorry situation and decided to stay at Lelia's Court. Despite publicly advocating marriage, in private Dickey had also concluded that he and Maxine should probably get divorced. In recognition of this, in his new novel *Alnilam* he made Frank Cahill a divorcee.

As Dickey continued to drink, he continued to worry about possible side effects like diabetes and blindness, and these also made their way into his novel. To learn more about blindness, in February he asked Robert Russell, an English professor at Franklin and Marshall College, to send him literature on the subject. Because he was also writing about night fighters, who for him epitomized another kind of blindness, he contacted his former pilot, Earl Bradley. On February 7, he told Bradley he wanted to discuss his "panoramic, Tolstoyan novel of the Pacific air war at night"[42] with him. He wrote another squadron pilot, Edward Traverse, to ask if he could record Traverse's memories of everything from the organization of cadets in Primary Training to the operation of aircraft. Since navigation by the stars figured into *Alnilam*, Dickey consulted his astronomy books, ordered numerous sextants from Davis Instruments in California, and began a Davis correspondence course on celestial navigation. To expedite his writing, he mastered a new technique of recording notes on tapes that he gave to his secretary to transcribe.

Dickey gathered valuable material for his novel in an unexpected way on a trip to Boone, North Carolina, around March 1973. Always a lover of masks, Dickey had been in touch with Appalachian State art professor William Dunlap, who was also a painter and sculptor. In Boone, Dunlap applied plaster to Dickey's face for a mold, peeled it off, and instructed Dickey to wash his face in the bathroom. Somehow Dickey managed to rub some dry plaster in his eyes and incur some minor alkaline burns. He could see light and dark, but had difficulty focusing on objects. Dunlap rushed Dickey to the emergency room of the local hospital. The doctor allayed Dickey's fears of blindness and ended up having a friendly conversation about *Deliverance*, which he had read. Nevertheless, Dickey decided he'd better go to the eye clinic in nearby Johnson City, so Dunlap drove him there, stopping along the way at bars for drinks and music— usually "Dueling Banjos"—on the jukeboxes. The eye clinic determined that Dickey's eyes had recuperated.

The hypochondriacal Dickey was dissatisfied with the prognosis and soon insisted that he had suffered total blindness. To an *Esquire* editor, who printed the first chapter of his novel, "Cahill Is Blind," he spoke of his harrowing experience with Dunlap. The introduction to "Cahill" read: "It was in sitting for the composition of this aluminum life mask [shown on *Esquire*'s cover] that poet James Dickey was temporarily blinded. Sculptor William Dunlap, artist in residence at Appalachian State University, was forming the plaster cast when calcium seeped through to Mr. Dickey's eyes and produced an alkaline burn that scalded his corneas. The poet was raced from Boone, North Carolina, to Johnson City, Tennessee, for medical treatment that saved his vision. The experience, which left him sightless for several hours, contributed to the store of feeling from which the poet's second novel proceeds."[43] In a letter to a Hollywood guitar-playing friend, Anthony Recupido, on March 26, 1973, Dickey claimed that he had been blinded for a week, embellishing his lie with a story about blind guitar player Doc Watson. Dickey had visited Watson, so his story went, and said: "Look, Doc, I don't have the experience of years of blind playing that you have." Watson supposedly replied: "That's all right, Jim, we'll keep everything right down in the low part of the guitar, near the nut."[44] Imagined blindness was merely another catalyst for Dickey's fantasies and writing.

Years later Dickey admitted that he had overdramatized the incident in Boone: "It really wasn't all that bad. But there were some moments of uncertainty. Actually, the stuff burned the cornea, so for a while, I had eyes, following hours of temporary blindness, like a newborn. I had been wearing glasses, but for several years after I didn't have to wear any."[45] Three months after "Cahill Is Blind" appeared, John Foster West, a Boone poet, wrote a letter about Dickey's eye trouble that was published in *Esquire:* "Can you imagine an artist with Dunlap's experience using a substance to cast a life mask that would endanger the subject's eyesight? Here's what really happened: The sculptor used simple molding plaster. Dickey and I had masks cast at the same time. We were instructed to keep our eyes tightly closed until we were led to a lavatory, where we could wash loose plaster from our faces. I followed instructions and had no trouble. Halfway to the bathroom, Dickey opened his eyes and got some plaster in them. Even so, he was in about as much danger of losing his eyesight permanently as your grandmother when she peels onions."[46] Dickey had suffered only minor discomfort and soon ordered more masks from Dunlap—a rubber one for his "blind guitarist" act and two aluminum ones to decorate his house.

In 1973, Dickey returned to the site of one of his early controversies: the University of Florida, where nearly twenty years before he had been fired after his provocative reading to the Florida Pen Women. He had vowed never to set foot on the campus again, but he agreed to teach there from April 20 to June 3. His motives for returning were hard to fathom. To Dave Smith, who would also teach at the University of Florida, Dickey once explained: "I . . . went back as a kind of guest-writer in residence, and did my dead-level best to alienate everyone, for I only took the latter job in revenge, and I hope I got a full measure of that."[47] The university's offer of six thousand dollars also attracted him. But perhaps the most significant factor was Paula Goff. Dickey's passionate love affair with Goff touched off fights at home and numerous unpleasant scenes at Columbia parties where Maxine would confront her. Conducting the affair on foreign soil would be easier, so he instructed Goff to join him after he settled into the Windmeadow Apartments.

As usual, Maxine orchestrated the move. Two students, Johnny Feiber and Ward Scott, who thought Windmeadow's Spanish-style buildings and acres of parking lots were a strange environment for the author of *Deliverance,* helped, and in the process got a glimpse of the Dickeys' dissolving marriage. What kept them together and apart seemed to be alcohol. One of Feiber's first chores was to drive to the liquor store. Expecting Maxine to give him a twenty-dollar bill for a bottle of Scotch and bottle of vodka, he was flabbergasted when she handed him six crisp one-hundred-dollar bills and told him to buy several cases of whiskey. Feiber wondered if they were stocking up for a party, but soon discovered that they rarely gave parties. And before long Maxine was back in Columbia, and Paula Goff was in Gainesville.

In his poetry classes, which were held at night, Dickey made an impression consistent with his *Deliverance* persona. On the first night, wearing a safari hat, camouflage fatigues, and a big wrist compass, he showed up twenty minutes late with a girl in tow. Everybody stared at the compass until he explained that it was a gift from Burt Reynolds. With the men he was generally popular, although his drunken braggadocio could be tiring; with the women he was less popular because of his condescending remarks and hostile gestures. In one of the first classes that Goff attended, she spoke up for a poem that Dickey had criticized, and a scuffle ensued in which Dickey slapped her. Some of the students wondered if he was joking; it was difficult to tell. Goff was not pleased (it was the first time he had slapped her face), and neither were others in the class. Those who knew of Dickey's previous troubles with women at the university must have experienced déjà vu, especially when some of the students complained to the chairman. Although he wasn't fired again, most members of the English Department were as relieved by his second departure as by his first.

Despite or because of the tumult in his classes, the number of students swelled to about forty. Aspiring writers from around Florida frequently visited. As was his custom, Dickey meted out savage criticism and sincere encouragement. J. Bruce Nunley, who took his class, always felt thankful for Dickey's help. Dickey not only gave him useful practical criticism of his poetry; he urged him to apply to Florida's graduate creative writing program and gave him advice regarding his personal life. Although Dickey cultivated a reputation as a womanizer at parties, Ward Scott never saw him successfully seduce a woman. Referring to an older woman who came to class, he told Scott the sort of lie that betrayed his real feelings for at least one woman: "That's my third wife; she was a prostitute."[48] With the rebukes of the Pen Women still on his mind, he preferred offending to seducing the Florida women. Scott, who liked to talk to Dickey about their mutual literary acquaintances—Andrew Lytle, Peter Taylor, and John Crowe Ransom—witnessed another of Dickey's misogynistic outbursts at a party where a number of librarians crowded around the famous writer. Rather than acknowledge their presence, he talked about gory scenes he had witnessed while training as a marine. He and his comrades, he said, had discovered a man hanging by a building while marching in boot camp. He boasted that he could take any amount of stress, even the ghastly sight of a hanged comrade, and that he had continued with the drill as if nothing had happened. The women were aghast. To unnerve them further, he implied in a mysterious voice that he could still see the ghost of the dead marine. Later, as if suffering delirium tremens, he told Scott that he heard ghostly voices speaking over the telephone.

Both Feiber and Scott felt Dickey was living in a fictitious world styled after *Deliverance*. To Feiber, who was a former all-state Gator running back and

Vietnam veteran, he said he had played end on the Vanderbilt football team, tried out for the Olympics as a hurdler, and parachuted to safety after the plane he piloted over the Pacific was shot down by the Japanese. Once when Scott came to Windmeadows, Dickey was dressed in hunting camouflage gear. While Goff dutifully typed in the background, he carried his blowgun, which he said pygmies used in Africa, into the parking lot and shot darts at a Dumpster. He seemed obsessed with Burt Reynolds. He took credit for Reynolds's current popularity, and told Scott that he had saved Reynolds from a long prison sentence after he had killed his romantic rival for the heir of the Folgers coffee fortune. To Laura Chambless, who wrote an article, "The Many Faces of James Dickey," for the *Tampa Tribune*, Dickey spoke further of Reynolds, claiming that they were such good friends that he had given Reynolds a blowgun.

If Dickey wanted to get revenge on the university, he did so at a poetry reading that made his earlier reading to the Pen Women seem innocuous. Harold Hanson, a physics professor working in the administration, had the dubious honor of introducing him. A nervous hush descended on the audience as Dickey ambled toward the podium. Many expected some act of retribution. According to one spectator, a "bombed" and defiantly unrepentant Dickey muttered that he was going to read "Sheep Child," and lingered salaciously over the descriptions of farmboys sodomizing sheep.

Dickey got another opportunity to avenge perceived wrongs committed against him when on May 19 he traveled to the luxurious Greenbrier hotel in White Sulphur Springs, West Virginia, to address the American Association of Advertising Agencies. The debacle at the University of Florida in the mid-1950s had been followed by five frustrating years in advertising. At the time, his advertising jobs resembled circles in Dante's *Inferno*. Would he scandalize the advertisers at The Greenbrier as he had the academics in Gainesville? To remind him of his years when he'd sold his soul to the devil, there were former Atlanta colleagues like Jim Gonia and Howard Axelberg from Liller, Neal, Battle and Lindsey. Both men partied with Dickey in a suite on President's Row the morning before he was scheduled to lecture. Luckily, the intervening decades had tempered Dickey's caustic memories of his business career. Gonia and Axelberg noticed no overt hostility. Slurping straight gin and bourbon from water tumblers, Dickey remained in jolly spirits.

On Saturday morning the conference participants gathered in The Greenbrier amphitheater to hear the invited speakers: film director Billy Friedkin, BBDO chairman Tom Dillon, McCaffrey and McCall chairman Jim McCaffrey, and Dickey. Following the first lecture, the master of ceremonies apologized for the absence of the next speaker, explaining that Dickey had been unable to rouse himself after the night's revels. Suddenly the audience heard the distinct notes of "Dueling Banjos" plucked on a guitar in the back of the amphitheater. Many thought it was Muzak, but the tune got louder and louder. Craning their necks, they saw a large man rising from his seat who said: "Thank you folks. I'm James Dickey, your next speaker."[49] Considering his condition six hours before, his appearance seemed nothing less than miraculous. Near the end of his lecture, in which he compared copywriting and poetry writing, he declared: "I would like very much at this time to go on public record to pay my debt to advertising. It taught me one thing about writing poetry that I don't believe I would have learned without it. And, this is not a joke. It taught me to get into the subject quicker. And I've never forgotten it."[50] Dickey read a few of his poems, and the audience gave Dickey a standing ovation.

Surrounded by The Greenbrier's splendors, Dickey glamorized his advertising years, implying that the money and knowledge he had acquired outweighed the drudgery. His bonhomie at the conference had another source besides parties with former colleagues. As a fiftieth birthday present, his friend Marie Tyler McGraw had rented a cabin in a nearby state park and arranged for Dickey to spend several idyllic days with her. Dickey relaxed by throwing acorns in McGraw's basket as he chatted about literature. He chose an odd book to read in this Edenic environment: Celine's *Journey to the End of the Night*, which documents the grim experiences of a misanthropic slum doctor during and after the First World War. In their talks, some of which concerned Nazis and Nazi collaborators, McGraw could not help but realize that her friendship with Dickey was doomed. He seemed fascinated by the Nazis' power over people, while her own political views had crystallized into a radical position she defined as Christian Socialist. Years later, trying to come to terms with Dickey's appeal, she said: "Ladies love outlaws. There's a real attraction . . . to the guy who is outrageous, to the guy who wants to pull you away from everyday life."[51] The attraction, however, was fading, and after their tryst in the cabin they rarely met.

Dickey returned from McGraw to Goff, and on June 2, shortly before his term in Florida ended, traveled north to accept an honorary doctorate from Moravian College and to deliver the University of Virginia baccalaureate address. The gist of his talk at UVA, "Upthrust and Its Men," like the gist of his conversations with McGraw, was masculine power. "Upthrust" had obvious sexual connotations, but Dickey was thinking of "thrust" as an aeronautical term referring to rocket power, too. His ideal of "upthrust," he explained, was embodied in the life of astronaut Ed White, the first American to walk in space and to use the phrase "the blue planet." White's adventurous spirit was what Dickey offered as an antidote to the boredom, anxiety, sterility, crime, pollution, and overpopulation in the modern world. He warned: "The really terrible danger to us—of which the drug problem and that of alcoholism are only symptoms—is the habit of mind that not only permits these things to happen, but encourages them, and in certain cases attempts to justify them intellectually."[52] Dickey turned his commencement address into an oblique confession.

Other exemplars of "upthrust," according to Dickey, were Robert Kennedy and Lewis Medlock. As he resketched what Norman Mailer had called "the existential hero," Dickey also redefined the classic notion of a tragic hero for the Space Age. Most of his heroes of "upthrust," he neglected to point out, had also suffered calamitous "downthrusts." Kennedy had been assassinated, White had been killed in a training accident, and Medlock had crashed on his canoe trip. In his own risky pursuit of "upthrust," Dickey had suffered numerous calamities, too. Was he secretly repudiating his own prescription against modern ills as hubristic and hinting at his own failures as an "upthruster"? Dickey once again was unable to disentangle himself from the problems and contradictions he proposed to correct.

Dickey demonstrated the tragic, sordid, and farcical aspects of his "upthrust" philosophy during a reunion several months later with Al Braselton. On Anabuse after completing his alcoholic treatment at the Peachtree Hospital, Braselton had returned to his advertising work and resolved some of his romantic difficulties. On his first vacation since divorcing his wife, Polly, he looked forward to introducing his new girlfriend to the Dickeys at their Litchfield condominium in Pawley's Island, which they had bought earlier in the year with money earned from *Deliverance*. In mid-October Braselton drove from Atlanta to South Carolina's marshy coast and entered the former indigo plantation. A guard dressed handsomely in dark livery sauntered from a crumbling brick gatehouse to check their name on the guest list. They passed by tennis courts and live oaks draped with Spanish moss. The main plantation house loomed like a Civil War relic from a manicured lawn. Modern, three-story condominiums built from cyprus-stained pine jutted above the flat land. Spotting the Dickeys' XKE Jaguar and Cadillac, Braselton parked and approached the condo called "Root-Light."

At first Braselton feared that Maxine, who had been close to Polly, might reject his girlfriend. On the phone Maxine had insisted that he and his girlfriend sleep in different rooms. Maxine appeared in her bulky muumuu and Dickey in his underwear with a guitar in his hand. Both held drinks. Despite their casual appearance, they exuded hospitality. Dickey startled the girlfriend by kissing her on the mouth, and made Braselton slightly uncomfortable by giving him a protracted Russian-style bear hug. Dickey complimented the girlfriend on her beauty in a courtly way and gave the newcomers a tour of the condo. Bookshelves scaled the white walls. White rugs, pastel furniture, and modern art decorated the rooms. A large picture window opened out onto an abandoned rice canal. When Dickey spoke of the ancient alligator that lumbered from the canal in the mornings, Maxine hollered: "Yeah, you see alligators all the time."[53] Dickey continued the tour.

After Braselton deposited his bags in his room, Dickey announced that they would dine at the clubhouse, which required formal dress, and later play guitars. Dickey had always told Braselton that, unlike Robert Bly, he didn't believe a poet had to "dress funny" to earn respect, so he surprised his friend by donning a garish shirt, bright green tie, and old corduroy coat for dinner. Before the foursome left for the club, Maxine gave Braselton a Tab, his drink of choice after going on the wagon. He recalled: "Before I drank it, I knew it had a great dose of bourbon in it. And I don't know why she did it."[54] As at the *Deliverance* party, the Dickeys seemed bent on undermining his pledge of abstinence. Partly out of nervousness, partly out of politeness, Braselton drank the spiked Tab and went to dinner.

At the clubhouse Dickey resumed his discussion of Braselton's alcoholism where he had left it the previous year. He commented to Maxine: "Well, he seemed to handle that all right. I'll tell you one thing: Old Al ain't no more an alcoholic than I am. But there's one thing worse than being an alcoholic, and that's being a dried-up alcoholic. Look what it did to F. Scott Fitzgerald."[55] Dickey mentioned seeing William F. Buckley, who was visiting his parents' house in Camden, and expecting to see Robert Penn Warren, who was coming to Litchfield in a week (Maxine planned to buy Warren's books and put them in the clubhouse library). They strolled through the rambling, one-story clubhouse and stopped briefly in the library, which seemed full of wealthy Republican businessmen. Braselton remembered the hush in the clubhouse as they watched Nixon's televised announcement that Gerald Ford would replace Spiro Agnew, who on October 10 had resigned the vice presidency because of income tax fraud.

Braselton's first drink had whetted his thirst. Feeling mellow after his fourth, he listened to Dickey, who was already drunk, brag to some friends about the screenplay he and his son Chris were writing about Thermopylae, a Greek pass where three hundred Spartan soldiers led by King Leonidas held off Xerxes's Persian army. "There was 13 [sic] men, none of your modern candy-asses, 13 of them stood off the Persian hordes," Dickey said with historical license. Because of problems with his esophagus, he hardly touched his food. He merely drank and talked about Thermopylae. At one point Maxine interjected: "Christ! The green tie is lying in the roast beef!" Dickey replied: "I'm going home, Maxine. . . . I can't take any more of this shit."[56] Braselton's girlfriend, who had been drinking steadily too, offered to walk Dickey to the condo. Braselton and Maxine finished their dinner and on the way home picked up the two stragglers.

The next day the two couples played mixed-doubles on the local tennis courts, and afterward Braselton trounced Dickey in a singles match. Resenting the loss, Dickey regained his composure on a walk along the beach and in a graveyard near the Episcopal Church. At one point, Dickey pulled Braselton aside and said: "It's wonderful to see you as a couple so much in love."[57] Braselton was touched. At six o'clock that night they both read poems to a group of residents in white flannels and blue blazers who had gathered in a little amphitheater by a swimming pool. Drinking ensued, and then they returned to the clubhouse for dinner. As before, Dickey got very drunk, barely sampled his food, and left early with Braselton's girlfriend.

Despite Dickey's kind words about his new romance, Braselton suspected he might try to avenge his loss on the tennis court. Because he distrusted Dickey with any woman, he borrowed Maxine's keys and drove her Cadillac to the condo. He later wrote: "I tiptoed into the house. And sure enough, my worst anticipation was realized, because I went to our bedroom and . . . there was [his girlfriend] . . . naked in sort of a passed-out position, and Jim was naked beside her. He was . . . fingering her [and] . . . talking all the time, sort of a strange monologue. Occasionally he would slap her. And I stood outside the door. I was horrified, but I was fascinated. He was going on about, 'Well, who is your real man?' And he would slap her. And she said, 'No, Jim, that hurts.' So I knew she was aware." Braselton went downstairs and made a stiff drink. When he returned, his girlfriend was still naked on her stomach, and Dickey was still slapping her and quizzing her about her "real man." Finally Braselton walked into the room and said: "Well, this is a pretty scene. What's going on here?"[58] For a moment, Dickey was speechless.

Gathering his wits, Dickey jumped up with a flurry of unconvincing explanations. In the kitchen over more drinks, Braselton said he was terribly disappointed that his best friend would betray his trust by seducing his girlfriend. Dickey kept trying to deflect his friend's anger. "Women are women and men are friends," he said, hoping an appeal to male solidarity would win forgiveness.

Meanwhile, Maxine, sans Cadillac, had walked home. At the condo she shouted at Braselton for leaving her stranded at the club. When he told her what had happened, she redirected her fury at her husband. Braselton remembered: "She got mad as hell at Jim. . . . Just mad as hell. But she said, 'Well, I know he wasn't screwing her. Because he's been impotent for four years.' And, I thought, Oh God, now we're getting to it."[59] (Dickey may have been impotent with Maxine, but with other women he was still sexually vigorous.) As the troubled foursome hashed out their differences, Maxine began to blame Braselton's girlfriend for flirting with her husband and Braselton for bringing her. Braselton was the one, she implied, who had planted the seductive apple in their Edenic garden. Braselton concluded that no matter how indiscreetly Dickey acted, Maxine would eventually rally to his side.

After drinking and bickering through most of the night, Braselton woke up with a hangover and renewed his drinking. He refused to speak to his girlfriend and insisted on leaving for Atlanta. Dickey convinced him to drive to Columbia in the Jaguar; the girlfriend could drive with Maxine in the Cadillac. The women could be women, and the men, he hoped, could be friends. According to Braselton, they continued to skirmish: "I was drinking on the way back. I was very drunk. And at one point I was so mad at Jim, I said, 'Let's just kill ourselves.' And I grabbed the wheel as if to turn the car off the road. We were going very fast. Jim was able to control it since I was very weak, and he was a powerful person. Later on I talked to him . . . full of remorse. I was blaming myself, and he said, 'You know when you jerked that wheel, you almost destroyed American literature.' And he was serious. He said, 'Thank goodness I was stronger than you were.'"[60] With American literature and the Jaguar still intact, the two men moved to safer topics—one of their favorite writers, Albert Camus, who wrote obsessively about suicide and died in a car crash. In Columbia, unable to drive to Atlanta on his own and unwilling to stay with the Dickeys, Braselton checked into a hotel. Finally an Atlanta friend arrived to take him home.

For Braselton the consequences of his long-anticipated vacation were dire. He began drinking uncontrollably; his auspicious romance collapsed; his friendship with Dickey was in tatters. Ashamed of his relapse, he blamed himself for the Litchfield fiasco and returned to the alcoholic hospital. In a letter to Dickey written on November 3, 1973, he admitted that he simply could not take a first drink. Once again he underwent the horrors of drying out so that he could go back to his advertising work. He told Dickey that he had returned temporarily to Polly and asked his old friends Jim and Maxine to accept him, too, without embarrassment. He didn't see them for another year, but Braselton would have a chance to once again resurrect their friendship—a friendship sorely tested by the hangover of *Deliverance*.

28. A Double Vision (1973–1974)

If Dickey had been disillusioned by the aftermath of *Deliverance*, he had plenty of other reasons in 1973 to feel dispirited. As the Watergate scandal unfolded, the American government imploded. Dickey's family in Atlanta seemed to be imploding as well. On July 11, Dickey wrote Gordon Lish that their Atlanta business interests had been threatened by "the sword of Damocles."[1] Dickey's devoted sister-in-law, Patsy, was going through a bitter divorce from Tom. Her children petitioned Dickey for help. Dickey was also upset about a number of deaths indirectly caused by *Deliverance*. Speaking to an *Atlanta Constitution* reporter in mid-August, he accepted some of the responsibility for the eight people who had drowned on the Chattooga River: "They are just out for a lark, just like those characters in *Deliverance*. They wouldn't have gone up there if I hadn't written the book. . . . There's nothing I can do about it. I can't patrol the river. But it just makes me feel awful."[2] Dickey warned all those who planned to canoe or raft down the Chattooga to take extreme precautions.

W. H. Auden's death from a heart attack in Vienna on September 28, 1973, deepened his gloom. Because Dickey had romanticized his association with Auden after serving with him on the Pulitzer Prize committee, he took his death as a bad omen. In letters and interviews Dickey predicted that he himself would die soon, and lamented that he would never finish his life work. He compulsively chanted the litany of doomed poets in his generation: Delmore Schwartz, Weldon Kees, Winfield Townley Scott, Dylan Thomas, Anne Sexton, Randall Jarrell, Sylvia Plath, John Berryman, Theodore Roethke. He believed his name would soon be on the list. In an October interview with the *Pittsburgher* magazine, he said either a drunk driver, an airplane explosion, a bout of cancer, or—as with Auden—a heart attack would bring him to an untimely end.

Amid his public and personal woes, Dickey found ballast in his teaching. He was pleased that one of his first creative writing graduate students, David Tillinghast (Richard's brother), finished his novel *A Blue Moon* and passed his oral exam for the Ph.D. in July 1973. Another promising student was Bill Baer. A New Yorker, Baer began his Ph.D. in 1973 and finished in 1979. He admired Dickey's casual style in class, his guitar playing in blue jeans and sneakers while students sang, but most of all the inspirational way he taught poetry. "He was the best teacher I ever had, far and away,"[3] Baer recalled. Flushed with excitement by his classes, Baer regularly went to the library and signed out all the books Dickey had mentioned. Dickey referred to Baer as "the Yankee boy" and "the classicist" because of his background and aesthetic tastes. Later, Baer became an accomplished poet and the founding editor of the journal *The Formalist*. It was Dickey's assignments that steered Baer away from free verse toward formal verse.

Skip Eisiminger, who studied with Dickey during the 1973 fall semester, also felt that teaching brought out the best in Dickey. Realizing the privilege of working with such a renowned writer, for the sake of posterity Eisiminger kept detailed notes of Dickey's classes. "Though teaching is self-destructive," Dickey asserted on one occasion, "I'm a writer who consents to teach, and I can't abide a class that doesn't talk back." To foster his students' critical faculties, he urged them to "read poetry with your nerves . . . kinetically. Your shoulder muscles should tighten when you read of a spear being thrown, and your heart should beat in time with the quivering spear stuck in the living chest. When that shaft stops, so should your heart." To improve his students' skill with similes, he gave bawdy examples of his own: "Screwing your wife is like striking out the pitcher"

or "Humping that whore was like waving your arm in a warm room." His combination of candor and cajolery won the students' attention.

Dickey was always quick to pounce on clichés and sententiousness. Pointing
to a hackneyed phrase in a student's poem, he once said: "Dammit, the winds
have never done anything but 'lash the four corners of the earth.' We don't need
a poet to tell us that." About a poem that echoed Wallace Stevens he complained: "This has the true academic stink. If you generalize, do it without the
whiff of cliché; say something true but not recognized before. I'd rather you try
to bring back to poetry some of the territory poets like Eliot and Stevens have
relinquished to prose. Of course, I don't want a classful of Jim Dickeys. A man
doesn't want friends to echo him; he wants original responses, counters to his
love." In warning his students against echoing famous poets, Dickey himself
echoed a famous poet, Robert Frost, who in "The Most of It" had called for
"counter-love" and "original response" to the world.

In Dickey's course, Eisiminger produced couplets, epitaphs, haiku, ballads,
and an epistolary poem to the comet Kohoutec in six quatrains using only one
adjective. The following semester he completed a fantasy poem and embarked
on the customary exercise in revision, which demanded fifteen drafts of one
poem. He found the assignments helpful and appreciated Dickey's exuberant
comments. "Yeah, right, I'm talkin' to ya," he would say when he approved, or in
a more literary vein: "Here's Hemingway's iceberg . . . ; this deadpans it like
Kafka . . . ; this has Pasternak's soil and fate." His harsh critiques made his praise
all the more satisfying. But Eisiminger resented Dickey's practice of anony-
mously submitting his own poems to the class for evaluation because it took
valuable time away from student work. Dickey had developed an elaborate ritual
to disguise the authorship of his poems, which were in fact meant to demonstrate different forms like the sonnet or villanelle. He told the class that the poems had been written by a mysterious, disfigured man named Silverskin.
Through correspondence with the phantom writer, Dickey had learned that
Silverskin came from Argentina, where his skin had turned silver from a rare
disease he had contracted while working in underground silver mines. (Dickey
probably based his persona on one of the characters in Joseph Conrad's
Nostromo, a novel set near South American silver mines.) At the end of the
spring semester in 1975, Dickey decided to reveal Silverskin to his class. He
arranged for his student David Havird to make a dramatic entrance wearing a
costume and the silver life mask that Dickey had donned on the cover of
Esquire.

Dickey's course on contemporary British and contemporary American poetry
was similarly unconventional. Regularly wandering from the syllabus, Dickey
liked to dispense Jehovah-like judgments on the Western canon: Homer was
"bloody damn good," Virgil was best "with the tears of things," Dante could be
admired for "incidental beauties if not for his whole system," Milton "misses the
gut world of things," Byron was the ultimate romantic "drinking wine from a
skull," and Keats was "fine but better read about than read." When he approached twentieth-century poets, Dickey's judgments grew more caustic: "T. S.
Eliot's autotelic art is a lot of bull, and to the man who says Wallace Stevens is a
great poet, I say screw 'em—I utterly and thoroughly detest his abyss-hopping,

his bombinating in a void!" Dickey often baffled his students, as he did everyone else, with his odd mix of damnings and blessings. But he made them think.

Dickey's classes offered him a stage on which to strut and preach. Students laughed and scratched their heads at their teacher's paradoxes: "For all Dickey's vanity, he was surprisingly unpolished in appearance. His pants were often too long; when they were, he just rolled them up and he didn't hesitate to pull them past his knee if he had to scratch. His gestures were often nervous; he'd rub his Phi Beta Kappa key for minutes on end." To students like Eisiminger, Dickey appeared to be a "fabulous grandfather" full of eccentricities: "His rubber-spade tongue would slide along the inside of his cheek and flick out several times to show his approval. But of all his personal characteristics, his hair-parting habits were most interesting. With little consistency, Dickey would lay a great slab of hair up and over his bald crown right to left one day and vice versa the next."[4] The students concluded that Dickey's performances were improvisations on a set script.

Outside the classroom, as on a reading trip to the University of Georgia on October 1, Dickey courted danger and death with reckless abandon. The trip to Georgia began ominously. Despite inclement weather at the Athens airport, English Department chair Coleman Barks decided to fly in fellow professor James Colvert's Bonanza airplane to Columbia to fetch Dickey. A forecaster had assured Colvert, who piloted the plane, that the weather in South Carolina would be suitable throughout the day for instrument landings, but when he landed in Columbia, the weather was so bad he wondered if he could make the return flight. Dickey wasn't concerned. He wanted to fly, and, to help with the navigation, he pulled out an old-fashioned circular slide rule. It had gotten him through all sorts of terrible weather in the Pacific, he said, and it surely could get them to Athens, Georgia.

No equipment could get them to Athens; the airport had closed. The trio sat in Columbia until about three in the afternoon, and then, as the weather improved, took off for Georgia. Colvert remembered: "We lifted off in a light drizzle and entered the cloud cover at about 600 feet, climbing and turning toward the airway to the south. We were still in the soup when I levelled off at my assigned altitude. Dickey was in the copilot's seat, holding his E6B [slide rule] . . . and looking out at the gray fog swirling around the wingtips. I was astonished when he leaned over after a time and said, 'I'll take her.' But not nearly as astonished as I would have been if I had known then that he was not and never had been a pilot. I had read somewhere years before that he flew P-61 Black Widow night fighters in combat during WWII, and I had always assumed that this was so." Colvert deflected Dickey's request to take the controls by telling him that they should wait until they were out of the clouds. He had no intention of letting Dickey fly the Bonanza.

Fortunately, the plane never escaped the clouds. As it neared Athens, Colvert told the airport controller that he would make a "look see" approach, and return to South Carolina if the weather failed to improve: "We began a descent on the approach course at Athens and levelled off at 300 [feet]—the absolute minimum altitude—dragging along looking for light spots below. Just as my navigation instruments showed that we had passed the end of the invisible runway, Dickey shouted that he could see it, and yelled something like, 'Turn right, there's a hole there.' This struck me as a most curious thing for a former P-61 pilot to be saying; no pilot—not even a Bonanza pilot—would ever try to execute a turning dive through a wavering hole in the clouds from 300 feet. I wondered if Dickey had ever tried such a trick in a Black Widow." In the end, they could not land and had to fly to Anderson, South Carolina, rent a car, and drive to Athens. For their fifty-mile road trip Dickey bought a six-pack of beer at a convenience store and quickly consumed it.

At the Athens airport, where they turned in their rental car and waited for a ride to the university, Dickey held out his wrist to Colvert: "See this watch, pilot? Burt Reynolds gave it to me. One day on the set Burt said, 'Dickey, you're one hell of a writer,' and took his watch off, handed it over, and said, 'Here, take it. I want you to have it as a token of my admiration.' Well, pilot, you are one hell of an instrument pilot, and I want to give you my old E6B as a token of my admiration." Playing along with the ruse (he realized Dickey's E6B was new), Colvert pointed out that his calculator must be too valuable a souvenir to give to a stranger. Dickey insisted that Colvert take it, and surprised Colvert by asking where he might buy another one. Colvert guided him to Clark's Flying Service, where Dickey paid twenty dollars for a replacement.

In the fine arts auditorium Dickey was similarly histrionic. He stood with feet apart, arms folded across his chest, and stared at the audience until it grew silent. In a contemptuous tone he bellowed: "Shi-i-i-i-i-t-t-t." The rowdy students broke into wild applause. Later, playing the guitar and impersonating William F. Buckley at a party given by the English department chair, Dickey turned away from Colvert without speaking to him, perhaps because he had just told the story he would often repeat about commandeering the plane to the Georgia reading. According to Colvert: "His story was that the pilot was young and inexperienced (I was 52 at the time and had been flying since 1943) and had become confused in the bad weather. He was obliged, he said, to take control of the airplane to prevent what could have been a disaster."[5] About a decade later, Dickey visited Athens for another reading. Colvert reintroduced himself, but Dickey again feigned ignorance. Colvert reminded him of their adventure in the Bonanza. Dickey said he was bad at remembering names and looked away at the crowd.

When Robert Penn Warren and his wife, the writer Eleanor Clark, came to Columbia in late October 1973, Dickey seemed just as mercurial. Warren was there to read and also to pick up the USC Award for Distinction in Literature, which had been invented by George Garrett and Jim Mann (Allen Tate, Robert Lowell, and Archibald MacLeish were among the other recipients). Feeling upstaged by Warren at a party at his house, Dickey found a copy of *Eye-Beaters*, read "Under Buzzards" (which was dedicated to Warren), and gave a rousing introduction to "Blood": "This is a poem about screwing—you've been screwing, and you're drunk; you wake up, and there's blood all over the sheets, the room, and you think, My God, has someone been murdered—because, you know, you're drunk, you've been passed out; but then you realize, because you've been screwing, that she's having her period, and it's not the blood of death, but the blood of life—the blood of life."[6] Dickey explained to David Havird that the events in the poem had taken place in Allen Tate's house. Dickey's tipsy mother-in-law braced herself against the couch for the reading of the bloody poem.

On November 18, at Drury College in Springfield, Missouri, for a reading, Dickey was similarly ungovernable. Among doting students gathered at the airport to welcome him, he flaunted a pornographic novellete, *The Stud Hustler*, while railing against the North Dakota citizens who had banned *Deliverance*. Before even seeing the campus, he declared: "I want to get my ticket out of here. Getting in was like swinging on a vine." To make civil conversation his hosts asked about his plans for the near future. Continuing in his Tarzan role, he spoke of hunts on a South Carolina island, travels to Alaska, and a trip to Adelaide, Australia. Why did he want to go back to Australia? the students wondered. Dickey replied: "I really like Australia; my wife's from there. There's no Jews or niggers there—no mongrelization, as we say in South Carolina. I was in Australia during the war, and there was this sort of freedom there becuz you weren't trying to compensate for others. . . . You know sentimental liberalism would allow black power but it wouldn't allow the white man his power. The ideal situation is separation. The blacks themselves want it more than anything else. . . . Coexistence isn't possible. . . . Thomas Jefferson sold us down the river in the Declaration of Independence. He overlooked the obvious fact of racial and ethnic grouping, and the basis of that grouping is 'we are together and you are opposed to us.'"[7] When Tom Shapcott, the Australian poet he had socialized with in Adelaide, visited him in March of 1975, Dickey mythologized Australia in a similar way: "Your Aborigines, you keep them in place. . . . We all make our political manoeuvres these days; but you don't let them become a *problem*."[8] As with the liberal Shapcott, with the liberal Drury students Dickey pretended to wave the Confederate flag of an unregenerate redneck.

In a less misanthropic mood, Dickey played the guitar with students at an English Department goat roast where wine, beer, roast pig, and squirrel were also available. For the rest of his stay he acted out variations on his usual routine. He left one party hand-in-hand with a young Drury alumna, accompanied a xylophone player with his guitar at another, bragged about winning a Pulitzer Prize for *Buckdancer's Choice*, drank beer for breakfast, conducted a salacious radio interview, and in an English class aired his literary opinions about the "bogus masterpiece" *Moby Dick*. Determined to irritate the students, he asked them why they had chosen Drury over other colleges like UCLA, the University of Chicago, and the University of Wisconsin. He exhorted them to go where outstanding professors taught, adding: "There are no outstanding people at Drury." In another class he was similarly truculent. Asked to explicate his poem "Foxblood," he replied: "I really don't know what the hell it's about. . . . I used to hunt a lot. I hit my finger with a hammer, and a blister formed on the half-moon of my fingernail. I thought it might be related to hunting, and that's 'Foxblood.'" He then took up the subject of *Deliverance*-burning again: "Who in hell ever heard of Drake, North Dakota, before? But I'll probably wait it out just a bit before deciding to make a public stand. They burned 60 copies of *Deliverance*. What a little shit-ass town is doing with 60 copies of my book. . . ." At the November 19 reading, Dickey continued his besotted monologue. He stumbled onto the Drury stage, mumbled his Marlon Brando imitation, read his poem "Blood" "for all you menstruating females out there," and snubbed the audience by refusing a request to read from *Deliverance*. A reporter for the college newspaper concluded his account of Dickey's appearance with two sentences: "James Dickey was an experience for Drury: a glimpse of a talent both blooming and wasted; a renowned author who became a racist and s.o.b. before our eyes. He flew out of Springfield at 7 A.M. Tuesday, a six-pack already under his belt."[9] If he had set out to purge his demons at Drury, he had accomplished his task with his characteristic excoriating flair.

Back in Columbia, Dickey assumed a more dignified pose to accept the Order of the South Award at a ceremony before the USC-Clemson football game. At a formal luncheon, Rev. Robert Oliver cited Dickey's outstanding contribution to Southern culture and welfare, and declared that The Southern Academy of Letters, Arts, and Sciences was proud to honor such a distinguished Southerner. Near the end of November, a few days after receiving the award, Dickey tried to alter the stereotype he so assiduously cultivated at places like Drury. He was not a raw, ham-fisted redneck, but "a bookish, rather shy person," he told Marshall Swanson for the *Gamecock*. Although the article paid homage to Dickey's bogus accomplishments as fighter pilot and football star, it also observed: "Dickey's campus reputation as a flatterer of young coeds and a two-fisted swashbuckling redneck may be more surface veneer than real personality traits."[10] Over the succeeding years, as Dickey realized the extent to which his image as a swashbuckling redneck was eroding his reputation as a serious writer, he increasingly set out to counter it. Nonetheless, he never made it easy for audiences to distinguish between his real personality and his impersonations. He revelled in the mystique—what Keats called "the egotistical sublime"—that his chameleon disguises afforded him.

Dickey's dire letter about Maxine's health must have startled Robert Penn Warren when he opened it in mid-January 1974. During Warren's visit to Columbia, Maxine had seemed robust, but by January, according to her husband, she was nearly dead: "Maxine has been deathly ill. At one time there were indications that she might have as many as four potentially fatal diseases at the same time." Several recent tests gave Dickey some cause for hope: "The danger of the high blood pressure and coronary problem seems to be over-rated, the diabetes . . . either receded or did not exist in the first place, the test for cervical cancer came back blessedly negative (though Maxine had to have a kind of exploratory operation), and now remains only the gravid liver, which she is combatting with a fine mixture of fury and temperance."[11] Maxine's troubles prompted Dickey to new worries about his own health. In February, he decided to visit his doctor, Donald Saunders, at the Columbia Clinic for an extensive checkup. Particularly anxious about possible diabetes and cirrhosis, he was mollified by Saunders's report on February 26, 1974, that his blood sugar, cholesterol, and triglycerides, and four out of five of his liver functions, were normal. But Saunders cautioned that the one abnormal liver function was serious and that he needed to cut back on alcohol. For the moment Dickey heeded his doctor's advice.

The Dickeys tried to put aside their health crises to entertain another writer friend, William Styron, near the end of January. Returning from a trip to Haiti,

Styron and his wife, Rose, stopped in Columbia and went to Litchfield for the customary music, archery, cocktails, literary chat, and oysters. Dickey brought Styron to his poetry class and announced: "Now . . . this course concerns the human sensibility and imagination and how these manifest themselves in words, whether in poetry or prose-fiction. . . . Today we've got with us one of the great novelists of the century; he's with us today and today only. Let's take advantage of it."[12] The students needed little prodding. They bombarded Styron with questions about suicide, dreams, and the furor incited by his Pulitzer Prize–winning novel *The Confessions of Nat Turner*. Styron addressed the students' concerns as diplomatically as possible. Later, as a token of thanks, Dickey gave Styron a bow and arrow. Styron promised to reciprocate with a juicy Virginia ham.

Dickey began 1974 full of confidence about his projects, new and old. *Slowly Toward Hercules*, he had told Warren, was quickly moving toward completion and would be "the best I have done to date."[13] To reassure Stewart Richardson that he was making satisfactory progress on the novel he was now calling *Alnilam*, on January 4 he mailed him a three-page letter with detailed plans for it and for its sequel, *Crux*. He promised to send a first draft of *Alnilam* by April 1974 or at least by June. Both his editor and agent were even more eager to receive the manuscript when the Franklin Mint offered one thousand dollars and a guarantee of fifteen thousand dollars to publish a deluxe, thirty-to-forty-dollar leather-bound edition. On January 14, Dickey sent the first chapter about Cahill's blindness to Richardson, but after the promising start his novel ground to a halt. Before long he renegotiated his contract to extend his deadline to July 1976.

Deaths in his family contributed to Dickey's writing difficulties. On March 12, 1974, he went to his father's hospital bed knowing that the event he had imagined in poems like "Approaching Prayer," "The Hospital Window," "Sled Burial, Dream Ceremony," and "Gamecock" would finally occur. Patsy Dickey had stayed with Eugene Dickey most of the previous night. Because of a stroke, one of Eugene's eyes had stopped moving by morning. According to Dickey, his father had gone blind from a lack of oxygen in his brain, but nevertheless had asked his assembled family: "Is Jim here with his guitar?" Dickey replied: "I'm here, but my guitar is out in the car. I can go get it." Dickey got his guitar and played his father's last request, the Baptist hymn "Just a Closer Walk with Thee," which his father had learned in the Baptist Church before spurning Christianity. Dickey recalled: "The old atheist [was dead] . . . by the time I finished the second chorus." Eugene had opened his eyes briefly and died around 9:40 A.M. To Dickey his father had shown courage in his acceptance of the inevitable. "Pop, get up and out of there and let's go back up in the country," Dickey had said at one point. His father had replied: "No, Jimbo . . . that ain't the pitch no more. We had our time."[14]

Although father and son had repaired some of their grievances over the years, Dickey showed little outward grief. He wrote an Atlanta friend, Ashley Walker, that he had left the hospital and gone to a restaurant with her mother: "I don't remember the occasion as being at all grim, and it was not, because of your mother. . . . She gave me the most imaginative and *interesting* account of how it feels to go blind from diabetes that *you* can imagine."[15] The account of diabetic blindness had been so enthralling that Dickey forgot about his father's death.

Dickey explored this sort of distracting experience more fully in his poem "Last Hours," where an enthralling story about the serial killer Ted Bundy relieves his brother's thoughts about his own death.

Kevin Dickey noticed his father's nonchalant attitude toward Eugene's demise at the funeral. Dickey kissed Eugene on the head as he lay in a canopy bed, but otherwise appeared blithely indifferent to him. Kevin remarked: "Everyone was sitting around talking like a cocktail party and nobody was really paying much respect to my grandfather. . . . What . . . really struck me about the whole thing was that no one seemed to really care very much." How the funeral home exhibited his grandfather also struck Kevin as odd. Fully dressed in a suit, he lay in a Victorian room with one arm tucked inside the bed covers and one arm underneath the covers. "Couldn't they have just put him in some pajamas or something for God's sake?"[16] Kevin asked a cousin. Dickey may have been referring to this family tradition of lying in state in "Sled Burial, Dream Ceremony" when he imagines "the dead southerner . . . with the top of his casket / Open, his hair combed" and a funeral arranger reaching "inside the coffin" and placing "The southerner's hand at the center // Of his dead breast."[17] Seeing his grandfather so exposed, Kevin decided—against his Aunt Maibelle's protests—that there would be no open-casket funerals for his mother or father.

Chris Dickey echoed his brother's observations: "My father had built such a screen of contempt around his own father that he barely talked about him in life and seemed to forget about him in death. . . . He was no more missed than a piece of furniture that had been moved to storage."[18] As a boy Dickey had been repulsed by his father's cockfighting, and even though Eugene was a lawyer in name and a substantial landowner in fact (at his death he had holdings in Louisiana as well as in Atlanta), Dickey consistently dubbed him a weak-willed failure. Eugene's death and funeral had little effect on Dickey's usual round of classes and readings. On March 18, reading at the Folger Shakespeare Library in Washington, D.C., he incorporated his father's death into his routine. After Katie Loucheim introduced him, even though she kept her remarks brief, he trotted out his favorite line about having her preach at his own funeral and excused his late arrival by saying that he had just left his father's funeral. The sympathetic audience felt sorry for the bereft poet. Drinking beer with *Washington Post* reporter Henry Mitchell at the Folger guest house afterward, he didn't seem especially mournful. He was similarly buoyant the following night at the University of Maryland's Tawes Recital Hall. To the English professor who introduced him as a "one-book novelist of distinction," he bellowed, "Jackass!" and, predictably, "Let me have your name, sir. I want to make a private arrangement with you to speak at my funeral."[19] A writer for a local paper who had attended the reading the previous night realized that Dickey was lying about his father's funeral. Twenty minutes late, he again claimed that he had just rushed from his father's funeral. The journalist found out from the student who shepherded Dickey from his hotel that he had simply overslept.

Marcia Kass, who interviewed Dickey after the reading, heard him mention his father's death only in the context of some sarcastic asides about women. In a discussion of *Deliverance* and his new project, a TV adaptation of Jack London's *Call of the Wild*, he told Kass that women were inclined to love men they feared.

He then proclaimed, "Look, baby, I'm not *a* male chauvinist. I'm *the* male chauvinist," and told a story about a nurse who had cared for his dying father: "It took a woman to do that. Don't talk about chauvinism: there are some things like that that a woman does much better than a man could possibly do." In an attempt to win sympathy from Kass, Dickey mentioned the death threats he had received from parents of children who had drowned on the Chattooga: "I only got four death threats last week. I think we're moving out of the woods now." His father's death, like the Chattooga drownings, simply provided fodder for excuses, stories, and homilies. "If you believe the image he tried to project," Kass concluded after watching Dickey vanish with several six-packs, he is "the wickedest, orneriest bastard to ever write poetry."[20]

Dickey sought to project a somewhat different image in April during Robert Lowell's visit to USC. Those who had helped arrange Lowell's reading expected a literary dogfight. Approaching the Business School auditorium with Don Greiner, Dickey paused to say: "Don, tonight it's as if Will Shakespeare and Ben Jonson were meeting at the Mermaid Tavern. And only time will tell which of us is Shakespeare."[21] Dickey, however, went out of his way to display Southern hospitality toward Lowell. Preempting David Havird, who was supposed to introduce Lowell and present him with the USC Award for Distinction in Literature, Dickey delivered an emotional peroration in which he praised Lowell as America's Milton and asked the audience to give him a standing ovation. Dickey customarily referred to Milton as a "stuffed goat," but this time he intended his reference to Lowell's early model as a compliment.

A feeble Lowell—he would be dead in two years—was visibly moved when the stalwart Dickey gave him a bear hug. Lowell acknowledged this adulation in an unexpected way: he read Dickey's "Adultery." Was Lowell trying to embarrass or outshock the poet who loved to shock? Lowell said he chose "Adultery" as an example of a poet's good prose style, so Dickey appeared pleased. Lowell proceeded to read his own poems, and before he finished, Dickey jumped to his feet to applaud. The audience's clapping was so tumultuous that Lowell decided to end the reading prematurely. Afterward Lowell expressed bemusement at Dickey's friendliness. As Havird drove him to Dickey's house in his red Volkswagen Beetle, Lowell said he couldn't understand why Dickey attacked his confessional poetry yet celebrated him as Milton's heir. Havird explained that in class Dickey had called Lowell his oldest friend and rival. That also puzzled Lowell, since their friendship had begun shakily in the mid-1960s.

During his drive to Lelia's Court, Lowell made adulatory references to *Deliverance*, which he was reading, and complimented Dickey's intelligence. He was surprised that Dickey was so learned. At an earlier party, Dickey seemed bent on reinforcing the image so many intellectuals—including Lowell—harbored of him as a Viking berserker. Having gotten terribly drunk, in Maxine's company he tried to seduce the girlfriend of Jim Mann's younger brother, William, who was a USC student. Maxine was furious, and when Havird asked Maxine whether he should help the diminutive woman, who was assisting Dickey down the stairs, Maxine retorted: "Let him help his own goddamn self."[22] Although no stranger to such domestic dramas, Lowell registered surprise at the way Dickey vacillated between boorishness, charm, and sophistication.

After his trip, Lowell thanked his host for his "almost royal entertainment" in Columbia. "The scene I somehow take away is sitting on your landing, a brown-ish, hot lake, a swept feeling, a feeling of summer inches away—a large hospital-ity." Dickey now shared a privileged place in Lowell's Southern pantheon. "You and Peter Taylor," Lowell wrote nostalgically, "are almost the last of the South for me."[23]

In 1974, another film project took Dickey away from his Southern home. Like other scripts to follow, this one appealed to his wallet as well as his imagi-nation. During the summer of 1973, Dickey had begun a screenplay based on Jack London's *Call of the Wild* for Hollywood producers Malcolm Stuart and Chuck Fries. London's novel, which deals with conflicts between the city and wilderness comparable to those in *Deliverance*, was a likely choice for Dickey. Like London, Dickey romanticized nature even while acknowledging its Darwinian brutality. Recognizing the two writers' similar obsessions, Malcolm Stuart had conceived of the plan to ask Dickey to write a screenplay after find-ing a copy of *Call of the Wild* in a Los Angeles bookstore. Suspecting that the last film version of the novel had been made in the 1930s with Clark Gable, he phoned an NBC executive to pitch his idea. The executive asked about screen-writers. Stuart said he wanted Dickey, and the executive assured him that if he could get Dickey, she could get a contract. Stuart called Dickey in Columbia and was greeted with a barrage of shouts and screams. Wondering whether Dickey was angry or deranged, he gradually realized that he was ecstatic. Dickey finally said: "I don't know you. And if you are lying about this I'll track you down and kill you. But if I can write it, it will give me the greatest pleasure of my life."[24] Stuart relayed the good news to NBC, and before long Charles Fries Productions, with Stuart as vice president of the film, offered Dickey forty thou-sand dollars to write a screenplay based on *Call of the Wild*.

Dickey's version of the events leading up to the film was quite different. Drinking martinis with Cecil Smith, a *Los Angeles Times* television critic, he said:

Well, one day there came a call from Charles Fries Productions. It seems Chuck Fries wanted me to write a two-hour TV spectacular. What about? says I. Anything you want, says he. Now writers don't get chances like that very often—the freedom to do anything you want. It was something I couldn't turn down.

I talked it over with my wife Maxine and I told her that I had always wanted to take a story that people think they know very well from child-hood or adolescence, whatever, and do that story in such a way that they realize they really didn't know it at all. I said I wanted to do Jack London's "The Call of the Wild" in my own way.

It's a wonderful story. If you get rid of Jack's Nietzschean pseudo-philosophizing about the laws of power, survival of the fittest, that sort of thing, get it down to the sheer narrative drive, well, then I thought it would make an extraordinary film. I called up Chuck Fries and his producer Malcolm Stuart, and told them so and they bowled me over by saying: "Let's go!"

Dickey said he watched the MGM film with Clark Gable and Loretta Young, but it was "utter tripe—it was totally unrelated to what Jack London's story was all about."[25] He also mentioned Charlton Heston's abortive adaptation of the story, which had been filmed in Norway and never released.

Following his preliminary talks with Fries and Stuart, Dickey seemed more concerned with finding a dog big and ferocious enough to play Buck than with completing his script. His sister-in-law, Patsy, gave advice: "Metromedia could breed a Saint Bernard and a collie and no doubt come up with an authentic Buck in time for the filming of the story for television. My second suggestion would be to find the biggest damned Arctic wolf known to man, break him to the sled and use him. The wolf is often bred to a domestic working dog to create a finer-breed sled dog."[26] Perhaps because of Patsy's mention of a collie, Dickey began telling interviewers that his Call of the Wild was going to be no Lassie.

NBC's fear of Heston's version being distributed slowed production. When these worries subsided, Dickey redoubled his efforts on the script and submitted a draft in late 1974. Because the NBC executives judged the script to be too rough, on December 20 Stuart sent Dickey a letter with five pages of revisions. He urged Dickey to rewrite the narration as if Jack London or he himself were telling the story, reveal Buck's thoughts and feelings more fully, make Buck's reversion to the wilderness more dramatic, and develop Thornton into a more sympathetic character. Stuart wanted the final script in time for filming to begin during the winter of 1974–75. Dickey procrastinated, using as an excuse his son Kevin's ruptured appendix, which he told Stuart on February 5, 1975, had nearly been fatal. (Kevin had had a routine appendectomy.) On February 18, having completed the revisions, Dickey informed Stuart: "As far as I am concerned at this moment in time the thing is done."[27] Stuart should go ahead with production.

Difficulties still remained, chief among them Dickey's request for a role in the film. He hoped to act alongside Charles Bronson, who would play the lead role of Thornton. Bronson, however, had already committed himself to other films. Dickey proposed teaming up with Burt Reynolds, Marlon Brando, or George C. Scott. One day when USC colleague Ward Briggs came to the house with Maxine after shopping, Dickey said that Scott had just called to say he wanted to act in Call of the Wild. Maxine laughed off the idea, and told Briggs never to lie to someone he loved. Stuart, Fries, and associate producer Tony Ganz had no intention of offering Dickey a role, or offering a role to Reynolds since he was too expensive. They also had no recollection of Dickey's alleged contacts with other Hollywood stars. What they remembered was the difficulty of getting Dickey to finish the script.

Just as Jacques de Spoelberch had flown to Columbia to squeeze a final draft of Deliverance from Dickey, Ganz flew to Columbia to expedite Call of the Wild. In his midtwenties, Ganz had worked closely with Stuart from the film's inception. In order to play midwife to the procrastinating Dickey, Ganz spent a week at Lelia's Court. Because Dickey's drinking made work nearly impossible after midday, Ganz discussed the script in the morning. Dickey dictated lines of dialogue to his assistant, Shaye Areheart, and asked Ganz if the lines were satisfactory. Ganz usually nodded. If he vetoed a line, Dickey was generally compliant.

As Dickey's drinking escalated, he became more unmanageable, work petered out, and the melodrama of Dickey's marriage commenced. Ganz likened the scenes he witnessed to a 1940s Hollywood cartoon. On one occasion Dickey chased Maxine with hunting arrows, threatening to kill her. Ganz learned that a broken corner on a kitchen countertop had been recently glued after Dickey swung at her with a skillet and missed. Like most guests, Ganz quickly grew fond of Maxine, but recoiled from the murderous vaudeville.

On his trip to Hollywood to work on *Call of the Wild* from August 15 to 19, 1974, Dickey proposed another movie idea to Fries and his associates. Thinking of his recently deceased father and the mixture of cowardice and courage he had inherited from Eugene, Dickey wanted to focus on a character's arduous but ultimately triumphant struggle against his pusillanimous tendencies. The epigraph Dickey eventually chose for the screenplay came from John Berryman: "A man can live his whole life in this society, and never know whether he is a coward or not."[28] Dickey's new movie would dramatize a struggle in which the main character discovered his heroism. The protagonist would be Sheriff Gene Bullard, his first name deriving from Eugene Dickey, his last name from one of Dickey's air corps acquaintances and the character Dickey played in *Deliverance*. Dickey gave the Hollywood producers a rough outline of his new film, which he originally called *Crownfire* and later *Gene Bullard*. He explained that he would introduce Bullard as a former athlete who avoids violence and who normally drives a meter maid to check for parking violations around the small North Georgia town of Ellijay. His mainstay would be a tough young woman named Beth Culclasher (Culclasure was the maiden name of Paula Goff, on whom Beth was modeled). Bullard's antagonists would be a motley assortment of small-town criminals: Joby, the son of deeply religious Baptist parents who were killed in a car crash when he was eighteen; Makens, a maniacal, sadistic monster who'd committed a number of bizarre sex crimes; Leon, a comically moronic ex-convict; and Jimbo, a forty-five-year-old escaped convict whose name had obvious resonance with Dickey's. Like the men in *Deliverance*, those in *Gene Bullard* would be Dickey's personae. Charles Fries was interested, and before long Dickey commenced work on the new script.

During the fall of 1974, Dickey directed most of his attention to promoting a monolithic coffee-table book, *Jericho: The South Beheld*, which he had written sporadically over the previous two years. The book had been a collaborative venture; Dickey had composed a narrative tracing an imaginative journey around the South, and the artist Hubert Shuptrine had provided watercolors to accompany but not necessarily follow Dickey's prose. The bulk of the book was art; there were 101 paintings in the 165 pages. According to Dickey, *Jericho* was the ultimate coffee-table book. It was so large (16' 5" x 13") and so heavy (7 lbs.) you didn't have to have a coffee table; it could serve as one.

As with so many of Dickey's narratives, the plot of *Jericho* was picaresque and mythic. One model for his adventure was Joyce's *A Portrait of the Artist as a Young Man*. Like Joyce's Stephen Dedalus, who counsels his soul to fly above the nets of nationality, language, and religion, Dickey endows his imagination with the wings of "pure spirit" and asks his readers "to hover, to swoop, to enter into the veer of the land and rivers, to zigzag over the landscape of people, to live the trembling of the Web of custom and family." Like Dedalus and his mythic fore-bear who built wings to escape the Minotaur's labyrinth, Dickey's spirit soars over the "net" or "web" of his culture in order to behold it more clearly. The re-sults of these beholdings resemble Joycean epiphanies, or what Dickey, punning on the old name for films, calls "flickers." They are supposed to reveal the real South beneath the stereotype of "the magnolia-and-moonlight South." Dickey begins by focusing on one oyster shell in a Saint Augustine wall. In this wall, reminiscent of the biblical Jericho's first walls, he construes the birth, death, and resurrection of the South. On his inspired travels he beholds alligators and rat-tlesnakes in Florida, trees cut for turpentine in Georgia, azalea gardens blossom-ing in Mobile, people "sweating like glass" in New Orleans, the "slow, masturbatory rhythm" of oil rigs in Texas, a potter gardening naked in Oklahoma, a hitchiker playing bluegrass music near Nashville, coal miners tun-neling through mountains in West Virginia, the ghost of Jefferson repeating his Agrarian ideals in Virginia, a black man fishing in "the hauntedness" of South Carolina, and his brother, Tom, digging Civil War relics outside Atlanta.

Shuptrine's first group of pictures depict simple, subdued scenes—a broken anchor leaning on driftwood, an old capstan, a rusted cannon in weeds, two hunting dogs in a snowy cornfield, a battered farm wagon, a pail of apples, a win-ter orchard. Image after image is awash in earth colors. Soft browns, greens, rus-sets, oranges, whites, and grays dominate and evoke a quiet, melancholy mood. Dickey's next prose sketch shifts abruptly to a builder from "Jericho Tech" (Georgia Tech) who wields a slide rule like Blake's demonic Urizen over the "commercial Utopia" of Atlanta. The next sketch shifts to a happier scene of a blind man on a porch playing a Baptist hymn as his family sings. As in the book's first section, Dickey returns to scenes visited already in his poems and prose. He stops at a marble quarry reminiscent of "In the Marble Quarry." He meets red-necks who kill for love and turn dogs loose on a racoon chained to a log in a pond, a tough girl playing softball in Georgia, a messianic preacher, a juvenile delinquent who robs banks with a cap gun, a mulatto child conceived in slave quarters who becomes a heavyweight champion. Traveling through the South, Dickey meets himself and his fictions at every turn. Regarding the storytelling tradition that enabled his own career, he exclaims: "We are the most outrageous and creative liars in the world, and we take our time to make the lies a lot more interesting than the truth."[29] Dickey's South, in the end, is a series of double vi-sions, of "creative lies" and actual places.

Jericho, which became one of the most lucrative coffee-table books ever pro-duced, was the brainchild of *Southern Living's* editorial director, John Logue, a former sports writer who had met Dickey at the Bitsy Grant tennis courts in Atlanta in the late 1950s. To guarantee *Jericho's* success he had modeled the book on an art book by Andrew Wyeth. Still, he harbored doubts. Oxmoor House, the book-publishing division of the Progressive Farmer Company in Birmingham, Alabama, was relatively unknown—it was founded in 1969— and certainly small compared to New York and Boston publishers. Emory Cunningham, a soft-spoken man from Walker County, Alabama, who presided over the Progressive Farmer, had published cooking, gardening, and travel books; *Jericho* would be his first art book. On reading Dickey's text, Cunningham had reservations. In particular, he objected to the "masturbatory" oil wells. Logue assured the president that their book would be highly remunerative, and eventually Cunningham passed along Logue's optimisitic predictions to his board members.

According to Dickey, the Oxmoor editors wanted a "view of the South through the eyes of the corporate Southerner . . . , pictures of objects such as the Mason-Dixon Line marker, Appomattox Court House, Colonial Williamsburg, football . . . , the Alamo."[30] Neither Dickey nor Shuptrine, whose paintings Logue had admired at the annual Plum Nelly Art Show, wanted anything to do with "corporate" visions. On February 27, 1973, Logue wrote Dickey a four-page letter that made concessions and outlined details. He said that Oxmoor had little interest in the suburban Southerner commuting to work in his car pool, but wanted the collaborators to focus on the Southern past and how it survived in the present-day South. Dickey was to write about Shuptrine's subjects or the way he painted them and finish the manuscript by March 1, 1974. About Oxmoor's plans for the book, Logue promised that *Jericho* would get more publicity than any book published in the South since *Gone with the Wind*.

Dickey, Shuptrine, and Logue got together in the spring of 1973 to discuss ideas (at this meeting Dickey suggested the prophetic title *Jericho*). Shuptrine returned to Highlands, North Carolina, to explore a fifty-mile radius around the town and paint whatever he found. The publisher, however, told him that to attract a wide array of advertisers he had to visit all sixteen states in the South. Shuptrine received a list of things he had to paint. In a rare moment of agreement, Dickey gave his collaborator helpful advice: "Paint what the hell you want to and forget about that list."[31] Shuptrine had no desire to render commercial products like ski boats and Mercury motors and well-known tourist sites. He wanted to concentrate on the hinterlands or at least on neglected objects in well-known places. In Annapolis, he painted a single tole lantern, in Williamsburg a country butter churn, in Charleston a humble indigo tub. No ski boat appeared in *Jericho*.

The logistics of collaboration evolved in unexpected ways. Shuptrine asked Dickey if slides of his paintings might help inspire his narrative (he had done little writing on *Jericho* by then). Dickey vehemently refused any such contributions. "No way," he said. "I'm not about to write commentary about your art. I'll send you some text pieces and then you do paintings of the text pieces." Shuptrine replied: "No way. I'm not about to illustrate your writing." Dickey smiled approvingly: "That's the answer. It's been done the other way many times. We'll do it differently for the first time. We'll have a double vision."[32] Because Logue knew both artists would work best independently, he approved of the unusual arrangement. Logue stipulated, though, that Dickey write something about all the Southern states. If some states were excluded, the book might lose potential buyers. At the end, when Logue noted that he had failed to include Florida, one of *Southern Living*'s most profitable markets, Dickey retorted: "I can cover Florida in three words: Peroxide and gonorrhea." Dickey eventually made Florida and its oldest town, Saint Augustine, his starting point. He also softened his stance toward Shuptrine, agreeing to write a passage about the black fisherman in the boat that eventually appeared on the book's cover. But when he found out that Shuptrine's name would appear ahead of his, he was furious. He felt betrayed by Logue, who overruled his objections, and in later years nursed a grudge against Shuptrine.

Initially Oxmoor intended to print five thousand copies of *Jericho*. Because of *Southern Living*'s advertising campaign, which had garnered twenty thousand orders by September 3, 1973, the publisher revised its plans. Dickey did what he could to increase demand for his book. One of the first places Logue got a chance to witness Dickey's promotional skills was at a Washington, D.C., meeting of the American Booksellers Association during the summer of 1974. Relegated to a smallish room at the end of a line of booths, the Oxmoor people lamented their prospects. Dickey, however, had worked out a strategy. The night before the conference started, exuding confidence, he strode into a room of about twenty bookseller representatives. Sporting a large, dark brown safari hat, a knife almost as big as a machete on his belt, and cowboy boots, he sat down in front of them and filled a tall iced-tea glass up to the brim with Scotch. The representatives were mesmerized. Dickey said: "I'm going to tell you how to sell this book. *I'm going to sell it*."[33] Having seen a mock-up of *Jericho* and the sort of charisma Dickey would utilize on the book's behalf, many of the representatives concluded that they had a winner.

To tap the enthusiasm for the book, which seemed to grow by the day, the public relations manager Rick Rush organized a one-hundred-thousand-dollar two-month book tour as grueling as any of Dickey's previous barnstorming trips. Shuptrine, his wife, Phyllis, Rush, Dickey, and one of Les Adam's assistants in charge of publicity, Betty Ann Jones, traveled to New York in July to attend a party where the itinerary would be announced. It was on this occasion that Shuptrine began to have grave doubts about Dickey's alcoholic "great white hunter" act as a promotional gimmick. American Library Association members, publishers, and numerous booksellers eager to arrange book signings for *Jericho* crowded into the hotel room to hear Jones map out the trip. They waited a long time for Dickey to arrive. Finally Rush, whose main assignment was to act as Dickey's chaperone, fetched Dickey from his hotel room. Looking like a dapper desperado, Dickey sauntered into the room forty minutes late. He wore a big Mexican hat with gold coins around the brim and a Mexican shirt embroidered with lace, which he continued to wear, clean or dirty, for the entire tour. A young woman in peasant dress who looked like "the queen of Rabun Gap" followed him. Hubert rose from his seat as the young woman approached. "Hubert, feel her ass. I assure you it's worth it!" Dickey said so that others nearby could hear. The audience gasped. As Dickey plucked his guitar, Jones went to the podium to discuss the itinerary.

Jones handed a schedule to Shuptrine, who approved of the various signings and interviews, and to Dickey, who commented: "Well, it looks alright to me, but you haven't left enough time for fucking."[34] The speechless Jones, who had hoped to keep relations with Dickey professional, turned livid. Dickey's behavior improved little as the day progressed. That evening, trying to distance himself from his collaborator, Shuptrine sat on the other side of the table at a fancy Italian restaurant. He noticed that Dickey's girlfriend gobbled up broiled chicken halves as if she hadn't eaten in a week, while Dickey slurped a little soup and continued drinking. Dickey got so drunk that Rush had to escort him from the restaurant. Making his way through the outdoor café, Dickey overturned a table with a canvas umbrella and upended another table. Everyone felt relieved when he was safely on the street.

The *Jericho* tour began with a 6:30 A.M. taping session with Dickey's friend George Plimpton at Walden Books in New York on September 4, but it was not until September 30 that the daily whistle-stops started. (To accommodate his tour schedule, Dickey dismissed all his October classes without consulting USC English Department chair William Nolte and threatened to quit USC altogether when he learned that he would have to take a leave-without-pay for the month.) The first *Jericho* events were in Birmingham, Alabama. Here Dickey and Shuptrine attended TV, radio, and press interviews as well as autographing parties. They continued their promotional efforts in Houston, New Orleans, Dallas, Atlanta, Columbia (SC), Charlotte, Greenville, Richmond, and Nashville. Rush had arranged a meeting on October 18 with South Carolina governor John West; and to ensure an even wider audience, he had booked appearances on *The Today Show*, Johnny Carson's *Tonight Show*, and *The Merv Griffin Show*.

Despite his initial promise "to sell" *Jericho*, Dickey resented the arduous promotional tour. "Don't let the ducks nibble you,"[35] he often told Shuptrine. While his partner was patient and talkative with admirers, Dickey was usually peremptory or mischievous. At the first large signing party in Birmingham, Shuptrine learned a lesson he never forgot on the trip. Dickey greeted the line of autograph seekers first, and, perhaps to get revenge for Shuptrine's name appearing before his on the title page, he signed his name with so many curlicues and loops and flourishes that Shuptrine had no space for his own signature. From then on Shuptrine made sure he was the first to sign his name. Dickey vented his jealousy in more-clandestine ways. In Atlanta, because a woman painter kept speaking to Shuptrine, Dickey took her copy of *Jericho* and wrote under his partner's signature: "Is a rotten son-of-a-bitch." "Here you go, ma'am," he said as he closed the book and politely handed it to her. Dickey also liked to titillate the book buyers. Approached by attractive women, he would write: "In memory of our passionate nights"[36] and then insert the appropriate city. The lines of customers were always long. In Birmingham, Anne Rivers Siddons, the Atlanta writer who would later pay homage to Dickey and Buckhead in her epic novel *Peachtree Road*, remembered that Dickey signed hundreds of copies of *Jericho* while she only signed a few copies of her most recent book.

The Shuptrines got advance warning of what to expect from Dickey from Maxine, who joined the group in Birmingham at the beginning of the tour. Maxine invited Phyllis for breakfast in her room after the men left for an interview. Wearing a frilly pink negligee, matching peignoir, two charm bracelets, earrings, and makeup, Maxine struck Phyllis as overdressed for the informal morning conversation. In a maternal voice Maxine quickly got down to business, apprising Phyllis of her husband's megalomania and constant drinking. She said the only thing that kept him sober, productive, and relatively organized was his teaching job at USC. On the road, he caroused like a fraternity boy. She usually refused to join him on these trips, she said, because neither she nor her husband enjoyed the other's company. Joining the wandering troupe at an Atlanta restaurant later in the tour, she demonstrated why she and her husband didn't travel together. She spotted him talking to a young girl in a corner, and slapped him as hard as she could on the face. Afterward, both husband and wife were happy to go their different ways.

Phyllis appreciated Maxine's advice, but nevertheless had to improvise with Rick Rush to keep Dickey functional. Each morning someone had to wake Dickey at six-thirty, put his feet on the floor, fill half a motel glass with Scotch, and help him get dressed. His clothes would often be dirty, a fact Dickey ignored partly because of his defective sense of smell. He ate no breakfast. If he hadn't quaffed exactly the right amount of Scotch, he would respond to the early morning TV or radio interviewers with "yes"-"no" answers, silence, or obscenities. The interviews over, Dickey usually lunched on soup, a saltine cracker, double martinis, and beer chasers. He often skipped dinner and organizational meetings to carouse or sleep. To maintain the ruse that he had a new woman in every city, he detailed his romantic adventures to Phyllis, who from the start suspected he was lying. On one occasion he told Phyllis about a torrid affair with his "protégé," Anne Sexton, at the University of Wisconsin. Because she had recently committed suicide, he moaned on one flight: "I'll never see those black hairs again."[37] He mentioned that he had an illegitimate twelve-year-old son in Denver; he wanted to help him, but Maxine refused. He spoke of his tryst with Paula Goff in New Orleans and how she had tied him to a hotel bed and tickled him with a feather duster. (Dickey and Goff had actually met at New Orleans's Pontchartrain Hotel; Goff wrote a poem titled "The World As a Lie, Coming True," which commemorated a scene in the hotel dining room where she drank Bloody Marys and discussed the possibility of marrying Dickey.) Hubert Shuptrine reflected: "I knew we were in for a damn long trip." His wife concurred.

In Atlanta the Shuptrines glimpsed at least one of the spurs behind Dickey's many stories that both romanticized and denigrated women. The revelation came after Dickey finished his martini-and-beer lunch with a reporter and retired to his room at the Marriott. Preparing to leave for the evening flight, Dickey's companions called his room repeatedly, but received no answer. It was reasonable to assume that Dickey was sleeping off the long night he had spent with John Logue at Atlanta's clubs. Or had he finally bolted from the tour, as the Oxmoor organizers had feared? Shuptrine knocked on Dickey's door. Nobody answered, so he contacted Rush, who opened the door with the extra key he always carried for such emergencies. The scene inside startled Shuptrine: "Dickey was lying on the floor, cursing, and banging his fists up and down, and the girl [in his bed] was saying, 'That's all right, Jim. I know you can do it. That's all right, Jim. I know you can do it.'" Exhaustion and alcohol had once again rendered Dickey impotent.

On the way to the Atlanta airport, Dickey struggled to reassert the image of himself that had been demolished by the woman at the Marriott. He first belittled her. "She was nothing but a whore. She expected too much," he said. Then he delivered a litany of his accolades: Vanderbilt track and football star, decorated combat pilot. . . . In the front seat Hubert and Rick Rush ignored him. In a boyish appeal for approval, Dickey turned to Phyllis: "When are you going to love me?" Trying to stare out the window, she replied: "I don't know, Jim." He persisted: "No, I'm serious, I want to know when you're going to love me?" Phyllis, who was thirty-eight at the time, answered sarcastically: "How about when I'm sixty-five and you're eighty." Dickey said: "I like that," and put his hat over his eyes and fell asleep.

By the time Dickey got to Los Angeles for an appearance with Johnny Carson on *The Tonight Show*, he had lost all patience with small talk about *Jericho*. Maxine joined the itinerant group once again and was given the unenviable job of keeping her husband sober. Dickey and Shuptrine met with Johnny Carson's assistants in the morning for a preparatory interview. The assistants selected questions and told Dickey and Shuptrine to repeat their answers when Carson eventually asked the questions written on cue cards. Later in the day, as they waited in "the green room" with Ethel Merman and Tony Randall, Dickey kept slipping out to drink. In a boisterous mood, he watched the monitor and imitated Randall, who starred in *The Odd Couple*. By the time the show's director signaled for Dickey to come on stage, he was drinking beer openly in the green room. Because of time constraints, Shuptrine had to stay behind. When Dickey took a seat, Carson observed jokingly that all you had to do to turn the book into a coffee table was put four legs on it. Carson proceeded with the prepared questions, but Dickey refused to give the rehearsed answers. Instead, he tried to steer the conversation toward apocryphal adventures in the Florida swamps hunting alligators. The nonplussed director returned to the green room and warned Shuptrine: "You may be going on next. That guy is out of his head!" In the end, Shuptrine remained seated, watching his partner fend off Carson's repeated attempts to discuss *Jericho*.

Dickey brought his tour to a close, appropriately enough, where he began his writing career—in Nashville. On October 30, he attended a black-tie luncheon honoring several authors. John Seigenthaler, the editor-in-chief of the *Tennessean* newspaper, acted as master of ceremonies. Five to six hundred people, including Seigenthaler's ninety-year-old mother, crowded into the large room. In his introduction Seigenthaler mentioned that his mother was one of Dickey's greatest fans and had come to hear him read. Looking harried and dejected (he had told the Shuptrines earlier in the day that Maxine was dying from uterine cancer), Dickey strode to the podium wearing his usual Mexican hat and shirt, a knife strapped to his hip, and flipped through his poetry book. The prolonged silence agitated the audience. Finally he stopped, looked up and said: "Alright, you assholes, I'm going to read you some literature."[38] He read "Sheep Child," savoring the salacious bits, as well as "Adultery," arguing that the only other option to adultery was spiritual death. Many were appalled. But according to John Logue, when Seigenthaler asked his mother, "Mama, how did you like it?" she supposedly responded: "I didn't like it, I loved it."[39]

After the black-tie affair in Nashville, Dickey returned to USC, and the Shuptrines continued touring for another month, relieved to be promoting *Jericho* on their own. In Atlanta, Dickey had talked to Shuptrine about collaborating on another coffee-table book about the ocean. "The ocean," he intoned over drinks, "we've got to get out on that ocean, Hubert."[40] In a few years, they considered joining forces on a coffee-table book about Appalachian culture, but personal differences and Shuptrine's post-*Jericho* troubles with Oxmoor House jeopardized their collaboration. Shuptrine's argument with Oxmoor arose from his contract, which stipulated that he get a bonus if *Jericho*'s initial print run of 150,000 sold out. In the month of October 1974, Oxmoor had sold over 100,000 copies at $40 per copy; on January 1, 1975, the price having climbed to $60 per copy, the book had kept selling; by 1981, some reports claimed that 170,000 copies had been sold. The *Houston Post* noted that Frank Sinatra alone had ordered 500 copies as Christmas gifts (Dickey quipped that he didn't know Sinatra had five hundred friends). The impressive figures notwithstanding, bookstores returned numerous unsold copies. Because it cost so much to hand bind *Jericho*—about $12 per book—approximately 25,000 additional copies were left unbound. Nevertheless, Oxmoor announced a colossal sell out. Shuptrine failed to get his bonus, brought suit, and ultimately prevailed. Considering *Jericho*'s financial windfall, Dickey's earnings also were modest. He complained vociferously about his niggardly contract on the tour, telling Shuptrine that he wanted "to see the color of their money."[41] His royalty agreement allowed him only $1 per book. After earning back his $25,000 advance, he saw the color of about $150,000 in all.

Dickey greeted *Jericho*'s financial and popular success, which had been helped by hundreds of newspaper reviews, with a combination of glee and embarrassment. With Lewis King and Al Braselton in Atlanta, he seemed eager to distance himself from the book. He knew that some highbrow critics would dismiss *Jericho* as hackwork. On November 30, Jonathan Yardley did exactly that in the *New Republic*, calling the book a "colossal ornament . . . for regional chauvinists to wallow in, sliding happily around in the red-clay murk of Dickey's prose."[42] Yardley was thinking of passages like the description of leaving Arkansas: "And then much east comes into us. With the change-magic of the Great River come back as we go over, we are somewhere else now. . . . Mountains, yes, but also big, never-level fields not with a lot of horses, but with a few, for all that field-space. A few, but these immortal."[43] To the benefit of Dickey's wallet, most readers ignored such muddled sentences, focused on Shuptrine's images, and skipped to more-evocative "flickers" about the South's places, people, and traditions.

While occasionally professing contempt for *Jericho*, Dickey continued to promote the book when he returned to Columbia. He badgered friends at *Newsweek* and *Time* to review it and planned to pitch the book to them on his way to a December award ceremony for *Jericho* held by *Playboy*, which had published excerpts. His concern for *Jericho*'s fate was evident in a letter he wrote the *New York Times* in November that berated the newspaper for not reviewing *Jericho* and for not putting it on its bestseller list: "The hard-cover edition of *Deliverance* was on your list for seven or eight months, and the combined sales of the book came to about seventy-five thousand, over a period of about a year. *Jericho* has done twice that in two months, and (the computers have spoken) bids fair to go well over half a million."[44] He hoped he could shame the *Times* into taking notice.

All Dickey's promotional activities on *Jericho*'s behalf left him run-down and ill by the end of 1974. When Al Braselton drove to Columbia to get his copy of

Jericho signed, Dickey said he had recently gone to the hospital for surgery to correct his intestinal problems. He was sober, gloomy, quiet, and still having problems digesting food. He seemed to look at life and his old friend from a posthumous distance. Braselton recalled: "He autographed my book . . . 'To Al Braselton, in memory.'" They spoke briefly, but Dickey was too tired to socialize. Maxine entered the room and said in a maternal way: "Jim, I think you'd better take a nap." He agreed, turned away from Braselton, and walked down the hall. "See you"[45] was all he said to his friend.

Jericho convinced many in the literary community that Dickey was pandering to the gods of commerce. The gods were certainly answering his prayers. By the end of 1974, the windfall from his various books was substantial; he had collected a $30,000 installment for *Alnilam*, over $50,000 in royalties from *Deliverance*, $26,000 from other publications, and about $100,000 from his readings, investments, and USC salary. After the *Jericho* tour, Andrew Lytle wrote a kindly letter admonishing him to withdraw to his "cave of making." At the beginning of 1975, he showed signs that he might acquiesce. When Nancy Duncan of Omaha Community Playhouse asked him to collaborate on a musical based on one of his favorite books, James Agee's *Let Us Now Praise Famous Men*, he declined. He turned down other offers as well, mainly so he could finish one of his most ambitious poems to date, *The Zodiac*.

29. "Star-Beasts of Intellect and Madness" (1975–1976)

As early as April 1973, Dickey reported to Stewart Richardson and Ken McCormick that he was writing "a major work, having to do with the human body and its relationship to the universe, as well as treating the artist and the self-destructiveness entailed in creativity." The advice he gave his editors about what to do with the manuscript in case he died "in a blown-apart aircraft commandeered by some political nut or criminal" was one measure of his high hopes for the poem. He passed along his usual instructions about making the poem noticeable: "The main point here is to raise a great deal of excitement about the *appearance* of the poem, which you and I will then, when the time is right and the excitement is sufficient, issue as a volume of poetry."[1] He wanted the editors to give advance notice to *Esquire*, the *Atlantic*, *Harper's*, *Playboy*, and *Time*. In April of 1975, he wrote the English poet W. S. Graham, whom he called "the finest poet to ever come out of the British Isles, and one of the finest in the world," that after his masterwork was published, he would share Graham's international reputation: "I have just completed a 29-page poem, *The Zodiac*. I think that it may be the piece of work to rival *The Wasteland*."[2] His editor friends, unfortunately, disagreed. Robert Shnayerson, the editor-in-chief at *Harper's*, spoke for the dissenting majority when he judged the poem too long, too elusive, and too opaque. Howard Moss at the *New Yorker* and Gordon Lish at *Esquire* agreed. Dickey was once again feeling the pangs of multiple rejections.

Dickey felt inordinately attached to *The Zodiac* because it was his most comprehensive confession. He told the poet R. T. Smith that he intended *The Zodiac* to be a "vindication of the daemonic poet, the desperately serious clown, hopeful genius, and wastrel": "It's an affirmation of the European imaginative tradition, the origin of all literature in the western world. It's the chronicle of the last ditch stand of a rootless man who has come home . . . , tried to relate himself to the starry heavens, and in a small bare room attempts to align his fragile body to the forces of creation. He will fail. He will die. But he is trying. His is the eternal delusion of the artist that he can read the universe. The triumph is in the trying."[3] The poem amounted to an allegory of Dickey's prodigal travels as bard, demon, clown, and wastrel.

As a midwife several times removed from the original poem, Dickey attempted to rewrite rather than translate Hendrik Marsman's "The Zodiac." Marsman had published "De Dierenriem" in Dutch, but Dickey used A. J. Barnouw's translation, which he had first read in a 1947 *Sewanee Review* and later in Barnouw's anthology of Dutch poetry, *Coming After*. Dickey had gravitated to the poem as a Vanderbilt student because he, like the poem's hero, had returned to his native land after an adventurous hiatus during World War II. The fact that Marsman was a casualty of the war made the poem even more poignant. Dickey's return to the South in 1968, his ritual of locating himself among the stars with sextants, and his alcoholic self-destructiveness rekindled his interest in Marsman. Referring to the original "Zodiac," Dickey said:

> I thought his idea for the poem was good but that the poem itself was not very good. I decided to use the idea, which is about an alcoholic sailor who comes home to write the ultimate poem that will link up the mortal human body with the heavens. The sailor believes that the poet is the person who will reveal the true relation of the mortal human body and the stars that something or someone called "God" has chosen to place in the particular relationship in which they find themselves, forming mythic figures which the poet believes add up to a form of universal celestial writing that only the poet can read and interpret through the divine medium of words. The sailor feels that the astronomer cannot read these symbols, nor can the astronaut, nor the philosopher, the metaphysician, nor the computer. The deciphering of the zodiac is in the hands of the poet, and his alone. It is the attempt of a drunken, half mad sailor who comes back to his home city of Amsterdam to have it out with God. . . . "The Zodiac" is an account of one dying man's attempt to read what he believes God has said—is saying each clear night to all of us.[4]

In a letter to his former student Ross Bennett, who had returned home to Australia, Dickey was more emphatic about the poet's godly aspirations: "The poem is really about one man's attempt to say the impossible *word*, the Lord's Logos itself. Every poet believes that by drunkenness or seizure (or both) he can arrive at the point of uttering a Word which in a new sense will create—rather than *recreate*—everything that is."[5] According to Dickey, alcoholic spirits allowed the poet access to divine spirits and to the supernatural assumption—some would say delusion—that the poet is the god of a new creation.

Other factors drew Dickey to Marsman's poem. In "The Zodiac" he found a new, compelling version of the heroic quest. Having emphasized the painful initiations and trials of the hero's "monomythic" journey in *Deliverance*, in *The Zodiac* he concentrated on the final stage—the disillusioning return. In his garret, which Marsman's translator describes as "A vacuum, an absolute white now, / Stained only by a faded wall paper," the weary traveler looks out on "the agonized obscurity / Of the dead city's hellish neon light." He suffers from the sort of metropolitan acedia common to wasteland figures in Baudelaire and Eliot. Because he deems the symbols in his poems "tokens of a vision dead," he seeks a new afflatus from God's "book of nature," specifically from the stars God has "written" in the form of constellations. Leaving his garret, Marsman's alter ego tours Amsterdam, fastening on images of time, illness, and decay. He chooses Cancer or the Crab as the most appropriate symbol in the zodiac for his dark thoughts, but re-creates it as a surreal lobster at time's "stations of the cross." Afflicted by the pangs mortal flesh is heir to, the lobster prays to Christ for immortal redemption. Because the creator of the lobster concedes that "the images of the gods were shattered" years ago, like a Dutch Wallace Stevens he struggles to cast off his nostalgia for orthodox religion and dig "deeper into earth's mystery" and into his own imagination for signs of God. Debating every idea he advances, he warns himself that he is on the verge of solipsism. He needs to escape the "insect plague / Of his own thoughts"—including the lobster, a relative of the spider—and embrace a simpler, more natural life.

Marsman's cosmic poet walks all night to his boyhood home, but finds little consolation among memories of his agonized mother, his otherworldly father, and his former self, who wrote murderous poems about unrequited love. Recalling his mother's advice to "Never look back at youth," he shifts his focus to his adult travels. These, unfortunately, have ended in paralyzing despair and loveless solitude. One of the few inklings of contentment comes when a friend arrives to drink and talk "About friends and poems, / Women and politics." Prospects improve in the final section when, his poetic inspiration returning, he prepares to embark on an epic that draws on "the immemorial European song / That sounded at the dawn of culture." If he can maintain his exalted mood, he will elevate his epic into the "firmament of intellect and dream"[6] and thereby rival God's heavenly creations.

Following the precepts of Ezra Pound, Robert Lowell, Robert Bly, and other modern translators, Dickey imposed his own voice and obsessions on Marsman's poem to create something radically different from the original. Marsman's persona broods quietly, imagines a strangely devotional lobster only once, and enjoys a social drink with a friend at the poem's end. Aware of the life-negating effects of introspection, he warns against coupling with the intellect's "cold womb" and becoming a solipsistic "hermaphrodite." Dickey transformed Marsman's hero into an image of his own drunken, garrulous self, careening between sublimity and bathos. Dickey's poet drinks to the point of delirium tremens and obsessively brags about supplementing God's zodiac with a new constellation—a lobster. He admits to impotence with women and a change in his sexual inclinations: "the seed he thinks he's got available to give / Some woman, fades back / Deep into his balls / . . . and some weird change comes on:

/ Our man may be getting double-sexed / Or something worse / or better." Has he become bisexual? Has his solipsism resulted in complete onanism? Dickey merely drops hints of his sexual quandaries.

In addition to overhauling the relatively innocent contents of Marsman's poem, Dickey shatters the approximations of iambic pentameter in Barnouw's translation. Using the long poems of Pound, Williams, and Charles Olson as models, he indents his long and short unmetered lines at different intervals in an attempt to revitalize the flat, archaic lines of the Marsman translation. He also tries to enliven his ruminations with vernacular outbursts. "Hot damn, here they come!" he shouts as he envisions his poetic images as drunken ants dancing on paper. "Shit, I don't know where I am," he worries in his room. "Well, son of a bitch / . . . Goddamn / I've misused myself   I've fucked up   I haven't worked / I've traveled and screwed too much," he confesses. The narrator keeps up an unremitting jeremiad against himself: "Christ / Would you tell me why my head keeps thinking / Up these half-assed, useless images?" He addresses God similarly: "Listen, you universal son of a bitch / I've heard it all   I've said it all— / You're talking to a poet now, so don't give me a lot of shit." Behind the speaker's accusations is the conviction that his life is as empty as the drained bottles that surround him; he has drunk himself into oblivion. If Dickey's sailor-poet hopes to utter God's Logos, he ends up babbling like an intoxicated bum on the street. If, like Lucifer, he wants to usurp God's place in the great chain of being, he is more "Like a man / Bartending for God" or, more accurately, for himself. He tries to reconnect with the stars and the cosmic mysteries they evoke, but he rarely escapes his besotted imagination to do so. He pledges to create "star-beasts of intellect and madness,"[7] but his poetic Zodiac is only intermittently sublime.

What Dickey desperately needed was what Eliot received from Ezra Pound while working on The Waste Land—a sober surgeon to cut, reorder, and reinvigorate his inchoate poem. Yet, even with a scrupulous editor, it is hard to conceive of The Zodiac so improved that it could justify the sort of claims Dickey made to a South Carolina reporter in the fall of 1976: "It has been rumored in literary circles that my book The Zodiac may be the greatest long poem to be written since Eliot's The Wasteland."[8] The poem does, in fact, allude to The Waste Land. "Oh God you rocky landscape   give me, Give / Me drop by drop / desert water at least,"[9] Dickey writes near the end of The Zodiac. The only refreshing water his doomed quester finds, however, is aquavit.

In life, as in art, alcohol continued to get the better of James Dickey. On leave from teaching in September 1975, his drinking landed him in jail and nearly got him killed. After visiting one of his favorite watering holes in Columbia, he drove the 1968 Jaguar he had given Chris, and which Chris had returned to him, into a utility pole on Garners Ferry Road near the Veterans' Hospital. South Carolina patrolman Kevin Mooney discovered him in his car, his head and face bleeding, and realized he was drunk. Fellow officer J. R. Swicher conducted a breathilizer test and concluded that Dickey was practically embalmed. In an account of the accident that made it into Time magazine, Swicher recounted: "He kept cursing me and said he was going to whip my ass."[10] When an ambulance arrived, the officers informed Dickey that they wanted the driver, who happened to be black, to examine him for injuries. Dickey angrily protested that he was not going to be checked by any "nigger."[11] Dickey took a swing at Mooney, who was in charge of making the arrest, and the two policemen handcuffed Dickey and pushed him into the squad car.

Dickey prepared a wittier version of his accident for his friends. He told Don Greiner that his first words on crawling out of his smashed Jaguar were: "Better DUI than DOA."[12] He told David Havird that he had, indeed, hit the cop with a punch. George Garrett heard that Dickey had crashed his car a little before dawn and "just hung there, all snarled up in the belt, and fell asleep until the cops came along." After he was booked at the Columbia jail, according to Garrett, Dickey called Maxine, who in turn called their lawyer. The lawyer assured her that Dickey would not lose his license. "But [the] Lawyer wanted to impress the seriousness of all this on Dickey, so he said he would wait until *after* breakfast to bail out Big Jim. Breakfast, a particularly repellent meal at the jail, was served at 7:00 A.M. Dickey was out and on the way home by 7:30 A.M." Several weeks later Ben Greer visited Dickey at his house and was surprised to hear him coopting scenes from *Slammer*, Greer's novel based on his experiences as a prison guard:

> Then all of a sudden Dickey goes into a long story about how he was once a trusty in prison, with the run of the place, and how one day he went into the empty room where the electric chair is kept. Sat in it. Strapped one arm in place. Sat there and imagined what it would be like to be electrocuted. Very moving scene.
>
> Only trouble was that it comes directly out of Ben Greer's first novel— *Slammer*. Ben is a real nice, polite Southern boy but this was going too far, taking his own story almost word for word. "Damn it, Jim!" Ben burst out. "There isn't any electric chair in the Columbia city drunk tank!" Dickey blinked briefly, sipped his bourbon, but kept a poker face. Never daunted.
>
> "Ben," he said quietly. "It's a *very small* electric chair. A lot of people don't even know it's there."
>
> Ever since then, we . . . have pictured Big Jim sitting on a little bitty electric chair, about the size of a potty chair, a very low-voltage model that would take a week and a half to kill you.[13]

The day after the accident, Maxine called David Havird and, without identifying herself, asked abruptly: "Where does Paula Goff live?" Havird pretended he didn't know. "Don't think about it; just answer, Where does Paula Goff live?" As it turned out, even though Havird knew Goff well, he didn't know her address. Convinced that Havird was trying to protect her husband, Maxine explained that she had been in Litchfield when the crash occurred. "Jim didn't even have the sense to call the lawyer," she snapped. According to Maxine, the lawyer had heard about the crash on the news and gone to the jail to bail out his client. Maxine wanted her husband to stay in jail longer, believing that the punishment might curb his recklessness. She discussed with Havird the story that Dickey had told about driving to the Italian restaurant Labrasca's, getting stuck in the wrong lane during five o'clock traffic, not being able to make a turn, and ending up near the Veterans' Hospital. As he talked to Maxine, Havird heard someone pick up another phone in the house. Maxine whispered that it was Jim and that he should hang up. Havird got off the phone. Around the time of the accident, Maxine told Chris that she was definitely leaving her "jackass" of a husband. Chris again encouraged her to get a divorce.[14]

Dickey was indeed headed for Labrasca's when he swerved off the road. During the afternoon before the mishap he had asked Paula Goff to join him for pizza. She drove to the restaurant and waited. Dickey failed to arrive, so she drove to Lelia's Court, and, not finding Dickey there, returned to Labrasca's. On the way she thought she saw Dickey in a police car. She returned to her West Columbia home, where her children, having heard of Dickey's car wreck on the news, were convinced that their mother had been in the accident as well. Goff dutifully went to the jail, posted the $132.50 bail, and took Dickey to Lelia's Court, where she cleaned his head wound and washed the blood from his fancy Mexican shirt. When Dickey's lawyer, Kirkman Finlay, came to the house, Dickey asked Goff to mix them both drinks.

Dickey tried to turn his collision with the utility pole to his advantage. He told the *Time* reporter that it should inspire "a couple of pretty good poems."[15] Although he wasn't badly hurt, he used the accident as an excuse to refuse unwanted invitations. When Doubleday asked him to read with Nikki Giovanni, Louise Glück, Carolyn Kizer, Mark Strand, Galway Kinnell, and Stanley Kunitz at an October 8 gathering called "Poets for Freedom to Read," he declined, citing his recent crash. A little like Tom Sawyer pretending to have died to get sympathy, he began circulating rumors that he was near death. In his fantasies, cancer rather than a utility pole was the agent of doom. A concerned Robert Dana wrote on November 23 to substantiate the rumor. He said that he had heard stories from Indiana to Florida that Dickey was dying of terminal cancer. Dickey reported cheerfully: "I am a long way from dying. . . . I do not nor have I ever had cancer. I hope that will always be the case."[16] In the aftermath of the crash, some friends encouraged Dickey to get medical help for his drinking. J. Watson Smoot suggested that he go to the Silver Hill Foundation's psychiatric hospital for alcoholics in New Canaan, Connecticut. Dickey would hear none of it.

As shades of the prison house and the tomb descended on him at the end of 1975, Dickey turned his attention to his sons and grandson. Although his comparison of grandchildren to mistresses—"You can enjoy 'em, but you're not stuck with them"[17]—was calculated to disturb, to show his affection for his five-year-old grandson, Tucky, he wrote a poem that resembled "Heaven of Animals" in its description of an innocent Tucky "killing" wild animals in his sleep with a pop-gun. On December 13, 1975, he sent "Tucky the Hunter" to Joan Raines, Theron's wife and business partner, with the hope that she could find a book publisher and illustrator. Happy that Inman Mays had helped Chris get a temporary job as a writer for the *Washington Post Guide to Washington*, Dickey now focused on Kevin's future. To help Kevin get into college, on November 4 he wrote the dean of admissions at the University of Virginia. Soon Kevin visited Charlottesville for meetings with the basketball coach, the dean, and other university officials. Dickey also wrote Scott Donaldson about the possibility of his son going to William and Mary.

Dickey helped and hindered his sons as his moods dictated. His competitive instincts were aroused by Chris's intellectual inclinations and by Kevin's athletic prowess. Chris once observed about his father: "He saw me as competition before I was born. He saw me as an extension of himself."[18] Chris was Oedipus, the mythical usurper. One of the reasons Chris decided to abandon his film aspirations was because he wanted to avoid competition with his father (after his master's in film he also realized that much of filmmaking had to do with raising money). As Chris evolved into a prominent journalist for the *Washington Post* and then for *Newsweek*, his father, while proud of his son's success, continued to compete and antagonize, to bless and damn. "My son is a journalist and a very good one," he told one interviewer. "He's a demon reporter and scooper of facts on the spot and all that sort of thing. That part of writing has no appeal to me at all. . . . Facts bother me. I like to make it all up."[19] In his hierarchy of values, the father's fantasies ranked higher than the son's facts.

Dickey confronted his other son in a more physical way—on the basketball court. Kevin had withdrawn from Saint Mark's School near Boston at the start of his second year and transferred to Winyah Academy in South Carolina. There he became the highest scorer in the academy's history. Dickey found out how good Kevin was in a father-son basketball game. Kevin recalled: "I was scoring left and right over Dad and I remember I had a breakaway layup and he had run down the court. He was waiting for me when I came down the floor and he went right underneath me and body-blocked me and took my feet right out from under me. I went down. I almost did a somersault in the air."[20] Stunned by this Dennis Rodman–like hit that could have seriously hurt him, Kevin decided to take more outside shots. When Kevin later became a highly successful doctor, his father invoked the same pecking order he had imposed on Chris. The poet, he stated on numerous occasions, was superior to the doctor, who could help people live but not make their lives worth living.

In 1976, Dickey continued to involve his family in his own work—namely, the two films, *Call of the Wild* and *Gene Bullard*. He went to Hollywood in March and returned after a rough cut of *Call of the Wild* had been completed. Dickey brought with him Maxine—Chris would join them—and an unlikely collaborator, Al Braselton, who at first balked at Dickey's request for help on the proposed spin-off of the movie—a TV series to be called *Thornton* (it was never made). On the flight west, Dickey chatted excitedly about Hollywood and all the money he had made and could make there. Maxine interjected that Braselton had been invited to ensure that Jim got his fair share from the Hollywood agents and producers. Noticing Charlton Heston get on the plane at the Dallas–Fort Worth airport, Dickey talked to him about their two versions of *Call of the Wild*, but he showed the most excitement when they crossed the mountains east of Los Angeles. He remarked to Braselton: "Have you ever seen anything so wild and untamed? I wonder what kind of animals live there? Me and you have got to go hunting up there one of these days."[21] In the airport, Dickey got lost as he greeted people like a movie star. Maxine and Braselton found the luggage, tipped the porter, and requisitioned the cab.

Once they arrived at the posh hotel, Dickey drank bourbon and spoke to Braselton about the way he depended on alcohol for enthusiasm. Maxine called the various people involved with *Call of the Wild* and *Gene Bullard*. (Dickey usually refused to take part in such mundane matters, choosing instead to goad Maxine: "Get on with your palaver. Hell, I could have had three of my Hollywood mistresses over here by now.")[22] Dickey was heartened by the way *Call of the Wild* was proceeding. Director Jerry Jameson and photographer Matthew Leonetti had done the filming during the 1975–76 winter in Jackson Hole, Wyoming. In the mountainous terrain that resembled the Klondike, John Beck played the tenderfoot prospector Thornton, Bernard Fresson the Frenchman who led him astray, Donald Moffatt a lost, snow-blinded prospector, John McLiam a rich miner with a lust for gambling, and Penelope Windust a saloon girl. The star, however, was Buck, a 140-pound mixed-breed dog borrowed from a Santa Clara ranch and trained to pull sleds. His fights with other sled dogs and responses to the prospector's harsh life were especially captivating. After seeing an early version of the film with Tony Ganz, Charles Fries, and Malcolm Stuart, Dickey remarked in an interview with the *Los Angeles Times*: "That dog'll tear the heart right out of you."[23] Dickey especially liked the film's quiet ending, in which Buck, having discovered the dead miners, gets bloody revenge on the killers and abandons his human masters. Dickey, however, had one objection— the film's "voice-over," which he found sententious.

Because *Gene Bullard* had languished at several film companies, Dickey was also in Hollywood to stir up interest in his screenplay. Fries and Stuart watched Dickey give a rousing summary of his script to Guy MacElwaine, a top executive at Warner Brothers. His description of the scene where a rattlesnake slides between a character's thighs and moonlit breasts so transfixed MacElwaine that he agreed to help produce it. Dickey's Hollywood agent, Robert Littman, brokered a deal with Fries and Warner Brothers that would pay Dickey $40,000 for the first draft of the *Bullard* screenplay, $20,000 for revisions, $35,000 for another draft if Warner Brothers and Fries went forward with the film, an additional $25,000 if they made the film, and a $30,000 bonus plus royalties if Dickey received sole screen credit. Glad to be working with the company that had made *Deliverance*, Dickey was also in a delicate position. Metro-Goldwyn-Mayer had already shown interest in the screenplay and paid Dickey $15,000 to work on it. Dickey had to get a "quit claim" before accepting Warner Brothers' offer. Luckily, MGM had already expressed discontent with Dickey for his failure to meet two 1975 deadlines.

By the early fall of 1976, the frustrations that had dogged Dickey during the composition of the *Deliverance* and *Call of the Wild* screenplays returned with a vengeance. Fries and Warner Brothers kept demanding changes to every final draft of *Gene Bullard* he submitted. In October 1976, bristling at the thought of studio executives tampering further with his screenplay, he refused to make any more revisions. And why hadn't he received the final $10,000 promised in his contract? He wrote Fries on October 1:

> I was nonplussed at this, as were both my agents because I had fulfilled my part of the bargain, that is to say my part of the contract. You then asked me to make extensive revisions in the script. This seemed excessive to me, but because of personal liking for you, Chuck, and for Mal and Tony, I put

a whole summer's work into the revisions you suggested. If that is not the fulfillment of a contract to write a screenplay I do not know where to find it. And still no forthcoming of the contracted payment. Now I am absolutely dumbfounded at the request to make additional changes without the slightest indication of the monies for work I have spent a year in doing. One puts one's time in on a project for which payment has been promised. Things like taxes come into the picture. . . . I am bewildered by all of this, but I can categorically guarantee that I will not touch the script of Gene Bullard again until I have received payment for the first draft. I'd as soon drop the whole project rather than proceed on this basis.[24]

The real problem with his script, which no amount of cosmetic surgery could correct, was the fundamental unbelievability of its gothic scenes and characters.

Like Deliverance, Gene Bullard expresses Dickey's anxieties about "manliness," but without the novel's finesse. A doctor questions Gene's ability to "act like a man" and catch the killers of his deputy: "You're bluffing, Gene. You always was one to put on a show. . . . You know you ain't gonna have to do nothing." Dickey's quandaries about "manly love" surface again in the bond between the criminals Joby and Makens, who talk about their homosexual relations on a work farm. Dickey's sadoeroticism erupts between Gene and his girlfriends, Beth and Lila. In the end, after witnessing devastating car wrecks, burning bodies, and decapitated family members tied to trees, Gene decides to marry his tough sweetheart, Beth, who proclaims: "You can tell your friends that Beth Culclasher Bullard said on her wedding day that, 'I brought to my bed a valiant husband, and bore him men. And I want that on my tombstone, too.'"[25] While the return of the men to their women in Deliverance was more subdued, it was also more convincing.

The amount of money Robert Littman was securing for scripts like Gene Bullard was substantial. On May 25, 1976, Littman wrote Dickey that he had closed a deal with Steve Tish and Columbia Pictures for The Spell. The contract promised Dickey $20,000 to start writing a treatment in August, $65,000 for the first draft of a screenplay if Columbia elected to go forward with the project, $30,000 for a second draft and revisions, $20,000 for a final draft, a $30,000 bonus if Dickey retained sole screenplay credit, and then royalties and future bonuses. Like so many screenplays in Hollywood, The Spell evaporated somewhere between the contract and the screen. Gene Bullard suffered the same fate. Rejecting Dickey's chary view of the script as potentially another Deliverance, Warner Brothers refused to film it. Fries and Stuart tried to "reactivate" it over the years but never had any luck. As Dickey's frustration with his Hollywood ventures increased, he soon parted ways with Littman.

The strain caused by his struggles with Hollywood may have aggravated Dickey's digestive problems. By September 1976, he realized that he was desperately ill and in need of major surgery. Other events added to his mounting anxiety. On September 22, Rosemary Daniell wrote him about her book, Fatal Flowers, which contained a searing account of their love affair. Maxine's health was also precarious. While Dickey coped with alcohol abuse remarkably well, Maxine was gradually succumbing to its destructive effects. Her liver became cirrhotic. A new friend to witness the Dickeys' desperate straits was Ben Franklin, a USC English professor who had arrived from the University of Michigan during the summer of 1976. Franklin, who was as healthy minded as his namesake, had met Dickey in early October at a welcoming party for new English Department members. Another colleague who came to the Dickeys' aid was the classics professor Ward Briggs. Briggs had first encountered Dickey in the mid-1960s as an undergraduate at Washington and Lee. At a Neruda conference held at USC in 1974, he had reminded Dickey of their earlier meeting in Virginia, when Dickey lashed out at his college dean's wife over dinner. (She had suggested that Kevin go to a special school that her two daughters had attended, and Dickey had muttered drunkenly: "There's nothing wrong with that boy that wasn't wrong with me at the same age, and there was nothing wrong with me at that age that wasn't cured by fucking every girl in North Georgia and South Carolina.")[26] Amused by Dickey's eruption at the time, Briggs soon realized the deleterious effects of Dickey's drinking on himself and Maxine.

One night in mid-October 1976, Maxine got out of bed and hemorrhaged in the bathroom. There was so much blood on the floor that Dickey initially thought a burglar had attacked her. At the hospital, doctors discovered that the blood vessels around her esophagus had burst and released nearly half her blood. She was in intensive care when her son Chris, who was living in Washington, and Kevin, who was in his first year at Washington and Lee, arrived to see her. About the gruesome night Dickey later told a journalist: "I held her in my arms, bleeding to death [between] blood-splattered suburban bathroom walls."[27] The doctors, fortunately, managed to stanch the bleeding.

Without Maxine managing the household, Dickey was bereft. On October 18, he wrote his CPA Talcott Stith about his domestic and financial problems and told him that Maxine had "always made deposits, kept records, paid taxes and issued checks for our living expenses and other purposes."[28] Dickey could do none of this, so he asked Stith to take charge. In the hospital Maxine remained relatively stable, which gave Dickey hope that she would recover and soon return to the house. On the night of October 27, he attended a USC reading by Elizabeth Bishop. Despite his derogatory remarks about her ("of course Elizabeth Bishop is no good,"[29] he wrote the biographer Jeffrey Meyers), Dickey was determined to have her sign his books and pose for a picture with him. She responded coldly: "Sir! I do NOT pose for pictures."[30] Others besides Bishop were startled by Dickey's preoccupation with photographs and signatures. Ward Briggs asked: "Aren't you going out to see Maxine at the hospital?" "No," Dickey responded, "I want to get Bishop to sign my books."[31] Dickey in fact did go to the hospital after the reading. No doubt sensing his priorities, Maxine wanted her mother rather than her husband to be with her. The altercation that ensued, in which Maxine screamed at him, may have contributed to her final collapse. Around eleven o'clock on the night of October 27, she hemorrhaged again and died on her way to the operating room. Hearing the sad news, Don Greiner and William Nolte drove directly to Dickey's house. Dickey opened the door, and said: "Well, she's gone."[32] The next day, Al Braselton called to enquire about Maxine. Dickey said in an exhausted, husky voice that she had expired "in an explosion of blood."[33] He told Braselton about clutching Maxine's body in his arms as she died. He asked his friend to drive to Columbia to comfort him.

Because alcoholics frequently die from esophagal bleeding—Jack Kerouac died in such a way—doctors sometimes call it "the Bowery bum's death." Maxine's two hemorrhages had been caused by "portal hypertension," a direct consequence of her cirrhosis. The blood traveling through her portal vein could not pass through her liver, so damaged was it by years of alcoholic abuse. Because of the increased pressure in the blocked vein, the blood sought a detour to the heart by way of the veins around the esophagus. Not used to so much blood, the esophageal veins burst. To stop the bleeding, the doctors inserted a tube into Maxine's throat and inflated it to put pressure on the veins. They secured the tube in an unforgettable way by putting a football helmet on Maxine's head and attaching the throat tube to the face mask. "That was one of the last images I have of my mother,"[34] Kevin remarked.

Chris was equally haunted by his mother's bloody death (the mother of the main character in his 1997 novel *Innocent Blood* dies in the same way), and by the fact that his father didn't call him in Washington to tell him about it. His aunt Patsy called. Chris had visited his mother for several days shortly before her death. Her hair matted with sweat, an oxygen tube taped beneath her nose, and various intravenous needles dripping liquids into her arms, she was hardly recognizable. Aware of her husband's inability to cope at home, Maxine had asked her mother to get a box of bills for Chris to take home; she didn't know who would pay them. Because of her festering anger toward her husband, Chris had to make up excuses to keep him away from the hospital. Assured his mother was improving, Chris returned to his job at the *Washington Post*. He called the hospital from his office to check on her, only to find out she was in great pain. The guilt over not being with his mother at her death only complicated Chris's feelings toward his father.

Maxine's untimely death at the age of fifty could have been averted, but her sons could not have changed her habits or the marriage that had provoked them. Chris had tried numerous times and failed. Doctors had warned Maxine of her cirrhotic liver, but, as Braselton pointed out: "She had continued to drink knowing almost certainly that it could kill her."[35] One of the reasons Dickey got so angry after Maxine died was because he knew her death was avoidable. The wife of Carl Zibart, who had become one of Maxine's close friends in Pawley's Island, where she and her husband vacationed, discovered how resentful Dickey was when she called to offer condolences. Dickey ranted over the phone: "She didn't have to die. The doctors warned her. I need her. I am lost without her. She knows everything. She had no business dying."[36] Was her death, to use one of her husband's favorite terms, a "virtual suicide"? Was it a "virtual murder"? Dickey occasionally admitted that he bore some of the responsibility for her demise. Shortly after her death, he told Chris in a moment of lachrymose agony: "Thirty years I was married to that woman. THIRTY YEARS. And I killed her. . . . I killed her. If I hadn't fucked around. If. But—and I loved her dearly—but if only there had been some good, natural sex at home." Chris told him bluntly that he would have slept with other women anyway. The fact that he had argued with her on her deathbed only compounded Dickey's guilt. In his memoir, *Summer of Deliverance*, Chris concluded acerbically: "I believed—I *knew*—that he had killed my mother. He belittled and betrayed her, humiliated her and forgot about her, then watched her over the course of a few years quietly, relentlessly poison herself with the whisky she had at her right hand all day long every day until she died."[37]

Many of the funeral guests gathered at the Dickey home the day before driving to All Saints Waccamaw Episcopal Church in Pawley's Island, where a service would be held. As they arrived, Dickey welcomed and offended them by turn. He hugged Al Braselton and Patsy Dickey, who had driven from Atlanta together, and told Al that he simply could not believe Maxine was dead: "You know, I feel like saying 'Maxine, hey Maxine, Al's here. Come on Maxine.' You know that you were one of her favorite people." Mrs. Tipton echoed these sentiments. Dickey's assistant Shaye Areheart seemed inconsolable; her eyes were red and swollen with grief. Jim Mann assisted by writing out directions to the Litchfield condominium and church. The mood in the house suddenly changed when the issue of Maxine's open coffin arose. Dickey remarked sardonically that he had no desire to view the "stuffed crow remains of Maxine down at the funeral home"[38] that night. Everyone fell silent. Kevin voiced his objection to seeing the open casket, too. When Dickey compared Maxine to a "dead dog by the road,"[39] Chris screamed with pain and anger.

Dickey's temper improved little overnight. Friends reuniting at the Lake Katherine house in the morning confronted a furious Mrs. Tipton about to hit her son-in-law for talking about Maxine's "gala coffin show."[40] She had lost her only daughter and was in no mood for her son-in-law's irreverent remarks. Tensions eased in Pawley's Island during the somber funeral inside the neoclassical, Doric-columned Episcopal Church. Dickey gave a moving rendition of the last section of Robert Penn Warren's *Audubon, a Vision*: "Tell me a story // In this century, and moment, of mania, / Tell me a story. // Make it a story of great distances, and starlight. // The name of the story will be Time, / But you must not pronounce its name. // Tell me a story of deep delight." The poem asks for a story's coherence and the sort of cosmic perspective that Dickey himself had tried to achieve in *The Zodiac*. It is a secular prayer for deliverance from the excess that led to Maxine's death. Dickey wrote Warren: "I could think of nothing of my own so fitting, or so likely to last, or to hang longer in the bearded oaks of Waccamaw Cemetery, at Litchfield, where we were all together."[41] For the formal part of the ceremony, John Templeton and another priest read the "Burial of the Dead" from *The Book of Common Prayer*.

The pallbearers—Michael Allin, Charles Guerry, Matthew Bruccoli, Bernie Dunlap, Calhoun Winton, and Al Braselton—carried the casket down the aisle and out to the grave. The sky was overcast. The coffin seemed heavy, and some of the pallbearers were unnerved by Maxine's body rolling from side to side as they stumbled over the rutted ground. Charles Guerry, one of Kevin's basketball friends, found the coffin unwieldy and remembered Dickey thanking them later: "I noticed that you men were struggling a bit. I was praying to the good Lord to lighten the load."[42] By a freshly dug hole the priest uttered his customary lines and threw a handful of dirt on the casket. In the family condominium, Dickey mused soberly to Braselton: "Well, I guess Maxine is going to spend the night in the ground tonight. I wonder if it's cold down there? She's going to have to get used to that." A woman standing nearby objected: "No, no, Jim, Maxine will be with her friends tonight." Dickey had the last word: "Well, wherever she is, she'll be giving them hell."[43] Braselton tried to cheer up Dickey on this grim Halloween day by discussing books he had been reading about Charles Ives.

"My whole world fell apart when Maxine died,"[44] Dickey told a reporter for the *Charlotte Observer.* Dickey recognized what others knew all along: Maxine had made his career as a writer possible. One of the Dickeys' closest friends, Matthew Bruccoli, once said: "Without Maxine Jim Dickey probably would not have become the successful literary figure he did become. She coped, she organized, she entertained, and she also raised very successful sons, whereas another woman would have given up on being a mother, faced with the difficulties she dealt with on a daily basis. She was totally devoted to Jim's career. . . . She was always dignified in situations that would have placed another woman in a humiliating position."[45] The lines from the English Renaissance poet Henry Constable—"I doo love thee as each flower / Loves the sunne's life-giving power"—that Dickey chose for Maxine's gravestone bore witness to his dependence on her. Now that his sun had vanished, he shriveled.

Three weeks after Maxine's death Dickey appeared to many as a rootless flower in a maelstrom. Reading at High Point College in North Carolina, where he had once studied as an aviation cadet, he made a public display of his abject mourning. Drunk and morose, he rambled on about the death of Maxine, the death of the South, and the uncontrollable drinking that would probably lead to his own death. His boast to reporters that he was drinking a fifth of liquor every day was also a plea for sympathy. To some in High Point's Memorial Hall, Dickey seemed delusional as he ranted against the modern South, contemporary books other than the ones written by his students, and magazines like the *New Yorker, Harper's,* and the *Atlantic Monthly.* He startled his audience further by telling them his wife had died during the previous week and that he had recently finished serving eighteen months in jail for manslaughter. A writer for the *Winston-Salem Journal,* Bill Collins, reported: "The Journal checked with police in Columbia, S.C., his hometown. A Columbia police investigator said he knew of no convictions of manslaughter and police records only show one charge of disorderly conduct listed against Dickey."[46] The newspaper also checked the date of Maxine's death and published it alongside Dickey's statement. The *Winston-Salem Journal* was not accustomed to the demonic logic of Dickey's fictions and probably knew nothing about his belief that he was partly responsible for his wife's death.

As he descended deeper into alcoholic despair, Dickey showed little besides contempt for all conventional ways of assuaging grief. Deriding religion as a pedestrian illusion, he substituted his own bizarre illusions in its place. To a reporter for the *National Observer,* who asked Dickey in early December whether he believed in an afterlife, he repeated earlier statements: "No. I saw Maxine lying there, and it could have just been a dead dog in the road."[47] His callous remarks belied his desperation; he could not accept the unalterable fact that Maxine had left him. He told the *National Observer* reporter that his grief was like a Caterpillar tractor he was trying to drag over the ground, yet he reached out to few people for help. Dickey's hostility toward others after Maxine died allowed him to savor his melancholy and guilt.

Dickey often thought about joining Maxine in Pawley's Island. He talked to the *National Observer* about suicide, and again recited the long list of his suicidal peers. Normally he lampooned Berryman, Plath, and Sexton; now he said sympathetically: "Their minds just eat 'em up. The level of intensity a poet lives at is such that it begins to get to him psychologically—till finally he's like an engine without a governor. So he destroys his body to get away from his mind." Should he put an end to his own mental agony as they had? "I've thought about my death a lot," he declared. "Once I thought I wanted to die by violence—get killed by a grizzly, maybe. But now I think I'd prefer to die by water, by drowning, not with others but alone. Just slip beneath it all."[48] Tired of the struggle to live without his wife, like Keats in "Ode to a Nightingale" or Frost in "Stopping by Woods on a Snowy Evening," Dickey brooded on an "easeful death." In the end he simply tried to drown his painful thoughts in alcohol.

Dickey found some relief when Doubleday published *The Zodiac* in a first edition of three thousand copies. He predicted the book would become a bestseller (it sold ten thousand copies) and give further evidence that he was "king of the cats." Dickey's hyperbolic claims for *The Zodiac* disguised his anxiety about the book's literary merit and about the state of his talent in general. In a letter to Dave Smith, he faced what he may have known all along: "*The Zodiac . . . of course* is a failure; there is no way that any poem which attempts to be a projection of booziness and confusion is ever going to be the kind of hand-fitted-together sort of 'success' that, say, *The Waste Land* is."[49] No matter what he really thought of *The Zodiac*'s merits, Dickey bullied family and friends to publish positive reviews. He told his son Chris, who now worked as an editor for the *Washington Post Book World*, to make sure that he printed something laudatory. "What's good for me is good for the family," he said. Chris protested. "Don't give me that shit," his father responded. "Just see that you do it—if you want those checks to keep coming in every month." Chris's parents hadn't sent any checks in two years. Rather than do what his father ordered, he withdrew from the reviewing process.

The reviews of *The Zodiac* were predictably mixed. Friends like Robert Penn Warren and Stanley Burnshaw published friendly words in the *New York Times Book Review* and the *Washington Post Book World,* and Peter Prescott compared the book favorably to other long modern poems like Berryman's "Homage to Mistress Bradstreet." Dave Smith in *Poetry* called it "an impressive failure,"[50] and many other critics agreed that the poem never fulfilled its lofty goals. This criticism—of ambition never quite achieved—would typify the reception given most of the books Dickey published for the rest of his life.

XII.

LA VITA NUOVA

30. Second Marriage (1976)

In early December 1976, reporters in Plains, Georgia, reminded President-Elect Jimmy Carter that Kennedy had summoned Robert Frost to write a poem for his inauguration and asked Carter if he would appoint a poet for his inauguration. Carter immediately suggested Dickey as a possibility. "I hate to knock other poets but he's the best poet I know," he said. Dickey learned of Carter's remark secondhand, and told the *Columbia Record:* "I don't think Carter would have mentioned to the press the possibility of inviting me to read unless he meant it, and he may or may not ask me, but I imagine that he will."[1] Later Carter joked that Dickey might stand a better chance of being his inaugural poet if he let him censor the poem. Dickey shot back, tongue-in-cheek, that he didn't believe in government censorship.

Dickey may not have known about Theron Raines's efforts on his behalf. When it looked like Carter would be elected president, Raines told a friend that if Carter won he would like Dickey to write a poem for the inauguration. The friend gave Raines the phone number of a film producer who worked for Carter. Raines contacted the producer, who was amenable to the suggestion. Raines called him again after the election, and the producer said, "Yes, I think we can do that."[2] As far as Dickey was concerned, no one ever formally asked him to write the poem; he decided to write it after reading Carter's comments in the newspaper: "When they printed the [inauguration] program and I saw my name on it I said to myself, 'I guess I am gonna do it so I better get crackin'."[3] In fact, Dickey had gone to Plains, Georgia, on December 3 for an appearance on *The Today Show* and probably consulted Carter or his aides about a presidential poem at that time.

Dickey had only about a month in which to compose what became "The Strength of Fields." To remove himself from memories of Maxine, he took his son Kevin to the Virgin Islands. According to Kevin: "Dad hardly ever left the room. He was drunk most of the time. It was an attempt to get us away from the house during a particular time of year that my mother loved—Christmas—and it was terrible."[4] The trip engendered a rift between father and son that widened over the following weeks and years. Unbeknownst to Kevin, other family members, and friends, Dickey had a secret: he planned to marry a student named Deborah Dodson, whom he had befriended during the fall. Perhaps because he knew how close Kevin had been to Maxine and how he would disapprove of a hasty marriage, in the Virgin Islands Dickey kept his marital plans to himself, drank, and worked on his poem.

Dickey was less discreet with students and strangers. According to the *State* reporter William Starr, several printed reports of his impending marriage had circulated by early December. In these Dickey had stated the principles that had guided his choice of a bride. "I don't care for those women's libber types," he growled sardonically. "I want a woman to be a slave to me."[5] Dickey chose an odd place to make his official announcement of marriage. On December 9, Dickey told his last poetry class of the term: "I'll remember this class. . . . You were with me in my need. When Maxine died. Yes! I'll remember . . . because I'm to MARRY this class. . . . Yes! . . . MARRY this class. Will the about to be Mrs. Dickey rise?" Deborah Dodson stood up, protesting: "Jim . . . , you didn't warn me." More like a drill instructor than a bridegroom, he commanded: "Sit Deborah. Congratulations later, class. I have much to say."[6] He proceeded with his lecture about the agonies and ecstasies of writing, with asides on suicidal poets and his wish to be buried by the Chattooga River. Some of the students cried and offered congratulations after class. Others fell silent before Dickey's operatic revelations. Charles Frazier, the future author of the bestselling novel *Cold Mountain*, thought the whole event was farcical and should have been kept private. Quiet and self-effacing, he was the antithesis of the histrionic Dickey.

According to Dickey, Deborah first became aware of him in high school after reading Peter Davison's 1967 article "The Difficulties of Being Major" in the *Atlantic Monthly*. She became more aware of him when she entered USC in the fall of 1969. Although she barely remembered going to one of his poetry readings in 1972, she met him there, and that same year spoke to him at Yevtushenko's USC reading. Having earned mainly As and Bs (as well as some Fs in theater) during her first two-and-a-half years at USC, she transferred to Coastal Carolina College, where she remained for the fall 1975 term, compiling As, Bs, and several incompletes. Afterward, she returned to USC.

Shaye Areheart claimed the honor of introducing Deborah to Dickey in late August 1976. In Dickey's office, helping him prepare for his first class of the fall semester, Areheart looked up to find a beautiful woman dressed in a black sheath dress standing in the doorway. She had signed up for Professor Dickey's poetry course but was concerned about her ability to keep up with the graduate students. She asked Areheart if her decision to enroll had been reckless. Areheart assured her that she had taken the class as an undergraduate, too. Deborah said: "I'd still feel better if I spoke to Doctor Dickey [sic]." Since Dickey was down the hall, Areheart told her to take a seat. When Dickey arrived, he puffed out his chest, sucked in his stomach, and exclaimed: "What do we have here?" Areheart replied: "This is Deborah Dodson. She signed up for your course."[7] Dickey spoke to Deborah for several minutes. Before long she was sitting in his poetry class. Dickey remembered thinking: "Who is this girl that looks like a fashion model or an actress, and how can she possibly know so much about Emily Dickinson?"[8] In the first class, Deborah asked from the front row: "Mr. Dickey, what are your hours?" "I knew the game was on,"[9] he later recalled. In mid-October, while Maxine was in the hospital, Jim Mann witnessed the "game" when he approached Dickey after class to talk. Ensconced in an intimate conversation with Deborah, Dickey asked Mann brusquely: "Can we have a few moments?" Mann stood to the side. More firmly Dickey said: "Alone?"[10] Mann took the hint and retreated.

Several months after their wedding, Dickey provided Maralyn Lois Polak at the *Philadelphia Inquirer* with other recollections of his fateful poetry class:

"Deborah just looked to me like a decorative little bric-a-brac in the classroom, a rather spectacular piece of student bric-a-brac. Pretty, distinctive-looking, very smart, a good student. I had no further interest than just lookin', which was quite a privilege. And then my wife of thirty years died. It wiped me out. Because everything had centered around her . . . I was pretty close to being totally demoralized by it. It was cataclysmic. . . . Then this marvelous girl just got me to understand she was there with me. That I was not going to be alone if I didn't want to be. She saved me, and I can never give her enough credit."[11] Over the next few years Dickey continued to tell friends that his new wife was his savior.

According to Dickey's version of his courtship, he and Deborah drifted together following Maxine's death. "Deborah sent flowers, and she was around the house after the funeral when people were trying to help," he said. Deborah had proposed living together to avoid gossip; Dickey would hear none of it. He told *People* magazine: "I would not live together with anyone. . . . I want a commitment. I consider myself a natural married man. Life would be all ego if you had nobody in on it with you. As I told my sons, Christopher and Kevin, 'Let's get the new life going.'"[12] Dickey informed William Starr that he had known Deborah for eight months before marrying her, even though, according to Areheart, they had become friends at the beginning of the fall term in 1976. Deborah had, in fact, gone to Maxine's funeral and accompanied Dickey to a Halloween party, which Shaye Areheart had organized. Several nights later she was at Lelia's Court to watch the election returns on television with Dickey, Bernie Dunlap, and Dunlap's wife. The Dunlaps left near midnight, and Deborah remained. Dunlap's wife commented: "My God, Maxine isn't even in the ground yet!"[13] Even before Maxine had died, USC professors had seen Dickey walking hand in hand with Deborah around campus. Ben Franklin, who had met Dickey just a week before, recalled: "I saw Jim in what I thought was a strange situation, walking hand in hand with what occurred to me was . . . an undergraduate woman. It turned out to be Deborah."[14] In hindsight, Franklin wondered if their friendship had been platonic; Dickey was certainly capable of asexual friendships with women.

Dickey's wedding on December 30, 1976, like his first, had few traditional trappings. A champagne brunch at the Wade Hampton Motel preceded a brief civil ceremony around noon before a justice of the peace at the Richland County Courthouse. According to Dottie Ashley, who reported the event for the *Columbia Record*, Dickey "seemed nervous as a caged leopard"[15] as he paced the courthouse corridor. Only four other people attended the wedding. Shaye Areheart was maid-of-honor, and her boyfriend, Jamie, was best man. Dottie and Franklin Ashley were the only others to witness the ceremony. Carrying a bouquet of yellow rosebuds and white carnations, and wearing a pin-striped suit with a white blouse and gold necklace, Deborah looked radiant beside her anxious husband. As she climbed the steps, she quipped: "This is the last chance to back out." Dickey retorted: "I ain't gonna take it, and you ain't gonna get it." Dickey later remarked that he liked getting married with working folks: "They're a lotta people around here with overalls, wrenches and machinery, and that's the way it ought to be."[16]

Dickey, who was fifty-three, told the press that he felt like a man restored by his youthful, vital bride, who was twenty-five. Like Dante following a young Beatrice, he was confident, at least among reporters, that Deborah would lead him to *la vita nuova*: "She's really very beautiful and I'm quite lucky. . . . I'm marvelously happy. . . . Since the death of my wife, I've been in a bad state of nerves and grief but I believe a new life is opening up, thanks to Deborah. We can now pick up the burden of writing and go on living."[17] For the time being, Deborah was content to sacrifice her career plans. She told the *State*: "I had planned to go to law school after finishing my degree at the university, but I'm going to postpone that for awhile now. I want to be free to travel with Jim."[18] To another reporter she said she would quit USC to join her husband on his "bardic drinking and hell-raising"[19] tours. Their immediate plans were to go on a working honeymoon to Hollywood with Shaye Areheart and her boyfriend so that Dickey could finish work on *Gene Bullard*. Although the honeymooners stayed in a luxurious hotel (Areheart recalled that the bill for the four of them at the end of two weeks was equivalent to her year's salary), from the start Deborah had to share her husband with others.

Returning from his depressing vacation in the Virgin Islands, Kevin was stunned to learn that his father had married: "I remember going down to a New Year's Eve oyster roast in South Carolina on the beach with my best friend at the time, Charlie Guerry. [He] walked up to me with a beer in his hand and said 'Congratulations . . . on your father's marriage.' He had gotten married between the time I left Columbia and the time I got to the beach." Because his father had married a woman he hardly knew so soon after his mother's death, Kevin found it hard to accept the news as anything but an insult to his mother and to himself. Afterward, he felt his father had shunted him as well as Chris aside in order to begin his new life: "Dad's loyalty was very clearly with Deborah at the expense of estranging both his sons."[20] Distraught by his mother's death, Kevin struggled with his classes at Washington and Lee. He reduced his course load for the spring term of 1977 and took off the following fall term. According to his father: "He dropped out of sight for a year. I never even did know where he was. He came back and his interests had changed."[21] During the summer and fall of 1977, Kevin visited relatives and friends in the Southeast and for several months collected marine animals in Panacea, Florida, for the Gulf Specimen Company. The rest of the time he worked in Columbia as a waiter. Despite his father's recollections of his son's exile, Kevin was always reachable.

Away from school, Kevin reconsidered his college and career goals. Because his basketball plans had not materialized (he was sixth man on the team) and because he wanted to attend a coed college near a larger, more progressive city, he decided to transfer to Emory. Once there he entered the premed program. Dickey sometimes explained his son's transfer by saying that while dissecting fish in the Virgin Islands, Kevin realized that he could make a lot of money by doing the same thing to people, so he decided to study medicine at Emory.[22] His decision probably had more to do with wanting to understand the illnesses that afflicted his parents. Relations with his father continued to fluctuate at Emory when Kevin finished his B.A. and entered Emory Medical School. During the summer of 1983, shortly after he finished his second year, Kevin called home about the National Board Exams, which he had just taken. His father and stepmother greeted the news by informing him that they were cutting off financial assistance. Despite Dickey's substantial earnings, he made Kevin pay his hefty med school fees himself. Kevin took out loans, which he was still repaying over a decade later.

Unlike Kevin, Chris learned of his father's decision to marry Deborah before it was a fait accompli. Chris had arranged to talk to his father about the marriage before Christmas in 1976. On the day his father was supposed to arrive in Washington, Chris called his room at the Georgetown Inn for hours, but got no response. Finally he went to the hotel and asked the bellboy to open his father's door. In a drunken stupor on the bed, Dickey asked his son: "Where am I?" Then he got on his knees, grabbed Chris around the waist, and exclaimed: "Don't leave me, son. Don't leave me." He told Chris that he was already married and that Deborah hadn't come because she thought he was a bum. He rambled on about different movies and, imitating the way Maxine had vomited blood at her death, shouted: "She *exploded* in my arms." He wept against the bed as he accused himself repeatedly of killing Maxine. He assured Chris that he would like Deborah, who was "rougher than a night in jail."[23] Chris called Deborah at the answering service where she worked, only to discover that his father had lied about being married. At dinner that night, in a more truthful mood, his father explained that he wanted to get married so he could have a daughter. The next day Deborah flew to Washington and met Chris in his *Book World* office.

One of the reasons for Dickey's secrecy about his marriage was the guilt he felt over spurning other women whom he had teased with marriage proposals. After a mock wedding ceremony with Paula Goff in New Orleans on the *Jericho* tour, Goff half-expected she would be chosen. Dickey had importuned Marie Tyler McGraw. To Mary Cantwell he had said: "Mah Mary, let me lay this on you. If we ever *could* marry, and I'm not sayin' we ever could, would you marry me?" She always said: "Yes." He asked her if she could cope in an academic community, be a good hostess, and use an adding machine like Maxine since he was "practically a conglomerate." Following the questions came a proviso: "The only person I'd marry if I didn't marry you would be some idealistic twenty-one-year-old I could train and teach and. . . . Now, mah Mary, don't get upset about a rival you haven't even got." As Cantwell painfully knew, she had plenty of rivals.

Cantwell was one of the main contenders right up until the end. A week after Maxine entered the hospital, Dickey called her, announced that Maxine was about to die, and asked her if she would marry him. At first Cantwell was stunned. She had enjoyed their affair and believed it would somehow continue unencumbered by the formality of marriage. Remembering another occasion several years before when Dickey claimed his wife was dying, she treated his grim prognosis with skepticism. She advised him to direct his attentions to his ill wife rather than to her. About a week after Maxine's funeral, Dickey met Cantwell in New York to discuss marriage face-to-face at a delicatessan near Sixth Avenue where they usually ate breakfast. She slipped her hands into Dickey's sheepskin jacket, hugged him, and then sat down for coffee. Dickey quickly got to the point: "Thank you for that lovely letter, mah Mary. . . . Of course I know you only wrote it because you want to marry me." Cantwell compared his eyes to those of a breeder at a horse auction. He continued: "Tell me about your daughter. I've got to know everything about her if you're going to be mah wife." Cantwell explained that her daughter was improving after seeing a psychiatrist about family troubles. Dickey voiced concern: "Mah Mary . . . there's somethin' awful wrong here. A child who hates her mother. And I just don't think I can take on your financial responsibilities." Cantwell was furious: "If you don't want to marry me, don't. . . . But don't you dare use my children as an excuse." Their talk stumbled along until Cantwell abruptly asked: "What is this? A job interview?" "What do you think it is?" Dickey replied. Cantwell's interview had a sequel at dinner the next night. Chugging martinis, Dickey wept about Maxine's death until his pink napkins were saturated. He whined about having to water the plants by himself, and bragged that there were plenty of women willing to console him. Back at his hotel room, he again spoke seriously of marrying Cantwell, but proposed that they wait a respectable interval after Maxine's death. "Mah Mary. We are *fated* to be man and wife," Dickey said. For the moment, he simply wanted to sleep with her. Cantwell demurred because she had not called a baby-sitter for her daughter and because she thought it improper so soon after Maxine's death. In Dickey's rebuke he implied that he could not marry a woman who failed at such simple tasks as scheduling baby-sitters.

Sloughing off the insult, Cantwell maternally tucked him into bed, read to him from one of his books, and listened to his youthful fantasies: "I keep thinkin', mah Mary . . . that if I get back into trainin', I could be an Olympic runner even now." Cantwell assured him that he could do anything he wanted. Dickey responded gently: "Mah Mary, thank you. You can't imagine what these last six weeks have been like. You've restored me." Years later Cantwell recorded in her memoir: "He was sleepy now, so I got up and turned off the light. 'Mah Mary,' he said in the dark, 'I want you to make me a statement. *Do you love me?*' 'I love you very much.' 'Would it hurt you a lot if we didn't marry?' 'Yes,' I said, 'it would hurt me a lot.'" Four weeks later, a friend called Cantwell to tell her about Dickey's marriage to Deborah. She hung up the receiver, took a long hot shower, and rushed to her psychiatrist, who told her in the midst of her sobs that she had fallen in love with her fantasy of James Dickey.

In hindsight, Cantwell decided that Dickey had been real for her only once and that was at the beginning of their affair when they quoted poetry to each other in Dickey's hotel. She told friends that her jilting was as painful as the loss of her father. Later on she chose to view the pain in religious terms: "I have paid the penance for failing my husband, I told myself. I have been absolved."[24] By accepting punishment from Dickey, who played a complicated god-father-husband role in her tortured psyche, she could go free. Her liaison over, she had no desire to renew contact with her bogeyman. When Deborah called on a visit to New York and told Cantwell that her husband wanted to see her, she hung up the phone.

Cantwell was only one among many who reacted to Dickey's marriage with shock. (She later purged her anger in "Hiatus," a short story about a woman's dream of murdering "the blonde man," which was published in the fall 1979 issue of *Mademoiselle*.) Don and Ellen Greiner learned about their close friend's nuptials when they brought a home-cooked dinner to Dickey's house at the beginning of the new year. Dickey announced: "I've invited Deborah. . . . We're married. Is that alright?" Ellen responded: "Jim, life is for the living."[25] Upset that he hadn't told them earlier and embarrassed by the way he introduced them to his new wife, both Greiners left as quickly as possible. Pegram Harrison, an Atlanta acquaintance of Dickey's from the 1950s, recalled a story that Kirkman Finlay told him about discovering the new alliance. Dickey had asked Finlay: "How long should a man wait to remarry after his wife has died?" Finlay responded: "Oh, maybe a year or two." Dickey next asked if there were any extenuating circumstances that might speed up the process. Finlay nodded: "Yes, of course. Perhaps if you need somebody to take care of the kids." The conversation wavered back and forth in this manner until Dickey mischievously proclaimed: "Well, I'd like you to meet the new Mrs. Dickey."[26] Deborah stepped out of the other room to Finlay's amazement.

Early on in their marriage, Dickey almost invariably sublimated Deborah into a "mythical deliverer" who'd plucked him from the abyss and restored him to happiness. He spoke of her as his muse, his mother, his former wife, his daughter. Later, when she toppled from the pedestal he had created for her, he addressed her in less endearing terms. As Chris Dickey pointed out, he became the father to "a prodigal daughter who's constantly leaving, constantly being welcomed back, who's going crazy, who's being thrown in jail, who's being institutionalized."[27] Some of Dickey's devotees initially shared his high hopes. Jim Mann wrote Dickey a congratulatory note the day after the wedding in which he said about Deborah: "I advised her that she would be marrying the greatest living poet in English, that the responsibility that she would be taking on would be an awesome one, and that she was an extremely fortunate young lady." Mann assured Dickey that Deborah was aware of her great good fortune and also assured him that he would continue writing magnificent poetry. In his despair over Maxine's death, Dickey had confided that he would never write again. Mann counseled: "You once told me how much creative energy one could derive from being married to a good woman, as had been your experience when you married Maxine. Now you have married another good woman, and why should not the imagination be unleashed all over again, in a new and exciting way—new experiments, new thresholds, new anatomies."[28] Mann's last phrases from Hart Crane were wishful thinking. If he had crossed a sublime threshold, Dickey would soon tumble into a pit.

Matthew Bruccoli caught glimpses of future troubles about two weeks after the wedding. Dickey called late at night and said he had moved into a hotel and consulted his lawyer about dissolving the marriage. The marital dispute that triggered such drastic measures may have been caused by Dickey's continuing friendship with Paula Goff. Around this time Goff went to see Dickey at Lake Katherine. Fearful and angry about a possible resuscitation of their affair, according to Goff, Deborah took a picture of Goff and Dickey in Gainesville and threw it on the floor. A catfight ensued. Goff picked up the picture, cutting her hand on the glass, and hurled it at Deborah. Goff said that she bled profusely and that Deborah tore some of her hair out, then got a fire poker. Shaye Areheart, who was working at the house at the time, called Bruccoli and asked him to come immediately to stop the fight. Goff was convinced that Deborah wanted to kill her and later said that Bruccoli had saved her life. Dickey simply stood on the sidelines like a spectator. According to Goff, he enjoyed the spectacle of two women fighting over him.[29]

Deborah was similarly jealous of Dickey's other women friends, and went to some trouble to find out which of them had been his lovers.[30] Looking back on her early years with Dickey, Deborah confessed that she had been uncomfortable "about being known as Jim's wife.... In fact, I was just spooky about it."[31] Dickey's age and fame and overbearing ways would have been hard for any twenty-five-year-old wife to handle. The comments to William Starr that were published in the *State* about wanting a "slave" for a wife may have spooked her further, especially when he asked her to read to him from *The Memoirs of Dolly Morton*, the anonymous book of Victorian pornography describing how a Virginia plantation owner turns his mistress into a sex slave so that he can satiate his lust for whipping (he whips his actual slave women as well).[32] Dickey wanted Deborah to quit her job and work for him. He told Starr in reference to her answering-service job: "She's going to cease and desist (from working) in the next few days."[33] In favor of her completing a B.A., he was nevertheless against her working once she received her degree. She would only have to work, he said sarcastically, if he went bankrupt. Starr pooh-poohed such a dire scenario, never suspecting that Dickey would nearly realize the possibility by the end of his life.

Close friends sympathized with Deborah's well-intentioned efforts to make her marriage work. She tried to take up where Maxine had left off, but numerous factors put Deborah at a disadvantage. She had neither Maxine's cheerful stoicism nor her old-fashioned acceptance of a woman's secondary position in marriage. She was of a younger generation; she had no intention of being Dickey's "slave." Dickey needed to be mothered, but Deborah had little of Maxine's domestic practicality. As for Deborah's need to be fathered, Dickey was unequipped to deal with Deborah's problems. According to one friend, Ward Briggs, Deborah had writing ambitions and hoped for the sort of happy, productive partnership that Elizabeth Barrett and Robert Browning had enjoyed. Dickey had other ideas. He didn't want literary rivals in his house; he wanted someone like Maxine to take care of all the domestic, business, and social chores. Refusing to let Maxine's example die, he insisted on keeping their house just the way she had left it, forbidding any new furniture or any rearranging of the old. "Houses are symbolic,"[34] Deborah once said. Her present house was haunted by the ghost of another woman and another marriage.

Deborah explained to her confidantes that she acted badly because she had little self-confidence. Dickey did not always correct her low opinion of herself. He would say that he had pulled her from the gutter.[35] Despite his alcoholism, Dickey sneered at those who used other drugs and sneered at alcoholics, too. Deborah told an interviewer several years into her marriage: "We really have learned to survive with each other."[36] But survival meant ferocious battles followed by precarious truces and more battles. Although it was not all Sturm und Drang—there were many happy, loving moments—both Dickeys realized that "survival" was less than an ideal goal for a marriage.

In the screenplay *The Sentence*, written a year after he married Deborah,

Dickey created a composite of his two wives in the character Laurette. In his introduction to her he records his disillusionment:

> When they were married, she was intelligent enough to be interesting, pretty enough to be haunting, passionate enough to make strangers pound angrily on motel-room walls demanding quiet.
>
> Her intelligence was all for show, and bored her. Her loveliness turned hard and her passion turned to ice. Her fascination with his kaleidoscope of interests faded into bitterness at being "exiled" to this place.
>
> Divorce, unfortunately, is frowned upon by Stanley's [her husband's] religion, and he bears the torment of a spiteful wife as best he can . . . as he bears the tedium of educating the next generation of suburbanites so he can spend an hour here, an hour there writing articles.[37]

For Dickey, marital sex always paled before the excitements of extramarital sex. As he put it with vulgar flair to his poetry class: "Screwing your wife is like striking out the pitcher." Not long after their wedding, Deborah admitted to friends that they rarely made love. After Bronwen was conceived in 1980, both Dickeys admitted to at least one Columbia friend that their sex life had virtually come to an end.[38]

By all accounts, including her own, Deborah had fragile underpinnings. She had been born in Greenville, South Carolina, the fourth of five children, and had suffered under an imperious, alcoholic father. "A lot of my problems in figuring out my life have to do with my upbringing," she said in an interview with *People* magazine. "The women around my family were victims. They accepted what was dished out to them."[39] Dickey attributed some of Deborah's problems to her early itinerant life. A building inspector for military bases, Mr. Dodson had uprooted his family on numerous occasions: "They went around to various air force bases, where she was raised. . . . Her father was an alcoholic. Her mother died when she was nine."[40] Dickey felt sorry for what he called Deborah's "very dysfunctional family."[41]

Deborah knew she needed psychiatric help during the first years of her marriage, but Dickey denigrated psychiatrists as overpaid charlatans. He had grown used to mayhem in his family, and, to a certain extent, his writing fed on it. Since he was one catalyst for her destructive behavior, he naturally had reservations about paying a psychiatrist to listen to Deborah's descriptions of their problematic marriage. Despite their troubles, there were signs during the first years of their marriage that Deborah might succeed at replacing Maxine. In 1979, one reporter observed of Deborah: "She types his letters and his poems, husbands his time, keeps up with his hectic schedule, shields him from unnecessary visitors, guides and chides with a gentle hand."[42] The guiding hand, however, was not always gentle, and Dickey's publicizing of Deborah's violence far and wide did little to soften her blows. Dickey elaborated to *Newsweek* reporter Pete Axthelm on what he had told Chris. Deborah, he said, could be "as rough on a man as a long drunken night in a South Georgia jail."[43] Millions of *Newsweek* readers now had access to their violent brawls. One of Dickey's most astute friends,

Richard Howard, felt that after Maxine's death the "governor" had been re-moved from Dickey's life. Without completely severing ties, Howard, along with many of Dickey's other friends, tried to avoid him.

31. Presidential Poet (1977)

Dickey usually insisted on a rigorous divorce between poetry and politics. He prided himself on his independence from national politics and contested anyone determined to tie him to a political party or ideological point of view. In 1976, he protested: "For some reason or other I've had the right-wing monkey put on my back. But I'm not right-wing; I'm not left-wing; I'm not any-wing."[1] Dickey conferred with prominent politicians like Eugene McCarthy and Jimmy Carter, but claimed that it was poetry and not politics that drew them together. Nonetheless, Dickey assiduously cultivated his alliance with Carter during his campaign for the presidency. He told reporters that he had engaged Carter in long conversations five or six times while Carter was Georgia's governor. This was undoubtedly an exaggeration since on August 4, 1976, the day Dickey be-gan sending Carter unsolicited advice on how to run his presidential campaign, he reminded Carter that they had met only once—for the Atlanta premiere of *Deliverance*. The only other significant contact between the two Georgians oc-curred when Dickey turned down Carter's invitation to become Georgia's poet laureate (Dickey was living in South Carolina at the time). Reintroducing him-self in his August 4 letter, Dickey went on to deliver an inspirational message to Carter that harked back to Donald Davidson and the Agrarians, but which also prophesied the political ideals of the 1980s and 1990s:

> The clue to our national and international salvation lies not in a futile yearning for a nebulous "unity," but in an emphasis on diversity, or the right—and eventual glory, given the right government—of differences. The South is not the East and the East is not the Pacific Northwest, nor is any one of these Alaska or Hawaii. What we should seek, as a political or-gan, is a reaffirmation of the principal difference, both local and individ-ual. As President—which you certainly shall become—you would do well to affirm cultural pluralism among the various ethnic and political groups of our nation. Men need, above all, pride: pride in themselves and pride in their heritage. I once did a film on this matter for USIA [United States Information Agency], narrated by Ben Gazzara. You could see this any time you wished to do so. It is called *Celebration*, loosely based on John Kennedy's book, *A Nation of Immigrants*, and it stresses the fact that in America ethnic groups do not lose their identity, and can celebrate these roots while still remaining a part of the American ethos.[2]

At the end of August, Carter wrote a short note thanking Dickey for his remarks about America's diversity. The pattern of lengthy sermon followed by brief thanks would characterize Dickey's correspondence with Carter over the subsequent months.

On September 29, 1976, Dickey apologized for writing Carter unsolicited letters and then, like a tough-minded football coach, told Carter that he would win by only a slim margin if he continued to conduct his campaign so apathetically. Why not aim for a landslide victory since that would give him more of a mandate to unify the nation? To achieve this goal Carter had to abandon his dull debating style and brandish a new, charismatic rhetoric: "The idea of talking to the issues and using a great many statistics that are unassimilable to the TV viewers, as the numbers—including decimals—fly past them, is to the point, but not to the ultimate point. Here the slide rule and the electronic calculator are of use to a minority of the population." Carter should also dispense with his quiet sincerity and imitate the zealotry of a Lewis Medlock, a Joel Cahill, or, for that matter, a James Dickey: "One can show a relatively low-key sincerity and move no one to the polls in affirmation. It seems to me, Jimmy, that you need in some manner to catch rhetorical fire, to come out louder and stronger with a greater and more emphatic stress on the key words of the key statements. Then people will have your words stay with them, and will vote accordingly. What we need is fire. And we need it now, for timing is imperative." Dickey reminded Carter of stirring lines by Kennedy and Lincoln, and urged him to find similar lines to ignite the voters' antipathy for Gerald Ford, whom he called "the prime Wooden-Indian of our time." If Carter could rouse the voters to rebel against the Republicans, Dickey predicted: "The next place you and I meet will be the oval office."[3]

Dickey proffered more advice on October 15, 1976. "Jim," as he now addressed Carter, should refrain from the sort of petty political haggling that Ford practiced in their televised debates. Dickey's letter must have struck Carter as otherworldly: "You might, for example, say something about the recent exploration on Mars which seems conclusively to prove that there is no life on the place where we most hoped it might be discovered. This makes the earth of infinite importance, because here thinking and feeling beings reside, and there is no evidence that they reside anywhere but in *our* minds and heads and in *our* dealings with each other. One of my favorite composers, Kurt Weill, wrote a song entitled *Lost in the Stars*. What we do here on the planet earth is of paramount importance, and I believe that if we conduct ourselves properly and solve our economic and political problems, we shall find ourselves not lost in the stars, but found there."[4]

If nothing else, Dickey's letters to Carter kept his name in the running for the position of inaugural poet. After receiving the nod from Carter, at times he feigned modesty about the president's request for his poetic services. "To read one poem at an inaugural gala is hardly enough to make one a poet laureate," he told one interviewer. Asked whether he would like to be an official laureate, he said: "No, I don't like official art at all."[5] In more self-aggrandizing moods, he made sure people regarded him as Carter's official poet. He liked to think of his new relationship with Carter in terms borrowed from *Deliverance*, as if he were a poetic Ed following a presidential Lewis. To Donna Landry at the *Washington Post* he explained how he had made an exception to his rule against writing occasional poetry (he had in fact made numerous exceptions) because "Jimmy Carter is the man destiny has cast in the role of deliverer."[6] He later informed Diana Loercher at the *Christian Science Monitor* that, as in *Deliverance*, he had based his inaugural poem on Van Gennep's theory of the rites of passage. Because Carter had returned after his triumph in the polls to Plains, Georgia, Dickey said: "I cast Jimmy Carter in his withdrawal from Washington and his return to his roots, his hometown, in the role of a mythical hero."[7] Just as he projected himself onto Lewis, in "The Strength of Fields" and in conversation he imagined Carter as his double: "Who would have thought that the Old South, downtrodden and beaten by war and the greater horror of Reconstruction, would have achieved the political initiative and ascendancy? Where else in history can you find it— the President and the poet, two Jimbos from Georgia?"[8] To a reporter for the *Baltimore Sun* Dickey said that while composing "The Strength of Fields" he deliberately envisioned taking the oath of office and running the country.

Dickey was not alone in celebrating Carter as a "deliverer." By the end of 1976, the nation had slumped into a morass of cynicism because of Vietnam and Watergate. Never before had the United States been so humiliated in a war; never before had a president resigned from office. After Kennedy's assassination, the walls of Camelot had come tumbling down, and with Nixon's resignation the presidency was in ruins. The humble, down-home, morally righteous Carter promised "A New Day," "A New Spirit," and "A New Beginning" for America. To begin his national deliverance, Carter organized a five-day People's Inaugural celebration. Six hundred Iowa farmers and their families, 106 Minnesota square dancers, 26 Crow Indians, and innumerable Irish musicians, bluegrass groups, country singers, Hollywood stars, and Georgia well-wishers would join about one million visitors in Washington for Carter's party. Carter, who would publish a book of poetry himself after leaving office, made sure that poets were invited, too. His assistants organized a Midday Muse Series at the Folger Shakespeare theater so that Richard Eberhart, Robert Hayden, Josephine Jacobsen, May Miller, Reed Whittemore, and Dickey could read.

Carter's request for Dickey to write an inaugural poem was not without controversy. Denise Levertov, Dickey's former executor, spoke for the opposition; she publicly attacked Dickey for his "redneck racism and sexism" and for his support "of the war in Southeast Asia." With Levertov's animadversion in mind, Donna Landry asked in the *Washington Post:* "What is born-again Baptist Jimmy Carter, who lusts only in his heart, to think of a man who has applauded adultery in his writing and claims not to understand 'moderate' men, only the 'excessives'?"[9] Having witnessed Dickey in his Great White Hunter hat telling a young woman he would sign her book "in memory of those many warm nights we spent together," another reporter, Roger Simon, commented: "Dickey has been chosen as the artistic conscience of the Carter administration. It does not seem, at first, to be a match made in heaven." Rather than repudiate his bumptious good ol' boy reputation, Dickey played it up to reporters. He told Simon: "After years of political disaster, they [the American people] are finally going to get a lasting solution. And they are going to get this solution by finally turning the country over to the good ol' boys!"[10]

In mid-January 1977, as poetic "deliverer" of the nation, Dickey gave an initial reading at the Folger theater and attended a reception at the Folger guest house around the corner on Third Street, where he was staying with Deborah, Shaye Areheart, and Shaye's boyfriend, Jamie. The events leading up to the next night's reading at the inaugural concert were exciting and tumultuous. Dickey shared a dressing room in the Kennedy Center with John Wayne and Paul Newman; Chevy Chase, Dan Akroyd, and John Lennon and his wife, Yoko Ono, were next door. Hoping to catch a glimpse of Paul Newman, Deborah, Shaye, and Jamie talked to Akroyd and Chase, who had brought a case of Coors to the dressing room for Newman. Before long all three performers—Dickey, Newman, and Wayne—were drinking Coors (Dickey later contended that he drank tequila with Wayne). Shaye and Deborah had to return to the guest house to get into their evening dress. Snow and traffic prolonged their trip, and by the time they returned to the Kennedy Center, as Shaye put it, Dickey was "quite snuckered." He looked up and exclaimed: "Oh, it's my girls. Paul, this is my wife Debba, and my assistant Shaye. I want you to give 'em a kiss."[11] To the "girls'" delight, Newman obliged.

At the inaugural concert on the evening of January 19, 1977, singers Johnny Cash, Linda Ronstadt, Loretta Lynn, and Beverly Sills; comedians Chevy Chase, Redd Foxx, and Dan Akroyd; and actors Jack Nicholson, Warren Beatty, John Wayne, Paul Newman, and Cher helped usher in Carter's New Spirit. Among the celebrities, Dickey gave a dramatic reading of "The Strength of Fields," which many praised. Patsy Dickey was ecstatic: "You looked like a Viking riding the bowsprit over a sea of humanity. . . . And the expression on Carter's face when you were introduced, Jim, was one of pride, deep affection— and no guile. He loves you."[12] Dickey reread "The Strength of Fields" during an NPR interview with Susan Stamberg in the Folger Shakespeare Library. Many listeners around the country commented on the beauty and appropriateness of Dickey's words.

At the party following the New Spirit concert Dickey mingled with Leonard Bernstein, Cher, and Paul Simon, but showed little interest in meeting John Lennon and Yoko Ono. Of all the celebrities he met, John Wayne was the most memorable. Dickey recalled: "We talked about Wayne's politics, his right-wing leanings. . . . He just said that he thought that we had a great country, and we should do everything we can to keep it like it is, keep the good institutions and the good things about it, [and] . . . not let radicals mess around with them too much." As for Carter's liberal spirit, Wayne quipped to Dickey: "You can consider me the voice of the loyal opposition."[13] Prior to their boozy chats in Washington, Dickey had often opposed Wayne, criticizing him as the apotheosis of what was wrong with American culture: "Everybody is so busy being cool, acting like John Wayne. I'll tell you . . . those John Wayne roles are responsible for a great deal of America's misconceptions of life. John Wayne projects an ideal of manhood that leaves out eighty percent of the personality. He's cool. He doesn't dare be tender or let anything touch him."[14] When Wayne died from lung cancer on June 11, 1979, Dickey changed his mind: "He was sensitive, much less callous than his movies showed him to be. And he was more intelligent. You could tell he could project that image—of being tough—but he was more than that. . . . He portrayed what every man would want to be. He got

578 / JAMES DICKEY

things done, no shadow of right or wrong. He projected an image of certainty, re-solve, moral rectitude that you can't argue with. The idea of a college professor arguing ethics with him is absurd. . . . His type has been undercut by what I call the 'dry rot of cynicism.' We have a nation of over-intellectual Hamlets—people who can't make up their minds."[15] Wayne had endeared himself to Dickey by ac-knowledging his desire to play Lewis in *Deliverance*. In the end, Wayne embod-ied Dickey's image of himself as a mix of tenderness and toughness.

Not all who saw Dickey read at the Kennedy Center were won over by his performance. Sheldon Kelly, who described the event in the *Reader's Digest*, thought Dickey looked uncomfortable before the television cameras and high-intensity lights. Others realized that he was drunk. Donald Branning wrote Dickey a caustic letter on January 21, first attacking him for calling Hemingway "one of the greatest phonies of all time, but . . . a *magnificent* phony,"[16] and then for his flamboyant reading. Dwight McDonald also sent a barbed riposte in which he dismissed Dickey's poem as doggerel and Dickey himself as a drunk. Dickey responded to McDonald defensively: "The title [of the poem] itself is better than the whole corpus of Agee's work. . . . As to being soused on that oc-casion, I was not that either, though I certainly would have had every excuse to be so, in view of the fact that I had had to share a dressing room with Paul Newman and—of all people—John Wayne for four hours."[17] Chris Dickey thought his father was both soused and embarrassing, and was particularly mor-tified when he broke ranks with everyone on stage singing "God Bless America" in order to whisper something obscene to Paul Newman.[18]

Writing a poem in a month for such an august occasion was no easy task, and Dickey accomplished it better than his critics allowed. As he later explained, his poem was meant as a tribute to Carter as well as to Stanley Hyman, the scholar who had originally written the essay in the *Sewanee Review* that contained the description of rites of passage and myths charting "a separation from the world, a penetration to some source of power and a life-enhancing return." His poem espoused values most of his audience were bound to share: humility, sensitivity, and simplicity. He chose to dramatize these ideals like a former inaugural poet, Robert Frost, with a scene in which an elderly man realizes his smallness in the cosmos on a walk beyond the city limits on a dark night. Dickey's persona searches the heavens for guidance like Frost in "Acquainted with the Night" and other poems, although the design of "The Strength of Fields" and its lofty rhet-oric are quite different from Frost's:

> The solar system floats on
> Above him in town-moths.
> Tell me, train-sound
> With all your long-lost grief,
> what I can give.
> Dear Lord of all the fields
> what am I going to *do?*
> Street-lights, blue-force and frail
> As the homes of men, tell me how to do it   how
> To withdraw   how to penetrate and find the source

Of the power you always had
    light as a moth, and rising
With the level and moonlit expansion
Of the fields around, and the sleep of hoping men.

As in "The Lord's Prayer," Dickey's supplicant asks God for a deliverance, but expects to receive it from small-town streetlights, freight trains, fields, and graves.

If Dickey baffled some listeners, it was partly because he shaped his archetypal journey as an idiosyncratic prayer. Dickey walks with Carter as Carter walks with God, and what the two men discover on their meditative dark night is pagan as well as Christian. Like participants in the fertility cults that preceded and influenced Christian rituals, they try to draw strength from nature and to bring new life from wintry death. Dickey's narrator calls for "More kindness, dear Lord / Of the renewing green."[19] Dickey recognizes that he, Carter, and everyone else are frail as moths in the cosmic scheme of things, and celebrates the president's desire—in a later president's words—to cultivate a "kinder, gentler America." The president's final promise, "My life belongs to the world. I will do what I can," however, came from an unexpected source. It was first spoken by a soldier at the end of the story "They Came" by the Welsh writer Alun Lewis. The soldier is stationed in the south of England, and as he watches a German bombing raid on the coast, he declares his devotion to his country's heroic cause. Carter's liberal principles, Dickey suggests, can only be implemented with similar devotion.

Dickey's noble poem limned an ideal that he, unfortunately, was not prepared to honor in Washington. His drinking led to vindictive indiscretions that were circulated as widely as his poem. Pete Axthelm recorded one of these in *Newsweek*. Dickey used his interview with Axthelm to pillory his former mentor, Andrew Lytle, who in many ways fit the description of the Agrarian Southern gentleman celebrated in "The Strength of Fields." Not mentioning Lytle by name, Dickey said he would never forgive "that man" who betrayed him at the University of Florida: "Many years ago I was teaching under him in Florida, and I got into such bad trouble that I had to leave town under cover of darkness. I left my wife, Maxine, behind, to join me when I could set up some new life. And that man treated her unkindly." Axthelm diplomatically left out some of the details, merely reporting that Dickey "filled in the tale, then worked up to his meeting with the old man only months ago. The man approached Dickey as a friend. 'You know, buddy-ro,' the poet told him cruelly, 'you never really had it. You failed.' Dickey exulted in the moral of the chilling story: 'Revenge is a real thing for a Southerner. We are people with emotions that endure.'" Axthelm concluded that "for those who suspected that there was more to the arrival of this Southern President in the Capital" besides "the down-home friendliness that is one part of his Southern heritage,"[20] all they had to do was talk to Dickey. Several years later, Dickey tried to make amends for his insults by telling Lytle's biographer, David Hallman: "I don't know where the misunderstanding that our relationship was less than friendly came from, but I certainly don't want to perpetuate it."[21]

Having insulted Lytle with a story that was half fiction, he insulted Deborah by discussing her violent temperament. To save face he said he admired all such women: "People who want to understand the South would do well to start with our women. Tough, loving, frail, powerful. They hold so many of our best secrets."[22] He was not so admiring after Carter's frosty, sunlit swearing-in ceremony on January 20. At a Folger party, Deborah found Dickey talking to a woman friend, reprimanded him for his drunkenness and flirtatiousness, and began hitting him.[23] The pressures of playing supportive spouse to a celebrity on such a public stage just weeks after getting married were already showing. Deborah must have resented the article in *Newsweek* on January 31 that compared her to a rough night in a Georgia jail. Looking dapper in his tie, jacket, and wide-brimmed hat, Dickey in the accompanying photograph stood beside a gorgeous and smiling Cher; Deborah was nowhere to be seen. To offset his remarks to Axthelm, Dickey trumpeted his Southern ideals of courtliness to Peter Behr of the *Baltimore Sun*. Queried about the change that a Southern president would bring to America, Dickey said: "I think there will be a turning around of the sensibilities of America, based on the traditional values which the South has always fostered. The word 'gentleman' is going to be important again. As to women, the word 'lady' is going to take on its age-old importance. I firmly predict a new courtesy. People are going to be kinder to each other in the great tradition of the South."

Over the next four years Dickey kept up a steady correspondence with President Carter. Among the most surprising letters that reached Carter was one written on June 15, 1977, not by Dickey but at Dickey's behest by Crown editor Lawrence Freundlich. It began breezily with a reference to Dickey's children's book, *Tucky the Hunter*, which Crown planned to publish, and then announced: "The second book of the contract is the occasion of why I am writing to you. We dream of James's being aboard the first NASA space-shuttle in 1979 or 1980, God willing. The mind of the poet confronted by the spectacle of this great deed is thrilling, I think. And I think you would agree. Would you be willing to use your influence or to put me in contact with someone who might convey your approval of James's space-shuttle passage?"[24] Dickey had conferred with Crown about a shuttle flight early in 1977, and the publisher's senior editor, Paul Nadan, had contacted NASA. NASA administrator James Fletcher wrote Nadan on March 15, informing him of Dickey's chances of becoming the first civilian aboard the shuttle: "Although we had decided that we would carry one or more non-scientist passengers on a relatively early Space Shuttle flight, we have not as yet determined how such a selection will be made. When we have made this decision, we will be happy to let you know. In the meantime, Mr. Dickey's name will be added to the list of those who have either volunteered themselves or been proposed by others to share this unique spot in history."[25] Eventually several nonastronauts did fly, but the 1986 *Challenger* disaster put such flights in jeopardy. By that time Dickey's alcoholism would have prevented him from passing the physical tests necessary for what would have been his ultimate flight.

Not long after the inauguration, Carter called on Dickey to represent the United States at a ceremony opening the Franklin and Jefferson exhibit at

Mexico City's National Museum of Anthropology. Honored to serve the president again, Dickey flew with Deborah to Mexico and began his week of ambassadorial duties on April 14 by attending a reception given by the Public Affairs officer, Leonard Baldyga. He attended parties, discussed the filming of *Deliverance*, conferred with cultural dignitaries, lectured on modern poetry at the anthropology museum, and went sightseeing. In his address on April 15 at the Franklin and Jefferson exhibit he praised America's two founding fathers for bettering the spiritual and practical lives of people all over the world. Clad in patriotic colors—a light blue jacket, deep blue tie, and red pants—Dickey stood before Mexico's most prominent leaders, who included President Portillo, and hailed the new spirit of understanding and cooperation between the two countries.

While in Mexico, Dickey also renewed his friendship with Octavio Paz, a poet he had known from his days as poetry consultant. To the press he remarked a number of times that Paz was Mexico's finest poet and deserved the Nobel Prize (Paz won the prize in 1990). At one of their meetings, they promised to translate each other's work. Two years later, when Carter visited Mexico, Dickey made a point of writing the president about the accomplishments of his earlier trip, and predicted that his statements about Paz would alter U.S. relations with its sometimes testy neighbor: "It might prove a telling point in Mexican-American relations for us to remember that I have gone on record—in Mexico, while acting there as your representative—as voicing this opinion [that Paz should get the Nobel Prize]. If in the future Paz does indeed receive the prize, which he almost certainly will, it should be a good fact to bring up in connection with cultural relations between our two countries."[26] Dickey's elation over meeting Mexico's most illustrious poets and politicians in 1977 was undercut by Deborah's disorderly behavior. She spent much of her time, he alleged, trying to purchase drugs and was in such bad shape by the end of the visit that he feared he would have difficulty getting her out of the country.[27] If he had any doubts about her substance abuse, the trip to Mexico City dispelled them.

Dickey hoped to meet Carter again during the spring of 1979. In March, Dickey joined South Carolina governor Riley and Senator Hollings in a campaign to get Carter to deliver the May commencement address at USC. The university president, James Holderman, planned to give Carter an honorary degree. Dickey wrote Carter: "It would be a good occasion for everybody down here in the May South Carolina sun, but most especially for Deborah and me. We send our regards to you and Rosalyn, there in your high position overlooking the world and the rest of us with our eyes turned upward toward you."[28] Dickey's image of Carter as a prophet on the mountain, however, could not divert the president from his other commitments. A short note from the White House blamed Carter's inability to attend USC on his heavy schedule.

Dickey continued to send Carter political advice. One of his longest letters was a response to Carter's summer energy speech in 1979, in which he had spoken about coping with shortages to a nation crippled by the oil crisis. Dickey's letter alternated between pep talk and literary lecture, nitpicking linguistic critique and visionary proclamation. He analyzed the president's rhetorical strategies—often disapprovingly—and instructed him to uplift the country by outlining a utopian ideal. He waxed moralistic and prophetic in his description of "a city of the sun" (a phrase he borrowed from Tommaso Campanella's book by that title about a utopian community), on which the nation should set its sights:

> First of all, you are dead on the center of the central target in *focusing* on the Energy situation. This very much needed to be done, and it needs continually to be emphasized. Your phrase "War on Energy" is slightly misleading, though, for it seems to imply that Energy itself is the opponent, and is some sort of entity that needs to be defeated instead of the source of continuing well-being and operating autonomy that we need. If the word "war" is desirable in this context, surely it is war *for* rather than *on* energy that we are engaged in, with the positive connotations that this shift in perspective implies.
>
> Next, I missed a firm statement as to your stand on nuclear power. The public sorely needs and wants to know what the country intends to do about this, and in your next major address, I think that you should allow consideration to giving this issue an important place. As for myself as a citizen, I believe very much that we must have nuclear power at almost all costs short of atomic holocaust itself, but of course the action followed will be defined by you in the stand you take. In connection with the new sources of energy, I think that you might also call even more attention to the possibilities of solar power, and step up both your programs and your public espousal of them; everybody is interested in the subject now, and most will support your proposals.
>
> All these things you already know to an extent I cannot possibly realize, and I bring them forward only as the opinions of a citizen. As a writer and necessarily therefore a sometime rhetorician, I am as usual chiefly concerned about the emphases, the slants, the vectors, the rhetorical tactics you command and employ. All of these factors contribute to the image you have at this time for the American people, and for the rest of the world. I have been most gratified by the forthrightness and the personal dramatic emphasis you displayed in the last of your debates with Ford, the Inaugural address, and now this newest declaration; it seems to me that you are presenting the figure of intelligent *force* that is above all other things needed in a president at this time. I would like to see more and more of this quality, and I think also that a certain *dominance* of attitude on your part—outspoken, vigorous, and above all decisive—would be very helpful to us all. In your last address, you gave the impression that the nation must take the energy crisis as a kind of renewal-point for its sense of solidarity and common purpose, but it is difficult to escape the unpleasant association that were we not driven by brute means and brute forces—the OPEC nations—to affirm this solidarity we would not feel inclined to do so. Your stern pronouncements about our moral laxity and selfishness are good points; they should be made, and they are true. But it is basically difficult to drive, cow and humiliate people to do things they ought to have been doing all the

time. There is bound to be a certain residue of resentment in a populace addressed in this manner, and it seems to me that the whole emphasis could be turned squarely toward the positive by a very memorably-stated spotlighting of the great resources of intellectual and spiritual power that we as a nation collectively and as individuals do in fact possess: a kind of hidden treasure: enormous, full of power and light and certainty and even a fierce and renewing kind of joy: above all, a sense of *going-toward* rather than escaping-from. It is a great deal better to lead people toward a goal, a kind of just city, a "city of the sun," than it is to attempt to intimidate a nation of sluggards and timorous wastrels into acting for its own good.

Having incorporated the title of one of his poems, "Power and Light," Dickey finished his letter with an aside on Joseph Conrad's *Youth*. He urged Carter to adopt Marlowe's role at the end of the novel by renewing the nation's heroic youthfulness at a time of "adversity, danger, vigor, pride, power and joy."[29] For all his earnest efforts to counsel the president in matters political and literary, Dickey received a note three sentences long thanking him for his encouragement and rubber-stamped JIMMY.

Determined to stay close to the political arena, the Dickeys continued to pledge support to the Carters. (On April 29, 1977, Dickey had sent Rosalyn, who had been ill, a telegram proposing that he and Deborah donate blood to her.) In a 1979 Christmas card, Deborah expressed hope that the president would call on them in 1980. In a triumphant mood, she revealed that she and her husband had quit drinking in July 1978. Although the Dickeys' temperance was always in flux, the Carters did call on them to participate in a White House reception saluting American poets in January 1980 and a White House celebration of Saint Patrick's Day. At the reception for poets, Dickey got so engrossed in George Plimpton's film about playing with the Detroit Lions football team that he nearly missed the party. He went unwillingly to read with Louise Glück and Simon Ortiz in the Red Room and to socialize afterward with David Ignatow, Theodore Weiss, Philip Levine, Maxine Kumin, Lucille Clifton, Marvin Bell, Stanley Kunitz, and Richard Eberhart. (In a letter to Robert Pinsky several weeks after the event, he characterized his fellow readers as "poetic deadwood, dead-weights, and dead-heads.") One of the few poets he enjoyed meeting was Pinsky, a future poet laureate who at the time was poetry editor of the *New Republic*. Dickey admired what he called Pinsky's "very fast, high-tension Jewish intellectual patter" and advised the younger poet to make it his "primary idiom."[30] For his part, Pinsky felt Dickey was surprisingly urbane, friendly, sober, and generous. But he also said: "I found his remarks on poetry very late-fifties: he liked chunky, Dylan Thomas–esque rhetoric and big, splashy conceptions. He was nice about some of my poems, but I never got very far into the art with him—never got past the obvious levels of his aesthetic to what made him capable of distinguished work within that aesthetic. My impression was of a decent soul, an alcoholic, a flamboyant entrepreneur, a self-indulgent, politically shrewd networker: a 'likeable' but inaccessible type more like a successful academic or good businessman than like most of the writers I have known."[31]

Dickey was undoubtedly looking for an advocate at the *New Republic*—Pinsky eventually published some of his poems there—and to that end carried on a sporadic correspondence with his new friend over the next few years.

If Pinsky had known of Dickey's treatment of James Wright at the reception, he would have had more reason to question Dickey's sincerity. Barely able to attend because of his debilitating cancer, Wright greeted Dickey with his customary friendliness and explained his dire condition. He was scheduled to enter the hospital in a week. (Within four months he would die.) Expecting sympathy from the friend to whom he had been so loyal over the years, Wright was shocked when Dickey grew inexplicably angry and turned away from him. How could Dickey be angry when he was the one suffering? Wright asked his wife, Anne. Was Dickey upset that a staunch supporter was about to abandon him? Did he blame Wright for trying to spoil his visit to the White House with bad news? Did he think his friend was simply whining? Near the end of January, Dickey sent Wright a short, valedictory telegram, saying: "I miss your voice."[32] Anne Wright, who was caring for her dying husband at the time, intercepted it, tore it up, and threw it in the trash.

Dickey's snub at the president's party may have resulted from feuds with the Wrights that had smoldered throughout the 1970s. The fact that Wright remained a devoted friend of Robert Bly irked Dickey. Dickey at first admired Anne (in the spring of 1968 in New York he presented the recently married couple with a trio of books by Edmund Wilson), but soon criticized her for coddling her husband. Early in 1975, Dickey deliberately antagonized both Wrights by recounting a drinking story involving their son, Franz. Anne had asked Dickey not to retell the story, and he had promised to abide by her wish. Her husband had been in a psychiatric ward during the fall of 1974, and she knew that it would upset him. Discovering that Dickey had reneged on his promise, on April 29, 1975, Anne scolded him in a letter. On May 6, Dickey responded: "The thing that is most destructive to your husband's personality is your constant over-protecting of him, and his willingness to reside in such a situation. What Jim wants most, and what I want most for him, is that he function as a fully responsible and creative human being, and that he take the responsibilities of an active man, and deal with them rather than hiding from them. I fear that you must be held responsible for a kind of emotional castration, the worst possible condition for a man of Jim's temperament. He wants desperately to be a man pulling his weight in the proverbial boat, and all of this coddling and copping-out is going to be the ruination of him if some change does not occur. It is not only going to be the ruination of a fine American poet but of his son Franz."[33] The rebuke infuriated Anne.

Dickey uncovered some of the reasons for his disappointment with Wright at Carter's reception in a letter to David Wagoner on April 21, 1980. Dickey had just heard of Wright's death: "Like you I don't know what to say or do but continue to remember Jim with love and honor and read his works. You did right not to come to the White House thing. For you would have beheld Jim there, not as Jim but as Jim's hoarse, diminished and obviously dying ghost, and would surely have been as appalled and saddened as I was."[34] At the White House, Dickey may have already been mourning Wright's loss and supplementing his grief with anger. Dickey was also preoccupied with his own health problems at the time. Asked in early 1980 to help reelect the president by organizing the "Poets and Writers for Carter and Mondale," Dickey said that he and his wife could never handle all the administrative work; a doctor had recently told him he would need surgery to remedy his malfunctioning esophagus. In his letter to the White House, he suggested that the only enticement the job offered was the possibility of taking on Lenny Bernstein, whose political views repelled him. He advised Carter's staff to contact *Poetry* editor John Nims, who had helped organize the recent gathering of writers at the White House.

Dickey continued to correspond with the president during the 1980 election year. In June, Dickey responded to a get-well card from the Carters with gratitude and a reaffirmation of his commitment "to be of service to you in whatever ways I may help."[35] Dickey repeated his offer in August 1980: "I stand ready to help in any way I can at this time, which is of such vital importance, and will not come again." Dusting off the mantle of presidential advisor, he tried to enlighten the president with a homily: "Timing is crucial in politics, as in most other things; what is done now will be what is done, and will have the results that it will have." He reiterated his qualifications as Carter's adviser: "My area is words, and in making them effective and memorable. That I can do, and make bold to assert that I can do it better than anyone else. I can stay clear of the inside of the campaign, and just look on with the rest of the populace by television and newspaper, or I can be part-way into the actual workings of it, or I can give it, with your permission and direction, a full, all-out commitment; in any case, that shall be as you wish, and as you indicate."[36] Like Robert Lowell, Dickey yearned for proximity to political power. He pretended to be Carter's humble servant, but his subservience was partially self-serving—it added luster to his stature as a writer. Carter looked favorably on Dickey's offer and on October 9, 1980, wrote him a personal note thanking him and promising to summon him if he could find anything specific for him to do.

Perhaps worrying that Dickey's association with Carter would only intensify the conservatives' attack on the president, Carter's people never called Dickey. The liberal and permissive days of the 1960s and 1970s were coming to an end, and Carter's hoped-for triumph over Reagan never came to pass. Undaunted by Carter's oversight, Dickey took matters into his own hands. He began a letter a little over a week before the November election: "Since I haven't heard from Jody Powell, and since time is getting short, I thought I had better send you what thoughts I have on the points you might want to emphasize in your debate with Reagan." He proceeded to lay out the issues he deemed crucial:

Though questions of an economic nature are of great concern, the issue of overwhelming importance is that of war, particularly of precipitous, foolishly-provoked and unnecessary war. The belief in the minds of many more than half the voters is that the election of Reagan would make such an eventuality much more likely, as I myself believe. In connection with this situation, and in furtherance of your own re-election, you need two things: the first of these is a simple, graspable, widely applicable and memorable metaphor to describe your position. This figure of speech should or might be the familiar one, urged on all citizens of driving as well as voting age, of *driving defensively*. The implications of operating an automobile so as not to *allow* any accidents to happen to one's own vehicle are obvious.

Having drunkenly crashed his Jaguar into a utility pole only a few years before, Dickey was speaking from rueful experience. Carter, he concluded, should link his defensive-driving metaphor to a key phrase: "If I am right, the phrase would be 'A passion for peace.'"[37] Was the aging Dickey becoming a "peacenik"? More likely, as in his work for Coca-Cola or Lay's potato chips, he was concerned with coming up with effective slogans to sell a product—the president in this case—rather than with expressing his own attitudes. The Carter administration had its own advertising agents and spin doctors, however, and chose to ignore Dickey's copious recommendations.

Dickey could not be silenced so easily. He reeled off letters that offered other packaging techniques and other appealing images that might facilitate Carter's message. In the era of TV sound bites and negative campaign ads, messages needed to be tailored to fit the medium, and Dickey was shrewd enough to recognize that the advertising business was a model for effective political campaigning. Reagan, however, had been in the advertising and acting business as well. The master of media—"the Great Communicator" as pundits later called him—prevailed. The schoolmarmish adage about driving defensively would have been no match for Reagan's visionary rhetoric about a revitalized America standing tall in the saddle and riding boldly toward a "city of the sun." As canny a mythmaker as Dickey, Reagan projected his Hollywood fantasies of American grandeur with the sort of dexterity Dickey hoped Carter would master. Although Reagan's messages may have been as thin as the celluloid from which they derived, they appealed to a nation still recovering from Vietnam and Watergate, and newly frustrated by the Iran hostage crisis that Carter had failed to resolve. Carter's liberal humanitarian ideals along with his foreign policy blunders made him appear soft, muddled, vulnerable, incompetent. America needed an "Energized Man," a "Deliverer," and found one in Reagan. Dickey could only stand back and envy Reagan's rhetoric, which in many ways resembled his own. After Carter left the White House, Dickey's contact with him virtually ended.

32. New Ventures (1977–1979)

Carter's appointment of Dickey as inaugural poet affected Dickey's career in several ways. It stamped him as America's preeminent poet. It boosted the sales of his books and the fees he could demand for readings. It also made him more aloof, multiplied his sycophants, and further numbed him to criticism that could have benefited his work. As Carter's "virtual" poet laureate, it became easier for Dickey to convince himself that all his books were masterpieces. A reading on February 4, 1977, at Dallas's Mountain View College typified the reception many audiences now granted Dickey. The college president, David Sims, introduced Dickey as "the first true successor to Walt Whitman as National Poet," and listed his mythic accomplishments. Beneath dimming lights in the community college's performance hall, Dickey appeared on a large screen as the sheriff in *Deliverance*. Deborah ushered her husband along with his books, manuscripts, big coat, and broad-brimmed safari hat toward the podium. Keeping to his routine, Dickey thanked President Sims for his fine introduction and asked him to speak at his funeral. Hungover from a birthday party held in his honor the day before, his voice quavered at first, but recovered. To reporters he described Deborah as his guardian angel. She seemed to fit the description as she kept autograph seekers at bay, protected his manuscripts, whisked him off for lunch, fended off a television camera crew's blinding lights at a book-signing session in the local bookstore, and helped him with string tricks before adoring fans at the hotel bar. Regarding his new notoriety, Dickey told a reporter he was reminded of Shakespeare's lines from *Julius Caesar*: "On such a full sea are we now afloat / And we must take the current when it serves / Or lose our ventures." Like Caesar, he rode his wave while it lasted.

In the spring of 1977, Dickey toiled at *God's Images*, a new coffee-table book. He sometimes said that Maxine's death had provided the original impetus to write the book, but he had actually discussed it with John Logue and its illustrator, Marvin Hayes, on March 25, 1976, half a year before she died. Hayes had already produced a series of etchings based on the Bible, and Logue had sent Dickey the relevant passages that he hoped Dickey would rewrite. The new book, according to Logue, would be even bigger in concept and marketability than *Jericho*, which by September 1976 had grossed about six million dollars and gone into a second printing of twenty-five thousand copies. After all, the new book's model would be the Bible, the biggest seller of all time. Oxmoor offered Dickey a lucrative contract: a thirty-thousand-dollar advance with 5-percent royalties. On October 11, 1976, Logue expanded his plans further; he proposed that Dickey write two coffee-table books, the first based on the Old Testament, the second on the New. A week after Maxine's death, Dickey had already written the book's introduction and about half of the text.

Along with *God's Images*, Dickey worked on his prison film, *The Sentence*. He had spoken to Charles Fries in Hollywood about writing a screenplay based on his 1975 crash into a utility pole, revealing how the plot would focus on the way a professor at a Southern university coped with arrest and incarceration. On June 30, 1976, he sent Malcolm Stuart a four-page outline. Intrigued, Fries and Stuart urged Dickey to write a brief summary for NBC. Dickey procrastinated; he didn't submit a ten-page treatment of the film until January 11, 1978. But NBC liked the idea and asked Dickey to write a script for a two-hour movie. Dickey had other movie ideas, too, many of which, like *The Sentence*, drew on his increasingly reckless life. He wrote a short summary of *The Breath*, which resembled Richard Connell's *The Most Dangerous Game* in describing a hunt by one man for another man. The protagonist, Quentin Dodson, is an eccentric, wealthy New Yorker not unlike Dickey (his hobby is collecting primitive weapons like blowguns). After engineers install escape-proof devices in his house, he goes to a bar, gets drunk with an unsavory group of men, tells them he keeps all his money at home, and gives them his address. A man named Garth attemps to rob his house and gets trapped. Over a loudspeaker Quentin promises

Garth thirty-five thousand dollars if he can survive the night. Choosing to stalk Garth with a poisonous blowgun, Quentin instructs his quarry to arm himself as well. When he finally confronts Garth "Quentin suddenly winks and puts the blowgun down. It develops that Quentin has never wanted to kill anyone; he only wanted the *game* of life and death."[1] Quentin offers Garth the thirty-five thousand dollars, which he refuses, and then Garth stabs Quentin in the stomach, killing him. Like the victim in Poe's "Cask of Amontillado," Garth discovers that he is permanently trapped inside Quentin's house.

The Breath took Dickey's contention that Deborah was like a rough night in jail and transformed it into drama. In the process, Dickey became Dodson, and the real Dodson became Garth. Dickey was the hunter—of animals and women—who pursued his prey just for the sake of it. His actual prey, however, did not always think his tactics were fun or funny. Deborah Dodson would sometimes wield the sort of primitive weapons—arrows, knives—that appear in *The Breath*. One of her more vehement shows of displeasure occurred during the early years of her marriage when she stabbed Dickey in the shoulder with a broadhead arrow. Recalling the attack, Dickey said that Deborah trembled with remorse as she drove him to the hospital. According to Dickey, while a doctor stitched his wound, a policeman asked: "Do you want to enter charges? This is a mad woman here." He responded calmly, "It's okay. I'll be alright,"[2] and went home. Dickey provoked Deborah's murderous attacks, but like Quentin in *The Breath* he wanted his dangerous games to end when he gave the proper signal. Deborah would not be refereed so easily. "She was pushed a long way,"[3] Paula Goff remarked sympathetically. Perhaps recognizing his provocative role, Dickey took no legal action. He remained married and continued to tell people, like a reporter for the *Jacksonville Journal-Courier* in March 1978, that his marriage was "the most fortunate thing that ever happened to me."[4]

In another proposed screenplay, *The Buzzer*, Dickey again wanted to explore his view of life as a highly competitive game in which he was the ultimate arbiter. The film would tell the story of a sensitive, withdrawn college basketball star who brings his team to the National Collegiate finals and quits right at the moment he has a chance to win the game. The plot reflected Dickey's ambivalence toward his literary stature—his temptation to quit and do something different while he was on top—but his more general desire to play, and probably lose, by following his own unpredictable whims. In yet another screenplay, *The Spell*, Dickey proposed to dramatize the sort of charismatic power that made him both desirable and vulnerable to women like Deborah and Paula Goff. A spellbinding minister, Joshua Daniels, gets off a bus in a Southern soybean field, walks to the house of Hannah Crewes, reveals his ecumenical views to her, and before long turns into a local demagogue who gets crucified between two pine trees.

On June 10, 1977, Dickey lost the woman primarily responsible for his complicated attitudes toward women—his mother. A prodigal son who treated most women with a mixture of adoration and contempt, childish dependence and independence, Dickey reacted to her death in predictable ways. According to Sheldon Kelly, who interviewed Dickey's brother and sister during the summer of 1977, Dickey retreated to his room in his family's West Wesley house to drink. His brother and sister wanted him to sober up, but he refused. How he got access to liquor mystified them (they later found vodka bottles hidden in nooks and crannies). He came to the funeral drunk, fidgeted during the service, and banged his guitar against the pew. Maibelle told Kelly: "It was like the scratching of fingernails on a blackboard. It was so sacrilegious. It was so disrespectful. And then Deborah dressed up in very dark reds of lip and deep purples of eye, and big Jim with his sheepskin coat and big leather hat. It was horrifying."[5] Maibelle's account was skewed by her close bond with her mother. Just before her mother was buried, she howled by the casket. While Tom, pale and grief stricken, stared at the ground, Jim put his arm around his sister to comfort her. She continued to wail and ultimately fainted.

To the end, Dickey's view of his mother was as irreverent as it was reverent. In deference to her memory, he decided to put an abrupt end to his drinking. He convinced Deborah to do the same. Normally alcoholics take anticonvulsant drugs when they quit, but Dickey refused to acknowledge the seriousness of his addiction, just as he brushed aside all normal treatments for it after Maxine's death. The result was nearly fatal. He suffered an alcohol-withdrawal seizure on Williams Street in Atlanta, bit off part of his tongue, and nearly bled to death. According to Al Braselton, who visited him shortly after his accident, Dickey suffered another seizure and bit his tongue a second time in the hospital. Tom Dickey, who had originally told Braselton about the seizure, had advised his brother to go to an alcoholics' hospital. Instead, he ended up at Grady Hospital under the care of Dr. John Stone, chief of emergency medicine, a respected cardiologist, and also a poet.

Once discharged from the hospital, Dickey stayed briefly with Deborah at Patsy Dickey's house. Fearing Tom and Maibelle might try to institutionalize him, Dickey insisted on returning to Columbia as soon as possible. Relations between Dickey and his two siblings worsened after their mother's death. If they communicated, it was usually about family business. In October 1977, Maibelle wrote her brother that she was sorting out their mother's estate taxes for the IRS, paying property taxes, and taking care of the West Wesley house, which was being painted and repaired so it could be sold. She reported that nearly all the Dickeys' Atlanta real-estate holdings were currently rented. To add to the family coffers, in 1978 she and Tom decided to sell their property in Louisiana. For the rest of Dickey's life, Maibelle sent him SSS dividend and rental-property checks. They rarely met.

Dickey found some consolation in his publisher's reaction to the manuscript of *God's Images*, which he had submitted near the end of the spring of 1977. On June 17, the president of the Progressive Farmer, Emory Cunningham, congratulated him on scaling new heights with his prose. John Logue praised the book as an extraordinary feat and passed along news that the book had received an auspicious reception at a recent American Booksellers Association Convention in San Francisco. Logue thought that *God's Images* might surpass *Jericho* in popularity. Dickey was pleased, but also worried about the book's critical reception. To Teresa Barker, a journalist for the *Tennessean*, he explained: "There has been such an epidemic of Jesus freaks—and then I come out and write about the Bible—I was concerned . . . it would be considered an attempt to get in on a fad, and it is not that. If the world had turned atheist, I would have written that book. It made no difference to me." While some wondered whether Dickey had found God, he was quick to disabuse them. He told Barker he definitely was not born-again: "My own religion is deliberately non-churchgoing. . . . I think the rituals are beautiful—I like them—and I could get to like them too much. As it is, the whole universe is my church."[6] As for the Bible, it was essentially its language and stories that attracted him.

When John Logue first broached the idea of another coffee-table book to Dickey, he did not have the Bible in mind. He proposed that Dickey collaborate on a wildlife book with Marvin Hayes. Hayes's biblical etchings changed his mind. Fearful of the way critics would respond to his tampering with one of the world's most sacred books, to spike their guns Dickey wrote in his foreword that his interpretation was merely one among many and that the Bible was "the greatest treasure-house of powerful, disturbing, life-enhancing images in the whole of humanity's long history."[7] In contrast to his collaboration with Shuptrine on *Jericho*, Dickey followed his partner's sketches of biblical scenes in his prose, and in his introduction praised his visionary art as comparable to William Blake's. Dickey reserved his tenderest praise for Maxine: "She was all her life a devoted dweller in the Bible, and now, through the flowering tomb, she resides among the superhuman reality of God's images. God bless you, my good girl, bride of the first night, and now of the first light."[8] For Dickey, his book was an act of redemption and atonement.

Dickey began his biblical narrative, logically enough, with the Creation. To consecrate that wondrous moment, he wrote prose in the fragmentary poetic style he now preferred: "Sky. Translucent infinite acre. Anxiety of water, when the hand of God passes over it. Here in the sleep-turning void, the pain waves have not begun. These are the star laws, moon-turning. The infinite hands are trembling. What is coming?" What comes is "the blue planet," a hot, biological soup that seems closer to Darwin's vision of origins than the Bible's. Speaking for God, Dickey prophesies that from the seas and jungles "great beasts will arise; this new place will be consecrated and fertilized by gigantic blood. The ground will shake with huge lizards. In the sea, monsters slide beneath the surface, up-coming to tear other monsters apart." In the second paragraph Dickey, who sometimes expressed his longing to be a god in his poetry, plays God more overtly. He asks himself why He is creating a world that includes such great terror and concludes: "I am trying something out. I don't have to do it, but the soft pain of the blue planet urges me on." As with his other attempts to write sublimely about the sublime, Dickey flirts with bathos. God declares portentously at the end of the first chapter: "I must do this thing. What I have done, I am doing. My hand passes over the deep waters, and the fish become." Following the Bible in word if not in spirit, Dickey next introduces Adam as a post-Freudian, post-Existentialist man rather than an innocent pastoralist in Eden. The fall into sex has uplifted rather than divided him. He is "healed of nothingness" while Eve, after a phallic encounter with a serpent, tries to speak for women through the ages by celebrating her sexuality. She says: "Lightning flows through our loins." Corresponding to Dickey's passages are Hayes's etchings of God's hands releasing the Earth, His fingers pointing at a miniature Adam, and a snake staring at an Eve that looks like a 1960s flower child who has just stripped off her shirt and bra. In addition to injecting modern ideas and sexual images into the biblical tales, Dickey stamps them with current pleas for racial harmony. The apostle Simon enjoins: "Let us do our best, black skin or white, to get up a hill with our load." Following the painful trials that transform heroes into gentler, wiser, poetic beings, Dickey offers a happy, apocalyptic end. Once again he constructs a narrative according to the "monomyth's" circular design; he concludes with a recapitulation of a pastoral Eden of sun, flowers, and grass.

High postal rates made God's Images too expensive to sell anywhere except in bookstores, so Oxmoor House decided on a relatively small print run of twenty-five thousand copies, which officially went on sale on October 15, 1977. By keeping the price low ($19.95), Logue hoped to have additional printings and to sell a hundred thousand copies by the end of 1977. Reviews—at least those that appeared in Christian magazines—were generally favorable. A group called Religious Media Today gave the book an award for Best Illustrated Work of the year. Some Christian critics, however, were disappointed by the book's sentimentality and earnest attempt to be au courant. Jane Dillenberger commented in Theology Today: "Hayes' illustrations sometimes become strained or stylish, at other times [they appear to be] expressions of the theology of the sixties and the new freedoms of the flower children." She was equally unimpressed by Dickey's prose poetry: "The poet's speech is often banal and [his] rhythms slack. The burden of the lines too often slips into an elevated, sentimental piety."[9] Despite the book's flaws, sales were brisk and were helped along on April 10, 1978, when the book was nominated for the Carey-Thomas Award—the award Jericho won for being the most significant publishing event in 1974.

Dickey facilitated sales on a tour through the South in February and March 1978. John Logue, who joined Dickey at several of his stops, confirmed that Dickey's promotional style had changed little since his Jericho trip. Despite his recent vow of temperance, he was drinking again as soon as he woke in the morning. In Richmond, he was more obstreperous than usual. Having perused Anne Sexton: A Portrait in Letters while Dickey signed God's Images in the Canterbury Book Store, in the hotel afterward Logue mentioned finding the letters about his friendship with Sexton. Dickey retorted: "Anne Sexton was looking for a demon all her life. And I was there all the time." The next morning, he fortified himself with beer before going to the local public radio station to discuss God's Images. When a caller mentioned Dickey's appearance in the Sexton book, Logue expected the worst. Dickey said: "You know Anne Sexton wrote so many poems about menstruation that I call her Ragtime Annie."[10] Logue thought of all the potential buyers of God's Images going to or from church—it was Sunday—and cringed.

To flaunt his irreverent attitude toward his book, Dickey made up a limerick he frequently recited in the voice of William F. Buckley at promotional events:

We've just rewritten the Bible
With images ancient and tribal
We hope it'll sell
From Heaven to Hell
If God doesn't sue for libel.[11]

His iconoclastic wit notwithstanding, at least some Christian groups reached out to Dickey. On November 23, 1977, during National Bible Week, Jimmy Carter invited him to the White House so that he and National Bible Week chairman Donald Seibert could present *God's Images* to Rosalyn Carter. In the spring of 1978, the Laymen's National Bible Committee elected Dickey to its thirty-member board of directors. Despite Dickey's ability to appeal to Christian groups, sales figures for *God's Images* never approached those for *Jericho*.

As *God's Images* demonstrated, Dickey was not as averse to the church and its literature as he sometimes pretended. When Deborah, who had been raised a Catholic, decided she wanted a formal wedding at Saint Joseph's, a Roman Catholic church in Columbia, Dickey acquiesced. Matthew Bruccoli, who had also been raised a Catholic, was asked to assist. The priest showed some reluctance to allow the ceremony until Bruccoli assured him that both Dickeys were serious about their intentions. The priest asked whether they planned to have children, and Bruccoli responded that they did, indeed, want a family. Six months after their secular wedding, the Dickeys were married in the church with Bruccoli serving as best man.

Some of Dickey's friends thought that his new attachment to the church and his preoccupation with the Bible had a salutary effect. Ward Briggs remembered an occasion before Dickey married Deborah when he told a date Briggs brought to a dinner party: "I'd like to take you to a motel room and beat you with a leather strap." Dickey was only half joking; he said the same thing to Jim Mann's fiancée and to other women as well. Now, according to Briggs, who became one of Deborah's closest friends at USC, Dickey was infused with a new righteousness and seemed almost paternal in his concern for Deborah: "He changed instantly one hundred and eighty degrees. He didn't want to hear any bad language; he didn't want to hear any dirty jokes; he didn't want to hear anything off-color."[12] Marrying in the Catholic Church was one way of accommodating Deborah and sanctioning their new life together. Deborah felt validated by Dickey's solicitude, but continued to strike back if he lapsed from his gentlemanly ways.

Dickey had another death to cope with at the end of the summer. Robert Lowell, whom he sometimes treated as the dearest of friends, died in a New York taxi cab on September 12, 1977. Dickey sent a telegraph to his second wife, Elizabeth Hardwick, whom Lowell was visiting after leaving his third wife, Caroline Blackwood, in England: "This man of words has no words. I like to think that Cal went in a great rush of pride in the wonderful accomplishment of his life and work. I can guarantee that I will have such a feeling for him when the same thing happens to me and as I do now. Please know that I am with you and Harriet always, now that all we can do is to love him forever."[13] To his USC classes he complained that the "Yahoo" Elvis Presley, who had also died recently, was stealing all the newspaper attention from Lowell. Dickey and critics had for years played up his rivalry with Lowell; now that Lowell was safely dead, Dickey wanted to emphasize their friendship. Their alleged competition, he said, had been manufactured by reporters: "It killed me when he died. And I wish to hell that the press would give over the supposed rivalry between Lowell and me. I loved the man. I had no rivalry with him. I'm not his opponent, but it's so fatally easy for journalists to do that. Here Lowell is the New Englander, I the Southerner, he the Classicist, I the Romantic. It's fatally easy to do that, when it should not be done, certainly not in this case."[14] To correct the misconceptions spawned by journalistic hacks, he told the *State* newspaper that he esteemed Lowell as a "great, tragic, caring poet" and "the most heartbreaking poet of our time. He could say to you in his writings that you were not alone in your suffering, that you were not alone in your pain, your mental illness. He was an understanding, compassionate man. . . . All we can do now is to love him forever, and I will."[15] But Dickey's retrospective feelings, like the kind he visited upon his dead wife in *God's Images*, were misleading. His friendly moments with Lowell were truces in a deliberate and often acrimonious battle he had waged for decades.

Now that many of his peers—Berryman, Plath, Sexton, Jarrell, and Lowell—were dead, Dickey had more reason to say, as he did to Mona Van Duyn, that he was "king of the hill"[16] or "king of the cats." The critics who used to envision him vying with Lowell or Berryman for the summit of Parnassus, however, were making way for other critics who argued that Elizabeth Bishop, John Ashbery, James Merrill, A. R. Ammons, Adrienne Rich, and a number of other poets were more deserving. Stung by these critical slights, Dickey vowed to disprove them even while conceding that his ambitious new projects might falter. In Nashville for an October reading, he told a journalist that he was unafraid of failing and that he had such monstrous plans for future works that his reputation was destined to take a beating.

On sabbatical during the 1978 winter and spring terms, the restless Dickey looked for opportunities to leave Columbia. In mid-January he traveled to Washington State for a number of readings. Not long afterward he went to George Mason University in Fairfax, Virginia, where he taught classes for the ailing writer John Gardner. He rented an apartment in a complex called Circle Towers (some called it the "Circular Ruins") and struck up a friendship with the fiction writer Richard Bausch, who taught at George Mason and lived down the street. Bausch had revered Dickey's poetry ever since he had read "The Last Wolverine" in the *Atlantic Monthly* while serving at Chanute Air Force Base in the mid-1960s. In 1978, Dickey endeared himself by unexpectedly suggesting a title for Bausch's first novel; he said he had been reading a lot of Catholic books in order to keep up with his wife, who was rediscovering her Catholic heritage, and had stumbled on a passage in Gerard Manley Hopkins about the real presence of Christ in the host. Dickey thought *Real Presence* fit Bausch's subject. Bausch was skeptical, but his publisher liked it.

Bausch had listened to Gardner lecture before, but a sober Dickey was far more charismatic. Pulling out books one by one from his vast briefcase, he awed Bausch as well as his regular students with his knowledge and entertained them with his wit. He taught two courses, an introduction to creative writing (English 396) and a seminar in creative writing (English 469). Sheldon Kelley, who sat in on some of Dickey's classes, agreed with Bausch's assessments. Alcohol made Dickey's moods shift abruptly; he could be scholarly one minute and childishly vulgar the next. Once, in order to demonstrate the heroic couplet for a class assignment, he rummaged through his briefcase for a book by Alexander Pope, failed to find it, and instead told a story: "When I stopped in a truck stop in Albuquerque, New Mexico, I had to go to the bathroom and lo and behold on the shithouse wall was the most remarkable and perhaps the most perfect heroic couplet. I'll repeat it now for you. Take note: 'How did I come to marry Ernestine? / I found her name on the rubber machine.' Think of it. Ernestine. Isn't that a lovely name!"[17] Dickey liked the name Albuquerque as much as Ernestine, and kept repeating it. The class looked on in stony silence as Dickey searched his briefcase again for Pope's poetry.

Dickey reached out to Gardner as he had to Bausch, occasionally driving to the Johns Hopkins hospital to visit Gardner during his cancer treatment. After Gardner's fatal motorcycle accident in 1982, he showed the same solicitude by trying to assuage the financial woes of the Gardner family. On September 22, he enlisted Jimmy Carter's help, explaining that Gardner's two children might not receive any money from their father's estate. Could Carter, even though he was out of office, prevail upon Reagan and the IRS to ease their tax burden? To strengthen his petition, Dickey cited the boxer Joe Louis and the writer Edmund Wilson as prominent citizens who had received similar relief from government officials. Deborah also wrote the former president, extolling Gardner as one of the best teachers in the world, a dedicated U.S. citizen, and a superb writer.

On March 6, 1978, Dickey traveled to Washington, D.C., to confer with poets rather than presidents. Along with twelve other former poetry consultants, he attended a Library of Congress reunion that was also a conference to evaluate the consultantship. John Broderick, chief of the Manuscript Division and supervisor of the library's poetry and literature programs, organized the event and was on hand to greet the participants. Daniel Boorstin, the current librarian, as well as Howard Nemerov, Elizabeth Bishop, Stanley Kunitz, Daniel Hoffman, and Stephen Spender convened in the library's paneled, book-lined Woodrow Wilson Room to discuss past problems and their possible solutions. Dickey lamented the dearth of poetry on cassette and video, and spoke with particular pride about initiating his program of taped readings. Bishop, who had grown wary of Dickey over the years, objected: "I don't like video tapes and I don't like recordings. I think it's more important for a student to sit home and read a book or write a poem than hear or see any of these things in the classroom. A poetry reading room seems a good idea, though the atmosphere would be so hush-hush I wouldn't enjoy it. Well, I can't stop progress, whatever that is."[18] At the Whittall Pavilion luncheon Dickey mingled with the other poets and then gravitated toward the newsmen. In a buoyant mood, he told them how happy he was to be on his "Olympian" summit again, and sermonized about the life-giving virtues of imaginative language. Later that night, the poets read for two and a half hours to an audience of more than a thousand people.

As his poems appeared less and less frequently in prestigious magazines, Dickey greeted minor awards with outbursts of gratitude. (In February, when he was inducted into Vanderbilt's Pi Kappa Alpha Fraternity as Brother Dickey, he told local reporters it was the most cherished honor he had ever received.) The number of reading invitations Dickey received proved he was still a crowd pleaser. On March 31, he appeared at Virginia Commonwealth University, from April 21–23 at the Jackson, Mississippi, Arts Festival, and he agreed to help inaugurate New York's Poetics Institute on May 9 by sitting on a panel and reading with Stanley Kunitz, Stanley Plumly, and M. L. Rosenthal. Sometimes, as in New York, a combination of insecurity and egotism incapacitated him. At the last moment he refused to participate with the other poets. Rosenthal, the event's organizer, had to scramble to find a substitute. In a May 16 letter to Rosenthal, Dickey blamed his absence on Deborah's unstable mental state, but added: "To be asked to appear on a bill with the likes of arrivistes like Stanley Plummer [sic] and never-weres like Stanley Kunitz, is a little bit more than I bargained for. I had been given the impression that the evening session was to be my own show. As Robert Frost used to say, 'I don't go if I ain't the show.' I have had enough of being victimized and traded upon by inferior poets, and will have no more of it. . . . Understand me, Mac, you owe me not one penny for my time."[19] He informed Rosenthal, however, that he *was* responsible for Dickey's $545.14 travel bill. The kindly Rosenthal wrote back that he had intended Dickey to be "the show" at the institute opening, and on August 23 wrote again to say that he was sorry their friendship had been compromised by the New York fiasco. To mollify Rosenthal, on September 11 Dickey offered to give a free reading at New York University during a promotional tour for Crown, which had just published *Tucky the Hunter*.

Sensing his slipping reputation among New York editors and publishers, early in 1976 Dickey urged friends to write letters supportive of his work to Gordon Lish at *Esquire* and Stewart Richardson at Doubleday. Occasionally he lashed out at the magazines that no longer favored his work. Asked about *Esquire* by a newspaper reporter in June 1977, Dickey did not mince words: "I hate it. . . . They're the last of the smart-ass magazines, and they're barely hanging on. I only stay there to help new poets get exposure."[20] Three weeks later, Lish, who would himself leave *Esquire* in 1977 to become an editor at Knopf, fired him as poetry editor. In a July 11, 1977, letter to Theron Raines, Lish wrote: "In view of Jim Dickey's stated feelings about Esquire and, further, the fact that the selection of poetry is and has been a task he's paid for but does not do, we're discontinuing the arrangement forthwith."[21] According to Lish, Dickey had enjoyed his *Esquire* title because it gave him another base in New York, but he did little as editor except recommend his friends for publication. As a result, Lish rejected most of the poems Dickey forwarded to him. After his dismissal, Dickey's rebukes of *Esquire* became harsher. At the Cosmos Club in Washington, D.C., with Sheldon Kelly, Dickey told some elderly ladies why he no longer worked for *Esquire*. "Ma'am," he said with false courtesy, "*Esquire* is nothing more than a popeye fuck book."[22] The ladies fell silent.

As Dickey lost publishing friends in New York, he pursued publishers elsewhere. In 1978, he discussed publishing his screenplays (*Escaped Shadows*), his fifty favorite guitar pieces (*The James Dickey Guitar Book*), and his uncollected poems with Matthew Bruccoli's firm, Bruccoli Clark. In July 1978, he joined the editorial board of the University of Idaho's relatively unknown journal *Ideogram*. If the glossy magazines snubbed him, he would return to the smaller magazines that had first embraced him. Dickey also tried to silence or manipulate those writers who were disseminating material harmful to his reputation. During the summer of 1978, his main target was Sheldon Kelly, who was doing research for his *Reader's Digest* profile. Dickey knew his siblings and intimate friends were talking to Kelly and feared the results might justify his critics' worst suspicions. When the *Reader's Digest* asked Dickey to cooperate with Kelly on May 30, 1978, he was of two minds. He wanted publicity, but perhaps not the kind Kelly would give. On July 15, 1978, Deborah called Al Braselton to say her husband was depressed and wanted to talk to a friend. Dickey took the phone, and soon got around to the subject of Kelly. Braselton tried to be reassuring: "Kelly is the perfect man to write a story about you. He's ex-airborne, a cowboy from Montana, bar-brawler, who happens to love James Dickey."[23] But when Braselton said that everyone in Atlanta was enjoying the opportunity to regale Kelly with James Dickey stories, Dickey called Kelly a son of a bitch. His principal worry, he confided, was that Kelly would expose his and Maxine's drinking problems.

One of the first things Dickey told Braselton on a visit to Litchfield after the phone conversation was that he was not an alcoholic. Dickey admitted needing a drink when he woke in the morning to inspire him to write, but assured Braselton that he was still in control of his consumption. Later Dickey justified his drinking with the pithy pronouncement: "I fault a man if he drinks too much before he's 40, but I fault him if he drinks too little after 40. I'm 55." Braselton noticed that Dickey kept sneaking drinks the whole time he was with him, and as he drank he slipped further into the role of rowdy teenager. Braselton commented: "I loved the child and the man and hated the adolescent. . . . Jim simply stayed in the adolescent mode more and more, which meant drinking more and more."[24] Having watched Dickey down six beers, three Bloody Marys, and eight double martinis before a poetry reading in the mid-1970s, Braselton decided that alcohol had killed the poetic child and threatened to kill the poetic adult in his friend.

With regard to Kelly, Dickey hoped that the forcefulness of his lies would predominate over the truths told by his Atlanta friends. The draft of Kelly's article that William Shulz at the *Reader's Digest* sent the Dickeys on August 8, 1979, proved that Dickey had little to worry about from the truth tellers. Dickey's tales of growing up in rural Georgia, starring as a 210-pound tailback on the high school football team, and piloting night-fighting planes in the Philippines and in Korea were preserved in mint condition. Other aspects of his mythic life were preserved as well. The draft contended that after his academic troubles in Florida, Dickey could have lived off his family's wealth—a net worth of one million dollars—but instead he chose poverty and poetry before getting a job in a New York advertising agency. As for his famous novel, it grew out of a treacherous white-water canoe trip down the Chattooga River. Many but not all of Dickey's fabrications were expunged from the final *Reader's Digest* article.

Talking to Braselton at Litchfield, Dickey must have realized that Kelly intended to do no harm. On their way to a country club for lunch, he spoke with his usual candor about such subjects as Hitler (he said he wanted to make a movie about the Nazi experience), homosexuality (he said when you have sex with a man "you fantasize a woman"), and Maxine (he had harbored no sympathy for her view of life as a series of grim obligations). Dickey said he once had shouted: "For God's sake, Maxine. Do you enjoy anything?" She had responded: "Yes, I enjoy having four or five stiff drinks and watching a basketball game on

TV."[25] Dickey roamed over other subjects as well: Beethoven's life, Einstein's theories about nature and God, Joyce's insubordinate meeting with Yeats, Picasso's theories of art, and his own contempt for urban Jewish writers. At lunch Dickey turned to his children. He spoke derisively of Chris getting his girlfriend pregnant at UVA and how Maxine had wanted Susan to get an abortion; he said he had objected to the ghastly procedure and now was glad to be the grandfather of Tucky. If Deborah felt left out of the conversation, Dickey didn't seem to take notice.

Braselton drove back to Atlanta hoping that his renewed friendship would survive his plan to write a biographical book about Dickey with the help of Kelly. Dickey, in fact, remained suspicious of both Braselton and Kelly, and asked various friends in Atlanta to act as informants. He had good reason to worry. While working on his *Reader's Digest* article, Kelly had learned about Dickey's pampered childhood, his military lies, his alcoholism, and many other aspects of his life, but chose to abide by Dickey's official story. From his many interviews he had construed a grim picture of the man he had once idolized: "There was a narcissism about him that was very apparent. His dalliance with Nazism . . . [was] a narcissistic evil [and] . . . had a great deal to do with the Nietzschean man."[26] Braselton had told Kelly about Dickey's fascination with Nietzsche's *ubermensch* and the Germanic ideals passed down by his grandmother. He had also told Kelly about Dickey's obsession with homosexuality and about his account of buggering a man earlier in his life. Reflecting on his own humiliating experiences with Dickey, Kelly speculated that Dickey's latent homosexuality arose from a sadomasochistic desire for subjugation. Kelly knew that the *Reader's Digest*, which had been leery of funding a story about Dickey, would not want to publish such controversial material. The article that appeared in November 1979 merely skimmed the surface of Dickey's career.

While Kelly worked on his article, Dickey confirmed some of Kelly's suspicions about his complexities in a frank interview with the English writer Paul Binding, who was composing a study of Southern writers, *Separate Country*. He confessed to Binding that he had a "Fascist reverence for force and the superman," but also a "persistent admiration for Quakerism and the pacifist ideal." To fill out his divided self-portrait, he said that he, like his wife, was a "convinced Catholic."[27] His admission of his newly found Catholicism, while in part a ruse, was another sign of his need for propriety, sanctity, and discipline in his disheveled life. He was also trying to articulate and organize his contradictory impulses in *Alnilam*, which addressed the issues of Nazism, the Nietzschean *ubermensch*, homosexuality, sadomasochism, and narcissism. (In Litchfield he had told Braselton that *Alnilam* was "My *Ulysses*, my multi-layered novel.")[28] Dickey's progress with his novel was so slow that he worried about forfeiting some of his $150,000 advance, and near the end of the summer he apologized to Stewart Richardson: "I regret and deplore the delay on the deliverance of the manuscript of *Alnilam*, but during the time I had set apart to write it, my entire family was wiped out."[29] He promised to mail the completed manuscript by the end of February 1979.

Hospital checkups in September 1978 convinced Dickey that his precarious health warranted a revision of his last will and testament. In the document he wrote on September 27 he made Matthew Bruccoli rather than Richard Howard his chief literary executor. In a letter recommending Bruccoli for USC's Russell Award several years later, Dickey explained that he had chosen Bruccoli as his executor because of his "combination of intelligence, tenacity, and loyalty: loyalty not only to me, personally, but to literature and research, and to those values we mean when we say cultural."[30] In his will he stipulated that Deborah should be consulted in estate matters providing she was still married to him at the time of his death. A divorce would nullify the agreement. On November 30, 1978, Dickey took further steps to settle his estate in case of imminent death. He signed a contractual letter to Kenneth Toombs, the USC librarian, stating that he agreed to the conditions worked out with Bruccoli for the deposit of his manuscripts at the USC library. "It is my intention," he wrote, "to make a formal gift of these manuscripts to the University of South Carolina at such time as the Federal tax laws are revised."[31] Despite his statement, Dickey indicated to Bruccoli that he never planned to give his papers to USC. Toombs, in fact, didn't want the papers in his library because he considered Dickey a disreputable writer. Because Bruccoli complained to the administration of Toombs's assessment, the provost arranged for the USC Caroliniana Library to house the papers "on deposit." During Arthur Young's tenure as librarian, Dickey asked Bruccoli to enter into negotiations for their sale, but Young felt Dickey's stature did not warrant their purchase. In the end, many at USC were disappointed when Dickey's papers went to Emory University.

Dickey dramatized some of his concerns about his health and domestic troubles in a step outline for a film, *The Olympian*, which he wrote in 1978 with North Carolina poet Tom Huey. Huey had formed a movie company, Upstream Productions, that agreed to pay Dickey fifty thousand dollars for the script and another fifty thousand dollars if the film was made into a TV film (it was never made). Another film he planned to write, *The Rising of Alna'ir*, also focused on the disturbing events that had recently befallen his family. Both screenplays, while embryonic in their development, reveal heroes passing through trials successfully but ending up bereft of their wives or lovers. They also reflect Dickey's estrangement from his sons and his difficulty giving up Maxine for Deborah.

As 1978 came to a close, Dickey distracted himself from depressing thoughts of death, decline, and estrangement by drinking and traveling. He read at the University of Miami on November 15, the U.S. Air Force Academy on November 28, and Nassau Community College on December 1. Early in 1979, at a Folger Shakespeare Library tribute to Shakespeare, he expressed his current mood by reading Shakespeare's "fearful meditation" on death, sonnet LXV:

> O, how shall summer's honey breath hold out
> Against the wrackful siege of battring days
> When rocks impregnable are not so stout,
> Nor gates of steel so strong but Time decays?

On January 23, 1979, he entertained an unlikely scheme to transcend "the wrackful siege of battring days" and perpetuate a legacy in outer space. Recalling that the Voyager spacecraft had been stocked with music for possible extraterrestrial civilizations, A.J. Vogl, an editor at Litton publications, asked Dickey to suggest music for a space flight to other solar systems. Dickey's choice was predictably eclectic. He picked Handel's *Water Music Suite*, Beiderbecke's "Royal Garden Blues," Bartók's *Concerto for Orchestra*, "Dueling Banjoes," recorded by Eric Weissberg and Steve Mandel, Mozart's *Concerto for Horn no. 1 in D Major*, and "Ragtime Annie," recorded by Doc and Merle Watson. Dickey didn't believe in life on other planets, but nevertheless sent Vogl his selection.

The death of his early mentor Allen Tate on February 9, 1979, only increased Dickey's preoccupation with time's "wrackful siege." Quoting a line from Tate's 1933 poem "Aeneas in Washington," he spoke to a Columbia reporter about Tate's imperishable mind: "Those of us who knew him personally as a very dear friend have suffered a great loss. But Allen's mind and his spirit are left with us. . . . Allen was the very last of his kind, the critic, essayist, the personal scholar, and finally the poet. . . . He was a marvelous, brilliant man."[32] Although Tate had encouraged Dickey in the early 1950s, their relations during the 1960s and '70s were sometimes acrimonious. Dickey had written a favorable review of Tate's poems for the *New Republic* in 1975, and Tate, who was suffering from emphysema, thanked him in October and in November called Dickey one of the most significant Southern poets of the past two generations. Tate, nevertheless, deplored Dickey's vulgarity.

On April 20, 1979, Dickey unleashed his inventive powers on Norwich University, the military school across the Connecticut River from Dartmouth College. He told the usual stories about being the "Crabapple Cannonball" on a North Georgia football team; fornicating with a dirt-poor cheerleader named Doris Holbrook who lived incestuously with her alcoholic father; and playing the sheriff in *Deliverance* at the insistence of Reynolds and Voight. Dickey did reveal something new to the Norwich cadets: He had recently finished his screenplay *The Sentence*, and it would be filmed later in the year. For his plot he had drawn heavily on *Deliverance* (the main character has a copy of the novel on his bookshelf) and the sort of rites of passage that informed his novel. Like Dickey's personae in *Deliverance*, his persona in *The Sentence*—Tennessee physics professor Stanley Hollis—is initiated into the netherworld beyond his civilized domain by a homosexual rape. Ed says of the rape in *Deliverance:* "A scream hit me, . . . it was a sound of pain and outrage, and was followed by one of simple and wordless pain."[33] Arriving in prison, Hollis hears a similar scream "of outrage and helpless pain."[34]

Dickey could have been referring to the mystique-driven Lewis Medlock or to himself when he said of the main character in *The Sentence:* "Stanley is not only extremely talented and inquisitive . . . , he is complex . . . , he is a mystery to everyone in the film, and will also be so to the audience."[35] Like Dickey he has a vast collection of books, operates a Davis sextant to figure out where he is, plays blues on the guitar, loves to fiddle with a slide rule, and regards teaching and learning as the most noble pursuits. He is a Quaker pacifist who abhors killing, capital punishment, and death of all kinds, but—like such notorious Quakers as Ahab or Nixon—he is also capable of deadly destruction. At a student party, he agrees to participate in an experiment in "cross-generation vice" by smoking marijuana while his competitor, a former high school band leader and current missionary named Lou Ann Robinson, drinks a fifth of Jack Daniel's. As he drives her home, he crashes his car, killing her and the other driver. A judge tells Hollis: "Dr. Hollis, you are a distinguished man in the community. . . . But you have committed a serious crime, one for which the law has no recourse other than sentencing you to six years in prison at the state facility at Firebreak Mountain." Dickey had his own sentencing in mind, although his prison term after crashing his Jaguar in Columbia was only four hours.

Dickey's story in *The Sentence* becomes a kind of allegory for his second marriage. The warden asks him to become a drug informer, but he refuses. After all, he is in prison because of an accident caused by his own drug use. He is also afraid of being killed by those who use drugs: "But that's not the main reason. I don't believe in lying and conniving and making deals. That's against my nature." Dickey had no such scruples, but protected his wife's drug use just the same. In *The Sentence* Dickey also wrote about his isolation from his sons. Because of his refusal to cooperate with the warden, Hollis is put in solitary confinement. Once he is released, during a literary conversation with the warden he quotes the German poet Stefan George about a prodigal son who comes home to tell his father "all about his sorrows, / And his wounded pride." Dickey hoped his estranged sons would do the same. Earlier in the script, Hollis questions one of his students as if he were Kevin. The young man wants to be a marine biologist, but Hollis wants to temper his scientific view with a more poetic one, so he reads Matthew Arnold's famous poem about the sea, "Dover Beach." Hollis finally excuses his students as if they were his children: "Go from me, my beknighted, over-specialized children, and become fully human."[36] In an interview with Elisabeth Beattie, Dickey once said of Kevin: "My son is a medical student, and he decries this [mystical, unscientific] attitude on my part. But I believe that I have more satisfaction in mysteries than he will ever have in explicit knowledge."[37] For Dickey, as for the Agrarians, science and poetry were antitheses, at least in arguments with his son.

The Sentence is partly indebted to Ben Greer's *Slammer* (1975), which also deals with the homosexuality and violence of prison life. Dickey gives Ben's name to the guard who hears Stanley's poetic recitations in solitary confinement, as if acknowledging the fact that Ben Greer was his poetry student before working as a prison guard. Greer was also Dickey's consultant during the writing of *The Sentence*. Dickey had offered to pay him fifteen thousand dollars for his assistance. Greer said he wanted his agent to draw up a contract, but Dickey responded: "You've got to trust me or there's nothing for you."[38] Greer grudgingly acquiesced, and they shook hands to ratify their agreement. Greer answered Dickey's questions about prison life, gave him advice about portraying characters, and tried to steer him away from melodramatic and unrealistic scenes. Since Dickey was more interested in describing his fantasies of prison, he rebuffed Greer's advice. He never showed Greer his completed screenplay and never paid him. Despite the pulp-fiction melodrama (the story concludes with strangulation, electrocution, and the prisoners' escape through a fence melted by cables attached to an electric chair), Dickey's new Hollywood agent, Evarts Ziegler, had hopes for the script in 1981. They went unfulfilled.

In composing *The Sentence*, Dickey may have had in mind Ezra Pound, another natural-born teacher and poet who had been imprisoned. As Dickey's poetic experiments and political statements veered closer to Pound's, Dickey decided to accept an invitation from the University of Idaho to deliver its fifth annual Ezra Pound lecture on April 26, 1979. Such luminaries as Buckminster Fuller, Marshall McLuhan, Hugh Kenner, and Robert Scholes had delivered the previous lectures. Taking his title from an image in Pound's *Cantos*, Dickey in "The Water-Bug's Mittens" attempted to distinguish Pound's valuable lessons from his "dismayingly wrongheaded" propaganda. Perhaps with his own bifurcated personality in mind, he stated that there were four Pounds: "the promotional and proselytizing" Pound, "the direct-observation and plain-statement" Pound, "the culture-plundering" Pound, and the translating Pound.[39] Pound-the-ideologue was a crackpot, but Pound-the-poet was a genius and an exhilarating model who overshadowed all those whom Dickey deemed talentless or mediocre imitators: Williams, Olson, Duncan, Zukofsky, Levertov, Rexroth, and Creeley.

Prior to the lecture in Idaho, a sober Dickey struck a less denunciatory pose with the local poet Ron McFarland. As he chatted about his public persona and his latest work, *The Zodiac*, he seemed both truthful and humble. Having admitted at a press conference that he was just an average college football player at Clemson, he tried to deflate other myths as well. He had been an indifferent advertising man, he said, and never wrote the jingle "Things go better with Coke," which many assigned to him. Asked whether his self-confidence had ever been shaken, he told McFarland: "I've never had it when it was not shaken. But if you let all that bother you, you just can't write, you won't try anything." Regarding his legendary drinking, he said he had quit and never missed it. His most revealing comment came when McFarland suggested that "the 'real James Dickey' is concealed by a self-created and media-assisted mask." Dickey replied with surprising honesty: "I suppose anybody would have a tendency to . . . partially invent or would partially have invented for him a kind of persona. . . . You don't know which the real one is. The person himself would be the least qualified to answer that."[40]

One thing Dickey did know was that many in the literary community reviled his exaggerated machismo. Over the next two decades he periodically stripped off his masks in an attempt to expose the vulnerable sensibility he had tried to conceal. He no longer wanted to be confused with one of his principal role models, Ernest Hemingway. In 1985, when the interviewer Hank Nuwer compared him to Hemingway, he protested: "If I have made a mistake, it is encouraging and allowing too much of that. My life is not at all that spectacular, nothing like his. I didn't go around killing elephants and lions and that sort of thing. I like to handle guns, and I like to hunt, but my success has not been spectacular."[41] In the same year he reemphasized his point to another journalist, Bruce Beans: "If you do the interview I want to stress . . . that I want as little biographical emphasis as can possibly be arranged. In connection with *Deliverance* I was foolish enough to give out a good deal more biographical information than was needed, with the result that the focus came to be on me rather than on the book I had written, and I have no wish to let that happen again. Thanks to my generosity—or garrulousness, it may be—the press built me up into some kind of

Hemingwayesque character, a real Natty Bumppo—or even Chingachgook—of the wilderness, a guitar player in the same league with Chet Atkins, an archer comparable to Howard Hill, and a number of other things that I emphatically am not."[42] If Dickey spoke honestly through one side of his mouth, through the other he could not help embellishing. In fact he was afraid of guns and didn't like to handle them. He could be generous and garrulous for sure, but he—not the press—concocted his mythic biography.

Dickey's reputation continued to flourish at USC. At the May 1979 graduation ceremony, the university chose him as its first Carolina Professor. USC president James Holderman made the announcement: "Jim Dickey is one of the most, if not the most, distinguished American poets. . . . This honor recognizes his contributions to literature which have brought renown to the University."[43] During the late spring and summer months Dickey made plans for a number of new projects. He told Doubleday editor Randall Greene he intended to visit relatives in Mineral Bluff to begin research for a new coffee-table book, *The Wilderness of Heaven*. Shaye Areheart had sent a contract in January 1978 that offered him a hundred-thousand-dollar advance. He translated the Swedish poet Lars Bäckström. He also got more involved in the National Institute of Arts and Letters. On June 11, he asked Malcolm Cowley to second his nomination of Matthew Bruccoli to the institute. He also urged his literary sparring partner Dwight McDonald to nominate John Simon (McDonald agreed, but not without a fuss) and contacted the scholar Harry Levin to support Simon.

After winning the National Book Award for *Buckdancer's Choice*, Dickey said: "If anyone enters into the writing of poetry for the purpose of awards, he's putting himself on and he's trying to put his readers on, too. That isn't what poetry's all about."[44] Nevertheless, in 1979 he worked out a strategy to win a Pulitzer Prize for his new poetry book, *The Strength of Fields*. He petitioned Doubleday to move the publication date from 1980 to 1979 so that he could take advantage of friends on the Pulitzer committee. He knew Jim Applewhite would be a judge, and he predicted that his other close friends Robert Penn Warren and Howard Nemerov would also serve. In May he told Stewart Richardson that if Doubleday could hurry the book through press: "We would be an absolute dead-sure certainty to win the prize." Upset by *The Zodiac*'s failure to win the 1976 Pulitzer—he had declined to sit on the Pulitzer committee so that his book would be eligible for the prize—he reminded Richardson that *Sorties* had almost won a National Book Award when the publication date of that book was timed to coincide with Stanley Burnshaw's service on the committee. (Burnshaw was on the 1971–72 committee with Frederick Morgan and John Lahr, but *Sorties* never made it to the final shortlist.) He assured his editor that they would "nail the matter air-tight shut with Applewhite, and the others, whoever they turn out to be, will surely follow."[45]

On June 5, Dickey apprised his agent, Theron Raines, of his scheme and prospects: "One of the judges [Applewhite] will vote for the book—in fact, he already has done so—another is a virtual certainty to do so, and the third a most likely probability. If we can get Doubleday to move the publication back to December, even if the publication date is the very last day of December, we will be eligible for the 1979 prize, and we will win it. This seems too good and too sure a thing to pass up, especially considering the fact that I probably will not have another collection for a good long time."[46] Doubleday published *The Strength of Fields* on December 14, 1979. The Pulitzer ultimately went to another poet. Dickey wrote Richardson: "I am still confused and dismayed about the failure of *The Strength of Fields* to win the Pulitzer Prize this time. Almost immediately after I got back [from Seattle], Rose Valenstein of the Pulitzer committee called me expressing the same feeling." About the committee, he said:

> I knew Jim Applewhite was on it, and I suspected that Helen Vendler of Boston University might also be on it, for they were the other two members of the committee the last time I was chairman and Jim and I gave the Prize to Howard Nemerov, over Ms. Vendler's violent objection. [In a letter written to Dickey on January 5, 1978, Vendler had said that she was happy to concur on the choice of Nemerov, but if Lowell had been alive she would have lobbied for *Day by Day*.] She wanted the Prize for Lowell, although he was dead; if I am not mistaken, there was something personal between her and Lowell, though I don't really know or care what. At any rate, I was right about this: Applewhite and Vendler were two of the members of the committee. The great surprise, however, was that Richard Howard was the chairman, and learning *that* floored me sure enough. Richard Howard's only distinction as a poet was that he received the Pulitzer Prize when I was chairman yet another time. . . . I have no idea how the judges voted, but I do know that Don Justice [who won the Pulitzer for his *Selected Poems*] is a very weak figure indeed, a compromise choice of some sort. I don't ask to be given prizes out of the gratitude of judges; I only ask that the best book win. I am quite convinced that *Strength* was easily the best book, and if there were any better ones around last year, one of them was certainly not anything by Donald Justice.[47]

Crediting himself for Howard's Pulitzer in 1970, Dickey fully expected Howard to return the favor in 1980. What he failed to realize was Howard's disaffection for his recent poetry. Dickey also hoped Vendler would support him. He had written her flatteringly when they served on the 1977 Pulitzer committee: "I am delighted to have you on the Pulitzer Committee for the selection of the prize in poetry. I have long admired your work, and can think of no one I'd rather join with in this enterprise."[48] Vendler, however, was not the type of woman to melt before his rhetorical charm; she felt *The Strength of Fields* was not of Pulitzer caliber. Applewhite was particularly disappointed by the book, since he had been such an avid supporter of Dickey's earlier poetry. Because Dickey had regarded Applewhite as one of his poetic "sons," he felt betrayed. Their friendship immediately cooled; they had little or no communication in the 1980s. On May 22, 1992, Applewhite was supposed to sit between Wilbur and Dickey at an American Academy of Arts and Letters ceremony (Applewhite was to receive the Jean Stein Award). Dickey failed to appear, and at the reception remained grumpy and aloof.

As Dickey's books went out of print—*Self-Interviews* in 1973, *Eye-Beaters* in 1977, *Sorties* in 1978—Dickey felt increasingly beleaguered. He was disappointed by the failure of *God's Images* to be another *Jericho*, and by the failure of *Tucky the Hunter* to sell as many copies as *God's Images* (it sold about fifteen thousand copies by May 30, 1979). He submitted the poem "A Saying Farewell—Homage to Nordahl Grieg" to Howard Moss at the *New Yorker* on May 28, 1979, acknowledging his "long hiatus" from the magazine. Moss rejected it. He submitted "For the Running of the New York City Marathon" several months later, and Moss rejected that as well. In 1979, Dickey submitted excerpts from *Alnilam* to the *Atlantic Monthly* and *Esquire*. The editors rejected them. The most painful indication of Dickey's sagging career was the demise of his "first-read" contract at the *New Yorker* on July 10, 1978. The *New Yorker* paid him $2,705.29 that had been accruing in his account, and essentially closed its doors to his poems. It published one poem in 1997 after he died and another with excerpts of Chris Dickey's *Summer of Deliverance* in 1998. Dickey reacted to the termination of his contract with indifference and contempt. He told friends that he had never wanted to be considered a *New Yorker* poet. To editor Liz Goldfarb, who wanted to publish some of his poems in her small journal in 1980, he wrote: "You needn't bother about *The New Yorker* contract system, for they have discontinued it. I was never comfortable with the thing, really, anyway."[49] In fact, the *New Yorker* had not done away with their contract system completely; they had merely nullified their contract with Dickey.

In contrast with his rosy accounts of his marriage to the press, Dickey felt as beleaguered at home as he did in the publishing world. His own marriage having dissolved around Thanksgiving 1977, Chris Dickey began hearing stories from Theron Raines about Deborah's violent attacks on his father. By that time Chris had given up on his efforts to be his father's keeper. Dickey had shown no interest in Chris's new job as a "Metro" reporter for the *Washington Post*, and Chris, in retaliation, withdrew further from his father's life. By 1979, Dickey's communication with his son was such that he had to contact Theron Raines to find out something about Chris's novel *The Colony*. (Chris had only formulated some ideas about a story concerning corporate dirty tricks in an American enclave in Mexico.) At Emory, studying for medical school, Kevin kept a similar distance from the troubles at Lelia's Court.

In the 1980s and 1990s, the indifference and hostility expressed by critics toward Dickey's work did little to curb his productivity. He published two new collections of poetry, three collections of previously published poetry, including his substantial *The Whole Motion: Collected Poems, 1945–1992*, two novels, two coffee-table books, a children's book, and two volumes of interviews and articles. He worked on several screenplays, began a new poetry book and a new novel, and continued to teach and tour as rambunctiously as ever. Nevertheless, only a small coterie of Dickey supporters believed that the quality of his work remained high. Many factors militated against his success. While his determination to experiment with new stylistic techniques in poetry and fiction was admirable, even he admitted his experiments periodically foundered. His alcoholism and his deteriorating marriage also contributed to his decline.

33. Under the Stone Snows of
Mount Saint Helens (1980)

In 1980, Dickey worked feverishly on his long-overdue novel *Alnilam;* he assured Stewart Richardson that the novel occupied him seven hours a day. Because he was nowhere near completion, he gave numerous excuses for his tardiness, the most unbelievable of them being the extra assignments he had accepted to stave off imminent poverty. He was so poor, he told Richardson, that he soon might not be able to afford steak even if surgery on his esophagus allowed him to eat it. He had been forced to schedule a spate of readings to pay the bill for the operation he would have in Seattle. From February to May he would read at William Rainey Harper College, Emory, the University of North Dakota, the Columbus Cultural Arts Center, and Southern Illinois University. In letters to his hosts, he demanded higher fees. To Clark Powell, who considered inviting him to read, he proclaimed: "The going rate for a reading—that is, for a single hour of my mortal time—is now five thousand dollars, which is double, exactly, what John Updike gets, what Truman Capote gets, and well above the fee of any other literary man or woman known to me. There are seven books being written on me at this time, and a good many more in prospect."[1] Such marketing tactics usually backfired. Emory only agreed to pay him a thousand dollars. In a letter written to Richardson on February 3, Dickey explained his dire situation: "I have had to fill up a lot of the time between now and May with reading and speaking dates, so that I won't go directly from the hospital to the alms-house. . . . But the novel is going fine, and now there comes the question of exactly in what stages you want to see it. I propose to send you a batch of manuscript every week, or every two weeks, to let you see what is happening to the story from point to point. I would like the closest connection with you on this, for it will be extremely helpful for me to know what your reactions are to the narrative as it unfolds bit by bit, as it would reveal itself to a reader, in his innocence, and—anticipation."[2] At the current stage of composition, Dickey still needed to figure out the motivations and goals of Joel Cahill's Alnilam Plot. Did Joel want a wholesale insurrection within the military? Did he want to initiate a global apocalypse?

Dickey had determined to bestow upon Joel the charisma of a dangerous utopian idealist. Like Hegel's and Nietzsche's "world historical" supermen, Joel would be the sort of zealot committed to altering the destiny of mankind. In deciding what sort of utopia Joel should espouse, Dickey told his editor:

For several years I have read avidly in this connection, and have here and there found hints of something like what I want—or Joel seems to want—particularly in Campanella's *City of the Sun* and in the odd, fascinating work of Ernest Junger, who was certainly the best of the writers under Hitler, who published an odd, unforgettable novel, while he was actually fighting in Hitler's army, called *Auf den Marmorklippen* (or *Marble Cliffs*), which you may have heard of, or read. We must be careful not to make Joel a crypto-Nazi, for that is too easy, so much after the fact, but to have elements in his Plot which prefigure a great releasing of energy, a kind of total marshalling of all human capabilities—in each individual case—such as has never before been experienced—or available—in human time. . . . I am sure the Alnilam Plot itself carries the potential of being a force of far greater power and authority, danger and excitement than, say, something like the John Birch Society (another "Plot" I have looked at and rejected, but which I thought worth scrutiny because it is a political scheme built around an individual *man*, a lost leader).[3]

Richardson must have been unnerved by the references to Joel's possible Nazi affinities.

To convince Richardson to be lenient about deadlines—he wanted an extension to 1981—Dickey deployed his own charismatic powers on his editor early in 1980: "You know, Sandy, how very deeply moved I am by your forbearance on the book. Since the time I began it my life has been through a series of upheavals as would cause God himself to weep in frustration. But those times are over now, thanks to your understanding and my marriage to Debba, and the road now is, if not absolutely straight and without obstacle, at least very much there. . . . God bless you, my good friend and great editor."[4] Having made little progress on the novel by the summer of 1980, Dickey again dipped into his ample reserves of sentimental praise. "I long for your company and the good aura you have about you," he told Richardson. "There is no way for me to tell you how much I owe to you as an editor, and as another human being in the world at the same time as I am. I will let all these things be unspoken, but will also reserve the possibility of putting them into words—real words—some time later on. Again, thank you so much, Sandy, for your existence."[5] Since Dickey began *Alnilam* in the early 1950s, his maudlin assessment of his "upheavals" could have applied to his entire career. He had every reason to suspect that the road toward *Alnilam* would *not* be straight and clear in the future, but for the sake of reassuring his editor he feigned optimism.

Dickey's confidence about the future was due in part to yet another pledge of temperance. Following a reading at Emory in mid-February, the *Atlanta Constitution* printed a laudatory article about Dickey's new civility and sobriety. With a Coke close at hand, he told the reporter: "Whatever drinking had for me has already passed. . . . I enjoyed it for a while . . . , but I found it was doing more against me than for me. I don't knock it at all; there are some definite benefits to (drinking). Morale, for instance. People say that the good feeling alcohol gives you is false—but all you have to do is live a human life to know that, in many instances, a false good feeling is better than none at all."[6] All year he did his best to abstain from drink. To boost his morale in a less deleterious way, he checked into a Columbia hospital for hair implants. Frustrated with his balding pate and his unsuccessful attempts to wind long strands of hair over it, he concluded that implants would help him look and feel younger.

Dickey's control over his persona was threatened by an unsuspected source in late winter. On March 11, 1980, his friend at the U.S. Air Force Academy, Jim

Gaston, proposed writing an exposé of Dickey's formative years as an air corps cadet and pilot. Dickey had lectured and read to the cadet wing in late November 1978, and Gaston had filmed his performance and incorporated it into an ambitious multimedia production about the Air Force Academy that utilized six slide projectors, two movie cameras, over eight hundred slides, a full symphonic orchestra, a ballet troupe, and thirty-five actors. Since Dickey had called his visit to the academy "a personal pilgrimage," Gaston and his collaborator, Bill Wallisch, had titled their show "Pilgrimage"; and on March 7, 1980, they had brought it to Columbia, South Carolina. After Dickey saw the show, he said haltingly: "I'm in your debt, not only for myself but for the other fellows in our squadron those 40 years ago. Don Armstrong and the others would be happy to know they have been so well remembered."[7] Dickey's halting speech may have been caused by guilt as well as gratitude, since his role in the film had been based on false pretenses. He had originally been invited to the Air Force Academy to talk about his experiences as a combat pilot, and in the film his words appeared next to those of a genuine pilot, Antoine de Saint-Exupéry. Because of Dickey's assertions about Armstrong, Gaston had depicted Armstrong as a kind of martyr, tortured and beheaded by the enemy, and had juxtaposed him with Lance Sijan, a pilot who, in contradistinction to Armstrong, actually had been tortured and killed (in Vietnam).

To persuade Dickey to cooperate with his literary exposé and give him permission to interview his air corps colleagues, Gaston argued that it would aid scholars, biographers, and Dickey, too, since Gaston assumed that Dickey wanted to write an autobiography. On May 8, knowing that Gaston would quickly uncover the systematic way he had lied about his military record, Dickey tried to dampen his good intentions without offending him: "I am much pleased that you would like to do some biographical work on me, but I feel that I shouldn't encourage you in this." His personality and personal experience, he contended, were superfluous compared to the literary works he had made from them. He admitted that his refusal to allow anyone to investigate his life aligned him with writers he generally discountenanced. "Oddly enough," he wrote Gaston, "I can think of only two writers who refused to have biographies done of them. These were Matthew Arnold and, perhaps not oddly, T. S. Eliot. Though I would not at this time be quite so adamant as those two gentlemen, I would stand somewhere near them." In order to deflect Gaston from his trail, Dickey flattered him by calling him the "only authentic war-hero"[8] he knew, and paid him a further compliment by saying that he wanted his grandson, Tucky, to attend the Air Force Academy. He promised to introduce Tucky to Gaston on a future visit to the campus (Dickey never made the visit). His kindly tactics worked; out of respect for his friend, Gaston refrained from writing about Dickey's air corps days.

In the summer of 1980, Dickey continued to fret about impending poverty. To help pay for his upcoming operation in Seattle, he asked Matthew Bruccoli to take charge of selling his papers. Bruccoli suggested a price of $350,000, and began negotiating with Emory. After showing initial interest in the purchase, Emory withdrew. Dickey now hoped that the Library of Congress might buy them, but in late September the library notified him that its budget did not allow for the purchase of large archives; it only accepted gifts. Still looking for a buyer, on December 8, 1980, Dickey told Janet Hughes at Arizona State that she should investigate the possibility of her university purchasing them. In late February 1981, Bruccoli informed Arizona State that the price was $300,000. The university replied that the amount far exceeded its resources. Dickey would have to wait another decade before receiving a satisfactory offer.

Having been unable to swallow properly for years, in May 1980 Dickey traveled to Seattle's Virginia Mason hospital for surgery on his blocked esophagus. An operation had been suggested as early as 1974 by Dr. John Converse, the husband of Gary Cooper's widow, who worked at the New York University Medical Center. He had urged Dickey to consult the specialist Dr. Lucius Hill. Dickey did, and was pleasantly surprised that the eminent physician admired his writing, but Dickey let his correspondence lapse until December 23, 1979. Now that a new operation had been perfected for correcting diaphragmatic or hiatal hernias (Dickey's intestine was strangling his esophagus), the time for surgery seemed propitious. The Virginia Mason hospital also had an attractive policy of letting patients settle into furnished apartments before and after surgery.

On May 15, Dickey flew with Deborah first to the University of Idaho to pick up an honorary degree and then to Washington for preliminary consultations with Dr. Hill. Hill explained the delicate operation and did his best to allay Dickey's fears. Seeking literary companionship, Dickey summoned William Matthews, David Wagoner, and several other Seattle poets to his new quarters. Matthews noticed that Dickey was extremely nervous about the operation, and with some justification since it had a low success rate. He appeared lonely and desperate for distraction. Matthews helped boost his confidence when a reporter, who had just finished an interview for a local newspaper, asked the two poets about a possible headline. Dickey suggested "Major Poet Comes to Town" and looked to Matthews for confirmation. Taking his glance as a cue, Matthews responded: "Yes, major poet."[9] Matthews and Dickey then played "quote for quote," reciting favorite passages from seventeenth- and eighteenth-century poems.

The prospect of surgery prompted Dickey to write another will, which differed from later ones in its generosity toward Deborah. In the mid-1990s, he would allocate few of his assets to her and make sure that she had nothing to do with his literary estate. In 1980, he consigned to Deborah his Oriental rug, musical and navigational instruments, whatever books she wanted, and the silver he had inherited from his mother. (In the 1990s Dickey complained to Al Braselton that she pawned the silver for drug money.)[10] She was to share his real estate with Kevin and Chris, and she could live at Lelia's Court or Litchfield if she remained unmarried. As for his literary estate, he instructed: "My wife, Deborah, is to serve as my Primary Literary Executor, with her principal advisor, Matthew J. Bruccoli, & if she should so desire, the added aid and advice of James Mann." (Dickey began regularly referring to Bruccoli as his sole literary executor from about 1990 to 1997, but Bruccoli remained skeptical of his appointment until Dickey's final will was revealed after his death in 1997.) The money from the sale of literary papers was to be divided equally between wife and sons. Much of the will dwelled on a future *Collected Poems*, even specifying that the cover should contain an illustration of an eclipsed sun. With regard to the un-finished *Alnilam*, it should be published in its fragmentary form with notes, or John Gardner should be asked to finish it. He asked that "James Dickey, American poet, 1923–1980" be engraved on his tombstone with the line, "What could I do but make the graveyards soar?" or "The spirit informs and wanders." He wanted Mike Russo and Ron Brentano to play "Dueling Banjos" at his fu-neral. Last but not least, he took precautions against those who might delve into the scandals of his life: "I authorize *no* official biography, though material may be consulted for critical & interpretive works dealing with my writings."[11] Both Dickeys signed the will.

On May 20, two days after Mount Saint Helens's cataclysmic eruption in Washington, Dr. Hill performed his operation. In his allegorical accounts of sur-geons battling Sleep and Death with short knives, Dickey could not help com-paring himself to Mount St. Helens. The volcanic mountain had been breached, he suggested, at the same time his body had been surgically opened. In a letter he wrote Stewart Richardson, he exclaimed:

> Well, I made it, though I was practically cut in half and stayed under—or out—for a long time. The operation not only entailed a release and dilation of the stricture that was preventing food and even liquid from passing from the esophagus to the stomach, but a kind of reorganization of all my diges-tive organs, which had been displaced by the stomach rising through the split place in the diaphragm and being in a place where it was never in-tended to be. There was a thorough check-out of all the organs—not only the digestive ones—for what they were looking for, the doctors later told me, was esophagal cancer and its possible spread to other areas. None was found, however, and the rest of the operation—or the "procedure," as we medical professionals call it—was successful, and I can eat normally, though still slowly. . . . But my God, it was strange! We left Idaho, where the good folk at the University were foolish enough to give me a degree, and were just *over* Mount St. Helens when the thing blew. The pilot was so ex-cited by all this he could hardly contain himself from flying into the crater, and he kept yelling to the passengers to get over there and look because "you won't see *this* every day," as though the eruption were a special service offered exclusively by Eastern Airlines. Then there was the period of uncer-tainty in Seattle. "The procedure" was scheduled for Friday, and everybody at the Clinic was sweating out the wind, for it was feared that it would shift and blow the ash up into Seattle, which might have clogged up the hospi-tal machinery, the anesthetic paraphernalia, and God knows what else. Luckily the wind off the sea held, and carried the ash back over Idaho.[12]

To Jim Gaston, who had wished him well, Dickey added further details of his surgery. He said that while anesthetized, "I was attempting to fly quite blind—under ether, without even eyesight or consciousness, much less instruments—through the stone snows of Mount St. Helens. . . . It was all a very strange experience, like a dream of combat where you don't even know whom or what you're fighting, but must be the battleground itself, either on the table or in some manner levitated, where the surgeons must go into action against the Dark Men, with only their short blades."[13] Etherized on the operating table, Dickey must have been thinking of blind Frank Cahill flying an airplane in *Alnilam*.

To local newspaper reporters like Frank Zoretich, Dickey described his ordeal in terms of death and resurrection: "Nobody who's come back to life can have greater incentive to enjoy just getting out into the sunlight, just walking around talking to people." He cast Dr. Hill in the role of his savior who deserved "hosannas of love and confidence." With his other *Deliverance* on his mind, Dickey tried—as he had done earlier at the University of Idaho—to dismantle the Hemingwayesque myths he had built around himself: "I'm not a great canoeist or whitewaterman. I love the wilderness, but I don't have a profound knowledge of it in the way that Thoreau had. I am an outlying suburban Southerner, therefore I sometimes go off into the wilderness like the *Deliverance* fellows. To me, as the city encroaches, the wilderness has more and more the quality of a vision, a Lost Paradise. It has a fascination for me in the same way that prize-fighting has for Norman Mailer, or the Gold Rush had for Jack London. I'm not a great macho figure—but I enjoy the vision of ultimate things, the zero situation, live or die."[14] Recuperating from what he often portrayed as a disembowelling, he was simply glad to be alive. He had no will or ability to strut.

Old friends contacted Dickey to wish him a speedy recovery. The poet Daniel Hoffman phoned just as Dickey was emerging from anesthesia and said: "Hang in there, Jim, we need you."[15] The groggy Dickey was ready with an answer. He said that Burt Reynolds and Jimmy Carter had called, but that Hoffman had been the only poet to do so. Some weeks later Dickey wrote Hoffman: "Befogged by drugs, lying under the surgical snows and pulverized (almost mythologized) stone of Seattle, I had no adequate words to thank you for the profound grace of your gesture in calling me." His call, Dickey averred, "meant . . . more than President Carter's, or even (God help us!) Burt Reynolds's! who read back to me, as though on cue, some of his lines from *Deliverance* ('Survival. That's the game. Now you get to play')."[16] Like his other alleged communications with Reynolds after *Deliverance*, the Seattle phone call was probably apocryphal.

Many poets besides Hoffman contacted Dickey at the hospital. William Stafford sent a poem and a letter, which Dickey later said "were the main things that went with me into the place where the doctors challenge the Dark Man with their short knives, and the main things that came out of it."[17] In another account of his hospital experience, Dickey told a Norton editor that Richard Hugo had been the first to telephone him. Dickey had been so moved by Hugo's solicitude that he'd wanted to drive to Missoula, Montana, to thank him. The volcanic eruption had intervened, and state police had prohibited traffic on the Montana roads. Unable to thank Hugo in person, on June 13 Dickey thanked him in a letter: "It may be that you won't believe me—though I hope you do—when I tell you that your messages from Montana were more effective medicine than all the knives, drugs, and radiocative magic of the doctors."[18] Dickey repaid Hugo by inviting him to read at USC on November 14, 1980. Not long after Dickey's operation, Hugo himself would go to Seattle's Mason clinic for surgery to remove a cancerous lung.

In his June 13 letter to Hugo, Dickey also made the startling admission that Ted Bundy, the notorious serial killer who had recently been apprehended and imprisoned in Florida, had been padlocked next to him on the plane from Idaho to Seattle. To his friend Liz Rosenberg he was more truthful. He said his surgery was "memorable . . . because I survived it, and because one of my nurses gave me a paperback of the life and adventures of a former neighbor of hers, Ted Bundy, the mass slayer of college girls now on Death Row in Florida."[19] In the hospital the stories about Bundy had distracted him from his pains and fears, as they would his brother, Tom, who went to an Atlanta hospital with terminal cancer in 1987.

To learn more about Bundy, in the early 1980s Dickey corresponded with C. Terry Cline, who wrote about Bundy's murders in *Missing Persons*. On a visit to New York after his operation, he bought a copy of *The Stranger Beside Me* by Ann Rule, a woman who had worked with Bundy on a crisis hotline and reported for a newspaper on some of his murder victims without ever suspecting that he was the murderer. During the fall of 1980, Dickey wrote Rule a letter praising her book. In their occasional correspondence over the next few years Rule intrigued Dickey with her reports of contacting Bundy in prison, where he was studying law books in order to defend himself. The idea of contacting Bundy so gripped Dickey that he began telling stories that Bundy had asked to see him and that he had, indeed, visited Bundy. The story had as much credibility as his others about prisons.

In Bundy, Dickey found several of his own salient traits magnified and gruesomely distorted. Rule's book made it clear that Bundy was a supreme liar, a camouflage artist, a man with many masks, a juggler of personalities. Referring to the many Bundys, Rule pointed out: "One [was] the perfect son, the University of Washington student who had graduated 'with distinction,' the fledgling lawyer and politician, and, the other, a charming schemer, a man who could manipulate women with ease, whether it be sex or money he desired, and it made no difference if the women were eighteeen or sixty-five. And there was, perhaps, a third Ted Bundy, a man who turned cold and hostile toward women with very little provocation."[20] Although Dickey's romantic machinations were tame by comparison, he schemed with similar finesse. Bundy, according to Rule, had killed many women because they resembled a woman he had loved, a woman of higher social status who had snubbed him. Dickey was fascinated by such a motive for revenge.

Dickey learned more about Bundy in a March 1983 issue of *Esquire*, which printed his article "The Poetics of Dress" as well as an article on Bundy. Dress, Dickey opined, "creates a new personality, for I am at an age where I have grown damned tired of the old one." In order to look "tough, gaudy, and phony" and to make strangers wonder "what person—what *other*—I might be,"[21] Dickey stated his preference for medallions, hats, denim, Latin American *guayabera* shirts, Civil War belt buckles, army-surplus fatigues with big pockets for compasses and knives, loggers' boots, and Puma running shoes. In a 1983 letter to Dave Smith that referred to the conjunction of the two *Esquire* articles, Dickey revealed how far his obsession with Bundy had progressed: "A woman [Rule] who was a friend of Bundy's during the time he was murdering all those girls around Seattle tells me that the famous man expressed an interest in getting together with me. Would you like to go down to Starke, Florida and sit on death row with me for a little while? I'm tempted to do it, not because I want to write about it, but because I'd like to see what such a fellow is like; you know, right *there.*"[22] As much as he would have liked to, Dickey never translated his fantasy into fact.

Dr. Hill rather than Bundy was responsible for restoring Dickey to health in Seattle. Pleased with the way Dickey had reacted to the operation, Dr. Hill suggested that he have a pH and pressure study in three months. Otherwise, he just needed to relax so his body could heal. On June 8, Dickey returned to Columbia, and by the end of the month he was eating and walking with only minor twinges of pain. He enthused to Liz and John Rosenberg: "I am so busy eating everything in sight for the sheer joy of feeling it go down my gullet unobstructed, that I have added nails, bobby pins, splinters of glass, nuts, bolts, and screws to my diet, and I don't even use ketchup. Believe me, our old friend Epicurus was right: the greatest pleasure is the absence of pain."[23] His pain had certainly abated, but during his remaining years he continued to have problems digesting food.

To build on what he considered his recent successes (he reported to friends that *The Strength of Fields* had entered its fourth printing and *The Zodiac* had sold out and would now be reissued in a special gift format), in mid-June Dickey applied himself to a new book he called *Deborah Puella*. Having turned down John Logue's proposal to collaborate on a coffee-table book about Southern cheerleaders—he sent back Logue's photographs on February 5, 1979—he took up the *Puella* poems, which had been intended for another coffee-table book. His letters to his publisher were full of promotional zeal. He told Stewart Richardson: "They are surely the best sustained sequence anybody has done since Rilke's *Orpheus* sonnets."[24] He sent Ken McCormick an equally enthusiastic claim: "It is the best poetry I have ever written, believe me. It may be strange and perhaps a little hermetic for some tastes, and it may take some getting used to, but the best of it makes my previous work seem thin and neat, and all the other poetry being written now at best off the true point and at worst irrelevant."[25] If Rilke's *Orpheus* sonnets provided models, according to Dickey, so did Valéry's *Le Jeune Parque* and numerous other books.

In mid-July Dickey contacted John O'Brien at the Deerfield Press to see if he wanted to select several of the *Puella* poems for a chapbook. He informed O'Brien that the original book publisher, The Golden Chalice Press, had "*apparently* turned the nineteen poems back over to me, to publish as a separate book without the photographs, and in any format or with any publisher I choose. . . . The poems were conceived as autonomous works, which are in no sense dependent on the illustrative material, but which could be read in reference to it. The poems are better—much better—standing alone, and I have changed the titles to allow the cycle to turn around the early girlhood of my wife Deborah, and I think the result will be a revelation to you or anybody else who reads them."[26] He urged O'Brien to contact The Golden Chalice Press and the *Atlantic Monthly* (where one of the poems had appeared) for permission to reprint the poems. Dickey then took matters into his own hands. On July 28, he told O'Brien that he had made all the required arrangements with his agent, with Golden Chalice Press, and with Doubleday for the release of the poems. O'Brien should proceed with the chapbook. In December 1980, Deerfield Press printed a limited edition called *Scion*.

It was not until December that Dickey got legal advice about wresting his poems from Bookie Binkley, the photographer who had originally commissioned them for the coffee-table book. On December 4, he informed Theron Raines: "Kirkman Finlay [Dickey's lawyer] says we owe Bookie nothing, and whatever we pay will be a matter of charity. The gist of what Kirk says is that I signed something which was supposed to have been subject to review by you, but since you say it was *not* subject to your review—that, in fact, you never even saw it—then that invalidates the contract I signed. According to Kirk, that consideration clears us from owing Bookie anything at all. What we give him, if anything, will be a matter of charity, or, if you like, a matter of morality, or what we choose to call morality."[27] Dickey's "charity" or "morality" would soon be tested in court.

In 1980 Dickey once again served on the Pulitzer Prize committee, this time as chairman. The two other members were the *New York Times Book Review* editor Nona Balakian and poet John Ashbery, whom Dickey had dismissed as a "non-poet"[28] a decade earlier. Dissent inevitably followed. Balakian, a survivor of the Armenian genocide, preferred the dark visions of Mark Strand, Louise Glück, and Galway Kinnell. Ashbery, a New York poet heavily influenced by abstract expressionism and avant-garde writing, voted to give the prize to his New York friend James Schuyler for his book *The Morning of the Poem*. Dickey's first choice was *Windrose, Poems 1929–1979* by Brewster Ghiselin. Dickey effected a compromise. Since Ashbery had found Ghiselin's lapidary style disappointing and since Dickey had placed Schuyler second on his list, the two men decided to give the prize to Schuyler. Dickey paid little attention to Balakian's choices.

Serving on the Pulitzer committee forced Dickey to alter his plans for *Puella*. He had originally wanted Doubleday to publish the book in 1980, but to make it eligible for the Pulitzer he urged his publisher to delay its release. He told Richardson that the only reason he had agreed to sit on the 1980 Pulitzer committee was because "one of the other members of the committee is to be John Ashbery, a kind of clique writer up there [in New York], and I thought it best that the award not go to one of his friends."[29] Dickey wanted the prize to go to one of *his* friends. During the judging process he had promised John Stone, the doctor he now called "My dear old Life Saver," that he would give his book *In All This Rain* special attention. He had grown closer to Stone after Kevin had spent the summer of 1980 working in the surgical emergency clinic at Emory's Grady Memorial Hospital. Later Dickey complained that, as Pulitzer chairman, he had no real authority. To his student David Havird, who expressed surprise over Schuyler's triumph, Dickey rejoined: "Anything to keep Mark Strand from getting it. . . . He's such a careerist."[30] A decade earlier, Dickey had written Strand: "I hope you do well in the NBA competitions. . . . You are one of the very good ones around, and that's the truth."[31] By 1980, Strand's reputation had eclipsed Dickey's, and Dickey, whose efforts on behalf of his own career had backfired, vowed revenge. As for Galway Kinnell, Dickey protested to another friend: "He is too obviously a spin-off from me for me to be comfortable in read-ing his work."[32] Although he admired some of Glück's poetry, in his view she was too obviously a spin-off of confessional poets like Plath and Sexton.

In an effort to rehabilitate his literary reputation, Dickey contacted some of America's and England's main arbiters of poetic taste. He wrote Helen Vendler, one of his antagonists, a chatty letter about George Herbert. He had just read something in the *American Scholar* about her book on the metaphysical poet, he informed her, adding that he admired Herbert and knew a lot about the con-temporary state of Herbert criticism. The next day he wrote Donald Davie, a leading English poet and critic who had recently accepted a position at his alma mater. Dickey offered a glowing assessment of Davie's career: "I have been fa-miliar with your work ever since Flannery O'Connor gave me a copy of your *Articulate Energy* on the front porch of her farm in Milledgeville, Georgia, and have since followed your writing as closely as I was able. In addition to your po-etry, which I consider by far the best of the group you are conveniently . . . asso-ciated with [the Movement, whose leading poet was Philip Larkin], your work on Pound is the best that has yet been done. . . . I hope the strongest warmth of which I am capable will come off this page."[33] Ranking England's top poets in other letters, Dickey rarely mentioned Davie.

Moved by Dickey's show of Southern courtesy, Davie replied with a friendly letter about how they had met at the Grosvenor Square embassy in London in the early 1960s when Cleanth Brooks was cultural attaché. Vendler sent a cooler message from Churchill College in Cambridge, England. With a veiled refer-ence to her past remarks about Dickey, she said that she was happier writing about a dead poet like Herbert since living poets often took offense at her judg-ments. Dickey was well aware of her stinging criticisms of his work. Along with a blurb he mailed Richard Tillinghast for his book, *The Knife and Other Poems*, he sent a warning: "The only danger you run from such an endorsement is that people like Helen Vendler, who for some reason detests me, will write you off as a follower of mine. But since Dave Smith is also a follower of mine or has cer-tainly been influenced to an almost unparalleled degree by my work, and since for some reason Ms. Vendler likes *him*, maybe you won't come in for dismissal by her, or even worse, for her always-wrong praise."[34] Dickey damned other critics of his work besides Vendler, usually for failing to appreciate his stylistic experi-ments. Attacked for political reasons, he could be similarly aggressive. During the summer of 1980, in a *Time* essay that playfully matched poet laureates with certain presidents, Lance Morrow aligned Dickey with Lyndon Johnson. Dickey was enraged. Although Morrow's tone was facetious—he paired the outspoken African-American poet Amiri Baraka with Nixon—Dickey fired off a rebuttal to the *Time* letters section. Why should he be associated with a president who was generally despised for his role in the Vietnam War? He bristled at Morrow's political innuendo: "I was poetry consultant to the Library of Congress during Johnson's Administration, but poets are not allowed to pick their Presidents. My political sympathies at the time were in no sense with the late President, but with then Senator Eugene McCarthy, who was and is a personal friend."[35] Still fuming, Dickey drafted another, more excoriating rebuke:

Johnson is irrevocably and forever the Viet Nam President, and that is the association your readers will inevitably make. I supported McCarthy because I felt he was right in his stand. What I may or may not have risked in taking such a stand while serving under Johnson is known to me, and not to you. How, exactly, do you know that I "realistically risked absolutely nothing" by doing what I did? And what do you mean by "posturing," and "a few fairly easy moral points with the antiwar movement"? If I had wanted to score points of this nature, either hard or easy, I would have been engaged in the various public demonstrations against the war that so many of my generation saw fit to participate in. I did none of this, whether you like it or not. You seem to look at literature and other such doings from the standpoint of career maneuvering, scoring points, and the rest. There is plenty of that around, to be sure, but I'll have none of it.[36]

How could the magazine that feted him in the 1960s and 1970s bracket him "with the most detested President of our time"? The vehemence of his letter betrayed the guilt he felt over frequently siding with Johnson's tough stand on Vietnam.

On September 4, Dickey left his political wrangling behind for a momentous five-day visit with Deborah to England. The ostensible purpose of the trip was a television broadcast. He was to participate in four BBC telecasts organized by William F. Buckley and directed by Malcolm Muggeridge about famous English authors like D. H. Lawrence, Somerset Maugham, and Graham Greene. Dickey joined Auberon Waugh and Robin Maugham (the novelist's nephew) in a series of witty and often contentious discussions. While not bantering before TV cameras, he visited famous places in London with Deborah and made a pilgrimage to the grave of Malcolm Lowry, the novelist who had died in Sussex after writing one of Dickey's favorite novels, *Under the Volcano*. Its moving portrayal of alcoholic hallucinations had influenced Dickey's *Zodiac* and had obvious relevance for his and his wife's afflictions.

The excursion to Sussex had unexpected consequences. As Dickey later revealed to Gwen Walti: "At that momentous time, my little girl, Bronwen, was thought of, or invented, in a rose-garden in Sussex, and, since Wales is the only part of the British Isles I have ever been able to stand, and feeling that we owed the islands *something* in connection with Bronnie, we named her as we did."[37] Deborah's memories of Bronwen's romantic conception were more explicit. She recalled taking a shower at about three in the morning to help her sleep. When she stepped out, the moon shimmered through the cottage window. Her husband beckoned her to their bed. Gazing at her moonlit body, he told her to keep her eye on the moon as he made love to her. The moment seemed so magical that she was sure she had gotten pregnant.[38] In honor of their moonlit night in the cottage among the roses, the Dickeys eventually decided to name their child Bronwen because it meant "white-breasted." The name would consecrate a bond between mother and daughter and, if what both Dickeys told friends can be trusted, the last sexual relations in their marriage.

As Dickey began a new family with Deborah, his son Chris took steps toward his own new family. On the "Metro" beat for the *Washington Post*, Chris had met Carol Salvatore in October 1978 at a lawyer friend's party. They had married in a civil ceremony in Philadelphia's City Hall in March 1980. A week later, now as a foreign correspondent for the *Post*, Chris had returned to El Salvador, where he was covering the bloody civil war. Against divorce on principle, Dickey made a lackluster show of support for the new marriage. He wrote Gwen Walti that "everybody in the family loved [Chris's first wife] but Chris."[39] Critical of his son for abandoning Tucky, who followed his mother to his grandmother's horse farm in Massachusetts, Dickey nevertheless wanted to attend the marriage ceremony in Philadelphia. Deborah refused, even after Matthew Bruccoli tried to persuade her to go. On January 1, 1980, Dickey did little to endear himself to Carol when he met her for the first time at Washington's Georgetown Inn. Despite Deborah's claim that he had all but quit drinking, he appeared drunk. He asked Carol about her people—Italian-Americans from Philadelphia—but as soon as she began to speak of her mother he cut her off in a heavy Southern accent. "Do you want to marry my son?" he asked. Flustered, she said, "Yes," to which he replied, "Good. . . . Because I want you to."[40] To Chris, his father seemed to be reciting lines from a script. On the way out of the hotel he tore up the copy of *The Strength of Fields* that his father had signed for him with wooden formality.

Chris and Carol reaffirmed their vows in a religious ceremony on October 1, 1980, in Moorestown, New Jersey. Carol's parents sent out engraved invitations, hired an orchestra, arranged for food, and set up a tent. Chris hoped his father and stepmother would stay away, but they decided to come: "My father was trying to keep his drinking under control, which made him nervous and talkative. In the limousine from the church he told my new in-laws what a fine wife and mother my *first* wife had been. He made Italian-American jokes. . . . Then, during the toasts to the bride and groom, Deborah made a toast to herself. She announced to the assembled guests that she was pregnant."[41] Chris was relieved when his parents returned to Columbia and he returned to Central America.

Three weeks after his son's wedding, Dickey traveled north with Deborah to lunch with William F. Buckley at his home in Stanford, Connecticut, speak at a *New York Quarterly* banquet honoring Richard Eberhart, and attend the tenth-anniversary benefit for Poets & Writers, Inc. (Other prominent guests were Lauren Bacall, William Styron, Abbie Hoffman, Leonard Bernstein, Norman Mailer, Joyce Carol Oates, and John Updike.) In New York he also discussed the publication of *Puella* with Shaye Areheart, who had taken a job at Doubleday on March 1, 1979, and with Ken McCormick. The most urgent matter on his publisher's agenda, however, was *Alnilam*. Doubleday had fired Stewart Richardson, and another editor, Randall Greene, had withdrawn from the project. McCormick wanted Dickey to pick an editor he respected. Dickey must have approved of Hugh O'Neill, because O'Neill replaced Richardson. Over the next six years the book moved from one editor to another like a hot brick.

In the final months of 1980, Dickey worked on *Puella, Alnilam, The Wilderness of Heaven*, and the *Deliverance* screenplay, which Southern Illinois University Press would soon publish. On the last day of the year he also completed a six-year correspondence course in celestial navigation (he soon told friends that shipping companies wanted to hire him as a navigator). Jim Acquitipace of Davis

Instruments in California—a company from which Dickey ordered numerous sextants—had served as Dickey's instructor, and to honor him Dickey asked if he could name one of the *Alnilam* characters after him (he never did).

Dickey had told various friends that after finishing *The Call of the Wild* he was through with screenwriting, although he might be tempted back if he could collaborate with his son Chris (Chris was not eager to do so). By the end of the year, in the midst of one of his many reversals, Dickey apprised friends like Mike Robertson, a cowboy poet, bear hunter, and ranch owner in British Columbia, that Hollywood wanted him to write a screenplay for a $36-million epic about the Klondike Gold Rush. He told Robertson that he hoped to see him when he scouted film locations in Alaska. He wrote another friend: "I am told it [the film] is the highest-budget film ever undertaken, and I have absolute carte blanche on the story itself and everything else except the acting and the directing, and I may even do some of that, too. Most of it will be shot in the Yukon territory and in Northern Alaska."[42] Jerome Hellman, the director of *Midnight Cowboy* and *Coming Home*, would make the film for United Artists.

In fact, during the spring Hellman had proposed working with Dickey to Theron Raines, and a few months later had discussed his ideas for a Gold Rush film with Dickey face-to-face in Columbia. Hellman, Dickey, and Raines later negotiated a contract with United Artists that would pay Dickey fifty thousand dollars for a treatment and two hundred thousand dollars for a script based on the treatment. No multimillion-dollar budget was ever formulated because the screenplay never made it past the treatment stage. Dickey was well aware of the precariousness of *Klondike*. At the same time he was heralding his new blockbuster, he was telling his agent to prepare for its demise. He notified Raines in December 1980 that the film's future depended on Michael Cimino's *Heaven's Gate*, which promised to be a financial disaster; it was. Steven Bach, head of production at United Artists, was deposed because of the millions squandered on *Heaven's Gate*. When Paula Weinstein and Anthea Sylbert replaced Bach, *Klondike*'s future became precarious.

As 1980 ended, Dickey stepped up efforts to deflect attention from his actual life as well as his invented life. Because of his hernia operation, he no longer resembled the bulky, boozy redneck he had played in *Deliverance*; he had slimmed from 250 pounds down to 190 pounds. To William Childress, who visited Columbia to write an article for a Saint Louis newspaper, Dickey reiterated his objection to journalists making him out to be another "damn Hemingway." Dickey may have been especially leery of such comparisons because of the unflattering portrait of Hemingway offered by his third wife, Mary, in *How It Was*. (In 1980, he told Mary he wanted to talk to her about her book over drinks or dinner in New York.) Hoping to expunge his reputation as a drinker and womanizer, Dickey gave Childress one of his standard lines: "I used to love drinking. . . . I enjoyed it immensely. But when it got to where it had nothing more for me, I dropped it like a hot rivet. You only get about 10 good minutes from drinking. The rest is a slow wearing off." About Deborah, who had an acting job for Educational TV, he gushed: "If I told you all the things I love about her . . . , you'd be here a hell of a lot longer than three days."[43] (A year before he had told the *State*: "She's the perfect poet's wife. . . . She's everything to me. She's an actress, writer, cook, companion, lover. And she's got a good critical sense. And we spend more time together than any other couple in history.")[44] Deborah reiterated her husband's halcyon view of their marriage while driving Childress back to his hotel: "I love Jim and admire him, and that's important. But to me, it's just as important that I *like* him. Jim is the only man I could ever love and like at the same time. Loving is easy. It's liking that comes hardest in any relationship. . . . You know, I simply have no complaints about the man, even after four years of marriage. . . . Well, maybe one. Jim works at his peak when he's alone. If I'm around, he's sure to take me by the arm and say, 'Sugar, what do you think of this?' One reason I work is so he can have the solitude he needs for his best writing."[45] The image of the dutiful, loving wife going to work to allow her husband the solitude his genius required was something both Dickeys wanted to believe. Despite periodic setbacks in his marriage, Dickey in fact was advancing on several fronts. He made progress with *Alnilam*, worked on the ambitious film project *Klondike*, and published his most ambitious poetry book since *The Zodiac*: the poetic sequence *Puella*, in which he imaginatively entered the lives of women.

XIII.

SLOWLY TOWARD *ALNILAM*

34. Second Fatherhood (1981–1982)

On sabbatical during the 1981 spring semester, Dickey began the new year by sorting out his business affairs in Hollywood. He fired his agent, Robert Littman, who had proposed parting ways in 1977. In his January 21 letter, he explained that he wasn't dissatisfied with Littman: "It is just that I don't believe that I am really very much in the way of a client for you, for my writing interests are only secondarily in doing films, and consequently there is little use in your seeking out projects for me which I keep turning down. You may be assured, however, that if I ever develop a real interest in writing for the films again, you will be the first to know; the first I would work with out there."[1] Dismayed, Littman wondered why his client had quit so suddenly. Did Dickey blame him for failing to get screenplays like *Gene Bullard* and *The Sentence* turned into movies? No matter what the reason for his defection, it was not because Dickey had lost interest in making films. He was in the midst of composing the screenplay for *Klondike*, and, to negotiate future Hollywood deals, he signed on Evarts Ziegler, an agent on Sunset Boulevard.

About the time Dickey abandoned Littman, Jerome Hellman invited Dickey to California for two weeks of collaborative work on *Klondike*. The Dickeys accepted Hellman's generous offer of a condominium with free maid service, a swimming pool, and access to a Malibu beach, and flew to California on February 15. At their story conference the next day, Dickey and Hellman began to fill a large notebook with ideas for their movie. To saturate himself in the details of his story, Dickey ordered twenty books from the UCLA library on the 1889–99 Yukon Gold Rush and other related topics. A researcher contacted Keith Tryck in Anchorage, Alaska, to gather information about purchasing claims, setting up mining camps, and extracting gold. Because one of his main characters was based on an unlikely gold digger—the poet Delmore Schwartz—Dickey wrote Schwartz's biographer, James Atlas, to find out whether Schwartz's family or literary executors would object to his name appearing in *Klondike*. Dickey told Atlas: "Though I met Schwartz only once, when he was very far gone, I have been as much fascinated by him as [Saul] Bellow has, or Dwight MacDonald has, or many others have. His super-intelligent, enthusiastic, creatively crazy personality is just right for this part, and if I were to tell you the actors ('stars') we have already turned down for the part you would accuse me of fantasy."[2] Dickey hoped Atlas would become an unofficial adviser for the film.

Hellman had other ideas. He warned Dickey to tread lightly on the Schwartz material, since he had heard from Saul Bellow that *Klondike* should not infringe on his novel *Humboldt's Gift*, which was based on Schwartz. Hellman also advised Dickey to refrain from soliciting outside help from people like Atlas and to destroy the notes he had made on Marlon Brando. Hellman's intention was not to silence Dickey, only to moderate his zealotry. By March 2, in fact, news of the film surfaced in the press. *Variety* announced that United Artists would produce *Klondike* and, although no budget had been established, the movie would be released in the spring of 1983. To celebrate their prospects, Hellman and his wife, Nancy Ellison, organized a party for the Dickeys. Russian director Andrei Kontchalovsky, Russian author Vassily Aksyonov, United Artists vice president Steven Bach, and actors Shirley MacLaine, Larry Hagman, Mrs. Aldous Huxley, Carroll O'Connor, and Ned Beatty were among the guests. Dickey exulted among the stars and was as mischievous as ever. At one point he tried on Hagman's ankle-length mink cape. The March 5 *Hollywood Reporter* carried news of the party along with a picture of Dickey.

Dickey's excitement about the new movie was hard to contain. Near the end of the winter he told the poet David Bottoms that Jon Voight, Dustin Hoffman, and Burt Reynolds all wanted roles in *Klondike*, but he didn't think any of them were right (Hellman denied any actors had been contacted at this early stage). Dickey was eager to impress Bottoms, whom he had befriended after Robert Penn Warren had chosen *Shooting Rats at the Bibb County Dump* for the prestigious 1979 Walt Whitman Award. Bottoms's poems detailing his rural Southern upbringing and his itinerant work as a country-and-western/bluegrass musician owed a good deal to Dickey, as Bottoms was quick to acknowledge. In 1981, while completing graduate work at Florida State University, Bottoms became one of Dickey's adopted poetic sons.

Much of Dickey's initial correspondence with Bottoms revolved not around movies or poetry but around music. Because Bottoms had played in The Lost Mountain Boys and other bands, he quickly engaged Dickey in technical discussions about banjo- and guitar-playing. Not to be outdone by a younger minstrel, Dickey wrote on January 23 that he had played guitar all his life and that by the time he went to Reed College in 1963 he could play on a par with his gifted students. To lower Bottoms's expectations of his present abilities, he said that he had little time to practice: "It is really impossible for me to play as well as I could when I was a teenager, or even when I was at Reed."[3]

In mid-May Bottoms got a chance to meet Dickey in person. He spent a merry day in Columbia playing guitars, drinking beers, and shooting bows and blowguns with his new mentor. (Bottoms was so enthralled by Dickey's blowgun that he ordered one after his visit.) He probably talked to Dickey about Ted Bundy—he often did—because Bundy had ended his killing spree on the Florida State campus in Tallahassee, where Bottoms was a student. Bottoms promised to buy Dickey books on Bundy, which were prominently displayed in the local shops. Dickey welcomed Bottoms and other young writers into his home as "sons" partly because his real sons had largely abandoned him. The sort of tensions that affected his relations with his biological sons, however, were not wholly absent from his relations with his protégés. Dickey still assumed a dominant and sometimes overbearing role and grew jealous when those like Bottoms or Dave Smith seemed poised to usurp his place in the literary limelight.

Toward his yet-to-be-born child, Dickey also expressed complicated emotions. He did so because he was convinced that the baby was going to be a boy, even though he desperately wanted a girl. He looked forward to the birth with foreboding. He told friends that the baby was due on the same day he had undergone his hernia operation (the baby was actually due on May 23; his operation had been on May 20). But the imminent birth also filled him with confidence and anticipation. Since he had conceived the child at the age of fifty-seven after periodic bouts of impotence, he repeatedly told friends that he was no mule; he was still capable of what he jokingly called "senile lust." The doctors, he believed, had determined that "the Little Hero" had a male heartbeat, so he decided to name the baby Talbot after his father's ancestors, the aristocratic English Talbots. Even three months after Deborah gave birth, Dickey assured those like Willie Morris that he would keep calling his child "Tal."

Knowing that Deborah would soon be cooped up with the baby, Dickey took her on a number of reading trips before her due date. In late January, they visited Columbus, Ohio, where his former air corps buddy Andrew Harbelis appeared surreptitiously at his reading. Heartened by his reunion, he asked Harbelis if he would be willing to give his name to one of the *Alnilam* characters. Harbelis agreed. The next day, January 28, Dickey read at Kenyon College, where he enjoyed talking to one of the editors still sympathetic to his poetry: Fred Turner of the *Kenyon Review*. Dickey also traveled to Radford College in Virginia and to a writers' conference in Oxford, Mississippi. His Oxford host, Willie Morris, had promised to introduce Dickey to Faulkner's niece, Dean Wells, who lived with her husband in Oxford. Although Dickey consistently fulminated against Faulkner as one of literature's largest stuffed goats, he was happy to attend a dinner party at the Wells's house and eat at the table where, he later claimed, Faulkner had written *Absalom, Absalom*.

During April and May, Deborah's pregnancy made travel more cumbersome, but the Dickeys continued to barnstorm—to Duke and St. Andrews Presbyterian College in North Carolina, Emporia State University in Kansas, Hilton Head in South Carolina, and Rice University for Monroe Spears's sixty-fifth birthday celebration. Dismayed that he couldn't command higher fees for his readings—he asked twelve thousand dollars for a multiple-day visit and five thousand for an individual reading—on April 29 he permanently severed connections with Bill Thompson, his long-standing booking agent at Lordly and Dame. "My situation is such that time is of more value to me than the money I get from these events,"[4] he explained. He was not, however, planning to stop reading, just as he was not planning to quit screenwriting when he fired Littman. On the same day he dismissed Thompson, he wrote Brian O'Shea, a vice president at W. Kessler Ltd. in Jackson, Mississippi: "My previous booking people have had nothing like your literacy, or your knowledge of what I in particular do; it would be a real pleasure to be associated with an agency where the people consider me as a being at least a *little* different from a dog act or a magician; a Watergate burglar or an ex-President."[5] On September 30, 1981, he sent a signed contract to O'Shea and instructed him to line up as many readings as possible.

It was around this time that Dickey began an intriguing correspondence with an imaginative boy, Robert "Beau" Geckle, the nephew of an English Department colleague. From Beau's letters Dickey gathered ideas for his second children's book, *Bronwen, the Traw, and the Shape-Shifter*. Geckle, who liked *Tucky the Hunter*, encouraged Dickey to write a story about a boy who enters a different world by flicking on the lights in his room, a world in which he must fight malevolent one-eyed monsters and armies of evil kings. A week after getting this advice, Dickey asked Geckle if he should include flying squirrels who change skins by day and by night as well as monsters who take different shapes in air, water, earth, and fire. In late February 1981, Geckle wrote back that the squirrels should keep the same skins day and night and that they should act as guides between the worlds of darkness and light. With regard to the combat scenes between the hero and the one-eyed monsters, these should take place in a cave where, for the sake of suspense, the hero should be on the verge of death and get saved by the flying squirrels. Geckle also offered suggestions on the monster's shape-shifting abilities. In air the monster should metamorphose into a giant hawk that makes sonic booms, in water into a giant starfish, in earth into a giant mole, in fire into a burning man. Enthralled by the fertile imagination of the young Geckle, Dickey incorporated many of his suggestions into *Bronwen, the Traw, and the Shape-Shifter.*

As Paul Christensen realized when he interviewed Dickey near the beginning of 1981 for the *Lone Star Review*, Dickey's hernia operation had made him a different man. Dickey was eerily quiet when Christensen entered his Lake Katherine home. Indeed, he was nowhere to be seen. While thumbing through some of the one hundred new books on and around the coffee table in the living room, Christensen suddenly heard shoe leather creaking behind him. Only then did he realize that Dickey had been staring at him from a distance. Dickey indicated that he was embarrassed by his physical condition, which Christensen described as "slack decrepitude." Nevertheless, Dickey arranged the microphones for the tape recorder and proceeded to talk for three hours about his work. Christensen was so impressed he divulged his secret desire to write Dickey's biography. Dickey responded that Christensen would grow to hate him if he realized how much mischief he had caused.

At lunch in a Columbia restaurant, Christensen ordered a glass of wine to relax after the long taping session. Expecting Dickey to begin gulping bourbon or double martinis, he was surprised by Dickey's polite request to join him. They drank Chablis together, and Dickey soon proposed that they have more. As the alcohol took effect, Dickey launched into an elated reminiscence of working with Burt Reynolds on *Deliverance.* Dickey must have promised his doctors as well as Deborah—who was not supposed to drink because of her pregnancy— that he would refrain from alcohol. Once they returned to Lelia's Court, Christensen watched Deborah approach her husband as if to give him a kiss, sniff his breath, and snarl: "You motherfucker; you goddamn son-of-a-bitch."[6] Rather than retaliate, Dickey sheepishly retreated.

After completing the interview in the afternoon, Dickey gave his new friend a tour of the house. With all the books, powerful bows, razor-sharp arrows, and other primitive weapons, the house struck Christensen as an odd combination of county library and medieval torture chamber. Outside, Dickey tried shooting some arrows at a target on the lawn and missed, and subsequently confessed to Christensen that his reputation as a skilled woodsman was a lie. He then told Christensen to put his hand on his shoulder and site down the arrow. Did he see the arrow bend from the bow's force as it streaked through the air? His initiation completed, Christensen packed his gear and said good-bye to Deborah. Dickey followed him out to the car so closely that their shoulders nearly bumped, stationed himself in front of the car door, and addressed him belly to belly: "You've seen a lot of me today. You've seen the real thing. When you get back to the typewriter, you can say that I'm nothing more than a broken-down old drunk. You can say anything you want. I can't stop you. But don't do it. It would be a waste of time and it would be untrue."[7] The interview that appeared in the summer issue of the *Lone Star Review* contained no surprises, so Dickey treated Christensen with typical largesse, calling it "the best I have ever done in the interview form."[8] He promised to reward Christensen with a blowgun and darts.

Dickey hoped that his *Puella* poems would convince his diminishing number of readers that he had evolved into a new poet. Determined to win over women poets and critics, Dickey again resorted to flattery. To Anne Stevenson, who was living in England, he wrote in March: "I hope you will permit me to say how much I have enjoyed the poetry of yours I have read. If I may, in a dream or otherwise, have said something derogatory or insensitive or off-the-point in a review—a dream one or a real one—I was surely wrong."[9] A decade earlier in *Sorties*, Dickey had reprimanded Stevenson—along with Sexton and Rich—for what he called their "quirky and offhand"[10] poems. On the same day he wrote Stevenson, he also tried to make amends with Adrien Stontenburg. He hoped she would not begrudge the fact that in 1970 he and Auden had awarded the Pulitzer Prize to Richard Howard: "Though Richard Howard was finally decided upon as the recipient of the prize, I have been over your poems many times since those days, and hardly ever over Mr. Howard's, and I thought I should write a note to you and tell you how much pleasure your work has given and gives me, and how very fine I think it is. For my money, the best women poets writing now are yourself, Mary Oliver of Provincetown, and Margaret Atwood of Canada."[11] In a follow-up letter on May 1, he flirtatiously asked her for a picture and information about her marital status, adding that she was not among the best female poets; she *was* the best.

In his advance campaign for *Puella*, Dickey tried to recruit sympathetic male reviewers as well. He wrote a fulsome letter to *Newsweek* book reviewer Walter Clemons in July, presumably hoping he would highlight *Puella* in his pages. He urged Peter Davison or James Atlas to review the book in the *Atlantic Monthly*. He directed friends to pressure Nona Balakian for reviewing space in the *New York Times Book Review*. Although he had treated her with indifference on the 1980 Pulitzer committee, he hoped as a woman she would look favorably on *Puella*. As for writing the review, he contacted his friends Richard Tillinghast, who had come from Harvard to read at USC in April, and Daniel Halpern, who was reissuing *Babel to Byzantium* at Ecco Press. His second letter to Tillinghast suggested a bargain: Dickey would recommend him for a job at Vanderbilt if he would produce a favorable review: "If the *Times* is willing for you to review [Charles] Wright's old poems they should be twice as willing to do mine. Sound them out on this, and let me know what you can do." He even offered Tillinghast a thesis: "The fact that a kind of new-wave movement, counter to Lowell's confessionalism, seems to be shaping up around the kind of thing that I have been trying to do over the years."[12] Tillinghast should cite the poetry of Smith, Bottoms, Lieberman, Atwood, and Oliver as evidence of Dickey's new wave.

Tillinghast, who sympathized with Dickey's sense of being besieged by academic critics, wanted to help. When Michael Blowen wrote an appreciative cover story about Dickey for the December 13 issue of the *Boston Globe Magazine,* Tillinghast approved, comparing the critics who had recently arrayed themselves against Dickey to a swarm of ticks on an Arkansas dog. (Blowen's article, like others at the time, attempted to revise the image of Dickey as a hirsute, hard-drinking tough guy from the hinterlands.) Projecting a new, gentler image to the press and seeking the aid of friendly critics like Tillinghast to bolster his reputation, in private Dickey seemed to be preparing for Armageddon. He told a friend in February 1981 that he was honing his weapons: "I have sharpened not only all the knives in the house, but also all the arrows, all the scissors, all the hatchets, the machetes, the blowgun darts, and everything else that will take an edge, until the house is like some place Charles Manson would go if he ever went to heaven."[13] He soon ordered more knives and "Nevr-Dull" knife polish from *Archery World* to make his blades even sharper. The women in Dickey's house felt he should get rid of the dangerous paraphernalia. When she got old enough to assert some control over her father's weapons, Bronwen hid the knives. On another occasion, Deborah threw them in Lake Katherine.[14]

During his readings and lectures, such as the ones he gave shortly before Christmas at Sea Pine Academy and the community library on Hilton Head Island, Dickey continued to batter away at the mythical life he had constructed for himself and that now entrapped him: "This pseudo-Hemingway projection some journalists have given me just ain't true. . . . I'm almost 60 now, and this image of me as the athletic, rugged outdoor fellow will just have to be curtailed somewhat. . . . I'm probably the most intellectual redneck there is, if that's an accurate term."[15] Two events near the end of 1981 convinced Dickey that his effort to shake off the Arkansas ticks and win new admirers was succeeding. He heard that Arizona State University was organizing a multigenre extravaganza based on the poems in *Puella,* and he heard from *Poetry* editor John Frederick Nims that the five *Puella* poems published in the magazine's March issue had won the prestigious Levinson Prize. Past winners, Nims informed Dickey, were Frost, Stevens, Crane, Cummings, and Dylan Thomas. Dickey was ecstatic. In November he wrote the donor, Mrs. Levinson: "Though I have had other awards, I can assure you that none of them, including the National Book Award or the Prix Médicis in France, means as much to me as this one does."[16] To be placed among such eminent poets allayed his worries about his recent stylistic experiments, as did the publication of more *Puella* poems in an upcoming *Kenyon Review.*

Dickey's real-life "puella" came into the world at 8:38 A.M. on May 17, 1981, when doctors delivered a small, healthy girl by Caesarean section. Melodrama and comedy attended the birth. Afraid she might die in the hospital, Deborah made Matthew Bruccoli promise to stay with her husband. Bruccoli fetched Dickey at his house early in the morning and drove him to the hospital. With a construction worker who was waiting for his own child to be born, Dickey began a friendly conversation about his engineering courses at Clemson. The obstetrician came out to announce the birth. Noticing that Bruccoli was younger than Dickey, he told Bruccoli that he had a new daughter. In his poem "Daughter," Dickey mythologized Bronwen into an elemental élan vital "shunting the glacier, whirling / Whole forests from their tops, moving // Lava, the flowering stone: moving the hand / Of anyone, ever." She is the eternal feminine, the godly anima or prime mover of all being. "Roll, real God. Roll through us,"[17] he chants in his Dylan Thomas–like hymn.

Shortly after Bronwen's birth Dickey told Willie Morris: "She came early, and weighed only five pounds and five ounces at birth, five ounces of which she promptly lost on her epic encounter with Air."[18] Dickey's prized name Talbot was quickly dropped, as was Hannah, the name of Dickey's distant grandmother, which he and Deborah had also considered. Having reconciled himself to having another son, Dickey was overjoyed to have a daughter and pleased by the publicity accorded the event by *Time* photographers. He repeatedly told friends that his wife had produced "a white goddess," an obvious but not entirely complimentary reference to Robert Graves's *The White Goddess*, a highly esoteric study of ancient tree myths—among other things—arguing that all male poets depend on a lunar muse that inspires as well as drives them mad. Dickey's enthusiasm for his second fatherhood ran unabated for months and, indeed, for the remaining years of his life. When Bronwen turned three months old, he told everyone she was a fat, fun, trouble-free baby, his "living poetry." To Liz Rosenberg he wrote: "She is the first consideration, no matter what *else* you may have to do, or want to do. This induces a rather odd frame of mind, but at the center of the frame is a very warm area which radiates out into the rest of one's activities, informs them with humanistic and mystical feelings, and is altogether to the good. We like Bronnie, and we can't imagine existence without her." Rosenberg, who was writing a novel about the South, had asked Dickey about Southern mores, and Dickey had answered that he "seldom paid any deliberate attention to any of them."[19] As a father to his "puella," however, he played the perfect, adoring Southern gentleman.

Dickey nominated Michael Allin to be Bronwen's godfather, but Allin had never been baptized. Since Deborah was a Catholic, the Dickeys had to get special permission from the local priest. The priest refused to grant it. Undaunted, Dickey decided to contact someone with more authority. On July 20, 1981, he wrote His Holiness John Paul II in the Vatican. "Though I am not a Catholic," he began, "my wife is, and very devout":

We have a new little girl, Bronwen, whom we want to raise as a Catholic. We also have a close friend, Michael Allin, whom we would like to be godfather to our daughter. I am quite convinced that, with his sincerity and love of our family, he would be ideal in this role, and for the rest of his life. But our main difficulty is that Michael Allin has never been baptized, and the local priest, here in Columbia, South Carolina, tells us that he cannot be our daughter's godfather because of this. From our standpoint this is regrettable, for if we looked the world over we could, I am sure, find no one so well qualified for this responsible position as Mr. Allin is. If in some way you could find a means by which Mr. Allin might become godfather to my daughter, I would be most grateful. Not knowing the Church doctrines, I am yet convinced that the precepts of Christ—kindness, forbearance and love—which Mr. Allin so perfectly embodies, may move you to intercede on his behalf against those forces which seem determined to keep the lives of my daughter and her proposed godfather from uniting in love, mutual responsibility and delight.[20]

He signed his request "Most sincerely, James Dickey." The pope, however, could not be persuaded. Because Matthew Bruccoli had gotten the local priests to permit him to serve as best man at the Dickeys' church wedding, he became Bronwen's godfather.

Like many women after pregnancy, Deborah found it difficult to lose weight. Her extra pounds, her stretch marks, and her wrinkled abdominal skin, which she compared self-deprecatingly to crepe paper, did little to stimulate her husband. She became acutely self-conscious and depressed about her looks. Her husband's friends, who dropped by to talk or watch TV, noticed that she often stayed in a back room to keep out of sight. If she emerged, like Dickey's invalid mother, she usually wore a nightgown, appeared listless, and sat quietly on the couch with Bronwen. She gradually began to take more drugs to assuage the fear that she was unwanted. One of the reasons Dickey rehired Paula Goff as his assistant in 1984 was because Deborah was unable or unwilling to do his secretarial work. With her husband's former mistress occupying the house for much of the day and Dickey showing little or no sexual interest in her at night, Deborah sought consolation from other sources.

Dickey's romantic interests—past or present, serious or playful—became more intolerable to Deborah with the loss of her sexual appeal. Her future indiscretions with men in Columbia's drug world were partly a way to win back the sense of self-worth that was slipping from her grasp. During the summer after Bronwen's birth, Deborah tried to sever at least some of her husband's connections with old girlfriends. She sent a letter to a former San Fernando Valley State student, rebuking her for writing her husband. Around this time, she also denounced Rosemary Daniell on the phone for her sensational exposé of her affair with "the Great Southern Poet."[21] *Fatal Flowers* infuriated Dickey as well. In 1981, he upbraided Daniell to a friend: "Rosemary Daniell is to me what Judith Exner was to John Kennedy—and, to hear her tell it, also to Sam Giancana and Frank Sinatra and God knows how many others, and the least and most and last of what I can say of her would be in the form of a plea to be delivered for all time from nondescript literary groupies."[22] Later in the decade, when Daniell had the temerity to send Dickey a copy of her poetry book, *Fort Bragg and Other Points South*, Deborah blasted her again.[23] In another fit of jealous wrath, she destroyed Dickey's notes and drafts of *The Indian Maiden* because they contained accounts of his affair with Robin Jarecki.[24]

Among the upheavals in his household, Dickey struggled to establish a normal routine. Having promised Hugh O'Neill that he would finish the first draft of *Alnilam* by summer's end, he returned to his novel, but realized that his new deadline was just as unattainable as the others. He managed to submit another detailed outline of the novel, but little else. O'Neill's response, which echoed others in the past from Doubleday, further frustrated Dickey. On August 13, 1981, O'Neill sent a list of objections to the work-in-progress: Joel vanished from the narrative before anyone really knew him; the dialogue was often stilted, long-winded, and superfluous; the light and dark sequences needed to be incorporated more fluently into the action; the plan to make Hannah a prostitute was a Southern cliché; and the final demolition of the planes seemed preposterous since the cadets valued machines and warfare so highly. To leaven his author's spirits after deflating them, O'Neill assured Dickey that the novel had potential. To make a genuine breakthrough, however, Dickey had to keep his expansive imagination in check.

On June 7, Jeffrey Meyers caught a glimpse of Dickey's curmudgeonly mood when he visited Lelia's Court. A prolific biographer who would also propose to write Dickey's biography, Meyers wanted to speak to Dickey about Randall Jarrell, whose death he was investigating. Meyers suggested that he bring his tennis racket, which spurred Dickey to reply: "I would certainly be very happy if you *did* bring your tennis racket, for though I never played with Frost and Pound, I did with Roethke and Jarrell, and I could beat them okay, in the old days."[25] When Meyers arrived, Dickey questioned him thoroughly about his game and, concluding he might lose, opted for a dart-blowing contest and a snake hunt. Meyers's first shot with the blowgun was a lucky one; he hit the bull's-eye—a pine knot in a board above the fireplace. Dickey reacted with extreme irritation and canceled the snake hunt. These initiatory tests out of the way, Dickey spoke insightfully about Jarrell as a pampered genius who had committed suicide out of frustration with his writing and lumped him with his peers—Berryman, Schwartz, Lowell, and Bishop—as another poetic failure.

Despite recent vows to refuse time-consuming readings, Dickey scheduled a number of them during the summer: at the Governor's School for the Arts and Humanities in South Carolina, Wofford College, the Charleston Poetry Society, the USC medical school, High Point, and Choate. On August 23, he also read at the College of Santa Fe to honor the birthday of the late Santa Fe poet Witter Bynner. To local reporters Dickey praised Bynner as a poet, scholar, and prankster. What most endeared Bynner to him was a hoax perpetrated in 1916. Using fictitious names, Bynner and Arthur Davison Ficke had coauthored a series of poems called *Spectra* to satirize the many schools of poetry in vogue at the time. Some in the Santa Fe audience thought Dickey's promise to lecture on "A Personal View of the Changing Nature of Poetry" (he was paid four thousand dollars to do so) was a hoax, too, since he never delivered it. In an argumentative mood, he told a reporter: "I don't like academia. . . . I don't want to make this another seminar."[26] He read poems like "The Sheep Child" and passages from *Deliverance* instead.

In July, Dickey demonstrated his own penchant for hoaxes. He had been outside his Litchfield condominium, he told Willie Morris, "with a super-redneck forest ranger who doubles as a groundskeeper and wants to be a mercenary soldier."[27] They had been discussing the latest issue of *Soldier of Fortune* magazine when a water moccasin squirmed through some marsh grass. The ranger, Wallace Maiden, agreed with Dickey's plan to act as a decoy. As soon as the poisonous, six-and-a-half-foot-long snake approached Maiden, the intrepid Dickey got off several shots with his blowgun, which killed it. To broadcast his feat he took pictures of the snake and sent them to friends, among them David Bottoms, who doubted it was a water moccasin. When the writer Tim McLaurin visited Dickey in Columbia, bringing with him the galleys of his first novel, one of the first things he noticed in Dickey's office was a photograph of the dead snake. A snake expert and former carnival snake handler, McLaurin inquired about the picture. Slightly altering his previous stories, Dickey boasted that it was of a deadly cottonmouth he had killed with his blowgun. At first McLaurin suspected that Dickey was testing his knowledge of snakes; then he wondered if Dickey actually believed what he said. Playing the role of courteous guest, the younger novelist refrained from disabusing his host of the snake's identity—it was a harmless banded water snake.

During the second half of 1981, a number of new film projects provided further diversions from the novel Dickey struggled to finish. He made plans to write a screenplay based on Peter Stansky and William Abrahams's book *Journey to the Frontier*, which elegized two idealistic upper-class poet-Communists, Julian Bell (nephew of Virginia Woolf) and John Cornford (great-grandson of Darwin), who had fought and died in the Spanish Civil War. Dickey thought that Peter Weir would be a perfect director for the film. On August 5, a more glamorous proposal came from Richard Roth, the man who would later produce *To the White Sea*. Roth sent Dickey a screenplay based on Jon Hassler's 1981 novel *The Love Hunter* and explained that he wanted Dickey to reshape the script with Robert Redford. On September 12, Redford made a clandestine trip to Columbia under the assumed name of Robert Miller to avoid publicity (frenzied, autograph-seeking women besieged him anyway). The next day Redford listened to Dickey's advice about rewriting the script at his home. Notes from the meeting reveal that, among other things, Dickey and Redford agreed to devise a new title for the film (the novel's title suggested something pornographic). They mulled over how to best present the drama in which one character (Chris) dreams of murdering his best friend (Larry) on a duck hunt in Manitoba and is wracked by feelings of humility and cowardice as he plans to marry Larry's wife, Rachel, after Larry dies of multiple sclerosis. To Gordon Lish, Dickey explained that Redford was convinced that they could "adapt a relatively mediocre novel . . . into something which is not mediocre."[28] Dickey was not so convinced and soon lost interest in the endeavor.

Another film proposal came from John Boorman in the fall. On October 5, in a letter encouraging Dickey to speak to Michel Ciment about *Deliverance* for a book he was writing on Boorman, the director suggested that Dickey write a screenplay based on his poem "Looking for the Buckhead Boys." Dickey wrote back that he was too busy to contemplate any more films. Twenty days later, however, he traveled to Beaufort, South Carolina, to make a PBS documentary on the Depression for WJWJ-TV. The pay—five thousand dollars—for narrating *One-Third of a Nation*, which his colleague Bernie Dunlap had written, was too tempting to refuse. And the subject intrigued him. He had grown up during the Depression, and in his personal mythology he had suffered as much as those who had once endured the run-down shacks they filmed in Beaufort.

Dickey's script for *Klondike*, which he returned to in early 1982, was inspired partly by the contradictory attitudes toward money that drove him toward and away from lucrative—but ultimately distracting—film projects. Lee Bartlett, who was annotating Dickey's correspondence with Ezra Pound for the journal *Paideuma*, may have been a catalyst for Dickey's soul-searching. Because Pound had inveighed so stridently against avarice and capitalism, Dickey in his letters to Bartlett tried to distance himself from his money-making stint in the advertising business, which he had discussed with Pound. He told Bartlett that he had written catch phrases for Coca-Cola, but neither "The pause that refreshes" nor "Things go better with Coke."[29] At the same time he downplayed his advertising prowess to Bartlett, to others Dickey played up a recent advertisement he had written for the Ogilvy & Mather advertising agency that had earned him five thousand dollars. In February, he proudly announced that his short piece "How to Enjoy Poetry," which was sponsored by International Paper as part of a campaign to improve reading and writing skills, would reach eighty million readers. It was appearing simultaneously in *Newsweek*, *Time*, the *New York Times*, *People*, *Psychology Today*, and *Rolling Stone*. His apology for poetry, which underscored the way it refreshed by offering a new perspective on the world, sounded like a Coca-Cola ad.

For Pound, as for the Agrarians, the craving for monetary wealth was incompatible with the quest for artistic beauty. To sacrifice one's artistic talents to Mammon and ephemeral commodities was a sin. For Dickey the Gold Rush in *Klondike* offered a convenient analogy for his own pursuit of wealth. The improbable main character, Delmore Schwartz, fit into his scheme mainly because Schwartz shared some of Dickey's self-defeating compulsions. Dickey did not choose him out of admiration for his poetry. He wrote Jeffrey Meyers in 1982: "I don't think Delmore ever said one single phrase of real poetry."[30] It was the sort of person Schwartz represented that made him appropriate for *Klondike*. In the screenplay Dickey upheld the sort of ethnic stereotype that Pound promulgated—the Jew as usurer, money-grubber, and gold digger—and, in a surprisingly confessional act, identified with the stereotype. Assessing the hubris behind his life in the 1960s and 1970s that had led inexorably to the tragic death of Maxine and the precipitous marriage to Deborah, Dickey also tried to assess and rectify the mistakes he had made in previous screenplays. Because he had relied so heavily on melodramatic fantasies in *Gene Bullard* and *The Sentence*, he went out of his way to learn the facts of gold mining and to make his 119-page treatment as historically accurate as possible. He even claimed to have panned and sluiced for gold in North Georgia (he supposedly worked five hours to collect thirty-six cents' worth of gold dust).

Dickey bestowed many of his own traits and interests on *Klondike*'s main character. Like Dickey, Victor is the second son in a family living in a prominent Southern city (Charleston). His family's shipbuilding business has allowed him a privileged upbringing. As an older man Victor cultivates habits that his family deems strange, such as finding out his geographical position by using sextants. Imaginative and eccentric, he sequesters himself in a shack at the shipyard, fiddles with a slide rule, and performs experiments with scientific gadgets. He has "thwarted engineering aspirations," just as Dickey's were "thwarted" after

Clemson. Victor ultimately renounces his family business out of loyalty to Delmore Schwartz, the symbolic mad poet who leads him—as other poets led Dickey—on a picaresque journey to strange lands full of promise and catastrophe. Victor first catches sight of Delmore on a trip to Seattle to procure lumber for his family's ships. (Dickey alleged that he first met Delmore Schwartz late in 1965 on a reading trip to Syracuse University.) In Seattle everyone is ablaze with gold fever and preparing to sail for the Klondike. Like Lewis Medlock, Thornton, and Muldrow, Victor romanticizes Alaska as one of the last frontiers. Among the clamoring voices Victor hears the "involved, enthusiastic, impatient, slightly manic" voice of Delmore. In a bar Delmore tells Victor he is going to the Klondike because he believes America owes him and his Jewish ancestors money. He convinces Victor to join him.

Delmore is a "charlatanistic spellbinder" who aspires to a cult following. In mocking Delmore's power over others, Dickey mocks his own: "Delmore is an adept of the mystical and doctrinal part of Pythagoreanism, particularly that dealing with the transmigration of souls, in which he confesses to believe without question, and a rigid practitioner of the Pythagorean rules of conduct: . . . to abstain from beans, not to stir fire with iron, not to sit on a quart measure, not to eat the heart, to smooth out the impress of the body from bedclothes, not to look in a mirror beside a light." Like Dickey, both Delmore and Victor have nearly total recall. Dickey also gives Delmore one of his paranoid obsessions; he is convinced that something is pursuing him from under ground or under ice. (Dickey said that his poem "Pursuit from Under" expressed the same fear.) On their trip north together in the *Humboldt* (a nod to Saul Bellow's novel), Delmore speaks in the voice of Dickey's other "deliverer," Medlock: "The whole gold-rush mania . . . is essentially childlike and naive, even innocent: the whole thing a game where one must make up the rules." Like the men in *Deliverance*, Victor and Delmore join forces in order to survive the outback. For the rich Charleston boy and the immigrant poet from the East Side of New York, the snowy wastelands of the North are as harsh and foreign as the war-torn Pacific Islands or the North Georgia woods were for Dickey. Dickey once again recapitulates his own rites of passage. "They are now survivors," Dickey writes after the two men climb Chilkoot Pass with all their heavy equipment and prepare for further trials in the tent city on Lake Lindeman.

When Victor and Delmore finally run the dangerous rapids on the Yukon River, Dickey writes in an aside, "I don't want to seem to trade on the white-water stuff in *Deliverance*," but the rest of *Klondike* resembles his novel in many ways. In Dawson City the two adventurers realize there are virtually no claims; all the promising ones have been mined. Finally buying a claim, they encounter the sort of environmental depredation at the end of *Deliverance*: "desecration in the midst of the most beautiful virgin scenery." The disasters begin after they build a dredger. One man gets run over and killed. The unwieldy machine self-destructs, flogging Delmore and another partner with a heavy, broken chain. A "Sam Peckinpah blood-ballet,"[31] which Dickey deliberately avoided in earlier scenes, erupts when the chain tightens around Delmore's throat, snaps his neck, and kills him. After burying his mining comrades, Victor discovers gold in the dredger's last load, returns to Dawson City where he sells his claim, and walks away from the Yukon. Like the survivors of the Cahulawassee canoe trip, he has learned a lesson amid calamity. He is a "victor," as his name implies, although his victory remains ambiguous.

Jerome Hellman read the treatment of *Klondike* and responded with a seven-page letter on March 26, 1982. His main worries centered around character development and story line. "In spite of all the wonderful texture that exists in details, the sum total is, in my judgment, finally neither sufficiently dramatic nor sufficiently involving. . . . It often seems we are relying on the uniqueness of the terrain and the larger events to cover over the fact that we really don't yet have an adequately well-developed or carefully thought-out story." Hellman rightly pointed out that Dickey had made no real use of Delmore's Jewishness. He existed more as a stereotype and alter ego than a distinct character. Hellman criticized Victor for similar reasons: "As far as the two of them as a team is concerned, they are often little more than voyeurs, rarely at the center of the action and consigned to walk aimlessly a good deal of the time, marveling at the sights and sounds around them."[32]

Hellman was still convinced that they had the blueprint for a marvelous film, but by July 1982 the project had been scrapped. Realizing his treatment was an improvement over *Gene Bullard* and *The Sentence*, Dickey was stunned and upset. Nearly a year later Hellman wrote Dickey an apologetic letter after Dickey invited him to his sixtieth birthday party: "I very much regret that our high hopes and enthusiasms over KLONDIKE didn't bear more fruit. It seems to me a more than usual array of difficulties, not necessarily of our own making, plagued us from the start."[33] Dickey later enumerated the difficulties: "We had a big producers' strike, or some big strike, that got in our way and halted the wheels. Then they had a big power shift in the studio and the person that had commissioned the film was ousted. The first thing the new person that came in did was to kill off all the previous guy's projects."[34] There had been a writers' strike from April to July of 1981 that had delayed work on *Klondike*. And when Weinstein and Sylbert, who replaced Bach at United Artists, demanded to see Dickey's treatment, Hellman refused to release it (he never circulated first drafts of treatments) and indicated that he would consult his lawyer since their demand went against his original agreement with Bach. Nothing was ever resolved, and the treatment—with its poetic gold miners and far-fetched Alaskan scenes—remained in limbo.

Early in 1982, Dickey channeled his hopes into a more feasible movie. CBS had proposed to make a documentary about the intertwined writing careers of Dickey and Robert Penn Warren. In late February the two poets conferred with CBS officials in New York and spoke further about their plans several days later at a USC symposium devoted to Warren's writing. Both writers agreed with director Marc Brugnoni that they should begin filming in the late spring at Warren's Connecticut house, move to Yale for a joint reading, and end in mid-June at Dickey's Litchfield condo. *Two Poets, Two Friends*, which resulted from their collaboration, presented endearing portraits of the two writers as they rambled through a New England field and rowed a boat on a South Carolina creek, all the while discussing poetry. As with his other recent movies, however, Dickey was in for a disappointment. CBS Cable abruptly folded after agreeing to broadcast *Two Poets, Two Friends.* In the end, PBS showed only a segment of the film on its *MacNeil/Lehrer News Hour.* Although his film projects had come to nothing, Dickey still had high hopes for the *Puella* poems he had been writing since 1977.

35. *Puella* Troubles (1981–1982)

The original coffee-table book for which Dickey wrote the *Puella* poems had first been conceived as a limited edition called *Flowering.* Each volume would be signed by Dickey and the young photographer Bookie Binkley, and would cost several hundred dollars. Binkley would model his pictures on the work of his teacher, the acclaimed photographer David Hamilton. With the help of his in-laws who lived in Columbia and several family friends, including the USC soccer coach, Binkley first pitched his idea to Dickey at his house on October 17, 1977. Binkley remembered the occasion vividly: Dickey had answered the door in a long robe that brushed the floor, his chest a tangle of gold chains, his hair disheveled. He had guided Binkley from room to room with a toy airplane in his hand, sputtering to imitate the engine. Eventually he landed his plane on a coffee table—an appropriate place to discuss the book.

Dickey's first query was about money. How much money did they plan to make on the book? How much would he get for producing thirty poems to go along with Binkley's thirty photographs? Settling on the sum of fifteen thousand dollars, Binkley agreed to pay Dickey in two installments. Binkley later declared in court: "I remember explaining to Mr. Dickey that this project was conceived for one purpose, and that was to make money, and was intended in every sense of the term to be a business venture. And this was explained to Mr. Dickey in great detail, and he understood and approved. Mr. Dickey knew that our purpose was to create a rare and unusual and beautiful book, something [that] would be sacred to the collector. It would be expensive; it would be plush, creatively and artfully done. . . . We wanted a rare book, and he liked that idea." Having agreed on terms, Binkley set up his slide projector and showed nearly one hundred slides of the girls he was considering for inclusion in the book.

Dickey vowed that "the pen would not touch the paper" until he received his first check, so on December 27, 1977, Binkley and his wife visited Dickey again, this time at his Litchfield condo. Dickey greeted them cordially and asked for the money. Binkley handed over an envelope with a check and slightly revised contract. Dickey perused the contract, agreed to it, and soon waxed effusive about their collaboration. Binkley recalled: "He assured us that this was going to be a great project and [told us] how excited he was about doing it and how he looked forward to getting started with it, and he just knew it was going to be a great success. He encouraged us a great deal, too, about going on with it, continuing with it at great speed."

Binkley photographed girls almost every day for a year and searched high and low for potential models for his book. He recalled: "At one time [I] contacted the superintendent of city schools in Winston-Salem, Dr. Adams, and asked him

if it would be possible for us to send out a mailer to the parents of girls between . . . the seventh through the 12th grade—in the city school system, letting them know that we were looking for girls of that age to photograph and
explained in some detail what the project was about, and he was very helpful
and agreed to do this for us. And we decided the best way to do that was to have
a seminar at the little theatre in Winston-Salem and invite on a Saturday all the
girls that wanted to come to this thing where my wife would do a little talking
about makeup." Because of her modeling career, Binkley's wife, Denise, helped
with the recruiting. Their best-known model was Brooke Shields. Many of the
models, however, were just attractive girls the Binkleys approached on the street
and dressed up in turn-of-the-century costumes.

In the early months of their collaboration, Binkley sent four or five pictures
at a time to Dickey, who wrote poems to accompany them. The Binkleys
searched for a calligrapher to copy the poems on special paper. They hired a
graphic artist to compose the outline of a girl's face on a box so that when the
book was pulled from the box, a girl's face would appear, her hair shaped like a
rose. They hoped to use the most expensive silk for the book jacket. Binkley,
who was in his early thirties, spent over $77,000 on studio expenses alone. The
total cost for requisitioning materials came to well over $100,000. To make
financial matters worse, for two years he sacrificed most of his regular studio
business.

Because his poems were coming slowly, Dickey was relieved by Binkley's decision to include nineteen rather than thirty photographs. On September 22,
1979, over a year past his deadline, Dickey had finished only a few of the poems.
In a letter to Binkley's business partner, Sidney Stapleton, he reviewed his desultory progress: "I have written out complete sketches of the settings, the activities, the attitudes and even the personality of each girl, and have written the
poem to and around these conditions. In addition, I have made the poems se-
quential, and the presentation of the photographs progresses from dawn to
night: from the girls running on the road to the girl asleep with the rose." It was
strenuous work, but titillating as well. "I have spent the whole summer with
these girls," he quipped, "and if you haven't spent the three hot months of the
year with nineteen teenage girls, you should try it, especially when you get to the
age of fifty-six!" Convinced that their limited edition of twenty-five hundred
copies would sell quickly, Dickey told Stapleton that the cover story about him
in the November 1979 Reader's Digest would serve as an advertisement: "This
will give us eighty-two *million*—by last count!—potential buyers, and we should-
n't have any trouble at all in being offered a demand far in excess of the supply,
a mighty fortunate situation for us, any way you look at it." He had visions of another *Jericho*.

To give further notoriety to *Flowering*, Binkley and Stapleton planned a number of previews in Winston-Salem, Charlotte, and New York. They hoped that
articles on *Flowering* in *Southern Living*, *Vogue*, *Harper's Bazaar*, *Cosmopolitan*,
and other magazines would further stimulate interest. In January 1980, they
threw a big party at Winston-Salem's sumptuous Graylin House, which had
once been owned by the president of the RJR tobacco company. They mailed fifteen hundred invitations, hired a chamber orchestra, decorated the reception

area with flowers and photographs, bought wine, hired a caterer, provided valet parking, and displayed a dummy of the book for the guests. To convince the wealthy partiers to order copies, they offered a discount: $175 per copy—$75 off the proposed list price. To introduce the sequence of poems, Dickey gave a reading. At the festivities, which cost about $2,000 to arrange, and at the dinner party in a fancy downtown restaurant, Dickey was witty, charming, and ebullient. Unfortunately, only two of the four hundred guests wrote checks for the book. After Dickey discussed the book on local television and radio shows, about fifteen additional subscriptions materialized.

In March 1980, having received what he believed were the finished poems, Binkley visited Dickey in Litchfield to make the final payment. On this occasion, with numerous watches strapped from wrist to elbow, Dickey brought out his blowgun and demonstrated how to shoot it. Slightly unnerved, Binkley handed him the second check for $7,500 and left. He was further perplexed in mid-May when Dickey mailed what he called his "final *final* version" of the poems. "Here is the definitive—and I *mean* definitive—version of *Flowering*," Dickey declared. "There will be no more changes, not even in proof-stage. These are the poems as I would like them to appear, and in the order in which they are in the version you already have. Please withdraw *immediately* the version of the manuscript which you are submitting to publishers, and show them these: they are what I want." Dickey's impending hernia operation had prodded him into making last-minute alterations.

Binkley should have taken the paltry number of subscriptions in Winston-Salem as an ominous sign. Financially taxed, desperately searching for a publisher to help with publicity and printing, he failed to get the necessary funding. Apprised of these developments on his return from Seattle, Dickey wrote Stewart Richardson: "As to the fate of *Flowering* . . . , it is my opinion at this stage that the publishers in Winston-Salem won't find a commercial house willing to take it on, for $250 a copy is a lot to ask for a book of photographs by an unknown photographer, even if the poems are by a poet who is not, let us hope, unknown. What I would really like is eventually to get the nineteen poems released to me so that I can then incorporate them into a new book with Doubleday."[1] A week later, on June 23, 1980, Dickey wrote Stapleton a dissembling note: "As to the actual arrangements, negotiations, possibilities of various publishers, I leave that entirely to you, for you are my publisher: my primary one, regardless of whoever else may come into the situation."[2] He also asked Stapleton to delay publication of the book until after 1980 so that it could compete for the Pulitzer Prize.

By September 1980, Dickey had concluded that *Flowering* was doomed. In October, Binkley and Stapleton warned Theron Raines and Dickey's lawyer, Kirkman Finlay, not to publish the poems elsewhere. In December, Binkley and Stapleton found out that Dickey had allowed the Deerfield Press to publish a limited edition of two poems without their permission. The more wrenching surprise came in 1982. Binkley's lawyer, James Humphreys, was in New York soliciting financial support for *Flowering* from a wealthy importer of Perrier and, while browsing in a bookstore, found a copy of *Puella*, recently published by Doubleday. He immediately contacted Binkley, who was shocked. Because

Humphreys refused to handle the case, Binkley hired Vernon Glenn and Kendell Few in Winston-Salem to sue Dickey for breach of contract.

To bolster their case, Few and Glenn acquired correspondence between Dickey, Theron Raines, Doubleday, and the various editors who had published his poems in journals. The lawyers informed them that Dickey had violated his contract with Binkley. Dickey responded to the lawyers' charges with scorn. He wrote Peter Balakian, who had published some of the poems in the *Graham House Review*: "The Golden Chalice Press doesn't even exist, and Binkley is attempting a rip-off because the *Puella* poems, or what became them, were originally commissioned by him and his partner, another Winston-Salem fellow named Sid Stapleton, for a book of photographs that Binkley was doing. However, when they could not get the book published, or finance it themselves, I went ahead and published the poems, for they were in no sense *dependent* on the rather mediocre pictures by which Binkley hoped to gain a reputation. . . . Kirkman Finlay, my lawyer, said that Binkley had no claim on either the poems or any rebate, since he had failed to fulfill his part of the bargain, which was to produce the book."[3] Dickey assured Balakian and the other nervous magazine editors that they had nothing to fear. This was small consolation after Binkley's lawyers sent them telegrams instructing them to come to Winston-Salem in late November 1982 to discuss the impending litigation.

Binkley's lawyers were convinced that Dickey had lied to the editors about his commitments to Binkley. To undermine his credibility, Glenn and Few hired Bill Moyers's daughter, then a student at Wake Forest, to scrutinize Dickey's printed statements about his life. It did not take long for them to discover Dickey's fabrications. Later, Few and Glenn confronted Dickey with their discrediting evidence. Realizing he had been caught in a net of his own invention, he blanched and tried to shrug off their questions.[4] As for Binkley's suit, Dickey decided the best strategy was a preemptive strike. On November 24, 1982, he filed suit in the South Carolina State Court to reform his December 27, 1977, contract and to charge Binkley with "non-fulfillment" of his obligations. Binkley subsequently filed his own suit in Columbia's Federal Court.

Lawyers Finlay, Manton Grier, and Clarke Dubose presented Dickey's case in court on September 15 and 16, 1983. Their goal was to change the wording of the statement: "I agree not to sell any of it [the text of *Flowering*] to any magazine, book or other publication without your written consent." As plaintiff, Dickey asked "that the agreement be reformed to provide that defendant's only contractual right is to publish his limited edition book using the captions, and that the agreement excludes any right in defendant [Binkley] to control the publication of the poems by plaintiff or to seek cash payments under any alleged right to give consent to publication." Grier opened the proceedings by questioning Binkley about his first contacts with Dickey. Binkley described his first trip to South Carolina to discuss the revised contract and reiterated his conviction that *Flowering* would be published as a limited edition even though all the major New York publishing houses had rejected it. Next on the stand was Theron Raines, who revealed that in March 1980 Binkley had agreed to go to Doubleday with the idea of printing *Flowering: An April 9th of Girls* as a trade edition rather than a limited edition. Grier read Doubleday's rejection letter, which stated that the book would be too expensive to produce. Doubleday was also uncomfortable with its theme and thought its vaguely pornographic photographs would sully Dickey's reputation.

As the trial developed, it became obvious that Binkley and Stapleton had abandoned their plan to publish a limited edition. Grier read a potentially damaging letter written by Stapleton to Raines on June 27, 1980, in which he proposed eliminating the photography altogether and just publishing Dickey's poems. Raines explained that Dickey had agreed to the plan of publishing *Flowering* as a trade edition but not to letting his collaborators publish a book of his poems. On July 7, 1980, Binkley's agent had given up on the trade edition idea and rightly declined to represent Dickey's poems. In August, Raines had approached Doubleday with the possibility of issuing Dickey's poems separately. A month later, Dickey had reiterated his desire to publish his poems with Doubleday, and on February 25, 1981, he had signed a contract to do so.

In the cross-examination, Few grilled Raines on the fact that Dickey had published the limited edition *Scion* with Deerfield Press and sold the *Flowering* poems to magazines such as *Ms.*, the *Atlantic Monthly*, *Poetry*, and the *Kenyon Review* without Binkley's permission. He inveighed against Raines for allowing Dickey to publish *Puella* before reforming the contract. Wasn't Dickey's lawsuit a bogus attempt to erase a crime after it had been committed? Dickey next took the stand. Asked to speak about his life, he referred to his early schooling, his athletic and military experience, his later academic jobs, and his eight honorary doctorates. Those in the courtroom accustomed to the biographical blurbs on his books about piloting one-hundred combat missions took notice: "I went through Primary Training in Camden, South Carolina where I was held back a class. They had some sort of jam-up on the basic schools that were there, and my flying was not suitable to the Air Force at that time, so I was eliminated from pilot training; but, I was determined to stay in aircraft. I went through aerial gunnery school in Fort Myers, Florida and my test scores qualified me for a new program called the Nightfighter Program and [I became] an Intercept Expert Radar Observer." Regarding his service during the Korean War, he said: "I was recalled into the Air Force as having a critical MOS, Military Occupation Specialty, and I spent at least until '53 in the Training Command in Mississippi but mainly in central Texas." Following these revelations, he described meeting Binkley in 1977.

Few dwelled on the contract that prohibited Dickey from selling his poems without Binkley's written consent, and depicted Dickey as an avaricious opportunist who kept Binkley's $15,000 payment, used the poems at readings to make $3,500 an hour (sometimes it was more), and made additional money by selling the poems to magazines (he earned $500 from one) and to Doubleday (his advance was $3,000). He had broken the contract by submitting the final draft of the poems two years after the deadline, he had proposed that Doubleday publish the poems one month after Binkley paid him the second installment of $7,500, and he had written Raines: "Make sure that whatever happens that they [Binkley and Stapleton] don't stop us from doing what we intend to do anyway by publishing *Puella*." Binkley's lawyer had warned Dickey of the consequences; Dickey had ignored them.

James Humphreys took the stand to corroborate Few's claims. Humphreys said he had written Dickey's lawyer, Kirkman Finlay, on October 29, 1980: "Bookie is not willing for the poems to be published now by Jim unless there is an adequate compensation to him for such permission. Bookie's contention is, and Jim should be on notice of this, that Jim's unauthorized use of the poems would be extremely injurious to Bookie and the damage would be irreparable." According to Humphreys, Binkley had agreed to let Dickey publish his poems elsewhere if Dickey returned $7,500. Dickey had offered Binkley less—about $3,000—and had suggested that Binkley take *Puella*'s royalties. Binkley was not interested.

On the morning of September 16, Sidney Stapleton told the court of his involvement with Binkley: how he had been in charge of hiring calligraphers, printers, designers, and publicity personnel. With regard to permissions granted Dickey to publish his poems in magazines, he said that he had allowed Dickey to revise a poem for the *Atlantic Monthly* (the elegy for James Wright), but had asked Dickey to acknowledge *Flowering* when the poem appeared, and Dickey had not. Stapleton testified that no other permissions had been granted. In his cross-examination, Grier tried to portray Stapleton and Binkley rather than Dickey as avaricious. Stapleton admitted that initially they had hoped to net $600,000 on the project; he and Binkley would each pocket $150,000. Dickey would earn no royalties, only his $15,000 advance. Rather than reinforce Binkley's claim that Dickey was a pirate, Stapleton's testimony suggested that the original partners were out to rob a poet.

Next Few called Binkley, who reiterated the monetary reasons for printing a limited edition, explained the contract revisions, and stated that he had never given Dickey permission to publish the poems anywhere except in the *Atlantic Monthly*. Few asked Binkley: "Have you ever given up your dream or intention to bring this matter to a conclusion?" Binkley responded curtly: "No, Sir." The case having concluded, Judge Harrison deliberated (there was no jury) and soon delivered his verdict: "A contract may be reformed on the ground of unilateral mistake where one of the parties is under mistake, either of the facts or the stipulations, and such mistake has been occasioned by the unequitable conduct, deceit, concealment or imposition of fraud on [the] part of the Defendant, inducing the Plaintiff's mistake. A contract may also be reformed where one of the parties is suffering under imbecility or other circumstances exists which would make it a great wrong to enforce the agreement." The judge ruled: "The record is devoid of any evidence tending to establish that Mr. Dickey is an imbecile or suffers from any other form of mental incapacity which would make it a great wrong to enforce the contract."[5] As for fraudulent actions on Binkley's part, the judge concluded that there were none. He had reviewed the contract revisions and decided that the misunderstandings did not warrant Dickey's request to alter the contract. Dickey had lost the case. Binkley's suit in Federal Court covered the same ground, but became entangled in copyright issues. The end result was that Binkley collected about $25,000 from Dickey. Binkley's victory was Pyrrhic. Legal fees consumed about a third of his award. Because he never published his photographs, he failed to recoup $60,000 of his original investment. Dickey did nothing to reconcile with Binkley after his loss, but he wrote Glenn an unexpected letter: "I like what I saw of you, and maybe there is some future in an association. How about becoming my lawyer, for example? What would be involved in this? Let me know what you think. . . . As Kafka says, 'From a real adversary endless strength flows into you.'"[6] Unaware that Dickey routinely tried to convert enemies into allies, Glenn found his query extraordinary and did not adopt him as a client.

In the spring of 1982, a year before these calamitous events, the *Puella* poems were to be the centerpiece of Dickey's poetic comeback; he would reinvent himself and retool his image for more liberal and feminist times. The poems would literally take center stage in a multimedia show on May 14 at Arizona State. Dickey's association with the show's director, communications professor Janet Larsen McHughes, went back a decade. On September 17, 1972, McHughes had sent her Northwestern Ph.D. dissertation, *A Phenomenological Analysis of Literary Time in the Poetry of James Dickey*, to Dickey and received one of his well-rehearsed compliments a month later: "Of everything I have read, I don't believe that any of it comes as close as your own interpretation does to what I actually had in mind."[7] Dickey urged her to develop her thesis into a book, and when she produced *Living Time: The Poetry and Prose of James Dickey*, he recommended it to the LSU Press. As a professor at Southern Illinois University in 1980, McHughes arranged a reading for Dickey in May and in June directed *The Passionate Myth: Poetic Tales of James Dickey*, a series of musical dramas based on "May Day Sermon," "Looking for the Buckhead Boys," "Falling," and other early Dickey poems. Dickey attended the performances with Deborah and complimented McHughes on her dramaturgy.

McHughes must have been puzzled by Dickey's initial refusal to attend her gala performance of *Puella* in Arizona. After all, the college had contributed fifteen thousand dollars toward the show's expenses, and to coincide with Bronwen's birthday, May 17, Arizona State was also publishing a special edition of *Puella* designed by a master of fine printing and bookmaking, John Risseeuw. Despite all these efforts on behalf of his poems, Dickey feared that the singing and dancing on the stage might cheapen them. He told reporters: "What is going to happen in Arizona in May is a risk. It is a gamble. . . . A writer does not want his work to be made to appear ridiculous, not after he has worked so hard."[8] McHughes, however, had already proved that she could adapt Dickey's poems successfully for the stage.

The main reason Dickey threatened to boycott the *Puella* extravaganza was because Arizona State had not yet offered him an honorary degree. He wrote McHughes on July 28, 1981, that he would probably get degrees in 1982 from Kenyon College and the University of Mississippi: "But if Arizona State were to offer a degree, and if there were any conflict between that and the other two universities, I would cancel those in favor of Arizona State."[9] When Arizona State finally promised Dickey the degree, his enthusiasm for *Puella's* prospects soared. He told Ken McCormick: "The state of Arizona is practically giving me the whole state—the Grand Canyon *first!*—what with honorary degrees, huge starlit amphitheaters to read the poems in, ballets 'interpreting' the poems, music, costumes, orchestras, and God knows what all."[10] He would attend to pick up his Ph.D. as much as to see the show.

McHughes had arranged to have ten music professors perform a fifty-minute score, and to have fifteen dancers and eleven actors dramatize the poems. She explained in her introduction:

> In tonight's performance, Deborah will take two journeys as part of her self-discovery. The first, comprising Act I, is Deborah's fantasy journey into time, as she attempts to understand who she is by experiencing former lives, events, and traditions that are her heritage. Her imagination carries her as far away as the middle ages, where she envisions her ancestors as part of a medieval tapestry. When she tried to become part of that pastoral scene, Deborah finds that she cannot fit; she is clearly a modern woman, although she had to go through the process of discovering her ancestral roots to understand that.
>
> In Act II, Deborah rejects ceremony (so prevalent in Act I), seeks identity through another woman friend and, in the process, realizes her sexuality, takes a lover, and gives birth. The birth of her child parallels the first scene of the performance, in which Deborah begins the process of transformation from teenager to woman, a process completed by her "making" of another "doll," her daughter.[11]

The story portrayed Deborah as lost and only recently emerging from a prolonged adolescence. By saying that Deborah viewed her daughter as a "doll," McHughes implied that Deborah was still a child.

The actual Deborah was dispirited and incensed by all the attention given to her private struggles. Her life, albeit a highly abstract version of it, was on stage. With Shaye Areheart and Dickey at her side, she denounced *Puella* and, according to her husband, ruined what could have been a happy occasion: "Deborah was so stoned [he claimed she was now using heroin], she acted like a poltroon. . . . She denied and repudiated everything and insulted everybody. And the whole thing was for her. I don't know what got into her."[12] Dickey was particularly offended by her claims that he had cheated Binkley by publishing the poems without repaying him or getting his permission. Deborah's complaints and denials were partly justified. Dickey had not written the poems specifically for or about Deborah. She was a model, for sure, but not the only one. Paula Goff was another; the many girls photographed by Bookie Binkley were others. And Dickey had acted culpably with Binkley.

Dickey applauded the way McHughes staged *Puella*. To the Arizona State people who made the show possible, he tried to gloss over his marital peccadillos. He wrote university president Russ Nelson: "In all our travels we have never been made to feel more welcome, nor have we enjoyed such a wealth of interesting association with so many open, friendly, and intelligent people."[13] The problems in Arizona, however, may have contributed to Dickey's return to heavy drinking. On a trip from New Smyrna on May 22 to receive an honorary degree from Kenyon College, he betrayed the image of the happy public man he tried to convey to the Arizona State president. He explained to Jeffrey Meyers what happened: "I came to the guest house [at Kenyon] from Florida, where I had been in residence at a new arts center, and I sat down to drink part of a six-pack and cool off before all the public show. There was a knock on the door, and this fat little woman came in with a packaged gown, and asked, 'Is this your aca-demic hood?' Rising, unshaven and very sweaty, but, I hope, grave, gracious and relaxed, I replied, 'Madam, I *am* the academic hood.' That was my introduction to Helen Vendler [who was also receiving a degree], though I understand she doesn't like me and doesn't mind saying so. Well, as the hippies used to say, that's what makes the soup thick."[14]

The fault lines in Dickey's marriage opened before a much larger audience than the one at Arizona State when *People* magazine printed an article about the Dickeys in its *Couples* section in August 1982. On July 6, Dolly Langdon had in-terviewed the Dickeys separately and together. Langdon tried to downplay the friction between them by depicting Dickey as a proud father and gracious hus-band: "These days the onetime two-fisted drinker and womanizer can be seen pramming his 15-month-old daughter, Bronwen, along the thoroughfares so his stunning wife, Deborah, 30, can go to graduate school." Deborah was quick to puncture the suggestion of marital unity. Still angry about *Puella*, both the book and its theatrical adaptation, she told Langdon that she felt "exploited, espe-cially when I'm not quite sure who I am or how I fit into his life." Worried that she was doomed to reside in her husband's shadow, she admitted that her mar-riage still hadn't evolved from their original teacher-student relationship. "Sometimes there's too much of that. He wants to captain the ship, my ship as well as his," she complained with feminist stridence.

According to Deborah, Dickey was used to a wife who functioned as both sec-retary and servant, who remained at home to attend to his every whim and need. She was experiencing the normal tug between career and family. A sister had confronted her with the question: "What if he leaves you?" Deborah knew that she would have to take care of Bronwen if Dickey, who was almost sixty, left or died. "I was terrified," she said, "because I felt like I couldn't even take care of myself." She added:

> Right now is a strained time for us. . . . I'm going back to school—to be-come a high school teacher—and I feel guilty. I feel like our child is suf-fering because I don't have as much time for her, and Jim is suffering because he is used to having his wife in attendance 24 hours a day. His first marriage was very much like that. Ours was too, until about a year ago when I decided I wanted to do something for myself. He's kind of reluc-tantly going along, making it very clear he would be happier if I didn't go. I'm not as sure of my directions as he is, but I'm just as stubborn. When I doubt, and I doubt a lot, I get gloomy. Then I start from the first premise— I love him. I know he loves me too. He means stability, the thing I hang on to.

The Dickeys' love for one another was, in fact, bedeviled from the start. Dickey mused: "I feel like the Henry James character who said that marriage should be such that there is no greater adventure than coming home."[15] Before long the adventures would draw the attention of police.

Deborah's struggle to begin a teaching career typified the pitfalls of her marriage. She had entered the USC master's program in education during the 1982 summer session. She showed real aptitude for her courses; the following spring semester she earned As in Teaching High School English and Literary Criticism. The College of Education approved her for student teaching in the spring of 1983, and she took a position at Columbia's predominantly black C. A. Johnson High School. To say Dickey "reluctantly" supported her would be euphemistic. On one occasion he blurted: "I didn't pay for you to go out and teach a bunch of niggers."[16] Later Deborah taught at nearby Columbia College. By this time her drug habit had eroded her composure and dedication to teaching. According to Don Greiner, "She could not control herself in the classroom," and soon left. She had had trouble controlling herself in Greiner's master's course as well. Although Greiner did not know she was an addict at the time, he observed of her contributions to his Modern American Literature class: "Once she got involved in the class discussion she couldn't stop talking. . . . The class was almost disintegrating."[17]

The *People* article did little to improve the Dickeys' deteriorating marriage. On October 20, 1982, Dickey told Gordon Lish that a convict who had been in solitary confinement for several years had been harassing Deborah because of the article. His solitary confinement apparently didn't preclude regular phone calls. Dickey said:

> I talked to him on the phone, and he says he is in protective custody, which means that he is extra-dangerous on his own or that he is a squealer or something equally reprehensible, such that the other cons are after him. Neither one of these possibilities is much in the way of a character-reference, but the disturbing thing is that he is due for release in seven months, and is already making noises about coming down here to see his "only friends!" Needless to say, we want to do everything possible to discourage him. . . . I don't want to have to resort to police, but neither do I want the guy around here, under any circumstances. I don't want to turn my back on a suffering fellow human being—murderer or squealer—but neither do I want to have to confront him on a face-to-face basis.[18]

Dickey liked to bamboozle Lish with outrageous lies and was probably doing so again, even though his prison fantasies originated in real events and real feelings. His fears, aroused by Deborah and her drug friends, some of whom were ex-convicts, would intensify over the years.

Dickey worked hard during the summer of 1982 on *Alnilam* and on Jack Leigh's photography book *Oystering: A Way of Life* (Dickey wrote the foreword and helped with the editing). Afterward, he took his family to Paris for a much-needed week-and-a-half vacation. The day before he left, he sent his editor, Hugh O'Neill, another one hundred pages of his novel along with a customary note: "In case our aircraft blows up or we are gunned down at a cafe by either Palestinians, Jews, Armenians, Turks, Greeks, or just criminals . . . publish what you have of the novel."[19] If he died, he suggested that O'Neill piece together his notes the way Edmund Wilson had assembled Fitzgerald's posthumous *The Last*

Tycoon. In the grip of travel fears, he filed a court document on July 29, 1982, designating Deborah's sister, Deirdre Dodson Young (she usually went by Elaine), as Bronwen's legal guardian.

Once they had arrived safely in Paris, Dickey played tour guide, escorting Deborah to the Eiffel Tower, the Louvre, the Jeu de Paume, the Sorbonne, and other famous sites. (His secretary, Leslie Bates, who stayed with them in the Hotel du Louvre Concorde, helped take care of Bronwen.) They dined in the city's sumptuous restaurants and visited bookshops. Dickey was especially glad to see his old friend Marcel at Le Pont Traversé. He tried to look up old writer friends such as Julien Green, whom he wrote two days before flying to France: "I can truthfully say that your own writing and the example of your life I take from your *Journal* has had a great and good effect on my own work, and on my standards and values. I learned to read French by reading your *Journal*."[20] Momentarily free of the public scrutiny that dogged them in the States, Deborah relaxed and enjoyed herself. Around the time of their Paris trip they even considered trying to conceive another child. They discussed names: "Galen" for a girl, "Talbot"—once again—for a boy. Since their trip to England had produced a girl, they may have hoped that another transatlantic voyage would be similarly productive.

Dickey had to confront the mixed reviews of *Puella,* which had been published on April 29, 1982, when he returned to the States. Some critics refused to accept that Dickey, who seemed so determined to present himself as an icon of unadulterated masculinity, should spend a whole book ruminating on a young girl (*puella* in Latin means "young wife," "sweetheart," or "girl"). Was Dickey pretending to be a feminist? He discussed his ideas of womanhood and their relevance to *Puella* in an interview witih Terry Roberts: "I don't think there's a deeper part of nature than a woman. The blood of women is connected with the moon, the heavens, everything. They bear the very seed of meaning and existence. I wrote about the mysteriousness of coming of age, the stirring of the juices. Mainly, though, the feeling of fragility and mystery that there must be. And if it's not that way, I hope no female will tell me it's not."[21] Dickey alleged that his sequence of poems charted the mystery of Deborah's existence. Along with Deborah, another woman who influenced Dickey's conception of feminine mysteries—Paula Goff—also took issue with *Puella.* Because her name sounded like the Latin *puella,* because Dickey often addressed her as Puella, and because he had convinced her that *Puella* would be "her book," she chafed at the dedication to Deborah. Other women less personally involved with the book concluded that Dickey was more interested in women as poetic "white goddesses" than in their actual day-to-day roles in a culture traditionally ruled by men.

While some critics, most notably Gordon Van Ness, praised the "psychological depth and richness"[22] with which Dickey endowed his idealized girl, others questioned the value of idealizing women as archetypal "male-imagined" goddesses. The highly stylized way in which Dickey wrote about his mythical girl also drew fire. One of the most devastating attacks came from the poet Dana Gioia, who called the book "an unqualified disaster." For his first exhibit he cited the opening lines of "Deborah, Moon, Mirror, Right Hand Rising": "The image Dickey conjures up here could have been very beautiful—a young woman preparing for bed catches the reflection of the moon rising behind her face in a hand mirror. But his language obscures the image with a profusion of tired verbal tricks—arbitrarily compounded words ('After-glowing in the hang-time'), hopelessly vague description ('the wide-open collisionless color'), and clumsy wordplay ('All pores cold with cream'). These strained, self-conscious local effects dominate the language of *Puella* so completely that it is frequently impossible to make out the general sense of a passage—the whole is so hidden by its parts. . . . The more one scrutinizes the language of *Puella*, the more it seems improvised and approximate, nothing but pure, old-fashioned sound and fury."[23] Gioia concluded that Dickey's strength had always been in dramatic narratives rather than linguistic acrobatics.

Dickey set out to justify *Puella*'s modus operandi in his lecture "The G.I. Can of Beets, The Fox in the Wave, and the Hammers over Open Ground," which he delivered at a November 1982 SAMLA (South Atlantic Modern Language Association) meeting in Atlanta. Borrowing a distinction between denotative and connotative poets made by Winfield Townley Scott, he implied that his early poetry had deployed language in a clear, realistic way to tell a story; his later poetry jettisoned narrative and replaced it with a highly metaphoric style. In *Puella* he wanted to handle language like a magician rather than a bricklayer: "Recently I have tried, as the athletes say, to work out with the magical side of language: to break away from an approach that I felt was tending toward the anecdote, and depending too much upon it for whatever value this dependency might give it. Perhaps, in the latest poems, this has been a mistake, but even if it has, I can still say that by the attempt I have been made aware of ranges of expression, of possibilities, of departures, of 'new thresholds, new anatomies,' that I previously had no idea existed."[24] Many of his former admirers concluded that Dickey's "new anatomies" were inscrutable. Donald Hall wrote Dickey on December 16, 1982, that he had tried to read the book four times and had finally given up: "It feels opaque to me, it resists me, it does not let me inside. This could mean that you have done something that fails, that resists me because it has in fact an impenetrable surface. . . . Or on the other hand it could mean that you are doing something new, something that I cannot get to."[25] Dickey tried to ignore these complaints and dwell on the few good reviews and his Levinson Award from *Poetry*. On September 24, 1982, he wrote Jeffrey Meyers: "The reviews so far have been extraordinary, the best I have ever had."[26] But as he proved in his angry confrontation with Dana Gioia several years later, Dickey was all too aware of the less-than-complimentary ones.

If Dickey intended to address his wife's troubled upbringing and its pathological effects on her in *Puella*, the poems nevertheless began as responses to Binkley's numerous photographed girls, whom Dickey had never met. Dickey had simply unified all the different girls under the name Deborah. (Near the end of his life he admitted that the book had little to do with Deborah: "I just wanted to write about young girls. Actually, I just wanted to use language in a different way."[27]) Half-expecting the baffled response of his audience, Dickey provided an extensive explication of his sequence in a long letter to Shaye Areheart at Doubleday. He hoped his comments would help the publisher promote the book. What his comments reveal is that he never abandoned the mythic superstructure inherent in his "anecdotal" narratives. Once again the cyclical journey—the rites of passage—of the mythic hero governed *Puella*'s plot: "The whole book is intended to be cyclic, or at any rate semicyclic, beginning before dawn and running on through the following midnight." It begins "with a kind of ritual getting-rid-of the effects and environments of childhood" in a ceremonial burning of a doll and dollhouse; progresses through ritualistic experiences in which the narrator "link[s] up with the enormous forces of the universe" in all their mysterious, awe-inspiring, and terrifying sublimity; and ends with an invocation as well as "an affirmation of the imagination, of the mind's associational powers, so that literally the whole universe can result, or build up from, a single thought." The costumes that Dickey's "puella" puts on and takes off are essentially ceremonial masks that allow her to assume different roles. They allow her to imagine her past as well as her future. When Dickey says that one poem, "The Lyric Beasts," "is intended as a defense of illusion, and also a depiction of the essential detachment and cruelty of art, and the unearthly beauty that it may give to the human body,"[28] he is resuscitating favorite themes.

Dickey liked to lampoon Anne Sexton and Sylvia Plath for their poems on menstruation, but in *Puella* he imitates them. His second poem describes Deborah's onset of menstruation and the awareness of temporal cycles that accompanies it. She falls into a disturbing knowledge of birth, loss, and death. Despite her new self-consciousness, she maintains a spirited resistance to the harsh pressures of reality and strives for what Yeats called "tragic joy." Scenes follow of Deborah as a drunken bridesmaid racing another bridesmaid (shades of Dickey's drunken footraces). Dickey depicts her as a sister in a field of raucous crows contriving to "counterpraise" everything that afflicts her, a girl in her underwear about to dive into a creek, a horseback rider like Plath in "Ariel" leaving "earth / And a hoofmark in midair," a young woman (again like Plath) delighting in the "High-risk and conglomerate frenzy"[29] of bees and flowers, a contemplative, old-fashioned graveyard visitor communing with dead ancestors, a sexy woman arousing male lust, a waif full of saintly manic-depressive energies, a pianist trying to honor the great composers with her playing, and—finally and improbably—as the landscape talking to James Wright. From these various snapshots, cut up and shuffled as they are, Deborah appears as a sprightly, troubled, imaginative young girl seeking stability and joy in a destabilizing world.

Dickey, who liked to call himself the oldest adolescent alive, found in Deborah's adolescence an objective correlative for his own. His paean to Deborah's early years suggests a need to identify with the feminine side of his personality that he, bowing to peer pressure, had denigrated as "sissy" when he himself was an adolescent. The poem may not offer any overtly androgynous or feminist vision; nevertheless, its frequent echoes of Sexton, Plath, and even Emily Dickinson indicate a willingness to incorporate their concerns. He confided to a reporter that he hoped the poems would express "above all, a sort of passionate and involved male tenderness."[30] Following the principles of Jung, he aimed to unify yin and yang, *puer* and *puella*. Like Joyce's Leopold Bloom, he presented himself as a "womanly man." Although Valéry, Rilke, Mallarmé, Hopkins, Hart Crane, and Dylan Thomas may have influenced *Puella*'s byzantine rhetoric and jangling sound effects, Joyce had the most noticeable impact, just as he did on *Alnilam*. Dickey's "mythic method," like that of Joyce and his imitators, articulated a quest for an intelligible order through multiple personae, time shifts, and fragmentary epiphanies. The baroque linguistic inventiveness, the preoccupation with female sexuality young and old, the integration of genders into an archetypal figure, the affirmation of fluidity over rigid order, and the collagelike design of the story harked back to Joyce. *Puella*'s end, which prescribes "*unending / invention*,"[31] recalls the idiosyncratic, inconclusive ends of *Ulysses* and *Finnegans Wake*. To a certain extent Deborah is Dickey's Molly Bloom and Anna Livia Plurabelle, his "eternal feminine" representing "a plurality of belles." If Dickey had created a clearer, more engaging portrait of his universal woman with his skewed diction and syntax, *Puella* could have been a tour de force.

36. The Poet at Sixty (1982-1985)

On October 15, 1982, Dickey instructed Areheart to send *Puella* to Richard Hugo, who was chairing the 1982 Pulitzer Prize committee. With an old friend in charge, once again Dickey entertained hopes for a Pulitzer. By the end of October, Dickey learned that Hugo had died. He expressed his melancholy frustrations to Dave Smith, a great admirer of Hugo's poetry. He wanted to go to Montana to give some commemorative readings and get a plaque erected in Hugo's honor, but remarked: "Fat lot of good that'll do, though, death being what it is. But we go on, until we can't. Right now, you and I go on."[1] With Hugo gone, Dickey asked Smith for continued support. Addressing Smith as "My best, my old Pulling Guard," Dickey urged him, just as he had recently urged David Bottoms, to knock down his adversaries. For Dickey the literary world, especially with the bruising reviews of *Puella* appearing, was as combative as a football game, and one that he was losing.

Because Smith's reputation was in the ascendant, Dickey viewed Smith as both friend and rival. When Robert Penn Warren worked during the fall to get Smith elected to the National Institute of Arts and Letters, Dickey gave Smith a qualified endorsement: "He is a rather good poet, I think, soft-spoken and sincere, but his pieces seem to me to blur into one another. But I do like his work, and I will be more than glad to back his play."[2] He seconded Smith's nomination in 1988 as well (Smith failed to get elected both times). Smith's reservations about Dickey's post-1970s poetry sometimes irked him, and as Smith's reputation grew, so did Dickey's ambivalence toward him. In 1995 Dickey vehemently protested a suggestion by Emory's Special Collections Library that Smith read at the opening of the Dickey archive (Dickey was gravely ill at the time). Two years later, discussing a replacement for Dickey at USC shortly before his death, Dickey opposed Smith's candidacy.

Dickey got a chance to confront some of his adversaries in a formal way at a *Firing Line* debate on November 30, 1982. Before an audience of three hundred in the USC Law School auditorium, Dickey teamed up with William F. Buckley and *National Review* columnist Joe Sobran to support the resolution that "women have it as good as men." Opposing them were three women: public relations executive Muriel Fox, psychoanalyst Dr. Erica Freeman, and lawyer Harriet Pilpel. The women cited statistics to prove that, in terms of economic and emotional well-being, women still lagged behind men. The men argued that Fox, Freeman, Pilpel, and women like them were essentially "America's leading victim lobby." Dickey attacked the women and the women's movement they advocated by saying that their doctrines attempted to "erode the biological polarity between the sexes," thereby "making the split between women and men deeper and deeper. [Feminism] sets aside the important fact of the maleness of men and the femininity of women, and the survival of the race depends on that fact."[3] For Dickey, whose biological ability to procreate had become problematic, men and women were still defined almost entirely by their genetic endowment and reproductive functions.

Despite his old-fashioned view of the sexes, Dickey was characteristically upbeat about his performance in the debate. He told his longtime friend Lester Hardwick: "I think Bill and I . . . got somewhat the best of it. All the girls wanted to do was talk percentages and statistics—how many women on top, really *top*, executive positions in this country—and so on. But statistics bore a television audience, or indeed any audience, and Bill and I concentrated on what is wrong between men and women, which is plenty."[4] His remarks about the successful women he faced and his attitude toward women in general amused and appalled many in the USC audience. Virginia Fox, the president of Southern Educational Communications, wrote on December 9 that she hoped Allah would one day show Dickey the light. She underscored the obvious fact that victims have oppressors. Dickey replied a few days later: "My particular remarks . . . were not about victims and oppressors, but about the uncertain relation between men and women themselves, the loss of depth-communication, the unsayable, the beyond-statistics relation, what Goethe called the entelechy, the vital force urging toward fulfillment."[5] Others who watched the debate when it appeared on TV in 1983 scolded Dickey for his reactionary views. On June 23, Toni Carter ridiculed his notion that women worked only because they wanted to work. Were all women so well-off that they could choose? Dickey tried to deflect these missiles with apologies and qualifications. He told Carter that he only meant that men had always expected to work and that women had not. Responding to Joe Chan, who questioned him about his refusal to endorse the Equal Rights Amendment, he was less than candid: "Please do not assume that because I am undecided about the ERA specifically, I am undecided about equal rights in general for women; I am not. I believe very strongly in the equality of men and women."[6] Those in his Columbia audience who had read Dickey's sarcastic quip about wanting to marry a "slave" after Maxine died had reason to question his sincerity.

Dickey's social conscience had evolved fitfully over the decades. When he felt cornered, as he did in the early 1980s, he often took up the cudgels of his unenlightened forebears. He showed little intention of amending his attitudes toward either women or blacks. Around the time of the Buckley debate, after lunching with Ward Briggs at California Dreaming in Columbia, Dickey met

Elizabeth Adams in a crowd of people. President Reagan had just appointed her husband ambassador to Malawi. "Now listen," Dickey said, "I've talked to your husband about this ambassadorship to Malawi, and he and I see eye to eye on almost everything. And he has agreed with me not to touch that apartheid system they've got there in Malawi. It's worked for years and shouldn't be changed." Adams replied that apartheid was terrible and, in any case, Malawi did not have the apartheid system. Briggs cringed as Dickey proceeded with sublime indifference: "No, that apartheid is good. And I tell you why. Your husband and I both agree that there never has been a nigger equal to a white man and there never will be."[7] Dickey astonished those within earshot, which was probably his intention.

Jeffrey Meyers paid Dickey another visit on December 29, 1982, and later reported: "I was struck by the contrast between his affable, generous, even courtly self in letters and on the phone and, when the veneer of Southern politeness was stripped off, his aggressive boastfulness in person." Because Meyers was on his way to Key West to do research for a Hemingway biography, Dickey sneered at Hemingway and other writers like Roethke and Jarrell for falling prey to mental illness: "Like a cornered buccaneer, Jim angrily cut and slashed his way through the literary world. He said Pound was a swamp that one could sink in, and strongly disagreed when I praised Ginsberg's intellect. He scorned and pitied Mailer, dismissing him as a pathetic exhibitionist. He disliked poets in groups and sneered at politically biased poetry about the death of President Kennedy or the liberation of El Salvador. He didn't read contemporary poetry and knew of no younger poets he could praise. . . . He rather defensively remarked that he taught courses at the University of South Carolina in modern poetry . . . to give the bumpkins some sense of the poets he liked."[8] Meyers concluded that Dickey's scalding insults originated from a deep-rooted insecurity that had grown deeper over the years. The fact that some of his coveted books had been stolen from his house earlier in the month contributed to his blustery mood. On December 9, he sent an announcement to *Bookman's Weekly* and *Antiquarian Bookman:* "I appeal to readers and collectors of rare books worldwide to help me recover my books. These include, but are not limited to, first edition copies by Robert Penn Warren, Allen Tate, Randall Jarrell, John Berryman, and W. D. Snodgrass."[9] Dickey offered a reward, but never retrieved his books.

The year Dickey turned sixty began with much fanfare. Following the example of Jimmy Carter, the new governor of South Carolina, Richard Riley, commissioned Dickey to write a poem for his inauguration. In January, to an assembled multitude of politicians and their families, Dickey celebrated "the palmetto state" and its new governor with "For a Time and Place." Like his essay "A Starry Place Between the Antlers," his poem wove images of South Carolina's flora, fauna, and geography—from the mountainous west to the marshy east—into an attractive quilt:

> We peer also from the flat
> Slant sand, west from estuary-glitter,
> From the reed beds bending inland

> At dawn as we do, to the high-ground hard-hurdling
> Power of the down-mountain torrent: at the blue ridged glance
> From the ocean, we see all we have
> Is unified as a quilt.[10]

To get better acquainted with the governor, Dickey invited him to his literary birthday party at USC in February along with Robert Penn Warren, Richard Howard, Norman Mailer, Saul Bellow, John Updike, John Simon, Monroe Spears, Harold Bloom, R.W. B. Lewis, and numerous other writers and professors.

As his marriage and reputation floundered, Dickey greeted USC's gesture with particular gratitude. The university honored him with a series of scholarly panels on his work: on February 1, Bernie Dunlap discussed the film *Deliverance*; on February 2, former students Franklin Ashley, Ben Greer, and Susan Ludvigson recalled his inspiring teaching; later that day Richard Riley held a birthday banquet at the Governor's Mansion; that night Harold Bloom and Richard Howard lectured on Dickey's poetry. Bloom, who focused obsessively on the Oedipal battles between poets, quibbled with Robert Hill about the sociopolitical bearing of Dickey's middle poetry (Bloom maintained that it was predominantly introspective and apolitical). Bloom's contrariness erupted more forcefully when John Simon read a paper on February 4. Simon drew laughs by portraying Bloom and his wild-eyed, theory-driven Yale colleagues as the new Horsemen of the Apocalypse, and, according to Simon, Bloom "got up and elephantinely marched or staggered or gallumphed out."[11] Upset by Simon's witty jabs, Bloom refused to attend the final breakfast at the Dickeys' house until he was assured that Simon would not be there. On February 4, the last day of the symposium, Monroe Spears also lectured. Addressing the topic of "Dickey as Critic and Literary Figure," Spears defended Dickey's experiments in *The Zodiac* and *Puella*. According to Dickey's faithful mentor, these books represented an advance in an exemplary career. Summing up Dickey's life work, he harked back to discussions about creative lying he had had with his former student at Vanderbilt. Dickey's writing, Spears pointed out, was characterized by "a strong sense of place, a love of storytelling, a love of ceremony and ritual, and a preposterous lying which outrages the reader but shows a truth deeper than the truth."[12] Dickey may not have been entirely happy with Spears's characterization of him as an outrageous liar, but was pleased that such a distinguished scholar complimented his two most maligned books.

The grand finale of Dickey's birthday symposium came in the form of a banquet on February 4, sponsored by university president James Holderman. Columbia mayor Kirkman Finlay introduced Dickey's reading by recalling a New Year's Eve party he hosted where Dickey shunned the other illustrious guests to entertain a lovely blonde woman who sat at his knee. During a lull in the after-dinner conversation, the guests heard the woman ask Dickey in a mellifluous Southern accent whether he had ever picked cotton. "No," he responded, "but I have known in a Biblical sense those who have." Finlay may have been thinking of Dickey's poem "Slave-Quarters," where the white master "knows" the slave "in a Biblical sense," but otherwise was just ribbing Dickey for his reputation as a womanizer. About the jokes, compliments, and critiques directed at him during the conference, Dickey told a reporter that he felt like a bard transfixed by many needles. All the analysis reminded him of an anecdote about Emerson lending a copy of Plato's *Dialogues* to a hardscrabble New England farmer. After keeping the book for several months, the farmer returned it. Emerson asked him what he thought of the book. "It's all right, I guess," the farmer said. "But he's got a lot of my ideas in that book." Dickey concluded: "There are a lot of my ideas here today. . . . And everybody's right who's favorable."[13] He was pleased that even those whom he had offended—like Susan Ludvigson—were favorable.

Partly because of the financial worries brought on by Bookie Binkley's lawsuit, Dickey went back to barnstorming for poetry. During the winter and spring he read at Albright College, the University of North Texas, Savannah College of Art and Design, Fairleigh Dickinson, New York's West Side YMCA, and the Guggenheim Museum. In late March 1983, he also appeared at Clemson for a three-day conference. Here he reunited with his friend Larry Lieberman, who recalled:

Halfway through lunch, several husky older men came into the [Holiday Inn] restaurant, walked past us, and Jim looked shocked and half-hid his face. Then, he whispered to us that one of the men had been his football coach many years before at Clemson. Shortly after, the former coach came over to our table and greeted Jim, not quite sure it was he, saying, "Hey, aren't you that poetry feller?" Jim, grinning and blushing a little, nodded yes. The coach exchanged a few pleasantries with Jim. Briefly, they discussed old times. All the time, Jim was in his seat, and the coach stood over him. But then as the coach turned to leave, Jim stood up to shake hands and say goodbye, and as Jim unfolded to his full height, the coach stood back—as if he'd forgotten Dickey's size—and said, as his parting words: "Say, you don't look like one of them poets. You should have been a trucker or longshoreman." And out the door he went. Jim was just beaming, as if he'd been paid the highest compliment you can imagine.[14]

Rock Norman confirmed Dickey in his quest to be a poet without looking like one.

In July, Dickey struck a more Byronic pose at the Colorado Mountain Writers' Workshop and Aspen Writers' Conference, where he also read and taught. On this trip he met a lovely Texan woman, Patricia Muske, who had accompanied a friend. Muske had fallen in love with Dickey's poetry years before as a teacher in Houston's prestigious Kinkaid School, but had not heard him read before the Aspen conference. Following the reading, Dickey invited her and some others to the Jerome Hotel Bar for drinks. The next night Dickey asked her to join him at the conference picnic. Subsequently, they met almost every day for lunch and dinner. At one of their first dinners, Dickey enchanted her with tales about his football heroics at Clemson and his military service in

Texas during the Korean War. Muske told him about inheriting and operating a three-thousand-acre cattle ranch built by her great-grandfather in 1865 after his return from the Civil War. The ranch quickly became a focal point for Dickey's fantasies. Over the next decade he frequently expressed his desire to marry Muske, whom he called "Rawhide and Jasmine." He wanted to run the Texas ranch, and—presumably after conquering his fear of horses—transform himself into a glamorous cowboy. As a backup scenario, he proposed marrying Muske in North Georgia, decking her hair with bridal flowers, and spending his remaining years with her as a princely rustic.

To manage the Texas ranch Dickey would also have had to overcome his stinginess. Muske was appalled when Dickey, who was paid several thousand dollars at the Aspen conference, insisted that she pay the sixteen-dollar dinner bill. An apologetic Dickey cited his daughter's college tuition as an excuse. Only later did Muske realize that Bronwen was two years old. At the dinner table Muske finally prevailed, and Dickey dutifully paid his portion of the bill. Despite his miserliness, Dickey charmed Muske with his conversation. Deborah, who was in Aspen, was not pleased by this budding friendship. She overheard her husband profess his love to Muske on the phone, and for the next six months wrote embittered letters and made threatening phone calls to Muske in Texas. At one point she became so distraught that she told Muske she was coming to Houston to decapitate her. Dickey could provide little consolation; he told a fearful Muske that Deborah was just crazy enough to do it.[15]

Drawn together by their common German lineage, which they often discussed, Dickey and Muske cultivated an erratic, long-distance romance for about a decade. Appreciative of Dickey's kindness and intelligence, Muske was well aware of his irascible moods. Before traveling to Rice for Monroe Spears's retirement party in 1986, he called Muske and brusquely announced: "I'll be in Houston, but don't try to get in touch with me."[16] Having professed anxiety about Deborah discovering a possible tryst, he in fact did call Muske in Houston. Miffed by his previous phone call, Muske refused to see him, but later sent him yellow roses. Several years later, in 1990, they renewed their friendship at writers' conferences in Chattanooga and Birmingham, where Dickey was his gallant, sensitive, funny, besotted self. In May 1995, while visiting New York for a National Institute of Arts and Letters meeting, Dickey introduced Muske to Jackie Onassis. (Shaye Areheart, who worked with Onassis at Doubleday, had first introduced Onassis to Dickey.) Onassis, Muske remembered, was rather shy and hung on Dickey's every word. Watching the film Howard's End with Muske, Dickey proceeded to cry, remarking that the Schlegel women reminded him of his mother. Muske had witnessed other lachrymose displays in hotel rooms when Dickey bemoaned the way Deborah was ruining her life with drugs and inflicting her problems on Bronwen.

In the late 1980s, Dickey's marriage proposals to Muske seemed more serious. He alleged that Deborah, after binging on alcohol and other drugs, had hit him on the head with a paperweight. Dickey tried to express his love for Muske, who was more muse than mistress, in several poems. He told her that he had written four poems for her—"Daybreak," "Two Women," "Vessels," and "Meadow Bridge"—which he collected in The Eagle's Mile. Even his claims about the poems, however, smacked of unreality. "Daybreak" focused on Dickey—he portrayed himself as "no different from cloud, among the other / See-through images"—rather than on Muske. "Vessels" elegized Dickey's dead brother, Tom, and "Meadow Bridge" described an unremarkable bridge. In "Two Women," rather than proclaim his love, he declared:

> Woman, because I don't love you,
> Draw back the first
>
> Of your feet, for the other will fall
> After it, and keep on coming. Hold back
>
> A little your printed pursuit, your
> Unstemming impurity.[17]

With Muske as with other women, Dickey both beckoned and rebuffed. The two remained Platonic lovers and confidants, cheering each other up on the phone during hard times.

Along with a screenplay based on an August *Newsweek* article regarding a rash of teenage suicides in Plano, Texas (Olmeyer Communications paid him forty thousand dollars for the treatment), several older projects occupied Dickey's attention in mid-1983, among them *The Wilderness of Heaven*, another coffee-table book, whose deadline was in October. Near the beginning of August 1983, Shaye Areheart had mailed reproductions of the paintings by Hubert Shuptrine that Dickey was supposed write about, but Dickey had repudiated them: "I think it would be better for me to work out my own interpretation of Appalachia, as I did with the South in *Jericho*. I really want more subject matter than Hubert's pictures would afford me, so I am going ahead on that basis."[18] He informed Shuptrine of his modus operandi, and told him to paint whatever he liked. Fearing a fractured, incoherent book, on August 25, Shuptrine asked Dickey to supply him with a rough outline of his narrative to guide his painting. If Dickey insisted on leading, Shuptrine graciously agreed to follow. Dickey finished his story of Appalachia quickly, sent a draft to Hugh O'Neill by the end of October, and completed revisions in December.

Dickey brought another book to completion in late 1983. On October 15, Bruccoli Clark published *Night Hurdling*, a potpourri of Dickey's articles, poems, commencement addresses, interviews, and afterwords. In his introduction Dickey made the startling admission that all the disparate writings had one goal, to delineate a self-portrait, but he also acknowledged: "Perhaps in the end the whole possibility of words being able to contain one's identity is illusory. . . . Perhaps the whole question of identity itself is illusory." Readers must have wondered about Dickey's identity after reading the first article, "The Enemy from Eden," which describes how to make an eight-foot blowgun from aluminum tubing and killer darts from sharpened pieces of coat hanger. The article, which had first appeared in *Esquire* as "Blowjob on a Rattlesnake," had little to do with the sexual connotations or the actual facts of snakes. "Snakes," Dickey wrote, "hate you and the human race instinctively hates them. All the naturalists in the world, pleading for better treatment of serpents, are not going to change that feeling."[19] Snakes, to this superstitious view, were mythic totems rather than real reptiles. Dickey was more convincing and incisive in his literary commentaries on Robert Penn Warren's angst, F. Scott Fitzgerald's poetry, Jack London's stylistic vices and narrative virtues, and Vachel Lindsay's suicidal decline.

In October and November of 1983, Dickey returned to the reading circuit, making stops at the Governor's School for the Arts in South Carolina, the Folger Shakespeare Library, George Mason University, Northern Virginia Community College, Westchester Community College, Colgate University, and the Alabama School of Fine Arts. He resumed his role as drunken bard partly out of frustration with the critical reception of his books and partly out of a desire to win back his audience's attention. After business meetings with his agent and publisher in New York, on November 4 he put on a vintage display at Colgate University. At the airport terminal, he met his host, the talented Armenian-American writer Peter Balakian, whose aunt Nona edited the *New York Times Book Review*. It was 10:30 A.M., and he was already staggering with too much drink. Mixing affection with avarice, he complimented Balakian's poetry, declared he had come "on the cheap" for the "human relation," and brusquely demanded his one-thousand-dollar check. With money in hand, he asked if Balakian had any six-packs in the car. Balakian had no beer, no cash to buy beer, but nevertheless stopped at a convenience store on the drive to campus and explained his desperate situation to the clerk. To his surprise the man handed over several six-packs. Dickey started guzzling and soon insisted that Balakian pull to the side of the road. Pointing vaguely at shadows in a nearby meadow, he claimed that deer would emerge from the woods. If he only had his blowguns, they could hunt them. Disturbed by his guest's prattle, Balakian convinced him that they should continue to campus.

Upon entering a department building at Colgate, Dickey began taunting and flirting with the secretaries. He imitated old actors like Jimmy Stewart, Humphrey Bogart, and James Cagney. Balakian was mortified and worried that Dickey would jeopardize his upcoming tenure decision. On the way to his house, Balakian spoke of playing on the Bucknell football team, and Dickey told stories about playing under the famous Clemson coach Frank Howard. Dickey demanded that Balakian pull to the curb again so that he could tell a story. When he was eighteen, he began, his father called him in for questioning. "Son, do you like to eat?" his father asked. He answered: "Yes." "Son, do you like to drink?" Dickey again said: "Yes." "Son, do you like to fuck?" Once again he said: "Yes." His father concluded: "Boy, you're just like me. You like the joys of this sweet life."

Having told his bawdy tale, Dickey allowed Balakian to drive to his house, where he began speaking of "niggers." Balakian found the racial slurs, which Dickey's drinking had unleashed, offensive and told Dickey they should go to the auditorium for the reading. Ignoring the weather—it was drizzling and muddy outside—Dickey said he wanted to practice some football pass patterns in the yard. In a turtleneck with a giant gold medallion flopping on his chest, he played quarterback, shouting commands like: "Run a down-and-out!" Balakian, who was wearing a tie and jacket, complied, and Dickey threw a wobbly pass.

After a few more awkward passes, Dickey decided he was suitably warmed up for the poetry reading.

Five hundred eager, rowdy students awaited Dickey in the auditorium. The president and the dean of Colgate, who admired Dickey's work, were also there, as were many of Balakian's colleagues. Dickey entered, grinning and leering, and threw his big hat to the crowd. Several props, including a bed from a student play that had been scheduled for the night of the reading, remained near the podium. Dickey couldn't resist commenting that he had never read beside a bed before, that he didn't know what to do with it, but maybe by the end of the night somebody would show him. The audience howled. He next recited some Rodney Dangerfield "I can't get no respect" jokes, and told one about a middle-aged couple having trouble with their sex life. One night they performed so badly, a Peeping Tom booed. He followed up with more sex jokes, which seemed to make light of his own inadequacies. When Dickey finally got around to read, he was as spellbinding as ever. After every poem he bowed to encourage applause. His performance over, Dickey and Balakian proceeded to the dean's elegant house for a lavish reception, where Dickey spoke politely to the president's wife about German literature and to the other professors about their interests. Balakian and the scholar Terrence Des Pres then escorted Dickey to Des Pres's house. Although the rain had turned to snow, Dickey again insisted on playing football. Noticeably drunk, he threw the ball even more sloppily than before.

Throughout his brief visit, Dickey often complained that Deborah, who had called several times to check on him, was paranoid and jealous. Their marital discord was obvious, as was Dickey's profound insecurity. He reminded Balakian of Norman Mailer, whom Dickey had tried to see on his recent visit to New York (he claimed Mailer was a great fan of his article about blowgunning rattlesnakes). Dickey had one last opportunity to pose as *l'homme moyen sensuel* when Des Pres and his wife, Liz, drove him to the airport to catch his night flight. In a brash voice, he declared that Liz needed "a real man" like himself. Balakian, who had been a loyal advocate of Dickey's work, even to the point of writing a favorable review of *Puella,* was glad to bid him farewell.[20]

In 1984, Dickey found in the writer Truman Capote a mirror-image for his own alcoholic behavior. On November 13, in an elegiac tribute delivered to the National Institute of Arts and Letters, he embraced Capote as a fellow Southerner who both indulged and transcended his self-destructive appetites. Capote's recent death, Dickey confessed, had shocked and terrified him. Alluding to newspaper obituaries, Dickey seemed to be worrying about his own: "The journals I read, some of them quoting friends and acquaintances of the deceased, were of the opinion that though Capote was a writer of real ability who had produced a bestseller from which a movie was made [*In Cold Blood*], he had ruined himself—his talent along with his health—for money and publicity." Dickey took exception to this dire assessment. He condoned Capote's careerism, his love of the "International-Cafe-Society, jet-set, Beautiful-People," his homosexual escapades, and his drunkenness; and he relished and apologized for Capote's fabulous, Gatsby-like panache: "If there is any magic in American life, it is to be found where great sums of money are spent in groomed and luxurious settings which exist for exposure and pleasure: a corrupt and debilitating magic, but the only one in which our culture truly believes." How could pedestrian critics understand and judge the complex demons that drove a Capote or, for that matter, a Dickey? "The notoriety, the campy put-on quality of some of the episodes, the cattiness, the public fights, the lawsuits—all of those things were regarded by many as evidence of a falling-off, a sell-out, a deterioration, a waste, a betrayal, an outrage, a tragedy. But were they? Were they *entirely* so?" In questioning Capote's critics, Dickey sought to undermine his own.

Capote, Dickey argued, had the power to remove himself from his scandalous acts, analyze them, and then articulate them with scientific precision. The "self-styled, self-made, self-taught country boy" had taught himself "to concentrate: to close out, and close in, to close *with*. His writing came, first, from a great and very real interest in many things and people, and then from a peculiar frozen detachment that he practiced as one might practice the piano, or a foot position in ballet." The nearly absolute absorption in a subject and nearly total recall of its details were abilities Dickey shared with his dissolute peer. His commemorative poem paid homage to Capote's ability to detach himself from the chaos around him. Capote's meditative withdrawal also involved a withdrawal from alcohol:

> What you hold,
> Don't drink it all. Throw what you have left of it
> Out, and stand. Where the drink went away
> Rejoice that your fingers are burning
> Like hammered snow. . . .
> Behold him
> With your arms: encircle him,
> Bring him in with the forge and the crystal
> With the spark-pounding cold.[21]

Dickey's acceptance of Capote was grounded in his own attempts to renounce drink, retreat into the fiery cold of his imagination, forge new art, and win back his audience. To facilitate his retreat to his "Cave of Making," Dickey rehired Paula Goff as his secretary. Ever willing to help her mentor, Goff, who was not well-off, agreed to work for free since Dickey complained he had little money after losing his lawsuit to Bookie Binkley. Deborah again had to confront one of her husband's former girlfriends on a daily basis. Often kind to Paula—she gave her advice about makeup and clothes—Deborah still found the situation hard to bear. Periodically she would get so upset that she would ask the police to escort Paula from the premises.[22]

Because Dickey and Deborah received fewer and fewer invitations to social gatherings, for the sake of camaraderie Dickey came to depend on three or four close friends in Columbia. During his sixty-first year he began a tradition of "power lunches" that he continued until the last year of his life. One day, while Dickey collected his mail at the English Department before an afternoon class, Don Greiner and Ben Franklin invited him to one of their regular lunches at the Faculty House on the Horseshoe. Franklin had befriended Dickey at a number of dinner parties at the Franklins' house, at which he was always polite and always without Deborah. Having just returned from a two-year Fulbright professorship at the University of Athens, Franklin looked forward to catching up with his old friend. Dickey enjoyed the lunch so much that he suggested meeting again, and soon they gathered every Tuesday and Thursday. They became known as the "Haggard Heroes." (Dickey celebrated the triumvirate with a heroic couplet adapted from Samuel Johnson: "Where culture's haggard heroes find repose / And safe in intellect defy our foes.") Because there were four chairs at each Faculty Club table, Dickey suggested inviting a "mystery guest" each week whose identity would be kept secret. The guest would be expected to contribute to their conversations, which usually pertained to literature, music, movies, and sports. Franklin played master of ceremonies, addressing the guest with formulaic aplomb: "Now we want you to feel no pressure. Feel at home. We were hoping that you would inform or entertain us, and following lunch we three will get together and vote on whether to invite you back."[23] The mystery guest lunches were usually high-spirited affairs. Sometimes Bronwen attended, but usually the guests were students or other professors.

Dickey treated these gatherings as one of his only outlets for friendly banter and private conversation. He often unburdened his marital agonies, confident that his two friends were not taking notes and keeping journals (they were not). He rarely missed a lunch, and if he had other commitments, he always informed his two friends in advance. He always ordered the same number of beers (two Heinekens, although at the start he sometimes ordered two martinis) and the same food (one bowl of she-crab soup). Because his hiatal hernia still hindered digestion, he occasionally frightened his friends by gagging on his lunch (during one of the more serious incidents, he vomited on the table). Dickey liked to ask about the books the others were teaching. Once when Greiner mentioned he was teaching Henry James's late, labyrinthine novel *The Golden Bowl*, he was astonished by Dickey's recollection of specific scenes and characters. Dickey showed the same command of nearly all the books Franklin taught. A close friend of Anaïs Nin and other writers, Franklin said: "I have never met anybody in literary circles like Dickey."[24] With Franklin and Greiner, Dickey felt comfortable enough to cast aside his various disguises and communicate his intelligence and anxieties in a forthright way.

At the lunches Dickey kept his friends abreast of his writing projects, chief among them *Alnilam*. In 1984, he hoped his friend George Plimpton would publish an excerpt in the *Paris Review*. He was fond of saying at the time that he had written over seven hundred pages in which nothing had happened, but high drama was imminent (in 1982, Dickey told other friends that he had already written one thousand pages). Nowhere near completing a final draft, on December 17, 1984, he signed another amended version of his original 1971 contract that extended his deadline to May 1, 1985. Although Dickey made progress with *Alnilam* in 1985, he knew he would fail to meet his new deadline as well. Therefore, on April 10, 1985, he signed another agreement that called for the manuscript in August of 1985. By mid-May 1985, he had written a staggering twelve hundred pages. August and his deadline passed, but by October he had mailed all fifteen hundred pages to his editor. Many wondered what had taken him so long. He told William Starr at the *State* that the death of Maxine, the marriage to Deborah, and the birth of Bronwen had slowed him. More importantly: "I've never felt I was subject to the exigencies of publishers. I've never felt it incumbent on me to produce another best seller. I've worked on the novel, but a lot of other things too. And remember, poetry remains at the center of everything for me."[25] Dickey may not have consciously aimed at bestsellerdom, but he and his publisher counted on substantial sales.

Keeping his novelistic ambitions in check was a self-defensive strategy. He went out of his way during the spring of 1985 to court best-selling writers, but as he did so he wore the mantle of the marginalized poet. One of the mass market authors he contacted was John Jakes, best known for such blockbuster historical romances as *North and South*. Dickey thought they should get together because, he wrote Jakes: "It is always good for someone who lives mainly in the back pages of obscure poetry magazines—mainly there, as I say, but not entirely—to meet someone new who operates up there among the gold-giving Masses."[26] The bitterness caused by such failures as *Flowering, Klondike,* and his other film treatments piqued Dickey's envy for the monetary success of a Jakes and also made him contemptuous of it. He responded to *Writer's Digest,* which had asked him to fill out a short questionnaire about his writing career: "I do not think it likely that a publication whose favorite word is 'market' . . . would be so naive as to suppose that a writer would set his own work aside to do something for nothing, particularly for a publication such as yours, whose emphasis is not on quality but the exploitation of a medium for profit."[27] At the same time Dickey spurned the exploitation of his medium for profit, he actively capitalized on his waning celebrity—even to the point of hawking souvenirs like signed photographs and "authentic" "Dueling Banjos" guitar picks. He often reminisced to reporters and friends about his earlier days when his literary future was so full of promise. On January 16, 1985, while giving a reading during the Founder's Day ceremonies at Berry College in Rome, Georgia, he waxed nostalgic about his first inspiring trips to see Flannery O'Connor. Crippled by disease, she had kept working and now served as an example of stoic resolve. As he returned to the back pages of little magazines, he expressed a new modesty. Questioned about what he would be if he hadn't been a writer, he told a reporter: "I would be a football coach of a moderately successful high school team . . . and I would coach track in the spring."[28] His humility, however, disguised the writerly ambitions that still burned within him.

37. Descent into Chaos (1985–1987)

Dickey's celebrity status went undiminished in some quarters. Early in 1985, he was asked to serve on an international panel of nine judges for the Ritz Paris Hemingway Award, which had been formally established on January 11. The brainchild of Pierre Salinger, the award was sponsored by the Sultan of Brunei and Mohamad al-Fayed, the proprietor of the Ritz and father of Dodi (Princess Diana's lover, who was killed in a car crash after leaving the Ritz a decade later).

Jack and Patrick Hemingway were directors. The award of fifty thousand dollars would be given to the author of the best novel of the year in English or in English translation. In late March, Dickey flew to Paris to join Salinger, who presided over the judges, and cast his ballot at the Ritz (Dickey voted for Marguerite Duras's *The Lover,* which won). Dickey hoped Deborah would accompany him to the awards dinner on March 29 and purchased a plane ticket for her. In the end she refunded it.

The highlight of Dickey's trip was his reunion with William Styron, who also served as a judge. As a practical joke, Styron identified himself as an Atlanta FBI agent in a phone call to Dickey's room at the Ritz. Because of his and his wife's recent confrontations with law officers, Dickey was at first spooked, but then shrugged off the prank. Styron had no idea of Dickey's distress. Having ordered a series of drinks from the Ritz bar via room service, Dickey reeked with sweat and alcohol when he hugged Styron at the door. His face glistening, his T-shirt soaked, he said: "You know, I've just been talking to Maxine." Trying to remain nonchalant, Styron responded: "That's interesting." Dickey continued: "She said to me, she said, 'I know Bill's coming to visit you. Give him a big hug from me.'"[1] Dickey appeared dead serious as he described how he had conversed with Maxine's spirit all afternoon. His eerie communing was a sign and a symptom of his problem-fraught marriage to Deborah.

Dickey's traveling had other macabre consequences during the spring of 1985. Exhausted and unable to concentrate, in one of his classes he began bleeding from the nose. With a dramatic gesture, he wiped his nose with his hand. It continued to bleed. Forgoing a Kleenex or handkerchief, he wiped his nose with the other hand. Then, like a mock Christ, he held out two bloody hands to his students and declared: "Don't say I never bled for you!"[2] (Dickey registered his propensity for nosebleeds as early as *The Entrance to the Honeycomb* and again in *Alnilam.*) His classes continued to provide a convenient stage on which to perform, and they continued to give order to his erratic life. Striding into the room with his customary hat, white jersey, Northwestern University windbreaker, faded blue jeans, sneakers, numerous watches, and gaudy necklace, he could always muster the sort of attention from students that he formerly enjoyed in the literary community.

An opportunity to speak to a larger audience came in the middle of 1985 when Ted Koppel invited Dickey to participate in the July Fourth edition of ABC's news show *Nightline.* Earlier in the year at Berry College he had tried to avoid reporters' political questions. With Koppel he was more willing to stray into the political arena, but when he discussed the political significance of Independence Day, he did so from a poetic perspective. He merely quoted a poem about July Fourth fireworks by Winfield Townley Scott and remarked on America's good fortune to have Jefferson, Madison, Adams, Washington, and Hamilton as its Founding Fathers. Thankful for the exposure that *Nightline* provided, Dickey remained cagey when offered similar platforms. On November 18, Time-Life Books asked him to contribute some war letters to a World War II anthology; he refused out of fear of exposing his war record. He also refused to cooperate with Bruce Beans, who approached him during the same month about a feature article for the *Washington Post Magazine*. Beans had asked about his flying experience. Dickey had responded with his standard rebuke: journalists should address his writing and not his life.

Some of Dickey's antipathy for political commentators and journalistic fact finders continued to spill over into his already contentious relationship with his son Chris. Dickey disapproved of Chris's dangerous forays for the *Washington Post* into Libya in 1985 and 1986 (Chris was in Tripoli when Reagan ordered the bombing raids in April 1986). Proud of Chris's new job as a *Newsweek* reporter and Mideastern bureau chief in Cairo (he took the job in May 1986), Dickey remained largely incommunicado, as if refusing to acknowledge the worth of journalistic writing and his own role in impelling his son toward far-flung posts around the world. Dickey's relations with his other son remained similarly strained. On May 13, 1985, when he and Deborah attended Kevin's graduation from Emory medical school, Dickey seemed more interested in driving around Atlanta in search of youthful haunts than spending time with his son. He neither socialized nor dined with Kevin.

Dickey undoubtedly felt guilty about the burdens he had placed on Kevin. Despite family adversities, Kevin had distinguished himself academically and extracurricularly. From 1983 to 1985 he had been a Joseph P. Whitehead Memorial Scholar; from 1982 to 1984, vice president of the student body; and in 1985, president of his class. Kevin's postgraduate career would be similarly distinguished: as an intern and resident in Emory's general surgery (1985–87), as a resident in diagnostic radiology at the University of Vermont's medical school (1988–92), and, after receiving a radiology fellowship from Yale, as an award-winning, well-published professor at Yale's prestigious medical school. As Dickey's life slipped deeper into chaos, he regarded his two sons' successes with respect as well as envy—and almost always from a distance. Like the father searching for his youthful self in *Alnilam*, Dickey on his tour of Atlanta must have wondered where and how he had gone wrong.

In mid-May, Dickey got another chance to explore his tangled roots at a University of Georgia symposium called "Roots in Georgia: A Literary Symposium," which included readings, panel discussions, films, lectures, and parties. Erskine Caldwell, whose Jeeter Lester in *Tobacco Road* had afforded Dickey a comical Doppelgänger in high school, attended the festival, as did the younger writer Wyatt Prunty, who had admired Dickey's poetry since his undergraduate days at the University of the South in Sewanee. For Prunty, after World War II Dickey and Richard Wilbur had presented the same sort of options to poets that Whitman and Dickinson had several generations earlier. (In his own poetry Prunty had set out to fuse Dickey's gothic romanticism with Wilbur's stately formalism.) Prunty had listened to Andrew Lytle's Dickey tales, so he was well prepared for his encounter in Athens. Wearing a formal suit and tie for his reading, Dickey radiated courtliness, but the next day he cavorted in bohemian motley—a lime green silk suit, purple T-shirt, lucite hawk feather medallion, broad-brimmed hat, and two digital watches. At lunch with Peter Taylor, Dickey was lucid, relaxed, and rather aloof. Afterward, when Prunty courteously remarked: "It's good to get to know you," Dickey shot back: "You don't really know me at all." Taylor always told Prunty that Dickey could be the most loyal and tender of friends. Prunty witnessed some of Dickey's virtues in theatrical form at his own poetry reading. While leaving the auditorium, Prunty's seventy-year-old mother tripped on some gravel and suffered a concussion. Dickey quickly worked his way into the middle of the crowd surrounding her, knelt down, and intoned: "Darlin, darlin, are you alright?" Mrs. Prunty said she was more embarrassed than hurt. Dickey enjoined: "Don't be embarrassed. When I do something like this, they take me to jail!" "I'd hate to go to jail," she responded. Dickey assured her: "Don't worry, I'd go with you."[3] Mrs. Prunty went to the hospital instead, and Dickey stayed at the symposium.

Dickey had another ailing woman to care for near the end of 1985. When he and Deborah flew to New York in early November, he told Norman Mailer, whom he had recently seen at a National Institute of Arts and Letters meeting, that he could not party with him because Deborah was on medication and had to go to bed. During his five-day visit he managed to socialize with other friends—Jerome Hellman, John Simon, Gordon Lish, and Herman Gollob. He also played pool with George Plimpton, losing all his games, and on November 6 attended a *Paris Review* party, where he probably spoke to some of the staff about an excerpt from *Alnilam* that the journal planned to publish. During the last days of December he traveled again, this time to an MLA conference in Chicago, where Larry Lieberman introduced his reading and where he met Lieberman's friend Gary Adelman, a University of Illinois professor who had gone blind from diabetes and who had served as one of the models for *Alnilam's* Frank Cahill. The invitation to the MLA convention may have boosted his expectations for future readings. On December 5, an agency called Capital Speakers offered to arrange readings and lectures for him. He responded four days later that he wanted to hear more about their proposal: "I am averaging $7,500 for an hour at present, but would like to go to $10,000. If you can offer any engagements in that range, I would be willing to talk about it. But the schedule is filling up fast. So, do let me hear from you soon."[4] Dickey's average fee had actually plummeted to around $1,000. Nevertheless, on January 3, 1986, he reached an agreement with Capital Speakers. Dickey's fee would be listed at $12,500, and after the agency's commission he would keep $10,000. No college or civic group, however, wanted to pay that much to hear Dickey read.

Dickey's frequent claims of destitution and demands for exorbitant fees originated in his pretense of always having been a "poorboy." They were also spurred by Deborah's medical bills and drug purchases. As her addictions worsened, her quest for a cure took her to many of Columbia's psychiatrists—so many, her husband joked, that she had exhausted the city's supply. Others observed that she changed psychiatrists to get her drug prescriptions refilled.[5] Dickey's gross income from all his writings in 1986—$27,563—was only a fraction of what he had earned during the boom years of the 1970s, and this also convinced him that he needed to earn more money. The fact that most of his current invitations came from the South was one measure of his stock in the larger marketplace. He often appeared at smaller venues. In March 1985, he read at the Writers' Workshop in Asheville, North Carolina, for $1,500. At a May 9–11 conference on Eastern Comparative Literature at NYU directed by David Hertz and Anna Balakian, he pocketed only $400 and $200 for expenses. In June, he accepted the paltry sum of $200 to read at the Association of Departments of English at USC. Only a few loyal friends like Joyce Pair, who had started the *James Dickey Newsletter* at De Kalb Community College in 1984, paid him more substantially and kept inviting him back for repeat performances.

Dickey demonstrated some of his frustration with his diminished status by demanding accolades even more vociferously than he had in the past. Supposed to accompany John Irwin and Daniel Hoffman in 1985 at an April 4–6 symposium honoring Monroe Spears's retirement from Rice, he got drunk on beer and champagne and refused to enter the auditorium unless his hosts promised him an honorary degree. His hosts told Dickey that they could not honor his request on such short notice. Dickey stood his ground. Why should Spears be honored and not himself? Realizing how intractable Dickey was, a professor promised to discuss the matter with the provost in the morning and hurried Dickey through the door. English professor Alan Grob, who had organized the symposium, delivered opening remarks in which he asked Spears and his wife Betty to stand, and praised Spears for his many academic accomplishments. He then read a prepared introduction for Dickey. Having already made a commotion at the back of the auditorium, Dickey moved toward the stage, noticed his former colleague Wilfred Dowden sitting by the aisle, and asked for a hand, and then for both hands. Pulling himself up the railing, Dickey lumbered toward the rostrum, where someone had placed a number of his briefcases. Unaware that Dickey would take an interest in his introduction to Spears, Grob shuddered as Dickey began rereading it with mock solemnity. Once again he asked Spears and his wife to stand. If he wanted to avenge the humiliations he had suffered at Rice in the early 1950s, which arose from not having a doctorate, he did so after his own fashion.

In 1986, Dickey returned with a new sense of urgency to his long-overdue novel. Since *Alnilam* revolved around the fiery crash of Joel Cahill's airplane, Dickey must have deemed the explosion of the *Challenger* space shuttle on January 28, 1986, a grim coincidence. Gayle Combest, who worked with Dan Rather at CBS, had remembered Dickey's accounts of Apollo missions in *Life* and decided to ask him for comments. Dickey quickly composed a eulogy for the shuttle astronauts that Rather read at the end of his special late-night report, "Disaster in Space":

> Put them on the list of men and women who counted, these searchers and seekers, these astronauts and teachers who died today in what became the spaceship disaster; they died in the blue and silver furnaces of their spacesuits. Think about them, who they were and the way they were: dreamers, explorers, adventurers forcing themselves past the point of danger and deep fatigue, to expand our understanding of what is up there and out there. They may never have known the nature of the trouble that killed them. For them, no more cries of "Wow, what a view!"; no more jokes with Mission Control; no more thumbs up for cheering crowds; no more phone calls from the President. They will not see their parents and their wives or husbands and their children meeting them—gone with the rush of the engines and the exploding sky—gone, but theirs were lives that mattered.[6]

Dickey later asked Combest for a transcript of Rather's special report, claiming he had not heard it on TV and that he had recently been asked by a publisher to write a small book, primarily for children, about the meaning of the *Challenger* calamity.

During the spring of 1986, Dickey was relieved to find out that a disaster of a more personal nature would not come to pass. He had worried about the "tell-all" book for which Al Braselton had received a contract. Braselton had already written in rough draft a memoir of their stormy friendship. Although the draft was fragmentary, it exposed Dickey's many lies—about his privileged Atlanta background, his athleticism, his air corps missions, his advertising career, his sexuality, and his abilities as an outdoorsman. The manuscript testified to Dickey's genius but also to his narcissism, alcoholism, sadoeroticism, interest in Nazism, and cruelty toward family and friends. On April 15, Braselton wrote a long, heartfelt, apologetic letter to Dickey. He accepted responsibility for his long silence, attributing it to his crises and suicidal depressions over the past five years. He had found a doctor who had prescribed a helpful antidepressant and looked forward to new advertising projects and a possible movie deal with Paramount based on a book by a local widow's husband. Most importantly, he wanted bygones to be bygones: "On the far side of youth we don't have time except for the absolute truth, both with ourselves and others. That's why I want to clear the slate with you all, come clean about my problems and let you know what a profound and beneficial influence you have been on me. Before I met Jim I was a *New Yorker* cartoon caricature, a typical Atlanta go-getter adman jerk. Jim introduced me to the world of literature and I have been trying to educate myself ever since. My life has been immeasurably enriched because I knew Jim Dickey and I apologize for any grief I may have caused you in any petty attempts I may have made to exploit our friendship in a seedy and contemptible book contract. I can assure you that this has long been abandoned and you need not fear that it will ever be resurrected."[7]

In late June, South Carolina honored Dickey by making him the first living writer to be inducted into its Academy of Authors, which had been founded several years before by Paul Talmadge, the vice president and academic dean of Anderson College. Dickey was pleased by the honor, even though he was inducted with two dead, little-read poets, Julia Peterkin and William Gilmore Simms: "I'm very flattered indeed. . . . I'm usually not much of a joiner, but I'll certainly join [the Academy of Authors]."[8] On June 28, 1986, at an Anderson College banquet, he spoke of his devotion to writing. "My real wish is just to put down one word after another until I die," he said. He proclaimed to his audience that the true poet was the one who would go on writing even if a megaton bomb blew up in his living room. Clad in blue jeans, green polo shirt, and green blazer and drinking a Moosehead beer, he articulated similar views at a more informal talk in the Holiday Inn. Regarding his failures and perseverance, he argued: "Every writer is a failed writer. We're all amateurs at this. We don't live long enough to be anything else."[9] He told journalists that he had been thinking of Thomas Wolfe as one of the exemplary failures because he had been editing a collection of Wolfe's stories for the last six months. (Actually he had written a foreword for Charles Scribner's 1987 edition of *The Complete Short Stories of Thomas Wolfe*.)

Dickey's reference to a bomb going off in his living room was more than an empty rhetorical gesture. It belied the marital disruptions he faced at home. Deborah's drug habit now brought her into regular contact with the Columbia underworld. Her violent threats and attacks on her husband showed no signs of abating. It was around this time that Officer Kevin Mooney, who had arrested Dickey when he crashed his Jaguar a decade earlier, drove to the house because Deborah had menacingly brandished a knife at her husband.[10] Not that Dickey was entirely the innocent victim. His provocative remarks, his insistence on having Paula Goff work in the house, his lack of sexual responsiveness, his flirtatiousness with other women all must have contributed to the explosive situation. His drinking only made things worse.

Briggs was privy to both Deborah's drug problem and the criminal element it attracted to the Dickey home. Before Dickey's induction into the Academy of Authors in Anderson, Deborah tried again to cure her substance abuse by checking into a local hospital for detoxification. Because Dickey planned to take Bronwen to the ceremony in Anderson, he asked Briggs to house-sit. To make the job look attractive, Dickey told him that he could play his guitars, read his books, and take his sailboat out on the lake. Briggs thanked him for the kind offer, but asked why he had chosen this weekend among so many others when he was out of town. Dickey responded: "We love you and know how much you love the house." "Now I wouldn't be in any physical danger out there, would I?" Briggs asked suspiciously. "No. Why should you be?"[11] Dickey answered. Sensing something was amiss, Briggs decided to contact Deborah. Startled by the news, Deborah told him to stay away from Lelia's Court because her main drug supplier planned a "hit" that weekend. "What do you mean?" Briggs asked. Deborah said the man was going to break in, steal televisions and other appliances, and then pawn them for drug money. "If he comes and there's somebody in there he's not expecting, he'll just kill him. He'll shoot first and ask questions later,"[12] Deborah informed the appalled classics professor. Briggs knew that the person Deborah described was one of the most feared drug pushers in Columbia. He had served a long jail sentence for killing and cutting the heads off three local college students who had insulted him. The Columbia police at one point showed Deborah photographs of the beheaded students to dissuade her from consorting with such a man.[13] Briggs certainly had no intention of confronting him alone in his friend's house.

Dickey considered his scheme to get Briggs into his house over the weekend a lark. He may also have wanted to test Briggs's loyalty while revealing the sort of horrors that he now had to face. Briggs puzzled over his friend's motives just as he puzzled over Deborah's need to ally herself with such criminals. Years later he speculated about her fearsome drug friend: "He was her protector and supplier. She would go into the worst sections of town [often with Bronwen], and people would respect her."[14] Her self-respect shattered, she associated with those Dickey abhorred. To proper Columbia society, her life had become a sordid exercise in self-abasement. In her eyes, she gained supportive allies among society's outcasts. Sharing needles and blood was her rite of passage into a community beyond the one that had rejected her. According to Briggs: "She honestly believed these guys loved her. These were the only people in the world who cared for her. And it was true."[15] Except for Briggs, Deborah's sister Elaine, and Dickey himself, Deborah had few close friends in Columbia's respectable community.

Dickey's attitudes toward his wife's drug habit and unsavory associates varied from sympathy and curiosity to pity and outrage. When she visited the black neighborhoods for drug purchases, he sometimes insisted on going with her. As their van or Volvo passed local residents, he would say in a loud voice so that people on the street could hear: "Look at that worthless nigger. Look at that shiftless nigger."[16] Once when her main supplier called the house and Bronwen answered the phone, Dickey shouted into the receiver: "Listen, nigger. You call this house one more time and I'll kill you with my bare hands."[17] Briggs, who was in the room at the time, had never seen Dickey act particularly aggressively. His threat was a sign of his fear as well as his anger.

The conflicts between Dickey and Deborah intensified during the 1980s with tragic predictability. As he treated her more as a prodigal daughter rather than as a wife, she retaliated with her fists or with more potent weapons. She was strong enough to inflict considerable damage. After one of their squabbles near the beginning of 1986, Deborah told Briggs that she had hit her husband on the head with her fists.[18] Afterward, Dickey began suffering headaches and blurred vision in his left eye. By June, the headaches grew more severe. Near the end of the month, when Jim Mann dined with the Dickeys at the Palmetto Club, the pain was so excruciating that he twice went to the bathroom to vomit. Mann recommended that Dickey immediately see a doctor.

The next day, on June 30, Dickey told doctors what he soon told the press: "I just began developing bad headaches. And I thought at first it was eye strain because I had just had my glasses changed and I was doing a lot of eye work."[19] Doctors at Richland Memorial Hospital checked his glasses and took a CAT scan of his brain. They found a massive blood clot under his skull called a subdural hematoma and decided to operate that night.[20] According to Dickey, the doctors said: "You must have taken a hell of a lick to the head."[21] An hour before the operation he told Patsy Dickey, who was at his bedside: "You may lose me." Well aware of her former brother-in-law's penchant for melodrama, she retorted: "I'll be damned if that's so."[22] Chastened, Dickey began discussing his upcoming residency at the Atlanta library.

As Dickey recuperated from the operation to remove blood on his brain, a long line of students traipsed through Dickey's hospital room to wish him a quick recovery. Kevin, Chris, and their two wives watched the endless procession with resignation and dismay. One plump woman lifted Dickey's spirits by addressing him as Dr. Dickey—the title he had worked so hard to legitimize with honorary degrees. During a break in the visits Chris bent over his father's bandaged head and whispered: "Did Debbie do this?" His father hesitated and then faintly said: "No. I don't know how it happened."[23] His conspiratorial tone resembled Burt Reynolds's response to Jon Voight's alibi at the end of *Deliverance*. Chris suspected that his father had concocted a similar alibi to protect Deborah, who might be subject to criminal investigation. Chris was used to such subterfuge. Usually when he inquired about the state of his father's marriage, his father glossed over all crises. Several years later, his health again precarious, Dickey told his son that in fact Deborah *had* caused the hematoma. Deborah, on the other hand, consistently denied the charge, attributing the head wound to the boom on the small sailboat that Dickey liked to sail drunkenly on Lake Katherine, a stumble down some stairs at Litchfield, or a fall against a night table as he got out of bed at Lelia's Court.

Dickey treated his surgery with characteristic drama. To Bill Starr at the *State* he repeated lines he had used to describe his hiatal hernia operation six years before: "I was consorting with the brothers, Sleep and Death, and another fellow named Lazarus. I tried to bring him out with me . . . , but he was waiting for someone else."[24] To his friend Hank Lazer he joked: "I now have ten holes in my head instead of just the seven we're all born with."[25] Tom Dickey sarcastically echoed his brother's quips; he said Jim's head now resembled a bowling ball. Regarding the cause of his hematoma, Dickey had many explanations. He told some of his friends that Deborah had hit him with a frying pan. To others he accused her of wielding a heavy lamp. To still others he said she had used a book end, a golf club, a baseball bat, a hammer. Matthew Bruccoli got a completely different story. Dickey said he had intervened in a brutal fight at a gas station in order to protect a child who was being beaten by an older man. During the struggle, the old man had brained him with a tire iron. Bruccoli doubted the story just as he doubted many of Dickey's stories. For her part, Deborah took the incident more seriously. She was afraid she *could have* caused the blood clot and during surgery grew acutely anxious that she might be responsible for her husband's untimely death.[26]

Shortly before he died, Dickey was still reluctant to put all the blame on Deborah. He admitted that he had received "repeated blows to the head" over a period of time, but added: "I don't remember any one punch. . . . She gets mad. She cannot control herself. She'll do any kind of mayhem to the other person. She wants to hurt you. She'll kill you if she can. It's violent; it's terrifying."[27] When friends heard that Dickey was being terrorized by his wife, they were at first incredulous. How could the man who so often posed as a Nietzschean strongman be so incapable of self-defense? Lunching with Ward Briggs after surgery, he delivered a jeremiad against Deborah. He cited past assaults like the arrow-piercing incident and vowed to put an end to them. He complained that Deborah woke up every day at eleven-thirty to embark on "The Great Narcotics Hunt."[28] He alleged that she had gobbled up all his postsurgery painkillers. "Every day I must make excuses for her, lie for her, and do her work, in addition to spending every afternoon looking after Bronwen. This is a situation for which my life up until now has ill-prepared me." He told Briggs that he planned to institutionalize her and rehire Paula Goff, who had been dismissed on July 8 after typing the final draft of *Alnilam*. "No purer heart beats in this world,"[29] he said of Goff.

To remove Dickey from the mayhem at home, Chris urged his father to visit him in Cairo. His father's response, although humorous, was typically condescending. He implied that Chris was inviting him to become an apprentice journalist for *Newsweek*. "I told him I didn't think I'd make a very good journalist," he announced to the *Chicago Tribune*. "I'd rather make things up."[30] His subtle rebuke of his son's writing and his refusal to visit merely aggravated Chris's sense of estrangement. Dickey, in fact, did take steps to get out of Columbia. Having agreed twice in 1986 to serve a ten-day residency in the Atlanta-Fulton Public Library system, finally in late August he was well enough to do so. He greeted James Taylor, a librarian from the Buckhead branch of the library, at the airport. Showing few signs of postoperative distress, he swaggered from the plane with two guitars, entertained Taylor with his Brando impersonation, and expressed enthusiasm for his upcoming half-dozen readings and discussions at McGuire's Bookshop, Manuel's Tavern, and local libraries. Relieved that his recent brain surgery had not affected his ability to perform, Dickey returned to his hard-drinking ways. Every day after picking him up at the Ritz-Carlton Hotel, Taylor was instructed to buy a six-pack of Schlitz malt liquor. To make the purchase seem legitimate, Dickey said he wanted beer to offer the music agent he expected any day in his hotel. A recording contract for his guitar playing, he implied, was imminent. Dickey may have concocted the lie to compensate for his dismal first reading in the Atlanta-Fulton Library's two-hundred-seat auditorium. Only about fifteen people attended. Insulted, Dickey confronted the cavernous space by talking about the way he used to fill up auditoriums at Harvard and the Library of Congress. To placate Dickey, Taylor took him to Manuel's Tavern, where he seemed more at home among the painted mirrors advertising "Miller on Draft" and "Pabst on Tap." Dressed in a sleeveless red mesh shirt, blue jacket, khaki pants, and sunglasses, he drank beer and, before reading in the hot, crowded tavern, stripped down to his fishnet underwear. Pausing in the middle of poems, he amused the crowd with the aside that had become an alcoholic tic: "Isn't that good? I'm sorry, but it is."[31] His fans gave "the Bard of Buckhead," as they liked to call him, a standing ovation.

Dickey soon took steps to move farther away from Columbia. On October 15, 1986, he asked his department chair, George Geckle, if he could take a leave of absence to teach at Southwest Texas State University during the fall of 1987. He had read and lectured at Southwest Texas at least three times over the previous ten years, and now the English Department offered him fifty thousand dollars to teach for a semester. Geckle granted permission. Prof. Jack Rosenbalm in Texas announced that Dickey would come; the English Department scheduled his classes and gathered student applications for them. In the spring of 1987, Rosenbalm heard a rumor that Dickey had changed his mind. Rosenbalm called Dickey to find out why he was reneging on his agreement, and Dickey explained that Deborah's drug problems were so severe that he could not leave home.

Embittered by Deborah's addictions and seemingly oblivious to his own, Dickey stepped up his denunciations of drugs. Drug abuse was "the worst thing that has ever happened to the human race," he told the *Chicago Tribune* early in 1987. It preyed on "the two worst sides of human nature. One is the desire for physical pleasure at any price. The other is the profit motive."[32] Dickey made similar comments at his "power lunches" with Ben Franklin and Don Greiner, and spoke frankly about his wish to divorce Deborah. He continued his threats of divorce for the next ten years. Realizing their friend's anguish, they asked him why he didn't go ahead with the divorce. Dickey always responded: "I love her."[33] His old-fashioned notion of a man's duty to stand by his wife "'til death do us part" and his profound love for Deborah, whose weaknesses resembled his own, seemed unshakeable. Some gave a different explanation for Dickey's refusal to divorce—if he went to court, his unsavory conduct would be made public, and he might have to send Bronwen to a foster home. Over the next few years Dickey periodically expressed such worries. At one point Jim Mann was called upon to vouch for the Dickeys' fitness as parents before the Department of Social Services (in the end he didn't testify). Around 1991, Dickey told Ben Greer that the authorities were regularly testing his blood and that if alcohol was detected, they would take away Bronwen.

Despite his domestic strife, Dickey proved to be a devoted father to his daughter. He tried to spend as much time with her as possible. He taught her to swim in a neighbor's pool and encouraged her dancing, even though he once said of ballet: "I cannot watch it without embarrassment."[34] Occasionally he woke her to watch the sun rise over Lake Katherine (Dickey recounted such a moment at the beginning of *Bronwen, the Traw, and the Shape-Shifter*). He playfully established the Whitewings Aviation Company with her. Deferring to her organizational skills, he made Bronwen the Whitewings president and reserved the roles of chief engineer and test pilot for himself. Having spent hours with her constructing model airplanes on the kitchen table, by January 1987 he and Bronwen had amassed a substantial fleet of planes with such names as *The Elliptic*, *The Cirrus*, *The Familiar*, and *The Dolphin*, and test flown most of them in the front yard. He told a reporter: "I love little girls. . . . I never have raised anything but boys. I know how to do [things] with them—roughhousing and carrying on, sports and all that. With little girls you have to have a delicacy I really didn't know I possessed. But you love them so much, you acquire it the best way you can."[35] Although she witnessed his vices, Bronwen brought out her father's virtues.

Dickey displayed his devotion to his daughter most publicly when he published *Bronwen, the Traw, and the Shape-Shifter* on September 10, 1986. As if recreating Bronwen as Alice in Wonderland, Dickey began with a highly idealized portrait. In mellifluous, rhymed quatrains, he removed mother, father, and daughter from the sordidness of their actual life in Columbia and transported them to an Edenic house and rose garden overlooking a beautiful river:

> Her mother'd look up from her planting
> In her light-blowing dahlia blouse
> As Bronwen came over the flagstones
> In her sunflower hat from the house.
>
> She would kneel in the brown of the garden
> With the pines and their jack-strawing straw
> And dig round the roses and tulips
> With the tingling three prongs of her traw.[36]

The menacing force of the "All-Dark," the monstrous "Shape-Shifter" associated with it, and the strange flying squirrels that beckon Bronwen to their magic kingdom are all enchanting, allegorical symbols that bear little resemblance to the truly dark forces Bronwen faced at home. Once again Dickey imposed on a semifictitious character his own sense of life as a mythical journey—a departure from home, an initiation into a source of power and "otherworld" of trials, and a return with lessons learned. Bronwen's rites of passage involve fighting the four elements with only her magic trowel, subduing them, and restoring the sun from its nightly slumber. She is the life force, the animating spirit that assures the diurnal cycle. Dickey's actual daughter also had to fight to survive and flourish in a nightmarish environment. *Bronwen, the Traw, and the Shape-Shifter* testifies to her strength without ever naming the specifics of her duress.

The evolution and fate of Dickey's new book were not as sunny as its plot. Random House and several other publishers turned it down before Deborah urged Matthew Bruccoli to publish it at Harcourt Brace Jovanovich, with whom he worked. The publisher offered a modest advance—five thousand dollars— and printed twenty thousand copies. Sales were brisk for several months—by December 30, 1986, ten thousand copies had sold—but then slackened. His publisher estimated that only about two thousand dollars in royalties would accrue by the spring of 1987. Pleased with what he called the "mystery, suspense, and strange beauty"[37] of Richard Jesse Weston's illustrations (he had sent Weston a picture of Bronwen wearing a sunflower hat in a rose garden to help him with his paintings), on October 29, 1986, Dickey contacted Weston about doing a sequel to be called *Bronwen, the Cunicorn, and the Nomain.* The sequel never materialized. Because *Bronwen's* final sales figures were disappointing, the publisher quietly remaindered it.

Perhaps sensing that *Bronwen* might not sell well, Dickey promoted the book with his usual fervor. He signed books in Columbia, Charleston, Gainesville (GA), and Atlanta. He sent a copy to the South Carolina governor's wife and spoke about the book at a dinner at the governor's mansion in early October. He informed Dan Rather that he would be in New York from October 16 to 19: "If you and the functionaires at CBS would like, I might be able to come on one of your programs for a few minutes and talk about my new children's book, *Bronwen, the Traw, and the Shape-Shifter.* . . . It would be good to be on a program for your network and talk about something cheerful and not the sad circumstances that had occurred before my other words, the ones about the shuttle explosion, went out over your waves."[38] Dickey had copies sent to Ted Koppel, Tom Brokaw, Barbara Walters, Johnny Carson, and most of the country's major newspapers and magazines from the *New York Times* to the *Reader's Digest.* Reviews of *Bronwen* were mixed. Many complimented the illustrations while complaining that the poetry was too overwrought for children. The book, however, had an afterlife; director John Gallogly adapted it for a brief stage run at Theatre West in California during March of 1998.

Throughout the early weeks of 1987, after finally submitting *Alnilam* to his publisher, Dickey worked hard correcting the proofs so that he could return them to Doubleday on February 25. He left Columbia briefly in January to collect an award from Clemson's President Lennon and in February to read at McNeese State in Louisiana, where his friend the poet Leon Stokesbury taught. In March, he made a longer trip to Washington, D.C., to celebrate the fiftieth anniversary of the poetry consultantship and the inauguration of its replacement: the poet laureateship. He had written Robert Penn Warren a year before to congratulate him on the honor of being named the first U.S. poet laureate and was crestfallen to hear that Warren could not come to Washington because of several debilitating throat operations.

On the last two days of March, thirty of America's most distinguished poets congregated in the Library of Congress—Anthony Hecht, Richard Eberhart, Daniel Hoffman, Maxine Kumin, Stanley Kunitz, William Meredith, Howard Nemerov, William Jay Smith, and William Stafford among them. The older poets invited protégés such as Jay Parini, Edward Hirsch, Ellen Bryant Voight, Michael Blumenthal, Dana Gioia, Gjertrud Schnackenberg, and Jane Kenyon. The first evening of readings began with a sumptuous, candlelit banquet in the Great Hall. Uncowed by such formalities, Dickey read "The Sheep Child." Surveying the multitude of aged bards, Stephen Spender commented: "We will probably not meet again until we enter Purgatory." "Or Parnassus," Dickey added. "That's where good poets go." Asked what he would call such an august meeting, Dickey said with a grin: "I'd call it a Parnassus of poets."[39] The *New York Times* printed his comments several days later.

Dickey's behavior in his old haunt was less than Parnassian. At one of the banquets, Daniel Hoffman's wife, who had been sitting next to Dickey, suddenly rushed to her husband to warn him that Dickey was about to collapse. Hoffman notified John Broderick, Dickey's former library colleague who had organized the reunion, and Broderick quickly found a wheelchair. Worried that he would be pushed ignominiously past all the tables, Dickey refused to get in the chair. Hoffman had to assure Dickey that they would avoid embarrassment by making a quick getaway through a back exit. This they did. Their first stop was the library's first-aid room. Soon a limousine whisked Dickey to the George Washington Emergency Room, where Ronald Reagan had been revived after he had been shot by John Hinkley. Doctors quickly determined that the anti-inflammatory drug Naprosyn, which Dickey had been taking with large quantities of alcohol, had disoriented him. They recommended rest. Dickey dutifully went to his hotel room, napped, and then returned to the reunion.

William Jay Smith and several other poets suspected that Dickey had staged his moment of dyspepsia to get attention. Moments before his collapse, talking to Smith about the possibility of contributing a blurb to Smith's *Collected Poems,* Dickey had seemed fine. The fact that Smith had invited Dana Gioia may have aggravated him as much as the Naprosyn and alcohol. Dickey—to Gioia's surprise—had read his unfavorable review of *Puella* in the relatively unknown Arkansas journal *Nebo.* Gioia recalled: "Dickey was already drunk, but his flushed face, slurred speech, and lumbering movement suggested a decline beyond the effects of alcohol. The robust outdoorsman-poet of the tabloids was nowhere visible. His solid frame now seemed at once both shrunken and bloated. His eyes were vague and watery. Worst of all, there was an alarmingly deep indentation on his upper forehead as if he had sustained some serious head injury. He said almost nothing and hardly attended to what the others said to him." Dickey mumbled Gioia's name to himself in a thick Southern accent, as if trying to place it, and suddenly waved his fists, splashing his drink: "Goddamn! You reviewers are all the same. You just don't understand. I am *not* Dick Wilbur!

I gotta grow. Goddammit, I am *not* Dick Wilbur! When you gonna understand that? You're all the same. I gotta grow. Gotta try things. All you want is the same damn thing. You're all the same. Gotta give me room! I gotta grow. Goddammit, I am not Dick Wilbur!" The other guests nearby stared in disbelief. Deciding a rational discussion about the merits and demerits of *Puella* was impossible, Gioia reached for Dickey's hand, shook it, smiled, and said: "How nice to meet you, Mr. Dickey."[40] He then walked away as Dickey returned to the bar.

Shortly before *Alnilam* appeared, Dickey's old hunting partner Terry Miller, who had just returned from a one-week bow-and-arrow bear hunt in Canada, asked if Dickey would like to join him for a similar hunt. As he had proved at the consultants' reunion, Dickey was no longer capable of such outdoor exertions and turned down the invitation. Out of concern for his flagging health, in May he again forswore alcohol. With Charles Trueheart of the *Washington Post*, who visited Columbia to do an interview about *Alnilam*, a tired, phlegmatic Dickey blamed his frailties on his recent brain surgery. He swore to Trueheart that he would no longer punish his body with booze. He sipped ginger ale while discussing his long-awaited novel, which he called "a study of the sources of power, the nature of persuasion itself, [and] the mysteriousness of causes."[41] Interested readers could find an excerpt from the novel, "The Captains," in April's *Esquire*. As he did for all of his books, Dickey sought to pave the way for what he hoped would be a critical and commercial success.

38. A Blind Ulysses (1987)

On June 5, 1987, Doubleday published *Alnilam* in a first printing of 125,000 copies that seemed calculated to match the massiveness of the book itself—682 pages. The promotion was sizeable as well; Doubleday reportedly spent a six-figure sum. Like *Deliverance*, *Alnilam* had started as a single image—in this case, of a ghostly man created by back-to-back, rotating airplane propellers—metamorphosed into a poem, and during its thirty-seven-year gestation accumulated heft and complexity. Its early poetic incarnation, "Joel Cahill Dead," had appeared in the 1958 summer issue of the *Beloit Poetry Journal*. The brief poem had limned the crucial event—Joel's crash into a wildfire and a farmer's attempt to rescue him:

> Like a man sent for, he ran,
> Waving his arms, and yelled through his sooty kerchief
>   In a curving voice around
> The boy who stood, amazed, beside the plane,
> Exhaled in fire, his shirt at the shoulders smoking,
> Who got then down upon one ragged knee.

The farmer and his wife drag the burning boy to the house, which is itself threatened by fire, and lay him on a peacock quilt where he "dies" into an imaginary otherworld. As with Marcel at the beginning of Proust's *Remembrance of Things*

Past, a lantern transports him. Dickey puns on "lie" to indicate Joel's preference for his inventions over the real world of military routines governed by his commander. Joel

> stiffened, then, remembering the Colonel,

> To whom he must affirm
> That he had less than no excuse to lie
>   Alone, in a carven bed, to hear a woman weep,
> To fade in and out of his open eyes,
> And see a forest, blazing, in the teeth
> Of a cock's-combed, motionless flame,

> Turned down, to bother no one while he slept
> In its fluted veil of glass.[1]

Drafts of "Joel Cahill Dead" equate Dickey and Joel more obviously. In one Joel is on his first solo flight in a Stearman aircraft and crashes into a bridge above a dam. Dickey's near crash as a trainee on the Camden runway also occurred on his first solo flight in a Stearman. Dickey could be reflecting on the genesis of his own mythopoetic imagination in the lines about Joel learning to "generate the song" while "strapped in the seat of terror."[2] Many of Dickey's poetic "songs" and stories originated in similar ways.

Fourteen years after publishing his poem and a year after signing a contract for his novel, Dickey wrote a brief explanation of *Alnilam*'s idiosyncratic style for the *New York Times Book Review*. "The method of presentation," he pointed out, "is unlike that of any other novel I have encountered in that it is divided into two parallel planes of observation and interpretation. The protagonist is a blind man; his actions and reactions happen on one side of the page, and the same events as they would appear to a person of normal sight are given opposite them." His goal, he explained, was to restore "the sense of bodily flight, lost to us somewhere in the air since the Wright brothers and other very early aviators, though fleetingly experiencable at any time by beginning flyers in light aircraft. Flight is the only true new *sensation* that men have achieved in modern history, and I am trying to render some of the feeling, compounded of danger, physical balance, and detachment, that flying should be able to claim, or reclaim." If the novel's form had a contemporary feel, like other modernist texts the central story derived from ancient Greek and Judeo-Christian mythology. Frank Cahill was another Oedipus or Tiresias whose blindness enhanced rather than precluded his insights. "A father-son search takes place," Dickey said about his novel, "and this bit by bit becomes a kind of discovery of the sightless father's own identity, much to his grudging horror and equally grudging recognition." The book explored "the connection between political power and personal mystery, and between religion, cultism, exhilaration, and cruelty."[3] Like many of his most successful poems, *Alnilam* followed the ritual action of a mystery cult. Joel Cahill was the "god" of the cult, a Dionysus or Christ, and the cadets his soldier-apostles. By superimposing his own identity on Joel's, Dickey examined the political and religious ramifications of his own quests for power.

In a letter written to Stewart Richardson on January 14, 1974, Dickey vowed to write a thousand pages and warned: "It is very important that the *style* be right, for we are going a very long way, and the style *must* be right to sustain such a long narrative."[4] By 1986, his manuscript was well over one thousand pages, and his new editor, Carolyn Blakemore, was displeased with both its length and style. The book's two columns, she argued, posed severe problems for readers and typesetters alike and would make for an extremely expensive book. On January 23, 1986, she sent Dickey seventeen pages of questions and suggested revisions. Dickey brushed her caveats aside: "As to this being a 'designer's and a typesetter's nightmare,' that is not my concern, nor is the 'cover price of the finished book.'" As a precedent for difficult typesetting, Dickey cited e. e. cummings's *Complete Poems 1904–1962* and recommended his editor look at it. Having pioneered the "split-line" technique in poems like "Falling," he now contended: "The split page will be much commented on, much attacked and at least somewhat praised. . . . It will immediately be much imitated."[5] To bolster his argument, he told Blakemore that all the other editors assigned to *Alnilam* over the past decade—Richardson, Greene, O'Neill, Areheart, Kate Medina—had encouraged his experimental technique. On February 27, Dickey responded with a seventeen-page letter of answers to her proposed amendments.

Angered by Blakemore's criticism, Dickey threatened to take the novel to another publisher. Although his agent had been supportive and patient during *Alnilam*'s prolonged development, Dickey vented his spleen at him as well. "Theron Raines is not doing a goddamned thing,"[6] he complained to his colleague Ben Greer. As he contemplated strategies to circumvent Doubleday, Dickey asked Greer to call his agent Julian Bach to see if he would represent him and sell *Alnilam* to another publisher. On the phone with Greer, Bach at first pretended he had never heard of Dickey, but then agreed to read the manuscript. In the end, Dickey's editor accepted his experimental format, the novel stayed with Doubleday, and Dickey stayed with Raines. Nevertheless, Blakemore pointed to a problem that many critics would mention in their reviews: Frank Cahill was too much of a cipher. Dickey told his editor that Frank was supposed to be incomprehensible: "He needs no one and he wants no one . . . ; his insistence on autonomy is absolute, and with his blindness it becomes obsessive, almost maniacal. . . . [He is] determined to be a law unto himself, a kind of king. . . . The reader should see that he is a man who never should have married, and is, as he feels himself to be, someone so entirely intent on self-sufficiency and autonomy as to be a kind of monster. It is the breaking down of this shell, which in its way is responsible for many of Cahill's better qualities—his courage, for example, and his stoicism, his self-reliance and even his creativity—that is the true subject of the story."[7] Dickey apologized for the problem without correcting it and also indicated how *Alnilam* combined two self-portraits: one of Dickey's younger self and one of his older self.

As early as 1973, Dickey had declared: "What I want to do now [after the great success of *Deliverance*] as far as novels are concerned is to write a resounding and interesting failure. Which I think this [*Alnilam*] is going to be."[8] Doubleday, obviously, was not in the business of underwriting resounding failures. Vowing never to write a sequel to *Deliverance*, Dickey had actually reconstructed the earlier novel's plot in a labyrinthine way. Just as the four men in the earlier novel undergo a departure from the relative safety of their Atlanta homes, an initiation into a realm of power and danger, and a return to their homeground, so Frank Cahill leaves Atlanta, travels to a military base where he learns of his estranged son's dangerous cabal, and returns home vaguely enlightened. Because of his blindness and stubborn rejection of help, Frank's mission—like that of the canoers—approximates an epic struggle. *Alnilam* was yet another of Dickey's many attempts to articulate the way his army air corps experience had changed his life. Again he chose to universalize his youthful rites of passage according to what Joseph Campbell and James Joyce called the "monomyth."

Dickey liked to tweak friends and interviewers about *Alnilam*'s literary precedents to suggest that it was the culmination of many lesser efforts. He told a *Washington Post* reporter in 1987 that he "wanted to do for air what Melville did for water [in *Moby-Dick*]."[9] He also wanted to do what Antoine de Saint-Exupéry did for flying in *Wind, Sand and Stars* and what John Hersey did for World War II bomber pilots in *The War Lover*. In 1977, he declared he was writing an "enormous multifaceted, multilayered type of book, a Nobel Prize type of book . . . rather like [Joyce's] *Ulysses*."[10] He also compared *Alnilam*'s bulk and discursiveness to Thomas Mann's *The Magic Mountain*, which also explored the illness and even criminality of artists. Faulkner's novel, *A Fable*, about a Christ-like World War I soldier and his disciples in the French army, served as a model, as did such little-known stories as "The Pupil" and "The Search" by the British aviator Rollo Wooley. Dickey claimed that Richard Hillary's *Falling through Space*, a novel about a British pilot's crash and recuperation during the Blitz, was another precursor, as was the British novel *Journey to the Frontier*. Dickey liked to point out that Joel Cahill shared his initials with John Cornford, the young British poet who dies in the Spanish Civil War in *Journey to the Frontier*, and that Joel shared his initials with Jesus Christ as well.

Laying out his many models as provender for critics, Dickey claimed his novel's superiority or, fearing critics might accuse him of being derivative, feigned ignorance of them. Two decades after acknowledging *Ulysses*, he asserted: "[Joyce's novel] never crossed my mind."[11] With regard to Mann's voluminous tome, *Alnilam* was "30 pages shorter than *The Magic Mountain*, but not as boring. Remember that 70-page discourse on free-masonry? Like two graduate students who never got around to taking the final exam." The discourses in *Moby Dick* about whales and whaling, Dickey stated, were just as boring. Saint-Exupéry's book was "too aesthetic, too abstract." Hersey's suffered from the opposite malady—it was too detailed, too technical. Faulkner was consistently verbose, and *A Fable*, in particular, "was a failure."[12] To his dismay, critics would find many of these faults in *Alnilam*.

Despite his avowals and disavowals, *Alnilam* bears a close kinship to *Ulysses*. More by coincidence than by intention, the first American edition of *Ulysses* was 768 pages long, exactly the same length as the first paperback edition of *Alnilam*. Joyce orchestrated a running counterpoint between Leopold Bloom's circular walk around Dublin and Odysseus's ancient journey from Ithaka to Troy and back to Ithaka; Dickey did something similar with Frank Cahill's journey from Atlanta to Peckover and back to Atlanta. Like Joyce, who mockingly deflated his Homeric antecedents (Leopold Bloom is no Greek warrior just as Molly Bloom is no steadfast Penelope), Dickey takes a similarly sardonic view of his characters. Because Bloom's son, Rudy, died in childhood, Bloom searches for a surrogate son and welcomes Stephen Dedalus, who, being disillusioned with his own father, finds a surrogate father in Bloom. In *Alnilam* Frank Cahill's son, Joel, has died (at least he is presumed dead), and this prompts his father's peripatetic search. To accentuate Frank's difficult journey, Dickey offers a mythic parallel: Christ's descent from the cross, harrowing of hell, and rise into heaven (Cahill travels on Friday, Saturday, and Sunday in imitation of Christ's death on Good Friday and resurrection on Easter Sunday).

Having lost contact with his son after his marriage dissolved, Frank knows almost nothing about Joel, just as Odysseus, who has been away from Ithaka for years, knows little about Telemachus. In *The Odyssey*, Odysseus and Telemachus ultimately reunite; in *Ulysses*, Stephen and Bloom unite as well. In *Alnilam*, father-son relations are not so propitious. Frank merely speaks to friends and acquaintances about his son at the air corps base and recovers evidence of his son's death. Although Joel reappears in a Christ-like way to the apostlelike cadets, the skeptical Frank enjoys no such revelation. In *Alnilam*'s modernist world of shifting identities, Frank plays God-the-Father hoping to conjure up his son; he also plays the legendary Greek hero Daedalus, who builds a labyrinth, escapes from it, and suffers the loss of a son to a fiery crash. During the composition of *Alnilam*, Dickey had lost a wife to alcoholism, virtually lost another to drugs, and watched in dejection as his sons renounced him. His novel expressed his dark vision of family matters through the blind Frank Cahill.

In writing *Ulysses* Joyce comically brought the divine and heroic spheres of *The Odyssey* down to earth. Joyce's book teems with human and humane correlatives to the world that the original Odysseus inhabited. The secular Bloom is charitable in his treatment of animals and fellow Dubliners; "love" is at the heart of his credo. Frank Cahill is a different animal altogether. He treats his half-savage dog Zack with respect, but is strangely indifferent when Zack is decapitated by an airplane propellor. He feels a paternal bond with his son, but he never really sheds his long-standing indifference to him. He often seems to forget why he is searching for information about his son on the base. Others—including editors and reviewers—also wondered why he was on the base. The Alnilam group believes Frank came because Joel prophesied he would come, but by the end of the novel the group is debunked as a foolishly zealous cult. Sometimes friendly, Frank usually greets people not with a gracious handshake, as Bloom or Odysseus might, but with a bone-crushing one to prove his strength. Frank exists in his own self-absorbed, masculine world somewhere between the secular humanism of Bloom and the primitive warrior-ethic of Odysseus. Although his son possesses some traditional heroic qualities, Frank has few. He is a violently egocentric antihero with an "iron monomaniacal will,"[13] as Dickey admitted to Carolyn Blakemore. He is a modern "grotesque" who personifies the cruel, indifferent, largely meaningless universe he finds around him.

Just as Joyce projected youthful and mature aspects of his personality onto Stephen and Bloom, so Dickey projects his identity as an aviation cadet onto Joel and his identity as an artist, father, and husband onto Frank. Out of a need to disguise past failures, Dickey usually resisted attempts to link his failure to become a pilot with Joel's crash at Peckover. With even his closest literary friends, such as James Wright, he invented complicated lies to protect himself from such suspicions. In the summer of 1958, responding to Wright's queries about "Joel Cahill Dead," Dickey wrote:

> It was a poem I conceived and wrote very quickly. It is actually a scene from a novel that I suppose I shall never finish, called *The Table of the Sun*. That actual Joel Cahill was a boy named Pike, who was in Primary Training with me in Hemmet, California, in 1942. He went against his flight-plan and flew over a forest fire, crashed, and was killed. A farmer (or someone who lived in the country around Hemmet) rescued him from his plane, in a kind of clearing the fire had burned out within itself, and took Pike inside his house, where Pike died before anybody could get to him. This incident stuck with me for years, not so much because I was especially close to Pike, but because fatal accidents were comparatively rare in such an early phase of flight training, and because the circumstances were extraordinary. There was an investigation, some thought it was suicide, etc.[14]

Dickey ended by complimenting Wright's appraisal of the poem: "You are dead right about one thing. I want the poem, or any poem I write, to *embody* the experience: to come as near as it can to *being* the experience."[15] Dickey's poem and exegesis, however, embodied his fantasies. In 1942, he was a student at Clemson, not an aviation cadet; his primary flight training was in 1943 at Camden; the cadet who crashed his plane on his solo flight was named Peck, not Pike; Dickey didn't go to California until 1944, and when he did, he went as a radar operator to Hammer Field, not to the apocryphal "Hemmet." Near the end of his life Dickey maintained that he had flown over fire, albeit without disastrous consequences: "I did exactly that . . . pretty much for the same reason that Joel might have done it, to see if I could do it. It's extremely terrifying. That's where I got the idea."[16] Once again Dickey pretended to be a daredevil pilot.

Dickey's quest for his former self resembles that of his favorite poet, Theodore Roethke, in "The Lost Son," the title poem of one of his best-known books. Like Roethke, Dickey explores those events and images that connect him umbilically to an Edenic childhood. Through his alter ego Frank, he returns obsessively to early marble games, model airplanes, roller skates, bicycles, and track stars in pre–World War II Atlanta. He keeps recalling the "flash" of one sprinter in particular—probably the notoriously fast Atlanta runner Bobby Pair—who exemplifies the competitive zeal and athletic grace he reveres. Frank reminisces about his grammar school tours of the Atlanta waterworks, Rickenbacker crashing a plane near Atlanta, and his brother Perrin starring as a welterweight boxer before he died of Graves's disease at the age of twenty-five. These and many other such events have analogues in Dickey's youth. His E. Rivers class as well as his family on Sunday afternoons took similar sight-seeing tours; in high school he was well aware of Rickenbacker, the illustrious World War I combat pilot who founded Eastern Airlines and who crashed a commercial plane near Atlanta; Dickey also had a brother who was a star athlete and a brother who died young.

Dickey underscores his close connection with Joel by making his middle name Wesley; Dickey spent his childhood on West Wesley Road. Joel attends college for one year before entering the Army Air Corps; Dickey attended college for one semester before entering the Army Air Corps. Joel is twenty years old; Dickey was twenty when he undertook Primary Flight Training at Camden. Joel evinces a keen interest in philosophy and astronomy; Dickey had a passion for both subjects. Joel suffers planter warts on his feet; during his military years Dickey contracted warts and other foot ailments that dogged him until he died. Joel relishes decadent Victorian poets like James Thomson and charismatic romantics like Shelley. He and his followers routinely quote lines from Shelley's "Prometheus Unbound," and to make himself more mysterious Joel appropriates Thomson's cryptic initials, B. V., which refer to Shelley's middle name "Bysshe," and a partial anagram, "Vanolin," which comes from "Novalis," a pseudonym for the German poet Hardenberg. At Joel's age Dickey pored over Thomson's and Shelley's poems in Louis Untermeyer's anthology of American and British poetry. One of Joel's favorite poems is Thomson's "The City of Dreadful Night" (after Joel's death the Alnilam cadets chant Thomson's lines about striding through a black, starless desert: "No hope could have no fear"); the gloomy poem was also one of Dickey's favorites. If Joel had lived, he would have become an artist; Dickey survived the war and fulfilled his promise. Joel's Alnilam cult with its coded language was as inspiring as it was destructive; so was the top-secret science of radar and its correlative—which had a similar mystique for Dickey—poetry.

Joel was partly based on Dickey's son, Chris, although Dickey confessed to the *Washington Post* that the correspondence was only approximate: "Chris is not that fanatical or that charismatic." Dickey was writing not so much about Chris as about his image of Chris and his distance from the real Chris. "He doesn't communicate much," Dickey complained about his son. "I read his stuff [in *Newsweek*]."[17] The sense of frustrated mutual devotion between father and son resonates throughout the plot, just as it did a decade later in Chris's *Summer of Deliverance*. Once asked to define the reason he wrote *Alnilam*, Dickey said: "The main thing I want to do . . . is to write the ultimate novel of fathers and sons; the mysteries, the frustrations, the revelations, and, in the end, the eventual renunciation and reconciliation."[18] Dickey's relationship with Chris followed the same zigzagging course. On one level *Alnilam* is a long search for atonement through a confession of fatherly sins. "The whole point of *Alnilam*," Dickey said, "is that the father, Frank, is so self-centered that he has no interest in the son. He abandoned him when he was a child. He hasn't given him a thought. . . . And when he's named as next-of-kin by the son, instead of the mother who raised the boy, he's struck by this."[19] Dickey was similarly struck by Chris's fidelity and desire for reconciliation.

Some of the specifics of Frank's blindness toward his son, which is as emotional as it is visual, derived from his frightening mask-making session in North Carolina with Bill Dunlap. Others came from Marian Leith, the librarian at

Raleigh, North Carolina's Library for the Blind, whom he wrote on May 23, 1972, to learn "in more detail about blindness, about becoming blind, about how one learns to live with it, and so on."[20] Sometimes Dickey liked to say he was thinking of Milton's blindness when describing Frank's, at other times Paula Goff's father's blindness. He was also dramatizing his own fears of going blind from diabetes. In a 1981 letter urging Shaye Areheart to consider Gary Adelman's manuscript *Smiler* at Doubleday, he revealed another source: "I draw heavily on Gary's diabetic history and his blindness for details in *Alnilam*; in fact, it was he who suggested the business about the gold lines going across the occluding vision of Cahill, which device is now, by the way, actually being used by doctors . . . in their diagnosis of some kinds of diabetic blindness!"[21] As with many diabetics, Adelman's retinal capillaries had bled, forming scar tissue that ultimately blinded him in 1964. A year before *Alnilam* appeared, Dickey asked Adelman if he could dedicate the book to him. Adelman was at first uncomfortable with the idea; he hardly knew Dickey and didn't remember discussing his diabetes or blindness with him. Out of courtesy rather than vanity, he agreed to Dickey's proposal and was surprised when Dickey reneged on it without giving any explanation.

Blind to the world and, like Dickey, further disconnected because of an ineffective sense of smell, Frank tries to piece together an image of his son from the stories others tell him. The handful of his son's possessions he collects—a cracked pair of goggles, a burned zipper from his flight suit, a wire from his plane, a few of his teeth, a blood stain—afford little knowledge. With so few souvenirs, he depends largely on his imagination. If *Alnilam* is a long apology for its author's egotistical self-reliance, it is also a testimony to the way he and everyone else reconstruct the world. Many of the characters in *Alnilam* support Dickey's thesis that the world is essentially a lie we compose from sense experience. Frank is an ersatz poet. Early in the novel he explains to Boyd McLendon, the bus station manager who rents him a room: "What goes out with colors, and all that, comes back in your ears and your hands, mainly. You start to put things together in another way and, just a little at a time, but more and more, you come to the notion that you can have the world be anything you want it to be, because it's all in your head anyway." A hunter who keeps a deer and a boar hanging in a meat cellar, McLendon has just tricked Frank into believing that he has a dead "doar," a hybrid deer and boar. Rather than scoff at the notion, Frank enjoys what his friend has made up: "I can make a whole world for that thing, and put him in there with the others I've got. . . . The doar has just been made up, and made; he's true, now."[22] Frank, like the creator of "The Sheep Child," pushes the making process of *poesis* to sublime and ridiculous extremes.

By necessity, Frank must invent the people around him. Meeting McClintock McCaig, Joel's flight instructor, he "invented him, putting together an image, adding to it, changing it." When McClintock discusses Stearman airplanes, Frank thinks: "Airplanes . . . ; let me make one up, so that I can follow this." The authoritarian Colonel Hoccleve, who may have played a role in Joel's fiery plane crash, condemns Frank near the novel's end for his troublemaking and prevaricating: "You bluffed your way in here because your son was killed; a son you had given not the slightest damn about for twenty years. Your whole attitude, and I daresay your whole existence, is bluff. You've lied, you've given people to assume and believe what was in no way the truth, and on the basis of these things you've caused a good deal of trouble where none need have been. I'm looking for an explanation for all this, but I have a pretty good idea I won't get one, because you don't know yourself."[23] If this sort of denunciation was aimed at him, Dickey usually retorted that he was not one self but many selves, and that the poet consciously lied while others did so unawares.

War and other traumatic events are catalysts for heroic lies in *Alnilam*. Dismissive of the young, starry-eyed Alnilam cadets, Frank nevertheless understands their desire to re-create the world. While his apocalypses are confined to his head, they clamor for apocalypses on a grander scale. Like Blake, Wordsworth, or Shelley at their most romantic, the cadets hope for a great war like the American or French Revolution that will annihilate the old, oppressive regimes and initiate a new sociopolitical heaven on earth. One particularly idealistic cadet, Malcolm Shears, states near the novel's end: "One of the reasons for war is to make heroes; there's nothing else like it. . . . With the momentum we get from the war we can do anything we like, go any direction with it we want to. We can make this fucking world over, and then walk off and leave it. There won't be anything else; only nihilism and music."[24] Dickey revealed to his doctor friend John Stone that he was quoting one of his favorite German writers, Gottfried Benn: "Though also a Nazi, he said he really only wanted—'Adam and Eden and an Earth / Of nihilism and music.' Not a bad paradise, eh?"[25] It was a paradise for the sort of decadent aesthetes Dickey esteemed as a youth. Although the name Malcolm Shears echoes the name of Dickey's teacher Monroe Spears, Dickey admitted: "I got the name Shears from the movie *The Bridge on the River Kwai*. That was the name of the character William Holden played."[26] Shears in the movie lied about his war experiences and was forced to return to the war zone on a dangerous mission he would have preferred to avoid. For Dickey he was another alter ego, another doomed romantic who believed he could transform the world as he wished. As in *Deliverance*, in *Alnilam* Dickey betrays an acute awareness of his own penchant for making up lies.

In both novels, Dickey also acknowledges his sexual ambiguity. Frank's odyssey originates in a kind of oasis in Atlanta where the lotus eaters and oxen of the sun are beauty queens and muscle-bound weight lifters. An aura of homoeroticism hovers over Frank's Willow Plunge swimming pool. Memories of the Nashville pool where Dickey swam as a Vanderbilt student, and where he falsely claimed he lifeguarded, mingle with memories of beauty contests and coin-tossing events at Atlanta's Venetian swimming pool. Dickey loved such contests—male and female—and while living at Westminster Circle even entered one.[27] Like Ed rhapsodically describing Lewis's godly body in *Deliverance*, at Willow Plunge Frank lavishes attention on his Mexican-American companion's "eighteen-inch biceps stretching the rolled-up sleeves of a T-shirt he had bought a half-size too small, so that the definition of his almost brassiere-worthy pecs would be inescapable."[28] Frank sponsors contests for both beautiful women and beautiful men, and speculates that the women, who don't really attract him, come out on

Sundays to "try their god-damned best to get their hands on all that slick mus-cle." The lifeguard contradicts him: "Well, I can tell you for a fact . . . I never met a girl who liked those guys. Queers, yes. Girls, no."[29] Frank is ambivalent about the sleek, well-tanned muscle men. He mocks Karl Kesmodl, a particu-larly muscular bodybuilder who parades his stuff at Willow Plunge (Dickey mod-eled him on Harry Johnson, a future Mr. America he claimed to have known as a young man). Kesmodl is a "clumsy goon" who can't swim. But Frank also sym-pathizes with him—he can't swim either.

Frank Cahill's vacillations apply to women as well. Like Julian Glass in *The Entrance to the Honeycomb* and the voyeur in "The Fiend," he takes adolescent pleasure in peeping at disrobed women through a special one-way window he has installed. Yet he also finds them "so disillusioning that he thought of remov-ing the glass and returning to fantasy, which was better."[30] When the mood strikes, he entraps women in the dressing room by locking all the doors just as the young Dickey trapped dates by locking car doors. Frank is especially horri-fied by one woman, who could have stepped out of a Flannery O'Connor story; she takes off her clothes and unstraps her right leg at the knee. Frank expresses Dickey's ambivalence in other ways as well—most memorably during his one moment of sexual intimacy in the book—when he beats Hannah on the bottom with his son's slide rule. Like Julian Glass, Frank finds little besides sadism sexu-ally fulfilling.

A propensity for sadomasochism unites Frank and Joel. Like Dickey as a teenager, Joel reads pulp fiction like *Terror Tales* and *Horror Stories* about women getting mauled by muscular, masked men. Carolyn Blakemore suggested cutting this section, but Dickey objected: "Certainly, it is in line with Joel's sexual sadism. . . . [Frank] Cahill has an idea what it is about, though; there can't be any mistake about that."[31] Frank understands Joel's sexual inclinations because he feels them toward both women and men. His approach to men often resem-bles his brutish dog's—he is wary and ready to break anybody's hand with his vicelike grip—yet he spends almost all his time with men. Are father and son bi-sexual as well as sadistic? McLendon points out to Frank that his son periodically stripped for the gay Dr. Iannone, who prepared a creosote bath for Joel's psoria-sis: "If you ask me, I think he [Iannone] was lookin' for somebody to fuck him. . . . Your boy must'a turned him down, maybe."[32] And maybe not. Dickey leaves Joel's sexuality as ambiguous as his father's.

Dickey asserted that two of the women in *Alnilam*—Hannah Pelham and Lucille Wick, who works in the Supply Department and is more crassly whorish than Hannah, were entirely fictitious: "I just made them up. I think Hannah is a great character, though. I got very interested in her."[33] In fact, Hannah—the name of his alleged relative, the niece of Zachary Taylor—was based in part on his mistress Robin Jarecki. Like Hannah, Robin suffered nosebleeds and felt compelled to reside in a cold apartment (she was with Dickey at Wisconsin's "frozen Berkeley"). Hannah also resembled Paula Goff, whose maiden name was Culclasure. In an earlier draft of the novel—a draft that Goff typed—Hannah is introduced as "Hannah Culclashure, the wild mountain flower of the cotton mills."[34] Dickey sometimes referred to Paula as Hannah or his "cotton mill girl." Dickey added the "h" to his character's name for the sake of easier pronunciation, but after typing the manuscript Goff insisted that he expunge her maiden name. He complied, changing it to Pelham.

Much else about Goff's relationship with Dickey remained intact in *Alnilam*. Goff once made up a story about a girl's reformatory in which a sadistic matron beat the bare bottoms of her delinquent "girls." Dickey listened to the tale with boyish glee and implored her to tell the story again and again. Not content to simply listen to sadomasochistic tales, Dickey reenacted them with Goff. Dickey played the flagellant, and Goff, who felt that spanking fulfilled Dickey's fantasies of patriarchal domination, the delinquent girl. Submissive to Dickey's fantasies and practices, Goff derived no pleasure from them.[35] To his death Dickey prized the sadoerotic scene in which Frank beats Hannah and she bleeds through the nose. "That's a great scene," he said. "That's one of the best scenes in there. The sex scene when she starts bleeding on him."[36] Flagellation was one way Dickey stimulated his jaded sexual appetite.

Dickey once told Goff that in *Alnilam* he was offering an etiology of his demonic character. The cruelties that Frank inflicted—both bodily and verbally—arose from the authoritarian demon in Dickey that he wanted to purge or at least explain. The verbal abuse Dickey visited upon Goff from time to time amounted to a test of loyalty to her master—a painful rite of passage undertaken by an initiate. Goff knew that other women, including Deborah, were subjected to similar rites. "He always said he would lead her [Deborah] through the fire,"[37] Goff recalled. Goff also knew that Dickey's sadomasochism began long before their affair. She had read "the spanking novel"[38]—*The Entrance to the Honeycomb*—that he kept in the silver cabinet in his house. She speculated that his will to dominate had something to do with his Germanic forebears and the rigorous way his *grossmutter*—grandmother Burkhardt—had demanded excellence and submission.[39]

As in Dickey's fervid pursuits of fame, ecstasy, wealth, and sex, in *Alnilam* sublime flights precipitate tragic falls. Dickey's personae catalog his losses. Frank loses his wife, son, and dog. The cadets lose their idol, Joel. McLendon's speech about losing his family resonates with Dickey's dirges in the late 1970s about losing his father, mother, and wife: "Everybody's dead. . . . My wife, Shirley Dell, died about six years ago. She cut her hand openin' a can in the kitchen—right back yonder—and it wouldn't heal up. She had a bad time; they finally had to cut her whole arm off, and she never did come out of it. She bled to death in the hospital."[40] Maxine had bled to death, too, and Dickey's Germanic grandmother had been an amputee. McLendon says that his baby boy, whom he was going to name Tal after his brother Talbot, had died. Dickey also had intended to name his baby Talbot.

In the scene where the poetically inspired cadets destroy their planes and cohorts at the Peckover graduation ceremony, Dickey traces his own early metamorphosis from a military aviator to a freedom-loving, charismatic poet. The cadets may seem ridiculous with all their palaver about the immortality of Alnilam, but Dickey suggests that once he was like them. He, too, made his poet-pilot ideal into a kind of god. Through one of the more reflective and humane characters, the gay Dr. Iannone, Dickey puts his youthful enthusiasms into a historical perspective. The doctor addresses the question of how such diverse figures as Hitler, Mussolini, Julius Caesar, Napoleon, and Jesus exert their power over millions: "They give people the notion that they can make life different in some way, and that the people who help them, who join in with them, will be different, will be made different, will exist in a new way, a way they couldn't have thought of by themselves. If you can sell people that notion they will do what you say; not anything on earth will stop them. There's not a person in the world who really likes himself, the way he is; anything at all would be better for him than the way he is. Most men wouldn't say that in so many words, but deep down they feel it; they know it's the truth."[41] In his self-excoriating moods, Dickey said the same thing about himself. He created lies and personae willy-nilly because they provided alternatives to who he was and how he lived. Dickey told Paula Goff that he intended his novel to be a journey toward self-revelation. By examining the creative and destructive aspects of his youthful compulsions and their adult consequences, he hoped to achieve redemption.

In June, as part of his book tour, Dickey signed copies of *Alnilam* in Charleston's Chapter Two Book Store. R. Z. Sheppard met him there and took him to Sullivan's Island for an interview. They gazed over the porch at marsh grass and boats that seemed to float through the grass. Sheppard did his best to hide his disappointment with *Alnilam* in the review he wrote for *Time*. He applauded Dickey's "talent for mating small details, his audacious lyric power and technical risks," and his way of portraying "the artist as an inspired liar." On Sullivan's Island, by contrast, Dickey belittled his Hemingwayesque lies and false public persona. He had hung up his hunting weapons, he told Sheppard, and would no longer sacrifice his art for his image: "The work is the im-*paw*-dent thing. . . . That's all that's going to be left. Otherwise it's just a faded photograph album with a picture of yourself with a rhinoceros head or a marlin hanging on a scaffold."[42] He quietly sipped a glass of milk. Sheppard later admitted that it had been hard to criticize the book because the magazine had included a profile of Dickey. He now felt that the experimental style needed to be less self-conscious and more spontaneous. Most reviewers agreed.

Jay Parini's response was characteristic. In a *USA Today* review, he called *Alnilam* "a massive, puzzling, occasionally brilliant, often hackneyed novel of World War II." The plot was "second-rate Robert Ludlum"—"windy, often incoherently organized, and—sometimes—downright bad."[43] The father and son protagonists were sketchily drawn. In E. M. Forster's terms, they were "flat" rather than "round." Forgetting what he once said of Hemingway—"He cannot create an interesting woman that you believe in. They're either whores, or bitches, or they're sentimental pastoral love objects"[44]—Dickey created women in *Alnilam* who were for the most part sluttish, ignorant love objects. Dickey tried to shrug off the negative reviews and solicit positive ones. He wrote Harold Bloom in 1987 to thank him for editing a book of essays on his work: "Have you read my big new novel, *Alnilam*, yet? I'd be interested to know what you think, should you get around to it."[45] The praise he'd hoped for from critics of Bloom's stature was intermittent or nonexistent. Since he had put so many years into his highly ambitious, experimental novel, Dickey was crestfallen.

At times Dickey grew belligerently defensive of his novel. One day in the USC English Department mailroom, he snarled at Ben Greer: "I want you to stop runnin' down my book in every god-damned bar in town." Greer asked him what he meant. "You know what I'm talkin about. . . . I thought you were my friend. Of all the people in the world, I never thought it would be you." With secretaries and colleagues listening, Greer suggested they discuss the matter in Dickey's office. "No, no," Dickey countered. "We are going to do it right here, right now. Besides you might use some of that Kung Fu shit on me." Greer had been studying martial arts, but rather than flip Dickey on the floor or kick him in the chin, he explained that he had merely told some graduate students at a bar that *Alnilam*, despite its patches of good writing, would never sell like *Deliverance*. Somewhat mollified, Dickey walked away in silence, then turned to have the last word: "Listen Ben, the future of my book will not be decided here or now."[46] The next day Dickey pretended to have forgotten the altercation. In a few years he asked Greer to give him advice on martial arts and the Oriental mind for his novel *To the White Sea*. As with *The Sentence* he again promised to pay Greer fifteen thousand dollars for his help. Perhaps recalling his colleague's insurbordinate remarks about *Alnilam*, he again reneged.

Doubleday was as disappointed as Dickey over the lackluster and hostile responses to *Alnilam*. Dickey's friend, the editor Herman Gollob, felt the rejection more keenly than most; forecasting a bestseller, he had called for the large initial printing. The book, in fact, sold reasonably well, but came nowhere close to selling out; by October 31, 1987, 52,453 copies had been returned to the publisher from bookstores. In Canada, 2,859 copies had been sold. Dickey struggled to fight off despair by returning to alcohol. The civil, milk-sipping image Dickey imparted to Sheppard in June was in total eclipse by October 15–17 when he attended a Florida Council of English Teachers Conference, "Magnolias and Manuscripts, Our Southern Literary Heritage." Pam Shelden, the vice president of the council, had invited him to Pensacola and promised to promote *Alnilam* by organizing a book-signing party and press conference. Dickey demanded ten thousand dollars, but agreed to come for five thousand dollars partly because he wanted to visit friends at Gulf Shores, a town near Pensacola.

Some of Shelden's colleagues treated Dickey's impending arrival on October 16, 1987, more as a security risk than a gala event. Mary Ann Cox, a supervisor of language arts for a local school district, had heard numerous rumors of Dickey's escapades in Gainesville and advised Shelden to devise a battle plan to keep Dickey in check. Shelden drew up a schedule of two-hour "watches," assigning a different "keeper" to each watch. Cox would take the lunch shift the day of Dickey's reading, Shelden the next shift, and Sandy Young, a vice president of the council, the next. Shelden also hoped that the council's hospitable gestures—ceramic magnolia gifts, historical tours of Pensacola, a Mardi Gras party, lavish meals—would appease Dickey. Dickey got off the plane drunk and surly. Used to being watched by "keepers" and to outfoxing them, on Friday afternoon, during Sandy Young's "watch," Dickey said he was going to his hotel for a nap. Instead, he went to a store to buy alcohol, contacted the daughter of his friends in Gulf Shores, and got roaring drunk with her and two of her pals. Discovering that her charge had escaped, Young reported the situation to Shelden, who soon caught up with Dickey and his three teenage compatriots in the Hilton lobby. It was nearly time for Dickey's reading, so Shelden ushered him down a long hall toward the banquet room. Dickey gulped his drink and staggered forward. "Where are we going?" he wanted to know. Shelden informed him that all the teachers were waiting in the hall. Dickey balked. Realizing that he might be too drunk to read, the diminutive Shelden grabbed his arm and asked him whether he intended to carry out his duties. He glared back: "Young lady, you've just made the biggest mistake of your life. You have insulted me." Her mind more on logistics than possible insults, Shelden said she would go to the banquet hall, make an excuse for Dickey, and postpone the reading. He retorted: "I will expose you from the podium. I can say whatever I like." Shelden tried to control her anger as she guided Dickey to the banquet area.

Dickey refused to eat anything at dinner except a little bread pudding, which he prodded with his fork. Soon two teenage girls wearing tank tops and an ill-clad boy with his fly open approached Dickey. One of them shouted: "Let's blow this place. Let's have some real fun." Referring to some of the English teachers, who were understandably surprised by Dickey's motley entourage, one of the teenagers said: "What are these bitches looking at?" Mortified and furious, Shelden threatened to get the security guard to remove the intruders. After they left under their own power, Mary Ann Cox suggested that she take Dickey outside for a sobering walk. Dickey consented, so Cox walked him up and down the hall as he did "sloppy drunk" impersonations of Marlon Brando. On returning to the hall, Dickey sat down and blurted at Shelden, who was preparing to deliver a flattering introduction she had written days before: "You're too pushy. What you really want me to do is fuck you." Shelden simply patted him on the hand. During her introduction at the podium, she glared at him as if delivering a challenge more than a heartfelt testimonial. Her comments over, he stumbled to the dais, fell off, righted himself, put his suitcase on the podium, and watched it fall to the floor. The evening had declined into a slapstick Marx Brothers routine.

Dickey tried to regain his composure, but only managed to slur in a drunken drawl: "Well, what do you'all want me to do?" As he read from *Buckdancer's Choice* and *Deliverance*, the officers at the head table refused to look at their highly touted and highly paid guest speaker. The more applause he received from the teachers, the clearer Dickey's voice became. Soon the officers grudgingly looked his way. Since Dickey had been scheduled to read for only twenty minutes, after forty-five the MC gave him a cue. Dickey snapped: "Go sit down. I'm not through. I'll let you know when I'm through." Earlier, when an overweight woman shifted at her table and spoke, he was similarly caustic. "Sit your fat ass down and shut up," he commanded. Shelden realized that everything Dickey did was intended to shock, including a poem about two fighters beating and bloodying their faces, which he explained was a dream about beating up his wife.

After the reading Dickey made his way to the book-signing and cocktail party in an upper suite of the Hilton. Shelden instructed the bartender to give Dickey nothing stronger than 7UP, which angered him. Meanwhile, Dickey's teenage friends had returned. This time Shelden called the security guard and ordered them out the door. Dickey dutifully autographed copies of *Alnilam* (Doubleday had sent several cartons of the novel), signing one for Shelden with something along the lines of "Don't try so hard." On the way to the airport, Dickey further disappointed her by giving his ceramic magnolia to one of the teachers. For her part, Shelden didn't want any souvenirs of the evening either and soon got rid of her copy of *Alnilam*.[47] Along with letters of sympathy from disgruntled colleagues, Shelden received an apologetic letter from Dickey at the end of October 1987 in which he confessed: "The occasion is one I had difficulty with, since my only brother is dying of cancer, and it is hard to perform in public under such conditions. I am grateful for your forbearance, and for the sympathy and understanding of your colleagues. . . . Human beings have the only remedy for others of their kind, which is sympathy. Many thanks for your gracious hospitality."[48] Shelden was not mollified and guessed that he was using his brother's illness as an excuse. On October 23, while lecturing on the "Varieties of Creativity" to a crowd of several hundred at UNC-Charlotte, Dickey showed that he could behave civilly despite his brother's dire condition. He also showed the sort of antagonism that lingered in his relations with his sibling. He dedicated his lecture to Tom with a testimonial as well as a snub. "He knows I write," Dickey said, "but he's never heard me read."[49] He made Tom sound like a bumpkin. Tom, of course, had heard him read.

On November 20, Dickey also spoke of Tom's cancer in a heartfelt letter to his son Chris. Apologizing for not writing more letters to Chris, he described how the cancer had metastasized all over Tom's body in spite of the various drugs and therapies: "It is a terrible thing, and the utter hopelessness is the worst of it. That, and the way the memory fills up with images of him when he was happy." Along with the loss of his brother, Dickey worried about losing his son in one of the world's combat zones. He complained about Chris's lack of communication: "Do know how proud I am of you, and what great joy I take in your human qualities, and what you have done with them, and are doing. There is a scene in *Alnilam*—I am writing this part of the film now—where the image of an extraordinary young man, the most extraordinary I could imagine, comes up on the galvanized tin wall of a tool shed. There is no doubt as to the identity of that face."[50] His father's intended compliment notwithstanding, Chris thought the alleged equation between himself and Joel was, at best, far-fetched.

On December 8, 1987, Tom Dickey lost his struggle with colon cancer and died in Atlanta's Piedmont Hospital. The elegy Dickey wrote for Tom, in which Ted Bundy played the role of a savior at death, testified to a frightening resemblance between the two brothers' imaginations. Once again Dickey paid homage to his brother in a backhanded way. Dickey told Dave Smith, who published the poem in the *Southern Review*, that because his brother was a Civil War buff he had brought Shelby Foote's three-volume history of the war to the hospital. Tom, however, was more interested in *The Bundy Chronicles*. Just as Ted Bundy's horrendous life had delivered Dickey from his mortal fears in the Seattle hospital, so Bundy had worked his magic on Tom in Atlanta. Dickey explained to Smith: "I want to envision the death-bed situation in which the dying father, in his delirium, sees his own daughter as the murderer's victim and himself as the murderer."[51] The reversal of predator and prey, especially as it applied to filial relationships, had haunted Dickey for decades.

Dickey began his poem by aligning Tom with the doomed Southern cause and, in particular, with two Confederate commanders, Stonewall Jackson and

686 / JAMES DICKEY

James Longstreet. Could Tom forget his pain and fear by losing himself in the war-haunted South? According to Dickey, the old generals no longer had the power to command his attention:

> No more munitions,
> No more projectiles, Tom. The South cannot win; but here,
> Here in the paperback
> Is something else. In your daughter's hand for some reason
> Known only to women is the step-by-step
> Chronicle of Theodore Bundy. I repeat: Longstreet has failed
> To help your life,
> Your death. The stranger is beside you. It is Bundy moving
> As Longstreet moved, but now through the hauntedness
> Of Florida State.

It had been Ann Rule's *The Stranger Beside Me* that had captivated Dickey's imagination at the Mason clinic. Now he recommended the Bundy story to Tom: "Take it where you find it / On your deathbed, Tom: where it comes to you / From anywhere. Longstreet has dissolved / Into the hauntedness. Follow now: follow / The other murderer." Dickey's concept of a deliverer had come a long way since Lewis Medlock.

Replacing an eminent Civil War general with a mass murderer of women was calculated to disturb Dickey's family and readers in general, as was casting Tom's daughter as the victim of a Bundy-like father: "Listen: there is one more girl / Walking innocently home: home / To the sorority house. She is your daughter reading / To you: she is the final / Unprotected girl."[52] Whether Tom goes along with Dickey's grim fable is left ambiguous. All that is certain is that, having experienced a catharsis wrought by Bundy on a similar hospital bed, Dickey counsels his brother to follow his example. Tom's daughter, Dorian, in fact did read to her father about Bundy. Her father was strangely captivated, and Dorian became fixated on Bundy after her father died.[53]

Buffeted by the sad news of his brother's death and, not long afterward, by the news of his father-in-law's death, Dickey nevertheless forged ahead with a number of new books. He gathered together poems by fifty of his former students for an anthology, *From the Green Horseshoe*, to celebrate his twenty years of teaching at USC. He continued to work on the poems he would collect in his last book, *The Eagle's Mile*. His main focus, however, was on the film treatment of *Alnilam*. On August 4, he had received over ten thousand dollars from Rockingham Productions for signing a contract to write a screenplay. He was as exultant as ever at the possibility of a blockbuster movie, but would soon experience the disillusionment to which he was all-too accustomed.

XIV.

TO THE WHITE SEA

39. Fortunes Rising, Fortunes Falling (1987–1992)

Amid his gloom at the end of 1987, Dickey took special pride in a telegram from Arthur Schlesinger announcing that Dickey had been elected to the American Academy of Arts and Letters. Organized in 1904 to honor fifty elected members, it was one of the most prestigious organizations for writers, artists, composers, architects, and dramatists in the country. Hankering after the Nobel Prize, Dickey found his chair assignment auspicious. It was number 15, the same chair occupied by Nobel Prize–winner John Steinbeck. The academy also elected his friend William Styron and a writer whose theories of myth had influenced his work more than any other—Joseph Campbell. In citing Dickey for the honor, academy member Howard Nemerov said: "James Dickey has done distinguished work in poetry for some 30 years. Original—sometimes to the point of eccentricity—his knowledge and regard for the tradition, as exemplified by his attentive and incisive criticism, of his own work and that of our contemporaries is, nevertheless, unquestionable."[1] The academy's chancellor, John Updike, formally inducted Dickey in May of the following year.

Now that *Alnilam* was finished, Dickey made desultory progress with his screenplay. He produced his initial story line in August 1987, and sent his director, John Guillermin, a rough draft of Act One on November 16. He mailed another forty pages on January 20, 1988. In January he wrote Guillermin: "My enthusiasm for the project grows, the more I write on it. If we do this film as you and I conceive it, people who watch it will understand that they have never really seen a movie before."[2] Dickey was pleased to be working with Guillermin. He admired his World War I film *The Blue Max*, which dramatized an irreverent, swashbuckling German pilot's conflicts with his fellow aviators. (Guillermin also achieved fame by directing *King Kong*, *Tarzan's Greatest Adventure*, and *The Towering Inferno*.) Aware that Guillermin would revise his script, he nevertheless urged the director to give his utmost scrutiny to what he had written. During the subsequent months Dickey and his director deliberated and clashed over alterations, just as he had done with John Boorman in the early 1970s. Dickey objected most stridently to Guillermin's demand to play up the homosexuality of the Alnilam group, but ultimately complied with it.

Unable to find financial backers for *Alnilam*, by mid-1989 Guillermin abandoned the film. On July 17, 1989, Dickey sent a dolorous letter with the final screenplay to Theron Raines: "It has been a long and debilitating struggle to get the material into this shape, and the disappointment over Guillermin is rather difficult to deal with, though I'll survive as best I can. As you know, I am not one of these people who don't mind their films not being made, so long as they are paid for the screenplay and its various drafts. Despite the money I would not have gone into this if I had thought Guillermin was not going to be able to make the movie; but it's too late to worry about that now."[3] He hoped Raines would find someone else in Hollywood to direct the film. Adding to his discontent was a royalty statement from Doubleday suggesting that *Alnilam* had not made back its advance.

Dickey's anguish over these setbacks was made more acute by his concern for Bronwen. Proud of her achievements as a dancer and student—she received almost all As on her second-grade report card from Brennen Elementary School— he was ashamed of her squalid home life. Deborah's troubles were taking their toll on her education. On April 11, 1988, Brennen's principal wrote her parents a stern letter about her numerous unexcused absences and notified them that state law required that the school take legal action against those parents whose children accumulated so many absences. He wanted to know why Bronwen was missing class. On April 17, Dickey wrote a contrite letter explaining that Bronwen's mother had "suffered some physical setbacks"[4] and had been hospitalized. Bronwen was needed at home. The matter passed.

In the spring and summer of 1988, Dickey had reason to hope for a better future. Deborah had shown improvement and a willingness to take over office work in late April. Bronwen's ballet skills would be highlighted at a recital in Columbia's Keenan High School theater on May 22. On June 3, Chris's son, Tucky, graduated from his school in Newport, Rhode Island, an event his grandfather proudly attended. Later in the year, after Chris had accepted the post of *Newsweek* bureau chief in Paris, Deborah made plans for a trip to France. The rifts in the family seemed to be healing. Dickey was also proud of his protégé Paula Goff for getting a teaching job at Midlands Technical College and for winning the first fellowship from the South Carolina Academy of Authors. Her epic sequence of dream poems, *Help from the Other Side,* which Dickey had helped to inspire two decades before, now filled three filing cabinets. Lucrative offers arrived for Dickey to read at Georgia College, USC's Carolina Journalism Institute, and the Governor's School in Greenville, South Carolina.

On May 15, Dickey flew to Pitzer College in California, where he had given a commencement address in 1965 at the end of the college's first year of operation. In his second commencement address, he returned to familiar themes. What he had affirmed about the sanctity of the individual he now felt even more strongly. Once again he waved the Agrarian banner, inveighing against computers and all other modern machines that he believed threatened the imagination. He cited Saul Bellow's long story "Seize the Day" and its indictment of Americans dying of alcohol, drugs, or boredom. Undoubtedly thinking of his and Deborah's self-destructive habits, his advice was simple: "The solution for me is still wonder: amazement, mystery." Science, he argued, should lead to an appreciation of God, or at least to the Sioux Indians' concept of God—the Great Mystery.

Dickey's surge of optimism also extended to his new novel about a U.S. tail gunner shot down over Japan during World War II. In early March, with the hope of refamiliarizing himself with the country he had known as a soldier in 1945, he flew to Tokyo for a ten-day visit. He had conceived the novel the previous year, and on his trip he tried to imagine the sort of fiery destruction his protagonist would have confronted in a firebombed Tokyo. On August 6, 1987, he had sent a plot outline of the novel he was calling *Thalatta* to Theron Raines. The title, he informed his agent, was another form of *thalassa*, the Greek word for sea, and it came from an account by the Greek general Xenophon of his war with the Persians. After fighting through Persian territory to the Black Sea, the Greeks triumphantly cried: "Thalatta!" As if retracing the Greek military journey as well as Cahill's trip to snowy Peckover, Dickey proposed to tell the story of a downed aviator's bloody trek from the inferno of Tokyo to the snowy island of Hokkaido in the northern Japanese archipelago. "In the case of my man," he explained to Raines, "the first sight of the sea 'with ice in it' of northern Hokkaido signifies the protagonist's coming 'home' to the cold and desolation that are his true *patria*."[5] In 1987, amid the summer heat of Columbia, Dickey set forth on what eventually became *To the White Sea*.

Due to the financial disappointment of *Alnilam*, Doubleday had no interest in another Dickey novel. Raines forwarded the proposal to Houghton Mifflin, where editor Marc Jaffe and his colleagues had a much different reaction. Trying to acquire major writers, especially those they had once published, they immediately saw *Thalatta* as a way to bring Dickey back to the company. Unfazed by *Alnilam*'s misfortunes, Houghton agreed to pay Dickey a $500,000 advance. Astonished by the windfall, Dickey increased it tenfold and sometimes even more in boasts to friends. Dickey hoped the company would also publish his poetry, but in August 1988, after consulting Peter Davison, he decided to return to Wesleyan. Substantial sums from the sale of *Thalatta*'s foreign rights added to Dickey's coffers (Germany, for instance, paid $78,000). The novel also found enthusiastic supporters in Hollywood. Richard Roth heard about the novel on a visit to Theron Raines after the abstract had gone to Houghton. He soon agreed to produce a movie of it for Universal Studios.

In October, Dickey could take pride in another of his long-standing projects coming to fruition. Oxmoor House printed fifty-five thousand copies of his third coffee-table book, *Wayfarer, A Voice from the Southern Mountains*. The book had undergone a decade of reincarnations. Dickey's original title was *The Wilderness of Heaven*, his original collaborator Hubert Shuptrine, his original publisher Doubleday, and his original publication date around 1982. In late November 1980, Shuptrine had flown to Columbia in his brother's private plane to discuss the book with Dickey, and then returned to his rented cabin in the North Carolina mountains, where he had already painted about half the one hundred landscapes and portraits. Dickey openly admitted to Morrison that the coffee-table book was not a priority: "I would not be telling you the entire truth if I said that it [*Wilderness*] meant as much to me as the poetry I'm writing, or even the novels. . . . But it's something I want to do. It's not a frustrating or a time-consuming sort of book like the novel. But I want to write something where there is not all that big a stake in the game—something like *Jericho*—so I can relax and have a good time." Despite his nonchalance, Dickey was as committed to preserving his vision of Appalachian culture in print as Shuptrine was in paint. "I have traveled a lot," Dickey said, "and I don't know a place on earth that is more distinctive, more strange, more haunting than Appalachia. The people there live in a strange sort of world that couples the most absolute, brute fact with fantasy, ghosts, and all sorts of imaginative constructions."[6] Shuptrine agreed. He also wanted to portray Appalachia as both heavenly and wild, beautiful and violent.

The standoff between poet and painter that had resulted in *Jericho* soon threatened to scuttle *The Wilderness of Heaven*. Dickey's condescension grated on Shuptrine. Because Dickey had refused to visit his North Carolina cabin, Shuptrine had been forced to bring his artwork to Lelia's Court. Examining Shuptrine's paintings, each of which he planned to sell for twenty-five thousand dollars, Dickey gave a few approving grunts and pulled out a photograph album by Eliot Porter. He pointed to a scene of fog settling around some mountains. "All you have shown me here are portraits," he scoffed. "A book titled *The Wilderness of Heaven* ought to have some wilderness in it."[7] Dickey next told Shuptrine what scenes to paint. Shuptrine dutifully took notes and tried to ignore his collaborator's heavy-handed manner.

Troubles dogged the project from the start. Dickey had *Puella*, *Alnilam*, and screenplays to write. When Shuptrine finally received the *Wilderness* text, he deemed it "totally inappropriate"[8] because it had nothing to do with his paintings. In 1986, his patience with Dickey exhausted, Shuptrine annulled his Doubleday contract by paying back his thirty-thousand-dollar advance. Because Doubleday decided that Dickey's contract should be cancelled and that he should repay his advance, a demand he vehemently resisted, Dickey returned to Oxmoor with a new collaborator—William A. Bake, an acclaimed photographer with a master's from Emory and a doctorate from the University of Georgia. He had published his pictures in three other Oxmoor art books: *The American South, Four Seasons of the Land*; *The American South, Towns and Cities*; and *The Blue Ridge*. His work had also appeared in *Southern Living, Natural History, Life, Audubon*, and *Reader's Digest*. The photographs he took for *Wayfarer* expressed the Appalachian landscape and its people with the same lyricism and gritty naturalism that informed Dickey's prose. Having agreed to follow the modus operandi governing *The Wilderness of Heaven*, Bake took his photographs with little thought for Dickey's text. Luckily, the writing and images meshed. The ramshackle farms and gnarled, weather-beaten mountain folk who inhabited them, the guitar and banjo pickers among dogs and horses, the eerie gray-blue mountains and snow-ringed lakes, the colorful flora and fauna all contributed to Dickey's narrative of tough people living among rugged beauty.

To a certain extent Dickey in *Wayfarer* made amends for his less-than-flattering portrayal of Appalachian culture in *Deliverance*. If James Agee's prose style in *Let Us Now Praise Famous Men* influenced the novel, Agee's devotional attitude toward hardscrabble folk informed the coffee-table book. Rather than depict the Appalachian mountaineers as rapacious sodomites, he aimed for a more balanced view. They are violent, but they are also clever, self-reliant masters of innumerable crafts and skills. He paid them the highest compliment by imitating their dialect. His narrative voice recalled some of the rustic voices Robert Frost recorded so deftly in poems about similar people (Frost's characters, after all, lived at the other end of the Appalachians). Dickey's wayfarer, walking at night without any accoutrements, resembled many of Frost's personae who go on similar nocturnal jaunts in New England. In *Wayfarer* Dickey returned to his father's home ground in North Georgia—he dedicated the book "To the remainder of my father's family—Fannin County, Mineral Bluff, Georgia."

Dickey begins his tale with an encounter between an Appalachian native and a stranger who is conspicuous mainly because of his absence from the conversation. Like Ed and Bobby in *Deliverance*, he is lost in his new, heavenly, vaguely menacing environment. Dickey re-creates the rural dialect just as convincingly as he did when depicting the mountain folk in *Deliverance*, but now he dwells more realistically on the actual encounters he and his two canoeing partners—Lewis King and Al Braselton—had with them. The natives are helpful rather than heinous. The Gentry-like narrator in *Wayfarer* begins: "I seen you in the last light, and I come on down. There's a fork up north of here, up above this-here road, and after I seen you walkin' down here, goin' the wrong way, on toward where don't nobody live, I thought I'd just make the turn on the switchback and meet up with you, to see what you was doin' up here by yourself, fixin' to be walkin' along in the dark. That ain't what you want to be doin'." In *Deliverance* the hillbillies say more or less the same thing to Ed and Bobby, but with different intentions.

The initial scene recalls Frost's poem "The Road Not Taken," where two roads diverging in a yellow wood force the traveler to choose between them. For Frost the roads connote different careers; for Dickey they refer more to splits in his personality and background. Examining his city and country roots, as he did in *Deliverance*, Dickey projects his cultured self onto the wayfarer and his more primitive self onto the mountain man. Once again he tries to track his confusing mix of civility and savagery to its origin. While he stresses the mountaineer's kindness, he also points to his dubious past. Is there a killer beneath the mountain man's welcoming face? Dickey lets the man address this supposition as if it were an accusation: "Don't be afraid of nothing'; I ain't never killed but one man in my life, and that was a damned accident, which anybody'd tell you it was except my third cousin Boyce Landrum, and he don't know nothin' about anything; he just don't like me." The native instructs the wayfarer to follow him through the dark woods, where he undoubtedly wonders whether he will descend into an inferno or climb purgatorial mountains toward a wilderness heaven.

At home, the mountain man discussing cockfighting resembles Dickey's father. Talk of blood sports serves as a prelude to a feast of quail, chicken, pumpkin, squash, cornbread, grapes, churned butter, and wild gooseberry pie that the man's wife, Alma, prepares for the wayfarer. As the story progresses, the wayfarer falls ill. His hosts nurse him back to health with home remedies like pine needle tea, moonshine blended with honey, and a shirt soaked in turpentine and lard. A deft quilt maker, Alma spreads one of her creations on the wayfarer to cure him. Like a medicine man or magician, her husband performs the sort of string tricks Dickey loved to do himself. He waxes lyrical about dulcimers, guitars, fiddles, and drums, and eventually introduces the wayfarer to a number of local musicians. Their repertoire of songs about millers beating girls to death and about other disasters undercuts any sentimenal preconceptions of them as "noble savages."

At times Dickey's narrator in *Wayfarer* seems to converse with characters in *Deliverance*. When Lewis discusses the legal repercussions of shooting Bobby's rapist, he says: "I can almost guarantee you that he's got relatives all over the place. Everybody up here is kin to everybody else, in one way or another." Dickey's *Wayfarer* narrator says: "It ain't so; ain't nothin' to that. But we've all got close connections; the blood goes way on out from every one of us." He could be addressing one of the *Deliverance* hillbillies when he says of his whiskey-running, murdering third cousin, Boyce Landrum: "He had to run it if he wanted to do anything with it besides drink it, because he was too dumb to make it." The *Wayfarer* hillbillies, like those in *Deliverance*, have a feudal sense of loyalty and justice. "You know, I might kill Boyce Landrum myself," the narrator says, "and if he don't stop tellin' them lies about me, I might have to. But ain't nobody else gonna say nothin' about him, or do nothin' to him. Him and me, we got the same blood runnin' through us." The advice he gives the wayfarer at the end sounds like the sort that Lewis gives his fellow canoers in *Deliverance*: "Remember everything you seen up here, and everything you heard, because we're losin' it; we're gonna lose it all." Although there is no dam and no inundation in *Wayfarer*, there is a similar prophesy of environmental doom.

The wayfarer espouses many of Dickey's conservationist sentiments. No longer a killer of animals on hunts, he says: "Some of the time I hunt, but now I'm gettin' on in life, I'd rather just walk around, and go sit by a creek." He also believes rivers—especially the Chattooga that "comes through them rocks like a freight train"—are among nature's sublimest creations. His approach to nature has become aesthetic rather than predatory. As if following Frost's naturalist in "Directive," who guides an anonymous traveler toward a forest spring and instructs him to "Drink and be whole beyond confusion," Dickey's guide directs his fellow traveler toward a pool among ferns for a drink and gives him a magical "fairy stone." Delivered from sickness, he can return home. The water and stone will serve as mementos of his host and his rugged domain. Having remained silent throughout the story, at the end the wayfarer is moved to recite a passage from John Crowe Ransom's poem "Antique Harvesters," which bears witness to human transience within the larger cycle of nature.

Although *Jericho* traced a more encompassing journey through the South, it also ended with a quotation from Ransom's "Antique Harvesters" and also displayed an Agrarian devotion to the cultural and agricultural fecundities of the South. In *Jericho* Dickey also echoed Frost. He ended his "Epilogue" with a directive to his fellow traveler: "Come down, reader, and be whole here."[9] Building on his previous books, Dickey in *Wayfarer* also tried to rectify past flaws. Unlike *Jericho* and *God's Images*, *Wayfarer* rarely strives for highfalutin poetic diction; the dialect of its main speaker exudes local color and crackling, down-home vitality. Reviews were generally positive, and from late September to mid-December 1988, Dickey and Bake promoted the book on an extensive tour through the South, with stops at Columbia, Atlanta, Greensboro, Charleston, Nashville, Birmingham, Charlotte, Miami, Jacksonville, Memphis, Lexington, and Louisville. Partly due to a slump in the economy, the book did not meet the publisher's expectations. It sold about one-fourth as many copies as

Jericho. Dickey's royalties for the financial year ending on May 31, 1989, were depressingly low—$2,825. Although he had received a large advance, he was convinced he was being cheated. He sent an embittered letter to Theron Raines about Bake's royalties, which he claimed were five times more than his. Soon Dickey's royalty complaints became irrelevant. On February 7, 1991, Oxmoor remaindered the book.

At sixty-five, Dickey no longer had the stamina of his earlier barnstorming years. Besides his teaching and writing, he had other appointments to fulfill. On October 29, 1988, along with John Jakes, William Price Fox, Ben Greer, Gen. William Westmoreland, boxer Joe Frazier, and Gov. Carroll Campbell, he helped open Columbia's State Museum. Worn out by the *Wayfarer* tour, he often grew morose. On November 15, he told Gordon Van Ness that he had dreamed of dying of a heart attack by the front door of his house. Gripped by such fears, his thoughts naturally turned toward his estate, which he was beginning to envision as a kind of Fortune 500 company. He now proposed that Van Ness join Deborah, Chris, Kevin, and Matthew Bruccoli on his board of executors. Having in 1987 submitted an insightful, well-researched Ph.D. thesis at USC on Dickey's early poetry, Van Ness was now one of his favored sons. Dickey taught him how to use a sextant, encouraged his poetry writing, and usually leveled with him about his life. Their trusting friendship was such that on November 22, 1988, Van Ness proposed writing Dickey's biography. For years Dickey had dogmatically refused to authorize any biography, but in this case he gave his consent. Before launching forth, however, Van Ness suggested that he publish Dickey's journals from the 1950s. Resisting the idea at first, on January 5, 1990, he gave his blessing to the project that eventually became *Striking In*.

When Van Ness questioned Dickey about his lies, such as his assertion that his brother had run bootleg whiskey out of the North Georgia hills, Dickey indicated that he was merely exercising his imagination. At the end of 1988, Dickey attributed his compulsive inventing to another source. In a letter to Gore Vidal, he complimented Vidal's new book, *At Home*, for the attention it brought to Frederic Prokosch. Prokosch, Dickey avowed, had had a great influence on his own writing and the way he interacted with the world. He told Vidal: "I make no real distinction between fact, fiction, history, reminiscence and fantasy, for the imagination inhabits them all. That is the place that Frederic Prokosch occupies: a kind of all-place. You yourself do the same, from Tarzan on up. As Whitman says, it all tastes good to me."[10] Despite the weariness brought on by travel, domestic turmoil, and numerous duties, Dickey's imagination still flickered with its mischievously creative flame.

As the 1980s ended, the claim that Dickey had become a regional poet with only a local following had some merit. Almost all the offers to make public appearances came from the Southeast. He was asked to attend the opening of Columbia's Ira and Nancy Kroger Center for the Arts on January 14, 1989, to receive an honorary degree from Atlanta's Oglethorpe College in May, and to teach some classes and read at Wilmington's Cape Fear Academy in October. His audience shrinking, Dickey continued to lash out in unexpected ways. When the young photographer Curt Richter met him at the first Honors

696 / JAMES DICKEY

Convocation of the Fellowship of Southern Writers in Chattanooga on April 6, Dickey was too busy to pose for pictures that were to hang in the Lupton Library at the University of Tennessee. He arranged for Richter to take photographs of him in New York around May 17. An hour late and drunk, Dickey met Richter on the scheduled day at the Mayflower Hotel. On their way to Dickey's room, Dickey punched Richter in the chest and asked belligerently: "How ya doin?" Dumbfounded, Richter responded that he would be doing much better if he hadn't been hit. "Are you homosexual?" Dickey next asked. Richter said he wasn't and asked Dickey why he wanted to know. Dickey explained he could only assume Richter was homosexual because Richter was escorting him to his room. Once in the room Dickey collapsed, crushing the bellows of Richter's camera. He next lumbered into the bathroom, urinated in the bathtub, and on his way back—Richter having fixed his camera—crushed the bellows again. Richter canceled the session.[11]

From August 9 to 13, a scholar interested in the North-South issues affecting Dickey's reputation visited him in South Carolina. Ernest Suarez, who had written a Ph.D. dissertation on Dickey at the University of Wisconsin, was convinced that Dickey's literary fortunes had suffered from what amounted to another War Between the States. The interview, which he conducted at Dickey's Litchfield condo and later published in the journal *Contemporary Literature*, focused on the way liberal critics from the North during and after the Vietnam War had undermined Dickey's status as a major Southern writer. On April 18, 1989, Dickey had agreed to Suarez's request for an interview, but warned: "The Vietnam War is over, and the only words that have survived in regard to it are those by the combatants, not those of the poetical lemmings who sought to substitute their supposedly good intentions for the ability to write. I don't give a fiddler's fuck . . . as to what any or all critics say or have said about me."[12] To the end of his life Dickey vehemently denied that his political views had contributed to the vagaries of his reputation. Wary and at times downright contemptuous of Suarez's interpretation of his literary rise and fall, at Litchfield he was consistently cordial. He talked for hours with Suarez, took him out to dinner, strolled on the beach with him, consumed a good deal of Wild Turkey, and generally had a good time.

Dickey's star continued to shine at USC, but on June 23 he wrote the poet C. K. Williams that he planned to resign; he was sixty-six. His star shone elsewhere, too, as his new contracts at Houghton Mifflin and Wesleyan attested. Other publishers beckoned with lucrative offers. During the summer of 1989, Birch Lane Press in New Jersey offered him an advance, which he turned down, of seventy-five thousand dollars for a book of reminiscences about his Atlanta childhood. He was still in good standing at the American Academy and National Institute, whose meetings he regularly attended. Requests for articles still came from Northern editors; on July 7, he signed a contract for fifteen hundred dollars to write about South Carolina's "Low Country" for Condé Nast editor Michael Shnayerson. Northern reporters continued to regard him as a spokesman for Southern literature. When Robert Penn Warren died on September 15, a reporter from the *Boston Globe* asked Dickey for comments, and he obliged, calling Warren a great writer whose roots were in the frontier and folk, but who coupled primitive instinct with the most sophisticated intellect. Dickey would have said the same of himself.

Perhaps the most telling sign of Dickey's vestigial influence in the North came from the university where Warren had taught—Yale. In July, the director of Yale University Press, John Ryden, asked Dickey to judge the annual Yale Younger Poets contest. The job would entail reading some forty or fifty manuscripts culled from about seven hundred submissions, selecting a winner each year by June 1, and writing an introduction to the book. For his services he would earn two thousand dollars. On July 26, he wrote Ryden: "The series is the best of all gateways to the slopes of Parnassus for new American poets, and has been so since its beginning. In other words, as a poet who struggled hard to get onto those slopes years ago, I realize the importance of what I am being asked to do, and can say in response that I will do the best I can, given my abilities and orientation."[13] On August 17, 1989, Ryden thanked him for accepting and in late September formally announced that Dickey would be the new judge of the prestigious series. Although Dickey had not been a Yale Younger Poet himself—many of his peers such as John Ashbery, Adrienne Rich, W. S. Merwin, and John Hollander had won the contest—by becoming the series' judge he joined an eminent list that included Auden, James Merrill, and Stanley Kunitz. His friend at Yale, John Hollander, praised the appointment: "James Dickey is a poet of the first importance, a literary essayist and novelist of strength and renown, and a knowledgeable and sophisticated critic of poetry. . . . He will bring to the series the high standards and acute personal taste which have distinguished the judging of his best predecessors."[14]

His own fortunes improving for the moment, Dickey made an effort to support Deborah in her ongoing search for vocations and avocations. He encouraged her to write fiction and to begin a screenplay based on Judith Thurman's biography, *Isak Dinesen: The Life of a Storyteller*. When she proposed getting a volunteer job at the Workshop Theatre in Columbia, he assured her that she had all the necessary talent to be an actor. Doubts and inertia, however, undermined her initial enthusiasm. Dickey showed his characteristic impatience with Deborah's vacillations at a lunch with Ward Briggs. After Deborah expressed uncertainty about her acting abilities, Dickey snapped: "If you can't do that, forget it."[15] Dickey's veering between affection and denunciation could only add to Deborah's confusion.

To friends like Don Greiner, Dickey continued to complain about Deborah's "narcotics" habit and the frightening people with whom she associated. He continued to threaten divorce. With his marital woes never far off, he struggled to make headway with *To the White Sea*, as he was now calling his novel. On October 18, he wrote optimistically to his editor, Marc Jaffe: "Despite most of the chaos down here—the hurricane, and my wife's being in the hospital [earlier in the year Deborah had been to the Hazelden Center in Minnesota for drug and alcohol addiction], though she is better—I am pushing hard on the book, and can see the story through to the end, I think. You mentioned March [1990] as a possible touch-down point, and I will try to keep to that. I do want to ride the unresearched impulse, because if I get trammelled in facts it might clip the wings, and I had rather fly to the end, and then come back and readjust, if need be. These are all peculiar habits, but they are those that work for me, and I cast myself on their particular flood, for better or worse."[16] Dickey planned to discuss his "peculiar habits" more fully with Jaffe when he came to New York on November 14 for Robert Penn Warren's memorial service.

Frugality also compelled Dickey to "ride the unresearched impulse." He didn't want to do the research himself, and he didn't want to pay a researcher to do it for him. A year after making his pitch for fantasy, he told Jaffe that he was extremely pleased that a student researcher, Tim Williams, had volunteered to dig up helpful information about air force equipment and wartime Japan. The industrious Williams traveled to the Smithsonian Institute in Washington, D.C., and brought back descriptions of B-29 bombers, which Dickey used at the beginning of the novel. Dickey bragged to Jaffe that most of Williams's research corroborated his guesses. To Dickey's chagrin, following *To the White Sea*'s publication, a scholar of the aerial campaigns against Japan, Kevin Herbert, pointed out that many of his guesses about the workings and flights of B-29s were erroneous.

In late 1989, depressed in part by her failure to find any sort of meaningful work and by the continuing difficulties in her marriage, Deborah went into another tailspin. Dickey canceled his plans to fly to New York for Warren's memorial service and canceled his appointment with his editor. On February 27, 1990, he complained to Jaffe:

A few months ago my wife's narcotic habit increased by geometrical proportions, so that there was not a day—or, especially, a night—when I knew where she was, what people she was among, or whether I and the child [Bronwen] would ever see her again. She abandoned her family all but completely, and entered the dope culture at the very lowest point, where there are only pushers, pimps, whores, hit-men and other murderers, and in consigning all such to the eleventh circle of the Inferno, where everything is frozen solid with vice. There seemed to be nothing I could do, except to try to protect the child and keep her life going, move forward with the teaching as best I could, and write whenever I had a minute amongst all the pity and terror. But at last the situation became so unmanageable—and violent—that there was no choice but to have Deborah committed in order to save her life, for she was, most of the time, all but comatose with cocaine and heroin, usually in bizarre combinations. The people on the law end of things were all for prosecuting her, but as it turned out she was sent to a drug rehabilitation center for three weeks, at the end of which time she was remanded to my custody on a kind of work-release arrangement, whereby, if she falters again, and goes back to night-town, she will not be returned to treatment, but will go to prison. It is probably the case that such a threat constituted the only workable means of turning Deborah's head toward the light: toward *any* kind of light at all. She has been home a couple of weeks now, closely monitored by the courts, and seems to be making some progress toward rehabilitation, though, having been married to her for 13 years or so, I would not bet on what she will do, once the legal restrictions are removed. However, they obtain for the next six months, and for that time she will have to keep herself in line. I'm hoping that it all works out, for the little girl loves her very much, and wants her whole, as do I. We'll have to see, I guess, what the future gives us.[17]

Like Dickey's many vows of temperance, Deborah's rehabilitation would only be temporary.

Dickey took concrete steps to establish a better home for Bronwen and for himself around the time of Deborah's most recent debacle. He paid a visit to Carolee Guilds, who had divorced her husband, Jack (in 1975 Jack had left USC to become dean of arts and sciences at the University of Arkansas), and returned to her Lake Katherine house. Dickey said: "I really want to get out of my life as it is. I really want to get a divorce. . . . Would you marry me, if I go ahead with the divorce, [and] help me to raise Bronwen?" He told her that he and Bronwen were in "mortal danger" because of the murderers and criminals Deborah attracted to the house. According to Dickey's plan for his new life with Guilds, she could keep her house while living with him across the lake. Anytime she wanted to see her children, she could simply return to her house. But he wanted her to take care of Bronwen and him at Lelia's Court. "You think this over and I'll be back in a few days to get your answer," he told her, moving toward the door. "Well, that's fine Jim," she replied. "I look forward to your coming back, but I could give you my answer right now." Dickey was eager to hear it. Guilds chose her words carefully as she explained that she could raise Bronwen just as she had raised her own three children, but she couldn't agree to dividing herself between two houses: "No. I just don't see where that's any good basis for a marriage." Dickey never came back to propose marriage again.

Dickey's proposal was more serious than his proposals to other women, but it was uttered out of desperation. On one of the few occasions that he returned to Guilds's house, he merely stood in silence in her hallway and stared at her. Guilds assumed that the horrors in his own house had rendered him speechless. On another occasion he invited her to Litchfield. Wary of his romantic intentions, she refused. While she loved him for his literary intelligence and charm, she also knew that she could never tolerate his boorish conduct. His debonair visits when he acted like Rhett Butler, leaning jauntily on a pillar outside her door with his hat cocked at an angle, or when he burst into her living room to reenact scenes from *Deliverance*, were one thing. His drinking—she refused to serve him any alcohol in her house—and his reputation as a philandering minstrel were another. Resuming their close friendship in the mid-1990s, he once said: "You really don't know me. There's another side of me you've never seen." She shrugged off his confession with a few jokes. But he was insistent: "I would be too afraid to marry you because I'm afraid I might turn to be that other person. . . . I can't stand the thought of being cruel or rude to you."[18] Dickey wisely refrained from any more marriage proposals to the lovely, well-mannered Guilds.

Dickey forged ahead with his novel, writing late at night and early in the morning. "I can promise you one thing," he said near the end of a letter to his editor, "*To the White Sea* will be published in 1991 . . . no matter what the conditions are." He resorted to his customary flattery to deflect his editor's impatience: "Let me say one thing more. You are the best editor I have ever had, by far, among a great many. I had rather cut off my own head with a dull razor than fail you in this way or any other; you can be convinced that I will not. You are my rare unswerving company, and I will deliver what we both want, come what may."[19] Despite his rhetoric and promises, the book was not published until 1993.

As a nightmarish pall descended on the Dickey household, Deborah often counted on friends to take care of Bronwen. It was not unusual in the early 1990s for her to ask Ellen Greiner to pick up Bronwen at afternoon dance school and feed her supper. A series of phone calls would ensue. Deborah would promise to fetch Bronwen at seven o'clock and call at ten to say she could not come. Could Ellen drive her home or to her sister Elaine's house? Bronwen, who turned nine in 1990, was mortified. Deborah would call several days later to thank the Greiners for their help. According to Don: "One felt trapped between one's love of Jim and concern for Bronwen and [one's awareness of] . . . being taken advantage of by Deborah."[20] Dickey felt trapped by conflicting loyalties as well. In his matter-of-fact, nonjudgmental descriptions of Deborah's activities at his "power lunches," his love for his wife and curiosity about her lifestyle seemed to outweigh his anger. He spoke with equanimity about her stealing and pawning, claiming that he had developed an affinity for the low-life districts where he had to buy back the pilfered cameras, bows and arrows, typewriters, guitars, and sextants.[21] As in his letter to Jaffe, he treated his trips to "night-town" (a phrase from Joyce's *Ulysses*) as something literary—a combination of Dantesque descent and pulp-fiction fantasy.

Dickey demonstrated his odd blend of hilarity, sangfroid, and sympathy toward his wife after one of her "night-town" visits. Informed that the police had stopped Deborah in her Volvo and found cocaine in the car, he notified Elizabeth Adams, who in turn called Jim Mann to request his help. Mann drove to Dickey's house only to find his mentor treating the dire situation as a farce. Dickey shouted into the phone to Deborah's AA partner, who had called and expressed shock at the news: "What do you mean you can't believe it? It was inevitable!" Matthew Bruccoli, who had also been summoned to the house, drove Dickey and Mann to the police station in his black Cadillac. On the way, Dickey seemed blithely unconcerned about his wife's incarceration. He talked about space travel and the possibility of sentient beings on other planets. "The universe needs the human race because we are the only ones to interpret it," he told Mann. At the police station, like a character in a grade-B crime movie, he announced in an ominous tone: "And three men detached from the Cadillac onto the curb on the hot summer night." As Bruccoli waited in the car, Dickey approached the desk sergeant and declared with similar fanfare: "Dickey's my name." Failing to evoke a laugh, he said he wanted to see his wife. The sergeant directed him to the "lock-up," where he spoke to Deborah about her calamitous night. Emerging from the building, he watched a tow-truck drag Deborah's expensive Volvo station wagon up the street. He was "just as blasé as when he went in,"[22] Mann recalled. He borrowed thirty dollars from Bruccoli (he later paid him back), redeemed the car from the tower, chatted with him in a friendly way, and asked Mann to drive the car to Lelia's Court.

During the early 1990s, Dickey regularly involved his friends in similar family crises. He called Ward Briggs about five times to ask for "refuge" when he felt especially menaced by either Deborah or her drug friends. Like a hero hounded by murderous villains in a crime thriller, he assured Briggs that the police had promised him—as well as Briggs, who always had to drive to Dickey's house—"safe passage."[23] Once on Bronwen's birthday, Dickey called the Greiners and asked them for "refuge"; Deborah, he said, was on a drug "rampage" and he needed a safe place to have a party. The Greiners invited him to their house. Dickey loaded Bronwen's presents into the car, and set off around dinnertime. At the table that night, Dickey turned to Bronwen and said with envy and sadness: "This is a real family."[24] In the TV room Dickey helped his daughter with her homework, and later they slept in the Greiners' daughter's room. The next morning Dickey repacked the car with Bronwen's presents and drove her to school.

One of the reasons Dickey worked so hard on his novel during the spring and summer of 1990 was his conviction that he needed money. (Deborah spoke to the local newspaper about her husband's discontent with his USC salary—$80,267—citing that he received no allowances for travel, housing, utilities, or other living expenses.) Deborah's legal and medical bills, never mind the money she spent on the drugs that necessitated them, were exorbitant. In a May 15 letter to Jaffe, who was trying to be as understanding as possible about the slow progress of To the White Sea, Dickey again placed the blame for his financial and literary troubles on Deborah. He began by thanking Jaffe for a recent message:

> Surely there have been but few letters written from an editor to an author which have been so heartening as your note to me. In fact, it came at a very dark time indeed; the darkest of all. You seem to understand, even from that distance, the unrelieved difficulty that obtains here, though there would have to be a great deal of description for me to be able to make you understand just how bad it has been. Things seem a little better now, though there is still much trafficking with legality, with police, magistrates, counselors and other supervisory agencies. In a matter of days it will be decided as to whether my wife goes to trial, but we have reason to hope that she will be given something called pre-trial intervention, and if she satisfies the conditions over a period of time, she—and the family—will be able to resume at least the semblance of a normal life.

In the maelstrom caused by Deborah's drug abuse, Dickey had managed to finish only the first fifty pages of To the White Sea. He pointed out to Jaffe: "Even this much was hard to manage; the section was accomplished mainly in police stations and waiting rooms and other places not generally thought conducive to creative writing."[25] Dickey's exaggerations revealed his real desperation.

It was during one of Deborah's recuperative periods that Dickey invited Ward Briggs, who had loyally come to his aid during recent emergencies, on an outing to celebrate the family's improved prospects. Because Briggs was such a close family friend, the Dickeys planned to treat him to a dinner at their favorite restaurant, California Dreaming. Briggs put on a tie and jacket and drove to

Lelia's Court around six-thirty in the evening. What he confronted was hardly indicative of family unity. Dickey had donned a surgical smock to work on some poetry in the dining room. Deborah had just experienced a drug-induced seizure on a shopping trip to Woolworth's. Treated by paramedics on the scene, she refused to take the ambulance to the hospital and instead drove home. Because Dickey was supposedly taking care of Bronwen, Deborah asked him about her. Dickey replied that he didn't know where she was. He had left her in her room, but when he looked there he couldn't find her. Furious and panicking, Deborah called the police and told them "her baby" was missing. Treating the situation as a possible kidnapping, Dickey commanded Briggs to "secure the perimeter" of their property and look for signs of "forced entry." Deborah added that Bronwen often went to a neighbor's swimming pool or played in a nearby field, and suggested that Briggs look there. Making the situation worse, Dickey declared that poisonous snakes in the field could have killed Bronwen.

After a lengthy, futile search, Briggs returned to the house just as a policewoman pulled into the driveway. "Are you Mr. Dickey?" she asked. Hot and irritated by the *Deliverance*-like drama, Briggs shot back: "No, my name is Burt Reynolds." She showed no sign of detecting his irony or anger. "Is Mr. Dickey in?" she asked. He led her to the door, and when he walked down the hall, he saw Deborah and Bronwen in one of the bedrooms. Deborah's anger, mixed now with tears, had returned. What her husband had done to Bronwen was terrible, she wailed. It was tantamount to child abuse. Briggs told her that a policewoman had arrived. Quickly putting an end to her weeping, she emerged from the bedroom and in a friendly way thanked the officer for coming to the rescue. Fortunately, the crisis had passed. Bronwen had been taking a bath, and her husband had failed to look for her in the bathroom. The polite officer said she was glad everything had been resolved and turned to Briggs, saying with a straight face: "Thank you Mr. Reynolds for your help." The first act of the soap opera had ended.

To escape his wife's reprimands, Dickey told Briggs that he wanted to "get the hell out" of his house. The others could stay behind. The family outing in tatters, Briggs drove to the restaurant while Dickey kept repeating his vow to end his marriage: "This is it. I'm divorcing. I'm going to tell her. This is it. I'm just going to get in my car and drive." Only slightly calmer at the restaurant, he said: "I'm going to call her before the meal. I'm going to do it. Have you got a quarter?" As usual Dickey had no money, so Briggs gave him a quarter and directed him to the phone. When Dickey returned, although he had been drinking heavily at home, he downed three martinis and two beers, told a story about Jonathan Winters, suddenly turned pale, gasped for air, and began beating his chest. Fearing Dickey was suffering a heart attack, Briggs wanted to call an ambulance. Dickey dismissed the idea and, finally relaxing, blamed his troubles on his recurrent hiatal hernia. Convulsions again wracked Dickey's chest as he told another story. By this point, Briggs had lost all patience with Dickey's disturbances and shouted angrily: "Stop it! Stop it! Go to the men's room!" Dickey obeyed. His retching fit over, he and Briggs left the restaurant. On the way back to Lelia's Court, Dickey returned to his litany about divorce. "I'm going to get in my car and just drive,"[26] he said. Like a character in *Waiting for Godot*, Dickey threatened to go many times, but always stayed.

Friends and family members outside of Columbia tried to alleviate Dickey's burdens without much success. In July 1989, to no avail, Chris urged his father to come to Paris. In June 1990, when Deborah suffered another drug crisis, Dickey's nephew Tom Dickey, a successful manager of IBM's Real Estate Services and an avid outdoorsman who lived in Georgia, proposed taking Bronwen to Disney World. Dickey agreed to the plan and suggested that Bronwen first familiarize herself with his nephew's family by spending a week with them in August; then she could go to Florida in the spring of 1991. In his letter expressing gratitude to Tom, Dickey gave some of the details of Deborah's condition: "Deborah is in a place which is a combination of a de-tox establishment and a mental hospital, and we are trying to fend off the criminal charges by this means and any others her lawyer can dream up. She is in very bad shape, and can use all the help she can get. This interest in Bronwen on your part will be such a help, and I can tell you that it pleases me."[27] Despite these friendly gestures, Dickey's domestic anguish continued.

During the summer of 1990, *To the White Sea* advanced at an excruciatingly slow pace. In a July 3 letter to Theron Raines, Dickey again blamed his writing difficulties on his wife: "Deb is in the hospital again, this time on a make-or-break basis."[28] When he traveled on July 6 to the Governor's School in Greenville, South Carolina, he brought Bronwen with him. Even at this humble institution, he asked one of the directors—Virginia Uldrick—to write the USC president commending his reading and lecture. Every testimonial, it seemed, was necessary to assure his employers that he was a benefit rather than a liability to the university. He got another chance to act as USC's ambassador from September 12 to 14 at UNC Wilmington, where he taught a seminar and read at a gathering for the Advancement of Public Education. The generous offer—six thousand dollars—was rare. The man who invited him, Robert Tyndall, had been an admirer of Dickey's writing since meeting him with Carolyn Kizer at UNC Chapel Hill in the 1970s. Arriving at the Wilmington airport, Dickey seemed little changed. He wore a bush hat and blue jeans, and he was drunk. On the way to his room near the beach, he told Tyndall to stop at an ABC liquor store, where he bought a half-gallon bottle of Jim Beam, some of which he shared with his host. Flamboyant as ever, he made Tyndall sing an old song before agreeing to go to dinner, and, when he found out the university's chancellor would be joining them, he joked: "I hate that son-of-a-bitch! I'm never going to dinner with him!" Dickey eventually charmed his dinner company, and later gave a dazzling reading to an audience that showed its appreciation with a standing ovation.[29]

In the midst of his marital upheavals, Dickey assembled what would be his last poetry book, *The Eagle's Mile*, which Wesleyan published in October 1990. Dickey must have thought he had come full circle. His association with Doubleday over, he had returned to the publisher that had helped make him one of the most highly regarded poets of his generation. Despite his battles with Deborah and virtual estrangements from Kevin and Chris, he dedicated the

book to them as well as to Bronwen and his grandchildren. It was one way to indicate to the world that he was still, in principle, a devoted family man. To promote his book he resorted to well-worn tactics. He wrote his publisher: "Of all
the books I have written, this one has had by far the best early press; believe me,
I am astonished at what people say, though there will doubtless be some adverse
comment later on."[30] Some critics did, in fact, give Dickey high marks for his
new book.

John Updike was the most prominent writer to find evidence in *The Eagle's
Mile* of a partial return of Dickey's former strengths. He led the charge with his
blurb on the book jacket: "James Dickey is the high flier of contemporary
American poets. In *The Eagle's Mile* he is flying higher than ever."[31] Writing for
the *New York Times*, Herbert Mitgang seconded Updike's assertion: "James
Dickey continues to extend his vision as a major American Poet."[32] In his *World
Literature Today* review, Dickey's Vanderbilt friend Bill Pratt also applauded
Dickey's stirring rhetoric and visionary flights. Even one of his staunchest detractors, Fred Chappell, noted that in patches *The Eagle's Mile* successfully brandished "the High Bardic, the vatic, the transcendent—the Pindaric Grandiose"
style that originally made Dickey famous. Writing for Dickey's hometown newspaper, the *State*, Chappell offered a balanced appraisal: "When he is good, he is
good to a fine extreme. . . . When he is bad, he writes as badly as anyone else
who attempts such tall flights. He must have foreseen the risks; he must have
known that nonsense, silliness, and dull rhetoric are the abysses that gape beneath the poet as high-soaring glider pilot."[33] Chappell felt on the whole that
The Eagle's Mile was a victory for Dickey's grandiloquence.

The slim book struck other reviewers as a hodgepodge of occasional poems
and translations. Not counting what he called his "collaborations and rewrites,"
there were only twenty-six new poems, many of which were short and written in
the early 1980s. While title poems of his early books had appeared in the *New
Yorker* and *Poetry*, "The Eagle's Mile" appeared in the *Hastings Constitutional Law
Quarterly*, which had commissioned it for five hundred dollars. As if to make
amends for this unusual venue, Dickey boasted that he wrote 130 drafts before
submitting it. Considering Dickey's periodic troubles with the law, the poem's
place of publication and subject were unusual for other reasons. The poem commemorated Justice William Douglas; it was an elegy celebrating the judge's life
and ideals. But Douglas had not yet died by January 5, 1980, the day Dickey
mailed the poem to the law quarterly. Like the astronauts who accommodated
Dickey's already-finished Apollo poem by landing on the moon, Douglas died
precisely two weeks after the elegy was submitted. Dickey's poem was also unusual in that it revealed nothing about Douglas's position as associate justice of
the U.S. Supreme Court (Douglas served for thirty-six years, the longest term in
U.S. history). In the poem the judge appears as an eagle flying over the
Appalachian mountains in order to escape civilization, which the law has made
possible. Famous for his defense of civil liberties and ecological issues, Douglas
expresses an attitude toward the law and the untamed outback similar to that of
Lewis Medlock.

In "The Eagle's Mile" Dickey blends fanciful sketches of his father—a lawyer who preferred the Appalachian wilderness to the courtroom—with Douglas and himself. The title comes from William Blake, another iconoclast who had little truck with conventional law. In citing Blake in his epigraph—"The Emmet's Inch & Eagle's Mile"—Dickey indicates the sort of qualities he plans to eulogize. He portrays Douglas not only as a soaring eagle looking down upon the world from a sublime height, but also as an emmet (an ant) who inches through the underbrush. He is the sort of man Dickey wanted to be: a high flyer who contemplated universals and united them to particulars. Douglas's shifting identities do not stop there. He is also a male deer walking the Appalachian Trail, as well as Adam waking to Eden for the first time. "Let Adam," Dickey implores, "far from the closed smoke of mills / Of every flame, true-up with blind-side outflash / The once-more instantly / Wild world." The line exemplifies the alliterative melody and exotic rhetoric of Dickey's book.

Dickey's calculated mistiness creates suspense and mystery in some of the poems, but often is simply vague. In "Night Bird" he dwells on a "gleam of air" on somebody's—we don't know whose—neck:

there is no limit

To what a man can get out of
His failure to see:
this gleam

Of air down the nape of the neck, and in it everything
There is of flight
and nothing else,
and it is

All right and all over you
From around
as you are carried

In yourself and there is no way
To nothing-but-walk—

No way and a bidden flurry
And a half-you of air.

Sound and sense in these "spaced-out" phrases are as nebulous as the bird itself.

Other poems strive to embody insubstantial subjects in insubstantial ways. In the first, "Eagles," Dickey rather than Douglas takes wing through the void. He addresses the bird: "Where you take hold, I will take // That stand in my mind, rock bird alive with the spirit- / life of height, / on my down-thousands / Of fathoms, classic // Claw-stone, everything under." Unlike Yeats's Chinamen in "Lapis Lazuli," who gaze upon past and present civilizations from a mountain height, Dickey finds less joy than tragedy beneath him. "My sympathy," he says, is "grovelling / In weeds and nothing." With a glimpse at his domestic tribulations, he sees a wasteland rather than a paradise at his feet. Taking a long, cold look at himself in "Daybreak," he sees vaporous images projected by his imagination: "You gaze straight into // The whole trembling forehead of yourself / Under you, and at your feet find your body / No different from cloud, among the other / See-through images." Fantasies of heroic athleticism characterize "The Olympian," a rewrite of his unsuccessful screenplay *The Olympian*. Dickey portrays himself as an out-of-shape, pizza-eating, beer-drinking, middle-aged man who enters his own "secret Olympics." The race is all in his imagination: "I blazed I felt great I was a great / Plaster stadium-god lagging lolloping hanging / In there with the best."[34] As in his previous athletic fantasies, he beats his Olympic opponent and collects a gold medal.

Dickey's dependence in *The Eagle's Mile* on "rewrites" was one sign of his struggle to find new inspiration. David Havird correctly pointed out that a number of the poems were indebted to the Spanish poet Vicente Aleixandre and that Dickey, as if conscious of his flagging powers, refused to acknowledge this: "I tried myself to explore it [the debt] with Dickey, but he was very reticent. Quite a number of those poems are free reworkings of Aleixandre, but there's no credit given whatsoever. And 'Immortals'—including the last poem in the book 'Word'—are much more than reworkings or 'rewrites.'"[35] When the *Memphis State Review* accepted some of these "rewrites," Dickey insisted they not be called translations: "You can understand that I don't want these poems to be presented as translations or adaptations of other translations, which they are not. They are original poems—and much better than *the* originals, I can tell you."[36] His denials to the contrary, Dickey had used Barstone and Garriston translations of Aleixandre, and then improvised on them.

Dickey was even more evasive with David Spider of Raccoon Books: "I rewrote them first in Spanish, then translated them into English, making the final product very unlike the original."[37] His improvisations had found takers at small literary journals like the *New York Quarterly* and *Verse*. James Anderson of Breitenbush Publications in Portland expressed interest in issuing a collection to be called *Immortals*. Dickey articulated his controversial methods of translation most succinctly to Ben Belitt, a translator of Pablo Neruda and other Spanish poets: "Since Pound at least, a new kind of curious form, which I try to experiment with myself, has come into existence. This is neither a translation or a completely original poem, but a kind of hybrid which for want of a better name I am tempted to call 'the rewrite.'" Rewrites, Dickey predicted, would engender "the most profound change that our poetry will undergo during the next phase of things."[38] In fact, dozens of prominent poets from Pound to Robert Lowell and Robert Bly had been rewriting poems in the way Dickey explained. Usually, however, they acknowledged their sources.

One of the few honors Dickey received in the 1990s, which brought with it the impressive title of Grand Master, came at the behest of some of his publishing friends in Birmingham, Alabama. Pleased to be associated with such past grand masters as Andrew Lytle, Edward Albee, Peter Taylor, and Eudora Welty, Dickey looked forward to the awards ceremony at a three-day *Writing Today* conference beginning March 7, 1991. *Birmingham Southern* and *Southern Living* magazines were sponsoring the event at Southern College of Technology in Alabama. One of those involved in the proceedings, John Logue, welcomed and congratulated him at the airport. Logue also organized a dinner, to which Dickey invited Patricia Muske (Deborah stayed at home). Pleased to see Dickey again, she was also bewildered by the way he slipped so quickly from Southern gentleman to Southern redneck. After talking at length with their gracious black waiter about a Foreman-Holyfield boxing match, rather than leave a tip he told the waiter to ask the restaurant owner to give him $10. Embarrassed by his condescending tone, Muske watched the waiter's face tighten with disdain. Was Dickey really that destitute? A month before, on February 9, he had collected $5,000 for a reading at St. Andrews Presbyterian College. In addition to his regular sources of income, in 1991 his sister, Maibelle, began sending him monthly checks of $675 from the family real estate holdings at 94 Broad Street and 107 Peachtree Street in Atlanta. He also had been receiving $120,000 installments from his advance for *To the White Sea.*

By the mid-1990s, Muske's tolerance for Dickey's indiscretions had worn thin. His literary talk could astonish, his flirtatiousness charm, and his wit amuse, but his mean-spirited remarks had a cumulative effect. Weary of his "nigger" and "Jew" jokes, she rebuffed him in 1996 when he made one of his more serious proposals of marriage. "I'm going to make you happy," he promised at the time. "How are you going to make me happy?" she asked skeptically. He insisted: "I'm just going to make you happy." Nonplussed, she retorted: "In the fourteen years I've known you, you've only spent fourteen dollars on me." Dickey mumbled over the phone, "This isn't going too well,"[39] and hung up.

Dickey's behavior in the early 1990s was part of an alcoholic routine from which he rarely deviated. On his visits to Ben Franklin's house one or two Sundays each month, he drank two quart bottles of beer and always listened to jazz records, beginning with Bix Beiderbecke's "Royal Garden Blues," which he played at full volume.[40] Sometimes he made phone calls he couldn't make at home. One time he called Paula Goff to vent his anger with Deborah. "I'm going to divorce her!"[41] he bellowed into the phone. As always, Franklin found it hard to understand Dickey's continuing devotion to Deborah. "I love that Deborah. She's so promiscuous,"[42] Dickey said, no doubt thinking of his own former promiscuity. Before long, however, Dickey heeded his friends' advice and took preliminary steps toward divorce by getting a "divorce kit." Deborah discovered it, and in a preemptive strike she asked *him* for a divorce.[43]

To Franklin, Deborah was an enigma flitting on the shadowy borders of his friendship with Dickey. One of the only times Deborah came to his house with her husband was to borrow twenty-five dollars. Franklin later concluded that the money was for a quick fix.[44] But why would Dickey—the highest-paid member of the English Department—need to borrow such a small sum from him? Franklin wondered. Where did Dickey's money go? Did Deborah siphon all of it off to drug pushers and psychiatrists? Dickey always acted as if he were impoverished, even making Franklin buy him lunch. And yet on one of his Sunday visits Dickey boasted that he had just made three million dollars on the film rights for *To the White Sea*. (The same Sunday he told Don Greiner that he had sold the rights for eight million dollars.) Dickey's poverty seemed to be a habitual ruse.

Realizing how disheveled the Dickey family had become, at the end of 1990 the Franklins tried to provide relief by inviting them to Christmas dinner. They invited Ward Briggs to join them. Having seen Dickey sitting in abject drunkenness on the front of his car in the Kroger parking lot several days before Christmas, Franklin knew that Dickey could use some down-home hospitality. So that Dickey would think he was the honored guest, Franklin asked him to read some of his poems. At the appointed hour on Christmas day, the Dickeys failed to appear. After two hours of waiting, the Franklins saw Deborah tear up the driveway in her van, deposit her husband, and tear back to the road. Dickey's condition was no better than it had been in the supermarket parking lot. He stumbled drunkenly into the house with his arms filled with books. The two Franklin daughters, who were in their early twenties, were aghast. As Dickey enacted scenes from *Deliverance* and mumbled his poetry unintelligibly, his hosts scowled with anger, pity, and embarrassment. During a pause in the conversation at dessert, Dickey leered: "I wonder if anybody would like to hear a good racist joke?"[45] One of the Franklin daughters rushed upstairs in tears, the other to a neighbor's house.

Deborah's drug habit became general knowledge in Columbia. The *State* reported that police had arrested her at 2:30 P.M. on March 25, 1991, during a routine patrol for drug users.[46] The article about her arraignment at the Richland County Courthouse read like an episode from one of the tawdry soap operas her husband liked to concoct: "Tears flowed down the face of the wife of writer James Dickey on Tuesday when her private battle with cocaine became public in a Richland County courtroom. Deborah Dickey, 39, admitted being caught injecting cocaine with a stranger in an abandoned house at 2314 Pendleton St. Ronald Middleton, 29, of 1311 Maple St., injected the cocaine for Dickey because she did not like doing it herself, said 5th Circuit Assistant Solicitor Duffie Stone."[47] Deborah's attorney, Alvin Neal, acknowledged that Deborah was addicted to cocaine and that she was participating in an out-patient drug-treatment program. She was allowed to go free on a personal recognizance bond.

At an April 30 court session, circuit judge Carol Connor suspended a two-year prison term on condition that Deborah serve two years' probation. She would have to submit to drug testing and drug treatment, which she had already started. Deborah looked distraught and embarrassed, nervously brushing her hair and glancing out a window at the courtroom's entrance. Her husband stared at the walls and ceiling.[48] At one point, he stood and told the judge that he wanted to help his wife overcome her drug habit. With the sort of eloquence he had admired in his father's *Classics of the Bar*, he vowed: "I will stand beside her until death and mourning."[49] He stood by her for a few more years.

It was at about this time that Dickey tried to involve Elizabeth Adams in Deborah's recuperation. Deborah was not only harming herself with cocaine and other substances; by associating with violent drug pushers, she was putting herself and her whole family in jeopardy. According to one friend, her cohorts had beaten her up in a restaurant on Gervais Street and had threatened to do so in a local graveyard.[50] Dickey hoped Adams, a respected member of Columbia society, could lead his wife out of her inferno. Adams's attempts to befriend Deborah, unfortunately, proved futile. According to Adams, Deborah assumed that there was a romantic bond between her and Dickey. In late-night phone calls to apprise Adams's husband of the situation, Deborah vented her paranoid suspicions. Her calls to Elizabeth were just as hysterical. When Deborah threatened to kill Elizabeth if she continued to see Dickey, Elizabeth backed off.[51]

Despite the efforts of police officers, lawyers, doctors, drug counselors, and her husband to direct Deborah toward a more productive life, Deborah continued to reel out of control. After a drinking spree on July 4, 1991, she crashed her Dodge van in North Carolina. A close friend recalled that she and her husband had driven to Asheville to retrieve Bronwen from summer camp. Dickey, who had also been drinking, had found Deborah passed out inside the van. When she woke, a woman nearby commented that she was in no shape to drive. Deborah ignored her and, on her way to the hotel, careened off the road and plunged down a steep embankment toward some woods. Police arrived to make an arrest. Although he was not driving, Dickey was cited as an accomplice because the van was registered in his name. The Dickeys left the van in Asheville, collected Bronwen, and flew home.[52]

After one of Deborah's drug suppliers had smashed the windows of her Volvo in a fit of resentment, Dickey had bought the bright red van to make his wife more conspicuous to police in Columbia's "night-town." Deborah now wanted to buy a less noticeable car. Her husband insisted on getting the van rebuilt, so he asked Ward Briggs to accompany him to Asheville to retrieve it. With conspiratorial glee, he told Briggs that they would do three things in North Carolina: they would get the van, view the accident scene, and have "a homosexual encounter." At his regular Thursday lunch group before the trip, Dickey repeated to Greiner and Franklin his plan to have "a homosexual tryst" with Briggs. Briggs was happy to help with the car, but fended off Dickey's whimsical advance. He told Dickey he would not have time for an overnight stay in a hotel because he needed to return on Sunday evening for a Columbia softball game. Dickey replied with mock grumpiness: "OK. I'll bring you by the hotel where it damn well ought to happen."[53] Briggs knew that Dickey's proposition was a bluff.

On the small commuter plane into Asheville, Dickey's spirits remained high. "I have just two questions," he said to the flight attendant. "What movies do you have on this flight? And when do we land in Tulsa?"[54] In Asheville, Dickey wrote a large check for the van repairs and, as Dickey promised, drove to the accident scene. Briggs was amazed that the Dickeys had survived such a perilous drop into the woods. Passing the hotel, Dickey repeated his homosexual jokes and then drove at ninety miles per hour back to Columbia, stopping only briefly at a knife store to buy a penknife. To Briggs's surprise, they arrived home just in time for his softball game. He was surprised again in January of 1992 when the Dickeys managed to get the charges against them dropped. Both seemed to have inherited the "luck of the drunk."

Dickey's stability, friends noted, was intimately connected to Deborah's. As Deborah floundered, so did he. About a year after driving her van off the road,

Dickey suffered a kind of copy-cat accident. He flipped his MG into a ditch on Columbia's Kilbourne Road. Luckily, some students helped pull the car from the ditch before police arrived. All these calamities hampered Dickey's progress with *To the White Sea,* and to a certain extent fueled the misogynistic, Ted Bundy–like rage he was instilling in the main character, Muldrow. Wasn't a woman responsible for most of his current afflictions? Wasn't his fight for physical and literary survival comparable to his battle against the Japanese? *To the White Sea* gave him an opportunity to purge his murderous demons.

Physical ailments unrelated to Deborah also afflicted Dickey. On June 18, 1991, he complained to Marc Jaffe that he had a "semi-gangrenous situation"[55] in his foot, which would probably require partial amputation of a toe. The pain was so intense that he took about forty Darvosets, along with propoxiphene, over a three-day period. The toe problem was the result of a toenail fungus that had bothered him most of his life and that he had never properly medicated. He usually blamed the problem on his mother's failure to buy comfortable shoes for him as a boy, but it was more likely the result of jungle rot contracted in the Philippines. Because doctors had amputated his diabetic grandmother's leg, he feared he would have a similar operation. Amputations—usually of heads—had obsessed him for decades.

To Jaffe, Dickey also claimed that he would need further surgery on his esophagus to correct his digestion. In his ruinous state, he nevertheless promised his editor on August 1 to complete his novel soon or die trying: "I feel I shouldn't go into the reasons for my delay, for fear that I might depress you with the details of my situation, so disheartening, so endlessly complicated with legalities, with medical solutions that don't work, with lawyers, doctors, psychiatrists, policemen, judges, probation officers, and God knows who or what else, that to lay all this on you would be an extreme unkindness, so I won't."[56] On December 18, 1991, he apologized again, although now he said his delay was due to the arduous task of collecting his poems for *The Whole Motion.*

Dickey had other distractions in 1991. On July 30, he accepted Cleanth Brooks's invitation to join Fred Chappell as a judge for the Hanes Poetry Prize given by the Fellowship of Southern Writers. In October, he published his fourth and final coffee-table book, *Southern Light* (his circular narrative, which followed the sun from dawn to dusk, was accompanied by glossy photographs of landscapes taken by Jim Valentine). In November and December, Dickey went on another book tour, submitting to the usual round of book signings and cocktail parties in Atlanta, Nashville, Birmingham, Charlotte, and Columbia. In November, he spoke at the University of Arkansas in Monticello, Lee College in Texas, the Harbour Front in Toronto, De Kalb Community College, and the Book Fair in Miami. On November 13, he gave an address at SAMLA, "LIGHTNINGS, or *Visuals,*" in which he described how images, when sufficiently brooded on, become mantras conjuring up stories.

In February 1992, Dickey told Theron Raines that Deborah showed signs of improvement and that he was optimistic of a permanent solution. Nevertheless, because he still feared she would squander his income on drugs, he decided to set up a trust fund so Bronwen would have money for college. His sons supported the plan. In all the depressing turbulence of his life, Bronwen remained the constant object of his devotion. Ben Franklin told him, "Jim, Bronwen is your great-est creation," and he replied: "I couldn't agree more."[57] With regard to his other creation of the moment, *To the White Sea*, Dickey was cheered by encouraging signals from his publisher. Despite his missed deadlines, in 1992 Houghton re-leased another portion of his advance (Raines, after taking his cut, sent Dickey seventeen hundred dollars). Dickey tried to accelerate his writing and to find magazines that would publish excerpts (the *Atlantic Monthly* declined, but the *Southern Review* and *Playboy* accepted).

Since Dickey always contended that poetry was at the center of his creative wheel, he considered the publication of *The Whole Motion: Collected Poems, 1945–1992* to be the main event of 1992. In July, the month Wesleyan released the collection, Dickey hailed his masterwork with a typical combination of hu-mility and promotional braggadocio: "When you look at all of it gathered there, 475 pages, almost 50 years, then you do have some trepidation. And when you open up the book, you know the blood in your stomach sinks. You think you're going to read those poems and say, 'You know, this is not as good as I thought.' Luckily, that didn't happen when I read through them again. I have to say, in all honesty, this is better than I thought—sometimes a lot better." Put on the de-fensive by years of carping critics, Dickey reiterated his insistence that, like the restlessly inventive Picasso, he never wanted to repeat himself. He told William Starr at the *State* that he had deliberately taken risks, tinkered with new styles, and even courted ridicule in his endless pursuit of fresh sublimity. Did he feel a sense of closure now that his book of 235 poems was complete? He told Starr: "I don't have all the answers. I never did. . . . I'll tell you I never wanted wisdom. What I want is perpetual adolescence. What excites me about life is the open-ing up of the new. If I thought I had some kind of maturity or wisdom and knew all there was to know, I would have no sense of discovery. And I value that above all." Nevertheless, he admitted to a sense of fulfillment: "There were times when I'd go on a plane trip and think it would be a damn shame if my airplane would blow up, because I have all these things to finish. I was worried then, but I'm not now. I don't feel a compulsion to give up family, food, health, recreation and everything else in order to worry about leaving something unsaid. I'll leave plenty unsaid. But I'm prepared to stand on what I've said."[58] He would soon sacrifice family, food, health, and recreation, but not because of his compulsion to write.

Hoping for a tidal wave of acclaim, Dickey found that his lifework created hardly a ripple in the critical community. David Biespel in the *Washington Post Book World* summed up the general response. He lauded the poems from Dickey's 1957–67 period and lamented those that came after: "By the 1970s Dickey's work had declined, and it's hard to find anyone who doesn't agree that his poetry is now uneven; the grace and control of that remarkable decade reveal them-selves only here and there in poems that retain, to paraphrase the poet, a one-drink-too-many tone and energy." The best poems, Biespel averred, drew on the grief and joy Dickey had felt as an Army Air Corpsman and survivor of war. Like so many other believers in Dickey's invented selves, Biespel was not entirely ac-curate in citing the basis for his views. "To appreciate Dickey," he argued, "you . . . have to remember that Dickey was a night-bomber pilot during World

War II and the war in Korea, flying over a hundred combat missions." There was an integrity to "James Dickey's unified vision,"[59] Biespel asserted, even though that integrity was compromised by a quarter-century of failed experiments.

The most complimentary reviews came from Dickey's home turf. With a glance at the critical skirmishes surrounding Dickey, Starr extolled the book as evidence of Dickey's gargantuan status: "This imposing, challenging, death-defying volume solidifies the case for James Dickey as one among a very few commanding poets of the second half of this century, a giant whose stature comes from his refusal to remain above the fight."[60] Dickey agreed with this portrait of himself as an embattled giant. On July 21, about a week after Starr's review appeared, Dickey dusted off his Hemingwayesque persona and visited Key West's week-long Hemingway Days Festival to accept the first Conch Republic Prize for Literature. In a fit of pique, he at first refused to go because the organizers sent him economy-class plane tickets; he demanded first-class tickets, not only for himself, but for Deborah and Bronwen. On receiving new tickets, he consented to accept the one-thousand-dollar honorarium. In Key West he read from *To the White Sea*, a novel he imagined Hemingway would have liked, and after telling his audience that as a septuagenarian he felt confident he had mastered his poetic idiom, he read from *The Whole Motion*. It was on this visit or another about the same time that he judged the festival's much-publicized Hemingway lookalike contest.

Dickey resembled Hemingway in ways that had little to do with aggressive masculinity. Both writers had traveled an arc from magnificent productivity to alcoholic decline. The sales of *The Whole Motion* reflected Dickey's current status better than any testimonials to his endurance as a giant or fighter. By April 1994, most of the hardback copies had sold, but the paperback sales had slowed. After paying Dickey an advance of forty-five hundred dollars, which was high by Wesleyan's standards, the publisher announced that it had no intention of reprinting the hardback. The failure of the book to win any significant awards or attract any significant critical attention rankled Dickey more than he was prepared to admit. In 1991, he had tried to brace himself for critical neglect by telling his class what Conrad Aiken had once said about publishing a new book: "Waiting for the reaction is like dropping a feather into the Grand Canyon and listening for the echo."[61] He admonished his writing students to repudiate the desire for fame and fortune and simply create poems that endured. His advice was noble, but difficult to follow. His closest friends at USC attributed his renewed drinking to the fact that his lifework had fallen into the void with hardly an echo.

40. Into the Desolation of Reality (1992–1994)

During the summer of 1992, when talk resurfaced about a sequel to *Deliverance*, Dickey adamantly stuck by his past refusals, even though a new movie would have made his name more visible. As for Burt Reynolds's eagerness to make a sequel, Dickey scoffed: "I don't believe in repeating myself. There will never be a

Son of Deliverance."[1] He threatened to take legal action to enforce his decree. Thinking of the second *Gone with the Wind,* he made up a rhyme: "Peggy Mitchell's dead, and you're no equal / You're *Scarlet's* deal. Murder by sequel."[2] In 1992, however, he did allow a theater director the right to resurrect one of his poems—"May Day Sermon"—for the stage. John Gallogly, who had credentials as a screenwriter as well as an actor, approached Dickey early in the year about adapting his poem. Gallogly directed Theatre West, a small Los Angeles company started in 1962, and planned to have the talented actress Bridget Hanley, who had made a name for herself in the television shows *Harper Valley P.T.A.* and *Here Come the Brides,* play the part of the high-strung Baptist preacher who narrates Dickey's iconoclastic sermon. Hanley was nervous about her ability to do justice to the preacher's oratory. After she first read the script in front of Dickey, she knelt at his feet and asked: "Are we still friends?" He responded with kingly authority: "My dear, you are an artist."[3] Although at first skeptical of the project, during a trip to Los Angeles in mid-November 1992, Dickey gave his blessings to Gallogly and Hanley.

Dickey returned to Los Angeles to attend one of the performances of *May Day Sermon* in early December, and was impressed by the minimalist staging and the fever pitch at which Hanley delivered her lines. Little besides a pulpit, Bible, and illuminated cross accompanied her sadoerotic monologue of youthful transgression and redemption. Remembering the furor over the poem's sexual contents when it first appeared in the *Atlantic Monthly,* Dickey was overjoyed and somewhat bemused by the critical response to the play. T. W. McCulloh praised the production as "a striking kaleidoscope of curious and commanding images wound through the Preacher's story of a young country woman's release from the pain of bondage by both religious hypocrisy and a male-dominated society that still exists, particularly in the narrow world of Dickey's South."[4] Some critics, such as Clifford Gallo of the *Daily News of Los Angeles,* even concluded that Dickey, by celebrating a woman's escape from her sadistic father to enjoy untrammeled sex with a motorcyclist, was a born-again feminist.

May Day Sermon's run ended in mid-December 1992, but later Theatre West took the play as far afield as South America and Scotland. Gallogly also hoped to make a film of Hanley's performance for television. Dickey considered bringing the play to New York. On May 18, 1992, Norman Mailer had asked Dickey if he had any plays for a festival at the Actors Studio he was helping to organize. At first Dickey said he had nothing, but in June he suggested that Theron Raines put Gallogly in touch with Mailer about *May Day Sermon.* Dickey had other instructions for Raines. Again apologizing for the homosexual emphasis in his *Alnilam* screenplay, he told Raines to send it to Terence Malik, who he felt would be an ideal director. Dickey was cheered by his possible involvement in other film projects. On October 13, a Dickey scholar with experience in film, Robert Kirschten, wrote Raines to acquire exclusive rights for a two-year period to produce any and all documentary films about Dickey. He had already lined up a Los Angeles director, Gretchen Somerfield, and begun fund-raising for the film he planned to call *James Dickey: American Poet.*

Several days before his seventieth birthday, Dickey received outpatient treatment at Columbia Providence Hospital for the hiatal hernia that continued to pester him. In a dour mood when William Starr called on his birthday, Dickey searched for reasons to celebrate. He commented wryly that the little black book he'd once filled with the names of girlfriends was now full of doctors' names: "I've got esophageal problems resulting from some major surgery I had for a hiatal hernia in Seattle in 1980. Nothing would go down my gullet. You can die of hunger or thirst. And God, it's a savage operation—it's like getting hit by a truck—and the doctors can't completely correct it, so I have to go back to the hospital for outpatient surgery every few months. And I've got a bad back. I was born with one extra vertebrae, and it affects a sciatic nerve in my leg, and sometimes it just shuts down on me. But who wants to go on and on about all that?" Dickey's hypochondriacal gloom lifted slightly when close friends offered a spate of birthday testimonials, some of which appeared in the *State*. Matthew Bruccoli generously proclaimed: "He is America's greatest living writer. Certainly its greatest living poet. . . . He still has the ability to retain the knowledge of a book he picked up only once 20 years ago and bring it up instantly. In my life I've never known anyone like him. He is a genius."[5] Students paid tribute by visiting his home. His son Chris called from Paris. English Department colleagues organized a surprise luncheon with a birthday cake, and USC president John Palms came to pay his respects.

Dickey's main effort at the beginning of 1993 was to complete *To the White Sea*. Early in the summer he met with Marc Jaffe in New York to work on revisions. Dismayed by what he called Dickey's "undercurrent of throttled violence"[6] and his identification with the sociopath Muldrow, Jaffe soon realized that Dickey's ferocity was mainly a pose. He grew to admire Dickey's professional diligence. Helping to establish rapport between them was the fact that Jaffe had served as a marine in the Pacific during World War II and also had fathered young children in a second marriage. With regard to revising *To the White Sea*, Jaffe urged Dickey to cut the scene where Muldrow kills a small child he entertains with string tricks, as well as the scene where he kills a young girl and sticks her head on a waterwheel. Dickey spared the child from strangulation, but merely changed the decapitated girl to an old woman.

In late September 1993, while Dickey was on sabbatical, Houghton launched Dickey's third novel with a barrage of publicity. Dickey was as optimistic as ever about the marketability of his new book. He told Don Greiner and Ben Franklin, to whom he had given typescripts of the novel, that he was convinced it would sell as well as *Deliverance*. In a 1993 conversation with Willie Morris and Joyce Pair, he suggested that readers would find Muldrow irresistible. "There is going to be a whole resurgence of Muldrow . . . because everyone wants to be *Muldrow*,"[7] he said. With his old Vanderbilt roommate, John Hall, at an American Booksellers Association conference in Florida, he was similarly buoyant. Muldrow's quirky personality would fascinate readers and especially women readers, who would admire his resourcefulness and self-reliance. Was Dickey being facetious? Hall was not so sure. Following the disappointments of *Alnilam*, *The Eagle's Mile*, and *The Whole Motion*, one thing *was* certain: Dickey wanted to win back the mass audience he had enjoyed in the 1970s.

One way Dickey strove for popular success in *To the White Sea* was by simplifying the heroic quest that had dominated his earlier novels. He kept the circular journey of Lewis Medlock and Frank Cahill intact by implying that Muldrow ends at his beginning; Muldrow travels to northern Japan, where the ice and snow recall his homeground in northern Alaska. His literal journey is straight-forward: He parachutes into Tokyo and heads north. Following the picaresque tradition, Dickey has Muldrow engage in a series of dramatic trials that evince his brutal efficiency. Like his forebears Medlock and Cahill, Muldrow encapsu-lates many of Dickey's real and imagined traits. Muldrow is full of obsessions, idiosyncrasies, and what Medlock called "mystiques." Like Cahill, he carries around in his memory a few key images redolent of terror and beauty (the red wall in his house by Alaska's Brooks Range, the blue ice of calving glaciers, the murderously cunning wolverine and lynx). Even his ordinary acts carry the im-press of his odd personality. In the strength contest he has with another fire-bomber before flying to Tokyo, he insists that his opponent hang from a beam with a "pinch grip" because only he has perfected it. His puerile machismo soon turns pathological. Among his enemies in Tokyo, he at first kills out of necessity. Later he kills to satisfy his sadistic whims.

Muldrow's journey can be read as a kind of allegory of Dickey's life, even though Alaska and Hokkaido seem utterly different from Dickey's Southern lo-cale. At its most basic level, the story articulates Dickey's conviction that life is a Darwinian power struggle, "red in tooth and claw," that ends in death. He had written about a similar journey in the 1964 poem "Sled Burial, Dream Ceremony," where a dead Southerner travels by train from his warm, rainy homeground to the cold, snowy "otherworld" of the North. Muldrow retraces the Southerner's route on Japanese soil, passing from fiery Tokyo to frozen Hokkaido. Like some of the *ubermensch* characters in Jack London's and Herman Melville's writings, as Muldrow travels into the white wastes he becomes the embodiment and oracle of the godless, amoral universe that engulfs him.

The threat of death and the struggle to overcome it had always stirred Dickey's imagination, but during the 1980s and 1990s his precarious health and violent marriage gave him more-visceral reasons for brooding on these topics. *To the White Sea* is a war novel about visiting revenge on Dickey's former enemies, the Japanese, but it is also a novel about visiting revenge on women. Muldrow has killed a college girl from Kansas whom he met in Point Barrow, Alaska, be-fore he goes on his Japanese rampage. His murderous misogyny, as Dickey read-ily admitted, allies him with Ted Bundy, who was so good at impersonating a normal, intelligent, caring young man that friends like Ann Rule found it hard to believe that he was one of the most prolific serial killers in history, even after overwhelming evidence led to his conviction. Muldrow is a similar chameleon fascinated with disguise, with blending in with the crowd or landscape, with camouflaging his predatory intentions. And like Bundy, he has honed his skills with horrifying mastery.

Asked by Alex Chadwick on NPR's *Morning Edition* why he was attracted to a character like Muldrow, Dickey at first deflected the question and then ex-plained that he wanted the reader to feel ambivalence toward Muldrow—to ad-mire him because he was an American trying to survive in enemy territory and to condemn him because "the American military has loosed on the Japanese civilian population the equivalent of Ted Bundy." Chadwick asked if Dickey had ever known a Muldrow. He replied that Muldrow was imaginary, "but, like the characters of any author, there are certain parts of your own personality that come to the fore and you . . . exaggerate those. As the German poet Goethe says, 'The strength of my imagination as a poet and a novelist is the fact that I cannot imagine any crime which I myself would not be capable of committing.'" "Do you think there's some part of you that's capable of Muldrow's acts?" Chadwick asked. Dickey disabused him quickly: "No. No, of course not. The difference is there's a part of my own character that is capable of thinking about Muldrow's action and using him as material for a novel."[8] Dickey later remarked that he was interested in Bundy because he seemed "to have been a complete sociopath . . . , somebody without a conscience, without any conscience."[9] Dickey was no Bundy, but even some of his family members called his unconscionable acts sociopathic.

Ted Bundy targeted a particular type of woman because of the resemblance she bore to a woman who had once romantically wounded him. Muldrow is a similarly wounded, vulnerable man. He suffers a physical wound late in his journey. Oddly enough, he admires the combativeness of his assailant—a goat— even to the point of comedy. He says masochistically: "I liked my knocked-out teeth and my thigh gored to the bloody bone."[10] The goat-goring parallels a sexual wounding and the mythic goring of Adonis, whose loves were divided between Persephone and Aphrodite. At the end of *To the White Sea*, Muldrow recuperates from his goring with a primitive tribe that specializes in ritual killings and communions with animals. Because of his identification with caged animals (in Japan, Muldrow is one), he develops a deep hatred for the tribe. They behead a bear, triggering memories of Muldrow's beheaded comrades, so he kills a tribal member he met on a goat hunt, puts the corpse in a bear cage, and releases a bear cub. Such are Muldrow's paradoxes: he searches for a primitive, tribal, animalistic ethos, but when he encounters it, he abhors it; he admires the amoral, bloodthirsty conduct of animals like the fisher marten and wolverine, but when humans treat animals in amoral ways, he reacts with moral indignation.

By making Muldrow both predator and prey, Dickey admitted to the roles he played in his marital conflicts and, for that matter, in his conflicts with most people. His predatory ways—with women, with money, with fame, with other writers—made him prey to recriminations. His marriage was the crucible in which his contraries fused most dramatically. The literary evolution, which amounts to a horrific devolution, of Medlock to Cahill to Muldrow highlighted Dickey's growing cynicism about marriage. Sometimes—as at the 1993 Atlanta Book Fair with Willie Morris and Joyce Pair—Dickey emphasized the connections among the three novels by telling stories that juxtaposed Muldrow's bloody knife work, Zack's consumption of Cahill's blood, and Medlock's bloody shooting of the hillbilly. As for marriage, Lewis returns to his wife like a wounded soldier to convalesce; Cahill abandons his wife and tender sexuality for voyeurism and sadism; and Muldrow kills rather than marries women.

In Muldrow Dickey's real life and fantasy life achieved a frightening apotheosis. Muldrow is a mixture of memory and desire, fear and obsession. As in

Deliverance, Dickey draws on his youthful reading of Edgar Rice Burroughs's Tarzan books and science-fiction stories of travel to distant planets. Although Muldrow may resemble Sylvester Stallone's self-reliant Vietnam War veteran Rambo or Clint Eastwood's Civil War veteran and "one man army" Josie Wales, Muldrow is another avatar of Tarzan (while composing *To the White Sea* Dickey had praised Gore Vidal for *his* youthful devotion to Burroughs and Tarzan). Like Tarzan, who is part English lord Greystoke and part African gorilla, Muldrow is a sophisticated man who learns from animals how to be a killer in a menacing, foreign land. Both of Tarzan's parents die before a mother gorilla adopts him; Muldrow's parents (like Dickey's) have died, too. Muldrow also shares Tarzan's ambivalent disposition toward animals. He likes hunting them and eating their raw flesh, but he also feels sentimental and friendly toward them.

Because Muldrow is as solipsistic as Frank Cahill, there is only one point of view in the novel—Muldrow's. His scatalogical disgust for humanity, which resembles that of Jonathan Swift, emerges early in *To the White Sea* when he hides in the Tokyo sewer. To Muldrow, Tokyo *is* a sewer, and he wants American fire-bombers to destroy it so he can escape: "If the fire didn't come down on Tokyo, it was only a question of time before somebody would find me, if I didn't drown in the flood of Tokyo shit, and no matter how hard I found or however many I might be able to kill, I would lose. I would have my balls cut off, I would have my head cut off, and that would be it."[11] In his poem "The Firebombing," Dickey had expressed guilt about not feeling guilt over the destruction of Japan. Rather than guilt, fear and hatred dominate Muldrow.

Muldrow's story begins on March 8, 1945. Dickey chose this date because on the night of March 9, Gen. Curtis LeMay ordered more than three hundred B-29s to drop 1,650 tons of napalm on Tokyo's civilian population. The damage and casualties from this raid alone were catastrophic. March was also significant in Dickey's war memory for personal reasons. His squadron cohorts Donald Armstrong and James Lally crashed on March 16, 1945, and Lally was beheaded shortly afterward. Early in his trek north, Muldrow witnesses a beheading on a Japanese air base that harks back to the one Dickey described in "The Performance." Only this time the act is more barbaric than heroic and ritualistic: "The American's head fell forward, but not off. Blood jumped in front of him at least a yard, and before he went down the Jap with the sword hit him again, and this time the head came off and rolled over. The body jerked and lay there pouring out blood, and one of the other Japs came over and kicked it a couple of times, hard." To satisfy his eye-for-an-eye sense of justice, Muldrow cuts the head off a Japanese woman by a waterwheel. Like Dickey, who had more-current reasons to be obsessed with beheadings, Muldrow is haunted by what he sees at the air base. One of his most disturbing visions is of deer heads "cut off and lined up"[12] in the snow.

Muldrow's experiences and obsessions merge with Dickey's at a number of other points. Muldrow is an excellent runner and spear thrower who appreciates such activities for their aesthetic qualities. Dickey once approached track with the same perspective. Like Dickey, Muldrow is fascinated by equipment, the more primitive the better. He learns to become a B-29 gunner at Buckingham

Field in Fort Myers just as Dickey did during the first months of 1944. Sgt. Hough, who teaches Muldrow how to tinker with a truck engine at Buckingham Field, is loosely based on a Sgt. Carter, with whom Dickey used to talk during gunnery training. Muldrow navigates by the stars, as Dickey learned to do with sextants in the 1970s. He also shares Dickey's reverence for ice. Dickey often told friends that he picked ice cubes off the floor, washed them, and reused them because in the Philippines ice was such a rare commodity. For Dickey ice also had symbolic value. Although he admitted he never saw a glacier crack, in *To the White Sea* the blue ice exposed by cracks is supposed to connote the "ultimate strangeness" and "unexpected beauty" at the heart of Muldrow and, ultimately, at the heart of the cosmos. "Looking into the heart of the glacier is like looking into him [Muldrow], because he has that, just a heart of ice,"[13] Dickey said.

In addition, Muldrow shares Dickey's passion for knives; he considers the flash off a blade his signature "mark." He adores them because they are primitive, and, like Dickey, rejects guns (even though he was a tail gunner) because they are too modern and frightening. Admiring certain animals for their totemic properties, Muldrow, like Dickey, is no expert naturalist. He confesses: "I didn't know which birds and animals were there, or even what some of the trees were."[14] Speaking for Dickey, Ed says the same thing in *Deliverance*. Muldrow's father, like Dickey's, knows more about the wilderness. Dickey situated Muldrow's father in the lonely wastes of the Alaskan tundra, he admitted, "because my father was the loner of loners."[15] Muldrow says the same thing of his father in the novel: "My father had been the loner of all loners."[16] On one level *To the White Sea* is both an elegy for and exorcism of Dickey's dead father. As Dickey himself approached death, he testified to his father's blood lust and solitude while enshrining his naturalistic principles.

Like Dickey, Muldrow is vulnerable to panic when his cleverly camouflaged self is threatened with exposure. Driving through the northern city of Morioka, he fears he will be discovered by the Japanese hordes: "The only panic was mine, and I didn't have any camouflage: no hillside, no pine straw, no rocks, no bushes, no snow. It is terrible to be exposed like that." As if hoping to fly again after falling from his plane, Muldrow kills a swan, plucks its feathers for warmth, sews some of them for insulation into a makeshift snowsuit, and at the end of his journey covers himself with the feathers to both disguise himself in the snowy landscape and transcend it. Both Dickey and Muldrow are drawn to rituals, whether profane or sacred, that empty consciousness and create a feeling of inspired invisibility. On meeting an American Zen Buddhist from Saint Louis, Muldrow mocks the organized rituals of the monks (in the end they betray him), but also sympathizes with their contemplative exercises designed to "understand the secret of the void . . . , the place of the spirit. . . . Pure emptiness. Nothing. Nothingness." He searches for and ultimately finds such a spiritual void on Hokkaido.

As Muldrow gazes at the sea that is the last barrier to his final destination, he talks to himself as Dickey undoubtedly did: "I told my self not to fake it, not to make things up. I want so much for the land to be there that it was almost like I was trying to think it into the real world, whether it wanted to come or not:

land, a whole island where the real snow was, the real space." Hokkaido is a place, he says, where "no concealment, no notion of hiding, no stalking, no camouflage"[17] exists. The "death" there is both literal and figurative. As in the poetry of Yeats and Stevens, the "death" initiates a kind of apocalyptic cleansing of all human artifice followed by a union with reality. As in Eliot's poetry, the "death" makes possible a resurrection into a spirit world of imagined voices. In this case, Muldrow's spirit speaks with Dickey's voice about the way things are on their most fundamental level. Contradictorily, Dickey also suggests that Muldrow in this white void or "zero condition" attains the perfect camouflage. Simply by closing his eyes, he "dies" into the landscape and becomes a genius loci. Dickey elaborated on this point in an interview: "If you find the perfect one [i.e., the perfect disguise], you cease to be but you become where you are, you become the place. So, covered with his own blood and swan feathers, he walks out there where the posse's shooting at him. He's got the perfect [camouflage]. At last he's got it, and he becomes the landscape of cold and desolation and wind and snow that he loves so much."[18] He becomes an incarnation of body and spirit, ground and air.

Muldrow's end, in its language and themes, is laden with poetic and religious significance. The old hermit-falconer Muldrow lives with on the island seems to have migrated there from a poem by Yeats. Yeats would have admired at least some aspects of the warrior-aesthetic espoused by Muldrow and the falconer. If Muldrow does not exactly "perne in a gyre" like a Yeatsean falcon when he dies, he certainly identifies with that other favorite Yeatsean bird: the swan. His blood sacrifice, in which he covers himself with swan feathers, and his execution by the posse deliver him into a timeless moment at the "cycle's center," as Dickey called it in "The Heaven of Animals." His voice, Heidegger might say, is now the voice of being.

The passage where Muldrow metamorphoses into a genius loci is one of the most evocative in the book. It is prose poetry of a high order. In death Muldrow ascends to no bucolic otherworld of angelic shepherds and green pastures, as he might in a traditional elegy. On the contrary, he represents reality in all its splendor and brutality. He says, almost posthumously: "I knew I had it. I was in it, and part of it. I matched it all. And I will be everywhere in it from now on. You will be able to hear me, just like you're hearing me now. Everywhere in it, for the first time and the last, as soon as I close my eyes." "It" refers to the elemental world, but "it" also refers to Dickey's book, his voice as an author, and the voice of the character he created. Muldrow advises us as Walt Whitman once did in Song of Myself. If we want to find him, we must look under our boot soles or in the air over our heads. If we listen to the physical world, according to Dickey, we will hear Muldrow's tale told by predators and prey, "full of sound and fury," signifying everything.

Muldrow's final statements summarize a vision of the world that Dickey began to articulate in his first book, Into the Stone. Muldrow alludes to the book as he tries to elucidate his vision: "It was being able to see into the snowbank, into the stone. To see beyond what any human, any man who has ever been born, could see. Like I tell you, out of the snowdrift, into the snowdrift, into the stone."[19] As he dies, he attains the sort of superhuman consciousness that Yeats associated with the full moon. Yeats's poem "Meru," which Dickey knew well, may have provided some of the impetus behind Muldrow's withdrawal from the lies and illusions of conventional civilization, his destructive trek toward a cold, desolate reality, his association with the hermit, and his final recognition of natural cycles:

> Civilization is hooped together, brought
> Under a rule, under the semblance of peace
> By manifold illusion; but man's life is thought,
> And he, despite his terror, cannot cease
> Ravening through century after century,
> Ravening, raging, and uprooting that he may come
> Into the desolation of reality:
> Egypt and Greece, good-bye, and good-bye, Rome!
> Hermits upon Mount Meru or Everest,
> Caverned in night under the drifted snow,
> Or where that snow and winter's dreadful blast
> Beat down upon their naked bodies, know
> That day brings round the night, that before dawn
> His glory and his monuments are gone.

Muldrow would have put it more simply, but he would assuredly agree with Yeats's vision of ravening and uprooting.

When a *Newsweek* photographer came to Lelia's Court to take pictures for a review of *To the White Sea*, as soon as Dickey and his guest walked into the yard they disturbed an underground yellow jacket's nest. The angry bees "came boiling up out of the ground and darkened the sky,"[20] Dickey recalled. In the August 30 *Newsweek*, uncowed by his recent bee stings, Dickey looked suitably Muldrow-like. On his porch overlooking Lake Katherine, he posed in camouflage gear, his smiling face partly eclipsed by a huge survival knife. The *Newsweek* review was one of the most laudatory. Malcolm Jones praised the novel as a first-rate adventure story as "relentless and mesmerizing as *Deliverance*."[21] Other reviewers were enthralled by Muldrow's escapades, but many found the main character chilling, inhuman, and even uninteresting. In the *New York Times*, Christopher Lehman-Haupt faulted the novel's lack of dramatic tension: "What stimulated much of the moral horror of *Deliverance* was that the canoeists were not only forced against their will to commit a murder but also put in the position of having to conceal their crime. But Muldrow kills so mechanically that his acts lack any moral resonance. Mr. Dickey's Japan is an alien world almost reminiscent of a World War II Hollywood movie, where subhuman yellow people chatter and swarm like so much vermin."[22] Jonathan Yardley wrote in the *Washington Post*: "Since the wayfarer is in all respects unengaging . . . one is hard pressed to say anything more urgent than, 'Who cares?'"[23] Others, like Thomas Mallon in *GQ*, were disgusted by the "farrago of pomposity and gore. Muldrow speaks in grunting, know-it-all pronouncements . . . that soon have a reader crying 'Papa *mia!*' and the plot is a veritable slayfest of knifing, shooting and decapitation. . . . The book remains a revolting performance from which most readers will eventually beg deliverance."[24] In almost all the negative reviews, the critics used *Deliverance* as a club with which to beat *To the White Sea*.

In a way the harsh reviews amounted to a judgment on Dickey's entire career, since the novel was a coda that drew together themes and even individual lines from his previous poems and novels. Brad Leithauser in the *New Yorker* called *To the White Sea* "a kind of rucksack stuffed with images and activities that have preoccupied him since the start of his poetry career, a third of a century ago. Once again, here are rivers, drainpipes, caribou, parachutes, pine trees, woodsmoke, cat's cradles, the glinting of knives, naked women seen through windows, bows and arrows, the belt of Orion."[25] These wide-ranging attacks were especially difficult for Dickey to repel, although in candid moments he echoed some of his critics' reservations. One such moment came while reading a portion of the novel to Bernie Dunlap in 1993 before Dunlap left USC for Wofford College. In a burst of fellow feeling, Dunlap assured Dickey that the novel would have the same critical success as *Deliverance*. Dickey gave him a quizzical look that betrayed his doubts. Dunlap also had doubts as soon as he read the book in its entirety.

When a writer for *People* magazine, Bill Shaw, visited Columbia near the end of 1993, Dickey seemed oblivious to the bad reviews. He was in high spirits as he showed his guest his arsenal of twenty bows, hundreds of arrows, dozens of knives, six guitars, numerous sextants, and, according to Dickey's count, thirty-five thousand books (actually, about eighteen thousand). Although he assured Shaw that he had never killed a deer during his forty years of hunting, he played up his Muldrow persona by affirming that he "flew more than a hundred B-29 bombing missions in World War II, dropping gasoline and napalm on the Japanese in the South Pacific [and] . . . more bombs in the Korean War."[26] Dickey almost never claimed he had flown B-29s, but with Shaw he grafted his previous fantasies as a pilot onto the B-29 firebombings in *To the White Sea*.

To the White Sea failed to meet Houghton Mifflin's high expectations in the U.S. market. German, French, and Japanese publishers, however, paid handsome advances and garnered healthy sales. Dell paid a substantial fee for paperback rights, and Universal Studios proceeded with their plan to make a film from the novel. On June 11, 1992, they had signed an option. David Peoples, who had written the screenplays for *Unforgiven* and *Blade Runner* and who was starting to work with his wife, Janet, had agreed to compose the script. Euphoric about Universal's offer, as usual Dickey inflated it. While his older friends had heard him say he had sold the rights for $8 million, he told Gordon Van Ness that he had refused the $8 million offer because his agent believed he could get even more. Universal actually had offered Dickey $500,000. He must have received $100,000 after signing the agreement because Universal soon signed an extension on the option that provided an additional $100,000 (they promised to pay Dickey the remaining $400,000 if the film was made between May 28, 1996, and December 9, 1997). A year after Universal made its original offer, Dickey was the beneficiary of another financial windfall. On June 13, 1992, Emory University confirmed its purchase of Dickey's papers for a sum in excess of $100,000. Linda Matthews, head of Emory Special Collections, and Steve

Ennis, who was in charge of cataloging the archive, had worked hard to finalize the deal. In addition to the large sums from Hollywood, Emory, and foreign publishers, Dickey earned $5,000 from an Audio Publication contract to tape-record *To the White Sea*, $9,000 from *Architectural Digest* to write an article on Shinto models (he delivered the article on January 19, 1994), and substantial fees from several readings. Once again his coffers brimmed.

Neither lucrative contracts nor a handful of good reviews, however, could resurrect Dickey's literary reputation to its former grandeur. The poet and critic R. S. Gwynn gave a disheartening account of Dickey's career in a 1994 *Sewanee Review* article, the details of which seemed incontrovertible: "Twenty-five years ago Hyatt Waggoner, in *American Poets: From the Puritans to the Present*, listed Dickey . . . as one of the key postmodernist poets. By the time of David Perkins's two-volume *A History of Modern Poetry* (1976, 1987) discussion of Dickey's work had shrunk to two brief paragraphs. Most recently Dickey merits a grand total of four sentences in the 894 pages of the new *Columbia History of American Poetry* (and that is only for the ecological 'correctness' of one poem, 'For the Last Wolverine'), and he is not mentioned in the *Columbia Literary History of the United States* (1988). In the late sixties and early seventies, Dickey would have been included in the reading list of virtually any course in contemporary poetry; but, after the appearance of *Deliverance* and Dickey's acting debut in the film version, his stock began to decline. Today the mere mention of his name summons up sniffy dismissals." Gwynn contended that Dickey's critical misfortunes were due to two decades of sloppy writing: "If a poet does not publish any work of unquestioned merit in a whole quarter of a century, no amount of spin control can save his reputation from a downward spiral."[27] Others, like Ernest Suarez, blamed Dickey's spiral on his political foes.

In 1993, perhaps because of the publication of Suarez's *James Dickey and the Politics of Canon*, Dickey decided to resuscitate his dormant feud with Robert Bly. Dickey villified Bly and Bly's pet cause, the men's movement, which might otherwise have aroused his sympathy, in the *Atlanta Journal-Constitution*: "Bly is the funniest and most pathetic thing I ever heard of. He has these poor fat businessmen hopping around on one foot doing the dance of the primitive heron, and then they go out beating tom-toms and he has them wearing loincloths. Can you imagine anything more foolish and self-conscious? He lectures and reads in some long costume made in the Peruvian Andes. I don't know what it is, but I say this: If you can write poetry, you don't have to dress funny—and he can't write. He's never written a memorable line in his life. It's pathetic, someone like him spending his whole life on something he doesn't have any aptitude for."[28] Dickey, of course, loved to dress up in exotic garb; identified with totemic birds and animals; and wrote about "fat businessmen" going off into the woods to discover their inner savagery. Despite their affinities, and perhaps because of them, Dickey's horns remained locked with Bly's.

In mid-October at the Southeastern Booksellers Association convention in downtown Atlanta, Dickey had another chance to brandish his horns at Blyish enemies who were partly responsible for his declining reputation. Drinking double vodka martinis with Willie Morris in the Hyatt Regency, he talked about the South, especially the Civil War. If a few battles had turned out differently, he averred wistfully, America would have become a different place. To show where his sympathies lay, he displayed his Confederate Army–issue CSA (Confederate States of America) belt buckle that his brother had unearthed at Antietam. He bemoaned the dilemma of being sandwiched between Southern rednecks who ridiculed literature and Northern liberals who ridiculed Southerners, declaring that, like Muldrow, he wanted "to get in there and fight because that is what I was bred to do." His friend Joyce Pair chided him: "Robert Bly was right; you love killing." Dickey gloated: "That's the God damned truth."[29] Safely out of range of his accusers, Dickey continued to play the enfant terrible.

Dickey temporarily forgot his detractors on September 17, 1993, when USC launched a three-day tribute to Dickey's career. The university had much to celebrate: Dickey's seventieth year, his quarter century of teaching at the university, and his publication that month of To the White Sea. USC announced that Dickey would now hold the honorary title of "Distinguished Professor." According to the State, Dickey "in turn disclosed his intention to turn over all of his personal and working papers to the institution where he has taught for the past 25 years." (The State reporter knew nothing about the already completed sale of his papers to Emory.) The tributes to Dickey began with a fifty-dollar-per-person dinner and reception at the Capital City Club. As master of ceremonies, George Plimpton delivered a humorous narration of Dickey's life. Only half-aware of Dickey's inventions, Plimpton saluted his friend's World War II experiences as a pilot by noting that he "won the least deserved Purple Heart in history." Other witty toasts and roasts followed. Regarding the awards ceremony scheduled for the weekend's football game, Plimpton quipped: "Jim had planned to go out on the field at halftime, look up at the 74,000 people in the stands, and say how surprised he was to see that so many people would come out just to see a poet honored." The new USC president, John Palms, hailed the legendary Dickey as well: "The fires and light of appreciation for his passion, his intellect and his caring burn brightest with those closest to home." Surrounded by adoring fans, Dickey told a reporter: "I'm humbled by what is before me tonight. . . . I'm excited and a little astonished at all this."[30] The evening drew to a close with Dickey's reading from To the White Sea, which had become a bestseller at some of the local bookstores.

A flurry of testimonials from Dickey's colleagues graced the Columbia papers. Matthew Bruccoli called Dickey "America's most eminent man of letters." Ron Baughman asserted: "He'll be remembered as America's greatest poet. . . . He's as intellectually challenging as [T. S.] Eliot, as sophisticated as [Wallace] Stevens, as deeply involved with nature as [Robert] Frost, and more lyrical than any of them." Don Greiner boldly prophesied: "He is America's greatest living poet, and 25, 50 years from now, his poetry will be taught in universities throughout the land. . . . He's the most brilliant literary mind I've ever known."[31] Much of the hoopla was generated by Dickey's novel, Universal Studios' contract, and Dickey's statement to the press that he was already working on two more novels.

The lectures and panels began auspiciously on Saturday. Richard Howard chaired the first series of papers on Dickey's criticism and teaching; Joyce Pair and Gordon Van Ness contributed. Later that afternoon in Gambrell Hall auditorium, R. W. B. Lewis sat on a panel with Richard Calhoun and Robert

Hill to discuss Dickey's fiction. On Sunday morning Robert Kirschten moderated a roundtable assessment of Dickey's career. In the afternoon Monroe Spears chaired a panel on Dickey's poetry that included Susan Ludvigson and Elizabeth Adams. Dickey, Deborah, and Bronwen sat at the front of the Richland County Library auditorium as the seventy-seven-year-old Spears reminisced about getting to know Dickey at Vanderbilt. After he sat down, Ludvigson began her paper. Suddenly a commotion broke out in the front row.

Betty Spears, who had been sitting beside her husband, sobbed with panic and grief. Her husband had slipped from his chair and lay sprawled on the floor. He had suffered a massive heart attack. Someone rushed to call 911. Fortunately, Don Saunders, a cardiologist and director of the USC School of Medicine, was sitting several rows behind Spears. Realizing that Spears had developed a condition called ventricular fibrillation—his heart was quivering, not beating—Saunders sustained him with CPR until an ambulance arrived. By doing so, he saved Spears's life. Medical personnel tried to shock his heart back to a normal rhythm, but failed. They drove him to the Baptist Medical Center, where, after an hour and a half, doctors finally stabilized his heart.

Treating the incident as an Oedipal drama, Dickey wandered through the auditorium groaning to friends: "I've killed my teacher; I've killed my teacher."[32] The audience milled in disbelief. The symposium's remaining events—a staging of Bridgit Hanley's *May Day Sermon*, a screening of *Deliverance*, and the award ceremony planned for Saturday night's USC–Louisiana Tech football game—were postponed or cancelled. Supposed to fly to New York on September 19, then to Los Angeles, San Francisco, Seattle, and Atlanta on a promotional tour for *To the White Sea*, Dickey told the press that he would stay in Columbia to monitor Spears's condition. He waited a month before beginning his tour. On October 26, he went to Texas, and four days later to the West Coast Florida Book Fair in Sarasota. He also attended the Miami Book Fair and Eckerd College in Saint Petersburg. In New York at an American Academy of Arts and Letters meeting, he spoke with fiction writer Janet Peery about developments in the filming of *To the White Sea*. (There to receive an award for her book of short stories, *Alligator Dance*, she sat between Updike and Dickey.) He gave her a cagey look when he revealed that Brad Pitt would be the star. She thought he was joking. "Oh really, that's wonderful," she replied. Suddenly realizing that Peery didn't know who he was, Dickey said: "I'm glad to introduce myself. I'm Burt Reynolds. I was in one of those James Dickey movies."[33] They both laughed and continued to talk merrily.

In January 1994, spectators at the world's most famous sporting event—the Super Bowl—must have been surprised to find a poem by James Dickey in their programs. Many probably didn't recognize the name, or, if they did, they undoubtedly linked it—as Dickey did for Peery—with Burt Reynolds and *Deliverance*. Several months before the game, an NFL representative had offered Dickey three thousand dollars to compose a poem about returning a punted football. In his letter to Phil Barber, who had commissioned the poem, Dickey explained that in "Breaking the Field" he wanted "to give the essential fluidity and anarchy of the punt-return situation, as opposed to the rigidity, the straight-line formulations of the scrimmage, the rehearsed formations, and so on."

Dickey also wanted to make the punt returner a spokesman for his own agony on and off the literary playing field. Catching the ball and surveying the clashing bodies, Dickey's alter ego sees "Not many friends / But the right ones." What is important, he decides, is the little "green daylight . . . beyond friends and enemies."[34] In letters to actual friends, Dickey frequently asked them to be "blockers" for his literary runs. In his Super Bowl poem he addressed them similarly.

After taking Deborah and Bronwen on a trip to Rome, from February 13 to 20, where he had waxed nostalgic among the ruined grandeurs of the past and acted as a tour guide for his family, Dickey reunited with one of his former "blockers" at USC. On March 22, in an introduction to a reading by Henry Taylor, he reminisced about their long friendship: "I first met Henry Taylor when he was an undergraduate at the University of Virginia many years ago. I gave something called the Peter Rushton Seminars on Hart Crane, and I noticed this boy in a raccoon coat. I remember that struck me as strange. And I thought, 'Now, this guy is either gonna yield somethin, or he's gonna yield nothin. It's all in the raccoon coat.' And it happened that enwrapped in the raccoon coat was Henry Taylor. . . . He has justified my hopes for him a thousand times over." Dickey mentioned Taylor flying an airplane to the Washington airport in the late 1960s to take him to a reading in Virginia: "I thought my goodness, look here. Here a poet gets an airplane to take another poet to a reading himself. And so I did the reading, and I never have known from that day to this how Henry Taylor managed to commandeer an airplane for a poetry reading." Dickey concluded with jokes about horses: "I've always been scared to death of them; they're too damn big for me, but anyway, Henry understands 'em . . . [and tonight] Henry comes to us on the winged steed Pegasus. . . . Now I own the back part of the horse. I own the back part, or some would say, *am*. Now, the front part of the horse, the part that has the wings, belongs to Henry."[35] Taylor, in fact, never owned a raccoon coat and never commandeered a plane; Dickey was probably thinking of the small plane he took to a reading Taylor organized at Roanoke College in 1967. The drunken introduction was complimentary, but in more sober moods Dickey treated Taylor as a poetic son who, like Dave Smith, had become a rival. (Taylor had won a Pulitzer Prize in 1985 for *The Flying Change*.) Discussing possible poets to fill his position after he retired or died, Dickey explicitly disapproved of Taylor's candidacy.

Dickey had other small duties in the spring. From May 11–13 he served in a Virginia Center for the Book Writing Life Residency in Richmond. Since his life over the past decade had resembled one of Edgar Allan Poe's gothic tales, in between readings and book signings he took ghoulish pleasure in sitting for his picture at the local Poe museum, where he hunched over a desk with a stuffed raven on his shoulder, pretending to compose a poem. On May 14, he visited Appalachian State University in Boone, North Carolina, to pick up yet another honorary degree. In a letter to Chancellor Francis Borkowski on October 1, 1993, he said that the degree would be his fifteenth, but because his roots were in the mountains "none would be more welcome" than the present one. Appalachian State not only offered him a degree, it asked him to give the commencement address. In his lecture, "The Eyes of the Egg," he again harked back to the Agrarians' warnings about science's devastating effects on the natural environment. He began with references to the atomic device exploded at Los Alamos and read a two-page account of the test site by John Hay. Hay focused on an old adobe Indian hut obscured by modern houses and manicured lawns, which for him—and for Dickey—represented the original, mysterious forces and elements that led to the creation of the world. Modern culture, according to their mystic view, was comparable to the atomic blast, obliterating nearly all signs of life's fundamental mystery. To Dickey the adobe hut symbolized not only an omphalos at the center of creation, but also "the subversive element: the woman." The commencement turned into a double-edged panegyric to Deborah, who for Dickey was subversive of aridity by bringing him a daughter and subversive in other ways as well. Bronwen appeared in the lecture as the thirteen-year-old girl who put on her wall a copy of "The Egg" by the French presurrealist painter Odilon Redon. For Dickey, eggs—and Deborah and Bronwen who carried them—were fertility symbols in the modern wasteland.

During the summer, Deborah, who was in and out of the hospital for various treatments, contrasted sharply with her husband's portrait of her as an Indian earth mother tending the élan vital by an adobe hearth. When Chris and his wife made a rare visit to Columbia, Deborah seemed on the verge of a nervous breakdown. On a drive from Columbia to Litchfield with Bronwen and Chris's son, James ("Tucky"), Deborah sat beside Chris in his rented Lincoln Town Car, periodically clutching a Bible as she spoke fervently about her drug problems. "I just love you all so much," she kept saying to the skeptical Chris. In Litchfield, Deborah's mood shifted. Feeling embarrassed by Chris's wife, Carol, she complained that Carol was prettier and better dressed than her and apologized profusely for her looks. The others reassured her that she looked fine. According to Chris: "She wouldn't believe us, and wouldn't quit apologizing. And now she was launched on a whole flood of apologies, each of them more sensational. She was talking about her drinking and her drugs and the men she'd been with. She was starting to call herself names, and each new confession, each new apology, was a little more humiliating for my father to hear and for him to see that I was hearing." To silence her, Dickey interrupted: "You have brought murderers into our lives. . . . You have endangered my life, and Bronwen's life, and your own." Before his accusations and Deborah's apologies became more salacious, Chris suggested they all go to dinner.

On the second day Deborah's condition worsened. Returning from lunch in Charleston, Chris watched his father stagger down the steps. "Don't go up there," he said drunkenly to Chris, who wanted to talk with Deborah. "You don't want to see." That night, using his laptop computer to explore the on-line newspaper archives, Chris got a better understanding of the Poeish nightmare his father and stepmother had been living. For the first time, he learned of Deborah's 1991 cocaine arrest in Columbia. The discovery marked a turning point in their relations. As he tried to organize a visit by Bronwen to Paris over the 1994 Christmas vacation, Deborah grew increasingly volatile. "Deborah would call in the middle of the night," he recalled, "and we would hear her electronically filtered rage smoldering on the speaker of the answering machine in the next room; or she would send faxes scrawled as if the pen were held in a clenched fist, words written and scratched out, and scrawled again." She accused Chris of persecuting her. Why wouldn't he leave her and her family in peace? As her fury grew more murderous, she told his father's secretary and maid that she would take out a contract to have Chris killed.[36]

When fellow Vanderbilt alumnus Jane Pepperdine asked Dickey to read at the Paideia School in Georgia, she also got a glimpse of Dickey's marital travail. At the airport, he seemed to be a man struggling to maintain decorum. Fashionably dressed in a suit, he joked: "I look just like a banker." Unlike most bankers, he soon divulged the gruesome facts of his wife's heroin addiction. Consuming martinis, beer, and wine, he told Pepperdine how wonderful it was just to sit down at a table for a meal. Deborah was incapable of fixing him meals. Eating almost nothing at dinner, Dickey drank and stayed up most of the night telling hilarious stories to Ron Schuchard and Sally Fitzgerald. With the seven hundred young students, whose questions he welcomed in a discussion at the Paideia School, he was similarly boisterous and endearing.[37]

Late in July 1994, Dickey left Deborah behind for a week-long conference in London on "The American South." Christina Patterson had asked him to participate in the affair, which included plays, art exhibitions, jazz and Cajun concerts, and readings. After haggling over fees, on July 23 Dickey discussed literature with Dave Smith before an audience at the Voice Box in London's South Bank Centre. That night he joined Smith and Ellen Bryant Voight for a poetry reading. In between the scheduled events—the National Film Theater screening of *Deliverance* on July 25, the American embassy party on July 27—Dickey amazed Smith by chasing after punk women and discomfited Voight by making risqué remarks about Christina Patterson. Seeing Dickey in the Grafton Hotel bar drinking while the other writers proceeded to breakfast, Reynolds Price asked: "Why don't you come to breakfast?" Dickey responded: "This is my breakfast."[38] An acquaintance heard that when Dickey was told he would feel better if he stopped drinking, he offered the quick rejoinder: "My doctor told me to drink lots of fluids."[39] Reynolds noticed that the alcohol had little effect on him; he remained clearheaded and friendly. His fluid diet, however, would soon have devastating consequences.

41. The Heart of the World (1994–1997)

As Dickey explained to his friend Robert Kirschten, "the hammer fell" in late October 1994. Apart from Chris, who had noticed his father's red, swollen ankles during the summer, few people suspected that Dickey was really sick. Even Ben Franklin and Don Greiner had little inkling of his deteriorating health. The shock came one warm afternoon as the two men sat in the garden section of the USC Faculty House, waiting for Dickey to arrive for lunch. It was getting late—almost twelve-thirty—but they were confident Dickey would appear. He was often late, and if he had to postpone, he always notified them. Suddenly they saw Dickey hobbling across the Horseshoe. Franklin waved his handkerchief, thinking his friend was drunk. Dickey nodded. It took him about five minutes to walk to the garden area by the fountain; he grasped the tables to negotiate the last few yards. On the step by his friends' table, he looked up and plaintively said: "Help me." According to Greiner: "He was yellow to the point his eyeballs were yellow. The sweat was just pouring off [him] . . . in large drops." Even for the ninety-degree day, the sweat saturating his shirt and hat was inordinate. His friends stared in fear and astonishment.

Realizing Dickey needed immediate medical help, Greiner suggested driving him to the student health center. Dickey refused to hear of it. "No, no," he said. "This university is paying me to teach and I'm going to teach."[1] Greiner offered to take him to the hospital rather than the health center; Dickey again refused. Franklin insisted that they call Dickey's doctor. The answer was the same. When the waitress came to the table, Dickey ordered a double martini. Then he ordered another one. At about one-thirty, Dickey announced he was going to teach his class. Franklin and Greiner helped him out of the Faculty House and drove him to the Humanities Complex, where he taught, and Franklin wrote the number of his own classroom on the board, instructing the students to contact him in the event of a crisis. Franklin went to his class, and Greiner returned to the provost's office. In about an hour, they heard that Deborah had tracked down her husband and taken him to Richland Hospital.

On October 25, the day Dickey entered the hospital, Deborah told reporters that her husband was suffering from "pancreatic problems." Deborah spoke more truthfully when she said: "He is in serious condition. He's fighting, he's doing the best he can. He is clear-minded except for the sedation they have to give him, but his mind is very much intact."[2] She asked for friends to send prayers and notes. In fact, Dickey's liver had finally stopped functioning after years of alcohol abuse. He had a severe case of hepatitis, which had inflamed his liver and destroyed its ability to metabolize bile. The bile had flooded his bloodstream, causing jaundice. His colleague Keen Butterworth was shocked by Dickey's appearance in the hospital: "He looked so bad—so emaciated and frail—I thought he'd be in the coffin in a month. He did too."[3] Matthew Bruccoli, who never knew whether Dickey was conscious or unconscious during his visits, considered his friend's prospects dire as well, especially after nurses declared: "Your friend is not going to leave here."[4] Deborah's sister, Elaine, came from another hospital where she worked as a nurse, and made Dickey as comfortable as possible. Within ten days Dickey had recovered sufficiently to go home. By November 14, however, he had suffered a relapse and had to be readmitted. Doctors spent another five days treating his hepatitis.

Deborah tried to help her husband as best she could. In her desperate messages to Chris and Kevin, she claimed that nobody could be trusted at the hospital. Dickey had fallen down, banged his head, and bled profusely, and nobody had helped him. She had tended to his wounds herself. A nurse had made a bloody mess with a needle (Deborah supposedly kept the needle and hid it as evidence for a possible lawsuit). Others realized that Deborah was now acting as her husband's watchdog. Carolee Guilds asked the hospital staff about visiting Dickey and learned that she first had to get Deborah's permission. She never visited. Ward Briggs, who went to see Dickey every other day, noticed not only Dickey's deterioration, but Deborah's frenzy. She grew increasingly agitated, which he attributed to the high dose of methadone she was taking to cure her heroin habit. On one occasion she insulted the staff by calling them "stupid nig-gers" and got into a fight with her husband's doctor.[4.1] Despite all the turmoil, Dickey's condition improved. Bruccoli, who had once joked that he wanted to send Dickey's liver to the Harvard Medical School for examination as a natural wonder, was as awed as the doctors by Dickey's fortitude. Dickey soon an-nounced his plans to resume teaching.

Because of the troubles surrounding his first visits to Richland Hospital, when Dickey suffered another setback, he checked into Providence Hospital on November 28. At home, Deborah was unfit to properly care for her sick hus-band. She had no medical training, and her craving for drugs was such that, according to a friend, she absconded with some of her husband's medica-tion.[5] Dickey relied more and more on his African-American maid, Mayrie MacLamore, who had cooked and cleaned for him since 1987. She visited him in the hospital religiously. At home, she administered his medicines—Duphalac, Colace, Prilosec—and badgered him into eating his vanilla pudding and drinking his Ensure. Fiercely loyal to her boss, she lightened his mood with friendly banter. Regaining enough strength to play the guitar, he obsessively sang "The Cacklin' Head." "Oh, you don't like my Blues," he would say, and Mayrie would reply with mock irritation: "Sing whatever you want to sing." He kept singing, and she kept needling.

Now that Dickey was sedentary much of the time, MacLamore became the target of his pranks. One night when she came to help him, he sat slumped in his stuffed armchair, eyes closed like a corpse. She exclaimed: "Oh Lord, please don't let this happen to me. Not now!" He suddenly opened his eyes: "Well, Mayrie. Do you understand? I just died on you." She retorted: "Listen Dickey, stop it." Sometimes he would quiz her about her private life. An undaunted pro-ponent of marriage, he asked her: "Will you ever marry?" "If I marry, I can't work for you," she responded. Dickey concluded that she'd better not marry; he needed her desperately to stay alive. She worked seven days and seven nights at the Dickey house. "It didn't pay well," she acknowledged. "I just enjoyed the work." During his last years he often spoke to MacLamore, a devout Christian, about God, death, and his mother's religious devotion. She counseled: "You aren't going until the good Lord is ready for you." About God, she quipped: "So you finally learned him." Dickey said: "That's the man who woke me up." She said: "Don't you know it."[6] His frail health having relegated him to childlike de-pendence, he treated her as surrogate mother, nurse, and playmate.

Dickey shared his friends' awe at his power to resurrect himself. Nevertheless, the hepatitis had numerous side effects, as he readily admitted: "It just depletes your system so much, it takes you years to recover from it. The main thing it did to me was take all the calcium out of my system, or almost all of it. I had enor-mous dental bills. It cost me ten thousand dollars to keep my teeth in my head. I lost fifty pounds in a week [actually, Dickey's weight plummeted from 230 to 160 pounds]. I wasn't supposed to live. I was supposed to die. In fact, I did die at Richland County Hospital, twice. I flat-lined on the monitor, watching the monitor with the doctor. The second time I went under, the last I heard was the doctor say, 'We've lost him.'" Dying, Dickey said philosophically, was like relax-ing: "It's not at all frightening. You have a sense of relief. . . . Everything just sort of goes, and that's it."[7] Dickey was finally sober and determined to set his affairs in order. The first sign of his resolve was his new attitude toward Deborah. Up to the end of 1994, according to Chris: "The scene at home was violent. It was dangerous. It was insane. It was a scene of constant, frightening abuse. . . . Dad would call up and he would literally sound like a man with a gun at his head."[8] Following his hospitalization, Dickey spoke with a new confidence and lucidity. Chris asked about Bronwen coming to Paris. Dickey responded: "She's going." Chris was incredulous. "But Debbie—" "You just let me take care of that,"[9] his father replied. Bronwen, indeed, visited her stepbrother in Paris before Christmas 1994.

Now that his father seemed willing to take command of his life, Chris decided to intervene more actively on his behalf. He reflected: "The cycle of destruction between Debbie and my father was much more extreme, but not so much different in nature from the cycle of destruction that existed between my mother and my father, and I had always thought that if I can get my mother away from my father that it would be better for both of them."[10] Chris spent the Christmas holiday with his in-laws in Florida, then drove to Columbia with his wife, Carol, to speak to his father about separating from Deborah and sending Bronwen to prep school. What awaited was both sad and frightening. No doubt guessing Chris's intentions, Deborah glowered at the door like Cerberus at hell's gate and shrieked obscenities and paranoid accusations: "You almost killed your father, you son of a bitch, and that bitch wife of yours. . . . Your father wanted to be sitting in a chair when you came, and he waited up and waited up, and then he fell down when I was trying to get him back to bed. You almost killed him. . . . You are not coming in this house." The drive from Florida had taken an hour longer than expected. Chris pushed past Deborah to talk with his father. From that point on Chris was as committed as his father to rectifying the dismal situation at Lelia's Court. He got his father to say on tape that he wanted his daughter to go to prep school and that he wanted to live in an environment more conducive to his recuperation: "It's hard to get well being ripped and torn to pieces emotionally all the time. And to have to fight off your wife because your son is coming to visit you, who you haven't seen in thirteen years or thereabouts. It's not right." He warned Chris to guard the tape. "Don't let Deborah get hold of it. It would be worth my life. And she would actually kill me. She's not above it."[11] Dickey was genuinely scared.

Before the taping session was over, Deborah, who had been on an errand, entered the house and, suspecting that Chris and Bronwen were conspiring against her, ordered Chris to leave. He refused, and she unleashed another diatribe. Chris got as close to her face as he could and told her no one was going to listen to her or obey her any longer. Fearing Chris would strike her, she broke down and cried on his shoulder. In his attempt to bring order to his father's house, Chris looked into having Deborah institutionalized. A lawyer counseled against it. If Deborah were put away, the state might take custody of Bronwen. For her part, Deborah redoubled her efforts to drive Chris away from his father. When Chris, with the help of his brother, Kevin, and Matthew Bruccoli, made plans to transport Dickey to a liver specialist in Charleston, Deborah did what she could to foil them.

Bruccoli worked hard to convince Dickey to keep the Charleston appointment. At first Dickey refused to make the trip by car, so Bruccoli contracted the USC plane. Dickey changed his mind; he wanted to be driven in a private ambulance. Bruccoli dutifully requisitioned an ambulance. Then Dickey returned to the original plan of driving in a car. Ever loyal, Bruccoli agreed to be the escort, but when he arrived at the Dickeys' house, plans had to be altered once again because Deborah now insisted on coming. After much procrastination, they left Columbia an hour late and had to drive over the speed limit the whole way to Charleston. Chris, who had been staying in a local hotel, took charge at the hospital, helping his father urinate and undress for his examination. He was horrified by his father's skeletal physique and the liquid in his abdomen that rippled when the doctor tapped his skin. The doctor was guardedly optimistic. He believed he could keep Dickey alive if he totally renounced alcohol. One drink could kill him, he said, and if he survived, the doctor would have nothing further to do with him. The doctor ordered him to join Alcoholics Anonymous. Refusing to do so meant he would be ineligible for the liver transplant that his friends and family hoped he could get. Dickey promised, with Deborah's help, to join AA.

As Dickey got better, rumors began to swirl about the severity of his and Deborah's recent crises. A writer for *Atlanta* magazine reported: "Because his liver is diseased, the rest of his body has begun to fail. His heart is weak. His feet have open sores, his arms and ankles are scaly. Large purple sores cover his skin. He has lost more than 50 pounds."[12] Dickey's friends rallied around him, but it was not always easy. When Dickey invited Don Greiner and Ben Franklin to his house during the first week of January 1995, Deborah confronted them at the door. Fearing that Dickey might die while he was in Helsinki for the winter and spring terms, Franklin wanted to at least say good-bye. Her husband was sleeping, Deborah said. Finally Dickey heard his friends over the din of the television in the back room and told them to come see him.[13] Deborah's hostility toward outsiders, on one level, was understandable; she wanted to protect her ailing husband from stress. And because friends and family wanted Dickey to drive her from the house, she wanted to do the same to them.

Paula Goff also became one of Deborah's targets. As before, Deborah used the occasion of her husband's illness to curtail Goff's secretarial duties. She forced Goff to move out of the house to Dickey's USC office the day he got ill— October 25, 1994—and made the banishment more complete by calling her at USC and threatening to come to the English Department with a knife to chase her from the building. Goff decided to quit that day.[14] Although Goff remained devoted to Dickey, she did not need any more distress in her life. In 1993, she had moved into a trailer park in West Columbia. Because of several heart attacks and seizures, she was forced to accept disability compensation. She later admitted that she would have been much happier if she had never met James Dickey.

By mid-January 1995, Dickey was well enough to teach one class of ten students in his home. They gathered in the glassed-in porch that had been added onto the house several years before. One of Dickey's former students, David Miller, taught his other class on campus. Deborah told reporters that her husband was making good progress: "He is slowly but very, very surely returning to good health. He is walking and exercising every day. . . . He is spiritually advanced and has embraced a spiritual way of life more so than he has done before. . . . He is very grateful for the fact that (although) things were very bleak for a while, they turned out very well."[15] To close friends Dickey elaborated on his "spiritual" advancement. In his struggle with hepatitis, he told Al Braselton that he had remembered a film by the Nazi propagandist Leni Riefenstahl, called *Triumph of the Will*. He jokingly said that he had triumphed in a similar way by mustering all his spiritual reserves and willing death away as it rose to clutch him. Knowing his father's repugnance for AA and similar counseling programs, Chris was surprised in March to see his father hold up a red plastic key tag carrying the AA motto "90 Days Clean and Serene." In the Charleston doctor's office, the doctor complimented his father for disavowing alcohol. Dickey affirmed that the AA sessions had been his salvation. Later, Chris asked him what it was like to stand up and confess his alcoholism to a group of fellow alcoholics. His father replied that he had made no such confession; he had gone to a few meetings with Deborah and borrowed her key tag. He mockingly repeated the doctor's words, "That was the finest thing you ever did," and added his own, "It certainly is—to put one over on you, you asshole." He told Chris: "I never did like that fella. My liver is the best thing I have got to show right now. It's a hundred percent. And I won't do a Mickey Mantle on him. Or a J.R. or whatever that guy's name is. No, we ain't gonna need that."[16] Along with his renewed liver came the renewal of his caustic irreverence.

Dickey exposed both his frailty and impishness at a World War II conference, "The Last Good War," organized by his colleagues George Geckle and Bill Fox at USC. A prominent group of writers—Joseph Heller, William Styron, Paul Fussell, Mickey Spillane, William Manchester, Mary Lee Settle, Albert Werthelm—agreed to discuss such topics as "America, Then and Now" and "Revisionist History and World War II" from April 12–14. On April 13, in the Business School auditorium, walking unsteadily and breathing heavily, Dickey all but exhausted himself as he read a short passage from *To the White Sea*. Styron, who spoke the same night as Dickey, recalled: "He looked like warmed-over death."[17] Dickey had enough energy, however, to talk to a *State* reporter, Michael Bonhour, about his contempt for World War II revisionists, his term at Clemson, "which at that time meant the grueling discipline of a military school plus the demands of Coach Frank Howard," and about all the friends he had lost as a night fighter pilot. Bonhour said of Dickey and his peers: "Some worry that the truth will be inalterably twisted once the generation that fought the war is gone."[18] Dickey relished the twisting even while pretending to renounce it.

The return of Dickey's mischievous antics got him into trouble with a student during the spring. In one of his classes, he made an offensive remark to a woman who subsequently filed a complaint. Having grown up in an era before accusations of sexual harassment became commonplace, Dickey found it extraordinary that she should complain to the chair of the English Department. He had made hundreds of such remarks in the past. And what could he possibly do, being impotent and virtually sedentary? The student, however, was so incensed by the comment that she dropped the class and insisted that her name be permanently expunged from the class roll. The chair, having consulted with the dean, informed Dickey that after the spring term he could no longer teach students in his house. Despite his illness, he would have to make the arduous trek to a campus classroom. The change in venue seemed innocuous enough, but as Dickey's health worsened, the journey became life-threatening. Dickey had other troubles at home as well. In a phone conversation with Al Braselton, he lamented Deborah's relapse into cocaine addiction in March. Doctors encouraged her to return to her rehabilitation program, but Dickey said she had refused.

Dickey regularly made light of his deteriorating condition with reporters, who were not always aware he was joking. Interviewed by Robert Morris, a haggard Dickey pretended to endorse drug-induced suicide: "For Dickey, the best thing about surviving his latest death struggle seems to be his getting another shot at orchestrating his own demise. He contemplates a Kevorkian-styled LSD trip. Although he says he has never taken the hallucinogen [in the 1960s he *had* admitted to taking LSD], he figures it might be a good way to go." He told Morris: "I would rather die feeling I was mixing with the universe than die caught like a rat in a trap."[19] By May 1995, his drug schemes notwithstanding, Dickey had managed to renounce his drug of choice—alcohol—permanently. He also told friends that Deborah, having gone "cold turkey," was finally free of heroin and cocaine.

As spring turned to summer, the Dickeys entertained better prospects. Accepted by all the prestigious New England prep schools to which she applied, Bronwen flew back to Paris for a vacation with Chris before preparing to go to Choate. Dickey made progress with his writing—he was working on a sequel for *Alnilam* and new poems—and also made plans to take a vacation with Chris, not in Europe but in Africa. After two decades of frustrating, intermittent communication, he and Chris were reestablishing rapport. Dickey acknowledged how destructive alcohol had been to himself, his family, and everyone associated with him. In July, he told a writer for *Reckon* magazine that, while alcohol had enhanced his confidence for years: "I am forever off drinking. *God could not get me to drink, Him and Jesus combined. That's over.*" Dickey decried his lack of judgment in the past and advised his interviewer: "You ought to quit, too. Don't let it do to you what it did to me." He steadily gained strength.

During his convalescence, Dickey spent most of his time reclined in a corduroy armchair in his living room, a wide-screen Mitsubishi television showing old movies to his right, and a three-foot wall of books stacked for easy access around his chair. "I must have read over three hundred books in four or five languages," he told the writer for *Reckon*. About his new novel, *Crux*, he was convinced "it should work out very well."[20] In the summer of 1995, he was also cheered by a project initiated by Catherine Fry, the new director of the University of South Carolina Press. Fry had met Dickey in the early 1980s as an employee of LSU Press, and had been a long-standing admirer. Out of a desire to honor his career, she developed an idea for a James Dickey poetry series but was unsure how he would respond. Would he be willing and well enough to edit it? Several months after her March 1995 arrival in Columbia, Matthew Bruccoli arranged a lunch at McGrady's restaurant so that Fry could speak to Dickey about the series. Dickey embraced her proposal wholeheartedly.

Fry set about raising funds and finding an editor for the four poetry books she planned to publish each year. The current Academy of American Poets director, William Wadsworth, helped in both areas. He suggested a number of editors and also an academy grant. Fry convinced Richard Howard to serve as series editor and garnered the academy's Eric Matthew King grant, which promised nine thousand dollars per year. Dickey signed an agreement on December 13, 1995, to allow the series to begin in the spring of 1996. In the meantime, he got involved with Fry in other ways. He called her daily to talk about books, Deborah, his illness, and whatever else was on his mind. He urged her to publish an anthology of poems selected from the Yale Series of Younger Poets, a collection of his Yale introductions, and an anthology of the most important poems ever written in the world. He had already made the selection for the "greatest poems" anthology and come up with a title—*One for One*. Fry, however, felt the book would have few buyers.

As Dickey's affection for Fry grew, he could be peremptory in his demands to see her. He might say on the phone: "I want you to come over here right now!" or "Goddamn it, come over here!" Or he might scare her into driving to his house: "I'm going to starve because Mayrie [the maid] hasn't fed me."[21] Having flirted with her years before at LSU, he continued to do so at USC. When he began divulging his sexual fantasies, however, she told him she was not interested. Hoping she would serve as his caretaker, Dickey often proposed marriage. Since she was the same age as Deborah, Fry concluded that Dickey regarded her as Deborah's replacement, and never seriously considered it. She also realized that despite all his complaints, he still loved Deborah.

At the end of the 1995 summer, Dickey told friends that Deborah had suffered another relapse, this time on heroin.[22] With Deborah's seemingly incurable addictions and his own failing health weighing on him, on August 22, 1995, he signed his official Last Will and Testament. In it he divided his personal property among his children. He appointed Nations Bank as his personal representative and Matthew Bruccoli as his literary personal representative with "full and complete authority" over the literary portion of his estate. Kevin and Chris were to serve as Bronwen's guardians. The provisions he had made for Deborah in his past wills were eliminated. To Al Braselton, who visited in mid-September, Dickey revealed some of the reasons for cutting Deborah from his estate. He said that he had recently found her in a heroin-induced stupor, put her in the hospital, and threatened to lock her up for good in an institution. But Dickey expressed sympathy as well as antipathy. He didn't want a divorce, he told Braselton; he still loved Deborah and wanted to keep the family together.[23]

Dickey was his old gracious self with Braselton. He played his guitar, took Braselton for rides in his blue Mazda Miata, talked about the film version of *To the White Sea*, and asked Braselton to come live with him in Columbia. Braselton was heartened to find his friend responding well to his medicine, his weight back in the 190s, his color returning after the yellowing of jaundice. The criminal, the tragic, the abominable—and their healing abilities—continued to fascinate him. On the phone before Braselton's visit, Dickey talked about his and his brother's interest in Ted Bundy. As with his other friends, Dickey convinced Braselton to stay up late watching "Inside the Criminal Mind" on the Arts and Entertainment channel. His obsessions with Bundy-like killers distracted him from the pain caused by his physical and domestic ills.

Around this time, despite his inveterate opposition to divorce, Dickey tried to resolve his marital crises once and for all. He claimed that Deborah had squandered Bronwen's first year of tuition (twenty-five thousand dollars) on drugs. According to other members of the family, she had written about twenty thousand dollars in bad checks.[24] Deborah had a habit of writing bad checks at local Kroger and Piggly-Wiggly supermarkets—she would simply forge her husband's signature[25]—but to sacrifice Bronwen's education fees, which he had already complained were too high, was unconscionable. In a denunciation of his wife and her drug friends, Dickey revealed the reasons moving him toward divorce:

> Her values were all geared to . . . getting dope. Any way she could get it. . . . I kept putting her in one institution after another, and one psychiatrist after another, to keep her out of jail. They finally put her in a place here, a half-way house. . . . She busts out of that and goes down in the district and makes a deal. The guy gets mad at her and breaks all the windows out of the car. . . . She comes back and in another day she's back down in the district in a car with no windows, a black eye. [She] just wanted to get the dope. She'd go through anything to get it. I said: "The buck stops here. Can't go on this way."[26]

Dickey confronted the prospects of divorce and declining health with sardonic jokes and a determination to endure. To expel rumors of his imminent demise, he told William Starr at the *State:* "People are trying to rush to interview me before I croak. God only knows where the press gets some of its ideas. That garbage about me having liver cancer. . . . Cancer I don't have."[27] To give evidence of his vitality, he told Starr he was teaching, writing poetry and prose, and playing the guitar. In one of the prose pieces he wrote at the end of 1995, he recalled being "yellow on white, jaundiced, made motionless by an all-but destroyed liver"[28] in a hospital bed. Since Chris had sent him a photograph of the Ngorongoro Crater in Africa and proposed visiting it with him, he imagined himself as another Ed Gentry perched in an acacia tree with bow and arrows, waiting for a gazelle to come to a watering hole. The gazelle, like the hyena in Hemingway's story "The Snows of Kilimanjaro," seemed to be a harbinger of death: "The gazelle appeared, materializing from the veldt. He was moving toward me. When he put his head down to drink I would release, dead or alive."[29] Hemingway's story, which depicted a dying writer's life as a series of drunken lies and his lover as a "rich bitch . . . and destroyer of his talent,"[30] had other relevance for Dickey. He identified with its self-loathing and misogyny, and depicted Deborah similarly—as a wild animal stalking his monitor.

Dickey's greatest test of endurance came at Emory's opening of the James Dickey archive. The ceremonies, which commenced with a banquet at the Houston Mill House on October 11, were marked by snafus. After flying to Atlanta with Ward Briggs, Dickey, who had to be transported in a wheelchair, got stuck in the airport elevator. Dickey and Briggs eventually made their way to the Ritz-Carlton Hotel in Buckhead, where Kevin Dickey and Bronwen were also staying (Chris was on assignment in Bosnia). Because one of the librarians assumed Kevin would bring his father to the banquet, Dickey was left stranded at the hotel. He arrived angry and an hour late for the honorary dinner.

Dickey soon relaxed with Bronwen on his left and the president of Emory University, William Chace, on his right. Friends, family, and Emory officials paid tribute. Al Braselton opened with remarks about his long friendship with Dickey. Lewis King also contributed, as did Tom Dickey, Jr., David Bottoms, President Chace, Emory vice provost Joan Gotwals, Kevin, Brownwen, and Inman Mays. Appreciative but visibly weary, Dickey delivered a few unrehearsed remarks, beginning with his customary: "Oh my, here I am, a man of words without adequate words."[31] Steve Ennis and Joan Gotwals then presented Dickey with an award. The next day, Ennis drove Dickey from his hotel to the Woodruff Library so Dickey could talk informally with students. As he often did, he asked his audience to name the twentieth-century's top poets (he invariably put Rilke and Yeats first) and chatted about the movie version of *To the White Sea*. He seemed curious about his vast collection of papers. Confronted by his past, he desperately wanted to believe that he was still a writer brimming with virile energy. He refused a wheelchair and, gasping for breath every fifty feet, insisted on walking through the library to the car. That night, his energy nearly depleted, he read at Emory's M. C. Carlos Museum and signed books in the library's Special Collections department. As he autographed his two last novels, former advertising colleague Inman Mays talked with him about the possibility of Clint Eastwood starring in *To the White Sea*. When Mays tried to help him out of his chair, Dickey repeated a phrase he had often used in Mays's company— *noli mi tangere* (don't touch me). He wanted to stand on his own. The next day Dickey was so fatigued that he had to ask Briggs to pack his suitcases at the hotel. He could only sit on the bed and give directions.

Around the time of the archive opening, having watched Dickey stay up past midnight drinking ginger ale and telling stories at a USC party for writer Jim Barnes, Keen Butterworth wrote: "His real problem is loneliness. Debbie is in a half-way house, trying to dry out. She can't come home. And Bronwen is away at school. So at night he's there by himself. The maid and secretary come in the morning, but leave after supper."[32] Dickey craved company and grew depressed in isolation. He might tell friends that he was glad Deborah was out of the house, but in fact he missed her and welcomed her calls and visits.

As if following Emory's example, USC also honored Dickey during the fall of 1995. The university assigned *Deliverance* to all freshman classes and showed the film several times in the University theater. In early November, looking gaunt, Dickey appeared at the Kroger Center for the Arts before several hundred USC students to discuss the novel. He cautiously climbed the steps to the stage, wheezing for air. The students whistled and shouted in appreciation. Clad in his customary turtleneck and neck chain, he struggled to get enough breath to answer their questions. Did he feel justified using such upsetting scenes and foul language in *Deliverance*? He said he did. Would there be a sequel? Definitely not.

Who were the models for the novel's characters? He said he had based Lewis largely on himself, but admitted that the characters resembled old friends. He read from the novel for about fifteen minutes. To round out the tribute, Keen Butterworth and Gordon Van Ness delivered testimonial speeches.

Near the end of 1995, Dickey also composed a moving commencement address, which he delivered on December 18 to twenty-seven hundred degree candidates at the Carolina Coliseum. In "The Weather of the Valley: Reflections on the Soul and its Making," which adapted Keats's definition of life as a "vale of soul-making," Dickey reflected on his career and values: "My main commitment throughout my life has been to works of the imagination, and to the teaching of subjects related to them. I have always believed that teaching is the second greatest occupation that the human mind and energy can undertake. . . . The *most* important preoccupation . . . is learning."[33] He spoke of reading Trumbull Stickney's poems on Okinawa and how one of his lines—"his island shivered into flowers"—struck him like an epiphany. At that moment he was born as a poet and vowed to dedicate the rest of his life to the art of writing.

Stickney undoubtedly facilitated Dickey's poetic birth, but he offered other stories of that momentous occasion as well. In May of 1977, at a Walt Whitman festival in Camden, New Jersey, he told a reporter that he once brought a copy of *Leaves of Grass* on a night flight during the war, turned on the automatic pilot, and lost himself in Whitman's great poems: "I was born as a writer on that night flight. . . . I think he is my great father as a writer."[34] (Dickey never had control of the automatic pilot in a P-61 Black Widow.) In his USC commencement address, Dickey was similarly romantic in his portrait of Deborah as a Botticellian beauty, a tutelary spirit, and an enchanting muse. He gave no indication of the rancor that had destroyed his marriage. He said Deborah had taught him how to read John Donne in depth. Gazing upon Deborah now, he realized that Donne was right in his poems about mature beauty. The aging process had made "the most beautiful woman I had ever seen even more beautiful."[35] In public Dickey continued to remain stubbornly faithful to his ideals.

In a letter written on the day after Christmas, Dickey expressed comparable sentiments to Gwen Walti about *their* early romance. Talking with friends, he also beatified Maxine. Separated by death or distance from the three women, Dickey let his nostalgia re-create them. Despite his public homage to Deborah, he was not always so charitable. Driving to the airport with Steve Ennis after his Emory visit, he recited some doggerel: "I married in my age a wife. / She was my own but not the first. / She gave the best years of her life. / I hope no one gets the worst."[36] At his "power lunches" in the fall, which constituted nothing but two glasses of chocolate milk, Dickey told Ben Franklin and Don Greiner that he had "locked up" Deborah in a hospital, called his lawyers, and ordered them to draw up divorce papers. His colleagues were skeptical of his ability to follow through with the divorce, yet he had, indeed, begun proceedings and stipulated that Deborah not be allowed in the house (a stipulation he periodically neglected).

With Deborah at a clinic in Statesboro, Georgia, Dickey was more relaxed and more vulnerable. Still mentally sharp and formidable in conversation, he desperately sought out company. Carol Fairman, his new assistant who typed as well as paid the bills, provided a welcome antidote to his solitude. He tried to alleviate his loneliness and health worries by working on his poems and novel, but, like walking, they often proved too taxing. Determined to show signs of continued productivity, he announced that his next book would appear in 1996. It would include poems he wrote in his notebooks between the ages of twenty-nine and thirty-six. (It was not really "his" book, but his early notebooks edited by Gordon Van Ness in *Striking In*.) He described himself as an "overseer" of the film version of *To the White Sea* (the film was really out of his hands). Discussing old age with reporters, he said he had attained a mastery comparable to Segovia's on the guitar. Most of his time was spent watching TV, meeting students and colleagues, reading books, and talking on the phone. When Chris and Kevin visited Litchfield for Christmas in 1995, their father seemed confident he would overcome what doctors had diagnosed as fibrosis of the lungs. Kevin examined his father's chest X rays, and predicted that the fibrosis would kill him.

To the surprise of close friends, Dickey filed his divorce papers with the Richland County Court on January 18, 1996. An "Obligations of Each Party" agreement gave custody of Bronwen to Dickey. Deborah would receive a $213 monthly installment as beneficiary of his retirement plan, $25,316 as her portion of Dickey's property, $40,000 in death benefits from his life insurance, 10 percent of future movie rights for *To the White Sea*, and $8,333 in alimony payments each year. In November, a financial declaration pertaining to the divorce estimated his total assets at $800,000 and his total income for 1996 to be $187,000. After prolonged legal maneuvers, on November 8, 1996, Dickey and his wife agreed on final terms. Legal problems, however, persisted. By early January 1997, Deborah having been out of the house for over a year, the divorce was ready to be finalized.

In February 1996, Dickey's sanguine mood had suffered a momentary setback. In a conversation with Al Braselton, he said he had just started using an oxygen machine because of his failing lungs. "I'm not going to be with you much longer,"[37] he said glumly. Hoping to get a more objective diagnosis, Braselton called Dickey's maid, who said her boss was simply depressed. Believing his stamina would improve once his liver recovered, Dickey found it hard to accept his doctors' recent description of his pulmonary fibrosis (what they called "usual interstitial pneumonitis"). The fibrosis had developed independently from the liver cirrhosis to the point that he could not breathe for more than a few minutes without oxygen tubes in his nose. When he took them out, which he liked to do, he felt like a scuba diver without tanks. The oxygen machinery was cumbersome. Carol Fairman had to transport it to his class and to his lunches in the Faculty Club. At one lunch, a tube leaked. As he suffocated, he panicked. Fairman held the tube as best she could while Don Greiner ran for scotch tape.

Dickey's attitude toward his health was complex. He vacillated between witty denial, stoical resignation, and flamboyant melancholy. On February 2, to the forty or so guests who attended the party for his seventy-third birthday, he set out to prove that he still possessed his former energy. Stationed in his thronelike armchair in the living room, he held court for three hours, talking to each guest in turn. When Hubert and Phyllis Shuptrine inquired about his health in late

March 1996, they were surprised by his optimism: "It is true that I have been a little bit under-average physically for the last year and a half, since jaundice moved in. I was supposed to die, and, I think, *did* die at least once or maybe twice, when the hospital monitor flat-lined. From that time on, though, I have been convalescing, and now, except for shortness of breath and a comparative lack of appetite, I am more or less okay again. During the down-period I kept on functioning, and only missed a month or so of classes, when the disease was doing its worst. But the recovery is, I believe, good news, though I am not all the way back yet. But the signs are good." Dickey also gave the Shuptrines insight into his marital crises: "Deborah and I have had to split up because of her dreadful addiction to hard drugs. The story is long and sordid, and I won't bother you with it. At present she is in a rehabilitation center in Georgia, but with such a history as hers it is doubtful that anything can be done. I am very much on her side, but my efforts on her behalf have never resulted in her improvement, and I am extremely doubtful as to whether the intervention of yet another group of professionals will prove beneficial, either. All this is terribly sad, for she has a number of outstandingly positive qualities. If she would bring these more into play, things would be better, better for us all."[38] Dickey ended by reminiscing nostalgically about their collaboration on *Jericho*. He hoped Shuptrine would send him some new sketches, and stated—as he had never done before—that he was a great admirer of all Shuptrine's work.

As Dickey tried to mend old friendships, he also approached Paula Goff. Because the hard-working Mayrie MacLamore needed time away from the Dickey household, she welcomed Goff's return. During the spring of 1996, usually at night, Goff brought Dickey food—often salads and stuffed bell peppers—which were an improvement over the TV dinners that MacLamore fixed. Goff also acted as his nurse, emptying his urine bottle, helping him into bed, and keeping him company as he watched *Law and Order* on TV from eleven o'clock to midnight. Dickey was as oblivious as ever to the financial burden he put on Goff. Happy to be with Dickey again, she willingly used her food stamps to buy his groceries; he didn't offer her money. Sometimes he didn't even provide MacLamore with enough money to buy Ensure, which he drank daily. MacLamore had to ask friends like Carolee Guilds to go to the store and buy it for her. Goff continued to visit from Good Friday until May 12, 1996. On that night they watched Tom Cruise and Jack Nicholson in *A Few Good Men*. After Nicholson's haughty speech to Cruise in which he declaims, "You can't take the truth," Dickey made a similar speech to Goff. Crushed by his animosity and confused by his motives, Paula left and never saw him again.[39]

Dickey's reunions with other friends who had strayed during his ill-fated marriage to Deborah were less histrionic. His former student Michael Allin, who was working on his book about the first giraffe transported to France (*Zarafa*), renewed his close ties over the phone. Dickey was also happy to hear from one of his most successful students, Pat Conroy. At the end of 1995, Conroy sent a copy of his bestselling novel *Beach Music*, inscribed to: "My splendid teacher and mentor who set me on fire with a love of writing. No one has written in our language as well as you. No one has spoken to me so indelibly. I'm still your boy."[40] On April 8, he thanked Conroy for his generous words and sent him a progress report about his recuperation in which he vowed: "I will win out, yet."[41] Dismissing physiotherapists and helpful diets, Dickey planned to orchestrate another "triumph of the will."

Dickey tried to sound upbeat on April 15 at a lunch with John Palms and *Time* reporter Lance Morrow, with whom he had reconciled. When David Havird visited Dickey in May and was visibly distressed by his haggard physique and oxygen tubes, Dickey pulled out the tubes with a flourish and insisted that he didn't need them. As Dickey's body betrayed him, a spirit of loving-kindness, as Thomas Hardy called it, became more noticeable. Encouraging to students like Havird in the past, now his concern seemed more sincere. In a letter to the struggling writer Michael Hanson, he sounded like a penitent who had renounced the less noble motives that had once driven his career:

> There were periods when there didn't seem to be any hope at all. But during that night of the soul I discovered one thing that has never betrayed me, and has gotten me through such periods, and everything else. It is this. A writer with standards can only go on and produce a life-work on one basis, and that is love. If you love words, and if you love writing, you will do it. If you don't then you won't, because there are many other more lucrative . . . occupations. But they are not more involving to the real writers: he already has the terms of his appeal. Speaking from my own case, I wrote for years without publication and without *thought* of publication. I was just fascinated with what I was doing, and if that fascination ever leaves me I will not write any more. It is a very simple situation.[42]

Empathy had always been one of Dickey's virtues—sometimes in eclipse, sometimes in the ascendant. In his debilitated state, it reasserted itself.

Dickey was pleased to have one of the smaller literary magazines that had sustained him early in his career reward him in 1996. On May 30, University of Chicago dean Philip Gossett informed Dickey that he had won the one-thousand-dollar Harriet Monroe Poetry Award, which had been judged by James Reiss, the poet who had helped edit *Self-Interviews*. Many other major contemporary poets—Berryman, Warren, and Bishop among them—had won the prize named after the founder of *Poetry* magazine. Because Dickey's health made travel difficult, he proposed that Gossett send a representative to give him the award at a special USC ceremony at Thomas Cooper Library. Such an arrangement was not feasible, so Dickey accepted the honor by mail.

After Paula Goff stopped seeing Dickey, Carolee Guilds began making frequent visits. Guilds never forgot the time of her rendezvous: four o'clock on the afternoon of July 29, 1996. To prepare for her on this and later occasions, Dickey cut his nails, shaved, and bathed. Concerned about his debilitated state, she soon brought him meals from the S & S cafeteria—soups, congealed salads, Jell-O, and other easily digestible foods—and petitioned Chris to hire somebody to cook and care for him at night. Dickey's love for the companionable Guilds flourished once again, and soon he renewed his proposals of marriage. Recognizing that he was still romantically and legally bound to Deborah, Guilds brushed them aside. While Guilds was in the house, he constantly spoke to Deborah on the phone, assuring her that everything would be all right and that he still loved her. Hanging up the receiver, he would turn to Guilds and say, "I'm going to get married to you; I'm committed,"[43] and continue to play the irrepressible suitor.

Dickey distracted himself from his physical and romantic problems with the screenplay of *To the White Sea*. He had drafted brief scenes as possible aids for the screenwriters and mailed them to Richard Roth on December 28, 1995. He received a draft of the David and Janet Peoples' script several months later, and on July 23 he responded with numerous suggestions. He insisted on having Muldrow hide in the sewer pipe at the beginning (he offered to write the scene himself), complained that key episodes had been shortened and minor ones lengthened, and recommended that a reference to the Kansas girl, whom Muldrow had killed, appear in the first third of the film. As for the end, he proposed that the posse wander aimlessly over the frozen landscape after assassinating Muldrow to emphasize his mysterious disappearance. A week later, Dickey forwarded more advice about the train scene, the beheading at the waterfall, and the voice-over, which he hoped would not interfere with the story as it had in *Call of the Wild*.

In his day-to-day life, Dickey opened himself to others as he had not done in his decades of drinking. He doted on Bronwen, who came home from Choate, where she had made the honor roll and excelled at ballet. He conducted long, tape-recorded sessions with Chris, who had flown from Paris in July to gather information for *Summer of Deliverance*. He worked on a film to promote USC and conferred with lawyers about his divorce. Perhaps it was loneliness compounded with his inability to rush from one place to another that made him want to sit for hours and talk. Friends like Jim Mann, who had known Dickey for twenty-five years, appreciated his accessibility. As he conversed, he gave signs that he had made peace with the various "imps of the perverse" that had caused so much havoc in his life. At times, he referred, overtly or obliquely, to his alcoholism, his compulsive lying, his penchant for sadomasochism, and his homosexual interests. At other times he withdrew behind well-rehearsed denials.

On August 5, chatting with Jim Mann as they watched a late-night World War II movie, Dickey returned to the topic of homosexuality. After a long search of his library, he had finally found George Painter's biography of André Gide. He read a passage about Gide going to a hotel in Algiers, leaving in a fit of moral righteousness when he discovered that Oscar Wilde and Alfred Douglas were there, and returning to the hotel out of a shameful recognition of his hypocrisy. At the moment of his return, Dickey said, Gide had proven himself a hero by finally acknowledging his homosexuality. Since Mann confessed he had no homosexual impulses, Dickey dissembled: "We hear all this about everybody having gay impulses. I just don't. I can't think about it without a sense of revulsion."[44] What revolted him when sober, however, had often titillated him when drunk. Dickey went on to speculate that homosexuality was not genetic but a result of the classic Oedipal relationship of a son with a mother. He had grown up in such an Oedipal situation—his Clemson and World War II letters overflow with amorous declarations to his mother—and he had given homosexual impulses to the alter egos in his novels and often pretended to be homosexual with friends or acquaintances.

Denials colored Dickey's views of his health as well. At summer's end, he insisted on teaching twice a week even though he was much weaker than the previous semester. Carol Fairman found the job of ferrying him to and from campus increasingly nerve-racking. Finally she convinced him to put aside his vanity and use a wheelchair, which made the trips easier. Nevertheless, all activity—especially his work on the USC film—exhausted him. At a conference celebrating Fitzgerald's one hundredth birthday in September, Dickey suffered another crisis. Wanting to contribute to Matthew Bruccoli's efforts on behalf of Fitzgerald's legacy (Bruccoli, a renowned Fitzgerald scholar, had turned over his private collection of twelve thousand books and papers to USC earlier in the year), on September 24 Dickey participated in a one-hour televised discussion with Joseph Heller. He also wrote two tributes to Fitzgerald, one in prose, the other in poetry. In "The Slow Surprise and the Deepening of Art" he praised Fitzgerald's high aesthetic standards, and in his poem "Entering Scott's Night," which the New Yorker published posthumously, he welcomed the thought of joining Fitzgerald in death.

Dickey's poem about passing on to an otherworld of literary ghosts was almost prophetic. On September 25, at a luncheon honoring Fitzgerald's friend Budd Shulberg at John Palms's house, Dickey nearly lost consciousness while Fairman spent several minutes changing his oxygen tank. Dickey, as well as those who watched in horror, thought he might die. With oxygen once again pulsing into his lungs, he gradually stabilized. As a result of the frightening incident, he regretfully gave up his Tuesday and Thursday "power lunches" and stopped going to his office after class. Fairman admitted at the time: "I feel such a grave responsibility for his very life when I take him away from the big machine in his home. Those oxygen tanks and controls are not failsafe. I am constantly afraid, and will be taking a CPR course soon to give me more confidence in my ability to handle an emergency."[45] Fairman had turned from literary assistant to part-time nurse. Continual stress, lack of benefits, and concern for Dickey's welfare convinced Fairman that she should resign. She was not easy to replace. Dickey's obstinate demands—his new assistant had to be a woman; she had to be young; she had to be attractive; she had to work for a low wage; she had to act as servant, business manager, nurse, and secretary—made the hiring process difficult. By early January 1997, however, Meg Richards had accepted the job.

On November 20, 1996, Dickey wrote Marc Jaffe that he felt better now that the doctors had put him on steroids. Crux, he informed his editor, was going forward; he had finished a publishable section called "Vines." Jaffe asked to see a proposal for the new novel. Dickey never sent one, but at the end of 1996 he did have the twenty-five-page beginning of Crux typed. His fragment began with the Alnilam character Harbelis watching flying fish glide over waves beside a troopship bound for the Pacific, just as Dickey had done on the USS Anderson over fifty years before. For Harbelis, as for Dickey, the fish were reminiscent of his failure to become a pilot; the fish always hit the water shortly after takeoff. As Dickey began his new novel, he returned to the military disappointments that had spurred his literary career: his washing out and reclassification as a radar observer in the Army Air Corps. Harbelis sarcastically testifies: "A Radar Observer is a half-made pilot; or half-ass. We've been at the controls, though, at least a little. Blazek is my pilot, my full-ass pilot." Harbelis gloomily concludes that the main reason he is going to war is because of "washing out of pilot training." He views his overseas assignment as a punishment: "He had been held back in Primary because of the destruction of the aircraft that Joel had ordered, and that he, Shears and the others had carried out." The opening pages of *Crux* read like a thinly veiled memoir of Dickey's World War II experiences. The narrator recapitulates Dickey's training at gunnery school in Florida, where he shot .50-cal. machine guns from B-17s at aerial targets; his lessons in radar in Boca Raton, where "the trainees were searched and marched . . . into bare classrooms and were handed notebooks and pencils"; his first impressions of the unwieldly-looking P-61s at Hammer Field; and his encounter with the Japanese training aircraft when "the target throttled back, and you went right under him."[46] Unwilling to forget his failure to become a decorated war pilot, at the end of his life he was more prepared to write about it realistically.

Although Dickey said little to Jaffe about *Crux*, while working on *Alnilam* he had compiled copious notes for the novel he had once called *Crux Meridionis* or *Crux Australis*. His plan was to trace the journey of Harbelis and Shears from U.S. bases to a New Guinea replacement depot and on to the Philippines, Okinawa, and Japan. Shears was to become "progressively more impressive, more learned, more intellectual, and more fanatical" until his men regarded him as "something of an airborne Lawrence of Arabia." He would cultivate a rare, powerful mystique by lying about the facts of his life, and—to enshrine his legend—die mysteriously in the Pacific. Dickey identified with Shears, but also with the more humanitarian Harbelis, the Ishmael of the Ahab-like Alnilam group that dies in an unspecified holocaust in the Pacific. Dickey hoped to end *Crux* with Harbelis on rest leave in a hotel near Mount Fujiyama, drinking whiskey or martinis and mumbling the secret language of the Alnilam cabal. Harbelis "plays in a ping pong tournament, and goes to a Japanese school where the children dance and sing around him, and give him American flags, and he is told by the schoolmaster about the strafing of the children before the peace was signed, when they came running out of the school waving American flags, and the A-26's shot them down." In 1945, Dickey had gone to Mount Fujiyama on rest leave and participated in many of these activities, too. Overcome by the absurdity and horror of the war, Harbelis would stare up at Mount Fujiyama and cryptically proclaim: "It was not impossible, like the mountain." He would keep alive the Alnilam group's hope of changing the world into a place as immensely beautiful and sublime as Mount Fujiyama. While sketching out *Crux* Dickey had a similar hope—if not for the world, then for his novels. "I truly believe that *Alnilam* and *Crux Australis*," he declared, "will create a new sensibility for mankind. . . . If I can bring this thing off, Tolstoy will seem a minor writer."[47] Unfortunately, fate would deny him his wish.

Dickey told the USC English Department that he planned to take a sabbatical and a medical leave-of-absence during the 1997–98 academic year. He also implied that the 1997 spring term would be his last. Like the math teacher in his early poem "Mangham" who suffers a stroke during class but refuses to quit teaching, Dickey doggedly fulfilled his commitment to teach. Because his breathing was so arduous, over the Christmas vacation Chris asked Don Greiner as acting provost to allow his father to meet students at home. The journey from Lelia's Court to campus had become too perilous. Greiner called the dean and department chair, who agreed that Dickey should be granted permission. Realizing his friend was near death, Matthew Bruccoli arranged for the Instructional Services Department to tape his last classes. Although Dickey had refused such intrusive and possibly incriminating equipment in the past, he now agreed to have his teaching preserved on tape. On Tuesday, January 14, he met his first group of students for the term. Coughing and retching for several minutes, he finally got enough breath to speak. As usual his mind ranged eloquently over many topics— from the poet's use of the unconscious to the necessity of imaginative lying, from the identity of God to the poet's role as a secondary God. Gathered around the feeble poet, the students sat in rapt attention as he lectured:

> Flaubert says somewhere that the life of a poet is a hell of a life, it is a dog's life, but it is the only one worth living. You suffer more. You also live so much more. You live so much more intensely and so much more vitally. And with so much more of a sense of meaning, of consequentiality. . . . For the poet everything matters, and it matters a lot. That is the realm where we work. Once you are there, you are hooked. If you are a real poet, you are hooked more deeply than any narcotics addict could possibly be on heroin. You are hooked on something that is life-giving instead of destructive. Something that is a process that cannot be too far from the process that created everything. God's process. . . . What this universe indubitably *is* is a poet's universe. Nothing but a poetic kind of consciousness could have conceived of anything like this. That is where the truth of the matter lies. You are in some way in line with the creative genesis of the universe. In some way—in a much lesser way, of course. We can't create those trees or that water or anything that is out there. We can't do it. But we can re-create it. We are secondary creators. We take God's universe and make it over our way.[48]

Romantics, symbolists, and modernists had articulated these ideas before, but Dickey gave them his own impassioned inflection.

As Dickey spoke to what would be his last class, he resembled the apparitional Kurtz at the end of *Heart of Darkness,* whose oracular voice remained grave, profound, and vibrant despite the fact that he was dying. Like Kurtz he had gratified "his unlawful soul beyond the bounds of permitted aspirations." As Conrad's Marlow said of Kurtz, his voice "was an affirmation, a moral victory paid for by innumerable defeats, by abominable terrors, by abominable satisfactions. But it was a victory!"[49] Struggling to rise above his own tragic circumstances, Dickey encouraged his students one last time to fight for poetic victory just as he had done throughout his life.

On the day after teaching his class, Dickey succumbed to feverish chills. Paramedics rushed to his house and found him shaking uncontrollably. At

Providence Hospital, doctors at first were optimistic. He had a slight chest infection that could be cured in a day or two. To friends like Ben Franklin who visited him, Dickey seemed unfazed. He was certain he could go home on Monday. By Thursday he wasn't so sure and complained that his medicines had done little good. When his former student and friend Lynn Cansler walked into his room, he was distraught. "How did you know I was here?" he asked. She didn't divulge her source (she had learned his whereabouts from Meg Richards). Mustering what vocal energy he could, he said: "You get out of my room! You get out of the hospital!" "You are cruel, Jim. You are cruel,"[50] she replied. She left the room sobbing. In his vulnerable state, Dickey believed that she had harmful intentions. The hospital staff moved him to a safer room, gave him a new phone number, assigned a policeman to guard his door, and only allowed visitors with Dickey's permission to see him.

Was Dickey, the compulsive impersonator of Marlon Brando, enacting a *Godfather* fantasy in the hospital? Was he playing the role of a Mafia boss in need of armed guards to fend off enemies? Cansler was clearly upset; her tears and accusations testified to that. But she said later that she had gone to the hospital to offer help; she even wanted to offer Dickey a lung if it would keep him alive. Her outburst in the hospital displayed the mix of grief and anger that many felt. After all, Cansler had been a friend of both Dickey and his wife. His first overtures to her had been seductive. "Baby, don't you ever cut that red hair,"[51] he had told her when she first entered his classroom in 1972. She had given him some of her artwork and other presents like a white buffalo and a stuffed rabbit. She had celebrated Thanksgiving with him and participated in Alcoholics Anonymous with Deborah.

After a difficult night, Dickey regained some of his strength on Friday. With Don Greiner, he had enough breath to recite all of Frost's "After Apple-Picking." Greiner, who had written his dissertation on Frost, spoke one line and Dickey the next until they reached the final passage about love and death:

One can see what will trouble
This sleep of mine, whatever sleep it is.
Were he not gone,
The woodchuck could say whether it's like his
Long sleep, as I describe its coming on,
Or just some human sleep.

For the poet born on Groundhog Day, Frost's poem provided a fitting conclusion. He reached out to Greiner, hugged him, and said he loved him. Numerous other visitors stopped by on Friday. Carolee Guilds came and conferred with a woman who had information about a healthier diet that she hoped to prepare for him as soon as he got out of the hospital. Matthew Bruccoli visited, as did John Palms and several others from USC who spoke to Dickey about finding someone to teach his class. Dickey found this especially galling—he was forfeiting his prized vocation—and on the phone he threatened his temporary replacement. (He said he would break the neck of the professor, who happened to be gay, if he found out the professor was propositioning his students.)[52] The turbulence of

Friday aggravated his condition. That night he weakened. Apprised of their father's plight, Kevin, Bronwen, and Chris all made plans to fly to Columbia.

After the drama of his first two days in the hospital, Dickey was glad to have
Carol Fairman by his side on Saturday night. She had intended to make a brief
visit, but when she saw how he was suffering, she asked him if he would like her
to spend the night. Dickey replied with gusto: "Yes." She went home to gather
her effects and around nine o'clock replaced Mayrie MacLamore. Dickey's face
lit up at the sight of Fairman's pillow and overnight bag. He had often teased her
about staying overnight at Lelia's Court. "At last," he whispered, "we'll spend
the night together." They both laughed. Fairman stretched out on the reclining
chair, but neither she nor Dickey could sleep. He frequently thrashed in his bed,
clenching his fists and striking the air as he fought for breath. Fairman felt desperately helpless. She remembered a line in which Emily Dickinson compared
dying to a wild night and concluded it was also a terribly solitary night.
Occasionally she gave Dickey a sip of water and swabbed his forehead with a wet
towel. She reported his worsening condition to the nurse's station, which was directly across from his room; the nurses said nothing could be done. From time to
time, the head nurse checked on Dickey, reprimanding him for not keeping his
bottom covered with his smock. In a childlike voice, Dickey said he was sorry.
Around nine o'clock the next morning, Fairman said: "Mr. Dickey, Mayrie is
here. I'm going home. I'll be back. Your family is coming around noon." Dickey
grew suddenly agitated. "When will you come back?" he demanded. She promised to return around four or five o'clock in the afternoon. "Thank you for the
night,"[53] he said politely.

Because Dickey continued to lose weight, doctors considered feeding him in-
travenously, but all the other medications he was taking made it impossible. His
heart raced in an effort to absorb more oxygen into his blood. Because of claus-
trophobia, he couldn't sleep with the oxygen apparatus to help him breathe. He
could hardly say more than one or two words at a time. On Sunday, Ben Franklin
saw Bronwen and Kevin by their father's bed and decided it was no time to intrude on the family vigil. At one point, Dickey seemed to have lost consciousness. Carolee Guilds, who had come earlier in the day, leaned close and said in
a friendly voice: "Jim Darling." Remembering their *Peter Pan* routine of calling
each other "Jim Darling" and "Mrs. Darling" (at other times he called her "My
Lady" or "The Lady"), Dickey perked up enough to hear his children say they
loved him.

Other visitors paid their final respects on Sunday. Matthew Bruccoli cut his
visit short because he found his friend's agony too much to bear. Ward Briggs recounted a story Dickey had once told him about a happy dream in Georgia.
Guilds talked to him about leaving all his illness behind and going to Joseph
Conrad's imaginary country, Costaguana, in South America, where Dickey
could play Nostromo to Guilds's Emilia, the incorruptible woman of intelligence
and charm to whom Nostromo confesses his crimes in hopes of absolution before
he dies. Although Dickey had made it clear to Guilds that he didn't want
Deborah in his hospital room, Deborah called from Georgia and said she would
arrive the next morning. Dickey's children conferred with doctors, who were

prepared to attach their father to a ventilator. "Let me die my own death, and not the death of doctors,"[54] Dickey had often said, quoting Rilke. They honored his wish.

Dickey's sons also let him die without any religious rites. Earlier on Sunday, Guilds had told one of the Sisters of Providence Hospital that she wanted a priest to visit Dickey from Trinity Cathedral. The Sister promised to send a message to the church. The Rev. Patsy Moore, who had once taught Kevin at Heathwood Hall, came to the hospital, but Kevin told her that his father would not be receptive to emissaries from the church. Guilds was distressed when Moore told her what had happened; she was convinced that Kevin was simply unaware of his father's recent turn toward Christianity. Guilds pointed out: "I had already taken the communion to Jim one time earlier, so I knew that he would be receptive."[55] She had done so surreptitiously about a month before he entered the hospital. Keeping some of the wafer and wine from communion in her mouth, she had kissed Dickey on the lips in order to pass on the symbolic body and blood of Christ. Guilds subsequently became a licensed lay minister so that she could formally administer the last rites in such situations.

Many of Dickey's discussions with Guilds after their July reunion had revolved around religion. Guilds noticed that he often picked up a picture of his mother that he kept beside him and spoke of her faith. During one of their talks about his near-death experience in the hospital, Guilds asked: "What did you see or realize or feel? What happened?" Dickey responded: "Nothin. I was just dead. Dead." He said he was an atheist who didn't believe in any sort of afterlife. Guilds recoiled: "Jim, I can't believe you said that, that you think that." He reiterated his conviction, so Guilds told him about suffering a heart attack when she was younger and how she had felt her spirit leave her body and rise through a tunnel of light to a warm, radiant, loving place above the clouds where silhouetted figures shook their heads to indicate it was not her time to die. She had felt forlorn drifting back through the ceiling and waking in her sickbed. Dickey explained that his father had been an atheist. "Did you have to carry on his bad ideas all of your life?" she asked. She proposed researching everything he had written for references to eternity, heaven, and God. "Well, why don't you write a paper and do research. Everybody else is," he replied sarcastically. Their acrimonious exchange about religious belief, she noticed, was not entirely futile. Afterward she found Dickey watching Christian television shows. Once he admitted to her that he had moments when he felt in touch with God and the whole of creation. On one of her visits to the hospital, just as she was about to go, Dickey tried to allay her fears of his apostasy. "Don't worry about what I said about Jesus. I know Jesus. *I'm* Jesus," he told her with a devilish look in his eyes. Guilds returned to his bed and squeezed his hand. "Jim, I'm not worried. I know you know Jesus, because you are the Jesus that lives in you." She was delighted by what she took to be his conversion.

Before Guilds left Sunday evening, Dickey pleaded for her help. He mustered all his strength to utter one line: "You have to help me for I cannot help myself." Later he said, as if hallucinating: "Fire. . . . Fire!" He fumbled for Guilds's hand as well as the buttons on the panel by his bed. Guilds thought he wanted a nurse:

"Are you hot? Is it too hot?" He was not hot. When a nurse arrived, Dickey clearly said to Guilds: "Show the lady the center." By his bed Guilds prayed quietly for Jesus to intercede on Dickey's behalf. Even though she had planned to stay with Dickey and MacLamore, whom she had brought to the hospital Sunday night, Guilds felt it was time to say "Goodbye," so she kissed him on the forehead, squeezed his hand, and said: "I love you."[56] She explained she had to go home, but that she would return at six o'clock in the morning to relieve MacLamore. Dickey would always tell Guilds to stay a little longer. This time he said nothing.

Like the black servants who waited on him as an infant, MacLamore brought Dickey drinks and helped him go to the bathroom. At one point, struggling for breath, he stuttered: "Mayrie, don't leave me now because you're the only one I depend on to help me. You're still a part of my family. So don't leave me." As his body relaxed, according to MacLamore, he found enough oxygen to talk about a trip to Jamaica. Having routinely promised to pay for the trip so that MacLamore could visit a friend on the island, Dickey said: "You remember that trip you asked me for?" She did. "As soon as I get this money we're going to Jamaica," he told her. They both laughed, knowing the trip would always remain a fantasy. A nurse checking on Dickey said: "My goodness, he's mighty happy." MacLamore explained that it was because he was talking about Jamaica. Dickey responded: "That's my Mayrie. That's the one that took care of me the years I was sick. I had no one else to depend on." As he entertained thoughts of Jamaica, he grew calm, as if he had been transported to a sunny beach under windblown palms with the green-blue Caribbean glinting in the distance. MacLamore saw no signs of struggle. If her memory had invented a story for Dickey's last hours (Dickey could barely say one word all day), it was the sort of creative lie that Dickey approved.

MacLamore's beeper suddenly disturbed Dickey's reverie. When she explained she had to go to the phone, he grew frantic. "Oh don't leave me. Don't leave me," he supposedly said. She replied: "But I've got an emergency call. You hold on until I come back." "I'm not going to be here, Mayrie," he complained. "Oh yes you is," she said. The call was from one of her children, who wanted to know how Dickey was faring. She explained that only a miracle could keep her boss alive through the night. She walked back to the room a few minutes before 11:15 P.M. and stood by his bed. Dickey was serene until he gripped her hand. She said: "Mr. Dickey?" He gasped one last time: "Don't leave me." In poetry and prose he had imagined serial killers like Ted Bundy ferrying the dying to the otherworld. Faced with the reality of that final, lonely journey, he took the hand of his loyal African-American maid. By coincidence, it was Martin Luther King, Jr., Day—the day set aside to memorialize America's tangled racial history. MacLamore stood by Dickey during his last moment. Having watched his breathing cease, she left the room and told the security guard by the door: "Mr. Dickey has passed." The guard said: "There's nothing I can do." "There's nothing you can do!" she nearly screamed. "The man just died!"[57] Next she walked down the hall and got a nurse, who said she would have to call someone else to pronounce Dickey dead. MacLamore then phoned Bronwen, Al Braselton, Carol Fairman, Meg Richards, and Carolee Guilds to tell them the sad news.

42. Last Rites (1997)

On Monday, January 20, 1997, the day of Bill Clinton's second inauguration as president, Dickey's death reached the country's news organizations. On the *Jim Lehrer News Hour* the poet Stanley Plumly testified to Dickey's literary importance. In a discussion of his life and writing, the hoary legends reared their heads. The dozens of obituaries in the nation's prominent magazines and newspapers recycled—sometimes with variations—Dickey's fanciful life as a football star, fighter pilot, advertising executive, archery champion, professional guitarist, big-game hunter, and poet laureate. The *Southern Partisan* called him America's greatest contemporary poet. Other elegists dropped the qualification and hailed him as the greatest poet in American history.

Bronwen, who was fifteen, wrote one of the most moving obituaries. Published in *Newsweek* on March 24, it described her visit to the hospital on the Sunday her father died. Rather than the vibrant father she knew as a young child, she had confronted a skeleton wracked with pain. His fingers had turned purple from oxygen depletion. His two watches—a Citizen Wingman and an Ironman Triathlon—ticked in rhythm with his dying pulses. He looked at his daughter through a thicket of plastic tubes, his eyes watering without the strength to cry. She remembered their exuberant times together—throwing knives, shooting arrows, watching movies—and fled in tears from the gnarled, emaciated figure before her. Struggling to maintain her composure, she walked back to his bed to say she needed him to stay alive. He told her that he had always needed her in his life. She squeezed his hand and told him she loved him.

After Dickey's death, his family let it be known that it did not want visitors or gifts. Because the house had been burglarized in the past, Kevin and Chris were wary of intruders. They hired Lt. Kevin Mooney, the Columbia police officer responsible for arresting Dickey in 1975, to guard the house against possible vandals. Ignoring these defensive measures, Elizabeth Adams brought roses and a cake. She noticed that there were no other flowers. Because their father's death happened unexpectedly, the children worked frantically to organize a private funeral and public memorial service. They had to decide where their father would be buried. Would it be in the family crypt in Atlanta where Dickey's brother, parents, and eventually his sister were buried? Maibelle, who would die in 1998, called Kevin to inquire about the burial arrangements. He informed her that his father would lie by his mother in the All Saints Waccamaw graveyard at Pawley's Island. She responded bitterly: "Good, because we don't have any room for him over here."[1] About a week before Dickey's seventy-fourth birthday, a Presbyterian minister, John LeHeup, performed the funeral service at All Saints. A former football player and English major, he had frequently visited Dickey to talk about books. Because Dickey had bestowed his enthusiasm for literature on so many, LeHeup said in his eulogy that he deserved God's grace. Chris's eulogy, like the memoir he would publish, acknowledged the "long stretch, about twenty years, when things were not good, when Kevin and I were prodigal sons of a prodigal father,"[2] but it also applauded the reconciliation that had occurred during his father's final years.

The funeral on Friday afternoon, January 24, was limited to family members and close friends. Patsy Dickey, who had been mugged in Columbia's Holiday Inn before the funeral, came with her children, Tom and Dorian. Kevin's family attended, as did Chris and his son, James, who flew in from his military post in South Korea. Deborah was also there. Although the other Dickeys tried to make her feel welcome, she seemed lost and unwanted. At one point in the ceremony she asked: "What do I do now?" Fearing the funeral would be spoiled by family squabbles, Patsy reached out and pulled her into line. Carolee Guilds, who took the death especially hard, grieved with the rest. Among the most inconsolable was Mayrie MacLamore. Weeping uncontrollably, she nearly collapsed outside the chapel and needed to be supported by two of the mourners. As Patsy wept by the casket, Deborah observed, "You loved him too," and added: "Oh I regret so much. All of this is my own fault."[3] In the cemetery, Deborah expressed her sorrow more tersely to Al Braselton and Lewis King. "I guess I blew it,"[4] she said. With the help of rehabilitation and religion, Deborah had been sober for a year.

Ben Franklin, Matthew Bruccoli, Michael Allin, Don Greiner, Braselton, King, and Chris's son served as pallbearers. Bearing the casket over the oak roots and humped earth in Waccamaw's graveyard, Braselton recalled hauling canoes in North Georgia during the years that had been so formative to *Deliverance*. King, as it turned out, had the same memory. Later they reflected wryly that nothing had changed; their friend had never liked lugging canoes, and once again he relaxed while they carried the weight on their shoulders. His friends buried Dickey next to Maxine, where he had often been seen after her death sitting by her grave and writing. He had changed his instructions for his funeral. Asked by Bill Moyers in 1976 how he wanted to die, Dickey had replied that he wanted to be killed by a grizzly bear and buried in a hole—without a coffin—on the west bank of the Chattooga River near Woodall Shoals with a gravestone inscribed:

JAMES DICKEY, 1923 TO 19 WHATEVER
AMERICAN POET AND NOVELIST,
HERE SEEKS HIS DELIVERANCE[5]

Now he asked for "James Dickey, 1923– , Poet, Father of Bronwen, Kevin and Christopher." His children also decided to engrave an eye like the one on the cover of the first edition of *Deliverance*, and at the bottom of the stone, "I move at the heart of the world," from his poem "In the Tree House at Night."

The following Monday, January 27, USC held a memorial service on the Horseshoe. Writer friends like Dave Smith, Jim Seay, Elizabeth Spencer, and David Bottoms converged with seven hundred others to pay tribute. After a dispute over the amount of the award, Chris, Kevin, and Bronwen accepted the Thomas Cooper Award from the vice provost for libraries, George Terry. Don Greiner was afraid he might weep as he made the introductory remarks. He read a note from his assistant's eleven-year-old daughter that urged him not to go "head-hanging," but, instead, to celebrate the day despite his anguish. In that spirit, Greiner dedicated the service to Dickey's life and writing.

Ward Briggs told a story that captured both the ordinary, all-American nature of Dickey's imagination and his complex view of the world:

> Jim called me up one night when he was alone and a little afraid, and he asked me to come stay the night with him, as I had done before and as I would do again. When I got there he told me he had a dream, that he was back in high school playing football and he had scored the first touchdown, and then he scored the second touchdown.
>
> He was carried off the field and that night went to a party where the most beautiful girl in all the state of Georgia fell in love with him. They ended the evening by the side of a country road with the top down and moonlight showering them.
>
> He said to her, "This is the greatest day of my life, but I can't be happy." She said, "Why not?" and he said, "This is just a dream; it's not real." She said, "Sure it's real, Jim. It's all real within the dream."
>
> He asked me when the end came, whenever that would be, to lean over to him on the bed and tell him, "It's all real, Jim, in the dream," and I promised I would. A little more than a week ago, I was in his room and I grabbed his hand at the end of our conversation, and I said, "Just remember, Jim, it's all real in the dream." And he said, "I know it is," and he squeezed my hand.[6]

Pondering Dickey's complicated life, the main speaker at the memorial service, Pat Conroy, declared: "A whole city of men lived in that vivid, restless country behind James Dickey's transfixing eyes."[7] Matthew Bruccoli also spoke, praising the range of Dickey's writing and his devotion to teaching. David Bottoms read "Buckdancer's Choice," and one of Dickey's students, Julie Bloemeke, read "The Heaven of Animals." A gospel chorale sang "Swing Low, Sweet Chariot," "Amazing Grace," and, as Dickey had requested, "Shall We Gather at the River." English Department chair Robert Newman gave the concluding remarks, and finally the Zassoff Boys played "Dueling Banjos."

Not all the reactions to Dickey's death were eulogistic. Many, including Chris Dickey and Mary Cantwell, soon published memoirs that rebuked him for the pain he had inflicted on those who tried to love him. Despite the agony of her marriage, Deborah continued to feel irrevocably bound to Dickey. Having established a drug-free life in Statesboro, Georgia, where she taught English as a foreign language, she deemed her years with Dickey a great privilege; she would never again be in such close proximity to genius.[8] She had descended into the inferno, and ascended to stabler ground. Her marriage, in a legal sense, had continued; the divorce had never been finalized. Supposed to sign the final papers in January, Dickey was ill and still waffling. According to Chris, Deborah and her lawyer had stalled, even though the division of property was clearly decreed. Chris and Kevin could have taken their stepmother to court to retrieve what had been allowed her by the Dickey estate, but decided against it. Their main concern was Bronwen. They wanted to guarantee her financial welfare at Choate and, later, at college. On August 15, 1997, all parties agreed on a solution. Chris, Kevin, and Bronwen would be the beneficiaries of the estate, and Deborah would receive her husband's retirement benefits (about $170,000). The document specified: "She shall indemnify and hold the Estate of James L. Dickey, III, harmless thereon."[9] Dickey had made more money during his life than most poets of his or any other generation, but little remained in his bank account when he died.

Although royalties from past books, the sale of papers and property, and future revenues from the film version of *To the White Sea*, which the Coen Brothers had agreed to make, guaranteed a substantial income to his survivors, James Dickey's legacy had more to do with moral than monetary values. It had to do, as Fitzgerald said of J. Gatsby, with the "foul dust [that] floated in the wake of his dreams." Like Gatsby, Dickey showed how the romantic desire "to suck on the pap of life [and] gulp down the incomparable milk of wonder" could be ecstatic as well as tragic, energizing as well as debilitating, childish as well as profound. Dickey wrote compulsively about the heroic quest for "something commensurate to his capacity for wonder,"[10] and in his life he showed how the will to kick free from all judicious restraints led to a pitiful denouement. His story, like Gatsby's, was in some respects a quintessential American tragedy. Both men attempted to realize their dreams of wealth, fame, romance, and power. It is no wonder that, as an old man reflecting soberly on his life, Dickey identified with Gatsby and Fitzgerald in his poem "Entering Scott's Night." The books he published in the 1960s and early 1970s ensured Dickey a place among the exemplary ghosts in Fitzgerald's night. The books that followed, while demonstrating a heroic willingness to take risks with different genres and styles, were testaments to the cautionary tale of flawed genius that was James Dickey's life.

ENDNOTES

ABBREVIATIONS

A *Alnilam* (Pinnacle Books ed.) **AB** Al Braselton, **AL** Andrew Lytle.
BF Ben Franklin, **BTB** *Babel to Byzantium*, **BTS** *Bronwen, the Traw, and the Shape-Shifter*.
CD Chris Dickey, **CP** *The Whole Motion: Collected Poems, 1945–1992*.
D *Deliverance*, **DG** Don Greiner, **DH** Donald Hall.
GC Al Braselton's *The Ghost Canoe* manuscript, **GI** *God's Images*.
HH Henry Hart.
J *Jericho*, **JB** John Boorman, **JD** James Dickey, **JDS** Jacques de Spoelberch,
JM James Mann, **JW** James Wright.
KD Kevin Dickey, **KM** Ken McCormick.
MD1 Maibelle Dickey (James Dickey's mother), **MD2** Maibelle Dickey (Dickey's sister), **MD** Maxine Dickey.
NH *Night Hurdling*.
P *Puella*.
RB Robert Bly.
SH *Squadron History: 418th Night Fighters*, **S-I** *Self-Interviews*, **S** *Sorties*,
SOD *Summer of Deliverance*, **SI** *Striking In*, **SIP** *The Suspect in Poetry*,
SR Stewart Richardson.
TWS *To the White Sea*.
VC *The Voiced Connections of James Dickey*.
W *Wayfarer*, **WB** Ward Briggs.

In the Notes, "with" means an interview or conversation with someone (which I have in transcribed or paraphrased form), and "to" means a letter to someone. I've given page numbers for the transcripts of my interviews with James Dickey, which were conducted in August 1996.

Most of the letters and unpublished manuscripts cited in this book are in the Emory Special Collections Library. A smaller collection is housed in the James Dickey Papers, Special Collections, Washington University Libraries in Saint Louis. Papers related to Dickey's term as poetry consultant are in the Library of Congress. Many of Dickey's letters to James Wright are in the University of Minnesota Special Collections Library, although carbon copies of some of them exist at Emory. Dickey's letters to Donald Hall are at the University of New Hampshire Library, and those to Anne Sexton are at the Harry Ransom Humanities Research Center, at the

University of Texas, Austin, although carbon copies of some of these are at Emory. Dickey's letters to William Carlos Williams are at the Yale Collection of American Literature, Beinecke Rare Book and Manuscript Library. Theron Raines, Dickey's literary agent, also has a collection of papers in his New York office. Dickey's letters to Jimmy Carter are in the Jimmy Carter Library in Atlanta. Letters from Dickey to Andrew Lytle are in Vanderbilt University's Special Collections Library. A letter by Louis Untermeyer is published by arrangement with the Estate of Louis Untermeyer, Norma Anchin Untermeyer, c/o Professional Publishing Services Co. This permission is expressly granted by Laurence S. Untermeyer.

INTRODUCTION

1. Kirby, *The Atlanta Journal-Constitution* (Jan. 21, 1997): E6. **2.** *The Carolinian* (Apr. 1997): 25. **3.** *S*, 89. **4.** *BTB*, 200, 203, 206. **5.** *S*, 217, 219. **6.** *S*, 222–23. **7.** JD with HH, Apr. 25, 1996. **8.** VC, 121. **9.** Suarez, *Contemporary Literature* (summer 1990): 131, 132. **10.** *Contemporary Literature:* 131. **11.** Yeats, *Mythologies* (New York: Macmillan, 1959), 334, 337. **12.** Goff with HH, Aug. 26, 1996. **13.** JD with HH, Jul. 15, 1996. **14.** Campbell, *The Mythic Image* (Princeton: Princeton UP, 1974): 490. **15.** VC, 164. **16.** *NH*, 91. **17.** Ellmann and Feidelson, *The Modern Tradition* (New York: Oxford UP, 1965), 17–18. **18.** *Alnilam* abstract ms., Emory archive. **19.** Keats to Richard Woodhouse, Oct. 27, 1818. **20.** GC, 61, 62, 65, 69. **21.** Vanderbilt, *Alumnus* (Sept.–Oct. 1967): 15. **22.** VC, 24–25. **23.** Patsy Dickey, "Requiem for Jim," Mar. 13, 1979. **24.** VC, 119. **25.** VC, 120. **26.** Wilbur to HH, Sept. 21, 1995.

I. ORIGINS
1. Cityfolk and Countryfolk

1. Goff with HH, Aug. 8, 1996. **2.** JD with HH, Aug. 5, 1996, 2. **3.** *Yemassee* (winter/spring 1998): 7. **4.** *SOD*, 33. **5.** WB with HH, Sept. 18, 1997. **6.** *The Washington Post*, May 24, 1987, F6. **7.** JM with HH, Nov. 6–7, 1993. **8.** AB with HH, June 5, 1997. **9.** VC, 247. **10.** MD2 with HH, Feb. 14, 1997. **11.** *S-I*, 89. **12.** Lewis to HH, Oct. 26, 1995. **13.** MD2 to HH, Aug. 24, 1994. **14.** VC, 232. **15.** JD to Meg Stock, May 25, 1981. **16.** AB, GC, 46. **17.** *D*, 37–38. **18.** JD with HH, Aug. 5, 1996, 22. **19.** Van Ness, *SI*, 154. **20.** VC, 214. **21.** DiSanto, *Portrait of the Poet as Teacher* (Davidson: Briarpatch), 18. **22.** *The State Magazine*, Jan. 25, 1987, 8. **23.** JD to JW, Aug. 30, 1961. **24.** VC, 102. **25.** MD2 with HH, Mar. 10, 1997. **26.** VC, 101. **27.** JM with HH, Nov. 6–7, 1993. **28.** JD with HH, Aug. 5, 1996, 21. **29.** JD with HH, Aug. 5, 1996, 20. **30.** *The Casting* ms., Emory archive. **31.** Goff with HH, Aug. 8, 1996. **32.** *S-I*, 26. **33.** VC, 214. **34.** *Time* (Dec. 13, 1968): 75. **35.** *Yemassee*, 1998, 7. **36.** Darden Pyron, *Southern Daughter, The Life of Margaret Mitchell* (New York: Oxford UP, 1991), 62. **37.** CP, 260–61. **38.** Kelly with HH, Mar. 23, 1996. **39.** JD with HH, Aug. 5, 1996, 23.

40. JD to JW, Sept. 6, 1958.   **41.** JD with HH, Aug. 5, 1996, 29.   **42.** AB, GC, 9.   **43.** AB, GC, 16.   **44.** JD to MD1, Mar. 11, 1943.   **45.** AB, GC, 16.   **46.** AB, GC, 17.   **47.** Ellis, *Rocky Mountain News* (Apr. 16, 1986): 96.   **48.** JD with HH, Aug. 5, 1996, 25.

II. THE INVISIBLE STUDENT

2. "A Good Old Scout" (1929–1936)

1. Kelly with HH, Mar. 23, 1996.   **2.** Screenplay, Emory archive.   **3.** Patsy Dickey, *Creative Loafing* (Aug. 23, 1986).   **4.** Blackwood, Nov. 8, 1995.   **5.** JD with HH, Aug. 5, 1996, 9.   **6.** A, 98–99.   **7.** JD to James Coleman, Mar. 24, 1971.   **8.** JD to Virginia Kirkland, Apr. 8, 1970.   **9.** George Montgomery to HH, Aug. 28, 1995.   **10.** JD with HH, Aug. 5, 1996, 32–33.   **11.** CP, 83.   **12.** Richard Lamb with HH, May 19, 1994.   **13.** *The River's Overflow*, 24.

3. An Athlete's Masks (1936–1941)

1. *Buckhead Atlanta* (Aug. 18, 1975): 1.   **2.** *The Casting* ms., Emory archive.   **3.** Barnwell with HH, May 20, 1994.   **4.** S-I, 152.   **5.** Barnwell with HH, May 20, 1994.   **6.** *The Washington Post*, Mar. 19, 1974, B2.   **7.** Danny Romine, *The Charlotte Observer*, Aug. 2, 1981, E1.   **8.** NH, 254–55.   **9.** A, 632.   **10.** Sheldon Jaffery, *Selected Tales of Grim and Grue from the Horror Pulps* (Bowling Green: Bowling Green State UPP, 1987), 5.   **11.** AB, GC, 3.   **12.** Barnwell with HH, May 20, 1994.   **13.** Ron Goulart, *The Dime Detectives* (New York: The Mysterious Press, 1988), 175.   **14.** Kenneth Robeson, *Doc Savage No. 13—Land of Always-Night* (New York: Bantam, 1966), 6.   **15.** JD to MD, Aug. 21, 1951.   **16.** Barnwell with HH, May 20, 1994.   **17.** S-I, 151.   **18.** Robert Lowrance, *JD Newsletter*, Fall 1984, 8–9.   **19.** NH, 184.   **20.** NH, 184.   **21.** NH, 185.   **22.** VC, 62.   **23.** NH, 200.   **24.** *The Casting* ms.   **25.** Baldwin Spencer and F. J. Gillen, *The Native Tribes of Central Australia* [sic] (London: Macmillan, 1938), 259.   **26.** *The Casting* ms.   **27.** SI, 42.   **28.** *The Casting* ms.   **29.** *The Casting* ms.   **30.** Barnwell with HH, May 20, 1994.   **31.** Barnwell with HH, May 20, 1094.   **32.** JD with HH, Aug. 5, 1996, 39–40.   **33.** Barnwell with HH, May 20, 1994.   **34.** Notebooks, Emory archive.   **35.** CP, 152.   **36.** CP, 280.   **37.** Betsy Fancher, *Georgia*, Oct. 1972, 31, 40.   **38.** JD with HH, Aug. 5, 1996, 40.   **39.** Barnwell with HH, May 29, 1994.   **40.** CP, 212–14.   **41.** CP, 153.   **42.** North Fulton High School Annual, 1941.   **43.** Michele Ross, *The Atlanta Journal* (Apr. 27, 1982): B1.

4. Postgraduate Blues (1941–1942)

1. JD to McCallie, May 25, 1981.   **2.** JD with HH, Aug. 5, 1996, 42.   **3.** AB, GC, 16.   **4.** J. Daniel Hanks, *Story of Darlington School* (Rome: Commercial Pub. Co., 1991), 3, 10.   **5.** Montgomery to HH, Aug. 28, 1995.   **6.** Frank Rogers with HH, Mar. 22, 1996.   **7.** Carl Warren to HH, Nov. 21, 1995.   **8.** R.

Bryan Ellis with HH, Mar. 27, 1997.   **9.** JD with HH, Apr. 25, 1996.   **10.** JD with HH, Aug. 5, 1996, 36, 41.   **11.** *VC*, 109.   **12.** JD with HH, Aug. 5, 1996, 35.   **13.** Rogers with HH, Mar. 22, 1996.   **14.** Notebooks, Emory archive.

5. A Cadet's Rites of Passage (Fall 1942)

1. O'Neil, *Life* (Jul. 22, 1966): 68, 74.   **2.** Henry Mitchell, *The Washington Post*, Mar. 19, 1974, B2.   **3.** JD to George Plimpton, Jan. 23, 1980.   **4.** JD with HH, Aug. 5, 1996, 42.   **5.** *The Tiger* (Aug. 22, 1942): 2.   **6.** JD to parents, c. Sept. 1, 1942.   **7.** JD with HH, Aug. 5, 1996, 42–43.   **8.** *SI*, 136.   **9.** *SI*, 122.   **10.** Ellis Melette, *Old Clemson* (1981): 41.   **11.** JD to MD1, Sept. 11, 1942.   **12.** MD1 on envelope of JD letter, Sept. 11, 1942.   **13.** JD to MD1, Sept. 21, 1942.   **14.** JD with HH, Aug. 5, 1996, 26.   **15.** JD to father, Oct. 4, 1942.   **16.** Arnold Levine to HH, Sept. 6, 1995.   **17.** *The Tiger* (Oct. 15, 1942): 4–5.   **18.** JD to JW, Oct. 3, 1958.   **19.** JD with HH, Aug. 5, 1996, 27.   **20.** *CP*, 276, 277.   **21.** *CP*, 320.   **22.** *CP*, 390, 391.   **23.** *VC*, 168.   **24.** *NH*, 282.   **25.** Major Farr, *The Tiger* (Dec. 3, 1942): 2.

III. JOURNEY TO WAR

6. The Failed Pilot (1943–1944)

1. *VC*, 12.   **2.** JD, qtd. in Gordon Van Ness, *Ritual Magic* (Columbia: USC Ph.D. thesis, 1987, unpub.), 32.   **3.** JD to parents, Feb. 28, 1943.   **4.** JD to MD1, Mar. 11, 1943.   **5.** JD to parents, Mar. 4, 1943.   **6.** JD to MD1, Mar. 16, 1943.   **7.** JD to MD1, Apr. 8, 1943.   **8.** JD to MD1, May 10, 1943.   **9.** JD to father, May 18, 1943.   **10.** JD to MD1, May 31, 1943.   **11.** JD, "The Rebel Soul," Emory archive, c. May 31, 1943.   **12.** JD with HH, Aug. 5, 1996, 46–47.   **13.** JD to MD1, Jun. 23, 1943.   **14.** JD to MD1, Jul. 4, 1943.   **15.** JD to MD1, Jul. 9, 1943.   **16.** JD to MD1, Aug. 23, 1943.   **17.** JD to MD1, Jun. 10, 1945.   **18.** JD to MD1, Jan. 26, 1944.   **19.** JD to MD1, Aug. 23, 1943.   **20.** JD with HH, Aug. 5, 1996, 48.   **21.** JD with HH, Aug. 5, 1996, 47.   **22.** Court transcript, *Dickey v. Binkley* (Columbia: South Carolina State Supreme Court, Jun. 18, 1984), 66–67.   **23.** JD to Tom Dickey, Oct. 28, 1943.   **24.** *CP*, 386.   **25.** JD with HH, Aug. 5, 1996, 50.   **26.** JD with HH, Aug. 5, 1996, 49.   **27.** Buckley and Woods, *Poetry of the Victorian Period* (Glenview: Scott, Foresman, 1965), 585–86.   **28.** JD with HH, Aug. 5, 1996, 52.   **29.** JD with HH, Aug. 5, 1996, 51.   **30.** JD with HH, Aug. 5, 1996, 12.   **31.** JD with HH, Aug. 5, 1996, 12, 53.   **32.** JD with HH, Aug. 5, 1996, 53.   **33.** JD to Tom Dickey, Mar. 28, 1944.   **34.** JD to MD1, Jun. 11, 1944.   **35.** Gwen Walti to HH, Jan. 31, 1996.   **36.** JD to parents, Jun. 11, 1944.   **37.** Gwen Walti to HH, May 22, 1997.   **38.** JD with HH, Aug. 5, 1996, 55.   **39.** JD to MD1, Jul. 22, 1944.   **40.** JD to MB1, Dec. 9, 1944.   **41.** JD with HH, Aug. 5, 1996, 56.   **42.** *SI*, 26–27.   **43.** *VC*, 251.   **44.** JD with HH, Aug. 5, 1996, 54.   **45.** Dr. Iannone with HH, Aug. 2, 1996.   **46.** *A*, 735.   **47.** JD to MB1, Jul. 22, 1944.   **48.** Earl Bradley to HH, Feb. 4, 1997 and Jun. 21, 1994.   **49.** JD to parents, Oct. 5, 1944.   **50.** JD with HH, Aug. 5, 1996, 54, and JD with HH, Aug. 6, 1996, 78.   **51.** *A*, 227, 238,

497. **52.** JD to father, Oct. 16, 1944. **53.** Oct. 20, 1944. **54.** JD to John Simon, Jul. 6, 1979. **55.** JD, Military Records, Emory archive.

7. The Brain of the Plane (1945)

1. *The Houston Post*, Aug. 23, 1972, AA12. **2.** Bradley to HH, Feb. 4, 1997. **3.** *Crux* ms. Emory archive, 4. **4.** JD with HH, Aug. 5, 1996, 58. **5.** Vaughn diary, Jan. 17, 1944. **6.** Bradley to HH, Jun. 21, 1994. **7.** *CP*, 59–60. **8.** JD with HH, Aug. 5, 1996, 59. **9.** JD with HH, Aug. 5, 1996, 60. **10.** *SI*, 166. **11.** George Kamajian to HH, Jul. 31, 1994. **12.** JD to MB1, Apr. 1, 1945. **13.** Campbell, *The Flaming Terrapin* (London: Jonathan Cape, 1924), 14. **14.** Kamajian to HH, Jul. 31, 1994. **15.** JD to MD1, c. Sept. 1945. **16.** *The Casting* ms., Emory archive. **17.** Bradley to HH, Jun. 21, 1994. **18.** JD with HH, Aug. 5, 1996, 63. **19.** JD to Tom Dickey, Apr. 11, 1945. **20.** JD to family, c. Apr. 1945. **21.** Logan with HH, Jun. 30, 1994. **22.** Kamajian to HH, Jul. 31, 1994. **23.** Darrel Campbell to HH, Jan. 26, 1996. **24.** Bradley to HH, Feb. 4, 1997. **25.** *Poetical Remains*, Emory archive. **26.** Logan to HH, Nov. 5, 1994. **27.** Vaughn diary, Feb. 18, 1944. **28.** JD to Tom Dickey, Mar. 2, 1945. **29.** *Poetical Remains*. **30.** VC, 249. **31.** *Poetical Remains*. **32.** *SH*, 89. **33.** Vaughn diary, Mar. 16, 1945. **34.** JD with HH, Aug. 5, 1996, 59. **35.** Harold Whittern to HH, Dec. 18, 1996. **36.** VC, 16. **37.** Vaughn, Jan. 8, 1996. **38.** Campbell to HH, Jan. 26, 1996. **39.** Kamajian to HH, Nov. 11, 1995. **40.** "Tacloban," Emory archive. **41.** *S-I*, 92. **42.** *CP*, 59. **43.** Vaughn to HH, Jan. 8, 1996. **44.** *S-I*, 92. **45.** *CP*, 58. **46.** *CP*, 95. **47.** Medical exam request, Apr. 6, 1945, Emory archive. **48.** Campbell to HH, Jan. 26, 1996. **49.** JD to MD1, Mar. 10, 1945. **50.** JD to MD1, May 7, 1945. **51.** JD to MD1, Apr. 2, 1945. **52.** JD to MD1, May 7, 1945. **53.** JD to MD1, May 11, 1945. **54.** JD to MD1, Apr. 11, 1945. **55.** *SH*, 95. **56.** JD to MD1, May 7, 1945. **57.** JD to Tom Dickey, May 23, 1945. **58.** JD to father, May 28, 1945. **59.** Vaughn diary, May 27, 1945. **60.** *CP*, 226. **61.** *S-I*, 151. **62.** JD to MD1, c. Jun. 4, 1945. **63.** JD to MD1, Apr. 2, 1945. **64.** JD to father, Jun. 5, 1945. **65.** JD to Tom Dickey, Jun. 13, 1945. **66.** JD to MD1, Jun. 18, 1945. **67.** VC, 252. **68.** Bradley to HH, Jun. 21, 1994. **69.** JD to MD1, Jul. 30, 1945. **70.** JD with HH, Aug. 5, 1996, 60. **71.** JD with HH, Aug. 5, 1996, 63–64. **72.** Vaughn diary, Aug. 8, 1945. **73.** JD with HH, Aug. 5, 1996, 64. **74.** Bradley to HH, Jun. 21, 1994. **75.** Earl Turner with JD, *Vetletter*, USC (Oct. 1978): 2. **76.** JD with HH, Aug. 5, 1996, 62. **77.** Logan to HH, Nov. 5, 1994. **78.** Bradley to HH, Feb. 4, 1997. **79.** Records of Army Air Forces, Nat. Archive, Box 3031. **80.** *CP*, 197–98. **81.** Ernest Suarez with JD, *Contemporary Literature* (summer 1990): 122–23. **82.** JD with HH, Aug. 5, 1996, 62. **83.** Bradley to HH, Apr. 14, 1997. **84.** Bradley to HH, Apr. 14, 1997. **85.** JD, "Eye of the Fire," Emory archive, 9–10, 12. **86.** *SH*, 114–15. **87.** JD with HH, Aug. 5, 1996, 64. **88.** Samuel Eliot Morison, *Oxford History of the American People* (New York: New American Library, 1965), 409. **89.** JD to father, c. Oct. 18, 1945. **90.** JD to father, c. Nov. 1945. **91.** JD to mother, Sept. 29, 1945. **92.** *Stars and Stripes*, Dec. 6, 1945, 1. **93.** JD to MD1, Oct. 30, 1945. **94.** Bradley, Jun. 21, 1994. **95.** Paul Fridley, Military Records,

Emory archive. **96.** Logan to HH, Nov. 5, 1994. **97.** *CP*, 101. **98.** JD with HH, Aug. 5, 1996, 65. **99.** Military Records, Emory archive. **100.** Richard Calhoun and Robert Hill, *James Dickey* (Boston: Twayne, 1983), 3. **101.** 99, *SI*, 157. **102.** Ernest Suarez in *Dictionary of Literary Biography Yearbook* (Detroit: Gale Research, 1997), 137. **103.** JD to AL, Nov. 7, 1954.

IV. BECOMING A POET

8. Vanderbilt University (1946–1950)

1. *Vetletter* (Oct. 1978): 2. **2.** Walti with HH, Mar. 22, 1997. **3.** Walti with HH, Mar. 22, 1997. **4.** *S-I*, 33. **5.** Louis Rubin, *I'll Take My Stand* (Baton Rouge: LSU Press, 1930), 62. **6.** *I'll Take My Stand*, 260–61. **7.** *I'll Take My Stand*, 174. **8.** Paul Conkin, *Gone with the Ivy* (Knoxville: U of TN Press, 1985), 313. **9.** *D*, 51–52. **10.** W. J. Cash, *The Mind of the South* (New York: Knopf, 1941), 380. **11.** *Mind of the South*, 18–19. **12.** *Mind*, 45, 50. **13.** *Mind*, 228. **14.** *S-I*, 34–35. **15.** Donald Davidson, *Regionalism and Nationalism in the United States: The Attack on Leviathan* (Chapel Hill: UNC Press, 1938), 283. **16.** Pratt to HH, Dec. 28, 1995. **17.** David Arnett with JD, *Contemporary Literature* (Summer 1975): 299. **18.** JD to Donald Davidson, Mar. 26, 1957. **19.** Davidson, *Still Rebels, Still Yankees* (Baton Rouge: LSU Press, 1957), 210. **20.** *Gone with the Ivy*, 444. **21.** Winton in Robert Kirschten, *Critical Essays on James Dickey* (New York: G. K. Hall, 1994), 69. **22.** *Critical Essays*, 70. **23.** *Critical Essays*, 70. **24.** *S-I*, 29. **25.** *Vetletter* (Oct. 1978): 2. **26.** JD to father, c. Nov. 1945. **27.** Monroe Spears, *The Southern Review* (Fall 1994): 751. **28.** JD to Posterity, Apr. 24, 1981. **29.** *S-I*, 30. **30.** *S-I*, 31. **31.** Spears, *The Southern Review*, 751–52. **32.** *S-I*, 32–33. **33.** Kelsie Harder to HH, Aug. 13, 1995. **34.** Harder to HH, Aug. 13, 1995. **35.** JD to Margarite McEachern, Jan. 21, 1969. **36.** Poem sent to HH by Anne Locke, Mar. 12, 1997. **37.** Locke to HH, Mar. 12, 1997. **38.** Locke to HH, Mar. 12, 1997. **39.** Locke to HH, Mar. 12, 1997. **40.** Flicky Ford to HH, Jun. 24, 1996. **41.** JD with HH, Aug. 5, 1996, 66. **42.** JD with HH, Aug. 5, 1996, 66. **43.** JD to JW, Oct. 3, 1958. **44.** JD to Richard Howorth, Jan. 22, 1981. **45.** *S-I*, 36–37. **46.** *Gadfly* (winter 1947): 59. **47.** Ed Hodges, *Durham Morning Herald*, Apr. 12, 1981, D3. **48.** Dickey, *Veteran Birth* (Charlotte: Palaemon Press, 1978). **49.** Qtd. in Van Ness, *Ritual Magic*, 127. **50.** Notebooks, Emory archive. **51.** Notebooks, Emory archive. **52.** Notebooks, Emory archive. **53.** *S-I*, 65. **54.** Notebooks, Emory archive. **55.** Notebooks, Emory archive. **56.** JD to Strickland, Oct. 19, 1970. **57.** JD with HH, Aug. 5, 1996, 27. **58.** *D*, 28–29. **59.** JD with HH, Aug. 5, 1996, 67. **60.** JD with HH, Aug. 5, 1996, 68. **61.** Winton, *Critical Essays*, 74. **62.** JD with HH, Aug. 5, 1996, 66. **63.** JD to MD, c. 1948. **64.** JD with HH, Aug. 5, 1996, 70. **65.** *S-I*, 39. **66.** JD with HH, Aug. 6, 1996, 70. **67.** *S-I*, 39. **68.** JM with HH, Nov. 6-7, 1993. **69.** JM with HH, Nov. 6–7. **70.** Winton with HH, Aug. 6, 1994. **71.** Winton, *Critical Essays*, 74. **72.** Winton, *Critical Essays*, 75. **73.** Winton, *Critical Essays*, 75. **74.** Winton, *Critical Essays*, 75. **75.** JD, *Symbol and Image in the Shorter Poems of Herman*

Melville (Nashville: Vanderbilt Univ. master's thesis, 1950, unpub.), 3–4. **76.** JD, master's thesis, 66. **77.** JD master's thesis, 59–60. **78.** Carl Zibart with HH, Jun. 9, 1997. **79.** JD with HH, Aug. 5, 1996, 66. **80.** *D*, 90. **81.** John Hall with HH, Jul. 14, 1995. **82.** Bill Pratt to HH, Dec. 28, 1995. **83.** Notebooks, Emory archive. **84.** Pratt to HH, Dec. 28, 1995. **85.** *S-I*, 40. **86.** *The Sewanee Review* (April–June 1951): 290. **87.** *The Sewanee Review:* 291. **88.** Patsy Dickey with HH, Nov. 15, 1997. **89.** Patsy Dickey, ms. for *Creative Loafing* article, "Requiem for Jim" (Mar. 13, 1979). **90.** JD to Pratt, Jan. 8, 1959. **91.** JD with HH, Aug. 5, 1996, 67. **92.** Pratt to HH, Feb. 23, 1997. **93.** JD with HH, Aug. 5, 1996, 71.

V. A KING IN THE CLASSROOM

9. Rice Institute (1950)

1. JD with HH, Aug. 5, 1996, 27. **2.** JD with HH, Aug. 5, 1996, 71. **3.** Edward Lewis to HH, Sept. 1, 1994. **4.** Pat Carr to HH, "James Dickey at Rice" ms. **5.** JD with HH, Aug. 5, 1996, 72. **6.** *VC*, 173–74. **7.** *VC*, 261. **8.** *SI*, 68. **9.** *SI*, 65, 160. **10.** Notebooks, Emory archive. **11.** Notebooks, Emory archive. **12.** Notebooks, Emory archive. **13.** *SI*, 96, 103, 97–98. **14.** *SI*, 113.

10. The Korean Distraction (1951–1952)

1. JD to James Coleman, Mar. 24, 1971. **2.** JD to Willie Morris, Jan. 10, 1972. **3.** *S-I*, 41. **4.** JD to father, Jul. 20, 1945. **5.** "Willie Morris in Conversation," *Mississippi Review*, no. 3 (1974): 130. **6.** JD to MD, Mar. 19, 1951. **7.** JD to MD, Apr. 25, 1951. **8.** JD to MD, c. 1951. **9.** JD to MD, May 4, 1951. **10.** JD to MD, May 4, 1951. **11.** JD to MD, c. mid-May, 1951. **12.** MD to JD, Jul. 2, 1953. **13.** JD to MD, Apr. 25, 1951. **14.** *Mississippi Review:* 130. **15.** Albert Murray with HH, Oct. 26, 1996. **16.** JD to MD, Aug. 4, 1951. **17.** Military Records, Emory archive. **18.** JD to MD, Aug. 15, 1951. **19.** JD to MD, Aug. 28, 1951. **20.** JD to MD, Aug. 21, 1951. **21.** *SI*, 131. **22.** Notebooks, Emory archive. **23.** *SI*, 152. **24.** JD to MD, Oct. 5, 1951. **25.** JD with HH, Aug. 7, 1996, 34. **26.** *SI*, 149. **27.** *SI*, 113. **28.** JD to MD, Sept. 28, 1951. **29.** Notebooks, Emory archive. **30.** Simone de Beauvoir, *The Marquis de Sade* (New York: Grove, 1953), 82. **31.** *Marquis de Sade*, 16. **32.** HH with WB, Nov. 14, 1998. **33.** *SI*, 211. **34.** Notebooks, Emory archive. **35.** JD to Willard Thorp, Dec. 26, 1953. **36.** *SI*, 135. **37.** Notebooks, Emory archive. **38.** Notebooks, Emory archive. **39.** *SI*, 169. **40.** Notebooks, Emory archive. **41.** JD to MD, Jul. 26, 1952.

11. Return to Academe (1952–1954)

1. George Garrett with HH, Oct. 23, 1993. **2.** JD with HH, Aug. 6, 1996, 77. **3.** Tom (no last name given) to JD, May 11, 1957. **4.** Carr, "Dickey at Rice." **5.** *S-I*, 42. **6.** MD to JD, Jul. 2, 1953. **7.** JD with HH, Aug. 6, 1996, 76–77.

8. JD with HH, Aug. 6, 1996, 78.   **9.** Lester Mansfield, "Existentialism," *The Rice Institute Pamphlet* (Oct. 1954): 20, 23.   **10.** *SI*, 58.   **11.** JD with HH, Aug. 5, 1996, 72.   **12.** Wilfred Dowden with HH, Sept. 30, 1994.   **13.** JD to Willard Thorp, Dec. 26, 1953.   **14.** JD to Robert Highfill, Jan. 5, 1954.   **15.** JD to Monroe Spears, Jan. 12, 1954.   **16.** JD to AL, Apr. 3, 1954.   **17.** AL to JD, Mar. 21, 1954.   **18.** JD to AL, May 7, 1954.   **19.** AL to JD, c. 1954.   **20.** JD to AL, c. 1954.   **21.** AL to JD, c. 1954.   **22.** JD to AL, Apr. 1, 1954.   **23.** JD to AL, c. Apr. 1954.   **24.** AL to JD, May 2, 1954.   **25.** JD to AL, Jun. 20, 1954.   **26.** AL to JD, Jun. 14, 1954.   **27.** AL to Eugene Dickey, Jun. 14, 1954.   **28.** JD to AL, c. Jun. 1954.   **29.** AL to JD, c. Jun. 1954.   **30.** JD to AL, c. 1954.   **31.** JD to MD, Jun. 17, 1954.   **32.** JD to AL, c. 1954.   **33.** JD to MD, Jun. 24, 1954.   **34.** JD to MD, Jun. 24, 1954.

12. Travels in Europe (1954–1955)

1. *SOD*, 71.   **2.** MD to her mother, Aug. 2, 1954.   **3.** JD to AL, c. 1954.   **4.** JD to AL, c. 1954.   **5.** JD to AL, Nov. 7, 1954.   **6.** JD to JW, Aug. 4, 1959.   **7.** JD with HH, Aug. 6, 1996, 2a.   **8.** DiSanto, *Portrait of the Poet as Teacher*: 22.   **9.** WB with HH, Sept. 18, 1977.   **10.** T. S. Eliot to Mrs. James Gussow, Dec. 19, 1954.   **11.** T. S. Eliot to JD, Mar. 9, 1955.   **12.** JD to AL, Aug. 15, 1954.   **13.** JD to AL, Sept. 25, 1954.   **14.** JD in *Creative Loafing* (Oct. 16, 1993): 15.   **15.** JD to AL, Sept. 25, 1954.   **16.** JD with HH, Aug. 6, 1996, 2a.   **17.** JD to AL, Sept. 25, 1954.   **18.** JD to AL, Sept. 25, 1954.   **19.** JD to AL, Nov. 7, 1954.   **20.** JD with HH, Aug. 6, 1996, 3a.   **21.** JD to Pratt, Nov. 3, 1954.   **22.** *VC*, 20.   **23.** John Edwardson to HH, Oct. 8, 1994.   **24.** MD to her mother, Oct. 26, 1954.   **25.** MD to her mother, Nov. 3, 1954.   **26.** JD to MD1, Mar. 24, 1955.   **27.** JD with HH, Aug. 6, 1996.   **28.** MD to her mother, Feb. 28, 1955.   **29.** JD to Pratt, Jan. 28, 1954.   **30.** JD to AL, c. 1954.   **31.** JD to Monroe Spears, c. 1954.   **32.** MD to her mother, Mar. 21, 1955.   **33.** JD with HH, Aug. 6, 1996, 25a.   **34.** *CP*, 98.   **35.** JD to Richard Wilbur, Oct. 25, 1955.   **36.** MD to her mother, Apr. 20, 1955.   **37.** JD to Jacob Wise, Apr. 22, 1955.   **38.** "To Gweno," Wash. Univ. archive.   **39.** JD to Pratt, Jun. 11, 1955.

13. Uncle Ez and the Pen Women Scandal (1955–1956)

1. Bill Pratt to HH, Apr. 14, 1997.   **2.** Pratt, "The Greatest Poet in Captivity," *The Sewanee Review* (Fall 1986): 627.   **3.** Pratt to HH, Apr. 14, 1996.   **4.** JD with HH, Aug. 6, 1996, 4–5a.   **5.** JD, qtd. in *Colorado Daily*, Aug. 2, 1968, 2.   **6.** JD to John Logue, Apr. 9, 1973.   **7.** *Colorado Daily*, 2.   **8.** Pratt to HH, Apr. 14, 1997.   **9.** JD with HH, Aug. 6, 1996, 6a.   **10.** JD to Pound, "Ezra Pound and James Dickey," *Paideuma* (Fall 1982): 293.   **11.** Pound to JD, *Paideuma*: 294.   **12.** *Paideuma*: 296.   **13.** JD to Pratt, Sept. 6, 1955.   **14.** JD to Pratt, Aug. 20, 1955.   **15.** JD with HH, Aug. 6, 1996, 6a.   **16.** Lucy Trowbridge to HH, Jul. 25, 1995.   **17.** Clinton Trowbridge to HH, Jul. 25, 1995.   **18.** John Lyons to HH, Jun. 20, 1995.   **19.** JD to MD, Apr. 8, 1956.   **20.** Madison Jones with HH, Apr. 19, 1997.   **21.** Walter Sullivan to HH, Sept. 27, 1995.   **22.** S-

I, 43.   **23.** JD to AL, Nov. 7, 1954.   **24.** "The Father's Body," *Poetry* (Dec. 1956): 145–49.   **25.** Harder to HH, Aug. 13, 1995.   **26.** Lucy Trowbridge to HH, Jul. 25, 1995.   **27.** Smith Kirkpatrick with HH, Aug. 21, 1994.   **28.** *Paideuma:* 298.   **29.** *Paideuma:* 301.   **30.** *Paideuma:* 305.   **31.** *Paideuma:* 308.   **32.** JD to William Jay Smith, Mar. 11, 1956.   **33.** JD to JW, Aug. 6, 1959.   **34.** GC, 107–8.   **35.** JD to Pratt, May 7, 1957.

VI. *INTO THE STONE:* THE ADVERTISING YEARS
14. Coca-Cola and Jingle Jim (1956–1959)

1. JM with HH, Nov. 6–7, 1993.   **2.** Pratt to HH, Jan. 10, 1996.   **3.** Patsy Dickey with HH, May 2, 1997.   **4.** Thad Horton with HH, Apr. 30, 1997.   **5.** JD with HH, Aug. 6, 1996, 8a.   **6.** JD to MD, c. Apr. 1956.   **7.** JD with HH, Aug. 6, 1996, 8a.   **8.** Apr. 10, 1956.   **9.** "Selling His Soul to the Devil," *TV Guide* (Jul. 14, 1979): 18.   **10.** JD with HH, Aug. 6, 1996, 9–10a.   **11.** JD with HH, Aug. 6, 1996, 10a.   **12.** JD to Gordon Lish, Sept. 17, 1981.   **13.** Pratt to HH, Apr. 17, 1997.   **14.** Violetta Brown with HH, May 20, 1997.   **15.** JD to MD, Jun. 1, 1956.   **16.** Brown with HH, Jun. 2, 1997.   **17.** Brown with HH, May 20, 1997.   **18.** JD to MD, Jun. 7, 1956.   **19.** Brown with HH, May 20, 1997.   **20.** JD to JW, Oct. 3, 1958.   **21.** JD with HH, Aug. 6, 1996, 10a.   **22.** Mark Bollmann with HH, May 5, 1997.   **23.** VC, 202.   **24.** JD with HH, Aug. 6, 1996, 11a.   **25.** Inman Mays, "The Devil and James Dickey" ms., 3.   **26.** Mays with HH, Mar. 7, 1995.   **27.** Howard Hyle with HH, Apr. 29, 1997.   **28.** Mike McDonald with HH, Apr. 30, 1997.   **29.** Doug Smith with HH, Jun. 26, 1977.   **30.** Thad Horton with HH, Apr. 30, 1997.   **31.** Jonis Gold with JD, May 4, 1997.   **32.** JD with HH, Aug. 6, 1996, 14a.   **33.** JD, "Air-Slash" ms., Emory archive, 2.   **34.** "Air-Slash," 3.   **35.** AB with HH, Mar. 3, 1995.   **36.** "The Archer's Author," *Archery World* (Apr.–May 1973): 35.   **37.** *S-I*, 44.   **38.** JD to Pratt, May 27, 1957.   **39.** JD to Williams, c. Fall 1957.   **40.** Williams to JD, Oct. 4, 1957.   **41.** JD to Williams, Nov. 22, 1957.   **42.** *The Atlanta Journal*, Apr. 24, 1988, H2.   **43.** *The Atlanta Journal*, H2.   **44.** JW to JD, Aug. 19, 1960.   **45.** JD to JW, Aug. 6, 1959.   **46.** JD to JW, Oct. 3, 1958.   **47.** JD to DH, Apr. 2, 1957.   **48.** JD to DH, Jul. 29, 1957.   **49.** JD to DH, Jul. 29, 1957.   **50.** JD to DH, Oct. 9, 1957.   **51.** JD to DH, Nov. 16, 1957.   **52.** *Paideuma:* 303.   **53.** Franklin Ashley with HH, Feb. 23, 1997.   **54.** JD to DH, Feb. 18, 1958.   **55.** JD to DH, Apr. 9, 1958.   **56.** JD to JW, Mar. 18, 1958.   **57.** Mays, "The Devil," 8.   **58.** *The Sewanee Review* (Apr.–Jun. 1958): 297.   **59.** JW to JD, Jul. 6, 1958.   **60.** Jul. 19, 1958.   **61.** JW to JD, Jul. 20, 1958.   **62.** JD to JW, Mar. 18, 1958.   **63.** JD to JW, Jul. 23, 1958.   **64.** JW to JD, Aug. 8, 1958.   **65.** Nov. 3, 1958.   **66.** JD to JW, Feb. 27, 1959.   **67.** JD to DH, Mar. 23, 1959.   **68.** *The Sewanee Review* (Apr.–Jun. 1958): 314.   **69.** Qtd. by JW to JD, Jul. 25, 1958.   **70.** JD to Berryman, Jul. 8, 1958.   **71.** JW to JD, Jul. 25, 1958.   **72.** RB with HH, Dec. 14, 1994.   **73.** RB to JD, Aug. 15, 1958.   **74.** RB to JD, Nov. 14, 1958.   **75.** RB to JD, May 5, 1959.   **76.** JD to JW, Mar. 18, 1958.   **77.** Box 146, folder 9, Emory archive.   **78.** JD to JW, Jul. 26, 1958.

79. JD to JW, Jul. 26, 1958.   **80.** JD to JW, Aug. 17, 1958.   **81.** JD to JW, Aug. 17, 1958.   **82.** JD to JW, Aug. 17, 1958.   **83.** JW to JD, Aug. 20, 1958.   **84.** AB with HH, Mar. 3, 1995.   **85.** JW to JD, Aug. 20, 1958.   **86.** JW to JD, Aug. 25, 1958.   **87.** JD to JW, Aug. 27, 1958.   **88.** *The Sewanee Review* (Apr.–Jun. 1958): 300.   **89.** JD to JW, Sept. 6, 1958.   **90.** Richard Hugo to JD, Sept. 16, 1958.   **91.** Hugo to JD, Sept. 16, 1958.   **92.** Hugo to JD, c. 1958.   **93.** JW to JD, Sept. 11, 1958.   **94.** Wheelock to JD, Dec. 19, 1958.   **95.** Wheelock to JD, Jan. 9, 1959.   **96.** JD to JW, c. early Feb., 1959.   **97.** DH to JD, Jan. 19, 1959.   **98.** JD to JW, Jun. 15, 1959.   **99.** JD to W. J. Smith, Oct. 3, 1958.   **100.** JD to Wheelock, May 27, 1959.   **101.** JD to JW, Oct. 12, 1959.   **102.** RB with HH, Dec. 14, 1994.   **103.** JD to JW, Nov. 27, 1959.   **104.** JD to JW, Nov. 27, 1959.   **105.** JW to JD, Nov. 19, 1959.   **106.** JD to HH, Dec. 5, 1996.   **107.** JD to Wheelock, Nov. 17, 1959.   **108.** Pendergrast notes for *For God, Country, and Coca-Cola* to HH, Oct. 19, 1992.   **109.** JD's application to Liller, Neal, Emory archive.   **110.** JD to DH, Mar. 23, 1959.   **111.** JD to JW, Oct. 12, 1959.   **112.** JD to JW, Oct. 12, 1959.   **113.** JD to Merrill, Dec. 6, 1959.

15. Potato Chips and Canoe Trips (1959–1961)

1. Richard Hodges with HH, Oct. 12, 1994.   **2.** JD to Thomas Hart, Jan. 15, 1982.   **3.** JD with HH, Aug. 6, 1996, 13a.   **4.** RB to JD, Feb. 6, 1960.   **5.** JD to JW, Mar. 21, 1960.   **6.** Ford grant, Emory archive.   **7.** Ford application.   **8.** Notebooks, Emory Archive.   **9.** JD to Gioia, Jan. 20, 1982.   **10.** JD to Cox, Dec. 7, 1972.   **11.** *D*, 19.   **12.** GC, 27, 114, 72.   **13.** GC, 103, 36.   **14.** GC, 77–78.   **15.** GC, 34, 72.   **16.** GC, 103–4, 28–29.   **17.** *NH*, 239.   **18.** JD, qtd. by Paul Hendrickson, *The National Observer* (Dec. 4, 1976): 24.   **19.** VC, 111.   **20.** JD with HH, Aug. 6, 1996, 14a.   **21.** GC, 112.   **22.** GC, 52.   **23.** *D*, 69.   **24.** CP, 142–44.   **25.** *D*, 7.   **26.** *D*, 34.   **27.** GC, 127.   **28.** GC, 55–56.   **29.** GC, 57.   **30.** *D*, 45.   **31.** GC, 117–19.   **32.** GC, 127.   **33.** GC, 126, 117–20.   **34.** GC, 56.   **35.** GC, 81.   **36.** Mays with HH, Mar. 7, 1995.   **37.** Cantwell with HH, May 29, 1998.   **38.** GC, 79.   **39.** GC, 84.   **40.** *D*, 83, 84.   **41.** CP, 80–81.   **42.** *D*, 163, 169, 171, 171.   **43.** JD to JW, Mar. 21, 1960.   **44.** Van Duyn with HH, Feb. 2, 1997.   **45.** JD to Maryrose Carroll, Nov. 15, 1996.   **46.** JD to JW, Mar. 21, 1960.   **47.** JW in Kirschten, *Critical Essays*, 29–30.   **48.** JD, qtd. by Katz, *The Denver Post*, Apr. 23, 1986, C1.   **49.** *S-I*, 85.   **50.** CP, 49.   **51.** *S-I*, 85.   **52.** CP, 54, 55.   **53.** CP, 52, 61.   **54.** Fancher, *Georgia* (Oct. 1972): 31, 30.   **55.** JD to JW, Nov. 20, 1960.   **56.** JD to DH, Feb. 21, 1961.   **57.** CP, 177.   **58.** JD to Gioia, Jan. 20, 1982.   **59.** Notebooks, Emory archive.   **60.** Cromartie with HH, Apr. 21, 1997.   **61.** DH to JD, May 28, 1961.   **62.** JD to DH, Sept. 14, 1961.   **63.** Wilbur to HH, Sept. 21, 1995.   **64.** DH in *The Paris Review* (Fall 1991): 168.   **65.** Guggenheim application, Emory archive.   **66.** JD to Gioia, Jan. 20, 1982.   **67.** JD to JW, Jul. 10, 1961.   **68.** JD to DH, Jul. 15, 1961.   **69.** Verill with HH, Apr. 21, 1997.   **70.** JD to JW, Aug. 30, 1961.   **71.** JD to JW, Aug. 30, 1961.   **72.** JD to Gioia, Jan. 20, 1982.   **73.** Kelly with HH, Mar. 23, 1996.   **74.** JD with HH, Aug. 6, 1996, 20a, and JD with HH, Aug. 5, 1996, 27.   **75.** Fancher,

Georgia, 31.   **76.** JW to JD, Jul. 17, 1961.   **77.** JD, qtd. by Polak, *Philadelphia Inquirer*, Jun. 19, 1977, 7.

VII. BARNSTORMING FOR POETRY
16. Return to Europe (1961–1962)

1. JD to DH, Sept. 7, 1961.   **2.** JD to DH, Sept. 14, 1961.   **3.** JD to DH, Oct. 18, 1961.   **4.** Wilcox with HH, Nov. 9, 1995.   **5.** Wilcox to HH, Mar. 2, 1996. **6.** Wilcox to HH, Mar. 2, 1996.   **7.** Wilcox to HH, Mar. 2, 1996.   **8.** Daniell, *Atlanta* (Jan. 1998): 38.   **9.** Daniell, *Fatal Flowers* (New York: Henry Holt, 1980), 162–63.   **10.** Daniell, *Atlanta* (Jan. 1998): 30.   **11.** Daniell, *Fatal Flowers*, 163.   **12.** Daniell, *Atlanta* (Jan. 1998): 38.   **13.** Daniell, *Fatal Flowers*, 163–64.   **14.** *Fatal Flowers*, 166.   **15.** Daniell with HH, Nov. 6, 1995. **16.** Daniell, "Surrealist" ms., Emory archive.   **17.** Daniell, *Fatal Flowers*, 168–69.   **18.** Daniell with HH, Nov. 6, 1995.   **19.** Terry with HH, Mar. 25, 1996.   **20.** Daniell with HH, Nov. 6, 1995.   **21.** RB with HH, Dec. 14, 1994. **22.** JD to DH, Oct. 18, 1961.   **23.** *SOD*, 107.   **24.** *SOD*, 109.   **25.** JD to father, Jun. 9, 1962.   **26.** *SOD*, 114.   **27.** CD with HH, Mar. 21, 1998.   **28.** JD to Merrill, Apr. 16, 1962.   **29.** Emory archive, Box 133.   **30.** Arnett, *Contemporary Literature*: 287.   **31.** JD, qtd. by Wood, *Charleston News and Courier*, May 31, 1979, A14.   **32.** JD to RB, Jun. 30, 1962.   **33.** JD to RB, Jun. 30, 1962.   **34.** JD to JW, Jul. 30, 1962.   **35.** JD with HH, Aug. 6, 1996, 25a. **36.** Raines to JD, Aug. 10, 1962.   **37.** VC, 151.   **38.** JD to JW, Jul. 30, 1962. **39.** MD's diary, Emory archive.   **40.** Oglethorpe commencement, May 14, 1989, Emory archive.   **41.** JD to RB, Aug. 21, 1962.   **42.** JD with HH, Aug. 6, 1996, 27a.   **43.** MD's diary, Emory archive.   **44.** JD to DH, Aug. 27, 1962. **45.** *S-I*, 168–69.   **46.** Untermeyer to JD, Feb. 7, 1966.   **47.** *S-I*, 102.   **48.** *CP*, 73–74.   **49.** *S-I*, 108.   **50.** *CP*, 79.   **51.** *CP*, 80.   **52.** *CP*, 87.   **53.** JD to Pratt, Nov. 9, 1961.

17. A Southerner in Oregon (1963–1964)

1. JD to JW, Jan. 10, 1963.   **2.** Katherine Camp with HH, Dec. 8, 1995.   **3.** JD with HH, Aug. 6, 1996, 31a.   **4.** JD to Raines, Jan. 28, 1963.   **5.** JD to DH, Jan. 10, 1963.   **6.** Roger Porter with HH, Jul. 19, 1995.   **7.** Hugo to JD, c. 1963.   **8.** Porter with HH, Jul. 19, 1995.   **9.** David Casseres with HH, Nov. 17, 1995.   **10.** Warshow with HH, Feb. 5, 1998.   **11.** Rawley to HH, Jul. 23, 1995.   **12.** Holden with HH, Oct. 4, 1995.   **13.** Kipnis with HH, Oct. 26, 1995.   **14.** Kipnis with HH, Nov. 14, 1995.   **15.** JD with HH, Aug. 6, 1996, 31a.   **16.** Ullman with HH, Mar. 18, 1997.   **17.** Ullman with HH, Mar. 18, 1997.   **18.** Ullman with HH, Mar. 18, 1997.   **19.** Rawley to HH, Jul. 23, 1995. **20.** Brentano to HH, Sept. 26, 1995.   **21.** DH to HH, Aug. 11, 1994.   **22.** JD to DH, Feb. 13, 1963.   **23.** DH to HH, Aug. 11, 1994.   **24.** DH, *The Paris Review* (Fall 1991): 168–69.   **25.** JD to DH, Jul. 28, 1963.   **26.** *S*, 218.   **27.** *S*, 219–21.   **28.** JD with HH, Aug. 6, 1996, 2.   **29.** Pincus with HH, Dec. 3,

1997.   **30.** VC.   **31.** David Keller with HH, Sept. 6, 1998.   **32.** Childress, May 27, 1981, Emory archive.   **33.** Hugo to JD, Apr. 19, 1963.   **34.** Hugo to JD, May 22, 1963.   **35.** Hugo to JD, Jul. 8, 1963.   **36.** Hugo to JD, Jul. 15, 1963.   **37.** JD with HH, Aug. 6, 1996, 3–4.   **38.** Wagoner, *Collected Poems, 1956–1976* (Bloomington: Indiana, UP, 1976), 67.   **39.** AB to JD, Jun. 21, 1963.   **40.** Ullman with HH, Mar. 18, 1997.   **41.** Taft to HH, Dec. 14, 1997.   **42.** JD to DH, Dec. 20, 1963.   **43.** Lescher with HH, Jul. 30, 1997.   **44.** Lescher with HH, Jul. 30, 1997.   **45.** JD with HH, Aug. 6, 1996, 11.   **46.** *Deliverance* ms., Emory archive.   **47.** JD, qtd. in *Florence Morning News*, May 21, 1972, D1.   **48.** *Deliverance* ms., Emory archive.   **49.** *Deliverance* ms.   **50.** *Deliverance* ms.   **51.** *Deliverance* ms.   **52.** Bruce Weigl and Terry Hummer, *The Imagination as Glory* (Urbana: U. of Illinois P, 1984), 165.   **53.** JD with HH, Aug. 6, 1996, 11.   **54.** JD to Merrill, Sept. 15, 1963.   **55.** Van Etten to JD, Feb. 1, 1964.   **56.** JD with HH, Aug. 6, 1996, 45.   **57.** Simon with HH, May 26, 1996.   **58.** Burnshaw with HH, Jul. 7, 1998.   **59.** Arnett, *Contemporary Literature*: 295.   **60.** Brooks with HH, Sept. 20, 1996.   **61.** MD to JD, Feb. 3, 1964.   **62.** Van Duyn with HH, Feb. 2, 1997.   **63.** *SOD*, 130.   **64.** JD to JW, Apr. 5, 1964.   **65.** RB with HH, Dec. 14, 1994.   **66.** JD to JW, Apr. 5, 1964.   **67.** Hugo to JD, Feb. 10, 1964.   **68.** Lockwood to JD, Apr. 2, 1964.   **69.** MD1 to JD, Apr. 29, 1964.   **70.** MD1 to JD, Jun. 2, 1964.   **71.** MB1 to JD, Oct. 29, 1965.   **72.** *NH*, 350, 347.   **73.** Rawley to HH, Jul. 23, 1995.   **74.** Merrill to JD, May 18, 1964.   **75.** JD to RB, Mar. 23, 1965.   **76.** JD to DH, May 11, 1964.   **77.** JD to DH, May 21, 1964.   **78.** DH to JD, Jun. 9, 1964.   **79.** JD to DH, Jun. 17, 1964.   **80.** Levertov to JD, Jul. 16, 1964.   **81.** JD to RB, Aug. 2, 1964.   **82.** *SIP*, 10–11.   **83.** *SIP*, 74, 16–17, 51, 54, 20, 21, 34, 45, 26, 56.   **84.** Lescher to JD, Apr. 19, 1965.   **85.** Lescher with HH, May 28, 1996.   **86.** Lescher to JD, Jul. 30, 1965.   **87.** JD to Brooks, Aug. 14, 1965.   **88.** JD with HH, Aug. 6, 1996, 53.   **89.** Sept. 29, 1965.   **90.** JDS to JD, Nov. 19, 1965.   **91.** King to JD, Apr. 14, 1964.   **92.** JD to MD, Aug. 8, 1964.   **93.** JD to DH, Sept. 26, 1964.   **94.** King to JD, Oct. 23, 1964.

18. California Sojourn (1964–1965)

1. *NH*, 202.   **2.** CD with HH, Mar. 21, 1998.   **3.** *CP*, 276.   **4.** *SOD*, 129–30.   **5.** *S-I*, 49.   **6.** ApRoberts to HH, Aug. 2, 1996.   **7.** Broesamle, *Suddenly a Giant* (Northridge: Santa Susana Press, 1993), 31.   **8.** JD with HH, Aug. 6, 1996, 31a.   **9.** Blakeslee to HH, Sept. 20, 1996.   **10.** Finestone to HH, Feb. 9, 1996.   **11.** Clendenning to HH, Aug. 16, 1996.   **12.** Clendenning to HH, Aug. 16, 1996.   **13.** VC, 24.   **14.** Graves to HH, Aug. 18, 1996.   **15.** *S-I*, 161.   **16.** CP, 237–38.   **17.** "In Fannin County" ms., c. Dec. 1963, Emory archive.   **18.** Suarez, *Contemporary Literature*, vol. 31, no. 2 (1990): 124–25.   **19.** Peters to HH, Apr. 26, 1997.   **20.** Graves, *The Kenyon Review* (Nov. 1966): 663–70.   **21.** *BTB*, 250–51.   **22.** VC, 29.   **23.** DH to JD, Nov. 18, 1964.   **24.** Levertov to JD, Feb. 24, 1965.   **25.** JD, *American Scholar* (fall 1965): 656.   **26.** JD with HH, Aug. 6, 1996, 5.   **27.** DH to HH, Aug. 11, 1994.   **28.** Levertov to JD, May 21, 1966.   **29.** *NH*, 353.   **30.** JD to MD, Jun. 16, 1965.

31. JD to CD, Jul. 10, 1965.   **32.** JD to Gaines, Apr. 10, 1970.   **33.** VC, 22.
34. JD with HH, Aug. 6, 1996, 6.   **35.** WB with HH, Sept. 18, 1998.

19. A Frozen Berkeley (Spring 1966)

1. JD to Rideout, Jan. 3, 1966.   **2.** Greiffer to HH, Sept. 26, 1997.   **3.** Keller
with HH, Sept. 6, 1998.   **4.** JD to Rideout, Jan. 3, 1966.   **5.** Rideout with HH,
Sept. 4, 1995.   **6.** Rideout with HH, Sept. 4, 1995.   **7.** Rodman to HH, Oct.
12, 1996.   **8.** Dembo to HH, Sept. 20, 1995.   **9.** Cromie, *Chicago Tribune*,
Mar. 15, 1966, sec. 2, 2.   **10.** Cross, *Milwaukee Journal*, Mar. 20, 1966, sec. 5, 4.
11. JD with HH, Aug. 6, 1996, 12–13.   **12.** JD with HH, Aug. 6, 1996, 14.
13. S, 68.   **14.** JD with HH, Aug. 6, 1996, 14.   **15.** CP, 395, 397, 399.   **16.**
S, 70–71.   **17.** CP, 262–63.   **18.** CD with HH, Mar. 21, 1998.   **19.** JD with
HH, Aug. 6, 1996, 17.   **20.** Diane Wood Middlebrook, *Anne Sexton* (Boston:
Houghton Mifflin, 1991), 250.   **21.** Sexton to JD, Dec. 12, 1965.   **22.** Sexton
to JD, c. Dec. 1965.   **23.** Sexton to JD, c. Feb. 1966.   **24.** Middlebrook, *Anne
Sexton*, 251.   **25.** Sexton to JD, Mar. 1966.   **26.** Davison with HH, Sept. 6,
1995.   **27.** CD with HH, Mar. 21, 1998.   **28.** Allin with HH, Jan. 14, 1997.
29. NH, 109–10.   **30.** JD to Lowell, Nov. 20, 1965.   **31.** JD, qtd. by Fancher,
Georgia (Oct. 1972): 30.   **32.** U. of Wisconsin Press Release, Mar. 15, 1966,
Emory archive.   **33.** RB to JD, Nov. 21, 1966.   **34.** RB, *American Poetry* (New
York: Harper & Row, 1990), 177.   **35.** VC, 15.   **36.** RB, *American Poetry*, 174.
37. VC, 32, 34.   **38.** RB to JD, Jun. 28, 1966.   **39.** JD to RB, Jul. 16, 1966.
40. RB, "The Collapse," *The Sixties* (spring 1967): 79.   **41.** VC, 128.   **42.** RB
with HH, Oct. 22, 1997.   **43.** GC, 290.   **44.** JD to KM, Aug. 24, 1970.   **45.**
RB with HH, Dec. 14, 1994.   **46.** RB with HH, Oct. 22, 1997.   **47.** CP, 193,
198, 194.   **48.** CP, 207, 234.   **49.** VC, 25.   **50.** CP, 216, 224.   **51.** CD with
HH, Mar. 21, 1998.   **52.** JD with HH, Aug. 6, 1996, 20.   **53.** Cody to HH,
Jun. 28, 1996.   **54.** MD1 to JD, Jul. 29, 1966.

VIII. IN POETRY'S CATBIRD SEAT
20. First Term (1966–1967)

1. JD, qtd. by Kenneth Ikenberry, *Washington Sunday Star*, Sept. 11, 1966, D21.
2. Aarons, *The Washington Post*, Sept. 10, 1966, D6.   **3.** William McGuire,
Poetry's Catbird Seat (Washington D.C.: Library of Congress, 1988), 52.   **4.**
VC, 59.   **5.** JD with HH, Aug. 6, 1996, 8–9.   **6.** JD to Burnshaw, Nov. 11,
1966.   **7.** JD to Pratt, c. 1967.   **8.** Pratt to JD, Feb. 27, 1967.   **9.** Pratt to HH,
Feb. 3, 1996.   **10.** Henry Taylor with HH, Aug. 7, 1994.   **11.** Taylor with HH,
Aug. 7, 1994.   **12.** Taylor with HH, Aug. 7, 1994.   **13.** Poetry Consultant's
Annual Report, Library of Congress archive, 2.   **14.** JD to Swain, Dec. 12,
1966.   **15.** CP, 248.   **16.** BTB, 203, 206–207.   **17.** JD, qtd. by Danny
Romine, *The Charlotte Observer*, Aug. 2, 1981, E1.   **18.** CP, 288–90, 294.   **19.**
JD to Williams, Nov. 15, 1966.   **20.** JD to Dwelle, May 8, 1967.   **21.** JD,

Annual Report 1967, Library of Congress. **22.** DH to HH, Aug. 11, 1994.
23. JD to Stafford, Oct. 28, 1970. **24.** Mrs. Plummer to JD, Mar. 1967. **25.**
GC, 162–63. **26.** WB with HH, Sept. 18, 1997. **27.** Lieberman with HH,
Apr. 6, 1996. **28.** JD to Hart, May 8, 1967. **29.** Wolf, *The Washington Post,*
May 9, 1967, A22. **30.** CP, 246. **31.** VC, 149. **32.** NH, 78. **33.** MD2 to
JD, May 18, 1967. **34.** Suarez, *Contemporary Literature:* 125. **35.** JD with
HH, Aug. 6, 1996, 23–24. **36.** GC, 157. **37.** JD to Janeway, Jun. 12, 1969.
38. Harder to HH, Aug. 13, 1995. **39.** Lieberman to JD, Jun. 25, 1967. **40.**
Harder to HH, Aug. 13, 1995. **41.** Suarez with HH, Jun. 20, 1995. **42.**
Harder to HH, Aug. 13, 1995.

21. Second Term (1967–1968)

1. JD to JW, Aug. 28, 1967. **2.** RB to Di Capua, Sept. 23, 1967. **3.** RB to JD,
Oct. 30, 1967. **4.** RB to Straus, Dec. 20, 1967. **5.** RB to JD, Dec. 20, 1967.
6. JD, qtd. by Shaw, *The Crimson* (Nov. 9, 1967): 2. **7.** Lowell to JD, Sept. 15,
1966. **8.** VC, 246. **9.** JD to JW, Aug. 28, 1967. **10.** Lieberman to JD, Nov.
2, 1967. **11.** *Virginia Quarterly Review,* vol. 71, no. 1, 1995, 97–98. **12.** Miller
with HH, Sept. 3, 1995. **13.** JD, qtd. by Neal, *The Daily Oklahoman,* Jun. 18,
1968, N1. **14.** CD to JD, Oct. 30, 1967. **15.** CD to JD, Oct. 30, 1967. **16.**
SOD, 147. **17.** CD with HH, Mar. 21, 1998. **18.** JD to CD, Nov. 7, 1967.
19. Nov. 3, 1967. **20.** JD to CD, Nov. 7, 1967. **21.** JD, qtd. by Olivia
Skinner, *St. Louis Post-Dispatch,* Nov. 15, 1967, F2. **22.** Updike to HH, Sept.
8, 1993. **23.** JD to Eleanor Taylor, Mar. 7, 1984. **24.** Broderick to HH, Mar.
14, 1996. **25.** Updike to HH, Sept. 8, 1993. **26.** JDS to JD, Nov. 7, 1967.
27. NH, 337. **28.** S, 179. **29.** Guilds with HH, Nov. 14, 1998. **30.** JD to
USC, Dec. 19, 1967. **31.** JD to Matheson, Dec. 15, 1967. **32.** Morris with
HH, Mar. 31, 1997. **33.** Smith to JD, Jan. 27, 1968. **34.** JD to Smith, Feb.
21, 1968. **35.** JD, qtd. by Price, *New York Times Book Review,* Mar. 23, 1997,
31. **36.** Price, *New York Times Book Review,* 31. **37.** Powell, "James Dickey—
Poetry, Music, and Deliverance," *Brandon Sun,* c. late 1974. **38.** JD to Beaver,
Oct. 1, 1968. **39.** JD with HH, Aug. 6, 1996, 28, 29. **40.** Sandy, "Corn Soup"
ms. to HH. **41.** BTB, 160. **42.** Mays, "The Devil," 21. **43.** Mills, *Chicago
Sun-Times Book Week,* May 5, 1968, 4. **44.** Lipton, *Los Angeles Free Press,* Feb.
4, 1972, 7. **45.** *Poetry's Catbird Seat,* 304. **46.** James Reiss with HH, Jan. 27,
1996. **47.** Reiss with HH, Jan. 27, 1996. **48.** Reiss to HH, Jan. 30, 1996.
49. Reiss with HH, Jan. 27, 1996. **50.** JD with HH, Aug. 6, 1996, 38. **51.**
Reiss to Raines, Aug. 6, 1969. **52.** JD to KM, Aug. 3, 1969. **53.** S-I, 10–11.
54. Smith to JD, c. Jun. 1968. **55.** Smith to *The Atlantic Monthly,* Aug. 15,
1968. **56.** Moore with HH, Aug. 1, 1997. **57.** *Poetry's Catbird Seat,* 306.

IX. TENURE IN SOUTH CAROLINA

22. "A Starry Place Between the Antlers" (1968)

1. MD, qtd. by Bruton, *The State,* Jun. 2, 1968, E3. **2.** NH, 323–24. **3.** NH,
20–21. **4.** NH, 23, 25. **5.** Reg Murphy, *The Atlanta Constitution,* Nov. 2,

1968, 4.   **6.** Rubin to HH, Jan. 5, 1998.   **7.** JD with HH, Aug. 6, 1996, 34.   **8.** MacFarlane to HH, Apr. 19, 1997.   **9.** JD to Raines, Sept. 22, 1968.   **10.** JDS to JD, Oct. 7, 1968.   **11.** *Time*, Dec. 13, 1968, 75.   **12.** JD, qtd. by McClellan, *Johnson City Press Chronicle*, Feb. 19, 1972, no p.   **13.** Kunhardt to HH, Nov. 17, 1995.   **14.** Kunhardt to HH, Nov. 17, 1995.   **15.** *Life* (Nov. 1, 1968): 26.   **16.** Schirra to HH, Oct. 17, 1995.   **17.** JD with HH, Aug. 6, 1996, 46.   **18.** *Life*: 26.   **19.** Kunhardt with HH, Oct. 26, 1995.   **20.** Mays, "The Devil" ms., 12.   **21.** CP, 314–15.   **22.** GC, 160.   **23.** S, 55–56.   **24.** *Time* (Dec. 13, 1968): 75.   **25.** Kanfer with HH, Sept. 25, 1995.   **26.** *Time*: 92.   **27.** Kanfer with HH, Sept. 25, 1995.   **28.** JD to Wilbur, Sept. 16, 1968.   **29.** Wilbur to JD, Sept. 18, 1968.   **30.** Lockwood to JD, Oct. 22, 1968.   **31.** JD to Boss, Mar. 16, 1969.   **32.** McHugh, *Columbia Record*, Nov. 30, 1968, C2.   **33.** Redman, *Portfolio* (Nov. 1980): 13.   **34.** VC, 211.   **35.** Redman, *(Portfolio)*: 12.   **36.** Redman, *Portfolio*: 13.   **37.** JM with HH, Nov. 6–7, 1993.   **38.** JM with HH, Nov. 6–7, 1993.   **39.** Adams to HH, Nov. 15, 1997.   **40.** Stapleton, *Southern World* (Nov.–Dec. 1979): 25.   **41.** Garrett with HH, Oct. 23, 1993.   **42.** JD to CD, Mar. 16, 1969.   **43.** John Kimmey to HH, Jan. 5, 1998.   **44.** Bruccoli with HH, Sept. 14, 1997.   **45.** DG with HH, Sept. 15, 1997.   **46.** Dunlap with HH, Sept. 30, 1997.   **47.** JD to Hollins Alumnae Club, Jan. 23, 1969.   **48.** JD to Burnshaw, Feb. 5, 1969.   **49.** CP, 299.   **50.** JD to Burnshaw, Jul. 10, 1969.   **51.** JD to Thorp, May 22, 1970.   **52.** JD to Howard, Jun. 17, 1970.   **53.** JD to Bexley, Sept. 4, 1969.   **54.** JD to KM, Feb. 28, 1969.   **55.** JD to KM, May 23, 1969.   **56.** Seay with HH, Jan. 3, 1996.   **57.** JD to Allen, Feb. 5, 1969.   **58.** JD to CD, Mar. 16, 1969.   **59.** JD to CD, Mar. 16, 1969.   **60.** JD to Buckley, Nov. 21, 1972.   **61.** Martin to HH, Dec. 18, 1997.   **62.** Morris with HH, Mar. 31, 1997.   **63.** Martin to HH, Dec. 16, 1997.   **64.** JD to KM, Mar. 4, 1971.   **65.** Gollob with HH, Nov. 15, 1995.   **66.** Morris with HH, Mar. 31, 1997.   **67.** JD to CD, Mar. 16, 1969.   **68.** Smart with HH, Jul. 22, 1995.   **69.** Smart with HH, Jul. 22, 1994.   **70.** McGraw with HH, Nov. 2, 1996.   **71.** CD with HH, Mar. 21, 1998.   **72.** JM with HH, Nov. 6–7, 1993.   **73.** JD to Smart, May 21, 1969.   **74.** JD to Janeway, May 22, 1969.

23. To the Moon and Hollywood (1969)

1. Buckley with HH, Nov. 7, 1997.   **2.** Byron Janice with HH, Oct. 7, 1997.   **3.** NH, 156.   **4.** CP, 315–17.   **5.** Crawford, *The Oxford American*, issue 16 (1997).   **6.** Mitchell to HH, Mar. 4, 1998.   **7.** Mitchell to HH, Mar. 4, 1998.   **8.** Crowther with HH, Feb. 17, 1998.   **9.** JD, qtd. by Pease, *The Milwaukee Journal*, Nov. 9, 1969, sec. 1, 18.   **10.** JD to Wouk, Aug. 24, 1969.   **11.** JD to Kinnell, Sept. 24, 1969.   **12.** JD, qtd. in *Tennessee Poetry Journal*, vol. 2, no. 2: 17.   **13.** JD to Applewhite, Jul. 24, 1969.   **14.** JD to Fiedler, Aug. 1, 1969.   **15.** JD to Wilbur, Jul. 31, 1969.   **16.** JD to Wilbur, Sept. 16, 1968.   **17.** S, 44.   **18.** JD to Unterecker, Sept. 16, 1969.   **19.** S, 26.   **20.** S, 84, 101, 90, 39.   **21.** S, 18.   **22.** JD to Neumeyer, Mar. 16, 1970.   **23.** JD to Lowell, Oct. 15, 1969.   **24.** Lowell to JD, c. Oct. 1969.   **25.** JD to Lowell, Oct. 29, 1969.   **26.** JD to Lowell, Nov. 13, 1969.   **27.** JD to Manns, Mar. 19, 1970.   **28.** JD to Larner, Mar. 19, 1970.   **29.** JD to Lowell, Dec. 10, 1969.   **30.** JD to Ann Stanford,

Jan. 30, 1970. **31.** SOD, 161. **32.** Morris, *The Hampden-Sidney Poetry Review* (winter 1979), no p. **33.** Frady with HH, Dec. 19, 1997. **34.** Howard with HH, Dec. 5, 1995. **35.** Howard with H, Dec. 5, 1995. **36.** JD to Howard, Jul. 15, 1981. **37.** JD to Howard, Jan. 23, 1970. **38.** JD, qtd. by Hopkins and Miles, *The Atlanta Constitution*, Jan. 1, 1970, A1. **39.** JD to Richmond, Jan. 9, 1970. **40.** JD to Klingman, Jan. 21, 1970. **41.** JD to SR, Sept. 30, 1970. **42.** JD to Howard, Jun. 17, 1970. **43.** Shaw, *Poetry* (Jul. 1971): 230. **44.** Leibowitz, *The New York Times Book Review*, Nov. 8, 1970, 22. **45.** JW to JD, Mar. 5, 1970. **46.** JD to JW, Mar. 16, 1970. **47.** CP, 332–35. **48.** JD to Sheldon, Mar. 19, 1970.

X. *DELIVERANCE*

24. A Bestseller (1970)

1. JD to JDS, May 23, 1969. **2.** JDS to JD, Jun. 18, 1969. **3.** JD to JDS, May 31, 1969. **4.** JDS to JD, Jun. 18, 1969. **5.** JD to JDS, Aug. 6, 1969. **6.** JD to Noble, Aug. 22, 1969. **7.** JD to Rahv, Dec. 17, 1969. **8.** JD to Stegner, Dec. 10, 1969. **9.** JD to Ellen Lane, Jun. 20, 1971. **10.** GC, 68. **11.** JD to Donaldson, Mar. 18, 1970. **12.** GC, 128. **13.** JD, qtd. by Coulbourn, *The Atlanta Journal-Constitution Magazine*, Mar. 15, 1970, 38. **14.** JD, qtd. by Curran, *Family Week*, Mar. 7, 1974. **15.** GC, 39–40. **16.** JD to JDS, Jun. 26, 1971. **17.** JD, qtd. by Coulbourn, *The Atlanta Journal-Constitution Magazine*, Mar. 15, 1970, 40, 43. **18.** Kelly with HH, Mar. 11, 1996. **19.** D, 233. **20.** D, 199, 214, 227–28, 215. **21.** Judith Crist, *Take 22* (New York: Viking, 1984), 139. **22.** JB with HH, Nov. 17 1995. **23.** Roper, *North Georgia Journal* (summer 1995): 20. **24.** Arnett, *Contemporary Literature*: 291. **25.** JD to Exley, Apr. 13, 1970. **26.** JD to John West, Oct. 20, 1972. **27.** D, 11, 14, 220. **28.** D, 8, 11. **29.** JD to Paul Binding, Jan. 31, 1979. **30.** D, 11. **31.** GC, 2. **32.** Greer with HH, Sept. 20, 1997. **33.** D, 30, 23, 37, 78, 98. **34.** Conrad, *Heart of Darkness* in *Modern British Literature* (London: Oxford UP, 1973), 114, 111, 165. **35.** Arnett, *Contemporary Literature*: 295. **36.** D, 231. **37.** JW to JD, Mar. 15, 1977. **38.** D, 235. **39.** D, 236. **40.** JD, qtd. by Roper, *North Georgia Journal*: 22. **41.** JD to Meyer, Apr. 10, 1970. **42.** JD to Cavell, Mar. 26, 1971. **43.** JD to Oates, Mar. 22, 1971. **44.** JD, qtd. by Tom Burke, *Esquire* (Jan. 1972): 155. **45.** D, 230. **46.** JD to Vince, Jun. 10, 1970. **47.** JD with Weiser, Nov. 16, 1973, Emory archive. **48.** JD to KM, Apr. 8, 1970. **49.** JD to Stevenson, May 22, 1970. **50.** JD to Stevens, Apr. 8, 1970. **51.** JD to Neumeyer, Apr. 10, 1970. **52.** JD to Ullman, Jun. 19, 1970. **53.** JD, "Adultery," c. 1970. **54.** Cantwell, *Speaking with Strangers*, 29, 30, 33. **55.** Cantwell, *Speaking*, 34, 48. **56.** *Speaking*, 71–72. **57.** *Speaking*, 84–85. **58.** Cantwell with HH, May 29, 1998. **59.** *Speaking*, 106, 32. **60.** JD to Thompson, Apr. 10, 1970. **61.** JD to Thompson, Jul. 10, 1970. **62.** Greer with HH, Sept. 20 1977. **63.** JD with HH, Aug. 8, 1996. **64.** Goff, qtd. in *Portfolio* (fall 1984): 20. **65.** Goff with HH, Aug. 8, 1996. **66.** Goff with HH, Aug. 8, 1996. **67.** Rorem, *The Later Diaries of Ned Rorem* (San Francisco: North Point, 1983), 323. **68.** Rorem with HH, Oct. 9, 1997. **69.** JD to

Rorem, May 18, 1970. **70.** JDS with HH, Oct. 9, 1995. **71.** R. H. W. Dillard with HH, Aug. 29, 1996. **72.** Chappell to HH, Sept. 30, 1997. **73.** Louis Simpson, *A Revolution in Taste—Studies of Dylan Thomas, Allen Ginsberg, Sylvia Plath, and Robert Lowell* (New York: Macmillan, 1978), 31. **74.** Crowther, *Oxford American*, issue 16 (1996): 14. **75.** Crowther with HH, Oct. 23, 1993. **76.** JD to Garrett, Jun. 29, 1970. **77.** JD to Whitehead, Aug. 11, 1970. **78.** JD to Beckerman, Apr. 8, 1970. **79.** JD to Stevens, Apr. 8, 1970. **80.** JD to Taft, Nov. 2, 1970. **81.** JD to Hill, Oct. 26, 1970. **82.** JD to Bottoms, Aug. 18, 1981. **83.** Amy Burk with HH, Sept. 23, 1998. **84.** GC, 124. **85.** JD to Morris, Nov. 19, 1970. **86.** JD to KM, Nov. 23, 1970.

25. Making the Movie (1971)

1. JD to Calley, Aug. 6, 1970. **2.** *NH*, 83. **3.** *D*, 8, 12. **4.** JD to Heyen, Aug. 11, 1970. **5.** JD to Abrahams, Aug. 20, 1970. **6.** JD with HH, Aug. 6, 1996, 51, 50. **7.** JD to Du Bois, Oct. 12, 1970. **8.** Michel Ciment, *John Boorman* (London: Faber, 1986), 129. **9.** JD with HH, Aug. 6, 1996, 51. **10.** Orme to HH, Nov. 3, 1997. **11.** JB with HH, Nov. 17, 1995. **12.** JD to Edwin Peeples, Jan. 1, 1971. **13.** JB to JD, Dec. 10, 1970. **14.** JD to JB, Nov. 25, 1970. **15.** JB to JD, Dec. 10, 1970. **16.** JD to JB, Dec. 29, 1970. **17.** JD to JB, Dec. 29, 1970. **18.** JD to JB, Jan. 18, 1971. **19.** JD to JB, Jan. 18, 1971. **20.** JD to JB, Jan. 18, 1971. **21.** JB with HH, Nov. 17, 1995. **22.** JD with HH, Aug. 6, 1996, 48. **23.** JD, qtd. by Trimble, *Arkansas Democrat Gazette*, Oct. 14, 1979, F5. **24.** Ciment, *John Boorman*, 129, 132. **25.** JD to Brentano, Mar. 6, 1971. **26.** Ciment, *John Boorman*, 129. **27.** JD to RB, Jan. 15, 1971. **28.** JD to Kuzma, Feb. 8, 1971. **29.** RB to JD, Feb. 25, 1971. **30.** JD to RB, May 10, 1972. **31.** JD to Du Bois, Apr. 8, 1971. **32.** Reynolds, *My Life* (New York: Hyperion, 1994), 150. **33.** Crist, *Take 22*, 138. **34.** *SOD*, 166. **35.** Crist, *Take 22*, 139. **36.** Reynolds, *My Life*, 151. **37.** JD with HH, Aug. 6, 1996, 52. **38.** Terry with HH, Mar. 25, 1996. **39.** JD, qtd. in Blackburn, *Archery World* (Feb.–Mar. 1972): 10. **40.** Crist, *Take 22*, 140. **41.** Blackburn with HH, Nov. 1, 1995. **42.** JD, qtd. in Blackburn, *Archery World:* 10. **43.** Ciment, *John Boorman*, 132. **44.** JD, qtd. by Ebert, *New York Times*, Mar. 26, 1972, 13. **45.** Reynolds, *My Life*, 151–52. **46.** Crist, *Take 22*, 139. **47.** Hubert Shuptrine with HH, Jul. 21, 1996. **48.** Voight, qtd. by Burke, *Esquire*, Jan. 1972, 157–58. **49.** Burke, *Esquire*, 150. **50.** Terry with HH, Mar. 25, 1996. **51.** JB with HH, Nov. 17, 1995. **52.** Reynolds, *My Life*, 152–53. **53.** JB with HH, Nov. 17, 1971. **54.** Reynolds, *My Life*, 153. **55.** JB, qtd. in *Los Angeles Times*, *Calendar*, Feb. 20, 1972, 54. **56.** JB, *LA Times*, 54. **57.** JD to JDS, Jun. 26, 1971. **58.** GC, 136. **59.** KD with HH, Jul. 26, 1997. **60.** Reynolds, *My Life*, 154–55. **61.** JD to SR, Jul. 26, 1971. **62.** Reynolds, *My Life*, 157. **63.** McKinney, qtd. by Coulburn, *The Atlanta Journal-Constitution Magazine*, Jul. 25, 1971, 18. **64.** Reynolds, *My Life*, 157. **65.** *SOD*, 180. **66.** Fancher, *Georgia*, Oct. 1972, 47. **67.** Reynolds, *My Life*, 158. **68.** JB with HH, Nov. 17, 1995. **69.** JD with HH, Aug. 6, 1996, 60–61. **70.** VC, 129. **71.** JD to Drinnon, Jul. 27, 1971. **72.** Ciment, *John Boorman*, 130. **73.** JD to JB, Sept. 5, 1971. **74.**

JD to Patterson, Nov. 9, 1971.   **75.** JB to JD, Sept. 28, 1971.   **76.** JD to Voight, Mar. 14, 1972.   **77.** *NH*, 84.   **78.** JD to Russo, Jul. 5, 1971.   **79.** *NH*, 85. **80.** *VC*, 68.   **81.** *VC*, 55.   **82.** JD to KM, Feb. 10, 1997.   **83.** *NH*, 142, 145.

XI. THE SECOND ACT

26. King of the Cats (1971–1972)

1. Bruccoli, *Notebooks of F. Scott Fitzgerald* (New York: Harcourt Brace Jovanovich/Bruccoli Clark, 1980), 58.   **2.** JD to Cid Corman, Oct. 4, 1971. **3.** JD to Aleda Shirley, Nov. 9, 1971.   **4.** JD to *Playboy*, Oct. 25, 1971.   **5.** Paul Mariani, *Dream Song* (New York: Norton, 1990), 407.   **6.** S, 3, 3, 124, 23, 26, 45, 51, 69, 85, 69, 52, 77, 97, 105, 106, 104, 73, 89.   **7.** Mays, "The Devil," 18. **8.** Broyard, *The New York Times*, Dec. 17, 1971.   **9.** Shaff, *Minneapolis Star Tribune*, Jan. 9, 1972.   **10.** Kessler, *Los Angeles Times*, Jan. 16, 1972.   **11.** JD to KM, Oct. 4, 1971.   **12.** JD, qtd. in *Subject to Change* (Oct. 26, 1978): 21.   **13.** JD to KM, Jan. 29, 1971.   **14.** *The State*, Nov. 30, 1971, B1.   **15.** JD to Stern, Nov. 25, 1970.   **16.** JD to Austin Briggs, Nov. 2, 1970.   **17.** JD to Atwell, Sept. 11, 1972.   **18.** JD to Univ. of Michigan, May 14, 1975.   **19.** JD to Thurston, Sept. 22, 1976.   **20.** JD to Gatenby, Nov. 7, 1980.   **21.** JD to Kilroy, Jul. 22, 1981.   **22.** JD to Donaldson, Dec. 22, 1984.   **23.** JD, qtd. by Stockton, *News and Courier*, Mar. 19, 1971, D1.   **24.** Hunter with HH, Sept. 19, 1995. **25.** Hunter with HH, Sept. 19, 1995.   **26.** MD, qtd. by Casey, *The Washington Post*, Nov. 20, 1971, E1.   **27.** Conroy with HH, Aug. 29, 1997.   **28.** Conroy to JD, Sept. 18, 1980.   **29.** *The Atlanta Constitution*, Oct. 14, 1974, B2.   **30.** Conroy with HH, Aug. 29, 1997.   **31.** Conroy with HH, Aug. 29, 1997.   **32.** Conroy to JD, Apr. 17, 1992.   **33.** Greer with HH, Sept. 20, 1997.   **34.** Richard Bausch with HH, Feb. 18, 1995.   **35.** GC, 17.   **36.** JD to Haffenden, Nov. 16, 1973.   **37.** JD to Hamilton, Dec. 7, 1982.   **38.** JD to Berryman, Jan. 20, 1971.   **39.** Yevtushenko, qtd. by Putney, *The National Observer*, Feb. 12, 1972, 6.   **40.** VC, 116.   **41.** Dolmetsch with HH, Jul. 31, 1994.   **42.** JD to Howard, Oct. 19, 1970.   **43.** *National Observer* (May 6, 1971): 22.   **44.** Lea with HH, Jan. 24, 1994.   **45.** JD to Quarry, Nov. 2, 1970.   **46.** JD to Hayes, Aug. 6, 1969.   **47.** *The Dartmouth*, May 26, 1972, 1.   **48.** Eleanor Taylor with HH, Apr. 17, 1996.   **49.** Styron obituary for JD, Jan. 27, 1997.   **50.** Styron with HH, Oct. 12, 1996.   **51.** Styron, Oct. 12, 1996.   **52.** *The Sewanee Review*, vol. CVI, no. 3 (1998): 473.

27. Premieres and Their Aftermath (1972–1973)

1. Mays, "The Devil," 18.   **2.** Mays, "The Devil," 19.   **3.** Richard Howard with HH, Dec. 5, 1995.   **4.** Mays, "The Devil," 19.   **5.** GC, 88, 89.   **6.** Fancher, *Georgia*, 30.   **7.** JB with HH, Nov. 17, 1995.   **8.** JD, qtd. by Harden, *Washington Sunday Times Advertiser*, May 8, 1977, E4.   **9.** Andrew Sabel, draft of 1973 article, Emory archive, 3.   **10.** JD to Bellow, Jun. 13, 1996.   **11.** GC, 95, 141.   **12.** GC, 98.   **13.** GC, 99, 283.   **14.** JD, qtd. by Maschal, *The*

Charlotte Observer, Oct. 8, 1972, D1.   **15.** Garrett with HH, Oct. 23, 1993.
16. JD to JB, Sept. 22, 1972, and Sept. 12, 1972.   **17.** JD to JB, Sept. 12, 1972.
18. JB to JD, Sept. 16, 1972.   **19.** Roper, *North Georgia Journal*, 20.   **20.** VC,
106.   **21.** Rickman with HH, Jun. 26, 1996.   **22.** JD to Gluck, Sept. 5, 1972.
23. Garrett with HH, Oct. 23, 1993.   **24.** Garrett, Oct. 23, 1993.   **25.** Garrett
to JD, c. Jul. 1969.   **26.** Garrett with HH, Oct. 23, 1993.   **27.** Garrett with
HH, Oct. 23, 1993.   **28.** JD to Allen Archery Co., Sept. 14, 1971.   **29.**
Worcester Evening Gazette, Nov. 9, 1972, 31.   **30.** *The State*, Nov. 2, 1972, A1,
A7.   **31.** Barnwell with HH, May 20, 1994.   **32.** JD to Rorem, Feb. 17, 1972.
33. JD to Shuptrine, Apr. 9, 1973.   **34.** *Denver Post*, Sept. 19, 1993, F6.   **35.**
The Gamecock, Feb. 1, 1973, 2.   **36.** *Melody Maker*, Apr. 21, 1973, 15.   **37.**
Santora with HH, Feb. 2, 1996.   **38.** U.S. District Court of Southern District
of New York, transcript of *Combine Music Corp vs. Warner Bros.*, Feb. 3, 1975, 3.
39. Court transcript 3–5.   **40.** GC, 6–7.   **41.** GC, 7.   **42.** JD to Bradley, Feb.
7, 1973.   **43.** *Esquire*, Feb. 1976, 67.   **44.** JD to Recupido, Mar. 26, 1973.
45. VC, 241.   **46.** *Esquire*, May 1976, 26.   **47.** JD to Smith, Jun. 12, 1981.
48. Scott with HH, Oct. 16, 1995.   **49.** Gonia with HH, Jun. 11, 1997.   **50.**
Greenbrier lecture, Emory archive.   **51.** McGraw with HH, Nov. 2, 1996.
52. *NH*, 178.   **53.** GC, 175.   **54.** GC, 179.   **55.** GC, 179–80.   **56.** GC,
184.   **57.** GC, 186.   **58.** GC, 189–90.   **59.** GC, 217, 191.   **60.** GC, 193.

28. A Double Vision (1973–1974)

1. JD to Lish, Jul. 11, 1973.   **2.** *The Atlanta Constitution*, Aug. 14, 1973, B4.
3. Baer with HH, Jul. 18, 1996.   **4.** Eisiminger, *Pembroke Magazine*, no. 12
(1980): 162–65.   **5.** Colvert to HH, Dec. 12, 1995.   **6.** Havird to HH, May 2,
1998.   **7.** *The Drury Mirror*, Nov. 30, 1973, 5.   **8.** Shapcott, *Biting the Bullet*,
165.   **9.** *The Drury Mirror*, 5.   **10.** JD, qtd. by Swanson, *The Gamecock*, Nov.
29, 1973, 4.   **11.** JD to Warren, Jan. 7, 1974.   **12.** *The Gamecock*, Jan. 28,
1974, 4.   **13.** JD to Warren, Jan. 7, 1974.   **14.** JD with HH, Aug. 6, 1996,
63–64.   **15.** JD to Walker, Jul. 22, 1981.   **16.** KD with HH, Jul. 26, 1996.
17. CP, 222.   **18.** SOD, 209.   **19.** JD, qtd. by Kass, *The Diamondback*, Mar. 21,
1974, 10.   **20.** Kass, *Argus/Dimension*, Mar. 29, 1974, 3.   **21.** DG with HH,
Sept. 15, 1997.   **22.** Havird to HH, Mar. 13, 1998.   **23.** Lowell to JD, May 18,
1974.   **24.** Stuart with HH, Apr. 16, 1998.   **25.** Smith, *Los Angeles Times*,
May 5, 1976, sec. 4, 1, 22.   **26.** Patsy Dickey to JD, May 1, 1973.   **27.** JD to
Stuart, Feb. 18, 1975.   **28.** *Gene Bullard* ms., Emory archive.   **29.** J, 15, 24, 65,
113.   **30.** Morrison, *Atlanta Weekly* (Feb. 1, 1981): 12–13.   **31.** JD to
Shuptrine, Jul. 21, 1996.   **32.** Shuptrines with HH, Jul. 21, 1996.   **33.** Logue
with HH, Oct. 27, 1995.   **34.** Shuptrines with HH, Jul. 21, 1996.   **35.** Phyllis
Shuptrine to HH, Jul. 25, 1996.   **36.** Shuptrines with HH, Jul. 21, 1996.   **37.**
Phyllis Shuptrine to HH, Jul. 10, 1996.   **38.** Shuptrines with HH, Jul. 21, 1996.
39. Logue with HH, Oct. 27, 1995.   **40.** *The Atlanta Constitution*, Oct. 24,
1974.   **41.** Shuptrines with HH, Jul. 21, 1996.   **42.** Yardley, *The New Republic*
(Nov. 30, 1974): 43.   **43.** J, 27.   **44.** JD to *The New York Times*, Nov. 31, 1974.
45. GC, 229.

772 / JAMES DICKEY

29. "Star-Beasts of Intellect and Madness" (1975–1976)

1. JD to SR, Apr. 12, 1973. 2. JD to Graham, Apr. 8, 1975. 3. JD to Smith, Feb. 3, 1975. 4. *The Columbia Record*, Sept. 30, 1976, B6. 5. JD to Bennett, May 30, 1979. 6. *The Sewanee Review* (Apr.–Jun. 1947): 238–51. 7. CP, 365, 348, 359, 373. 8. JD, qtd. by Ashley, *The Columbia Record*, Sept. 30, 1976, B6. 9. CP, 372. 10. *Time*, Sept. 29, 1975, 46. 11. Mooney with HH, Jul. 31, 1998. 12. DG with HH, Sept. 15, 1997. 13. Garrett, *Whistling in the Dark* (New York: Harcourt Brace, 1992) 69–70. 14. *SOD*, 195. 15. *Time* (Sept. 29, 1975): 46. 16. JD to Dana, Dec. 11, 1975. 17. *Houston Chronicle*, Oct. 13, 1974. 18. CD with HH, Mar. 21, 1998. 19. *Yemassee*, winter–spring 1998, 11. 20. KD with HH, Jul. 26, 1997. 21. GC, 247. 22. GC, 289. 23. Smith, *Los Angeles Times*, May 5, 1976, 22. 24. JD to Fries, Oct. 1, 1976. 25. *Gene Bullard* ms., Emory archive, 103, 140. 26. WB with HH, Sept. 18, 1997. 27. Redman, *Portfolio* (Nov. 1980): 11. 28. JD to Stitch, Oct. 18, 1976. 29. JD to Meyers, Sept. 24, 1982. 30. DiSanto, *Portrait:* 23. 31. WB with HH, May 11, 1998. 32. DG with HH, Sept. 15, 1996. 33. GC, 234. 34. KD with HH, Jul. 26, 1997. 35. GC, 235. 36. Zibart with HH, Jun. 9, 1997. 37. *SOD*, 203. 38. GC, 238. 39. AB with HH, Sept. 2, 1998. 40. GC, 239. 41. JD to Warren, May 12, 1980. 42. Guerry with HH, May 4, 1998. 43. GC, 241. 44. Romine, *The Charlotte Observer*, Aug. 2, 1981, E1. 45. Bruccoli with HH, Sept. 14, 1997. 46. *Winston-Salem Journal*, Nov. 19, 1976, 13. 47. Hendrickson, *National Observer*, Dec. 4, 1976, 24. 48. *National Observer*, Dec. 4, 1976, 24. 49. JD to Smith, Nov. 17, 1980. 50. *Poetry*, Mar. 1981, 352.

XII. LA VITA NUOVA

30. Second Marriage (1976)

1. Carter and Dickey, qtd. by Ashley, *Columbia Record*, Dec. 6, 1976, A1. 2. Raines with HH, Nov. 9, 1996. 3. JD, qtd. by Loercher, *The Christian Science Monitor*, Oct. 5, 1977, 19. 4. KD with HH, Jul. 26, 1997. 5. JD, qtd. by Starr, *The State*, Dec. 31, 1976, B1. 6. Di Santo, "Portrait," 26. 7. Arehart with HH, Oct. 15, 1996. 8. JD, qtd. by Langdon, *People* (Aug. 1982): 41. 9. Gordon Van Ness with HH, Jul. 17, 1995. 10. JM with HH, Jul. 28, 1998. 11. Polak, *Philadelphia Inquirer*, Jun. 19, 1977, 7–8. 12. Langdon, *People:* 41. 13. WB with HH, Sept. 18, 1997. 14. BF with HH, Sept. 17, 1997. 15. Ashley, *Columbia Record*, Dec. 31, 1976, 2. 16. Franklin Ashley, *People* (Jan. 17, 1977): 30. 17. *Chattanooga News-Free Press*, Dec. 31, 1976. 18. Deborah, qtd. by Starr, *The State*, Dec. 31, 1976, B1. 19. Langdon, *People:* 41. 20. KD with HH, Jul. 26, 1997. 21. JD with HH, Aug. 7, 1996, 8. 22. Prunty with HH, Jul. 20, 1996. 23. *SOD*, 202–3. 24. Cantwell, *Speaking with Strangers*, 105, 108, 110, 111, 113. 25. DG with HH, Sept. 15, 1997. 26. Harrison with HH, Feb. 9, 1996. 27. CD with HH, Mar. 21, 1998. 28. JM to JD, Dec. 31, 1977. 29. Goff with HH, Apr. 21, 1998. 30. Carolee Guilds with HH, Nov. 14, 1998. 31. Langdon, *People:* 41. 32. WB with HH, Nov.

14, 1998.   **33.** *The State*, Dec. 31, 1976, B1.   **34.** Langdon, *People:* 41.   **35.** Deborah Dickey phone call to HH, Apr. 27, 1998.   **36.** Langdon, *People:* 41. **37.** *The Sentence* ms., Emory archive.   **38.** Elizabeth Adams with HH, Sept. 17, 1997.   **39.** Langdon, *People:* 41.   **40.** JD with HH, Aug. 6, 1996, 71.   **41.** JD with HH, Aug. 6, 1996, 71.   **42.** Sid Stapleton, *Southern World,* Nov.–Dec. 1979, 24.   **43.** Axthelm, *Newsweek* (Jan. 31, 1977): 25.

31. Presidential Poet (1977)

1. *The State*, Apr. 12, 1976, B1.   **2.** JD to Carter, Aug. 4, 1976.   **3.** JD to Carter, Sept. 29, 1976.   **4.** JD to Carter, Oct. 15, 1976.   **5.** VC, 161.   **6.** JD, qtd. by Landry, *The Washington Post*, Jan. 19, 1977, B1.   **7.** JD, qtd. by Loercher, *The Chrstian Science Monitor*, Oct. 5, 1977, 19.   **8.** Landry, *Post*, B1.   **9.** Landry, *Post*, B1.   **10.** Simon, *Times-Picayune*, Jan. 21, 1977, sec. 1, 15.   **11.** Arehart with HH, Oct. 15, 1996.   **12.** Patsy Dickey to JD, Jan. 21, 1977.   **13.** JD with HH, Aug. 6, 1996, 73.   **14.** VC, 39.   **15.** *The State*, Jun. 13, 1979, D5. **16.** Landry, *Post*, B3.   **17.** JD to McDonald, Jun. 26, 1979.   **18.** CD with HH, Mar. 21, 1998.   **19.** CP, 378–79.   **20.** Axthelm, *Newsweek:* 25.   **21.** JD to Hallman, Jul. 6, 1984.   **22.** Axthelm, *Newsweek:* 25.   **23.** JM with HH, Nov. 6–7, 1993.   **24.** Freundlich to NASA, Jun. 15, 1977.   **25.** Fletcher to Nadan, Mar. 15, 1977.   **26.** JD to Carter, c. Feb. 1979.   **27.** JD with HH, Aug. 6, 1996, 35.   **28.** JD to Carter, Mar. 6, 1979.   **29.** JD to Carter, Jul. 18, 1979.   **30.** JD to Pinsky, Feb. 1, 1980.   **31.** Pinsky to HH, Sept. 12, 1995.   **32.** JD to JW, Jan. 20, 1995.   **33.** JD to Anne Wright, May 6, 1975.   **34.** JD to Wagoner, Apr. 21, 1980.   **35.** JD to Carter, Jun. 23, 1980.   **36.** JD to Carter, Aug. 12, 1980.   **37.** JD to Carter, Oct. 24, 1980.

32. New Ventures (1977–1979)

1. *The Breath* ms., Emory archive.   **2.** JD with HH, Aug. 7, 1996, 14.   **3.** Goff with HH, Aug. 8, 1996.   **4.** JD, qtd. by Laurence, *Jacksonville Journal-Courier,* Mar. 24, 1978, 15.   **5.** Kelly with HH, Mar. 23, 1996.   **6.** JD to Barker, Oct. 27, 1977.   **7.** GI, no p.   **8.** Foreword.   **9.** Dillenberger, *Theology Today*, Jan. 1979, 508.   **10.** Logue with HH, Oct. 27, 1995.   **11.** Morrison, *Atlanta Weekly,* Feb. 1, 1981, 22.   **12.** WB with HH, Sept. 18, 1977.   **13.** JD to Hardwick, Sept. 13, 1977.   **14.** VC, 172.   **15.** JD, qtd. by Starr, *The State*, Sept. 14, 1977, A3. **16.** Van Duyn with HH, Feb. 2, 1997.   **17.** Kelly with HH, Mar. 23, 1996. **18.** *Poetry's Catbird Seat*, 18–19.   **19.** JD to Rosenthal, May 16, 1978.   **20.** JD, qtd. by Polak, *Philadelphia Inquirer,* Jun. 19, 1977, 7.   **21.** Lish to Raines, Jul. 11, 1977.   **22.** Kelly with HH, Mar. 23, 1996.   **23.** GC, 263.   **24.** GC, 264, 269, 23.   **25.** GC, 268.   **26.** Kelly with HH, Mar. 23, 1996.   **27.** JD in Binding ms., Jan. 31, 1978, Emory archive.   **28.** GC, 264.   **29.** JD to SR, Aug. 24, 1978.   **30.** JD to David Cowen, Feb. 26, 1982.   **31.** JD to Toombs, Nov. 30, 1978.   **32.** JD, qtd. by Starr, *The State*, Feb. 10, 1979, A15.   **33.** *D*, 100.   **34.**

The Sentence ms., Emory archive, 28. **35.** JD to Stuart, Mar. 17, 1978. **36.** *The Sentence* ms., 10, 19, 35, 50, 6. **37.** JD, qtd. by Beattie, *Carolina Lifestyle*, May 1982, 45. **38.** Greer with HH, May 14, 1998. **39.** *NH*, 29, 35. **40.** *Slackwater Review* (winter 1979–80): 17–18. **41.** *VC*, 237. **42.** JD to Beans, Nov. 29, 1985. **43.** *The Columbia Record*, May 16, 1979, B7. **44.** *VC*, 41. **45.** JD to SR, May 29, 1979. **46.** JD to Raines, Jun. 5, 1979. **47.** JD to SR, Jun. 17, 1980. **48.** JD to Vendler, Jul. 14, 1977. **49.** JD to Goldfarb, Jul. 30, 1980.

33. Under the Stone Snows of Mount Saint Helens (1980)

1. JD to Powell, Aug. 20, 1980. **2.** JD to SR, Feb. 3, 1980. **3.** JD to SR, Feb. 3, 1980. **4.** JD to SR, Feb. 3, 1980. **5.** JD to SR, Jun. 17, 1980. **6.** JD, qtd. by Green, *The Atlanta Constitution*, Feb. 18, 1980, B1. **7.** JD, qtd. by Starr, *The State*, Mar. 10, 1980, B16. **8.** JD to Gaston, May 8, 1980. **9.** Matthews with HH, Jan. 19, 1996. **10.** AB with HH, May 17, 1999. **11.** JD, will and last testament, Emory archive, May 22, 1980. **12.** JD to SR, Jun. 17, 1980. **13.** JD to Gaston, Jun. 30, 1980. **14.** JD, qtd. by Zoretich, *Seattle Post-Intelligencer*, Jun. 22, 1980, F10. **15.** Hoffman with HH, Dec. 20, 1997. **16.** JD to Hoffman, Jun. 11, 1980. **17.** JD to Stafford, Jun. 18, 1980. **18.** JD to Hugo, Jun. 13, 1980. **19.** JD to Rosenberg, Feb. 3, 1981. **20.** Rule, *The Stranger Beside Me* (New York: Norton, 1989), 169. **21.** *Esquire* (Mar. 1983): 100, 103. **22.** JD to Smith, Mar. 4, 1983. **23.** JD to Rosenbergs, Jul. 3, 1980. **24.** JD to SR, Jun. 17, 1980. **25.** JD to KM, Sept. 9, 1980. **26.** JD to O'Brien, Jul. 17, 1980. **27.** JD to Raines, Dec. 4, 1980. **28.** JD to Seldon Rodman, Nov. 23, 1970. **29.** JD to SR, Jun. 17, 1980. **30.** Havird to HH, Aug. 19, 1996. **31.** JD to Strand, Feb. 5, 1971. **32.** JD to Clark Powell, Aug. 20, 1980. **33.** JD to Davie, Oct. 31, 1980. **34.** JD to Tillinghast, Jul. 8, 1981. **35.** JD to *Time* (Oct. 6, 1980): 9. **36.** JD to *Time* (no date). **37.** JD to Walti, Nov. 5, 1981. **38.** WB with HH, Sept. 18, 1997. **39.** JD to Walti, Nov. 5, 1981. **40.** *SOD*, 215. **41.** *SOD*, 219. **42.** JD to Tom Goldpaugh, Feb. 5, 1981. **43.** JD, qtd. by Childress, *St. Louis Post-Dispatch*, Dec. 4, 1980, G1, G3. **44.** *The State*, Sept. 23, 1979, 11. **45.** Childress, *Dispatch*, G3.

XIII. SLOWLY TOWARD *ALNILAM*

34. Second Fatherhood (1981–1982)

1. JD to Littman, Jan. 21, 1981. **2.** JD to Atlas, Mar. 6, 1981. **3.** JD to Bottoms, Jan. 23, 1981. **4.** JD to Thompson, Apr. 29, 1981. **5.** JD to O'Shea, Apr. 29, 1981. **6.** Christensen with HH, Sept. 15, 1995. **7.** Christensen with HH, Sept. 15, 1995. **8.** JD to Christensen, Apr. 29, 1981. **9.** JD to Stevenson, Mar. 10, 1981. **10.** *S*, 53. **11.** JD to Stontenburg, Mar. 10, 1981. **12.** JD to Tillinghast, Dec. 14, 1982. **13.** JD to Raye and Bill (no last names given), Feb. 5, 1981. **14.** Elizabeth Adams with HH, Sept. 17, 1997. **15.** JD, qtd. by Dolan, *The Florida Times-Union*, Dec. 27, 1981, G6. **16.** JD to Levinson, Nov. 6, 1981. **17.** CP, 447–48. **18.** JD to Morris, Jul. 16, 1981. **19.** JD to Rosenberg, Jul. 22, 1981. **20.** JD to Pope John Paul, Jul. 20, 1981. **21.** Daniell with HH, Nov. 6, 1995. **22.** JD to Ted Morgan, Jan. 16, 1981. **23.** Daniell with HH, Nov. 6, 1995. **24.** JD with HH, Aug. 6, 1996, 13. **25.** *The Virginia Quarterly Review* (Summer 1998): 452. **26.** JD, qtd. by Eichstaedt, *The New Mexican*, Aug. 23, 1981, A1. **27.** JD to Morris, Jul. 16, 1981. **28.** JD to Lish, Sept. 17, 1981. **29.** JD to Bartlett, Jan. 25, 1982. **30.** JD to Meyers, Sept. 24, 1982. **31.** *Klondike* ms., Emory archive, 54, 24, 28, 29, 35, 58, 83, 100, 66. **32.** Hellman to JD, Mar. 26, 1982. **33.** Hellman to JD, Jan. 25, 1983. **34.** JD with HH, Aug. 7, 1996, 8.

35. *Puella* Troubles (1981–1982)

1. transcript of *Dickey v. Binkley* case, South Carolina State Supreme Court, Jun. 18, 1984, 196, 109, 203, 251, 252, 206–7, 256, 257, 259, 323, 318, 321. **2.** JD to Stapleton, Jun. 23, 1980. **3.** JD to Balakian, Sept. 24, 1982. **4.** Vernon Glenn with HH, Oct. 2, 1995. **5.** transcript of *Dickey v. Binkley*, 3, 7, 66–67, 68, 133, 165, 213, 396, 397. **6.** JD to Glenn, Jul. 25, 1986. **7.** JD to McHughes, Oct. 19, 1972. **8.** JD, qtd. by Montini, *The Arizona Republic*, Apr. 11, 1982, F1. **9.** JD to McHughes, Jul. 28, 1981. **10.** JD to KM, Apr. 13, 1982. **11.** McHughes, *Puella* intro., Emory archive. **12.** JD with HH, Aug. 7, 1996, 10. **13.** JD to Nelson, May 26, 1982. **14.** JD to Meyers, Sept. 24, 1982. **15.** Langdon, *People* (Aug. 1982): 37–41. **16.** WB with HH, Sept. 18, 1997. **17.** DG with HH, Sept. 15, 1998. **18.** JD to Lish, Oct. 20, 1982. **19.** JD to O'Neill, Aug. 13, 1982. **20.** JD to Green, Aug. 12, 1982. **21.** *NH*, 233. **22.** Van Ness, *JD Newsletter* (fall 1989): 9. **23.** Gioia, *Can Poetry Matter?* (Saint Paul: Graywolf, 1992), 191–92. **24.** *NH*, 133. **25.** DH to JD, Dec. 16, 1982. **26.** JD to Meyers, Sept. 24, 1982. **27.** JD with HH, Aug. 7, 1996, 10. **28.** JD to Arehart, no date, Box 135, Emory archive. **29.** *P*, 20, 24, 26. **30.** JD, qtd. by Beattie, *Carolina Lifestyle* (May 1982): 45. **31.** *P*, 48.

36. The Poet at Sixty (1982–1985)

1. JD to Smith, Oct. 29, 1982. **2.** JD to Warren, Sept. 15, 1982. **3.** JD, qtd. by Corvini, *The State*, Dec. 1, 1982, B1. **4.** JD to Hardwick, Dec. 14, 1982. **5.** JD to Fox, Dec. 15, 1982. **6.** JD to Chan, Jun. 23, 1983. **7.** WB with HH, Sept. 18, 1997. **8.** Meyers, *The Virginia Quarterly Review* (summer 1998): 454. **9.** JD to *Bookman's*, Dec. 9, 1982. **10.** CP, 454. **11.** Simon with HH, May 26, 1996. **12.** Romine, *The Charlotte Observer*, Feb. 13, 1983, F7. **13.** Romine, *The Charlotte Observer*, F1. **14.** Lieberman to HH, Jul. 21, 1998. **15.** Muske with HH, Sept. 24, 1996. **16.** Muske with HH, Sept. 24, 1996. **17.** CP, 435–36. **18.** JD to Arehart, Aug. 5, 1983. **19.** *NH*, xi, 2. **20.** Balakian with HH, Jun. 13, 1994. **21.** Academy, *Proceedings*, 69–75. **22.** WB with HH, Aug. 12, 1998. **23.** BF with HH, Sept. 17, 1977. **24.** BF with HH, Sept.

17, 1997. **25.** JD, qtd. by Starr, *The State*, Oct. 13, 1985, F7. **26.** JD to Jakes, Apr. 16, 1985. **27.** JD to *Writer's Digest* (Sept. 3, 1985). **28.** JD, qtd. by Marks, *Rome News-Tribune*, Jan. 17, 1985, 1.

37. Descent into Chaos (1985–1987)

1. Styron with HH, Oct. 12, 1996. **2.** JD, qtd. by Hodges, *The Tampa Tribune*, Jun. 2, 1985, G1. **3.** Prunty with HH, Jul. 20, 1996. **4.** JD to Capitol speakers, Dec. 9, 1985. **5.** JM with HH, Jul. 28, 1998. **6.** *CBS News Special Report*, Jan. 28, 1986, Emory archive. **7.** AB to JD, Apr. 15, 1986. **8.** *The Columbia Record*, Jun. 19, 1986, A15. **9.** JD, qtd. by Hartung, *Anderson Independent-Mail*, Jun. 29, 1986, 1. **10.** Mooney with HH, Jul. 31, 1998. **11.** WB with HH, Sept. 18, 1997. **12.** WB with HH, Sept. 18, 1997. **13.** WB with HH, Sept. 18, 1997. **14.** WB with HH, Sept. 18, 1997. **15.** WB with HH, Sept. 18, 1997. **16.** WB with HH, Sept. 18, 1997. **17.** WB with HH, Sept. 18, 1997. **18.** WB with HH, Sept. 18, 1997. **19.** JD, qtd. by Bryant, *The Columbia Record*, Oct. 1, 1986, C1. **20.** *Columbia Record*, C1. **21.** *Columbia Record*, C1. **22.** Patsy Dickey, ms. for *Creative Loafing* article on JD. **23.** *SOD*, 224. **24.** JD, qtd. by Starr, *The State*, Jul. 24, 1986. **25.** JD to Lazer, Sept. 10, 1986. **26.** WB with HH, Sept. 18, 1997. **27.** JD with HH, Aug. 7, 1996, 14. **28.** WB note, Jul. 28, 1986. **29.** WB note, Jul. 28, 1986. **30.** JD, qtd. by Hirsley, *Chicago Tribune Magazine*, May 10, 1987, 13. **31.** JD, qtd. by Graham, *The Atlanta Constitution*, Aug. 26, 1986, D1. **32.** *Chicago Tribune*, May 10, 1987, 10. **33.** BF with HH, Sept. 15, 1997. **34.** *NH*, 234. **35.** JD, qtd. by O'Briant, *The Atlanta Constitution*, Feb. 28, 1986, C2. **36.** *BTS*, no p. **37.** JD to Pamela Tehrani, Sept. 24, 1985. **38.** JD to Rather, Oct. 10, 1986. **39.** JD, qtd. by Robertson, *The New York Times*, Mar. 31, 1987, C13. **40.** Gioia, "How Nice to Meet You, Mr. Dickey" ms., to HH. **41.** JD, qtd. by Truehart, *The Washington Post*, May 24, 1987, F6.

38. A Blind Ulysses (1987)

1. "Joel Cahill Dead," *Beloit Poetry Journal* (summer 1958): 18–19. **2.** "Joel Cahill Dead" ms., Washington Univ. archive. **3.** JD to *The New York Times Book Review*, Jun. 24, 1972. **4.** JD to SR, Jan. 14, 1974. **5.** Blakemore to JD, Jan. 27, 1987. **6.** Greer with HH, May 14, 1998. **7.** JD to Blakemore, Jan. 27, 1987. **8.** VC, 107. **9.** JD, qtd. by Truehart, *The Washington Post*, May 24, 1987, F7. **10.** VC, 148. **11.** JD with HH, Aug. 5, 1996, 3. **12.** JD, qtd. by Claffey, *The Boston Globe*, Jun. 16, 1987, 69–70. **13.** JD to Blakemore, Jan. 27, 1986. **14.** JD to JW, Sept. 6, 1958. **15.** JD to JW, Sept. 6, 1958. **16.** JD with HH, Aug. 5, 1996, 11. **17.** JD, qtd. by Trueheart, *The Washington Post*, May 24, 1987, F6. **18.** *Pages*, Gale Research, 1976, 14. **19.** JD with HH, Aug. 5, 1996, 3. **20.** JD to Leith May 23, 1972. **21.** JD to Areheart, Feb. 5, 1981. **22.** A, 51–52. **23.** A, 127–28, 592. **24.** A, 723. **25.** JD to Stone, Aug. 6, 1980. **26.** JD with HH, Aug. 5, 1996, 8. **27.** *SOD*, 84. **28.** A, 18.

29. A, 18.   **30.** A, 22.   **31.** JD to Blakemore, Jan. 27, 1986.   **32.** A, 687.
33. JD with HH, Aug. 5, 1996, 10.   **34.** A ms., 416, Goff to HH, Sept. 21,
1996.   **35.** Goff with HH, Aug. 8, 1996.   **36.** JD with HH, Aug. 5, 1996, 10.
37. Goff with HH, Aug. 8, 1996.   **38.** Goff with HH, Aug. 8, 1996.   **39.** Goff
with HH, Aug. 8, 1996.   **40.** A, 219.   **41.** A, 739.   **42.** *Time*, Jun. 29,
1987, 71.   **43.** Parini, *USA TODAY*, May 29, 1987, 70.   **44.** *Subject to
Change*, Oct. 26, 1978, 21.   **45.** JD to Bloom, Jul. 22, 1987.   **46.** Greer with
HH, May 14, 1998.   **47.** Shelden with HH, Jan. 18, 1996.   **48.** JD to
Shelden, Oct. 30, 1987.   **49.** JD, qtd. by Romine, *The Charlotte Observer*, Oct.
25, 1987, B4.   **50.** JD to CD, Nov. 20, 1987.   **51.** JD to Smith, Dec. 18, 1993.
52. *The Southern Review* (fall 1994): 696–97.   **53.** Patsy Dickey with HH, Nov.
15, 1997.

XIV. *TO THE WHITE SEA*

39. Fortunes Rising, Fortunes Falling (1987–1992)

1. Nemerov, qtd. by Ashley, *The State*, Dec. 4, 1987, A16.   **2.** JD to Guillermin,
Jan. 20, 1987.   **3.** JD to Raines, Jul. 17, 1989.   **4.** JD to school principal, Apr.
17, 1988.   **5.** JD to Raines, Aug. 6, 1987.   **6.** Morrison, *Atlanta Weekly*, 11, 22.
7. *Atlanta Weekly*, 23.   **8.** Shuptrines with HH, Jul. 21, 1996.   **9.** *W*, 3, 5, 107,
73, 79, 81, 97, 83, 85, 157.   **10.** JD to Vidal, Dec. 14, 1988.   **11.** Richter with
HH, Sept. 19, l996.   **12.** JD to Suarez, Apr. 18, 1989.   **13.** JD to Ryden, Jul. 26,
1989.   **14.** *The State*, Sept. 24, 1989, F6.   **15.** WB with HH, Sept. 18, 1997.
16. JD to Jaffe, Oct. 18, 1989.   **17.** JD to Jaffe, Feb. 27, 1990.   **18.** Guilds with
HH, Nov. 14, 1998.   **19.** JD to Jaffe, Feb. 27, 1990.   **20.** DG with HH, Sept.
15, 1997.   **21.** DG with HH, Sept. 15, 1990.   **22.** JM with HH, JD with HH,
Aug. 6, 1996.   **23.** WB with HH, Sept. 18, 1997.   **24.** WB with HH, Sept. 15,
1997.   **25.** JD to Jaffe, May 15, 1990.   **26.** WB with HH, Jun. 24, 1998.   **27.**
JD to Tom Dickey, c. summer 1990.   **28.** JD to Raines, Jul. 3, 1990.   **29.**
Tyndall with HH, Aug. 21, 1998.   **30.** JD to Wesleyan UP, c. 1990.   **31.**
Updike, qtd. on book jacket, *The Eagle's Mile*.   **32.** Mitgang, *The New York
Times*, Oct. 27, 1990, 16.   **33.** *The State*, Dec. 9, 1990, 5F.   **34.** CP, 446,
434–35, 432, 435, 450.   **35.** Havird to HH, Aug. 19, 1996.   **36.** JD to *Memphis
State Review* (May 29, 1990).   **37.** JD to Spider, Jul. 6, 1990.   **38.** JD to Belitt,
Jan. 19, 1987.   **39.** Muske with HH, Aug. 7, 1997.   **40.** BF with HH, Sept. 17,
1997.   **41.** BF with HH, Sept. 17, 1997.   **42.** BF with HH, Sept. 17, 1997.
43. WB note, Feb. 1, 1992.   **44.** BF with HH, Sept. 17, 1997.   **45.** WB with
HH, Aug. 13, 1998.   **46.** *The State*, May 1, 1991, B1.   **47.** *The State*, May 1,
1991, B1.   **48.** *The State*, May 1, 1991, B1.   **49.** *The State*, May 1, 1991, B1.
50. WB with HH, Aug. 12, 1998.   **51.** Adams with HH, Sept. 17, 1997.   **52.**
WB with HH, Sept. 18, 1997.   **53.** WB with HH, Sept. 18, 1997.   **54.** WB
with HH, Aug. 12, 1998.   **55.** JD to Jaffe, Jun. 18, 1991.   **56.** JD to Jaffe, Aug.
1, 1991.   **57.** BF with HH, Sept. 17, 1997.   **58.** JD, qtd. by Starr, *The State*, Jul.
12, 1992, F1.   **59.** Biespel, *The Washington Post Book World*, 8 Nov. 22, 1992, 8.
60. Starr, *The State*, Jul. 12, 1992, F4.   **61.** *The Modesto Bee*, Jan. 27, 1991, 4.

40. Into the Desolation of Reality (1992-1994)

1. *The State*, Sept. 3, 1992, A2. **2.** *Creative Loafing* (Dec. 14, 1991): 29. **3.** *The State*, Mar. 8, 1998, F4. **4.** *The State*, Dec. 13, 1992, F1. **5.** *The State*, Feb. 3, 1993, B1. **6.** Jaffe with HH, Jul. 28, 1997. **7.** *Creative Loafing* (Oct. 16, 1993). **8.** Transcript of NPR interview with JD, Sept. 21, 1993, 21. **9.** JD with HH, Aug. 8, 1996, 46. **10.** *TWS*, 258. **11.** *TWS*, 35. **12.** *TWS*, 105, 145. **13.** JD with HH, Aug. 5, 1996, 16. **14.** *TWS*, 110, 135. **15.** JD with HH, Aug. 5, 1996, 13. **16.** *TWS*, 213. **17.** *TWS*, 209, 193, 228, 261. **18.** JD with HH, Aug. 5, 1996, 17. **19.** *TWS*, 275, 271. **20.** *The Atlanta Journal-Constitution*, Sept. 26, 1993, M4. **21.** *Newsweek* (Aug. 30, 1994): 54. **22.** Lehman-Haupt, *The New York Times*, Sept. 13, 1993. **23.** Yardley, *The Washington Post Book World*, Aug. 29, 1993. **24.** GQ (Sept. 1993): 107. **25.** Leithauser, *The New Yorker* (Sept. 27, 1993): 103. **26.** Shaw, *People* (Jan. 31, 1994): 82, 80. **27.** *The Sewanee Review* (winter 1994): 154–56. **28.** *The Atlanta Journal-Constitution*, Sept. 26, 1993, M4. **29.** *Creative Loafing* (Oct. 16, 1993): 23. **30.** *The State*, Sept. 18, 1993, B7. **31.** *USC Times*, Sept. 10, 1993, 6–7. **32.** Howard with HH, Dec. 5, 1995. **33.** Peery with HH, Mar. 28, 1997. **34.** JD to Barber, Dec. 4, 1993. **35.** Taylor to HH, May 20, l995. **36.** *SOD*, 238, 241, 244. **37.** Pepperdine with HH, Jun. 13, 1996. **38.** Price with HH, Feb. 9, 1999. **39.** Richter with HH, Sept. 19, 1996.

41. The Heart of the World (1994-1997)

1. DG with HH, Sept. 15, 1997. **2.** *Gamecock* (Oct. 31, 1994): 1. **3.** Butterworth to HH, Oct. 23, 1995. **4.** Bruccoli with HH, Sept. 14, 1997. **4.1** WB with HH, Sept. 18, 1997. **5.** WB with HH, Sept. 18, 1977. **6.** MacLamore with HH, Sept. 21, 1997. **7.** JD with HH, Aug. 5, 1996, 1. **8.** CD with HH, Mar. 21, 1998. **9.** *SOD*, 246–47. **10.** CD with HH, Mar. 21, 1998. **11.** *SOD*, 248, 250. **12.** Morris, *Atlanta* (Aug. 1995): 56. **13.** BF with HH, Sept. 17, 1997. **14.** Goff with HH, Apr. 21, 1998. **15.** Deborah, qtd. in article sent to HH by Ashley Brown, Feb. 28, 1995. **16.** *SOD*, 253. **17.** Styron with HH, Oct. 12, 1996. **18.** *The State*, Apr. 14, 1995, A1. **19.** Morris, *Atlanta*: 57. **20.** *Reckon* (winter 1996): 76. **21.** Fry with HH, Dec. 15, 1997. **22.** AB with HH, Sept. 22, 1995. **23.** AB with HH, Sept. 22, 1995. **24.** CD with HH, Mar. 21, 1998. **25.** WB with HH, May 20, 1999. **26.** JD with HH, Aug. 7, 1996, 14–15. **27.** JD, qtd. by Starr, *The State*, Nov. 26, 1995, F1. **28.** *The State*, Nov. 26, 1995, F1. **29.** JD, qtd. by Starr, *The State*, Nov. 26, 1995, F1. **30.** Hemingway, *The Complete Short Stories of Ernest Hemingway* (New York: Collier, 1987), 45. **31.** Mays, "The Devil," 31. **32.** Butterworth to HH, Oct. 23, 1995. **33.** "Weather of the Valley," *All the Rights and Privileges* (Columbia: USC Press, 1998), 37. **34.** *Sunday Times Advertiser*, May 8, 1977, E4. **35.** "Weather," 41. **36.** Ennis with HH, Oct. 20, 1995. **37.** AB with HH, Feb. 10, 1996. **38.** JD to Shuptrines, Mar. 29, 1996. **39.** Goff with HH, May 4, 1998. **40.** *The State*, Nov. 26, 1995, F1. **41.** JD to Conroy, Apr. 8, 1996. **42.** JD to Hanson, Jun. 3, 1996. **43.** Guilds with HH, Nov. 14, 1998. **44.** JM with HH, Aug. 6, 1996. **45.** Fairman to HH, Sept. 25, 1996. **46.** *Crux* ms., Emory archive, 6, 11, 20, 27.

47. *Crux* notes, Emory archive.   **48.** *SOD*, 269–70.   **49.** *Heart of Darkness*, 161, 165.   **50.** Cansler with HH, Sept. 8, 1997.   **51.** Cansler with HH, Sept. 8, 1997. **52.** Ed Madden with HH, Nov. 16, 1998.   **53.** Fairman with HH, Aug. 21, 1998. **54.** *SOD*, 266.   **55.** Guilds with HH, Nov. 14, 1998.   **56.** Guilds with HH, Nov. 14, 1998.   **57.** MacLamore with HH, Sept. 21, 1997.

42. Last Rites (1997)

1. KD with HH, Jul. 26, 1997.   **2.** CD obituary to HH, Feb. 21, 1997.   **3.** Patsy Dickey with HH, Nov. 15, 1997.   **4.** King with HH, Nov. 10, 1997.   **5.** *NH*, 93.   **6.** *The Carolinian* (Apr. 1997): 24.   **7.** *The Carolinian:* 25.   **8.** Deborah phone call to HH, Apr. 27, 1998.   **9.** WB document, Aug. 15, 1997.   **10.** *The Great Gatsby* (New York: Charles Scribner's Sons: 1925), 2, 112, 182.

INDEX

PERMISSIONS

Jimmy Carter Library, Yale Collection of American Literature: Beinecke Rare Book and Manuscript Library, Harry Ransom Humanities Research Center: The University of Texas at Austin.

Excerpts from obituary for James Dickey reprinted by permission of William Styron.